The Caribbean

written and researched by

Nicky Agate, Arabella Bowen, Maureen Clarke, Dominique De-Light, Gaylord Dold, Natalie Folster, Sean Harvey, Tom Hutton, Sarah Lazarus, Karl Luntta, Fiona McAuslan, JoAnn Milivojevic, Matthew Norman, Lesley Rose, Nelson Taylor, Polly Thomas, Adam Vaitilingam and Claus Vogel

www.roughguides.com

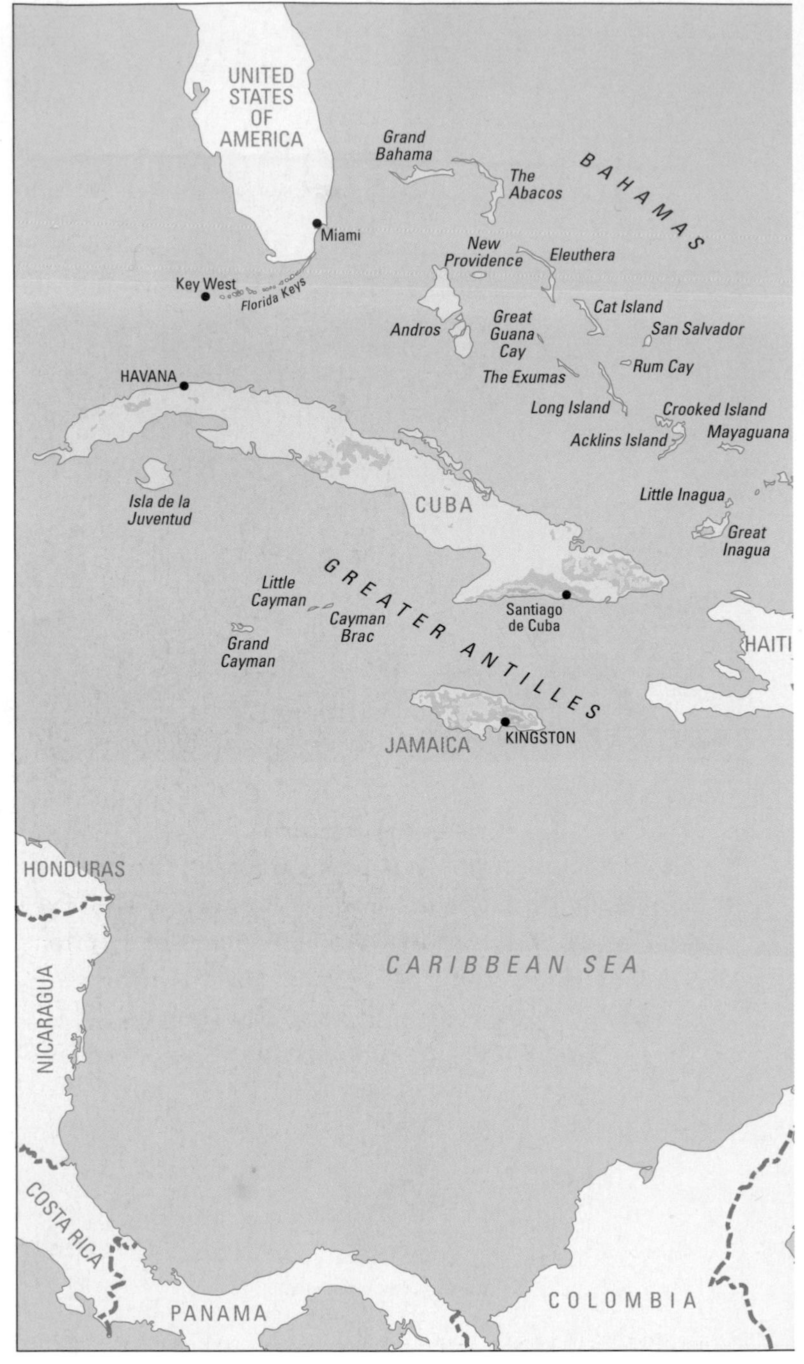

UNITED STATES OF AMERICA
Miami
Key West
Florida Keys
Grand Bahama
The Abacos
BAHAMAS
New Providence
Eleuthera
Andros
Great Guana Cay
Cat Island
San Salvador
The Exumas
Rum Cay
Long Island
Crooked Island
Acklins Island
Mayaguana
HAVANA
Isla de la Juventud
CUBA
Little Inagua
Great Inagua
GREATER ANTILLES
Little Cayman
Cayman Brac
Grand Cayman
Santiago de Cuba
HAITI
JAMAICA
KINGSTON
HONDURAS
NICARAGUA
CARIBBEAN SEA
COSTA RICA
PANAMA
COLOMBIA

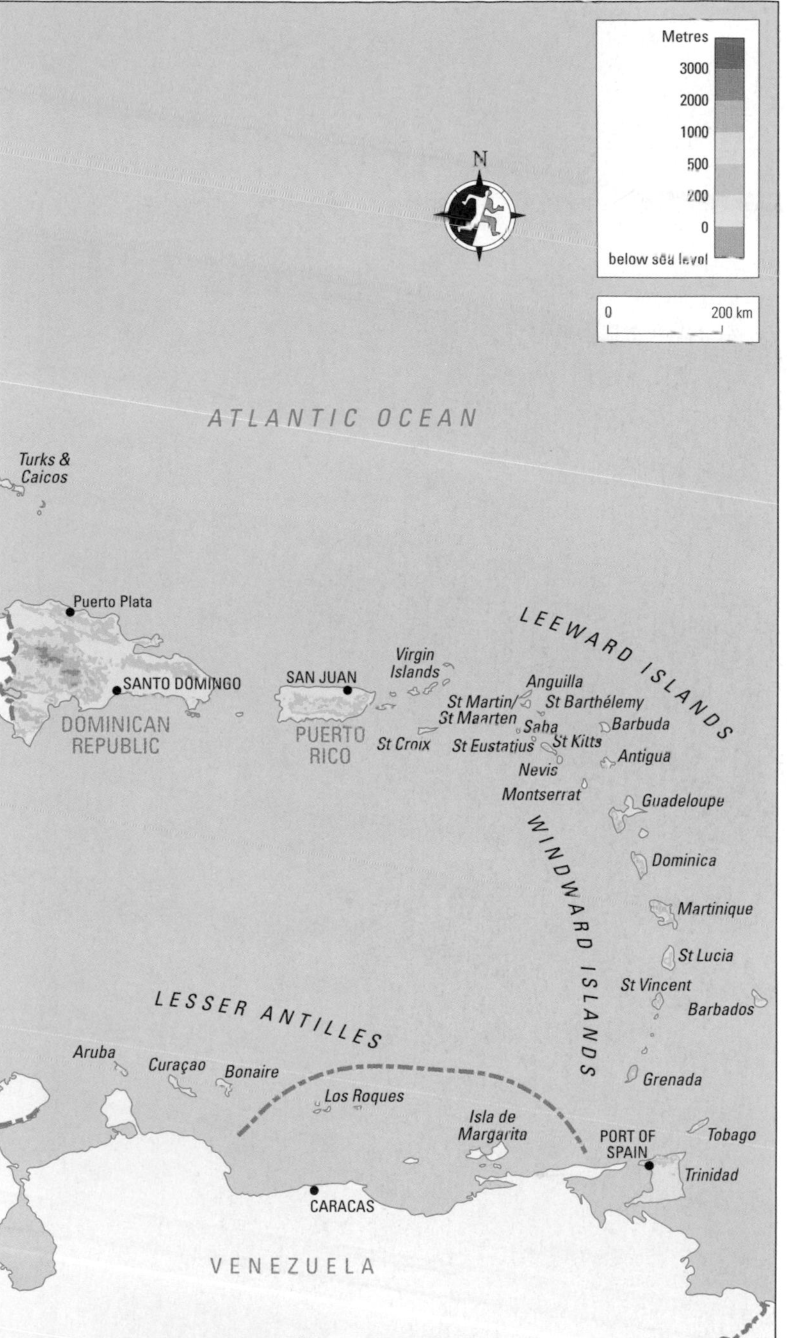
Metres
3000
2000
1000
500
200
0
below sea level
0
200 km
N
ATLANTIC OCEAN
Turks & Caicos
Puerto Plata
SANTO DOMINGO
DOMINICAN REPUBLIC
SAN JUAN
PUERTO RICO
Virgin Islands
St Croix
LEEWARD ISLANDS
Anguilla
St Martin/ St Maarten
St Barthélemy
Saba
Barbuda
St Eustatius
St Kitts
Antigua
Nevis
Montserrat
Guadeloupe
WINDWARD ISLANDS
Dominica
Martinique
St Lucia
St Vincent
Barbados
Grenada
LESSER ANTILLES
Aruba
Curaçao
Bonaire
Los Roques
Isla de Margarita
PORT OF SPAIN
Tobago
Trinidad
CARACAS
VENEZUELA

Introduction to the

Caribbean

Palm trees swaying over white-sand beaches, pellucid waters with teeming reefs just a flipper-kick from the shore and killer rum cocktails brought right to your lounge chair – this is the Caribbean, as per everyone's favourite tropical fantasy. The ultimate place to flop on the sand and unwind, the region offers sun, sand and corporeal comforts aplenty, and has long seduced those after life's sybaritic pleasures.

Given these obvious draws, a holiday in the Caribbean – anywhere in the Caribbean – is commonly proffered as the ultimate getaway. But buying into this postcard-perfect stereotype – and failing to recognize the individual idiosyncrasies of the islands that make up the archipelago – is the biggest mistake a first-time visitor can make. Drawing on the combined traditions of Africa and those brought here by Spain, Britain, France, Holland and the 500,000 people who arrived from India as indentured workers after the abolition of slavery, no other area in the Americas exhibits such a diverse range of cultural patterns and social and political institutions – there's a lot more on offer here than sun, sea, sand and learning to limbo.

Culturally, this relatively small, fairly impoverished collection of islands has had an impact quite out of tune with its size, from the Jamaican sound-system DJs who inspired hip-hop, to the Lenten bacchanalia that have come to define carnivals worldwide. Over the last five hundred years, each country or territory has carved out its own identity (some much more recently than others, with the onset of mass tourism and the advent of the all-inclusive), and it's hard to think of worlds so near and yet so disparate

Fact file

• The combined **population** of the Caribbean islands is just over 38 million; Great Inagua in the Bahamas has a population of less than 1000 people but is home to 60,000 pink flamingos, spoonbills and ducks.

• **Tourism** is by far the region's biggest business, with between fifteen and twenty million visitors each year. With over two million visitors annually, the DR is the most popular destination; Saba, with around 9000, is the least-visited.

• The Caribbean Sea is the **fifth largest body of water** in the world, with a total area of 970,000 square miles (slightly bigger than the Mediterranean).

• The **highest point** in the region is the Dominican Republic's Pico Duarte, at 3125m above sea level – it even gets some snow in winter. The DR also holds the Caribbean's **lowest point**: Lago Enriquillo, some 39m below sea level.

• With an estimated 390,000 people diagnosed HIV-positive, **HIV/AIDS infection rates** in the Caribbean are among the highest in the world, second only to sub-Saharan Africa.

• St Lucia has produced two **Nobel prize winners**, the poet Derek Walcott and the economist Sir Arthur Lewis.

as the sensual *son* and *salsa* of Cuba compared to the dance-hall and Rasta militancy of neighbouring Jamaica or the poppy zouk of Martinique and Guadeloupe. **Sport** rivals music as a Caribbean obsession, and though golf is well represented by the scores of world class courses, the region's game of choice has traditionally been cricket, introduced by the Brits and raised to great heights by the Windies team, who led the world for much of the 1970s and 1980s. Wins are rather less common these days, but cricket remains central to the Caribbean psyche, with international matches known to bring their host islands to a complete standstill. Other popular spectator sports include football, which has made massive inroads since Jamaica's Reggae Boyz qualified for the 1998 World Cup, and baseball, firmly entrenched in Dominican Republic, Puerto Rico and Cuba.

Each island has a strong **culinary** tradition, too, and while you might come here to sample Caribbean classics such as Trinidadian roti, Grenadian "oil-down" or Dominican mountain chicken (actually a very big frog), you can also enjoy croissants and gourmet dinners in the French islands, Dutch delicacies in the Netherlands Antilles and piles of good ol' burgers and fries in Puerto Rico and the Bahamas – and on every island with a fair-sized tourism industry you'll find "international" restaurants of every ilk alongside hole-in-the-wall shacks selling local specialities.

The Caribbean's natural attractions are equally compelling, its **landscapes** ranging from teeming rainforest, mist-swathed mountains and conical volcanic peaks to lowland mangrove swamps, lush pastureland and savannah plains. The entire region is incredibly abundant in its **flora**, despite the sometimes volcanic or scrubby interiors on certain islands. Heliconias and orchids flower most everywhere, while hibiscus and ixoras brighten up the hedgerows, and the forest greens are enlivened by flowering trees such as poinsettia and poui. Not surprisingly eco-tourism abounds, whether it be hiking through the waterfall-studded rainforest of Dominica or St Lucia, high-mountain treks in Jamaica, or birding in Trinidad, which has one of the highest concentrations of bird species in the world. The sea here is as bountiful as the land; besides taking in superlative **diving** and **snorkelling** around multicoloured reefs and sunken ships that play host

Rum

Tipple of choice for the region, **rum** is an integral part of Caribbean life – even the smallest village has a rum shop where old men nurse glasses of overproof "whites" and water and put the world to rights. Everyone has their favourite brew, ranging from home-brewed firewaters such as Tobago's babash or Jamaica's jancro batty (strictly for masochists), to weaker, cocktail-friendly whites from Trinidad and Tobago or sweet, rich, oak-aged concoctions like Cuba's Matusalem – best drunk after dinner, and never to be adulterated with a mixer.

Rum-making has remained much the same over the centuries. Yeast is added to sugarcane juice or molasses to kick-start fermentation (which converts the sucrose to alcohol); this "dead wash" is then boiled, and the evaporating alcohol is collected. After a little blending and the addition of water, the white rums are ready to bottle; smoother brown rums are aged in oak barrels, which colour the spirit to varying shades of brown. It's a simple process, but consider that it takes some ten to twelve tonnes of cane to produce half a bottle of pure alcohol, and you'll understand the prevalence of those endless fields of swaying cane.

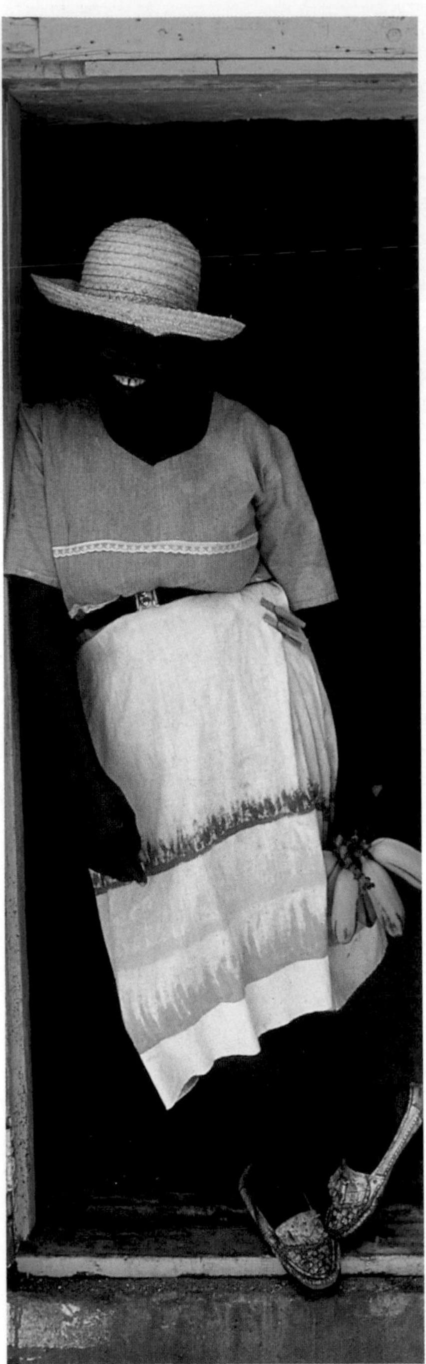

to technicolour tropical marine life, you can turtle-watch on innumerable beaches that see nesting leatherbacks and hawksbills, go whale-spotting from St Lucia, Dominica and the Dominican Republic, or frolic with giant manta rays offshore of Tobago and stingrays in the Caymans.

Beyond their cultural and physical richness, the Caribbean islands share a similar history of **colonization**. The first known inhabitants, farming and fishing Amerindians who travelled from South America by way of dugout canoes around 500 BC, were swiftly displaced by **Christopher Columbus**, the Italian explorer who "discovered" the region for Spain in the late fifteenth century, touching down on the Bahamas, Cuba, Hispaniola and Jamaica, and mistakenly assuming that he had found the outlying islands of India, bestowing the title "West Indies" to the region. Seduced by fantasies of innumerable riches, other European countries soon jumped on the bandwagon. The Spanish were followed by the **British**, **French** and **Dutch**, who squabbled over their various territories for most of the sixteenth century, their colonization of the

islands hindered by **pirates** and state-licensed **privateers** who plundered settlements and vessels without mercy.

Nonetheless, European colonies were established throughout the region, and by the seventeenth century, the islands had begun to be developed in earnest. The British proved most adept at establishing huge plantations of **sugarcane** – estates which required far more labour than the colonists themselves could provide, and which gave rise to the appalling business of the **slave trade**. Plantation life for slaves was one of unimaginable barbarity, and eighteenth-century **rebellions**, combined with Christian tenets of humanity and charity, engendered the first moves toward emancipation – between 1833 and 1888 slavery was abolished in the Caribbean.

While the fenced-off all-inclusive enclave is still going strong today, the region now has as many budget-oriented bolt holes as it does luxury resorts, and as many possibilities for adventurous travel as it does for staid beach holidays.

Post-emancipation, conditions for all but the planter elites remained abysmal, and the establishment of unions and subsequent labour strikes led, by the 1930s, to the creation of political parties throughout the region. This in turn nudged the islands to call for independence from their colonial rulers, increasingly so after World War II. The early twentieth century also saw **tourism** start to take root. Wealthy Brits and North Americans had patronized palatial resorts since the late nineteenth century, and the glitterati followed in the footsteps of Noel Coward and Errol Flynn to Jamaica and Ernest Hemingway to Cuba, thus creating the air of exclusivity which remains inextricably tied to the Caribbean today. But with the introduction of long-haul air travel in the 1960s, tourists began to arrive en masse. While the fenced-off all-inclusive enclave is still going strong today, the region now has as many budget-oriented bolt holes as it does luxury resorts, and as many possibilities for adventurous travel as it does for staid beach holidays.

Where to go

Spanning an arc from southern Florida to Venezuela on the South American coast, the islands of the Caribbean are made up of two main chains which form a 3200 kilometre mile breakwater between the Caribbean Sea to the south and the Atlantic Ocean to the north. Running south from Florida, the mostly limestone **Greater Antilles** (Cuba, Jamaica, Cayman Islands, Dominican Republic and Haiti, Puerto Rico and the Virgin Islands) comprise the largest and most geographically varied of the two chains, with white-sand beaches aplenty as well as rain-forest-smothered peaks that are remnants of submerged ranges related to the Central and South American mountain systems. Dryer, somewhat flatter and boasting as many black-sand beaches as white, the volcanic **Lesser Antilles** are further subdivided into the **Leeward Islands** (Anguilla, St Martin/St Maarten, St Barts, Saba, St Eustatius, St Kitts, Nevis, Antigua, Barbuda, Montserrat and Guadeloupe) and **Windward Islands** (Dominica, Martinique, St Lucia, Barbados, St Vincent, the Grenadines, and Grenada). North of the Greater Antilles, the Bahamas, and Turks and Caicos Islands sit alone, as do Trinidad and Tobago and the "ABC islands" (Aruba, Bonaire and Curaçao), just off the Venezuelan coast, though the latter are also an

How to pick a beach

Finding a beach that suits your tastes shouldn't be hard, given that Caribbean beaches can be as varied as the islands themselves. Spectacular swathes of sand are ten-a-penny here, but for the archetypal stretch of powdery white sand, lapped by warm clear water and generously endowed with coconut palms, you'll want to head to low-lying corraline islands such as Antigua (said to boast 365 beaches – one for every day of the year), the Bahamas (which has pink sand as well as white), or, in no particular order, Barbados, Aruba, Cayman Islands, Virgin Islands, Anguilla, and the Turks and Caicos. If you're after desert-island solitude, you'll be hard-pressed to find any: the best spots were snapped up long ago by developers who've added everything from hotels, bars and restaurants to watersports, and usually charge a fee for use of the facilities.

Those willing to travel off the beaten path might consider checking out the Caribbean's stunning grey- or black-sand beaches (the happy result of age-old volcanic activity), many of which are relatively undeveloped and surrounded by lush tropical foliage – St Lucia, Grenada, St Vincent, Guadeloupe and Martinique are all solid contenders, while the larger of the Windward Islands have all the types of beach.

Remember that many islands have coastline on the Atlantic Ocean as well as the Caribbean Sea; beaches on the Atlantic side typically have rougher waves and cooler, green-tinged depths, while those on the Caribbean are usually calmer, warmer and properly conform to the classic "white-sand-and-palms" image.

Though we've not covered **Haiti** in this edition of the guide, out of safety concerns for travellers, it's longtime spell over foreigners is hard to deny. Perhaps the most culturally fascinating destination in all the Caribbean, Haiti is well known for its African-derived artistic traditions, its common practice of voodoo religion, and as the site of a successful slave rebellion, which overthrew the colonial government some two centuries ago. Not that that solved everything politically; military dictatorships and "Presidents-for-life" have followed, as has the occasional contested election. It remains, too, in the economic doldrums, its teeming capital Port-au-Prince comprised of many depressed barrios – if beautifully set against a protected bay – and much of its green and lovely countryside not at all set up for the casual traveller.

autonomous part of the Kingdom of The Netherlands. Together with Saba, St Eustatius and St Maarten, these islands are collectively known as the **Netherlands Antilles**.

Deciding which of the islands to visit, however, is the fifty-million-dollar question. Obviously, you'll need to consider what you want from your holiday. If you're after two weeks of sunbathing and swimming and don't plan on doing any exploring, then you've the freedom to allow a travel agent to pick the cheapest deal available – or just flip through this book and pick which sounds the most appealing. If variety is on your agenda, bigger islands which boast a diversity of landscapes – Cuba, Jamaica and the Dominican Republic – offer more scope for adventurous travel, with possibilities for hiking, rafting, eco-pursuits and cultural tours as well as beachlife, and probably demand a single-island trip. However, as **island-hopping** can be relatively easy, either by short plane trips or the occasional ferry, it's well worth seeing more than one island, especially if you've picked a destination in the Lesser Antilles.

Of the Caribbean islands, two are not covered in this guide; at the time of writing Montserrat was still recovering from recent volcanic activity, while unrest in Haiti has made travel to that country inadvisable.

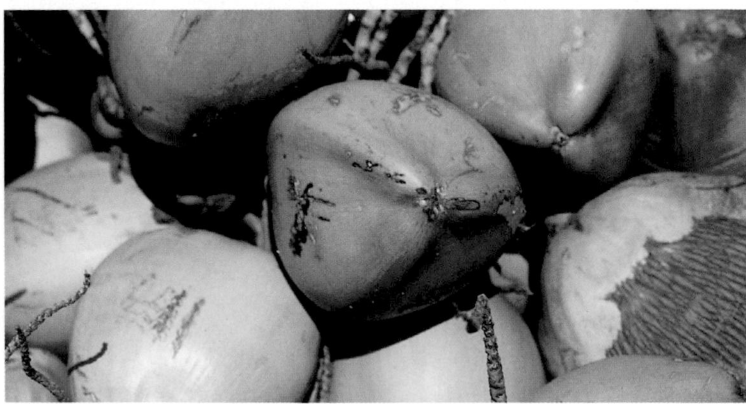

When to go

As visitors mainly flock to the Caribbean to swap snow, rain and wind back home for the sun and warm waters of the tropics, it'll come as no surprise to find that the region's busiest time is the northern hemisphere's **winter** (roughly Nov–Feb). During this high season, the daytime heat doesn't reach blistering proportions, and is tempered by cool breezes and balmy evenings, while rain is generally restricted to brief early-afternoon showers. The downside to this, however, is that the beaches and attractions are busy, hotels are often full, and flights can get oversubscribed, with fares at a premium. Prices for almost everything may decrease in the slow **summer** season, but it's not an ideal time to visit the Caribbean: days are oppressively hot and humid and nights are muggy. Late summer also sees the start of the **hurricane season**, which runs roughly from July to November, and even if there's no big blow, this usually means a lot of **rain**. While there's never really a bad time to holiday in the region, the Caribbean is best enjoyed in the **shoulder seasons** (early Nov and Feb through June), when flights and hotels are plentiful (and less expensive), and the weather dependable. Spring is also the season for catching one of the Caribbean's many pre-Lenten carnivals.

Carnival mentality

Balmy temperatures, stunning outdoor venues and a bacchanalian worldview – the Caribbean is a fabulous place to **party**, and there's an extensive programme of annual events that cater to the hedonistic urge. The festival calendar may kick off with Christmas **Junkanoo** parades throughout the region, but the real deal is pre-Lenten **Carnival**, of which Trinidad's is the main event, bursting with pure, unbridled energy and with the emphasis on participation. Buy a costume and "play mas" in a costume band with five thousand revellers, or get coated in mud, paint or oil at the rawer, early-hours Jouvert parade. Carnival culture runs pretty much year-round, too, with substantial events in March (Jamaica, St Thomas), July (St Lucia, Barbados, St Vincent, Cuba, Antigua and Barbuda) and August (Grenada). Other major happenings with a uniquely Caribbean flavour include Jamaica's **Reggae Sumfest** (Aug), held next to the sea and under the stars – the ultimate way to enjoy the cream of reggae performers in their home ground. Caribbean scenery provides the perfect backdrop for other music, too, and there are major **jazz** festivals featuring international performers in Barbados (Jan), St Lucia (May), Jamaica and Aruba (June), while Dominica stages the World Creole Music Festival each October. Although you may not be here for the big events listed above, rest assured that as every island has its own sizeable roster, there'll be something going on whenever you visit; see individual chapters for lists of major festivals and events.

Average daily temperatures and monthly rainfall

	Jan	Feb	Mar	Apr	May	June	July	Aug	Sept	Oct	Nov	Dec
Havana, Cuba												
Max °C	25	25	27	29	29	30	32	32	30	29	27	25
Min °C	19	19	20	21	22	23	24	24	24	23	21	20
Rain (mm)	71	46	46	58	119	165	125	135	150	173	79	58
Kingston, Jamaica												
Max °C	30	30	30	31	31	32	32	32	32	31	31	31
Min °C	19	19	20	21	22	23	23	23	23	23	22	19
Rain (mm)	23	15	23	20	102	86	86	89	97	178	76	36
Port of Spain, Trinidad												
Max °C	31	31	32	32	32	32	31	31	32	32	32	31
Min °C	21	20	20	21	22	22	22	22	22	22	22	21
Rain (mm)	69	41	46	53	94	193	218	246	193	170	183	125
St John's, Antigua												
Max °C	28	28	29	30	31	31	31	31	32	31	29	28
Min °C	21	21	21	22	23	24	24	24	23	23	23	22
Rain (mm)	122	86	112	89	97	112	155	183	168	196	180	140
Santo Domingo, Dominican Republic												
Max °C	29	29	29	30	30	31	31	31	31	31	30	29
Min °C	19	19	20	21	22	23	23	23	23	22	21	20
Rain (mm)	51	44	44	68	187	152	179	157	165	170	96	70

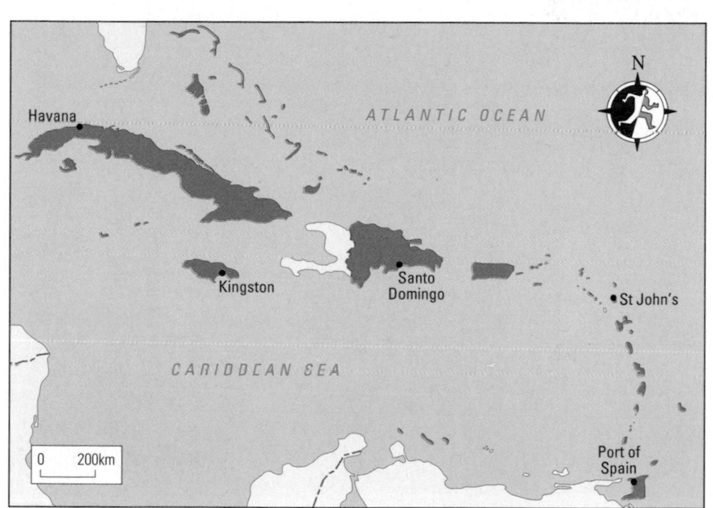

26 things not to miss

It's not possible to see everything that the Caribbean has to offer in one trip – and we don't suggest you try. What follows is a selective and subjective taste of the region's highlights: spectacular natural attractions, thrilling ocean activities and rich cultural traditions. They're arranged in five colour-coded categories to help you find the very best things to see, do, eat and experience. All highlights have a page reference to take you straight into the guide, where you can find out more.

01 **Swimming with dolphins, the Bahamas** Page **85** • Swim, feed and frolic among dolphins off the coast of Grand Bahama.

02 Antigua's Carnival Page **524** • One of several raucous Carnivals celebrated throughout the Caribbean; with ten straight days full of colourful costumes, steel-drum bands and lots of dancing, it's *the* social event of the year.

03 The Pitons, St Lucia Page **623** • Towering over Soufrière, St Lucia's oldest town, these distinctive twin peaks are, rightfully, the island's most photographed sight.

04 **Willemstad, Curaçao** Page **807** • Literally one of the Caribbean's most colourful capitals, Willemstad's Dutch heritage is apparent along its narrow winding streets and attractive waterfront.

05 **Cuban music** Page **165** • The sounds of the Caribbean are every bit as important as the sights – be sure to check out some *salsa* and *son* in Cuba's dance halls, or even on its streets.

06 **Boiling Lake, Dominica** Page **591** • If the island's ultimate hike leading to the lake fails to impress, the eerie sight of its steam-enshrouded waters most certainly will.

07 **Places you've never heard of** Page **483** • Far off the beaten track lie islands like tranquil Saba, one of the unspoiled gems of the Caribbean.

08 Bonaire Marine Park Page **801** • Home to everything from angelfish to moray eels and just one of the Caribbean's spectacular marine habitats.

09 Seven Mile Beach, Grand Cayman Page **218** • Lovely strands of coast like this lengthy one help make the Cayman Islands known for more than just offshore banking.

10 Jamaican nightlife Page **247** • From sweaty dance halls to laid-back jam sessions, the island's phenomenal music scene is bound to keep you busy, night after night.

11 Barbados surf Page **664** • Though difficult and treacherous to swim in, the Atlantic waves along the island's little-explored east coast make Barbados a popular surfing destination.

12 Beach bumming Page **563** • Flop down on your own patch of sand, like these sun-worshippers in Martinique, and savour the freedom of not having to do anything at all.

13 Fresh seafood Page **44** • Don't miss the region's countless seafood options, including succulent fresh lobster, a mainstay of menus everywhere from high-end eateries to charming beachside shacks.

14 La Soufrière, St Vincent Page **681** • A hike to the summit on the rainforest-cloaked trails on this active volcano will reward those who make it with nearly indescribable vistas.

15 Scuba diving Pages **57, 207 & 795** • While most of the Caribbean isles boast sunken wrecks, reefs and colourful ocean creatures in spades, Bonaire, the Bahamas, and the Cayman Islands are the high points for in-the-know diving enthusiasts.

16 Street food Page **726** • Be sure to visit food stalls in places like Trinidad and Tobago for *roti* and the like – they're often the top spots to sample local cuisine and rub elbows with the locals.

17 Caribbean sunsets Seal the memory of your Caribbean vacation with the spectacular sight of a tropical sunset.

18 Old Havana, Cuba Page **157** • Untouched for years by tourism, the faded grandeur of Havana's old town is unmatched in the region.

19 Sea kayaking in the Exumas Page **99** • Kayaking around this island chain – stopping off at whichever deserted beach strikes your fancy – is a rewarding adventure for first-time paddlers and experienced explorers alike.

20 Bomba's shack, Virgin Islands Page **435** • Quiet and unassuming most of the time, this ramshackle bar comes alive every full moon to host an all-out bash.

21 The Baths, Virgin Islands Page **440** • Clamber about in this alien landscape, where gigantic boulders form striking grottoes, pools and underwater caves.

22 Old San Juan, Puerto Rico Page **363** • The preserved colonial buildings of the city make for excellent wandering, amidst old fortresses, convents and the odd historic museum.

23 Snorkelling Page **48** • Snorkelling through the Caribbean's underwater world is often as rewarding as diving – and far cheaper, especially if you bring your own gear.

24 Windsurfing at Cabarete, Dominican Republic Page **335** • The world class conditions, along with a plethora of schools and rental centres, make this lively coastal town the best place to windsurf in the western hemisphere.

25 Plantation inns, St Kitts Page **506** • Exuding old-world ambience, inventive inns like *Rawlins* – housed in a former sugarcane plantation – are a refreshing break from the usual beachside accommodations.

26 El Yunque, Puerto Rico Page **371** • There's great rainforest scenery on islands like Grenada, St Lucia, and Puerto Rico, the latter is home to El Yunque, the largest rainforest in the US and excellent for birdwatching opportunities.

contents

Using the Rough Guide

We've tried to make this Rough Guide a good read and easy to use. The book is divided into four main sections, and you should be able to find whatever you want in one of them.

colour section

The front colour section offers a quick survey of the Caribbean Islands. The introduction aims to give you a feel for the place, with suggestions on where to go and when. Next, our authors round up their favourite aspects of the Caribbean Islands in the things not to miss section – whether it's great food, amazing sights or a spectacular festival. Right after this comes a full contents list.

basics

The Basics section covers all the **pre-departure** nitty-gritty to help you plan your trip. This is where to find out which airlines fly to your destination, what paperwork you'll need, what to do about money and insurance, internet access, food, public transport, car rental and overland travel – in fact just about every piece of **general practical information** you might need.

guide

This is the heart of the Rough Guide, divided into user-friendly chapters, each of which covers a specific country or region. Every chapter starts with a list of **highlights** and an **introduction** that helps you to decide where to go, depending on your time and budget. The introduction prefaces the **minibasics** section, which is full of specific practicalities and is followed by a brief **history**. Chapters then move on to **detailed coverage** of your destination. Introductions to the various towns and smaller regions within each chapter should help you plan your itinerary. We start most **town accounts** with information on arrival and accommodation, followed by a tour of the sights, and finally reviews of places to eat and drink, and details of nightlife. Longer accounts also have a directory of practical listings.

index + small print

Apart from a **full index**, which includes maps as well as places, this section covers publishing information, credits and acknowledgements, and also has our contact details in case you want to send in updates and corrections to the book – or suggestions as to how we might improve it.

Map and chapter list

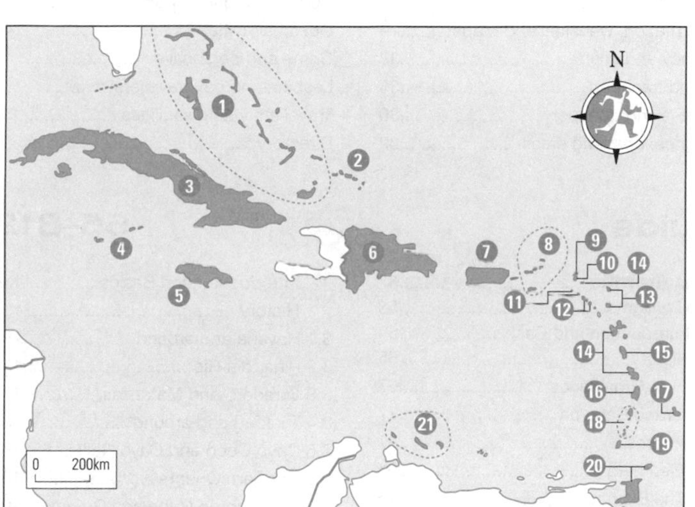

contents

colour section i–xxiv

basics 9–54

guide 55–812

index and small print 813–826

map symbols

maps are listed in the full index using coloured text

International boundary
Provincial boundary
Chapter division boundary
Motorway
Major paved road
Minor paved road
Unpaved road
Tunnel
Footpath
Railway
Ferry routes
Waterway
Wall
Church (regional maps)
Synagogue
Marshland
Waterfall
Springs
Mountains
Mountain peak
Viewpoint
Crater
Cave
Ruins
Fortress
Monument
Museum
Stately home
Reef
Diving site
Shipwreck
Turtle nesting site
Lighthouse
Windmill
Golf course
Gardens
Petrol station
Airfield
Airport
Accommodation
Restaurant/café
Campsite
Information office
Post office
Telephone
Hospital
Building
Church (town maps)
Park
Forest
Beach
Salt pond

Basics

Basics

Getting there

Given the ocean-bound nature of the Caribbean, for many visitors flying is the only viable option. Flights to the Caribbean tend to operate through a major US East Coast hub: Miami, or New York, though San Juan, Puerto Rico, is also well connected. Similarly, most cruises to the region depart from the US East Coast, making a flight to the US an inevitable part of the itinerary.

Airfares always depend on the **season**. In the Caribbean, high season is from mid-December to April, with fares peaking during the holiday season. Fares drop during the "**shoulder**" seasons – May to July – and you'll get the best prices during the low, wet season, August to November. Of course, prices vary wildly depending on your destination and it is inevitably much cheaper to vacation in countries hosting the transit hubs of major airlines, such as Puerto Rico, Jamaica, Trinidad and Barbados. Note also that flying on weekends is more expensive; price ranges quoted below assume mid-week travel.

You can often cut costs by going through a **specialist flight agent** – either a **consolidator**, who buys up blocks of tickets from the airlines and sells them at a discount, or a **discount agent**, who in addition to dealing with discounted flights may also offer special student and youth fares and a range of other travel-related services such as travel insurance, rail passes, car rentals, tours and the like. Some agents specialize in **charter flights**, which may be cheaper than any available scheduled flight, but departure dates are fixed and withdrawal penalties are high. Booking flights well in advance, or taking advantage of web-only offers and airline frequent-flyer programmes, can often knock a couple of hundred dollars off the price of your flight. Another way to vastly reduce the price of your Caribbean holiday – especially if you book last-minute, accept charter flights and don't insist upon particular accommodation – is to book with a tour operator who can put together a package deal including flights and accommodation at an especially arranged price, and perhaps tours of the island or even a wedding ceremony as well.

If you intend to take in the Caribbean as part of a world trip, a **round-the-world ticket (RTW)** offers the greatest flexibility. Many international airlines are now aligned with one of two globe-spanning networks: the "Star Alliance", which includes Air New Zealand, Lufthansa, SAS, Singapore Airlines, Thai, Varig and Air Canada; and "One World", which combines routes run by American, British Airways, Cathay Pacific, LanChile and Qantas, among others. Both networks offer RTW deals requiring a minimum number of stopovers. Fares depend on your point of origin, the class you fly in and the number of continents or the distance you travel. For details on inter-island transport, see p.36.

Booking flights online

Many airlines and discount travel **websites** offer you the opportunity to book your tickets online, cutting out the costs of agents and middlemen. Good deals can often be found through discount or auction sites, as well as through the airlines' own websites.

Useful websites

Ⓦ **http://travel.yahoo.com** Incorporates a lot of Rough Guide material in its coverage of destination countries and cities across the world, with information about places to eat, sleep and so forth.
Ⓦ **www.cheapflights.com** Bookings from the UK and Ireland only. Flight deals, travel agents, plus links to other travel sites.
Ⓦ **www.cheaptickets.com** Discount flight specialists.
Ⓦ **www.expedia.com** Discount airfares, all-airline search engine and daily deals.
Ⓦ **www.flyaow.com** Online air travel info and reservations site.
Ⓦ **www.gaytravel.com** Gay online travel agent,

concentrating mostly on accommodation but with cruises and flight offers too.

Ⓦ **www.hotwire.com** Bookings from the US only. Last-minute savings of up to forty percent on regular published fares. Travellers must be at least 18 and there are no refunds, transfers or changes allowed. Log-in required.

Ⓦ **www.lastminute.com** Bookings from the UK only. Offers good last-minute holiday package and flight-only deals.

Ⓦ **www.priceline.com** Name-your-own-price website that has deals at around forty percent off standard fares. You cannot specify flight times (although you do specify dates) and the tickets are non-refundable, non-transferable and non-changeable.

Ⓦ **www.skyauction.com** Bookings from the US only. Auction tickets and travel packages using a "second bid" scheme. The best strategy is to bid the maximum you're willing to pay, since if you win you'll pay just enough to beat the runner-up regardless of your maximum bid.

Ⓦ **www.travelocity.com** Destination guides, hot web fares and best deals for car rental, accommodation and lodging as well as fares. Provides access to the travel agent system SABRE, the most comprehensive central reservations system in the US.

Ⓦ **www.travelshop.com.au** Australian website offering discounted flights, packages, insurance and online bookings.

Flights from the US and Canada

Most American airlines operate their Caribbean **flights** from the East Coast of the US and from Toronto, except for American Airlines, which flies from most major US cities to their Caribbean hub in San Juan. Additional direct flights include a US Airways Saturday service to St Lucia from Philadelphia and Northwest's once-weekly summer service from Detroit to San Juan and Montego Bay; in Canada you can fly direct from Toronto to Grand Cayman, Barbados, Antigua and San Juan. Flights from New York average around five hours, from Miami three hours and from Toronto five hours.

Airfares **peak** around Christmas and New Year, when they can reach US$900–1000/CAN$1380–1535 from the East Coast of the US and Toronto, and from January to April when you can expect to pay up to US$800/CAN$1230, more for some flights from Canada – but for which you'll get the best weather. Amounts drop during **shoulder season** when you'll pay around US$700/CAN$1125, and the best prices are available during the (wet) **low season**, from August to November – you should be able to get a regular fare for around US$650/CAN$1000. Count on paying an extra US$300 or so to fly from the West Coast of the US. Note also that flying on weekends ordinarily adds at least US$50 to the round-trip fare.

Package tours can often be the most economical option and range from combined flight and accommodation deals to specialist tours. For details on scuba-diving tours see p.48.

Airlines

Unless otherwise specified all phone numbers work in both the US and Canada.

Aces Airlines Ⓣ1-800/846-2237, Ⓦwww.acescolombia.com

Aeroflot US Ⓣ1-888/340-6400, Canada Ⓣ416/642-1653, Ⓦwww.aeroflot.com

Aeromexico Ⓣ1-800/237-6639 or 713/939 0077, Ⓦwww.aeromexico.com

Air Canada Ⓣ1-888/247-2262, Ⓦwww.aircanada.ca

Air Jamaica US Ⓣ1-800/523-5585, Canada Ⓣ416/229-6024, Ⓦwww.airjamaica.com

Air Sunshine US Ⓣ1-800/327-8900, Ⓦwww.airsunshine.com

AirTran Airways Ⓣ770/994-8258, Ⓦwww.airtran.com

American Airlines Ⓣ1-800/433-7300, Ⓦwww.aa.com

American Trans Air Ⓣ1-800/225-2995, Ⓦwww.ata.com

Bahamas Air US Ⓣ1-800/222-4262 or 305/526-2001, Ⓦwww.bahamasair.com

BWIA International Ⓣ1-800/538-2942, Ⓦwww.bwee.com

Cayman Airways Ⓣ1-800/GCAYMAN or 345/949-2311, Ⓦwww.caymanairways.com

Chalk's Ocean Airways US Ⓣ1-800/4CHALKS, Ⓦwww.chalksoceanairways.com

Continental Airlines domestic Ⓣ1-800/525-0280, international Ⓣ1-800/231-0856, Ⓦwww.continental.com

Delta Air Lines domestic Ⓣ1-800/221-1212, international Ⓣ1-800/241-4141, Ⓦwww.delta.com

Gulfstream International Airlines Ⓣ954/226-3000

or 1-800/231-0856, Ⓦwww.gulfstreamair.com
Iberia Ⓣ1-800/772-4642, Ⓦwww.iberia.com
JetBlue Ⓣ1-800/538-2583, Ⓦwww.jetblue.com
Lacsa Costa Rica Ⓣ1-800/225-2272, Ⓦwww.taca.com
LanChile US Ⓣ1-800/735-5526, Canada Ⓣ416/862-0807, Ⓦwww.lanchile.com
Lynx Air International US Ⓣ1-888/596-9247 or 954/772-9808, Ⓦwww.lynxair.com
Mexicana Ⓣ1-800/531-7921, Ⓦwww.mexicana.com
North American Airlines Ⓣ718/656-6250, Ⓦwww.northamair.com
Northwest/KLM Airlines domestic Ⓣ1-800/225-2525, international Ⓣ1-800/447-4747, Ⓦwww.nwa.com
Pan American Airways Ⓣ1-800/FLY-PANAM, Ⓦwww.FlyPanAm.com
Spirit Airlines Ⓣ1-800/772-7117, Ⓦwww.spiritair.com
Suriname Airways Ⓣ1-800/432-1230 or 305/599-1196, Ⓦwww.slm.firm.sr
Taca International Airlines US Ⓣ1-800/535-8780, Canada Ⓣ416/968-2222, Ⓦwww.taca.com
United Airlines domestic Ⓣ1-800/241-6522, international Ⓣ1-800/538-2929, Ⓦwww.ual.com
Universal Airlines Ⓣ718/441-4900, Ⓦwww.universalguyana.com
US Airways domestic Ⓣ1-800/428-4322, international Ⓣ1-800/622-1015, Ⓦwww.usairways.com

Charter flight operators

Air Transat Ⓣ1-800/470-1011, Ⓦwww.airtransat.com. Charter flights from Toronto, Montreal, Calgary and Vancouver to various Caribbean locations.
BelAir Transport Ⓣ954/524-9814. Flies from Fort Lauderdale to the Bahamas.
Bimini Island Air Ⓣ954/938-8991, Ⓦwww.flybia.com. Charters from Fort Lauderdale to the Bahamas.

Travel agents

Airtech Ⓣ212/219-7000, Ⓦwww.airtech.com. Standby seat broker with space-available Caribbean fares.
Goway Travel Ⓣ416/322-1034 or 1-800/387-8850, Ⓦwww.goway.com. Full-service travel agency with comprehensive website.
Skylink US Ⓣ212/573-8980 or 1-800/247-6659, Canada Ⓣ1-800/759-5465, Ⓦwww.skylinkus.com. Consolidator.
STA Travel Ⓣ1-800/777-0112 or 781-4040, Ⓦwww.sta-travel.com. Worldwide specialists in independent travel; also student IDs, travel insurance, car rental and so on.
TFI Tours International Ⓣ212/736-1140 or 1-800/745-8000, Ⓦwww.lowestairprice.com. Consolidator.
Travao Ⓣ1-800/872-8800, Ⓦwww.thetravelsite.com. Consolidator and charter broker with offices in New York City and Orlando.
Travel Avenue Ⓣ1-800/333-3335, Ⓦwww.travelavenue.com. Full-service travel agent that offers discounts in the form of rebates.
Travel Cuts Ⓣ1-800/667-2887, US Ⓣ1-866/246-9762, Ⓦwww.travelcuts.com. Canadian student-travel organization.
Worldtek Travel Ⓣ1-800/243-1723, Ⓦwww.worldtek.com. Discount travel agency for worldwide travel.

Specialist tour operators

Adventures Abroad Ⓣ604/303-1099 or 1-800/665-3998, Ⓦwww.adventures-abroad.com. Adventure specialists.
Ambiance Vacations Ⓣ1-800/861-1109, Ⓦwww.ambiancevacations.com. Good-value operator using scheduled flights and with properties on most islands.
AmeriCan Adventures Ⓣ1-800/873-5872, Ⓦwww.americanadventuress.com. Budget adventure tours.
American Express Vacations Ⓣ1-800/241-1700, Ⓦwww.americanexpress.com/travel. Luxury vacations.
Caribbean Concepts Ⓣ206/575-0907 or 1-800/777-0977, Ⓦwww.caribbeanconcepts.com. Tour company with properties all over the islands but specializing in Anguilla.
Caribbean Journey Ⓣ602/820-7119 or 1-888/343-2101, Ⓦwww.caribbeanjourney.com. Personalized tours to most Caribbean islands.
Delta Certified Vacations Ⓣ1-800/654-6559, Ⓦwww.deltavacations.com. Vacations from most major US cities.
Ecosummer Expeditions Ⓣ1-800/465-8884 or 250/674-0102, Ⓦwww.ecosummer.com. Sea kayaking trips in the Bahamian Exumas.
Global Exchange Ⓣ415/225-7296, Ⓦwww.globalexchange.org. Cultural and eco-tours to Cuba.
Leisure Time Travel Ⓣ352/795-3474 or 1-800/771-2202, Ⓦwww.leisuretimetravel.com. Tour operator specializing in fly fishing and light tackle vacations to the Bahamas, Cayman Islands and Costa Rica.
Maupintour Ⓣ1-800/255-4266,

Ⓦwww.maupintour.com. Luxury tours including independent golf packages.
Suntrek Ⓣ1-800/SUN-TREK, Ⓦwww.suntrek.com. Small group tours including trek and cruise options.
TourScan Inc Ⓣ203/655-8091 or 1-800/962 2080, Ⓕ203/655-6689, Ⓦwww.tourscan.com. This Caribbean specialist scans over 200 brochures containing 10,000 Caribbean holidays and publishes the best-value options in their US$4 catalogues.
Tradewind Tours Ⓣ320/573-5501 or 1-800/860-8013, Ⓦwww.tradewindtours.net. A small, specialist travel agency focusing only on St Lucia and Barbados, and offering in-depth local knowledge as well as skilled and personal service.

Cruises from the US

Cruises are a popular way to visit multiple islands in a very short time – trips can last anywhere from a few days up to a week or more and ships usually stop for a day at each port. Plenty of corporate cruise lines ply the Caribbean, offering all-inclusive cruises that can scale the heights of luxury (and costs) but can also be relatively affordable: a seven-day spin on a not-so-swanky ship in the region could set you back just US$700–900. One drawback of choosing a cruise is that you only get to visit the tourist ports, making it difficult to know what the island is like in anything more than a superficial sense. Cruises can, however, be more reasonably priced than their package tour counterparts – prices for cruises from Florida for seven nights range from US$600 for the Western Caribbean, US$700 for the Eastern region and slightly more for the southern islands.

The internet is a good place to start your research. **Websites** such as Ⓦwww.cruise.com and Ⓦwww.cruisereviews.com are helpful resources for deciding which cruise is best for you, taking into account price range, size of boat and length of trip. Travelocity .com (Ⓦwww.travelocity.com) also provides useful reviews of the major cruise companies. While some companies offer cruises only, there are still many others that negotiate rates with major airlines allowing for fly/cruise options from most major airports in the US and the rest of the world.

Cruise lines

The fares quoted are for single person/double occupancy "inside" (no ocean views) cabins, outside of the high season (when prices can jump by US$300–500) and are exclusive of port charges, which add an extra US$200 or so.
Carnival Cruiselines Ⓣ1-888/CARNIVAL, Ⓦwww.carnival.com. A youthful cruise line with a big emphasis on fun, offering seven nights from Miami, Orlando or Fort Lauderdale from US$599.
Disney Cruise Line Ⓣ1-800/951-3532, Ⓦwww.disneycruise.disney.go.com/. Seven nights from Key West from US$829, including a trip to Disney's own Bahamian island.
Holland America Ⓣ1-877/932-4259, Ⓦwww.hollandamerica.com. Family cruise line, with hefty scheduled entertainment for both adults and kids. Weeklong cruises from Fort Lauderdale from around US$700.
Princess Cruises & Royal Caribbean Ⓣ1-800/PRINCESS, Ⓦwww.princesscruises.com. Seven-day luxury cruises (including spas and scuba diving) from Florida for upwards of US$649.
Radisson Seven Seas Ⓣ1-877/505-5370, Ⓦwww.rssc.com. Fifteen-day cruises from Florida to LA via the Caribbean and South America, starting at US$5471 for two people.
Regal Cruises Ⓣ1-800/270-7245, Ⓦwww.regalcruises.com. A rare opportunity to cruise straight from New York to the Bahamas for upwards of US$669.
Silversea Ⓣ1-800/722-9955, Ⓦwww.silversea.com. Top-notch cruises and fly/cruise options from all over the world – all-inclusive packages start at around US$4100.
Windstar Cruises Ⓣ1-800/258-7245, Ⓦwww.windstarcruises.com. Luxury sailing ship cruises to the Virgin Islands, the French Antilles and the West Indies from US$3850.

Cruise travel agents

Accent on Cruising Ⓣ972/661-5151 or 1-800/317-3157, Ⓦwww.accentoncruising.com. Agents for Radisson, Royal Caribbean. Celebrity, Princess and Silversea.
Adventure Travels Ⓣ1-800/327-8967, Ⓦwww.preferr.com. Agents for Carnival, Celebrity, Holland America, Princess, Radisson, Windstar, Royal Caribbean and Silversea.
Cruise Discounters Ⓣ1-800/268-0854, Ⓦwww.cruisediscounters.com. Discount agent for most major cruise lines.

Flights from the UK and Ireland

The majority of British and Irish visitors to many Caribbean islands, such as Barbados, Jamaica and Trinidad and Tobago, are on some form of **package tour**. This is usually the simplest way of going about things, and even if you plan to travel independently and organize your own accommodation, a seat on a charter can be the cheapest way to reach your destination. But charters do have their drawbacks, especially if your plans don't fit exactly into their usual two-week straitjacket. As an alternative, several airlines fly **direct** scheduled flights from London to many Caribbean destinations, and you can find comparable fares with other carriers that require a stopover in the US. For former Dutch colonies like Aruba, Bonaire, Curaçao, Saba, St Eustatius and St Maarten, try KLM via Amsterdam for £580–700, or for Guadeloupe and Martinique – both former colonies of France – you can fly from London with Air France via Paris for £400–700, depending on the time of year.

There are no direct flights from Ireland to a number of islands, including Antigua and Barbados, but there are good connections via London or via New York or Miami (see "Flights from the US and Canada", p.12).

Many islands in the Caribbean are popular **package tour** destinations, and as such there are legions of operators to choose from. If you're planning to do little more than stay in one place and soak in the sun, then a package holiday might be your best option. There are many specialist companies that can arrange flights as well as accommodation ranging from self-catering apartments to all-inclusive hotels (meals and drinks are included in the room price). Many operators offer specialized tours geared toward a wide range of interests: from couples wishing to get married in the Caribbean to diving enthusiasts and spa-seekers.

Airlines

Unless otherwise specified all phone numbers work within the UK only.

Air France UK ⓣ0845/0845 111, Republic of Ireland ⓣ01/605 0383, ⓦwww.airfrance.co.uk, ⓦwww.airfrance.ie
Air Lib ⓣ0825/805 805, ⓦwww.air-liberte.fr
British Airways UK ⓣ0845/77 333 77, Republic of Ireland ⓣ1800/626 747, ⓦwww.britishairways.com
BWIA International ⓣ020/8577 1100, ⓦwww.bwee.com
Caribbean Star Airlines ⓣ020/8571 7533, ⓦwww.flycaribbeanstar.com
Continental UK ⓣ0800/776 464, Republic of Ireland ⓣ1890/925 252, ⓦwww.flycontinental.com
Cubana ⓣ020/7734 1165, ⓦwww.cubana.cu/ingles/index.html
Delta UK ⓣ0800/414767, Republic of Ireland ⓣ1800/768 080 or 01/407 3165, ⓦwww.delta.com
Dutch Caribbean Express Aruba ⓣ297/883 8030, ⓦwww.flydca.net
Iberia Airlines UK ⓣ0845/5601 2854, Republic of Ireland ⓣ01/407 3017, ⓦwww.iberiaairlines.co.uk
KLM UK ⓣ08705/074 074, Republic of Ireland ⓣ353/212 4331, ⓦwww.klmuk.com
Lufthansa UK ⓣ0845/7737 747, Republic of Ireland ⓣ01/844 5544, ⓦwww.lufthansa.com
United Airlines UK ⓣ0845/8444 777, ⓦwww.ual.com
Virgin Atlantic Airways UK ⓣ01293/747 747, ⓦwww.virgin-atlantic.com

Charter flight operators

Air 2000 ⓣ0870/240 1402, ⓦwww.air2000.com. Charter airline affiliated with First Choice and Unijet, but bookable by independent travellers also.
Britannia Airways UK ⓣ0870/607 6757, ⓦwww.britanniaairways.com. Charter airline operating with Lunn Poly and Thomas Cook.
Monarch Airlines ⓣ01582/400 000, ⓦwww.flycrown.com. Charter flights to Grenada and Tobago.

Travel agents

Apex Travel Dublin ⓣ01/241 8000, ⓦwww.apextravel.ie. Specialists in flights to Australia, Africa, the Far East, US and Canada.
Aran Travel International Galway ⓣ091/562 595, ⓦwww.iol.ie/~arantvl/aranmain.htm. Good-value flights to all parts of the world.
CIE Tours International Dublin ⓣ01/703 1888, ⓦwww.cietours.ie. General flight and tour agent.
ebookers ⓣ01/241 5689, ⓦwww.ebookers.com. Ireland-based online booking agency that trawls all

major airlines for the best fares.
Flightbookers ⓣ0870/010 7000, ⓦwww.ebookers.com. Low fares on an extensive selection of scheduled flights.
Go Holidays Dublin ⓣ01/874 4126, ⓦwww.goholidays.ie. Package tour specialists.
Joe Walsh Tours Dublin ⓣ01/872 2555 or 676 3053, Cork ⓣ021/427 7959, ⓦwww.joewalshtours.ie. General budget fares agent.
Lee Travel Cork ⓣ021/277 111, ⓦwww.leetravel.ie. Flights and holidays worldwide.
McCarthy's Travel Cork ⓣ021/427 0127, ⓦwww.mccarthystravel.ie. General flight agent.
North South Travel UK ⓣ & ⓕ01245/608 291, ⓦwww.northsouthtravel.co.uk. Friendly, competitive travel agency, offering discounted fares worldwide – profits are used to support projects in the developing world, especially the promotion of sustainable tourism.
Premier Travel Derry ⓣ028/7126 3333, ⓦwww.premiertravel.uk.com. Discount flight specialists.
Rosetta Travel Belfast ⓣ028/9064 4996, ⓦwww.rosettatravel.com. Flight and holiday agent.
STA Travel UK ⓣ0870/160 0599, ⓦwww.statravel.co.uk. Low-cost flights and tours for students and under-26s, though other customers welcome.
Trailfinders UK ⓣ020/7628 7628, ⓦwww.trailfinders.co.uk, Republic of Ireland ⓣ01/677 7888, ⓦwww.trailfinders.ie. One of the best-informed and most efficient agents for independent travellers.
Travel Cuts UK ⓣ020/7255 2082, ⓦwww.travelcuts.co.uk. Canadian company specializing in budget, student and youth travel, and round-the-world tickets.

Specialist tour operators

British Airways Holidays ⓣ0870/242 4245, ⓦwww.baholidays.co.uk. Using British Airways and other quality international airlines, offers an exhaustive range of package and tailor-made holidays.
Caribbean Chapters ⓣ020/7722 0722, ⓦwww.villa-rentals.com. Villa rental specialist that will organize holidays that take in two different islands or towns.
Caribbean Expressions ⓣ020/7431 2131, ⓦwww.expressionsholidays.co.uk. Specializing in hotel holidays to most Caribbean islands, including diving packages to St Lucia, Tobago and the Cayman Islands, and yacht charters (from £3000 for two) in the Virgin Islands.
Caribtours ⓣ020/7751 0660, ⓦwww.caribtours.co.uk. Long-established operator offering tailor-made breaks – including trips designed for families, spa-seekers, island hoppers and honeymooners – using scheduled flights to the Caribbean.
Complete Caribbean ⓣ01423/531031, ⓦwww.completecaribbean.co.uk. Tailor-made holidays on most islands for families, couples, adventureseekers, with accommodation in villas and hotels.
Discover the World UK ⓣ01737/218 803, ⓦwww.discover-the-bahamas.co.uk. Well-established operator specializing in the Bahamas.
Hayes & Jarvis UK ⓣ0870/898 9890, ⓦwww.hayes-jarvis.com. Specialists in long-haul holidays, particularly with diving destinations. Exotic weddings organized.
Journey Latin America UK ⓣ020/8747 8315, ⓦwww.journeylatinamerica.co.uk. Specialists in flights, packages and tailor-made trips all over the Caribbean.
Just Grenada ⓣ01373/814214, ⓦwww.justgrenada.co.uk. The only company focusing exclusively on holidays in Grenada, with knowledgeable staff who have stayed at most properties and know the area well.
Kuoni Travel UK ⓣ01306/742 888, ⓦwww.kuoni.co.uk. Flexible package holidays with extensive presence in the Caribbean and good family offers.
Thomas Cook UK ⓣ0870/566 6222, ⓦwww.thomascook.co.uk. Long-established one-stop 24-hour travel agency for package holidays or scheduled flights.
Trips Worldwide ⓣ0117/311 4400, ⓦwww.tripsworldwide.co.uk. Tailor-made holidays to the "alternative Caribbean" include rainforests, culture, birdwatching and plenty of activities. Website lets you create your own itinerary.
Tropic Breeze ⓣ01752/880977, ⓦwww.tropicbreeze.co.uk. Vacations ashore and afloat in St Kitts and Nevis, Antigua, Grenada, the Grenadines and the British Virgin Islands. Two-week yacht charters from £900 per person, including flight, in the low season, to £1500 per person at peak times.

Cruises from the UK and Ireland

Cruises aren't as good value an option from outside of the US, as you will have to fly state-side before getting on a boat, but there are several cruise operators that work with major airlines to give you an all-in package deal.
Celebrity Cruises UK ⓣ0800/018 2525, US ⓣ1-800/722-5941, ⓦwww.celebritycruises.com.

Cruises with an emphasis on high-end pampering, including spas and art classes. Seven nights from Fort Lauderdale, Baltimore or San Juan from £429 (cruise only).

Fred Olsen Cruises UK ⓣ01473/742424, ⓦwww.fredolsencaribbean.co.uk. An extensive range of Caribbean cruises; 14 nights from £1950, including a flight from London or Manchester.

Royal Caribbean International ⓦwww.royalcaribbeaninternational.com. A rich variety of cruises throughout the Caribbean – seven nights from £429 – with additional flight options from throughout the UK and Ireland.

Flights from Australia and New Zealand

There are no direct flights from Australasia to the Caribbean, and the best option for travellers is to fly to the US, the UK or the Netherlands – all of which have interests in the Caribbean – in order to avail themselves of the best possible selection of routes and fares. The most straightforward **routes** involve flying to the US – usually the West Coast or Canada – and then transferring to an East Coast hub such as Miami, or to the American Airlines hub in San Juan, for onward transportation to the Caribbean islands. Fares tend not to vary much year-round, so expect to pay up to A$250 0/NZ$2940 and A$3000/NZ$3530 from Sydney, more at Christmas and New Year; add around A$500/NZ$590 to fly from Darwin or Perth. A viable alternative, if you have the time, is to buy a **Round-the-world ticket (RTW)** – though a sample itinerary leaving from Sydney and stopping in the US, Venezuela, Trinidad, Jamaica, England, Greece and Thailand before returning to Sydney could set you back around A$6000/NZ$7055. For RTW travel specialists, see under "Specialist agents" overleaf .

Cruising from Australia is not really an option, and travellers wishing to sail the Caribbean will have to book with a specialist travel agent in their home country and fly to meet the cruise ship, usually to Florida. Prices for a fifteen-day cruise start at around A$1800/NZ$2100, including one night in Miami but excluding flights. For cruise travel specialists, see "Specialist agents" overleaf.

Airlines

Air Canada Australia ⓣ1300/655 767 or 02/9286 8900, New Zealand ⓣ09/379 3371, ⓦwww.aircanada.ca

Air France Australia ⓣ1300/361 400 or 02/9244 2100, ⓦwww.airfrance.com

Air New Zealand Australia ⓣ13 24 76, New Zealand ⓣ0800/737 000, ⓦwww.airnz.com

Air Pacific Australia ⓣ1800/230 150, New Zealand ⓣ0800/800 178, ⓦwww.airpacific.com

Alitalia Australia ⓣ1300/0361 400, ⓦwww.alitalia.com

America West Airlines Australia ⓣ02/9290 2611 or 1300/364 757, New Zealand ⓣ0800/866 000, ⓦwww.americawest.com

American Airlines Australia ⓣ1300/650 747, New Zealand ⓣ09/309 0735 or 0800/887 997, ⓦwww.aa.com

British Airways Australia ⓣ02/8904 8800, New Zealand ⓣ09/356 8690, ⓦwww.britishairways.com

BWIA International Australia ⓣ02/9285 6811, ⓦwww.bwee.com

Cathay Pacific Australia ⓣ13 17 47, New Zealand ⓣ09/379 0861 or 0508/800 454, ⓦwww.cathaypacific.com

Continental Airlines Australia ⓣ02/9244 2242, New Zealand ⓣ09/308 3350, ⓦwww.flycontinental.com

Delta Air Lines Australia ⓣ02/9251 3211, New Zealand ⓣ09/379 3370, ⓦwww.delta-air.com

Finnair Australia ⓣ02/9244 2299, New Zealand ⓣ09/308 3365, ⓦwww.finnair.com

KLM Australia ⓣ1300/303 747, New Zealand ⓣ09/309 1782, ⓦwww.klm.com

LanChile Airlines Australia ⓣ1300/361 400, New Zealand ⓣ09/309 8673, ⓦwww.lanchile.com

Lauda Air Australia ⓣ02/9251 6155, New Zealand ⓣ09/308 3368, ⓦwww.laudaair.com

Lufthansa Australia ⓣ1300/655 727 or 02/9367 3887, New Zealand ⓣ09/303 1529 or 008/945 220, ⓦwww.lufthansa.com

Northwest Airlines Australia ⓣ1300/303 747, New Zealand ⓣ09/302 1452, ⓦwww.nwa.com

Qantas Australia ⓣ13 13 13, New Zealand ⓣ09/357 8900, ⓦwww.qantas.com.au

TAP Air Portugal Australia ⓣ02/9244 2344, New Zealand ⓣ09/308 3373, ⓦwww.tap-airportugal.pt

United Airlines Australia ⓣ13 17 77, New Zealand ⓣ09/379 3800 or 0800/508 648, ⓦwww.ual.com

Varig Brazilian Australia ⓣ02/9244 2179, New Zealand ⓣ09/308 3375

Virgin Atlantic Airways Australia ⓣ02/9244

2747, New Zealand ⓣ09/308 3377, ⓦwww.virgin-atlantic.com

Travel agents

Anywhere Travel Australia ⓣ02/9663 0411 or 018/401 014, ⓔanywhere@ozemail.com.au. Worldwide fare discount agent offering personalized service.

Destinations Unlimited New Zealand ⓣ09/373 4033, ⓦwww.etravelnz.com. Cruises, packages, flight deals and more.

Flight Centres Australia ⓣ02/9235 3522 or 13 16 00, New Zealand ⓣ09/358 4310, ⓦwww.flightcentre.com.au. Long-established independent travel agent that books everything from cheap flights to cruise ship specials.

Thomas Cook Australia ⓣ13 17 71 or 1800/801 002, ⓦwww.thomascook.com.au; New Zealand ⓣ09/379 3920, ⓦwww.thomascook.co.nz. Covering everything from package tours to travel cash, flight-only tickets and RTW deals.

Trailfinders Australia ⓣ02/9247 7666, ⓦwww.trailfinders.com.au. Discount flights, car rental, tailor-made tours, rail passes and RTW tours, especially for the independent traveller.

Specialist agents

Adventure World Australia ⓣ02/9956 7766 or 1300/363 055, ⓦwww.adventureworld.com.au; New Zealand ⓣ09/524 5118, ⓦwww.adventureworld.co.nz. Agents for a vast array of international adventure travel companies, including some that organize cruises from Australasia to the Caribbean.

Caribbean Bound Australia ⓣ02/9267 2555, ⓦwww.caribbean.com.au. Agents covering most major Caribbean islands.

Caribbean Destinations Australia ⓣ03/9614 7144 or 1800/354 104, ⓦwww.caribbeanislands.com.au. Specializing in hotel accomodation throughout the Caribbean, as well as holidays geared towards festivals.

Contours Australia ⓣ03/9670 6900 or 1300/135 391, ⓦwww.contours.com.au. Tours and independent travel, concentrating on island stays and flights throughout the Caribbean.

Creative Cruising ⓦwww.creative-cruising.co.nz. NZ-based cruise holiday operator offering an array of fly/cruise packages that include hotel stays.

Cruiseworld ⓣ08/9322 2914, ⓦwww.flightworld.com.au. Agents for the American Express range of cruise holidays.

Harvey World Travel ⓣ02/9267 7866, ⓦwwww.harveyworld.com.au. Huge franchise operation with 340 branches in Australia that books Caribbean cruises and flights.

Silke's Travel Australia ⓣ1800/807 860 or 02/8347 2000, ⓦwww.silkes.com.au. Gay and lesbian specialist travel agent with cruises to the Caribbean.

STA Travel Australia ⓣ1300/360 960, ⓦwww.statravel.com.au, New Zealand ⓣ0508/782 872, ⓦwww.statravel.co.nz. Specialist agent for students and young people,, with great flight deals and knowledgeable staff.

Student Uni Travel Australia ⓣ02/9232 8444, ⓦwww.sut.com.au. Multi-destination tickets, cheap flights and more.

Red tape and visas

Island-specific advice about visas and entry requirements is covered at the beginning of each chapter, where necessary. As a broad guide, citizens of the US, Canada and Great Britain do not need a visa for stays of less than thirty days; however, nearly every country requires that your passport be valid for at least six months from your date of entry. Some demand proof of onward travel (such as an air ticket) or sufficient funds to buy a ticket. As all visa requirements, prices and processing times are subject to change, it's always worth double-checking with the embassies.

For **proof of identity**, most islands in the Caribbean have in the past required only a birth certificate as well as a driver's licence or one other form of government-issued photo ID. In the aftermath of September 2001, however, it is advisable to carry a passport and an onward/return ticket, regardless of whether or not they require a visa.

Caribbean embassies and consulates abroad

Anguilla

The UK handles consular responsibilities.
Australia British High Commission, Commonwealth Avenue, Yarralumla, ACT 2606 ⓣ02/6270 6666, ⓦwww.uk.emb.gov.au
Canada British High Commission, 80 Elgin St, Ottawa, ON K1P 5K7 ⓣ613/237-1542, ⓦwww.britain-in-canada.org
New Zealand British High Commission, 44 Hill St, Thorndon, Wellington ⓣ04/924 3888, ⓦwww.brithighcomm.org.nz
UK Foreign and Commonwealth Office, Old Admiralty Building, London SW1A 2PA ⓣ020/7008 0232 or 0233, ⓦwww.fco.gov.uk
US British Embassy, 3100 Massachusetts Ave, Washington DC 20008 ⓣ202/588-6500, ⓦwww.brit-info.org

Antigua and Barbuda

Australia handles consular responsibilities.
Canada Embassy of Antigua and Barbuda, 112 Kent St, Ottawa, ON K1P 5P2 ⓣ613/236-8952.
UK and Ireland Antigua and Barbuda Diplomatic Mission, 15 Thayer St, London W1U 3JT ⓣ020/7486 7073, 7074 or 7075, ⓕ020/7486 9970, ⓦwww.antigua-barbuda.com
US Embassy of Antigua and Barbuda, 3216 New Mexico Ave NW, Washington DC 20016, ⓣ202/362-5122, ⓕ202/362-5225.

Aruba

The Netherlands handles consular responsibilities.
Australia Consulate General of the Netherlands, 120 Empire Circuit, Yarralumla, ACT 2600 ⓣ02/6273 3111, ⓦwww.netherlandsconsulate.org.au
Canada Royal Netherlands Embassy, Constitution Square Building, 350 Albert St, Suite 2020, Ottawa, ON K1R 1A4 ⓣ613/237-5030, ⓦwww.netherlandsembassy.ca.
Ireland Royal Netherlands Embassy, 160 Merrion Rd, Dublin 4 ⓣ01/269 3444, ⓦwww.netherlandsembassy.ie
New Zealand Royal Netherlands Embassy, PO Box 840, cnr Ballance and Fetherston St, Wellington ⓣ04/471 6390, ⓦwww.netherlandsembassy.co.nz
UK Netherlands Diplomatic Mission, 38 Hyde Park Gate, London SW7 5DP ⓣ020/7590 3200, ⓕ020/7225 0947, ⓦwww.netherlands-embassy.org.uk
US Consulate General of the Netherlands, 303 E Wacker Drive, Suite 2600,Washington DC 20008 ⓣ202/244-5300, ⓕ362-3400, ⓦwww.netherlands-embassy.org

Bahamas

Canada High Commission for the Commonwealth of the Bahamas, 50 O'Connor St, Suite 1313, Ottawa, ON K1P 6L2 ⓣ613/232-1724, ⓕ232-0097, ⓔottawa-mission@bahighco.com
UK and Ireland Bahamas High Commission, 10 Chesterfield St, London W1X 8AH ⓣ7408 4488.
US The Embassy of the Commonwealth of the Bahamas, 2220 Massachusetts Ave NW,

Washington DC 20008 ⓣ202/319-2660, ⓕ319-2668.

Barbados

Australia Consulate-General, 4 Warren Rd, Double Bay, NSW 2028 ⓣ02/9327 7009.
Canada High Commission for Barbados, 130 Albert St, Suite 1204, Ottawa, ON K1P 5G4 ⓣ03/236-9514, ⓕ230-4362.
UK and Ireland Barbados Diplomatic Mission, Great Russell St, London WC1B 3JY ⓣ020/7631 4975, ⓔ barcomuk@dial.pipex.com
US Barbados Embassy, 2144 Wyoming Ave NW, Washington DC 20008 ⓣ202/939-9200, ⓕ332-7467.

British Virgin Islands

The UK handles consular responsibilities.
Australia British High Commission, Commonwealth Avenue, Yarralumla, ACT 2606 ⓣ02/6270 6666, ⓦwww.uk.emb.gov.au
Canada British High Commission, 80 Elgin St, Ottawa, ON K1P 5K7 ⓣ613/237-1542, ⓦwww.britain-in-canada.org
Ireland British Embassy, 29 Merrion Rd, Ballsbridge, Dublin 4 ⓣ01/205 3822, ⓦwww.britishembassy.ie
New Zealand British High Commission, 44 Hill St, Thorndon, Wellington ⓣ04/924 3888, ⓦwww.brithighcomm.org.nz
UK Foreign and Commonwealth Office, Old Admiralty Building, London SW1A 2PA ⓣ020/7008 0232 or 0233, ⓦwww.fco.gov.uk
US British Embassy, 3100 Massachusetts Ave, Washington DC 20008 ⓣ202/588-6500, ⓦwww.brit-info.org

Cayman Islands

The UK handles consular responsibilities.
Australia British High Commission, Commonwealth Avenue, Yarralumla, ACT 2606, ⓣ02/6270 6666, ⓦwww.uk.emb.gov.au
Canada British High Commission, 80 Elgin St, Ottawa, ON K1P 5K7 ⓣ613/237-1542, ⓦwww.britain-in-canada.org
Ireland British Embassy, 29 Merrion Rd, Ballsbridge, Dublin 4 ⓣ01/205 3822, ⓦwww.britishembassy.ie
New Zealand British High Commission, 44 Hill St, Thorndon, Wellington ⓣ04/924 3888, ⓦwww.brithighcomm.org.nz
UK Foreign and Commonwealth Office, Old Admiralty Building, London SW1A 2PA ⓣ 020/7008 0232 or 0233, ⓦwww.fco.gov.uk
US British Embassy, 3100 Massachusetts Ave, Washington DC 20008 ⓣ202/588-6500, ⓦwww.brit-info.org

Cuba

Australia Consulate General of the Republic of Cuba, IPI House, Ground Floor, 128 Chalmers St, Surrey Hills, NSW 2010 ⓣ02/9698 9797, ⓕ8399 1106, ⓔconsulcu@optusnet.com.au
Canada Embassy of the Republic of Cuba, 388 Main St, Ottawa, ON K1S 1E3 ⓣ613/563-0141.
UK Embassy of the Republic of Cuba, 167 High Holborn, London WC1V 6PA ⓣ020/7240 2488, ⓕ7836 2602, ⓔembacuba.lnd@virgin.net
US Cuban Interests Section, 2630 16th St NW, Washington DC 20009 ⓣ202/797-8518, ⓕ986-7283.

Dominica

Australia handles consular responsibilities.
Australia Department of Foreign Affairs and Trade, R.G. Casey Building, John McEwen Crescent, Barton, ACT 0221 ⓣ02 6261 1111, ⓕ6261 3111, ⓦwww.dfat.gov.au
UK and Ireland Dominican High Commission, 1 Collingham Gardens, London SW5 0HW ⓣ020/7370 5194, ⓕ7373 8743, ⓦwww.dominica.co.uk
US Embassy of the Commonwealth of Dominica, 3216 New Mexico Ave NW, Washington DC 20016 ⓣ202/364-6781 or 6782, ⓕ364-6791, ⓔembdomdc@aol.com

Dominican Republic

Australia Consulate of the Dominican Republic, 343A Edgecliff Rd, Edgecliff, NSW 2027 ⓣ & ⓕ02/9363 5891.
Canada Embassy of the Dominican Republic, 2727 Steeles Ave West, Suite 301, Toronto, ON M3J 3G9 ⓣ416/739-1237.
UK and Ireland Embassy of the Dominican Republic, 139 Inverness Terrace, Bayswater, London W2 6JF ⓣ020/7727 6285, ⓕ7727 3693, ⓔgeneral@embajadadom-london.demon.co.uk
US Embassy of the Dominican Republic, 1715 22nd St NW, Washington DC 20008 ⓣ202/332-6280, ⓕ265-8057, ⓦwww.domrep.org

Grenada

Canada Consulate of Grenada, 439 University Ave, Suite 930, Toronto, ON M5G 1Y8 ⓣ416/595-1343, ⓔgrenadatour@sympatico.ca
UK and Ireland Grenada High Commission, 1

Collingham Gardens, London SW7 0HW ⓣ020/7373 7809, ⓕ7370 7040.
US Embassy of Grenada, 1701 New Hampshire Ave NW, Washington DC 20009 ⓣ265-2561.

Guadeloupe

France handles consular responsibilities.
Australia Embassy of France, 6 Perth Ave, Yarralumla, ACT 2600 ⓣ02/6216 0100, ⓦwww.france.net.au
Canada Embassy of France, 42 Promenade St, Sussex, Ottawa, ON K1M 2C9 ⓣ613/789-1795, ⓦwww.ambafrance-ca.org
Ireland Chancery, 36 Ailesbury Rd, Dublin 4 ⓣ01/260 1666.
New Zealand Embassy of France, 34-42 Manners St, Wellington ⓣ04/802 1590.
UK Embassy of France, 58 Knightsbridge, London SW1X 7JT ⓣ020/7201 1000, ⓕ7201 1004, ⓦwww.ambafrance.org.uk
US Embassy of France, 4101 Reservoir Rd NW, Washington DC 20007-2172 ⓣ202/944-6200 or 6187, ⓦwww.ambafrance-us.org

Jamaica

Canada Consulate-General of Jamaica, 214 King St West, Suite 402, Toronto, ON M5H 1K4 ⓣ416/598-3008, ⓕ598-4928.
UK and Ireland Jamaica High Commission, 1–2 Prince Consort Rd, London SW7 2BQ ⓣ020/7823 9911, ⓦwww.jhcuk.com
US Embassy of Jamaica, 1520 New Hampshire Avenue NW, Washington DC 20036 ⓣ202/452-0660, ⓕ452-0081, ⓦwww.emjam-usa.com

Martinique

France handles consular responsibilities.
Australia Embassy of France, 6 Perth Ave, Yarralumla, ACT 2600 ⓣ02/6216 0100, ⓦwww.france.net.au
Canada Embassy of France, 42 Promenade St, Sussex, Ottawa, ON K1M 2C9 ⓣ613/789-1795, ⓦwww.ambafrance-ca.org
Ireland Chancery, 36 Ailesbury Rd, Dublin 4 ⓣ01/260 1666.
New Zealand Embassy of France, 34-42 Manners St, Wellington ⓣ04/802 1590.
UK Embassy of France, 58 Knightsbridge, London SW1X 7JT ⓣ020/7201 1000, ⓕ7201 1004, ⓦwww.ambafrance.org.uk
US Embassy of France, 4101 Reservoir Rd NW, Washington DC 20007-2172 ⓣ202/944-6200 or 6187, ⓦwww.ambafrance-us.org

Puerto Rico

The US handles consular responsibilities.
Australia US Embassy, Canberra ⓣ02/6214 5819, ⓦwww.usis-australia.gv/embassy
Canada Embassy of the United States of America, 490 Sussex Drive, Ottawa, ON K1N 1G8 ⓣ613/238-5335, ⓕ688-3097, ⓦwww.usembassycanada.gov
Ireland US Embassy, 42 Elgin Rd, Ballsbridge, Dublin 4 ⓣ01/000 7122, ⓦwww.usembassy.ie
New Zealand US Embassy, 29 Fitzherbert Terrace, Thorndon, Wellington ⓣ04/462 6000, ⓦhttp://usembassy.org.nz
UK US Embassy, 24 Grosvenor St, London W1A 1AE ⓣ020/7499 9000, ⓦwww.usembassy.org.uk
US US Department of State, 2201 C Street NW, Washington DC 20520 ⓣ202/647-4000, ⓦwww.state.gov

Saba

Same as Anguilla (see p.19).

St Barts

France handles consular responsibilities.
Australia Embassy of France, 6 Perth Ave, Yarralumla, ACT 2600 ⓣ02/6216 0100, ⓦwww.france.net.au
Canada Embassy of France, 42 Promenade St, Sussex, Ottawa, ON K1M 2C9 ⓣ613/789-1795, ⓦwww.ambafrance-ca.org
Ireland Chancery, 36 Ailesbury Rd, Dublin 4 ⓣ01/260 1666.
New Zealand Embassy of France, 34-42 Manners St, Wellington ⓣ04/802 1590.
UK Embassy of France, 58 Knightsbridge, London SW1X 7JT ⓣ7201 1000, ⓕ7201 1004, ⓦwww.ambafrance.org.uk
US Embassy of France, 4101 Reservoir Rd NW, Washington DC 20007-2172 ⓣ202/944-6200 or 6187, ⓦwww.ambafrance-us.org

St Eustatius

Same as Anguilla (see p.19).

St Kitts And Nevis

Australia handles consular responsibilities.
Australia Australian Department of Foreign Affairs and Trade, R.G. Casey Building, John McEwen Crescent, Barton, ACT 0221 ⓣ02/6261 1111, ⓕ6261 3111, ⓦwww.dfat.gov.au

Canada Honorary Consulate of St Kitts and Nevis, 133 Richmond St West, Suite 311, Toronto, ON M5H 2L3 ⓣ416/368-6707.
UK and Ireland 10 Kensington Court, London W8 5DL ⓣ020/7937 9522.
US Embassy of St Kitts and Nevis, 3216 New Mexico Ave NW, Washington DC 20016 ⓣ202/686-2636, ⓕ686-5740, ⓦwww.stkittsnevis.org

St Lucia

Australia handles consular responsibilities.
Australia Australian Department of Foreign Affairs and Trade, R.G. Casey Building, John McEwen Crescent, Barton, ACT 0221 ⓣ02/6261 1111, ⓕ6261 3111, ⓦwww.dfat.gov.au
Canada 130 Albert St, Suite 700, Ottawa, ON K1P 5G4 ⓣ613/236-8952, ⓕ236-3042, ⓔechcc@travel-net.com
UK and Ireland 1 Collingham Gardens, London SW5 0HW ⓣ020/7370 7123, ⓕ7370 1905, ⓔhcslu@btconnect.com
US Embassy of St Lucia, 3216 New Mexico Ave NW, Washington DC 20016 ⓣ202/364-6792, ⓕ364-6723.

St Vincent And The Grenadines

Australia handles consular responsibilities.
Australia Australian Department of Foreign Affairs and Trade, R.G. Casey Building, John McEwen Crescent, Barton, ACT 0221 ⓣ02/6261 1111, ⓕ6261 3111, ⓦwww.dfat.gov.au
Canada Consulate of St Vincent and the Grenadines, 333 Wilson Ave, Suite 601, Toronto, ON M3H 1T2 ⓣ416/398-4277.
UK and Ireland St Vincent Diplomatic Mission, 10 Kensington Court, London W8 5DL ⓣ020/7937 9522, ⓔhighcommission.svg.uk@cwcom.net
US Embassy of St Vincent and the Grenadines, 3216 New Mexico Ave NW, Washington DC 20016 ⓣ202/364-6730, ⓕ364-6736.

Trinidad And Tobago

Australia Consulate-General of the Republic of Trinidad and Tobago, Unit 2, 72 New South Head Rd, Vaucluse, NSW 2030 ⓣ02/9337 4391, ⓕ9337 4564, ⓔconsgett@aol.com
New Zealand Honorary Consul of Trinidad and Tobago, Level 26, 151 Queen St, PO Box 105-042, Auckland ⓣ09/302 1860, ⓕ302 0923.
UK and Ireland Trinidad & Tobago High Commission, 42 Belgrave Square, London SW1X 8NT ⓣ020/7245 9351.
US Embassy of Trinidad and Tobago, 1708 Massachusetts Ave NW, Washington DC 20036 ⓣ202/467-6490, ⓕ785-3130.

Turks And Caicos

The UK handles consular responsibilities.
Australia British High Commission, Commonwealth Avenue, Yarralumla, ACT 2606 ⓣ02/6270 6666, ⓦwww.uk.emb.gov.au
Canada British High Commission, 80 Elgin St, Ottawa, ON K1P 5K7 ⓣ613/237-1542, ⓦwww.britain-in-canada.org
Ireland British Embassy, 29 Merrion Rd, Ballsbridge, Dublin 4 ⓣ01/205 3822, ⓦwww.britishembassy.ie
New Zealand British High Commission, 44 Hill St, Thorndon, Wellington ⓣ04/924 3888, ⓦwww.brithighcomm.org.nz
UK Foreign and Commonwealth Office, Old Admiralty Building, London SW1A 2PA ⓣ020/7008 0232 or 0233, ⓦwww.fco.gov.uk
US British Embassy, 3100 Massachusetts Ave, Washington DC 20008 ⓣ202/588-6500, ⓦwww.brit-info.org

US Virgin Islands

Australia US Embassy, Canberra ⓣ02/6214 5819, ⓦwww.usis-australia.gv/embassy
Canada Embassy of the United States of America, 490 Sussex Drive, Ottawa, ON K1N 1G8 ⓣ613/238-5335, ⓕ688-3097, ⓦwww.usembassycanada.gov
Ireland US Embassy, 42 Elgin Rd, Ballsbridge, Dublin 4 ⓣ01/668 7122, ⓦwww.usembassy.ie
New Zealand US Embassy, 29 Fitzherbert Terrace, Thorndon, Wellington ⓣ04/462 6000, ⓦhttp://usembassy.org.nz
UK US Embassy, 24 Grosvenor St, London W1A 1AE ⓣ020/7499 9000, ⓦwww.usembassy.org.uk
US US Department of State, 2201 C Street NW Washington DC 20520 ⓣ202/647-4000, ⓦwww.state.gov

Health

In general, travelling in the more developed areas of the Caribbean won't raise many health concerns. You can count on food being well and hygienically prepared, and tap water in hotels and restaurants that's safe to drink. The preventive measures you need to take elsewhere will depend on the areas you visit but some general advice is given below. Note, however, that the quality of medical care and facilities varies widely throughout the Caribbean. While it is excellent and readily available in places such as Aruba, the Bahamas, Barbados, Cayman Islands, Martinique and Guadeloupe, others – particularly in rural areas on islands like Jamaica and the Dominican Republic – may consist of only a small, poorly equipped clinic. In any event, it's a good idea to make sure that your medical insurance covers you abroad or else take out an insurance policy that includes medical coverage (see p.27 for more on insurance).

Inoculations

No specific inoculations are required to enter any of the Caribbean islands, unless you're arriving from a country where yellow fever is endemic, in which case you'll need a vaccination certificate. (Consult your doctor or a travel clinic for advice on specific shots.) Islands that require yellow fever inoculations include Antigua, Bahamas, Cayman Islands, Cuba, Grenada, Guadeloupe, Jamaica, St Kitts and Nevis, St Lucia, St Vincent, and Trinidad and Tobago.

It's also worth making sure that you're up to date with **polio, tetanus** and **typhoid** protection; the latter is particularly recommended for those planning to visit rural areas of Puerto Rico, Cuba, Dominica and the Dominican Republic. Inoculations against **hepatitis A and B** are also strongly advised.

Malaria and dengue fever

The Caribbean is not a malarial zone, but cases of **malaria** have been reported in the Dominican Republic, mainly along the Haitian border. While the risk to travellers is small, if you intend to travel in this area it's a good idea to take a course of prophylactics (usually chloroquine), available from a doctor or travel clinic.

There are slightly higher rates of **dengue fever**, another mosquito-borne illness whose symptoms resemble those of malaria but include extreme aches and pains in the bones and joints, along with fever and dizziness. The only cure for dengue fever is rest and painkillers, and like malaria the only precaution you can take is to avoid mosquito bites (for details, see p.24).

Stomach problems

The most common food-related illness for travellers is **diarrhoea**, possibly accompanied by vomiting or a mild fever. Its main cause is a change in diet whereby bacteria you're not used to are introduced into your system. In many cases, the condition will pass within a few days without treatment. In the meantime, rest up and replace the fluids you've lost by drinking plenty of water – or for persistent diarrhoea – an oral rehydration solution, readily available from your home pharmacy, should do the trick. Barring that, you can make a home-made solution by dissolving half a teaspoon of salt and eight teaspoons of sugar in a litre of boiling water. If symptoms last more than four or five days, or if you are too ill to drink, seek medical help immediately.

Travellers should note that dairy products aggravate diarrhoea and should be avoided.

Food and water

While stomach disorders aren't likely to be a big problem in the Caribbean, taking a few common-sense precautions will lessen the chances greatly. Steer clear of unpasteurized dairy products and unrefrigerated food, and wash and peel fresh fruit and vegetables. When buying street food, stick to obviously popular food vendors and restaurants, and wash your hands well before you eat.

Drink only bottled or boiled **water**, or carbonated drinks in cans or bottles. Avoid tap water, fountain drinks and ice cubes. If you are outside of cities and this is not possible, make water safer by both passing it through an "absolute 1-micron or less" filter as well as adding iodine tablets to the filtered water. Filters and tablets are available from travel clinics and good outdoor equipment stores.

Swimming or bathing in rivers and lakes has risks as well, particularly giardia, a bacterium that causes stomach upset, fever and diarrhoea, and **schistosomiasis**, a freshwater flatworm found in parts of Antigua, the Dominican Republic, Guadeloupe, Martinique, Puerto Rico and St Lucia that can penetrate unbroken skin; both are treatable with antibiotics. If you suspect that you have either of these, seek medical help.

Ciguatera

Ciguatera is a form of poisoning caused by eating infected reef fish, and sporadic outbreaks have been reported throughout the Caribbean. Symptoms include nausea, numbness, diarrhoea, abdominal pains, muscular weakness and vomiting, and can last up to two weeks. As infected fish are indistinguishable from healthy ones, the only way to reduce most of the risk is by avoiding commonly affected fish such as grouper, amberjack, snapper, and barracuda in particular. Travellers who suspect that they have ciguatera should seek immediate medical assistance.

Bites and stings

Bites and stings can lead to infection, so keep wounds clean and wash with antiseptic soap. Take steps to avoid insect bites by wearing a generous layer of bug spray during the day and remaining in well-screened areas at night; in cheaper hotels, use a mosquito net or, in an emergency, wear clothes that cover as much of your body as possible. You should also bring insect repellent (preferably containing DEET) and use it on exposed areas of skin at all times, though especially from dusk until dawn when malarial mosquitoes are active. **Sand flies**, often present on beaches at dusk, are tiny but possessed of a painful bite; they ignore most repellents but can typically be avoided if you use Avon Skin-So-Soft.

There are some **snakes** in the Caribbean, but very few are poisonous. One notable exception is the fer-de-lance, found on Martinique, St Lucia and Trinidad, and identifiable by its pointed head, yellow underside and chin, and orangish-brown triangular markings. Fortunately, most snakes will slither away before you know they are there. However, to be safe you should wear thick socks and boots when hiking through undergrowth or rainforest. If you do get **bitten**, note the snake's appearance, immobilize the bitten limb as much as possible and seek medical help immediately.

You're more likely to encounter the many **spiny black sea urchins** that inhabit reefs and bays; if you tread on one, remove as much of the spine as possible, douse the area in vinegar (or even urine) and see a doctor. Take care to avoid the purple **Portuguese man o' war**, a rare but toxic jellyfish whose trailing tendrils leave red welts. Similarly, never touch coral; you'll kill the organism on contact and come away with a painful, slow-healing rash. In both instances, washing with vinegar or iodine will help; again urine can be used if nothing else is available, and should pain persist consult a doctor. For stingray and stonefish stings, alleviate the pain by immersing the wound in very hot water – just under 50°C – while waiting for medical help.

Heat trouble

The Caribbean's position near the equator means that the sun's rays in the region are very strong – use a high-factor sunblock (SPF 15 or more) and apply it liberally at least every two hours and after swimming or exercise. Keep sun exposure to a minimum, especially between the hours of 11am and 4pm; wear a hat and a shirt, drink plenty of water and make sure children are well covered up.

Dizziness, headache and nausea are symptoms of **dehydration** and should be

Manchineel trees

Take care to avoid manchineel trees, which grow to around 12 metres tall and are recognizable by their small dark green leaves and tiny apple-like fruit. Both the fruit and its milky sap are poisonous. Don't touch any part of the tree and avoid taking shelter under its boughs in the rain: the sap will cause blisters if it drips on you. On the more popular beaches manchineel trees have notices nailed to their trunks warning visitors of the potential danger. However, caution is advised on quieter beaches where these trees are less likely to be identified.

treated by lying down in a shaded place and sipping water or other hydrating fluids. Should symptoms persist, or if you are suffering from hot, dry (but not sweaty) skin – potentially a sign of **heatstroke** – seek medical assistance immediately.

AIDS and HIV

The Caribbean has the highest regional prevalence of **AIDS and HIV** outside of sub-Saharan Africa. Haiti is the worst-afflicted area, with the Bahamas and the Dominican Republic close behind. With regard to sex, the same common-sense rule applies here as anywhere else; condomless sex is a serious health risk, and it's worth bringing **condoms** from home as those sold in some areas (ie Cuba, the Dominican Republic) are of poor quality.

Medical resources for travellers

Websites

Ⓦ **www.cdc.gov/travel/** US Department of Health and Human Services travel health and disease control department, listing precautions, diseases and preventive measures by region, as well as a summary of cruise ship sanitation levels.

Ⓦ **www.fitfortravel.scot.nhs.uk** UK NHS website carrying information about travel-related diseases and how to avoid them.

Ⓦ **www.istm.org** The website of the International Society for Travel Medicine, with a full list of clinics specializing in international travel health.

Ⓦ **www.masta.org** Comprehensive website for Medical Advisory service for travellers abroad (see also listing on p.26).

Ⓦ **www.tmvc.com.au** Contains a list of all Travellers Medical and Vaccination Centres throughout Australia, New Zealand and Southeast Asia, plus general information on travel health.

Ⓦ **www.travelvax.net** Website detailing everything you could ever want to know about diseases and travel vaccines.

Ⓦ **www.tripprep.com** Travel Health Online provides an online comprehensive database of necessary vaccinations for most countries, as well as destination and medical service provider information.

In the US and Canada

Canadian Society for International Health 1 Nicholas St, Suite 1105, Ottawa, ON K1N 7B7 Ⓣ613/241-5785, Ⓦwww.csih.org. Distributes a free pamphlet, "Health Information for Canadian Travellers", containing an extensive list of travel health centres in Canada.

Centers for Disease Control 1600 Clifton Rd NE, Atlanta, GA 30333 Ⓣ404/639-3534 or 1-800/311-3435, Ⓕ1-888/232-3299, Ⓦwww.cdc.gov. Publishes outbreak warnings, suggested inoculations, precautions and other background information for travellers. Useful website plus International Travelers Hotline on Ⓣ1-877/FYI-TRIP.

International Association for Medical Assistance to Travellers (IAMAT) 417 Center St, Lewiston, NY 14092 Ⓣ716/754-4883, Ⓦwww.sentex.net/~iamat, and 40 Regal Rd, Guelph, ON N1K 1B5 Ⓣ519/836-0102. A non-profit organization supported by donations, it can provide a list of English-speaking doctors in the Caribbean, climate charts and leaflets on various diseases and inoculations.

International SOS Assistance Eight Neshaminy Interplex Suite 207, Trevose, PA 19053-6956 Ⓣ1-800/523-8930, Ⓦwww.intsos.com. Members receive pre-trip medical referral info, as well as overseas emergency services designed to complement travel insurance coverage.

Travel Medicine Ⓣ1-800/872-8633, Ⓕ1-413/584-6656, Ⓦwww.travmed.com. Sells first-aid kits, mosquito netting, water filters, reference books and other health-related travel products.

Prescriptions

Be aware that even on islands with good medical facilities and well-stocked pharmacies you may not be able to find the **exact medication** that you take at home, or even a viable alternative. To be safe, bring any prescribed medicine in its original container and make sure you have enough for the length of your trip, as well as a copy of the prescription itself. The US State Department also advises bringing a letter from the prescribing doctor explaining why the drugs are needed.

In the UK and Ireland

British Airways Travel Clinics Twenty-eight regional clinics (call ☎01276/685 040 for the nearest, or consult Ⓦwww.britishairways.com), with several in London (Mon–Fri 9.30am–5.15pm, Sat 10am–4pm), including 156 Regent St, London W1 ☎020/7439 9584, no appointment necessary. There are appointment-only branches at 101 Cheapside, London EC2 ☎020/7606 2977; and at the BA terminal in London's Victoria Station ☎020/7233 6661. All clinics offer vaccinations, tailored advice from an online database and a complete range of travel healthcare products.
Communicable Diseases Unit Brownlee Centre, Glasgow G12 0YN ☎0141/211 1074. Travel vaccinations including yellow fever.
Dun Laoghaire Medical Centre 5 Northumberland Ave, Dun Laoghaire, Co. Dublin ☎01/280 4996, Ⓕ280 5603. Advice on medical matters abroad.
Hospital for Tropical Diseases Travel Clinic 2nd Floor, Mortimer Market Centre, off Capper St, London WC1E 6AU (Mon–Fri 9am–5pm by appointment only; ☎020/7388 9600; a consultation costs £15 which is waived if you have your injections here). A recorded Health Line (☎0906/133 7733; 50p per min) gives tips on hygiene and illness prevention as well as listing appropriate immunizations.
Liverpool School of Tropical Medicine Pembroke Place, Liverpool L3 5QA ☎0151/708 9393. Walk-in clinic Mon–Fri 1–4pm; appointment required for yellow fever, but not for other jabs.
MASTA (Medical Advisory Service for Travellers Abroad) London School of Hygiene and Tropical Medicine. Operates a recorded 24-hour Travellers' Health Line (UK ☎0906/822 4100, 60p per min; Republic of Ireland ☎01560/147 000, 75p per min), giving written information tailored to your journey by return of post.
Trailfinders Immunization clinics (no appointments necessary) at 194 Kensington High St, London (Mon–Fri 9am–5pm except Thurs to 6pm, Sat 9.30am–4pm; ☎020/7938 3999).
Travel Health Centre Department of International Health and Tropical Medicine, Royal College of Surgeons in Ireland, Mercers Medical Centre, Stephen's St Lower, Dublin ☎01/402 2337. Expert pre-trip advice and inoculations.
Travel Medicine Services PO Box 254, 16 College St, Belfast 1 ☎028/9031 5220. Offers medical advice before a trip and help afterwards in the event of a tropical disease.

In Australia and New Zealand

Travellers' Medical and Vaccination Centres Ⓦwww.tmvc.com.au; 27–29 Gilbert Place, Adelaide ☎08/8212 7522; 1/170 Queen St, Auckland ☎09/373 3531; 5/247 Adelaide St, Brisbane ☎07/3221 9066; 5/8–10 Hobart Place, Canberra ☎02/6257 7156; 147 Armagh St, Christchurch ☎03/379 4000; 5 Westralia St, Darwin ☎08/8981 2907; 270 Sandy Bay Rd, Sandy Bay, Hobart ☎03/6223 7577; 2/393 Little Bourke St, Melbourne ☎03/9602 5788; 5 Mill St, Perth ☎08/9321 1977, plus branch in Fremantle; 7/428 George St, Sydney ☎02/9221 7133, plus branches in Chatswood and Parramatta;
Shop 15, Grand Arcade, 14–16 Willis St, Wellington ☎04/473 0991.

Insurance

It is always sensible, and often necessary, to take out an insurance policy before travelling to cover against theft, loss and illness or injury. Before buying a new policy, however, it's worth checking whether you are already covered: some all-risks home insurance policies may cover your possessions when overseas, and many private medical schemes include cover when abroad. In Canada, provincial health plans usually provide partial cover for medical mishaps overseas, while holders of official student/teacher/youth cards in Canada and the US are entitled to meagre accident coverage and hospital in-patient benefits. Students will often find that their student health coverage extends during the vacations and for one term beyond the date of last enrolment.

After exhausting the possibilities above, you might want to contact a specialist **travel insurance company**, or consider the travel insurance deal we offer (see box below). A typical travel insurance policy usually provides cover for the loss of baggage, tickets and – up to a certain limit – cash or cheques, as well as cancellation or curtailment of your journey. Most of them exclude so-called dangerous sports unless an extra premium is paid: in the Caribbean this can mean scuba-diving, whitewater rafting, windsurfing and trekking, though probably not kayaking or jeep safaris. Many policies can be chopped and changed to exclude coverage you don't need – for example, sickness and accident benefits can often be excluded or included at will. If you do take medical coverage, ascertain whether benefits will be paid as treatment proceeds or only after return home, and whether there is a 24-hour medical emergency number. When securing baggage cover, make sure that the per-article limit – typically under US$730/£500 – will cover your most valuable possession. If you need to make a claim, you should keep receipts for medicines and medical treatment, and in the event that you have anything stolen, you must obtain an official statement from the police.

Rough Guides travel insurance

Rough Guides offers its own travel insurance, customized for our readers by a leading UK broker and backed by a Lloyds underwriter. It's available for anyone, of any nationality and any age, travelling anywhere in the world.

There are two main Rough Guide insurance plans: **Essential**, for basic, no-frills cover; and **Premier** – with more generous and extensive benefits. Alternatively, you can take out **annual multi-trip insurance**, which covers you for any number of trips throughout the year (with a maximum of 60 days for any one trip). Unlike many policies, the Rough Guides schemes are calculated by the day, so if you're travelling for 27 days rather than a month, that's all you pay for. If you intend to be away for the whole year, the Adventurer policy will cover you for 365 days. Each plan can be supplemented with a "Hazardous Activities Premium" if you plan to indulge in sports considered dangerous, such as skiing, scuba-diving or trekking.

For a policy quote, call the Rough Guide Insurance Line on US toll-free ⓣ1-866/220 5588, UK freefone ⓣ0800/015 09 06; or, if you're calling from elsewhere ⓣ+44 1243/621 046. Alternatively, get an online quote or buy online at ⓦwww.roughguides.com/insurance.

Information, websites and maps

Advance information on many of the Caribbean islands can be obtained from the tourist information offices listed below. Once you've arrived at your destination, you'll find most major towns have visitor centres of some description that will give out detailed information on the local area and can often help with finding accommodation. Free newspapers in many areas carry news of events and entertainment.

Recommended **maps** of individual islands are detailed at the beginning of each chapter where appropriate. The most detailed map of the Caribbean is the World Map: Caribbean, published by GeoCenter International.

Tourist offices abroad

Local **tourist information offices** are discussed in the individual chapters. Note that in some cases public relations firms handle tourist requests from abroad.

Anguilla

Ⓦwww.anguilla–vacation.com
UK Carolyn Brown River Communications, PO Box 2119, Woodford Green, London IG8 0GZ Ⓣ020/8506 6614, Ⓕ8505 8974.
US Keating Public Relations, 343 Millburn Ave, Millburn, NJ 07041 Ⓣ973/376-9300, Ⓕ376-8020.

Antigua and Barbuda

Antigua and Barbuda Department of Tourism, Ⓦwww.antigua-barbuda.org
Canada 60 St Claire Ave East, Suite 304, Toronto, ON M4T 1N5 Ⓣ416/961-3085, Ⓕ961-7218.
UK 15 Thayer St, London W1U 3JT Ⓣ020/7486 7073, 7074 or 7075, Ⓕ7486 9970.
US 610 Fifth Ave, Suite 311, New York, NY 10020 Ⓣ212/541-4117 or 1-888/268-4227, Ⓕ212/541-4789.

Aruba

Aruba Tourism Authority, Ⓦwww.aruba.com
Canada 5875 Highway #7, Suite 201, Woodbridge, ON L4L 1T9 Ⓣ905/264-3434, Ⓕ264-3437.
UK The Copperfields, 25 Copperfield St, London SE1 0EN Ⓣ020/7928 1600, Ⓕ7928 1700.
US 5901 N Cicero, Suite 301, Chicago, IL 60646 Ⓣ773/202-5054 or 1-800/TO-ARUBA, Ⓕ773/202-9293.

Bahamas

Bahamas Tourism Centre, Ⓦwww.bahamas.com
Canada 121 Bloor St East, Suite #1101, Toronto, ON M4W 3M5 Ⓣ416/968-2999, Ⓕ968-0724 or 6711.
UK and Ireland Three, The Billings, Walnut Tree Close, Guildford, Surrey GU1 4UL Ⓣ01483/448900, Ⓕ571846.

Caribbean Tourism Organisation

A useful general resource is the **Caribbean Tourism Organisation** (CTO; Ⓦwww.doitcaribbean.com), an international development agency that promotes tourism throughout the Caribbean with an eye toward sustainable tourism and preserving local culture and the environment.

Caribbean Tourism Organisation offices

Barbados Sir Frank Walcott Building, Culloden Rd, St Michael, Barbados Ⓣ246/427 5242, Ⓕ429 3065.
Canada 512 Duplex Ave, Toronto, ON M4R 2E3 Ⓣ416/485-8724, Ⓕ485-8256.
UK 42 Westminster Palace Gardens, Artillery Row, London SW1P 1RR Ⓣ020/7222 4335, Ⓕ7222 4325.
US 80 Broad St, New York, NY 10004 Ⓣ212/635-9530, Ⓕ635-9511.

US c/o Nassau/Paradise Island Promotion Board, One Turnberry Place, 19495 Biscayne Blvd, Suite #804, Aventura, FL 33180 ⓣ305/931-1555, ext 213 or 1-888/627-7281.

Barbados

Barbados Tourism Authority, ⓦwww.barbados.org
Canada Suite 1010, 105 Adelaide St West, Toronto, ON M5H 1P9 ⓣ416/214-9880, ⓕ214-9882.
UK 263 Tottenham Court Rd, London W1P 9AA ⓣ020/7636 9448.
US 800 Second Ave, New York, NY 10017 ⓣ212/986-6516 or 1-800/221-983, ⓕ212/573-9850.

Bonaire

Tourism Corporation Bonaire, ⓦwww.infobonaire.com
Europe Basis Communicatie BV, Mariettahof 25–29, PO Box 472, NL-2000 AL Haarlem, The Netherlands ⓣ23/5430 704, ⓕ5430 730.
US Adams Unlimited, 10 Rockefeller Plaza, Suite 900, New York, NY 10020 ⓣ212/956-5912 or ⓣ1-800/266-2473, ⓕ212/956-5913.

British Virgin islands

BVI Tourist Board, ⓦwww.bvitouristboard.com
UK Banks Hoggins O'Shea FCB, 55 Newman St, London W1P 3PG ⓣ020/7947 820 ⓕ7947 8279.
US 370 Lexington Ave, Suite 1605, New York, NY 10017 ⓣ212/696-0400 or 1-800/835-8530, ⓕ212/949-8254.

Cayman Islands

Cayman Islands Department of Tourism, ⓦwww.caymanislands.ky/
Canada 234 Eglinton Ave East, Suite 306, Toronto, ON M4P 1K5 ⓣ416/485-1550 or 1-800/263-5805, ⓕ416/485-7578.
UK 6 Arlington St, London SW1 1RE ⓣ020/7491 7771, ⓕ7409 7773.
US 420 Lexington Ave, Suite 2733, New York, NY 10170 ⓣ212/682-5582 ⓕ986-5123.

Cuba

ⓦwww.cubatravel.cu
Canada Bureau de Tourisme de Cuba, 440 blvd Dorchester Ouest, #1402, Montreal PQ H2Z 1U7 ⓣ514/875-8004.
UK Cuba Tourism Office, 154 Shaftesbury Ave, London WC2H 8JT ⓣ020/7240 6655.
US Cuban Interests Section, 2639 16th St NW, Washington DC 20009 ⓣ202/797-8609 or 1-800/752-9282.

Curaçao

ⓦwww.curacao-tourism.com
Europe Curaçao Tourist Board, 3011 BP Rotterdam, The Netherlands ⓣ10 414 2639.
UK Axis Sales & Marketing Ltd, Curaçao Representation UK, 421a Finchley Rd, London NW3 6HJ ⓣ020/7431 4045, ⓕ7431 7920.
US Curaçao Tourist Board (no address), ⓣ1-800/445-8266, ⓔjoel@aventura.npipb.com

Dominica

Dominica Tourist Office, ⓦwww.ndcdominica.dm
UK Mitre House, 66 Abbey Rd, Bush Hill Park, Middlesex EN1 2QE ⓣ020/8350 1000.
US Dominica Tourist Office, 800 Second Ave, Suite 1802, New York, NY 10017 ⓣ212/ 949-1711, ⓕ949-1714.

Dominican Republic

Office of Tourism for the Dominican Republic, ⓦwww.dominicana.com.do
Canada 35 Church St, Unit 53, Toronto, ON M5E 1T3 ⓣ416/361-2126/27 or 1-888/494-5050.
UK 18–20 Hand Court, High Holborn, London WC1V 6JF ⓣ020/7242 7778.
US 12174 Greenspoint Drive, Houston, TX 77090 ⓣ281/875-3888 or 1-866/752-5200.

Grenada

ⓦwww.grenada.org
Canada Consulate General of Grenada, Phoenix House, 439 University Ave, Suite 930,Toronto, ON M5G 1Y8 ⓣ416/595-1343, ⓕ595-8278.
UK Grenada Board of Tourism, 1 Battersea Church Rd, London SW11 3LY ⓣ020/7771 7000, ⓦwww.grenadagrenadines.com
US Grenada Board of Tourism, 800 Second Ave, Suite 400-K, New York, NY 10017 ⓣ212/687-9554 or 1-800/927-9554, ⓕ212/573-9731.

Guadeloupe

ⓦwww.antilles-info-tourisme.com/guadeloupe/offto-bt.htm
US Guadeloupe Tourist Office, 161 Washington Valley Rd, Suite 205, Warren, NJ 07059 ⓣ1-888/448-2335.

Jamaica

Jamaica Tourist Board, ⓦwww.jamaicatravel.com
Canada 303 Eglinton Avenue East, Suite 200, Toronto, ON M4P 1L3 ⓣ416/482-7850, ⓕ482-1730.
UK 1–2 Prince Consort Rd, London SW7 2BZ ⓣ020/7224 0505, ⓕ7224 0551.
US 801 Second Ave, 20th Floor, New York, NY 10017 ⓣ212/856-9727, ⓕ856-9730.

Martinique

ⓦwww.martinique.org
Australia 25 Bligh St, Level 22, Sydney, NSW 2000 ⓣ02/9231 5244, ⓕ9221 8682. **Canada** Martinique Tourist Office, 2159 Rue Mackay, Montreal PQ H3G 2J2 ⓣ514/844-8566, ⓕ844-8901.
Ireland Maison de la France, 10 Suffolk St, Dublin 2 ⓣ01/679 0813.
UK Maison de France, 178 Picadilly, London WIJ 9AL ⓣ020/7493 6594.
US Martinique Promotion Bureau, 444 Madison Ave, 16th Floor, New York NY, 10022 ⓣ212/838-7800 or 1-800/391-4909, ⓕ212/838-7855.

Puerto Rico

Puerto Rico Tourism Company, ⓦwww.gotopuertorico.com
Canada 41–43 Colbourne St, Suite 301, Toronto, ON M5E 1E3 ⓣ416/368-2680 or ⓣ 1-800/667-0394, ⓕ416/368-5350.
UK and Spain Calle Serrano, 1-2 Izq, 28001, Madrid ⓣ34-91/43-2128, from UK free phone ⓣ800-898 920, ⓕ34-91/577 5260.
US 666 Fifth Ave, 15th Floor, New York, NY 10003 ⓣ212/586-6262 or 1-800/223-6530, ⓕ212/586-1212.

Saba

ⓦwww.sabatourism.com
Germany Dutch Caribbean Travel Center, Karlstrasse 12, D-60329 Frankfurt/Main ⓣ49 69/240 0183, ⓕ2427 1521, ⓦwww.dutch-caribbean.com
All other countries Netherlands Kabinet van de Gevolmachtigde Minister van de Nederlandse Antillen, Badhuisweg 173–175, 2597 JP 's-Gravenhage ⓣ70/351-2811, ⓕ351-2722.

St Barts

ⓦwww.st-barths.com
For all inquiries, contact your country's French Tourist Board office.

St Eustatius

ⓦwww.statiatourism.com
See under St Maarten.

St Kitts and Nevis

St Kitts and Nevis Tourism Office, ⓦwww.interknowledge.com/stkitts-nevis
Canada 365 Bay St, Suite 806, Toronto, ON M5H 2V1ⓣ416/368-6707, ⓕ368-3934.
UK 10 Kensington Court, London W8 5DL ⓣ020/7376 0881.
US 414 East 75th St, Suite 5, New York, NY 10021 ⓣ212/535-1234 or 1-800/526-6208, ⓕ212/734-6511.

St Lucia

St Lucia Tourist Board, ⓦwww.stlucia.org
Canada 8 King St East, Suite 700, Toronto, ON M5C 1B5 ⓣ416/362-4242 or 1-800/869 0377, ⓕ416/362-7832.
UK 421a Finchley Rd, London NW3 6HJ ⓣ020/7431 3675, ⓕ7431 7920.
US 800 Second Ave, 9th Floor, New York, NY 10017 ⓣ212/867-2950 or 1-800/456-3984, ⓕ212/867-2795.

St Maarten

St Maarten Tourist Office, ⓦwww.st-maarten .com
Canada 703 Evans Ave, Suite 106, Toronto, ON M9C 5E9 ⓣ416/622-4300, ⓕ622-3431.
US 675 Third Ave, Suite 1806, New York, NY 10017 ⓣ212/953-2084 or 1-800/786-2278, ⓕ212/953-2145.

St Martin

ⓦwww.st-martin.org
Australia Maison de la France, Level 20, 25 Bligh St, Sydney, NSW 2000 ⓣ02/9231 5244, ⓕ09221 8682, ⓦwww.franceguide.com
Canada French Government Tourist Office, 30 St Patrick St, Suite 700, Toronto, ON M5T 3A3 ⓣ416/593-6427.
Ireland Maison de la France, 10 Suffolk St, Dublin 2 ⓣ01/679 0813, ⓕ679 0814.
UK Maison de la France, 178 Piccadilly, London W1J 9AL ⓣ09068/ 244 123 (60p/min), ⓕ020/71493 6594.
US French West Indies Tourist Board, 44 Madison Ave, New York, NY 10022 ⓣ1-900/990-0040 (95¢ per min).

St Vincent and the Grenadines

St Vincent and the Grenadines Tourism, Ⓦwww.svgtourism.com

UK 10 Kensington Court, London W8 5DL Ⓣ020/7937 6570.

US 801 Second Ave, 21st Floor, New York, NY 10017 Ⓣ212/687-4981 or 1-800/729-1726, Ⓕ212/949-5946.

Trinidad and Tobago

Ⓦwww.visittnt.com

Canada The RMR Group, Taurus House, 512 Duplex Ave, Toronto, ON M4R 2E3 Ⓣ416/485-7827 or 1-888/535-5617, Ⓕ416/485-8256.

UK Mitre House, 66 Abbey Rd, Bush Hill Park, Enfield, Middlesex EN1 2QE Ⓣ020/8350 1000.

US Cheryl Andrews Marketing Inc, 311 Almeria Ave, Coral Gables, FL 33144 Ⓣ305/444-7827 or 1-888/595-4868, Ⓕ305/447-0415.

Turks and Caicos

Turks and Caicos Tourist Board, Ⓦwww.turksandcaicostourism.com

Canada 512 Duplex Ave,Toronto, ON M4R 2E3 Ⓣ416/440-0212, Ⓕ485-8256.

UK Mitre House, 66 Abbey Rd, Bush Hill, Enfield, Middlesex EN1 2QE Ⓣ020/8350 1017.

US 11645 Biscayne Blvd, Suite 302, North Miami, FL 33181 Ⓣ305/891-4117 or 1-800/241-0824, Ⓕ305/891-7096.

US Virgin Islands

USVI Department of Tourism, Ⓦwww.usvi.net

Canada 703 Evans Ave, Suite 106, Toronto, ON M9C 5E9 Ⓣ416/622 7600, Ⓕ622-3431.

UK Molasses House, Clove Hitch Quay, Plantation Wharf, London SW11 3TW Ⓣ020/7978 5262, Ⓕ7924 3171.

US 1270 Avenue of the Americas, Suite 2108, New York, NY 10020 Ⓣ212/332-2222 or 1-800/372-USVI, Ⓕ212/332-2223.

Websites

There is a wealth of **information** about the Caribbean on the web. For details of internet access within the region, see p.41.

BBC Caribbean
Ⓦwww.bbc.co.uk/caribbean
Audio news reports, including the week's highlights, plus arts, entertainment and sports coverage.

CANA On-Line
Ⓦwww.cananews.com
Daily sports, news, business and features stories on the English Caribbean.

Caribbean Aviation
Ⓦwww.caribbeanaviation.com
Very up-to-date and comprehensive website detailing charter and scheduled airlines serving the Caribbean.

Caribbean Information Office
Ⓦwww.caribbeans.com
Travel, accommodation, packages and airline information.

Caribbean On Line
Ⓦwww.caribbean-on-line.com
Extensive coverage of airlines, car rental, restaurant reviews and accommodation throughout the islands.

Caribbean Travel and Life
Ⓦwww.caribbeantravelmag.com
Comprehensive web version of the print magazine, with reader forums, custom trip planning, classifieds and resort information.

Cruise Critic
Ⓦwww.cruisecritic.com
Detailed reviews of cruise ships serving the Caribbean.

Sunhead magazine
Ⓦwww.sunheadmagazine.com
Excellent politics/arts/youth culture 'zine for young people in the Caribbean.

Turquoise Net
Ⓦwww.turq.com
In-depth site covering everything from maps to hotel listings, weather, books and travel tips.

Travel bookshops and map outlets

In the US and Canada

Adventurous Traveler Bookstore 102 Lake St, Burlington, VT 05401 Ⓣ1-800/282-3963, Ⓦwww.adventuroustraveler.com

Book Passage 51 Tamal Vista Blvd, Corte Madera, CA 94925 Ⓣ1-800/999-7909, Ⓦwww.bookpassage.com

Complete Traveller Bookstore 199 Madison Ave, New York, NY Ⓣ212/685-9007.

Distant Lands 56 S Raymond Ave, Pasadena, CA 91105 Ⓣ1-800/310-3220, Ⓦwww.distantlands.com

Elliot Bay Book Company 101 S Main St, Seattle, WA 98104 Ⓣ1-800/962-5311, Ⓦwww.elliotbaybook.com

Forsyth Travel Library 226 Westchester Ave, White Plains, NY 10604 Ⓣ1-800/367-7984, Ⓦwww.forsyth.com

Globe Corner Bookstore 28 Church St,

Cambridge, MA 02138 ⓣ1-800/358-6013, ⓦwww.globecorner.com
GORP Books & Maps ⓣ1-877/440-4677, ⓦwww.gorp.com/gorp/books/main.htm
Map Link 30 S La Patera Lane, Unit 5, Santa Barbara, CA 93117 ⓣ805/692-6777, ⓦwww.maplink.com
Rand McNally ⓣ1-800/333-0136, ⓦwww.randmcnally.com. Around thirty stores across the US; dial ext 2111 or check the website for the nearest location.
Travel Books and Language Center 4437 Wisconsin Ave NW, Washington DC 20016 ⓣ1-800/220-2665, ⓦwww.bookweb.org/bookstore/travelbks
The Travel Bug Bookstore 2667 W Broadway, Vancouver V6K 2G2 ⓣ604/737-1122, ⓦwww.swifty.com/tbug
World of Maps 1235 Wellington St, Ottawa, ON K1Y 3A3 ⓣ1-800/214-8524, ⓦwww.worldofmaps.com

In the UK and Ireland

Blackwell's Map and Travel Shop 50 Broad St, Oxford OX1 3BQ ⓣ01865/793 550, ⓦhttp://maps.blackwell.co.uk/index.html
Easons Bookshop 40 O'Connell St, Dublin 1 ⓣ01/873 3811, ⓦwww.eason.ie
Heffers Map and Travel 20 Trinity St, Cambridge CB2 1TJ ⓣ01223/568 568, ⓦwww.heffers.co.uk
Hodges Figgis Bookshop 56–58 Dawson St, Dublin 2 ⓣ01/677 4754, ⓦwww.hodgesfiggis.com
James Thin Booksellers 53–59 South Bridge, Edinburgh EH1 1YS ⓣ0131/622 8222, ⓦwww.jthin.co.uk
John Smith & Son 100 Cathedral St, Glasgow G4 0RD ⓣ0141/552 3377, ⓦwww.johnsmith.co.uk
The Map Shop 30a Belvoir St, Leicester LE1 6QH ⓣ0116/247 1400, ⓦwww.mapshopleicester.co.uk
National Map Centre 22–24 Caxton St, London SW1H 0QU ⓣ020/7222 2466, ⓦwww.mapsnmc.co.uk
Newcastle Map Centre 55 Grey St, Newcastle-upon-Tyne NE1 6EF ⓣ0191/261 5622.
Ordnance Survey Ireland Phoenix Park, Dublin 8 ⓣ01/8025 349, ⓦwww.irlgov.ie/osi
Ordnance Survey of Northern Ireland Colby House, Stranmillis Ct, Belfast BT9 5BJ ⓣ028/9025 5761, ⓦwww.osni.gov.uk
Stanfords 12–14 Long Acre, London WC2E 9LP ⓣ020/7836 1321, ⓦwww.stanfords.co.uk. Maps available by mail, phone order, or email. Other branches within British Airways offices at 156 Regent St, London W1R 5TA ⓣ020/7434 4744, and 29 Corn St, Bristol BS1 1HT ⓣ0117/929 9966.
The Travel Bookshop 13–15 Blenheim Crescent, London W11 2EE ⓣ020/7229 5260, ⓦwww.thetravelbookshop.co.uk

In Australia and New Zealand

The Map Shop 6–10 Peel St, Adelaide, SA 5000 ⓣ08/8231 2033, ⓦwww.mapshop.net.au
Mapland 372 Little Bourke St, Melbourne, Victoria 3000, ⓣ03/9670 4383, ⓦwww.mapland.com.au
MapWorld 173 Gloucester St, Christchurch ⓣ03/374 5399 or 0800/627 967, ⓦwww.mapworld.co.nz
Perth Map Centre 1/884 Hay St, Perth, WA 6000, ⓣ08/9322 5733, ⓦwww.perthmap.com.au
Specialty Maps 46 Albert St, Auckland 1001 ⓣ09/307 2217, ⓦwww.ubdonline.co.nz/maps

Money and costs

The US dollar is widely accepted in the Caribbean along with local currency – albeit at a less-than-favourable exchange rate. In fact, the US dollar is the official currency in the Virgin Islands, Turks and Caicos and Puerto Rico. The British pound, however, is not used in the former British colonies, and while French islands such as Guadeloupe and Martinique do accept pounds, the euro is the preferred currency.

As the majority of Caribbean islands are fairly developed, at least in the touristed areas, travellers' cheques and credit cards are accepted. ATMs accept debit and credit cards linked to the Cirrus, Plus and Visa networks, while most hotels will change money, though at less favourable rates than banks. In less developed areas, it's best to carry **local currency** as few establishments will take credit cards and ATMs are rare. (See individual chapters for information specific to the islands.)

Cash and travellers' cheques

If you are going to be away from urban or tourist centres or shopping in local markets and stalls, cash is a necessity – preferably in small denominations of local currency.

In countries that do not have the euro as their official currency, you will find that your euros will not be accepted; the same applies to British pounds and Canadian dollars, at least outside of major tourist hotels and restaurants.

As a general rule, US **travellers' cheques** are accepted in resorts – those issued by Visa are best, although in countries where the euro is used (Martinique, Guadeloupe, Curaçao, Saba, St Barts, St Martin/St Maarten and St Eustatius) you might be better off using cheques in euro denominations. Outside of hotels you may have trouble cashing any cheques at all, as they have become an obsolete method of payment.

If you are in doubt, though, or simply want some peace of mind, you can generally cash travellers' cheques in bureaux de change in city centres and airports, as well as in resorts. Remember, though, that unless you are willing to seek out an exchange office every day, you will still end up carrying a fair amount of cash on your person once you have cashed the cheques.

The usual fee for travellers' cheque sales is one or two percent, though this fee may be waived if you buy the cheques through your bank. It pays to get a range of denominations so that you're not stuck with more cash than you need. Some outlets offer better rates for cheques than for cash and most charge a commission. Keep the purchase agreement and a record of cheque serial numbers safe and separate from the cheques themselves. In the event that they're lost or stolen, you'll need to report the loss to the issuing company; refer to the list of phone numbers provided with the cheques; most companies claim to replace lost or stolen cheques within 24 hours.

Credit and debit cards

Credit cards are a handy back-up and can be used either at ATMs or over the counter at banks. **MasterCard** and **Visa** are the most commonly accepted in the Caribbean; other cards may not be recognized and US-issued cards are not accepted in Cuba at all. Remember that if you use your credit card to obtain **cash advances**, you'll pay credit-card rates of interest on the cash from the date of withdrawal; there may be a transaction fee on top of this.

If you want the security of travellers' cheques without the hassle of carrying large amounts of cash or waiting for exchange offices to open, consider using your ATM card – many ATMs in the region now take US and European **debit cards** (linked to Cirrus, Plus or Maestro) at a minimal fee –

check with your bank for details. Make sure you have a personal identification number (PIN) that lets you access your account from overseas. A complete list of ATMs on the Cirrus and Maestro networks can be found at www.mastercard.com; for those on the Visa Plus network, log on to http://visaatm.infonow.net

A compromise between travellers' cheques and plastic is **Visa TravelMoney**, a disposable pre-paid debit card. Load up your account with funds before leaving home and when they run out, simply throw the card away. You can buy up to nine cards to access the same funds – useful for couples or families travelling together – and it's a good idea to buy at least one extra as a back-up in case of loss or theft. There is also a 24-hour toll-free customer assistance number.

The card is available in most countries from branches of **Thomas Cook** and **Citicorp**. For more information, check the Visa TravelMoney website at http://usa.visa.com/personal/cards/visa_travel_money.html

Wiring money

Having **money wired** from home using one of the companies listed below is never convenient or cheap, and should be considered a last resort. It's also possible to have money wired directly from a bank in your home country to a bank in the Caribbean, although this is somewhat less reliable because it involves two separate institutions. If you go this route, your home bank will need the address of the branch bank where you want to pick up the money and the address and telex number of its main island office. Money wired this way normally takes two working days to arrive, and costs around US$40/£25 per transaction.

Money-wiring companies

American Express
www.moneygram.com
Australia 1800/230 100
New Zealand 09/379 8243 or 0800/262 2631
UK and Republic of Ireland 0800/6663 9472
US and Canada 1-800/926-9400

Thomas Cook
www.us.thomascook.com
Canada 1-888/823-4732
Republic of Ireland 01/677 1721
UK 01733/318 922 or 028/9055 0030
US 1-800/287-7362

Western Union
www.westernunion.com
Australia 1800/649 565
Republic of Ireland 1800/395 395
New Zealand 09/270 0050
UK 0800/833 833
US and Canada 1-800/325-6000

Costs

Your **daily budget** in the Caribbean depends, of course, on where you are travelling and how comfortable you want to be. The **cheapest destinations** are likely to be Dominica, Trinidad and Tobago and the Dominican Republic, where you can get by sleeping in the cheapest accommodation, travelling by bus and eating food from street stalls and supermarkets on about US$30/day, possibly less. A couple of other islands, such as Barbados and Trinidad and Tobago can be visited on around US$50/day, or US$100/day with a little luxury; however, most Caribbean islands will be around US$125/day, with a few – such as Bonaire – setting you back US$150/day or more. Remember that **incidentals** such as car rental, room and departure tax, local driving permits and guides – never mind island-hopping, whale watching, fancy dinners or scuba diving – really add up but are some of the most enjoyable facets of a Caribbean holiday.

Island transport

Public transport on the larger Caribbean islands is generally cheap, though not wholly reliable in many cases. Most tourists tend to travel in taxis or rental cars – often a hair-raising experience given the erratic nature of Caribbean driving, but worth it for the independence granted. Those unprepared to risk the roads themselves might consider taking the bus – bus routes usually cover all main destinations on most islands, and many minor ones besides, and are much used by the locals. Be aware, though, that many bus drivers don't adhere to a timetable and will leave only when the bus is full. For island-specific details, see individual chapters.

Buses and taxis

Buses tend to operate a frequent, if erratic, service between 6am and 8pm on the more populated islands of the Caribbean, stretching to 10pm or even midnight in more developed locales. There is often limited or no service on a Sunday. The buses themselves are usually small minivans which the drivers like to pack to the gills before departure – given that whatever bus services are available are cheap (rarely more than US$3, usually closer to 50¢) they are very much used by the locals.

Taxis are plentiful throughout the Caribbean; drivers are often very knowledgeable and act as tour guides and advisors, even accompanying single women to street parties and the like (for a fee), as well as serving as chauffeurs. Sometimes the only way to identify a taxi is by checking the number plate for a designated letter or colour. Usually taxis are not metered and fares are regulated by the various island governments (although some taxi drivers may ignore the official rates and set their own, especially longer trips). Lists of sample taxi fares are available from tourist offices, but you should always agree to a rate before you start your journey. Don't be afraid to negotiate, either, as this is often customary.

Car rental

Car rental is straightforward on most Caribbean islands, with major companies operating on many and local outfits offering stiff competition in terms of price. On many of the islands you will need to buy a local, temporary driving permit, usually valid for three to six months and costing US$15–25 (see box overleaf). Car rental will cost on average US$200–350 per week for a compact automatic with air conditioning. Be prepared to be refused, or at least charged a hefty surcharge – sometimes as much as the regular rate again – if you are under 25. Be aware that on most Caribbean islands vehicles drive on the left, with the exceptions being Aruba, Cuba, the Dominican Republic, Guadeloupe, Martinique, Aruba, Bonaire, Curaçao, Saba, and St Eustatius.

Driving conditions and local driving patterns vary widely. Many roads are narrow or winding, signs may not be in English or there at all, some routes may be little more than dust tracks and inaccessible after rain or without a four-wheel-drive vehicle, and in some places domestic animals roam freely. **Defensive driving**, therefore, is a must. Be prepared to use your horn – and your hand gestures – liberally.

Many hotels and resorts will either rent bicycles to guests or have a company nearby with whom they can arrange preferential rates (US$10–25/day with discounts for weeklong rentals). Similarly, scooters and motorbikes are available; some local car rental agencies have motorbikes and scooters for hire. Count on paying around US$20 per day or US$130 per week for a scooter; US$25 per day or US$160 per week for a motorbike.

Local driving permits

Visitors planning to drive in the Caribbean will need to obtain a local driving permit on the following islands. You'll need to show a current driver's licence, and often an international driver's licence as well.

Anguilla Available from car rental companies for US$20.
Antigua and Barbuda Available from car rental companies for US$20. Valid for three months.
Barbados Required only if you do not have an international licence. Available from the airport, local police stations and car rental companies for US$5.
British Virgin Islands Available from car rental companies or Police Headquarters for US$10.
Grenada Available from the police at La Carenage or at car rental companies for EC$30.
St Kitts and Nevis Available from the Police Traffic Department for EC$50. Valid for one year.

Inter-island transport

One of the joys of Caribbean travel is the ease with which travellers can journey between islands, taking in two or three different cultures in one trip. Most islands are well connected by local and international airlines, although some – Cuba, for example, or Dominica – are less well served than most. Many of the bigger airlines offer airpasses costing from US$300 for three stopovers to US$600 for unlimited Caribbean travel within an airline's range – see opposite for details of specific deals.

If you plan simply to travel between groups of islands – the Caymans, for example, the Virgin Islands or the Grenadines, the many **small airline companies** operating there run a regular and reasonable service. Alternatively, you might consider travelling by **ferry**: there is a high-speed service between St Lucia, Martinique, Dominica and Guadeloupe and another between St Barts, Saba and St Maarten – full details of inter-island ferry services are given on p.38.

Airlines

Abaco Air ⓣ242/367 2266, ⓦwww.oii.net/abacoair. Service between the Bahamas, Florida and the Turks and Caicos islands. Scheduled seats cost US$33–69 each way.
Air Anguilla ⓣ264/497 2643. Runs scheduled daily flights between Anguilla and St Thomas, and charter flights between Tortola and San Juan, and Anguilla and St Maarten.
Air Caraibes ⓣ059/082 4700, ⓦwww.aircaraibes.com. Serves St Barts, St Maarten, St Lucia, Dominica, the Dominican Republic, San Juan, Guadeloupe and Martinique.
Air Culebra ⓣ787/268 6951, ⓦwww.airculebra.com. Operates flights between Puerto Rico and most Caribbean islands.
Air Jamaica ⓦwww.airjamaica.com. Operates flights to Barbados, Bonaire, Curaçao, Grand Cayman, Grenada, Cuba, Jamaica, the Bahamas, the Dominican Republic and St Lucia.
Air Santo Domingo ⓦwww.airsantodomingo.com. Operates between Santo Domingo and San Juan.
Air St Kitts-Nevis ⓣ869/465 8571. Charter service offering flights to most neighbouring islands.
Air St Thomas ⓣ340/776 2722 or 1-800/522-3084, ⓦwww.airstthomas.com. Service between St Barts, St Thomas, San Juan and Virgin Gorda.
Air Sunshine ⓣ954/434 8900 or (US & Canada) ⓣ1-800/327-8900, ⓦwww.airsunshine.com. Operates between the US Virgin Islands, Puerto Rico

and the British Virgin Islands.
BWIA International ⓣ1-800/538-2942, ⓦwww.bwee.com. Regular service throughout the Caribbean.
American Eagle ⓣ1-800/433 7300, ⓦwww.aa.com. Service between the American Airlines San Juan hub and most Caribbean destinations.
Caribbean Star ⓣ268/480 2561, ⓦwww.flycaribbeanstar.com. Operates between Antigua, Anguilla, Barbados, Grenada, Nevis, Trinidad and Tobago, St Kitts, St Lucia, St Maarten, St Vincent and Tortola.
Caribintair ⓣ509/298-3041, ⓦwww.caribintair.com. Operates between the Dominican Republic, Trinidad and Tobago, and the Virgin Islands.
Carib Aviation ⓣ269/462 3147, ⓦwww.candoo.com/carib/indx.html. Charter flights between Antigua, St Kitts and Nevis.
Cubana ⓣ05/255 3776. Major Cuban airline flying inter-island and to Canada, and operating a code-shared London–Havana–Kingston–London flight with Air Jamaica.
Dutch Caribbean Airlines ⓣ 297/883 8080, ⓦwww.flydce.com. Service between Aruba, Bonaire, St Maarten and Curaçao.
Fly BVI ⓣ284/495 1747, ⓦwww.fly-bvi.com. Charter flights between Puerto Rico, the British Virgin Islands and the US Virgin Islands.
Gulfstream International Airlines (in US) ⓣ1-800/231-0856 or (in Bahamas) ⓣ242/394 6019, ⓦwww.gulfstreamair.com. Service from San Juan, St Thomas, St Croix, St Maarten, Tortola and Virgin Gorda, Bahamas, and between St Thomas and St Croix.
Inter Island Express ⓣ787/253 1400 in San Juan; from US ⓣ1-866/747-5263, ⓦwww.interislandexpress.com. Small San Juan-based charter airline serving most islands in the region.
Interisland Airways ⓣ649/946 4999. Flights throughout Turks and Caicos, Haiti and the Dominican Republic.
LIAT ⓣ268/480 5625, ⓦwww.liatairline.com. Services Anguilla, Antigua, Barbados, Dominica, Nevis, Mustique, Port of Spain, San Juan, St Croix, St Kitts, St Lucia, St Maarten, St Thomas, St Vincent, Tobago, Union Island and Tortola.
Lynx Air International ⓣ954/772 9808, ⓦwww.lynxair.com. Flights between Florida and the Bahamas, Turks and Caicos and Cuba.
Mustique Air ⓣ784/458 4380, in US ⓣ1800/526-4789, ⓦwww.mustique.com. Flies between Barbados and the Grenadines and costs US$120–140, with reduced rates for seniors. Flights between St Vincent and Mustique cost US$20 each way, between St Vincent and Union Island, US$30.
Nevis Express ⓣ869/469 9755, ⓦwww.nevisexpress.com. Scheduled flights between St Kitts and Nevis and San Juan.
Sky King Air ⓣ649/941 5170, ⓦwww.skyking.tc. Provides service between Turks and Caicos, Haiti and the Domincian Republic.
St Barths Commmuter ⓣ590/590 275 454. Ten-minute shuttle flights between St Barts and St Maarten.
SVG Air ⓣ784/457 5124, ⓦwww.svgair.com. Offers service between St Vincent and the Grenadines, St Barts, Grenada, Barbados, Martinique, Antigua, Trinidad, Tobago and St Lucia.
Trans Island Air 2000 ⓣ246/418 1650, ⓦwww.tia2000.com. Barbados-based airline with regular service between many Caribbean islands.
Windward Express Airlines ⓣ599/548 3085, ⓦwww.windwardexpress.com. Charter airline serving St Barts and St Maarten.

Airpasses

BWIA Air Pass

For passengers whose international flights are booked with BWIA, the airline offers a pass for travel between Antigua, Barbados, Georgetown, Grenada, Jamaica; Port of Spain and Tobago, Trinidad and Tobago; St Lucia; St Vincent; St Maarten and Caracas. Their Caribbean Traveller (economy: US$399, first class: US$599) allows travel to any of the above destinations in any 30-day period (except from Dec 19 to Jan 6). The itinerary must be booked in advance; no open returns and no backtracking is allowed.

LIAT Air Pass

LIAT operates between Anguilla, Antigua, Barbados, Dominica, Martinique, Grenada, Guadeloupe, Nevis, Trinidad, St Croix, St Kitts, St Lucia, St Thomas, St Vincent and the Grenadines, St Maarten, Tobago, the British Virgin Islands, San Juan and Puerto Rico, and offers three passes, valid only on their flights (not codeshares) all of which must have an itinerary booked in advance, with no open returns, and no backtracking. The passes are valid year-round and can be booked with Caribjet in the UK.
The Explorer (US$300). Allows a maximum of three stopovers in 21 days, returning to the originating destination to connect with the international flight.
Caribbean Super Explorer (US$575/£340). Unlimited travel to all of LIAT's destinations for 30 days.

Airpass (US$98 per sector). European travellers buying this airpass in conjunction with their international ticket can avail of three to six US$98 stopovers in 21 days.

AIR ALM Caribbean Airpass

ALM's Caribbean destinations are Aruba, Bonaire, Curaçao, Jamaica,Trinidad and Tobago, the Dominican Republic, Puerto Rico and St Maarten.

The Visit Caribbean Airpass Costs US$695 for a 30-day period and may be used for five destinations including one foreign gateway (Caracas, Maracaibo, Miami and Valencia) to the Caribbean.

Dutch Caribbean Airpass Choose between the so-called Mango deal (US$140, two from Aruba, Bonaire and Curaçao) and the Cantaloupe deal (three from Aruba, Bonaire, Curaçao and St Maarten).

American Eagle Caribbean Explorer

American Airlines and American Eagle offer Caribbean Explorer fares, which allow travellers from the US, Canada and Mexico who fly to the American/American Eagle hub in San Juan to then hop to 23 other Caribbean destinations. Fares are non-refundable, must be booked seven days in advance and travel must begin within fourteen days of arrival in San Juan. Holiday blackouts apply in December and January.

Air Jamaica Caribbean Hopper Program

The Caribbean Hopper Program allows a passenger originating in the US to visit three or more islands for US$399 for economy class and US$699 for first class for travel within their Caribbean and Central American network, which includes Jamaica, Providenciales, Grand Cayman, Nassau, Havana, Bonaire, Barbados, Grenada and St Lucia. Tickets must be purchased along with the US-originating flight and are valid year-round on Air Jamaica and Air Jamaica Express (economy only) for stays between three and thirty days. Backtracking is not allowed.

Ferries

While there is no ferry service that covers the entire Caribbean, there are a number of ferries that run between certain islands. We've listed some of the more useful lines below.

Between Bonaire and Curaçao

There is a twice-daily ferry service operated by **Flamingo Fast Ferries** (☎599/717 7001 on Bonaire); there is no service between Curaçao or Bonaire and Aruba.

Between St Maarten, Saba and St Barts

The Edge (☎599/514 2640) is a high-speed ferry, leaving Wed–Sun; the crossing takes one hour and costs US$40 one way or US$60 return.

The Voyager (☎590/87 10 68 or 599/542 4096, ⓦwww.voyager-st-barths.com) travels between the islands on Thursdays. The round-trip fare is US$57 (one-way US$39) and the journey takes one hour.

Between the Dominican Republic and Puerto Rico

Ferias del Caribe (in DR ☎809/433 7300, in San Juan ☎809/832 4800) connects Mayaguez, Puerto Rico and Santo Dominigo, departs Mon, Wed and Fri from Mayaguez and Tues, Thurs and Sun from Santo Domingo. It costs US$144.

Between Guadeloupe, Martinique, Marie Galante and the lesser French West Indies

Brudey Frères (Guadeloupe ☎502/90 04 48, Martinique ☎596/70 08 50, Marie Galante ☎590/97 77 82, ⓦwww.brudey-freres.fr) and **Deher Freres** (Guadeloupe ☎502/99 50 68) operate a regular service between the islands.

Between Guadeloupe, Marie Galante, Les Saintes, Dominica, Martinique and St Lucia

Express-des-Isles (in Guadeloupe ☎502/83 12 45, in Martinique ☎596/63 12 11, ⓦwww.express-des-iles.com) is a high-speed catamaran operating daily in the Southern Caribbean.

Between Anguilla and St Martin

Ferries depart daily from Anguilla beginning at 7.30am approximately at regular half-hour intervals. The last day ferry departs Marigot Bay, St Martin at 5.40pm. The day ferry costs US$10 plus US$2 departure tax.There is one evening ferry that departs Anguilla at 6.15pm. The return ferry departs St Martin at 7pm. Evening fare is US$12 plus US$2 departure tax.

Phones, post and email

What follows is general advice about communications across the Caribbean region; island-specific information on phone, mail and internet facilities is given at the beginning of each chapter.

Post

Post offices in cities and major towns offer a wide range of services; those in villages are much more basic, with shorter opening hours and often infuriatingly slow service. Most resorts and hotels sell stamps and have a postbox – if you are staying in such an establishment, this can often be the most convenient way to send a letter home. Mail to Europe and North America normally takes from one to two weeks, but it can take up to one month depending on the departure and destination points. Travellers can receive mail via poste restante, in any Caribbean country except Dominica. The system is universally fairly efficient (if you're going to be abroad for a while) but tends to be available only at the main post office in cities, not in small towns and villages. Most post offices hold letters for a maximum of one month, though some hold them for up to three.

Phones

You should be able to **phone** home from most islands in the Caribbean without any problems. Islands usually have both payphones that accept coins and those that require phone cards, which are usually available from shops everywhere.

Local calls in the Caribbean are usually very cheap, while many tour companies, hotels and activity providers will have free call numbers that you can dial from any public or private phone.

Avoid calling long-distance from hotels unless you have a cheap long-distance phone card with a free or local access number; even then check to see if the establishment charges for such calls. Some larger resorts have been known to charge upwards of US$1 per minute for local dialling.

Calling home from abroad

One of the most convenient ways of phoning home from abroad is via a **telephone charge card** from your phone company back home. Using a PIN number, you can make calls from most hotel, public and private phones that will be charged to the telephone card account. Since most major charge cards are free to obtain, it's certainly worth getting one at least for emergencies; enquire first, though, whether your destination is covered, and bear in mind that rates aren't necessarily cheaper than calling from a public phone.

In the **US and Canada**, AT&T, MCI, Sprint, Canada Direct and other North American long-distance companies all allow their customers to make credit-card calls while overseas, which are then billed to their home number. Check with your phone company to see if they provide service from the Caribbean; If they do, remember to ask for the toll-free access code.

In **the UK and Ireland**, British Telecom (Ⓣ0800/345 144, Ⓦwww.chargecard.bt.com) will issue free to all BT customers the BT Charge Card, which can be used in 116 countries; AT&T (dial Ⓣ0800/890 011, then the toll-free number 888/641-6123 when you hear the AT&T prompt to be transferred to the Florida Call Centre, 24hrs) has the Global Calling Card; while NTL (Ⓣ0500/100 505) issues its own Global Calling Card, which can be used in more than sixty countries, though the fees cannot be charged to a normal phone bill.

To call **Australia and New Zealand** from overseas, telephone charge cards such as Telstra Telecard or Optus Calling Card in Australia, and Telecom NZ's Calling Card, can be used to make calls abroad, which are charged back to a domestic account or credit card. Apply to Telstra (Ⓣ1800/038

000), Optus (☎1300/300 937), or Telecom NZ (☎04/801 9000).

Mobile phones

If you want to use your **mobile phone** abroad, you'll need to check with your phone provider to see whether it will work there, and what the call charges will be. Should it not work, you might want to consider renting a phone from Cable and Wireless (www.caribcell.com), which provides mobile service for most of the Caribbean: Antigua, Anguilla, Barbados, the Cayman Islands, Dominica, Grenada, Jamaica, St Kitts and Nevis, St Lucia, and St Vincent and the Grenadines; they also rent mobile phones on these islands for a sizeable deposit, connection fee and rental fee. However, any dual-band digital mobile phone with an 800MHz band that is primed for **roaming** can work on their network. The Cable & Wireless network does not support GSM mobile phones. A three-minute call to the US and Canada costs around US$4.50, to Europe US$5. A US$200 credit card deposit is required and a monthly service charge of US$18.60 is also applicable.

Intra-Caribbean mobile phone service

In Antigua, St Vincent and St Lucia, maritime mobile phone users can sign up for Cable & Wireless's **Intra Caribbean Roaming Marine Plan**, which offers roaming service on one cell phone number throughout Antigua, Dominica, St Lucia, Grenada, St Kitts and Nevis, and St Vincent and the Grenadines. There is also an Intra Caribbean forwarding service for land-based mobile phone users.

Cable and Wireless numbers

Anguilla ☎264/493 3100
Antigua ☎268/480 2628
Barbados ☎246/292 4000
British Virgin Islands ☎284/494 4444
Cayman Islands ☎345/949 7800
Dominica ☎767/448 1111
Grenada ☎473/440 1000
Jamaica ☎876/926 9700
St Kitts and Nevis ☎869/465 1000
St Lucia ☎758/453 9922
St Vincent ☎784/457 2016
Turks and Caicos ☎649/946 2200

Calling home from overseas

To **phone abroad** from the following islands, you must first dial the international direct dialling or IDD code (listed below), followed by the country code, the area code and then the phone number.

International direct dialling codes when dialling from

Anguilla ☎011
Antigua ☎011
Aruba ☎00
Bahamas ☎011
Barbados ☎011
Bonaire ☎00
British Virgin Islands ☎011
Cayman Islands ☎011
Cuba ☎119
Curaçao ☎00
Dominica ☎011
Dominican Republic ☎011
Grenada ☎011
Guadeloupe ☎00
Jamaica ☎011
Martinique ☎00
Nevis ☎011
Puerto Rico ☎011
Saba ☎00
St Barts ☎00
St Eustatius ☎00
St Kitts ☎011
St Lucia ☎011
St Maarten/St Martin ☎00
St Vincent and the Grenadines ☎011
Trinidad and Tobago ☎011
Turks and Caicos ☎011
US Virgin Islands ☎011

International country codes

Australia ☎61
New Zealand ☎64
Republic of Ireland ☎353
UK ☎44
US and Canada ☎1

Email

One of the best ways to keep in touch while travelling is using a **free internet email address** that can be accessed from anywhere, for example YahooMail or Hotmail – accessible through Ⓦwww.yahoo.com and Ⓦwww.hotmail.com. Once you've set up an account, you can use these sites to pick up and send mail from any place that provides internet access – cafés, hotels and so on. If you're taking a **laptop** with you, Ⓦwww.kropla.com is a useful website giving details of how to plug your lap-top in when abroad, phone country codes and information about electrical systems in different countries.

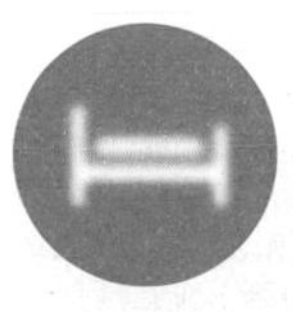

Accommodation

Accommodation choices in the Caribbean range from basic guesthouses with no hot water through genteel bed and breakfasts and boutique hotels – usually slightly away from the cruise ship ports and main tourist drag – to moderately priced family resorts, "fun" all-inclusives for couples or families set right on the beach, all the way up to luxury hotels with spa facilities and ultra-exclusive, remote, eco-resorts serving five-star cuisine.

True **budget accommodation** in much of the Caribbean is hard to come by, especially in the more exclusive islands. If most of your budget will go toward getting to the Caribbean, then Cuba, the Dominican Republic and the rural parts of Trinidad and Tobago have some of the lowest costs of living and accommodation in the region, as tourism is still developing. Be aware, though, that youth hostels and camping facilities are practically non-existent, and private rooms in local houses are usually not an option, except in places like Cuba and the Dominican Republic.

Most tourist offices will happily provide a list of accommodation but bear in mind that establishments often have to pay to be included on these lists. Generally, however, tourist boards will not recommend specific accommodation, nor will they book it – for this, you either have to go through a travel agent or do it yourself. The **web** is a great place to look for accommodation choices, as you can often check out rates, photographs of properties and rooms, and special offers and amenities before you decide on a place. The website of the Caribbean Tourism Organisation, Ⓦwww.doitcaribbean.com/accommodation/index.html, is a good place to start your independent search.

Prices are much cheaper **off-season**, and many establishments will give a reduced price for longer stays in the low season. It's worth asking around and bargaining a little, as desperate hoteliers will sometimes upgrade rooms or drop the hefty accommodation tax in order to get tourist custom. The more popular destinations may, however, have a seven-night minimum stay, especially in the high season.

Hotels

The range of Caribbean **hotel** accommodation is astounding, not only within islands but often within resorts themselves. Be aware that if you seem to be getting an extraordinary deal for a top-name resort, you may well end up in a small room far from the beach and other amenities – ask to see the room, or at least ask for a description in writing – before you sign anything or pay. Hotel buildings themselves range from modern, purpose-built resorts to old plantation mansions, and the most basic hotel rooms will usually have a mosquito net and possibly a sink; prices increase with minor amenities

Accommodation price codes

All accommodation listed in this guide has been graded according to the following **price categories**. Rates are generally for the least expensive double or twin room in high season, and do not include tax, except where this is explicitly stated. For islands that quote prices in currencies other than US dollars, we've converted the local price to US dollars, unless we've stated otherwise.

❶ up to US$25	❹ US$75–100	❼ US$160–200
❷ US$25–50	❺ US$100–130	❽ US$200–250
❸ US$50–75	❻ US$130–160	❾ US$250 +

such as a bathroom, air-conditioning, or cable TV and a phone, and increase exponentially with the range of extras available: plunge pools, fridges stocked with drinks, mountain or sea views, beachfront access and outdoor showers and hammocks. Whatever your preference, there's probably a hotel in the Caribbean that has what you're after.

All-inclusives

Pioneered in Jamaica, **all-inclusive hotels** are resorts where a single price covers the room, all meals, snacks and tips, and often all drinks and sports (though scuba diving can be an exception). The advantages of staying at an all-inclusive are the product offered, which can be excellent value, along with the convenience of not having to reach for your wallet every time. The main disadvantage is that there's not much incentive for guests to get out and sample the wide variety of local restuarants and bars – or get a feel for the islands themselves. At the smaller resorts, especially, the appeal of having everything provided in one place can wear off quickly. It's also worth bearing in mind that all-inclusives do little for the local economy: the chains are invariably foreign, much of the food they serve is imported and guests don't frequent local businesses.

Apartments and villas

One of the best ways to save money if you're travelling as a family or in a group is to rent a **villa or apartment** for the length of your stay. Accommodation ranges from secluded, one-bedroom apartments on a remote stretch of beach to palatial villas built for parties and group weekends. They are typically self-catering, with well-equipped kitchens or kitchenettes, and can stand alone or as part of a "holiday village" where you share amenities such as a laundry, restaurant and shop with other holiday-makers but retain the privacy and independence of your own cottage. Independently leased apartments – as opposed to those which form part of a "village" – can cost anything from US$250 per week for a beachfront one-bedroom in the Dominican Republic to US$1500 per week for a two-bedroom, two-bathroom property on St Lucia or US$1500 per night for a five-bedroom waterfront estate with decks and a huge pool in Barbados. Property owners tend to stipulate the maximum number of guests allowed (reckon on two per room) but are sometimes flexible, allowing additional people to stay at a fee. Extras can include anything from a maid who cleans daily or weekly (often included in the price of the more exclusive places) to free use of a car, or at least discounted car rental.

Caribbean villa rental agencies

Caribbean Way 3883 St Jean Blvd, Suite 501, Dollard-Des-Ormeaux, Quebec, H9G 3B9, ⓣ514/620-6989 or 1-877/953-7400, ⓕ514/620-4054, ⓦwww.caribbeanway.com. Representing over 600 villa properties, some on six private islands, with photos, information and booking available online.

Island Hideaways 3843 Highland Oaks, Fairfax, VA 22033 ⓣ703/378-7840 or 1-800/832-2302, ⓕ703/378-4722, ⓦwww.islandhideaways.com. Agents representing private island hideaways throughout the Caribbean with an emphasis on luxurious, unique properties.

The Owners' Syndicate 6 Port House, Plantation Wharf, Battersea, London SW11 3TY ⓣ020/7801

9801, ⓦ www.ownerssyndicate.com. Villa specialists with properties on Anguilla, Antigua, Barbados, Grenada, Jamaica, Mustique, Nevis, St Lucia, Tobago and the Virgin Islands.
Villa Connections ⓣ 01625/858158, ⓦ www.prestburytravelgroup.co.uk. Established for 15 years and offering a choice of over 300 villas all over the Caribbean. Several properties are available on private islands.

Guesthouses

Guesthouses, usually with basic rooms and shared bathrooms, and rarely on the beach, can nonetheless be a welcome bargain option for Caribbean travellers on a budget and usually cost no more than US$30/night. In areas where there are no campsites and little choice of private rooms in family homes, these locally owned places often work out to be the least expensive places to stay.

In recent years, a number of boutique guesthouses, or bed and breakfast operations – small, intimate and luxurious, operating more along the lines of miniature hotels – have been cropping up on some of the more exclusive islands. They make a lovely alternative to large-scale resorts and, while they might not be the most private places in the region, they are often friendly, accommodating and very stylish.

Alternative accommodation

Unregulated camping is illegal, or else strictly controlled on many Caribbean islands, in an effort to protect the beauty and wildlife of the region's indigenous rainforests. The few regulated campsites in existence are covered in the individual country chapters.

In Cuba, visitors have the option of "camping" in rudimentary cabins set in countryside areas called *campisimos*; there is at least one in every province, and at little more than US$5 per cabin they are excellent value.

Food and drink

Caribbean food and drink can be a delight and a shock to the Western palate, with its polar extremes of heavily fried foods and fresh fruit, but it's a varied cuisine that's well worth seeking out. A blend of African, Indian, Arab, Chinese, Spanish, French, Dutch and British influences, Caribbean cooking draws on a wide range of ingredients: African groundnuts, yams, okra and oxtail; East Indian curries and rotis; French Creole and bouillabaisse; and Spanish sofritos and citrus fruits.

Fruits and vegetables

Amongst the many **fruits** on offer, some of the best are the familiar favourites: bananas, grapefruits and oranges all tasting more sweet, juicy and flavoursome than any of our imported equivalents. Juices made from citrus fruits, and fresh-baked banana breads are available everywhere. More exotic fruits include the milky white pulp of the **soursop**, from which a breakfast juice is made; the **carambola** or **star fruit**, which is de-seeded and then eaten whole or sliced in salads or as a garnish for drinks and meat dishes; **guava** – often used to make breakfast jelly – and **coconuts**, which produce milk when ripe and a refreshing coconut-flavoured water when green.

Vegetables tend to be versatile and filling, like the **yucca**, **breadfruit** or **callalloo** – a spinach-type vegetable in Jamaica, where it is used like turnip or greens, and a leek-like plant in the Eastern Caribbean, also known as **dasheen** and often used to thicken soup.

Plantains, sweet when ripe and mealy when green, are prepared as a side dish to rice and beans or fried and made into chips, a delicious accompaniment to a local beer or a cocktail at sunset. Also popular is **christophene**, whose pale green and crisp flesh is much used in Chinese, Latin American and West Indian cooking; **calabaza**, a generic term for West Indian pumpkins, which are often similar in texture to butternut squash; **cassava**, a root vegetable that comes in bitter and sweet forms; and **okra**, a finger-shaped vegetable that is often added to soups and stews.

Meat and seafood

Meat – with the exception of goat – is expensive and most islanders survive on vegetables and delicious variations of chicken and fish; in Cuba, however, **pork** is a major feature of most cooking.

Unsurprisingly, the region's **seafood** is excellent, cheap and easy to come by. Popular Caribbean fruits of the sea include lobster, crab, shrimp, blue marlin, kingfish and flying fish – all of which should be sampled at a local weekend fish fry, which is a great opportunity to fill up on the freshest fish for very little money, while soaking in some atmosphere, music and some local rum. The fish is cooked by the road, barbecued, fried or grilled and served with hot cakes – heavy, grilled patties of unleavened bread.

By and large, **soups and stews** are variations on a theme, based on what's available at the local market on a given day – spiked with onions and peppers and bulked out with "tubers" or root vegetables. No stew would be complete without a bottle of Caribbean **hot sauce**, developed by the Carib and Arawak Indians who combined hot pepper juice, cassava juice, brown sugar, cloves and cinnamon to produce a thick, tangy sauce for slathering over barbecued fish, chicken and the like.

Cooking styles

Cooking styles in the Caribbean islands are as diverse and heterogeneous as the various nations that have populated the region over the years. Generally, French and Spanish styles predominate, with lots of garlicky, tomato sauces served over fish, and meat cooked very simply in an oven or on an open grill. Vegetables usually come on the side, as do rice and beans.

Yet despite similarities in cuisine, most of the islands have distinct leanings that show through in the most local of dishes and from top-notch restaurants to street-side stalls. **Criollo cooking** is popular on Spanish-speaking islands such as Puerto Rico, Cuba and the Dominican Republic, and makes liberal use of cilantro and mixed seasonings like *adobo*. Chefs in the Netherlands Antilles add Indonesian touches such as soy sauce, satay and nasi goreng, while old French colonies in particular have a tendency to cook in a Creole style, in which chives, bouquet garni and tomato are made into a delicious, thick sauce and applied liberally to fish and chicken.

Jerk cooking is also common throughout the Caribbean, and originated with the African slaves who came to the islands in the 1600s, coated meat in spice mixtures (jerk) using island-grown ingredients such as ginger, thyme, allspice, hot peppers and green onion and then marinated it before cooking it very slowly in a pit, smoker or on a barbecue grill.

Drinking

Rum is the liquor of choice in the Caribbean, and most islands distil their own brand. You'll find rum distilleries, factories and museums all over the islands, from Jamaica and Barbados to Trinidad and Tobago, with the most famous brand, Bacardi, being made in Puerto Rico. Rum comes in three distinct varieties: **white rum**, a sweet, fruity drink used as the base for the popular Caribbean cocktail, Ti-Punch; **ambered rum**, which is white rum aged in barrels of oak, from which it gets its darker colour and slightly more dense flavour; and the richest rum of all – **old rum**, aged for three to six years in barrels of oak from North America that once contained bourbon or whisky.

Caribbean **beers** are refreshing and moderately light, somewhere between their European and American counterparts. Particularly good are Jamaica's Red Stripe, St Lucia's Piton lager and ubiquitous regional favourite, Carib, which is brewed on Trinidad and Tobago. Others include Antigua's pale lager Wadadli, the Barbadian and Bahamian lagers Banks Beer and Kalik, and the Dominican Kubuli, made with the island's spring water.

Fantastic **fruit juice** concoctions are a great alcohol-free alternative: the quality of Caribbean citrus fruits is very high, and limes, lemons, oranges and grapefruits are available freshly squeezed in most cafés and restaurants, as well as by the side of the road. The roadside is also the place to buy delicious coconut water – vendors simply sell you the unripe coconut with a hole drilled through to the delicious sweet water inside, and a straw. Tropical fruit juices such as pineapple, mango and papaya are also widely available, as is a delicious cranberry-coloured beverage made from the flowers of the slightly sour sorrel plant, and the almost creamy, milky-white juice of the prickly and dark-skinned soursop.

Tea and **coffee** are readily available but – with the exception of strong, rich roasts from Jamaica and Dominica – tend to be of negligible quality; instead, many islanders will drink a cup of milky hot chocolate made from the shavings of a locally grown cocoa stick with their breakfast.

There are also some local forms of **soda**: the ubiquitous Tang, which comes in different flavours, Jamaican cream soda and home-made ginger beer, for which the island is justly famous.

Public holidays and festivals

Each island will have its own unique holidays, saint days, Constitution, independence and festival or carnival days during which nobody works – except for employees of specific tourism enterprises, such as hotel workers and resort staff. For island-specific information refer to individual chatpers.

Opening hours for most tourist attractions are daily 9am to 4 or 5pm, although some businesses close early on a Saturday – specific opening hours vary from place to place and island to island. Caribbean **banks** are usually open from 8 or 9am to 2 or 3pm Monday to Thursday, with extended hours (often until 5pm) on Fridays. Weekend banking is practically non-existent.

Public holidays

The main **public holidays** celebrated throughout the Caribbean, during which virtually all shops and offices close, are:

January 1 New Year's Day
Good Friday
Easter Monday
May 1 Labour Day
Whit Monday
Dec 25 Christmas Day
Dec 26 Boxing Day

Bear in mind that islands ruled by European countries will celebrate the national holidays of the governing country; for example, Bastille Day is celebrated in Guadeloupe and Queen's Day in the Netherlands Antilles.

Carnival

Celebrated throughout the region, Caribbean **carnival** is an elaborate spectacle, when your senses are assaulted by the best in Caribbean culture and camaraderie. It has its roots in the pre-Lenten **carnevale** of early Italian Roman Catholicism, a time when Catholics were meant to finish up the meat in their pantries in preparation for the fasting period of Lent. The Italians chose to go out in style with a wild costume festival (*carne vale* "farewell to flesh"), and the practice soon spread to France, Spain and Portugal and then to the Americas as they were colonized by Catholic Europe. In the Caribbean itself, carnival has grown from a two-day festival into a season of hedonism and debauchery stretching from February to August. These days more than ever it's all about spectacle, and with each passing year costumes are more flamboyant, dance routines more daring and headdresses more precariously balanced as each island seeks to throw the ultimate Caribbean carnival, probably at its peak on islands such as Trinidad and Tobago and Guadeloupe.

Sports and outdoor activities

The biggest spectator sports down this way are cricket, soccer and, in certain cases like Cuba, Puerto Rico and the Dominican Republic, baseball. If you're looking to participate, there's plenty of resort space with top-notch golf courses, tennis and other leisure activities. More actively, numerous islands have, if not mountainous and/or rain-forested interiors, at least a few good areas to explore on hikes; bike trips and horseback riding are other enjoyable options.

Cricket

Cricket is respected and exalted throughout parts of the Caribbean, and the West Indies team is among the very best on the planet. Those interested in the game as it is played here should check out Ⓦwww.caribbean-cricket.com for details of players, match play and an excellent news section. Another good source of information is the official site of the West Indies cricket board, Ⓦwww.windiescricket.com. The top islands for watching the sport are Jamaica, Antigua and Barbados.

Baseball

In the Dominican Republic **baseball** is the national spectator sport. Many of the top American major league players have come from here, including Alex Rodríguez, Sammy Sosa and Pedro Martínez. A professional winter season runs from mid-November through mid-February, after which the winner goes on to compete in the **Caribbean Series**. In addition to the professional season, amateur winter seasons take place in San Francisco de Macorís, San Juan de la Maguana, San Cristóbal and a few other towns.

The Cuban national league, the **Serie Nacional de Beisbol**, takes place over a regular season that usually begins in October and finishes with the playoffs in March and April. Every provincial capital has a baseball stadium and, during the season, teams play five times a week, so there's a good chance of catching a game if you're in the country during the summer months.

Like the Dominican Republic, Puerto Rico has produced many ballplayers who've succeeded in the US major leagues, among them the great Roberto Clemente. The island competes in the Caribbean Series against teams from Venezuela, Mexico and the Dominican Republic, and the season runs from November to March.

Hiking

An excellent way to see some untouched, and often protected, indigenous wildlife, as well as enjoying the sunshine, is to go **hiking**. The lush rainforests of Puerto Rico, Dominica, Antigua, the Dominican Republic and St Lucia, the coastal hikes of St Croix or the huge national park that constitutes most of St John in the US Virgin Islands, are all highly recommended. For more detailed information about hiking, see the individual island chapters.

The rules of cricket

The **rules of cricket** are so complex that the official rule book runs to twenty pages. The basics, however, are by no means as Byzantine as the game's detractors make out. There are two teams of eleven players. A team wins by scoring more **runs** than the other team and dismissing the opposition – in other words, a team could score many runs more than the opposition, but still not win if the last enemy **batsman** doggedly stays "in" (hence ensuring a draw). The match is divided into innings, when one team **bats** and the other team **fields**. The number of innings varies depending on the type of competition: one-day matches have one per team, Test matches have two.

The aim of the fielding side is to limit the runs scored and get the batsman "out". Two players from the batting side are on the pitch at any one time. The bowling side has a **bowler**, a **wicketkeeper** and nine **fielders**. Two umpires, one standing behind the stumps at the bowler's end and one square on to the play, are responsible for adjudicating whether a batsman is out. Each innings is divided into **overs**, consisting of six deliveries, after which the wicketkeeper changes ends, the bowler is changed and the fielders move positions. The batsmen score runs either by running up and down from wicket to wicket (one length = one run), or by hitting the ball over the boundary rope, scoring four runs if it crosses the boundary having touched the ground, and six runs if it flies over. The main ways a batsman can be dismissed are: by being "clean bowled", where the bowler dislodges the bails of the **wicket** (the horizontal pieces of wood resting on the stumps); by being "run out", which is when one of the fielding side dislodges the bails with the ball while the batsman is running between the wickets; by being caught, which is when any of the fielding side catches the ball after the batsman has hit it and before it touches the ground; or "LBW" (leg before wicket), where the batsman blocks with his leg a delivery that would otherwise have hit the stumps.

The best plan is to start early in the morning and cover plenty of distance before the midday heat sets in, or else choose a hike that goes through forest. Some of the mountain trails in the Caribbean are badly marked and even dangerous; check with the relevant tourist authority about conditions before you head off, and be sure to tell someone where you are going if you are planning to hike alone. There are also plenty of **tour companies** that offer private hiking trips if you'd prefer to travel with a group.

Remember to bring plenty of water, a hat, a spare pair of socks, a jumper, a map, compass and first-aid kit, sunblock, a sandwich and some high-energy snack foods, insect repellent, sunglasses and a camera. Many Caribbean trails have waterfalls and swimming holes along the way, so bring a bathing suit if a dip might be on the agenda.

Camping is illegal on many Caribbean islands; on the few where it is allowed, permission is usually required in advance from the relevant government department and a fee is payable.

Ocean activities

The Caribbean's vast, clear waters make the region a veritable playground for watersports. The quality of diving and snorkelling in many places is superb, thanks to the sheer abundance of marine life, and there are excellent opportunities for sport fishing, waterskiing, windsurfing, parasailing, jet-skiing, kayaking, glass-bottomed boat trips and sailing, most of which are usually offered by the major resorts for free. Resorts are also packed with operators offering dive trips and snorkelling excursions; the most reputable are listed throughout the Guide.

Scuba diving and snorkelling

Wall dives, wreck dives, under-mountain dives, coral gardens, pinnacles, muck dives and slopes all await the **scuba diver** in the Caribbean. The most famous site of all is off Virgin Gorda, where the wreck of the *HMS Rhone* has lain since 1867. Other famous wrecks are to be found off St Croix and St Lucia; Stingray City on Grand Cayman is renowned for the scores of ray fish that populate the site and are willing to be fed by hand. Also highly regarded are Saba's underwater lava flows and black sand, or the amazingly accessible reefs of Bonaire and St Lucia. Bonaire is perhaps the finest of all the dive islands, as its entire perimeter has been protected as a marine park since 1979 and eco-friendly regulation is very much enforced.

Each of the islands famous for diving is well equipped in terms of instruction courses and diving package deals and many people choose to become certified as divers on their Caribbean holiday. Instruction ranges from r**esort courses** for beginners that last a day (US$50–150) to the more advanced **open-water certification**, which can take three to five days and varies more in price (starting around US$300). You'll need a clean bill of health and at least a week where you can dive every day; remember you cannot fly until 24 hours hours after your last dive, due to the difference in air pressure.

If you want to go out to sea, check with dive operators as they often take **snorkellers** on their trips. Most resorts provide free snorkelling gear; if yours doesn't it's worth bringing your own as buying equipment in the Caribbean can be expensive.

Scuba holiday operators

Island Holidays/Dive4Less ⓣ770/461 4838 or 1-888/246-6452, ⓦwww.diveforless.net. Guaranteed lowest prices for scuba-diving holidays in the Caribbean.

Scuba Safari PO Box 8, Edenbridge, Kent TN9 7ZS, ⓣ01352/851 196, ⓦwww.scuba-safaris.com. UK-based company offering diving holidays to Turks and Caicos, Saba and the Cayman Islands.

Scuba Voyages 595 Fairbanks St, Corona, CA 92879 ⓣ909/371-1831 or 1-800/544-7631, ⓦwww.scubavoyages.com. All-inclusive diving packages to Bonaire, Dominica, Saba, St Lucia, St Vincent and Tobago.

Snooba Travel Ltd PO Box 31487, London W4 2QW ⓣ020/8987 3111, ⓦwww.snooba.com. Snorkelling and diving trips all over the Caribbean.

US Dive Travel ⓣ952/953-4124, ⓦwww.caribbeandivetravel.com. Family-run operation offering Caribbean-wide holidays.

Fishing

The Caribbean boasts some good **sport fishing**, an expensive though potentially dramatic pastime. The waters around the Bahamas and the Turks and Caicos especially offer countless fishing opportunities, among them deep-sea fishing for wahoo, tuna and marlin and shark; bottom-fishing for reef fish such as grouper, snapper and parrotfish; and fly-fishing for bonefish. Also recommended is big-game fishing along the southern coast of the Dominican Republic, around Trinidad and Tobago, and off the northern coast of Cuba. Throughout these islands you'll find plenty of charter boat operators offering fishing excursions as well as fully equipped boats for rent. Most boats take groups of up to six in number, and can cost anywhere from US$400–1000/day.

Sailing

Needless to say, the Caribbean is a major **sailing destination**. Those not fortunate enough to visit the region on their own sailboats will find a slew of charter operators offering all manner of trips, from rum-soaked party cruises and luxurious yacht charters to relaxed day trips of island-hopping. Resorts, too, often rent out small sailboats for use close to shore. For details on specific islands refer to the individual chapters.

Crime and personal safety

With a total of 35 countries making up the region, each with different levels of population, development and standards of living, it's difficult to do anything but generalize about safety standards in the Caribbean. On the whole, though, the region is politically stable and safe. If you don't venture outside the resorts and heavily touristed areas, you might believe that it is also economically prosperous – though this is not necessarily the case, as it is heavily reliant on tourist trade for survival and large pockets of poverty do exist.

However, certain common-sense measures should be observed when travelling in the region. For tourists, the most common hazards are **bag snatching** and **pickpocketing**, so always make sure you sling bags across your body rather than letting them dangle from one shoulder, keep cameras concealed whenever possible, don't carry valuables in easy-to-reach places and always take a minimum of cash out with you. Needless to say, don't leave bags and possessions unattended anywhere, especially at the beach. Most **resorts** and **hotels** in the Caribbean are very safe; guests should nonetheless use room safes when they're available. Also avoid leaving personal possessions on view in a rental car, even in the trunk, as these are also a prime target.

Violent street crime – such as tourist assault and even rape – while rare on most islands, has been reported throughout the region. Incidents tend to take place at weekend "jump-ups" or **street parties**, where locals and tourists mingle freely and many visitors make the mistake of ostentatiously displaying their wealth. Visitors should take extra care at street parties and during **carnival** time, when everything seems like one big heady mix of music, alcohol and people.

That said, criminals can attack at any time, and are more likely to do so at night: **women** especially should take care after dusk and try not to wander through unpopulated areas alone at any time. Avoid deserted beaches or poorly lit areas at night, and make sure that any taxi you take is officially licensed – look for identification, take down the licence number and check the plates for the identifying "H" symbol (if there is one – see individual chapter entries for details of taxi travel). For advice for women travellers, see p.54.

As an additional precaution, visitors should know that **car theft** has been on the increase, so be sure to check all documentation carefully – sometimes vehicle leases or rentals may not be fully covered by local insurance, and car thieves often target rental cars. If you are unlucky enough to be the **victim** of theft or other offences, report the incident immediately as you'll need a police report to make any insurance claim.

Visitors should also be aware that heavy **drug** trafficking and production is a major problem in many Caribbean countries – the Bahamas and the Dominican Republic have been included on the US government's list of major narcotics producers. Penalties for committing a crime in the Caribbean can be extremely harsh, and those for drug use, possession and trafficking are severe and usually include jail sentences and heavy fines.

Certain islands in the Caribbean – especially Cuba, Jamaica and the Dominican Republic – are known for both their potent **marijuana** and the lax attitude of the authorities regarding recreational marijuana use: Jamaica's local **marijuana** crop brings in more cash than its tourist industry. However, the consumption or possession of marijuana is not legal on any of the islands, and as governments of individual countries try to crack down on drug trafficking in general, penalties are likely to be harsh.

Lesbian and gay travellers

Like any other large region, attitudes towards homosexuality in the Caribbean differ from place to place. The Bahamas take the lead in terms of positive attitude, with the government openly condemning homophobia, although there still isn't much of a gay scene. Trinidad and Tobago has had a gay rights group since 1994, and the fairly sizeable community is quite visible, especially during Carnival. In Puerto Rico and Jamaica, gay and lesbian visitors are not only accepted but sustained by a lively gay social scene. On many islands, such as Aruba, Bonaire and Curaçao, there is no organized gay life as such, but because of the free-thinking Dutch influence on these islands, a live-and-let-live attitude prevails. Barbados, the British Virgin Islands and Saba operate in a similar fashion. Martinique has an emergent and fairly open gay community and St Lucia has several gay-friendly resorts, though attitudes in towns and cities may be less friendly.

Other islands, however, are much less tolerant: in the Cayman Islands, a gay cruise ship was turned away from the port; attitudes in the US Virgin Islands – with the exception of St John's nude beach – and in Dominica are fairly intolerant. In Cuba public displays of affection between gays are very much frowned upon, although there is a nascent gay scene, albeit an underground one.

Contacts for gay and lesbian travellers

In the US and Canada

Alyson Adventures PO Box 180129, Boston, MA 02118 ⓣ1800/825-9766, ⓦwww.alysonadventures.com. Adventure holidays all over the world, including gay scuba diving packages to the Caribbean.

Damron Company PO Box 422458, San Francisco, CA 94142 ⓣ415/255-0404 or 1-800/462-6654, ⓦwww.damron.com. Publisher of the *Men's Travel Guide*, a pocket-sized yearbook full of listings of hotels, bars, clubs and resources for gay men; the *Women's Traveler*, which provides similar listings for lesbians; and *Damron Accommodations*, which lists over 1000 accommodations for gays and lesbians worldwide.

Envoy Resorts and Tours 1649 N Wells St, Suite 201, Chicago, IL 60614 ⓣ312/787-2400 or ⓣ1800/44ENVOY, ⓦwww.envoytravel.com/rainbow.html. Gay-specific information and travel

services, including gay cruise ship bookings.
Ferrari Publications PO Box 37887, Phoenix, AZ 85069 ☎602/863-2408 or 1-800/962-2912, ⓦwww.ferrariguides.com. Publishes *Ferrari Gay Travel A to Z*, a gay and lesbian guide to international travel; *Inn Places*, a worldwide accommodation guide; the guides *Men's Travel in Your Pocket* and *Women's Travel in Your Pocket*, and the quarterly *Ferrari Travel Report*.
International Gay & Lesbian Travel Association 4331 N Federal Hwy, Suite 304, Ft Lauderdale, FL 33308 ☎1-800/448-8550, ⓦwww.iglta.org. Trade group that can provide a list of gay- and lesbian-owned or -friendly travel agents, accommodation and other travel businesses.
Out and About Travel Providence, RI ☎1800/842-4753, ⓦwww.outandaboutravel.com. Gay- and lesbian-oriented cruises, tours and packages.

In the UK

ⓦ**www.gaytravel.co.uk** Online gay and lesbian travel agent, offering good deals on all types of holidays. Also lists gay- and lesbian-friendly hotels around the world.
Dream Waves Redcot High St, Child Okeford, Blandford DT22 8ET ☎01258/861 149, ⓔdreamwaves@aol.com. Specializes in exclusively gay holidays, including skiing trips and summer sun packages.
Madison Travel 118 Western Rd, Hove, East Sussex BN3 1DB ☎01273/202 532, ⓦwww.madisontravel.co.uk. Established travel agents specializing in packages to gay- and lesbian-friendly mainstream destinations.

In Australia and New Zealand

Gay and Lesbian Travel PO Box 208, Darlinghurst, NSW 1300 ☎02/9380 4115, ⓦwww.galta.com.au. Directory and links for gay and lesbian travel worldwide.
Parkside Travel 70 Glen Osmond Rd, Parkside, SA 5063 ☎08/8274 1222 or 1800/888 501, ⓔhwtravel@senet.com.au. Gay travel agent associated with local branch of Hervey World Travel; covers all aspects of gay and lesbian travel worldwide.
Silke's Travel 263 Oxford St, Darlinghurst, NSW 2010 ☎02/9380 6244 or 1800/807 860, ⓔsilba@magna.com.au. Long-established gay and lesbian specialist, with the emphasis on women's travel.
Tearaway Travel 52 Porter St, Prahan, VIC 3181 ☎03/9510 6344, ⓔtearaway@bigpond.com. Gay-specific business dealing with international and domestic travel.

Gay resources on the web

Gay and Lesbian Travel ⓦwww.galta.com.au. Directory and links for gay and lesbian travel in Australia and worldwide.
Gay Caribbean ⓦwww.gaycaribbean.net. Covers accommodations, meetings and social events throughout the Caribbean, with links to individual islands.
Gay Dive ⓦwww.gaydive.com/home.htm. Provides summaries about attitudes on individual islands as well as information on dive sites and gay-friendly accommodation.
Gay Places to Stay ⓦwww.gayplaces2stay.com/caribbean.html. Information about accommodation in Bonaire, the Cayman Islands, St Croix, Jamaica, St Kitts, Puerto Rico, Saba and St Martin.
Gay Travel ⓦwww.gaytravel.com. The site for trip planning, bookings and general information about international travel.

Travellers with disabilities

Cruise lines and top Caribbean resorts have made big steps over the course of the last decade toward catering for disabled travellers, with many cruise ships now offering cabins that have been fitted out for wheelchairs and the number of wheelchair-accessible cabins having increased by 60 percent between 1999 and 2002. Of course, a lot remains to be done, and some islands, such as Dominica, have virtually no facilities, accommodation or restaurants that cater to travellers with disabilities, save in the top resorts. Remember that while Caribbean legislation is nowhere near as stringent as American or European law when it comes to accessibility for all, tourism has taken a downturn in recent years and many of the larger resorts are ensuring that their premises can cater for most special needs in order to fill beds. Especially at the top end of the market, it shouldn't be too difficult to find accommodation and operators who can cater for your particular needs. The important thing is to check beforehand with tour companies, hotels and airlines that they can accommodate you specifically.

Contacts for travellers with disabilities

In the US and Canada

Directions Unlimited 123 Green Lane, Bedford Hills, NY 10507 ⓣ914/241-1700 or 1-800/533-5343. Tour operator specializing in custom tours for people with disabilities.

Mobility International USA 451 Broadway, Eugene, OR 97401, voice and TDD ⓣ541/343-1284, ⓦwww.miusa.org. Information and referral services, access guides, tours and exchange programmes. Annual membership US$35 (includes quarterly newsletter).

Society for the Advancement of Travelers with Handicaps (SATH) 347 Fifth Ave, New York, NY 10016 ⓣ212/447-7284, ⓦwww.sath.org. Non-profit educational organization that has actively represented travellers with disabilities since 1976.

Travel Information Service Moss Rehabilitation Hospital, 1200 West Tabor Rd, Philadelphia, PA 19141 ⓣ215/456-9600. Information and referral service for disabled travellers – they cannot book accommodation, and only accept queries by mail or telephone.

Twin Peaks Press Box 129, Vancouver, WA 98661 ⓣ360/694-2462 or 1-800/637-2256, ⓦwww.twinpeak.virtualave.net. Publisher of the *Directory of Travel Agencies for the Disabled* (US$19.95), listing more than 370 agencies worldwide; *Travel for the Disabled* (US$19.95); the *Directory of Accessible Van Rentals* (US$12.95) and *Wheelchair Vagabond* (US$19.95), loaded with personal tips.

Wheels Up! (no address) ⓣ1-888/389-4335, ⓦwww.wheelsup.com. Provides discounted airfare, tour and cruise prices for disabled travellers; also publishes a free monthly newsletter and has a comprehensive website.

In the UK and Ireland

Access Travel 6 The Hillock, Astley, Lancashire M29 7GW ⓣ01942/888 844, ⓦwww.access-travel.co.uk. Small tour operator that can arrange flights, transfer and accommodation. Personally checks out places before recommendation and can guarantee accommodation standards in many countries – for places they do not cover, they can arrange flight-only deals.

Disability Action Group 2 Annadale Ave, Belfast BT7 3JH ⓣ028/9049 1011. Provides information about access for disabled travellers abroad.

Holiday Care 2nd Floor, Imperial Building, Victoria Rd, Horley, Surrey RH6 7PZ ⓣ01293/774 535, ⓦwww.holidaycare.org.uk. Providers of a £5 booklet about accessible cruise holidays and information about financial help for holidays.

Irish Wheelchair Association Aras Cuchulainn, Blackheath Drive, Clontarf, Dublin 3 ⓣ01/833 8241, ⓕ833 3873, ⓦwwwiwa.ie. Useful information about travelling abroad with a wheelchair.

Tripscope Alexandra House, Albany Rd, Brentford, Middlesex TW8 0NE ⓣ08457/585 641,

Ⓦwww.justmobility.co.uk/tripscope. This registered charity provides a national telephone information service offering free advice on UK and international transport for those with a mobility problem.

In Australia and New Zealand

ACROD (Australian Council for Rehabilitation of the Disabled) PO Box 60, Curtin, ACT 2605 Ⓣ02/6282 4333; 24 Cabarita Rd, Cabarita, NSW 2137 Ⓣ02/9743 2699. Provides lists of travel agencies and tour operators for people with disabilities.
Disabled Persons Assembly 4/173–175 Victoria St, Wellington, New Zealand Ⓣ04/801 9100. Resource centre with lists of travel agencies and tour operators for people with disabilities.

Disabled travel advice on the web

Access-Able Ⓦwww.access-able.com. Online resource for travellers with disabilities, including detailed information on cruise lines that cater for disabled travellers.
Jim Lubin's Disability Resource Ⓦwww.makoa.org/index.html. Extensive database of links for disabled travel around the world.

Directory

CHILDREN While many people see the Caribbean as an adult-oriented, honeymoon and cruise ship destination, an increasing number of all-inclusive resorts cater for children, offering kids' meals, activities and watersports. Be sure to check with your accommodation about bringing children as some hotels prefer couples-only. When children are catered for, however, facilities can range widely from the odd banana boat rides, evening disco, afternoon tennis match or tortoise race to comprehensive activity programmes involving nature walks, arts and crafts, pool games and even field trips.
CIGARETTES Smoking is legal and very much on display in the Caribbean, although you are unlikely to see many locals enjoying the infamous hand-rolled Cuban and Dominican cigars. Many of the larger resorts will have non-smoking areas, but visitors should ensure they request a non smoking room when they book – the alternative can often smell like a freshly filled ashtray. Smokers wanting to take advantage of duty-free prices are advised to do so in their home airport, as Caribbean airports can be small and dingy, with minimal – if any – choice.
ELECTRICITY Most islands in the Caribbean use 110V (US) sockets, some have 220/240V (UK) only and some have both. Larger hotels will usually have an adaptor, but you should bring your own just in case. (See box overleaf.)
GETTING MARRIED The Caribbean is one of the most popular wedding destinations in the world, as well as one favoured by many honeymooning couples. You can't, however, simply turn up and expect to be married straight away – islands have different requirements about the length of stay prior to the ceremony. Some require a notarized letter declaring the single status of the bride and groom or an affidavit for couples under the age of 18. Residency requirements can be anything from newly arrived to fifteen days. Island tourist offices will give information on marriage requirements on their island, although many of the classier establishments will arrange everything for you. If in doubt, contact the tourist office of your chosen destination – or check their website for details.
HURRICANES The hurricane season begins around June or July, lasts six months or so and is most threatening between August and October. If a hurricane watch is posted, it means hurricane conditions are possible within the next 36 hours; if a warning is posted, conditions are expected usually within 24 hours. Advice about dealing with watches and warnings is usually posted in hotels and guesthouses, but should you be away from your accommodation, get indoors and stay away from windows. Be aware, too, that a tornado will often follow a hurricane.
TIME All islands in the Caribbean are on Atlantic Time, one hour ahead of Eastern Standard Time and four hours behind Greenwich Mean Time.
TIPPING Tipping rates, which can vary in the islands, are covered more specifically in the individual chapters. Hotels normally include a

Electricity

Anguilla	110v	**Guadeloupe**	110/220v
Antigua and Barbuda	110/220v	**Jamaica**	110/220v
Aruba	110v	**Martinique**	220v
Bahamas	120v	**Puerto Rico**	110v
Barbados	110v/220v adaptors	**Saba**	110v
		St Barts	220v
Bonaire	120v	**St Eustatius**	110/220v
British Virgin Islands	110v	**St Kitts and Nevis**	230v
Cayman Islands	110v	**St Lucia**	220v
Cuba	110v, some 220v	**St Martin/St Maarten**	110/220v
Curaçao	110/220v	**St Vincent and the Grenadines**	220/240v
Dominica	220v	**Trinidad and Tobago**	115/220v
Dominican Republic	110v	**Turks and Caicos**	110v
Grenada	220/240v	**US Virgin Islands**	120v

service charge in their bills but if your accommodation doesn't include the charge, or if you want to make sure that the staff get tipped (and not the management), aim to give around US$1 a night per guest to housekeeping staff directly and per bag to porters. (Note: staff at all-inclusives are not meant to be tipped at all.) Restaurants often add 10–15 percent automatically to their bills, as do most taxi drivers, but the percentages vary from island to island and in Jamaica and Puerto Rico a tip of up to 20 percent can be expected.

Women travellers Though violent attacks against women travellers are rare, many women find that the constant barrage of hisses, hoots and comments in parts of the Caribbean (Puerto Rico, Cuba, the Dominican Republic and the French-influenced islands, for instance) comes close to spoiling their vacation. Whatever you do, don't be afraid to seem rude; even the mildest polite response will be considered an indication of serious interest. Be aware too that a woman on her own in a restaurant or bar will be seen as fair game; usually a firm "no" works in deterring unwanted attention. In any event, never be afraid to ask for help if you feel lost or threatened.

Guide

Guide

Bahamas

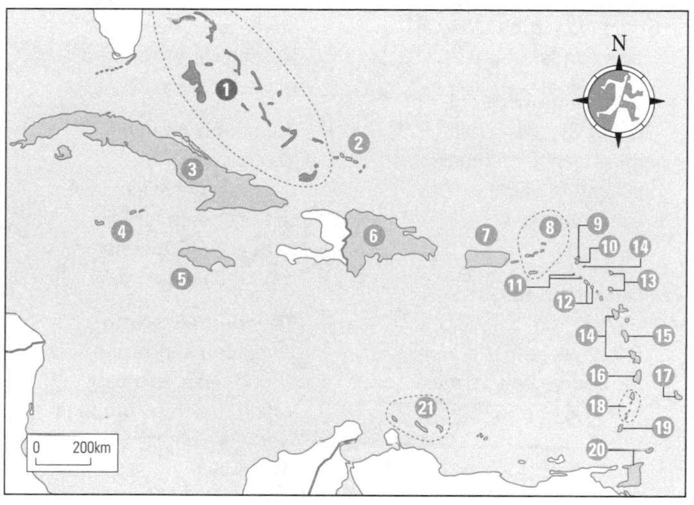

Bahamas Highlights

* **Sea kayaking in the Exumas** Glide through turquoise waters, stopping for a picnic along the way. See p.99

* **Atlantis hotel, Nassau** Fourteen-acres of Las Vegas–style entertainment edged by glorious pink sands. See p.75

* **Swimming with dolphins** Commune with these gentle creatures in peaceful Sanctuary Bay, Grand Bahama. See p.85

* **Out Island Regatta** Sloops from all over the Bahamas gather in April for George Town's main event. See p.96

* **The Exuma Land and Sea Park** Nature lovers will thrill to the fertile coral reefs, untouched beaches and native wildlife here. See p.99

* **Straw Market** Pick out hand-carved turtles and shark-tooth necklaces at Nassau's lively open-air market. See p.72

* **Junkanoo Festival** Thousands of masquerading revellers take to the streets for this hedonistic Christmas celebration. See p.64

* **Thunderball Grotto** If you can handle the strong tides, this captivating undersea grotto is worth the effort. See p.99

Introduction and Basics

Graced with beautiful beaches of pink sand, evocative windswept panoramas and countless opportunities for diving, snorkelling and fishing, the islands of the Bahamas are well established as one of the world's top draws for both intrepid explorers and casual vacationers. An island chain beginning a mere 55 miles east of Miami, Florida, the Bahamas offer an array of tourist hotels, all-inclusive resorts, and even rustic lodges, making staying there a relatively simple endeavour. Indeed, more than three million travellers each year choose the islands as their prime destination for outdoor sports, sun worship, casino gambling and, on some of the slightly more remote spots, eco-tourism.

In total, the Bahamas include around seven hundred islands, no more than thirty of which are inhabited, as well as smaller cays (pronounced "keys") and rocks – an impressive **arc** stretching from just beyond the Atlantic coast of Florida to the outlying waters of Cuba, where Great Inagua lies only sixty miles offshore. Although deeper

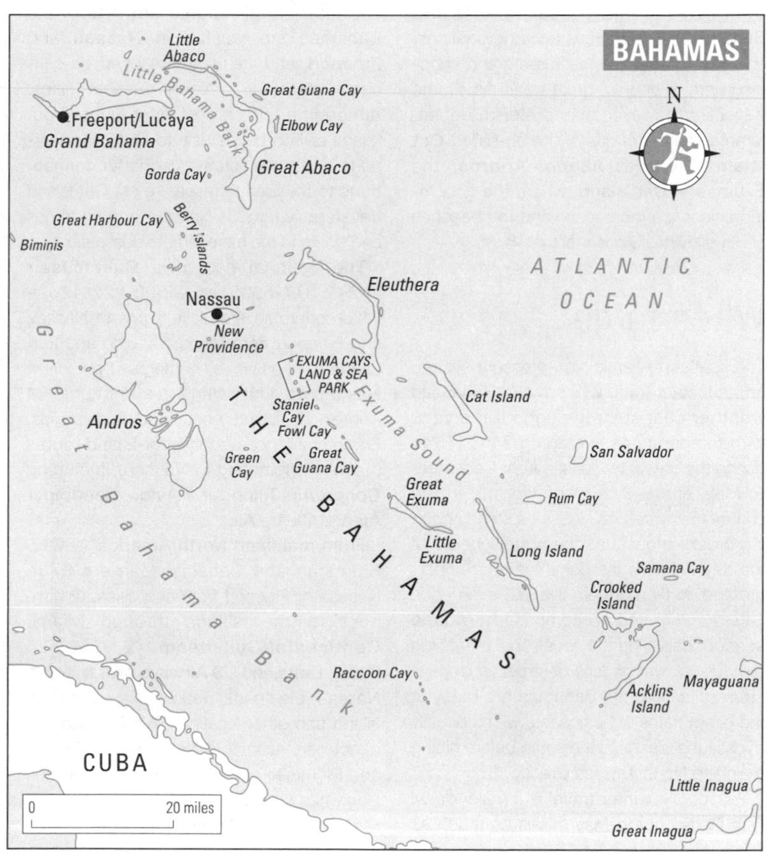

oceanic troughs surround some of the islands, most are encircled by **shallow, crystalline water** that reflects a light turquoise hue during the day and glows with purple luminescence at night. This combination of shallow and deep water makes **diving** and **snorkelling** both challenging and intriguing, with numerous reefs waiting to be explored just beyond the shores of the gorgeous, uncrowded beaches.

Where to go

The islands' most popular destinations are **New Providence** – site of the capital **Nassau** – nearby **Paradise Island**, and **Grand Bahama** and its vacation towns of **Freeport** and **Lucaya**. Both New Providence, with its **Cable Beach** and **South Beach** resort areas, and **Grand Bahama** offer glamorous accommodations, enticing nightlife, fine restaurants and shopping and, of course, great beaches. Some travellers, however, may prefer the quiet, remote charms of one of the so-called **Out Islands** such as **Abaco**, **Andros**, the **Exumas** or **Cat Island**, where the accommodations are more rustic and the beaches and reefs virtually deserted.

When to go

The southern Atlantic high-pressure system and constant trade winds make Bahamian **weather** consistent throughout the year, with temperatures averaging 24°C (75°F) during the dry winter season from December to May, and 5–8 degrees warmer in the summer rainy season. Just as a steady cooling breeze moderates the hottest hours of the day, nights in the Bahamas are temperate and, in the northern islands, even cool. Late summer and fall comprise **hurricane season**, delivering the occasional menacing tempest as well as less destructive tropical storms. Luckily, the Bahamas are rarely in the direct paths of hurricanes, which usually bypass the islands to the south before hitting mainland North America directly.

Predictably, **winter travel** is a major draw, with December-to-May prices as much as 25 percent higher than during the rest of the year. **Late spring** and **early summer travel** are popular with bargain hunters, divers, and anglers and sailors drawn by the summer round of fishing tournaments and regattas. Travelling during the Christmas **holiday season** can be bustling and wearisome, with tourists thick on the ground and many locals taking trips to the North American mainland. Likewise, college students often crowd the major resorts during Spring Break in February and March, while other travellers escape to the Bahamas during **late summer** and **autumn** to enjoy a respite in that relatively tranquil period, the odd hurricane notwithstanding.

Getting there

The major **international airports** of the Bahamas are located in **Nassau** and **Freeport**, and are usually reached via connecting flights from North American cities. Although a few carriers offer flights from Miami or Fort Lauderdale to **Out Island** airports, and some hotels offer **charter connections** to the island's resorts, most Out Island travellers fly through Nassau, or take ferries and boats to the more remote destinations.

The national carrier is **Bahamasair** (Ⓣ242/377-5505 or 1-800/222-4262), which offers several daily flights to Nassau and Freeport from Miami, Orlando and Fort Lauderdale, as well as numerous flights from Nassau to Out Island destinations on Andros, Cat Island, Abaco and other islands. Some smaller carriers fly **inter-island routes** (usually originating in Nassau), including **Congo Air**, **Taino Air Service**, **Sandpiper Air** and **Cleare Air.**

From **mainland North America**, several American and Canadian carriers fly to Nassau or Freeport from hub cities, or connect to the islands through Miami. **Continental-Gulfstream** (Ⓣ1-800/525 0280), **Delta** and **US Airways** offer flights to Nassau, Eleuthera, Treasure Cay, Paradise Island and other locations. **Air Canada** has direct connections to Nassau from Toronto and Montreal, and many other flights to the Bahamas via US hubs. American Airlines' regional carrier **American Eagle** serves

Nassau from Miami with regular daily flights, while smaller carriers typically fly a Florida-to-Bahamas route and include **Pan Am Air Bridges, Lynx Air International**, **Twin Air** and **Chalks International.**

From the **UK**, the major carrier is **British Airways**, offering direct flights to Nassau at least twice weekly from London Gatwick, while **British West Indian Airways**, **Virgin Atlantic**, **Bahamasair** and **Caledonian** also offer competitive fares for flights to Nassau through Miami. Similarly, other European travellers most often connect to the Bahamas via Miami. For phone numbers of airlines see pp.12–18 and 36–37.

Cruise lines such as **Disney, Carnival** and **American Canadian Caribbean** make calls at **Prince George Wharf** in Nassau, where visitors can enjoy the city's colonial centre and do some shopping, though most ships only dock there for a day or two.

Money and costs

The local currency is the **Bahamian dollar (B$)**, divided into 100 cents. Coins come in denominations of 5, 10, 15, 20 and 50 cents, as well as $1 and $2. Notes are issued in denominations of $1, $3, $5, $10, $20, $50 and $100. The Bahamian dollar is on a par with the US dollar, and both currencies are accepted throughout the country. Because all hotels and tourist facilities freely exchange both US and Bahamian currency, there is little need to formally change US dollars before travelling here. Big islands like New Providence, Grand Bahama and Abaco have major **banks** and financial institutions near the tourist centres, and offer numerous **ATMs** as well.

Many **Out Islands** have few, if any, banks and most have no ATMs, so it's best to visit these more remote islands with credit cards and travellers' cheques. **Credit cards** are widely accepted throughout the islands, except at some of the more isolated lodges, and are almost always required to reserve and rent automobiles.

Costs on the major islands are comparable to US prices. **Hotels**, save for motel-style lodges in downtown areas of major cities, average at least US$95–125 per night for a double room, while luxury resorts charge up to 25 percent more. Some Out Island lodges are less expensive, though the costs of **food** and **transportation** in the Out Islands are greater because goods and services are imported. Many resorts and hotels offer **all-inclusive packages** or **three-day/seven-day rates**, which can reduce costs considerably, and at least a few hotels at every destination offer **self-catering** options, which may also lower costs, especially for longer-term stays.

Information and websites

The best source of **information** on the Bahamas is the Bahamas Ministry of Tourism; you can contact the branch nearest you before you leave home. Once in the Bahamas, you can visit the local tourist offices at Nassau and Grand Bahama airports and in the main towns.

Information on the Out Islands is available from the **Bahamas Out Island Promotion Board** (☎305/931-6612 or 1-800/688-4752, Ⓦwww.bahama-out-islands.com), which distributes small maps of each Out Island as well. All major bookstores carry scale maps of the Bahamas.

Websites

Ⓦ**www.bahamas.com** The Bahamas Ministry of Tourism site, covering everything from travel info, water-sports and accommodation to local cuisine.

Ⓦ**www.bahamasdiving.com** Includes lists of diving operators and live-aboard operators, information on diving training and links to dive-specific features.

Ⓦ**www.bahamasnet.com** Comprehensive website with details on accommodation, activities and restaurants, and a calendar of events.

Ⓦ**www.thenassauguardian.com** Website of one of the two leading dailies, with the usual departments plus links to other local papers.

Getting around

In general, travelling around the Bahamas is a breeze. The islands are well linked by inter-island **flights** as well as **boats** and **ferries**, while on the islands themselves **taxi** and **bus** service is generally excellent.

By plane

Inter-island **transportation** is usually done by air, especially on the national carrier **Bahamasair** (☎242/377-5505 or 1-800/222-4262), which flies regular routes between Nassau and the Out Islands, while smaller, Nassau-based carriers offer charter services to the Out Islands and other destinations. Many hotels and resorts have their own **charter services** to bring passengers from Florida and elsewhere.

By boat

The traditional way of exploring the Bahamas is by **ferry or mail boat**, the latter a form of transit still favoured by locals. The Bahamas government operates nineteen mail boats, which also carry cargo and passengers between Nassau and all the Out Islands – trips that can vary from a few hours to most of a day. Call the **dockmaster** on Potter's Cay, Nassau (☎242/393-1064) for details and schedules.

The very efficient **Bahamas Fast Ferry** (☎242/323-2166) runs from Nassau to Harbour Island and Central Eleuthera, while the equally speedy **Bahamas SeaRoad/SeaLink** (☎242/323-2166) connects Nassau with Eleuthera and Andros. Individual **boat rental** is also a good option for inter-island transit, with many marinas featuring choice spots for anchorage.

By taxis and bus

Once on an island, **taxis** are abundant, especially on New Providence and Grand Bahama, while larger islands like Abaco and Eleuthera offer efficient taxi service in major tourist zones. What's more, most airports in the Out Islands (except some to the far south) draw at least a few taxis to meet every flight. Taxis on New Providence and Grand Bahama are metered, but it's wise to establish a set fare before heading out. (Many taxis can be hired for an hourly rate of US$45.) Out Island taxis, except in Marsh Harbour on Abaco, are rarely metered, and are usually hired for long-distance hauls between resorts. Again, it's always a good idea to establish the fare in advance.

Bus service in Nassau is generally excellent, with **jitneys** serving most of the city as well as the outlying regions of New Providence for the same low fare.

Guests at resort hotels may find renting **bicycles** a convenient and inexpensive way to explore some islands, with motor scooters and motorcycles for longer trips a possibility. Large resorts often rent guests **golf carts** to drive around the grounds, and where cays or towns prohibit motor vehicles – such as Treasure Cay and Hope Town on Abaco – golf carts are the vehicle of choice.

By car

Most major hotels offer **car transport** for their guests upon arrival at the airport, and almost all the major **car rental** agencies are found on New Providence and Grand Bahama, including **Alamo**, **Avis**, **Budget**, **Dollar** and **Hertz.** Nassau and Freeport are home to many local agencies that rent older cars for lower rates, though rarely with the added convenience of toll-free reservation services. Many Out Islands either lack car-rental agencies altogether or only have a few older, less reliable vehicles at expensive rates. In any case, rental cars are hardly needed on the smaller, more remote islands.

Visitors who **drive** in the Bahamas must have a valid driver's licence and liability insurance, and must take care to stay **on the left**.

Accommodation

Although there are relatively few inexpensive places to stay in the Bahamas, the islands do offer many **accommodation** choices for travellers. Honeymooners and large families will find plenty of options among the large and small hotels, resorts, bed and breakfasts, inns and lodges. Popular among snowbirds are **all-inclusive resorts** like Club Med (☎1-800/258-2633) and Sandals (☎1-800/SANDALS), while families and groups of friends may care to vacation at **rental villas**, **vacation homes** and **long-term condos**, most of which offer self-catering, adequate privacy and reduced rates for longer stays.

Every island has a fair number of **tourist hotels**, which can vary in quality, though almost all feature swimming pools, beach access, aquatic sports, island tours and in-house restaurants. On larger islands like New Providence, Grand Bahama, Abaco and Eleuthera, some of these hotels rival any in the world for luxury and nightlife.

Scattered throughout the islands are traditional **Bahamian guesthouses**, anything from converted two-storey homes to small motels surrounding a pool and verandah. Some guesthouses can be pretty basic, especially in the more southerly islands, while others are luxurious and spacious. Adventurers and anglers often prefer to stay at a **dive resort** or **fishing lodge**, many of which are located at Out Island destinations. Yachters on the other hand may simply remain on board ship at one of the many **marinas** around the islands.

Food and drink

Traditional Bahamian **meals** may include seafood like grouper, conch and snapper (usually broiled or baked in a tomato sauce), along with tropical fruits like guava and papaya. As former members of a British colony, Bahamians have adopted many traditional **English dishes**, or adapted them to suit local tastes. These include macaroni and cheese, peas and rice, boiled potatoes and other vegetable dishes. A **Bahamian breakfast** may consist of anything from fried eggs, bacon, toast, tomato and coffee to more Caribbean-influenced dishes like johnny cakes with coconut. Lunch tends toward seafood stews and soups or large conch salads.

With tourism expanding to the Bahamas, many different types of **imported culinary styles** have flourished here as well. On New Providence and Grand Bahama, you can find restaurants serving **Continental**, **Mediterranean** and **Greek** cuisine, and even **Mexican** and **pan-Asian** dishes, in elegant surroundings with excellent service and fine wines. Many of these restaurants are located at major hotels and resorts and require reservations, while other eateries in Nassau, Paradise Island and Grand Bahama operate independently and cater to a more eclectic crowd.

Every town or settlement in the Bahamas has its share of **take-away** restaurants, featuring traditional offerings like **fried chicken**, **french fries** and **deep-fried seafood**. Most Out Island restaurants serve fairly simple and uniform fare, usually fish, conch or fried chicken, with fresh Bahamian **lobster** a rare treat. Island **desserts** are often delightful, especially the coconut concoctions, rice pudding, gingerbread and fruit cocktail.

Bahamians are not much for **drinking** wine or liquor, though the national **beer**, Kalik, is a fine elixir enjoyed throughout the islands. Fruit juice and soft drinks are popular, and major brands like Coke and Pepsi are predictably ubiquitous. **Fast-food** chains have also invaded the Bahamas, and the major islands all feature at least one pizza or hamburger joint from each chain.

Phones, post and email

Batelco is the national telephone company of the Bahamas, and it maintains excellent **phone service** for all but the most isolated islands. **Public phones** are available in all tourist areas, though some Out Islands phones may be out of service for long periods. **Long-distance calls** may be made from public phones by using **phone cards** or through the local long-distance operator.

Postal service to and from the Bahamas is fairly reliable. Postcards from the islands to North America, Europe and South America require a 50-cent stamp, while airmail letters cost 65 cents per half-ounce.

Modem connections and **email** are a still-developing feature of most Bahamian telephone networks, so it's worth checking availability in advance with your hotel or resort.

The **country code** for the Bahamas is ☎242.

Opening hours, festivals and holidays

Most Bahamian **shops** are typically open Monday to Saturday 9am–5pm. **Banks** are generally open Monday to Thursday 9am–3pm and Friday 9am–5pm; Out Island banks may have very limited opening hours and be open one or two days per week. While Bahamian stores are permitted to open on Sunday, almost none does, making Sunday a very quiet day, at least for commerce. Otherwise, **shopping** is best in the morning when the crowds are few and the temperature mild.

The Bahamian year features many important **festivals** and **holidays**, reaching its peak during the Christmas holiday season. Celebrated on December 26 and again on New Year's morning, **Junkanoo** is a lively national festival, especially colourful in Nassau, where thousands of revellers descend on Bay Street dressed in elaborate costumes and dance wildly through the night and into the early morning.

The **Eleuthera Pineapple Festival** occurs in early June in Gregory Town, while during spring and summer countless **fishing tournaments** and **regattas** take place, including the famous **Bahamas Family Island Regatta** at George Town in the Exumas during the last week of April. Long Island and Abaco also feature popular regattas.

Bahamians, especially those in Fox Hill in Nassau, celebrate **Emancipation Day** in the first week of August, partaking in parades and food, as well as cultural events. Fireworks and parades highlight **Independence Week**, which culminates on July 10. Bahamian **tourist centres** provide lists of the many festivals, holidays and craft shows that occur year-round.

Public holidays

Holidays that fall on Saturday or Sunday are generally observed on the preceding Friday or the following Monday.

January 1 New Year's Day
March/April Good Friday, Easter Monday
Whit Monday
First Friday in June Labour Day
July 10 Independence Day
First Monday in August Emancipation Day
October 12 Discovery Day
December 25 Christmas Day
December 26 Boxing Day

Crime and safety

During the 1980s and early 1990s Nassau suffered a small wave of gun violence, mostly as a result of the drug trade. These days things have calmed down and the tourist-friendly zones around Nassau, Cable Beach, Paradise Island and Freeport-Lucaya are fairly **safe**. Nevertheless, **petty crimes** like hotel-room theft and pickpocketing do occur. Visitors should exercise caution in Nassau after dark and avoid suburbs like Over-the-Hill and Fox, which still have problems. Drug dealers may also frequent touristed areas, and visitors should be aware that Bahamian **drug laws** are harsher than those in North America or Europe, with long prison sentences always a possibility.

The streets of Nassau and Freeport tend to empty out rather early in the evening, and visitors, especially women, should avoid venturing out alone there after dark. Places like the neighbourhood Over-the-Hill in Nassau have experienced a recent spurt of **gun violence**, and tourists should exercise reasonable precautions before heading out alone.

The **emergency number** for police and ambulance is ☎911.

Outdoor activities

Sunny weather, sandy beaches, exquisite reefs, shallow water, steady winds, and proximity to the gulf stream make the Bahamas an ideal choice for all manner of **sports** and **outdoor activities**. Islands like **Bimini** are rightfully regarded as great spots for **fishing** (especially for wahoo, tuna, barracuda, shark, grouper and snapper), while many Out Islands like Andros, Cat Island and Abaco are famous for their **bonefishing** – so named after the silvery catch. Likewise, the islands' shallow, calm waters have made **sailing** a popular activity, especially on New Providence, the Exumas, Abaco and Eleuthera.

Nearly every resort, hotel and lodge offers a full range of aquatic sports, including **diving**, **snorkelling**, **boating**, **sea kayaking**, **windsurfing**, **parasailing** and **swimming**, with the cost often included in with accommodation.

Golf and **tennis** are provided at resorts and hotels on the major islands, with the best golf courses being located at Cable Beach in Freeport, and on Paradise Island. **Biking**, **hiking** and **eco-tours** are growing in popularity as well, and a number of operators specialize in trips to isolated spots throughout the islands. **Birdwatching** is a major draw, especially for seabird species like the rare **Bahamian parrot** on Abaco, and the **flamingos** on Inagua. There's also **horseback riding** at stables on New Providence and Grand Bahama.

Shopping

Offering savings of 30–50 percent below international retail prices, **duty-free shopping** is a popular way to find bargains for jewellery, perfume, watches, china, crystal and liquor, with the tourist zones of Nassau and Freeport providing particularly good buying opportunities. Nassau's Bay Street is famous for its **Straw Market**, offering a wide array of mats, baskets, hats, dresses, T-shirts and hand-crafted items at bargain prices. While many items at the market are cheap imports, others may be genuine, so a close inspection of the merchandise is usually worthwhile. As one of the better shops, Nassau's **Plait Lady** (☎242/356-5584) guarantees its items are 100 percent Bahamian-made. While Straw Market purchases are subject to negotiation, **bargaining** is not a typical Bahamian custom.

The Bahamas are also known for their **Androsian batik** fabrics made by a small operation in Andros Town on a remote Out Island. Although the factory is fascinating to visit (see p.88), **batik** items are available at many outlets in Nassau, Freeport and major Out Islands like Abaco and Eleuthera.

Cigars and **local art** are often worthwhile purchases as well, with Bahamian painters, water-colourists, woodcarvers and jewellers creating original works for sale in **galleries** throughout Nassau and Freeport.

History

The name Bahamas probably comes from the Spanish "Baja Mar", meaning "shallow seas", an apt description of the area attributed to Columbus. After the European discovery of the islands in 1492, they remained a backwater until a few **English settlers** from Bermuda arrived on Eleuthera in 1647. Soon after, farmers colonized New Providence and established Charles Town, whose name was changed in 1690 to **Nassau** to honour England's new ruler, William, Prince of Orange and Nassau.

With the islands ruled by a series of incompetent royal governors, Nassau gradually slipped into chaos and piracy, becoming home to such notorious figures as **Blackbeard**, who preyed on Spanish and French shipping lines. Not until the arrival of Royal Governor Woodes-Rogers in 1717 was piracy finally curtailed.

During the American Revolution, many **Loyalists** came to the Bahamas from the North American colonies, settling in Abaco, Eleuthera, Exumas and Long Island and creating an economy and society based on **plantations** run by slave labour. However, their cotton and tobacco crops failed due to crop diseases and lack of demand. After the **abolition of slavery** here in 1834, island residents turned to salvaging, sponging, fishing and subsistence farming to make a living.

During the American Civil War, Nassau became a boomtown built on **blockade running**, later turning to **rum-running** during America's Prohibition of the 1920s and early 1930s. **Tourism**, popular since the mid-nineteenth century, gained a further foothold after World War II with the advent of modern air travel, air conditioning and telephones.

On July 10, 1973, after 325 years of British rule, the Bahamas became an **independent**, **democratic state** supported in large part by tourism, banking and fishing.

Bahamian music

The native **music** of the Bahamas is a combination of African and Caribbean rhythms, often played on drums and various skin or pipe instruments. **Rake'n'scrape** music, prominent on the Out Islands, features rough guitars and percussion instruments made from ratchets and saws; **calypso** and **reggae** are also popular.

1.1

New Providence

NEW PROVIDENCE and PARADISE ISLAND are the undeniable heart of the Bahamian archipelago. Despite its tiny size – 21 miles long and 7 miles wide – New Providence has more than two-thirds of the country's population and is home to the capital **Nassau**, a thriving city of around 100,000 residents. Initially gaining renown for its sheltered harbour and strategic location on the shipping route from the New World to Spain, the island has during its nearly 230-year history been a refuge for pirates and privateers, site of illicit smuggling, haven for fishermen, and formidable centre of tourism, with nearly two million visitors now arriving annually.

Stretching east to west, New Providence offers a wealth of lovely, uncrowded **beaches**, while on its northeastern shore Nassau runs six blocks deep and features the shopping arcade **Bay Street**, located along **Prince George Wharf**. A lengthy toll bridge east of downtown Nassau connects to **Paradise Island**, a glitzy tourist enclave that includes the mega-resort *Atlantis*, as well as many other hotels, shops, restaurants and spas. The island's main highlight is **Cabbage Beach**, covering most of the north coast and featuring deep blue water and trade winds that cool even the hottest of afternoons.

Although much of eastern New Providence has been covered by urban sprawl, the areas west of Nassau include stunning stretches of beach, though the main draw of **Cable Beach** is increasingly peppered by exclusive resorts, private estates, condominiums and time-shares. More worthwhile, the **western shores**, twelve miles of sand from Cable Beach to the **western point**, are the most dazzling parts of the island, with isolated **Love Beach** near Compass Point a particularly appealing spot.

Beyond the western point is exclusive **Lyford Cay**, where celebrities like Sean Connery live in hermetically sealed luxury. New Providence's **south shore** has few notable beaches, and even fewer hotels, though diving and snorkelling draw many enthusiasts to the shore's outer reef and reef walls.

Although the **central interior** of New Providence is marshy scrub, several local **eco-tourism** operators offer kayaking on **Lake Killarney** and combination biking-kayaking tours as well.

Arrival, information and island transport

Nassau International Airport (☎242/377-7281), the hub of Bahamian air transport, is located on the west-central part of New Providence, a fifteen-minute taxi ride from downtown Nassau and only ten minutes from Cable Beach. While there are no buses from the airport, there are plenty of **taxis**, with the average fare to Nassau around US$18 for two people, and many hotels provide **limousines** for arriving guests. Both taxis and limos congregate just outside the arrival area, adjacent to customs and immigration. In addition, the Ministry of Tourism operates a small **information booth** at the airport.

In downtown Nassau, there are two information booths that provide useful maps and brochures. The smaller one can be found near the Straw Market on Bay Street (Mon–Fri 9am–5pm; ☎242/356-7591), while the larger office is located in Rawson Square, about two blocks east of the market (Mon–Fri 8.30am–5pm, Sat 8.30am–4pm, Sun 8.30am–2pm; ☎242/326-9781).

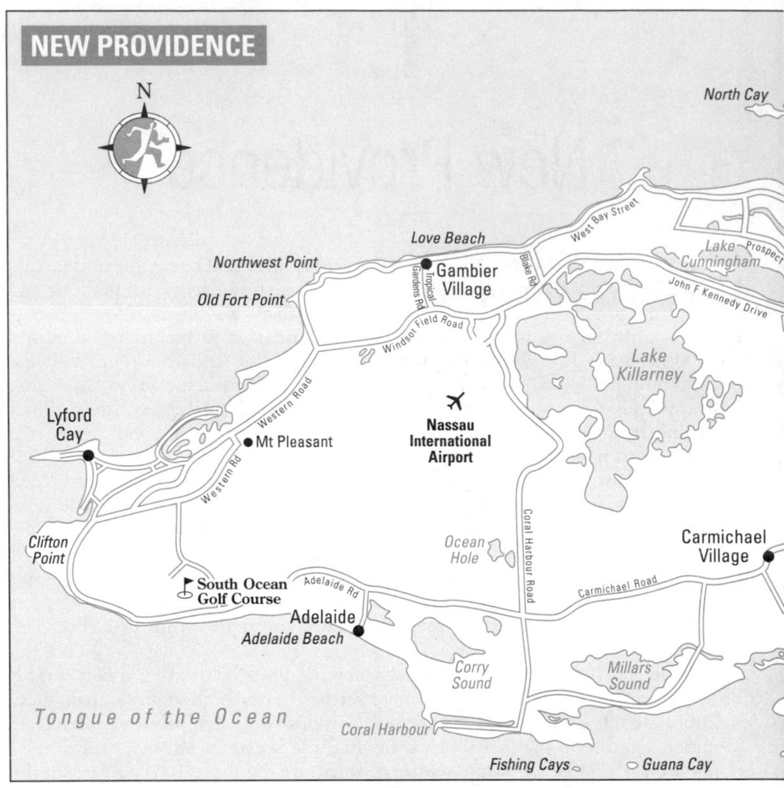

Getting around New Providence and Paradise island is rather easy, considering that both islands are fairly compact and centralized, and few destinations are ever more than fifteen or twenty minutes apart. **Taxis** are ubiquitous, with almost all hotels and resorts having taxi stands, and are typically owned by independent operators, most of whom are experienced and friendly (dispatchers reached at ⓣ242/322-5111 and 323-4555). If you're travelling early in the morning, make a **taxi reservation** the night before.

Bahamian buses are known as **jitneys** and serve all parts of Nassau and Cable Beach for 75 cents. Downtown Nassau's central **bus stop** is near the corner of Frederick and Bay streets, across from the *British Colonial Hotel*, and the popular #10 line runs west from downtown to Cable Beach and Compass Point. The major **car rental** agencies are all located in Nassau, though there are also a number of locally owned – and cheaper – agencies throughout the city. You can rent **motor scooters** and **bicycles** at local outlets as well.

Nassau

Originally a harbour base named Charles Town, **NASSAU** is the modern-day face of the Bahamas, visited by most everyone who comes down this way, not least for its service as a transport hub. Though dingy in parts, enough historical flavour has been preserved to make such a stop here worthwhile. Much of this atmosphere comes from its development during the so-called Loyalist period from 1787 to 1834, when many of the city's finest colonial buildings were built. Before this build-up, Nassau had largely been a haven for pirates, privateers and wreckers, situated as it was on key shipping routes between Europe and the West Indies.

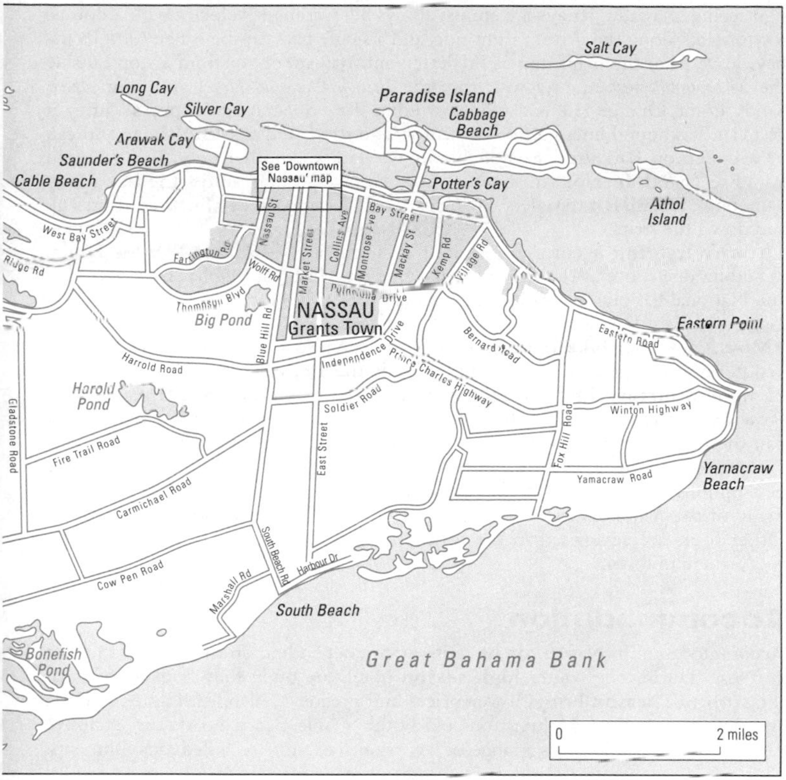

But it was really the development of the tourist industry here that put Nassau firmly on the map. After alternating periods of decline and prosperity in the nineteenth and early twentieth century, the spike in trade and construction that followed World War II led directly to Nassau's emergence as a global centre for tourism and **finance**. By the mid-1950s, with the dredging of the harbour and the construction of the international airport, Nassau began to host more than a million visitors a year, and a decade later, after the construction of the **Paradise Island Bridge** and the development of Cable Beach, the city was receiving twice as many more.

Getting around

With its centrally located historic area of no more than six square blocks, Nassau is great for **walking**. **Taxis** are also readily available throughout the city, with Bahamas Transport and the Taxi Cab Union (☎242/323-5111 or 323-4555) as the most reliable companies. Any driver can be enlisted to give informal **tours**, with the cost usually running about US$60 for three people and two hours of sightseeing. Nassau's **jitneys** are almost always 32-passenger vehicles with a double row of seats along the driver's right side, and a single row on the other. All #10 jitneys leave from the main stop at Frederick and Bay streets, or from a stop outside the *McDonald's* restaurant across from the *British Colonial Hotel*, and connect to Sandy Point, Orange Hill and Compass Point. Try to catch an "**express**" jitney if you can. Eastbound lines go from downtown to the Paradise IslandBridge and can be accessed on Bay Street east of the Straw Market. Another good way to reach Paradise Island, **ferries** run from Prince George Wharf across the bay (daily 9am–6pm; US$2). For travellers stayingon Cable Beach, a **free shuttle** operates up and down the strip.

If you're **renting a car**, Avis has four locations in Nassau and Paradise Island, including one office at the airport, while Budget, Hertz and Dollar have two each and National has one airport location. Local operator Orange Creek Car Rentals is located on West Bay Street.

Most hotels offer **bike rentals**, though you can also rent a **scooter** at Knowles Scooter and Bike Rental, located just outside the *British Colonial Hotel*, or take a 25-minute **surrey ride**. Surrey masters congregate near the wharf gangway at Rowson Square and, for US$10 per person, will take you on a horse-drawn tour past the Bahamian Parliament and other major sights of old Nassau.

If you're **touring** New Providence, Majestic Tours (T 242/322-2626) is one the best options for historical, snorkelling and boating expeditions, and has booths in many of the major hotels in Nassau, as well as Cable Beach and Paradise Island. Other tours are advertised in the tourist magazine *What's On*, available almost everywhere in town.

Accommodation

Accommodation in Nassau can be quite pricey, depending on the time of the year you visit. During the winter **high season** hotels are often fully booked, whereas the **summer season** brings lower prices and greater availability. The downtown area offers expensive and luxurious old hotels, Cable Beach boasts the exclusive resorts, and Orange Hill has a range of less expensive, more secluded establishments.

Breezes West Bay St, Cable Beach T 242/327-5356, W www.superclubs.com. An all-inclusive package hotel (part of the Superclubs chain), serving up countless activities, including a full range of aquatic sports and even ice skating. 9

British Colonial Hilton Nassau 1 Bay St T 242/322-3311 or 1-800/742-4276, W www.nassau.hilton.com. Built in 1922 and rebuilt a year later after a fire, this is the most elegant and expensive hotel in town, with 305 rooms that get pricier the higher up you go, and exorbitant suites at the top. Great restaurants and beach activities. 5

Buena Vista Hotel Delancy St T 242/322-2811. Housed in a venerable, rambling mansion a mile from the beach, this charming hotel features copious flower decorations, sizeable rooms and one of Nassau's better restaurants (see review p.73). 3

Dillet's Guest House West Nassau T 242/325-1133, W www.islandeaze.com. Within walking distance of the beach, a 60-year-old Bahamian house nestled on an acre of gardens and hammocks, with tasteful rooms, breakfast and dinner service, and tea at 4pm. 5

El Greco Hotel West Bay and August streets T 242/325-1121. Centrally located across from the beach and near downtown, with 26 rooms positioned around a pool and courtyard. Moderately priced. Single 4, double 5

Graycliff West Hill St T 242/322-2796, W www.graycliff.com. Perched on a hill above Nassau, a Georgian Colonial pile with pricey "garden rooms" and private cottages where Churchill and the Beatles slept. While expensive, the hotel has one of the city's top restaurants. 8

Holiday Inn Nassau West Bay St T 242/356-0000 or 1-800/HOLIDAY, W www.holiday_inn.com /nasjunkanoo. Three blocks from downtown Nassau on a public beach, with five floors of standard rooms, heated pool, jacuzzi and restaurant. 7

Mignon Guest House 12 Market St T 242/322-4771. Clean, six-room budget choice with air conditioning and shared baths. 2

Nassau Beach Hotel West Bay St, Cable Beach T 242/327-7711 or 1-888/627-7278, W www.nassaubeachhotel.com. Classic hotel from the 1940s with 403 rooms, six restaurants, watersports facilities and access to a golf course. ❼

Orange Hill Beach Inn West Bay St at Blake Rd, Love Beach ☎242/327-7157, Ⓦwww.hotelguide.com. Four miles west of Cable Beach, an isolated spot offering motel-style rooms, central pool and relaxed bar. Downtown Nassau and the airport are only a short bus ride away. ❺

Parthenon Hotel West St ☎242/322-2643, Ⓕ322-2644. A quiet option in downtown, the *Parthenon*'s 18 rooms are in a two storey L-shaped building that overlooks a garden. Continental breakfast is available for US$3. ❸

Radisson Cable Beach Casino and Golf Resort West Bay St, Box N-4914, Nassau ☎242/327-6000 or 1-800/333-3333, Ⓕ242/327-6987. Bringing a touch of Las Vegas to the Bahamas, this 700-room high-rise hotel draws many guests with gambling and golf, but also boasts 18 tennis courts, a health club, three pools and abundant watersports. Though uniform, the rooms are comfortable. ❻

Villas on Crystal Cay Silver Cay ☎242/328-1036. Marriott property featuring 21 luxurious, single-level villas with one or two bedrooms, Italian tiled bathrooms, great views and steep prices. ❽

Historic Nassau

The heart of **historic Nassau** is bustling **Rawson Square** on Bay Street, just across from Prince George Wharf, where the major cruise lines dock. The square is a small but authentic crossroads of old Nassau, where tourists, government workers, hawkers and musicians congregate – especially during Christmas **Junkanoo** festivities, when up to 30,000 onlookers arrive.

Just west and north of the square, the **Hairbraider's Centre** features Bahamian women braiding hair for about US$1 a strand. Across Bay Street, just south of Rawson Square, **Parliament Square** is the centre of Bahamian government, with buildings from the early 1800s and including the Opposition Building, House of Assembly and Senate, where a statue of **Queen Victoria** looks down sternly from

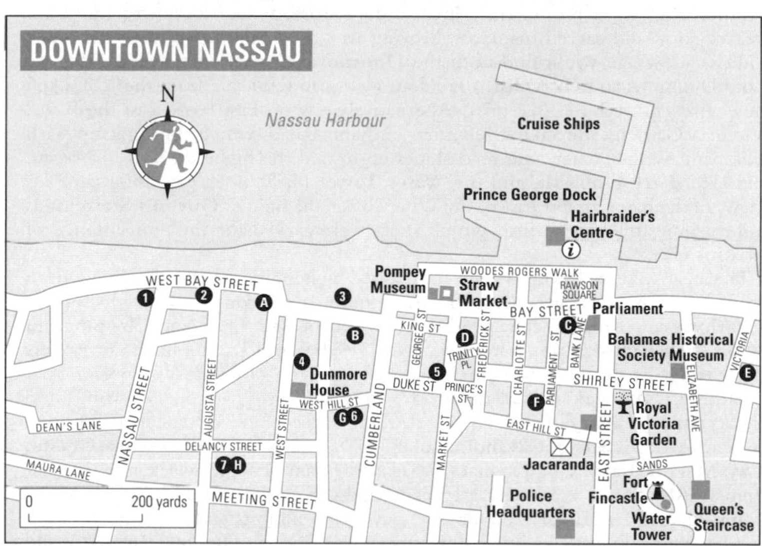

ACCOMMODATION				EATING & DRINKING			
Buena Vista	7	Graycliff Hotel	6	Buena Vista	H	Gaylord's	E
British Colonial Hilton Nassau	3	Holiday Inn Nassau	1	Café Matisse	C	Graycliff	G
El Greco Hotel	2	Mignon Guest House	5	Conch Fritter's	B	Green Shutters Restaurant & Bar	F
		Parthenon Hotel	4	Europe Restaurant & Bar	A	Silk Cotton Club	D

the steps. Behind the Senate is the **Supreme Court** building, and its lovely **Garden of Remembrance** honouring Bahamian casualties of two world wars.

Back on Bay Street, a few blocks west of Prince George Wharf, is Nassau's justly famous **Straw Market**. Filling much of a square block, the open-air squeezes in 150 vendors peddling everything from beads, totes and T-shirts to shark-tooth necklaces and expensive hand-carved wooden turtles. Just behind the market, the waterfront area is bounded by **Woodes-Rogers Walk**, worth a quick stroll for the view of the teeming harbour.

Just west of the Straw Market, the **Pompey Museum**, on the corner of Bay and George streets (Mon–Fri 10am–4pm; US$1; ⓣ242/236-2566), is located in a former bank called Vendue House, later renamed to honour a rebellious slave who hid out on Exuma during the 1830s. One of the city's oldest buildings, it houses a collection of artefacts and documents tracing the history of Bahamian slavery.

Hillside area and west

South of Rawson Square, roughly bounded by Elizabeth Avenue to the east and Cumberland Street on the west, the **Hillside area** has a charming historical flavour enlivened by small **cafés** that offer refreshing drinks, full-fledged lunches and much local colour.

A block south of Parliament Square is the **Nassau Public Library and Museum**, an octagonal former city jail (daily; free) whose crowded rooms house a remarkable collection of maps, photographs and engravings. Across from the library on the south side of Shirley Street is the delightful **Royal Victoria Garden**, where you're free to wander among three hundred species of tropical plants on the former grounds of its namesake hotel, now a crumbling ruin. Following East Road, which runs along the eastern edge of the grounds, the road forks at East Hill Road. A right turn here will take you along a stretch containing much of Nassau's historic **architecture**, most prominently **Jacaranda House**, a two-storey structure with peaked roofs and carved mansards. Moving west, East Hill Road turns into West Hill Road, where you'll find both the **Dunmore House**, built in the 1790s by Lord Dunmore, and **Graycliff**, a fabulous Georgian residence from the 1720s and now an exclusive hotel (see p.70). Alternatively, stay on East Road past the Royal Victoria Gardens and take a left turn on Sand Road, which will link up with Elizabeth Avenue, where the road slopes up toward the highest points in Nassau: the 1793 **Fort Fincastle** and the **Water Tower** (daily; free), providing fabulous views of the harbour. Just east of the Water Tower, the unique **Queen's Staircase** is a deep limestone gorge into which stairs were carved for the convenience of Nassau's elite.

The areas west of downtown are best visited by hopping on the #10 jitney from in front of the *British Colonial Hotel*. A mile or so from downtown is **Fort Charlotte**, on a magnificent overlook between Nassau Street and Chippingham Road (daily 9am–4.30pm; free). Begun in 1787 by Lord Dunmore, the fort offers daily tours by guides occasionally sporting period costumes. Opposite Fort Charlotte is **Arawak Cay**, a manmade island and local hangout featuring food shacks where native cooks sell conch salad and cracked and fried conch. Connected to Arawak Cay is **Silver Cay**, home to one of Nassau's most famous sights, **Crystal Cay Marine Park**, Chippingham Road (daily 9am–4.30pm, weekends closes at 4pm; US$16; ⓣ242/323-1036), a 16-acre hands-on experience of local marine life, complete with an underwater observatory, shark exhibits and 100ft observation tower, where you can take in breathtaking views of Nassau Harbour, Paradise Island and Cable Beach.

Cable Beach

Five miles west of downtown Nassau, and named for the first underwater phone cable that reached here in 1892, **CABLE BEACH** is home to numerous hotels, restaurants and sports facilities, along with a major golf course and tennis courts. Two of the top hotels, *Breezes* and *Sandals*, are all-inclusive resorts, though the other major establishments also feature an array of eateries, shops, pools, bars and beach activities.

Along the beach, whispering **casuarina trees** line the sands, and offshore lie **North Cay** and **Long Cay**, which make nice day trips for snorkellers and picnickers. At the end of Cable Beach is **Delaporte Point Beach**, a chic assortment of Venice-style apartment condos, fancy shops and restaurants.

Eating and drinking

Thanks in part to its international influx of tourists, Nassau's **restaurants** feature a wide variety of cuisines, highlighted by Bahamian seafood prepared by local chefs using fresh ingredients. Every large hotel also has its own restaurants, some of them world-class. The tourist magazine *What to do: Where to dine* contains a complete listing of restaurants, diners and take-aways.

Bahamian Kitchen Trinity Plaza at Market St ☎242/325-0702. The top Bahamian restaurant in downtown Nassau, with wonderful grouper, snapper and conch dishes for US$10 per entree.

Buena Vista *Buena Vista Hotel*, Delancy St ☎242/322-2811. Expensive Continental cuisine and a fabulous wine list enhanced by nineteenth-century surroundings.

Cafe Johnny Canoe outside *Nassau Beach Hotel*, West Bay St, Cable Beach ☎242/327-3373. Kitschy, people-watching spot good for fried chicken, meat loaf and macaroni and cheese, along with a decent bar.

Cafe Matisse Bank Lane and Bay St ☎242/356-7012. Upscale, business-oriented bistro with an eclectic menu of seafood and pasta, highlighted by duck filled ravioli and seafood pizza. Occasional Thursday or Sunday night jazz.

Caripelago Bean and Berry Restaurant Royal Palm Mall, West Bay St, Cable Beach ☎242/327-4749. Casual spot for fried chicken or Bahamian seafood like grouper with mango sauce. Coffee and tea served on the terrace.

Chez Willie West Bay St ☎242/322-5364. Just west of the *British Colonial Hotel*, this expensive and cordial French restaurant serves delicious mussels and steak tenderloin.

Conch Fritters Bar and Grill Marlborough St ☎242/323-8778. Convenient location and excellent, inexpensive food, namely breakfast with johnny cakes and omelettes, and lunch of burgers and conch.

Dickie Mo's West Bay St, Cable Beach ☎242/327-7854. Seafood and Bahamian specialties in a mostly outdoor restaurant where the waitresses wear sailor suits. A popular night-time hangout.

Europe Restaurant and Bar West Bay St ☎242/322-8032. On the bottom floor of the *Ocean Spray Hotel*, a dark Vienna-style pub featuring wiener schnitzel, rich pork dishes and numerous imported beers.

Gaylord's Dowdeswell St near Victoria Ave ☎242/356-3004. In a charmingly ornate 1870s mansion, an upscale Indian restaurant with delicious samosa and tandoori. Special vegetarian dishes are also available.

Graycliff West Hill St ☎242/322-2796. Located in the eponymous hotel, with four dining rooms loaded with art and a 300,000-bottle wine cellar.

Green Shutters Restaurant and Pub Parliament St ☎242/322-3701. A centrally located English pub serving shepherd's pie, steak and kidney pie, bangers and mash and English ales on tap.

Mamma Lyddy's Place Market St at Cockburn St ☎242/328-6849. Authentic Bahamian restaurant in a tangerine-coloured house featuring Junkanoo art, serving English-style dishes like macaroni and cheese, creamed corn and coleslaw.

Sun and... Lakeview Rd and Shirley St ☎242/393-1025. Expensive, dinner-only establishment east of downtown, with a peculiar name but serving excellent soufflés, salmon and veal. Its gardens, rock pools and jacket-only policy lend an upscale appeal.

Swiss Pastry Shop West Bay St, across from *Sandals* ☎242/327-5368. An excellent quick stop in Cable Beach for coffee, sweets and pastries.

Nightlife and performing arts

Generally, **nightlife** in Nassau and on Cable Beach resembles a charming version of 1920s tourism, with the major resort hotels hosting a variety of bars and clubs. The biggest "floor show" in town is *Kings and Knights* at the Nassau Beach Hotel, where King Eric and his Knights perform steel drum music with **limbo** and **fire dancing**, while the *Drumbeat Club* on West Bay features **Junkanoo music** and limbo as well. Every hotel on Cable Beach has its own **disco**, with the most lively being the *Fanta-Z Disco* at *Sandals*. Also popular is the bar at *Cafe Johnny Canoe* on Cable Beach, and *Conch Fritters* on Marlborough Street, across from the *British Colonial Hotel*. Major dance clubs include *The Zoo*, west of Nassau, the *Rock and Roll Café*, on Cable Beach, and the new *Bahama Boom Beach Club*, downtown near the wharf. The *Silk Cotton Club* on Market Street is famous for its jazz music, while *Cocktails and Dreams* is a quiet nightclub on the beach, just west of the *British Colonial*. Smaller clubs include the *Pacific Bar* on Victoria Street, *Millie's Place* just off Devaux Street and the *Drop Zone*, catering to locals and tourists alike.

On Mackey Street, the **Dundas Centre for the Performing Arts** (Ⓣ242/393-3728) provides a year-round schedule of music, theatre and dance, featuring both local and foreign artists. The magazine *What's On* contains a section on the latest nightlife offerings.

Diving and aquatic sports

It's no surprise that Nassau offers many premier **diving**, **snorkelling**, **fishing** and **sailing** opportunities. Long, deep reefs and drop-off walls line the south shore of the island, and shallow reefs fringe the western side as well. The main diving centre is **Coral Harbour** along the south shore, where six dive operators maintain shops and boats, including **Bahama Divers** (Ⓣ242/393-1466), **DiveDiveDive, Ltd**. (Ⓣ242/362-1143) and the largest, **Stuart's Cove Dive South Ocean** (Ⓣ242/362 4171). Every operation also offers snorkelling and swimming trips and combination snorkel-picnic packages, as do most hotels and resorts. All offer similar rates, starting with with one-tank dives for around US$35.

The shallow waters around New Providence are renowned for their **sport fishing**, especially for grouper, snapper, deepwater amberjack, blackfin tuna, bonito and blue marlin. One reliable operator is the Charter Boat Association (Ⓣ242/363-2325), with a fleet of ten vessels. Other operators charter fishing boats out of Nassau's harbour and include Chubasco Charters, Born Free Charters and Marine Adventure Company.

Sailing is an expensive Nassau pastime, with Brown's Boat Basin, East Bay Yacht Basin, Lyford Cay, Nassau Harbour Club and Nassau Yacht Haven as the major marinas where boats may be chartered. Sailboats are available for rent at most marinas and yacht harbours. Rates vary widely, depending on the size and type of vessel, and whether it's crewed, and you'll need to reserve in advance and provide proof of experience. Marinas to try include **Brown's Boat Basin** (Ⓣ242/393-3331), **East Bay Yacht Basin** (Ⓣ242/394-1816), **Lyford Cay** (Ⓣ242/362-4131), **Nassau Harbour Club** (Ⓣ242/393-0771), **Nassau Yacht Haven** (Ⓣ242/393-8173) and **Atlantis** (Ⓣ242/363-3000).

Paradise Island

Three hundred yards across the Paradise Island Bridge from Nassau's harbour, **PARADISE ISLAND** consists of 686 acres of hard-pack coral and wind-blown limestone oolite sand, and until the mid-1960s was Nassau's boat-building centre and supported a population of wild hogs and domesticated pigs. This former "**Hog Island**" also acted as a get-away for rich tourists, home to places like the posh *Ocean*

Club, a 59-room Georgian charmer with a central courtyard garden and tennis courts.

In 1967, when the Paradise Island Bridge linked the island with Nassau, a small airport was built at the island's eastern end, and *Resorts International* created a huge hotel complex catering to package tourists. With a recent second bridge now assisting the increased traffic flow, Paradise Island has become a hugely popular destination, with a spate of resorts, hotels, casinos and beaches submitting it to accusations of being overbuilt. Still, the island has some quiet backwaters, namely a marvellous **north coast** where pink sands meet the soft turquoise of the Atlantic Ocean.

Around the island

Almost all visitors to Paradise Island arrive through Nassau International Airport, though in 1989 the **Paradise Island Airport** was opened: a small-jet port serving commuter airlines, which will soon be expanding to accommodate larger planes as well.

Only four miles long and half a mile wide, Paradise Island tapers to a point on its western end where there is a small **lighthouse**. The best **beaches** are on the north side facing the Atlantic Ocean, while the south side mainly features marinas, docks and wharves. From the Paradise Island Bridge, drivers encounter a huge roundabout, the northern axis of which leads to the **Atlantis** hotel and its casino. North of the hotel is **Cabbage Beach**, two miles of fabulous pink sand, and further east, separated by a small anvil-shaped headland, is **Snorkeler's Cove Beach**, a striking and often deserted stretch where one can snorkel in peace.

Two main east–west roads cross the island: the first, **Paradise Island Drive**, heads east from the roundabout, passing the *Ocean Club* and other resorts and restaurants, and leads to the island's eastern end, home to private residences, a few exclusive hotels, the airport and a golf course. The only sights in the vicinity are **Versailles Gardens** and **The Cloister**, built to resemble medieval ruins by the developers of the *Ocean Club*. The other street, **Paradise Beach Drive**, running west from the roundabout, heads out to Club Med and provides access to **Pirate's Cove Beach**, a secluded, windswept stretch, and **Paradise Beach**, two miles of sand that live up to the name.

Since many people simply walk to their destinations, **getting around** Paradise Island is quite easy. The **Casino Express**, a shuttle bus making the rounds of the major hotels for a US$1 fare, is based at the *Atlantis* hotel. For longer trips or when it is hot, **taxis** circulate on the main roads and carry passengers across the Paradise Island Bridge for shopping in Nassau. **Water taxis**, **ferries** and **boats** leave from **Hurricane Hole** to shuttle tourists into Nassau.

Accommodation

Most **accommodation** is quite expensive, though a few small **hotels** and **guesthouses** offer affordable rates with adequate privacy and solitude.

Atlantis Casino Drive ⓣ242/363-3000 or 1-800/321-3000, ⓦwww.Atlantis.com. A huge, package-tourist hotel with 2119 rooms, 230 suites, 21 eateries, 17 bars, 9 swimming pools and a giant outdoor aquarium with snorkelling. 9

Comfort Suites Casino Drive ⓣ242/363-2234 or 1-800/451-6078, ⓕ242/363-2588, ⓦwww.comfortinn.com. A three-storey pink hotel with 320 junior suites, nicely furnished rooms with a king-size bed, sofa, cable TV and bathroom. There is a pool and spa, and Cabbage Beach is nearby. 7 per person.

Howelton Rose House Casuarina Drive ⓣ242/363-3363. Known as the "Pink House", an old Georgian home with four slightly dowdy rooms, but with plenty of historic charm, and breakfast served on its front porch. Located on a plot of land in the middle of *Club Med*, and one of the few quiet, private hotels on the island. 5

Ocean Club Paradise Island Drive ⓣ242/363-3000 or 1-800/321-3000, ⓦwww.oceanclub.com. Once a private estate, now a venerable and stunning hotel between miles of gorgeous beach and exquisite gardens, with a great restaurant and jaw-dropping prices. 9

Eating and drinking

Only a handful of **restaurants** on Paradise Island are unconnected to hotels or resorts, making dining a rather expensive endeavour. Still, Paradise Island has many of the best restaurants in the Bahamas, serving some of the most innovative dishes around. *Atlantis* seems to feature places to eat around every corner: the elegant *Villa d'Este* has freshly made pasta, *Atlas Bar and Grill* hamburgers and ribs, the *Bahamian Club* steaks and grilled seafood, and the *Clock Tower* pizza and salad.

At the *Paradise Harbour Club*, the *Columbus Tavern* has a nice harbour view and especially good lobster, steak and crème brûlée.

Apart from hotels, the choices narrow considerably. At the Paradise Island Shopping Center, *Anthony's Caribbean Grill* has surprisingly good pizza, lobster and chicken, but the only really authentic eatery around is the *Island Restaurant*, just off Paradise Beach Drive, which has inexpensive breakfasts of boiled fish, johnny cake and grits, and lunches of grilled fish sandwiches.

Nightlife

As you might expect, most Paradise Island **nightlife** is centred around the resorts, with almost all hotels having their own watering holes, some with piano bars and **live music**. The *Atlantis* features Las Vegas-style entertainment with a dozen bars and lounges, notably *Club Pastiche* and *Dragons Lounge and Dance Club*. Other hotels also have prominent bars and lounges featuring music and dancing, such as the *Oasis Lounge* in the *Club Land'Or*, and *Le Paon* in the *Sheraton Grand Resort*. For more relaxed fun, the *Blue Marlin* at Hurricane Hole serves lunch and dinner in an outdoor setting and occasionally features music like Junkanoo, steel band and limbo for around US$10.

Outdoor activities

Paradise Island **beaches** are famous for their swimming and sunbathing. At the far western edge of the island, **Paradise Beach** is nicely secluded, though lined with resort properties that charge swimmers a small fee. More spectacular is three-mile-long **Cabbage Beach**, one of the longest in the Bahamas, a sunny pink stretch that links the inlet at the *Atlantis* to Snorkeler's Cove. Because of the trade winds along the beach, **parasailing** has become very popular here, often resulting in a brilliant display of sails outlining the glowing horizon.

East of Cabbage Beach, many in-shore **snorkellers** head to **Snorkeler's Cove**, though more intrepid enthusiasts pay a visit to **Rose Island**, **Southwest**, **Razorback** and **Booby Rock reefs**, easily reachable from Hurricane Hole. Several boat operators also offer half- and full-day adventures out to these reefs, with Barefoot Sailing and Sea-Island Adventures running a regular schedule of snorkelling and swimming excursions. The island's only **diving** operator is Diver's Haven at Paradise Island Ferry Terminal (☎242/363-3333), with five instructors, three boats, PADI certification and various snorkelling trips.

1.2

Grand Bahama

Fifty five miles east of Miami, **GRAND BAHAMA** looks from the air to be a flat, dry slab of bleached limestone bristling with tall, thin pine trees and edged by a ribbon of powdery white sand and multihued bands of blue-green water. Accessible by daily ferry service and direct flights from several major American cities, the island is ninety-six miles long and seventeen miles wide, and has a range of appealing features: gorgeous white **beaches**, aquamarine **seas**, and an exotic profusion of lush **coral reefs** and **undersea gardens**. The island's **interior landscape** is as stark and rugged as its coastline is colourful and brilliant, with seemingly barren forests revealed up close to be teeming with life – home to numerous species of birds, lizards, plants and trees. Although the sun-dappled stands of pine, with an understorey of emerald-green thatch palm, are accessible on old logging roads that may be explored on foot or mountain bike, the rest of the interior is a vast monotony of unkempt bush and swamp that is decidedly less picturesque.

Despite the natural surroundings, most of the half-million annual visitors to Grand Bahama rarely stray far from the urban conglomeration of **Freeport** – located three miles inland from the south coast – and its seaside suburb **Lucaya**, which together are home to most of the island's 47,000 residents. Not surprisingly, the local economy is geared almost entirely to the **tourist trade**. Here, you can golf, gamble or just relax poolside at any number of all-inclusive resorts.

Outside the city, between Pelican Point and Sweeting's Cay, there are seven oceanic **blue holes** to entice divers and snorkellers. East of Freeport, the **Lucayan National Park** encompasses walking trails, limestone caves and mangrove creeks that can be explored by kayak. West of Freeport, **Deadman's Reef** offers lush snorkelling opportunities accessible from the powdery white beach at **Paradise Cove**.

Some history

After the tragic deaths of native Lucayans at the hands of **Spanish conquistadors**, Grand Bahama remained virtually uninhabited for several hundred years. Bands of **pirates** and **privateers** often lurked at the west end to ambush ships sailing through the Florida Channel and heading to Europe loaded with gold and other treasures, and many Spanish galleons and British men-of-war wrecked on the reefs encircling the island.

During the American Civil War, the island experienced a sudden spurt of growth when the village of West End briefly became a staging ground for Confederate **blockade runners** smuggling guns and supplies into the southern states, just as it later became a base for **rum runners** during Prohibition in the 1920s.

When American businessman **Wallace Groves** acquired the rights to harvest timber on Grand Bahama around 1950, the island was still nearly empty and undeveloped, but the tycoon set about creating a **winter playground** for the rich and famous, almost overnight. However, by the 1970s and 80s, the novelty and glamour of the once-burgeoning casinos and hotels began to fade, and Freeport and Lucaya were left mainly to continuous waves of college students on Spring Break and to cruise-ship day-trippers.

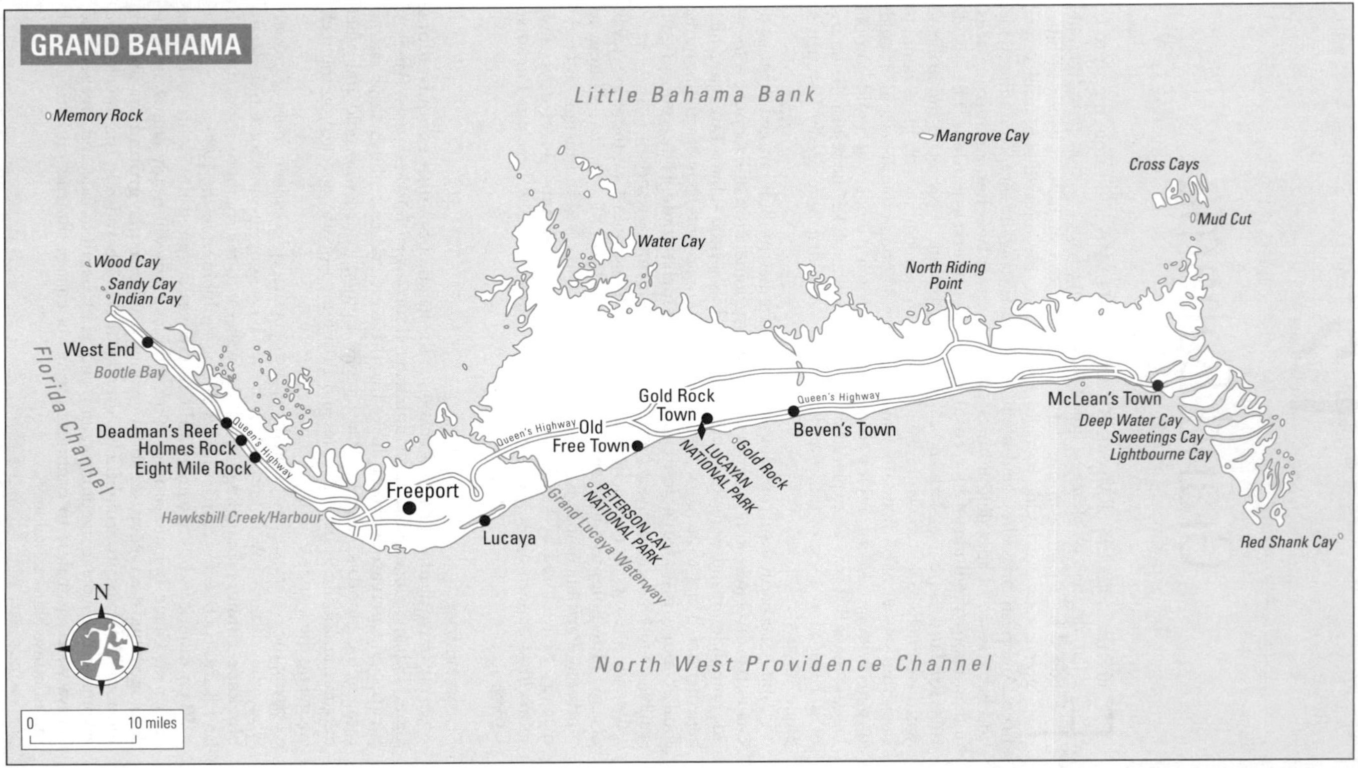

GRAND BAHAMA
Little Bahama Bank
Memory Rock
Mangrove Cay
Cross Cays
Mud Cut
Water Cay
Wood Cay
Sandy Cay
Indian Cay
North Riding Point
West End
Bootle Bay
Florida Channel
Deadman's Reef
Holmes Rock
Eight Mile Rock
Queen's Highway
Gold Rock Town
Old Free Town
Beven's Town
McLean's Town
Deep Water Cay
Sweetings Cay
Lightbourne Cay
Red Shank Cay
Gold Rock
LUCAYAN NATIONAL PARK
PETERSON CAY NATIONAL PARK
Grand Lucaya Waterway
Freeport
Lucaya
Hawksbill Creek/Harbour
North West Providence Channel
N
0
10 miles

After some years of decline, Grand Bahama has enjoyed a dramatic **economic rejuvenation** in the last five years fuelled by a number of giant, five-star resort complexes, helping the island shake off its image as Nassau's poorer, more unsophisticated cousin. Whether this latest tourism boom can translate into long-term stability and prosperity, however, remains to be seen.

Arrival and information

If you're **arriving** in Grand Bahama by airplane, cruise ship, commercial ferry or mail boat, you will first encounter Freeport/Lucaya. Otherwise, there are three marinas licensed as official ports of entry for private yachts, and only one other official island port, the marina at Old Bahama Bay at the west end of the island, 25 miles from Freeport.

By air

Grand Bahama International Airport (☎242/352-6020) is located on the northern outskirts of the city, but does not offer public bus service into town. Although many hotel packages include **free transfers** to and from the airport, you will likely have to take a taxi or rent a car. Taxi ranks and car-rental agencies are found at the front entrance to the terminal (see listing in "Getting around", below), and the usual taxi fare to Freeport hotels is around US$10, and to Lucaya US$15.

By boat

If you arrive by cruise ship, ferry from Florida or on the mail boat from Nassau, you will come ashore at Freeport Harbour, five miles west of Freeport proper. Several **cruise ships** call here every week, including the *MSV Discovery Sun*, a quadruple-decker passenger ferry/cruise ship taking a daily five-hour route between Fort Lauderdale and Freeport, with casino, swimming pool, buffet meals, games and floorshow (US$179 round-trip; ☎1-800/937-4477 in Florida, 1-800/866-8687 in the US and Canada and ☎305/597-0336 elsewhere, Ⓦwww.discoverycruiseline.com). The ticketing office in Freeport is located at the Tanja Maritime Centre (☎242/352-2328), on Queen's Highway near the Port Facility.

There are five full-service **marinas** in Freeport/Lucaya, three of which are official ports of entry to the Bahamas. Dockage rates range from 75 cents to US$1.50 per foot/per day. All have electricity and fresh-water hookups, as well as showers, bathrooms and laundry facilities.

Information

The Grand Bahama Island Tourism Board (PO Box F 40251, Freeport, Grand Bahama Island, Bahamas; Ⓦwww.grand-bahama.com) has **information booths** at the airport, the cruise-ship dock and in the Port Lucaya Marketplace, and a main office in Freeport's International Bazaar. Copious maps, brochures and activity guides are available in most hotel lobbies, shops and restaurants around town, with free **maps** of Grand Bahama, Freeport and Lucaya available almost everywhere. Finally, the *Grand Bahama Island Snorkelling Map* is on sale at the UNEXSO shop in Lucaya.

Getting around

Most visitors rarely venture beyond the resorts of Freeport/Lucaya, where the major attractions can easily be reached by foot, bicycle, motor scooter, public bus or organized bus tours. Complimentary **shuttle buses** to beaches, restaurants and the town centres of Freeport and Lucaya are offered by most hotels, and dinner shuttles are also available from some of the restaurants on the outskirts of town.

For those who want to roam further, a variety of transport options are available. **Car rentals** start from around US$80 a day plus gas, and include companies like

Avis at the airport (☎242/352-7666) and Port Lucaya (☎242/373-1102), Brad's (☎242/352 7930), Dollar-Rent-a-Car (☎242/352-9325), Hertz (☎1-800/654-3131 from North America, otherwise ☎242/352-3297), and Thrifty (☎242/352-9308).

Bahama Buggies (☎242/352-8750, ©buggies@batelnet.bs) rents bright-pink **dune buggies** for US$50 a day plus optional $15 insurance, while **motor scooters** can be rented for US$50 per day in the parking lot across from *Reef Village* in Port Lucaya, at *Running Mon Resort and Marina*, at the *Island Palm Resort*, and can also be arranged through your hotel. Well-maintained single-gear **bicycles** can be rented by the hour, day or week in Lucaya at *Reef Village* and at *Running Mon* (☎242/352-6834). If you are planning to put in some heavy mileage, though, bring your own bike.

Taxis meet every arriving flight and cruise ship, and any hotel will call one for you, including companies like Freeport Taxi (☎242/352-6666) and the Grand Bahama Taxi Union (☎242/352-7101). A **passenger ferry** makes a ten-minute trip between Port Lucaya and the *Ritz Bay Resort* on Taino Beach (hourly 8am–11pm; US$3 one-way, US$5 round-trip), leaving from the dock behind the *Flamingo Bay Hotel* at Taino Beach and the dock at Port Lucaya next to the *Ferry House Restaurant*. The ferry is not licensed to carry luggage, so only day-packs and handbags are permitted.

Freeport/Lucaya and other nearby communities are well connected by a fleet of privately owned minivan **buses**. To travel between Freeport and Lucaya, catch the bus in front of Freeport's International Bazaar or on the corner of Seahorse Road and Royal Palm Way in Lucaya. Bus stops throughout the city are marked by pink and white shelters. On busy routes, the buses leave when they are full and a ride costs a mere dollar anywhere within the city limits. Buses to settlements east and west of Freeport/Lucaya leave regularly from the **main bus stand** in the parking lot of Winn Dixie Plaza in downtown Freeport.

Freeport and Lucaya

With only about 40,000 residents, **FREEPORT/LUCAYA**'s many roads often lead to nowhere, through undeveloped bush and grandly named but still-deserted subdivisions awaiting development. Even in the commercial centre of Freeport, the port-authority headquarters, banks and apartment complexes – large colonial confections in pink, blue and yellow – manage to poke out above the treetops, but are still separated by significant remaining stands of **pine forest**. A utilitarian town with no organic centre or street life – everyone lives in the suburbs – it's not a good place for strolling or sightseeing, though easy enough to navigate on foot for visiting shops and restaurants.

Freeport's main commercial district is centred on **The Mall**, located between **Ranfurly Circus** – named for a British royal governor who supported the city's development in the 1950s – and **Churchill Square**, about ten blocks north. Surrounding the city centre, The Mall is bound on one side by West Mall Drive, and on the other by **East Mall Drive**, where most of the hotels and restaurants are located. Tourist activity is focused on the south end of **East Mall Drive**, around Ranfurly Circus and the **International Bazaar**, a faded warren of tacky shops and cafes marked by red Japanese-style Torii gates. In addition to several serviceable but uninspired restaurants, a straw market and assorted souvenir stands, there are duty-free shops selling jewellery, perfume, Cuban cigars, rum, resort wear and crystal.

East from Ranfurly Circus on Sunrise Highway, and south on Seahorse Road, **Port Lucaya** and the beachfront hotels of **Lucaya** comprise a resort area with a more cheerful atmosphere than Freeport's, with carefully tended lawns and shrubbery, and tidy, candy-coloured shops and houses. A seaside suburb first developed in

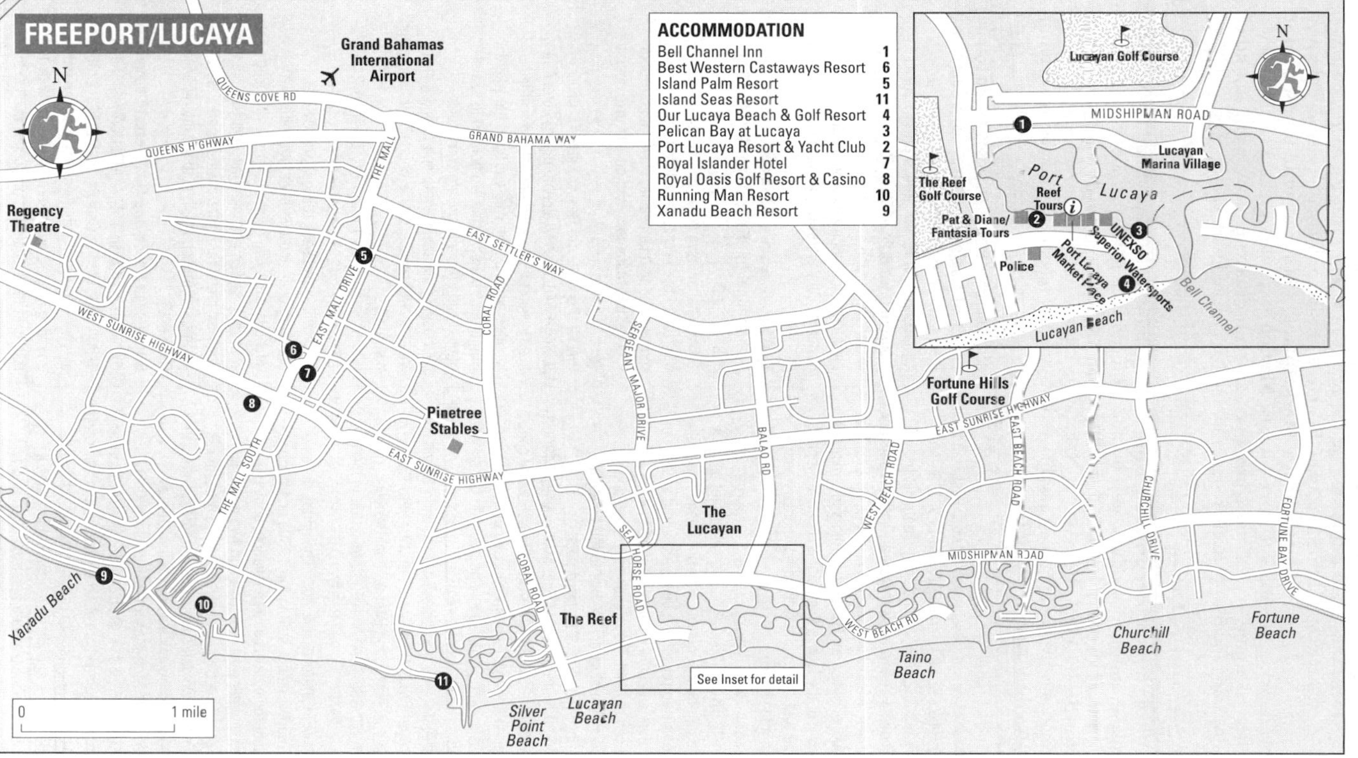
FREEPORT/LUCAYA
ACCOMMODATION
Bell Channel Inn 1
Best Western Castaways Resort 6
Island Palm Resort 5
Island Seas Resort 11
Our Lucaya Beach & Golf Resort 4
Pelican Bay at Lucaya 3
Port Lucaya Resort & Yacht Club 2
Royal Islander Hotel 7
Royal Oasis Golf Resort & Casino 8
Running Man Resort 10
Xanadu Beach Resort 9
Grand Bahamas International Airport
Regency Theatre
Pinetree Stables
The Lucayan
The Reef
Fortune Hills Golf Course
Xanadu Beach
Silver Point Beach
Lucayan Beach
Taino Beach
Churchill Beach
Fortune Beach
QUEENS COVE RD
QUEENS H'GHWAY
GRAND BAHAMA WAY
THE MALL
EAST MALL DRIVE
EAST SETTLER'S WAY
WEST SUNRISE HIGHWAY
EAST SUNRISE HIGHWAY
THE MALL SOUTH
CORAL ROAD
SERGEANT MAJOR DRIVE
SEA HORSE ROAD
BALAO RD
WEST BEACH ROAD
WEST BEACH RD
EAST BEACH ROAD
MIDSHIPMAN ROAD
CHURCHILL DRIVE
FORTUNE BAY DRIVE
See Inset for detail
0
1 mile
N
Lucayan Golf Course
The Reef Golf Course
Lucayan Marina Village
Port Lucaya
Reef Tours
Pat & Diane/ Fantasia Tours
UNEXSO
Superior Watersports
Port Lucaya Market Place
Police
Bell Channel
Lucayan Beach

the 1960s, Lucaya is dominated by the brand-new and massive *Our Lucaya Beach and Golf Resort*, fronting **Lucayan Beach**, with two golf courses. Across the street from *Our Lucaya* is **Port Lucaya Marketplace**, a busy, colourful tourist market overlooking the boats at **Port Lucaya Marina**, with shops selling clothing, jewellery, perfume, crystal and china, open-air stalls displaying straw work and other souvenirs, and several lively restaurants and bars packed with vacationers.

Accommodation

When choosing **accommodation**, keep in mind that Freeport lies several miles inland, and although there are a number of nice hotels in town, it is not an especially attractive place. If you do stay here, you can take one of the complimentary **shuttle buses** to the beach at Xanadu or Lucaya (five and ten minutes away by car, respectively). The main advantage of staying in Freeport is generally lower room rates than those found in Lucaya.

Freeport

Best Western Castaways Resort East Mall Drive ⓣ242/352-6682 or 1-800/700-ISLANDS, ⓕ242/352-5087, ⓔcastaway@batelnet.bs. Recently renovated with 139 attractive rooms and suites overlooking the pool or street, an excellent budget option for Freeport, within a few minutes' walk of the town's main sights. Features a pool, bar and restaurant, with complimentary beach shuttle service. ④

Island Palm Resort East Mall Drive ⓣ242/352-6648, ⓕ352-6640, ⓔispalm@batelnet.bs. A decent budget choice, with bright and cheerful rooms surrounding a courtyard and a small pool. Offers an outdoor bar, restaurant that becomes a disco at night, motor scooter rentals, and complimentary shuttle bus to the beach at Lucaya's *Island Seas Resort*. ④

Royal Islander Hotel East Mall Drive ⓣ242/351-6000, ⓕ351-3546, ⓔroyalisland@hotmail.com. A small gem with a palm-shaded courtyard, restaurant, jacuzzi, pool and poolside bar serving light meals. Rooms are nicely appointed, and hotel provides free transportation to Xanadu Beach. ⑤

Royal Oasis Golf Resort and Casino Ranfurly Circus, next to the International Bazaar ⓣ242/350-7000 or 1-800/545-1300 in the US and Canada, ⓕ242/350-7002, ⓦwww.theroyaloasis.com. The gaudy doyen of Freeport hotels, built in the 1960s and currently undergoing extensive renovation, adding a giant freshwater pool, waterfall and two waterslides. Features a casino, twelve tennis courts, fitness centre, two golf courses, seven restaurants and 965 guest rooms also being updated. ⑦

Running Mon Marina and Resort Kelly Court ⓣ242/352-6834, ⓕ352-6835, ⓦwww.running-mon-bahamas.com. A bit off the beaten track, with 31 clean rooms with rattan furniture, terracotta tiled floors and kitchenettes. Site includes a dipping pool, pleasant bar, restaurant and full-service marina. Bicycle, motor scooter and boat rentals available on site. Complimentary transit to downtown Freeport and Xanadu Beach. ⑤

Xanadu Beach Resort and Marina Sunken Treasure Drive ⓣ242/352-6782, ⓕ352-6299, ⓦwww.xanadubeachhotel.com. Overpriced monument to 1980s kitsch on a litter-strewn patch of beach. Only worth visiting as a last resort. ⑤

Lucaya and adjacent beaches

Bell Channel Inn King's Rd ⓣ242/373-1053, ⓕ373-2886, ⓦwww.bahamasvg.com/caribdiv.html. Located at the rear of the *Port Lucaya Marina*, with dated rooms offering unappealing views, but in-room fridges, bar, restaurant, and on-site dive operator. ④

Inn at Old Bahama Bay ⓣ242/346-6500, ⓕ346-6546, ⓦwww.oldbahamabay.com. A new luxury resort with several hundred secluded wooded acres on the western tip of the island. Sumptuous guest rooms are housed in pastel-gabled cottages with private verandahs overlooking the sands. Watersports and fishing trips, as well as spa, tennis courts, golf course and bistro. ⑨

Island Seas Resort Silver Point Drive ⓣ242/373-1271, ⓕ373-1275. Small, isolated beachfront hotel with a pleasant, relaxed atmosphere, featuring one- and two-bedroom suites with kitchens and living quarters, large swimming pool with rock garden and waterfall, swim-up bar and open-air restaurant. Offers watersports, bicycle rentals and free shuttle bus to the International Bazaar. ⑥

Our Lucaya Beach and Golf Resort Seahorse Rd ⓣ242/373-1333 or 1-877/OURLUCAYA in the US, 1-800/848-3315 in Canada, ⓕ242/373-2396, ⓦwww.ourlucaya.com. Five-star resort matching anything on Nassau or Paradise Island, with 1350 rooms in three seafront complexes, each designed to appeal to different tastes. Site's 372 acres include two golf courses, seven acres of white sandy beach, nine swimming pools, four tennis courts, fourteen restaurants and bars, fitness centre, spa and casino. 5

Pelican Bay at Lucaya Seahorse Rd ⓣ242/373-9550, ⓕ373-9551, ⓦwww.pelicanbayhotel.com. Small, lovely hotel built around a quiet courtyard with a swimming pool, jacuzzi and open-air bar serving light meals. Elegant rooms have tile floors, refrigerators and balconies furnished with adirondack chairs, while luxury suites have kitchens as well. All guests have access to the beach at *Our Lucaya* resort across the street. 6

Port Lucaya Resort and Yacht Club Seahorse Rd ⓣ242/373-6618, ⓕ373-6652, ⓦwww.portlucaya.com/resort. Located across from Lucayan Beach, featuring boat slips outside each of the hotel's 160 rooms, and balconies overlooking the swimming pool or marina. Also with jacuzzi and on-site restaurant. 5

Eating and drinking

In general, hotel **restaurants** have most of the area's best food options, with *Our Lucaya* resort especially good for its thirteen eateries with eclectic cuisine. There are a few popular local **cafés**, but most residents prefer takeout – traditional dishes or fast food – to dining out. Dining in Freeport/Lucaya is predictably expensive, though there are a few cheap eateries around, if you look for them.

Cally's in the Port Lucaya Marketplace. Serving tasty and affordable Greek and Bahamian dishes, including Greek salad and savoury grilled vegetable wraps. Cheerful and relaxed atmosphere, with indoor and outdoor seating on the wooden verandah.

Calypso Café ground floor of the *Country Club, Royal Oasis* resort. A cheerful, busy place for breakfast or lunch, with plentiful buffets; coffee and pastries à la carte.

Churchill's Chophouse in the *Manor House, Our Lucaya* resort. An elegant glass-and-mahogany dining room open for dinner only, serving steak, lobster and other seafood dishes and a fine selection of vintage wines.

The Ferry House on the waterfront at Port Lucaya ⓣ242/373-1595. Featuring an imaginative menu with dishes like grouper braised in Nassau Royale sauce and shrimp with a ginger glace, as well as staples like chicken and pasta. Elegant dining room is sunny and inviting at breakfast, and candlelit with harbour views at dinner.

Geneva's Place East Mall Drive at Kipling ⓣ242/352-5085. Popular and lively local eatery serving Bahamian and American food at reasonable prices.

Irie's behind Breaker's Cay, *Our Lucaya* resort. A cosy, colonial-Caribbean house featuring Cuban, Jamaican, Puerto Rican and Haitian cuisine, with traditional stews and seafood dishes like snapper steamed in banana leaf and served with plantains and voodoo fritters. Expensive.

The Main Sail at the *Running Mon Resort* ⓣ242/352-6833. Boasting the island's most extensive wine list, an imported Austrian chef, and a circular dining room with verandah overlooking the marina and channel. Varied menu changes daily and may include lobster bisque, salmon with dill, beef stroganoff and, of course, wiener schnitzel. US$20–30.

The Prop Club on the beach at Breaker's Cay, *Our Lucaya* resort. A casual restaurant and sports bar decked out like an airplane hanger. Inexpensive menu features margarita pizza, chicken, ribs and tropical drinks. With a pool table and nightly music and dancing.

The Pub at Port Lucaya outside Count Basie Square. A busy, outdoor patio restaurant serving a moderately priced international menu.

Sugar Mill Bar and Grill poolside at *Reef Village, Our Lucaya* resort. Cheap and tasty lunch and dinner fare served al fresco, including deli sandwiches, salads, burgers, hot dogs and tropical drinks.

Willy Broadleaf ground floor of Breaker's Cay, *Our Lucaya* resort. A series of themed dining rooms offering breakfast, lunch and dinner buffets, with eclectic Middle Eastern and Indian dishes, Mexican favourites, fresh pasta, crepes, and sweets like baclava and Bahamian guava duff. Expensive. Breakfast US$20, dinner $38.

Zorba's Port Lucaya ⓣ242/373-6137. Providing tasty and inexpensive Greek favourites like souvlaki, pitta wraps and salads, with a no-frills seating area.

Grand Bahama tours and outdoor activities

Boat excursions

Pat and Diane/Fantasia Tours booth at *Port Lucaya* resort ⓣ242/373-8681. Organizes an array of daily boat cruises, including a four-hour trip to Peterson Cay National Park for swimming, snorkelling and picnicking. US$59, kids $35.

Reef Tours at Port Lucaya Marketplace ⓣ242/373-5880. Offers several daily tours aboard a glass-bottomed boat, lasting about an hour and costing US$25, kids $15. As a second option, the catamaran *Fantasea* departs each morning on a two-hour trip. $30 per person.

Smiling Pat's Adventures ⓣ242/373-6395, ⓔpath@grouper.batelnet.bs. Provides different outings every day, from all-day boat excursions to Abaco and Peterson Cay National Park to beach-hopping trips and spear-fishing expeditions.

Diving and snorkelling

East End Adventures ⓣ242/373-6662, ⓔeastendsafari@yahoo.com. A quality outfitter offering a seven-hour "Blue Hole Snorkelling Safari", which explores the marine life of blue holes off the eastern end of Grand Bahama, followed by a barbecue lunch on a deserted cay. Group size is limited to eight. Adults US$85, kids $35.

Paradise Cove at Deadman's Reef ⓣ242/349-2677. Twenty minutes away on a secluded beach, a place to snorkel over lush reefs, float in a glass-bottomed kayak or relax on the sand. A snack bar and grill serves tasty beach food as well. Includes transport to and from your hotel, lunch and equipment usage. US$30, kids $23.

Superior Watersports ⓣ242/373-7863. Uses a large motorized catamaran for hour-long snorkelling trips along Treasure Reef, departing four times daily. Another catamaran departs daily at 11am for a five-hour "Robinson Crusoe Beach Party", including 90 minutes of snorkelling followed by a full buffet lunch and volleyball on a deserted beach. US$59, kids $39.

Underwater Explorer's Society (UNEXSO) based at Port Lucaya ⓣ242/373-1244 or 1-800/992-3483

Nightlife

There is no shortage of things to do **after dark** in Freeport/Lucaya. One popular and fun way to spend the evening is on one of the numerous **sunset dinner** or "**booze cruises**" leaving nightly from Port Lucaya. Otherwise, you can usually find a beachside **bonfire** and **fish fry** almost any night of the week at one of the major hotels or restaurants. Inside *Our Lucaya Resort* (bars daily 6pm–2am; ⓣ242/373-1333), the *Manor House*'s swank *Churchill Bar* features live jazz Thursday through Sunday nights, and in the *Royal Oasis Resort and Casino* (ⓣ242/352-6721), the casual *Johnny B Bar*, poolside at the *Country Club*, has nightly live music as well.

There are several lively **bars** in the Port Lucaya Marketplace, patronized mainly by beach bums and yacht cruisers. In Freeport, locals and visitors mix on the dance floor at *Club 2000* (Thurs–Sun 10pm–3am; ⓣ242/352-8866) and at *Amnesia* (ⓣ242/351-2582), both on East Mall Drive near the International Bazaar. For visual refreshment, there are two **cinemas** on East Mall Drive with several daily showings: Columbus Theatres (ⓣ242/352-7478 or 7577) and RND Cinemas (ⓣ242/351-3456). Finally, two local **amateur drama** societies put on plays throughout the year, the Freeport Player's Guild and the Regency Theatre (both at ⓣ242/352-5533), located in the same theatre on Regency Boulevard, just west of the Ruby Golf Course.

and 954/351-9899 in the US, Ⓕ242/373-1244, Ⓦwww.unexso.com. Well-established operation with equipment rental, courses and day or night snorkelling and diving trips, including swimming with dolphins and sharks, and visits to wrecks, reefs and blue holes.

Xanadu Undersea Adventures Ⓣ242/352-3811, Ⓕ352-4731. Offers a full range of guided diving excursions and certification courses.

Other outdoor activities

The Dolphin Experience ticket booth at UNEXSO Ⓣ242/373-1250 or 1-888/365-3483, Ⓕ242/373-3948, Ⓦwww.dolphinexperience.com. One of the most popular tourist activities on Grand Bahama. Departing from the UNEXSO dock, a twenty-minute boat ride leads to Sanctuary Bay, where the dolphins live in a quiet cove. Three experiences are offered: petting dolphins, swimming with them, and spending the day assisting their keepers. US$39–179.

East End Adventures Ⓣ242/373-6662, Ⓔeastendsafari@yahoo.com. Offers excellent all-day excursions to the unspoiled eastern tip of the island, visiting fishing villages, bumping along bush trails and sampling wild fruit before arriving at Sweeting's Cay for a conch cracking demonstration. Final destination is the pristine beaches of Lightbourne Cay for picnic lunch, sunbathing and snorkelling. Group size limited to eight people. US$110, kids $55.

Kayak Nature Tours Ⓣ242/373-2485, Ⓦwww.bahamasvg.com/kayak.html. Runs enjoyable paddling excursions, including day trips in Lucayan National Park, kayaking/snorkelling tours to Peterson Cay National Park (US$69), strenuous trips to the tiny remote settlement of Water Cay ($110) and guided, cycling nature tours as well ($69). Tour group sizes are limited and tours include transport and picnic lunches.

Pinetree Stables Ⓣ242/373-3600, Ⓔpinetree@batelnet.bs. Offers a pleasant, two-hour guided trail ride through a pine forest and along the beach. Twice daily rides, no experience necessary. US$65; reservations required; closed Mondays.

The rest of the island

The two main attractions outside Freeport – Lucayan National Park and Paradise Cove – lie on opposites sides of the town. Straddling the Queen's Highway 25 miles to the east, **Lucayan National Park** (daily 9am–4pm; $3; Ⓣ242/352-5438) encompasses forty acres of mixed forest, limestone caverns and sinkholes, mangrove creeks, a spectacular beach and several nature trails all less than a mile long. A trail from the parking lot on the north side of the highway leads to a six-mile-long **underwater cave system**, one of the world's longest. One of them, Ben's Cave, is named for Grand Bahamian Ben Rose, the first diver to explore the entire cave system. Others have died trying to repeat this feat, but certified divers may explore the underwater stalactites and stalagmites of the tunnels with a permit obtainable from the Bahamas National Trust (Ⓣ242/359-1821, Ⓔexumapark@aol.com), and UNEXSO (Ⓣ242/373-1244, Ⓦwww.unexso.com) offers guided expeditions. The opening of Ben's Cave, accessible by a steep staircase, is home to a large colony of bats and is closed to visitors in the summer months when they nurse their young. Nearby, in Burial Mound Cave, another limestone sinkhole, divers discovered the skeletons of four indigenous Lucayans.

Heading west from Freeport along Queen's Highway, a sign on the left marks the turn-off to **Paradise Cove** (Ⓣ242/349-2677, Ⓕ352-5471, Ⓦwww.paradisecove-bahamas.com or Ⓦwww.deadmansreef.com) at **Deadman's Reef**, and a beautiful stretch of white sandy beach backed by tall grass and bush, with great snorkelling around the teeming reef just offshore. Deadman's Reef is the site of an important archeological find – the remains of a Lucayan settlement from the twelfth or thirteenth century that was discovered in 1996. It is, however, closed to the public.

Practicalities

In Paradise Cove, the Smith family operate two well-maintained, two-bedroom beachfront cottages (US$125 per night), a one-bedroom apartment ($100) and a two-bedroom villa ($175) for rent within steps of the water (Ⓣ242/3420-2677). The family also runs a friendly and relaxed **snack bar** and rents snorkelling gear and glass-bottomed kayaks, and runs day excursions from Freeport/Lucaya.

Kayak Nature Tours (Ⓣ242/373-2485, Ⓦwww.bahamasvg.com/kayak) offers a unique view of Lucayan National Park on its easy paddling **kayak expeditions** through a mangrove creek, followed by a guided nature walk and picnic lunch on the beach ($69). Public buses also pass by three times a day.

1.3

Andros

Bahamians call **ANDROS** their "Big Back Yard", an appropriate description considering the thick bush that dominates the island, which in the north consists mainly of tropical and deciduous trees like **Andros pine** and **lignum vitae** – the latter virtually the national tree of the Bahamas – and in the south, a mix of mangroves, mud flats and tidal swamps. Not surprisingly, amid this rugged natural terrain, there are seemingly as many **birdwatchers** as there are birds, making the island an essential stop for avian enthusiasts.

However, what really makes Andros unique is its magnificent **barrier reef**, the third longest in the world after those in Australia and Central America. Running parallel to the island's east coast for 167 miles, the Androsian reef is a massive inner bar of **elkhorn coral** that lies 10-200ft underwater and helps protect the island from tropical storms and hurricanes. It's also a truly spectacular place to explore, whether you **dive**, **snorkel** or **fish**, with an outer wall that plunges down spectacularly through a myriad of canyons, caves, blue holes and sand chutes. In the shallower waters inshore, the sights are just as stunning, featuring a bright assortment of reef fish, starfish, sea cucumbers and southern Manta rays, among countless other species.

The island is divided into three zones: **North Andros**, home to most of the population; Central Andros, better known as **Mangrove Cay**; and **South Andros**, the most lightly populated and remote section. Aside from the north end, many parts of the rest of the island received electricity only in the last twenty years, and still have a rather poor, antiquated road system. This gives the region a rather charming and isolated character, a rustic appeal for those with the patience to deal with it.

Arrival, information and getting around

Located 25 miles west of New Providence, Andros is easily accessed by airplane or ferry from Nassau or mainland Florida. Bahamasair (☎242/339-4415 or 1-800/222-4262 in the US) is the main carrier between Nassau's International Airport and any of the four airports on Andros. Some other, smaller carriers are Congo Air (☎242/377-8329), Lynx Air International (☎1-888/596-9247) and Major Air (☎242/352-5778).

Ferries and **mail boats** are a cheap and easy way to reach Andros from Nassau. Ferries can make the 25-mile journey in just under three hours, although, depending on your destination and route, they may sometimes take up to seven hours. Fares are US$30 one-way. For ferry schedules and for information on accessing government mail boats, contact the **dockmaster's office** at Potter's Cay in Nassau (☎242/393-1064).

Tourist information offices are located throughout the island, though the best site is at Fresh Creek (☎242/368-2286), located opposite the city park on the south side of the creek. Other offices are at Mangrove Cay (☎242/369-0544) and South Andros (☎242/369-1688).

There are only a few good options for **getting around** the island, mainly because there are so few roads, and major settlements are widely separated. **Renting a car** can be a frustrating endeavour, and is typically best forsaken in lieu of **walking** and **bicycling** as cheaper, easier alternatives.

Taxis present another travel option, meeting all incoming flights at the airport, though cab companies on Andros are mainly individual operators who can vary dramatically in service and price. With no official tour operators on the island, most taxi drivers also double as **tour guides**, and offer informal sightseeing jaunts, particularly on North Andros, for around US$300 per day for two people. Some hotels and resorts may also include a complimentary taxi service for guests.

North Andros

The most prominent activity on **NORTH ANDROS**, and the major draw for many of the island's visitors, is the sport of **bonefishing**. Although many of the creeks, flats, bights and rivers here sport countless numbers of hungry bonefish, the **North Bight** is the focus of the fishing scene, about thirty miles from Andros Town airport.

You can always find a great assortment of fishing boats parked at the wharf at nearby **Nicholl's Town**, a small burg of six hundred residents living in breeze-block and tin-roofed homes and scattered wooden shacks, lying near the island's north tip along a beach fringed by tall palm trees. To the east lies the pleasant fishing village of **Lowe Sound**, which has a guesthouse for visitors, several small bars and restaurants, and a few recommended bonefishing guides like Arthur Russell (Ⓣ242/329-7372).

Less appealing, the town of **San Andros**, further south along the east coast, consists of a few concrete houses surrounded by pine forest, with a nearby harbour at **Mastic Point**. Both settlements are tiny and virtually without services. On the island's rugged west coast, the tiny fishing village of **Red Bays** is the only real settlement, reachable by a bumpy, unpaved fifteen-mile road from San Andros.

South of San Andros airport, the delightful *Small Hope Bay Lodge* is the island's premier diving and fishing destination, while two miles south of Small Hope Bay is **Fresh Creek**, which actually encompasses two distinct settlements connected by a lovely single-lane bridge. The first, **Coakley Town**, is home to a few shops, restaurants and bars, as well as a large lighthouse on a cape. The town also has the only full-service marina around, the Andros Lighthouse Yacht Club and Marina, though the *Chickcharnie Hotel* offers slips as well. Across the bridge, **Andros Town** has a tourist office, a pleasant park with a few disused tennis courts, and the **Androsia Batik Factory** (Mon–Sat 8am–5pm; Ⓣ242/352-2255), one of the few commercial enterprises on Andros. Operated by the Birch family, which also owns *Small Hope Bay Lodge*, the factory produces colourful batiks, which make fashionable dresses, blouses, pants, T-shirts and scarves, as well as excellent wall hangings.

The rough road south from Fresh Creek to Cargill Creek runs through bush and pine scrub, and is devoid of settlements. Still, the towns of **Cargill Creek** and nearby **Behring Point** are in the midst of prime bonefishing country, and worth making the effort to visit if you don't mind the drive.

Practicalities

As you might expect, most of the activities and **tours** of North Andros are based around bonefishing, and often organized by the island's **lodges** and **resorts**. The Andros Lighthouse Yacht Club and Marina in Fresh Creek (Ⓣ242/368-2305 or 1-800/688-4752, Ⓕ242/368-2300) is built around a central patio, with a hotel overlooking an eighteen-slip marina, and offers bonefishing and island tours. Also in Fresh Creek, *Coakley House* (Ⓣ242/368-2013) is a large self-catering villa operated by the *Small Hope Bay Lodge* (below), while *Point of View Villas* (Ⓣ242/368-2750 or 1-800/688-4752, Ⓕ242/368-2761, Ⓦwww.pointofviewbahamas.com) offers exclusive, expensive accommodations. Further north, on an island off Staniard Creek, *Kamalame Cay* (Ⓣ242/368-6281 or 1-800/688-4752, Ⓕ242/368-6279) is a private resort with many upscale facilities. At Cargill Creek, the best lodges are *Andros Island Bonefishing Club* (ⓣ242/368-5167 or 1-800/688-4752), *Cargill Creek Fishing Lodge* (ⓣ242/368-5129 or 1-800/533-4353), and the rustic favourite *Charlie's Haven* (ⓣ242/368 4087).

Unquestionably, though, the island's premier diving and snorkelling lodge is *Small Hope Bay Lodge* in Calabash Bay (ⓣ242/368-2013 or 1-800/223-6961, ⓦwww.smallhope.com, ⓔshbinfo@smallhope.com), a limestone and pine resort with a converted old boat for a bar and batik décor in the rooms. Diving and snorkelling trips are available, along with a beachside hot tub, kayaks, bonefishing, saltwater flyfishing and reef fishing. **Dining** is excellent here, as it is at most of the lodges. Other good choices for meals include *The Conch Sound Resort* and *Green Windows Inn* in Nicholl's Town, and in Fresh Creek, *Hank's Place*, known for its great fried chicken.

Mangrove Cay and South Andros

Most of the hotels and resorts in central and southern Andros are located directly on the beach, typically a rather narrow strip of soft, white sand. Offshore, the barrier reef is close enough for **snorkelling** and features stunning, close-up views of Caribbean spiny lobster, natural sponges, southern Manta rays, parrotfish and iridescent displays of coral.

In central Andros, around **MANGROVE CAY**, the main settlement of **Little Harbour** is most interesting at its northern end, known as **Moxey Town**. With a tiny dock for harvesting fishing catches and bringing in ferries, Moxey Town has a few restaurants and bars, and good access to the offshore reef as well. The main diving centre on Mangrove Cay is the *Seascape Inn* (see below), with special snorkelling and diving packages, kayak dives and weekly night trips for advanced divers.

A few miles beyond Mangrove Cay, **SOUTH ANDROS** features thirty miles of coastal road edging white sands and coconut palms, and premier birdwatching and nature-hiking opportunities on its inland terrain. From **Drigg's Hill** to the north (where the ferry from Mangrove Cay disembarks), it's a slow and bumpy 25 mile trip to the road's southern end at Mars Bay. **Congo Town** is the site of the airport, offering a few places to eat, an ocean walk through coconut palms and, in the town centre, a **cemetery** where many of the island's founding families are buried. Everything west of here is mangrove and dense bush.

There are many attractive vistas on the road south and several worthwhile stops, namely **Long Bay**, departure point for long hikes into bromeliad- and orchid-covered hinterlands, **High Rock**, site of a magnificent blue hole perfect for diving and swimming, and little **Duncombe's Court**, a hole-in-the-wall village with a few restaurants. **Mars Bay**, at the road's southern terminus, is a pleasant little burg with a quaint town square and a busy fishing dock, where loads of grouper and conch are stacked for cleaning and shipment.

Practicalities

As with North Andros, most of the **activities** and **accommodation** to the south are centred around hotels and resorts. A prime spot for beauty and isolation, the refurbished *Seascape Inn* in Moxey Town (ⓣ242/369-0342 or 1-800/688-4752; ❺) offers both rooms and cottages, excellent breakfasts and dinners, and a popular bar. In Kemp's Bay, the *Royal Palm Beach Lodge* (ⓣ242/369-1608 or 1-800/688-4752, ⓕ242/369-1934, ⓔrahmings@batelnet.bs; ❸) has ten rooms, a courtyard, palm tree décor and a small bar and restaurant. The area's premier luxury resort, located between Drigg's Hill and Congo Town, is *Emerald Palms by the Sea* (ⓣ242/369-2661 or 1-800/688-4752, ⓕ242/369-2667; ❺), featuring twenty rooms and two suites. Bonefishing, hiking, blue-hole swimming, and kayak tours are all available, along with diving equipment rental. The resort also offers a fine restaurant serving an eclectic blend of European and Bahamian cuisines, though the area has a few other good **dining** options as well. Congo Town's *Square Deal* and *Flamingo Club* are solid choices, and in Drigg's Hill, the *Blue Bird Club* (☎242/369-4546) offers decent food and nightly dancing. In Kemp's Bay, *Big J's on the Bay* (☎242/369-1954) is the most popular place to eat, while *Cabana Beach Bar* and *Lewis' Bar* are good watering holes.

Alice Town

Just fifty miles east of Miami, Florida, is the world-famous fishing destination **Alice Town** on North Bimini. Capital of the tiny Bimini island chain, Alice Town is also one of the most well-known party sites anywhere in the Bahamas. Popularized by Ernest Hemingway, who described it as a hard-drinking fishing refuge, the town's numerous hotels and marinas continue to provide plenty of activity for anglers, divers and snorkellers, as well as a freewheeling, somewhat ribald atmosphere somewhat reminiscent of the town's glory days.

With more than two hundred hotel rooms in a six-block-square area, Alice Town has a number of notable **fishing clubs** and **resorts**. Best known is the *Compleat Angler Hotel*, King's Highway (☎242/347-3122; 3), where Hemingway drank, fought and wrote the novel *To Have and Have Not*. It houses a collection of Hemingway memorabilia including rare photographs of the author. Almost as famous, the original *Bimini Big Game Fishing Club and Hotel*, King's Highway (☎242/347-3391), has hotel rooms, two penthouse suites and twelve cottages, and offers marina services along with excellent food and drink. Both the *Bimini Bay Guest House* (☎242/347-2171), an Art Deco treasure, and the *Bimini Blue Water Resort* (☎242/347-3166), where Hemingway wrote in a cottage called the Anchorage, also offer comfortable surroundings and fine food.

King's Highway, the only paved road on the island, is lined with many good **restaurants**, swinging **pubs**, and garish souvenir stands. Primary **air service** to Alice Town is provided by Pan Am Air Bridges (1000 MacArthur Causeway, Miami, Florida; ☎242/347-3024 or 1-800/424-2557), although charter services to North Bimini, namely Bimini Island Air (☎954/938-8991), operate out of Fort Lauderdale as well.

1.4

Eleuthera

Derived from an ancient Greek word for "freedom", the name **ELEUTHERA** was given to the island by a small band of European settlers who landed on its beaches in 1648, fleeing religious persecution in Bermuda. A set of four closely related islands, the Eleutheran group's most prominent member is the long, thin island of **Eleuthera** itself, over a hundred miles long but less than two miles wide. The most populous of the Out Islands, Eleuthera has ten thousand residents scattered in a dozen fishing villages spread along its coastline, though not much goes on, outside of some ocean activities and laid-back solitude.

Eleuthera Island

In the middle of Eleuthera, the genteel community of **Governor's Harbour** is one of the earliest settlements in the Bahamas. To the north, the **Hatchet Bay Cave** is a good spot for amateur explorers, while beyond that, **Gregory Town**, built on a steep hillside surrounding a deep horseshoe-shaped harbour, is the self-proclaimed pineapple capital of the Bahamas. To the south of Governor's Harbour are the picturesque fishing villages of **Tarpum Bay** and **Rock Sound**.

Outside of a handful of comfortable resorts, there are few organised tourist facilities on Eleuthera, which is part of its appeal for many visitors – that and the many **empty beaches** fit for swimming, strolling, snorkelling, shell-collecting or sunbathing.

By comparison, attractive **Harbour Island** – or Briland, as it also known locally – bustles with activity, highlighted by the historic burg of **Dunmore Town**, which boasts several luxury resorts, restaurants, bars, dive outfitters and the stunning, three-mile **Pink Sand Beach**. Unlike Harbour Island, nearby **Spanish Wells**, which occupies the whole of **St George's Island**, is a working-class settlement with a large fleet of fishing and lobster boats. It too has a long white-sand beach, but a very modest tourist trade.

Arrival and information

On the main island of Eleuthera, there are **airports** at Rock Sound, Governor's Harbour and North Eleuthera, with daily service from Nassau and Florida. Bahamas Fast Ferries (US$55 one way, $100 round-trip; ⓣ242/323-2166, ⓦwww.bahamasfastferries.com) operates daily **ferry** service between Nassau, Harbour Island and Spanish Wells, and twice-weekly service to Governor's Harbour. Government **mail boats** call once a week at Rock Sound, Governor's Harbour, Hatchet Bay, Spanish Wells and Harbour Island.

There are Ministry of Tourism **information offices** in Governor's Harbour (ⓣ242/332-2142, ⓕ332-2480) and Dunmore Town on Harbour Island (ⓣ242/333-2621, ⓕ333-2622), theoretically open during regular business hours, but in practice more sporadically. Tarbox Publications offers an excellent, well-detailed four-sheet **map** of Eleuthera, Harbour Island and Spanish Wells, including their respective beaches and other local attractions (US$10), available at the *Rainbow Inn* and other local shops.

Accommodation

Cartwright's Oceanfront Cottages Tarpum Bay, ⓣ242/334-4215. Offers three cosy two- and three-bedroom cottages on the waterfront at the western edge of town, with a homey and eclectic décor and a great view of the sea. ❺
Cigatoo Resort Governor's Harbour ⓣ242/332-3060 or 1-800/467-7595 in North America, ⓕ242/332-3061, ⓦwww.cigatooresort.com. Has 24 clean, bright and modern rooms set in nicely landscaped grounds around a swimming pool, with tennis courts and a bar and restaurant. ❺
Cocodimama ⓣ242/332-3150, ⓕ242/332-3155, ⓦwww.cocodimama.com. Two miles south of Governor's Harbour airport, a small beach resort with three two-storey cottages on the beach. Twelve spacious, well-decorated rooms feature Balian art, clay-tile floors and private balconies with hammocks. Windsurfing, kayaking and snorkelling gear available for guest use. Closed Sept–Nov. ❼
The Cove Eleuthera ⓣ335-5142, ⓕ335-5338, ⓦwww.thecoveeleuthera.com. A small, casual resort two miles north of Gregory Town, with a white-sand beach in a sheltered cove and bicycle rentals, snorkelling gear, bar, restaurant, tennis courts and a dramatic coastline to explore by kayak. Features 24 comfortable rooms with ceramic-tiled floors, some with kitchenettes. ❻
The Duck Inn Governor's Harbour ⓣ242/332-2608, ⓕ332-2160, ⓦwww.theduckinn.com. Located on the waterfront, this has three charming wooden cottages from the early 1800s, with an outdoor barbecue, kayaks for guest use and an orchid nursery complete with rock grotto. Cottages sleep two to eight. ❺
Nor'Side Resort Rock Sound ⓣ242/334-2573. Perched on a high bluff overlooking the Atlantic, a cluster of four hexagonal cottages with eight studio apartments, sand-floored bar and a restaurant serving the best home-cooked Bahamian meals on the island. ❺
Rainbow Inn ⓣ242/335-0294, ⓣ1-800/688-0047 in Canada and the US, ⓦwww.rainbowinn.com. Ten miles north of Governor's Harbour airport, a relaxed resort with hexagonal cottages built around a swimming pool overlooking the sea, and rooms with kitchens and private decks. Facilities include tennis courts, free bicycle use, kayaks, hobie cats, snorkelling gear and hammocks. Closed Sept 1–Nov 15. ❻

Eating

Cocodimama ⓣ242/332-3150. Part of a small resort, with romantic seating on a wide terrace overlooking the sands, serving Italian and Bahamian cuisine and featuring dishes like gorgonzola cheese salad, grouper in a white wine, and crepes with Cointreau and ice cream. Breakfast, lunch and dinner service; US$50.
Mate and Jenny's ⓣ242/332-1504. Just off the highway in South Palmetto, with a dark and cosy interior, rafters strung with yachting pennants and a pool table. Offers delicious conch pizza, seafood, steak, sandwiches and potent tropical cocktails. Closed Tuesdays.
Pammy's Queen's Highway, Governor's Harbour. A popular local spot with fine, home-style Bahamian food like fried chicken, conch fritters, burgers and sandwiches, with traditional side dishes like coleslaw, fried plantains, peas 'n' rice and macaroni and cheese.
Rainbow Inn ⓣ242/335-0294. Atmospheric, hexagonal resort restaurant, among the nicest on the island, with excellent American-style seafood and sublime, home-made key lime pie. Dinner only; closed Sun-Mon.
Rosie's Café and Bakery Located in James Cistern, serving fine breakfasts and lunches at reasonable prices. Also sells delicious home-made bread and banana-and-pineapple loaf.

Harbour Island

Two miles off the northeastern side of Eleuthera, **HARBOUR ISLAND** is a tiny, green island – three miles long and half a mile wide – with a handful of charming sights. The island's main attractions are undoubtedly its spectacular **Pink Sand Beach**, running the length of the Atlantic side without any high-rises to block the view, and its only settlement, the serene village of **Dunmore Town**. On a low hill overlooking the harbour, the burg's neat, narrow streets are lined with clapboard cottages, flower boxes and white picket fences, evoking a quaint New England seaside town. However, the place was actually built by **Loyalist exiles** and their American colonial slaves at the end of the eighteenth century, evident in some of the well-preserved buildings of that era and a few ancient cannons. Although the island is easy enough to navigate **on foot**, most locals buzz around on **golf carts**, which can be rented on the dock when you arrive, arranged through your hotel, or rented from Ross's Garage (Ⓣ242/333-2064 or 2122, Ⓕ333-2585).

Accommodation

Most **hotels** charge an additional 20 percent fee for taxes and gratuities. If you're **renting** a place to stay, Island Real Estate (Ⓣ242/333-2278 or 2377, Ⓕ333-2354, Ⓔislandrealest@batelnet.bs) handles bookings for more than eighty properties, ranging from self-catering studio **apartments** to beachfront **villas** staffed with a cook and housekeeper.

Bahama House Inn Ⓣ242/333-2201, Ⓕ333-2850, Ⓦwww.bahamahouseinn.com). Charming bed and breakfast with seven guest rooms in a rambling late eighteenth-century mansion with a view of the harbour. No kids under 12; ❻ including breakfast.

Coral Sands Hotel Ⓣ242/333-2350, Ⓕ333-2320, Ⓦwww.coralsands.com. The largest, most modern hotel on the island, offering choice rooms with expansive ocean views and mahogany four-poster beds and cheaper rooms with quaint décor and patios or balconies. Also tennis courts, swimming pool, bar and restaurant. ❽

Dunmore Beach Club Ⓣ1-877/891-3100 or 242/333-2200, Ⓕ242/333-2429, Ⓦwww.dunmorebeach.com. On eight beachfront acres, featuring seven guest cottages with old-fashioned décor in chintz and wicker, as well as reading room, convivial bar, small dining room and tennis court. Cottages ❾

The Landing Ⓣ242/333-2707, Ⓕ333-2650, Ⓦwww.harborislandlanding.com. Elegant historic inn overlooking the harbour, with restored guest rooms evoking the colonial era with four-poster beds, dark wood floors, antique furnishings and original art. ❽

Royal Palm Hotel Ⓣ242/333-2738, Ⓕ333-3177, Ⓦwww.royalpalmhotel.com. Provides basic, carpeted motel units with ceiling fans and some with kitchens. ❹

Tingum Village Hotel Ⓣ242/333-2161. Several rustic, self-catering cottages and apartment units set in a quiet grove of coconut palms, with close beach access and the famous *Ma Ruby's* restaurant. ❺

Eating

Dinner **reservations** are recommended for all eateries, and required for many of the most formal and expensive **restaurants**. On Bay Street along the waterfront are several **kiosks** selling fresh conch salad and hamburgers and chips, and offering fine harbour views.

Angela's Starfish Restaurant Barracks Hill Ⓣ242/333-2253. Simple local eatery that receives rave reviews for its seafood dinners.

Arthur's Bakery Crown at Dunmore. Sunny café serving fresh cinnamon buns, home-made bread and soft jazz music for breakfast and lunch.

Browser Café Murray St Ⓣ242/333-3069. Charming little courtyard café with great coconut french toast and omelettes, Bahamian tuna and grits, boiled fish and souse for breakfast, and home-made soups and chowder, salads and sandwiches for lunch. Daily specials include grouper with fried plantains. Inexpensive.

Gusty's Barracks Hill. Serves seafood with live music several nights a week and is renowned as a hangout for Caribbean icon Jimmy Buffett.

Hammerheads Bar and Grill Harbour Island Marina Ⓣ242/333-3240. Attractive lunch and dinner spot overlooking the marina, serving finger food, salads, sandwiches, jerk chicken, strip steak, veggie quesadillas and cocktails.

Ma Ruby's at Tingum Village Ⓣ242/333-2161. Provides tasty meals of seafood, salads and sandwiches on a pleasant terrace surrounded by greenery. Famous as the inspiration for Jimmy Buffett's tune "Cheeseburger in Paradise".

Sports and outdoor activities

Ocean Fox Dive Shop (ⓣ242/333-2323, ⓕ333-2500) offers **snorkelling** and **diving** excursions, **boat rentals** and **fishing** charters, as does Valentine's Dive Center (ⓣ242/333-2080, ⓦwww.valentinesdive.com). Robert Davis presents ninety-minute **historical tours** of Dunmore Town (US$100; ⓣ242/333-2337) for up to three people, along with **horseback riding** on the beach (US$20 for a half-hour, $30 for a full hour).

1.5

The Exumas

Encompassing more than 365 islands, cays and rock outcroppings, **THE EXUMAS** stretch over one hundred miles along the eastern edge of the Great Bahama Bank. Bound on one side by the bank's shallow, clear waters, and on the other by the deep waves of Exuma Sound, the island chain is predominantly oriented toward fishing and farming, though the tourist trade continues to make slow but steady progress. Not surprisingly, the most compelling reasons to visit the Exumas are to **sail**, **snorkel**, **dive** or **kayak**, as the surrounding waters are lush with undersea gardens and iridescent coral reefs, and abundant with multi-coloured sea life.

A bit less stunning than the luminous turquoise sea around them, the Exumas are mainly low-lying chunks of honeycombed **limestone**, rimmed by bright, powdery sand and covered with dense vegetation. While the outlying reefs and bars glow with swirling blue and white tones, the **cays** themselves are a dun-coloured landscape marked by pristine expanses of soft white beaches, towering silhouettes of coconut palms and dunes covered with tangled vines and exotic blooms.

The largest islands in the Exuma chain are **Great Exuma** and **Little Exuma** at the southern end, which have been settled and farmed for two hundred years, giving them an authentic pastoral character. North of Great Exuma, there are a few small fishing settlements on sleepy **Little Farmer's Cay**, on **Great Guana Cay** at **Blackpoint**, and on inviting **Staniel Cay**, which famously hosts a New Year's Day regatta with three days of festivities. North of Staniel Cay, a lengthy array of mostly uninhabited cays extends thirty miles, with the highlight being the **Exuma Land and Sea Park**, a protected sanctuary of extraordinary beauty.

Arrival and information

George Town International Airport is located eight miles north of town, and receives two daily **flights** from Nassau, in the early morning and late afternoon, while American Eagle flies from Miami daily at noon. Long Island's *Stella Maris Resort* provides direct, one-way flights from George Town for its guests (US$100; ⓣ242/338-2050), and charges US$450 to charter the entire five-seat plane.

Unless you're arriving by private yacht, your port of entry will likely be George Town or Staniel Cay, with **ferries** and **mail boats** arriving at the government dock in the centre of George Town, within walking distance of most hotels. The *Sealink* ferry (ⓣ242/323-2166) leaves Nassau on Tuesdays at 2am, arriving at 12.45pm, and departs George Town at 6pm, returning 4am Wednesday morning. The well-maintained *Grand Master* mail boat (US$40 one-way; ⓣ242/393-1064) departs Nassau on Tuesdays at 2pm, arriving in George Town early Wednesday morning, and depending on tides and cargo, returns Wednesday night or Thursday morning, arriving in Nassau twelve hours later.

Located in the centre of George Town above Thompson's Car Rental, the **Bahamas Ministry of Tourism** provides useful information (Mon–Fri 9am–5pm; ⓣ242/336-2440, ⓕ336-2431) and a wide selection of **maps**, brochures and magazines.

Great Exuma and Little Exuma

Conjoined at the southern end of the Exumas by a narrow bridge, **GREAT EXUMA** and **LITTLE EXUMA** are home to all but a few hundred of the island chain's three thousand residents, most of whom live in the capital **George Town**, a bustling little hub offering plenty of hotels, restaurants and nightly entertainment, and popular with yacht sailors and venturesome tourists. Nonetheless, the town's most appealing sights lie offshore, including the azure and emerald depths of **Elizabeth Harbour** and its offshore cays such as **Stocking Island**, with its long windswept beach, and **Crab Cay**, site of the ruins of a Loyalist plantation. In late April, George Town's biggest social event of the year occurs, the **Out Island Regatta**, drawing crews from across the Bahamas to race their sloops.

North and south of town are several modest settlements like **Rolle Town** and **Williams Town**, which make a pleasant day trip by car or bicycle, and provide access to prime bonefishing and deep-sea **fishing grounds**.

Getting around

Although many different types of **transportation** are available in George Town, it's also worthwhile to simply **walk** and explore the islands on foot. **Hitchhiking** is also easy on the Exumas, and many residents rely on it for travelling and commuting to work. However, to explore the cays north of Great Exuma, a boat or water taxi is required.

Taxis

While there are no public buses on the Exumas and no shuttle services from the airport, **taxis** meet every flight and any hotel will call one for you, with the eight-mile trip to George Town costing around US$25 for two passengers. Two reliable and courteous operators are "J.J." (Ⓣ242/345-5005, cell 357-0757), who drives an antiquated white limo, and Leslie Dames (Ⓣ242/357-0015), who pilots a minivan decked out like the *Starship Enterprise*.

Rental cars, bicycles and scooters

Great and Little Exuma are easily explored by **rental car**, as the island roads are relatively flat and uncrowded. Three companies with reasonable vehicles are Airport Rent-a-Car (Ⓣ242/345 0090 or 358 8049), Thompson's Rentals (Ⓣ242/336-2442), in the centre of George Town, and Uptown Rent-A-Car (Ⓣ242/336-2822), across the street. All charge around US$70 a day, plus a $200 deposit.

Birdsong and picturesque rest stops make travelling by **motor scooter** or **bicycle** a fun way to get around, especially heading south from the capital. You can rent well-maintained 21-speed bikes at Starfish The Exuma Activity Centre (Ⓣ242/336 3033) for US$15 for a half-day and $100 per week. The Exuma Dive Centre (Ⓣ242/336-2390) and Prestige Cycle Rentals (Ⓣ242/345-4250), opposite Regatta Park, rent **motor scooters** for US$35 a day or $175 per week.

Boat travel

You can also **rent a motor boat**, **sailboat** or **kayak** to explore the coastline and the numerous cays offshore. Exuma Dive Centre (Ⓣ242/336-2390) rents 17ft boats for US$80 a day or $400 per week, while Minns Water Sports (Ⓣ242/336-2604, Ⓕ336-3483) offers similar package deals, with discounts for rentals of three days or more. Both companies restrict use of their boats to Elizabeth Harbour, so if you want to travel further, you must make special arrangements.

Accommodation

Rates for **hotel rooms** in the Exumas tend to be higher than for those in North America, with most of most of the larger hotels adding a mandatory **service charge** of ten to fifteen percent. Despite this, there are a number of good options for cheap, comfortable accommodation. If you're planning to visit during the Out Island Regatta in late April, you must book months in advance or be prepared to rough it on the beach.

George Town

Bahamas Houseboats ⓣ242/336-BOAT, ⓕ336-2629, ⓦwww.bahamashouseboat s.com. Economical, 35ft floating apartments with large windows, air conditioning, fully equipped galleys, CD players, outdoor barbecues and water slides on the top deck. Each comes with a motorized dinghy to get to shore. Daily rates from US$300 (three-day minimum) or US$1750 per week.

Club Peace and Plenty ⓣ242/336-2551 or 1-800/525-2210 in the US, ⓕ242/336-2093, ⓦwww.peaceandplenty.com. Comfortable rooms with wicker furniture, satellite TVs, and balconies overlooking the pool or Elizabeth Harbour. ❻, plus minimum US$21 added daily fee.

Marshall's Guesthouse ⓣ242/336-2328, ⓕ336-2081. *Marshall's* offers ten basic rooms in the centre of town. Closed for renovation in early 2002 with plans to reopen later in the year. ❸

Minns Cottages ⓣ242/336-2033, ⓕ336-2645. Quiet cottages in a shady grove with screened-in porches, nice ocean views, tiled floors, fully equipped kitchens and satellite TV. Within easy walking distance of the town centre on the northern outskirts. One-bedroom unit ❹

Regatta Point ⓣ242/336-2206, ⓕ336-2046, ⓦwww.regattapointbahamas.com. Pleasant accommodation on a private and secluded point of land, located at the end of Kidd Cove past the wharf. Credit cards not accepted. ❺

George Town outskirts

Coconut Cove Inn ⓣ242/336-2659, ⓕ336-2658. A mile and a half north of town, a small beachfront hotel with twelve modern rooms featuring private balconies, most with ocean views. Also restaurant, palm-shaded terrace, beach bar and shuttle buses to and from George Town. ❻

Coral Gardens Bed and Breakfast ⓣ242/336-2880, ⓦwww.bahamasbliss.com. Inexpensive B & B five minutes away from the beach, perched on a breezy hilltop at Hooper's Bay with views of both coasts of Great Exuma. Offers three rooms with refrigerators and shared baths (US$65) and beachfront apartment sleeping up to six (US$95). Includes breakfast and rental car access for US$40 per day. ❸

Hotel Higgins Landing ⓣ242/336-2460, ⓦwww.higginslanding.com. Luxurious hotel on Stocking Island with five timber guest cottages furnished with antiques, each with a private ocean view. Rate includes breakfast, supper and watersports. ❼

Peace and Plenty Beach Inn ⓣ242/336-2250 or 1-800/525-2210 in the US, ⓕ242/336-2253, ⓦwww.peaceandplenty.com. Quiet retreat a mile and half north of town, featuring sixteen well-appointed rooms with private balconies and ocean views, as well as beach access, pool, restaurant, outdoor bar and shuttle to and from George Town. ❻, plus minimum US$21 added daily fee.

South of George Town

Club Peace and Plenty Bonefish Lodge Hartswell ⓣ242/345-5555 or 1-800/525-2210 in the US, ⓕ242/345-5556, ⓦwww.ppbonefishlodge.com. Handsome timber and stone lodge with wraparound verandah overlooking Little Exuma. The most luxurious hotel on Great Exuma, featuring eight rooms with tile floors, ceiling fans, deep balconies and ocean views, as well as restaurant and bar. Fishing packages include lodging, meals, bonefishing guides and use of kayaks, bicycles and snorkelling equipment. Three nights and two days US$998 per person, seven nights and six days $2562. ❾

La Shanté Beach Club Forbes Hill, Little Exuma ⓣ242/345 4136. Spectacular beachside setting in a secluded cove, with three double rooms and one bedroom apartment, offering basic accommodation without ocean views. Restaurant serves lunch and dinner on a terrace overlooking the beach. Doubles ❹, one-bedroom apartment ❻

Master Harbour Villas ⓣ242/345 5076 or 357 0636, ⓕ345-5140, ⓦwww.exumabahamas .com/masterharbour. Three miles south of George Town and set in a grove of coconut palms, three white clapboard cottages on a rocky shore overlooking Crab and Redshank cays, with high ceilings, overhead fans and motor-boat rental for guests. One-bedroom villa ❻; two-bedroom ❽; and four-bedroom ❾

Eating

Although many of the appealing **restaurants** in the Exumas can be found in George Town, there are other good choices scattered around the islands as well. South of George Town, *La Shanté Beach Club*, on the beach in Forbes Hill, makes a good spot for lunch, while in Williams Town, *Mom's Bakery*, *The Arawak Club* and *Santana's Grill* all serve tasty snacks and simple seafood meals. North of George Town, *Big D's Conch Spot*, on the beach at Steventon, is a local favourite, and *Kermit's Hilltop Tavern* in Rolle Town and *The Fisherman's Inn* in Barreterre are also worth a try.

The Bistro at February Point ⓣ242/336-2661. A mile south of George Town, on a terrace at the edge of a white sandy beach, an alfresco restaurant with delicious seafood and meat dishes for lunch and dinner, as well as Wednesday night pizza. Free transfers to and from George Town for supper. Moderate to expensive.

The Chat and Chill Open-air beach bar at Volleyball Beach on Stocking Island. A cheap and breezy place for burgers, seafood, cool drinks and a swim. Daily 11am–7pm.

Cheater's Restaurant and Bar ⓣ242/336-2535. No-frills roadhouse two miles south of Georgetown on the Queen's Highway, serving tasty home-style Bahamian food. Lunch and supper Mon–Fri 10am–11pm, and Sat 8am–11pm for breakfast as well. Tuesday night fish fry with rake 'n' scrape music. US$8–24.

Club Peace and Plenty Restaurant ⓣ242/336-2551. Located off the hotel lobby (see p.97) and set in a glassed-in alcove with a nice view of Stocking Island, featuring fish, lobster and steak. Open for breakfast, lunch and dinner. Expensive.

Coconut Cove Inn ⓣ242/336-2659. One of the best restaurants in the Exumas, with an extensive menu, cosy atmosphere and attentive service. Offers delicious pizza, pasta, and steak and seafood platters. The chef will prepare your day's catch, and the beachside *Sand Bar* serves sandwiches and snacks Fri 3–9pm. Breakfast daily 7.30–9.30am, dinner Tues–Sun 6–9pm; reservations recommended before 4pm. Moderate to expensive.

Eddie's Edgewater Club ⓣ242/336-2050. Popular, inexpensive local spot overlooking Victoria Pond and offering native dishes, pool tables and live music Mondays and Saturdays.

Hamburger Beach Snack Bar at *Peace and Plenty* beach club on Stocking Island. An array of inexpensive hotdogs, burgers, soft drinks, beer and ice cream. Daily 11am–3pm.

Sam's Place ⓣ242/336-2579. Upstairs in a grey timber building overlooking the marina, the best place in George Town for breakfast, specializing in Bahamian boiled breakfasts and American-style bacon and eggs and pancakes. Also good lunchtime seafood, sandwiches and burgers, great oceanside views, and quick and friendly service.

Two Turtles Inn ⓣ242/336-2545. Outdoor patio bar overlooking the wharf, a great place for lunchtime sandwiches, salads, burgers and conch dishes. Friday night barbecues with live entertainment.

Outdoor activities

Several outfitters based in George Town offer an array of **outdoor activities**. Starfish The Exuma Activity Center (ⓣ242/336-3033 or 1-877/398-6222 in Canada and the US, ⓦwww.kayakbahamas.com) offers guided **history** and **eco-tours** of Elizabeth Harbour, Crab Cay and Stocking Island by boat, along with **cycling trips** on quiet island byways and paddling excursions through the cays off George Town. Day trips include beachside picnics and snorkelling, and full-moon, sunset and sunrise **paddling excursions** are also available, as well as two- to six-day kayaking and camping trips.

The Exumas are one of the best places in the world to **snorkel** and **dive**. Exuma Scuba Adventures (PO Box 29055, George Town, Exuma ⓣ242/336-2893 or 357-2259, ⓦwww.exumascuba.com) operates out of *Club Peace and Plenty*, while the Exuma Dive Center (PO Box EX-29102, George Town, Exuma ⓣ242/336-2390, ⓔexumadive@BahamasVG.com) offers snorkelling and diving excursions and rents watersports equipment.

The islands also offer superb **deep-sea fishing** and **bonefishing** waters, and a number of good fishing guides are based in George Town and the surrounding area:

Cely's Fly Fishing (☎242/345-2341), Cooper's Charter Service (☎242/336-2711), Fish Rowe Charters (☎242/345-0074) and Abby MacKenzie (☎242/345-2312). Fishing expeditions and day trips to the cays of Barreterre, including **Leaf Cay** – home to a colony of giant iguanas – can be arranged through Captain Martin (☎242/358-4057) or Rev. A.A. MacKenzie (☎242/355-5024).

Staniel Cay and around

Tidy, green and nicely painted **STANIEL CAY** has a noticeably prosperous air, owing largely to its popularity with yacht cruisers and expatriate residents with money and clout. The gateway to the **Exuma Land and Sea Park**, the cay has an airstrip, two marinas, library, volunteer-run clinic, and several restaurants and shops, though its main highlight is the renowned **New Year's Day Regatta**, which includes warm-up events like a public cookout, children's boat race, fireworks and Junkanoo festivities. There's also live music and a Long Drive Contest in which golf balls are hit into the sea. To qualify for the event, you must participate in Happy Hour beforehand.

Just offshore from Staniel Cay is the spectacular **Thunderball Grotto**, where columns of stalactites and stalagmites surround a chamber filled with colourful fish, as shafts of sunlight pour in through holes in the roof. Named for the James Bond film that was somehow filmed here in the early 1960s, the undersea cavern can only be accessed by diving or snorkelling through a strong underwater current. Unless you are an expert, go with a guide – or just rent the movie.

The Exuma Land and Sea Park

Beginning five miles north of Staniel Cay, the **Exuma Land and Sea Park** (c/o Bahamas National Trust, see p.85) encompasses fifteen sizeable cays and many smaller outcroppings over 176 square miles – 22 miles long and 8 miles wide. Bound on the east by the deep waters of Exuma Sound, and on the west by the shallow reefs and sandbars of Great Bahama Bank, the park was established in 1958 as a marine conservation area by the **Bahamian National Trust** – a non-profit agency overseeing the preservation of the country's environment. Arresting the destruction of the islands' ecology and bio-diversity, the BNT protects and replenishes the native flora and fauna, while relying completely on private donations to operate.

The park presents many striking contrasts of form and colour, from low rocky islands rimmed by brilliant white sands, to lush coral reefs and undersea gardens abundant with tropical sea life, to windswept beaches enclosed by rolling dunes and

Sea kayaking in the Exumas

One of the best and most popular ways of exploring the Exumas is by **sea kayak**, with several outfitters offering guided expeditions through the cays. Starfish The Exuma Activity Center (see overleaf) rents kayaking equipment and offers excellent **day trips**, in which a leisurely journey precedes a picnic lunch on one of the several small islands enclosing Elizabeth Harbour.

Further north in the Exumas, Ibis Tours (PO Box 208, Pelham, NY 10803 ☎914/738-5334 or 1-800/525-9411 in the US, ©info@ibistours.com) runs eight-day **guided expeditions** through the Exuma Land and Sea Park from March to May (US$1600, not including airfare to Nassau). Starting at Staniel Cay and travelling toward Norman's Cay at the park's southern end, the trip allows plenty of time for snorkelling, swimming and sunbathing on the many beaches along the way. The kayaks are equipped with sails to lessen the exertion required.

The park volunteer programme

If you're interested in marine conservation and would like to spend at least two weeks working in this beautiful and remote region of the Bahamas, the Land and Sea Park runs a strenuous **volunteer programme**. Facilities at Warderick Wells are limited, so be prepared to sleep on your boat or bring a tent (mooring and camping fees are waived). While there is access to drinking water, showers and a kitchen, you must bring your own food and provisions. Contact the warden at least a month in advance, outlining your skills and availability.

tall stands of coconut palms. There are no commercial developments, resorts or restaurants within the park boundaries, and the major events are the spectacular dawn and dusk, along with resplendent evenings under an opulent canopy of stars.

The **park headquarters** (Mon–Sat 9am–noon & 3–5pm, Sun 9am–1pm; Ⓣ242/359-1821) are housed in a brown wooden building in the middle of the park, on the north end of Warderick Wells Cay, where you can find an interesting display on the natural history of the Exumas, as well as assorted **maps**, information sheets and reference books.

Twenty miles north of Staniel Cay, serenely beautiful **Warderick Wells Cay** is well worth the considerable effort it takes to reach it, offering stunning vistas of undulating ridges and valleys, vivid green foliage, inland lakes, sheer coastal cliffs, quiet sandy coves, and a distant silhouette of cays extending to the horizon. Seven miles of well-marked hiking trails criss-cross the island, leading through groves of thatch palm and silver buttonwood, past limestone sink holes, and along a broad tidal creek-bed to lookout points and Loyalist plantation ruins. A dozen white beaches dot the secluded palm-fringed coves on the leeward side of the island.

The Northern Exumas

Although the northern boundary of the Land and Sea Park lies at the Wax Cay Cut, the Exuma chain continues to the northwest for another ten miles. The **Northern Exumas**, however, are most easily reached from Nassau, forty miles to the west. Three companies offer day trips to the cays, departing from the dock on Paradise Island. Island World Adventures (Ⓣ242/394-8960, Ⓕ363-1657) makes a daily excursion to Saddleback Cay in a 45ft speedboat, Out Island Voyages (Ⓣ242/394-0951 or 1-800/241-4591, Ⓕ242/394-0948, Ⓔbalymena@bahamas.net.ba) offers sailboat journeys out to the cays, and Powerboat Adventures (Ⓣ242/327-5385, Ⓕ393-7029, Ⓔinfo@poweradventures.com) leads a full-day outing to the Sail Rocks and Allan's cays, including snorkelling, a barbecue lunch on the beach, and a visit with the islands' resident giant iguanas.

Arrival and getting around

Unless you're piloting your own watercraft, getting to the park takes money and effort. The park is best accessed from Staniel Cay, from which you can **rent a boat** from operators like the Staniel Cay Yacht Club (Ⓣ242/355-2024, Ⓕ355-2044, Ⓦwww.stanielcay.com), which rents 13ft and 17ft Whalers for US$85 and $235 per day, including fuel. Local fishermen also offer trips to the park, such as Captain Bill Hirsch (PMB 935, 12555 Biscayne Blvd, North Miami, Florida 33181; Ⓣ305/944-3033, Ⓕ944-8033, Ⓦwww.myknottymind.com), who runs 45-minute excursions to Warderick Wells for US$100 and offers **guided park tours** aboard his yacht *M/Y Knotty Mind* for US$450 per day. From Nassau, Captain Paul Harding of Diving Safaris Ltd (Ⓣ242/393-2522 or 393-1179) offers direct **floatplane** flights to Warderick Wells or any other location in the park.

Accommodation

Although Staniel Cay offers sufficient choices for **accommodation**, there are no such options within the boundaries of the Land and Sea Park, though there are dozens of soft beaches on which you can pitch a tent. Fees for **camping** are US$5 per night; drop your payment at park headquarters or mail it in after you leave.

Happy People Marina ⓣ242/355-2008, ⓕ355-2025. Adequate motel-style rooms (❹) on the Staniel Cay waterfront and a nice two-bedroom apartment (❸).

Sampson Cay Club and Marina ⓣ242/355-2034. Just north of Staniel Cay on small cays bordering the Land and Sea Park, a newly renovated club with five cottages, grocery store, restaurant and bar. Rent a 13ft Boston Whaler to explore the park, for US$80 per day. Call for cottage rental rates.

Staniel Cay Yacht Club and Marina ⓣ242/355-2024, ⓕ355-2044, ⓦwww.stanielcay.com. Featuring five cute wooden cottages with coffeemakers, small refrigerators and verandahs overlooking the water, with cottages sleeping four to seven people also available. ❺

Eating

Club Thunderball. North of Staniel Cay and overlooking Thunderball Grotto, an eatery serving native dishes for lunch and dinner and offering a pool table and weekend dancing. Closed Mon.

Happy People Restaurant and Bar ⓣ242/355-2008. Next to the hotel and marina, a popular local hangout famous for impromptu performances by Jimmy Buffett. Open for breakfast, lunch and dinner, and serving Bahamian dishes, sandwiches and burgers. Call in advance.

Staniel Cay Yacht Club Restaurant and Bar ⓣ242/355-2024. Near the dock, a colourful and relaxed eatery with a nautical theme, offering American and Bahamian food and home-made desserts. Breakfast Mon–Sat 8–10am, Sun 8–9.30am; lunch Mon–Sat 11.30am–3pm; dinner 7.30pm only, reserve by 5pm. Moderate.

1.6

Cat Island and San Salvador

A world away from the up-tempo lifestyle and commercialism of a place like Nassau, **CAT ISLAND** and **SAN SALVADOR** offer an isolated example of Bahamian life before the advent of modern tourism. Still retaining the traditional farming and agriculture of the old Bahamas, the islands have nonetheless experienced economic difficulties in recent years, with their young workers leaving for service jobs in New Providence and Grand Bahama and the population shrinking to new lows in the last few decades. Nevertheless, they both have considerable attractions for visitors, from splendid stretches of **pink sand beaches**, to exquisite snorkelling and diving, to intimate and comfortable lodges far from the bustle of more populated islands.

Arrival and information

During holiday seasons or Junkanoo, **flights** to the islands are hard to get, so try to reserve early. Bahamasair departs for **Arthur's Town airport** from Nassau on Tuesdays, Thursdays and Sundays (one-way fare US$70; ⓣ242/377-5505 or 1-800/222-4262 in the US), and leaves for **New Bight airport** on Mondays and Fridays. Air Sunshine (ⓣ1-800/327-8900) and Island Express (ⓣ954/359-0380), both in Fort Lauderdale, also serve New Bight. In the south, *Hawk's Nest Resort* (ⓣ242/342-7050 or 1-800/688-4752) has a private airstrip, though pilots must clear customs first in New Bight, along with a marina for arriving yachts. *Fernandez Bay Marina* is a good alternate choice.

There are no formal **information** services on either Cat Island or San Salvador, but excellent material is available through Nassau's Ministry of Tourism (ⓣ1-800/224-2627, ⓦwww.bahamas.com), or the Out Island Tourist Board (ⓣ305/931-6612 or 1-800/688-4752, ⓦwww.bahama-out-islands.com).

Cat Island

Lying 130 miles southeast of Nassau, the small and boot-shaped **CAT ISLAND** is a relaxed and unspoiled site with sparkling beaches, pristine lakes, and even a few sizeable hills and mountains. The **southern boot** of the island presents great opportunities for diving, with steep cliffs and offshore reefs, while the entire **east coast**, accessible only by dirt roads, offers a continuous strand of idyllic seaside, with hidden coves and rugged shores. The **west coast**, with its mud creeks and estuaries, is great for bonefishing. The major settlements are charming **Arthur's Town** in the north, pre-Hollywood home of Sidney Poitier, and **New Bight** in the south, a sprawling burg two miles long. Cat Island is served by a single good paved road, the **Queen's Highway**, which runs the length of the 48-mile island.

Although the most popular beach is **Fernandez Bay**, just north of New Bight, the Atlantic beaches are wilder, harder to reach, and home to big waves and high winds – a tempting challenge for windsurfers and swimmers. Near New Bight, a dirt road leads toward marvellous **Sandy Point Beach**, while further south, **Greenwood Beach** stretches for ten miles, its pink sands unmatched for their beauty. Towering over the island terrain, **Mount Alvernia** stands 206ft above sea level, the highest point in the Bahamas, and provides accommodating views of the headlands of the east coast.

Attractions like **hiking** and **birdwatching** are both excellent in the southern boot, where ponds and lakes abound, and the island's major celebrations include the annual **Cat Island Regatta** in August, attracting hundreds of yachters, and the **Rake 'n' Scrape** festival in late June, appealing to music lovers throughout the Bahamas.

Accommodation

Arthur's Town, Bennett's Harbour and New Bight all have a good number of options for **accommodation**, from small and cheap motels to older resorts and lodges popular with divers.

Fernandez Bay Village New Bight ☎242/342-3043 or 1-800/940-1905. Bahamian-style wood-and-stone lodge with access to nearby Skinny Dip Beach and justly popular gardens and dining room. ❽

Greenwood Beach Resort Port Howe ☎242/342-3053 or 1-800/688-4752. The premier dive resort in the area, offering twenty isolated rooms on ten miles of pink sand, along with swimming pool, dive shop, restaurant and bar. ❺

Hawk's Nest Resort and Marina Devil's Point ☎242/342-7050 or 1-800/688-4752. Set on four hundred acres of beachfront, featuring ten ocean-view rooms and two houses with two bedrooms. ❻ per person.

Eating and nightlife

Although much **dining** and **nightlife** centres on the major resorts, which offer formal meals in elegant surroundings as well as beachside buffets, most of the major settlements also have a good selection of road-side **eateries**, small **cafés** and **restaurants**, and decent **bars** and **pubs**. In New Bight, the *Bridge Inn Bar and Restaurant* and the *Blue Bird Restaurant and Bar* host locals and visitors for fried chicken, seafood, rake 'n' scrape music and dancing, while in the far north at Smith's Bay, *Hazel's Seaside Bar* is a relaxed spot for a quiet drink at sunset.

San Salvador

Two hundred miles east of Nassau, small **SAN SALVADOR** is the easternmost island in the Bahamas. Only twelve miles long and five wide, this low-lying island features saline lakes and brine ponds surrounded by palmetto brush, a beautiful shore of uninterrupted white sands, and a **western reef** that offers some of the best diving and snorkelling in the country. Despite this, its renown for aquatic sports is a relatively recent phenomenon. Although it was the original place where Columbus first encountered the New World, San Salvador remained a backwater until diver Bill McGehee promoted the beauty and diversity of its western reef in the 1970s, and *Club Med* later added its own endorsement, building a resort north of **Cockburn Town** (pronounced "Coburn") in 1992. Though it's the main settlement on the island there's little to keep you in Cockburn, other than a few accommodation options (see p.105).

Typical **island tours** take in the lovely **East Beach**, **Dixon Hill Lighthouse**, and the **Bahamian Field Station** (for prime birdwatching and hiking), each taking about four hours and available through the two major resorts (see p.105). Likewise, either resort can arrange **sport fishing** and **underwater photography** – which is quickly becoming something of a cottage industry in San Salvador.

△ Patterns in the sand

Practicalities

Bahamasair offers twice-weekly **flights** from Miami and Nassau to Cockburn Town, while Florida-based Air Sunshine flies to Cockburn Town out of Fort Lauderdale. Both *Club Med* and *Riding Rock Inn* provide charter **air service** for their guests.

There are only a few choices for **accommodation** on San Salvador, most clustered around Cockburn Town. *Club Med Columbus Isle* (ⓣ242/331-2000 or 1-800/453-2582) is a local branch of the French-based chain, as well as one of the world's better dive resorts, while less prominent *Riding Rock Inn*, southwest of the airport (ⓣ242/331-2641 or 1-800/272-1492; 7 per person), also features diving packages, as well as cottages and furnished rooms with patios (single 4). Cockburn Town has a number of grocery stores, **restaurants** and **bars**, though most visitors predictably dine at the big resorts.

1.7

The Abacos and Loyalist Cays

The northernmost of the Bahamian islands, **THE ABACOS** are sometimes called the "isles of the old-time Loyalists" because of their association with Tory expatriates fleeing the American Revolution. Located two hundred miles east of Miami and 75 miles north of Nassau, the Abacos stretch some two hundred miles in length, though they are rarely more than four miles wide at any point. Even so, they remain the most accessible of all the Bahamian Out Islands, making them the chain's most developed, visited, and affluent.

The **mainland** is actually composed of **Great Abaco** and **Little Abaco**, two distinct islands separated by a tiny gap. In the far north, a group of smaller cays begins with **Walker's Cay** and runs southeast to **Cherokee Sound** – a lengthy chain well worth visiting for its superb diving, snorkelling and fishing. Most visitors, however, prefer to concentrate on the areas near Great Abaco's main town, **Marsh Harbour**, and the old-English charm of nearby **Elbow Cay**, **Green Turtle Cay** and **Treasure Cay**, which provide not only glimpses of early Loyalist settlements, but also enchanting coastlines, radiant bays and inlets, and terrific aquatic sports.

The pine-covered Abacos have a temperate-to-subtropical **climate**, with cool winters and mild, windy summers, and an average yearly rainfall of 50-60 inches. Sailors may find ideal yachting in the shallows of the western coast, a fascinating landscape of mangrove islands, rocks, and cays known collectively as **The Marls**. On the east side, **fringing reefs** and several **deep canyons** offer excellent diving, with most choice locations just north of Marsh Harbour.

Some history

Abaco's first wave of settlement came in 1783 when **Loyalist emigrants** from New York, the Carolinas and Florida came to stay after the American Revolutionary War. Some original settlers were black Americans who arrived near present-day Treasure Cay, founding the village of Carleton. The Loyalists, about two thousand in all, eventually colonized all the areas around Marsh Harbour, bringing with them their New England **architecture** of clapboard houses, steeply pitched roofs, and tiny gardens surrounded by picket fences. This **Abaco style** survives today in the island's bright plantings of oleander, hibiscus and bougainvillea, its complex and narrow streets, and its grand old tradition of boat-building.

Arrival, information and getting around

The main entry point for most visitors to Great Abaco and the Loyalist Cays is **Marsh Harbour International Airport**, though other **airports** are located at Treasure Cay and Walker's Cay, the latter serving only the exclusive resort based there. Bahamasair (Ⓣ242/377-5505) offers flights to Marsh Harbour from Nassau (three daily), West Palm Beach (Fri–Mon & Wed) and Miami (Thurs–Sat), with most flights continuing on to Treasure Cay airport as well. American Eagle (Ⓣ954/367-2231 or 1-800/433-7300) also has daily flights to Marsh Harbour from

Miami. As an alternative, two Nassau **mail boats** make the journey to Great Abaco (one-way; US$30); contact the **dockmaster** at Potter's Cay dock in Nassau (☎242/393-1064) for schedules and information.

The **tourist information office** (☎242/367-3067) for the Abacos can be found in Marsh Harbour on Queen Elizabeth Drive, in a small shopping centre in the heart of town. The Out Islands Tourist Board (☎305/931-6612 or 1-800/688-4752) offers complete information and maps about the island, and the glossy periodical *Abaco Life* (PO Box 37487, Raleigh, NC 27627, ☎919/859-6782) publishes regular features on island history, events and the like, and sells an excellent **map** for US$3. For yachting information, send for a copy of the *Cruising Guide to the Abacos* (Steve Dodge, White Sound Press, 1615 W. Harrison, Decatur, IL 62526).

The **car rental agencies** located around Marsh Harbour have a very limited selection, and reservations should be made well in advance. A&P Auto Rentals (Don McKay Boulevard, ☎242/367-2655) and H&L Rentals (Shell Station downtown, ☎242/367-2840) both offer subcompacts and midsize vehicles. Nearly every hotel and resort rents **bicycles**, **motorcycles** and **motorscooters**, with many visitors choosing motorscooters for day trips to the southern Abacos.

Marsh Harbour and around

Home to four thousand residents, **MARSH HARBOUR** is the third largest town in the Bahamas and the main focus of tourism in the Abacos. Featuring most of the hotels, inns, marinas and diving operations on the island, the town is an essential hub for ferries connecting with the rest of the Loyalist Cays. The settlement lies on a peninsula just off the smoothly paved **Great Abaco Highway**, which runs south through Great Abaco to **Cherokee Point** and **Little Harbour**. North of town, the road becomes **S.C. Bootle Highway**, another smooth stretch that runs north and west toward Treasure Cay and Little Abaco.

Marsh Harbour has most of the **services** available in any small town in Florida, including an excellent post office, bookstore, grocery stores, specialty shops, travel agencies and laundries. Most visitors come to boat, swim or snorkel, and stay at one of the lodges located near **Bay Street** on the waterfront, though some adventurers reserve a day or two to **kayak** in the **Marls** on trips conducted by naturalist guides.

To get around you can use the numerous **taxis** in town, which are metered at US$1.50 per mile (though you should always establish a fare with the driver before setting off) or **bicycles**, **motorcycles** or **motorscooters**, which can be rented at most resorts, or at R&L Rent-a-Ride (☎242/367-4289), at the entrance to *Abaco Towns-by-the-Sea*.

The Town

Founded in 1784 by Loyalists, Marsh Harbour spent many years as a **logging**, **sponging** and "**wrecking**" town, with boat-building as a secondary industry. These days, **tourism** has replaced logging as the town's major source of income, and its marinas are now lined with expensive yachts and surrounded by the swank vacation homes and retirement castles of a new breed of North American expatriates.

For the most part, Marsh Harbour is a quiet place, its **nightlife** restricted to a few local bars and lounges and most of its activity taking place at the **resorts** near the **harbour**, where **Albury Ferry Dock** transfers tourists to boats journeying out to the Loyalist Cays. The town's only conventional "sight" is an exotic yellow edifice known as **Seaview Castle**, the creation of one Evans Cottman, an author and doctor who settled here in 1944, building this crenellated fantasy as his home. Nearby **Bay Street**, along the harbour, offers a pleasant walk, and leads to an area known as **Dundas Town**, inhabited mostly by Bahamians of African descent, as well as a number of Haitian immigrants. **Don McKay Boulevard** is

Abaco National Park

Located only 35 miles south of Marsh Harbour on the Great Abaco Highway, **Abaco National Park** comprises 2500 acres reserved to protect the **Bahama parrot**, which nests in holes in the island's limestone surface. Vivid with bright green, red, white and blue colours, the parrots are known as "rainbows in the sky" to local residents. As an endangered species, they are found only on Abaco and Great Inagua, and the campaign to preserve their habitat as a national park was a notable success for ecological conservation.

Heavily forested, Abaco is the best island for **birdwatching** in the Bahamas, and in the park you can expect to see warblers, West Indian woodpeckers, yellowthroats, flycatchers, swallows and Cuban Emeralds. The park's 32 square miles feature hardwood forests, nature trails and wild Atlantic coast scenery, and notable fauna include butterflies, egrets, herons, spoonbills and rare hummingbirds, which inhabit a landscape filled with bromeliads and orchids. **Day trips** can be arranged at travel agencies and resorts in Marsh Harbour.

the town's major thoroughfare, home to a number of shopping centres, travel agencies, fast-food joints, ice cream shops and even a few authentic Bahamian restaurants as well.

Accommodation

Abaco Beach Resort and Boat Harbour PO Box AB-20669 ☎242/367-2158 or 1-800/468-4799. Elegant and relaxed resort with eighty oceanfront rooms, six two-bedroom cottages and a large marina, along with pool, swim-up bar, tennis courts and diving rentals. Double 7

Abaco Towns-by-the-Sea PO Box AB-20468 ☎242/367-2227 or 1-800/357-7757. Seaside property with 64 two-bedroom villas with garden and ocean views, and on-site tennis courts and large swimming pool. 6

Conch Inn Marina and Hotel PO Box AB-20469 ☎242/367-4000 or 1-800/688-4752. Located on Bay Street, a motel-style inn with nine pleasant rooms with private baths and small verandahs. Hotel marina has 75 slips and an excellent dive shop. 4

Different of Abaco Casuarina Point, PO Box AG-20092 ☎242/366-2150. The premier eco-destination in the Abacos, a unique lodge 25 minutes south of Marsh Harbour, with 28 well-furnished cabana rooms, lake, hot tubs, beach, pool and access to boating and bonefishing. Packages are offered, starting at US$800/double for four days.

Pelican Beach Villas Pelican Shores Rd, PO Box AB-20304 ☎1-800/642-7268. On an isolated peninsula, six two-bedroom villas with kitchens, TVs and rattan furniture, with an 87ft marina and access to a snorkelling reef. Good base for day trips to neighbouring cays. 6

Eating and drinking

Many of Marsh Harbour's **resorts** feature excellent **restaurants**, including *Angler's* in *Abaco Beach Resort*, specializing in seafood like lime grouper, lobster pate and curried conch, and the *Jib Room* at *Pelican Shores*, serving prime lobster, ribs, steaks and seafood. Other **eateries** present a range of options, from fine dining by the sea to greasy spoons in the middle of nowhere.

Bayview Restaurant on the Water Bay St, Dundas Town. Just west of the harbour, featuring prime rib, Sunday champagne brunch and lots of Bahamian-style seafood.

Bistro Mezzomare Queen's Highway ☎242/367-4444. Upscale and sophisticated spot for great Italian food in a marina setting.

The Conch Inn Bay St ☎242/367-4000 or 1-800/688-4752. Famous for its fabulous breakfasts of jumbo French toast, and great dinners of calypso grouper and stuffed jalapeños, and fine gumbos and stews.

Mangos ☎242/367-2366. Housed in a large cedar home with cathedral-sized ceilings, serving scrumptious pork tenderloin with mango sauce, grilled chicken with garlic and ginger, veal piccata and cracked conch and ribs, among other specialties.

Mavis Country Kitchen Don McKay Blvd. The top authentic Jamaican and Bahamian diner in town, offering dishes like souse pot and jerk chicken.
Sapodilly's Harbour View Marina. Despite having picnic tables for dining, the restaurant's menu features a superb blue-cheese mushroom burger for lunch, and typically tasty catch-of-the-day for dinner.

Sharkee's Island Pizza across from *Abaco Towns-by-the-Sea.* The town's top choice for rich, filling pizza.
Wally's Bay St ⓣ242/367-2074. Bahamian colonial house filled with Haitian art, featuring burgers and conch salad for lunch, dinners with grilled lamb chops and cracked conch, and great drinks like the Goombay Smash. Closed Sun & Mon.

Treasure Cay

Although **TREASURE CAY** is now an exclusive resort, it began life as humble **Carleton Point**, a settlement of six hundred Loyalists who in 1783 fled the newly formed United States, hoping to develop a major commercial and agricultural centre at the northern end of the former Sand Banks Cay. Although this didn't necessarily occur, Treasure Cay has grown rapidly in recent years, and now supports an array of time-share villas, condos and upscale resorts. Not really a cay at all, but a slender **peninsula**, Treasure Cay has its own schools, churches, stores, post office, banks, health clinic and marina. Its beachfront, stretching four miles along the **Sea of Abaco**, is not as spectacular as other Bahamian beaches, but it is good for swimming and sunbathing.

North Americans make up the bulk of the year-round residents of Treasure Cay, who maintain more than 150 expensive vacation and retirement homes. The **marina** is a favourite with yacht sailors, who make use of its huge dock, featuring a marina store, dive shop, boat rentals, pool, bar and restaurant. Between Treasure Cay's beach and the outer island of **Whale Cay** are several eye-catching turquoise banks that are especially lovely at dawn and dusk.

Practicalities

Most guests arrive at **Treasure Cay International Airport** from Nassau or West Palm Beach. Because of its small size, no one rents vehicles on Treasure Cay, though small **golf carts** are available from the resorts or at the marina for about US$35 per day. In any case, considering the amount of diving, fishing and sightseeing **tours** available, there's little need for motorized transport.

The centre of activity is the *Treasure Cay Beach Hotel Resort and Marina* (PO Box AB-22183 ⓣ242/365-8250 or 1-800/327-1584; ❻), offering beautifully furnished **hotel** rooms, suites, condos and small, self-catering villas and providing reduced guest rates for golf, tennis and dive packages. Located on the sands, *Banyan Beach Club* (PO Box AB-22158 ⓣ242/365-8111; villa US$1900/week) has condos with two or three bedrooms and ocean views. Several private agencies also offer **cottages** and **condos for rent**.

Options for **eating** and **nightlife** are quite limited on Treasure Cay outside of the major resorts, with a few exceptions: *Cafe La Florence* (ⓣ242/367-2570), a bakery, serves good quiche and cinnamon rolls; *The Spinnaker*, on the dock at *Treasure Cay Resort*, specializes in johnny cake for breakfast, burgers for lunch, and the catch-of-the-day for dinner; and north of the cay, *Touch of Class* is easily the best Bahamian restaurant.

Sports and outdoor activities

Home to Abaco's only **golf course**, Treasure Cay features many resorts and villas with **tennis courts**, some lighted for night play, and **package tours** from local operators. Divers Down at Treasure Cay (ⓣ242/365-8465 or 1-800/327-1584) is a full-service vendor offering group dives, night dives, certification and snorkelling trips; C&C Boat Rentals, at the marina, rents **watersports** equipment, including sunfish boats, windsurfers and hobie cats; and Sidney Hart Sightseeing (☎242/365-8582) leads small groups on shelling, picnicking and snorkelling trips. A number of **fishing guides** are also based at the marina, some providing day packages, spearfishing, bottom fishing and boat tours. Not surprisingly, many world-famous **fishing tournaments** take place off Treasure Cay in May and June every year.

Little Abaco

Shaded by pines and casuarinas, the S.C. Bootle Highway through **Little Abaco** passes a number of quiet beaches. The scenery here is much the same as on Great Abaco, although there are more rocky hills and the forest is denser. By the time you pass Cedar Harbour, the shores are overtaken by rock-shallows, and finally heavy mangroves.

Cedar Harbour is the largest settlement on Little Abaco – though that isn't saying much. *Nettie's Snack Bar* offers a pleasant place for conch and fried fish. Eight miles west in **Fox Town**, local Gladys Saunders operates the *Tangelo Hotel* (☎242/365-2222), which has twelve plainly furnished and basic rooms with A/C, TV and both double or twin beds for US$65. The small restaurant serves basic fish dishes for US$8. The end of the line is tiny **Crown Haven**, a quiet tumbledown village with a wooden wharf and a struggling lobster business.

Taxi rides to Little Abaco from Marsh Harbour are quite expensive, averaging about US$60 (somewhat less from Treasure Cay). If you want to stay at the *Tangelo*, call ahead, and the owners will send a car for you.

The Loyalist Cays

Beyond Great and Little Abaco, the **Loyalist Cays** are arranged in a great half-moon that runs from southeast to northwest of Marsh Harbour, beginning with **Elbow Cay** and followed by **Man o' War**, **Great Guana** and, opposite Cooper's Town on Great Abaco, **Green Turtle Cay**. As almost perfectly preserved "New England" towns, Elbow Cay and Green Turtle Cay feature exquisite Atlantic beaches and scenic inlets and bays, understandably making them the most popular of all the Loyalist Cays.

Elbow Cay and Hope Town

Six miles southeast of Marsh Harbor, five-mile long **Elbow Cay** is home to six hundred residents, many with family histories going back centuries. **HOPE TOWN**, the only settlement, has a population of 450 and is located at the cay's northern end, traversed by two narrow lanes known as **Back Street** and **Bay Street** – which locals call Up Along and Down Along. The village features a picturesque assortment of one hundred brightly painted clapboard houses huddled against the sand dunes, each surrounded by quaint picket fences and flower gardens. As there are no cars on the island, visitors and residents must walk or take **golf carts** for longer journeys.

While the town's biggest attractions are its scenic bays and inlets, it does have a few interesting sights, including the historic **Elbow Cay Lighthouse**, a candy-striped pole visible for miles, and the **Wyannie Malone Museum**, housing an eclectic collection of island memorabilia. In the centre of Hope Town, the **Byrle Patterson Memorial Garden** offers solace amid pines, gazebos and dolphin sculptures, while at the north end, the **Cholera Cemetery** and the **Old**

Cemetery provide a fascinating glimpse of local history. Hope Town also serves as a good base for visits to the natural sanctuaries of the **Pelican Cay Land and Sea Park** and **Sandy Cay National Sea Park** nearby.

Elbow Cay provides plenty of opportunity to engage in a wide range of **outdoor activities**. Dave's Dive Shop and Froggies Out Island Adventures offer scuba, snorkelling, picnicking and boating **excursions**, while other operators provide packages for fishing, windsurfing and surfing.

Practicalities

The few options for **arriving** in Elbow Cay are all nautical. From Marsh Harbour, Albury's Ferry Service makes seven daily round-trips to Hope Town, a twenty-minute **ferry ride** that costs US$12, or $6 for kids. Private yachts can dock at numerous marinas.

For **accommodation** in Elbow Cay, there are several worthwhile options. Overlooking the harbour and the town, **Hope Town Harbour Lodge** (Ⓣ242/366-0095 or 1-800/316-7844; ⑤) offers twenty rooms, watersports rentals, a pool, lounge and an excellent restaurant. Near the lighthouse opposite the town, the luxury villas of **Hope Town Hideaways** (Ⓣ242/366-0024 or 1-800/688-4752; ⑦) sit on eleven beautiful acres and come with all amenities. On the southern tip of the island, **Sea Spray Resort and Marina** (Ⓣ242/366-0065 or 1-800/688-4752; one-bedroom villas US$700/week) provides villas with kitchens and patios, a good dockside restaurant, pool and access to watersports.

All the resorts feature a good selection of **restaurants**, though one of the most renowned local eateries is *Cap'n Jack's* near the harbour. Serving three meals a day and open late for drinks, the restaurant is locally famous for its great conch burger and macaroni and cheese, with live music on Wednesday and Friday nights. Also worth seeking out are Vernon's Grocery, up the hill from *Cap'n Jack's*, serving tasty sandwiches and flavourful key lime pie, and *The Harbour's Edge*, a reasonably good choice for breakfast.

Green Turtle Cay and New Plymouth

Eight miles north of Treasure Cay, **Green Turtle Cay** is the most popular of the Loyalist Cays, a striking array of bays, inlets and sounds, with one very well-preserved New England-style village, **NEW PLYMOUTH**. Although the cay's leeward shore is certainly eye-catching with its rugged natural features, its Atlantic coast is also appealing, with white sand beaches rimmed by close-in reefs ideal for **snorkelling** and **diving**. However, the cay's charms and beauty are far from hidden or unknown. Because New Plymouth is only a ten-minute ferry ride from the Treasure Cay dock, the town usually teems with sightseers and day-trippers. Not surprisingly, with a permanent population hovering around 350, many of the town's residents work in the fishing, boat-building and tourist trades. Several operators offer **boat rentals** and **sport fishing**, as well as **diving packages**, including Brendals Dive Shop (Ⓣ242/365-4411) on White Sound.

Lying on the south side of **Black Sound**, New Plymouth perches dramatically on a hillside leading north to **White Sound**, another of Green Turtle's stunning bays. While simply wandering the town's streets is enjoyable, there are a handful of interesting sights as well, including the **Albert Lowe Museum**, housed in a 200-year-old colonial house and displaying a fine collection of photographs, model ships and paintings. In the museum's basement, more art is viewable at the **Schooner's Gallery**, while on the outskirts of town, at the head of Black Sound, the **Alton Lowe Studio** is the best gallery in the area.

Arrival and transport

Arrival in Green Turtle Cay is strictly by water transport, usually by **ferry** or **private boats**. Green Turtle Ferry (☎242/365-4166) operates out of Treasure Cay, making eight daily ten-minute crossings beginning at 8am. AIT (☎242/365-6010) operates a ferry from Green Turtle Dock, two miles south of Treasure Cay airport, and both companies offer **charter service** with advance notice.

The most popular forms of **transit** on the cay are **golf carts**, **motor scooters** and **bicycles**, which can be rented at Cay Cart Rentals (☎242/365-4406), C&D Rentals (☎242/365-4161) or almost any resort. There are two **taxi services** on the cay, Omri and McIntosh Taxis (☎242/365-4406 for both).

Accommodation

The major **resorts** on Green Turtle Cay are located either around White Sound or in a cluster between New Plymouth and Gilliam Bay. Some isolated **cottages** are available in the far north of the island, or on the Atlantic shore closer to New Plymouth. Rental agencies include *Coco Bay Cottages* (☎242/365-4464) and *Linton's Beach and Harbour Cottages* (☎242/365-4003). **Apartments** can also be rented in downtown New Plymouth through local agents.

Bluff House Beach Hotel ☎242/365-4247. On a hill 80ft above White Sound, with hotel rooms, townhouse suites and large villas, as well as two miles of beach, tennis courts, boat rental and a marina. ❺

Green Turtle Club and Marina ☎242/365-4271. At the north end of White Sound, featuring 32 poolside rooms and eight villas, along with a full-service marina, English pub, restaurant and beachfront. ❼

New Plymouth Inn ☎242/365-4161. The most famous accommodation in New Plymouth, a restored 150-year-old building that once housed a sea captain and his family, and now features elegant gardens, enclosed porches, on-site bar and saltwater pool. Available for rental through agents in town. ❺

Eating

Green Turtle Club ☎242/365-4271. An exquisite experience dining on the resort's charming patio, with reservations expected for dinner. Lunch and dinner are served outdoors as well, without reservations.

Islands Restaurant and Grill inside Lowe's Foods on Parliament Street. A tiny space serving fine baby-back ribs, jalapeño poppers and T-bone steaks, as well as wonderful desserts.

McIntosh Restaurant and Bakery. A favourite downtown choice for delightful breakfasts and lunches.

Miss Emily's Blue Bee Bar. In central New Plymouth, a place full of ambience and history, famous for its "Goombay Smash" drinks and business-card lined walls.

New Plymouth Inn ☎242/365-4161. The fanciest spot to dine in New Plymouth, serving breakfast, lunch and dinner in a pleasant garden.

1.8

Long Island

Virtually untouched by tourism, the 3200 residents of **LONG ISLAND** live in a dozen or so small fishing settlements along a seventy-mile strip, a narrow sliver of land rarely more than two miles wide, separating Grand Bahama Bank from the Atlantic Ocean. Running along the spine of the island, the central road connecting its villages – **The Queen's Highway** – only became passable when it was resurfaced in 1991, the same year electricity and telephones arrived.

A varied **landscape** of steep rocky cliffs, sheltered coves filled with turquoise water, idyllic green pastures with grazing goats, and historic churches in quaint seaside villages, Long Beach offers eye-catching sightseeing, whether by car or bicycle. Along with its unspoiled rustic beauty, the island's key attractions are its excellent **diving** and **snorkelling**, superb **fishing** throughout the year, and many pristine **beaches**. These include the striking white sands that stretch for three miles along **Cape Santa Maria** at the north end of the island; **Guana Cay** with its terrific snorkelling, further south; and secluded **Lowes Beach** on the Atlantic side near the southern end.

Although most locals continue to make their living from fishing, the small burg of **Mangrove Bush**, at the southern end of the island, is home to a number of artisans constructing wooden boats – a longstanding tradition in the area. The **Long Island Sailing Regatta**, held in **Salt Pond** in mid-May for the past 35 years, is one of the main social events in the Out Islands.

Further along, two essential sights not to be missed include **Hamilton's Cave**, near the village of **Cartwrights**, a collection of underground chambers filled with colourful stalactites, stalagmites and pictographs, and the **Columbus Monument**, atop a rocky bluff at the northern tip of the island, offering a stunning panorama of the craggy terrain and white-sand fringes that Columbus first surveyed on his two-week Bahamian tour in 1492.

Arrival and transport

There are two **airports** on Long Island, one at Deadman's Cay in the centre of the island (ⓣ242/337-0877), the other at Stella Maris at its northern end (ⓣ242/338-2015). Daily flights come in at midday. Guests staying at the *Stella Maris Resort* (ⓣ242/338-2050) also have the option of taking the hotel's private, twice-weekly flights from George Town and Nassau (one-way US$102).

Two government **mail boats** serve Long Island: the *Mia Dean* departs Potter's Cay in Nassau Tuesdays at noon, reaching Clarence Town in southern Long Island twelve hours later, then leaves for Nassau Wednesdays or early Thursday mornings (US$45 one-way); and the *Sharice M* departs Nassau Mondays at 5pm, reaching Deadman's Cay, Salt Pond and Seymours in northern Long Island after fifteen hours, then leaves for Nassau on Wednesdays (US$45 one-way). Call the **dockmaster's office** on Potter's Cay for more information (ⓣ242/393-1064).

Two full-service **marinas** serve the island as well. The Stella Maris Marina (ⓣ242/338-2055) offers fifteen boat slips, electrical hookups, diesel and gasoline fuel, on-site mechanics, showers and access to resort amenities, while Flying Fish Marina (ⓣ242/337-3430, ⓔflyfishmarina@batelnet.bs) also has fifteen slips, fuel, laundry facilities, showers, provisions and a nice double guest room (US$125).

Getting around

Because there is no public bus service on Long Island, **taxis** meet every flight from the airport. However, if you plan to do your own exploring, you'll need to **rent a car** or a **motor scooter**, which can be arranged through your hotel or by Alfred Knowles (ⓣ242/338-5009 or 5091), on the north side, and Joe Williams (ⓣ242/338-5002), in Glinton's, who both offer cars for US$65 per day with unlimited mileage. With varied scenery and scant traffic, Long Island is a wonderful destination for **cyclists**. The two main resorts – *Cape Santa Maria Beach* and *Stella Maris* – have serviceable touring bikes for guest use.

Accommodation

Cape Santa Maria Beach Resort ⓣ242/338-5273 or 1-800/663-7090 in North America, ⓕ242/338-6013, ⓦwww.capesantamaria.com. On a sandy peninsula at the island's northern tip, with twenty double rooms in ten beachfront cottages featuring clay-tile floors, screened-in porches, on-site dining room, bar, fitness centre, watersports and fishing trips. Closed Sept & Oct. ⑨

Ellen's Inn Deadman's Cay ⓣ242/337-0888, ⓕ337-0333, ⓔellensinn@batelnet.bs. Featuring clean, homey rooms with shared kitchens and sitting rooms. US$100 a night, $450 per week.

Lochobar Beach Lodge Lochobar Bay ⓣ242/327-8323 or 337-3123, ⓕ327-2567, ⓦwww.thebahamian.com/lochobarbeach. Secluded, two-storey timber lodge housing two rustic studio apartments and a one-bedroom apartment sleeping up to five, with balconies or patios steps from the beach. ⑤

Sea View Lodge south end of Salt Pond ⓣ242/337-7517 or 337-0100. Good budget option, three one- and two-bedroom cottages with kitchens and satellite TV. Just off the Queen's Highway, providing choice views of Long Island Regatta in May. ④

Stella Maris Resort ⓣ242/338-2050 or 1-800/426-0466 in North America, ⓦwww.stellamarisresort.com. Featuring views of both coasts at the island's northern end, a friendly resort with several cottages and two dozen guest rooms with private verandahs. Also with three swimming pools, jacuzzi, tennis courts, fitness centre, bar, lounge and nice dining room. Several secluded beaches within walking distance, and free transport to others, along with snorkelling, diving and fishing packages. ⑦

Eating

Cape Santa Maria Resort ⓣ242/338-5273. Atmospheric dining room in glass-walled timber beach house. Menu has gourmet seafood dishes and imaginative American cuisine. Expensive; reservations required.

Harbour Restaurant Clarence Town ⓣ242/337-3247. Near the government dock, offering harbour views and tasty seafood, deep-fried dishes and adequate sandwiches. Open 10.30am–8pm.

Max Conch Bar and Grill Deadman's Cay ⓣ242/337-0056. Local favourite serving conch cracked, frittered and marinated, as well as fried chicken, burgers and fries, at outdoor kiosk with stools and tables.

Oasis Bakery and Restaurant one mile north of Clarence Town ⓣ242/337-3003. Nice spot for breakfast or lunch with tables set on wooden verandah overlooking a small pond. Highlights include fresh-baked bread, pastries and cookies, as well as cheap sandwiches, pizza, burgers and conch. Open Mon–Fri 8am–5pm, Sat 7.30am–5pm.

Stella Maris Resort ⓣ242/338-2050. Pleasant bar and dining room with nice oceanside views and elegant décor, and especially delicious breakfast buffet. Reservations recommended.

2

Turks and Caicos

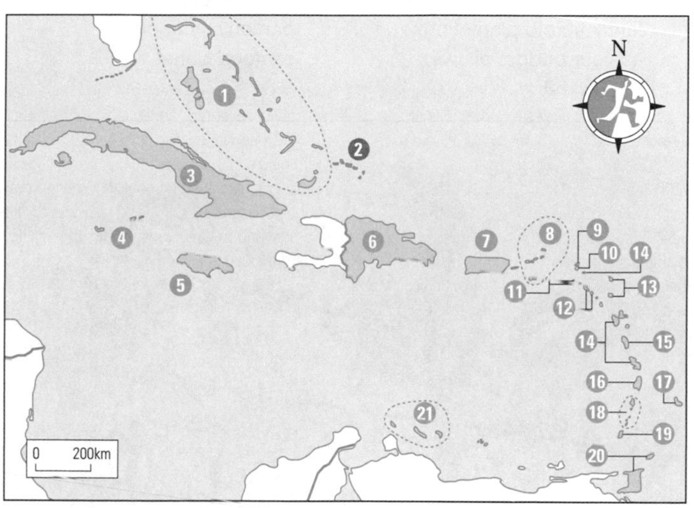

Turks and Caicos Highlights

* **Little Water Cay** Mingle with some prehistoric rock iguanas before snorkelling in the crystal waters. See p.123
* **Salt Cay** accommodation Choose between a festive guesthouse and a fantastic old plantation, as your budget allows. See p.133
* **Grand Turk** The quaint colonial streets of this languid island feature fine examples of local architecture. See p.131
* **Dora's** Island food at its best – *Dora's* on Providenciales offers a particularly good seafood buffet. See p.125

Introduction and Basics

Just twenty years ago, the Turks and Caicos Islands were one of the quietest and least-known destinations in the West Indies. Today, on the back of classy development on Providenciales, and great beaches and diving on all of the islands, they have become one of the most fashionable places to visit in the region.

The country comprises two groups of islands – eight inhabited and around forty uninhabited – separated by the Columbus Passage, a deep-water channel 22 miles wide and up to 6000 feet deep. To the east, the Turks Islands include **Grand Turk** and **Salt Cay**, the former the long-time home to government, the latter a tiny island named for the salt industry that once dominated the country. To the west, the chain of Caicos Islands includes inhabited **South**, **Middle** and **North Caicos** – each with its own charms – and the fast-growing island of **Providenciales**, known as Provo and home to the great majority of the nation's tourist development.

The major attractions on all of the islands are concentrated along their coasts: truly sensational white-sand beaches that stretch for miles, and world-class diving, snorkelling and deep-sea fishing and bonefishing. Inland, there's not much to see other than low-lying scrubby vegetation and, particularly in the Turks Islands, large expanses of featureless salinas, from which Bermudian settlers and traders harvested salt during the islands' early development.

Where to go

Most visitors head to **Provo**, which receives nearly all of the country's international flights and has the major hotels and restaurants. Even if you plan to stay there, however, you should consider excursions to one or more other islands. Particularly recommended are **Grand Turk**, a terminally calm, easy-going place and just a thirty-minute flight away, notable for its great colonial architecture, the National Museum and more fantastic diving and beaches – or a boat trip around the spectacular **Caicos Cays** to **Middle** or **North Caicos**, where you can check out some dramatic caves or the remains of an old plantation house.

Getting there

All international flights arrive on the island of Providenciales. American Airlines **flies** there three times daily from Miami taking ninety minutes. It also operates weekend flights from JFK in New York. The flight takes three and a half hours. British Airways flies once a week from London, stopping in Nassau en route. The flight leaves Heathrow on Sundays at 9.55am and takes ten and a half hours. Air Canada flies in from Toronto on Saturdays. Bahamas Air leaves Nassau on Tuesdays, Thursdays and Saturdays, for a two-hour flight. Finally, Air Jamaica flies in from Montego Bay from Friday to Monday. All four airlines turn round and fly out the same day.

Money and costs

The official currency of the Turks and Caicos Islands is the **US dollar**.

Costs are fairly high as most food, drink and other items are imported. There is a government room tax of 7–9 percent, and most hotels and restaurants automatically add a 10–15 percent **service charge**, so check your bill to ensure you're not paying twice. **Tipping** is customary, with 15 percent being average.

Getting around

Travelling between the islands of the Turks and Caicos is relatively easy, especially if you're starting from Provo; three local **airlines**, TCA (☎649/946-4255), Inter-Island

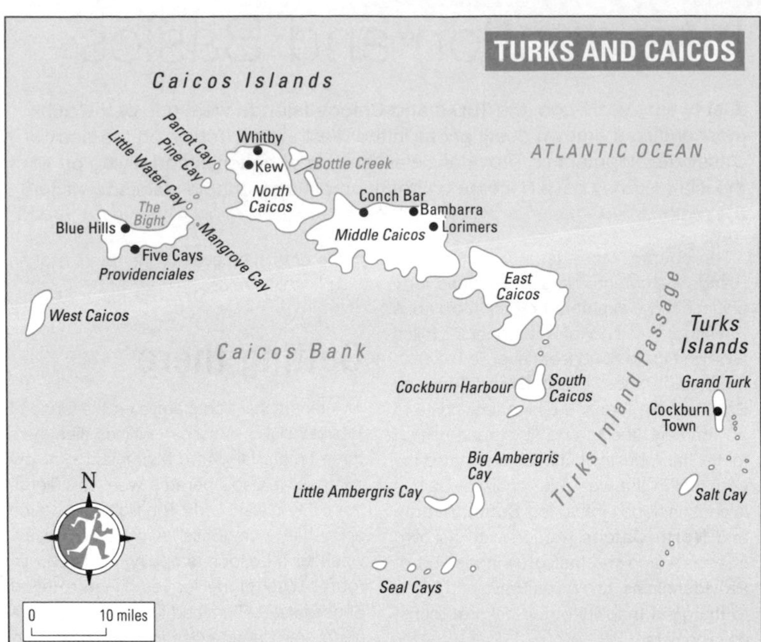

(☎649/946-4381, Ⓦwww.interislandairways.com) and the generally more reliable Skyking (☎649/946-4594 or 941-5464, Ⓦwww.skyking.tc) offer frequent connections. Skyking has nine daily scheduled flights each way between Provo and Grand Turk taking thirty minutes, three stopping in South Caicos to pick up and drop off in both directions. Round-trip fares cost around US$120. Normally, there are daily flights, too, between Provo and North and Middle Caicos (around US$60 round-trip) and between Grand Turk and Salt Cay (US$30).

Each of the islands has a **taxi** service, and there will invariably be a taxi waiting for passengers at the airports. For **car and jeep rental**, typically around US$60 a day, it's best to try in Providenciales (see p.121) or Grand Turk (see p.131). Elsewhere you may struggle to get a rental; it's worth asking at your hotel.

The **country code** for the Turks and Caicos Islands is ☎649.

History

The earliest inhabitants of the Turks and Caicos Islands were Amerindians, whose sites and relics have been found dotted across the islands; particularly important finds include those at the Conch Bar Caves in Middle Caicos (see p.129) and a canoe paddle recently discovered in North Creek in Grand Turk. The Amerindian period is well documented at the National Museum in Grand Turk (see p.132).

There is a major debate about the first European visitor. While the island of San Salvador in the Bahamas (see p.102) has probably the strongest claim to be where **Christopher Columbus** first set foot in the Americas in 1492, there are many exponents of the theory that it was in fact Grand Turk that saw his ships pull up to shore.

With Spanish slaving ships raiding the island for Amerindian labour for the gold-mines of South America, by 1513 the population had been reduced to zero. As for the colonial powers, ownership of the Islands passed between Spain, France and Britain, but none was interested in setting up base. Between 1690 and 1720 Providenciales and the Caicos Cays were used as hiding places by **pirates**, and stories of buried gold and jewels still bring treasure hunters to the Islands.

By the late seventeenth century, though, it was a new "treasure" that drew occasional visitors: **salt-rakers** from Bermuda, who had discovered the ease with which salt could be produced from shallow salt-water ponds or salinas which were constructed across the islands. This was particularly true in Salt Cay, Grand Turk and South Caicos, where large numbers of trees were chopped down to discourage rainfall (resulting in the largely bare landscape that endures today). "White gold", as the stuff came to be known, was a highly lucrative crop, much of it sent off to Newfoundland for salting cod, and some of the remaining grand houses on Salt Cay are testament to that profitable era. By 1781 the rakers had established a permanent settlement in Grand Turk.

Meanwhile, the Caicos Islands became inhabited only after the American War of Independence, when thousands of defeated **Loyalists** fled from the southern states such as Georgia and the Carolinas. Some were granted large tracts of land by the British government, from Providenciales to Middle Caicos, in recompense for what they had lost in North America. Around forty Loyalists arrived during the 1780s, bringing with them more than one thousand slaves, and began farming cotton.

Though immediately successful – **Caicos cotton** was said to be among the finest in the world – the cotton industry went into decline after just a generation, with hurricanes and pests taking a heavy toll. Though a few planters moved to the Turks Islands and went into salt, almost all of the planters had left the country by the mid-1820s, leaving their slaves behind to a subsistence existence of farming and fishing, much like the original population of Amerindians.

For the next century, the economy was sustained by the remnants of the salt industry, but there was little population growth and the pace of life was extremely slow. Things began to change with the arrival of a group of American investors in the 1960s, who laid the foundations for **tourist development**, building a small airstrip on Provo and erecting the first hotel – *Third Turtle* – in Turtle Cove. A trickle of foreign visitors began to arrive, turning into a steady stream once *Club Med* insisted on a proper airport to service their Grace Bay resort in the mid-1980s, and then a small flood with the arrival of further resorts through the 1990s.

2.1

The Caicos Islands

The **CAICOS ISLANDS** form a rough semi-circle, running from the lovely and uninhabited island of West Caicos up through the major tourist centre of Providenciales and a chain of tiny islands – the Caicos Cays – to North Caicos, then down through the largest island of Middle Caicos and uninhabited East Caicos, to the once busy but now largely ignored island of South Caicos.

North and Middle have their individual charms and can be easily accessed from Providenciales by plane (see p.117) or via a fabulous boat trip from Leeward Marina that takes you round the Caicos Cays (see p.122) – a highlight of any stay in the islands.

Providenciales

Providenciales is where the country's tourist industry has boomed. With little in the way of cultural life or historical interest, for decades only a handful of visitors made their way here, attracted particularly by the superb opportunities for diving and fishing in the offshore waters. Tourism began to heat up in the 1980s with the arrival of *Club Med*, and rocketed through the 1990s as investors spotted the great potential for resorts. The opening of *Beaches* in the late 1990s (part of the enormously successful *Sandals* resort chain) put Provo on the map as far as large-scale tourism was concerned, but it remains an easy-going getaway nonetheless.

There's no town to speak of on the island. Downtown, as the business centre is known, is a rather ugly group of shops and offices that you'll pass through on your way from the airport. The three original settlements (which can loosely be described as villages) are little visited by tourists: **Blue Hills**, a pretty residential area that runs alongside the sea north of the airport; **Five Cays**, a drab collection of homes and shops on the south of the island; a similar cluster around the *Beaches* resort known as **The Bight**.

For many visitors, particularly those staying at the all-inclusives on the north coast, the only sightseeing worth venturing out for is a wander along the six miles of magnificent beach on **Grace Bay**. It's a spectacular stroll beside a turquoise sea, with occasional shade beneath the casuarina trees, and however large the crowd outside the hotels, you'll invariably find a deserted spot to pitch camp.

More adventurous visitors will want to take advantage of the **boat trips** that run to the Caicos Cays from Leeward Marina (see p.122), where you can spot rock iguanas, hunt for sand dollars and make a picnic on a deserted island.

Arrival and getting around

Nearly all visitors arrive at **Luddington Airport**, roughly in the centre of the island, where there's always a string of taxis waiting outside; a ride to the hotels along Grace Bay costs US$12–20. There are also a couple of car rental desks here as well.

A **bus service** operates along the island's main artery, Leeward Highway, but it does not run to the airport or by any timetable. If you want to explore the island for a day or two it's worth renting a **car** (or a jeep if you want to make a trip to Malcolm Roads – see p.124); try Rent-a-Buggy (☎649/946-4158), Provo Rent-a-Car (☎649/946-4404) or Avis (☎649/946-4705). Expect to pay US$55–60 a day including insurance. **Scooters** can be rented from Scooter Bob's (☎649/946-4684) for US$30/day.

For **taxis**, try Nell's (☎649/231-0051 or 941-3228) or Provo Taxi (☎649/946-5481).

Accommodation

Due to the resort boom of the past decade there are plenty of **hotels** on Provo, though most are at the top end in terms of price and quality (and none is covered below). By far the most popular are the **all-inclusives** – *Beaches*, *Allegro* and *Club Med* – but there are several other excellent options, such as *Sibonne*, dotted along the north coast.

If you're thinking of renting a **villa**, Lynnette Simpson at Elliot Holdings (☎649/946-5355, ⓕ946-5176, ⓦwww.ElliotHoldings.com) has a superb range of places starting from around US$1500/week.

Airport

Airport Inn Airport Rd ☎649/941-3514, ⓕ941-3281, ⓦwww.tcnational.tc/hotel.htm. Far from the beach (though they'll provide a free ride to get there), this is the cheapest option on Provo, with nineteen clean and tidy rooms going for US$75 a day with air-conditioning, US$65 a day if not. Some rooms have kitchenettes, all have cable TV, and there's a local restaurant and bar on site. Fifteen percent discount on car rental. ③

Turtle Cove

Erebus Inn Turtle Cove ☎649/946-4240, ⓕ946-4704. Perched just above Turtle Cove marina, with fine views out to sea, the *Erebus* is a pleasant enough place (though it could do with a lick of paint), offering 21 good-sized and air-conditioned rooms, all with cable TV and either a patio or a balcony, clay tennis courts and a restaurant and large, attractive bar. ④

Turtle Cove Inn Resort Turtle Cove ☎649/946-4203, ⓕ946-4141, ⓦwww.TurtleCoveInn.com. Right by the marina, and a ten-minute walk from the nearest decent beach, but a relaxed and reasonably priced little place near a couple of good restaurants. The friendly *Tiki* bar is popular with locals, and there's a small, shaded pool. ④

Grace Bay

Allegro Grace Bay ☎649/946-5555, ⓕ946-5522, ⓦwww.allegroresorts.com. Rather hideous when approached from the road, this 186-room all-inclusive compensates guests by being on a superb stretch of Grace Bay. It also features the nation's only casino, aimed at casual blackjack and roulette players. There are two restaurants: a casual open-air place on the ground floor and a smart Italian one upstairs (make your reservation early), as well as a piano bar. Rooms have rattan furniture, colourful throws, A/C and fans, and there's a large pool, as well as tennis courts, a fitness centre and good watersports facilities. ⑥

Beaches Grace Bay ☎649/946-8000, ⓕ946-8001, ⓦwww.beaches.com. This superb all-inclusive resort – part of the impressive *Sandals* chain – is aimed at families, with top-class facilities for entertaining children, including a Pirate's Island, a Sega centre and their own restaurant and disco. Rooms are spacious, colourful and evenly distributed across a wide area, all within a short walk of the glorious beach and a number of pools. Watersports facilities are top-notch, while nine excellent restaurants range from Italian and French to Caribbean and Japanese, some catering to adults only. ⑧–⑨

Comfort Suites Ports of Call ☎649/946-8888, ⓕ946-5444, ⓦwww.comfortsuitestci.com. One of the cheapest options in the Grace Bay area and not a bad spot, the *Comfort Suites* are a ten-minute walk from the beach and right by the Ports of Call shopping area and restaurants. There are one hundred rooms, all with either a king bed or two double beds, plus cable TV, a fridge, telephone and A/C. ④

Coral Gardens Grace Bay ☎649/941-3713, ⓕ941-5171, ⓦwww.coralgardens.com. This small block of smart and good-value one -, two- and three-bedroom condominiums is popular with repeat visitors to the island. All condos are good-sized, with private balconies, sea views, fully equipped kitchens and daily maid service. Close to a good snorkelling site. ⑤–⑥

Sibonne Grace Bay ⓣ649/946-5547, ⓕ946-5770, ⓦwww.Sibonne.com. One of the best and best-value options on the island, this small boutique hotel sits beside a magnificent stretch of white sand and houses the *Bay Bistro*, one of Provo's finest restaurants (see p.126). The two-storied and attractively landscaped hotel has 27 medium-sized rooms, all with A/C, and a tiny pool. 6–7

Leeward Marina and boat tours

At the eastern end of the island, neat little **Leeward Marina**, overlooking the first of the Caicos Cays (see box, opposite) that stretch around to North Caicos, is home to most of the boat tour groups. You can just about make out the mangrove swamps of Mangrove Cay directly across the channel and, looking to your left, the sandy beaches of Little Water Cay where rock iguanas strut their stuff. If it's a calm day, it's worth renting a kayak from the Big Blue (US$20 per hour for a double; ⓣ649/946-5034) for an hour or two of cruising across to the cay and stopping on a deserted sandbank or beach to look for shells.

If you're feeling less energetic, there are a number of professional operators based at the marina who run excellent **sailboat or speedboat trips** to Little Water Cay to see the iguanas and to other nearby cays for shelling and picnics, normally stopping for some excellent snorkelling en route. Even more adventurous, and definitely worth trying, are the speedboat trips that go around all of the cays to Middle Caicos, where you can visit the Conch Bar caves (see p.129). The journey takes about ninety minutes each way, and you'll stop off to see the iguanas and to do some snorkelling.

The main **speedboat operators** are Silver Deep (ⓣ649/946-5612) and J&B Tours (ⓣ649/946-5047). Both run similar trips for similar prices; expect to pay around US$50 per person for the visit to Little Water Cay and US$120 for the trip to Middle Caicos. Big Blue (ⓣ649/946-5034) runs slightly pricier tours, with more emphasis on "eco-adventures", like visiting mangrove swamps or nature trails on Middle Caicos.

Sailing trips are run by Sail Provo (ⓣ649/946-4783) and Beluga (ⓣ649/946-4396) on comfortable catamarans or trimarans; as well as trips to the cays and snorkelling and shelling trips, both offer sunset cruises for around US$50 per person.

The Caicos Conch Farm

Tucked away in the wilds of Leeward east of the marina, the **Caicos Conch Farm**, on Leeward Highway (Mon–Sat 9am–4pm; $6, $3 for children), is the only one of its kind in the world. Started in 1984, the farm is responsible for rearing queen conch – a giant sea snail, famous for its gorgeous pink shells and pearls – for export and for sale in the islands. Conch – pronounced *konk* – are subject to numerous predators in the sea, including sharks, stingrays, porcupine fish and octopus. At the farm they are protected, first in large hatcheries and then, as they grow towards adulthood at three to five years, in pens at sea.

Twenty-minute **tours** of the farm are given frequently – if you arrive mid-tour you can still join in; the guide will fill you in afterwards on the parts you missed.

Long Bay and the Hole

Just a short drive along the road that runs west of the Conch Farm, **Long Bay Hills** is a developing residential area on the south side of the island with an impressive stretch of sand. Unfortunately, millions of conch shells washed in by the prevailing winds make access to decent swimming awkward, though you'll notice that some local house owners have tried to clear a path out to the ocean. Even then, however, the water is shallow for some way out and the sand more silty than you'll find on the north shore.

The Caicos Cays

Strung out in a chain between Providenciales and North Caicos are a dozen tiny islands, of which all but two are uninhabited. Though there are airstrips for the private planes of the millionaire residents of Pine Cay and Parrot Cay, the most likely way to set foot on any of the cays is by taking a boat trip from Leeward Marina (see opposite) – one of the undoubted highlights of any visit to the country. All beaches are open to the public and, on all the uninhabited islands, you're pretty much free to wander around at your leisure.

Five minutes by boat from Provo, the nature reserve of **Little Water Cay** is home to several thousand rock iguanas. These reptiles – unique to the region – were once found throughout the islands, but development and destruction by man and dog has led to their virtual extinction elsewhere. Here, wooden boardwalks have been put up across the cay to allow you access to the heart of their protected habitat. You'll see dozens of them – up to two feet long – sunning themselves on the beach or foraging around in the scrub.

Northeast of the cay, **Water Cay** is fringed by small sandy cliffs and fantastic white sand, while the adjoining **Pine Cay** has a small hotel and about 35 private homes dotted around its beaches and interior providing winter retreats for their wealthy and mostly US-based owners. The twelve-room *Meridian Club* hotel (Ⓣ203/602-0300, Ⓕ602-2265; US Ⓣ1-800/331-9154, Ⓦwww.meridianclub.com) is one of the finest of its kind in the world, priding itself on being simple but classy ("barefoot elegance" is the apposite slogan), with nature trails crossing the cay, and kayaks, snorkelling, fishing and diving all available for guests. Rooms cost US$825/650 in winter/summer based on double occupancy, and no children under 12 are allowed.

Beyond Pine Cay as you head east, **Fort George Cay** once housed a fort erected in the eighteenth century by the British to deter pirates from concealing themselves and plunder pinched from Spanish galleons sailing further south. The fort is long gone, though two of its iron cannons can be seen by snorkellers in shallow water just off the northwest shore.

Last in the chain and closest to North Caicos, **Parrot Cay** (formerly known as Pirate Cay, and thought to have been a refuge for pirates including Calico Jack, Anne Bonney and Mary Read) saw a multimillion-dollar hotel (Ⓣ649/946-7788, Ⓕ946-7789; Ⓦwww.parrot-cay.com) with all mod cons open its doors in the late 1990s. With fifty rooms and six villas, some with private swimming pools, and a fabulous spa, the place is altogther grander (and, most would say, rather snootier) than the *Meridian Club* on Pine Cay. Prices starting at US$400 a room/$2000 a villa mean that it's for the rich only, and in true copy-cat style a bunch of celebrities have beaten a steady trail here since it opened to the likes of Paul McCartney. Bruce Willis and Donna Karan are building holiday homes on the cay.

Follow signs to the hidden and rather dramatic **Hole** (always open; free), where the cap of the limestone rock has crumbled away – probably the result of wave action many centuries ago – leaving an eighty-foot drop down to a wide green pond. You can clamber around the edge – brave souls have been known to scramble down for a swim in the icy water – but beware there are no ropes or other protection, so make sure to keep small children well away.

Blue Hills and Malcolm Roads

West of Long Bay, Leeward Highway cuts straight across the island to its tiny commercial centre downtown. Just before you reach downtown, turn off to the right for what is perhaps the prettiest drive on the island. After about half a mile, take the right fork leading onto a coastal road that passes **Blue Hills**, the most attractive of Provo's original settlements. As well as an astounding variety of churches, and a graveyard where all the graves face out to sea, there are some great bars on the beach serving fish and conch snacks and lunches.

If you've got a jeep, at the end of Blue Hills you can turn left to join a more substantial road a few hundred yards inland (the continuation of the road you avoided earlier by forking right). Continue west towards Malcolm Roads beach and Northwest Point. Where the road divides, take the left turn (ignoring signs for the white elephant Crystal Bay condominium project) down a diabolical track about four miles long to Malcolm Roads. As you crawl down this rocky road, look out for osprey nests, large bundles of twigs and sticks, assorted palms and cacti that characterise the island's original vegetation, and great views over the bays as well as the virtually inaccessible inland ponds known for their spectacular birdlife.

The beach at **Malcolm Roads** is one of the most beautiful spots in the country. The surf often crashes in on the magnificent beach here, and you can expect to have it to yourself, though you may see dive boats moored offshore at some great dive sites. Bring water as there's no shelter and no facilities; you can also clamber around some rocky outcrops to find tiny coves for swimming. Steer clear of the small group of thatched, wooden tiki-huts that were put up here for a French gameshow in the early 1990s; untended since then, and blown about by occasional hurricanes, they have fallen into disrepair, with rotten floor boards and rusty nails a peril to the unwary.

Five Cays, Chalk Sound and the south

There's little in the way of tourist development on the south side of the island, where you'll find one of Provo's original settlements at Five Cays (named for the small group of rocks just offshore) and the gorgeous Chalk Sound national park and semi-circular Taylor Bay.

To get there from downtown, turn down the main road virtually opposite the airport road. A left turn at the gas station leads to **Five Cays** – an uninspiring and unkempt jumble of houses, schools and small businesses. Make sure you stop at the excellent *Liz's Bakery* (daily 6am–6pm) on the main road for some freshly baked breads, cakes and pasties.

Continuing south on the main road towards the island's main dock at South Dock, a turn to the right just before you reach the sea leads to the gloriously milky blue **Chalk Sound**, a stunning lagoon in a national park; bear in mind, though, that it's not a great place to swim because of the silty bottom. The Sound is protected from the sea on its southern side by a narrow peninsula, which is indented with a series of bays, overlooked by grand and very expensive private homes. **Sapodilla Bay** is the first and largest of the bays, with a handful of yachts normally moored just offshore. At the eastern end of the bay, reached by a rocky path just west of the run-down *Mariner's Hotel*, are a number of inscriptions in the rock that were carved by shipwrecked sailors in the early nineteenth century.

Beyond Sapodilla Bay, **Taylor Bay** has a perfect crescent of sand. Like Chalk Sound and Sapodilla Bay, however, it's not a great place to swim.

Watersports and diving

The **diving** around Provo is as good as you'll find anywhere. Although the best wall diving is a lot further from shore than you'll find in Grand Turk, there is a great variety of excellent sites here, including those at Northwest Point and at West Caicos, between sixty and ninety minutes by boat from Turtle Cove marina. There are also good shark and other dives to be found closer by off the island's north shore.

Reputable **operators** include the longstanding Provo Turtle Divers (Ⓣ649/946-4232, Ⓦwww.ProvoTurtleDivers.com), which also offers snorkelling tours and glass-bottomed boat rides, Caicos Adventures (Ⓣ649/941-3346, Ⓦwww.caicosadventures.tc), and Big Blue Unlimited (Ⓣ649/946-5034, Ⓦwww.bigblue.tc), which also run whale-watching trips in February and March when humpback whales pass by and kayaking tours of the cays near Provo. Expect to pay around US$55/90/130 for a one-tank/two-tank/three-tank dive, US$60 for a night dive or $160 for a resort course which includes a two-tank dive. A four- or five-day open-water certification course, involving four or five two-tank dives, costs US$400–450.

The best places to **snorkel** on Provo close to shore are near the *Coral Gardens* hotel and at Smith's Reef, just east of the entrance to the Turtle Cove marina. At both places you'll find good reefs just offshore. Alternatively, ask the dive operators when they have a snorkelling trip going out (normally US$35 per person) or take one of the island/snorkelling trips offered by the outfits at Leeward Marina (see p.122).

Other **watersports** are not well catered for, although the larger hotels all have good facilities for their guests. If you're not staying at one of those, your choice is likely to be rather limited, though you can rent windsurfers, hobie cats and kayaks from a rental outlet on the beach outside the Ocean Club on Grace Bay.

Fishing charters offer superb deep-sea fishing for marlin, wahoo, tuna and shark, difficult but exhilarating bonefishing in the shallow flats around the islands and bottom-fishing for grouper, snapper and parrotfish. For deep-sea fishing, try Sakitumi (☎649/946-4065) or Gwendolyn (☎649/946-5321) at Turtle Cove marina and expect to pay US$850/550 for a full/half-day's fishing for up to six people or US$150 if they'll take you on your own. For bonefishing or bottom-fishing, try Catch the Wave (☎649/941-3047) or Silver Deep (☎649/946-5612), both at Leeward Marina. In July there's a huge billfish tournament, with boats coming from around the world to hunt for the biggest blue marlin in the sea.

Golf and tennis

There is a magnificent **golf** course at Provo Golf and Country Club (☎649/946-5991), where you'll pay US$120 each for 18 holes and a cart or US$70 for nine holes. Many of the hotels have private **tennis** courts, and the public are welcome to hire the courts at the *Erebus Inn* (see p.121).

Eating and drinking

There is a good range of places to **eat** in Provo, from fine French and Italian restaurants to local hostelries dishing up traditional island food. As you'd expect, seafood has pride of place on most menus, but there's plenty to keep you happy if you're a meat-eater. Vegetarians will struggle to find much in the way of variety.

Downtown

Angelas Leeward Highway, opposite the turn-off for Turtle Cove ☎649/946-4694. New York-style deli, with a great range of bread, meat and cheese, plus sandwiches, muffins and snacks. There's a separate branch in the Ports of Call village. Mon–Fri 6am–5pm, Sat & Sun 6am–3pm.

Dora's Leeward Highway ☎649/946-4558. Dora has run this place – best of the native restaurants – for over a decade and still dishes out excellent and relatively inexpensive fare from curried chicken, lobster and goat to beef stew and creole snapper or grouper. Monday and Thursday have a seafood buffet where, for US$22, you get a great selection of conch fritters, lobster, turtle and fish. Open all day.

Hey Jose! Central Square, Leeward Highway ☎649/946-4812. Longstanding island favourite for Mexican dishes (enchiladas, burritos and fajitas) and pizzas at US$10–20 per head. Cocktails are excellent, particularly during Friday happy hour (5.30–7pm), when trademark margaritas go for US$3.50 a shot. Lunch and dinner Mon–Sat.

Tasty Temptation Butterfield Square, Downtown ☎649/946-4049. This established bakery sells a great selection of plain or filled croissants, rolls and sandwiches from around US$5 as well as giant muffins and good coffee. Mon–Fri 6am–3pm.

Turtle Cove

Banana Boat Turtle Cove ☎649/941-5706. Pleasant family-friendly place at Turtle Cove marina, with a moderately priced range of fish and seafood platters, including excellent cracked conch

and snapper or grouper in a spicy creole sauce.
Sharkbite Turtle Cove ⓣ649/941-5090. This great spot overlooking the marina offers tasty meals from almond-crusted grouper in curry sauce (US$17.50) to fish and chips ($9.95) and burgers ($10 up). Alongside the restaurant there's a long and busy bar, and a handful of games to keep the kids occupied.

Grace Bay

Bay Bistro *Sibonne Hotel*, Grace Bay ⓣ649/946-5396. Sip a cocktail at the bar and watch a fabulous sunset before sidling into this easy-going bistro that has quickly earned a reputation as one of the finest places to eat on the island. The fish and lobster are superb whether marinated in ginger and soy or simply pan-fried on the grill, and there's a smaller selection of fine cuts of beef or lamb. Finish with the lemon *crème brûlée* – it's huge, but you'll manage it. Starters cost $5–10, mains $16–35). Lunch and dinner Wed–Mon.
Caicos Café Caicos Café Plaza, near Ports of Call, just east of *Allegro* hotel ⓣ649/946-5278. Beautifully lit with candles and fairy lights and decorated with Haitian art, this semi-outdoors French-owned restaurant serves superb fresh meals. Starters include conch salad (US$9) and tuna carpaccio ($12), while mains always feature fresh local fish and lobster ($20–27) and imported steaks. Finish things off with a Caicos Coffee, strong and infused with plenty of kahlua and whipped cream.
Lattitudes Ports of Call ⓣ649/946-5832. Happy hour starts at 5pm after which Californian but long-time resident Jeff Rollings starts dishing out top-notch pizzas, ribs, steaks, fish and burgers in a relaxed setting. All dishes under US$15. Dinner only.

Leeward

Gilley's at Leeward Leeward Marina ⓣ649/946-5094. Right on the marina, *Gilley's* prides itself on its full breakfasts from US$5.95 and tasty lunches of cracked conch, conch salad and fish and chicken sandwiches from around $10.

Nightlife and entertainment

Nightlife on Provo is fairly quiet. However, if you're up for dancing, the nightclub *Stardust and Ashes* (on Leeward Highway near the turn-off for the *Allegro* hotel) has something going on each night from Tuesday to Saturday, including a mellow jazz night on Tuesday, a late late "island party" night on Friday and salsa and merengue at Saturday's Latin night. For more sedate fun, you can head to the casino at the *Allegro* to try your hand at blackjack and roulette.

The biggest party of the year is held around "Provo Day", which takes place in late July and early August. There is a beauty pageant, a regatta and a parade of floats and a big weekend party with live music and stalls (normally around the ballpark in Downtown) selling beer and local food like souse and conch fritters.

Listings

Banks Both Scotiabank and Barclays have branches in Downtown. Hours are Mon–Thurs 8.30am–2.30pm, Fri 8.30am–4.30pm.
Emergencies ⓣ911
Internet access There are no internet cafés, but most hotels will let you log on for a modest charge.
Laundry Pioneer Cleaners, Butterfield Square, Downtown (ⓣ649/941-4402)
Medical services Associated Medical Practices, Leeward Highway (ⓣ649/946-4242, ⓦwww.doctor.tc); Grace Bay Medical Centre, Grace Bay (ⓣ649/941-5252)
Police ⓣ649/946-4259
Post office Airport Rd (Mon–Fri 8am–noon & 2–4pm)

North Caicos

NORTH CAICOS is the most lush and in many ways the most beautiful of the nation's islands. Receiving more rainfall than anywhere else, the vegetation is denser and taller here than on the other islands, and many islanders keep vegetable patches and grow fruit trees, including tamarind, papaya and sapodilla. As you'd expect, the beaches are great, too. Although property speculators have pushed land prices to dramatic heights in the hope that North Caicos will become the next Provo, tourist development to date is pretty low-key, with just a few small hotels on the north coast.

Getting there and getting around

There are no international flights to North Caicos, and most people arrive by **plane** from Providenciales with Skyking, TCA or Inter-Island Airways (see p.117–18). Scheduled ferry service from Providenciales to the island has been suspended, though boats do make trips from Leeward Marina as part of day excursions from Providenciales (see p.122).

Similarly, there is no tourist office on the island nor any formal car rental facilities, although it's worth asking at your hotel if they can arrange a rental for you (they normally can). There are **taxis** at the airport to meet incoming flights. If you want to tour around by taxi, M&M (Ⓣ649/946-7338) charges US$25 per hour.

Accommodation

Most of the **hotels** on North Caicos are scattered along the lovely sandy beaches of Whitby; the *Bottle Creek Lodge* is a delightful newcomer on the other side of the island.

Bottle Creek Lodge Bottle Creek Ⓣ649/946-7080, Ⓦwww.bottlecreeklodge.com. Comfortable eco-friendly accommodation in two cottages and an apartment, overlooking the turquoise creek that divides North from Middle Caicos. Not ideal for the beach, but a very relaxed place which has free sailboats and kayaks for exploring Middle Caicos and nearby cays. The owners will also arrange expeditions around the island. Based on double occupancy, expect to pay US$130 a night from May to mid-Dec. ❼

Pelican Beach Hotel Whitby Ⓣ649/946-7112, Ⓕ946-7139. Laid-back and longstanding small hotel with excellent ocean views from the air-conditioned upstairs rooms and unpretentious but comfortable furnishings and decoration. There's a cosy bar, and you can expect to find good local food at the roomy restaurant. ❻

Prospect of Whitby Whitby Ⓣ649/946-7119, Ⓕ946-7114, Ⓦwww.clubvacanze.com. Probably the nicest place to stay on the island, this is an Italian-run all-inclusive hotel on a fabulous beach. Just 23 good-sized and air-conditioned rooms keep an intimate feel, while the restaurant is excellent and scuba diving, windsurfing and tennis are included with the package. ❾

The island

At the west end of the island, **Sandy Point** is a small fishing community and your likely arrival point if you're coming by boat from Provo. Just offshore lie three prominent rocks known as **Three Mary Cays**; one of them has a huge osprey nest, whose occupant is often seen gazing imperiously over passing vessels. Back on land, and a short drive from Sandy Point, birdwatchers can douse themselves in bug spray and make for **Cottage Pond**, a small nature reserve with a deep sinkhole and inhabited by local ducks, grebes and other birds, or (a little further east) for **Flamingo Pond**, a large expanse of brackish water where you can normally spy a flock of flamingos (though it's hard to get close to them, and you'll need binoculars for a decent view).

On the north side of Flamingo Pond, **Whitby** is home to the island's main hotels and guesthouses and fringes onto a number of excellent white-sand beaches with good snorkelling just offshore. On the western edge of Whitby, the powdery sands of Pumpkin Bluff Beach are magnificent while, on the eastern side of the village, Pelican Point is a good place to snorkel.

South of Whitby, the road leads inland to the farming settlement at **Kew** – the only one of the original settlements in the country not based on the coast – named for the botanical gardens in London and home to many of the island's most productive fruit and vegetable growers. There's also a post office, church and general store.

A mile to the west of Kew, the extensive though unspectacular ruins of **Wades Green Plantation** are currently under restoration, and you're free to wander around the remains of the massive kitchen, overseer's house, stables and walled garden plots. Built in 1789 by Wade Stubbs, the plantation developed high-quality cotton and was a rare success story for the area; upon his death in 1822, Stubbs owned over 8000 acres on North and Middle Caicos and Providenciales as well as 384 slaves, many of whom took his surname. Today, Stubbs is one of the most common names in the islands.

On the eastern side of the island is **Bottle Creek**, North Caicos's largest settlement, whose houses spread out along the ridge that overlooks the creek between North and Middle Caicos. The peace and quiet and the colours of the creek make this a gorgeous spot, especially if you're passing through by boat, though there's little specific sightseeing. A vehicle ferry crosses the creek on weekends; otherwise ask around in Bottle Creek for a ride to Crossing Place in Middle Caicos (five minutes by boat). Bear in mind that you'll want to arrange a taxi for the other end (see opposite).

Eating and drinking

Away from the hotels, there's not much in the way of restaurants or bars, and nightlife tends to be quiet.

Club Titters Bottle Creek ☎649/946-7316. This local place dishes up tasty and inexpensive fare all day, including grouper with peas and rice and cracked conch, and there's occasional live entertainment at weekends.

Pappa Grunt's Seafood Restaurant Whitby ☎649/946-7301. Expect to find lots of local fish and conch on offer here, served in a variety of ways, along with fried chicken and burgers. Most dishes cost US$6–10.

Pelican Beach Hotel Whitby ☎649/946-7112. Good mixture of local and international food, with plenty of fine grilled snapper and grouper served up with peas and rice as well as ribeye steaks and lobster salad for US$15–20. The place can lack atmosphere when its quiet, but there's a very easy-going vibe.

Prospect of Whitby Hotel Whitby ☎649/946-7119. Excellent food, often Italian but far more than basic pizza and pasta, at this all-inclusive, where non-residents can get a pass for dinner. The chef lays on daily specials that might include veal, lobster or fillet steak. Expect to pay upwards of US$35 for a three-course meal.

Middle Caicos

Home to just three hundred people, **MIDDLE CAICOS** is the country's largest island and one of its quietest. Despite the abundance of great beaches, especially at **Mudjin Harbour** near Conch Bar and further east at **Bambarra**, tourist development has been very slow and there are few facilities for visitors; you'll find just a handful of guesthouses and a couple of taxi drivers. If you're after peace and quiet, you couldn't find many better refuges in the country.

Middle Caicos was settled by **Lucayan Indians** between the eighth century and around 1540, by which time Spanish slave traders had killed or shipped off the local population for servitude in South American mines. The island remained uninhabited until Loyalists and their slaves arrived from North America after the Revolution. As elsewhere in the islands, the settlers' attempts at growing cotton made little progress and, within a generation, the settlers departed, leaving their former slaves to run the three north coast settlements that survive today.

Arrival, information and getting around

There are daily **flights** to Middle Caicos from Providenciales with TCA and Inter-Island Airways (see p.117–18), some of them stopping at North Caicos en route. There is also a ferry from Bottle Creek in North Caicos on Saturdays from 8am (US$2 per person, US$20 for a car), landing at Crossing Place in the west of the island.

You won't find a tourist office on the island or a car rental outlet, but there are a couple of local **taxi** drivers who prowl around the airport and will be delighted to take you on a tour of the island – reckon on around US$25 per hour. Try Earnest Forbes (☎649/946-6140) or Cardinal Arthur (☎649/946-6107). They'll also be happy to organize fishing trips for you on the shallow waters south of the island.

Accommodation

Other than private villas, there are just a couple of **places to stay** for visitors to Middle Caicos: the small but upmarket *Blue Horizon* resort or the pleasant little *Taylor's Guesthouse*.

Blue Horizon Resort Mudjin Harbour ☎649/946-6141, ⓕ946-6139, ⓦwww.bhresort.com. A handful of large and comfortable cottages perched on the hilltops above the harbour, with fine views over the coastline. It's a fabulously relaxed place, a short walk from a superb beach – sometimes pounded by waves, at other times blissfully calm – though don't come expecting much in the way of entertainment or nightlife. The staff will organize snorkelling or hiking expeditions on request. Meals available by reservation. Rooms cost US$150–225, $1000–1500 for a week.

Taylor's Guesthouse Conch Bar ☎649/946-6161, no fax. A good place for those on a tight budget, five minutes' walk from the beach. Inexpensive rooms are clean and well kept in a large, attractive wooden house, all with fans and TV. There's also a small restaurant on site. ❸

Around the island

One of the main draws in Middle Caicos is a series of limestone **caves** at Conch Bar. Formed over millennia by the action of water on the soft rock, the extensive network was once the home to Lucayan Indians, almost certainly here at the time of Columbus, and various of their artefacts – including tools and pottery – have been removed to the National Museum in Grand Turk (see p.132). Tours of the caves need to be arranged in advance, either through a tour company in Provo (see p.122) or by booking a tour with one of the Middle Caicos taxi drivers. Try Earnest Forbes on ☎649/946-6140.

If you are here on a tour, you'll probably spend some time at **Mudjin Harbour**, a short drive east of the caves. It's a dramatic setting with tall cliffs dropping down to the sea, a rocky promontory just offshore and waves often crashing onto a yellow-sand beach. As you go down to the beach there's a short trail off to the left that leads to the top of the cliff where you'll have fantastic views down the coast and across the scrubby, undeveloped interior of the island.

East of here the road leads to the small settlement of **Bambarra** where there is a large and very quiet white-sand beach framed by casuarina trees; at low tide you can wade out along a sandbank for half a mile to the delightful beach at Pelican Cay. Continuing further east, **Lorimers** – named for a local plantation owner – is one of the most remote settlements in the country, though there's little here of for visitors.

The high point in the island's calendar is **Middle Caicos Expo**, a great weekend party in August during which former residents return and others flood in to hear live bands and hang out at the beer tents set up on Bambarra beach.

Hiking and biking

The **Crossing Place Trail** makes Middle Caicos one of the best places in the country for hiking and biking. It's an ancient path that leads from Lorimers in the east around the north coast of Middle Caicos to Crossing Place in the west, from where it's possible to cross to North Caicos at low tide. After years of being overgrown, the path was recently cleared by the National Trust, and you can now follow the track for four and a half miles from Conch Bar to Crossing Place. Part of the path is on the beach and passes through Mudjin Harbour, with trail markers along the way. It's a great way of seeing the island, mostly along the flat and not particularly strenuous parts, though you may want to arrange for a taxi to pick you up at the end of the route.

There is also a seven-mile **biking trail** on pretty easy terrain from Conch Bar to Bambarra beach, with good snorkelling spots along the way. Bikes can be rented from Sport Shack in Conch Bar for around US$15 a day.

Eating and drinking

Given the tiny population of the island (and the fact that most of it consists of either elderly people or children), there's nowhere much to head to for a night out, other than a small bar in Conch Bar where local guys gather in the evening to drink beer and play dominoes. Plan quiet nights in your hotel, guesthouse or villa and lay in the beer from the grocery store in Conch Bar.

2.2

The Turks Islands

The small group of **TURKS ISLANDS** has just two inhabited islands: **Grand Turk**, the home of government, and tiny **Salt Cay**, with its population of under a hundred. Both places are quiet and quaint, showcasing attractive remnants of the colonial era, with great beaches and diving to keep you entertained during the day but little in the way of nightlife.

Grand Turk

Despite the government's best efforts, major development continues to elude the small but delightful island of **Grand Turk**. Frustrating as this is to the powers that be – who see their young people emigrating to Providenciales or abroad for jobs – those who make the effort to get here will find a charming and unspoiled island.

A series of expansive, muddy-coloured **salinas** dominate the centre of the island, testament to the salt trade that first brought development to Grand Turk. West of here and running beside the sea, Front Street has much of the country's finest colonial-era **architecture** as well as the tiny but superb **National Museum**, while the **diving** and **fishing** are world-class and the **beaches** magnificent. Consider renting a car or scooter for a day to tour the island, which will only take you a few hours to explore, or ask a taxi driver for a guided tour.

Arrival and getting around

There are no international flights into Grand Turk and you'll need to come in via Providenciales, from where there are more than a dozen **flights** a day (see p.117–18) costing US$60 each way.

Car rental can be arranged from Dutchies (Ⓣ649/946-2244) or Tony's (Ⓣ649/946-1879) for around US$55 a day; scooters from Val's (Ⓣ649/946-1022) for US$30 a day. Taxis are found at the airport or can be reached by phone – try K's (Ⓣ649/946-2239).

Accommodation

Though Grand Turk has none of the five-star hotels that you'll find on Provo, there's a good range of **places to stay**.

Osprey Beach Hotel Front St Ⓣ649/946-1453, Ⓕ946 2817, Ⓦwww.ospreybeachhotel.com. Comfortable and tranquil little place right on the beach, with sixteen tidy rooms, each with a patio or a balcony overlooking the sea. There's a small restaurant a short walk from the main hotel, and a tiny pool around which the owners hold occasional barbecues. ❺

Sadler's Seaview Apartments Duke St Ⓣ649/946-2569. Just three small units at this friendly little pad, with kitchens, TVs and ceiling fans, and a stone's throw from the sea. ❸

Salt Raker Inn Front St Ⓣ649/946-2260, Ⓕ946-2817, Ⓦwww.saltrakerinn.com. Under renovation at the time of writing, the faded colonial charm of the *Salt Raker* made it an old favourite for visitors to Grand Turk; it lies across the road from a good beach and an is incredibly peaceful place. The best rooms overlook the ocean; others are spread around the garden where the restaurant is located.

Check the website for the latest rates.

Turks Head Hotel Front St ⓣ649/946-2466, ⓕ946 1716, ⓦwww.grand-turk.com. Another charming colonial building from the 1840s, the *Turks Head* pulls in business travellers and tourists with its attractively furnished rooms and period charm, all just a short walk from the beach. At quiet times it can feel rather soulless, but the bar is normally busy with locals in the evening and there's a good restaurant on site. ❺

Around the island

Cockburn Town is the country's capital, but don't expect to find a bustling city. Although the government has spent a great deal to smarten the place up, it hasn't brought in the masses, with most of the tourists still coming here for diving more than sightseeing. Comprising a couple of streets of nineteenth-century homes and warehouses, it's rare to find much activity and the streets are often empty. Stroll down the main drags of **Duke Street** and **Front Street**, which run alongside the gorgeous blue ocean, and you might encounter a gaggle of smartly dressed children making their way to school or a languid cow munching from some overhanging foliage.

The island's **architectural highlights** are centred on these two streets. At the southern end of Front Street, the *Salt Raker Inn* and *Turks Head Hotel*, two of Grand Turk's best hotels, are fine examples of the wooden houses built in the 1840s by Bermudian shipwrights who came to the island to collect salt. Other colourful examples like the General Post Office line this area of Front Street, many of them constructed with ballast and timbers taken from the trading ships of the time, and covered with purple and orange bougainvillea, as well as the occasional Turk's-head cactus, recognizable by its red fez-shaped flower.

The Turks and Caicos National Museum

Continuing up Front Street from the hotels, you'll come to the **Turks and Caicos National Museum** (Mon–Fri 10am–4pm; US$5), chief among the island's highlights. Here you can examine the remains of the Molasses Reef wreck, the oldest recovered shipwreck in the Caribbean, dating from around 1515. Mistaking it for a treasure ship, some morons blew sections of it apart with dynamite looking for treasure after the wreck was discovered in the 1970s. Key remains on display include the enormous main anchor, cannon and other weapons, hand- and foot-cuffs of prisoners and some tools.

The exhibits upstairs span the islands' history from pre-Columbian times to the present, and include a room given over to artefacts – notably pottery – from the Lucayan Indians and another explaining the islands' reefs and aquatic life. Also on display are items recording key visits to the island, from astronauts John Glenn and Scott Carpenter, who splashed down near here in 1962 and were brought to Grand Turk for debriefing, to present-day British monarch Queen Elizabeth II and members of her family who have visited periodically over the past forty years.

Governor's Beach and around

Of the good **beaches** that line the west and east coasts, the pick of them is **Governor's Beach**, where the powdery sands shelve into a turquoise sea. To get there head south on the road from Cockburn Town, ignoring the turn-off to the airport, and continuing towards the Governor's residence, known as **Waterloo**. Just before you reach the imposing white walls, turn off to the right along a track that runs past the small nine-hole golf course in the grounds of the house (call ⓣ649/946 2308 to book a round for US$25). At the end of the track take the path through the bush to a superb stretch of white sand, backed by casuarina trees and fronting onto a magnificent turquoise bay. Be sure to take water, as there are no facilities on the beach and you're likely to have it to yourself.

Outdoor activities

Superb **diving** opportunities, many of them very close to shore, include fantastic deep and shallow dives at twenty sites along the five-mile wall that starts just off the west coast. You'll find magnificent coral formations, abundant reef life and plenty of shipwrecks.

The three **operators** are Blue Water Divers (☎649/946-2432, ⓦwww.grandturkscuba.com), Oasis Divers (☎649/946-1128, ⓦwww.Oasisdivers.com) and Sea Eye Diving (☎649/946-1407, ⓦwww.seaeyediving.com). All offer PADI certification courses, and are happy to take snorkellers along if they're going to train at a shallow site. **Snorkellers** should also make for the old pier at South Dock, not the most attractive place to dive but teeming with fish, and try to get on a boat ride to deserted Gibbs Cay where the snorkelling is fantastic and where you'll bump into some friendly southern stingrays.

Eating, drinking and nightlife

There's not much sophistication to **dining** out in Grand Turk, but there are plenty of decent options and prices are reasonable. Nightlife is quiet, though there's usually some late-night music and dancing at *Nookie Hill* on Friday and Saturday and occasional mellow guitar music at *Water's Edge*.

Calico Jacks *Turks Head Hotel*, Front St ☎649/946-2466. Good food from an experimental and eclectic menu, covering everything from grilled lobster (US$25) and fish and chips (US$9) to Thai curry (US$12) and stone-crab claws (US$22). Sit outdoors under the trees at lunchtime but remember the bug spray.

Regal Beagle Hospital Rd ☎649/946-2274. Shack-like restaurant dishing up tasty and inexpensive native lunches and dinners for US$4–10, such as conch fritters, stewed beef, goat curry and fried chicken.

Water's Edge Front St ☎649/946-1680. The best food on the island, served on a pier poking out into the gorgeous waters off the west coast, and usually busy at lunch and dinner. The well-tended bar is often lively, and the cracked conch, conch salad and grilled fish are a treat. Expect to pay US$20–25 for a three-course meal.

Salt Cay

Tiny **SALT CAY** is one of the loveliest islands in the country, both for its natural beauty and its historical appeal. Although it measures no more than six and a half square miles and is home to fewer than one hundred people, the island was a once an important source for the Bermudian salt rakers, whose relics still litter the place and provide much of the charm: fabulous old white-washed houses as well as the salt pans from which the "white gold" was laboriously scraped. Add to that some sugary white beaches (particularly along the north coast), great diving and snorkelling, and a small but fine range of accommodation, and you've got another great place to chill out.

Arrival, information and getting around

Flights with TCA and Inter-Island Airways leave from Provo for Salt Cay daily and cost US$120 return (see p.117–18). There are also daily flights between Grand Turk and Salt Cay, though these are less frequent and cost US$25 each way. The government **ferry** runs between Grand Turk and Salt Cay, leaving Grand Turk on Mondays, Wednesdays and Fridays at 3pm and costing US$4 per person.

There's no tourist office on the island and just a couple of taxis.

Accommodation

Salt Cay has a range of **accommodation** options to suit most budgets; magnificent as *Windmills* is, there's plenty of choice for those without money to burn.

Mount Pleasant Guest House ⓣ649/946-6927, ⓕ946-6927, ⓦwww.turksandcaicos.tc/mtpleasant. Superb value, this timber-beamed nineteenth-century salt trader's home on the great north coast beach has been catering mainly to divers for over a decade. There's a comfortable lounge/library for guests, and rooms are colourful and quiet. The restaurant and gazebo bar are the most popular on the island. Single 6, double 4

Salt Cay Sunset House ⓣ649/946-6942, ⓕ946-6942, ⓦwww.seaone.org. Another charming, old salt trader's home, with just three rooms ranging from US$70 to US$100. There's a big, communal living room, and good food served by the owners on the verandah. 3

Windmills Plantation ⓣ649/946-6962, ⓕ946-6930, ⓦwww.WindmillsPlantation.com. Fabulous and fabulously expensive, *Windmills* is built like a traditional West Indian plantation house. Wooden walkways connect the main house, with its wooden verandahs and gingerbread fretwork, to the other guest rooms, all furnished with superb antiques and custom-designed furniture that includes four-poster beds. The restaurant is five-star and the capable proprietors will arrange whatever activity you need. 9

Around the island

Like Grand Turk, the centre of Salt Cay is dominated by the flat, shallow **salinas** that supplied the island's once-thriving salt industry. Recognizing the commercial potential of raking up the salt, the salt traders built stone walls and sluice gates to create smaller ponds so that the water would evaporate more quickly under the baking sun. Windmills were built to speed up the process, but it was fiercely hard manual work scraping the salt into piles. Trading ships from Bermuda carrying limestone rocks as ballast (later used to build the traders' smart houses) then transported the rough salt to trade along the eastern seaboard of the fledgling United States.

For centuries, salt was the source of the island's wealth, but the industry was the subject of stiff international competition and went into decline for decades before it finally ground to a halt in the 1960s. Nothing much has happened since, and Salt Cay's population has slowly melted away, the remaining people mostly elderly or children, their numbers supplemented by a trickle of tourists.

On the west side of the island, **Balfour Town** is the principal settlement, home to government buildings, the local school and a couple of stores. It's also where you'll find the **White House** dominating the shoreline, the most spectacular of Salt Cay's two-storey jalousie-windowed limestone houses, built by local salt magnate Joshua Harriot after the great hurricane of 1812 had flattened his wooden home with a 15ft tidal wave. Elsewhere you'll see more recent and pastel-coloured wooden houses, with little courtyards and low stone walls to keep stray cattle at bay.

The island's best **beach** runs along the entire north coast, a magnificent swathe of sand, with massive elkhorn coralheads in a couple of places just offshore harbouring schools of fish and perfect for snorkelling. The rocky east coast is dominated by sharp-edged ironshore limestone, with a series of small bays dotted along it. It also has the island's highest point at Taylor's Hill, 60ft above sea level.

For **divers** there are a handful of good sites five minutes by boat off the west coast of the island, where you'll find spotted eagle rays and a wealth of brightly coloured fish as well as deep-water gorgonians and black coral trees. Ten miles further south, the encrusted wreck of *HMS Endymion*, an eighteenth-century British warship complete with cannon, lies in thirty feet of water.

Eating and drinking

You'll do almost all of your eating and drinking at hotels and guesthouses, where prices are reasonable. The food at the *Mount Pleasant* (see opposite) is particularly good, and you should also make tracks to the *One Down, One To Go* bar in Balfour Town for a drink and a game of pool, and some local colour.

Outdoor activities

The island's principal dive operator, Salt Cay Divers (Ⓣ649/946-6906, Ⓦwww.saltcaydivers.tc), based at the *Mount Pleasant Guest House*, also rents bikes and organ-iszes horse-riding tours of the island. From January to March, humpback whales make their way to the nearby Mouchoir Banks to breed, and while a fortunate few will spot them blowing from the shore, you might be better off joining one of the whale-watching tours organized by Salt Cay Divers (and their Grand Turk equivalents, see p.133).

3

Cuba

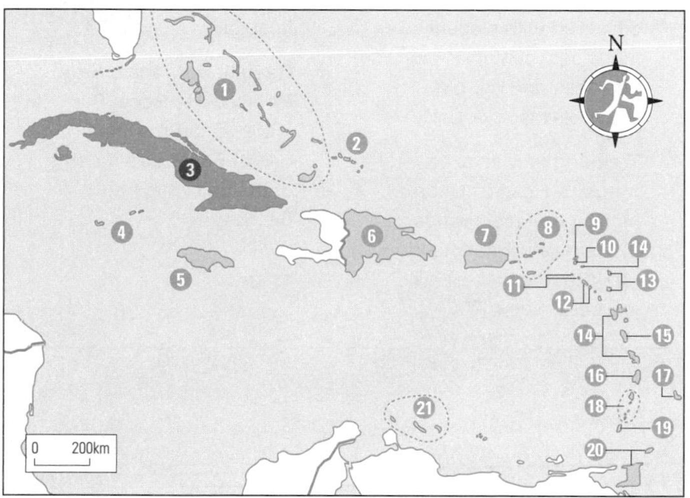

Cuba Highlights

- **Cuban music in Havana** Check out at least one of the excellent salsa, jazz or son groups that regularly make the rounds of the best-known clubs. See p.164
- **Habana Vieja** The old city, filled with elegant mansions, centuries-old churches and cobblestone plazas. See p.157
- **Trekking in Sierra Maestra** Head to Cuba's highest mountain range for its revolutionary landmarks and excellent hiking trails. See p.202
- **Viñales valley** Bizarre limestone hillocks lend this valley a dreamlike air. See p.169
- **Baracoa** Isolated by verdant mountains, quirky Baracoa has retained much of its charm and hospitality. See p.193
- **Castillo del Morro San Pedro de la Roca** This colossal fort makes for one of Santiago's most dramatic sights. See p.201

Introduction and Basics

Isolated from the Western world for over thirty years, Cuba burst back onto the international tourist scene a decade ago and hasn't looked back since. Shaped by one of the twentieth century's longest-surviving revolutions, until recently Cuba's image had been inextricably bound up with its politics, rather than its long satiny beaches, offshore cays and jungle-covered peaks. Now, the country is changing and Cuba today is characterized as much as anything by a frenetic sense of transition as it shifts from socialist stronghold to one of the Caribbean's major tourist destinations, running on capitalist dollars.

Yet at the same time, it can seem to visitors that nothing has changed here for decades, even centuries: the classic American cars, moustachioed cigar-smoking farmers, horse-drawn carriages and colonial Spanish architecture all apparently unaffected by the breakneck pace of modernization. Newly erected department stores and shopping malls, state-of-the-art hotels and resorts are the hallmarks of this new, emerging Cuba. This improbable combination of transformation and stasis is symbolic of a country riddled with contradictions and ironies. In a place where taxi drivers earn more than doctors, and where capitalist reforms are seen as the answer to preserving socialist ideals, understanding Cuba is a compelling but never-ending task.

Despite favouritism toward tourists and the crippling **US trade embargo**, there is surprisingly little resentment directed at foreign visitors. In most of the country it's easy to come into **contact with the locals**: the common practice of renting out rooms and opening restaurants in homes allows visitors stronger impressions of Cuba and its people even in a short visit. It's a good thing, too, since Cubans are renowned for their love of a good time. Their energy and spirit are best expressed through **music and dance**, both vital facets of the island's culture. As originators of the most influential Latin music styles, such as *bolero*, *rumba* and *son*, which spawned the most famous of them all – salsa – people in Cuba seem always ready to party.

There are occasional reminders that Cuba is a highly bureaucratic one-party state. Going to the police, finding your hotel room double-booked or simply needing to make an urgent phone call can prove to be frustratingly complicated, making a certain determination and a laid-back attitude essential requirements for a pleasant trip here, particularly for exploring less visited parts of the country. Things are becoming easier all the time, though, with the introduction of a wider variety of more efficient services; unfortunately these improvements also mark an irreversible move away from what makes Cuba unique.

Where to go

No trip to Cuba would be complete without a visit to the capital city, **Havana**, whose time-warped colonial core, Habana Vieja, is crammed with architectural splendours dating back to the sixteenth century. West of the capital, **Pinar del Río** is the best area for getting close to nature. The most accessible resorts for walking are **Las Terrazas** and **Soroa**, but it's the peculiar *mogote* hills of prehistoric **Viñales** valley that attract the most attention.

The country's premier holiday destination and beach resort is **Varadero**, two hours' drive east of Havana, while on the opposite side of the province, the **Península de Zapata** boasts a potent mix of beaches, wildlife excursions and other attractions. Further east, **Trinidad**, a small colonial city, lures coach parties and backpackers in equal numbers. However, the most popular destinations in this central part of the country are the luxurious resorts of **Cayo Coco** and **Cayo Guillermo**. Beach-goers also won't want to miss **Guardalavaca**, on the northern coast of Holguín province, where

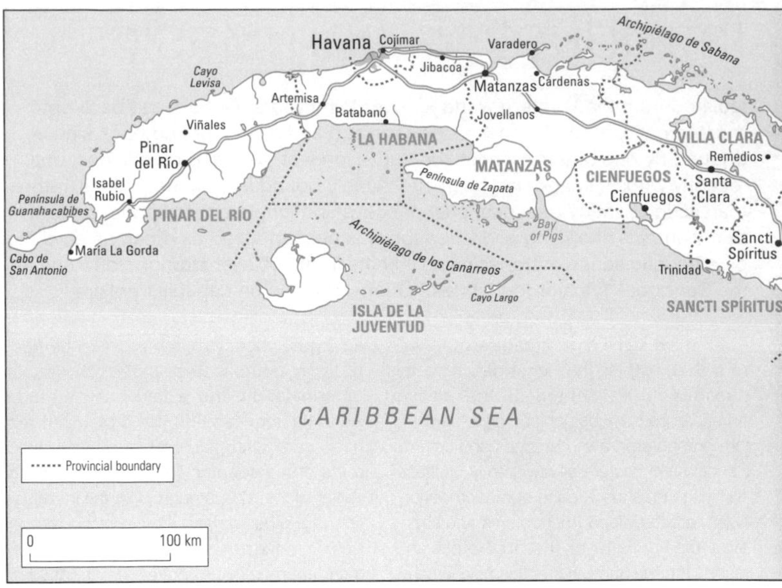

there are ample opportunities for watersports.

While **Guantánamo province**, forming the far eastern tip of the island, is best known for its infamous US naval base, it is the jaunty seaside town of **Baracoa** that is the region's most enchanting spot. The country's most vibrant and energetic city after Havana is **Santiago de Cuba**, on the island's southeast coast, which, like the capital, has a lively historic centre. Trekkers and revolution enthusiasts will want to follow the Sierra Maestra as it snakes west of here into **Granma** province, offering various revolutionary landmarks and nature trails. Finally, lying off the southwest coast of Havana province, luxurious and anodyne **Cayo Largo** is the only sizeable beach resort off the southern coastline of Cuba.

When to go

Cuba generally has a hot and sunny tropical climate. While the average annual temperature is 24°C (75°F), temperatures can drop to 15° (59°F) or lower in January and February (considered winter), especially at night and in the mountains. These months fall in the **dry season**, which runs roughly from November to April. May through October is considered the **wet season**, when you can expect it to rain at least a couple of days during a two-week holiday. Downpours don't usually last long, however, and are quickly followed by sunshine. September and October are the most threatening months of the annual **hurricane** season that runs from June to November.

The **peak tourist season** runs from about December to March and July to August (high summer). Prices and crowds are most rampant in summer when the holiday season for Cubans gets under way. As much of the atmosphere of the smaller resorts is generated by tourists, they can seem somewhat dull out of season – although you'll benefit from lower prices. The cities, particularly Havana and Santiago, are always buzzing and offer good value for money all year round.

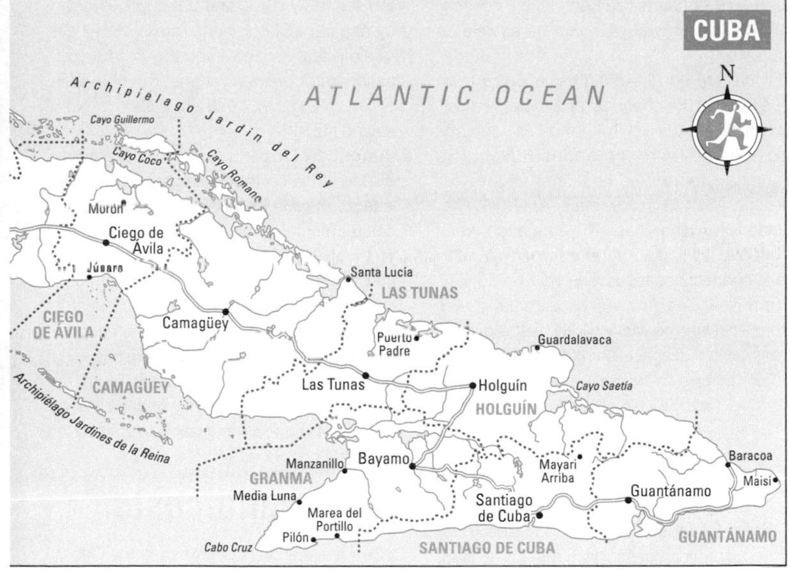

Getting there

The only airlines with **direct scheduled flights** to Cuba from the UK are Cubana, departing three times weekly from London Gatwick, and Air Jamaica, whose only flight leaves on Mondays, also from Gatwick. Though Cubana tends to offer the cheapest flights, it is notoriously unreliable and you should be prepared for delays or, more likely, overbooking. Return fares can be as little as £380 in low season and average about £450 in high season. Both Iberia and Air France run at least four flights a week from London Heathrow and Manchester with a change of plane in Madrid and Paris respectively.

There are no direct flights to Cuba from Ireland, so you'll have to change planes, usually in London, Paris or Madrid. Return flights to Havana from Dublin combining Aer Lingus and British Airways flights start at around £540. Alternatively you can make the whole journey with a single airline; Iberia flies from Dublin to Havana via Madrid for as little as £430.

Since the United States continues to maintain a trade embargo with Cuba **US citizens** are not allowed, by their own government, to travel there freely and must instead apply for a licence. If you think you have a case for being granted permission to travel, perhaps as a journalist, student or as part of a humanitarian mission, contact the Licensing Division, Office of Foreign Assets Control, US Department of the Treasury, 1500 Pennsylvania Ave NW, Washington DC 20220 (☎202/622-2480, ⓦwww.treas.gov/ofac. You can also get information from the Cuban government through the Cuban Interests Section, 2630 16th St NW, Washington DC 20009 (☎202/797-8609 or 797-8518). For most US nationals who want to visit Cuba for other reasons less acceptable to the US government, like tourism, travel involves catching a flight from a third country. The following are sample APEX fares for round-trip travel from Mexican and Caribbean cities to Havana: Mexico City (US$400); Cancún (US$280); Kingston or Montego Bay (US$226); Nassau (US$179).

Canadians of course are not directly affected by the US embargo and are free to travel to Cuba. Cubana has regular flights from Toronto and Montreal to Havana, as do a number of charter carriers. In low season, APEX fares for this route can be as little as US$210.

There are no direct flights to Cuba from Australasia. The cheapest and most straightforward route is via Tokyo to Mexico City, from where there are frequent flights to Havana; Japan Airlines offer flights for around A$2499 in low season. Otherwise, Canadian Airlines has six flights each week from Sydney to Toronto, from where you can take connections to Havana via Mexico City. From New Zealand, Air New Zealand flies from Auckland to Mexico City, with connections on to Havana, starting from NZ$2578.

For phone numbers of airlines see pp.12–17 and 36–37.

Entry requirements

Citizens of most Western countries must have a ten-year passport, valid for at least six months, a tourist card (*tarjeta de turista*) and an onward ticket. **Tourist cards** are valid for thirty days and although you can buy one from Cuban consulates you will get more efficient service if you buy it from your tour operator or travel agent. The charge in the UK is £15, in Australia A$35, in New Zealand NZ$44.

American citizens (see box below) can travel to Cuba on tourist cards purchased in Canada, Mexico or other countries, and the Cuban authorities will on request stamp the card instead of your passport when you enter and leave Cuba.

Note than you will pass through customs much more smoothly if you have entered the name of a state hotel on your tourist form as your destination. If you don't have an address you may have to pay on the spot for three nights' accommodation in a hotel of the state's choosing.

US citizens

Strangely enough, the letter of US law does not actually prohibit US citizens from being in Cuba, just from spending money there. In practical terms, of course, this amounts to a ban on travel, by all except those approved and "licensed" by the US government. While many Americans see the embargo as cruel and unusual, or at least dated, there are no signs of it being lifted any time soon. The Helms-Burton Act of 1996 allows for fines of up to US$50,000 and the confiscation of property of US citizens who visit Cuba without permission. This is in addition to the already standing threats contained in the Trading with the Enemy Act, which make fines of up to US$250,000 and prison terms of up to ten years theoretically possible. Things change quite often, depending on the direction of the prevailing political winds in the US; for the latest on the current situation, check out the Center for Cuban Studies' website (see box opposite).

Money and costs

Cuba's national unit of currency is the Cuban **peso** or, in Spanish, the *peso cubano*, divided into 100 **centavos**. Banknotes are issued in denominations of 50, 20, 10, 5, 3 and 1. At time of writing US$1 was worth 26 Cuban pesos. In 1995 the government introduced the **convertible peso**, which, though completely worthless outside Cuba, is interchangeable with the dollar and has exactly the same value.

You'll need to keep in mind that pesos, convertible pesos and dollars are all **represented by the dollar sign** ($). The most commonly used qualifiers are *divisas* for dollars and *moneda nacional* for pesos. Thus one peso is often written $1MN. Unless otherwise stated, any reference to pesos in this book will be to Cuban pesos, not convertible pesos, while the $ symbol is used to signify the US dollar only.

All official tourist-oriented facilities, including all state-run hotels, most state-run restaurants and pretty much all goods sold in shops, are charged in **US dollars**. You'll also be expected to pay in dollars for rooms in people's homes, meals in *paladares* (small, privately run restaurants) and most private taxis, though there is some flexibility in these cases. Entrance to cinemas and sports arenas, local buses, snacks bought on the street and food from *agromercados* are all paid for with pesos.

Hard currency is king in Cuba, so it's a good idea to arrive with a supply of dollars in low denominations. Although **travellers' cheques** are easily exchangeable in many banks, a significant number of shops and restaurants still refuse to accept them. Travellers' cheques issued by a US bank are unusable in Cuba, though American Express cheques issued outside of the US are accepted. **Credit cards** – Visa and MasterCard in particular – are more widely accepted, but in most small- to medium-sized towns plastic is useless as a method of payment. Moreover, no card issued by a US bank (including American Express, regardless of country of issue) can be used in Cuba. Credit cards are more useful for obtaining **cash advances**, most efficiently through branches of the Banco Financiero Internacional. There are very few **ATMs** in Cuba and most only accept cards issued by Cuban banks. **Bank opening hours** are usually Monday to Friday 8am to 3pm; at weekends, when most banks are closed, it is virtually impossible to obtain money.

Accommodation aside – for which you should expect to pay a minimum of US$15–25 – your **daily budget** can vary quite considerably. Eating street-vendor type meals, you can get away with a daily food budget of just US$5, or about 125 pesos. At restaurants and *paladares* allow US$5–15 for food; add at least another US$5 if you want to attend a live performance or go to a club. If you **travel** by tourist bus expect to pay upwards of US$15 per journey. Private taxis can sometimes work out cheaper than buses if you share them with three or four other dollar-paying travellers – this way, a 100km trip can cost as little as US$5–10 each. A rental car will add another US$50-70 a day.

Information, websites and maps

There is a shortage of printed travel literature in Cuba and getting hold of any kind of **tourist information**, particularly outside the major resorts, can be difficult. Before you leave home, therefore, it's worth contacting the nearest branch of the **Cuban Tourist Board (ⓦwww.cubatravel.cu/oficinas.asp)**, which has information for visitors.

Finding a trustworthy **map** once in Cuba is also difficult. The exception is the invaluable *Guía de Carreteras* (US$6), a national road map which also has basic street maps for Havana and Varadero.

All areas of the **media** in Cuba are subject to tight censorship and are closely controlled by the state, much to the dismay of many Cubans. *Granma*, the only national daily **newspaper**, openly declares itself the official mouthpiece of the Cuban Communist Party.

Getting around

Mastering Cuban transport can be a fascinating if sometimes frustrating experience, and understanding its nuances can take years. However, with the introduction of a

Websites

While the majority of **websites** on Cuba are US-based – many of them politically oriented and quite interesting – there is also an increasing number of Cuban state-run sites.

ⓦ**www.afrocubaweb.com** Fantastically detailed site covering absolutely anything even remotely connected to Afro-Cuban issues, from history and politics to music and dance.
ⓦ**www.cubatravel.cu** The Cuban Ministry of Tourism site with practical information and advice on a wide range of issues from customs regulations to accommodation and transport.
ⓦ**www.cubaupdate.org** An excellent source of information that details tours organized by the Center for Cuban Studies.
ⓦ**www.cubaweb.cu** The Cuban government's official site, in co-operation with a Canadian internet service provider, includes news reports from the Cuban press, plus information on travel, investment and many other subjects.
ⓦ**www.treas.gov/ofac** The US government's official contribution to the debate – with a detailed presentation of the terms of the sanctions against Cuba.

new bus service, a proliferation of car rental agencies and an increase in the fleet of state-run taxis, it's become much easier for the dollar-paying traveller to get around the country.

Hitching a lift in Cuba, or *coger botella* as it is known locally, is as common as catching a bus. Crowds of people wait by bridges and junctions along the major roads waiting for vehicles to stop. Drivers often ask for a few pesos, and tourists, though they are likely to attract a few puzzled stares, are welcome to join in. The usual precautions apply.

By bus

Bus travel, the most common method of transport, usually means long queues and overcrowding, and is further exacerbated by the complicated system of timetables and tickets. There are two separate services for **inter-provincial routes**, one operated by Astro, the other by Víazul. Though technically available to anyone willing to pay dollars, **Víazul** (☎7/81-14-13) is effectively a bus service for tourists. Although currently limited to just seventeen cities and resorts, it is the quickest and most reliable way to get around independently.

Most bus routes are still the exclusive domain of **Astro** (☎7/70-33-97). Even if you choose a destination covered by Víazul you may decide that the Astro fare (usually between half and two-thirds of the price of a Víazul ticket) justifies the less comfortable conditions.

Foreign passport-holders are obliged to pay for their **ticket** in dollars but by doing so they avoid the queuing and waiting-list ritual which dominates the public transport system. Most town or city bus stations have a separate office where dollar tickets are sold. Seats for dollar passengers are limited; to guarantee a seat you should arrive at the bus station at least an hour before departure. Before you do that, however, ring to check whether the bus is actually leaving, particularly if you are in a non-touristy area.

By train

Cuba is the only country in the Caribbean with a functioning rail system and though slow, trains are a good way of getting a feel for the landscape. You'll need your passport to buy a ticket, which you must do at least an hour before departure, direct from the train station. The **main line**, which links Havana with Santiago, also serves Matanzas, Santa Clara, Ciego de Ávila, Camagüey and Las Tunas. **Normal trains**, which are perfectly comfortable, leave once daily, stopping at all the main-line stations, and fares work out at around US$4 per 100km; Havana to Santiago, for example, costs US$35. The ***especial* service** runs every three days and is more expensive (US$43 from Havana to Santiago), but the trains are air conditioned and significantly quicker.

By car

The best way to get around the island is in your own **rental car**. Traffic jams are almost unheard of and away from the cities many roadways are almost empty.

There is a confusing array of car rental agencies, despite the fact that they are all state-run firms. Apart from **prices**, which are rarely less than US$35 a day and more often between US$50 and US$70, the essential difference between the agencies is the type and make of car. **Havanautos** (Calle 1ra esq. 0, Miramar, Havana ☎7/23-98-15 or 23-96-57, reservations ☎24-06-47 or 24-06-48) and **Transautos** (Calle 40-a esq. 3ra, Miramar, Havana ☎7/24-76-44, reservations 24-55-32) have the most branches throughout the island as well as the widest range of vehicles. For any chance of getting a car that isn't the most expensive model, it's essential to book at least a day in advance. All agencies require you to have held a driving licence from your home country or an international licence for at least a year, and that you be at least 21.

Driving is on the **right-hand side** of the road. There is only one **motorway** in the whole of Cuba - *el autopista* – and from Havana it cuts through the country down to the eastern edge of Sancti Spíritus province and in the other direction to the provincial capital of Pinar del Río; it fluctuates between six and eight lanes. Road markings are almost non-existent and the 100km/hr speed limit would undoubtedly lead to accidents were there more traffic. The main alternative route for most long-distance journeys is the two-lane **Carretera Central**, a more scenic though far more congested road with an 80km/hr speed limit. The quality of **minor roads** varies enormously and potholes are commonplace. Driving anywhere outside the cities is dangerous at night, but to mountain resorts like Viñales or Topes de Collantes it's positively suicidal. The high proportion of cyclists on the road (the vast majority without lights) and the amount of horse-drawn transport are also cause for caution.

By taxi

Taxis have become one of the most popular expressions of private enterprise. The official **metered state taxis** are the easiest to spot and getting hold of one by telephone isn't usually a problem. Cost depends primarily on the size of the car. For the smallest hatchback taxi in a provincial town you will be charged around 30 centavos per kilometre, whilst in Havana a saloon car can cost as much as 90 centavos per kilometre, with luxury taxis even pricier.

As ubiquitous are individually owned cars, predominantly 1950s American classics or Ladas, which are run as taxis by their owners. The local name for these is *máquinas* or *taxis particulares* but those that carry tourists are referred to throughout this guide as **private taxis**. Officially, drivers can charge in either dollars or pesos, depending on their licence, but most will try to charge tourists in dollars. Intra-city journeys typically cost between US$2 and US$5, but negotiation is part and parcel of the unofficial system. For longer trips, there is usually a specific area of a town, invariably next door to a bus station, where taxis wait for long-distance passengers. As a rough indicator, a driver will be looking for between US$20 and US$30 per 100km.

Peso taxis are known as *colectivos*, into which drivers fit as many passengers as possible. More akin to a privately run bus service, they are used almost exclusively by Cubans and can be flagged down from the roadside. It is generally accepted in Havana that a trip within the city in a *colectivo* will cost ten pesos. The rest of the country is similar.

Accommodation

Broadly speaking, **accommodation** in Cuba falls into two types: state and private. You'll find at least one state hotel in every large town, for which you should budget at least US$30 per room per night. Private accommodation, in *casas particulares*, works out cheaper at between US$20 and US$30. Only in major tourist areas like Havana will you need to pay more. At the higher-end state hotels, expect to pay US$100 or more a night. During low season, some hotels lower their rates by about ten percent.

State-owned **tourist hotels** are the most convenient type of accommodation in Cuba – you can usually get a room by turning up on spec, although reservations are recommended. On arrival, specify how many days you intend to stay to avoid having your room booked by someone else.

For many visitors, staying in *casas particulares* – "private houses" – is an ideal way to gain insight into the country and its people. Like a guesthouse, proprietors rent out rooms in their home. Most offer breakfast and an evening meal for an average of US$5. Touts (called *jineteros* or *intermediarios*) wait to meet potential customers at buses; note that if you're brought to a *casa particular* by one you can expect an extra US$5 per night. Many *casas particulares* operate **illegally** without paying taxes. They are usually no cheaper than their registered counterparts and, although you are not breaking the law by staying in one, if you encounter a problem you will get little sympathy from the authorities.

Campismos, or quasi-**campsites**, are an excellent countryside option, and all provinces have at least one. Not campsites in the conventional sense, they offer basic accommodation in rudimentary concrete cabins. At around US$5 a night per cabin they are extremely reasonable. For more details contact **Cubamar**, Calle 15 no. 752 esq. Paseo Vedado, Havana (ⓣ7/66-25-23 or 30-55-36, ⓔcubamar@mit.cma.net), which runs the best sites.

Food and drink

While you'll often be able to eat decently in Cuba, mealtimes are not the gastronomic delight enjoyed on many other Caribbean islands.

Restaurants are divided into two categories: state restaurants and small, privately run *paladares*. Covering both dollar establishments and peso eateries, **state restaurants** differ greatly in quality – the best offer up tasty meals in congenial settings while the worst are atrocious. Peso restaurants, which you'll find away from the tourist areas, cater essentially to Cubans. The quality tends to be poor, though you can occasionally get a passable meal very cheaply. As a visitor you're more likely to eat in the dollar establishments which, particularly in the large cities and tourist areas, have better-quality, more varied food – often including some international dishes, like Chinese and Italian. By way of contrast, state-run **road-side cafés** are unhygienic and poorly run and should be avoided.

Paladares are a godsend. Usually run out of a spare room in someone's home, they offer visitors a chance to sample good Cuban home cooking in an informal atmosphere. They are plentiful in Havana, and while most large towns have at least one, some smaller towns may not have any at all. Prices are uniform, with a meal costing US$5–10. They can seat no more than twelve people and are subject to tight restrictions on what they can serve: beef and seafood are prohibited (though you may be offered them anyway) and lamb and mutton are banned in some provinces. Chicken and pork are always on the menu and although there will be few, if any, set **vegetarian** options, *paladares* are more accommodating than state restaurants in terms of off-menu ordering, making them a good choice for non-meat-eaters.

Also privately run, from front gardens and driveways, the peso **street stalls** dotted around cities and towns are invariably the cheapest places to eat and an excellent choice for home-made snacks and impromptu lunches.

Breakfast in Cuba is commonly a bread roll eaten with eggs. **Lunch** also tends to be light, and following the locals' lead and snacking on maize fritters or *pan con pasta* – bread with a garlic mayonnaise filling – from the peso street stalls is the best bet for a midday meal. The basis for a typical **dinner** is fried chicken or a pork chop or cutlet. Although there is not as much **fish and seafood** as you might expect, what you can get is excellent, particularly the lobster, prawns and tuna. Note that apart from garlic and onion, spices are not really used in Cuban cooking. Accompanying your meal will almost always be **rice and beans**, known as *congrí*, *moros y cristianos* or *arroz con frijoles* depending on preparation. Other traditional **vegetable** side dishes are fried plantain, cassava and salad. The best places to buy **fruit** are the *agromercados*, where you can load up cheaply with whatever is in season. Particularly good are the mangoes, juicy oranges and sweet pineapples.

It's best to stick with **bottled water**, readily available from all dollar shops and hotels; otherwise tap water should be boiled. Canned **soft drinks** are widely available, and peso food stalls serve non-carbonated soft drinks made from powdered packet mix – these cost just a couple of pesos, though you should be cautious about the water they're made with. With the same caveat, try the *granizado* (slush) served from portable street wagons; *guarapo*, a super-sweet frothy drink made from pressed sugar cane; and, a speciality in the east of the island, *Prú*, a refreshing drink fermented from sweet spices and tasting a little like spiced ginger beer. **Coffee** is the beverage of choice for many Cubans, and is served most often as pre-sweetened espresso. **Tea** is less common but is available in the more expensive hotels and better restaurants.

As for alcohol, if you like *ron* (rum) you'll have plenty of options. Havana Club reigns supreme, but also look out for Caribbean Club and Siboney. Cuba is also famous for its **cocktails**, including the ubiquitous **Cuba Libre**. Made from white rum, Coke and a twist of lime, it's second only in popularity to the **Mojito** – white rum, sugar, sparkling water and mint. Lager-type **beer** (*cerveza*) is plentiful and there are some excellent national brands, particularly Cristal, Hatuey and Bucanero.

Phones, post and email

Although improvements have been made in recent years, the **telephone** system in Cuba is still fairly inefficient. **Payphones** are of two distinct types: the newer kind, dollar phones in glass-walled phone cabins, which only accept pre-paid phone cards (available in denominations of US$5, US$10 and US$20); and the older, less reliable type, which only accept 5c peso coins and are useless for international calls. The latter, however, are still the only kind of public phone in the majority of Cuban towns and villages. National rates are reasonable, starting at 5c per minute for calls within the same province. For **international calls**, the cheapest method is to call from a payphone - currently a payphone call to the US or Canada costs US$2 per minute, or US$4.40 per minute to Britain or Australia.

To make a call within the same province you will not need to dial the area code of the place you are calling but instead you will need the **exit code** for the place from where you are making the call. The exit code, available either through the operator or from the telephone directory, can itself depend upon where you are calling to. However, if calling from a prepaid card phone simply dial ⓣ0 followed by the area code and number.

For **interprovincial** calls you will need to dial first the appropriate prefix (usually 0 but there are a number of variations depending on where you are in the country) to get onto the national grid, then the area code, followed finally by the number. Some interprovincial calls are only possible through the operator. If you are consistently failing to get through on a direct line dial ⓣ00.

For international calls without the assistance of an operator, possible from the newer payphones but only on a relatively small proportion of private phones, dial the international call prefix, which is ⓣ119, then the country code, the area code and the number.

Cuba's **postal service** has seen a slight improvement in recent times; it now takes weeks instead of months for airmail to leave the island. If you send anything other than a letter, either inland or overseas, there's a significant chance that it won't arrive at all as pilfering is widespread within the postal system. You should also be aware that letters and packages coming into Cuba are sometimes opened as a matter of policy. **Stamps** are sold in both US dollars and pesos at post offices, from white and blue kiosks marked *Correos de Cuba*, and in many hotels. All large towns and cities have a **post office**, normally open Monday to Saturday from 8am to 6pm. The full range of postal services, including DHL and EMS, is offered in some of the larger hotels, usually at the desk marked *Telecorreos*.

The country code for Cuba is ⓣ53.

There are very few places in Cuba where the general public can get access to the **internet**, and private home connections are forbidden by law. The country's first **cybercafé** is in Havana, in the Capitolio Nacional (see p.159) and remains the most straightforward way to gain access, though there are also now a small number of ETECSA phone cabins providing internet facilities.

Communicating by **email** (as opposed to using the internet itself) has become significantly more commonplace in Cuba in recent years and though it remains rare in homes there are increasing numbers of *casas particulares* now with access to it. Nevertheless, there are very few places from where you can send or receive an email and outside the major cities and resorts it will be more or less impossible.

Opening hours, holidays and festivals

Cuban offices are normally open for business between 9am and 5pm Monday to Friday, with many of them closing for a one hour break anywhere between noon and 2pm. Shops are generally open 9am to 6pm Monday to Saturday, normally closing for lunch, while the shopping malls and department stores in Havana stay open as late as 8pm. Sunday trading is increasingly common, with most places open until noon or 1pm, longer in the major resorts. Banks generally operate Monday to Friday 8am to 3pm, but this varies.

Cultural **festivals**, like the International Theatre Festival and the International Festival of New Latin American Film have won Havana global applause. Lesser-known festivals celebrating dance, literature, and other arts, and a whole host of smaller events in other provinces are also worthwhile. If you're around in July, Cuba's main **carnival**, which takes place in Santiago, is unmissable; also well worth checking out are the carnival celebrations held in Havana.

Public holidays and festivals

Public holidays

January 1 Liberation Day. Anniversary of the triumph of the revolution.
May 1 International Workers' Day
July 25–27 Celebration of the day of national rebellion.
October 10 Anniversary of the start of the Wars of Independence.
December 25 Christmas

Festivals

January

Cubadanza Gran Teatro, Habana Vieja ⓣ 7/31-13-57, ⓔparadis@turcult.get.cma.net. Cuban contemporary dance festival featuring performers from around the country.
Havana Jazz Festival Teatro Nacional, Havana ⓣ7/ 79-60-11. See the best of Cuban jazz, including the legendary Irakere with Chucho Valdés, play around the town at different venues. International guest stars also feature.

July

Fiesta of Fire Festival Santiago de Cuba ⓣ226/2-35-69, ⓔupec@mail.info-com. etecsa.cu. Santiago's weeklong celebration of Caribbean music and dance culture takes place at the beginning of July.
Santiago Carnival Santiago de Cuba ⓣ 226/2-33-02, ⓔburostgo@binanet.lib.cult.cu. Cuba's most exuberant carnival holds Santiago in its thrall in the first two weeks of July with costumed parades and congas, salsa bands and late-night parties.
Havana Carnival ⓣ7/62-38-83, ⓔrosalla@cimex.com.cu. Festivities in Havana have been moved from February to late July/early August, with parades and street parties around the city centre for about three weeks.

August

Cubadanza Gran Teatro, Habana Vieja ⓣ7/31-13-57, ⓔparadis@turcult.get. cma.net. The summer season of the Cuban contemporary dance festival which draws performers from all over the country to Havana.

September

Havana International Theatre Festival Havana ⓣ7/31-13-57, ⓔparadis@turcult.get.cma.net. Excellent ten-day theatre festival showcasing classics and contemporary Cuban works at various theatres around the city.

December

International Festival of New Latin American Film Havana ⓣ7/55-28-54,ⓔrosalla@cimex.com.cu. One of Cuba's top events, this ten-day film festival combines the newest Cuban films with the finest classics, as well as providing a networking opportunity for leading independent film directors.

Crime and safety

Despite increasing worries about **crime**, Cuba is still one of the safest destinations in the Caribbean and the majority of visitors will experience a trouble-free stay. The worst you're likely to experience is incessant and annoying attention from touts and hustlers, known as *jineteros*. **Women travellers**, however, particularly those travelling solo, should brace themselves for non-stop male attention. While violent sexual attacks are virtually unheard of, unaccompanied women are generally assumed to be on holiday because they're looking for sex. Fortunately, the persistent come-ons will be more irritating than threatening.

The most common assault upon tourists is **bag-snatching** or **pickpocketing**, so take the usual precautions and only carry the minimum amount of cash you require. Also avoid leaving personal possessions on view in a rental car. Some **hotels** are not entirely secure, so put any valuables in the hotel security box, if there is one, or at least stash them out of sight. Registered *casas particulares* are, as a rule, safe. You should

The **emergency number** for the Cuban **police** differs from place to place. In Havana dial ☎82-01-16 or 60-01-06; in Varadero, Trinidad and Santiago dial ☎116.

always carry your **passport** (or a photocopy) as the police sometimes ask to inspect them.

The **police** are generally indifferent to crimes against tourists – and may even try to blame them for not being more vigilant. You may find it more useful to contact **Asistur** (☎7/33-85-27 or 33-89-20), the 24-hour assistance agency, based in Havana and Santiago, which can arrange replacement travel documents, help with financial difficulties and recover lost luggage.

Drugs, specifically marijuana and cocaine, are increasingly common in Cuba. The authorities take a very dim view of drug abuse and prison sentences are often meted out, even for possession of small amounts.

Health

Providing you take common-sense precautions, visiting Cuba poses no particular health risks. It is essential, however, to bring your own **medical kit**, including painkillers and any other supplies you think you might need as they are difficult to buy on the island and the choice is extremely limited.

Cuba's famous free health service does not extend to foreign visitors; in fact the government uses their impressive medical advances to earn extra revenue for the regime. There are specific hospitals, most of them run by Servimed (☎07/24-01-41 or 42) – the institution set up to deal with health tourism – which accept foreign patients. If you do wind up in hospital in Cuba, one of the first things you should do is contact Asistur (see above), who usually deal with insurance claims. For minor complaints you shouldn't have to go further than the hotel doctor. If you're staying in a *casa particular*, your best bet if feeling ill is to inform your host, who should be able to arrange a house-call with the family doctor.

As with much else on the island there are two types of **pharmacies** in Cuba: tourist pharmacies operating in dollars and peso pharmacies for the population at large. The majority are run by Servimed and you should ask for the nearest *clínica internacional* within which they are normally located.

Sports and outdoor activities

On the whole, participatory sports and **outdoor activities** in Cuba are still in the development stage. **Watersports** are the main exception, with dive sites all around the island. Featuring some of the richest and most unspoilt waters in the world, Cuba has great **scuba diving and snorkelling**. As well as reefs there are numerous underwater caves, tunnels and even wrecks. Most of the major beach resorts, including Varadero, Santa Lucía and Guardalavaca, have well-equipped diving centres. Varadero, with its three marinas and two diving clubs, is one of the best places for novice divers.

Hiking is another good option and all three mountain ranges in Cuba feature hiker-friendly resorts. Designated hikes tend to be quite short, rarely more than 5km, and trails are often unmarked and difficult to follow without a local guide. Furthermore, orienteering maps are all but non-existent. This may be all part of the appeal for the more adventurous but it is generally recommended that you hire a guide, especially in adverse weather conditions.

History

Cuba was inhabited for thousands of years before Columbus by Amerindians who had worked their way up through the Antilles from the South American mainland. The last group, the Taíno, who arrived sometime around 1100 AD, were a mostly peaceful people, largely unprepared for the conflict they were to face with the arrival of the Spanish.

On October 27, 1492, **Columbus** landed on the northeastern coast of Cuba. On his second voyage in 1494, he erroneously concluded that Cuba was part of the mainland of Cathay, or China. Not convinced that Columbus had discovered a western route to Asia, Spain's King Ferdinand sent an another expedition to the island, and in 1509 **Diego Velázquez** landed near Guantánamo Bay with three hundred men. Those Indians who were not killed died later from European diseases or the harsh living and working conditions forced upon them.

As Spain consolidated its American empire, Cuba gained importance thanks to its location on the main route to Europe. The population grew slowly, with African **slaves** being imported as early as the 1520s to replace the dwindling indigenous population; by the end of the sixteenth century there was almost no trace of the Taíno natives.

The economy came to be based heavily on **agricultural farming**. Cassava, fruits, coffee, tobacco and sugar were amongst the chief exports and the island slowly became a source of potentially significant wealth. The first half of the eighteenth century saw Cuban society become more sophisticated, as a clear Cuban identity emerged, distinct from that of Spain. By the end of the century the colony had established its first newspaper, theatre and university.

However, economic progress was restricted as the colony was forced to trade exclusively with Spain. This was to change with the **British seizure of Havana**. Engaged in the Seven Years' War against Spain and France, the British sought to weaken the Spanish position by attacking Spain's possessions overseas. On August 12, 1762, the British took control of Havana and opened up new markets in North America and Europe. Within a year, Cuba was back in Spanish hands, but the impact of the British occupation was enormous, as previously unobtainable products flowed into Cuba. In 1776 the newly independent US started trading directly with Cuban merchants.

In 1791 revolution in Haiti, then known as Saint-Domingue, destroyed the sugar industry there and Cuba became the largest producer of sugar in the region. Rising demand and rising prices, combined with scientific advances in the sugar industry and improved transportation on the island during the first half of the nineteenth century, transformed the face of Cuban society.

Meanwhile, as the size of the slave population increased, the conditions of slavery worsened, and **slave rebellions** became more common. The rebellions were symptomatic of an increasingly divided societal structure, one which pitted *criollos* against *peninsulares*, black against white, and the less developed eastern half of the country against the more economically and politically powerful west. A **reformist movement** emerged and grew more and more radical; in the early 1840s, the colonial government reacted with a brutal campaign of repression known as **La Escalera**. The authorities killed hundreds, soldiers were sent over from Spain, and the governor's power was increased to allow repression of even the slightest sign of rebellion.

In 1865 the **Reformist Party** was founded by a group of *criollo* planters, providing the most coherent expression yet of the desire for change. A revolution plotted by a group of landowners, headed by **Carlos Manuel de Céspedes**, got no further than the planning stage when the colonial authorities sent troops to arrest the conspirators. Pre-empting his own arrest on October 10, 1868, Céspedes freed the slaves working at his sugar mill, effectively instigating the **Ten Years War**, the first Cuban war of independence. The **Pact of Zanjón** (1878), signed by the Spanish, ended most of the hostilities but failed to address the fundamental causes of conflict, including political representation for the *criollos* and the end of slavery. It was not until 1886 that **slavery was abolished**, whilst in 1890, when universal suffrage was declared in Spain, Cuba was excluded.

No one did more to stimulate interest in Cuban independence than **José Martí**. From his base in New York he worked tirelessly, trying to gain momentum for the idea of an independent Cuba. In 1892 he founded the **Cuban Revolutionary Party** (PRC), which began to co-ordinate with groups inside Cuba as preparations were laid for a **Second War of Independence**. Martí was killed in his first battle, but the revolutionaries fought their way across the country until on January 1, 1896, they reached Havana province.

Riots in Havana gave the US the excuse they had been waiting for to send in the warship **Maine**, ostensibly to protect US citizens. On February 15, 1898, the *Maine* blew up in Havana harbour, killing 258 people; the US accused the Spanish of sabotage and so began the **Spanish-American War**. To this day the Cuban government remains adamant that the US blew up its own ship in order to justify its intervention in the war, but evidence is inconclusive.

On December 10, 1898, the Spanish signed the **Treaty of Paris,** handing control of Cuba, as well as Puerto Rico and the Philippines, to the US. In 1901 Cuba adopted a new constitution, devised in Washington without any Cuban consultation, which included the **Platt Amendment**, declaring that the US had the right to intervene in Cuban affairs should the independence of the country come under threat. The intention to keep Cuba on a short leash was made even clearer when at the same time a US **naval base was established at Guantánamo Bay**. On May 20, 1902, under these terms, Cuba was declared a **republic** and Tomás Estrada Palma, the first elected Cuban president, headed a long line of US puppets.

With the economy in ruins following the war, **US investors** moved in. Havana and Varadero became flooded with casinos, strip-clubs, hotels and sports clubs, as the island gained a reputation as an anything-goes destination, a reputation enhanced during the years of Prohibition in the US. However, the global economic crisis, which followed the Wall Street Crash in 1929, caused widespread discontent, and opposition to the government became increasingly radical – but was ruthlessly repressed. Amidst the chaos emerged a man who was to shape profoundly the destiny of Cuba.

A young sergeant, **Fulgencio Batista**, staged a coup within the army and replaced most of the officers with men loyal to him. He installed Ramón Grau San Martín as president, and then continued to prop up a series of Cuban presidents until in 1940 he was himself elected.

Batista was not, at least during the early years, the hated man that communist Cuba would have people believe. Some of his policies had widespread support and, despite the backing he received from the US, he was no puppet. By the time he lost power in 1944 Cuba was a more independent and socially just country than it had been at any other time during the pseudo-republic. Carlos Prío Socarrás led the country until 1952 when Batista, who had left Cuba after his defeat in 1944, returned to fight another election. On March 10, 1952, two days before the election, Batista, fearing failure, staged a **military coup** and seized control of the country. He abolished the constitution and went on to establish a dictatorship bearing little if any resemblance to his previous term as Cuban leader.

Amongst the candidates for congress in the 1952 election was **Fidel Castro**, a young lawyer who saw his political ambitions dashed when Batista seized power. Effectively frozen out of constitutional politics by Batista's intolerance of opposition, on July 26, 1953, Castro and around 125 others attacked an army barracks at **Moncada** in Santiago de Cuba. Castro regarded the attack "as a gesture which will set an example for the people of Cuba". The attack failed and those who weren't shot fled into the mountains where they were soon caught. Castro would certainly have been shot had his captors taken him back to the barracks, but a sympathetic police sergeant kept him in the relative safety of the police jail. A trial followed in which Castro gave what has become one of his most famous speeches, uttering the immortal words, "Condemn me if you will. History will absolve me." He was sentenced to fifteen years' imprisonment but had served less than three when, under popular pressure, he was released and sent into exile.

Now based in Mexico, Castro set about organizing a revolutionary force to take back to Cuba; amongst his recruits was an Argentinian doctor named **Ernesto "Che" Guevara**. They called themselves the **Movimiento 26 de Julio**, the 26th of July Movement. Waging a war based on guerrilla tactics, the rebels gained the upper hand against Batista's forces. The army surrendered to the rebels and Fidel Castro began a victory march across the country, arriving in Havana on January 8, 1959.

Though the revolutionary war had ended, this date marks only the beginning of what in Cuba is referred to as **the Revolution**. The **Agrarian Reform Law** of May 1959 set the tone, by which the land, much of it foreign-owned, was either nationalized or redistributed amongst the rural population. **Education** became the focus for the reshaping of the country, while **public health** saw great gains in the early years of the revolution and is an area that continues to elicit praise. As the decade wore on, the regime became more intolerant of dissenting voices, declaring all those who challenged government policy to be counter-revolutionaries.

During the first few years of the revolution, as Cuba–US relations soured and the revolution seemed to be swinging further to the left, the Cuban upper-middle and upper classes sought refuge overseas, predominantly in the US. Between 1960 and 1962 around 200,000 **emigrants** left Cuba, forming large exile communities, especially in Florida.

As huge sectors of Cuban industry were **nationalized** and foreign businesses, most of them US-owned, found themselves dispossessed, the US government retaliated by freezing purchases of Cuban sugar, restricting exports and then, in 1961, breaking off diplomatic relations. The US backed counter-revolutionary forces within Cuba as well as terrorist campaigns aimed at sabotaging the state apparatus. Finally, President Kennedy, opted for all-out invasion and on April 17, 1961, a military force of Cuban exiles, trained and equipped in the US, landed at the **Bay of Pigs** in southern Matanzas. However, the revolutionaries were ready for them and the whole operation ended within 72 hours.

In December of that year, in the face of economic and political isolation from the US, the Cuban leader declared himself a Marxist-Leninist. The benefits for Cuba were immediate as the **Soviet Union** agreed to buy Cuban sugar at artificially high prices whilst selling them petroleum at well below its market value. Then, in 1962, at Castro's request, the Soviets installed over forty **missiles** on the island. Kennedy declared an embargo on any military weapons entering Cuba. Krushchev ignored it, and Soviet ships loaded with more weapons made their way across the Atlantic. Neither side would back down and nuclear weapons were prepared for launch in the US. A six-day stalemate followed, after which a deal was finally struck and the world breathed a collective sigh of relief – the **Cuban Missile Crisis** had passed.

The **1960s** saw new economic policies aimed at reducing Cuba's dependence on sugar production. However, the mass exodus of professionals during the early years of the decade, coupled with the crippling impact of the US embargo, made this all but impossible. In the end, Cuba became even more dependent on sugar than it had been prior to the revolution.

In 1975 the government adopted its first **Five Year Plan**, setting relatively realistic targets for growth and production. With rises in the price of sugar on the world market and increased Soviet assistance, there were tangible improvements. The policy changes were carried on into the next decade as the economy continued to make modest improvements, though the mass exodus of 125,000 Cubans in the **Mariel boatlift** of 1980 demonstrated that, for many, times were still hard. As more private enterprise was permitted, however, Castro became alarmed at the number of people giving up their state jobs and in 1986 issued his **Rectification of Errors**. The economy returned to centralization and, with increasing sums being ploughed into defence, Cuba survived only with heavy Soviet support.

In 1989 the bubble burst. The collapse of the Soviet Union led to a loss of over eighty percent of Cuba's trade. In 1990, the government declared the beginning of the **Special Period**, a euphemism that essentially meant compromise and sacrifice for all Cubans. Public transport deteriorated dramatically as the country lost almost all of its fuel imports, strict rationing of food was introduced, and power cuts became frequent.

In 1992, the US government took advantage of Cuba's crisis to tighten the trade embargo further as thousands of Cubans risked their lives trying to escape the country across the Florida Straits. Forced to make huge ideological readjustments, the government embarked on one of its most ideologically risky journeys yet, when, in August 1993, the **US dollar** was declared legal tender. With this came other reforms as the Cubans sought to rebuild the economy by appealing to the worldwide **tourist trade**.

Former President Jimmy Carter's visit to Cuba in May of 2002 was the first visit to Cuba by a former or sitting US leader since 1959. While Carter promoted reconciliation with the US, and expressed his support for easing the embargo, President George W. Bush vowed to keep the embargo in place until Castro implements democratic reforms. Compounding the situation around the same time was the Bush administration's inclusion of Cuba in the "Axis of Evil".

The economic hardships following the collapse of the Soviet bloc and the measures taken by the government to deal with them have made Cuba's lack of social and **political freedoms** more apparent than at any time since the 1960s. However, whether Cuba is the country decried in right-wing circles as suffering at the hands of a dictator or, as more moderate pundits suggest, a country whose people would elect a similar government were they not denied the privilege, many Cubans support the ideologies of the revolution, even though they feel frustrated by their political impotence. So convinced are they that the present situation will last forever that it is not uncommon to hear people surmise that *if* Fidel dies, rather than *when*, things may change.

3.1

Havana and around

With five times as many inhabitants as the next biggest Cuban city, **Havana** is in a class of its own. Nowhere else are the contradictions which have come to characterize the country as pronounced as they are here in the capital. Restoration projects have returned some of the finest colonial architecture in the Caribbean to its original splendour, whilst whole neighbourhoods, overcrowded and dirty, wait for their first coat of paint in decades. There is a sense that Havana is on the move, with dollars pouring in, new nightspots appearing regularly and an increasing variety of products in shops which, not long ago, either didn't exist or stood empty. Yet, on the other hand, time stands still, or even goes backwards, in a city where 1950s Chevrolets, Buicks and Oldsmobiles cruise the roads and significant numbers of people seem to spend most of the day in the street or on their crumbling, nineteenth-century doorsteps. Although the tourist industry and US dollar are infiltrating every level of life in the capital, the city is far from a slave to tourism. Cuban **culture** is at its most exuberant here, with an abundance of theatres, cinemas, concert venues and art galleries. Along with Santiago, Havana is host to the country's most diverse **music scene,** where world-famous salsa and bolero orchestras and bands ply their trade while, bubbling under the surface, the newer rock and hip-hop subcultures are gaining momentum.

East of the city are the region's best beaches, including the top-notch **Playas del Este**. South of the city is the **Museo Ernest Hemingway**, the writer's long-time Cuban residence, while slightly further west, the impressive **Jardín Botánico Nacional** offers some picturesque scenery.

Havana

Founded on the western banks of a fabulous natural harbour, what was once the entire city of **HAVANA** now forms the most captivating part of **Habana Vieja**, the old city and the capital's tourist centre. This UNESCO-declared World Heritage Site is one of crumbling magnificence and restored beauty. Any sightseeing you do will fan out from here, taking in the fine museums, colonial buildings, elegant plazas, sweeping boulevards and narrow, atmospheric streets bristling with life.

Most visitors restrict themselves to Habana Vieja and **Vedado**, where many of the post-colonial mansions have been converted into public works and ministry offices or museums. The best way to appreciate Vedado's compact, quiet suburban streets is on foot. From here, you could walk the couple of kilometres to the famous **Plaza de la Revolución**, where giant monuments to the two most famous icons of the Cuban struggle for independence, Che Guevara and José Martí, present unmissable photo opportunities. Beyond Vedado to the west, on the other side of the Río Almendares, **Miramar** – modelled on mid-twentieth-century Miami – ushers in yet another change in the urban landscape. A commercial district is emerging on its western fringes, accompanied by a number of luxury hotels, whilst some of Havana's most sophisticated restaurants are scattered around Miramar's leafy streets.

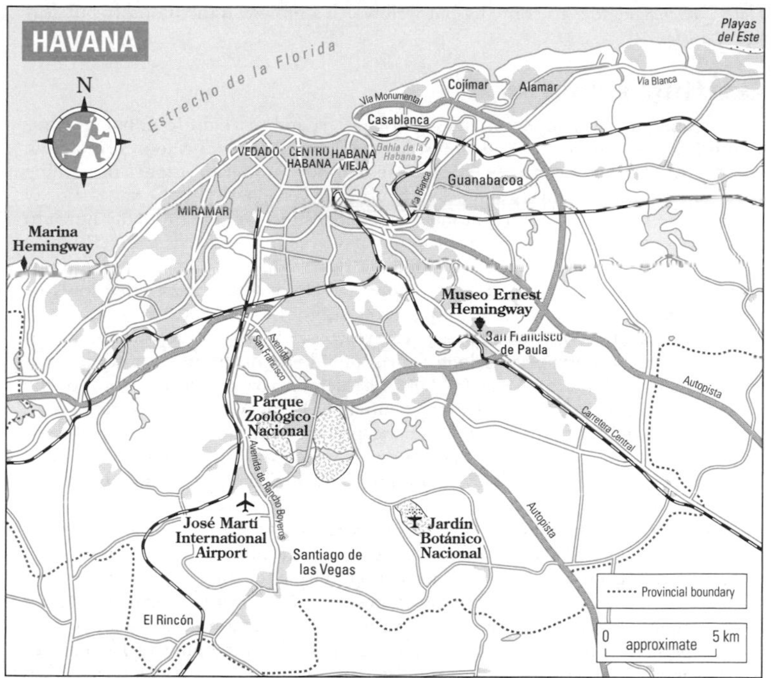

Arrival and information

All international flights land at **José Martí International Airport**, about 15km south of the city centre. The vast majority deposit passengers at Terminal Three where most of the airport services are concentrated, though there are **car rental desks** in each of the three terminals. It's most likely you'll take a **taxi**; the half-hour journey into Havana shouldn't cost much more than US$15.

Arriving by **bus**, you'll be dropped off at either the **Víazul terminal** (☎81-14-13 or 7/881-56-52), over the road from the city zoo, or the Astro-operated **Estación de Omnibus** (☎79-24-56), near the Plaza de la Revolución. Both bus stations are a US$3–5 taxi ride from most centrally located hotels, and there's a car rental desk at the Víazul terminal. **Trains** pull in at the **Estación Central de Ferrocarriles** (☎61-85-40 or 7/863-58-62) in Habana Vieja, where you'll probably have to find yourself a private taxi or one of Havana's army of bicitaxis. If you arrive on one of the two or three **cruise ships** that dock in Havana every week, you will disembark at the splendid **Terminal Sierra Maestra** (☎62-19-25), facing the Plaza de San Francisco in Habana Vieja.

The state-run **Infotur** operates several **information centres**, with the best-stocked found at Obispo e/ Bernaza y Villegas in Habana Vieja (daily 9am–7pm; ☎33-33-33), and in Playa at 5ta. Ave. y 112 (daily 9am–6pm; ☎24-70-36). You can book rooms and excursions through them, though for a better choice of **maps and guides**, head for El Navegante at Mercaderes no. 115 e/ Obispo y Obrapía, Habana Vieja (☎57-10-38).

The free weekly **listings guide,** *Cartelera*, comes out every Thursday and is available in most of the four- and five-star hotels, but the most reliable supplier is the

Hotel Nacional. Harder to come by, but well worth a browse, is the monthly publication *La Isla*..

Getting around

There's only one way to experience Habana Vieja and that's on foot, but **getting around** the rest of the city will almost inevitably involve a taxi ride of some kind. Most of the central sections of Havana are laid out on a grid system and finding your way around is relatively simple, particularly in Vedado, where the vast majority of streets are known by either a number or a letter: streets running roughly north to south are known either by an even number or a letter between A and P, whilst those running east to west have odd numbers. Habana Vieja is a little more complicated, not least because the narrower, more densely packed streets allow less forward vision; the obvious reference point is the seafront to the north.

There are plenty of official tourist **taxis,** which will take you across the city for around US$5. It shouldn't take long to flag one down in the main hotel districts and particularly along the Malecón, but to be certain you can always head for the *Hotel Nacional* in Vedado or the Parque Central in Habana Vieja. However, the most stylish way to travel, and no more expensive, is in any number of vintage pre-revolutionary cars found all over the city, most of which operate as both official and unofficial taxis. To take in the surroundings at a slower pace, **bicitaxis** (three-wheeled, two-seater bicycle cabs) are ideal though not necessarily any cheaper than a car; a fifteen-minute ride costs between US$2 and US$3. Another inexpensive option, three-wheeled novelty motor scooters encased in large yellow spheres and known as **cocotaxis** are usually found waiting outside the *Hotel Inglaterra*.

Buses are overcrowded and infrequent and there is no route information at bus stops, though if you decide to brave it, your journey will cost no more than 40 centavos (less than 3¢). For tourists, and looking more like something you would see touring around a theme park, the **Tren Turístico** (sometimes referred to locally as *el trencito*) runs from the Palacio de las Convenciones in Miramar all the way to Habana Vieja via the Malecón. Departure times are infrequent, though you can flag it down anywhere along the route; fares start at US$2.

Accommodation

Accommodation in the capital is abundant and in most of the main areas you'll find rooms starting from US$25 – as well as those at upwards of US$200 a night. You'd do well to make a **reservation**, particularly in high season (November to April) when the town is chock-full. Many visitors choose to stay in the state hotels in **Habana Vieja**, handy for many of the key sights and well served by restaurants and bars. Quieter **Vedado** features some of the city's more spectacular *casas particulares,* but you'll need transport to make the trip to Habana Vieja.

Habana Vieja

Caribbean Paseo del Prado no. 164 e/ Colón y Refugio ⓣ60-82-33, ⓕ60-94-79. Cheap option within easy walking distance of the Parque Central; rooms are a bit poky and many have no windows. ❸

Casa de Eugenio Barral García San Ignacio no. 656 e/ Jesús María y Merced ⓣ62-98-77. Deep in southern Habana Vieja, this exceptional large-apartment *casa particular* with very hospitable landlords is spotlessly clean and beautifully furnished with antiques. The three double bedrooms all have A/C and one has a TV. Price includes full breakfast. ❷

Casa de Fefita y Luís Aguacate no. 509, apto.403, e/ Sol y Muralla ⓣ61-32-10 or 7/867-64-33. On the fourth floor of a modern building in the heart of the old city, this small self-contained *casa particular* provides fantastic views over Habana Vieja. The double bedroom has A/C and the lounge has a TV, video and fridge-freezer. ❷

Hostal Conde de Villanueva (aka *Hostal del Habano*) Mercaderes esq. Lamparilla ⓣ62-92-93, ⓕ62-96-82, ⓔhconde@villanueva.ohch.cu. Despite its relatively small size this place boasts a fantastic cellar-style restaurant, a wonderful courtyard and a relaxing smokers' lounge and bar. ❺

Hostal Valencia Oficios no. 53 esq. Obrapía ⓣ67-10-37 and 7/861-64-23, ⓕ60-56-28, ⓔhostales@hvhc.ohcch.cu. Plain but pleasant rooms in a beautiful building that feels more like a large house than a small hotel. Attractions include a cobbled-floor courtyard with hanging vines. ❹

Inglaterra Paseo del Prado no. 416 esq. San Rafael, Parque Central ⓣ60-85-93 to 97, ⓕ60-82-54, ⓔreserva@gcingla.gca.cma.net. This classic nineteenth-century hotel superbly located on the Parque Central has become rather complacent and could do with some inspiration. However, the atmospheric interior is full of genuine colonial hallmarks and the rooms are of a high standard. ❺

Vedado

Bruzón Calle Bruzón no. 217 e/ Pozos Dulces y Boyeros ⓣ57-56-84. More like a youth hostel than a hotel; the lack of frills or hot water is balanced by the reasonable price. Near the Plaza de la Revolución. ❷

Casa de Angela Arenal Calle 6 no. 620 e/25 y 27 ⓣ3-72-09. A *casa particular* with three double rooms, one with private bath, in an airy white colonial house. The covered patio with a canopy of hibiscus, the pretty gardens and off-road parking make this an excellent choice. ❷

Casa de Mélida Jordán Calle 25 no. 1102 e/ 6 y 8, ⓣ3-52-19, ⓔmelida@qirazul.com. Extremely professional *casa particular* offering three top-quality rooms with mod cons. Beautiful grounds match the elegant 1950s house, while the friendly owners do their utmost to make you feel at home. ❷

Habana Libre Calle 23 esq. L ⓣ33-40-11, ⓕ33-31-41, ⓦwww.solmeliacuba.com.Large, slick city hotel with a terrace pool, three restaurants, numerous bars and a cabaret. ❼

Nacional Calle 0 esq. 21 ⓣ33-35-64, ⓕ33-51-71. The top choice of visiting celebrities, this handsome hotel looks like an Arabian palace and is deservedly recognized as one of Havana's best. Beautiful rooms, smooth service and excellent facilities. ❼

Habana Vieja

Bursting with centuries-old buildings and buzzing with a strong sense of the past, **Habana Vieja** – or Old Havana – is by far the richest sightseeing area in the city. Its narrow streets, refined colonial mansions, countless churches, cobblestone plazas and sixteenth-century fortresses make it one of the most complete colonial urban centres in the Americas. Yet there is much more to Habana Vieja than its physical makeup. Unlike many of the world's major cities, the tourist centre of Havana is also home to a large proportion of the city's residents, with some of its poorest families crammed into the very buildings that tourists ogle at.

The **Plaza de la Catedral** and the nearby **Plaza de Armas** are both good starting points for your visit, while for the other unmissable sights head up **Obispo**, Habana Vieja's busiest street, to the **Parque Central**. If you intend to do all your sightseeing in one fell swoop you might want to restrict yourself to a maximum of three or four museums, as the half-hearted displays and incoherent collections which occupy many of them can become disheartening, though several of the city's museums are quite excellent, most notably the **Museo de la Revolución** and the **Museo Nacional de Bellas Artes**.

A word of warning: Habana Vieja is the **bag-snatching** centre of the city, with an increasing number of petty thieves working the streets, so take the usual precautions. Even at night, however, there is very rarely any violent crime.

Plaza de la Catedral

The **Plaza de la Catedral**, in northeastern Habana Vieja, is one of the most architecturally coherent squares in the old city, enclosed on three sides by a set of symmetrical, eighteenth-century, aristocratic residences. The striking **Catedral de la Habana** (Mon–Sat 10.30am–4pm, Sun 9.30am–noon; Mass at 10.30am; free), hailed as the consummate example of the Cuban Baroque style, dominates the plaza with its swirling detail, curved edges and cluster of columns. While the less spectacular interior bears an endearing resemblance to a local church, it features lavishly framed portraits by French painter Jean Baptiste Vermay and other artwork.

Opposite the cathedral, the Casa de los Condes de Casa Bayona, built in 1720,

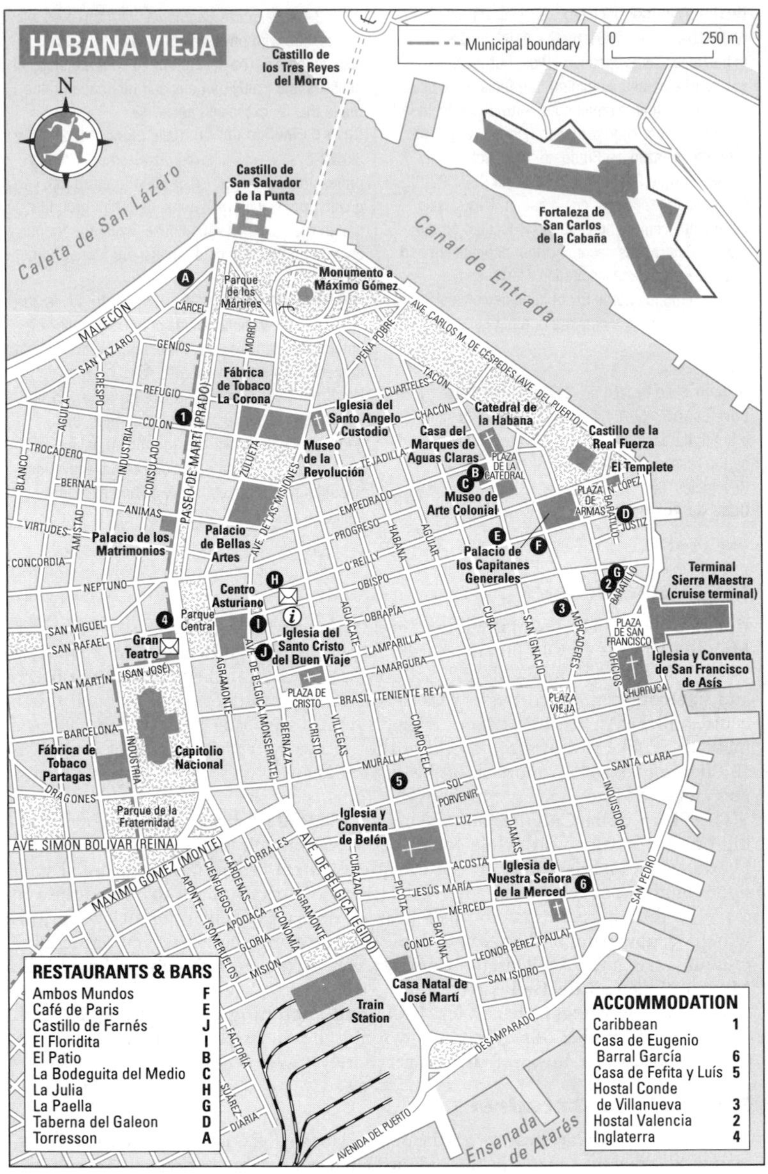

houses the **Museo de Arte Colonial** (daily 9am–7pm; US$2). Its comprehensive collection of well-preserved, mostly nineteenth-century, furniture and ornaments offers a clear insight into aristocratic living conditions during the later years of Spanish rule in Cuba. The predominantly European-made artefacts have been collected from colonial residences around the city and include mahogany dressers, gold and porcelain vases and crystal candlesticks. The most sophisticated of the colonial mansions on the plaza is the **Casa del Marques de Aguas Claras**. Its serene fountain-centred courtyard encompassed by pillar-propped arches and simple coloured-glass portals is actually part of the delightful *El Patio* restaurant (see p.163), so you'll need to eat there to see it.

Plaza de Armas and the Castillo de la Real Fuerza

A couple of blocks southeast of the Plaza de la Catedral, on San Ignacio and then on O'Reilly, the area around the **Plaza de Armas**, the oldest and most animated of Habana Vieja's squares, was where Havana established itself as a city in the second half of the sixteenth century. Based around an attractive landscaped leafy core, at its busiest the plaza seethes with tourists as live music wafts from *La Mina* restaurant in the corner.

The refined **Palacio de los Capitanes Generales**, on the western side of the plaza, was the seat of the Spanish government from the time of its inauguration in 1791 to the end of the Spanish-American War in 1898. It's now home to one of Havana's best museums, the **Museo de la Ciudad** (daily 9.30am–6.30pm; US$2, US$1 extra for guided tour), a fine representation of the city's colonial heritage. A number of the upstairs rooms have been precisely restored, including the sumptuous Salón del Trono (Throne Room) with its dark-red, satin-lined walls intended for royal visits (though in fact no Spanish king or queen ever did visit colonial Cuba). Most striking is the Salón Dorado (Gold Room), where the governor of the city used to receive his guests amidst golden furniture and precious porcelain.

There's more to see around the rest of the square, particularly in the **Museo Nacional de Historia Natural** (Tues–Fri 9.30am–5.30pm, Sat & Sun 9.30am–4pm; US$3), on the corner of Obispo and Oficios. The essentials are covered on the ground floor, where models and interactive video displays help tell the history of life on earth, while one floor up, Cuban wildlife is the dominant theme.

In the square's northeastern corner, the incongruous classical Greek architecture of **El Templete** church (daily 9.30am–6pm; US$1) marks the exact spot of the foundation of Havana and the city's first Mass in 1519. In the same corner, just beyond the northeastern border of the plaza, is the **Castillo de la Real Fuerza**, a heavy-set sixteenth-century fortress surrounded by a moat. It is placed well back from the mouth of the bay, a location which allowed the English, in 1762, to take control of Havana without ever coming into the firing-range of the fortress's cannon. Today the ground floor houses an excellent collection of ceramic art in the **Museo de la Cerámica** (daily 8.30am–6.30pm; US$1), where pre-Columbian-style vases sit alongside quirky modern pieces, such as a pottery typewriter.

Parque Central

From the Plaza de Armas a walk up busy Obispo leads to the **Parque Central**, straddling the border between Habana Vieja and Centro Habana and within shouting distance of the Capitolio Nacional. Although the speeding traffic detracts from the whole a little, the grandeur of the surrounding buildings, characteristic of the celebratory early twentieth-century architecture in this section of town, lends the square a stateliness that's quite distinct from the residential feel which pervades the rest of Habana Vieja. The attention-grabber is undoubtedly the **Gran Teatro** (☎62-94-73), between San Martín and San Rafael, an explosion of balustraded balconies, colonnaded cornices and sculpted stone figures striking classical poses. For a proper look inside, you'll have to attend a performance; these usually take place at weekends.

Capitolio Nacional

Just beyond the southwestern corner of the Parque Central looms the familiar-looking dome of the **Capitolio Nacional** (daily 9am–7.30pm; US$3). Opened in 1929 (and bearing a striking resemblance to the Capitol Building in Washington DC, though little is made of this in Cuban publications), it was the seat of the House of Representatives and the Senate prior to the revolution. The two ornate main chambers are now the centrepiece of visitor tours and the walk round, with or without a free tour guide, shouldn't take you longer than twenty minutes as only one floor is open to the public, much of it behind ropes. Nevertheless, the sheer size of the magnificent polished entrance hall known as the Salón de los Pasos Perdidos (The Room of Lost Steps) and the breathtaking gold and bronze Rococo-style decoration of the Hemiciclio Camilo Cienfuegos, a theatrical, echoing conference chamber, are enough to leave a lasting impression.

Fábrica de Tobacos Partagás

Behind the Capitolio stands the **Fábrica de Tobacos Partagás** (tours every 30 min Mon–Fri 9.30am–2pm; US$10), one of the country's oldest cigar factories, founded in 1849 and still churning out such famous makes as Cohiba, Bolívar and Partagás. Although steeply priced compared to most museum entrance fees, the 45-minute tour is easily among the most fascinating things to do in the city, with English-speaking guides taking you through the various stages of production – drying, sorting, rolling and boxing – all performed in separate rooms under one roof. There's even an area used as a kind of cigar school, from where, after a nine-month course, those who graduate will move upstairs and join the hundred or so workers making some of the finest cigars in the world. Here, a sea of expert workers – expected to produce between 80 and 250 cigars during their eight-hour shifts – are read to, from a newspaper in the mornings and from a book in the afternoons. It's entirely uncontrived and there's a very genuine sense of observing an everyday operation, with most of the workers almost oblivious to the flashing of cameras.

Museo Nacional de Bellas Artes

The **Museo Nacional de Bellas Artes** (Tues–Sat 10am–6pm, Sun 9am–1pm; US$5 for one building, US$8 for both) is the most spectacular of Havana's museums, containing by far the largest collection of art in the country. This has been divided between two buildings: the Art-Deco Palacio de Bellas Artes, opposite the Museo de la Revolución on Trocadero, is the showcase for exclusively Cuban art, while the rest of the world is represented in the Centro Asturiano, across Agramonte from the Parque Central.

The best way to tackle the **Cuban collection** in the **Palacio de Bellas Artes** is to take the lifts in the entrance lobby up to the top floor and walk round clockwise, as the exhibits are laid out in chronological order. The most historic pieces are on the gantry that runs most of the length of the first two rooms, including a great lithograph of nineteenth-century Havana by Eduardo Laplante. The rest of the top floor leaps straight into the twentieth century, beginning with paintings by Victor Manuel García (1897-1969), including *Gitana tropical*, a national treasure. Here also is the morbid work of Fidelo Ponce de León (1895-1949). Amongst the more modern stuff, the bewildering *Esta es la Historia* (This is history) by Gilberto de la Nuez (1913-93) charts the history of Cuba all in one image.

The grandiose **Centro Asturiano** is divided by country of origin, with collections from Britain, Italy, Spain and France, as well as Latin and North America rooms and a smaller Asian section. It's the Italian collection which is perhaps the most impressive, featuring Vittore Carpaccio's (c.1455-1525) *La recepción de un legado* (Receiving a bequest), one of the oldest paintings in the entire building. Most of the fourth floor is dedicated to the ancient art of Rome, Egypt and Greece, with highlights of the Egyptian section including a 3000-year-old tomb.

Museo de la Revolución

From the Parque Central it's a two-minute walk along Agramonte to Havana's most famous museum, the **Museo de la Revolución** (daily 10am–5pm; US$4), defiantly housed in the sumptuous presidential palace of the 1950s' dictator, General Fulgencio Batista. The events leading up to the triumph of the revolution in 1959 are covered in unparalleled detail, but your attention span is unlikely to last the full three storeys. Visitors work their way down from the top floor, which is the most engaging part of the museum and where you should concentrate your efforts. The events of the revolutionary war and the urban insurgency movements during the 1950s were surprisingly well documented, and there are some fantastically dramatic pictures, like one of the police assault on the Socialist Party headquarters. Some of the classic images of the campaign waged in the Sierra Maestra by Castro and his band of followers will look familiar, but even serious students of Cuban history will struggle to keep track of the chronology as they overdose on battle plans and miscellaneous firearms. Located outside, to the rear of the museum, is the **Granma Memorial**, where the boat which took Castro and his men from Mexico to Cuba to begin the revolution is preserved within a giant glass case.

Vedado

The cultural heart of the city, graceful **Vedado** draws the crowds with its palatial hotels – the backbone of so much of Havana's social scene – contemporary art galleries, concerts, restaurants, bars and nightspots. Threadbare but character-filled cinemas lie dotted throughout the area, with the names of the latest North American (and occasionally Cuban) films picked out in wonky and incomplete peg letters on billboards above the entrance. Loosely defined as the area running west of Calzada de Infanta up to the Río Almendares, Vedado is less ramshackle than other parts of the city and more intimate. Plenty of crowds lend a veneer of activity but look closely and you'll see that many people are actually part of a bus queue, waiting their turn to enter Havana's massive ice-cream parlour, *Coppelia*, or are *jineteros* keeping watch for the next buck. Vedado divides into three distinct, easy-to-negotiate parts intersected by four main thoroughfares: the broad boulevards of Avenida de los Presidentes (also known as Calle G) and Paseo, running north to south, and the more prosaic Linea and Calle 23, running east to west.

The most obvious part is modern **La Rampa** (Calle 23), and the streets immediately to the north and south, racing with battered Chevrolets and Buicks and landscaped in high-rise 1950s' hotels and utilitarian buildings. It's a relatively small space, but it dominates your immediate impression of Vedado, firstly because the peeling, 50-year-old, skyscrapers are such a rarity in Cuba and, secondly, because as a visitor you end up spending a fair amount of time here – confirming or booking flights, changing money in the hotels, souvenir-shopping in the street markets and dollar shops, or eating at the restaurants. Although it's an area for doing rather than seeing, you will find some worthy museums, including the **Museo Napoleónico** on San Miguel (Mon–Sat 10am–5pm; US$3, guided tour US$3 extra), a treasure trove of artefacts relating to the erstwhile French emperor. Nearby, the **Universidad de La Habana** comprises a series of beautiful buildings in verdant grounds, attended by well-behaved students who personify the virtues of post-revolutionary education.

Beyond here, to the south, the **Plaza de la Revolución** sports immense monuments to the twin heroes, José Martí and Ernesto "Che" Guevara, as well as the exhaustive **Museo José Martí** (Tues–Sat 10am–6pm; US$3, $5 including lookout point), which charts Martí's luminary career. The uncompromising sweep of concrete of the plaza itself forms a complete contrast to the area's other key attraction, the atmospheric **Necrópolis de Cólon** (daily 8am–5pm; US$1), one of the largest cemeteries in the Americas.

Vedado shows its third face further west and north. This quieter area is less distinct but broadly encompasses the area north of Calle 23 up to the Malecón, bordered to the west by the Río Almendares and stretching east roughly as far as Avenida de los Presidentes. Here, the back streets narrow and avenues are overhung with leaves from the pine, rubber and weeping fig trees planted in the mid-nineteenth century to create a cool retreat from the blistering tropical sun. Many of the magnificent late- and post-colonial buildings that line these streets – built in a mad medley of Rococo, Baroque and classical styles – have now been converted into state offices and museums, though others retain their role as lavish albeit stricken homes. Particularly noteworthy is the **Museo de los Artes Decorativos**, 502 Calle 17 (Tues–Sat 11am–7pm; US$2, $1 extra with guide, $3 extra with camera), a dizzying collection of fine furniture and *objets d'art*. Further afield, dotted around Linea, Paseo and Avenida de los Presidentes, are several excellent galleries and cultural centres, notably the **Casa de las Américas** (Sala Contemporánea Mon–Fri 10am–5pm; free; Galería Latino-americana Mon–Thurs 10am–5pm, Fri 10am–noon; US$2), set up to celebrate Pan-Americanism and displaying quality artworks from all over Latin America as well as hosting regular musical events.

Miramar and the western suburbs

Miramar and the western suburbs are Havana's alter ego: larger than life, with ice-white Miami-style residences, flash business developments, spanking new hotels and curvy Japanese cars streaking along wide avenues. The area is divided into four main suburbs: oceanfront **Miramar**, reached from the Malecón through the tunnel bridging under the Río Almendares; **La Sierra** to its immediate south; **Kohly** tucked underneath; and **Almendares** to the west; but you'll often hear the whole area referred to as **Playa** and sometimes addresses are listed as such. Although the houses and embassies are good for a gawp, most visitors who venture over the river do so for the **entertainment**, particularly the famous *Tropicana* cabaret in Marianao, and the international **restaurants**, which provide a welcome respite from pork, rice and beans. The **Marina Hemingway** on the outskirts of Miramar also pulls in scores of yachties.

Habana del Este

Many people omit the sights in **Habana del Este**, across the bay from Habana Vieja, from their itinerary, erroneously believing them to be inconveniently located, but those who do make it this far can trace a series of links in the city's history.

A visit to the castles and fortifications that collectively make up the **Parque Morro-Cabaña** is really worthwhile. Part of the Havana skyline, they dominate the view across the harbour and, along with the fortifications in Habana Vieja, comprise the city's oldest defence system. The **Castillo de los Tres Reyes Magos del Morro** (daily 8am–8.30pm; US$3, $2 extra for lighthouse) was built between 1589 and 1630 to complement the **Castillo de San Salvador de la Punta** on the opposite side of the bay, but the dual fortifications failed spectacularly when the British invaded overland in 1762 and occupied the city for six months. From the high parade grounds, studded with rusted cannons and Moorish turrets, you could easily spend an hour or so surveying the bay. A highlight of the visit is watching the sun set over the sea from the summit of the **lighthouse** that was built on the cliff edge in 1844.

Roughly 250m further east, the **Fortaleza San Carlos de la Cabaña** (daily 8am–11pm; US$3) needs more time to do it justice. Built as the most complex and expensive defence system in the Americas, the fortress was started in 1763 as soon as the Spanish traded the city back from the British. However, its defensive worth was never proved, as takeover attempts by other European powers had largely died down by the time it was finished. It took eleven years to complete and you can see why with one look at the extensive grounds, whose cobbled streets lined with houses (where soldiers and officers were originally billeted) now shelter a miscellany of workshops, artisans' boutiques and restaurants.

The easiest way to get to Habana del Este is to take a metered (US$4) or private taxi (US$2–3), or a bus (40c) from the bus stop near the Monumento Máximo Gómez – get off at the first stop after the tunnel. From the fortifications it's a brisk half-hour walk to the seventeen-metre-high **Cristo de La Habana**, the gigantic hilltop Christ figure, or a pleasant ride on the foot-and-bicycle ferry (1 peso) that leaves every thirty minutes from Avenida del Puerto e/ Sol y Luz, ten minutes' walk south from Plaza San Francisco and the main Sierra Maestra Terminal.

Eating

Havana offers the most varied eating scene in Cuba, even if the setting of many establishments is more notable than the food. The best restaurants tend to be in Miramar and the western suburbs, while numerous *paladares* dish up good-value portions of local fare. There are several **ethnic** restaurants in Havana; the most common are Chinese, Italian and Spanish. **Vegetarians** will find decent though predictable choices (pizza and omelettes featuring heavily) at most places, but vegans should resign themselves to a diet of salad and fries. Stick to the hotels for **breakfast** as elsewhere the choice is a bit patchy; the *Habana Libre* does a particularly fine buffet for about US$12. The best option for **lunch** is to grab a snack from one of the **street stalls** dotted around Centro Habana and Vedado, which sell tasty fritters and pizzas for just a few pesos each.

Habana Vieja and Centro Habana

Castillo de Farnés Ave. de Bélgica esq. Obrapía. With a refreshingly original menu by local standards, the Spanish cuisine includes the tasty *arroz indiana*, a mixed meat and rice dish, and well-prepared seafood.

El Floridita Monserrate esq. Obispo ☎57-12-99 or 7/57-13-00. Expensive seafood dishes in one of the most exclusive restaurants in the old city. It's another Hemingway heritage site and a velvet-curtain doorway leads through from the equally famous bar to an elegant circular dining area.

El Patio Plaza de la Catedral. The serenity of this leafy, eighteenth-century mansion courtyard goes a long way to justifying the above-average prices, as does the excellent choice of main dishes, with an emphasis on seafood, set vegetarian meals and plenty of optional extras.

La Bodeguita del Medio Empedrado e/ San Ignacio y Cuba ☎57-13-74 or 75. A Havana classic which relies more on its secret-hideout ambience and Ernest Hemingway associations than its standard, though fairly priced, *comida criolla*. Hemingway's usual tipple, a *mojito*, has become the house speciality.

La Julia O'Reilly no. 506a e/ Bernaza y Villegas. Top-quality cooking and flavourful *comida criolla* are the main attractions of this homey little *paladar*, which has pork dishes down to a science.

La Paella *Hostal Valencia*, Oficios no. 53 esq. Obrapía. Authentically prepared Spanish food including six different kinds of paella and an ample selection of light meals and aperitifs. Moderately priced.

Torresson Malecón no. 27 e/ Prado y Cárcel, Centro Habana. Chicken, pork and fish dishes for average prices in a basic balcony *paladar* overlooking the seafront with a good view of El Morro.

Vedado

Coppelia Calle 23 esq. L. Havana's massive ice-cream emporium contains several peso cafés and a dollar open-air area, serving rich sundaes with exotic flavours like coconut and guava. Closed Mon.

Doña Clara Calle 21 no. 107 e/ L y N. The best stall for lunch snacks at rock-bottom prices. Ice-cold soft drinks, *papas rellenas* and guava pies.

Nacional Calle O esq. 21. The US$18 all-you-can-eat buffet restaurant in this hotel's basement provides one of Havana's best feeds, with an extensive range of fish and meat and a welcome array of green vegetables.

Nerei Calle 19 esq. L. Elegant mid-range *paladar* where you can dine alfresco on escalope of pork or pork cooked in garlic or fried chicken, all served with yucca, fried banana and salad. The house speciality – rubbery squid – is best avoided.

La Roca Calle 21 esq. M ☎33-45-01. Although somewhat pricey, this tranquil seafood restaurant is great for a blow-out meal of lobster or grilled red snapper.

La Torre Calle 17 no. 55 Edificio Focsa piso 36. Mesmerizing views from the city's second tallest building are matched by the excellent French menu. Definitely worth splashing out US$40 or so to dine on foie gras, fillet of beef with rosemary, shrimps caramelized in honey, and profiteroles.

Miramar and the western suburbs

Club Almendares Calle 49c y 28a, Reparto Kohly. A country club-style venue with two restaurants. The popular outdoor pizza house serves excellent Italian-style thin-crust pizzas and pasta dishes for less than US$5, whilst the fancier *Restaurant Almendares* offers decent lobster, paella, fried rice and Cuban cuisine for upwards of US$7 per dish.

Villa Diana Calle 49 e/ 28a-47, Reparto Kohly. A classy establishment offering a US$12 set meal of grilled and roast meats, accompanied by some good live music.

Drinking, nightlife and entertainment

A typical night out in Havana is a giddy whirl of thumping salsa or soulful boleros, well oiled with rum, and often a hefty bill attached for you and all your newly acquired Cuban friends. What Cuba does best is **live music**, so you should definitely try to catch at least one of the excellent salsa, jazz or *son* groups that regularly do the rounds of the best-known clubs.

A more spontaneous night out is a bit difficult, as there's no single area with a buzz. **Bar crawls** involve a lot of walking, although the Plaza de la Catedral district is usually quite lively at night, with most of the attention focused on *El Patio* bar and restaurant. However, for sheer *joie de vivre* you can't beat Havana's best option – taking some beers or a bottle of rum down to the Malecón and mingling with the crowds beneath the stars. Another option is the **cinema**, a popular form of entertainment with Cubans, with plenty of atmospheric fleapits dotted around Vedado. As a visitor, you may be charged in dollars (US$2–3).

Bars and cafés

Ambos Mundos Obispo no. 153 esq. Mercaderes, Habana Vieja. Looking out over the Palacio de los Capitanes Generales, lolling on the tasteful garden furniture amongst the potted plants of this hotel's fabulous rooftop patio-bar is as relaxing an option as you could wish for in Habana Vieja.

La Bodeguita del Medio Empedrado e/ San Ignacio y Mercaderes, Habana Vieja. Made famous by Ernest Hemingway, this usually overcrowded but always atmospheric bar no longer attracts Havana's bohemian set, but retains some of the spirit of the 1930s and 1940s, despite the queues of tourists.

Café de Paris San Ignacio esq. Obispo, Habana Vieja. Popular with an even mix of tourists and locals, this simple little bar enjoys a party atmosphere stirred up by a live band on a nightly basis.

Taberna del Galeon Baratillo no. 53 e/ Obispo y Jústiz, Habana Vieja. Just off the Plaza de Armas (and a good place to avoid the frenzied atmosphere of the Obispo bars and the plaza itself), this place has an attic-like upstairs balcony above a rum and cigar shop. Open 10am–5pm only.

Cabarets, discos and live music

Cabaret Nacional San Rafael esq. Paseo del Prado, Habana Vieja. Below the Gran Teatro, this seedy basement cabaret and disco is more than just a pick-up joint, though it is certainly that too. The show starts around 11pm and the disco usually gets going at about 1am.

Casa de la Cultura Aguiar no. 509 e/ Amargura y Brasil, Habana Vieja ⓣ63-48-60. In the converted Convento de San Francisco, this centre for local talent runs a full programme of evening performances, ranging from folk music to rap. Entrance is usually between 2 and 5 pesos.

La Pampa Parque Maceo, Centro Habana. Distinguished by a music policy of swing and hip-hop, a rarity in Cuban clubs, *La Pampa* attracts an enthusiastic, finger-on-the-pulse local crowd. At just 20 pesos to get in, you can't go wrong.

Listings

Banks and exchange The *cambio* in the *Nacional* hotel has the longest opening hours (daily 8am–noon & 1–7pm); Banco Internacional de Comercio (Mon–Fri 8.30am–3pm) at Empedrado

Cuban music

Music forms the pulsing backdrop to virtually all entertainment in Cuba, and if you're looking to hear traditional Cuban music, like that popularized on the *Buena Vista Social Club* album – and in the documentary of the same name and that ensemble's subsequent tour – you won't come away disappointed. Along with Santiago and Varadero, Havana offers the best variety of places to soak up home-grown salsa, from lavish salsa palaces and open-air venues to hotel salons. Better still, you can also hear all the soulful *son* (which is the foundation, really, of most Cuban music), boleros and *guajiras*, as well as salsa (itself an offspring of *son)*, in any of the **Casas de la Trova** – atmospheric music halls specializing in traditional Cuban tunes that often have live groups – located throughout the country. For something a bit more riotous, Cuban street parties, held on holidays and at **carnival,** feature live bands, which expertly tease seductive moves from heaving crowds.

esq. Aguiar is the best bank in the old city for foreign currency transactions.
Car rental There's a concentration of rental agencies on or within a few blocks of the Malecón, between the Parque Antonio Maceo in Centro Habana and the Cupet-Cimex Tángana petrol station in Vedado. Micar is the cheapest and has offices at the Fiat showroom, Malecón esq. Príncipe, Centro Habana ⓣ33-58-10, and Calle 1era esq. Paseo, Vedado ⓣ55-35-35 (open 24hr).
Embassies Embassies in Havana include the Canadian Embassy, Calle 30 no. 518, Miramar, Playa (ⓣ 7/24-12-22; ⓕ 24-20-44); the British Embassy, Calle 34 no. 702–704, Miramar, Playa ⓣ 7/24-17-71, ⓕ 24-81-04); and the US Special Interests Section, Calle Calzada y L, Vedado, Havana ⓣ 7/ 33-35-31; ⓕ 33-37-00. There are no consulates or embassies for Australia or New Zealand; citizens are advised to go to either the Canadian or UK embassies.
Immigration and legal Asistur, Paseo del Prado no. 212 esq. Trocadero ⓣ33-89-20 or 33-83-39 or 7/867-13-15, ⓕ33-80-87 deals with insurance claims and financial emergencies and is open 24hr. There's also an office a few doors down at no.254 ⓣ33-85-27 or 7/867-13-14. Otherwise, try the Consultoria Juridica Internacional in Miramar at Calle 16 no. 314 e/ 3ra y 5ta ⓣ24-24-90 or 7/24-26-97 (Mon–Fri 8.30am–noon & 1.30–5.30pm).
Medical Call ⓣ40-50-93 to 94 or 57-70-41 to 43 for a state ambulance, or contact Asistur on ⓣ67-13-15 for a tourist ambulance. The Clínica Internacional Cira García in Miramar at Calle 20 no.4101 esq. Ave. 41 ⓣ204-0330 to 31 or 204-2673 is run predominantly for foreigners, while two floors are reserved for foreign patients at the Hospital Hermanos Ameijeras, San Lázaro no. 701 e/Padre Varela y Marqués González, Centro Habana, switchboard ⓣ57-60-77.
Pharmacies Farmacia Internacional at Ave. 41 no.1814, esq. 20 ⓣ24-50-51 in Miramar is one of the best-stocked in Havana.
Police The main station in Centro Habana is at Dragones e/ Lealtad y Escobar ⓣ62-44-12. In an emergency ring ⓣ82-01-16 or 60-01-06.
Post offices The branch at Ave. Salvador Allende esq. Padre Varela, Centro Habana (Mon–Sat 8am–6pm) offers peso services only. The branch in the Gran Teatro building, at Paseo del Prado esq. San Martín, offers fax and telegram services as well as poste restante facilities (daily 8am–6pm).
Taxis Havanautos offer a 24-hour pick-up service ⓣ24-24-24. Try also Turistaxi ⓣ33-66-66; Habanataxi ⓣ41-96-00; Panataxi ⓣ55-55-55.

Around Havana

East of the city, **Guanabacoa** is a quiet provincial town with numerous attractive churches and a fascinating religious history. However, for most people, the big attractions east of Havana are the boisterous **Playas del Este**, the nearest beaches to the city, where clean sands and a lively scene draw in the crowds. South of Havana, the **Museo Ernest Hemingway,** a perfect preservation of the great writer's home, is the most neatly packaged day-trip destination. Not far away, the sprawling **Jardín**

Botánico is the best bet for a relaxing escape from the city grime. Outside the city proper, public transport is scare and unreliable, and you'll really need a car to see many of these sights, though there are **local buses** to the Playas del Este (4 daily; 1hr) from the Parque de la Fraternidad in Habana Vieja.

Guanabacoa

Two kilometres inland along the Vía Monumental from the tunnel under the bay is the turn-off to **GUANABACOA**, a little town officially within the city limits but with a distinctly provincial feel. The site of a pre-Columbian community, and then one of the island's first Spanish settlements, it's the strong tradition here of Afro-Cuban religion which holds the most appeal for visitors, centred on a visit to the town's **Museo Histórico de Guanabacoa** (Mon & Wed–Sat 10.30am–6pm; US$2), at Martí no. 108 e/ Quintin Bandera y E.V.Valenzuela, two blocks from the understated main square, Parque Martí. The collection of cultish objects relating to the practices of Santería, Palo Monte and the Abakuá Secret Society give the museum its edge. One room is set up to reflect the mystic environment in which the *babalao*, the Santería equivalent of a priest, would perform divination rituals, surrounded by altars and African deities in the form of Catholic saints. There are also some interesting bits and pieces, including furniture and ceramics, relating to the town's history.

The most accessible and intact of the town's five **churches** is the run-down **Iglesia Parroquial Mayor** on Parque Martí, with its magnificent, though age-worn, altar. Otherwise, once you've checked out the Afro-Cuban-style knick-knacks in the **Bazar de Reproducciones Artísticas**, two blocks down from the museum at Martí no. 175, and eaten at *El Palenque*, the basic outdoor **restaurant** next door, you've done the town justice.

Playas del Este

Fifteen kilometres east of Cojímar, the Vía Blanca reaches Havana's nearest beaches – Playa Santa María del Mar, Playa Boca Ciega and Playa Guanabo – collectively known as the **Playas del Este**. Hugging the Atlantic coast, the three fine-sand beaches form a long, twisting, ochre ribbon, which vanishes in summer beneath the crush of weekending Habaneros and tourists. There's not a whole lot to choose between the beaches, although as a general rule the sand is better towards the western end.

There is an abundance of really good self-catering and hotel **accommodation** around the beaches, and if you're based in Havana for most of your holiday this could provide an excellent mini-break. Those craving creature comforts should head for the big hotels in Santa María, though budget travellers will find the best value in the inexpensive hotels and *casas particulares* in Guanabo. Other than the rather anonymous, all-inclusive *Club Arsenal* (☎7/97-12-72; ➐) there's nowhere to stay in Playa Boca Ciega. Although a number of **restaurants** serve cheap meals, these all tend to be rather alike, and your best bet is to eat at the *paladar* in Guanabo; otherwise, see if a *casa particular* can recommend somewhere.

Museo Ernest Hemingway

Eleven kilometres southeast of Habana Vieja, in the suburb of San Francisco de Paula, is **La Vigía**, an attractive little estate centred on the whitewashed nineteenth-century villa where Ernest Hemingway lived for twenty years until 1960 and wrote a number of his most famous novels. Now the **Museo Ernest Hemingway** (Mon–Sat 9am–4pm, Sun 9am–noon; US$3), it makes a simple but enjoyable excursion from the city. On top of a hill with splendid views over Havana, the single-storey colonial residence has been preserved almost exactly as Hemingway left it – with drinks and magazines strewn about the place and the dining-room table set for guests. Frustratingly, entrance into the rooms is forbidden, but by walking around the encircling verandah you can get good views of most rooms through the windows. In the well-kept gardens, Hemingway's fishing boat is suspended inside a wooden pavilion and you can also visit the graves of four of his dogs, next to the swimming pool.

The museum closes when it rains to protect the interior from the damp and to preserve the well-groomed grounds, so time your visit to coincide with sunshine. To get there by car, take the Vía Blanca through the southern part of the city and turn off at the Carretera Central, which cuts through San Francisco de Paula. Alternatively you can brave the M 7 *camello* bus, one of the converted juggernauts used for longer bus journeys in and around the city; catch it at the Parque de la Fraternidad and walk from the bus stop to the museum. A taxi to the museum from Habana Vieja or Vedado should cost about US$10.

Jardín Botánico Nacional

About a 25-minute drive south of the city, via the airport road (Avenida Rancho Boyeros) and then branching right on to Avenida San Francisco, is the entrance to the **Jardín Botánico Nacional** (Wed–Sun 8.30am–4.30pm; 60 centavos, US$3 for guided tour). The grounds are split into sections according to continent, with the different zones blending seamlessly into one another. Highlights include the collection of 162 species of **palm** from around the world, and the picture-perfect **Japanese Garden**, built around a beautiful little lake and donated by the Japanese government in 1989 on the thirtieth anniversary of the revolution. The Japanese Garden is also the best place to stop for **lunch**, in *El Bambú* (open 1–3.30pm), where US$10 lets you eat your fill from a tasty vegetarian buffet. Near the main entrance are the indoor **Pabellones de Exposiciones**, two large greenhouse-style buildings with raised viewing platforms and twisting pathways, one housing a fantastic collection of cacti, the other a jungle of tropical plants and flowers.

Although you can explore the botanical gardens yourself, a lack of information means you'll learn far more by taking the one- to two-hour **guided tour**, whether in the tractor-bus or having a guide in your own car (at no extra cost). There's usually at least one English-speaking guide available. Tours leave every hour or so from just inside the main entrance, near the useful **information office**. There's also a small **shop** selling ornamental plants. At weekends a bus takes passengers from here directly to the Japanese Garden (every 30min; US$1).

3.2

Pinar del Río

Despite its relative proximity to Havana, life in **Pinar del Río** is a far cry from the noise, pollution and hustle of the capital. The butt of a string of national jokes, native Pinareños are caricatured as the island's most backward country folk, a reputation that fits in with the slower, more relaxed feel to the province. Most of the highlights are well away from the population centres, the majority situated in and around the green slopes of the **Cordillera de Guaniganico**, the mountain range that runs down the length of this narrow province, invitingly visible from the *autopista* running alongside. Hidden within the relatively compact **Sierra del Rosario**, the eastern section of the *cordillera*, the peaceful mountain retreats of **Las Terrazas** and **Soroa** provide perfect opportunities to explore the tree-clad hillsides and valleys. Both are set up as centres for eco-tourism, though of the two Las Terrazas offers the chance to get a little bit closer to the local community. Most visitors head straight for what is justifiably the most touted location in Pinar del Río, the **Viñales valley**, whose unusual flat-topped mountains or *mogotes*, unique in Cuba, are worth the trip alone.

Las Terrazas

Eight kilometres beyond the signposted turn-off at Km 51 of the *autopista* is **LAS TERRAZAS**, a harmonious tourist resort and small working community forming the province's premier eco-tourism site. The motorway suddenly seems a long way behind as the road takes you into a thickly wooded landscape and up to a junction where, after a left turn, you'll reach a **toll booth** (US$2 per person; resort guests free) marking the beginning of the main through road for Las Terrazas. About 2km beyond the toll booth, another left-hand turn leads several hundred metres down to a complex of red-roofed bungalows and apartment buildings, beautifully set into the grassy slopes of a valley, at the foot of which is a lake. The cabins belong to the resident population, which numbers around a thousand and has lived here since 1971 as part of a government-funded conservation and reforestation project, covering some fifty square kilometres of the Sierra del Rosario. A large proportion of the locals work in tourism, either directly or indirectly, many as employees at **Moka** (Ⓣ82/78-601 to 603, Ⓕ82/78-126, Ⓔhmoka@teleda.get.cma.net; ❹, lakeside cabin ❺), a resort hotel that blends perfectly with its surroundings.

There are several official **hiking trails** around Las Terrazas, none more than 6km – the three best are covered in the box opposite. There is no better way to experience the diversity of the Sierra del Rosario than along these routes, which collectively offer the most comprehensive insight available into the region's topography, history, flora and fauna. Whilst you are free to follow the trails independently, it's generally better to hire a guide from **Rancho Curujey** (Ⓣ82/78-555), the complex's visitor centre, as you'll learn a lot more and you won't get lost – this is also where you can get hold of a map. Though the centre has no formal opening hours, it's generally a good idea to arrive at around 8.30am before staff disappear on hikes and excursions. To get to the restaurant and the one or two other buildings that make up Rancho Curujey, take the signposted right-hand turn off the main through road just before the left turn that leads down to the village and hotel. **Guides** cost between US$15 and US$35 per person on a pre-booked excursion, depending on the size of the group and your specific requirements. It works out considerably cheaper if you're in a group of six or more; you may be able to join another visiting group if you call a day or so in advance, or if you arrive at or before 9am.

Soroa

Sixteen kilometres southwest of Las Terrazas, the tiny village of **SOROA** nestles in a long narrow valley. It's very cosy, but as access into the hills is limited and the list of attractions brief, Soroa is best for a short stint rather than a protracted visit. Incidentally, you can get here from Las Terrazas without having to return to the *autopista*. Follow the main road through Las Terrazas until you reach a second toll booth, marking the other end of the resort, where you should turn left.

All of the official attractions are based around the **Villa Soroa** (☎85/21-22 or 20-41, ℗85/78-218; ④), a well-kept hotel complex encircling a swimming pool. Most of what you'll want to see is within ten minutes' walk of the reception building, but if you've driven up from the *autopista* the first place you'll reach, 100m or so from the hotel, is the car park for **El Salto** (open during daylight hours; US$2), a twenty-metre **waterfall** and one of Soroa's best-known attractions.

Back at the car park, follow the sign pointing in the direction of the small bridge to **El Mirador**, the most easily accessible local viewpoint. A thirty-minute hike scales an increasingly steep dirt track, though it's mercifully shady and a set of steps has been installed for the final stretch. There are a number of possible wrong turns on the way up; follow the track with the horse dung. At the summit you'll find vultures circling the rocky, uneven platform. **El Castillo de las Nubes** is the more developed of Soroa's two hilltop viewpoints and the only one you can drive to. The road up to the summit, which you'll have to follow even if walking as there are no obvious trails through the woods, is between the car park for El Salto and the hotel. It shouldn't take you more than twenty minutes on foot to reach the hilltop restaurant, housed in a building resembling a toy fortress with a single turret (the *castillo* – or castle – in question). It's worth stopping for a meal in the **restaurant** (daily 11.30am–4pm), as the views are fantastic.

Viñales

The jewel in Pinar del Río's crown, the **Viñales valley** is by far the most visited location in the province. Though only 25km from the provincial capital, Pinar del Río, the valley feels far more remote than that, with an almost dreamlike quality that's inextricably linked to the *mogotes*, the 160-million-year-old boulder-like hills, which look like they've dropped from the sky onto the valley floor.

Hiking trails at Las Terrazas

Ruta del Cafetal Buenavista (2.5km). The route follows a trail barely distinguishable amid the dense foliage on one of the more back-breaking hikes. There are occasional views of the complex below on the way up to the Cafetal Buenavista (daily noon–4pm), an excellent reconstruction of a nineteenth-century coffee plantation.

Sendero Las Delicias (3km). Starting on the same course as the Cafetal Buenavista trail, this path bypasses the turn for the coffee plantation and continues up to a *mirador* at the summit of the Loma Las Delicias, for some magnificent views.

Sendero La Serafina (5km). This trail, through rich and varied forest, is the best route for birdwatching and is much enhanced by going with a guide who'll be able to point out the red, white and blue *tocororo*, the endemic *catacuba* and the enchanting Cuban nightingale amongst the 73 species which inhabit the *sierra*.

Despite the influx of visitors, the region has remained largely unspoilt, with the tourist centres and hotels kept in isolated pockets of the valley, often hidden away behind the *mogotes*. Most of the locals live in the small **village of Viñales**, reached in a five-hour bus ride from Havana. If time is limited, concentrate your visit on the **San Vicente** region, a valley within the valley, much smaller and narrower than Viñales and home to the **Cueva del Indio** cave system. On the other side of the village, the **Mural de la Prehistoria** is by far the most contrived of the valley's attractions.

Accommodation

There's an even spread of good **places to stay** in Viñales, with average costs relatively low. Both *Los Jazmines* and *La Ermita* offer comprehensive programmes of **activities and excursions**, including horseback-riding, trekking and birdwatching.

Campismo Dos Hermanas on the road to the Mural de la Prehistoria ⓣ8/9-32-23. This *campismo*, buried within the *mogotes*, is better equipped than most, despite having no A/C or fans in its well-kept cabins. The cheapest of the official options, this is the place to come to share your stay with Cuban holidaymakers, but be prepared for the blaring music around the swimming pool in peak season. ❶

Casa de Doña Hilda casa no. 4, Km 25 Carretera a Pinar del Río ⓣ8/9-33-38. Three rooms for rent – the biggest (with bath, fridge and colour TV) is in its own small bungalow, next door to the main house where the two smaller rooms are located. A large dirt courtyard joins it all together, and parking is available. ❶

Hostel Inesita Salvador Cisnero no. 40 ⓣ8/9-32-97. Run by an elderly couple, the two rooms (one with A/C) in this *casa particular* in the heart of the village are in a separate apartment taking up the entire top floor of the house. With a wide balcony running around it, this is one of the best places to stay. ❶

La Ermita Carretera de Ermita Km 2 ⓣ8/93-60-71, ⓕ93-60-91. Gorgeous, open-plan hotel in immaculate grounds high above the valley floor. With some of the best views in Viñales, this tidy complex features three apartment buildings, a central pool, tennis court and a wonderful balcony restaurant. Rooms are attractive and reasonably well equipped. ❸

Los Jazmines Carretera de Viñales Km 25 ⓣ8/93-62-05, ⓕ93-62-15. The first hotel along the road into Viñales has an unbeatable hillside location; almost all the tasteful rooms in the colonial-style main building have panoramic views. Most rooms are in a separate, modern building, with a few housed in tile-roofed cabins. There's a pool, a well-stocked shop, two bars, small disco, and taxi and car rental. ❸

Mogote Dos Hermanas and the Mural de la Prehistoria

Less than a kilometre west of the village, the flat surface of the valley floor is interrupted by the hulking mass of the **Mogote Dos Hermanas**, the face of Viñales as seen on the front of most tourist brochures. It plays host to the misleadingly named **Mural de la Prehistoria** (daily 8am–7pm; US$2), hidden away from the main road down a dust track. Rather than the prehistoric cave paintings that you might expect, the huge painted mural, measuring 120m by 180m, desecrating the face of one side of the *mogote*, is in fact a modern depiction of evolution on the island, from mollusc to man. The bar, restaurant and souvenir shop just off to the side of the mural do nothing to alleviate the contrived nature of the place, although it's not an unpleasant spot to have a drink and a bite to eat. The **restaurant**'s speciality is roast pork cooked "Viñales-style", the highlight of an otherwise limited menu.

The Cueva del Indio

By taking the left-hand fork at the petrol station at the northeastern end of the village, you can head out of Viñales through heavily cultivated landscape to the narrower **San Vicente** valley, around 2km away. Past the lacklustre Cueva de San Miguel, it's a two-minute drive or a twenty-minute walk north to San Vicente's most captivating attraction, the **Cueva del Indio** (daily 9am–5pm; US$5), 6km north of the village. Rediscovered in 1920, this entire network of caves is believed to have been used by the Guanahatabey Amerindians, both as a refuge from the Spanish colonists and, judging by the human remains found here, as a burial site. The walls are marked with natural wave patterns, testimony to the flooding which took place during the caves' formation millions of years ago. Only the first 300m of the tunnel's damp interior can be explored on foot, before a slippery set of steps leads down to a subterranean river, where a tour guide in a **boat** steers you for ten minutes through the remaining 400m of accessible cave. The boat drops you off out in the open, next to some souvenir stalls and a car park, around the corner from where you started.

3.3

Varadero and Matanzas

V**aradero** is Cuban tourism at its most developed: a world apart from most of Cuba, but for its thousands of foreign visitors, the familiar face of the Caribbean. The Península de Hicacos, on which Varadero makes its home, reaches out from the northern coastline of the western **province of Matanzas** into the warm currents of the Atlantic as the ocean merges with the Gulf of Mexico. Its 25-kilometre stretch of fine white-sand beaches and turquoise waters are enough to fulfil even the most jaded sun-worshipper's expectations. On the opposite side of the province, the **Península de Zapata**'s sweeping tracts of unspoilt coastal marshland and wooded interior are easy to explore, thanks to an efficiently run tourist infrastructure. It's perfectly suited to a multitude of activities, including walking through the forests, birdwatching on the rivers, scuba diving in crystal waters and sunbathing on faultless beaches. The peninsula also boasts a recent history featuring an event as renowned as any other in the entire revolution – the invasion at the **Bay of Pigs**.

Varadero

Cuba's answer to the Costa del Sol in Spain or Cancún in Mexico, **VARADERO** is dominated by tourism and almost nowhere are you out of sight of a hotel. However, anyone hoping for a polished, Disney-style, resort will be disappointed. With hotels, shops and nightclubs spread out across the peninsula, there are areas where activity is more concentrated, but nowhere is there the buzz you might expect from the major holiday resort on the largest Caribbean island. None of this detracts from what most people come here for, namely the **beach**: a seemingly endless runway of blinding white sand. This is also the best place in Cuba for **watersports**, scuba diving, fishing and boat trips, with three marinas and two diving clubs offering a wide range of activities.

Varadero is divided into three distinct sections, though all are united by the same stretch of beach. The bridge from the mainland takes you into the **main town** area, where all the Cubans live and where nightlife, eating and entertainment are most densely concentrated. The streets here are in blocks, with *calles* numbering 1 to 65 running the width of the peninsula; dissecting them is **Avenida Primera**, the only street running the five-kilometre length of the whole town. The two-kilometre section of the peninsula west of the town, separated from the mainland by the Laguna de Paso Malo, is the **Reparto Kawama**, largely the exclusive domain of hotel guests. The majority of the all-inclusive luxury hotels lie **east of the town** on a part of the peninsula wholly dedicated to tourism.

Arrival, information and getting around

All international and most national flights arrive at the **Juan Gualberto Gómez Airport** (☎5/61-30-16), 25km west of Varadero. There's an information centre and several car rental agencies here, and although there's no public bus service many hotels pick up guests with reservations. It's worth talking to the driver or tour guide to see if there are any spare seats, or there are plenty of taxis which will take you to the centre of Varadero for US$25. Inter-provincial **buses**, whether Víazul (☎5/61-48-86) or Astro (☎5/61-26-26), arrive at the small **Terminal de Omnibus** on

Calle 36 and Autopista Sur. The daily services from Havana take two and three-quarter hours, or nearly six hours from Trinidad. There are many hotels within easy walking distance of the terminal, some less than five minutes away, and there are often two or three **taxis** waiting out front. If not, call Cuba Taxi on ⓣ5/61-93-61 or 61-95-60. At least half of central Varadero's hotels are within a US$5 ride of the bus terminal.

The three most prominent national tourist travel and **information** agencies are represented in the lobby of most hotels, whilst they each also have their own offices. All offer very similar services, including excursions and hotel bookings. The Rumbos **Centro de Información Turística** at Ave. 1era esq. Calle 23 (daily 8am–7pm; ⓣ5/61-23-84 or 66-76-30) is the best place for picking up written information. **Cubatur**, at Calle 33 esq. 1era (daily 8.30am–8.30pm; ⓣ5/66-74-01 or 66-72-17), is also helpful, whilst the travel agent for **Havanatur**, Tour y Travel, has the largest number of outlets on the peninsula, with the most central office at Calle 31 e/ 1era y Ave. Playa (daily 9am–6pm; ⓣ5/66-71-54 or 6-31-74).

Most people get around in **taxis**; there's a constant stream of them along Avenida Primera, and a taxi rank between calles 54 and 55, next to the Cubana office.

Accommodation

Varadero has no shortage of **accommodation**, but there isn't the variety you might expect, except at the more expensive end of the market. An overwhelming proportion of the hotels east of the town are all-inclusives, and the further east you stay the more restricted you are to your hotel grounds, as places become increasingly isolated. However, wherever you stay, the distance from hotel to beach is never more than a ten-minute walk. Locals continue to rent rooms in their houses in Varadero, despite the government ban on **casas particulares**, with prices at around US$20–30 per room. Touts offering to take you to one are never far away, though the bus station is as good a place as anywhere to find them.

Reparto Kawama

Hotel Kawama Calle 0 y Ave. Kawama ⓣ5/61-44-16 to 19, ⓕ66-73-34, ⓔreserva@kawama.gca.cma.net. Large, landscaped, all-inclusive complex, bordered by 300m of beach, centred on a neo-colonial terraced main building founded in 1930 as a gentlemen's club. Choose from private or shared houses, or modern apartments, all tastefully furnished. There's a fantastically chic restaurant and cosy basement cabaret. ⑧

The town

Barlovento Ave. 1era e/ 10 y 12 ⓣ5/66-71-40, ⓕ66-72-18, ⓔreserva@ibero.gca.cma.net. Stylish and sophisticated complex with over 200 rooms, yet retaining a harmonious atmosphere. There's an atmospheric lobby with a fountain, a captivating pool area enveloped by palm trees, plus tennis and basketball courts. ⑥

Dos Mares Calle 53 y Ave. 1era ⓣ5/66-75-10, ⓕ66-74-99. Untypical of Varadero, this agreeable little hotel is of the kind more often found in provincial colonial towns. Makes up for its lack of facilities with bags of character. ③

Pullman Ave. 1era e/ 49 y 50 ⓣ5/66-71 61, ⓕ66-74-95. One of the smallest and most adorable hotels in Varadero, whose main building features a castle-like turret. Very relaxing atmosphere and ideal if you want to avoid the hullabaloo laid on as entertainment at most of the other hotels on the peninsula. ③

Villa La Mar Ave. 3era e/ 29 y 30 ⓣ5/61-39-10 or 61-31-10. Sociable but unsophisticated concrete complex offering cheap rooms to both tourists and Cubans. ④

East of town

Beaches Varadero Carretera Las Morlas, off Autopista Sur ⓣ5/66-84-70, ⓕ66-83-35, ⓔvaradero@beaches.var.cyt.cu. A pastel-coloured, five-storey main building stands at the top of the spacious grounds of this tastefully designed hotel. The emphasis is on sophisticated comfort, with soft-cushion seats around the lobby bar, a relaxing lounge area and an airy piano bar. ⑥

Coral Ave. de las Américas e/ H y K ⓣ5/66-72-40 to 42, ⓕ66-71-94, ⓔjefres@coral.solmelia.cma.net. A busy complex featuring the region's largest landscaped swimming pool. Thankfully, the imposing architecture is balanced by plenty of trees and plants – also a tennis court, pool room, beauty parlour and watersports. Currently the best bargain amongst the all-inclusives. ⑨

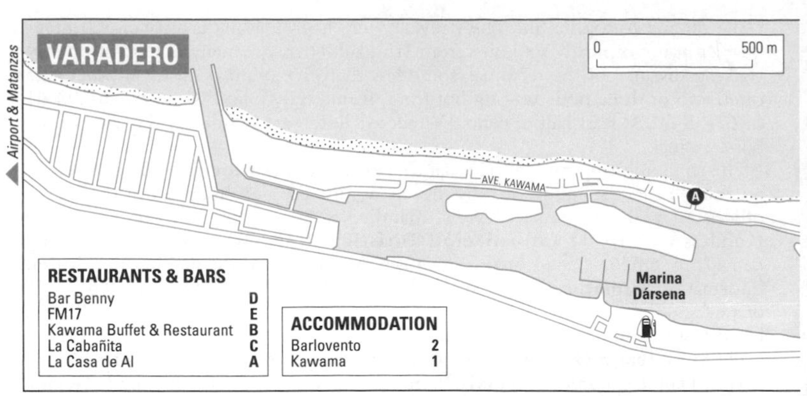

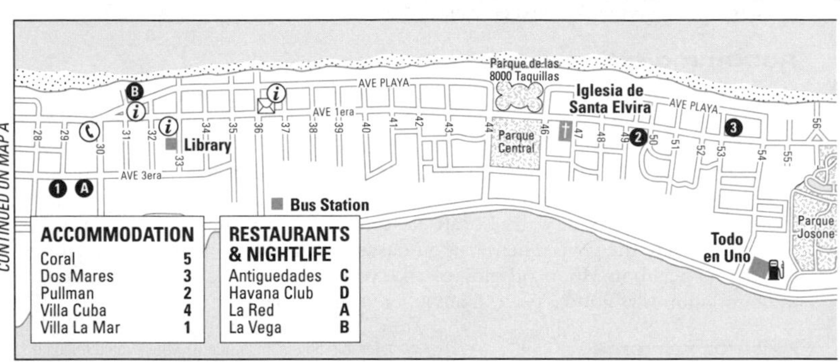

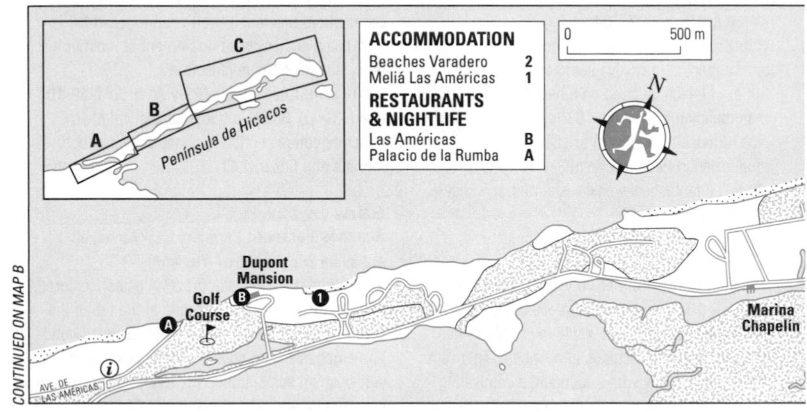

Meliá Las Américas Autopista Sur Km 7 ⓣ5/66-76-00, ⓕ66-76-25, ⓔmelia.lasamericas@america.solmelia.cma.net. This is the most stunningly designed complex on the peninsula, with paths weaving their way through the intricately landscaped grounds to a secluded part of the beach. Even the pool drops down a level whilst it twists itself around the pathways and pond. ⑦

Villa Cuba Ave. de las Américas ⓣ5/66-82-80,

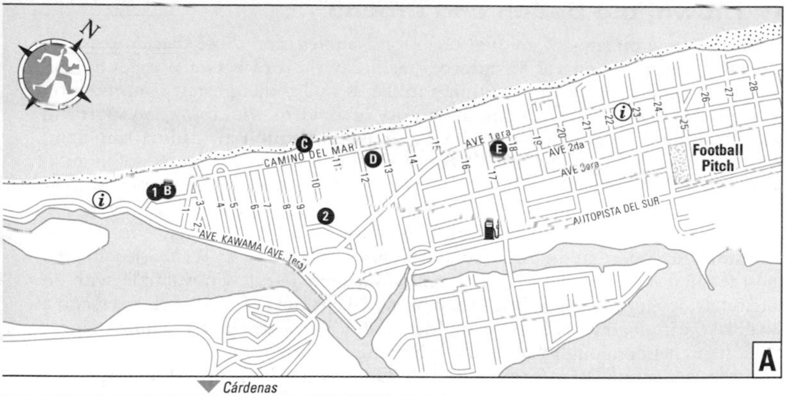

CONTINUED ON MAP E

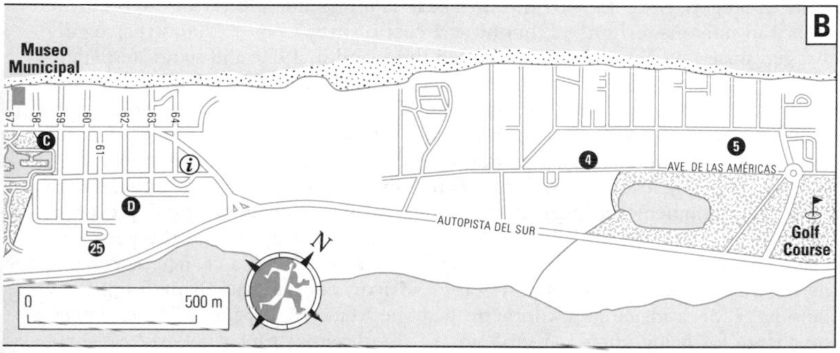

CONTINUED ON MAP C

☎ 66-82-82, ✉ reserva@vcuba.gca.cma.net. The main building of this impressive all-inclusive features staircases and gangways zigzagging through a network of different floors and platforms. Spread out around the open-plan complex, which stretches down to the beach, there are various smaller residences, some with their own swimming pool. ⑧

The Town, the beach and around

Varadero is low on sites of cultural or historic interest, and those that do exist are quickly exhausted. **Central Varadero**, specifically the area between calles 56 and 64, has the highest proportion of things to see, as well as the greatest concentration of shops and restaurants. Detailing the history of Varadero, with rooms on sport and wildlife thrown in for good measure, the **Museo Municipal** (daily 10am–5pm; US$1), at the beach end of Calle 57, contains exhibits of varying degrees of interest, including some eye-catching photographs of Fidel Castro, Che Guevara and their colleague, Camilo Cienfuegos, living it up in Varadero's hotels during the 1960s. Over the road from the grounds of the Museo Municipal is the entrance to **Parque Josone** (daily noon–midnight; free), sometimes referred to as Retiro Josone, the most tranquil and picturesque spot in central Varadero. The design is simple, with no intricately designed gardens, just sweeping well-kept lawns dotted with trees, and a small lake with its own palm-tree-studded island. There are three restaurants and a cafeteria to help prolong what would otherwise be a short visit.

To the east, about 2km from central Varadero, is the **Dupont Mansion** (daily noon–midnight), next door to the *Meliá Las Américas* hotel. Built in 1926 by the American millionaire Irenée Dupont at a cost of over US$700,000, it has hardly changed since Dupont and his family fled the island in 1959, and stands testament to the wealth and decadence of the pre-revolutionary years in Varadero. It was once open to the public as a museum, but these days to appreciate the splendidly furnished rooms you have to eat at the restaurant (see "Eating", opposite) or sip a cocktail in the dignified bar, from where there are fine views of the coastline.

At the eastern extreme of the peninsula, three square kilometres of land have avoided development and been declared the **Varahicacos Ecological Reserve**. Billed by its founders as "the other Varadero", it's the only part of the peninsula where you can experience relatively unspoilt landscapes, with a chance of viewing the flora and fauna up close. The reserve's **visitor centre** (daily 8am–5pm) is by the side of the road, about a kilometre past the Marina Chapelin. For individuals, the charge for being guided around any of the three set routes is US$2.50–3.50, but you can also arrange tailor-made excursions.

Of course, it's the **beach** which attracts most attention, a golden carpet of fine sand stretching from one end of Varadero to the other and bathed by placid, emerald-green waters. From the Dupont Mansion to the western tip of Varadero the beach is accessible to anyone, whether a hotel guest or not. There is actually very little to differentiate any one section of this ten-kilometre highway of sand from another, though there tends to be a livelier atmosphere on the stretch between calles 57 and 61, where the *Albacora* restaurant looks over the beach.

Eating

For an international holiday resort the quality and variety of food in Varadero's **restaurants** is remarkably mediocre, though the choice is wider than anywhere else

Water sports and activities

Most **water sports and activites** in Varadero are organized through one of the three following marinas: **Marina Dársena**, Vía Blanca, 1km from the Varadero bridge (⊕5/66-80-63, ⓕ66-74-56), which does good-value fishing trips around northern Varadero, lasting four, six or eight hours (daily; US$200-300); **Marina Chapelin**, Autopista Sur Km 12 (⊕5/66-75-50 or 66-78-00, ⓕ66-70-93), which does a two-hour "Jungle Tour" (hourly 9am–4pm; US$35), on two-person ski-bikes; and **Marina Gaviota** at the end of Autopista Sur, Punta Hicacos (⊕5/66-77-55 or 56), which runs fishing trips (9am–3pm; US$250 for up to four people, plus US$25 per extra person), with an open bar on board a motorized yacht.

outside Havana. It's well worth trying some of the restaurants in the deluxe hotels, where the quality of food is often higher, thanks to their more direct access to foreign markets, while even the all-inclusives usually open their doors to non-guests. Like *casas particulares*, *paladares* are forbidden by law in Varadero.

Reparto Kawama

La Casa de Al in the grounds of *Villa Punta Blanca*, Ave. Kawama. Better-than-average Spanish food in one of the most impressive restaurant buildings in Varadero.

Kawama Buffet Restaurant *Hotel Kawama*, Calle 0 y Ave. Kawama ☎5/66-71-56. Dine on a terrace overlooking the beach from a regularly changing menu which can include anything from pizza to rumpsteak.

The town

Antiguedades Ave. 1era e/ 58 y 59. The menu consists of only three or four expensive, but exquisite, seafood dishes, though the atmosphere more than makes up for the limited choice. From pictures of jazz greats and bygone Hollywood stars to a wall of old clocks and even a rocking chair hanging from the ceiling, nothing in this Aladdin's cave of a restaurant looks out of place.

La Cabañita Camino del Mar y 10. The inexpensive seafood served in this beachfront bungalow isn't as popular as you might expect, probably because the restaurant is located in a distant part of town.

La Vega Ave. Playa y 31. Hearty portions of paella and other rice dishes are the highlights on the menu at this reasonably priced restaurant, themed on a tobacco plantation ranch.

East of town

Las Américas Dupont Mansion, Autopista Sur Km 7 ☎5/66-77-50. One of the classiest and most expensive restaurants on the peninsula, with seating in the library, out on the terrace and down in the wine cellar. The international menu won't win any awards but is a cut above the average; more outstanding is the selection of cocktails and wines.

Drinking, nightlife and entertainment

Nightlife is almost entirely restricted to the hotels, most of which offer something more akin to a school disco, with music to match, than a fully equipped nightclub. The majority are open to non-guests, although some of the all-inclusives may restrict entrance to their own clientele. The most popular alternative to a night on the dance floor is an evening at the **cabaret**, almost all of which are, again, run by the hotels. There are considerable differences in ambience, but wherever you go the shows themselves are basically the same displays of kitsch glamour, overly sentimental crooners and semi-naked dancers. There are surprisingly few places to go for **live music** in Varadero, the hotels again being your best bet.

Bars and cafés

Bar Benny Camino del Mar e/ 12 y 13. This beachside bar sometimes hosts live music on the patio out front, whilst in the tiny cellar-style interior is a set of photos of Cuban musician Benny Moré.

El Galeón *Hotel Dos Mares*, Calle 53 y Ave. 1era. One of the most characterful bars in town, set just below street level and with a slight Mediterranean feel. A good place to come if you're fed up with hotel bars – this is just a straight-up, laid-back place to get a drink.

Clubs and discos

Havana Club Calle 62 y Ave. 2da. The biggest nightclub in town and a popular pick-up joint. Often the last place to close at night. Cover US$5. Daily 10pm–late.

Palacio de la Rumba end of Ave. de las Américas just beyond the *Bella Costa*. Often referred to simply as *La Rumba* and as lively a night as anywhere in Varadero. Having paid the US$10 to get in, there's an open bar and therefore a guaranteed night of lost inhibitions. Daily 10pm–5am.

La Red Ave. 3era e/ 29 y 30. There's a good mix of Cubans and foreigners at this popular and friendly club, which gets packed out at weekends. Cover US$3. Daily 10pm–4am.

Cabarets and live shows

Cabaret Kawama *Hotel Kawama*, Calle 0 y Ave. Kawama. One of the more stylish cabarets, set in a cosy underground jazz-style nightclub. Cover US$5 for non-guests. Mon–Sat 11pm–late.

Continental *Hotel Internacional*, Ave. de las Américas ☎5/66-70-38. You'll have to pay US$25 to see Varadero's best and most famous cabaret. Exceeded in reputation only by the *Tropicana* in

Havana, the exaggerated costumes and heartfelt renditions of cheesy love songs make this a classic show. There's a disco afterwards. Tues–Sun 9pm–3.30am.

Península de Zapata

Forming the whole of the southern section of the province is the **Península de Zapata**, a large nature reserve covered by vast tracts of wild and unspoilt swampland and dense forests. It's equally appealing as a more orthodox holiday destination, situated on the Caribbean side of the island, with over 30km of accessible coastline and crystal-clear waters. As one of the most popular day trips from Havana and Varadero, the peninsula has built up a set of relatively slick and conveniently packaged diversions. **Boca de Guamá** draws the largest number of bus parties with its **crocodile farm** and is the point of departure for the boat trip to **Guamá**, a convincingly reconstructed lakeside Taíno Indian village. The beaches at the **Playa Girón** and **Playa Larga** resorts, where the famous **Bay of Pigs** invasion took place in 1961, are less spectacular than those of Varadero, but there are enough palm trees and white sand to keep most people happy. There's a greater emphasis on scuba diving here, most of which takes place relatively close to the shore.

The travel agent and tour operator **Rumbos** runs most of the attractions and organizes all excursions on the peninsula; the best place to go for **information** is the Rumbos-run **La Finquita** (☎59/32-24), a snack bar-cum-information centre by the side of the *autopista* at the junction with the main road into Zapata. Rumbos also runs *buros de turismo* in the lobbies of the *Hotel Playa Larga* (☎59/72-94) and *Hotel Playa Girón* (☎59/41-10). **Public transport** in this area is virtually non-existent and unless you're content to stick around one of the beach resorts you're best off **renting a car** or scooter. Both Havanautos (☎59/41-23) and Transautos (☎59/41-26) rent out cars from Playa Girón, whilst scooters are available from either of the two beachfront hotels. That said, the hotels all run various excursions of their own and, if you take advantage, then having your own transport becomes less of an issue.

Boca de Guamá and Guamá

Eighteen kilometres from the *autopista*, down the Carretera de la Ciénaga, **Boca de Guamá** is a heavily visited roadside stop. Boca, as it's referred to locally, is famous for the **Criadero de Cocodrilos** (daily 9am–4.30pm; US$5), a crocodile-breeding farm, where a short path leads from the car park to the small swamp where the beasts are fenced in. The stars of the show are left more or less to themselves and you may have trouble spotting even one on the short circuit around the swamp. For a more dramatic encounter, it's best to visit at one of the twice-weekly feeding times, though unfortunately there is no regular timetable.

Boca also serves as the departure point for boats travelling to **Guamá**, the second part of the package usually offered to day-trippers. Located on the far side of the open expanse of the Laguna de Tesoro, Guamá is intended to recreate the living conditions of the Taíno, the last of the Amerindian groups to arrive in Cuba, around a thousand years ago. A perfectly straight canal lined by fir trees leads to the **Laguna de Tesoro**, the largest natural lake in Cuba. The first of the neatly spaced islets, where you'll be dropped off, is occupied by life-sized, posed Taíno figures, each representing an aspect of their culture. Cross the footbridge to reach the diminutive **museum** detailing Taíno life and featuring a few genuine artefacts.

Passenger **boats** seating 35 people leave Boca for the village at 10am and noon every day; alternatively you can cross in a five- or six-seat **motor boat** any time between 9am and 6.30pm. In either case, an English-speaking guide is available and the round-trip costs US$10 per person.

Playa Girón

Following the road down to and then along the coast, it's a drive of around 35km from Boca de Guamá to **Playa Girón**, where the course of Cuba's destiny was played out over 72 hours in April 1961. Aside from the hotel and beach, the main reason for stopping here is the **Museo Girón** (daily 9am–noon & 1–5pm; US$2), a two-room museum documenting the events prior to and during the US-backed invasion. Outside the building is one of the fighter planes used in the defence of the island, inside, there are depictions of life before the 1959 revolution, along with dramatic photographs of US sabotage and terrorism in Cuba immediately prior to the **Bay of Pigs**. The museum goes on to document the invasion itself, with some incredible photography taken in the heat of battle and, most poignantly, photographs of each of the Cuban casualties. To bring it all to life it's worth asking the staff if you can watch the museum's ten-minute documentary, filmed at the time of combat.

The **Hotel Playa Girón** (Ⓣ59/41-10 or 41-18, Ⓕ41-17, Ⓔreservas@pgiron.cyt.cu; ❺), a stone's throw from the museum, is the largest of all the tourist complexes on the peninsula, with most of its family-sized, fully furnished, bungalows facing out to sea. There's a diving centre, pool, tennis court, car rental and all the usual services. The beach is more exposed than that at Playa Larga, to the northwest, but it's blessed with the same transparent green waters.

3.4

Trinidad and around

While **Trinidad** attracts more tourists than many of Cuba's larger cities, its status as a UNESCO-declared World Heritage Site has ensured that, as in Habana Vieja, its marvellous architecture has remained unspoiled. Plenty of other Cuban towns evoke a similar sense of the past, but there is a harmony about central Trinidad's cobbled traffic-free streets, its jumble of colonial mansions and its red-tiled rooftops, that sets it apart. Wandering the streets of the colonial district in particular, there is something of a village feel about the place – albeit a large and prosperous village – where horses are as common a sight as cars. From Trinidad, most of the province's highlights are within easy reach. In fact, the city's proximity to the **Península de Ancón** and its Caribbean beaches, and the lush mountain slopes around the **Topes de Collantes** hiking resort, make it one of the best bases on the island for discovering the different facets of Cuba's landscape.

Trinidad

The historic centre of the city is the main attraction of **TRINIDAD**, and it's there that you'll spend most of your time. In general, if you're walking on cobbled stones you're in the UNESCO-protected part of the city, often referred to as the "old town". Beyond these streets there are a number of less feted but equally historic buildings, especially in the northern limits of Trinidad, where the absence of motor vehicles and the buzz of human activity lend the muddy streets a strong sense of the past.

Arrival and information

Inter-provincial buses use the **bus terminal** (☎419/44-48 or 24-04) at Piro Guinart e/ Maceo e Izquierdo, just inside the colonial centre and within easy walking distance of a number of *casas particulares*. Arriving on the coastal road by **car** from the west will bring you into town on Piro Guinart, which leads directly up to the two main roads cutting through the centre of the city, José Martí and Antonio Maceo. From Sancti Spíritus and the east, the Circuito Sur takes cars closer to *Las Cuevas* hotel, but a left turn at Lino Pérez will take you into *casa particular* territory. Incidentally, the Cuban phenomenon of towns and cities with **old and new street names** is particularly prevalent and confusing in Trinidad. All street signs show the new names, as used in the addresses listed here.

For **information**, try **Cubatur** at Maceo esq. Francisco Javier Serquera (daily 9am–7pm; ☎419/63-14), which has a desk for taxis and car rental, as well as being an agent for Inter-Cuba flights (☎419/62-12). **Rumbos** at Simón Bolívar e/ Muñoz y Rubén Martínez in the Mesón del Regidor complex (daily 8am–8pm; ☎419/44-14) has fewer facilities, but both can arrange excursions and help with other activities such as diving or horse-riding.

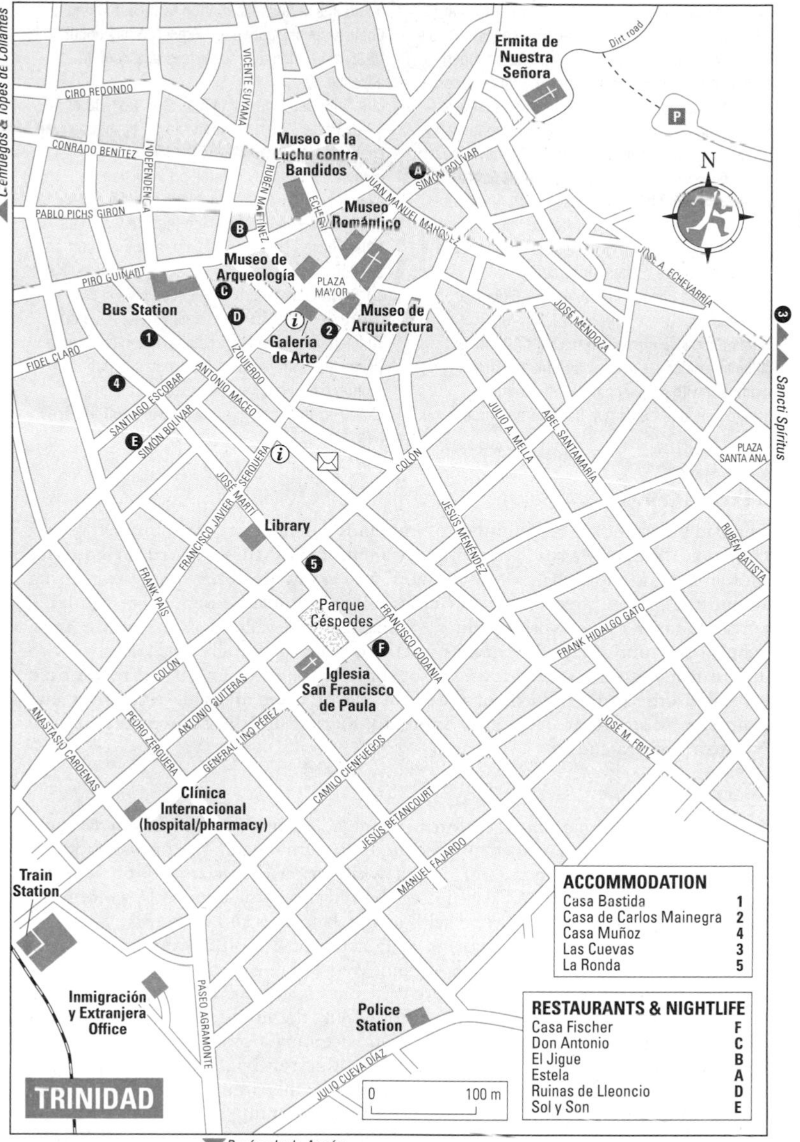

Accommodation

Trinidad has one of the best selections of **casas particulares** in the country and they're spread throughout the city, with a concentration on and around Maceo and José Martí.

Casa Bastida Maceo no. 587 e/ Simón Bolívar y Piro Guinart ☎419/21-51. One very spacious triple room with streetside balcony and one cramped double, both next to a pleasant outdoor terrace and with access to the roof. This was once also a *paladar*, and the meals are of excellent quality. ❶

Casa de Carlos Mainegra Rubén Martínez no. 21 e/ Simón Bolívar y Francisco Javier Serquera; no phone. Right on the Plaza Mayor, with one double bedroom to rent in a modest house with a plant-lined courtyard. This is a better place than some to try and negotiate a cheaper price. ❶

Casa Muñoz José Martí no. 401 e/ Fidel Claro y Santiago Escobar ☎419/36-73, ©juliotrinidad@mixmail.com. One of the finest colonial residences in Trinidad, this house is crammed with original nineteenth-century furniture, and features two bathrooms, three large bedrooms, a fantastic rooftop terrace, parking and English-speaking owners. Expect to pay about US$5 more than average prices and book in advance. ❷

Las Cuevas Finca Santa Ana ☎419/61-33 or 40-13 to 19, ℗61-61. A twenty- to thirty-minute walk east from the Plaza Mayor, this large cabin complex is superbly located on a hillside overlooking the town and coast. There's access to the cave network over which the site was built, a music-based show every night, a tennis court and the only pool in town. ❸

La Ronda José Martí e/ Colón y Lino Pérez ☎419/22-48 or 40-11. The only hotel in central Trinidad, this is an easy-going place near Parque Céspedes, with pleasing little rooms, a patio, rooftop bar and agreeable restaurant. More character than comfort, but no worse off for it. ❷

The Town

Trinidad boasts the highest number of museums per capita in the country, three on the central **Plaza Mayor**, including the memorable **Museo Romántico**, with another two no more than a few minutes' walk away. However, simply wandering around the narrow streets in the shadows of the colonial houses, whose shuttered porticoes form a patchwork of blues, greens, reds and yellows, is one of the highlights of any tour of Trinidad and it's worth conserving enough time and energy to do just that, even if it means missing out some of the museums. If you're prepared to walk a little further, north of the Plaza Mayor, there are wide-reaching views from the hillside that overlooks Trinidad, marked by the ruined **Ermita de Nuestra Señora** church.

Plaza Mayor

At the heart of the colonial section of Trinidad is the beautiful **Plaza Mayor**. Comprising four simple fenced-in gardens, each with a palm tree or two shooting out from one of the corners, and dotted with various statuettes and other ornamental touches, this is the focal point of the old town, surrounded by colourfully painted colonial mansions adorned with arches, balconies and terraces.

Overlooking the plaza on the corner of Echerrí and Simón Bolívar is the **Museo Romántico** (Tues & Thurs 8.30am–10pm, Wed & Fri–Sun 8.30am–5pm; US$2), containing one of the country's most valuable collections of antique furniture, packed into its fourteen rooms. Dating from 1808, the house itself is a magnificent example of elegant, yet restrained, nineteenth-century domestic Cuban architecture, built for the Brunet family, one of the wealthiest in Trinidad during the sugar-boom years. The contents have been gathered together from various buildings all over town, with highlights including the exquisite dining room, with its Italian marble floor, and the master bedroom featuring a four-poster bed and French wardrobe, miraculously constructed without nails or screws.

Working your way clockwise around the square from Echerrí, is the **Museo de Arquitectura** (daily 9am–5pm, closed Fri; US$2), a sky-blue and white building with a plant-decked courtyard, whose central theme is the development of domestic architecture in Trinidad during the eighteenth and nineteenth centuries. Its maps, pictures and exhibits needn't delay you for long, before nipping into the **Galería de Arte** (daily 8am–5pm), at the bottom end of the square, from where – through the open shutters upstairs – there is a perfectly framed view of the plaza.

Museo de la Lucha Contra Bandidos

A block north of Plaza Mayor, where Echerrí meets Piro Guinart, the **Museo de la Lucha Contra Bandidos** (Tues & Thurs 8.30am–10pm, Wed & Fri–Sun 8.30am–5pm; US$1) can be easily picked out by the dome-topped, yellow- and white-trimmed bell-tower that's become the trademark image of Trinidad. Displays here concentrate on the counter-revolutionary groups – the *bandidos*, or bandits – that formed during the years immediately following Castro's seizure of power in 1959. The most striking exhibits are in the central courtyard, where a military truck and a motorboat mounted with machine guns stand as examples of the hardware employed by and against the *bandidos* in their struggle to overthrow the revolutionary government. But even if the museum's contents don't appeal, it's well worth paying the entrance fee to climb the tower for the panoramic view over the city and across to the hills and coastline.

Ermita de Nuestra Señora

As it heads up and away from Plaza Mayor, Simón Bolívar leads out of Trinidad's historic centre and through a less pristine part of town; soon the road becomes a dirt track leading steeply up to the **Ermita de Nuestra Señora**, a dilapidated church marking the last line of buildings before the town dissolves into the countryside. There's nothing to see of the church but its ruins, but it's worth making the easy fifteen-minute walk up the hill for the views alone. Just beyond the ruined church you can easily cut across to the *Las Cuevas* complex, on the adjoining hillside, where non-guests can use the hillside **swimming pool** (US$1).

Eating, drinking and nightlife

With so many of the colonial mansions converted into **restaurants**, eating out is one of the easiest ways to soak up Trinidad's gracefully ageing interiors. Although the choice of food is almost exclusively restricted to *comida criolla*, the quality is, as a rule, far higher than in most of Cuba's larger cities. **Breakfast** isn't easy to come by in Trinidad, but *Hotel La Ronda* is usually willing to serve up eggs, bread, fruit and coffee for around US$4.

For **drinking**, you're best off in the restaurants listed below, many of which have separate bars. *Don Antonio* is as pleasant as anywhere and, on the same street, *Ruinas de Lleoncio* is open later and has an upstairs balcony bar. **Nightlife** in Trinidad is decidedly subdued. By far the liveliest place is **Parque Céspedes**, where an open-air disco is held every weekend, the modern salsa and pop music geared very much to the large crowd of young locals.

Restaurants

Don Antonio Izquierdo e/ Simón Bolívar y Piro Guinart. Open for lunch only, there's a fair selection here, from meat dishes to salmon or lighter meals such as tuna salad or vegetable omelette. The canopied courtyard and comfortable interior are equally appealing.

El Jigue Rubén Martínez Villena esq. Piro Guinart. Friendly place in a colonial residence, specializing in chicken dishes. Portions are on the small side, but are reasonably priced and of a high quality.

Estela Simón Bolívar no. 557 e/ Juan Manuel Marquez y José Mendoza. Although there are only three (meat-based) main courses on offer at this peaceful, backyard *paladar*, a feast of extras are laid on and the two-tier patio within high walls and under tree-tops makes this one of the most relaxing spots in town.

Sol y Son Simón Bolívar no. 283 e/ Frank País y José Martí. Choose from a number of spaghetti dishes, an array of fish, or plenty of chicken and pork plates. Everything is carefully prepared and full of flavour, served in a romantically lit courtyard. It's the best place to eat in the city.

Live music

Casa Fischer Lino Pérez e/ Gracia y José Martí. This old colonial mansion is one of the more reliable venues for live music. Folkloric nights are a mainstay and there are sometimes Cuban dance performances. Daily 9pm–1am; cover US$1.

Around Trinidad

From Trinidad some of the province's foremost attractions lie within easy reach. Probably the least energetic option is the twenty-minute drive to the **Península de Ancón**, one of the biggest beach resorts on the south coast, though still tiny by international standards. Another alternative is to head west out of the city for about 3km, then take a right turn onto the mountain road into the **Sierra del Escambray**, whose borders creep down to the outskirts of Trinidad. Here, 15km from the turn-off, is **Topes de Collantes**, a rather run-down resort that offers some excellent hikes in the surrounding national park.

There are organized **excursions** to the mountains, which you can book at either the Rumbos or Cubatur information centres in Trinidad. Alternatively, there are plenty of **private taxis** near the bus station on Piro Guinart in the city. A day trip to the mountains can be negotiated for US$20–30, depending on the car and the driver you pick, whilst a trip to the beach should only cost half as much.

Península de Ancón

The **Península de Ancón** – a five-kilometre finger of land curling out into the placid waters of the Caribbean, backed by rugged green mountains – enjoys a truly marvellous setting. Covered predominantly in scrub, the peninsula itself is not terribly impressive but does boast at least 1.5km of sandy **beach** and an idyllic stretch of largely undisturbed coastline. Shrubs and trees creep down to the shore and there is more than enough fine-grained sand, the best of it around the hotels, to keep a small army of holidaymakers happy. On the beach, the **Nautical Sports Centre** (daily 9am–5pm) rents out pedaloes, kayaks, surfboards and the like. Opposite the *Hotel Ancón* (see below), on the other side of the peninsula, **Marina Trinidad** (Ⓣ419/62-05) offers a selection of boat trips, including diving and fishing trips, for US$10–50 per person.

To **get there** from Trinidad, follow Paseo Agramonte out of town and head due south for 4km to the village of Casilda. Continue for another 4km, west along the northern edge of the Ensenada de Casilda, the bay clasped between the mainland and the peninsula, and you will hit the only road leading into Ancón. The taxi fare is around US$10 one-way but, every afternoon, the **Trinibus** from Trinidad's *Hotel Las Cuevas* makes the round-trip every hour or so for just US$2 each way.

Of the **places to stay**, *Brisas Trinidad del Mar* (Ⓣ419/65-00 to 07, Ⓕ65-65, ereservas@brisastdad.co.cu; ❺) is the newest, flashiest hotel on the peninsula and by far the most comfortable and luxurious place to stay around here. *Hotel Ancón* (Ⓣ419/61-20 to 26, Ⓕ61-51 or 61-47, ereserva@ancon.gca.cma.net; ❻), right on the best bit of beach, is an older, family-oriented all-inclusive where most activity on the peninsula is focused; facilities include a number of bars and places to eat, plus a pool, two tennis courts, a basketball hoop, volleyball net and pool tables.

Topes de Collantes

Rising to the northwest of Trinidad are the steep, pine-covered slopes of the Guamuhaya mountain range, more popularly known as the **Sierra del Escambray**. These make for some of the most spectacularly scenic – and dangerous – drives in Cuba, whether you're cutting through between Trinidad and Santa Clara, or over to Cienfuegos where most of the range, including its highest peak (Pico San Juan, 1140m), lies. Three kilometres from central Trinidad along the Trinidad–Cienfuegos coast road, a right turn takes you the 15km or so into the mountains to the scattered houses of Vegas Grandes village; immediately beyond is the resort of **Topes de Collantes**. Don't expect too much in the way of eating, entertainment or nightlife, but as a base for **hiking** this is the obvious starting-point for visiting the much larger area encompassed by the 175-square-kilometre Topes de Collantes national park.

The best way to take advantage of what's on offer is to follow one of the designated **trails**, the most popular of which heads to the **Salto del Caburní**, a 62-metre-high waterfall surrounded by pines and eucalyptus trees; at the base of the cascade is a small natural pool perfect for swimming. This 2.5-kilometre trek – which takes around three hours, there and back – begins at the northernmost point of the resort complex (see below) and takes you on one of the more clearly marked trails, down steep inclines through the dense forest to the rocky falls.

Unless you book a tour in Trinidad (which you can do through Rumbos or Cubatur), the place to get advice and maps – both absolutely essential as some of the trails are almost completely unmarked – is the **Carpeta Central** (daily 8am–5pm; ⓣ42/4-02-19), the park's **information centre**, a few minutes' walk from most of the hotels. English-speaking guides can also arrange **excursions** from a basic choice of four trails and you should be prepared to pay at least US$4 per person for each hike. Excursions, if booked directly through the Carpeta Central, cost US$16–25 per person and will usually include a lunch; there is normally a minimum of eight people required.

Practicalities

Although the rather worn-out resort is unlikely to lure you into staying the night, it might prove necessary. There are four **hotels** within the resort, two of which are permitted to rent rooms to non-Cubans. Best is the dated-looking *Los Helechos* (ⓣ42/4-01-80 to 89 ext. 2244, or 4-03-30, ⓕ4-03-01; ❸), whose rooms with balconies are surprisingly light and airy. There's a disco and a restaurant in a separate, marginally more run-down building, as well as a bowling alley and a large indoor pool. The only place to eat outside the hotels is in the limited-menu **restaurant** at Parque La Represa, a neat little patch of landscaped lawn tucked away in a corner of the complex and overlooking a stream.

△ Vintage car in Habana Vieja

3.5

Cayo Coco and Cayo Guillermo

Spanning the trunk of the island, 450km east of Havana, the provinces of Ciego de Ávila and Camagüey form the farming heart of Cuba, their handsome lowland plains given over to sugarcane, fruit trees and cattle pasture. Though the eponymous capitals of both provinces are well worth visiting, the main draws hereabouts are the paradisiacal **Cayo Coco** and **Cayo Guillermo**. These cays lie to the north of Ciego de Ávila and offer the twin pleasures of superb beaches and virgin countryside. And with one of the longest offshore reefs in the world, the cays offer excellent **diving,** while they are also home to a variety of wildlife, prompting the government to designate them an ecological protected zone.

There's a ban on locals visiting the resorts, so getting to the cays without the umbrella of a tour guide, state taxi or rental car can be a bit of a mission. Don't try to go in a private taxi, as your driver will have monumental hassle with the authorities before being routed back home, leaving you dumped at the barrier. All **road traffic** enters the cays along the causeway – where passports are checked and rental cars looked over to make sure they're not harbouring nationals – and then takes the fork for either Coco or Guillermo. **Flights** from Havana arrive daily at the airstrip on the west of Cayo Coco, from where hotel representatives whisk passengers off to their accommodation. **Tour buses** drop you off at the hotels.

Once on the cays, the best way to **get around** is by moped. Transautos rents mopeds, jeeps and sand buggies from its office at the *Sol Club Cayo Coco.* **Maps** of the cays are available from all the hotels and give a good impression of the islands but are distinctly lacking in specifics. There's no tourist office, but each hotel has a public relations officer who can provide general **information**.

Cayo Coco

With 22km of creamy white sands and cerulean waters, **Cayo Coco** easily fulfils its hyperbolic tourist-brochure claims. The islet is 32km wide from east to west, with a hill like a camel's hump rising from the middle. The best beaches are clustered on the north coast, dominated by the all-inclusive hotels (all built in the last decade), whose tendrils are gradually spreading along the rest of the northern coastline.

The big three **beaches** hog the narrow easternmost peninsula, which juts out of the cay's north coast. Spanning the tip, and home to the *Sol Club Cayo Coco*, **Playa Las Coloradas** is exceptionally picturesque, with fine sand and calm, shallow waters. It's a good place for watersports and is busy with cruising **catamarans and pedaloes** – a US$50 all-inclusive day-pass, which includes all meals and drinks, lets you join in. Three kilometres west, **Playa Larga** and **Playa Las Conchas**, divided by name only, form a continuous strip of silvery sand. They are arguably the best beaches on the island, although very crowded during the organized activities laid on by the *Hotel and Club Cayo Coco Tryp*. Non-guests are welcome to use the beaches during the day – access is through the hotel – though to use any of the facilities will cost US$40 for an all-inclusive day-pass; access is restricted at night.

For solitude, head west along the main dirt road to **Playa Los Flamencos**, demarcated by a stout stucco flamingo, which has 3km of golden sands and clear waters where tangerine-coloured starfish float through the shallows – this is a good place for **snorkelling**. The beach gets busy in the daytime but wandering away from the lively, expensive bar should guarantee some privacy.

Away from the beach strip, dirt roads – perfect for mopeds – allow easy access into the lush wooded **interior**, where hidden delights include sightings of hummingbirds and pelicans, some gorgeous lagoons and **Sitio La Güira**, a re-creation of an old Cuban peasant village. Although it's something of a novelty theme park, a number of interesting exhibits rescue it from tackiness; entrance is free, there is an on-site restaurant (see below), and riding and walking tours are offered (US$5 an hour for the horse; rates for a guide are negotiable).

Accommodation

With no towns or villages to offer *casas particulares*, **accommodation** on Cayo Coco is almost totally limited to a few plush **all-inclusives**, grouped together on the main beach strips. The only alternative is right at the other end of the scale, bedding down at the **beach hut** on Playa Los Flamencos (ask at the *Flamenco* bar).

Hotel and Club Cayo Coco Tryp Playa Larga ⓣ33/30-13-00, ⓕ30-13-75, ⓔhtcc@club.tryp.cma.net. The oldest and best hotel on the strip is actually two hotels combined into one, built to look like a colonial village and with accommodation in cobalt-blue and yellow buildings shaded by healthy palms. Although equipped with all the usual facilities, including baby club, nursery and beach activities, it feels more Cuban than the other four-stars on the strip. ❼

Meliá Cayo Coco Playa Las Coloradas ⓣ33/30-11-80, ⓕ30-11-95, ⓔmelia.cayo.coco@solmelia.com. Opulent hotel with deluxe chalet-style accommodation, a large pool, children's area and a full range of amenities, including sauna, gym and watersports. The theme nights and organized games give it the feel of a holiday camp, albeit a very upmarket one. ❽

Sol Club Cayo Coco Playa Las Coloradas ⓣ33/30-12-80, ⓕ30-12-85, ⓔsol.club.cayo.coco@solmelia.com. Palatial but anonymous glass-fronted hotel with three international-quality restaurants, sauna, gym, mini-club for kids and a multitude of sports, including free preliminary dive classes in the pool. ❼

Eating, drinking and nightlife

With all **food** and **drinks** included in your hotel bill if you're staying on the cays, you probably won't need to look elsewhere for meals, although there are a few places that cater for day-trippers. If you've paid for a day-pass at one of the hotels, you can dine there and go on to the hotel disco afterwards. *Sol Club Cayo Coco* has a disco with **live salsa** and tacky floorshows, but the one at *Hotel and Club Cayo Coco Tryp* is better, with a raucous palm-wood bar overlooking the sea at the end of a pier, and a house DJ alternating *salsa* with Europop.

Cueva del Jabalí. This natural cave 5km inland from the hotel strip takes its name from the one-time resident wild boar evicted to make way for the restaurant, which serves moderately priced roast pork and grilled meats. It's best during the day, when you can admire the peaceful countryside, but is more animated in the evening with a glittery cabaret. Closed Sun & Mon.

Playa Flamenco Bar. A friendly, though pricey, beach bar with trestle tables under a palm wattle roof, serving Cuban cuisine (and occasionally lobster) to the strains of a mariachi band.

Playa Prohibida Bar. A tiny beach bar serving tasty barbecued chicken and fish.

Sitio La Güira. A ranch restaurant in the midst of Cayo Coco's recreated village, specializing in *escabeche* – meats and fish prepared in a pickle made from oil, vinegar, peppercorn and herbs – and holding a *Guateque*, "a farm party with animation activities and lessons on typical dances". Closes at 10pm.

Cayo Guillermo

Bordered by pearl-white sand melting into opal waters, **Cayo Guillermo** is a quieter, more serene retreat than its neighbour, although there's a fair amount of hotel construction taking place and it may not remain so forever. It is here that the cays' colony of twelve thousand **flamingos** (celebrated in all Cuban tourist literature) gathers and, although they are wary of the noise of passing traffic, while crossing the causeway you can glimpse them swaying in the shallows and feeding on the sandbanks. As the presence of the birds testifies, there is a wealth of fish, notably marlin, in the waters and the cay's marina offers a range of deep-sea fishing expeditions. At only thirteen square kilometres the cay is tiny, but its 4km of stunning beaches seem expansive. It's quite a trek from the mainland if you are not staying overnight, but arriving early and spending a day lounging on the sands and exploring the offshore coral reef definitely merits the effort.

All the hotels and beaches are strung along the north coast, apart from gorgeous **Playa Pilar** on the western tip of the cay. This was Ernest Hemingway's favourite hideaway in Cuba and is named after his yacht, *The Pilar*. With its limpid waters and squeaky-clean beaches, Playa Pilar is the top beach choice on Guillermo, if not the entire cays, though there are no facilities other than a small beach bar. The two other beaches on Guillermo are **Playa El Medio** and **Playa El Paso** on the north coast, serving the *Sol Club Cayo Guillermo* and *Villa Cojímar* respectively. Popular with package-tour holidaymakers, both have shallow swimming areas and lengthy beaches, though El Medio also has towering sand dunes, celebrated as the highest in the Caribbean.

Practicalities

Accommodation on Cayo Guillermo is restricted to several slick all-inclusives largely patronized by Italians. *Club Villa Cojímar* on Playa El Medio (Ⓣ33/2-23-52; ❼) provides four-star services, with snazzy rooms, a large pool, two restaurants and ample sports facilities. Also on Playa El Medio, *Sol Club Cayo Guillermo* (Ⓣ33/30-17-60, Ⓕ30-17-48, Ⓔreserve@cguille.solmelia.cma.net; ❼) has similar facilities with pleasant, spacious rooms – some with a sea view. Brand-new **Iberostar Daquiri** (Ⓣ33/30-16-50, Ⓕ30-16-41, Ⓔinfo@iberostarcaribe.com; ❼) offers colonial-style bungalows and a private beach, and the usual amenities. **Day-passes** for all the hotels (inclusive of meals and drinks) will set you back US$40, but you can use *Sol Club Cayo Guillermo*'s stretch of beach for free. Outside the hotel **restaurants** you are limited to a floating bar and a beach restaurant on Playa Pilar, a simple wooden lean-to where you can eat excellent but pricey barbecued fish and lobster as skinny cats rub around your ankles. Opening times fluctuate, but service around lunchtime is usually guaranteed.

The **Marina Cayo Guillermo**, at the entrance to the cay near the *Club Villa Cojímar*, runs deep-sea fishing excursions for US$200/400 for a half/full day; dive trips to the best sites around Cayo Media Luna, the tiny crescent cay off Playa Pilar (each dive costs US$35); and yacht "seafaris" with time set aside for off-shore swimming and snorkelling.

3.6

Northern Oriente

Traditionally, the whole of the country east of Camagüey is known simply as the "Oriente". Running the length of the north coast, the three provinces that make up the **northern Oriente** – Las Tunas, Holguín and Guantánamo – form a mountainous landscape fringed by flatlands, with some of the country's most breath-taking peaks and stunning white-sand beaches.

Possibly the quietest and least dynamic province in Cuba, Las Tunas is justifiably overlooked by visitors pushed for time. By contrast, larger Holguín province has a variety of attractions, not least the **Guardalavaca** resort, whose beaches and lively atmosphere draw scores of holidaymakers. Of the three provinces it is undoubtedly Guantánamo, with the notorious US naval base at **Caimanera**, that is best known. Many Cubans living in this region are of Haitian and Jamaican origin – the result of late nineteenth- and early twentieth-century immigration – while an indigenous heritage is still visible in the far east. Although the provincial capital, small and quiet **Guantánamo town**, is a very ordinary place, it forms a useful jumping-off point for the seaside settlement of **Baracoa**, one of Cuba's most enjoyable destinations. Sealed off from the rest of the island by a truly awe-inspiring range of rainforested mountains – fantastic for trekking – Baracoa's small-town charm is immensely welcoming and a visit here is the highlight of many trips.

Guardalavaca and around

Despite being the province's main tourist resort, **GUARDALAVACA**, on the north coast 112km from Holguín, retains a charmingly homespun air. Surrounded by hilly countryside and shining fields of sugarcane, it combines small-scale intimacy with a vibrancy lent by its youthful visitors. Four hotels are centred on the lively **Playa Guardalavaca** and there's a more exclusive satellite resort at **Playa Esmeralda**, about 5km away. **Guardalavaca town**, which backs onto the resort, is little more than a clutch of houses, though the surrounding area has enough sights to keep you busy for a couple of days should you tire of sunning yourself on the beaches.

The beaches and local excursions

A 1500-metre-long stretch of sugar-white sand dappled with light streaming through abundant foliage, **Playa Guardalavaca** is a delight. One of its most refreshing aspects is that, unlike many resort beaches, it's open to Cubans as well as tourists, which gives it a certain vitality. A shady boulevard of palms, tamarind and sea grape trees runs along the centre of the beach, the branches strung with hammocks and T-shirts for sale. Groups of friends hang out chatting or resting in the shade, while children play in the water. Those seeking solitude should head to the eastern end, where the beach breaks out of its leafy cover and is usually fairly deserted. Midway along, a restaurant serves simple snacks and drinks, and there are stands renting out **snorkelling equipment** so you can explore the coral reef offshore.

A five-kilometre trip west from Guardalavaca, along the Holguín road, **Playa Esmeralda** – also known as Estero Ciego – boasts clear blue water, a smooth swathe of powdery sand speckled with thatched sunshades, and two luxury hotels hidden from view by thoughtfully planted bushes and shrubs. If you want unashamed, hassle-free luxury, where the intrusion of local culture is kept to a bare minimum, this is the place for you. The beach is owned by the hotels but is open to non-guests, although you'll have to pay for a day-pass (around US$40) for facilities, meals and drinks. Also in the resort is a **horse-riding centre**, opposite the hotels, with negotiable rates for treks into the countryside, and *Hotel Sol Club Río de Luna*'s **dive centre**, Easy Sport (ⓣ24/3-01-02), offering dives for US$50 and courses for between US$50 and US$500.

All the hotels arrange excursions to the fascinating **Taíno burial ground**, uncovered about 3km away in the Maniabon hills, which incorporates a re-creation of a Taíno village that really brings the lost culture to life. Close to Playa Esmeralda, at the Bahía de Naranjo, an offshore **aquarium** offers an entertaining day out. Visits can be arranged with the hotels. Alternatively, one of the most rewarding pastimes is to rent a bicycle or moped and head off into the countryside to enjoy stunning views over the hills and sea.

Accommodation

As a prime resort, Guardalavaca's **accommodation** consists of all-inclusive hotels at the top end of the price range, and while most deliver the standards you would expect for the price-tag, a couple fall slightly short. As the region has grown up with the tourist industry, there are no peso hotels nor any registered *casas particulares*, although you might be able to find unregistered accommodation in the houses near the beach.

The three hotels around **Playa Guardalavaca** are interconnected, with guests at each entitled to vouchers that allow them to eat in the restaurants of the others; *Delta Las Brisas Club Resort* is based at Playa Las Brisas, 1.5km to the east. All four of these offer free watersports, including kayaks, catamarans and diving classes in the hotel pools (open-water dives cost extra), although you have to pay for the jet-skis and rides on the inflatable yellow banana. The two hotels at **Playa Esmeralda** are decidedly fabulous, facing the low peaks of the Cerro de Maita mountains and with a full complement of facilities.

Playa Guardalavaca

Atlántico ⓣ24/3-01-80, ⓕ3-02-00. A costly makeover has almost brought the *Atlántico* into line with its more modern neighbours, and with big, airy rooms it's a reasonable choice. Twinned with *Atlántico Bungalow*, and guests are free to use the facilities there too. ❸

Atlántico Bungalow ⓣ24/3-01-95, ⓕ3-02-00. With spacious, well-appointed rooms laid out in "bungalow" blocks, a generously proportioned pool and good international food, this hotel makes for a comfortable stay, though it's a short walk from the beach. There's a large pool, non-motorized watersports, bars and restaurants, and a children's club. Those after peace and quiet might not appreciate the staff's relentless encouragement to join in the fun and games. ❺

Club Amigo Guardalavaca ⓣ24/3-01-21. As the oldest on the strip, this hotel is something of a poor relation, with slightly shabby rooms – it's telling that this is the only hotel on the strip open to ordinary Cubans. That said, the staff are friendly and what they lack in competence they make up for in enthusiasm. ❺

Las Brisas Calle 2 no. 1 ⓣ24/3-02-18, ⓕ3-00-18. There's a choice between rooms and suites within the hotel building or more privacy in newer, bungalow-style rooms, although all are equally luxurious (and the suites have jacuzzis). Four restaurants, three snack bars, a beauty salon, massage parlour, kids' camp and watersports, as well as mercifully restrained variety show-style entertainment. Non-guests can wallow in luxury for US$25 a day. ❻

Playa Esmeralda

Sol Club Río de Luna ⓣ24/3-00-30. The grander of Playa Esmeralda's two hotels whose spacious, well-appointed rooms (many with a sea view) are equipped with cable television and security boxes. Also tennis, sauna, gym, sailing school and excursions into the surrounding countryside. ❼

Sol Río de Mares ⓣ24/3-00-60. Large, comfortable rooms overlook a central swimming pool, and the hotel offers a range of facilities including two restaurants, three bars, extensive watersports and a pool table. The attractive lobby is filled with a mass of greenery, home to several tame birds. ❻

Guantánamo town and around

GUANTÁNAMO town is only on the tourist map because of the proximity of the US **Guantánamo naval station**, 22km southeast, but the base plays a very small part in the everyday life of the town itself. For the most part, this is a slow-paced provincial capital, marked by a few ornate buildings, attractive but largely featureless streets, and an easy-going populace. Many visitors come to see the US base and although you can get to the two lookout points, **Mirador Malones** and **Caimanera**, with a little groundwork, there really isn't a lot to see and you cannot enter the base itself.

Buses from Santiago, Baracoa, Havana and Holguín arrive at the Astro Terminal de Omnibus, Carretera Santiago, 2.5km out of town. Daily trains from Santiago, Havana and Las Tunas pull in at the central **train station**, housed in a squat Art Deco folly on Pedro A. Pérez. The main **hotel**, *Guantánamo*, at Ahogados esq. 13 Norte, Reparto Caribe (☎21/38-10-15; ❷), 5km from the centre, is a typical, hulking, old-style Cuban hotel. Much nicer is the intimate *Casa de los Sueños*, 500m further along the street, at Ahogados esq. 15 Norte (☎21/38-16-01; ❷), with three double rooms. *Casa de Elsye Castillo Osoria*, Calixto García no. 766 e/ Prado y Jesús del Sol (❷), is a friendly *casa particular* with a sunny courtyard.

There are several **restaurants** in the centre, though few are well stocked with food. *El Colonial* and *La Cubanita*, neighbouring *paladares* on Martí esq. Crombet, both serve adequate portions of pork or chicken with rice and beans for around US$5, while the *Guantánamo* hotel restaurant, *Guaso*, boasts a more interesting menu than most, with a house speciality of chicken "Gordon Blue" – stuffed with ham. The tastiest food, including fritters, milkshakes and hot rolls, comes from the **street stands** clustered at the south end of Pedro A. Pérez, while *Coppelia*, at Pedro A. Pérez esq. Varona, does bargain bowls of ice cream for a couple of pesos.

Mirador Malones

The more easily accessible of the two naval base lookouts, **Mirador Malones** is 32km from town, on the east of the bay, near Boquerón. At the top of a steep hill of dusty cacti and grey scrubs, a purpose-built platform is equipped with a restaurant and high-powered binoculars. From a distance of 6km, and at 320m above sea level, the view of the base is rather indistinct, but you can make out a few buildings and see the odd car whizzing past. The real wonder is the view of the whole bay area: dramatically barren countryside, luminous sea and unforgiving desert frequented by hovering vultures. You can arrange a trip with a guide through the *Guantánamo* hotel in town (see above; US$6 per person plus around US$15 for an unmetered taxi).

Caimanera

Bordered by salt flats that score the ground with deep cracks, **CAIMANERA**, 23km south of Guantánamo, takes its name from the giant caiman lizards that used to roam here, although today it's far more notable as the last point in Cuba before

Guantanamera: the song

Synonymous with the beleaguered history of the US naval base, Guantánamo is an enduring legacy of the struggle between the US and Cuba. In name at least, it's one of the best-known places in Cuba, thanks to the immortal song **Guantanamera** – written by Joseito Fernández in the 1940s as a tribute to the women of Guantánamo. Made internationally famous by North American folk singer Pete Seeger during the 1970s, it has become something of a Cuban anthem and a firm – if somewhat hackneyed – favourite of tourist bar troubadours the world over, a fitting fate for the song which includes words from José Martí's most famous work, *Versos Sencillos*.

you reach the US naval base. The village is a restricted area, with the ground between here and the base one of the most heavily mined areas in the world, although this hasn't stopped many disaffected Cubans from braving it in the hope of escaping to America. Until 1995, many who chanced it, along with those who were brought to the base after being rescued from makeshift rafts in the Florida Straits, were allowed into the US on humanitarian grounds, but illegal Cuban immigrants are now returned to Cuban territory. The village is entered via a **checkpoint** at which guards scrutinize your passport before waving you through. The lookout is within the grounds of the **Hotel Caimanera** (☎9/94-14-16; ❷), which has a view over the bay and mountains to the base – though even with binoculars (US$1), you only see a sliver of it. You can use the lookout without being a guest of the hotel but you must phone ahead to let them know you are coming: staff then alert the checkpoint of your imminent arrival. A taxi from town costs US$15–20, and you will need a guide, which you can arrange through the *Guantánamo* hotel.

Baracoa

In the eyes of many who visit, **BARACOA** is quite simply the most beautiful place in Cuba. Set on the island's southeastern tip and protected by a deep curve of mountains, its isolation has so far managed to protect it from some of the more pernicious effects of tourism creeping into other areas of the island. Surrounded by awe-inspiring countryside – whose abundance of cacao trees makes it the nation's **chocolate** manufacturer – Baracoa is fast becoming an absolute must on the travellers' circuit.

On a spot christened Porto Santo by Christopher Columbus, who arrived here in 1492 and, as legend has it, planted a cross in the soil, Baracoa was the first town to be established in Cuba, founded by Diego de Velázquez in 1511. The early conquistadors never quite succeeded in exterminating the indigenous population and direct descendants of the Taíno population are alive today, with Baracoa the only place in Cuba where they survive. Their legacy is also present in several myths and legends that are habitually told to visitors.

Half the fun of a visit to Baracoa is getting there. Before the revolution, the town was only accessible by sea, but the opening of **La Farola**, a road through the mountains that provides a direct link with Guantánamo, 120km away, changed all that and a flood of cars poured into town. Considered to be one of the triumphs of the revolution, the road was actually started during Batista's regime but was temporarily abandoned when he refused to pay a fair wage to the workers, and work was only resumed in the 1960s. Today, it makes for an amazing trip through the knife-sharp peaks of the Cuchillas de Baracoa mountains.

Arrival, information and getting around

The **airport**, Aeropuerto Gustavo Rizo (☎4/2-52-80), is near the *Porto Santo* hotel, on the west side of the bay, 4km from the centre; taxis wait to take you into town for US$2–3. **Buses** pull up at the Astro bus terminal, west on the Malecón, with services to and from Santiago (10–11 weekly; 6hr), Guantánamo (10–11 weekly; 4hr) and Havana (1 every other day; 20hr); it's a short walk down Maceo to the centre, or you can take a *bicitaxi* for ten pesos. The private peso trucks that arrive from over the mountains via La Farola drop off on Maceo.

There's no official **information** bureau in town, but the staff at the *El Castillo* hotel are extremely helpful. The best way to **get around** is on foot, as most of the places you'll want to see are within easy reach of the centre. To travel further afield, catch a *bicitaxi* or unmetered **taxi** from outside the tobacco factory at Calle Martí no. 214. There's little point relying on public transport – buses are scarce and always jam-packed. **Excursions** to the surrounding countryside can be arranged through the *El Castillo* hotel (see overleaf). For a less official trek, pay a visit to Castro at the

Fuerte Matachín museum (☎4/21-22), a knowledgeable town character who will be happy to negotiate a tailor-made trip for you.

Accommodation

In *El Castillo*, Baracoa has one of the most characterful **hotels** in Cuba, though the sheer volume of visitors means that this and the two other hotels in town are often full. However, the taxes on private accommodation are low and you'll find a number of superb **casas particulares**, all within a few streets of one another.

Casa de Sr Dulce Maria Máximo Gómez no. 140 e/ Pelayo Cuervo y Ciro Frias ☎4/22-14 (after 5pm). A charismatic little room, with one double bed and one single, as well as a private bathroom and a kitchen with fridge. Good for a longer stay. ❷

El Castillo Calixto García ☎4/21-25. Perched on a hill overlooking the town, this former military post, one of a trio of forts built to protect Baracoa, was built between 1739 and 1742 and is now an intimate, comfortable and very welcoming hotel. Glossy tiles and wood finishes give the rooms a unique charm, while the handsome pool patio (US$2 for non-guests) is the best place in town to sip *mojitos*. Reservations essential. ❷

Jorge M. Martinez Flor Crombet, no. 105 e/ Maraví y Frank País ☎4/23-76. A range of rooms all with private bathrooms, A/C and warm water, run by an enterprising man who also serves food and runs excursions. ❷

Ykira Mahiquez Maceo 168A e/ Céspedes y Ciro Frias; ☎4/24-66. Casual accommodation on a friendly street one block from the main square. The owner knows almost everyone in town with a room to let, so if her place is full she'll be able to point you elsewhere. ❷

The Town

Although many will be happy simply to wander through the town, enjoying its easy charm, there are several tangible attractions. Baracoa's most notable exhibit is **La Cruz de la Parra**, the celebrated cross which is reputed to have been erected by Christopher Columbus himself. It is housed in the picturesque **Catedral de Nuestra Señora de la Asunción**, on the edge of leafy **Parque Independencia**, a local gathering point. On the east side of town you'll find the **Fuerte Matachín**, one of a trio of forts built to protect colonial Baracoa, and now the site of the town museum (daily 8am–noon & 2pm–6pm; US$1). Further east is the main beach, **Playa Boca de Miel**, shingled in jade, grey and crimson stones, and a lively summer-time hangout. Converted from the second of the town's fortifications, which overlook the town from the northern hills, the **El Castillo** hotel is a peaceful retreat, while on the western side of town, the third fort, **Fuerte La Punta**, is now a restaurant and overlooks the **Playa La Punta** – the best bet for solitude seekers.

Baracoa has a strong tradition of local art, with reasonably priced originals sold at **La Casa Yara**, Maceo no. 120 (Mon–Fri 8am–noon & 1–6pm, Sat & Sun 8am–noon), along with coconut-wood jewellery, hand-made boxes and other trinkets. Art is also available from the **Casa de la Cultura**, at Maceo no. 124 – look out for paintings by Luís Eliades Rodríguez.

Eating and drinking

After the monotonous cuisine found in much of the rest of Cuba, **food** in Baracoa is ambrosial, drawing on a rich local heritage and the region's plentiful supply of coconuts. Tuna, red snapper and swordfish fried in coconut oil are favourite dishes and there is an abundance of clandestine lobster, as well as a few vegetarian specials. Look out for *cucurucho*, a deceptively filling concoction of coconut, orange, guava and lots of sugar, sold in a palm-leaf wrap. Other treats for the sweet-toothed include the locally produced Peter's chocolate and the soft drink *Prú*, widely available from *ofreta* stands, a fermented blend of sugar and secret spices that's something of an acquired taste.

Casa Tropical Martí no. 175 e/ Céspedes y Ciro Frias. A central *casa particular* with a cool interior and a friendly atmosphere that offers food to non-guests. Excellent swordfish and generous helpings of shellfish, when available, are served in a courtyard beside an ailing papaya tree.
La Colonial Martí no. 123 e/ Maraví y Frank País ☎4/31-61. A homey place offering standard, though well-prepared, Cuban dishes for US$6–8 per person. It gets very busy, so reservations are recommended – as is early arrival.
La Duaba Calixto García ☎4/21-25. The weekly buffet night at *El Castillo* hotel offers the best meal in town – a feast of Baracoan dishes featuring coconut, maize, local vegetables and herbs, all for US$10–15.
La Punta Ave. de los Martires, at the west end of the Malecón. An elegant 24-hour restaurant in the grounds of La Punta fort, serving traditional Cuban and Baracoan food, some spaghetti dishes and the house speciality, *bacan*, a delicious baked dish with meat, green bananas and coconut milk. There's a cabaret show on from 9pm to midnight, so arrive early if you want a peaceful meal.
Walter's Rupert López no. 47 e/ Céspedes y Coroneles Galano. This open-air restaurant offers an excellent view over the bay, perfect for watching the sun set over *El Castillo*, and serves satisfying portions of rice and beans with pork, goat or the catch of the day. Just don't expect speedy service.

Nightlife and entertainment

Baracoa has quite an active **nightlife**, perhaps surprisingly so for such a small town, though it's essentially centred on two small but boisterous venues near Parque Independencia. The most sophisticated option is twilight cocktails at *El Castillo* rooftop bar. Baracoa's small **cinema**, Cine-Teatro Encanto, Maceo no. 148, screens Cuban and North American films every evening.

485 Aniversario de la Fundación de la Ciudad Maceo 141, in front of Parque Independencia. Known by all as "el cuatro ocho cinco", this is *the* place to hang out in town. In a room reminiscent of a village hall salsa bands play for a mixed crowd of Cubans and visitors, while across the courtyard, a fire escape leads to a precarious roof-top disco where you've every chance of taking a dive over the edge. Downstairs 9pm–3.30am; upstairs 9pm until they decide to close.
Casa de la Cultura Maceo e/ Frank País y Maraví. A haven of jaded charm, with live music and dancing on the patio nightly. Tends to get going around 9 or 10pm.
Casa de la Trova Victorino Rodríguez no. 149B e/ Ciro Frias y Pelillo Cuevo. Concerts take place in a tiny room opposite Parque Independencia, after which the chairs are pushed back to the wall and exuberant dancers spill onto the pavement. Mon–Fri 9pm–midnight, Sat 9pm–1am.
La Terraza Calle Maceo 120. A lively open-air terrace bar whose varied repertoire includes magic shows and comedians, as well as dancing to western disco music with a smattering of salsa. Popular with Cuban couples and visitors. Cover US$1. Open daily 8pm–3am.

3.7

Santiago de Cuba and Granma

The southern part of Oriente – the island's easternmost third – is defined by the **Sierra Maestra**, Cuba's largest mountain range, which binds together the provinces of Santiago de Cuba and Granma. Rising directly from the shores of the Caribbean, the mountains make much of the region largely inaccessible, a quality appreciated by the rebels who spent years waging war here.

At the eastern end of the *sierra*, the romantic provincial capital **city of Santiago de Cuba** draws visitors mainly for its music, at its best in July when **carnival** drenches the town in rumba beats, fabulous costumes, excitement and song. This talent for making merry has placed Cuba's second city firmly on the tourist map, but there's much more to the place than carnival. Briefly the island's first capital, Santiago has a rich colonial heritage and played an equally distinguished role in more recent history, as the place where Fidel Castro and his small band of rebels fired the opening shots of the revolution. Further west, bordering Granma province, the heights of the Sierra Maestra vanish into awe-inspiring cloud forests, and although access to the **Parque Nacional Turquino** – around Pico Turquino, Cuba's highest peak – is often restricted, you can still admire it from afar. Unlike Santiago de Cuba, which is centred around its main city, the province of Granma has no definite focus. The small black-sand beach resort at Marea del Portillo gives Granma some sort of tourist centre, but the highlight of the province, missed by many, is the **Parque Nacional Desembarco del Granma**, lying in wooded countryside at the foot of the Sierra Maestra and easily explored from the beach of **Las Coloradas**.

Santiago de Cuba city

Nowhere outside Havana is there a Cuban city with such definite character or such determination to have a good time as **SANTIAGO DE CUBA**. Set on a deep-water bay and cradled by mountains, the city is credited with being the most Caribbean part of Cuba, a claim borne out by the laid-back lifestyle and rich mix of inhabitants. It was here that the first slaves arrived from West Africa, and today Santiago boasts a larger percentage of black people than anywhere else in Cuba. **Afro-Cuban culture**, with its music, myths and rituals, formed its roots here, with later layers added by French coffee-planters fleeing revolution in Haiti in the eighteenth century. Santiago's proximity to Jamaica has encouraged a natural crossover of ideas and it is one of the few places in Cuba to have a strong Rastafari following, albeit a hybrid one – devout Jamaican Rastas are teetotal vegetarians who don't wolf down huge plates of fried pork with lashings of beer.

The leisurely pace of life doesn't make for a quiet city, however, and the higgledy-piggledy arrangement of narrow streets around the colonial quarter rings night and day with the beat of drums and the toot of horns. **Music** is a vital element of *Santiaguero* life, oozing from the most famous Casa de la Trova in the country, not to mention numerous impromptu gatherings. Although music and the July carnival are good enough reasons to visit, the city offers a host of other attractions too. Diego Velázquez's sixteenth-century merchant house and the elegant governor's residence, both around **Parque Céspedes**, and the commanding **El Morro** castle at the entrance to the bay, reflect the city's prominent role in Cuban history. Added to this, the part played by townspeople in the **revolutionary struggle**, detailed in several fascinating museums, makes Santiago an important stop-off on the revolution trail.

Arrival, information and getting around

Flights arrive at the **Aeropuerto Internacional Antonio Maceo** (☎226/9-10 14), near the southern coast, 8km from the city. Metered and unmetered **taxis** wait outside and charge around US$10–15 to take you to the centre, while there is sometimes a bus that meets flights from Havana, charging around 5 pesos for the same journey. You can arrange car rental at the Havanautos desk at the airport or at agencies in town, including Cubacar on Avenida de los Defiles (☎226/5-45-68).

Inter-provincial buses pull in at the **Astro bus terminal** on Avenida de los Libertadores (☎226/2-30-50), 2km from the town centre. Next door, tourist buses arrive at the **Víazul bus depot** (☎226/12-84-84); there are daily services to and from Havana (15hr 30min). A taxi to the centre from either terminal costs US$3–4. Provincial buses use the **Terminal de Omnibus Intermunicipal**, on Paseo de Martí, north of Parque Céspedes (☎226/2-43-25).

Arriving by **train** (10 weekly services from Havana; 14hr) you'll alight at the station near the port, on Paseo de Martí esq. Jesús Menéndez (☎226/2-28-36), from where horse-drawn buggies and *bicitaxis* can take you to the centre for around US$3, while a taxi will cost around US$5.

Information

Santiago boasts an excellent **tourist information bureau** on the Plaza de Marte, at no. 5 Perez Carbo (Mon–Sat 8am–5pm; ☎226/2-33-02), with a wealth of information on the city's music scene, plus weekly events bulletins and cinema listings. You can also buy **maps** here, as well as from the Tienda Rialto shop below the cathedral, at no. 654 Santo Tomás, and the shop in the basement of the *Hotel Casa Granda*. Santiago's weekly **newspaper**, the *Sierra Maestra* (20 centavos), is available from street vendors and occasionally from the bigger hotels and has a brief **listings** section detailing cinema, theatre and other cultural activities.

Getting around

Although a large city, Santiago is easy to negotiate, as much of what you'll want to see is contained within the historic core around Parque Céspedes. Even the furthest sights are no more than around 4km from Parque Céspedes, making it an excellent city for **exploring on foot**. However, taxis are the best way to reach outlying sights, as the buses are overcrowded and irregular.

Metered taxis wait on the cathedral side of Parque Céspedes or around Plaza de Marte and charge between forty and eighty cents per kilometre, with a US$1.50 surcharge, while the **unmetered taxis** parked on San Pedro negotiate a rate for the whole journey – expect to pay about US$3–4 to cross town. A cheaper option for the brave – or foolhardy – are the **motorbike taxis** that hare round town as fast as their two-cylinder engines can carry them. These congregate at the corner of San Pedro and Aguilera, by the Casa de Cultura, and all rides within the city cost 10 pesos.

In the *Hotel Casa Granda* you'll find Havanatur (Mon–Sat 8am–5pm; ☎226/86-1-52), one of the two agencies in Santiago offering **city tours**. Its rival, Agencia de Viajes Rumbos (daily 8am–5pm; ☎226/2-22-22), opposite the hotel, is friendlier and can also make bookings at state hotels elsewhere in the country. Both agencies offer similarly priced **excursions** throughout the province.

Accommodation

Accommodation in Santiago is plentiful and varied. Except during carnival in July, when rooms are snapped up well in advance, you can usually turn up on spec, though making a reservation will save you the possibility of having to trudge around the city, especially as accommodation is spread over a wide area.

Hotels

Casa Granda Heredia no. 201 e/ San Pedro y San Félix ⓣ226/8-66-00, ⓕ8-60-35. A tourist attraction in itself, the beautiful *Casa Granda* is a recently restored 1920s' hotel overlooking Parque Céspedes. From the elegant, airy lobby to its two atmospheric bars, it has a stately, colonial air reflected in its tasteful rooms. ❻

Gran Hotel Enramada esq. San Félix ⓣ226/2-04-72. Whilst it no longer merits the "grand" of its title, the vaguely colonial exterior and faded interior charm is very appealing if you don't mind roughing it a bit – there's no hot water in the somewhat grubby bathrooms. Singles, doubles and triples all come with A/C, many with a tiny balcony overlooking the busy shopping street. ❷

Casas particulares

Casa Colonial Maruchi San Félix no. 357 e/ San Germán y Trinidad ⓣ226/62-74-87, ⓦwww.casacolonialmaruchi.turincon.com. Three A/C rooms in a colonial house with many appealing features, like brass beds, exposed brickwork and a well-tended patio. Sharing a bathroom is the only drawback. ❷

Casa de Eumelia Marisy Calle Clarín no. 3 e/ Aguilera y Heredia ⓣ226/2-05-09. Two light and fairly spacious rooms – one with two beds and both with A/C – in a comfortable house with a rooftop patio, communal refrigerator and laundry area. A good choice for self-catering accommodation. ❷

Casa de Giovanni Villalón Heredia no. 353 e/ Reloj y Calavario ⓣ226/5-19-72. This centrally located, gracefully shabby colonial house offers two rooms and a shared cold-water bathroom (though the owners will heat saucepans of water as required). ❷

Casa de Leonard Rodríguez Calleja Clarín no. 9 e/ Aguilera y Heredia ⓣ226/2-35-74. Two smallish, rather dark A/C rooms (with a shared, hot-water bathroom) in a wonderful eighteenth-

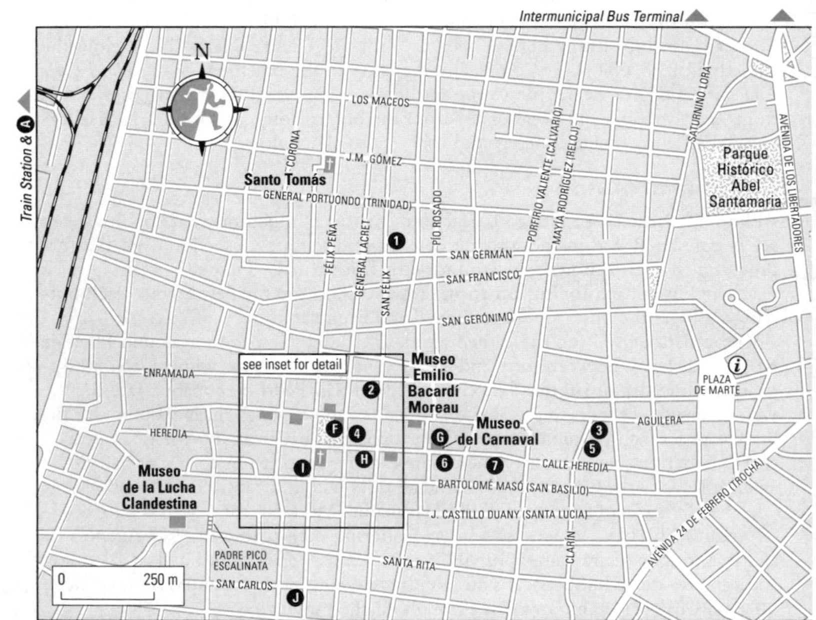

century house with period ironwork, wooden walls, high ceilings and red and blue stained-glass windows. Out back is a serene courtyard filled with leafy palm trees. ❷

Casa de Raimundo Ocaña y Bertha Peña Heredia no. 308 e/ Pío Rosado y Porfirio Valiente ☎226/2-40-97. A charming household with an attractive sunny patio, bedevilled by noisy passing traffic. Two rooms, one with A/C, share a bathroom with hot water. ❷

The historic centre and around

While many of the sights are gathered in the **colonial quarter** to the west side of town – and you will need at least a day to do this area justice – you'll also want to take some time to explore the newer suburbs out to the east and north. The other sights of interest are dotted randomly on the outskirts and can be squeezed into the tail end of a visit to other areas.

The colonial district's must-sees are clustered around the picturesque **Parque Céspedes**, the spiritual centre of Santiago. Originally the Plaza de Armas, the first square laid out in the town by the conquistadors, it is more of a plaza than a park, and is usually bustling with activity. A known pick-up spot, it also draws everyone from brass bands to old folk to tourists, and is great for people-watching. On its south side stands the handsome **Catedral de Nuestra Señora de la Asunción** (daily except Tues 8am–noon; Mass daily at 6.30pm, plus Sun 9.30am). The first cathedral in Cuba was built on this site in 1522, but repeated run-ins with earthquakes and pirates made their mark, and *Santiagueros* had to rebuild several times. The present cathedral was completed in 1818. A Baroque-style edifice, its twin towers gleam in the sunshine and its doorway is topped by an imposing herald angel, statues and four Neoclassical columns. Cherubs and angels are something of a theme in the interior, strewn across the ceiling and up the walls. The prize piece of the cathedral, though almost hidden on the left-hand side, is the tremendous

organ, now disused but still replete with tall gilded pipes. Lining the wall is a noteworthy frieze detailing the history of St James, patron saint of Santiago. A tiny **museum** (Mon–Sat 9am–5pm; US$1), in a small upstairs room round the cathedral's east side, has a small collection of calligraphic correspondence between various cardinals and bishops, portraits of all the past bishops of the cathedral and not much else. It's the only museum of its kind in Cuba and worth checking out if you're into that sort of thing.

On the north side of the square is the brilliant-white **Ayuntamiento**, or town hall, dating from the sixteenth century. During colonial times, the building on this site was the Casa del Gobierno, the governor's house, though the first two structures were reduced to rubble by earthquakes and the present building, erected in the 1940s, is a copy of a copy. It's not open to the public, but you can still admire the front cloister covered in shiny red tiles and fronted by crisply precise arches, with snowflake-shaped peepholes cut into the gleaming walls and shell-shaped ornamentation below the windows. The balcony overlooking the park was the site of Fidel Castro's triumphant speech on New Year's Day 1959.

The magnificent stone structure on the west side of the park, built in 1515 for Diego Velázquez, one of the first conquistadors of Cuba, is the oldest residential building in Cuba. It now houses the **Museo de Ambiente Cubano**, Parque Céspedes esq. Félix Pena (Mon–Sat 9am–5pm, Sun 9am–1pm; US$2, US$1 extra for each photo taken), a wonderful collection of early and late colonial furniture, curios, weapons and fripperies which offers one of the country's best insights into colonial lifestyles, and is so large that it spills over into the house next door. Much of what's on display is imported from Europe and shows off the good life enjoyed by the bourgeoisie, but the most interesting items are native to Cuba like the *pajilla* chair with latticework back and seat, invented in Cuba to combat the heat, and the reclining *pajilla* smoking chair with an ornate ashtray attached to the arm, made for the proper enjoyment of a fine cigar.

A couple of blocks southwest of Parque Céspedes, in the **El Tivolí** district, the **Museo de la Lucha Clandestina** (Mon–Sat 9am–5pm; US$2; English, Italian and Spanish guides available; no photographs), perched on the Loma del Intendente, is a tribute to the pre-revolutionary struggle. Spread over two floors of a reproduction of an historically important eighteenth-century house, the museum comprises a photographic and journalistic history of the final years of the Batista regime and is a must for anyone struggling to understand the intricacies of the events leading up to the revolution. The best exhibits are those that give an idea of the turbulent climate of fear, unrest and excitement that existed in the 1950s in the lead-up to the revolution. Adjoining the museum is the celebrated **Padre Pico escalinata**, a towering staircase of over five hundred steps, built to accommodate the almost sheer hill that rises from the lower end of Calle Padre Pico.

Heading east from Parque Céspedes lands you on the liveliest section of **Calle Heredia** with its craft stalls, music venues and museums, amongst them the quirky **Museo de Carnaval** at no. 301 Heredia (Tues–Sat 9am–5pm, Sun 9am–noon; US$2, plus US$1 per photo taken, US$5 for camcorder). Be sure to stop here if you can't make it for the real thing in July. Thoughtfully laid out on the ground floor of a dimly lit colonial house, the museum is a bright and colourful collection of psychedelic costumes, atmospheric photographs and carnival memorabilia. When the museum closes, the flamboyant carnival atmosphere continues with a free, hour-long **dance recital** (Tues–Sat 5–6pm, Sun 11am–noon), the Tardes de Folklórico (folklore afternoon), which is given outside, on a patio to the back of the museum.

In the street parallel to Heredia, on the corner of Aguilera and Pío Rosado, the suberb **Museo Emilio Bacardí Moreau** (Tues–Sat 10am–8pm, Sun 10am–6pm; US$2, US$1 extra for each photograph) is the one Santiago museum you should definitely visit if your time is limited. Styled along the lines of a traditional European city museum, it was founded in 1899 by Emilio Bacardí Moreau, then mayor of Santiago and patriarch of the Bacardi rum dynasty. Its colonial antiquities, excellent collection of Cuban fine art and archeological curios – including an Egyptian mummy – make it one of the most comprehensive hoards in the country.

East of the historic centre, Avenida de los Libertadores, the town's main artery, holds the **Moncada barracks** where Santiago's much-touted **Museo Histórico 26 de Julio** (Mon–Sat 9am–5pm, Sun 9am–1pm; US$1, US$1 extra for each photograph) fills you in on Fidel Castro's celebrated – though futile – attack on July 26, 1953. With a commanding view over the mountains, the building is peppered with bullet holes. It's a must-see, if only for the place it has in Cuban history. While the exhibits are not without flashes of brilliance when it comes to telling the story, they are otherwise rather dry.

Outside the city

Eight kilometres outside the city, presiding over the bay, is Santiago's most magnificent sight, the **Castillo del Morro San Pedro de la Roca**, or "El Morro" (Mon–Fri 9am–5pm, Sat & Sun 8am–4pm; US$4, $1 extra for a camera, $5 for a camcorder), a statuesque fortress built by the Spanish between 1633 and 1639 to ward off pirates. However, despite appearing to be indomitable – with a heavy drawbridge spanning a deep moat, thick stone walls and, inside, expansive parade grounds stippled with cannons trained out to sea – it was nothing of the sort, and in 1662 the English pirate Christopher Myngs, finding to his surprise that the fort had been left unguarded, made a successful rearguard attack. Ramps and steps cut precise angles through the heart of the fortress, which is spread over three levels, and it's only as you wander deeper into the labyrinth of rooms that you get a sense of how awesomely huge it is.

Eating, drinking and nightlife

As in most of the country, the majority of Santiago's **restaurants** fall back on the old favourites of pork or chicken accompanied by rice and beans, although many state restaurants, especially the ones at the top end, usually have a tasty seafood dish or two. However, you won't be stuck for places to try, with plenty of restaurants and cafés around the centre all serving decent meals at affordable prices. Away from the state arena, choice is very limited as high taxes and tight controls on what food can be served have pushed most of the **paladares** in town out of business, but some *casas particulares* make meals for their guests.

As for **bars**, since much of the action in Santiago revolves around music there are few places that cater specifically for drinkers, although the *Hotel Casa Granda* has two excellent bars. **Musical** entertainment in Santiago is hard to beat, with several excellent live *trova* (traditional Cuban music) venues – all a giddy whirl of rum and high spirits with soulful boleros and *son*. Keep an eye out for the superb Estudiantina Invasora *trova* group, who often play at the *Casa de la Trova* (see overleaf). You don't have to exert too much effort to find the best music; it often spills onto the streets at weekends. The best nights are often the cheapest and it's rare to find a venue charging more than US$5. Around **carnival** time in July, bands – including some of the biggest names in Cuban salsa – set up just about everywhere, with temporary stages in many of the open spaces, notably at the Guillermón Moncada Baseball Stadium on the Avenida de las Américas, and parks around the centre.

Discos tend to draw a young, sometimes edgy and high-spirited crowd, including many of the *jinetero* and *jinetera* types who hang out in Parque Céspedes trying to win your attention. It's a situation that attracts a lot of police interest and trouble spots are often closed without warning in a bid to stem the flesh trade. At those discos that are open, you can expect to pay between US$1 and $5 entrance.

Cafés and restaurants

Casa Granda Heredia 201 e/ San Pedro y San Félix. This hotel restaurant is the best place for breakfast, with an extensive hot and cold Continental, English and Caribbean buffet. Also scores highly for lunch and dinner, with lemon roast chicken, steak and lobster as well as some drinkable wines. Prices start from US$6.

Coppelia Ave. de los Libertadores esq. Garzón. Freshly made ice cream at unbeatable peso prices in an outdoor café that looks like a crazy golf course. Very popular locally, so arrive early before the best flavours sell out. Closed Mon.

La Corona Félix Pena no. 807 esq. San Carlos. Excellent bakery with an indoor café, serving up a wide variety of breads, sweets and pastries filled with custard or smothered in super-sticky meringue.

La Maison Ave. Manduley esq. 1 no. 52, Reparto Vista Alegre ☎226/4-11-17. A swanky restaurant in the La Maison fashion-house complex, serving good steaks, red snapper and seafood specialities including paella and "surf 'n' turf" grill. Prices start at US$8.

Bars and clubs

Bar Claqueta Santo Tomás e/ San Basilio y Heredia. Small but perfectly formed open-air club with excellent live music from the resident salsa group, Tierra Caliente. Closed Mon.

Barra Ron Caney Ave. Jesús Menéndez s/n, near the train station. Friendly staff and a silky smooth 15-year-old rum make this bar a top choice.

Casa de la Cultura San Pedro, opposite Parque Céspedes. Formerly a high-society club, this gracefully decaying venue is perfect for classic sounds. There's usually a band playing on Saturdays, a fairly regular rumba night, occasional classical music and, once a month, on the *Noche Tradicional* (traditional music night), a *trova* group.

Casa de la Trova Heredia no. 208. A visit to the famous *Casa de la Trova* is the highlight of a trip to Santiago, with musicians playing day and night to an audience packed into the tiny room or hanging in through the window.

Museo del Carnaval Heredia esq. Carnicería. An ebullient, open-air *folklórico* floorshow, with its roots in Santería, in which the dances and music of various *orishas* (deities) are performed. Tues–Sat 5–6pm, Sun 11am–noon.

Pico Real *Hotel Santiago de Cuba*, Ave. de las Américas y Calle M. Rooftop bar with a nightly fashion show (around US$25) followed by a small-scale salsa disco.

Pista Bailable Teatro Heredia, Ave. de las Américas s/n. Pumped-up salsa, *son*, bolero and merengue all get the crowd dancing at this unpretentious local club, with live music some nights.

Granma and the Sierra Maestra

Protruding west from the main body of Cuba, cupping the Bahía de Guacanayabo, **Granma** is a tranquil, slow-paced province, bypassed with impunity by those pressed for time. That said, a visit to the small, simple rural town of **Pilón** gives a worthy insight into life beyond the tourist trail. On the southwestern tip of Granma's coastline, **Las Coloradas**, where Fidel Castro and his revolutionaries came ashore on the *Granma*, is the highlight of any revolution pilgrimage, while nearby the **Parque Nacional Desembarco del Granma** has several excellent guided nature trails.

The **Sierra Maestra**, Cuba's highest and most extensive mountain range, stretches along the southern coast of the island, running the length of both Santiago and Granma provinces. The unruly beauty of the landscape – a vision of undulating green-gold mountains and remote sugar fields – will take your breath away. That said, once you've admired the countryside there's not an awful lot else you can do: national park status notwithstanding, much of the Sierra Maestra is periodically declared out of bounds by the authorities, who sometimes give the reason of an epidemic in the coffee crops but more often give no reason at all. Should you get the opportunity to go trekking here, seize it as there are some excellent trails, most notably through the stunning cloud forest of the **Parque Nacional Turquino** to the island's highest point, **Pico Turquino** (1974m).

Pilón

The tiny sugar town of **PILÓN**, 175km west from Santiago de Cuba, is a step back in time, with open-backed carts laden with sugarcane zigzagging across the roads and the smell of boiling molasses enveloping the town. There's little to do, but the two beaches, **Playa Media Luna**, with beautiful views over the Sierra Maestra and a rocky coastline good for snorkelling, and the narrow white-sand **Playa Punta**, are refreshingly different from those at the smart resorts. The small but engaging **Casa Museo Ceila Sánchez Manduley** (Mon–Sat 9am–5pm, Sun 9am–1pm; US$1), erstwhile home of revolutionary Ceila Sánchez, offers a rag-bag of exhibits, from Taíno ceramics to shrapnel from the wars of independence.

There's nowhere to stay or eat, though the local service station on the Marea de Portillo road sells sweets, snacks and cold drinks. Bus service from Santiago is erratic; if you don't have your own transport, the most dependable way to reach the town is to catch one of the *colectivo* trucks that leave from the Astro bus terminal on Avenida de los Libertadores.

Parque Nacional Desembarco del Granma

West of Pilón, the province's southwestern tip is commandeered by the **Parque Nacional Desembarco del Granma**, which starts at the tranquil holiday haven of **Las Coloradas**, 47km from Pilón, and stretches some 20km west to the tiny fishing village of Cabo Cruz. The forested interior of the park is littered with trails, but the most famous feature is the **Playa Las Coloradas**, on the western coastline, where the *Granma* yacht deposited Fidel Castro and his 81 comrades on December 2, 1956, on their clandestine return from exile in Mexico.

Named for the red colour that the mangrove jungle gives to the water, the beach is completely hidden and you can't see or even hear the ocean from the start of the path that leads down to the **Monumento Portada de la Libertad** (Mon–Fri 8am–5pm, Sat & Sun 8am–2pm; US$1, including guide), which marks the spot of the landing. Flanked on either side by mangrove forest hedged with jagged saw grass, the kilometre-long path presents a pleasant walk even for those indifferent to the revolution, and even the most jaded cynics will find the enthusiasm the guide has for his subject hard to resist. His compelling narrative (in Spanish) brings to life the rebels' journey through murky undergrowth and razor-sharp thicket.

The tour also takes in a life-size replica of the **yacht**, which the guide can sometimes be persuaded to let you clamber aboard, and a rather spartan **museum** with photographs, maps and an emotive quotation from Castro on the eve of the crossing that neatly sums up his determination to succeed: "*Si salimos, llegamos. Si llegamos, entramos, y si entramos triumfamos*" (If we leave, we'll get there. If we get there we'll get in, and if we get in we will win).

The only **accommodation** in the area is *Villa Las Coloradas,* on Playa Las Coloradas, which has simple, clean chalets with air conditioning and hot water, along with a restaurant and bar. Bookings should be made via Cubamar (Ⓣ7/66-25-23; ❶) and are essential at weekends, when this is a favourite target for Cubans. Las Coloradas is somewhat out of the way; if you are not driving, your best bet is to hitch from Pilón or arrange private transport in Santiago.

3.8

Cayo Largo

South of the mainland, the little-visited Isla de la Juventud (Island of Youth) is the largest of over three hundred scattered emerald islets that make up the **Archipiélago de los Canarreos**. Most visitors to the archipelago, however, are destined for its comparatively tiny neighbour **CAYO LARGO**, arguably Cuba's most exclusive holiday resort.

Some 140km east of the Isla de la Juventud, the cay is a narrow, low-lying spit of land fringed with powdery beaches, and is totally geared to those on package holidays. The tiny islet, measuring just 20km from tip to beachy tip, caters to the quickening flow of European and Canadian tourists who swarm here to enjoy the excellent watersports, diving and Club Med-style hotels. In November 2001, **Hurricane Michelle** wrought havoc on the cay; large-scale evacuations took place and some of the hotels were damaged beyond repair. At the time of writing some of the hotels have reopened but parts of the island still resemble a building site.

Arrival, information and getting around

The only way to reach **Cayo Largo** is by **plane**, and its airport sees numerous international arrivals, as well as domestic flights on a rickety Russian twenty-seater from Havana (2 daily; 40min); you'll be required to book accommodation along with your flight. The tiny Vilo Acuña airport is 1km from the main belt of hotels and courtesy hotel buses meet every flight.

Though there is no main **tourist office** on the cay, the representatives of various tour companies who share a desk at the *Sol Club Cayo Largo* offer general information and organize excursions. You can buy **maps** at all the hotel shops or from the post office in front of the *Isla del Sur* hotel and there's a **bank** on the corner of the village plaza. The cay is also relatively well represented on the web, with informative sites at Ⓦwww.cayolargodelsur.cu and Ⓦwww.cayolargo.net.

The island is small enough to negotiate easily and courtesy **buses** regularly do the circuit of the hotels, running from early morning to midnight. A free **ferry** leaves from the marina to Playa Sirena and Playa Paraíso twice daily at 9.30am and 11am, returning at 3pm and 5pm. There's also a speedboat service running intermittently, charging US$2. The best way to take in the east of the island is to rent a moped, dune buggy or jeep from the office at the *Sol Club Cayo Largo.*

Accommodation

Hotel standards are high and rooms are not overly cheap as they tend to be block-booked by overseas package-tour operators at a specially discounted rate. All the hotels are all-inclusive, and some group together to offer a range of shared facilities. A selection are reviewed below – the price codes represent what you'll pay if you book through a Cuban tour operator.

Isla del Sur Ⓣ5/4-81-11 to 18, Ⓕ4-81-60. Though its reception is sunny and pleasant and home to a lively bar, this is a slightly dowdy hotel with rooms strung along old-style, shadowy corridors painted a lurid green. With an almost exclusively Italian clientele, this is the cay's cheapest option. ⑦

Sol Club Cayo Largo Ⓣ5/4-82-60, Ⓕ4-82-65, Ⓔsol.club.cayo.largo@solmeliacuba.com. This luxury hotel consists of two-storey villas housing attractive, airy rooms painted in pretty pastels. It offers several bars, à la carte and buffet restaurants, a nightly cabaret, a huge luxurious pool, a health centre and two rooms especially adapted for disabled visitors. ⑧

Villa Coral ⓣ & ⓕ as for the *Isla del Sur.* This family-oriented hotel has graceful, pale yellow blocks with red-tiled roofs, divided by neat beds of sea shrubs and palms to ensure a sense of privacy. Rooms have spacious balconies while smart sun terraces and shaded seating surrounds an attractive circular pool. An Italian chef whips up delicious international meals at the hotel's *La Piazzoletta*, at which guests from other hotels can pay to eat. ⑦

Villa Lindamar ⓣ & ⓕ as for the *Isla del Sur.* Backing onto an ample stretch of beach lined with sun shades and loungers, the appealing, spacious, thatched cabins perch on stilts and overlook a garden of sea grass and hibiscus bushes. Each stylish *cabaña* feels self-contained and private – a definite plus. ⑦

Exploring Cayo Largo

Life on the cay began in 1977 when the state, capitalizing on the extensive white sands and offshore coral reefs, built the first of eight hotels that now line the western and southern shores. There is still ample room for development, however, and while plans are under way for more hotels, the cay has a long way to go before it is spoilt; indeed so sparse is the infrastructure away from the hotels that at times hanging out in the resort can seem rather monotonous. The artificiality which works well in the hotels fails somewhat in the **Isla del Sol village** on the west of the island, which has a distinctly spurious air: it's just a sparse collection of a shop, restaurants, a small museum, a bank and, behind the tourist facade, blocks of workers' accommodation.

There's rather more activity around the beaches to the south and along the hotel strip, where warm shallow waters lap the narrow ribbon of pale downy sand. Protected from harsh winds and rough waves by the offshore coral reef, and with over 2km of white sands, **Playa Sirena** enjoys a deserved reputation as the most beautiful of all the beaches and is consequently the busiest. There's a road to the beach from the *Sol Pelícano* but, as it's frequently covered by rifts of sand, you're better off catching one of the ferries or speedboats from the marina (see below). There's a café on the beach serving drinks, sandwiches and snacks. Further south along the same strand, **Playa Paraíso** is almost as attractive and popular as Sirena, with the added advantage that the shallow waters are ideal for children. Heading east, **Playa Lindamar** is a serviceable 5km curve of sand in front of the *Lindamar, Sol Pelícano* and *Villa Coral* hotels and is the only one where you can play volleyball and windsurf.

With over thirty dive sites in the clear and shallow waters around the cay, Cayo Largo is also known as one of Cuba's best **diving areas**. Particularly outstanding are the coral gardens to be found in the shallow waters around the islet, while other highlights of the region include underwater encounters with hawksbill turtles and sea green turtles, and trips to the tiny Cayo Iguana where the eponymous reptiles are tame enough to be fed by hand. The cay boasts two dive centres, one at the Marina Puerto Sol and the other on Playa Sirena, although both are managed by the marina and offer identical packages (ⓣ5/4-82-13, ⓦwww.puertosol.net). One dive costs US$35, including all equipment and transfer to the dive site, and prices per dive decrease with subsequent dives. The marina also runs catamaran excursions that include snorkelling at the coral gardens, a visit to Cayo Iguana, lunch, an open bar and paddling in the Fifth canal - an area where the deliciously warm waters of the Caribbean sea never exceed a depth of one metre (US$65).

Eating, drinking and entertainment

Although some hotels have two-way co-operative systems whereby their guests can eat at either hotel, most all-inclusive packages confine visitors to the buffet **restaurants** of the hotel they are booked into, where the food is a fairly standard range of international dishes. Of these, the *Sol Club Cayo Largo* has the largest selection and the cheeriest atmosphere. It also has an à la carte restaurant serving more sophisticated fare at which non-guests can pay to eat. *Villa Coral* has a pleasant and airy snack bar in a pink-tiled pool area, serving small pizzas, sandwiches and ice cream.

Down in the quiet of the village, the thatched *Taberna del Pirata* bar, on the plaza overlooking the picturesque harbour, is a great spot to enjoy the cooling sea breezes as you watch the sun go down. Next door, the *El Criolla* restaurant has a distinctive Wild West flavour with a wooden ceiling, cow-hide-covered chairs and some ornamental saddles. It serves classic Cuban chicken and pork dishes as well as lobster and shrimp cooked in a variety of ways. Other than the *Taberna del Pirata* bar, there is no **nightlife** on the island outside of the hotels. The bar in the reception of the *Isla del Sur* is open 24 hours a day and has a buzzy atmosphere. The *Sol Club Cayo Largo* is probably the liveliest spot at night, with a friendly lobby bar and a larger one by the pool that's mercifully set back from the stage where an entertainment team puts on nightly cabaret shows with enforced hilarity. Should you feel like providing the entertainment yourself, there's also a karaoke bar. For a cover charge of US$15, guests from other hotels can join in the festivities and drink at the open bars.

4

The Cayman Islands

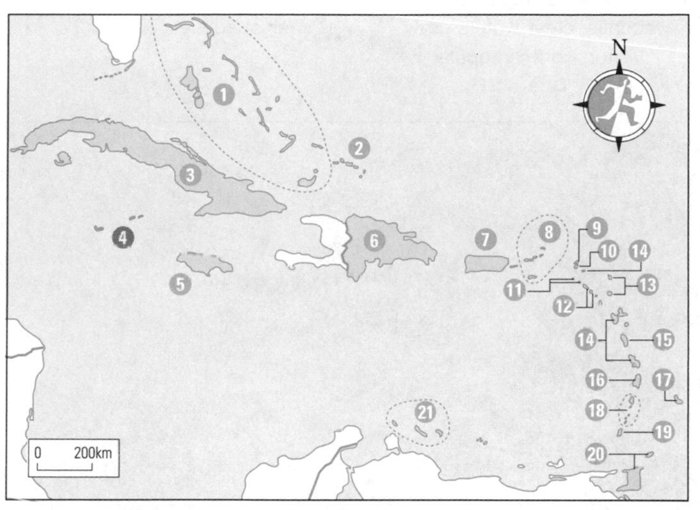

The Cayman Islands Highlights

* **Bloody Bay Wall** Swim amongst luminescent corals and colourful fish at Little Cayman's premier wall dive. See p.225

* **Seven Mile Beach** Powdery white sand and gentle, clear waters draw visitors to this popular stretch. See p.218

* **Stingray City**. Superb dive spot where you can get friendly with the local sting ray population. See p.215

* **Royal Palms beach bar** One of the best places in the Caymans for a cocktail at sunset. See p.221

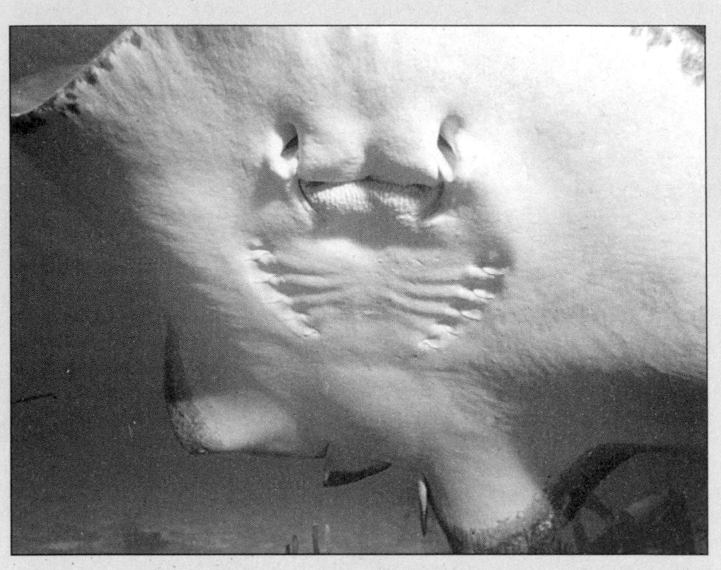

Introduction and Basics

Just south of Jamaica, the Cayman Islands have truly grown up the past thirty years, driven by tourism and banking. The Cayman Islands rank as the world's fifth largest offshore financial centre. Bank secrecy laws make it illegal to reveal the identities of accounts owners – unless of course, shady dealings are suspected. Through the years, regulations have been severely tightened making it nearly impossible to launder cash here.

On the tourism side of development, the islands have been a **scuba-diving** paradise since the 1960s. The Cayman Islands, like all islands, are essentially the tips of underwater mountains, and the submerged terrain around these islands is especially dramatic. The spectacular underwater walls, caverns and healthy coral reefs have made these islands one of the world's best spots for diving and snorkelling. Add to that their virtually crime-free ambience (thanks to tight government controls and the high per-capita income enjoyed by most Caymanians) and it's easy to see why so many people choose the Cayman Islands for a Caribbean holiday.

Though people from around the world visit to scuba dive and enjoy the tropical climate, **US travellers** predominate. The islands are just a 90-minute flight from Miami, Florida, and being a British territory, English is the official language – making these islands a quick, convenient and easy getaway for Americans. In fact, the hotels, fast-food chains, products and many of the service industry workers hail from the US (many Canadians also work here).

An abundance of natural attractions make the islands an ideal destination for those who enjoy watersports, birdwatching, laid-back day hikes, clear water and sandy beaches (Grand Cayman's **Seven Mile Beach** is among the finest in the Caribbean). If rousing casinos and wild nightlife are what you seek, these are not the islands to visit. There's no gambling of any kind here, and beach nudity is forbidden.

Grand Cayman is the **most developed** of the three islands and where you will find the largest choice of accommodation, restaurants and attractions. The sister islands Cayman Brac (pronounced "brack") and Little Cayman have far fewer choices in lodging and dining and most travellers to these islands choose all-inclusive meal packages. Compared to Grand Cayman, the pace is far mellower here. They've yet to put up stop lights on either island, and Little Cayman only recently got its first full-time police officer.

All three of the islands are **low-lying and arid**, though Cayman Brac does have a ridge that rises to 140 feet above sea level, the highest point of the three islands. The vegetation throughout is predominately scrub brush and mangrove. There are also colourful flowering plants and trees such as the **brilliant flamboyant tree** that grows as high as 50 feet and develops a blossoming orange canopy that spreads across the roadways. **Bougainvillea** flowers almost year-round, dotting island homes in vibrant swatches of fuchsia, white and lemon-yellow. A variety of tropical birds also flock to these islands, especially to Little Cayman.

Where to go

The Cayman Islands' premier diving attractions are the main reason to come here. Frolic with the friendly rays at **Stingray City** off Grand Cayman, or else head to **Bloody Bay Wall** just off Little Cayman for superb snorkelling and diving; snorkellers can explore the wall in about 15 feet of water while a short distance away divers can slip into a 6000-foot abyss.

When to go

The **average temperature** hovers around 24°C (75°F) in winter and 29°C (85°F) in the summer. If travelling during the holiday season (late Nov through early Jan), be sure to reserve hotels and vehicles a few months in advance. Off-season (April through mid-Nov) lodging rates can drop 20 percent or more and the islands are less crowded.

There are **two seasons**, "rainy" lasting from mid-May through October, followed by the "dry" season, November through April. Don't let the term "rainy season" deter you from visiting; in general you'll encounter brief afternoon showers followed by sun and higher humidity than in the drier months.

The Cayman Islands' western Caribbean location puts them **out of the general hurricane belt**, though they are not immune to these storms. Officially, the hurricane season begins June 1 and ends November 30.

Getting there

Flights from the US are plentiful, with major American airlines flying to Grand Cayman anywhere from two to four times a week; a few fly daily during high season. The national carrier, Cayman Airways, offers more non-stop flights between Grand Cayman and the US than any other airline, with daily service from Miami and regular service scheduled several times a week from Tampa, Florida and Houston, Texas. it also provides connecting regional service to Cayman Brac, and to Kingston, Jamaica.

All flights touch down first on Grand Cayman, with connecting flights to Cayman Brac and Little Cayman usually departing the same day. Round-trip flights from the US and Canada average about US$450.

From the UK, British Airways flies to Grand Cayman three times weekly from London Heathrow, with a stopover in Nassau, Bahamas. Fare start around £500.

Although there are no direct flights from **Australasia**, a number of airlines offer connecting service from Australia to Los Angeles, then on to Grand Cayman, including American Airlines, Delta, Air New Zealand and Qantas.

Island Air (Ⓣ345/949-5252, Ⓦwww.islandaircayman.com), based in Grand Cayman, offers scheduled daily service between all three islands. The flight between Grand Cayman and either of the sister islands is approximately 40 minutes.

Cayman Brac is served by Cayman Airways, which provides daily jet service.

For phone numbers of airlines see pp.12–17 and 36–37.

Money and costs

The official currency is the **Cayman Islands dollar (CI$)**, which comes in $1, $5, $10, $25, $50 and $100 notes; the coins are 1, 5, 10 and 25 cents. The Cayman dollar is based on 100 Cayman cents. The exchange rate is 80 Cayman cents for one US dollar and doesn't fluctuate. Both Cayman dollars and US dollars are accepted everywhere on the islands. All other currencies will need to be exchanged at either a bank or your hotel.

All prices in this chapter are in US dollars unless otherwise stated.

Credit cards and travellers' cheques

Travellers' cheques and all major **credit cards** are accepted in most places. Be aware, however, that some smaller restaurants, hotels and especially bed and breakfasts may not accept credit cards.

Although Grand Cayman has hundreds of licensed **banks**, only a handful provide customer banking service as most visitors know it. These include Barclays, Scotiabank, Bank of Butterfield, Royal Bank of Canada, Cayman National Bank, Canadian Imperial Bank of Commerce and British American. **ATMs** accepting Visa and MasterCard linked to the Cirrus system are located at Cayman National Bank and other banks, as well as at Owen Roberts International Airport on Grand Cayman. There is one bank on each of the sister islands, and money can also be exchanged at your hotel.

Though there are special deals and packages, the Cayman Islands are not a bargain hunters' paradise; **prices are fixed** and haggling is not the norm here. High-season prices kick in from late November and begin to drop in March.

Though a "tax-free haven", your visit will not be tax-free. There is a US$25 **departure tax** included in your airline ticket, a 10 percent **government tax** added to all hotel bills, and many hotels add 10 percent or more as a **service fee**. When making reservations, be sure to ask if the quoted rate includes these additional charges – some do, some don't.

The most expensive and desirable **accommodations** are along Seven Mile Beach in Grand Cayman. In high season, ocean-front rooms start upwards of US$200 per night and can skyrocket to more than US$1000 per night for deluxe suites. Despite some of the higher costs, you can still enjoy a stay here on a more moderate budget. Seek out one of the hotels located across the street from Seven Mile Beach, where you may not have a view from your room, but you'll save significantly and be just steps away from the sand.

Information, websites and maps

Once you arrive on Grand Cayman, you'll find a dizzying amount of brochures and maps at the **information booth** at Grand Cayman's Owen Roberts International Airport and at the North Terminal cruise ship dock in George Town Harbour. The Department of Tourism also has its headquarters in George Town at The Pavilion, Cricket Square, Elgin Avenue (Ⓣ345/949-0623, Ⓕ949-4053, Ⓦwww.caymanislands.ky). There are also some brochures and maps at the airport on Cayman Brac.

Websites

Ⓦ**www.caymannetnews.com** Online version of a local tabloid newspaper which has stories filled with insight as well as innuendo. A great place to get an insider's look at the islands.
Ⓦ**www.caypolitics.com** Perhaps most useful for the feedback section in which you can read about islanders' thoughts on international politics and local affairs.
Ⓦ**www.divecayman.ky** Details on dive sites, resorts and dive operators. An interactive dive map with pop-up windows that take you directly to a dive site with a full listing on what you will see there.

Phones, post and email

When making a **phone call**, watch out for hotel surcharges: they can be double the already expensive per-minute rate. A less expensive option is to purchase a phone card, available in most stores, and make your call on a public phone, readily available throughout the islands and in most hotel lobbies.

Post office hours are weekdays 8.30am–3.30pm and Saturday 8.30–11.30am. The main branch is in downtown George Town on Edward Street and Cardinal Avenue (Ⓣ345/949-2474). There are branch locations throughout the island, including one in the West Shore Plaza on West Bay Road in the Seven Mile Beach strip. The main post office on Cayman Brac is in West End, and there is one post office on Little Cayman. Stamps are widely available at grocery stores and most hotels.

Grand Cayman has all the latest high-tech communications infrastructure and devices. Satellite dishes dot most yards, cell phones, fax machines and computers are quite common as well. There are an ever-increasing number of Internet cafés on Grand Cayman, while there's one public Internet outlet on Little Cayman and none yet on Cayman Brac.

The **country code** for the Cayman Islands is Ⓣ345.

Food and drink

Thanks to the Caymans' historical connection to Jamaica, it's no surprise to find **jerked meats** as one of the island specialities – heavily spiced meats smoked over hard woods in enclosed barbecue grills. Also prevalent is **conch**, often served as ceviche – sliced thin and marinated in lemon or lime with bits of tomato and onion. **Turtle**, though not as popular as it once was, is part of traditional Cayman cuisine, often prepared in stews or as steaks.

Cayman-style **fish** can really be any fish pulled fresh from the sea and sautéed with pepper, onions and green peppers. Typical sides are plantains, yams, and rice and peas. **Heavy cake** is a real treat and can be found in small grocers and at some gas stations. Made of a grated cassava root, it is sweetened with sugar and has the consistency of fudge.

You can find **locally grown produce** such as mango, grapefruit, coconut, breadfruit; home-made goodies; and a buffet of local foods at the Farmer's Market (see p.220) just north of George Town. Though most restaurants specialize in Continental or international fare, traditional Caymanian cuisine occasionally appears on menus. You can also go to smaller local markets, both in George Town and some other Grand Cayman settlements, to get a truer taste of island food.

The **drinking water** is desalinated sea water and is fine on all three islands.

Public holidays and festivals

The main event on Grand Cayman is the annual **Pirates' Week** (see below), a ten-day celebration held in late October. Special events take place all over the island and include street dances into the wee hours, sports contests, a mock pirate invasion and glittering parades. George Town is centre stage for the major activities on the weekends. For details, check out Ⓦwww.piratesweekfestival.com. It's a popular event with islanders and tourists, so book hotel accommodations several months in advance.

Sports

Given the clear warm sea it's no surprise that watersports predominate, the greatest vari-

Public holidays and festivals

Public holidays

January 1 New Year's Day
February 13 Ash Wednesday
March/April Good Friday, Easter Monday
May 20 Discovery Day
June 17 Queen's Birthday
July 1 Constitution Day
November 11 Remembrance Day
December 25 Christmas Day
December 26 Boxing Day

Festivals

February

Little Cayman Annual Mardi Gras Festival Ⓣ 345/948-1010. This is small-town parade atmosphere at its best; many people visit during this time just to be a part of the festival.

April

Annual Batabano Carnival Ⓣ345/945-598. Held in downtown George Town , the carnival features parades and live soca and calypso bands, and street stalls offering tasty Caymanian and Caribbean delicacies.

Cayman Islands International Fishing Tournament Ⓣ345/945-3000, Ⓦwww.fishcayman.com. Anglers worldwide compete to catch blue marlin, yellowfin tuna, wahoo and the like for hefty cash prizes.

October

Pirates' Week Grand Cayman Ⓣ345/949-5078, Ⓦwww.piratesweekfestival.com. A ten-day event bringing together parades, regattas, treasure hunts and a mock pirate invasion.

ety being available on Grand Cayman. Scuba diving and snorkelling are by far the most popular; visibility can exceed 100 feet. There are numerous offshore reefs, and further out by boat lies the Cayman Trench, several miles deep and teeming with sealife. For those who prefer to stay dry, a glass-bottom boat or an air-conditioned submarine will shuttle sightseers down to this amazing world underwater.

There is as much to do on top of the water: **deep-sea fishing**, **bonefishing** on the flats around Little Cayman, **windsurfing** (especially good on the breezy East End of Grand Cayman), **jet skiing**, **parasailing**, **sailing**, and simply **swimming** or floating around on the salty sea. Children especially enjoy the **Grand Cayman turtle farm** where they can watch hatchlings and hold baby turtles (see p.218).

For those who like to swing a **golf** club, Grand Cayman has well-maintained and challenging courses including The Links at Safehaven (greens fees US$60), an 18-hole, par 71 championship course. At the *Hyatt Regency*, the Britannia Golf Resort (greens fees US$40–90) is the only Jack Nicklaus–designed course in the Caribbean and is actually two courses in one: a par 58 executive-style, or short, course, and a par 70 championship course.

The sister islands offer some distinct nature-based sports. Cayman Brac sets itself apart from the other Caymans with the many **hiking trails** that criss-cross the island. Be sure to wear sturdy shoes as some of the trails are over sharp ironshore coral, and bring water as it's easy to get dehydrated in the heat. On the less strenuous side, there's excellent **birdwatching** on Little Cayman where the centre of the island is dominated by a mangrove swamp. The National Trust building is situated right on the swamp and has viewing decks complete with telescopes. The red-footed booby, black frigate and snowy egret are commonly seen here. If you're unfamiliar with tropical birds, the volunteers inside the Trust building will be happy to orient you.

Scuba diving

Excellent conditions and unique terrain have made the seas around the Cayman Islands the domain of **scuba divers**. The underwater landscape is unique in the Caribbean region because of a massive trench (Cayman Trench) which plunges down some 25,000 feet. To scuba divers, diving this trench is akin to exploring the Grand Canyon. The walls of the trench explode with life – sea fans, barrel sponges and sea whips abound as does a plethora of marine creatures that crawl, hover and dart around the reefs. Given the popularity of the sport, dive operators and dive packages are abundant. If diving is your only quest, go directly to Little Cayman as conditions are more pristine.

There's a wide variety of **dive shops** on the islands. The following are just a few of the best.

Grand Cayman

Don Foster's Seven Mile Beach ☎345/945-5132 or 1-800/83-DIVER.
Eden Rock South Church Street ☎345/949-7243.
Red Sail Sports Seven Mile Beach ☎345/945-5965 or 1-877/RED-SAIL.
Sunset Divers ☎ 345/949-7111 or 1-800/854-4767.

Cayman Brac

Brac Aquatics South Side ☎345/948-1429 or 1-800/544-2722.
Reef Divers South Side ☎ 345/948-1642 or 1-800/327-3835.

Little Cayman

Conch Club Divers Blossom Village ☎345/948-1026 or 1-800/327-3835.
Reef Divers Blossom Village ☎948-1033 or 1-800/328-3735.

History

Christopher Columbus is the first European credited with discovering the islands in 1503, though frankly he stumbled upon them. While en route between Panama and Hispaniola he got blown west off course and recorded seeing two small islands (Little Cayman and Cayman Brac) "full of tortoise". Thus he dubbed them "Las Tortugas", Spanish for turtle, though the name didn't last. A few decades later in 1585, British explorer Sir Francis Drake passed through, recording that the islands were flush with "great serpent-like lizards". These were **caimans** – land creatures related to crocodiles after which the islands were renamed.

Except for the animals and marine creatures, the islands were believed uninhabited until seafarers began using them as **replenishment centres** in the sixteenth century. The islands had abundant supplies of fresh water and food, including sea turtles and wildfowl. English, Dutch, French and Spanish explorers and pirates all made use of the sustenance available here. Historians dispute whether pirates ever actually touched down on the islands, but legend has it that in the eighteenth century **Blackbeard** stashed his treasures in Cayman caves.

The **Spanish** and **British** were the two main colonial powers battling for control of the islands in this region (and elsewhere in Caribbean as well). The Cayman Islands became part of the British Empire in 1670 under the Treaty of Madrid. Nearby Jamaica and other islands were also part of that Treaty which bestowed Caribbean territories to the British. For the next two hundred years or so, the Cayman Islands were governed as a dependency of Jamaica. That ended in 1962 when Jamaica gained independence while the Cayman Islands preferred to remain a **British colony**.

Most of the original settlers were British, Irish and Scottish who came from Jamaica, some of whom brought their **African slaves** with them to farm the rocky land, make thatch rope and work the turtle industry. Many Caymanians also turned to the sea to earn a living as merchant marines. Those arduous labours are long gone, however, replaced by the offshore finance industry which took hold in the late 1960s, along with the development of the tourism sector. Today, **finance** and **tourism** are the mainstays of the Cayman economy, and most people work in one of those two industries.

4.1

Grand Cayman

With a total landmass of 78 square miles, **GRAND CAYMAN** is the largest, most populated and most developed of the three Cayman Islands. As such it receives the greatest number of visitors and certainly feels the most traditionally Caribbean, with a small colonial capital, a beautiful stretch of beach, and lots of typical resorts that will set your whole holiday up for you.

Each week thousands of cruise ship passengers shoulder their way along the narrow sidewalks of **George Town**, where duty free shops hawk everything from fine emeralds to Cuban cigars. Once you've covered downtown, it's easy to explore the rest of the island in a day or two. Of the outer districts, each certainly has its charm and a far mellower pace than George Town, but few really hold that much individual interest. **East End** does have some prime places for **diving**, and **Bodden Town** bears vestiges of its status as former island capital; perhaps best of all, **Seven Mile Beach**, just a ten-minute drive from George Town, is arguably one of the finest stretches of sand in the entire Caribbean, its fine powder and calm waters making an alluring destination. No place on the island is more than an hour from any other, so you can base yourself anywhere, and come and go as you please.

Getting around

The main roads around Grand Cayman were paved in the late 1990s and are in good condition. You might find it easiest to **rent a car** to get around on them, though the public bus service is efficient, and taxis are relatively comfortable, with fixed rates that aren't too astronomical.

By taxi

Taxis are available from the airport, all resorts and from the taxi stand at the cruise ship dock in George Town. Rates are fixed and posted at the downtown dock and at the dispatch stand at the airport. Cabbies rarely try to rip off visitors. Rates from the airport to the Seven Mile Beach resorts run about US$35 one-way.

Stingray City

Referred to as the world's best "12-foot dive", **Stingray City**, in Grand Cayman's North Sound, has become a definitive goal for divers and snorkellers in the Caribbean. Plunging in these shallow depths can be an unforgettable experience, the chance to mingle up close and personal with Atlantic southern stingrays in the wild.

The rays were first attracted to these waters by the scraps left by fishermen, who used the area to clean their fish. They weren't scared off either by locals who set up volleyball nets on the sandbar here, perhaps thinking more snacks would be involved. Local dive operators recognized the economic possibilities and began offering trips to Stingray City, and the opportunity to feed and touch these elegant creatures, with wingspans of up to five feet and skin like wet velvet. If you fancy doing the same, check out any number of boat operators throughout the island; excursions start at about US$35 per person and include snorkelling gear.

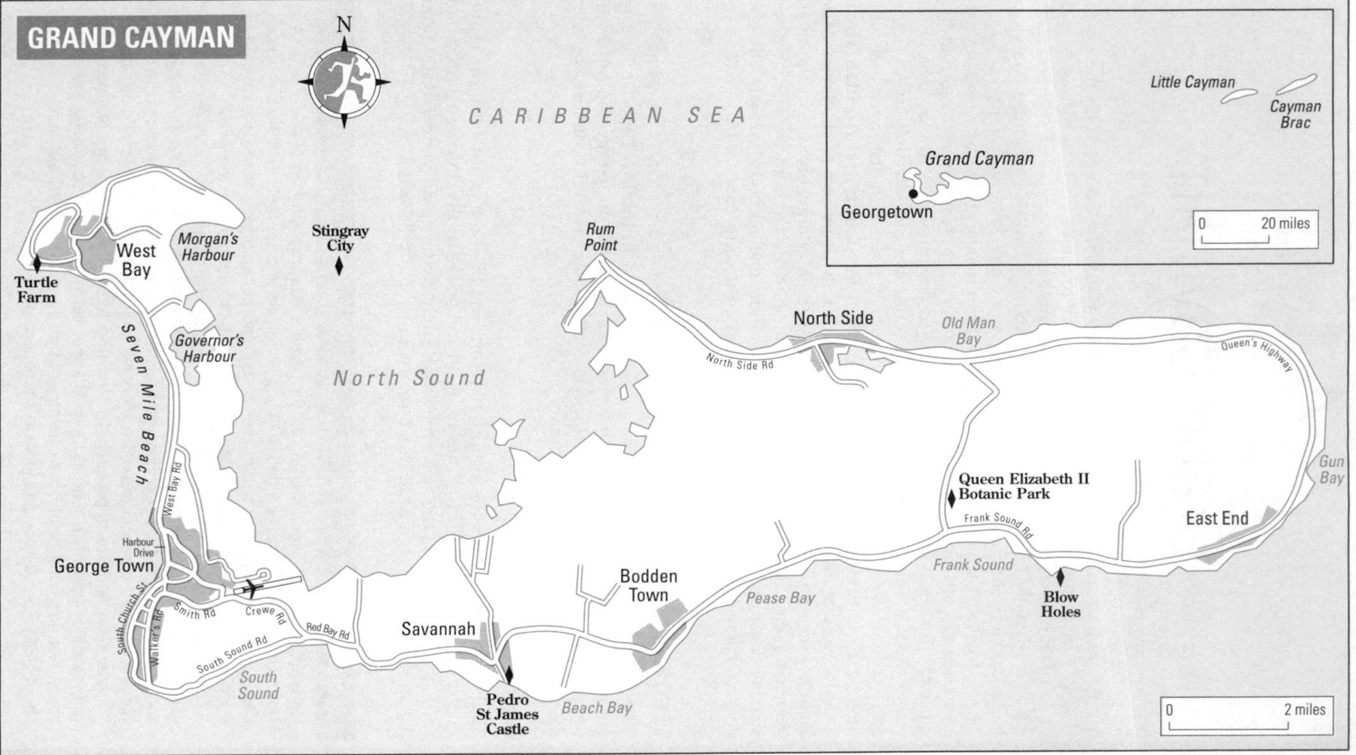
GRAND CAYMAN
N
CARIBBEAN SEA
Little Cayman
Cayman Brac
Grand Cayman
Georgetown
0 20 miles
Stingray City
Rum Point
Morgan's Harbour
West Bay
Turtle Farm
Governor's Harbour
Seven Mile Beach
North Sound
North Side
North Side Rd
Old Man Bay
Queen's Highway
Gun Bay
East End
Queen Elizabeth II Botanic Park
Frank Sound Rd
Frank Sound
Blow Holes
Pease Bay
Bodden Town
Savannah
Pedro St James Castle
Beach Bay
West Bay Rd
Harbour Drive
George Town
South Church St
Walker's Rd
Smith Rd
Crewe Rd
Red Bay Rd
South Sound Rd
South Sound
0 2 miles

By bus

The **bus terminal** is adjacent the public library on Edward Street in downtown George Town and serves as the dispatch point for all buses. The white and beige minibuses serve as the fleet and are distinguished by the large round colour-coded stickers initialled with the routes they cover. All districts are served by bus, though depending on where you want to go you may have to transfer. Rides cost CI$1.50–2. Because of all the stops they make, it will take longer as compared to driving your own car but you'll certainly get a dose of local culture by listening in on the conversations or joining in one yourself. Daily bus service generally begins at 6am and runs until midnight. If you're planning on using bus service past 10pm its best to make sure your route will be served; sometimes the bus service stops early

By car

Rentals are available across the street from the airport and at some hotels. Most agencies provide complimentary pick-up/drop-off. All the major US rental companies operate here – Avis, Budget, and Hertz – though Coconut Car rentals (☎345/949-4377), an island-based company, is often a few dollars a day cheaper than the others. Economy-size car rentals start at US$25 per day.

George Town and around

Downtown **George Town** is dense with tourists on cruise ship days (two to three times a week); otherwise it's a fairly quiet little town with business people running around in suits plying the financial trade. Still you're likely to spend a bit of time here, at least checking out the cigar and gem shops – which though duty- and tax-free, are still no bargain – or the decent museum and nearby colonial buildings.

The Town

To get oriented on Cayman history, begin downtown at the **Cayman National Museum**, Harbour Drive at Shedden Road (weekdays 9am–5pm and Sat 10am–2pm, closed Sun; US$5), which has served variously as a courthouse, place of worship and a jail. The 150-year-old building was refurbished as a museum in 1990, with the former jail converted into a gift-shop. Of the historical displays inside the museum, most interesting is the three-dimensional plastic model revealing the Cayman Islands as small peaks of massive underwater mountains.

From the museum, walk a few blocks north on Harbour Drive to **Elmslie Memorial Church**, built in 1920 by architect-shipbuilder Captain Rayan. His nautical heritage is evident in the structure's ceiling, which mimics the upturned hull of a schooner. North to Fort Street, and then right, you'll hit the **Legislative Assembly Building**, a modern construction reminiscent of a pyramid and the very first poured-concrete building on the island. There were no modern cement mixers, so the concrete was mixed in vats right on the street and poured pail by pail by a brigade of workers. If the assembly is in session, you're welcome to observe from seats in the upper gallery.

Bus schedule

Route 1 (yellow) and **Route 2** (lime green) run between George Town and West Bay every 15 minutes.
Route 3 (blue) operates between the depot in George Town and Bodden, running every 30 minutes.
Route 4 (purple) runs between the depot and East End.
Route 5 (red) operates from the depot to East End and North Side.
Route 6 (dark green) covers North Side to West Bay.
Route 8 (orange) runs from the depot to Hutland in North Side about every hour.

Next door is another Rayan building, the **Peace Memorial Town Hall**. Though once the hub of community activity, it's now used as an extra courthouse. Cross over Edward Street to Rayan's third civic project, the **public library**, which like the church has an upturned hull ceiling. Cool off inside while browsing books about the Caymans or purchase a used paperback from the rack at the front entrance (proceeds benefit the library).

Continue down Edward Street to the columned **post office**, built in 1939. There is no home delivery of mail on the islands, hence the two thousand post boxes at this location.

To get back to the bay, head down Cardinal Avenue, flanked by sparkling duty-free shops. On South Church Street, there's a small beach at **Eden Rock** where you can rent snorkel/scuba gear and swim out to one of the finest snorkelling reefs on the island. If you prefer not to get wet, *Atlantis* submarines will shuttle you down 100 feet in air-conditioned comfort. You can't miss the store, which has a yellow model submarine right on South Church Street. Tours generally start on the hour (US$70 per person), but it's best to call for reservations at ☎345/949-7700.

Seven Mile Beach and West Bay

Seven Mile Beach is a wide, powder-soft stretch of white sand that curls around the west side of the island. The waters are generally calm, warm, and crystal-clear – owing to the barrier reef that protects the shoreline from large waves and currents. The slope heading out to sea is an easy and gradual one, ideal for swimming or just wading in. It's by far the most popular beach around; even so, it never gets towel-to-towel. If you do want to slip away from the crowds, walk west to where there are fewer hotels.

The community of **West Bay** north of George Town begins at the northern edge of Seven Mile Beach and is the second largest district on the island. Though most of the area is residential, a few tourist attractions are around here, like the **Turtle Farm** on West Bay Road (daily 8.30am–5pm; ☎345/949-3893), which has thousands of green sea turtles on display, of which more than half are raised to meet the local demand for turtle meat. Those who are conservation-minded can sponsor the release of turtles into the wild. Tours are self-guided and take less than a half-hour to complete. At the time of publication, the farm was still recovering from Hurricane Michelle, which destroyed much of the seaside tanks and gift-shop; there's still plenty to see across from the original location.

The north and east sides

On the northeast side of the island the districts of **Savannah**, **Bodden Town**, **East End** and **Northside** offer the odd sight that reveals a fuller picture of life on Grand Cayman.

The first stop of note, fifteen miles on from George Town in Savannah, is the **Pedro St James Castle**, just a mile or so back from the main road; the signs are self-evident (daily 9am–5pm; US$8, US$4 children; ☎345/947-3329). The island's oldest stone building (built in 1870) and the birthplace of democracy in the Cayman Islands, it has been restored to traditional splendour, along with the sprawling grounds – full of tropical fruits and native flora. The **visitor centre** has a state-of-the-art multimedia theatre, with screens on which the story of the castle unfolds.

After leaving the castle, drive east to **Bodden Town**, Grand Cayman's original capital. The area has become a bit run-down and there's nothing really to see here, other than the kitschy **Pirates Cave**, in which the property's owners have placed fake treasure and pirate-bedecked mannequins. A curio shop in front charges a small admission fee.

Continuing down Red Bay Road, you'll pass a white lighthouse which has been transformed into a restaurant, a good place to stop at for lunch or a beverage. Just after the lighthouse, the road becomes Frank Sound Road, off which you can watch plenty of crashing waves offshore. As you work you way northeast, the road turns into **Queen's Highway** and enters **North Side**. Signs will direct you to **Rum Point**, a popular beach bar/resort where you are welcome to use the facilities on the sandy beach and snorkel about in the shallow waters.

On your way back to George Town, take the bypass at Old Man Bay and stop at the **Queen Elizabeth II Botanic Park** (daily 9am–6.30pm; US$7; ⓣ345/947-7873). You can easily walk the gardens within an hour, noting the signs that identify the varied plant life; the **colour garden** is a clever and pretty collection of similarly hued plants and flowers.

Accommodation

Most **hotels** are along Seven Mile Beach proper, which is located within the George Town district. There a few hotels scattered inland and in the other districts but if you are here for the beach, the hotels along the main drag are your best bet. As would be expected, resorts on the beach are pricier than those located elsewhere.

If you travel during high season, book several months in advance, and know that many hoteliers require minimum stays. Though there are some less expensive properties (around US$100/night), expect to pay at least US$150 per night for even the most modest accommodation.

Special **packages** (diving, fishing, golfing) are offered throughout the year; most are advertised on the tourist office's website (ⓦwww.caymanislands.ky).

Below is a range of what's available near downtown and Seven Mile Beach. A 10 percent government tax is added to all bills, and most properties also tack on a service charge of 10–15 percent. All rates apply to high season and are based on double occupancy.

George Town and Seven Mile Beach

Adams Guest House 84 Melmac Ave, George Town, Grand Cayman ⓣ345/949-2512, ⓕ949-0919, ⓦwww.adamsguesthouse.com.ky. Run by Caymanians, the simple, clean rooms all have a private entrance and bath, A/C, mini-fridge, toaster-microwave and satellite TV and are ideal for those on a budget. The guesthouse is on a residential street within one mile of downtown George Town (an easy walk), though for beaches, you'll need transportation. ④

Comfort Suites Seven Mile Beach ⓣ345/945-7400 or 1-800/517-4000, ⓔcomfort@candw-ky. This reasonably priced all-suites hotel includes kitchens and is within walking distance of restaurants, shops and the cinema. Each room has a data port for those who simply must connect to the outside world. ⑨

Holiday Inn West Bay Rd ⓣ345/946-4433 or 1-800/HOLIDAY, ⓦwww.holiday-inn.com. Located across the street from Seven Mile Beach and as such will save you plenty while not shirking on amenities. This five-storey resort hotel has 231 rooms, two restaurants and a wait staff that serves drinks poolside. A well-equipped fitness room is also on site. ⑥

Hyatt Regency Seven Mile Beach ⓣ345/949-1234 or 1-800/233-1234, ⓦwww.grandcayman.hyatt.com. This British colonial-style resort is one of the poshest properties on the island. The 236 rooms sit on lush landscaped grounds and an additional 53 suites are on the beach. Some of the rooms have step-out balconies while others have full ones; be sure to ask as the prices are the same. Amenities include a Jack Nicklaus-designed golf course, tennis, fitness centre, a Rum Point Ferry excursion and complete dive and watersports facilities. Rates start at US$415.

Sunset House South Church St ⓣ345/949-7111 or 1-800/854-4767, ⓦwww.sunsethouse.com. This popular full-service dive resort includes an underwater photo centre on site, gear lockers, and plenty of off-shore diving along the ironshore (no beach here). Hungry divers won't be disappointed as the restaurant serves scrumptious meals and the room rates include made-to-order full breakfasts. ⑥

Sunshine Suites West Bay Rd, Safehaven ⓣ345/949-3000, 1-877/786-1110, ⓦwww.sunshinesuites.com. Don't let the location behind a strip mall put you off from this pretty yellow all-suites hotel. Each suite has an efficient kitchen with full-size fridge, microwave and electric stove. A golf course, restaurants, dive centre and shopping are all within walking distance, and because it's across the street from the beach, the rates are lower (and include Continental breakfast). 6

Treasure Island Resort 269 West Bay Rd ☎345/949-7777 or 1-800/203-0775, www.treasureislandresort.net. A large open-air lobby filled with tropical plants and cosy couches is a lovely place to relax at this large resort. All rooms have mini-fridges and a private terrace or balcony. Amenities include three swimming pools, kiddie pool, hot tubs, dive shop, tennis courts and several restaurants. 9

Westin Casuarina Seven Mile Beach ☎345/945-3800 or 1-800/WESTIN-1, salesing@candw.ky. Marble baths and balconies that face the sea are the main attractions at this upscale resort. The luxurious spa is a perfect place to pamper sun-kissed skin and the highly rated open-air Cuban-Caribbean restaurant has a fine selection of cuisine and cigars. Rates start at US$550.

West Bay

Colbalt Coast Sea Fan Drive ☎345/946-5656 or 1-800/992-2015, www.colbaltcoast.com. Just a few miles north of bustling Seven Mile Beach is this jewel of place. It's along the ironshore so there's no beach here, but you can easily slip into the water from the large pier. Catering to scuba divers, the property is near the unspoilt North Wall, one of the island's best wall dive sites. A meal package is the way to go here as you are far away from anything other than the sea. 7

Bodden Town

Turtle Nest Inn ☎345/947-8665, www.turtlenestinn.com. Built in the tradition of a Spanish villa with a red-tile roof , white-washed walls and graceful arches, this intimate hotel has just eight rooms which include small suites and one-bedrooms. The swimming pool faces the sea and there's a small beach for superb snorkelling. A gourmet restaurant is also on site. 5

North Side

Retreat at Rum Point ☎345/947-9135, www.theretreat.com. These condos vary in style and amenities but all are on the sandy peninsula and have screened-in porches. The beach, though not as expansive as Seven Mile Beach, is lovely for swimming and short strolls. Ideal location for those who want a nice beach and seclusion. 9

Eating and drinking

Of the three Cayman Islands, Grand Cayman has by far the most dining choices in **cuisine**. There are gourmet dining choices galore and international cuisines like Thai, Chinese and Indian are also easily found. American fast-food choices include such familiar fare as Subway and Kentucky Fried Chicken. Most restaurants are on West Bay Road along the Seven Mile Beach corridor. Local food, such as jerked meats (spicy slow-barbecued chicken or pork), peas and rice (usually bland white rice and green peas) and fried plantain (a type of banana), is most common on menus in the outer districts.

The **Farmer's Market**, on Smith Road just north of George Town (Mon–Fri 9am–5pm), has a decent number of local delicacies. The self-serve lunch buffet at the **Fort Street Market** in downtown George Town, on Fort Street and Harbour Drive, has a fine selection of island dishes prepared by the chefs at *Champion House*. You can grab lunch at either of these two places for under US$10 per person, a real bargain hereabouts.

Almond Tree House North Church St, George Town ☎345/945-0155. Dining on the water's edge is the best seat in the house here. Seafood choices are the main event, and the coconut shrimp appetizer shouldn't be missed. Main courses start at US$17. Daily noon–midnight.

Bed Harquail Bypass, George Town ☎345/949-7199. The servers here may wear pyjamas (hence the name) but the cuisine is anything but casual. The well-prepared entrees include a delicious vegetable lasagna, prawns sautéed in a ginger lime sauce, various curries and meat dishes. Prices start at US$15.

Café Mediterraneo West Shore Centre on West Bay Rd, George Town ☎345/949-8669. The best seats in the house are the plush semi-private booths, perfect when sipping on one of the wines from the ample list. Tasty menu choices include nicoise salad, calzones filled with prosciutto, ricotta, spinach and tomato, pastas, steaks and rack of lamb. Main courses start at US$14. Daily 11.30am–10.30pm.

Casanova Fort Building, South Church St, George Town ☎345/949-7633. Complete with a mostly Italian wait staff, this traditional restaurant is an island favourite. Choose from an array of fresh pastas, ravioli, catch of the day, veal dishes and risottos, among others. Pasta dishes cost US$13 and up. Reservations are essential. Daily, no lunch Sunday.

Champion House Two 43 Eastern Ave, George Town ☎345/949-7882. Of the two restaurants at this address, be sure to go to *Champion House Two* at the back (*Champion House One* is a little seedy). *Two* serves fabulous island fare in a comfortable, air-conditioned setting with views of the garden. The menu features local fare such as turtle stew, ackee (a plant) and codfish, and curried goat. Main dishes start under US$10. Daily breakfast, lunch and dinner.

Coffee Grinder Seven Mile Beach Shops, George Town ☎345/949-4833. This café is a good choice for breakfast and lunch. Selections include freshly made pastries, soups, black-bean wraps and sandwiches, plus rich and full-bodied coffees. Prices range US$5–10. Daily 7.30am–6.30pm.

Grand Old House South Church St, George Town ☎345/949-9333. The outdoor ocean-side gazebos surrounded by palm trees provide an elegant backdrop for romantic dinners. The gourmet Continental cuisine won't disappoint and includes such expertly prepared dishes as roasted duck with coriander and anise seeds crowned on roasted polenta cake and glazed apples. Reservations are essential. Entrees start at US$22. No lunch on weekends.

Heritage Kitchen Boggy Sands Rd, West Bay (no phone). Well worth the 20-minute drive from downtown George Town. Indulge in fish tea (basically a fish stew touted as an aphrodisiac, US$5) or one of the freshly fried fish options (US$10). If you're brave, try one of the local hot sauces, made from the world's hottest pepper – the scotch bonnet. Mr Powell, who runs the kitchen, also owns the little museum next door which he may open for you if he's not busy. Fri and Sat 5pm–2am, Sun noon to late.

The Reef Grill at Royal Palms Seven Mile Beach, George Town ☎345/945-6358. Connected to a popular beach bar with live bands most evenings, the lovely outdoor garden setting is amid baby royal palms; there's a more formal dining room indoors. Seafood reigns supreme – the signature dish is a tender Chilean sea bass served with coconut rice. Reservations recommended. Entrees begin at US$17. No lunch.

Nightlife

The islands aren't exactly pulsing with nightlife but there are a few **discos, outdoor bars** and **dance clubs**. The best way to find out what's happening is to read the Friday edition of the *Cayman Compass*. Wednesday through Saturday live bands play soca and reggae at the outdoor beach bar *Royal Palms* (☎345/945-6385) on Seven Mile Beach across from the West Shore Centre shopping mall – there is no admission charge unless a high-profile band is playing. *Bed* (☎345/949-7199) on the Harquail Bypass also has live music in its tiny lounge. Slapping rounds of dominos are played by the locals especially on Friday nights at *Sunset House* (☎345/949-7111) on South Church just east of downtown George Town; the open-air bar is also a popular hangout for the scuba-diving crowd. *Legendz* (☎345/959-1950) on West Bay Road in the Falls strip mall has live bands and disco most nights.

Listings

Airports Grand Cayman: Owen Roberts International Airport (☎345/949-7733).

Banks Hours are generally Mon–Fri 9am–4pm; closed on weekends.

Bookshops Grand Cayman: Book Nook in Galleria Plaza on West Bay Road (☎345/945-4686); Hobbies and Books downtown in Piccadilly Centre on Elgin Avenue (☎345/ 949-0707); both are open Mon–Sat 9am–6pm.

Driving Drive on the left and wear a seatbelt. Visitor's licence required and available at rental agencies and at the central police station in George Town. Roads are in excellent condition and gas costs about US$3 per gallon.

Embassies There are no embassies on the Islands; the closest location is in Jamaica. For assistance, call the Department of Tourism main office at ☎345/949-0623; or the Government Administration Building ☎345/949-7900.

Hospital George Town Hospital on Hospital Road

☎345/949-8600 has a 24-hour emergency room and a decompression chamber.

Internet Access *Dickens Literary Café*, Galleria Plaza on West Bay Road (☎345/945-9195), Mon–Sat 8.30am–10pm; CyberCOMP Internet Centre, down town on South Church Street (☎345/946-6982), Mon–Sat 8am–6pm, Sunday noon–6pm. On Little Cayman, there are two computers for public use at McLaughlin's Car Rental (☎345/948-1000); there are none on Cayman Brac.

Supermarkets On Grand Cayman there are many well-stocked and conveniently located supermarkets, including Foster Food Fair, which carries gourmet and vegetarian products. The two locations with full pharmacies are Airport Centre (☎345/949-5155) and The Strand Plaza on West Bay Road (☎345/945-4748).

4.2

Cayman Brac

About eighty miles northeast of Grand Cayman, and accessible by a quick plane hop, lies tiny **CAYMAN BRAC**. With none of the fast-food outlets or tourist bustle of the larger island, the Brac (as it's colloquially known) offers the chance for an isolated Caribbean vacation, though growing numbers come here for outdoor activities such as scuba diving and hiking. As such, relatively few resorts cater to such vacationers, although those that do generally have the best access to the few **beaches** on the island; most are relatively brackish, with plenty of seagrass, save for the lone public beach, which is the best stretch around these parts, located on the same south side as most hotels and just a ten-minute bicycle ride away.

The best way to explore the Brac is to get on one of its numerous **trails**, the best of which traverse the bluff that runs along the island's spine and culminates with great ocean views on the eastern coast – a perfect place to catch the sunrise. The trails are accessible off the main road, marked by large white **Heritage Site signs** that designate the name of the trail. You'll need a car or motor scooter to reach most of the trails as few are within walking distance of the main hotels. You might also consider renting a **bicycle** to get around, though if you're serious about cycling, it's best to bring your own as most here are of the no-speed coaster-brake variety.

There's not much in the way of specific attractions on the island, other than the **Cayman Brac Museum** in Stake Bay (Mon–Fri 9am–noon & 1–4pm; free) where local history is on display, and the **Brac Parrot Reserve** near the bluff to the island's northeast – a tropical woodland where the rare, emerald-green Cayman Brac **parrot** has nesting colonies. A short nature trail threads its way through forty-odd species of native trees, including candlewood and mastic, plus varieties of cacti and orchids.

As well, the **scuba diving** here is supreme and most sites are a ten- to twenty-minute boat ride from the shore. It is possible to shore dive here, though it's easiest on the north side where the water is generally calmer. The marine life is abundant, among which you'll find schooling fish and vibrant parrot fish. Walls are encrusted with purple sea fans, massive barrel sponges and the occasional spotted moray and green eel.

As there is no main town or major developments outside the scattered hotels on the island, the place you choose to stay will go a long way toward determining what facilities are on offer. Neither are there miles-long strips of beautiful sand; most of the small beaches, located on hotel property, have a fair amount of seagrass in their waters; the **public beach**, a short ways north of the main hotels, is the best on offer.

Practicalities

Flights arrive at **Gerrard Smith International Airport** (☎345/948-1222), on the western tip of the island.

Because there aren't many restaurants here, most hotels offer a meal plan. Also, unlike the other two islands, many properties include taxes and service charges in their rates. Be sure to ask what's included as this varies property by property.

Hiking the Brac

The **hiking trails** are fairly easy to navigate on your own – and the longest is about three hours round-trip – though you can also request a free guide from the Brac Department of Tourism (Ⓣ345/948-1849) covering wildlife and local history. At the least, you can get hiking maps from the DOT, or from many hotels. Sturdy shoes are essential as many trails weave through sections of sharp ironshore; carry some water and consider a light long-sleeve shirt to reduce scratches from twigs. The caves all have easy accessible entryways, no spelunking required; just walk right in. Be aware that there will be bats dangling from the ceiling; bring a small penlight if you want a better glimpse. Avoid hiking at sunset as the mosquitoes are at their peak.

Brac Reef South Side Ⓣ345/948-1323, Ⓦwww.bracreef.com. Divers love this property for its reasonable rates, excellent dive and knowledgeable dive staff. The tiki bar is popular with locals and the illuminated dock attracts sea creatures at night, like tarpon, stingrays and the occasional fluttering squid. Packages include meals, diving, airport transfers, service charge and government tax. Rates for two are US$400.

Carib Sands South Side Ⓣ345/948-1121, Ⓦwww.caribsands.com. This condo complex wrapping around the beach offers a full-service dive shop and the island's only gourmet restaurant, *Captain's Table*. ⑦

Las Esperanza Stake Bay Ⓣ345/948-0531, Ⓔesperan@candw.ky. Located on the island's north side, this property has rustic but clean two- and three-bedroom apartments. There's a grocery and restaurant across the road, but you'll need a car to reach the beach and dive shops. ④

Walton's Mango Manor Stake Bay Ⓣ345/948-0518, Ⓦwww.waltonsmangomanor.com. This well-run B&B is on landscaped gardens steps away from a rocky but accessible swimming beach. Rooms come with private bath. Also available is a pretty two-storey beach villa perched right along the sea. ④

4.3

Little Cayman

On string-bean-shaped **LITTLE CAYMAN**, road signs read "iguanas have the right of way", fitting for an undeveloped island on which the two thousand or so of these primordial-looking creatures greatly outnumber people. Even more so than Cayman Brac, this least developed of the Cayman Islands attracts visitors looking for untrammelled seclusion, not to mention scuba and wildlife enthusiasts eager to take advantage of a top dive site and an inland nature sanctuary.

The mangrove-filled wetlands in the centre of the island are home to many birds, including West Indian whistling ducks, egrets, herons, frigates and a large nesting colony of red-footed boobies. In fact, this area has been preserved as a National Trust **bird sanctuary**; the visitor centre is just a few steps east of the airport and has a balcony offering panoramic views of the wetlands. To get a closer look, head to one of the scattered boardwalks along the lone main island road, across from the *Little Cayman Beach Resort* or the *Southern Cross Club*.

There's really not much else going on here, just the kind of atmosphere suitable for relaxation, though a small **museum** on the southern shore contains some artefacts of island life such as tools and documents from days past.

Diving and fishing

For divers, the famed **Bloody Bay Wall**, a mere ten- to fifteen-minute boat ride from most hotel docks, is hailed as one of the **world's best dive sites**; the walls here feature a sheer drop-off plunging miles down into the depths. These walls are lush with coral and sponge life; large groupers as well as elegant and triangle-shaped arrow crabs are common sights. Anglers can partake in deep-sea fishing as well as bonefishing on the flats. Hotels can arrange for gear and guides; alternately, you can try McCoy's Diving and Fishing, especially well known for its expert bonefisherman.

Practicalities

Edward Bodden Airstrip (☎345/948-0021), on the southwest end of the island, handles incoming flights. Once here, there's little need for a **vehicle**, though you might like one for a day. McLaughlin Rentals (☎345/948-1000) rents Suzuki jeeps starting at US$75 per day. You can easily drive around the island in an hour. **Bicycles**, available at most properties, are the best way to get around.

Hotel rates are based on double occupancy during high season, some including various meals, activities, taxes and services charges; check with each property to confirm what the rates include. Most of the properties have fewer than twenty rooms, and can feel quite cosy.

Conch Club Condos Blossom Village ☎345/948-1033 or 1-800/327-3835, @www.conchclub.com. These two- and three-bedroom condos sit right on the beach. Guests can use any of the facilities and partake in the meal at the sister hotel nearby. *Conch Club* itself has two pools, a dock and a jacuzzi. US$375 for up to four adults.

Little Cayman Beach Resort Blossom Village ☎345/948-1033 or 1-800/327-3835, @www.littlecayman.com. The island's only two-storey hotel, complete with spa, dive and photo shop, and fitness room. The rooms away from the bar are quieter at night. Rates begin at US$316 for two with modified meal plan (breakfast and dinner). 9

McCoy's Diving and Fishing Lodge Bloody Bay ⓣ345/948-0026 or 1-800/626-0496, ⓦwww.mccoyslodge.com.ky. The McCoys, among the few island-born families, run a rustic and economical lodge catering to anglers and divers. Elder Sam McCoy is probably the finest bonefisherman on the island. The property is on Bloody Wall, making the shore dives quite remarkable. Rooms for two are US$360 per night and include all meals, two-tank dives daily and unlimited shore diving.

Pirates Point Resort Preston Bay ⓣ345/948-1010. The island's finest chef keeps the repeat guest rate high at this well-run resort. Ten cottages dot the beach; rooms on the water don't have A/C. Rates are US$500 per night for two with two-tank dives daily, all meals and alcoholic beverages. Non-diver packages are also available.

Southern Cross Club Blossom Village ⓣ345/948-1099 or 1-800/899-2582, ⓦwww.southerncrossclub.com. This full-service diving and fishing resort is on a fine stretch of beach within kayaking distance of uninhabited Owen Island. The pretty pastel cinderblock cottages have two units in each. Rates include three-tank dives daily, service charge, government tax and all meals, and start at US$676 for two.

5

Jamaica

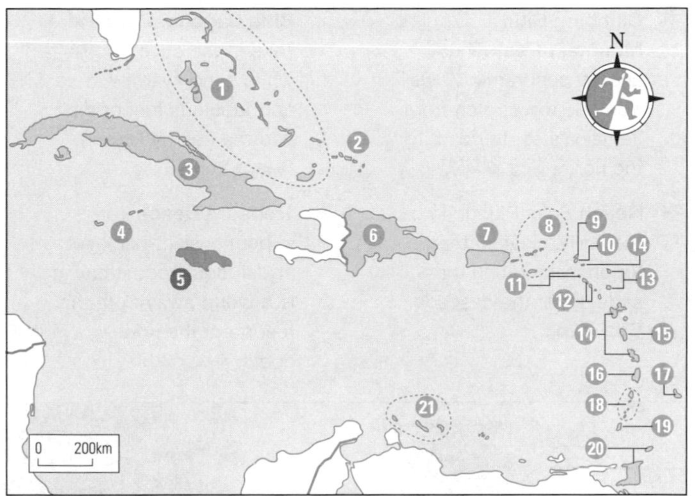

Jamaica Highlights

* **Jamaican nightlife** Whether it's reggae icons singing out under the stars or dancehall queens winding and grinding to ragga, Jamaican nightlife is unmissable. See p.247

* **Climbing Blue Mountain Peak** The superb panoramic views from the top stretch from Jamaica's south coast to the north. See p.257

* **Reach Falls** Plunge into the chilly, clear waters for an invigorating massage under the cascade. See p.263

* **Hellshire beach on Sundays** Best visited on Sundays, when the beach comes alive with booming sound systems, dancing and sizzling grills. See p.252

* **Frenchman's Cove and Blue Lagoon, Portland** Take in the cove's soft white sand, warm waters and fabulous reef or dip into the nearby lagoon. See p.260

* **Treasure Beach** This supremely laid-back yet stylish south coast bay is a world away from the resorts of the north coast. See p.290

Introduction and Basics

Rightly famous for its beaches and music, beautiful, brash Jamaica is much more besides. There's certainly plenty of white sand, turquoise sea and swaying palm trees, but there are also spectacular mountains and rivers, tumbling waterfalls and cactus-strewn savannah plains. Far more than just a resort, the island also boasts vibrant towns and cities such as sprawling Kingston, which inspired the music of Bob Marley and countless other home-grown reggae superstars.

Jamaica is a country with a swagger in its step – proud of its history, sporting success and musical genius – but also with a weight upon its shoulders. The island faces the familiar problems of a developing country, including dramatic inequality of wealth and social tensions that occasionally spill over into localized violence and worldwide headlines. As a result Jamaicans are as renowned for being as sharp, sassy and straight-talking as they are laid-back and hip. People don't beat around the bush here, and this can sometimes make them appear rude or uncompromising. Particularly around the big resorts, this direct approach is taken to extremes at times, with harassment reaching irritating levels.

But there's absolutely no reason to be put off. As a foreign visitor, the chances of encountering any trouble are minuscule, and the Jamaican authorities have spent millions making sure the island treats its tourists right. As the birthplace of the "**all-inclusive**" hotel, Jamaica is well suited to those travellers who want to head straight from plane to beach, never leaving their hotel compound. But to get any sense of the country at all, you'll need to do some exploring. It's undoubtedly worth it, as this is an island packed with first-class attractions, oozing with character, and rich with a musical and cultural heritage; if you're a reggae fan, you're in heaven.

Where to go

Most of Jamaica's tourist business is concentrated in the **resorts** of Montego Bay, Ocho Rios and Negril, which together attract hundreds of thousands of visitors every year. **Montego Bay** is a busy, commercial city with hotels lined up along its lively main strip, a stone's throw from a couple of Jamaica's most famous beaches. There's a great entertainment scene, especially during the annual August **Reggae Sumfest** festival. To the west is **Negril,** its low-rise hotels slung along seven miles of fantastic white sand and two miles of dramatic cliffs. It's younger, more laid-back, and with a longstanding reputation for hedonism that still carries a hint of the truth. East of MoBay, and the least individualistic of the big three, **Ocho Rios** embodies high-impact tourism – purpose-built in the 1960s to provide the ultimate package of sun, sand and sea. It's not an overly attractive place, and the beaches don't compare favourably with Negril and MoBay, but its tourist infrastructure is undeniably strong – the place is packed with shops, restaurants, bars and watersports – and you're right by some of Jamaica's leading attractions, including the famous **Dunn's River** waterfall.

Jamaica's quieter east and south coasts offer a far less packaged – perhaps more rewarding – experience, and there are plenty of real gems worth hunting out. In the island's **east**, lush, sleepy **Port Antonio** and its increasingly popular neighbour, **Long Bay**, provide gateways to some of Jamaica's greatest natural attractions, like the cascading **waterfall** at Reach. The **south coast** offers different pleasures, from gentle beach action at easy-going **Treasure Beach** – the perfect base from which to explore area delights such as the YS waterfalls – to boat safaris in search of local wildlife on the **Black River**.

Last, but in no way least, **Kingston** is the true heart of Jamaica, a thrilling place, pulsating with energy and spirit, that is home

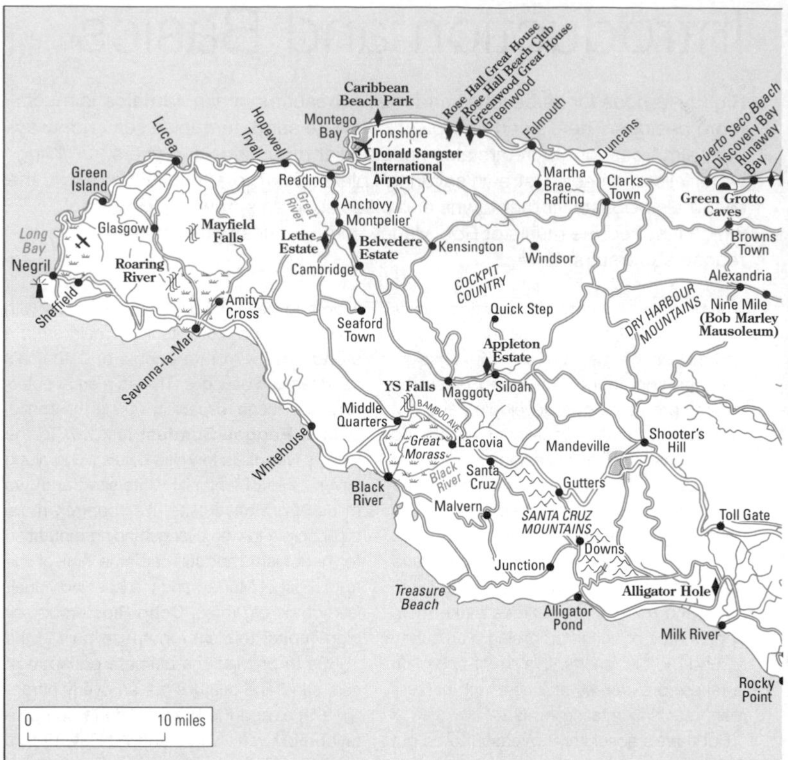

to more than a third of the island's 2.5 million people. This is not just the nation's political capital but the focus of its art, theatre and music scenes, with top-class hotels, restaurants and shopping, a clubbing scene that is second to none and legendary fried fish on offer at the fabulous Hellshire beach. A stunning backdrop to the city, the cool, coffee-smothered **Blue Mountains** offer plenty of hiking possibilities, while the nearby fishing village of **Port Royal**, once a pirate refuge, provides historic diversion.

When to go

Jamaica's tropical **climate** is at its most appealing during the peak mid-December to mid-April tourist season, when rainfall is lowest and the heat is tempered by cooling trade winds; it can also get quite cool at night at this time, so it's worth packing a sweater. Things get noticeably hotter during the summer, and particularly in September and October the humidity can become oppressive. September is also the most threatening month of the annual hurricane season, which runs officially from June 1 to October 31; however, on average, the big blows only hit about once a decade.

Prices, and crowds at the attractions and beaches, peak during high season. Outside this period it's quieter everywhere, and though the main resorts throb with life pretty much year-round, quieter areas like Port Antonio and Treasure Beach can feel a little lifeless. The good news is that in the off-season hotel prices fall by up to 25 percent, there are more bargains to be had in every field of activity, and a number of **festivals** –

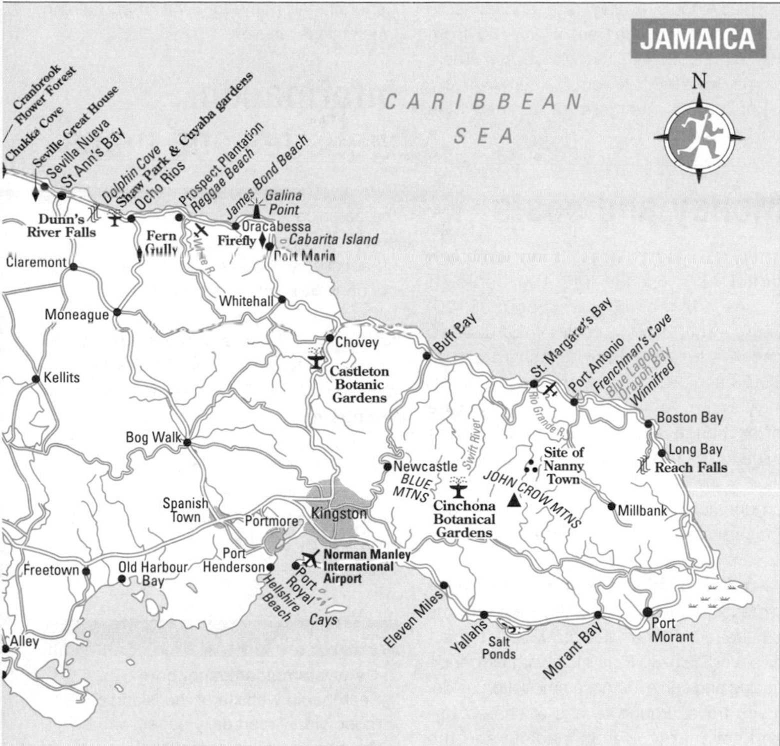

including the massive annual Reggae Sumfest in Montego Bay – inject some zip.

Getting there

As a regional hub, Jamaica is well served with direct flights from the US and UK. The majority of visitors purchase **packages** that include flight, accommodation and airport transfers, but there are plenty of good **flight-only** deals available for those who want to go it alone. Most airlines fly into Montego Bay, but many also land at Kingston as well – more convenient if you're heading for Port Antonio or the Blue Mountains.

Though cheap **flights** to Jamaica can be hard to come by, there are good deals available, particularly from the national carrier Air Jamaica, which flies direct to Montego Bay from the New York area (JFK and Newark), LA, Chicago, Miami, Atlanta, Phoenix, Philadelphia and Boston. American Airlines flies from Miami and New York; Northwest from Tampa, Detroit and Minneapolis; TWA from St Louis; and US Airways from Philadelphia. Air Canada flies to Montego Bay from Toronto, Montreal, Halifax and Winnipeg. Most of the airlines also land in Kingston. Air Jamaica's high- and low-season **fares** to Montego Bay average US$650/550 from New York; US$510/ $420 from Miami; and US$820/710 from LA.

The main carriers from the **UK** are Air Jamaica, which flies daily direct from Heathrow (nine weekly) and from Manchester (two weekly) to Montego Bay and Kingston, and British Airways, also to both airports but offering slightly fewer services per week. You can also book a charter flight with companies such as Airtours. Average high- and low-season scheduled fares are £550/430 from Heathrow, £560/440 from Manchester. There are no direct flights to Jamaica from Ireland.

For phone numbers of airlines see pp.12–17 and 36–37.

Money and costs

Jamaica's unit of currency is the **Jamaican dollar (J$)**, divided into 100 cents. It comes in bills of J$1000, J$500, J$100, J$50 and J$20, and coins of J$20, J$10 and J$5. It's worth keeping a sharp eye on J$100 and J$1000 bills, which look alarmingly similar. At the time of writing the **rate of exchange** is roughly J$48 to US$1 and J$69 to £1. This is prone to fluctuation, and as a result, the **US dollar** has emerged as an unofficial parallel currency, with prices for tourist-oriented goods and services usually quoted in US$.

Accommodation is likely to be the major expense, although extremely basic rooms can be found for as little as US$30. Expect to pay US$60–80 for a room with air-conditioning and cable TV. Accommodation aside, if you travel around by bus or shared taxi and get your food from markets and the cheaper cafés and roadside stalls, you can just about survive on a daily budget of around US$30 per day. Upgrading to one decent meal out, the occasional taxi and a bit of evening entertainment, expect to spend a more realistic US$40–60; after that, the sky's the limit.

Banking hours are generally Monday to Thursday 9am to 2pm and Friday 9am to 3pm or 4pm. **Cambios**, which are widespread throughout the country, are often more convenient, opening later and offering better exchange rates. FX Trader, with branches islandwide, is one to look out for; call ⓣ1-888/398-7233 to find the nearest outlet. **Exchange bureaux** at the main airports offer rates slightly lower than the banks, and at **hotels** the rate is invariably significantly lower.

Jamaica is not a cheap country to visit. Still, don't hesitate to **negotiate** on prices, particularly in taxis and at markets and roadside stalls. Even hotels and guesthouses are generally fair game for a bit of bargaining when things are slow.

Information, websites and maps

Before you leave home, it's worth contacting the Jamaica Tourist Board (JTB), which will send out brochures on the main tourist attractions, schedules of events, accommodation listings and a good road map. Once in Jamaica, you can get the same information from JTB desks at the Kingston and Montego Bay airports, and JTB offices in the main towns. Jamaica has no **entertainment listings magazine**, so to find out what's going on, you have to rely on the radio (particularly Irie FM), newspapers, and flyers and banners posted up around the towns. The best road **map** is *Discover Jamaica*, distributed free by JTB offices abroad and on the island.

Websites

ⓦ**www.jamaicagleaner.com**
Searchable website of the island's most widely read daily paper, with all the news and lots of features.

ⓦ**www.jamaicans.com**
All things Yard, from language, culture and music to cookery and tourist info, plus busy message boards.

ⓦ**www.jamaicatravel.com**
The Jamaica Tourist Board site, with lots of pretty pictures, resort rundowns and good links.

ⓦ**www.top5jamaica.com**
Links to the most popular Jamaican websites, divided by category.

Getting around

Buses and minibuses are inexpensive if not comfortable. Renting a car offers maximum independence but will eat heavily into your budget; if you just want to make the odd excursion or short trip, it can be cheaper to take a taxi, or even hire a private driver. For longer trips, internal flights are reasonably priced.

By bus

Jamaica's **buses** and **minibuses** can be a little disquieting: timetables are non-existent outside Kingston, drivers can show little interest in the rules of the road, and passengers are often squeezed in with scant regard for comfort.

On the other hand, public transport is a great way to meet people, and it's also absurdly cheap – about J$70 per 50 miles for a bus and J$100–140 per 50 miles for minibuses. Each town has a bus terminal of sorts, often near the market. The destination is usually written on the front of the vehicle, along with its name ("Nuff Vibes", "Tings Coulda Worse" and the like). The conductor shouts out the destination before departure, scouting the area for potential passengers and cramming in as many as possible. Buses and minibuses stop anywhere en route to pick up or drop off passengers (except in major towns, where they are restricted to bus stops and terminals). If you want to get off somewhere before the terminus, just tell the conductor; to get on a bus, stand by the side of the road and flag it down.

By car

If you can afford it, **renting a car** is the best way of seeing Jamaica. However, rental **prices** are high, starting at around US$70 per day in high season, including government tax (rates can go as low as US$40 a day at slow times). Third-party insurance is normally included in the price; if you don't have a credit card that offers free collision damage waiver, you'll have to pay another US$12–15 per day to cover potential damage to the car.

There are rental companies all over the island, with the best selection in Kingston, Montego Bay and Ocho Rios, and we've listed them throughout the chapter. Though local companies often offer the best rates, going with a known name will normally ensure guaranteed roadside assistance and a better vehicle; larger companies will also allow you to pick up and drop off in different major towns for no extra fee. Major international rental companies with offices in Jamaica are Budget (ⓣ868/952-3838, ⓦwww.budgetrentacar.com), Econocars (ⓣ868/926-9989, ⓕ978-1798), Hertz ⓣ868/979-0438, ⓦwww.hertz.com), Island (ⓣ868/926-8861, ⓕ929-6987) and Thrifty (ⓣ868/952-5825, ⓦwww.thrifty.com).

Driving in Jamaica is on the **left**, and (unless otherwise specified) speed limits are set at 30mph in towns and minor roads and 50mph on highways. Wearing front seatbelts is mandatory, and police frequently levy on-the-spot fines on those who don't wear them.

If you don't drive – or don't want to – it might be worth hiring a **local driver**, which will cost around US$100 a day.

By taxi

What passes for a taxi in Jamaica varies from the gleaming white vans and imported cars of the **Jamaican Union of Travellers Association** (JUTA; ⓣ868/927-4534, 926-1537 or 952-0623), the official – and expensive – tourist carriers, to beaten-up old Ladas. Licensed taxis carry red numberplates with "PP" or "PPV" on them, but there are also a number of rogue taxis. The authorities advise against using these.

On the whole, **fares** are hefty – around US$20 for ten miles, and you'll always pay a little more if you take a taxi licensed to a hotel. Meters are non-existent, so always establish a price before you get in (or over the phone if you're calling for one). The first quoted price may well be just an opener, particularly if you hail a vehicle on the street; don't be afraid to negotiate. Once a price is agreed, a tip is unnecessary.

Shared taxis or "route taxis" are usually crammed with as many passengers as the driver/owner can fit in, and operate on short, busy set routes around the main towns, picking up and dropping off people anywhere along the way in the same manner as the buses and minibuses. Prices are much closer to bus fares than to taxi rates.

By motorbike

Renting a **motorbike** or **scooter** can be an exhilarating way of touring the island. Outlets abound in the main resorts, and at US$30–40 per day, prices are very reasonable. Though in theory you'll need to show a driving licence, these are rarely asked for.

Under Jamaican law, all motorcycle riders must wear helmets.

By plane

If you're heading across country, it's well worth considering one of the **internal flights** provided by Air Jamaica Express (Ⓣ868/923-6664, Ⓦwww.airjamaica.com). They're quick and efficient, though not exactly a budget option; the one-way fare from Montego Bay to Kingston, for example, is US$83. Flights shuttle among the domestic airports at Tinson Pen in Kingston (Ⓣ868/924-8850), Montego Bay (Ⓣ868/952-4300), Port Antonio (Ⓣ868/913-3692), Negril (Ⓣ868/957-4251 or 4972), and Ocho Rios (Ⓣ868/726-1344).

Accommodation

Although Jamaica has many more accommodation options than most other islands, it's rare to find anywhere to stay for less than US$20 per night in the large resort areas, and you usually need to pay more than twice that for a place with reasonable security and comfort. Jamaica also has some of the world's finest luxury hotels, and there are plenty of options in the middle.

It is always worth **haggling** over the price of a room. Even in high season, a lot of hotels have surplus capacity. In low season, you have even more bargaining power. Prices in the resort areas tend to be more seasonal than elsewhere; in this chapter rates are for the low season (mid-April to mid-Dec) or most of the year.

Jamaica has no youth hostels and the **cheapest** places to stay are usually small, family-run **guesthouses** with pretty basic facilities. The low-cost rooms (US$20–35) that we recommend are normally clean and have some measure of security, though you can expect them to be cramped and box-like, with spartan furniture, shared bathrooms and a fan. Moving up in price, and into **hotel** territory, US$40–60 will normally secure a more tolerable place with a comfortable bed, hot water and, usually, a bar and maybe a place to eat. Once you're paying US$75, you can expect your hotel to have a swimming pool, a restaurant and air-conditioning; over US$100 you'll get a considerable degree of luxury.

Jamaica was the birthplace of the **all-inclusive** hotel, where a single price covers your room and all meals, and often all drinks, watersports and tips too. As it's pretty much unheard-of not to pre-book at these places, we've not listed any in the chapter, but if you do want to go all-inclusive, visit the websites of the two main operators in Jamaica, *Sandals* (Ⓦwww.sandals.com) and *Superclubs* (Ⓦwww.superclubs.com).

Throughout Jamaica, there are hundreds of **villas** available for rent, normally by the week. Ranging from small beachside chalets to grand mansions, these are typically self-catering places, often with maid service, and can make a reasonably priced alternative to hotels for families and groups. JAVA, the Jamaica Association of Villas and Apartments (Ⓣ868/974-2508, Ⓕ974-2967, Ⓦwww.villasinjamaica.com), represents scores of villas islandwide; you can book via their website.

Food and drink

From fiery jerk meat to inventive seafood dishes and ubiquitous rice and peas, the Jamaican diet is surprisingly varied, and the Rasta preference for natural cooking means you can get good vegetarian food fairly easily. Snacking is good, too, with beef, vegetable or chicken patties the staple fare, and there is a vast selection of fresh fruit and vegetables. Outside Kingston and the north-coast resorts, international eating options are limited.

The classic – and addictive – Jamaican breakfast is **ackee and saltfish**. The soft yellow flesh of the otherwise bland ackee fruit is fried with onions, sweet and hot peppers, fresh tomatoes and boiled, flaked salted cod. It's usually served with the delicious spinach-like **callaloo**, boiled green bananas and fried or boiled dumplings.

At most of Jamaica's cheaper restaurants and hotels, **chicken** and **fish** are the mainstays of lunch and dinner. Chicken is typically fried in a seasoned batter, jerked or curried, while fish can be grilled, steamed with okra and pimento pods, brown-stewed in a tasty sauce or "**escovitched**" – served in a spicy sauce of onions, hot peppers and vinegar. "**Jerking**" is the island's most distinctive cooking style. Meat – usually chicken or pork, but occasionally fish – is seasoned in a mixture of island-grown spices, including pimento, hot peppers, cinnamon and nutmeg, and then grilled slowly, often for hours, over a fire of pimento wood and under a cover of wooden slats or corrugated zinc sheets in a customized oil drum.

Rice and peas (rice cooked with coconut, spices and red kidney beans) is the accompaniment to most meals, though you'll sometimes get **bammy** (a substantial bread made from cassava flour), **festival** (a light, sweet, fried dumpling), sweet or regular **potatoes** (the latter known as Irish potatoes), yam, dasheen (like a yam, but chewier), Johnny cakes or fried or boiled **dumplings**.

Jamaica's water is safe to drink, and locally bottled **spring water** is widely available. For a tastier non-alcoholic **drink**, look no further than the roadside piles of coconuts in every town and village, often advertised with a sign saying "**ice-cold jelly**". Other soft drinks include Jamaica's own Ting (a refreshing sparkling grapefruit drink), Malta (a fortifying malt drink), throat-tingling ginger beers and fresh limeade. **Fresh fruit juices** – tamarind, June plum, guava, soursop, strawberry and cucumber – are always delicious if occasionally over-sweet. Jamaican **Blue Mountain coffee** is among the best and most expensive in the world, though the other local brews, such as High Mountain, Low Mountain or Mountain Blend, are also good.

The national **beer** is the excellent Red Stripe. Heineken is widely available, as is locally brewed Guinness, which competes with the sweeter Dragon as the island's stout of choice. Wray and Nephew make the classic white overproof **rum**: cheap, potent, available everywhere and best knocked back with a mixer of Ting. There are plenty of less caustic brands of white rum, the smoothest being C.J. Wray Dry. If you're after taste rather than effect, try gold rums and the older, aged varieties such as Appleton Estate 12-year-old.

Post and phones

Though fairly efficient, Jamaica's telephone system is expensive for overseas calls; local calls are far cheaper, but watch out for the shocking surcharges imposed by most hotels. You can bypass the high charges, though, by way of a locally available international calling card. The mail service is less dependable. Internet access is available in all of the major resorts for anything from J$150 to US$6 for half an hour.

Phones

Most hotel rooms have a **phone**, and phone booths litter the island; the latter accept **phonecards** only, available from hotels, post offices and gift-shops. The cheapest and easiest way to make international and local calls is to buy a Worldtalk **calling card**, they can be used from public, private and hotel phones for both international and local calls

All Jamaican telephone numbers (except some freephone ones) have **seven digits**. To dial locally (within the same parish), simply key in the number. To get a number in another parish, prefix the number with "1"; you also use the "1" prefix when dialling mobile (cellular) numbers.

To **phone abroad** from Jamaica, dial ☎00 + IDD country code (see p.40) + area code minus first 0 + number. For domestic and international **directory assistance** phone ☎114.

The **country code** for Jamaica is ☎876.

Mail

It's amazing how long it takes for mail to get across the island. Don't expect a letter from Kingston to the north coast (or vice versa) to arrive in less than a week. International mail is also slow – reckon on around ten days to a fortnight for airmail to reach Europe or North America. Most towns and villages have a **post office**, normally open Monday to Friday from 9am to 5pm; smaller postal agencies in rural areas keep shorter hours.

Opening hours, festivals and holidays

Jamaican business hours are normally 8.30am to 4.30/5pm Monday to Saturday, although some shops and offices close at noon on Saturdays. Sunday trading is rare. Museums normally close for one day a week, either Sunday or Monday, while most other places you'll want to visit are generally open daily.

Most of Jamaica's special events are timed to coincide with the winter tourist season. The main exceptions are Montego Bay's **Reggae Sumfest** in August and **Spring Break**, when young Americans take over the big resorts for a fortnight of raucous, beer-fuelled cavorting. April is **Carnival** time – though not on the same scale as Trinidad's, Jamaica's Carnival is a growing event. **Emancipation Day** and **Independence Day** celebrations – concerts, dance and theatre performances, and parades – are held in late July to early August; contact the Jamaica Tourist Board for details. The JTB's annual calendar of events is available from offices on the island and abroad, and is posted on the JTB website, ⓦwww.jamaicatravel.com.

Public holidays

January 1 New Year's Day
February Ash Wednesday
March/April Good Friday, Easter Monday
May 23 Labour Day
August 1 Emancipation Day
First Monday in August Independence Day
Third Monday in October National Heroes Day
December 25 Christmas Day
December 26 Boxing Day

Sports and outdoor activities

Sport is a Jamaican obsession – hardly surprising in a country that has produced so many world-class athletes. The island is also a great place to indulge your own sporting passion, with excellent watersports and top-class golfing in particular.

Cricket is the national game, and bringing it up in conversation is a sure-fire icebreaker. The atmosphere at matches is very Jamaican – thumping reggae between overs, and vendors hawking jerk chicken and Red Stripe. There are cricket pitches throughout the island; visit ⓦwww.windiescricket.com for schedules.

Scuba diving and snorkelling are concentrated on the north coast between Negril and Ocho Rios. The state of the reefs is variable, but there are still some gorgeous sites very close to the shore. The resort areas are packed with operators offering dive and snorkelling excursions; the most reputable are listed in the Guide.

Jamaica boasts no fewer than twelve **golf courses**, from the magnificent championship Tryall course near Montego Bay (ⓣ868/956-5681) – home to the annual Johnnie Walker International – to less testing nine-hole links in Mandeville and Port Antonio (ⓣ868/993-7645). All are open to the public, except during tournaments (Tryall sometimes closes to non-members in winter). **Greens fees** vary from US$10 to US$100 in winter, less in summer.

Crime and safety

While Jamaica's murder rate is undeniably high – the average is about a thousand per year – the JTB is keen to stress that you are more likely to be mugged in New York than Montego Bay. Nonetheless, robberies, assaults and other crimes against tourists do occasionally occur, and it's wise to apply the **precautions** you'd take in any foreign city.

Hustling can be a major annoyance in Jamaica. Especially in Montego Bay, young hopefuls aggressively (or humorously) accost foreigners in the street with offers of transport, ganja, aloe massages, hair-braiding and crafts. While an inevitable few street touts see tourists as easy prey for exploitation, most are just trying to make a living in an economically deprived country. Best advice is to keep things in perspective and employ a dash of humour.

Though tourism officials are loath to acknowledge it, many people do come to Jamaica in search of what aficionados agree is some of the finest marijuana in the world. If you're fairly young, expect to be offered **ganja** in the tourist areas; if you're not interested, calmly and firmly refuse. Bear in mind, too, that the possession, use, export or attempted smuggling of any quantity of ganja is **against the law** in Jamaica and carries stiff penalties.

> The **emergency number** for the Jamaican police is ☎119.

History

Jamaica's first inhabitants were Taíno (also called Arawak) Indians, who arrived from South America around 900 AD and led a simple life of farming and fishing until the arrival in 1494 of Columbus, who claimed the island for Spain. Spanish settlement began in 1510, first at Sevilla Nueva on the north coast and then at the site of today's Spanish Town, just northwest of Kingston.

Spanish Town was completely sacked by the British in 1596, and again in 1643. In 1655, fifteen British ships, having failed in their assault on the island of Hispaniola, turned their sights on neighbouring Jamaica. They quickly captured Spanish Town, but the Spanish weren't defeated until five years later, when the last of them fled to Cuba. In the process, the Spanish freed and armed their slaves, most of whom fled to the mountainous interior. The **Maroons,** as they were called, later waged successful guerrilla war against the British.

Under British rule, new settlers were enticed to Jamaica with gifts of land. The colonists established vast **sugarcane** plantations. In the eighteenth century, the island became the world's **biggest producer** of sugar. The planters amassed extraordinary fortunes, but their wealth was predicated upon the appalling inhumanity of **slavery**.

Despite heavy opposition from a West Indian lobby desperate to protect its riches in the colonies, pressure from the church finally brought about the **abolition of slavery** in 1834. Across the country, missionaries set up **"free villages"**, buying land, subdividing it and either selling or donating it to former slaves. Meanwhile, planters found another source of cheap labour by importing 35,000 **indentured labourers** from India in the 1830s.

Jamaica's sugar industry took another major blow in 1846, when a **free-trade-minded** British government passed the Sugar Duties Act, forcing Jamaica's producers to compete on equal terms with sugar producers worldwide. At the same time, the development of **beet-sugar** in Europe reduced demand for the West Indian product.

The economic downturn that followed abolition and the introduction of free trade in sugar took its toll on the freed slaves. Wages were kept pitifully low, taxes were imposed and unemployment rose as plantations were downsized or abandoned altogether. There were numerous **riots**, the most significant of which took place in 1865, when a major **rebellion** broke out in **Morant Bay** in St Thomas. Fearing islandwide insurrection, the governor ordered a show of strength from the armed forces. Little mercy was shown as 437 people were killed, while thousands more were flogged and terrorized. The brutal suppression caused horror throughout Jamaica and Britain and the governor was dismissed for his part in the atrocities. His assembly abolished itself, and in 1866, Jamaica became a **Crown Colony.**

The early twentieth century saw considerable economic prosperity. Inevitably, though, most of the new wealth bypassed the black masses, and serious poverty remained throughout the island. By the 1930s, as the **Great Depression** took hold worldwide, unemployment spiralled and riots became commonplace. **Strikes** erupted too, with a major clash in 1938 between police and workers at the West Indies Sugar Company factory in Frome leaving several people dead. Partly as a result of the Frome incident, strike-leader **Alexander Bustamante** founded the first **trade union** in the Caribbean in 1938 – the Bustamante Industrial Trade Union (BITU). An associated **political party** was born too, with the foundation of the People's National Party (PNP) by the lawyer **Norman Manley**. Both events gave a boost to Jamaican nationalism, already stirred by the campaigning of black-consciousness leader **Marcus Garvey** during the 1920s and early 1930s.

After serving as a major Allied base during **World War II**, Jamaica experienced newfound prosperity in the late 1940s, thanks to early tourism and the first **bauxite** exports. In 1944, a **new constitution** introduced universal adult suffrage, and first elections for a government that would work in conjunction with the British-appointed governor were held. Bustamante's newly formed **Jamaica Labour Party** (JLP) won, and gradually the island's two political parties drifted in different ideological directions, with the JLP adopting a basic liberal capitalist philosophy, and the PNP leaning towards democratic socialism.

The JLP stayed in power until 1955, when the PNP were elected on a manifesto that placed independence firmly on the agenda. Following the collapse of the short-lived West Indies Federation, Jamaica became an **independent state** within the British Commonwealth on August 6, 1962, with Bustamante as its first prime minister.

The early years of independence were marked by rising prosperity, as foreign investment increased, particularly in the bauxite industry. The JLP continued in power until the key **elections of 1972**, when the PNP – now led by Norman Manley's charismatic son **Michael** – swept to power. Manley set out to improve the conditions of the black majority, and his reforms included a minimum wage, the distribution of land to small farmers, and increased funding for the island's education and health-care sectors, all of which were financed by taxation, in particular of the internationally owned bauxite industry.

The bauxite companies promptly scaled down their Jamaican operations, and the ensuing economic decline was compounded by the 1973–74 oil crisis. Manley sought to promote a greater degree of **self-sufficiency**, rejecting closer ties with the US in favour of an alignment with Communist Cuba. US reaction was furious; economic sanctions were applied and it became increasingly difficult for Jamaica to attract foreign investment.

Politics became ever-more polarized during the Manley years. The opposition JLP, led now by **Edward Seaga**, launched blistering attacks on the "communist" administration. The 1976 election – won by the PNP again – saw a disturbing increase in **political violence**, particularly in the ghettos of Kingston. Despite criticism from human rights groups, Manley's response to the violence was to impose a **state of emergency** and severe anti-crime legislation was put in place. Jamaica entered the economic doldrums, and was forced to turn to the IMF for assistance.

Violence flared again during the 1980 election campaign, with hundreds of people killed in shoot-outs and open gang warfare. Amid the carnage, Jamaican voters turned to the JLP. In turn, the JLP turned to the US, but were still obliged to continue the cutback of government services begun under the PNP. The JLP's honeymoon with the Jamaican people proved short-lived; in 1989, Michael Manley and the PNP were returned to office. Ill health forced Manley's resignation in 1992; his successor, **P.J. Patterson**, the first black man to become Jamaica's prime minister, won the election of 1993 on a far less radical platform. The demands of the World Bank and the IMF continued to be met and a generally liberal economic policy followed.

Tourism, bauxite and agriculture remain the mainstays of the Jamaican economy, but the island carries a huge burden of **debt** to foreign banks, and much of the foreign currency earned is required to repay interest and capital on that debt. Consequently, education, roads and public transport have suffered, and the lot of the average Jamaican remains hard. **Crime**, though, is the key concern for most people. Kingston's "garrison communities" are these days delineated by the whims of drug dons rather than by political allegiances, and gun battles have resulted in far too many riots and curfews in the capital.

Despite these problems, there remains much to be positive about in Jamaica. Tourism remains strong, and Jamaican culture remains vibrant. Whatever the challenges, it is hard to quench the island's spirit, and while many islanders predict that "things will get worse before they get better", Jamaica's future, on balance, seems bright.

Music

Close your eyes practically anywhere in Jamaica and you'll hear music. Radios blare on the street, buses pump out non-stop dancehall and every Saturday night the bass of countless sound-system parties wafts through the air. Music is a serious business here, generating an average of a hundred record releases per week and influencing every aspect of Jamaican culture from dress to speech to attitude. Reggae and DJ-based dancehall dominate, but Jamaicans are catholic in their musical tastes: soul, hip-hop, jazz, rock 'n'roll, gospel and the ubiquitous country and western are popular.

Jamaica's music scene first came to international attention with **ska**, the staccato, guitar-and-trumpet-led sound heard in Millie Small's smash hit *My Boy Lollipop* and Desmond Dekker and the Aces' *007 (Shanty Town)*. By the mid 1960s, ska had given way to the slowed-down and more melodic **rocksteady** sound. Rocksteady didn't carry the swing for very long, though, and by the late 1960s it had been superseded by the tighter guitars, heavier bass and sinuous rhythm of **reggae.** Bob Marley's lyrics, drawn from the tenets of Rastafari, emphasized repatriation, black history, black pride and self-determination. Reggae became full-fledged protest music – anathema to the establishment, which banned it wherever possible.

The 1970s stand out as the classic period of roots reggae. But while **Burning Spear** was singing *Marcus Garvey* and *Slavery Days,* the era also offered a sweeter side: the angelic crooning of more mainstream artists like **Dennis Brown** or **Gregory Isaccs** found an eager audience, their style becoming known as **lovers' rock**. As the 1970s wore on, studio technology became more sophisticated and producers began manipulating their equipment to produce **dub** – some of the most arresting and penetrating music ever to emerge from Jamaica. With a remarkable level of inventiveness and often limited means, dub pioneers **King Tubby**, **Prince Jammy** and **Scientist** brought reggae back to basics, stripping down songs so that only bass, drums and inflections of tone remained. Snippets of the original vocals were then mixed in alongside sound effects (dog barks, gunshots). Before long, scores of **DJs** clamoured to produce dub voice-overs. The craft was mastered by **U-Roy**, who released talk-based singles to great success throughout the 1970s.

As the violent elections of 1976 and 1980 saw the pressure in Kingston building up, the sound systems multiplied and the DJs "chatted" on the mike about the times, analysing the position of the ghetto youth in Jamaica. But reggae struggled to find direction and purpose after the death in 1981 of Bob Marley; his legacy of cultural consciousness began to seem less relevant to the ghetto world of cocaine-running and political warfare.

Meanwhile the lewd approach and overtly sexual lyrics – or "slackness" – of DJs such as Yellowman became hugely popular, leading to the rise of **ragga** (from "ragamuffin", meaning a rough-and-ready ghetto-dweller), a two-chord barrage of raw drum and bass and shouted patois lyrics. Also known as **dancehall**, it is now the most popular musical form in contemporary Jamaica; names to look for include Beenie Man, Bounty Killer, Lady Saw, Elephant Man and Spragga Benz.

Dancehall, though, isn't to everyone's taste, and the battle between cultural and slackness artists continues. The culturally conscious lyrics and staunch Rastafarian stance of the late Garnet Silk, who burst on the scene in the mid-1990s, led the way for artists such as Capleton, Sizzla and Luciano, while singers such as Beres Hammond and Sanchez continue to release wonderful reggae tunes.

5.1

Kingston and around

Fast, furious and fascinating, **KINGSTON** is unlike anywhere else in the Caribbean. Given its troubled reputation, it's hardly surprising that few tourists visit, and though the scare stories are absurdly exaggerated, Jamaica's capital is not a place for the faint-hearted. With a population fast approaching one million, the city seethes with life, noise and activity; it's a side of Jamaica that couldn't be more different from the resorts. The live-for-today vitality of the place is tempered by a cool elegance and a strong sense of national history. In addition to being the seat of government and the island's administrative centre, Kingston is Jamaica's cultural heart, the city that spawned Bob Marley, Buju Banton, Beenie Man and countless other reggae stars, and it's *the* place to experience the best of local art, theatre and dance.

Though undeniable, the crime and violence in Kingston is largely confined to the ghettos, and as these are positively not places for casual sightseeing, you're actually no more at risk here than in any other big city. Take the usual precautions – don't walk the downtown streets alone, take cabs after dark, keep jewellery and valuables out of sight – and you're unlikely to run into any problems. If you do decide to visit, you'll find that not only is it easy to steer clear of the troubled areas, but that there's little of the persistent **harassment** that bedevils parts of the north coast.

A handful of interesting museums, galleries and churches can easily fill a couple of days of sightseeing; the island's best clubs, theatres and some great restaurants will take care of the evenings. In addition to the lovely Blue Mountains (see p.253), plenty of other attractions surround the city. The area is littered with historic sites, such as the forts of the English buccaneers in atmospheric **Port Royal**, while white-sand **Hellshire** and **Lime Cay beaches** are the perfect places for a dip in the ocean.

Some history

There was little development in Kingston until 1692, when thousands of Jamaicans fled a violent **earthquake** that devastated Port Royal. Kingston's population was further expanded in 1703, when more Port Royalists fled to the other side of the harbour after a devastating **fire**. In 1872, when Kingston replaced Spanish Town as Jamaica's capital, many wealthy families were already moving beyond the original town boundaries to the more genteel areas that today comprise **uptown** Kingston. Meanwhile the less affluent, including a growing tide of former slaves, huddled downtown and in the **shanty towns** that began to spring up on the outskirts of old Kingston, particularly west of the city.

Jamaica's turn-of-the-century boom, engineered by tourism and agriculture, largely bypassed Kingston's poor. The **downtown** area continued to deteriorate, neglected by government and hit by a catastrophic earthquake in 1907. Those who could afford to continued to move out, leaving behind an increasingly destitute population that proved fertile recruitment ground for the **Rastafari** movement during the 1920s and 1930s.

In the 1960s, efforts were made to give the old downtown area a face-lift. Redevelopment of the waterfront resulted in a much-needed expansion of the city's **port facility** and a smartening up of the harbour area. A mini **tourist boom** was sparked by the new-look Kingston (and by the growing popularity of reggae music abroad). But the redevelopment of downtown was only cosmetic. Crime soon proliferated, and tourists headed for the new beach resorts on the island's north coast as the city sank into a quagmire of unemployment, poverty and crime. Today there are hints that the capital's fortunes may be turning, with some serious attempts to tackle crime and improve economic fortunes; still, Kingston remains a divided city.

Arrival and information

All international and some domestic **flights** land at **Norman Manley International Airport** (☎876/924-8546 or 8452) on the Palisadoes – a strip of land that frames Kingston Harbour southeast of the city. A number of **car rental** firms have desks in the arrivals area; others will meet you there on request. Try Econocars, 11 Lady Musgrave Rd (☎876/927-6761), or Island, 17 Antigua Ave (☎876/926-8012).

A city **bus** runs from just outside the arrivals area to downtown roughly every half-hour (around J$30). However, as buses drop you downtown (not a good idea

for a new arrival toting suitcases), you're far better off opting for a **cab** – the fare for the thirty-minute journey to New Kingston is around J$700, and there are plenty of JUTA drivers around. You can **change money** in the arrivals lounge.

The domestic airport of **Tinson Pen** (☎876/978-8068; 923-6664 for Air Jamaica Express flights) is just to the west of downtown on the fringe of some of the city's less desirable communities. A cab into central Kingston from here should cost around J$300. Taxis usually meet the flights; otherwise, call one of the operators listed below.

The main office of the **Jamaica Tourist Board** (Mon–Fri 9am–4.30pm; ☎876/929-9200) is at 2 St Lucia Ave in New Kingston. It distributes maps and brochures and has a useful little library. There's a smaller branch at Norman Manley airport (☎876/924-8024; normally open to meet flights).

Getting around

Finding your way around Kingston is pretty straightforward. Downtown uses a grid system, while uptown is defined by a handful of major roads; the mountains to the northeast serve as a good compass. The heat and the distances between places mean you're not going to want to do a lot of **walking**, though the downtown sights are easily navigable on foot. It's not advisable to walk the streets at night in any part of the city; Kingstonians don't.

Taxis are the best way of getting around the city and reasonably cheap; a ride from New Kingston to downtown costs around J$250. Although it is standard practice to call for a taxi, particularly at night, they can almost always be flagged down on the main streets (look out for red "PP" or "PPV" plates). There's a bustling rank downtown at Parade and an unofficial one in New Kingston along Knutsford Boulevard. Reputable taxi firms include Blue Diamond (☎876/937-1604) and Eagle Force (☎876/923-4236).

Unfortunately, **public transport** in Kingston is not a viable option for visitors. Fares are absurdly cheap – no more than J$50 for any journey around the city – but overcrowding and the fact that all services radiate from terminals at less-than-salubrious Half Way Tree and at Parade mean it's not worth the hassle. If you want to take a **tour** of the city; see p.248 for details of reliable firms.

Accommodation

Most of Kingston's **hotels** are scattered around the uptown district of **New Kingston**, a convenient base for sightseeing and close to many of the restaurants, theatres, cinemas and clubs. Prices are not as seasonal as in the resort areas, and there are few discounts available during the summer. Although it is wise to reserve in advance, finding a room is rarely a problem.

Alhambra Inn 1 Tucker Ave ☎876/978-9072 or 9073, Ⓕ978-4338, Ⓔalhambra@cwjamaica.com. Pretty complex set back from the road near the National Stadium, with a pool, outdoor restaurant and lots of greenery. The rooms offer king-size beds, telephone, A/C and cable TV, and are superb value; rates include breakfast. ④

Altamont Court 1 Altamont Terrace ☎876/929-4497 or 4498, Ⓕ929-2118, Ⓦwww.cariboutpost.com/altamont. Excellent location in the shadow of the gleaming *Jamaica Pegasus* hotel, with a small swimming pool, hot tub, restaurant and bar. The comfortable rooms have A/C, cable TV and phone. ④

Christar Villas 99 Hope Rd ☎876/978-8066, Ⓕ978-8068, Ⓔchristar@n5.com.jm. Appealing rooms and self-catering studios and suites with satellite TV and A/C in a great location near the Bob Marley Museum. Gym, small pool, and restaurant and bar on site. ④

Courtleigh 85 Knutsford Blvd ☎876/929-9000, Ⓕ926-7744, Ⓦwww.courtleigh.com. A New Kingston old-timer that's fast eclipsing its competition as the best in town. The recently built high-rise contains a fully equipped business centre, restaurants, bars, a gym, a pool and a popular nightclub. Rooms are luxurious, with plenty of extras; some have balconies with great views. ⑥

Four Seasons 18 Ruthven Road ⓣ876/929-7655, ⓕ929-5964, ⓦwww.hotelfourseasonsja.com. Attractive converted Edwardian home in New Kingston. Rooms in the main house are more atmospheric than those in the new wing, but all have A/C, cable TV and phone. There's a pool, restaurant and bar on site. ❹

The Gardens 23 Liguanea Ave ⓣ876/927-5957, ⓕ978-6942, ⓦwww.forrespark.com. With a central location and a relaxing ambience, this delightful complex is one of Kingston's best choices. Expansive two-bedroom townhouses are set on grounds with gorgeous gardens and a pool. Rooms and apartments (sleeping four) with living room and kitchen are available, as are home-cooked meals on request. ❷

Hilton Kingston 77 Knutsford Blvd ⓣ876/926-5430, ⓕ929-7439, ⓦwww.hilton.com. Lively, glitzy complex dominating New Kingston, with a huge pool, nightclubs, restaurant and bar. Rooms afford good views and have A/C, satellite TV, phone and hairdryer. ❺

Holborn Manor 3 Holborn Rd, Kingston 10 ⓣ876/926-0296, ⓕ906-5281. Very basic but friendly family property in New Kingston. The somewhat dingy rooms have fan, phone and cable TV, and there's a dining room on site. ❸

Indies 5 Holborn Rd ⓣ876/926-2952, ⓕ926-2879. Compact, clean and appealing little hotel next to *Holborn Manor*, set on two levels around a garden courtyard and small restaurant. Rooms have A/C and phone – you pay a little more for a TV. ❸

Sunset Inn 1A Altamont Crescent ⓣ876/926-2017. Rather cramped but functional, and well located in the heart of New Kingston opposite *Altamont Court* hotel. Rooms have A/C, phone, cable TV and fridge; some have small kitchens. ❸

The City

Kingston's main sights are divided between the area known as "downtown", which stretches north from the waterfront to the busy traffic junction of Cross Roads, and "uptown", spreading up into the ritzy suburbs at the base of the mountains. **Downtown** is the industrial centre, its factories and all-important port providing most of Kingston's blue-collar employment. You may be surprised at how attractive and easy-going **Uptown** feels. Most of Kingston's hotels, restaurants, clubs and shopping centres are here, and it's where you'll spend most of your time. Some of the residential districts are simply beautiful, while the central high-rises suggest a modern city anywhere in North America.

Downtown

Flattened by an earthquake in 1907, **downtown Kingston** has lost most of its grand eighteenth-century architecture, though a handful of historic buildings can still be found along Rum Lane, Water Lane and King Street. Much of Kingston's economic strength still derives from its impressively huge natural **harbour**, one of the world's best but grimly polluted these days. Once buzzing with trading ships, the wind-whipped waterfront is a good spot to start exploring; it's also the departure point for the ferry to Port Royal (see p.249). The chief beneficiary of the city council's 1960s' effort to beautify downtown, the waterfront saw its historic buildings swept away and replaced by spanking new high-rises. Today these modern monuments define the eastern end of the waterfront's main strip, Ocean Boulevard. Housed in an unprepossessing iron building at the western end of Ocean Boulevard, the **Craft Market** (closed Sun) is the least expensive place on the island to buy souvenirs, and shopping here is usually a hassle-free experience.

The National Gallery

Just up from the waterfront, the air-conditioned **National Gallery**, at 12 Ocean Blvd on the corner of Orange Street (Tues–Thurs 10am–4.30pm, Fri 11am–4pm, Sat 10am–3pm; J$50; guided tours on request at J$800, call ⓣ876/922-1561), is one of the highlights of a visit to Kingston. The permanent collection here is superb, ranging from delicate woodcarvings to flamboyant religious paintings, while the Annual National Exhibition (normally Dec–Feb) showcases the best of contemporary Jamaican art.

Ten galleries on the first floor cover the **Jamaican School**, 1922 to the present. The school is generally deemed to have begun with Edna Manley's 1922 *Bead Seller*, a dainty little statue that married Cubism to a typical local image (the Kingston "higgler", or female street vendor) to create something distinctly Jamaican. Manley's sculpture and the dark, brooding local scenes of John Dunkley (1891–1947) dominate the first galleries. Dunkley and Manley paved the way for other Jamaican artists to paint what they saw around them.

The paintings of Carl Abrahams in the later galleries show a move towards abstraction that is capped by the Jamaican surrealism of Colin Garland and the ghostly images of David Boxer. Realism returns with the powerful re-creation of a Trench Town ghetto in Dawn Scott's *A Cultural Object*. An entire room houses the **Larry Worth Collection** of African-style sculpture and paintings by Shepherd Mallica "Kapo" Reynolds. Downstairs, the **A.D. Scott Collection** displays a selection of Edna Manley's sculptures alongside some of the finest works of the island's most important artists, including Gloria Escoffery and Barrington Watson.

Uptown

The phrase "Uptown Kingston" is used as a catch-all for areas of the city north of Cross Roads, including the business and commercial centres of **Half Way Tree** and **New Kingston** as well as residential areas such as **Hope Pastures**, **Mona** and **Beverly Hills**. The heart of **Uptown** is the high-rise financial district of **New Kingston**, found in an eccentric triangle bounded by Trafalgar Road, Old Hope Road and Half Way Tree Road.

Though there are no attractions of note in New Kingston itself, there are plenty of facilities ranged along the central Knutsford Boulevard, and chances are that you will stay and do much of your eating and drinking in or around this area. Some of the interesting sights are within walking distance; the rest are a short taxi ride away.

Devon House

Trafalgar Road forms a T-junction with Knutsford Boulevard, and then swings east toward Hope Road. Opposite the junction of Trafalgar and Hope Road is the immaculate **Devon House**, 26 Hope Rd (Tues–Sat 9.30am–5pm, tours run throughout the day, last tour at 4.30pm; J$200 including guided tour) – still the grandest house in the city.

Devon House was built in 1881 by Jamaica's first black millionaire, building contractor George Stiebel. Born in Kingston in 1820, Stiebel made his fortune goldmining in Venezuela, returning home in 1873 to snap up properties throughout Jamaica. Among these was Devon Pen, where he built the house that was his Kingston home until he died in 1896. Bought by the Jamaican government in 1967, it has gradually been furnished with West Indian and European antiques as well as more modern Jamaican reproductions. It makes for a diverting hour's exploration, in spite of the enforced tour, which can be rushed and monosyllabic – don't be afraid to take your time.

The landscaped grounds make a fine place for a leisurely stroll. The former stables now house a handful of expensive gift-shops, but chief attractions are the shop selling heavenly homemade "**I Scream**", and the *Brick Oven* bakery, which sells excellent gooey cakes and some of Kingston's best patties. There are also a couple of great restaurants here, detailed in "Eating"see p.246.

The Bob Marley Museum

For reggae fans, the **Bob Marley Museum** at 56 Hope Rd (Mon–Sat 9.30am–5pm, tours every 20min, last tour at 4pm; J$400; ⓣ876/927-9152, ⓦwww.bobmarley-foundation.com) is the whole point of a visit to Kingston, and even if you're not a serious devotee, it's well worth stopping by. Marley's Kingston home from 1975 until his death from cancer in 1981 is still much as it was when he lived here. During the hour-long guided tour you'll see legions of silver, gold and platinum discs and scores of awards as well as concert memorabilia. Upstairs there is a recreation of Wail 'n' Soul – Marley's tiny, shack-like Trench Town record shop. You'll also see Marley's kitchen, bedroom, stage outfits, and the room where he was almost assassinated during the 1976 election campaign – the bullet holes still much in evidence. The tour ends behind the house in the theatre that once housed Marley's Tuff Gong recording studio. There's moving footage of the "One Love" concert of 1980, at which Marley brought together rival political party leaders Michael Manley and Edward Seaga, and a film of interviews with Marley. There's an excellent photo gallery, too.

To the right of the museum entrance are a juice bar/restaurant and a series of high-quality, Rasta-oriented craft shops. A small shop at the back of the complex sells surprisingly stylish clothes and shoes from Marley's own Tuff Gong line.

Eating

After the sun goes down, the Kingston area is hard to beat for open-air eating. Uptown – which is where you'll want to be in the evenings – you'll find a wider choice of **restaurants** than anywhere else in Jamaica and an excellent standard of food. Most places offer variations on traditional Jamaican fare, but you'll also find good Chinese, Indian and Italian cuisine. If you want a meal with a view, head to Port Royal for the waterside restaurant at *Morgan's Harbour* hotel or any of the fish places dotted around the village. For informal lunches, head to the **food courts** at Sovereign Centre in Hope Road, Island Life Plaza on St Lucia Avenue, the huge Marketplace complex in the Constant Spring Arcade or the two Manor Plazas on Constant Spring Road. If you're after truly authentic **jerk chicken**, try any of the smoking oil-drum barbecues set up on street corners.

Akbar 11 Holborn Rd ☎876/922-3247. The best Indian food in town, in a tastefully decorated but rather dark air-conditioned indoor dining room. All the regular dishes, roti and plenty of vegetarian choices. The all-you-can-eat weekday lunchtime buffet (J$500) is well worth it if you're hungry.

Carlos Café 22 Belmont Rd. Friendly place off Oxford Road with appealing décor and excellent service. Decent and inexpensive, food ranges from salads and sandwiches to steaks, seafood and pasta.

The Grog Shoppe Devon House ☎876/929-7029 (closed Sun). A shady spot on the Devon House grounds serving standard Jamaican meals at lunchtime and more European fare (and prices) in the evening. There are regular theme nights, such as all-you-can-eat crab night; call ahead to check.

Heather's Garden Restaurant 9 Haining Rd. Solid Jamaican food in a quiet location with an extensive, medium-priced menu and a daily seafood speciality.

Hot Pot 2 Altamont Terrace. Popular spot for typical Jamaican meals in the heart of New Kingston, with excellent breakfasts, including cornmeal and banana porridge and saltfish combinations, and lunches of fish and bammy, curry goat, stewed beef and the usual Jamaican staples.

JamRock 69 Knutsford Blvd. A perfect and always busy combination of bar, hangout, restaurant and patisserie; favourite among Jamaican dishes is the sumptuous "Jerk Nyamwich", and you can also get salads, soups, burgers, sandwiches, excellent patties, pastries and espresso or cappuccino.

Mother Earth 13 Oxford Terrace. Centrally located and businesslike vegetarian restaurant doing a cracking trade. The menu changes daily; expect good Jamaican staples for breakfast and imaginative lunches with lots of pulses, soya and tofu. The patties are excellent, as are the natural juices and soya ice cream.

Norma's on the Terrace Devon House ☎876/968-5488. Upscale eatery, situated on the terrace of the old Devon House stables and serving gourmet Jamaican food with an international twist. Menu highlights include peppered beef salad, smoked marlin and seafood chowder; afternoon teas feature delectable pastries. It's also good for a late-night espresso accompanied by one of the superb desserts.

Our Place 102 Hope Rd. Laid-back place offers excellent Jamaican cooking and attracts a regular crew of lunchers. All the staples, from conch soup to curry goat, and evening specials such as janga night on Fridays. The bar is nice for a quiet drink.

Red Bones Blues Café 21 Braemar Ave ⓣ876/978-8262. Stylish, upmarket restaurant-cum-music venue with a distinguished but laid-back atmosphere, serving imaginative Jamaican-style food.

Drinking and nightlife

Kingston has legions of great places to get a **drink**, and many of them also double up as restaurants; *Carlos*, *JamRock*, *Red Bones*, *Our Place* and the *Grog Shoppe* (see above) are all good bets, as are hotel bars uptown. There are scores of **clubs** around town, ranging from state-of-the-art places featuring big-name DJs to more sedate in-hotel affairs. Anticipate a cover of around J$300. It's also worth keeping a look-out for posters advertising one-off club nights at places such as Mas Camp Village, or summer all-inclusive parties staged at private outdoor venues throughout the city; these are usually well attended and invariably lots of fun.

Live music in the capital is less predictable; some of the best shows are the annual round of Heineken Startime concerts, featuring the best of Jamaica's vintage artists. Kingstonians celebrate **Carnival** each April; it's similar to the Trinidadian event but on a far smaller scale and with a bigger ratio of reggae to soca. For more on Carnival, contact the JTB (ⓣ876/929-9200).

Bars

Chasers Café 29 Barbican Rd. Popular hangout with a decent beer selection. Monday offers karaoke, Tuesday is oldies night, there's disco each Friday night, and sports on TV throughout the week.

Friends on the Deck 51 Hope Rd. Easy-going and central outdoor bar under a mango tree, popular with a friendly, older set. Different snacks on offer each night, and low-key music from a DJ; women get half-price drinks each Thursday between 5pm and 8pm.

Harry's Bar 80 Constant Spring Rd ⓣ876/755-0514. Pretty, laid-back outdoor bar and restaurant set off from the road in gardens. The music mix includes reggae, alternative and rock, but not dancehall; and there's a dance floor and occasional live music.

Mingles *Courtleigh Hotel*, 85 Knutsford Blvd ⓣ876/929-9000. Indoor and outdoor sections of this hotel nightclub are pleasant places for a drink during the week, while the dance floor fills up on Friday and Saturday nights.

Peppers 31 Upper Waterloo Rd. Late-opening and permanently popular outdoor bar that pulls in post-work drinkers and then younger clubbers, who come for a snack or to dance to sound-system DJs.

Raquel's 38c Trafalgar Rd. Central and fairly smart, with lots of fish tanks and excellent service; good for a quiet drink or a meal.

Clubs

Asylum 69 Knutsford Blvd ⓣ876/929-4386. Fully refitted and packed with Kingstonians checking out the latest dances under the dry ice and UV glare. A different theme every night, so call head to see what's on. Wednesday nights, when more conscious reggae is played, are typically the best introduction.

Jonkanoo Lounge *Hilton Kingston*, 77 Knutsford Blvd ⓣ876/926-5430. Relatively sedate, as you'd expect from a hotel-based venue, but a good and very upmarket (if rarely crowded) disco with occasional live bands.

Mingles *Courtleigh Hotel*, 85 Knutsford Blvd ⓣ876/929-9000. Popular and central, this in-hotel club-cum-bar is usually a good bet, drawing a pleasant crowd for the Friday After Work Jam, with jerk chicken and DJs. Busiest is Saturday's Latin party, when Latin dance classes are held (7–9pm) and the place is packed.

Peppers 31 Upper Waterloo Rd ⓣ876/925-2219 or 969-2421. One of Kingston's most consistently popular venues, with a heaving outdoor dance floor, big-name stage shows every month and DJs most nights; usually packed and a lot of fun.

Theatre and cinema

Kingston's **theatre** scene is limited but buoyant, with a small core of first-rate writers, directors and actors producing work of a generally high standard. Most of the plays are sprinkled with Jamaican patois, but you'll still get the gist. **Comedies** (particularly sexual romps and political satire) are popular, and the normally excellent annual **pantomime** – a musical with a message, totally different from the English variety – is a major event, running from December to April at the **Ward Theatre** (☎876/922-0453) and, later, the **Little Theatre** (☎876/925-6129).

Kingston's **cinemas** invariably screen recent mainstream offerings from the States. Tickets are around J$250, and there's usually a snack interval in the middle of the show. Most of the cinemas are uptown and include the **Palace Cineplex** (☎876/978-3522) at the Sovereign Centre, the **Island Cinemax** (☎876/920-7964) at the Island Life Centre on St Lucia Avenue and the plush **Carib Cinema** at Cross Roads (☎876/926-6106).

Shopping and galleries

A multitude of American-style malls means that **shopping** in Kingston is nothing if not convenient. The major players are the New Kingston Shopping Centre on Dominica Drive, the Sovereign Centre on Hope Road and the multitude of malls on Constant Spring Road.

For **books**, the bookshop at the University of the West Indies in Mona is far and away the superior choice for both novels and books on Jamaica. Reggae fans are in shopping heaven in Kingston. There are **record shops** in most of the shopping malls, and downtown's Orange Street has several places stocking everything from dancehall to rocksteady and reggae classics.

For **souvenirs**, try the Crafts Market downtown (see p.244); for more expensive items, check out the gift-shops at Devon House, or Patoo in the Upper Manor Park Centre. It's also worth browsing the malls on Constant Spring Road, which hold excellent, reasonably priced craft shops.

Listings

Airlines Air Canada, Norman Manley Airport (☎1-800/813-9237 or 876/924-8211); Air Jamaica, 72 Harbour St (☎876/922-4661), Norman Manley Airport (☎876/924-8331); American Airlines, 26 Trafalgar Rd (☎876/920-8887), Norman Manley Airport (☎1-800/433-7300 or 876/924-8248); British Airways, 25 Dominica Drive (☎876/929-9020), Norman Manley Airport (☎1-800/AIRWAYS or 876/924-8187); BWIA, 19 Dominica Drive (☎876/929-4231), Norman Manley Airport (☎876/924-8364 or 8377); Cayman Airways, 23 Dominica Drive (☎876/926-1762), Norman Manley Airport (☎1-800/G-CAYMAN or 876/924-8092); Cubana, 22 Trafalgar Rd (☎876/978-3406), Norman Manley Airport (☎876/978-3410 or 3411).

Tours from Kingston

All of the places around Kingston can be explored on an **organized tour** from the city, a hassle-free means of seeing the sights. Kingston-based **Sun Venture** (☎876/960-6685, ⓕ920-8348, ⓦwww.sunventuretours.com) offers small-scale, individually tailored tours, including an interesting half-day city tour of the more conventional sights – the Bob Marley Museum, Devon House and the like – for US$35 per person for a group of four or more. Sun Venture is also your best choice if heading into the Blue Mountains. Funky, offbeat and extremely enjoyable **Nutourious Adventures'** tours of Kingston provide an insider's look at the capital and its environs and start at US$20 per person (☎876/927-7619, ⓔmmorris@bigplanet.com).

Ambulances Call ☎110 for a public ambulance, ☎876/926-8264 for a private one.
Banks The main banks have branches city-wide including: Bank of Nova Scotia at 2 Knutsford Blvd, 6 Oxford Rd and 125–127 Old Hope Rd; Citizen's Bank at the Sovereign Centre, 17 Dominica Drive and 15A Old Hope Rd; National Commercial Bank at 32 Trafalgar Rd, 133 Old Hope Rd and 37 Duke St. Most of those uptown have ATMs.
Embassies Almost all of the embassies and consulates are based in New Kingston. They include the British High Commission, 28 Trafalgar Rd (☎876/929-6915 or 7049); the American Embassy, 16 Oxford Rd (non-emergency ☎876/935-6042, emergency 935-6044, after-hours emergency 926-6440); the Canadian High Commission, 3 West Kings House Rd (☎876/926-1500).
Hospitals Kingston's public hospitals are the University Hospital at Mona (☎876/927-1620) and the Kingston Public Hospital downtown on North Street (☎876/922-0210). There are a number of private hospitals in New Kingston, including Medical Associates, 18 Tangerine Place (☎876/926-1400) and Andrews Memorial, 27 Hope Rd (☎876/926-7401).
Police The main station is at 79 Duke St (☎876/922-9321).
Post offices The GPO is at 13 King St downtown (☎876/922-2120) and there are a number of branches around town. Stamps can also be bought at most hotels.

East of Kingston

The main route east out of Kingston, Windward Road, follows the coastline. It scythes through an industrial zone of oil tanks and a cement works that towers over the ruined defensive bastion of Fort Rock – now the **Rockfort Mineral Baths**, where you can take a therapeutic soak for J$700. A mile or so further on, turning right at the roundabout takes you on to the **Palisadoes**, a narrow ten-mile spit of land that leads out past the international airport to the ancient city of **Port Royal**, from where it's a short hop to the tiny island of **Lime Cay**.

Port Royal

A short drive or ferry ride from downtown Kingston, **PORT ROYAL** captures the early colonial spirit better than any other place in Jamaica. Originally a tiny island, this little fishing village is now joined to the mainland by the **Palisadoes**, a series of small cays that silted together over hundreds of years and, with a bit of human assistance, now form a roadway and a natural breakwater for Kingston's harbour.

After wresting Jamaica from Spain in 1655, the British turned the island into a **battle station**, with five separate forts and a palisade at the north to defend against attackers coming over the cays. As added protection, they encouraged the buccaneers who had for decades been pillaging the area to sign up as **privateers** in the service of the king. Merchants took advantage of the city's great location to buy and sell slaves, export sugar and logwood, and import bricks and supplies for the growing population. The privateers wreaked havoc on the ships of Spain, and the fabulous profits of trade and plunder brought others to service the town's needs; brothels, taverns and gambling houses proliferated, and by the late seventeenth century, the population had swollen to six thousand.

The huge **earthquake** that struck the city on June 7, 1692, dumped sixty percent of Port Royal into the sea, killing two thousand people in seconds; within a week, a thousand more had died. Most of the remaining population fled for Kingston; almost all who remained later died or deserted when a massive fire swept the island in 1703.

Despite the destruction, Port Royal continued to serve as the country's **naval headquarters** until the advent of steam ships saw the British Navy close its dockyard in 1905. Though Port Royal still retains its naval traditions as home to the JDF naval wing and the Jamaican coast guard, it's a far less exotic place today, a small and tidy fishing village, proud of its very low crime rate and happy to serve up some of the tastiest fresh **fish** you'll find anywhere in Jamaica.

Getting there

Unless you're **driving**, the most pleasant and convenient way to get to Port Royal is on the little **ferry** that leaves regularly from the pier at the bottom of Princess Street in downtown Kingston, near the National Gallery. Services from Kingston start at 7am and finish at 7pm Monday to Friday, 6am to 7pm Saturday, and 11.30am till 6.30pm on Sundays; all ferries depart Port Royal half an hour later. The one-way fare is J$20, and journey time is about half an hour.

A **bus** (J$20; 25min) runs several times a day between the Parade and Port Royal Square, via Harbour View; if you decide to take a **taxi** it will set you back around US$25 in each direction.

The Town

Look back to sea as the ferry docks at Port Royal and you'll get not only a great view of the harbour, but a clear idea of the area's strategic military importance and a glimpse of its former limits.

What remains of Port Royal is easily navigable on foot. Five minutes' walk from the ferry terminal, behind the old garrison wall, are the decaying red bricks of the **Old Naval Hospital**, the oldest prefabricated structure in the "New World". The ramshackle structure now holds the offices of the National Heritage Trust.

Ten minutes' walk away and on the main Church Street, **St Peter's Church** (irregular opening hours) was built in 1726 and, apart from the roof, has survived largely intact. It's unremarkable apart from an intricately carved mahogany and cedar organ. More interesting are the ancient tombs in the small and rambling graveyard. A left turn out of the church leads down the main road to fascinating **Fort Charles** (daily 9am–5pm; J$140). Originally known as Fort Cromwell, Charles was the first of the five forts to be built here, though it never saw any action. In the courtyard, the **Maritime Museum** provides a lucid history of Port Royal and displays items – bottles, coins, cannonballs, shipwrights' tools and a set of ankle shackles used to restrain slaves – dredged up from the underwater city. Notice the National Geographic re-creation of the city at the time of the 1692 earthquake.

The raised platform on the other side of the small parade ground is known as **Nelson's Quarterdeck**; the great commander (incredibly still under 21) used to pace up and down here spoiling for a fight with the French. From the quarterdeck you can see how the land has built up around the fort as the sea has continued to deposit silt – over a foot per year – against the former island. The two structures that now stand between the fort and the water both date from the 1880s. The squat, rectangular **Giddy House** was an ammunition store, while the circular bunker beside it was the **Victoria and Albert Battery** – an emplacement for a nineteenth-century supergun that was fired only once, at a British soldier attempting to desert.

There are a couple of **beaches** around Port Royal, but both sea and sand are pretty dirty; if you want to **swim**, you're better off taking a boat out to Lime Cay (see below). Otherwise, the Buccaneer dive shop at *Morgan's Harbour Hotel* runs scuba certification courses (from US$300) as well as **diving** (US$65 per dive) and **snorkelling** (US$15 per hour) excursions to some of the best sites on the south coast, many centred around wrecked ships. You can also arrange deep-sea **fishing** (4hr US$400; 8hr US$650) and evening drop-line fishing (4hr; US$400) through the hotel.

Lime Cay

Just fifteen minutes by boat from Port Royal, **Lime Cay** is a tiny uninhabited island with white sand, blue water and easy snorkelling. It was here that Ivanhoe ("Rhygin") Martin – the cop-killing gangster and folk-hero immortalized in the classic Jamaican movie *The Harder They Come* – met his demise in 1948. Boats run regularly from *Morgan's Harbour Hotel* (see below) or you can ask the fishermen at the pier to take you – the going rate is J$250 per person round-trip. On Sundays,

△ Rafting on Martha Brae River

when a good-natured crowd of Kingstonians descend, food and drink stalls are set up on the beach; at other times, take your own picnic.

Practicalities

The best place to **stay** in Port Royal (and a five-minute drive from the airport) is the elegant and atmospheric *Morgan's Harbour Hotel* (Ⓣ876/967-8030 or 8040, Ⓕ967-8073; Ⓔmharbour@kasnet.com; ❻), all dark wood and seafaring charm with a pool and an open-air bar. Otherwise, ask in the town square about one of the private homes in the small housing development behind Church Street.

Morgan's Harbour Hotel has a good and reasonably priced restaurant, *Sir Henry's*, which affords marvellous views of the city and cooks up excellent seafood and "international" dishes. Several cheaper **eateries** near the ferry pier serve Port Royal's best fish; the most popular is *Gloria's Rendezvous* at 5 Queen St, where you can enjoy a tasty plate of fish and bammy and watch the pelicans and frigate birds fishing just offshore. Otherwise, there's *Buccaneer's Roost* around the corner, a patty store on the same block, and local women selling fried fish in the main square. At weekends, speakers are stacked up in the square for an outdoor **party**, playing dancehall on a Friday and oldies on Saturday; *Gloria's* occasionally has Sunday oldies parties.

Hellshire and around

Southwest of Kingston, a **causeway** connects the city to the bland but booming dormitory town of **Portmore** in the neighbouring parish of St Catherine. Portmore lies at the eastern fringe of the **Hellshire Hills**, an arid and scrubby expanse of "makko" thorn bushes and towering cacti that shelters the closest beaches to the capital. Virtually the only inhabitants are the migrant birds, a few conies and a handful of Jamaican **iguanas**, once thought to be extinct. From the small fishing community of Port Henderson, the signposted road to the Hellshire beaches runs under the flanks of the hills. Follow the road to **Hellshire beach** (no set hours; free), separated from the less enjoyable Fort Clarence beach (Mon–Fri 10am–5pm, Sat & Sun 8am–6pm; J$100) by a barrier reef that makes the Hellshire water a lot calmer. Hellshire buzzes at the weekends, with booming sound systems and a party atmosphere. Most Jamaicans come here for the **fish restaurants** as much as the sea and sand, and Hellshire fried fish, best eaten with vinegary home-made pepper sauce, beats anything you'll find in town; for excellent cooking and friendly service, try *Flo's* shack. On weekends, **watersports operators** offer jet-ski rental and snorkelling equipment, and there are horse rides for children.

5.2

The Blue Mountains and Portland

Towering behind Kingston, the **Blue Mountains** – named for the mists that colour them from a distance – are an unbroken, undulating spine across Jamaica's easternmost parishes. At 28 miles, the mountains form one of the longest continuous ranges in the Caribbean, and their cool, fragrant woodlands, dotted with coffee plantations, offer some of the best **hiking** on the island. The most popular hike is to **Blue Mountain Peak** – at 7402ft, the highest point in Jamaica – but there are dozens of other trekking possibilities such as the marked trails within the gorgeous Hollywell Recreational Park. Otherwise, **coffee** is the chief interest is here, and you can visit several of the estates producing some of the most expensive – and delicious – beans on earth.

On the other side of the Blue Mountains (here officially known as the **John Crow** range), the northeastern parish of **Portland** is justifiably touted as one of the most beautiful parts of Jamaica, with jungle-smothered hillsides cascading down to a postcard-perfect Caribbean shoreline. If you stay in parish capital **Port Antonio**, you'll be close to the lovely **Reach** waterfalls and fabulous swimming at the magical **Blue Lagoon**. Inland, you can hike in pristine tropical **rainforest** or take a gentle rafting trip on the **Rio Grande**.

Getting around the mountains

You'll need a **car** to get the most out of the mountains. The principal access road, the B1, cuts straight through the slopes, connecting Kingston with Buff Bay on the north coast; a right fork at the small village of **The Cooperage** leads to Mavis Bank, the main access point for Blue Mountain Peak. Landslides are inevitable in the wet season and you can expect bumpy roads throughout the year. You'll need to be extra-attentive when behind the wheel here. Though the roads appear wide enough only for a single vehicle, delivery trucks loaded with precariously balanced crates frequently barrel up the slopes, sounding their presence with blasts on the horn. It's wise to turn off the radio here and listen for oncoming traffic, and also toot your horn at every corner.

Public transport will only take you as far as the main settlements – from Papine in northeast Kingston, **buses** (roughly J$60) go to Newcastle via Irish Town (with the occasional minibus managing to get up as far as Hollywell), and to Mavis Bank via Gordon Town. Ask around in Papine square the day before you plan to travel, and avoid starting out on a Sunday. **Cycling** is an attractive option if you've got your own mountain bike (finding one to rent can be difficult). Several hotels run day-long biking expeditions, among them the *Mount Edge Guesthouse* (☎876/944-8151; US$60; see p.256). Blue Mountain Tours (☎876/974-7075 or 1-800/982-8238; US$89 including transfer, brunch, lunch and refreshments) will pick you up from Ocho Rios and Runaway Bay, drive you up into the mountains and let you freewheel sixteen miles or so down to a waterfall near Buff Bay.

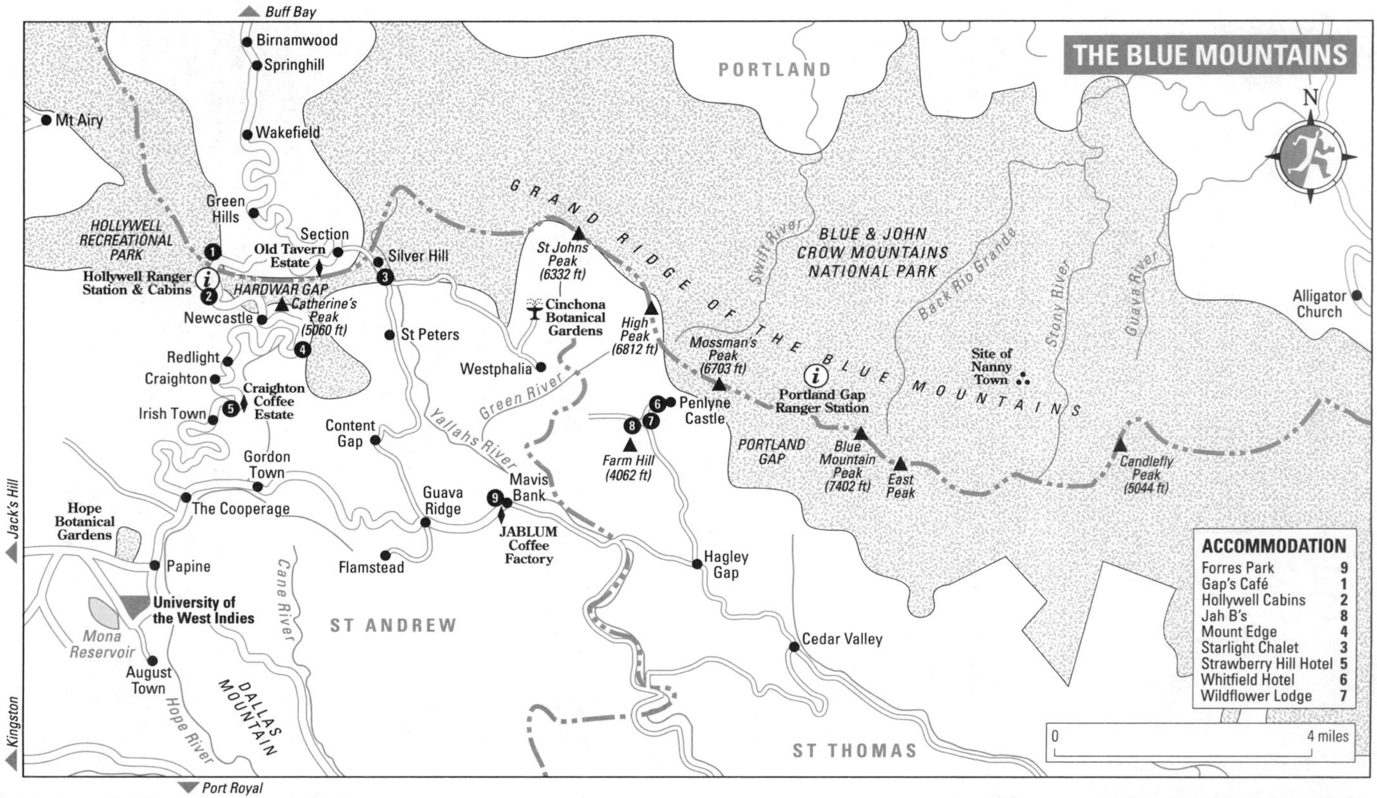

THE BLUE MOUNTAINS

ACCOMMODATION

Forres Park	9
Gap's Café	1
Hollywell Cabins	2
Jah B's	8
Mount Edge	4
Starlight Chalet	3
Strawberry Hill Hotel	5
Whitfield Hotel	6
Wildflower Lodge	7

0 4 miles

N

Buff Bay
Birnamwood
Springhill
Mt Airy
Wakefield
Green Hills
HOLLYWELL RECREATIONAL PARK
Hollywell Ranger Station & Cabins
Old Tavern Estate
Section
Silver Hill
HARDWAR GAP
Catherine's Peak (5060 ft)
Newcastle
Redlight
Craighton
Craighton Coffee Estate
Irish Town
St Peters
Content Gap
Gordon Town
The Cooperage
Hope Botanical Gardens
Papine
University of the West Indies
Mona Reservoir
August Town
Hope River
DALLAS MOUNTAIN
Cane River
ST ANDREW
Flamstead
Guava Ridge
Yallahs River
Green River
Westphalia
Cinchona Botanical Gardens
St Johns Peak (6332 ft)
GRAND RIDGE OF THE BLUE MOUNTAINS
High Peak (6812 ft)
Mavis Bank
JABLUM Coffee Factory
Farm Hill (4062 ft)
Penlyne Castle
Hagley Gap
Cedar Valley
ST THOMAS
PORTLAND
Swift River
BLUE & JOHN CROW MOUNTAINS NATIONAL PARK
Back Rio Grande
Stony River
Guava River
Mossman's Peak (6703 ft)
Portland Gap Ranger Station
PORTLAND GAP
Blue Mountain Peak (7402 ft)
East Peak
Site of Nanny Town
Candlefly Peak (5044 ft)
Alligator Church
Jack's Hill
Kingston
Port Royal

Papine to Section

At Papine in northeast Kingston, the city slams to an abrupt halt as it meets the southern edge of the Mona valley. From here, Gordon Town Road (B1) winds slowly upward into the riverine hills. The road forks at the tiny village of **The Cooperage**; turning right brings you toward Mavis Bank and ultimately Blue Mountain Peak (covered on pp.257), while the left fork leads up a winding road for three miles to the friendly settlement of **IRISH TOWN**. Just over 3000 feet above sea level, it's a small farming community dominated by one magnificent **hotel**, *Strawberry Hill* (ⓣ876/944-8400, ⓕ944-8408, ⓦwww.islandoutpost.com; ⑨). This is among the most attractive places to stay in all Jamaica, with beautifully landscaped gardens, a glorious decked pool providing panoramic city vistas, a sauna and a spa. It's fashionable amongst the glitterati, and Bob Marley was brought here to convalesce after being shot in 1976. Perched on the hillsides, the twelve luxury cottages – from studios to two-bedroom villas with full kitchens – offer fabulous views.

Even if you can't afford to stay here, **eating** at *Strawberry Hill* is a must. The setting on the Great House balcony overlooking Kingston is exceptional, and the menu offers an eminently successful combination of fresh local ingredients and sophisticated international-style cooking. The Sunday brunch is an immensely popular local institution and very reasonably priced at US$45. If you're after a less formal meal in Irish Town, the *Crystal Cove*, at the roadside just south of the village, offers excellent Jamaican cooking and lots of good-natured chat.

From Craighton, the road continues through the tiny village of **Redlight**, named for the former brothels that kept the Irish coopers entertained. There are a few basic bars and a couple of hole-in-the-wall stores where you can buy provisions. Four thousand feet up and multiple switchback turns from here is **NEWCASTLE**, an old British military base still used by the JDF as a training facility. The main road cuts across the **parade ground**, emblazoned with insignia of the various regiments stationed here during the past century or so. The views across the mountains and down to Kingston are dazzling, while behind you, immediately above Newcastle,

Hiking in the Blue Mountains

There's no charge to enter most parts of the Blue Mountains; however, visitors pay J$200 to enter the managed Hollywell Recreational Park area and walk its trails. Park information is available from each of the Blue and John Crow national parks' three **ranger stations**, located at **Hollywell**, **Portland Gap** and **Millbank**. Theoretically always open (though Hollywell is the liveliest and by far the most accessible), these can provide advice on weather conditions and trail access, and ordnance survey maps are on display. None of the ranger stations has a phone, but you can make prior contact through the administrative **park office** at Guava Ridge (ⓣ876/997-8044 or 8069; Mon–Fri 10am–4pm).

No matter where you're walking in the Blue Mountains, it's almost always advisable to use a **guide**; given the changeable weather conditions and poor hiking maps (in a terrain with few obvious landmarks), it's very easy to get lost. Security can also be a problem for unaccompanied hikers, particularly on the Kingston side of the mountains. A guide will ensure your safety, clear overgrown paths and provide an informed commentary. You can arrange a guide through any of the accommodation options listed in this section, but if you just want a day tour or guided hike, contact Sun Venture, 30 Balmoral Ave, Kingston 10 (ⓣ876/960-6685, ⓕ920-8348, ⓦwww.sunventuretours.com), which offers trips to the gorgeous Cinchona gardens, as well as various day-long mountain walks (US$60–80), and a hike up the peak trail, with a night at *Wildflower Lodge* in Penlyne Castle (US$130). Prices are based on groups of two to four people and transport is included.

Catherine's Peak (5060ft) marks the highest point in the parish of St Andrew.

For **accommodation**, just below Newcastle and clinging to the side of the valley, *Mount Edge* (ⓣ876/944-8151, ⓦwww.goactivejamaica.com; ❷-❸) is a laid-back counterculture-ish guesthouse-cum-restaurant. The simple rooms inside the main house, and separate but small units just outside, are perfect for backpackers, while the bar is a great place to chill out. Meals (cooked to order; call ahead for dinner) are also available, ranging from crab in coconut milk to crayfish. Otherwise, you can press on to the *Gap Café* (Mon–Thurs 10am–5pm, Fri–Sun 10am–6pm; ⓣ876/997-3032 or 023-7078, ⓕ923-5617, ⓔtinoc@cwjamaica.com) at **Hardwar Gap**, 4200ft above sea level and some two miles up past Newcastle. Constructed in the 1930s, it's a pretty, flower-wreathed place offering yet more fabulous views. It serves American and Continental breakfasts, and excellent lunches and dinners (J$300–700). There's also a small cottage for rent (US$80); it's nicely decorated and offers TV and a compact kitchen; breakfast is included in the rates.

Just beyond the café is the entrance to the 300-acre **Hollywell Recreational Park**, often bathed in mist but affording a spectacular unbroken view over Kingston, Port Royal and Portmore on a clear day. Easily accessible from the city, this "park within a park" is the busiest part of the mountains, latticed with enjoyable, well-maintained hiking trails. Call at the ranger station just past the entrance (where you pay your J$200 fee) if you plan to hike beyond the trails in the immediate area, best of which is the signposted Oatley Mountain jaunt (2 miles; 40min) an easy, varied circular hike through the tunnel-like jungle. If you want to **stay**, there are three cabins (❸), which you'll need to book well in advance through the Jamaica Conservation and Development Trust, 95 Dumbarton Ave, Kingston 10 (ⓣ876/920-8278 or 8282, ⓕ960-2850, ⓔjcdt@greenjamaica.org). These sleep four to six people, and the very basic facilities – foam-mattressed beds without bedding, indoor cooking range, fridge and cold shower – take second place to the marvellous setting, a Kingston view from your balcony, and complete seclusion. Rates vary from J$2500 for a cabin with two bunk beds, to J$3500 for one with three beds. You can also camp for US$5 per person. You may be able to buy local produce from vendors on the weekends, but it's safer to bring everything you'll need with you, or plan on taking all your meals at the *Gap Café*.

Section

Past Hollywell, the scenery becomes more beguiling as you wind your way higher, with fantastic clear views over mountain gaps planted with neat rows of coffee. The next break in the trees comes at **SECTION**, a friendly little settlement that's home to several small-scale coffee farmers – it's a great place to both enquire about a local hiking guide and buy some coffee (a pound of beans should cost about J$300). The small shop can supply you with beers and snacks, and if you want cheap and very basic **accommodation** (around US$30), ask at the Dennis family's cavernous concrete house opposite. The road forks at Section; the left turn winds seven miles down to the north coast at Buff Bay, while turning right and to the east takes you, via several switchback turns, toward **Silver Hill Gap**, a stunning spot some 5000ft above sea level and offering awesome views across coffee-planted peaks. The *Starlight Chalet and Health Spa* (ⓣ876/969-3116 or 985-9380, ⓕ906-3075, ⓦwww.jamaicamarketplace.com/starlight; ❸), is an isolated and extremely appealing **hotel** on a gorgeous flower-filled bluff. The rooms are modern and comfortable, with balconies and private bathrooms, and there's a sauna and steam room (US$25 per session); you can also have the full spa treatment including massage for US$70. Try the good, inexpensive Jamaican meals served up in the **restaurant**, which, like the attached bar, is open to non-guests; call ahead if you plan to eat. There are a couple of bicycles available for guests to use, and several short trails surround the property, one leading down the valley to a swimmable river; guides are available.

Mavis Bank and Blue Mountain Peak

Back down the hill at The Cooperage, the right-hand fork of the Gordon Town Road passes through the comparatively lively village of Gordon Town. Turn right at the bridge over the Gordon Town River, and a bumpy half-hour drive takes you to neatly arranged **MAVIS BANK**. Nestled in the Yallahs River valley, it's the last full-scale settlement on the route to Blue Mountain Peak. There's little to the tiny village itself; the main attraction is the government-owned **JABLUM coffee factory** (Mon–Fri 9.30–11.30am & 12.30–3.30pm; US$8; tours by appointment on ⓣ876/977-8015) on the west side. The factory is Jamaica's main Blue Mountain coffee-processing plant, and an engaging tour takes you through the whole process.

The main reason to visit Mavis Bank, however, is hiking up to Blue Mountain Peak. As only the sturdiest of Land Rovers can take the abominable road up to Penlyne Castle, where the peak trail starts, it's best to make arrangements in advance; contact Sun Venture (see p.248), which will take care of everything, or call one of the lodges at the base of the trail (see below), and arrange for a pickup, which costs J$1500 one-way per vehicle. You can **stay** at *Forres Park* (ⓣ876/927-8275 or 5957, ⓕ978-6942, ⓦwww.forrespark.com; ❸), a delightful collection of self-contained wood cabins set around a large house that holds simple, comfortable rooms with private bathrooms. **Meals** are available on request (non-guests are also welcome).

From Mavis Bank, it's a fabulous drive up to Penlyne Castle, just over five miles northeast. On the way up, you'll turn left through **HAGLEY GAP** – a one-street village where you can buy provisions and get a hot meal – after which you'll traverse one of the least road-like roads in Jamaica, with huge gullies carved through the clay by coursing water and a constant scree of small boulders in your path. At some 4500 feet above sea level, **PENLYNE CASTLE** is a completely different world, where wind whistles through eucalyptus trees and mists billow over the mountainside only to evaporate in the sun. You're unlikely to meet anyone save the odd coffee-grower or scallion farmer. The only buildings of note are the two hiking hostels; of these, *Whitfield Hall* (ⓣ876/926-6612 or 927-0986; bunks ❶, cabin ❸) is the most atmospheric, set in an old stone planters' house, with a grand piano, a log fire, low ceilings and a pre-war kitchen. You sleep in bunks or in a self-contained cottage. A few hundred yards down the road is the more comfortable *Wildflower Lodge* (ⓣ876/929-5394; bunk ❶, private rooms ❷, cottage ❸), a modern two-storey house set in gorgeous flowered gardens. Bedding choices include private double rooms with bathrooms as well as bunk beds and a self-contained cottage; there's also a gift-shop, cavernous kitchen and dining room. Another option, on the hillside just below *Wildflower*, is the simple, friendly guesthouse run by local Rasta Jah B (ⓣ876/773-6638), where bunk beds cost US$12 and meals are available. Whichever lodge you choose, it's a good idea to arrange to have a **hot meal** ready for your return. Any of the lodges will be able to provide a peak guide for around US$50.

The highest point on the island, **Blue Mountain Peak** (7402ft) seems daunting but isn't the fearful climb you might imagine – though it's hardly a casual stroll, either. It's magnificent by day, thrilling by night. From Penlyne Castle, the climb to the peak is around eight miles and can take anything from three to six hours depending on your fitness level. Most people start at around 1am and catch sunrise at the peak (at around 5.15 to 6.15am, depending on the time of year). If you synchronize your walk with a full moon, you'll get beautiful natural floodlighting – but take a flashlight anyway. Regular signposts make the route easy to follow without the aid of a guide, but in this remote area it's sensible to go with someone who knows their way. Don't stray onto any of the tempting "short cuts" – it's illegal, you'll damage the sensitive environment, and you'll almost certainly get lost.

The Portland Gap ranger station, around a third of the way up, offers the opportunity to refill your water bottles. From here it's another three and a half miles to the peak. At around 7000ft, the plateau at **Lazy Man's Peak** is where many hikers call it a day, but it's worth struggling on for another twenty minutes, as a far more spectacular panorama awaits you at the peak. As the sun burns off the mist, you can make out Cinchona and, on a good day, Buff Bay and Port Antonio's Navy Island to the north and Kingston, Portmore and coastal St Thomas to the south.

Portland

North of the Blue Mountains, **PORTLAND** is rightfully touted as the most beautiful of Jamaica's parishes – a rain-drenched land of luscious foliage, sparkling rivers and pounding waterfalls. Small-scale **Port Antonio** is the largest settlement, a relaxed country town with some inexpensive accommodation options. East of town lie a string of fabulous **beaches** and swimming spots, including the lovely Blue Lagoon. If you head into the interior, you can be poled down the **Rio Grande** on a bamboo raft or hike through the rainforest along the centuries-old trails of the Windward Maroons. An increasing number of visitors are venturing east of Port Antonio for the even more laid-back pleasures of **Long Bay** – with a growing young travellers' scene and the best surf in Jamaica – while the roadside vendors in **Boston Bay** offer some of the best jerk pork in the country in a lovely oceanside setting.

Some history

Portland's early economy was dependent on sugar, with large estates scattered around the parish. However, as the industry declined in the nineteenth century, the parish's fertile soil proved ideally suited for **bananas**. As the country's major banana port, Port Antonio boomed, ushering in an era of prosperity for the town and the region. Cabin space on the banana boats was sold to curious tourists, and the place became a favourite of glitterati such as William Randolph Hearst, J.P. Morgan, Bette Davis and Errol Flynn.

Celebrities still sequester themselves in Portland, and there's a burgeoning backpacker scene at Long Bay, but despite the revitalizing of areas such as Port Antonio's harbourfront, the area can't yet compete for the mainstream vacationer, losing out to the more accessible and better-marketed resorts of Montego Bay, Negril and Ocho Rios. Agriculture is still important, though, and the movie business periodically injects much-needed cash into the economy – films shot here include *Cocktail*, *The Mighty Quinn*, *Club Paradise* and *Lord of the Flies*. That said, the area is still a long way from the prosperity of its heyday.

Port Antonio

A magnet for foreign visitors during the 1950s and 1960s, the quiet town of **PORT ANTONIO** feels more like an isolated backwater these days. But that may change following the recent redevelopment of the harbour, which now boasts a waterside promenade and increased marina facilities; across the bay, the hotel and beaches at Navy Island (currently closed) are slated to receive some much-needed attention, too. At this point, however, there's not a lot to see, but "Portie" remains a friendly and beguiling place, with a bustling central market and a couple of lively clubs.

Arrival, information and getting around

Flights arrive at **Ken Jones Aerodrome**, six miles west of town in St Margaret's Bay, from where a taxi into town costs around US$10. **Buses** and **minibuses** from Kingston (3hr 30min) and Montego Bay (5hr) pull in at the main terminus by the seafront on Gideon Avenue, or by the town's central square on West Street (which also serves as the main **taxi rank**). If you're **driving**, the A4 highway runs straight into and through the town. The **Jamaica Tourist Board** office (Mon–Fri 9am–4pm; ⓣ876/993-3051) is upstairs at the City Centre Plaza on Harbour Street, although it just has a few brochures on hotels and attractions.

To get your bearings, head up to the *Bonnie View Hotel* (signposted off Harbour Street at Port Antonio's eastern outskirts), overlooking the entire town and providing great views. You can **walk** between the handful of sights in Port Antonio, while most places of interest outside town (and all of the beaches) can be reached by **public transport**. Shared taxis run along the main road as far as Long Bay; you'll pay around J$40 to Dragon Bay/Frenchman's Cove, J$50 to Boston Bay, and J$60 to Long Bay.

Since you'll want to get out of town a lot, renting a car is a good idea. Try Eastern Car Rentals at 26 Harbour St (ⓣ876/993-3624 or 2562) or Derron's, east of town at Drapers (ⓣ876/993-7111, ⓕ993-7253); both companies will deliver to your hotel. If you're just planning a single day trip it can work out cheaper to use a taxi; the main rank is in the central square. Alternatively, call the cheerful Mr Palmer (ⓣ876/993-3468 or 772-9648), the Port Antonio taxi co-operative (ⓣ876/993-2684) or JUTA (ⓣ876/993-2684).

Accommodation

Port Antonio has plenty of good **accommodation**, much of it far cheaper than in the more heavily visited north coast resorts.

De Montevin Lodge 21 Fort George St, Titchfield ⓣ876/993-2604, ⓕ715-5987, ⓔdemontevin@cwjamaica.com. Good value in a lovely old gingerbread house, a relic from colonial days. Clean, cool and simple rooms with balconies and shared or private bathrooms, and great food from the restaurant downstairs. ❷, en-suite ❸

Ivanhoes 9 Queen St, Titchfield ⓣ876/993-3043, ⓕ993-4931. Scrupulously clean and tidy no-frills guesthouse opposite the ruins of the old *Titchfield Hotel*. Each of the appealing, reasonably priced rooms has a private bathroom and a fan; meals are available. ❷

Jamaica Heights Spring Bank Road (off Boundbrook Road) ⓣ876/993-3305 or 2156, ⓕ993-3563, ⓦwww.jamaicaheights.com. By far the prettiest place to stay in town, this mellow guesthouse offers a grand view of the twin harbours. The spacious rooms have four-poster beds and big balconies. There's a pool, and meals are available, as are walks to nearby waterfalls. ❹

Ocean Crest 7 Queen St, Titchfield ⓣ876/993-4024. Friendly place with clean, homey units with TV, ceiling fan and private bathroom; there's a shared kitchen and TV lounge. Meals are available. ❷

Scotia Guesthouse 15 Queen St, Titchfield ⓣ876/993-2681. Very basic accommodations in an atmospheric wooden house. Most of the fan-cooled rooms share bathrooms; en-suite units cost a bit more. Rooms J$400, en-suite J$600.

Triffs Inn 1 Bridge St ⓣ876/715-4358, ⓕ993-2162, ⓔtriffs@in-site.com. Mid-range option in the centre of town, popular with Jamaican business travellers. Rooms have A/C, cable TV and private bathroom, and there's a decent restaurant attached. ❸

The Town

The obvious starting-point for a stroll around Port Antonio is its **central square**, with a landmark **clocktower** opposite the red-brick, two-storey Georgian **courthouse**, built in 1895 and fronted by an elegant fretworked verandah. On the other side of the road is the **Village of St George** shopping mall.

Due north from here, the **Titchfield peninsula** juts out into the Caribbean Sea, bisecting Port Antonio's **twin harbours**. The tip of the peninsula once held the British **Fort George**, whose ancient cannons and crumbling walls today form part of Titchfield High School. The short wander up from town takes you past the **De Montevin Lodge** hotel – high-Victorian gingerbread architecture at its best – and the ruins of the **Titchfield Hotel**, Port Antonio's first and once owned by Errol Flynn. Off Queen Street, a footpath leads down to small but pretty **Folly beach**, a nice spot for a swim or a drink at the open-air bar.

Back in the centre of town on West Street, which shoots off from the clocktower, **Musgrave Market** is the liveliest spot in town, crammed with stalls selling fresh produce, fish, meat, clothes and a handful of crafts and souvenirs. Farther up West Street (now called West Palm Avenue), **Boundbrook Wharf** is still the loading point for bananas being shipped to Europe and the United States. This is the place that inspired the banana boat song *Day O*, and the hulking freighter, which arrives on Friday afternoons and leaves the following day, is an impressive sight.

Eating

Port Antonio isn't a gourmand's paradise, but you can get good, inexpensive Jamaican **meals** at a handful of places around town. Patties are available from several outlets along West Street, and there's a branch of *Juicy Beef*, which sells lobster and chicken patties, on Willam Street (parallel to Harbour Street at the eastern end of town). The food court at the top of Village of St George also offers some passable lunch options, and you can get great baked goods at *CC's Bakery*, 25 West St.

Anna Bananas Allan Avenue. A seaside restaurant overlooking the bay, it's one of the best inexpensive places to eat in the area, with excellent, smiling service. Popular with tourists and locals alike, the food is reliable Jamaican; breakfast, lunch and dinner are served daily.

Dickie's Sweet Banana Stop On the A4 just west of Port Antonio. On a knoll as you round the far bend of Port Antonio's west harbour, this simple wooden house scaled down the cliffside is easily missed, but is one of the best choices around. The moderately priced four-course dinners are fabulous (order the morning before you want to eat); choices include ackee on toast, garlic lobster and steamed fish. You can also drop by for breakfast, lunch or afternoon tea.

The Hub 2 West Palm Ave. Just west of the main drag near the old train station, this is a popular place for afforable Jamaican food: rundown, liver or callaloo for breakfast, stew beef, stew peas, cow foot, chicken or baked chicken for lunch and dinner.

Lion's Hut Café 10 Queen St. Relaxed Rasta-oriented place with outdoor seating and delicious ital-style meals: ackee and callaloo breakfasts, steamed veg and brown rice, jerk chicken, and roast, escovitch or shredded fish. Great natural juices.

Port Antonio Marina West Street. With funky décor and a pretty harbourside setting, this is perhaps the most upmarket place in town. The moderately priced lunch menu offers pizzas, sandwiches, burgers, chicken wings and the like; there's good lobster and seafood for dinner.

Drinking and nightlife

The few places to head for a **drink** in town are often very quiet. The oceanfront Port Antonio Marina on West Palm Avenue (☎876/993-3209) is a breezy and pleasant place with a happy hour on Fridays and occasional **live entertainment**, and the terrace at the *Bonnie View Hotel* offers the town's best harbour views. Just out of town and right by the sea on Allan Avenue, the friendly *K-S Kozy Knook* is the archetypal Jamaican drinking hole; a similar scene is found in town at *The Hub* at 2 West Palm Ave.

With none of the bad-boy posturing of Kingston or the resort slickness of the north coast, **clubbing** in Portie is a laid-back and supremely enjoyable experience. Top spot has traditionally been the *Roof Club* at 11 West St (nightly; J$100), while options are *Club Xtacy*, on the top floor of the Village of St George, and the slightly more upmarket *Crystals*, at the western end of West Palm Avenue. All play dancehall, reggae, R&B, hip-hop and a splash of soca.

East of Port Antonio

The coastline east of Port Antonio is a fairytale landscape of jungle-smothered hills rolling down to fantastic beaches, from upmarket **Frenchman's Cove** and **Dragon Bay** to laid-back **Winnifred** and **Long Bay**. It also boasts the sublime **Blue Lagoon**, made famous by the eponymous 1980 movie. Further east, the

Rafting and hiking in the Rio Grande valley

Portland's interior – the **Rio Grande valley** – is a fantastically lush and partially impenetrable hinterland of tropical rainforest, rivers and waterfalls. The **Rio Grande** – one of Jamaica's major rivers – pours down from the John Crow Mountains through the deep and beautiful valley of real virgin forest, with none of the soil erosion and deforestation found on the south side of the Blue Mountains. The paucity of good roads means it's not a heavily visited area, but it does offer some marvellous hiking, as well as the chance to slide down the waters of the Rio Grande aboard a bamboo raft. Once just an easy way to transport bananas to the loading wharf in Port Antonio, **rafting** has been Portland's most popular attraction ever since Errol Flynn began organizing raft ing races for his friends in the 1950s. From the put-in point at **Berridale**, six miles southwest of Port Antonio, rafts meander down the river on a three-hour journey through some outstanding scenery before terminating at the Rafters' Rest complex at St Margaret's Bay. The raft captain stands at the front and poles the craft downstream, stopping periodically to let you swim or buy snacks from vendors positioned along the route. **Tickets** are sold at the put-in spot by Rio Grande Attractions Ltd (☎876/995-778; US$45 per raft), or by hotels and tour groups in Port Antonio. Because it's a one-way trip, **transport** can be a problem. If you're driving, you can leave your car at Berridale and have an insured driver take it down to Rafters' Rest for around US$5. A taxi to Berridale and back to Port Antonio from Rafters' Rest costs around US$10 each way.

If you fancy seeing the valley on foot, call into the **Valley Hikes** office, upstairs at shop 13, Village of St George (☎876/993-3881, ⓔvalleyhikes@cwjamaica.com). An eco-friendly, non-profit-making group employing valley citizens as guides, Valley offer a comprehensive package of walks and excursions, from a gentle two-hour stroll to McKenzie Falls to a strenuous climb up to the White River. Excursions in the lower Rio Grande valley cost US$20–35, but there are plenty of more adventurous (and costlier) options such as an overnight trip to Nanny Town (US$150), as well as horse riding and rafting.

smoking, sizzling jerk stands at Boston Bay are an essential stopoff en route to Reach Falls, a lavish natural cataract in the hills pounding down into a deep pool. A series of smart hotels vie for business with a handful of less expensive guesthouses, the latter mostly slung along the palm-fringed, wind-whipped beach at funky, laid-back Long Bay.

East to Winnifred

Just past Port Antonio's eastern outskirts, Allan Avenue swings past the **Folly Peninsula**, site of the sorry ruin of what was, briefly, one of the grandest houses in Jamaica. Built by an American banker in 1902, it stood for less than thirty years – a victim of shoddy construction. The remaining Grecian-style pillars retain an evocative look, and the ruins have appeared in music videos and films. Around the corner is the fantasy **Trident Castle**. Built by European baroness Zigi Fami, owner of the *Jamaica Palace* hotel, the castle is now the property of the *Trident Hotel* and is occasionally rented out for private functions.

Three miles east of Port Antonio is **Frenchman's Cove**. The formerly sumptuous hotel villas here have deteriorated, but the grounds are still beautifully maintained, and the **beach** (daily 9am–5pm; J$100), though small, is one of the most splendid in Jamaica. The curve of fine sand is enclosed by verdant hills, and a fresh-water river, its bottom lined by white beach sand, runs straight into the sea. Food and drink are usually available, and you can rent loungers or take a boat tour to nearby beaches or the Blue Lagoon (US$10 per person). The easily missed entrance is opposite the turn-off to the eighteen-hole San San Golf Course (☎876/993-7645).

The next option for a swim is privately owned San San beach, open to tourists for around US$5, but you're far better off pressing on to the **Blue Lagoon**. Enclosed by greenery-smothered cliffs, the remarkably turquoise lagoon is a result of several underwater streams running down from the mountains. The whole effect is very picture-postcard, and it's a peaceful place to swim. You can do so for free from a pebbly "beach", but if you're going to make a day of it, you're best off paying the J$120 entry fee to use the facilities at the purpose-built Blue Lagoon complex (daily 10am–10pm; ⓣ876/993-7791). An upmarket **restaurant** area hangs over the water (your entry fee is refunded if you eat), and snorkel gear is available to rent at US$9 for four hours.

There's more marvellous swimming a couple of miles east at **Dragon Bay**, where a protected sandy beach adjoins the *Dragon Bay Hotel*, half a mile from the main road and open to the public for a daily fee of J$150. It has a lovely protected cove to swim and snorkel in – the hotel also offers **scuba diving** (ⓣ876/993-8988) – and access to the thatched bar where Tom Cruise juggled his bottles in *Cocktail*. (The hotel was purchased by the *Sandals* chain in 2001, but at the time of writing the beach was still open to non-guests – ask locally for an update.) Supremely laid-back **Winnifred Beach**, two miles further east, is one of the biggest and most appealing on this side of the island, its wide, golden crescent of sand justly popular with Jamaicans. The small reef is perfect for snorkelling (bring your own gear) and protects the bay from the waves. At the eastern end, a small mineral spring offers a fresh-water rinse (the changing facilities are best avoided). Winnifred has good, unobtrusive food and drink facilities; the best is *Painter and Cynthia's*, tucked into the western corner and serving up delicious platefuls of ackee and saltfish, chicken and fresh fish.

The coast road swings away from the sea parallel to Winnifred; to get to the beach, take the road opposite the *Jamaica Crest Resort* and follow it for half a mile or so. You can park and walk down to the sand where the tarmac ends; if it hasn't been raining recently, you should be able to drive right down onto the beach.

Practicalities

There are several upmarket **accommodation** options on the coast east of Port Antonio, best of which is *Dragon Bay* (ⓣ876/993-7527, ⓕ993-8971, ⓦwww.dragonbay.com; ⑤). A classic Caribbean resort, it has 55 lavish acres, a gorgeous beach, and good facilities including tennis courts, pool, fitness centre, sauna, a dive shop and two restaurants. You stay in rooms or one-, two- or three-bedroom villas. Otherwise, green-conscious *Mocking Bird Hill* (ⓣ876/993-7267, ⓕ993-7133, ⓦwww.hotelmockingbirdhill.com; ⑤) boasts a lovely airy setting on a peaceful bluff above San San, with great Blue Mountain views too. The comfortable rooms have balconies, and there's a pool and a good restaurant. Italian-style *San San Tropez* (ⓣ876/993-7213, ⓕ993-7399, ⓦwww.sansantropez.com; ④) is another possibility. Its large rooms feature A/C and cable TV, and there's a pool and renowned restaurant on site. A less expensive option is *Drapers San*, right on the road at Drapers (ⓣ & ⓕ876/993-7118; ②), a funky, friendly, Italian-run guesthouse with an eclectic collection of rooms, some with kitchen, some with shared bathroom; all have fans and mosquito nets. Breakfast is included, and the owner is a great source of local information.

There's a good selection of **places to eat** this side of Port Antonio. With an impossibly romantic setting right on the water, the *Blue Lagoon* restaurant (ⓣ876/993-8491) serves jerk shrimp, honey conch and fresh fish and lobster for lunch and dinner. For a more formal meal, head to *Mille Fleurs* at *Mocking Bird Hill Hotel*, where the terrace restaurant offers imaginative dishes based on Jamaican staples. The Sicilian chefs at *San San Tropez* serve up home-made pasta, fantastic thin-crust pizzas and Italian-style grilled fish with tomatoes.

Boston to Long Bay

Though blessed with a perfectly good public beach, **BOSTON BAY**, further east along the A4, is better known for its collection of **jerk stands**. Jerking of meat originated in this part of the country, and the pork and chicken sold here is still reckoned to be the best in Jamaica. You'll pay around J$380 for a pound of chicken, and J$300 for a pound of pork; both are best eaten with a dollop of ketchup and jerk sauce and accompanied by roast yam, breadfruit or a hunk of fresh hardough bread.

Still owned by the widow of Errol Flynn, the rolling pasturelands below Boston Bay give way to **LONG BAY**, where a mini tourist industry – unusual on the barely developed east coast – is swiftly growing up. With its wide swath of surf-pounded honey sand, Long Bay for the last decade has been attracting a smattering of European backpackers, some of whom have settled here and opened guesthouses. Two simple, friendly beach bars, *Chill Out* and *Cool Runnings,* cater to the demand for entertainment. It's a far cry from the developed resorts on the north coast: tourists are outnumbered on the beach by local people, and there's a lot of ganja-wreathed hanging out. There isn't much to the village, which has grown up piecemeal on either side of the main road. The north end of the beach is Jamaica's premier **surf** scene, though you'd never know it from the paucity of board-rental outlets; the locals should be able to help you find a board, and they'll also know who will take you out **fishing**. **Swimming** is excellent here, too, but watch out for a dangerous undertow and rip tides; never swim out further than you can stand.

When you're able to drag yourself away from the beach, head a couple of miles further east to a signposted turn-off that swings inland from the coast road to spectacular **Reach Falls** (daily dawn to dusk; J$150), where the Drivers River cascades thirty feet into a wide, green pool. You can stand right underneath the falls for an invigorating water massage. From the base of the falls, tour guides will take you on a thirty-minute trek upriver through the rainforest (the charge is negotiable, but it's well worth doing). There's a small bar at the falls car park and, on weekends, stalls selling janga soup and roast corn; there are changing rooms and toilets, too.

Practicalities

There's a wealth of budget **accommodation** in Long Bay. Up the hill toward the east end of the bay is the simple, reliable and relaxed *Skanka Heights* (Ⓣ876/913-7318, Ⓔcoolrunnings@iricweb.net; ❶), a perfect backpackers' hangout which affords gorgeous views over the surrounding coastline. Rooms are in the main house or private cottages; all have fans, mosquito nets and access to the kitchen; meals – from pizza to Jamaican staples – are also available. Down on the beach, the owner has built a couple of African-style huts (Ⓣ876/913-7712, email as above; ❷) adjacent to his *Cool Runnings* bar; they have verandahs overlooking the water and private bathrooms. On the other side of the road, *Likkle Paradise* (Ⓣ876/913-7702; ❷) offers spotless rooms with fans and private bathrooms; guests can use the kitchen. Just up the road, *Monica's Hideout* (Ⓣ876/913-7113 or 7479; ❷) offers compact, self-contained one-bedroom cottages.

Evenings in Long Bay are usually centred around the appropriately named *Chill Out* beach bar and restaurant (Ⓣ876/913-7327), a French-run, open-sided thatch-roofed joint where you can get good **meals** or have a **drink** at the lively bar. A few steps west, on a lovely bit of beach, the appealing *Cool Runnings* offers tasty meals (fish in coconut, chicken in satay sauce, calamari fritters, pizza). There's usually good music, and occasionally parties or sound-system jams.

5.3

Ocho Rios and around

With its high-rise blocks, buzzing jet skis and duty-free stores, the classic resort town of **Ocho Rios** typifies the commercial feel of Jamaica's north coast. Home to a wealth of managed attractions – from the famous **Dunn's River Falls** to **Dolphin Cove** and a couple of lovely **botanical gardens** – the town is geared to the needs of cruise shippers and beach vacationers. East of town, the quiet coastal villages of **Oracabessa** and **Port Maria** boast a funky beach club and Noel Coward's former home, while west of town hotels line the shore at the resort-oriented coastal sprawls of **Runaway Bay** and **Discovery Bay**. The lush St Ann hills hold one of Jamaica's major draws, the **Bob Marley Mausoleum** at the singer's birthplace, Nine Mile.

Ocho Rios

The first town in Jamaica to be developed specifically as a resort, **OCHO RIOS** (usually just called "Ochi") abounds with neon-fronted duty-free stores, fast-food chains, bars, clubs and visitor-oriented restaurants. Local culture takes a back seat to the tourist trappings here, so it's not a good place to get an authentic flavour of Jamaica. It's not the best choice amongst the island's "big three" resorts for the classic Caribbean beach holiday, either – the strip of hotel-lined sand just can't compete with the beaches of Negril and Montego Bay, and the club and bar scenes are less vibrant. Nonetheless, the nightlife is improving, and Ochi compensates for its scenic deficiencies with a certain infectious energy.

Arrival and information

All **buses** pull in at the terminus behind Main Street. It's within walking distance of most hotels, but taxi drivers usually hang around plying for fares. If you're **driving** in from Montego Bay, the coast road forks as you enter town; left takes you onto the one-way section of Main Street, where the majority of hotels are located, while right takes you along DaCosta Drive, which connects with the bypass (the route to hotels east of town), and with Milford Road, which leads to Fern Gully and, eventually, Kingston. If you drive in from the east, you enter town via the bypass and there are numerous signposted exits onto Main Street. Domestic **flights** touch down at Boscobel Aerodrome, a thirty-minute drive from town; a cab to town should cost about US$25.

The main **JTB office** (Mon–Fri 9am–5pm, Sat 9am–1pm; ⓣ876/974-2582 or 2570) is in Ocean Village Plaza on Main Street.

Accommodation

There are numerous **lodging places** in Ochi, including many all-inclusive resorts (see p.234). However, there are options for those of a more independent bent, and the best, most central choices are listed below.

Carlene's by the Sea 85 Main St ⓣ876/974-5431. Fantastic value, this friendly place has pleasant rooms with cable TV and fans, and a great location with access to the sea. ❷

Hibiscus Lodge 83–87 Main St ⓣ876/974-2676, ⓕ974-1874. Set back from the road in beautiful gardens, this is the most attractive hotel in the town centre. The clean, pleasant cliffside rooms all

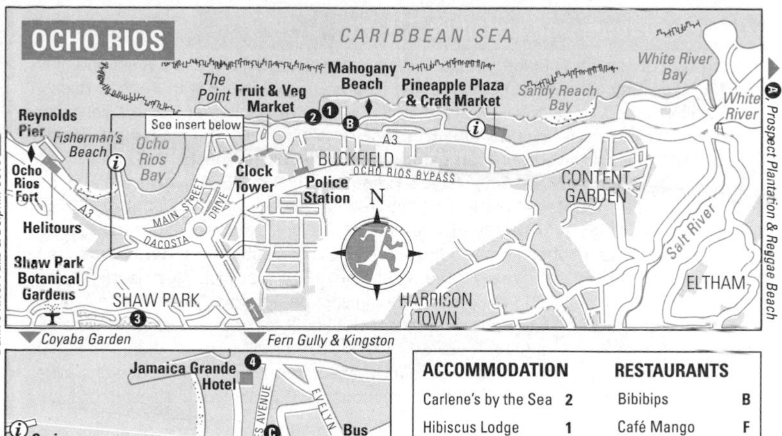

ACCOMMODATION		RESTAURANTS	
Carlene's by the Sea	2	Bibibips	B
Hibiscus Lodge	1	Café Mango	F
Little Pub Inn	5	Evita's	J
Little Shaw Park Guest House	3	The Healthy Way	I
Ocean Sands	4	Jack Ruby's	D
Pier View	8	Little Pub	E
Sandcastles	7	Ocho Rios Village Jerk Centre	K
Village Hotel	6	Passage to India	G
		Peppers	C
		Toscanini	A
		Veggie Kitchen	H

have balconies, and there's a pool, hot tub, tennis court, sun deck, sea access, excellent restaurant and a bar. Rates include breakfast. ⑤

Little Pub Inn 59 Main St ⓣ876/974-2324, ⓕ974-5825, ⓔlittlepub@reggaesun.com. The restaurant, entertainment and shopping mall make this one of the busier spots in town. Some rooms are split-level with platform beds, most have sloping ceilings, and all are spotless and inviting with A/C and satellite TV. Rates include breakfast. ③

Little Shaw Park Guest House 21 Shaw Park Rd ⓣ876/974-2177, ⓕ974-8997. Easy-going, family-owned place overlooking town, set in gardens with space for camping. Homey rooms with cable TV, fan; some share bathrooms, others have kitchen facilities. Meals are available. ②, camping ①

Ocean Sands 14 James Ave ⓣ & ⓕ876/974-2605, ⓦwww.oceansandsresorts.com. Hidden behind Main Street and right on the sea, this is a lovely base, with a slip of beach, a pool and restaurant/bar. Rooms are spotless, with A/C and private balcony, and rates include breakfast. Excellent value. ③

Pier View 19 Main St ⓣ876/974-2607, ⓕ974-1384. Busy, friendly and laid-back apartment development, next to UDC beach and popular with younger travellers. Standard rooms have fan, fridge and cable TV; you pay more for A/C and kitchen. All have access to the pool and sun deck. ③

Sandcastles 120 Main St ⓣ876/974-5626, ⓕ974-2247, ⓦwww.sandcastlesochorios.com. Backing onto the beach (guests get free access), these airy studios and one- or two-bedroom apartments each have A/C, cable TV and kitchenette. Good for families (the pool has a slide and kids' area). There's a restaurant and bar. ④

Village Hotel 54–56 Main St ⓣ876/974-3193, ⓕ974-8894, ⓦwww.geocities.com/villagehotel. Friendly, family-run property slap in the centre of town and a five-minute walk to the beach. Rooms have queen bed, cable TV, A/C and phone, and there's a pool, restaurant and bar. ④

Organized tours and activities

In terms of quality and choice, the Ocho Rios roster of **organized tours** is second only to Montego Bay. Scores of comparably priced operators (most with in-hotel desks) will whisk you off to Dunn's River Falls or the Marley mausoleum at Nine Mile. More interesting excursions include **tubing** along the White River from Spanish Bridge (3.5hr; US$49), and five-hour **jeep safaris** (US$60 including lunch), both offered by Chukka Cove (☎876/972-2506). **Horse-riding** trips (3hr; US$55) also are run by Chukka, as are **mountain-bike tours** (3hr; US$50). An innovation at Chukka is **gliding**; trips cost US$90 for twenty minutes. Costs for all trips cover return transportation from Ochi and refreshments. Hooves (☎876/972-0905) offers **horseback trail rides** around the Seville Great House at St Ann's Bay that include swimming your horse (2hr 30min; US$60); they also offer inland hacks (2hr "Bush Doctor" ride, US$50), and will do private rides on request. Ochi isn't far from the **Blue Mountains** (see p.253), and Blue Mountain Tours (☎876/974-7075 or toll-free on 1-800/982-8238) will transport you up into the mountains for a spectacular sixteen-mile downhill bike ride to a waterfall near Buff Bay on the north coast (US$89 including transfer, brunch, lunch and refreshments).

Yet more adventurous possibilities include the exhilarating ATV (or **quad bike**) tours in the St Mary interior offered by Wilderness Resorts (☎876/974-5189 or 4613). The valley tour (1hr; US$60) goes through the lush landscape that surrounds the Wilderness farm, while the country tour (2hr; US$103) takes you to Spanish Bridge with stops for swimming and photos. All trips include transport to and from your hotel, and can be combined with other Wilderness activities such as fishing, hiking and horse riding.

The Town

Home to most of the town's hotels, bars, banks, shopping plazas and restaurants, as well as the bustling craft market, Ochi's permanently busy Main Street holds little interest for sightseeing. You're likely to spend your days lazing on the **beach** – variously known as UDC, Mallards, Turtle and Ocho Rios Bay (daily 9am–5pm; J$50). Tucked under the tower blocks and accessible from the western end of Main Street near the *Pier View* and *Sandcastles* hotels, the white-sand beach is wide, fairly attractive and well maintained, with showers, changing rooms, bars and plenty of activity. Patches of sea grass and occasional pollution mean that this isn't one of the north coast's most appealing places to swim, however, particularly when it's overshadowed by docked cruise ships across the bay.

The only other stretch of sand in Ochi that's not the private domain of an all-inclusive hotel is **Mahogany Beach**, set at the eastern stretch of Main Street as it climbs uphill (turn off just past the *Hibiscus Lodge* hotel). This compact wedge of beach with calm, clean waters and good snorkelling also boasts a beach bar and grill, swimming pool, volleyball and basketball courts, all set in beautiful landscaped gardens. However, complaints from residents of the adjacent villa complex mean that proprietors come and go, and the nightly beach parties that once carried the swing here are held only intermittently; you may also have to pay an entrance fee during the day.

Dolphin Cove and Dunn's River Falls

Heading west of town along Main Street, a boardwalk allows easy pedestrian access to Ochi's two biggest, and best, organized attractions. The first, some ten minutes' walk from the centre, is **Dolphin Cove** (daily 8.30am–5.30pm; ☎876/974-5335, Ⓦwww.dolphincovejamaica.com). The main draw at the landscaped, theme-park style complex is the chance to interact with the trained bottlenose dolphins kept in a fenced-off section of the bay. There are three choices of "interactive programme":

Watersports

Although there isn't that much to see underwater at Ocho Rios's main beach – you'll find much richer pickings east of the harbour or at the reef at the bottom of Dunn's River (see below) – the sand is lined with **watersports concessions**. Prices are fairly high – even snorkel equipment can cost as much as US$20 per day, though bargaining usually brings this down a bit and you might get better deals toward the quieter, western edge of the beach. Touts roam the sand offering jet-ski rides (30min; US$50), banana boat rides (30min; US$25), water-skiing (about US$50 for three laps of the bay), and parasalling (10–15min; US$50). You can also take a glass bottom boat ride; many go along the coast toward Dunn's River Falls, at a cost of around US$20 per person plus entry to the falls. For **scuba diving**, try Resort Divers at 2 Island Plaza (☎876/974-5338), which also offers deep-sea fishing from US$300 per half-day.

Many private boats offer **pleasure cruises**. Day trips go to Dunn's River for snorkelling and climbing the falls, with an open bar and lunch or snacks; sunset cruises include drinks only. Most operators offer dinner cruises, too. Visitors usually book via the agents who stake out the beaches. One of the better operators is Red Stripe (☎876/974-2446), which runs a day cruise to Dunn's River (3hr; US$45) and a sunset soca cruise (2hr; US$25). All prices are per person; trips leave on Tuesday, Thursday and Saturday.

the "Touch Encounter" (US$35), in which you stand in knee-high water and get to stroke a dolphin and have your photo taken (US$12); the "Encounter Swim" (US$79), which gets you into the water to kiss and play with the animals; and the "Swim with Dolphins" (US$145), in which you spend a bit more time in the water, and get a dorsal pull. While it's all very organized, nothing much can take away from the delight of being so close to the dolphins. Elsewhere in the complex, there's a pool containing sharks and rays; a nature trail with stops for petting macaws, touching starfish and snakes; a small beach (you can hire snorkel equipment and canoes); a restaurant; and a great gift-shop. The entrance fee of US$15 allows you to stay and explore all day. Dolphin programmes start daily at 9.30am, 11.30am, 1.30pm and 3.30pm; it's advisable to book ahead, and you must arrive half an hour before the programme starts. There are changing facilities and lockers on site, but most people arrive in their bathing suits.

A couple of minutes' walk further west, **Dunn's River Falls** (daily 8am–5pm, last ticket 4pm; US$6, plus a tip for the guide) is Jamaica's best-loved waterfall and a staple of tour brochures. Masked from the road by restaurants, craft shops and car parks, the wide and magnificent 600ft waterfall cascades over rocks down to a pretty tree-fringed, white-sand beach that's far cleaner than the one in town. There's a lively reef within swimming distance, and snorkel gear is available to rent. With water running so fast you can hear it from the road below, the falls more than live up to their reputation, despite the concrete and commerciality. The main activity is climbing up the cascade, a wet but easily navigable hour-long clamber. The step-like rocks are regularly scraped to remove slippery algae, and visitors form a hand-holding chain led by one of the very experienced guides. Wear a **bathing suit** – you're showered with cool, clear water all the way up. Most people also rent "sticky feet" shoes (US$5). There's a restaurant and bar, craft and hair-braiding shacks and full changing facilities at the beach and at the top of the falls.

Shaw Park and Coyaba

From the main roundabout at Ochi's western outskirts, a twenty-minute walk starting along Milford Road takes you to two of Ochi's better-known pastoral attractions, both on the ill-maintained Shaw Park Road (turn right from Milford Road 100ft from the junction at the Shaw Park signpost). Some 550ft above sea level,

Shaw Park Botanical Gardens (daily 8am–5pm; US$4) afford stunning aerial views of town and do a cracking trade with cruise-ship passengers. The former grounds of a long-gone hotel, the 25-acre gardens are resplendent with unusual flowers, plants and trees – including a huge banyan – set amidst grassy lawns; there's even a near-perpendicular (but non-swimmable) waterfall. You can walk unaccompanied, but the knowledgeable gardeners-cum-guides will initiate you into the wonders of tropical horticulture. There's an on-site bar, and crafts and jewellery on sale at the gift-shop.

About five minutes further up Shaw Park Road, **Coyaba River Garden and Museum** (daily 8am–5pm; US$4.50) is another favourite tour bus stop-off, a meditative and restful miniature hothouse of lush, well-watered flower beds. Wooden walkways allow easy viewing of the tropical foliage, and the flower beds are bisected by streams teeming with fish and turtles, with glass panels providing views of the underwater goings-on. Housed in an elegant cut-stone building, the museum has a limited but thoughtful collection of exhibits spanning Jamaican history; special weight is given to St Ann's own Marcus Garvey and Bob Marley. There's a good café and gift-shop on site.

Prospect Plantation and Reggae Beach

A five-minute drive east of town, the former haunt of British planter Harold Mitchell has been reincarnated as a tourist attraction, **Prospect Plantation** (1hr 25min guided tours Mon–Sat 10.30am, 2pm & 3pm, Sun 11am, 1.30pm & 3pm; US$12; ⓣ876/974-2058). Designed to introduce the more sedentary visitor to the delights of tropical farming, the tour consists of sitting with 38 others on an open trailer and listening to an inaudible commentary while trundling through sugarcane patches and groves of coconut palm, pimento, lime, ackee, breadfruit, mahoe and soursop trees, stopping only to sample fruits, admire the bay views from Sir Harold's lookout, and potter around a stone church. You'll feel less like a member of a cattle herd if you do the tour aboard a **mountain bike** (1hr; US$12) or on **horseback** (1hr; US$20). Other **trail rides** cover the property and go down into White River gorge (1hr 30min; US$35), the site of Jamaica's first hydro-electric plant, while the "View Jamaica" trek goes down to the river and up into the hills (2hr 15min; US$50). You'll need to book all rides one day in advance, and the horses rest on Sundays.

A few minutes' drive east of Prospect along the A3 is **Reggae Beach** (Mon–Fri 9am–5pm, Sat & Sun 9am–6pm; US$5). A pretty curve of coarse yellow sand, it's cleaner than the strip in town, though there's also some sea grass. Pluses include brightly painted showers and changing rooms, rope swings from the trees, plenty of shade and a good snack shop. Friday after-work jams carry on till 1am, with a bonfire, DJs and live band; there's usually music in the daytime, too. As it's a fair drive from town, the place is pleasantly quiet during the week.

Eating

As many of Ochi's **restaurants** aim to please the foreign palate, Italian, Indian, Chinese and American fare is available in addition to the Jamaican staples, and there are a couple of excellent vegetarian options. There are several patty shops around town, including a branch of *Juicy Beef* by the clocktower, as well as numerous **fast-food** joints. For Jamaican food on the hop, head to the excellent *Island Grill* at 12 Main Street (opposite *Sandcastles* hotel), for jerk chicken and fish. Jerk stands also set up around the clocktower in the evenings.

Bibibips 93 Main St. Set back from the road, with tables overlooking the sea, this place serves excellent fish dishes as well as coconut curry chicken, seafood crepes, vegetable stir-fry, Rasta pasta, and all the usual Jamaican favourites. Service is excellent and prices are fair.

Café Mango Main Street, opposite the entrance to *Jamaica Grande*. Semi-open-air and inexpensive diner in a shady, central location. Jamaican and American breakfasts, also calamari, nachos, chicken wings, salads, some Mexican dishes, pasta and pizza. A nice spot for a long lunch or an outdoor dinner.

Evita's Eden Bower Road ⓣ876/974-2333. The best-advertised pasta on the north coast, served on a gingerbread verandah overlooking the bay. Huge choice of starters, salads and soups; main courses include pasta – even "Lasagne Rastafari" with ackee, callaloo and tomatoes – and seafood. Expensive, but worth the splurge.

The Healthy Way Ocean Village Plaza. Energetic and efficient vegetarian take-away, with a couple of tables, offering veggie/tofu burgers and patties, soups, Ital juices, fruit salad, cakes and a different main dish each day.

Jack Ruby's 1 James Ave. Reliable, affordable Jamaican food – ackee and saltfish or callaloo with all the trimmings, fish and lobster any style, Ital stew, cow foot, oxtail and chicken.

Little Pub 59 Main St ⓣ876/974-2324. American and Jamaican breakfast and lunch in a roadside café with a juice bar on site. Dinner – from filet mignon or surf 'n' turf to lobster thermidor – is dished up in the "entertainment area". Prices range from moderate to expensive.

Ocho Rios Village Jerk Centre just before the roundabout on DaCosta Drive. Renowned for the consistently good and sensibly priced jerk pork, chicken, fish and barbecued spare ribs as well as the piped dancehall, which draws in an evening crowd of drinkers.

Passage to India Soni's Plaza, 50 Main St ⓣ876/795-3182. Rooftop restaurant serving excellent Indian cuisine. The menu is pretty comprehensive. Breads are particularly good, as are the lassi yogurt drinks and desserts.

Peppers 3 James Ave. Popular place for a late supper; fish is served any which way, with bammy, festival or rice and peas. The outdoor seats are perfectly placed for soaking up the James Avenue shenanigans. Closed Tuesday.

Toscanini Harmony Hall ⓣ876/975-4785. A ten-minute drive east of the centre under the eaves of pretty Harmony Hall, and easily one of Ochi's best. Service is great, and the relatively expensive menu features all the Italian classics. Vegetarians are well served, and the puddings are sublime. Closed Monday.

Veggie Kitchen Shop 11, Island Plaza, Main Street. Delicious dairy-free vegetarian cooking: plantain porridge, ackee breakfasts, soups, patties, salads, veggie burgers and full hot meals for lunch or early dinner. Great natural juices. Closed Sunday.

Nightlife and entertainment

Despite its dedication to the tourist dollar, Ocho Rios is surprisingly short of good clubs and bars. Chris Blackwell's new Island Village development at the west end of town near the cruise ship pier should improve the nightlife scene with a branch of *Margaritaville* for alcohol-fuelled disco nights. There are a couple of clubs along James Avenue which are mostly the preserve of locals; it's best to go with a Jamaican companion, as the area can be a bit risky after dark. Otherwise, *Evita's* restaurant (see above) holds occasional theme nights with dancing, and if you fancy taking in a standard Caribbean-themed **floorshow**, try the *Little Pub*. Finally, the stellar **Ocho Rios Jazz Festival** brings Ochi to life every June, with concerts at venues around town – for more information call the tourist board or the Jazz Hotline (ⓣ876/927-3544) or visit ⓦwww.ochoriosjazz.com.

Amnesia Disco Above the Mutual Security building, 70 Main St. The new incarnation of the former *Acropolis* nightclub, with an indoor, air-conditioned dance floor and an outdoor bar area. Music policy is dancehall, R&B, hip-hop and dance; and entrance is J$200. Closed Monday and Tuesday.

Bibibips 93 Main St. Laid-back but upscale clifftop bar popular with Jamaicans. One of the best places in town.

Jamaika-Me-Krazy *Jamaica Grande*. Popular in-hotel disco with good sound and lights and a happy holiday crowd taking advantage of the all-inclusive bar. Cover US$30. Closed Tuesday.

Little Pub 59 Main St. Right in the centre of Ochi and one of the town's most enduring nightspots, with football games and boxing via satellite TV in the busy bar area, and different entertainment each night in the stage/dance floor area. Details are posted on a board outside; entrance fees vary.

Shopping

Shopping is big business in Ocho Rios. The town's three **craft markets** (daily 7am–7pm) have enticed many a hapless soul to leave Jamaica laden with "Yeh mon it irie" T-shirts and the like. Among the dross you'll find really nice T-shirts and sculptures. The main market is to the right of Ocean Village Plaza, while the smaller Pineapple Place and Coconut Grove markets are further east towards *Hibiscus Lodge* and the all-inclusive hotels. Don't miss the gorgeous **art gallery and shop** at Harmony Hall, ten minutes' drive out of Ochi on the way to Tower Isle. Set in a beautifully restored great house, it features works by renowned contemporary Jamaican artists, and a variety of crafts, books, aromatherapy oils and women's clothing.

East of Ocho Rios

As the clamour of Ocho Rios recedes, the A3 coast road switchbacks through the countryside toward the slow, close-knit communities of **Oracabessa** and **Port Maria**, where tourism is only just starting to take hold. Though ostensibly quiet, the area has long been a favourite haunt of the rich and famous. Noel Coward and Ian Fleming (creator of James Bond) both lived here in the 1950s and '60s, and their old homes, **Firefly** and **Goldeneye**, are still standing, with Firefly now a prime tourist site and Goldeneye the centrepiece of a luxury villa complex.

Oracabessa

Lit in the afternoons by an apricot light that must have inspired its Spanish name *Orocabeza*, or "Golden Head", **ORACABESSA**, some sixteen miles east of Ocho Rios, is a friendly one-street town with a covered produce market (main days Thursday and Friday) and a few shops and bars. A centre for the export of **bananas** until the early 1900s, Oracabessa became something of a ghost town when the wharves around the small natural harbour closed in 1969, taking with them the rum bars, gambling houses and most of the workers. The town snoozed quietly until the mid-1990s, when the **Island Outpost** corporation, owned by Chris Blackwell, bought seventy acres of prime coastal land and opened up the village's main draw, the **James Bond Beach Club** (Tues–Sun 9am–6pm; US$5), signposted just off Main Street along Old Wharf Road. Jamaica's most stylish beach, the pretty but tiny strip of white sand offers brightly painted changing rooms, a watersports centre, and a bar and restaurant. The expansive lawns are a regular venue for large-scale concerts.

East of the turn-off for James Bond Beach, Oracabessa merges into the residential community of **Race Course**. This is the site of **Goldeneye**, the unassuming white-walled bungalow in which Ian Fleming wrote almost all of the James Bond novels. Now an exclusive hotel, it's off limits to all but the very well-heeled.

Port Maria and Firefly

The diminutive capital of St Mary, **PORT MARIA**, nestled around a crescent bay some five miles east of Oracabessa, is one of Jamaica's most picturesque towns, but once you've taken in the bay view and strolled the few shopping streets, there's little to keep you here. Most people turn off the main road before getting into town and travel the precipitous route up the hill to **Firefly** (daily 8.30am–5.30pm; US$10), the Jamaican home of Noel Coward and his partner Graham Payn from 1956 to Coward's death in 1973. The house remains much as Coward left it, with the table laid as it was on the day the Queen Mother came to lunch in 1965. Coward died here and is buried on the property. It's worth going to Firefly for the view alone. The panorama takes in Port Maria bay and Cabarita Island to the east, with the peaks of the Blue Mountains poking through the clouds, while to the west lies **Galina Point** and **lighthouse**, the most northerly tip of Jamaica – you may even see Cuba on a clear day.

West of Ocho Rios

The coast road west of Ocho Rios swings past a couple of engaging attractions. Some eight miles west of town is the former site of Seville, Jamaica's first Spanish settlement, now an overgrown wasteland dotted with the crumbling remains of once-impressive buildings. The best way to see it is on horseback; see p.266 for details of the rides offered here by Hooves. Across the road is **Seville Great House and Heritage Park** (Tues–Sat 9am–5pm, 45min tours; J$150), one of the few sites on the island focusing on the lives, customs and culture of Taínos and Africans. There's more equine action at **Chukka Cove**, the most prestigious equestrian facility and polo ground in Jamaica – matches are open to observers most weekends; call for schedules (☎876/972-2506). The immaculate stables also offer fabulous three-hour beach rides as part of their roster of excursions (see p.266). A mile or so past Chukka Cove, a tiny paved road cuts inland toward the signposted **Cranbrook Flower Forest** (daily 9am–5pm; US$10 ☎876/770-8071), an exquisitely landscaped, 130-acre nature park with several grassy lawns, a fishing pond where you can catch your lunch and have it cooked for you, and a swift-running river with plenty of marvellous swimming spots. It's the perfect place for a picnic: bring your own or buy it on site.

Runaway Bay and Discovery Bay

Halfway between Ocho Rios and Falmouth, the neighbouring mini-resorts of **RUNAWAY BAY** and **DISCOVERY BAY** bask in isolated indolence. Dominated by lavish all-inclusives, neither demands much of your time unless you've checked into one of the hotels. Runaway is the more developed of the two, though beyond the hotel fences and Italianate marble lobbies, life jogs along at a slow pace. There's little obvious activity in town; for swimming, sugary-sanded **Cardiff Hall public beach**, opposite the Texaco petrol station, is popular with locals. At **Salem Paradise Beach**, at the Salem end of town, sound-system dances are occasionally held. Midway between the two bays are the **Green Grotto Caves** (daily 9am–5pm; US$20), a system of expansive limestone caves that's been made accessible to the public. The guides inject plenty of humour into their tours, but nothing really justifies the entrance fee.

Even more pacific than its neighbour, with fewer hotels, Discovery Bay is more a coastal clutch of shops, snack bars and houses than a town. But it does have the fantastic **Puerto Seco beach** (daily 8am–5pm; J$200), which, despite gleaming sand and crystal-clear water, is relatively deserted on weekdays.

Marley's mausoleum and the St Ann interior

Both the B3 from Runaway Bay and the inland road from Discovery Bay lead toward **ALEXANDRIA**, a tiny hamlet where you turn left for the only tourist attraction in the St Ann interior, Bob Marley's Mausoleum, at his former home of **NINE MILE**. Though the red-earthed pastures and sweeping hills and gullies of the Dry Harbour mountains are stunning, there are few specific points of interest. You'll need to have your own transport or charter a taxi to get here; a round-trip in a taxi from Runaway or Discovery bays should cost US$80–90, and from Ochi around US$100. From Alexandria, the narrow road off the B3 to the **Bob Marley Centre and Mausoleum** (daily 9am–6.30pm; US$12 ☎876/995-1763) winds through the hills past **Alva** and **Ballintoy**. You know you're in Nine Mile when you see red-gold-and-green flags flying high above a bamboo-fenced compound to the side of the main road. If driving, you'll be directed into the compound car park. There's also a vegetarian restaurant and as a small gift-shop selling tapes and high-quality Marley memorabilia. Led by a Rasta guide, the tour includes the wooden shack that Marley lived in between the ages of 6 and 13, an outdoor barbecue where Marley cooked up Ital feasts, and the Rasta-coloured "meditation stone", immortalized in the song *Talkin' Blues*. The **mausoleum**, a concrete building painted with Rasta colours and depictions of black angels, encases the marble slab that holds Marley's remains.

If you want to linger in Nine Mile, you can stay in the relatively basic **hotel** opposite the complex, run by extended members of the Marley family; rooms cost around US$35 and you can have meals cooked for you or use the kitchen yourself. The place comes alive every **February 6**, when Marley's birthday is celebrated with a sound-system jam and live show.

Bob Marley – king of reggae

Born February 6, 1945, **Robert Nesta Marley** was the progeny of an affair between 17-year-old Cedella Malcolm and 51-year-old Anglo-Jamaican soldier Captain Norval Marley, stationed in the Dry Harbour mountains. Marley's early years in the country surrounded by a doting extended family and by the rituals and traditions of rural life had a profound effect on his development. He clung to the African side of his heritage and revelled in the rich cultural life of downtown Kingston, where he spent most of his later life.

Fusing African drumming traditions with Jamaican rhythms and American rock guitar, Marley's music became a symbol of unity and social change worldwide. Between 1961 and 1981, his output was prolific. Following their first recording *Judge Not* on Leslie Kong's Beverley's label, his band, The Wailers (Marley, Bunny Livingstone and Peter Tosh), went on to record for some of the best producers in the business. In 1963, the huge hit *Simmer Down* meshed perfectly with the post-independence frustration felt by young Jamaicans, and the momentum of success began in earnest. International recognition came when the Wailers signed to the Island label – owned by Anglo-Jamaican entrepreneur Chris Blackwell. The first Island release was *Catch a Fire* in early 1973, and the eleven albums that followed all became instant classics. After the departure from the group of Peter and Bunny in 1974, Marley continued to tour the world with a new band – Bob Marley and the Wailers.

After being injured in a 1976 **assassination** attempt, Marley left Jamaica to recover and record in Britain and the States. Two years later, he returned to perform at the historic **One Love Peace Concert**. Marley ended his performance by enticing political arch-enemies Michael Manley and Edward Seaga on stage to join hands in a show of unity. But Marley's call for unity and freedom was not restricted to Jamaica; one of his greatest triumphs was performing the protest anthem *Zimbabwe* at the independence celebrations of the former Rhodesia.

In the midst of a rigorous 1980 tour, Marley was diagnosed as suffering from cancer; he died a year later in Miami, honoured by his country with the Order of Merit. The Bob Marley Foundation, administered by his wife, Rita, continues to sponsor the development of new Jamaican artists, and many of the Marley children have forged their own musical careers – look out for the marvellous **Junior Gong**. In the hearts of Jamaicans, though, the master's voice can never be equalled.

5.4

Western Jamaica

Home to two of the island's busiest resorts, western Jamaica is firmly on the tourist track. **Montego Bay**, once Jamaica's tourist capital, is losing out a bit to the hedonistic pleasures of **Negril** at the extreme western tip. In many ways, though, MoBay, as it's usually called, still delivers. Sitting pretty in a sweeping natural harbour and hemmed in by a dazzling labyrinth of protected offshore reefs, it remains the grand dame of Jamaican resorts and is particularly lively during its world-renowned summer reggae festival. Sybaritic Negril, boasting the longest continuous stretch of white sand in Jamaica and a front-row sunset seat, has a geographical remoteness that lends it a uniquely insouciant ambience. "Discovered" by wealthy hippies in the 1970s, it is still immensely popular with those who favour fast living and corporeal indulgence, and is easily the best place outside Kingston for **live reggae** and **nightclubs**. There are plenty of natural attractions around Negril, too, including the pleasant river walk at **Mayfield Falls** and the blue hole at **Roaring River**.

Montego Bay

Jamaica's second largest city, **MONTEGO BAY** nestles between the gently sloping Bogue, Kempshot and Salem hills, and extends some ten miles from the haunts of the suburban rich in Reading at its western edge to the plush villa developments and resort hotels of Ironshore and Rose Hall to the east. It's made up of two distinct parts: the main tourist strip **Gloucester Avenue** (rechristened by the marketing men as the "Hip Strip"), and the city proper, universally referred to as "**downtown**" – a split so sharp that most tourists never venture further than the dividing roundabout.

The "Hip Strip" wouldn't exist were it not for Montego Bay's prize asset: a dazzling bay with miles of coral reef (now designated a marine park) and some beautiful beaches. Much of the coastline has been snapped up by the hotels, but there are three main **public beaches** along the length of Gloucester Avenue, all with showers, changing rooms, snack outlets and watersports concessions and a minimal entrance fee. If you fancy a quieter day by the sea, you can head east of town to Ironshore, where the Caribbean Beach Park (Tues–Thurs 9am–6pm, Fri–Sun 9am–8pm; J$100) has a pretty swathe of white sand that's usually more or less deserted. There are changing facilities and showers, and a restaurant and bar; the huge grassy space out front is often used for stageshows. Shared taxis run here from Gloucester Avenue (J$40).

Arrival, information and getting around

More than eighty percent of visitors to Jamaica arrive at **Donald Sangster International Airport**, three miles east of the town centre and a mile from Gloucester Avenue. It has a 24-hour **cambio** and a branch of the NCB bank, a tourist-board desk (daily 9am–10pm) and numerous hotel, ground-transport and

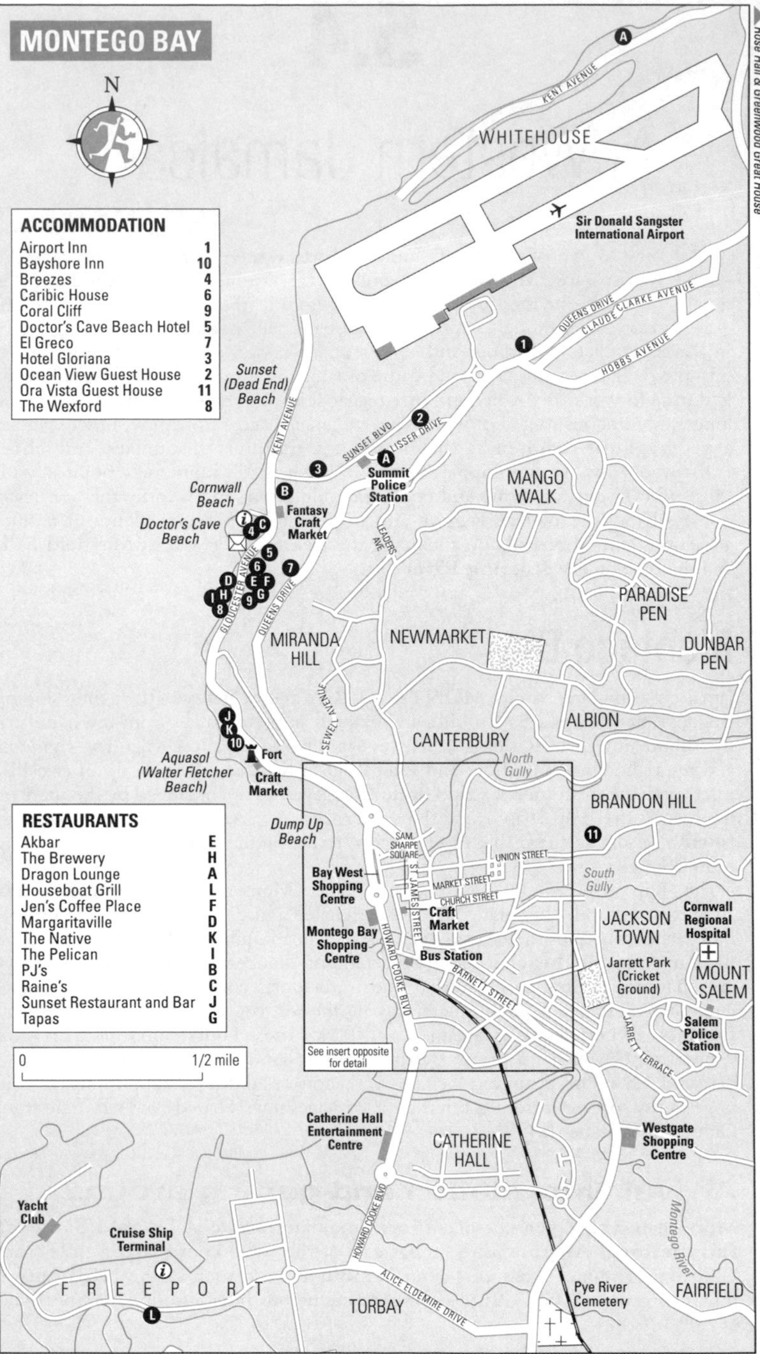

MONTEGO BAY
N
ACCOMMODATION
Airport Inn 1
Bayshore Inn 10
Breezes 4
Caribic House 6
Coral Cliff 9
Doctor's Cave Beach Hotel 5
El Greco 7
Hotel Gloriana 3
Ocean View Guest House 2
Ora Vista Guest House 11
The Wexford 8
RESTAURANTS
Akbar E
The Brewery H
Dragon Lounge A
Houseboat Grill L
Jen's Coffee Place F
Margaritaville D
The Native K
The Pelican I
PJ's B
Raine's C
Sunset Restaurant and Bar J
Tapas G
0
1/2 mile
Rose Hall & Greenwood Great House
WHITEHOUSE
KENT AVENUE
Sir Donald Sangster International Airport
QUEENS DRIVE
CLAUDE CLARKE AVENUE
HOBBS AVENUE
Sunset (Dead End) Beach
SUNSET BLVD
LISSER DRIVE
Summit Police Station
Cornwall Beach
Fantasy Craft Market
Doctor's Cave Beach
LEADERS AVE
MANGO WALK
GLOUCESTER AVENUE
QUEENS DRIVE
PARADISE PEN
MIRANDA HILL
NEWMARKET
DUNBAR PEN
SEWELL AVENUE
ALBION
CANTERBURY
North Gully
Fort
Aquasol (Walter Fletcher Beach)
Craft Market
BRANDON HILL
Dump Up Beach
SAM SHARPE SQUARE
UNION STREET
Bay West Shopping Centre
ST JAMES STREET
MARKET STREET
CHURCH STREET
South Gully
Craft Market
JACKSON TOWN
Cornwall Regional Hospital
Montego Bay Shopping Centre
HOWARD COOKE BLVD
Bus Station
BARNETT STREET
Jarrett Park (Cricket Ground)
MOUNT SALEM
Salem Police Station
JARRETT TERRACE
See insert opposite for detail
Catherine Hall Entertainment Centre
CATHERINE HALL
Westgate Shopping Centre
Yacht Club
Cruise Ship Terminal
HOWARD COOKE BLVD
Montego River
FREEPORT
ALICE ELDEMIRE DRIVE
TORBAY
Pye River Cemetery
FAIRFIELD
Lethe, Rocklands & Negril

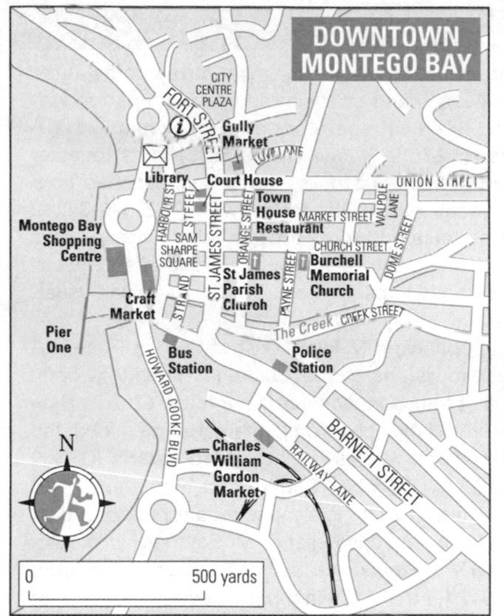

car rental booths. **Luggage trolleys** aren't permitted past immigration, but the official red-capped porters will carry your bags for a small charge (J$20 per bag). Larger hotels provide free airport transfers, but you can charter a **taxi** from any of the omnipresent JUTA drivers – the trip to Gloucester Avenue, Queens Drive or downtown should cost no more than US$10. If travelling *very* light you can take one of the local **shared taxis** that leave from the petrol station past the airport's car park, which charge J$30 for the same journey. There is no public bus service from the airport.

The main **Jamaica Tourist Board** office (Mon–Fri 8.30am–4pm, Sat 9am–1pm; ⓣ876/952-4425) is at the end of the access road to Cornwall Beach, just off Gloucester Avenue. For comprehensive information on Montego Bay check out ⓦwww.montego-bay-jamaica.com.

Unfortunately there is no public transport serving downtown Montego Bay or the strip, and consequently any tourist walking the streets will be assailed with offers by passing **taxis**. Be prepared to haggle and always settle the price before you get in. However, if you're spending most of your time on the strip, you can easily get around on foot.

Accommodation

The range of **accommodation** in Montego Bay is huge. This is prime **all-inclusive** territory, with the swankiest enclaves out at suburban Ironshore just east of town (see p.234). Most people, however, stay along the Gloucester Avenue **strip** – busy, buzzing and swarming with hustlers – and the best of the bunch there are listed below. Many hotels include free airport transfers in their rates, and more distant properties throw in a free beach shuttle. Unless otherwise stated, rooms have air conditioning, TV and phone.

Airport Inn Queen's Drive ⓣ876/952-0260, ⓕ929-5391. Two minutes from the airport, and clean and reliable. All rooms have kitchen facilities, and there's a pool and bar/restaurant. ❷

Bayshore Inn 27 Gloucester Ave ⓣ876/952-1046, ⓔkhruma@yahoo.com. Cheerful rooms above a great jerk restaurant at the less frantic end of the strip. Reduced-rate weekly rentals available. ❸

Breezes Gloucester Ave ⓣ876/940-1150, ⓕ940-1160, ⓦwww.superclubs.com. Fancy-looking all-inclusive that towers over Doctor's Cave Beach. Amenities are many – pool, hot tub, gym, watersports, tennis courts, games room, restaurants, bars, poolside grill and nightly entertainment – but the rooms are poky and the resort characterless. Very popular disco. Minimum stay two nights. ❾

Caribic House 69 Gloucester Ave ⓣ876/979-6073, ⓕ979-3521, ⓦwww.caribicvacations.com. Small hotel, popular with European backpackers, in a great location opposite Doctor's Cave Beach. Adequate rooms, some with ocean views, and reasonable rates. ❷

Coral Cliff Gloucester Avenue ⓣ876/952-4130, ⓕ952-6532, ⓦwww.coralcliffjamaica.com. Colonial-style hotel behind the complex's garish gaming lounge. Rooms are pleasant and clean,

Organized tours

Hundreds of **tour companies** operate out of Montego Bay; most have booths at the airport and offices along Gloucester Avenue and offer similarly priced trips to independent plantations and great houses. The **best operators** are slightly more adventurous: Barrett Adventures, Rose Hall (ⓣ876/995-2796, ⓕ979-8845), puts together customized packages to off-the-beaten-track waterfalls, farms and beaches from US$100 per person per day; Caribic Vacations, 69 Gloucester Ave (ⓣ876/979-3421), offers islandwide specialist and reggae tours and trips to Cuba. Alternatively, hire a **local driver** and do some independent sightseeing. Dale Porter, aka "Shaka" (ⓣ876/806-8147 or 375-7918), offers all-day tours for around US$100; he can usually be found outside *Caribic House Hotel*.

There are also a few less pedestrian options: ATV Tours, east of town at Rose Hall (ⓣ876/953-9598), offers **quad-bike excursions** in the St James interior (1.5hrs; US$50); you'll pay a bit more if you want transportation from your hotel. Chukka Blue (ⓣ876/979-6599 or ⓣ990-9166, ⓦwww.chukkablue.com) offers **tubing** along the White River in Ocho Rios (3.5hr; US$49), as well as five-hour **jeep safaris** (US$60 including lunch). **Horse-riding** trips (3hr; US$55) and **mountain-bike tours** (3hr; US$50) are also run by Chukka Blue. **River rafting** is a more sedate pleasure, best done along the Martha Brae River, 45 minutes' drive east of MoBay near Falmouth. You can either turn up at the Rafter's Village departure point (signposted from Falmouth's main square) and pay US$42 for a 1hr 15min trip on a two-person raft, or opt to be transported there and back, which costs US$45 per person; to book the latter, call ⓣ876/952-0889.

Tour sites

Listed below are the best tour sites and most popular organized excursions. Each can be seen independently as well as on a package.

Croydon in the Mountains Catadupa, St James ⓣ876/979-8267, ⓔthenry@infochan.com. Croydon Estate is a 132-acre working coffee and pineapple plantation in the foothills of the Catadupa mountains in the St James interior. A half-day tour (US$50) includes barbecue lunch and fruit tasting. Tours on Wednesday and Friday.

Hilton High Day Tour St Leonards, St James ⓣ876/952-3343, ⓦwww.montego-bay-jamaica.com/hilton. "High" because it once included a balloon ride, this tour (US$55) is now a little short on thrills but still very enjoyable. Visitors are bussed up Long Hill through Montpelier and Cambridge to the diminutive Hilton plantation house, whose small grounds contain a piggery and stables. Breakfast and lunch are included, as are a stroll around the village and local school, a bus ride to the German settlement of Seaford Town and its museum, and a drive back through the western outskirts of Cockpit Country. Tours on Tuesday, Wednesday, Friday and Sunday.

and there's a pool and restaurant. ④

Doctor's Cave Beach Hotel Gloucester Avenue ⓣ876/952-4355 or 4359, ⓕ952-5204, ⓦwww.doctorscave.com. One of the better strip hotels, across from Doctor's Cave Beach, with stylish décor, gorgeous tropical garden, pool, hot tub, restaurant, bar and small gym. Rooms are pretty uniform, but the friendly atmosphere wins a lot of points. Rates include breakfast. ⑤

El Greco Queen's Drive ⓣ876/940-6116, ⓦwww.elgrecojamaica.com. Sprawling complex of self-contained apartments perched high above the strip (access is via the lift of the adjacent *Montego Bay Club* resort). The modern suites have kitchens and balconies; tennis courts and pool are on site. Good value but lacking in atmosphere. ⑤

Hotel Gloriana 1–2 Sunset Blvd ⓣ876/979-0669, ⓕ979-0698. Cheap and cheerful place, popular with Jamaicans as well as tourists. Rooms are basic but nice, with fridges and balconies; units with kitchens are available. There's a pool, whirlpool, restaurant and bar. ②

Ocean View Guest House 26 Sunset Blvd ⓣ876/952-2662. Modest guesthouse between the strip and the airport offers basic rooms and a convivial atmosphere. Meals are available. ❷

Ora Vista Guest House Richmond Hill, Union Street ⓣ876/952-2576. Superb, friendly guesthouse overlooking downtown MoBay, with unrivalled atmosphere and great views. Rooms are simple, with no A/C, but clean and homey. There's a pool, bar, kitchen, sun deck and lounge. Excellent Jamaican food available. ❷

The Wexford Gloucester Avenue ⓣ876/952-2854, ⓕ952-3637, ⓦwww.montego-bay-jamaica.com/wexford. Strip old-timer near *Margaritaville* has recently undergone extensive restoration. Rooms are bright and clean, and there's a pool, bar and restaurant on site. ❹

The strip: Gloucester Avenue and the beaches

Occupying the whole of **Gloucester Avenue** and stretching north into **Kent Avenue**, Montego Bay's glittering oceanfront tourist strip builds to a bottleneck around Doctor's Cave Beach during the daytime, with hair braiders, taxi drivers and hustlers shadowing your every move and gift-shops competing for business. At night the action switches to MoBay's most happening joint, *Margaritaville*, and street vendors stake out jerk chicken stands and carts selling snacks. Gloucester Avenue is home to most of MoBay's tourist hotels and restaurants as well as the best beaches, bars and clubs, so even if you don't check into a strip hotel, you'll spend a lot of time here.

Starting at the roundabout that filters Howard Cooke Boulevard, Queens Drive and Fort Street traffic, the first stretch of Gloucester Avenue is a kind of no-man's land, split in two by an elevated section of a one-way traffic system and bordered by the only sizeable undeveloped beach in town. **Fort Street Craft Market** is a favourite haunt of persistent hair braiders but a relatively relaxed spot for a bit of bartering. Arranged around steep steps that make a useful shortcut to Sewell Avenue and Queen's Drive, stalls sell the usual array of carvings and T-shirts. Opposite the market, and still popularly referred to by its old name of Walter Fletcher Beach, **Aquasol Theme Park** (daily 10am–10pm; J$100) has the most comprehensive sports facilities of MoBay's three main beaches. It offers watersports (jet-skis US$50, glass-bottom boat rides US$10, snorkelling US$10; all per half-hour), tennis and basketball courts, and a go-kart track (five laps cost J$150 in a one-person kart, J$200 in a two-person kart). The wide expanse of sand, a decent seafood restaurant, and an attractive decked bar (which stays open until late every night) have made the beach popular with young tourists and the attendant hangers-on as well as Jamaican families. However, it's not the cleanest place to swim after a bout of wet weather.

Though Gloucester Avenue runs parallel to the sea, the sea is mainly obscured by the buildings. The only place to fully appreciate the sweep of the bay is from the strip's only **green space**, opposite the restaurants and bars at Miranda Ridge; there are a couple of benches from which you can watch the sunset. The bucolic illusion is rudely shattered just past the park at **Margaritaville** (daily 10am–3am; ⓦwww.margueritaville.com), a mini-lido-cum-restaurant-cum-bar that proudly displays the second-tackiest facade along the strip. (The Coral Cliff Gaming Lounge opposite, with its faux waterfall, must be seen to be believed.) *Margaritaville*'s bar and outdoor eating deck are built right over the sea; below there's a watersports area with boat berths and swimming platforms. On the roof there's a hot tub, sun deck, and – best of all – a 110ft water slide (US$5 or free to customers) which sluices down into the sea and draws hordes of tourists and locals alike.

The strip builds in intensity as it approaches the magnificent Doctor's Cave Beach, becoming a seamless parade of bars, cafés and identikit duty-free shops. **Doctor's Cave Beach** itself (daily 8.30am–5.30pm; J$135) is Montego Bay's premium portion of gleaming white sand and see-through water. The rapidly deepening waters really are the best in town, and following extensive refurbishment, facilities are excellent. On the downside, there's little shade (umbrella rentals are available but extortionate), and it gets very crowded on the weekend.

Past Doctor's Cave is the diminutive **Fantasy Craft Market**, tucked behind a row of duty-free stores and offering some bargains. Opposite the market, and with its own driveway off Gloucester Avenue, **Cornwall Beach** (daily 9am–5pm; J$80) is the most intimate and laid-back of MoBay's public beaches, but it looks a little rough around the edges following its competitors' ritzy face-lifts. It's a young person's beach, with music pumped out from giant speakers and topless bathing common (though theoretically prohibited). It's popular with the gigolo crowd, and female visitors should expect (usually good-natured) approaches. Set under a massive sea grape tree, the central bar is a lovely spot for a drink.

The hotels peter out as Gloucester becomes **Kent Avenue** (known locally as Dead End Road) at the junction with Sunset Boulevard and continues to hug the coast before ending abruptly at the wall marking the distant section of the airport runway. The adjacent **Buccaneer Beach** (or Sunset/Dead End Beach) is a thin but attractive strip of public sand; it's popular with Jamaicans, despite the racket of airplane landings and take-offs. The water is shallow and there are no facilities, but snorkelling is good and the view over the bay is fabulous, providing the best free sunset seat in town.

The last of the strip proper, **Sunset Boulevard** is home to a small complex of forlorn shops and bars, countless car rental outlets and the rather grand **Summit Police Station**. At the airport roundabout, the boulevard becomes part of **Queen's Drive**, a fast traffic route parallel to Gloucester Avenue. Pavements are sporadic and walking can be risky, though the views over the bay are fantastic.

Downtown: Sam Sharpe Square and the craft market

Downtown MoBay announces itself with its very own stretch of undeveloped shoreline opposite the dividing roundabout. **Dump-Up Beach** looks pretty enough, particularly from a distance, but this is one of the dirtiest parts of the bay. Shooting off from the roundabout, the main route into the centre of town is **Fort Street**, a clamorous thoroughfare with dancehall flooding out from storefronts and all manner of pushcarts and vehicles jostling for space with the thick human traffic. Past here, over the bridge across North Gully, you enter town proper. The lively covered fruit and vegetable market to the left is popularly known as the **Gully** (the correct name, William Street Market, is seldom used).

St James Street comes to an abrupt end at **Sam Sharpe Square**, the heart of downtown, with a central fountain and seemingly permanent stream of traffic. The square is bordered by a jumble of old and new architecture, including **The Cage**, built in 1806 as a lock-up for disorderly seamen and runaway slaves. Just outside is a **bronze statue** of national hero Sam Sharpe by Jamaican sculptor Kay Sullivan.

Charles Street waves toward the sea from Sam Sharpe Square, passing the brand-new Georgian-style **Town Hall** and weaving its way toward MoBay's main **craft market**. With 200-odd brightly-painted stalls selling a colossal variety of craft items, it's a good place to pick up some souvenirs and is surprisingly hassle-free. Otherwise, there's little to see downtown, and given the prevalence of pickpockets, it's not a great area for a wander.

Watersports

Montego Bay is justifiably famed for its deep turquoise waters and abundant reef systems, some close enough to swim to from the main beaches. Discarded rum bottles and tyres can be disconcerting, but the deeper reefs are alive with fish, rays, urchins and the occasional turtle and nurse shark. There are hosts of similarly priced **watersports operators** on each beach and within the larger hotels; we list the most reputable below. Information is available from the Montego Bay Marine Park office at *Pier One* (☎876/971-8082).

Diving and snorkelling

The following offer guided dives (around US$50), certification courses (from US$350) and equipment rental (from US$15). Like every other watersports operator in Montego Bay, they also rent **snorkel gear** for around US$10 a day; some also offer guided snorkelling tours of the best reefs.

Captain's Watersports and Dive Centre *Round Hill Hotel*, Hopewell ☎876/956-7050 ext 378.
Fun Divers Wyndham, Rose Hall ☎876/953-3268.
Jamaica Scuba Divers *Half Moon Hotel*, Ironshore ☎876/953-9266.
Resort Divers *Jack Tar Village* and *Holiday Inn* ☎876/940-1183 or 953-9699.

Boat trips

With an open bar and sometimes lunch, **boat trips** are always popular and usually fun, if bawdy humour is your bag. Most depart from the *Pier One* complex downtown and sail around the bay to the airport reefs, with a stop for snorkelling. Best of the bunch are *Calico*, the only wooden sailing ship in town (☎876/952-5860; 3hr daytime cruise, US$35; 2hr evening cruise, US$25) and *Tropical Dreamer* (☎876/979-0102; 3hr cruises; US$45), a catamaran that offers a wet 'n' wild cruise party including a stop at *Margaritaville* (see p.281) to ride the water slide; tours leave at 10am and 1pm Monday to Saturday.

Glass-bottom boats operate from all the main beaches and sail out to the airport reefs for around US$15 for half an hour. MoBay Undersea Tours (☎876/940-4465; 2hr; US$34) has semi-submersible vessels that take you ten feet underwater. Tours leave at 11.30am and 1.30pm from *Margaritaville.* If you'd rather go it alone, you can rent out the *Sharky*, a semi-sub that holds fourteen passengers, for US$300 per hour.

A fully equipped **sport fishing boat** costs around US$700 per day; try the *Irie Lady* (☎876/953-3268) or *No Problem* (☎876/936-6702, ©dptaylor@n5.com.jm). Captain's Watersports has several boats and also rents out *Stoshus*, a 36ft yacht (®www.montego-bay-jamaica.com/stoshus; US$120 per hour, US$600 per day).

Day trips from MoBay

Tourist town that it is, Montego Bay is within easy distance of a glut of managed attractions. Most are on the roster of tour companies, but all can also be seen independently. Most popular is **ROSE HALL**, six miles east from MoBay and site of the infamous **Rose Hall Great House** (daily 9.15am–5.15pm; US$15). It is said to be the former home of a voodoo practitioner who ruthlessly disposed of her husbands and still haunts the corridors. Built between 1770 and 1780 by planter and parish custos (mayor) John Palmer, the dazzling white stone structure is set back from the A1 and surrounded by gardens, woods and a swan-filled pond. The rather mechanical 45-minute tours that run every fifteen minutes make much of the vastly embellished legend of Annie Palmer, the "White Witch of Rose Hall". As the house was unoccupied and widely looted during the nineteenth century, almost all of its current contents have been transported from other great houses or from overseas. You can combine a trip to the house with a dip at Rose Hall Beach Club (daily 9am–6pm; US$6), an overpriced private enclave five minutes' drive further east. It offers a pretty beach, good swimming, and excellent watersports facilities (jet skis US$60 for 30min; snorkelling US$25 per hour; parasailing US$55; scuba diving US$40 per one-tank dive, US$90 for resort course). Five miles east from Rose Hall, the A1 opens up to a magnificent sea view at diminutive **GREENWOOD**. Perched on a hill overlooking the sea, the dull grey stone of **Greenwood Great House** (daily 9am–6pm; US$12) dominates the few houses and bars below. Surrounded by luscious flowering gardens, the house has managed to retain most of its original contents. Built in 1790 by relatives of the Barrett family of Wimpole Street fame, Greenwood contains their original library and a wonderfully eclectic collection of objects. The tour, which ends in a bar set up in the original kitchen area, is much more enjoyable than the breakneck run round Rose Hall, but is soured by a rather cavalier attitude to the property's slave history.

West of MoBay

On the west side of Montego Bay, the B8 winds inland at the small community of Reading, access point to a brace of well-signposted natural attractions. Set amid cool and vividly green hills, **Lethe Estate** (☎876/956-4947) offers a **jitney tour** of its grounds (US$12) as well as a 45-minute **rafting** trip down the gushing Great River. You'll pay US$68 per two-person raft if you need transportation from MoBay, or US$38 if you get here independently. Back on the B8, turn off at the small village of Anchovy for the **Rocklands Feeding Station** (daily 2–5pm; US$8; ☎876/952-2009), regularly visited by more than a hundred species of birds, including orange quits, vervains and the long-tailed doctor bird, the national bird. Hummingbirds will perch on your outstretched finger to drink sugar water here; feeding peaks at around 4.30pm, when the air thrums with tiny wings.

About three miles further along the B8 is **Montpelier**, a scattered rural community 2000ft above sea level and surrounded by citrus groves, arable land and cattle. Here, the B8 forks: to the right is an incredibly pretty route over the interior mountains to Shettlewood and on to Savanna-la-Mar in Jamaica's far west. The left fork takes you to **Belvedere Estate** (Mon–Sat 10am–4pm; US$10 ☎876/956-7310), an attractive and well-organized fruit and cattle farm that does good business with tour operators and can also be enjoyably explored independently. The standard tour of the estate is unusually imaginative, with a traditional mento band and samplings of jerk pork and sugarcane juice. The coconut, citrus and banana fields are impressive, and the waterfall and pool provide excellent swimming.

Eating

Montego Bay has its fair share of swanky **restaurants** alongside the more usual Jamaican eateries, though many offer bland "international" fare or watered-down Jamaican dishes at inflated prices. Pricier tourist restaurants almost always offer special deals; look out for flyers around town. Aside from notable exceptions such as *The Native*, Jamaican food is at its best from small-scale cookshops and restaurants. There are plenty of US-style **fast-food** outlets around town.

Akbar Gloucester Avenue ☎876/979-0113. The sister of the renowned Kingston purveyor of fine Indian cooking serves excellent curries in an air-conditioned dining room with tasteful Indian décor. Prices are moderate to expensive.

The Brewery Miranda Ridge, Gloucester Avenue. Late-opening spot above the strip. Extremely varied menu with daily specials, a big burger selection, lots of salads and excellent fajitas. Good value and pretty views over the bay.

Dragon Lounge Kent Avenue, Whitehouse. Laid-back terrace under almond trees specializes in fresh seafood, with some Chinese dishes. Proximity to the airport makes it perfect for plane-spotting, albeit somewhat noisy. Good mix of locals and tourists.

Houseboat Grill Freeport Road ☎876/979-8845. Fantastic, unique setting in a beautifully converted houseboat moored on Bogue Lagoon; you board by way of a rope-pulled launch, and a window in the floor allows perusal of the marine life gliding underneath. The menu is superlative and sophisticated, mixing Jamaican cooking with international dishes; the pepper shrimp with scotch bonnet beurre blanc is unmissable, and the desserts are pure indulgence. Best choice in town.
Jen's Coffee Place 166 Gloucester Ave. Friendly breakfast café and ice-cream parlour with reasonably priced pancakes, eggs and bacon and club sandwiches.
Margaritaville Gloucester Avenue. The loudest place on the strip. International menu with a Mexican flavour, and American-style service with the emphasis on fun. Hidden behind an aquatic wall mural, *Marguerites* (☎876/952-4777) next door has elegant décor, upscale atmosphere and a Continental menu specializing in seafood; there's a flambé grill for table-side cooking as well.
The Native 29 Gloucester Ave ☎876/979-2769. The best place on the strip for a sit-down Jamaican meal – take advantage of reduced-rate buffets and lunch specials. Try the "Boonoonoo's Platter" of ackee, curry goat, jerk chicken and escovitched fish, rice and peas and plantain.
The Pelican Gloucester Avenue ☎876/952-3171. Long-established restaurant popular with locals and tourists. Highlights include American/Jamaican breakfast, the daily lunch specials, and the rum pudding and coconut or banana cream pie for dessert.
PJ's 17 Kent Ave. Excellent open-air and inexpensive jerk centre, serving delicious platters of curried lobster, steamed fish and vegetables as well as jerk meats and all the trimmings.
Raine's St James Place, Gloucester Avenue. Popular kiosk café between Doctor's Cave and Cornwall beaches with all-day breakfasts, burgers, and home-made cakes.
Sunset Restaurant and Bar Gloucester Avenue. Tiny, easily missed place that's the only really authentic Jamaican bar and restaurant along the strip, as suggested by the local clientele. Recommended, especially the home-made ginger beer.
Tapas Corniche Road ☎876/952-2988. Innovative and delicious Mediterranean food in a place that's upscale but affordable, and blessedly detached from the strip; take the small road to the left of *Coral Cliff* hotel.

Drinking, nightlife and entertainment

Aside from the shenanigans at the permanently packed *Margaritaville*, Montego Bay is not particularly lively at **night**. Nonetheless, there are several places to sink a few beers or pickle yourself in rum punch, and the slot machines at Coral Cliff Gaming Lounge, opposite *Margaritaville*, are always busy; the bar is pretty lively, too.

Bars

Aguasol Gloucester Avenue. The beach bar here offers lovely views across the bay, sea breezes and a pool table.
The Brewery Miranda Ridge, Gloucester Avenue ☎876/940-2433. Friendly bar-cum-club, with a cosy indoor bar and great bay views from the verandah. Usually packed with young Jamaicans and large parties of American tourists. Tuesday and Friday are karaoke nights, and there's a daily Happy Hour (4–6pm). Look out for Saturday night promotions featuring well-known Jamaican DJs.
Dead End Bar Kent Avenue. Laid-back spot perfect for sunset- and plane-watching. Thursday night is given over to a beach party, with a comprehensive mix of reggae, soca and hip-hop. Sunday features classic reggae and rocksteady.
Houseboat Grill Freeport Road. This restaurant-on-a-boat has a cosy indoor bar downstairs and a breezy upper deck for a romantic cocktail under the stars. Excellent martinis, great bar snacks and friendly staff.
PJ's 17 Kent Ave. Outdoor bar attractively set under towering bamboo and silk cotton trees, with roller-blading rink, nightly live reggae and craft stalls. Hustlers are the only drawback to an otherwise entertaining scene.

Clubs

Hurricanes Disco *Breezes*, Gloucester Avenue. Flashy in-hotel club, with dancehall, Euro-techno and R&B until dawn. Heaving on Saturday, with the gigolos out in full force. Cover J$500, including all drinks and the first one hundred women get in for free.
Margaritaville Gloucester Avenue ☎876/953-4777. Hugely popular bar, club and restaurant that usually draws the biggest evening crowd. Lively themes each evening; Friday and Saturday are party nights, with a mostly Jamaican crowd and lots of dancehall,

R&B, hip-hop and even house; there's live music upstairs too. Fabulous bay views but an irritating token payment system for drinks, which include 52 different flavours of margarita. If you're looking for guaranteed action this is the place, and if you don't mind gigolos galore and sunburnt tourists it's great fun. Dance floor opens at 10pm; cover charge varies. Call ahead for pickups from local hotels.

Pier 1 Howard Cook Boulevard. Oldies on the boardwalk during the week (free) and a pumping club on the weekends; Friday is busiest, with upfront dancehall and R&B until dawn. The club's a bit rough round the edges but entertaining nevertheless. On Thursday and Sunday *Sharky's* party boat goes out to sea (9pm–midnight) for an all-inclusive cover of US$7.

Platinum Gloucester Avenue. Thoroughly Jamaican club, playing dancehall, hip-hop and R&B for a mostly local crowd. Best experienced in the company of somebody local.

Shopping

The best market is the huge Harbour Street complex (daily 7am–7pm), packed with straw and wicker work, belts, clothes, jewellery, T-shirts and woodcarvings. The Fort and Fantasy craft markets along the strip (daily 8am–7pm) are worth a look but tend to be a little more expensive with less variety. Also worth a look are Things Jamaican at 44 Fort St, and Irie Creations upstairs in the City Centre Mall. The **Bob Marley Experience** at Half Moon Shopping Village has the largest collection of Marley T-shirts in the world. Downtown, **record stores** offer custom-made reggae tapes (around US$3) as well as CDs and vinyl. Worth a visit is Federal Records, 14 Strand St.

Negril

Jamaica's shrine to permissive indulgence, **NEGRIL** has metamorphosed from deserted fishing beach to full-blown resort town in little over two decades. American hippies first started visiting what was then a virgin paradise in the 1970s, setting the tone for today's free-spirited attitude, but these days, the presence of deliberately risqué resorts like the infamous **Hedonism II** has ensured that Negril is widely perceived as a place where inhibitions are lost and pleasures of the flesh rule. The traditional menu of ganja and reggae draws a young crowd, but the north-coast resort ethic has muscled in too. All-inclusives of every ilk pepper the coast and hotels line every inch of the beach, while hustling has increased to an irritating degree.

But Negril shrugs off such minor issues and remains supremely chilled-out. Pristine miles of sand, comprehensive watersports facilities, open-air dancing to first-rate live music, a wide range of eating and drinking joints, gregarious company, and the best sunsets on the island are all on offer here. Many foreigners have stayed on permanently, blurring the distinctions between tourists and locals and making for a relaxed, natural interaction that's a refreshing change from other resorts.

Arrival, information and getting around

Buses from MoBay drop off passengers on the A1 (Norman Manley Boulevard) just before Negril's central roundabout; if you're staying on the boulevard (ie the beach rather than the cliffs), ask the driver to drop you off outside your hotel. Buses from Savanna-la-Mar terminate at the top end of Sheffield Road, where you can charter a **taxi** to the West End or beach for about US$5. Domestic **flights** land at Negril Aerodrome at Bloody Bay. Taxis wait there, but fares can be ridiculous – a reasonable price is between US$7 and US$10.

The **Jamaica Tourist Board office** is on the first floor of Coral Seas Plaza opposite the roundabout (Mon–Fri 9am–5pm, Sat 9am–1pm; ⊕876/957-4597). Pink JTB **information booths** are located at the main craft market by the roundabout and

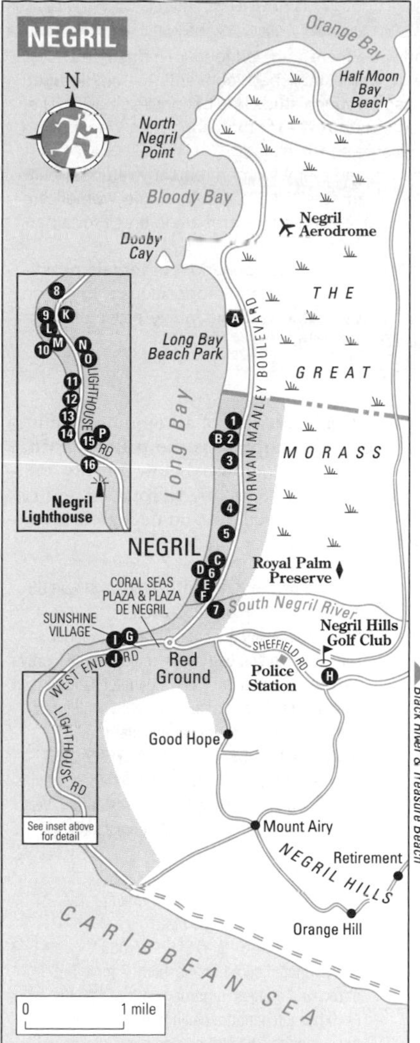

ACCOMMODATION		RESTAURANTS	
Banana Shout	14	3 C's Naturally	G
Catcha Falling Star	13	Alfred's Ocean Palace	C
The Caves	16	Beach Beans	F
Country Country	2	Blue Mountain Coffee Shop	E
Firefly	3	The Carrot	N
Home Sweet Home	8	Chicken Lavish	J
Kuyaba	6	Cosmo's	A
LTU Villas	15	Easy Rock Bar and Grill	I
Mariners Inn	11	Hunan Garden	B
Negril Tree House	1	Hungry Lion	O
Negril Yoga	7	Just Natural	K
Nirvana on the Beach	4	Kuyaba	D
Rockhouse	10	LTU Pub	P
Tensing Pen	12	Pickled Parrot	L
Whistling Bird	5	Rockhouse	M
Xtabi	9	Sweet Spice	H

on West End Road opposite *Tensing Pen* hotel. Alternatively, ⓦwww.negril.com is a great source of local information, and the Yacht Club (ⓣ876/957-9224, ⓦwww.yachtclub.com) on West End Road offers accommodation, watersports, bike rental and taxi services as well as informal advice.

You don't need a **car** if you're going to stay in town. **Shared taxis** run the length of the beach and West End Road all day every day; you can flag them down anywhere en route. A trip from the roundabout to the lighthouse or Bloody Bay costs between J$20 and J$50. **Chartering a taxi** can be expensive, but competition is high, so haggle – US$5 from the roundabout to Bloody Bay is reasonable. There is no local bus service to the roundabout from the beach or cliffs. Other than **walking**, the most popular modes of transportation are moped, motorbike and bicycle. Motorbikes rent for around US$40 per day, mopeds from US$30 and bicycles from US$10. You could also take a **water taxi** from the Yacht Club on the West End to the beach (US$5 each way) or, if you're staying on the cliffs, try flagging down a glass-bottomed boat on its way to the beach.

Accommodation

Negril has over two thousand **beds**, split between the cliffs and beach. Easily the more popular location, the **beach** reeks of commercial vitality. The quieter **West End** offers more privacy, but steep open-access cliffs make it a bad choice for those travelling with children. There are more budget options here and rates are often open to negotiation, especially if you're planning a long stay; check out ⓦwww.negril.com.

"Rent-a-dread"

Jamaica is a carnal kind of country, and while there's no sex tourism industry as such, monetary-based holiday liaisons are a well-established convention. Middle-aged women strolling hand in hand with handsome young studs has become so normal that pejorative epithets – **"Rent-a-dread"** or **"Rastitute"** – for the young men who make a career out of these cynical liaisons have entered the lexicon.

Negril is a centre for this kind of trade-off, and many women regularly return specifically to partake of an injection of "Jamaican steel". As a result, single women are almost unanimously assumed to be out for one thing only – prepare yourself for a barrage of propositions.

Male tourists are less involved in the holiday romance scenario, but **female prostitutes** are common and men should expect to be frequently propositioned. If you do choose to indulge, make sure that you practise safer sex; one in five prostitutes are HIV-positive, and STDs – including syphilis – are rife.

As Negril prohibits buildings taller than a palm tree, a lot of accommodation is in traditional circular palm-thatched **cottages**; also popular is the **pillar cabin**, a round cottage set on top of a stone column, with a shower below. Twenty-four-hour security is sensible if you plan to **camp**; if you're willing to rough it and risk it, there are plenty of cabins and campsites with few facilities and negligible security on the morass side of Norman Manley Boulevard.

The beach

Country Country ⓣ876/957-4273, ⓕ957-4342, ⓦwww.countrynegril.com. Brightly painted cottages set in a garden on a lovely stretch of beach. The rooms are spacious and have a fridge, A/C and ceiling fans. There are two good restaurants, including the only Chinese restaurant in Negril. ❺

Firefly Norman Manley Boulevard ⓣ876/957-4358, ⓕ957-3447, ⓔfirefly@jamaicalink.com. Pretty beachside rooms and fully equipped studios and cottages in a neat strip of garden. Outdoor whirlpool and genial beach bar. Rooms ❹, apartments and cottages ❺

Kuyaba ⓣ876/957-4318, ⓕ957-9765, ⓔkuyaba@cwjamaica.com. "Rustic cottages" set along a pretty landscaped track leading to the beach, with porches, A/C and fans; some have kitchenettes. There are more luxurious (and expensive) options in the main block. Good restaurant on site. ❸

Negril Tree House ⓣ876/957-4287, ⓕ957-4368, ⓦwww.negril-treehouse.com. An appealing complex of clean, comfortable rooms and villas with A/C, phone and cable TV. Two bars , a restaurant, a pool and watersports are on site. ❺

Negril Yoga Centre ⓣ876/957-4397, ⓦwww.negrilyoga.com. Yoga centre and guesthouse overlooking the Great Morass. Attractive cottages of varying degrees of comfort surrounded by greenery. Wholefood cooking and yoga classes available, and there's a communal kitchen. ❷–❸

Nirvana on the Beach ⓣ876/957-4314, in US 716/789-4753, ⓕ876/957-9196, ⓦwww.nirvananegril.com. Attractive wooden cottages with two bedrooms and kooky decorative touches, set in an unusually beautiful sand garden shaded by tall trees and dotted with sculptures and hammocks. Friendly atmosphere. ❻

Whistling Bird ⓣ876/957-4403, ⓕ957-3252, ⓦwww.negril.com. Pretty beach cottages set in a lovely garden with cook-to-order restaurant. Very private and alluring. Extremely genial staff. ❹

West End

All properties are on West End Road or its continuation, Lighthouse Road.

Banana Shout ⓣ & ⓕ876/957-0384, ⓦwww.negril.com/bananashout. Simple but attractive cottages in gardens or right on the cliffs. Each has kitchenette, ceiling fan, hammocks on the verandah. The cliff portion has a diving platform, sun deck, its own cave and exceptional sunset views; cliffside rooms are also treated to a nightly serenade from the band at next-door *Rick's Café*. Garden ❷, cliffside ❸

Catcha Falling Star ⓣ876/957-0390, ⓕ957-0629, ⓦwww.seastarinn.com/negril_catch. Attractive gardens crisscrossed by pathways, lots of grassy sunbathing spots and excellent sea access. Most of the split-level cottages have verandahs with hammocks, a few have waterbeds, and all have fridge and access to the communal kitchen. Rates include breakfast. ❺

The Caves ⓣ876/957-0270, ⓕ957-4939, ⓦwww.islandoutpost.com. Gorgeous small hotel set behind Fort Knox-style gates and patronized by celebrities who are helicoptered in. Funky cottage-style rooms are equipped with batik bathrobes and CD players. On-site facilities include a spa, hot tub and sauna. ⑨

Home Sweet Home ⓣ876/957-4478, ⓦwww.homesweethomeresort.net. Small, cheerful resort with swimming pool, hot tub, restaurant, cliffside sun deck. All rooms have ocean views. Popular with young Americans. ③

LTU Villas ⓣ876/957-0382, ⓦwww.negril.com/ltu. A great-value option offering spacious rooms in quiet gardens opposite one of Negril's best bars, the *LTU Pub*. Each room has a lounge, fridge and balcony; those with A/C cost a little more. ②

Mariners Inn ⓣ876/957-0392, ⓕ957-0391, ⓦwww.marinersnegril.com. Medium-size retreat with attractive rooms and apartments. Facilities include a dive centre, swimming pool and games room patronized by local pool wizards. Great sea swimming and a boat-shaped bar. Rooms ②, apartments ④

Rockhouse ⓣ876/957-4373, ⓕ957-0557, ⓦwww.rockhousehotel.com. Enviable location, Mediterranean styling, magnificent thatched bar/restaurant and saltwater pool are highlights. Thatched studios and villas have glass-doored patios overlooking the ocean, outdoor showers, fans, four-poster beds. Innovative and expensive restaurant. ④

Tensing Pen ⓣ876/957-0387, ⓕ957-0161, ⓦwww.tensingpen.com. Stylish and exclusive retreat in pretty clifftop gardens with imaginatively decorated bamboo and wood cottages and a well-equipped communal kitchen/lounge. Some of the cliffs are linked by a tiny suspension bridge. Breakfast included in the rates. Bungalows ④, cottages from ⑦

Xtabi ⓣ876/957-4336, ⓕ957-0827, ⓦwww.xtabi-negril.com. Lovely West End veteran with flowering gardens and a network of caves. Accommodations in wooden cabins with private sun decks and sea access or two-storey concrete cottages with kitchens. Also pool, open-air restaurant and bar, and countless swimming platforms. Rooms ②, seafront cottage ⑤

The Town

Negril doesn't really have a centre – just a roundabout feeding its three main roads – and most people leave the beach or cliffs only to change money, buy petrol or find a ride out of the area. However, **Sheffield Road** is the least tourist-oriented part of town and the closest approximation of a real heart, with the police station, market stalls, petrol station, restaurants and constant crowds dodging beeping mopeds. To the right of the roundabout are two **shopping plazas** – Coral Seas Plaza and Plaza de Negril; the car park in front is known as **Negril Square**, a base for taxi drivers, black-market currency touts and would-be guides. Nestled behind is **Red Ground**, a residential area that houses most of Negril's permanent population.

The beach

Negril beach is a near-perfect Caribbean seashore. The seven-mile stretch of whiter-than-white sand is lined by palms and sea grapes, the water is warm, translucent and still, and the busy reefs ornately encrusted. It's also packed with tourists, locals and holidaying Jamaicans. While it's great for lively socializing, the high concentration of human traffic inevitably draws plenty of vendors and hustlers. The hassle is constant and high-octane, and as well as the usual crafts, hair braiding and aloe massage, you'll be offered sex and drugs with alarming frequency.

Though hotels guard "their" portion of beach with security men and strings of floating buoys, by law the beaches are public up to the shoreline. The beach is roughly divided by the bank of all-inclusives at the outcrop splitting Long Bay and Bloody Bay. Beginning at the roundabout, **Long Bay** is the most heavily developed, by day a rash of bronzing bodies and flashing jet skis, by night a chain of disco-bars dedicated to reggae, rum punch and skinny-dipping. At the far end, the hotels give way to the grassy stretch of **Long Bay Beach Park**, with picnic tables, changing rooms, a snack bar and considerably fewer people.

The West End

The **West End** begins at the roundabout in the centre of town and meanders along the cliffs for some three miles, becoming Lighthouse Road at Negril lighthouse and winding inland to Orange Hill and ultimately Sheffield Road. The first stretch is the liveliest, with jerk shacks, bars, juice stalls and craft shops – including the official A Fi Wi Plaza **craft market** – lining the inland side and restaurants hanging over the sea's edge. There are a couple of ramshackle **beaches** where fishermen moor their canoes but the murky water makes swimming inadvisable. The road opens up a little once you get to the fancy Kings Plaza and Sunshine Village shopping malls, but the true West End begins over the next blind bend; the road narrows, the water clears and the hotels that carve up the rest of the cliffs begin in earnest.

As this is Jamaica's extreme westerly point, the **sunset view** from the West End is the best you'll see. Sunset-watching is an institution here; most bars and restaurants offer sunset happy hours and the half-hour or so before dusk is the closest the West End gets to hectic. Coach parties descend in droves upon undeservedly popular **Rick's Café**, where you pay for your drinks with plastic tokens, cameras click and local lads dive off the cliffs.

After *Rick's* the road becomes a country lane and the hotels are interspersed with near-wild coastline. A main point of interest is **Negril Point Lighthouse**, standing 100 feet above sea level at Jamaica's westernmost tip. Built in 1894, the 66-foot tower now flashes a solar-powered beam ten miles out to sea. Workers who live on site are usually willing to take you up all 103 leg-quivering steps to the top.

Around Negril

As most visitors to Negril are after a beach holiday rather than sightseeing, there aren't many managed attractions in the area. But if you fancy getting out of town, there are attractive options nearby. For some peaceful beachlife, head east out of town along Norman Manley Boulevard. Just outside Green Island, the nearest village to Negril, the unspoilt **Half Moon Bay Beach** (daily 8am till late; J$80 entrance, redeemable at the bar; ⓣ876/957-6467) is full of the paradisiacal charm that originally brought tourists to Negril. The wide curve of white sand has no braiding booths, jet skis or hassle, just a little sea grass and some small islets; nude bathing is perfectly acceptable and snorkel equipment cheap. The **restaurant** (daily 8am–10pm) serves excellent chicken, fish and sandwiches. On the way to Half Moon is **Rhodes Hall Plantation** (ⓣ876/957-6333, ⓦwww.fantasyisle.com), a 550-acre coconut, banana, plantain and pear farm with two private beaches – one a

The West End's top spots

Many **hotels** will let you swim from their piece of cliff for the price of a drink, and though they all look pretty similar, some stand out. *Drumville Cove* has a friendly attitude towards non-guests and a spectacular portion of cliff, while *Rockhouse* boasts a stylish saltwater swimming pool, a bar, excellent sea access and complete seclusion. The limestone cliffs are riddled with **caverns**, with a popular network below *Xtabi* hotel. The ever-popular *Pickled Parrot* watering hole is in prime position for the exploration of **Joseph's Cave**, one of the largest along the West End, made famous in the movies *Dr No*, *Papillon* and *20,000 Leagues Under the Sea*; the daredevil swings and waterslide above help to draw in the crowds as well. The cliffs are at their highest around *Rick's Café*, the venue of daily **cliff-diving** demonstrations; a less prominent place to have a go yourself is the *LTU Pub* next door. Past the lighthouse, the cliffs peter out, coastal winds whip the sea into a frenzy, and swimming becomes a little risky, but there is a sheltered spot just past the point where Lighthouse Road turns inland – turn straight onto the piece of undeveloped land and climb down the rocks.

shallow, sea-grassy reef beach with a freshwater mineral spring bubbling under the brine, the other a more conventional sugar-sanded curve. Volleyball and football/basketball pitches and a restaurant/bar are adjacent, but the main draw is **horse riding**. The well-kept mounts trot into the hills and along the beach (US$30–50, depending on length of ride).

Mayfield Falls

One of the most popular excursions from Negril heads into the low-lying **Dolphin Head Mountains** to the 22 mini-cascades and numerous swimming spots at **Mayfield Falls** (daily 9am–5pm; US$10). The falls are very hard to find independently, and most people visit as part of an organized tour run by one of two operators, Original Mayfield Falls (☎876/957-4729) and Riverwalk at Mayfield Falls (☎876/974-8000). Both offer tranquil guided walks through bamboo-shaded cool water with swimming holes every twenty yards. The tours (US$65 per person, plus tip) include transport from Montego Bay or Negril and lunch. Wear a swimming costume and bring flip-flops, as the stones are tough on bare, wet feet. Mosquitoes can also be a problem.

Roaring River Park

An easy escape about five miles north of Savanna-la-Mar is gorgeous **Roaring River Park** (daily 9am–5pm; US$10) near the small community of **Petersfield**, approached on a rutted road that you'll probably need directions to find, though there are plenty of signposts from town. Set in a former plantation and still surrounded by cane fields, a dazzling swimmable **mineral pool** and extensive **caves** have been developed with tourists in mind. A guide takes you on a trip round the caves and surrounding gardens. Steps, concrete walkways and lighting let you appreciate the full magnitude of the caverns. Bats flit about, and there are two mineral pools for a disquieting swim in pitch-blackness.

Eating

Negril caters to a cosmopolitan crowd and the classiest, albeit somewhat pricey, dining is likely to be found in hotel restaurants; the best of these are included in the listings below. Thanks to Negril's hippy associations, there are plenty of **vegetarian** options, and you'll also find a lot of **pasta**, as the area attracts a huge number of young Italians. Vendors based at the first stretch of West End Road sell roast or fried fish, jerk chicken and soup.

Sheffield Road

Sweet Spice The best place on Sheffield Road for cheap, delicious Jamaican food to take away or eat in.

The beach

Alfred's Ocean Palace ☎876/957-4735. Hearty American-style breakfasts are accompanied by live piano music. Crepes and sandwiches are served at lunch, and seafood, blackened chicken and pasta in the evenings.

Beach Beans *Mariner's Beach Club* hotel ☎876/957-4220. Inexpensive pizzeria and ice-cream parlour on the beach with really good coffee, milkshakes, sundaes and home-made cakes.

Blue Mountain Coffee Shop Deservedly popular breakfast joint. Excellent coffee, banana pancakes, callaloo omelettes served up cheaply.

Cosmo's ☎876/957-4330. One of the best, busiest spots on the beach, equally popular with Jamaicans and tourists. Excellent, moderately priced seafood – conch soup is a speciality – and the usual selection of chicken variations.

Hunan Garden *Country Country* hotel ☎876/957-4359. Excellent, though slightly pricey Chinese restaurant in attractive dining room. Eat in or take out.

Kuyaba ☎876/957-4318. Upscale thatch-roofed, open-sided restaurant with good food and regular crowds. The menu includes lobster and shrimp, crab and pumpkin cakes, vegetarian dishes and pasta. Good cocktails, too.

West End

3 C's Naturally Open-air diner at the beach end

of the West End, serving Jamaican breakfasts; salads, sandwiches, burgers and soups for lunch; local staples for dinner. Reliable and late-opening.
The Carrot Beautifully decorated restaurant with indoor and outdoor seating and a natural juice bar. Serves inexpensive Jamaican-style seafood and chicken cooked to perfection, great conch soup, vegetarian dishes and breakfasts. There's even an on-site herbal consultant.
Chicken Lavish Choice spot for domino players, serving chicken and fish, Jamaican and Chinese style; steaks and pork chops, too.
Easy Rock Bar and Grill Lovely setting right at the water's edge, with eating in the bar area or on the breezy rooftop. Inexpensive Jamaican standards with an English twist, and lovely breakfasts. Friendly owners, especially welcoming to solo women travellers.
Hungry Lion ☎876/957-4486. The best vegetarian food in town, with seafood as well. A walled courtyard affords privacy, and the fairly priced food is always good. Don't miss the coconut cream pie.
Just Natural Fresh and cheap Jamaican food, callaloo omelettes, pasta, burritos and vegetarian options are served in a beautiful shady garden.
LTU Pub Laid-back venue with cliffside dining. Eclectic menu offers seafood, stuffed jalapeño chillis, chicken filled with callaloo and cheese, and some German dishes.
Pickled Parrot Popular and efficient American-style bar and grill. The extravagant clifftop original serves large portions of tacos, fajitas and burritos alongside jerk chicken, seafood, formidable burgers and pizza.
Rockhouse ☎876/957-4373. Romantically set on a boardwalk right over the sea, with excellent service and an expensive menu that includes vegetable tempura, seafood linguine with garlic and conch fritters.

Drinking and entertainment

Most **bars** want you to spend the **sunset** with them and provide drinks promotions or happy hours as an incentive. As the cliffs give the best view, bars along the West End tend to be livelier at dusk, with the action moving to the beach after dark. The larger places are distinctly tourist-oriented; if you want some local flavour, try the **rum bars** and **beer shacks** along Sheffield Road or West End Road near the roundabout.

Jungles (see below) is the only proper **club** in town, but there's also week-night dancing at the **beach bars**, which use their portions of sand as dance floors. DJs play dancehall or Euro-disco, and the **live music** usually consists of a no-name reggae band singing Bob Marley covers. Ask around to see what's on each night.

Large **stageshows** featuring well-known reggae artists are advertised on roadside billboards and through a car-with-megaphone system. Main **venues** for large shows are *Roots Bamboo* on the beach and *MXIII* in the West End. *The Samsara Hotel* and *Central Park* (both on West End Road) have occasional live events. Stageshows rarely begin before 11pm and often go on until 3 or 4am; cover charge is usually about US$7.

Norman Manley Boulevard

Alfred's Ocean Palace Busiest bar on the beach with thrice-weekly live reggae and crowds of happy holidaymakers dancing on the sand. This is where all the action is, and it's great fun, but watch out for the hustlers, particularly on gig nights.
De Buss The trademark London bus used in *Live and Let Die* stands outside; inside there's piped or live music every night in a covered area and a section of the beach. The jerk chicken is famously good.
Errol's Small 24-hour beach bar with reggae videos, an overdose of fairy lights and hard-core drinking by guests who rent basic but adequate rooms in the yard behind the bar.
Jungles ☎876/957-4005. Negril's only true club is a fairly lavish place with a smoky, packed indoor dance floor downstairs and a breezy upper deck with pool, table tennis and a restaurant. Each night has a different theme and music. Cover charge US$10. Closed Mon and Tues.
Margaritaville Large beach bar with nightly bonfire, beach volleyball, two-for-one drink offers and big TV screens for sports fans. Karaoke on Sundays and Mondays and an all-inclusive party on Friday evenings (US$34 per person). Hugely popular with American students.
Risky Business Popular American-style beach bar complete with big-screen sports via satellite,

Thursday two-for-one drinks offers, and Ladies' Nights on Mondays and Saturdays (women drink for free).

West End Road

LTU Pub Very cool bar, vastly superior to next-door *Rick's*, offers cliffside drinking, diving, snorkelling and food to boot. Ask the barman to make you a Bob Marley – and then try and drink it.

Mi Yard High-rise bar that's tourist-friendly but positively Jamaican. Open 24-hours for music, dominoes, drinking and jerk; always packed after 2am.

Pickled Parrot The cliffside venue with water slide and swing gets very busy during the daily happy hour (3–5pm) and is an essential stop-off for sunset cruisers. If nude hedonists and seriously misbehaving swingers (don't ask) are not your chosen drinking companions, then this isn't the place for you.

Rick's Café Overpriced tourist trap puts on the West End's main sunset event. An appallingly tuneless band play reggae while local boys dive from the high cliffs.

Yacht Club Large thatched bar overlooking the sea. Cheap Red Stripe all day until 7pm, live music on weekends and wonderfully shady clientele. Come for a heavy drinking session with the hippies who "discovered" Negril and other local characters; the staff are helpful and friendly. It's surprisingly safe and often great fun.

5.5

The south coast

If you want to catch a glimpse of Jamaica as it was before the tourist boom, head **south**. Mass tourism has yet to reach the southern parishes – none of the all-conquering all-inclusives has opened here yet, and the beaches aren't packed with sun-ripened bodies – but there are some fantastic places to stay and great off-the-beaten-track places to visit. It takes a bit of extra effort to get here, but it's definitely worth it. The parishes that make up south-central Jamaica are immensely varied; the landscape includes mountains, cactus-strewn desert, lush jungle and rolling fields. To the west, in the beautiful parish of St Elizabeth, **Treasure Beach** – an extremely laid-back place with decent beaches and some lovely accommodation options – is the area's main draw. If you want to do some sightseeing, you can visit the **rum factory** at Appleton or the fabulous **YS waterfall**, or drive around the tiny villages of the attractive **Santa Cruz Mountains**. **Black River** is the main town – an important nineteenth-century port that today offers popular **river safaris** and a handful of attractive colonial-era buildings. New roads have opened up large parts of the south coast in the last few years and it's now possible to drive along large stretches of it without losing sight of the sea. The scenery is often wild and unspoilt down here, though you'll need a car to see most of it; buses and minibuses tend to stick to the main, inland roads, making side-trips down to coastal villages as required.

Treasure Beach

The easy-going, snoozy little community of **TREASURE BEACH** has become the main tourist centre on the south coast, particularly popular with a hip bohemian crowd. It has a good range of **accommodation** options, including a delightfully eclectic collection of villas and beach cottages to rent. There are also some great places to **eat** and a couple of diverting attractions, while the bays here boast some pretty **beaches**. The **Santa Cruz Mountains** rise up from the sea just east of Treasure Beach and run northwest, providing a scenic backdrop for the village and protecting the area from rainclouds coming from the north. As a result, Treasure Beach has one of the **driest** climates on the island, with a scrubby, desert-like landscape. This is farming country nonetheless, and you'll see plantations scattered around the area.

Treasure Beach itself is made up of a string of loosely connected fishing settlements. The chances are that you'll stay on the long sandy sweep of **Frenchman's Bay**, where tourism has displaced fishing as the main industry, or smaller **Calabash Bay**, where brightly coloured fishing boats are pulled up on the beach below the newly constructed hotels and guesthouses. To the east, **Great Bay** remains a fishing village with just a couple of guesthouses and some lovely beaches, while west of Frenchman's Bay the road runs past **Billy's Bay**, home to several of the classiest villas in Treasure Beach, some shacks and a lot of goats.

Arrival, information and getting around

Public transport links with Treasure Beach are not great, although several **minibuses** and **shared taxis** (around J$70) run daily from Black River; a regular taxi costs around US$30 each way. If you're **driving**, there are two approaches to the village. Most traffic arrives via the road from Pedro Cross, passing the police station and post office north of the village. A turn-off to the left leads to Great Bay, while the main road continues towards Calabash Bay, where most of the recent tourist development has taken place. The newer, coastal road from Black River runs into the village from the west past a string of small bays and intermittent guesthouses.

Treasure Beach has a comprehensive website, ⓦwww.treasurebeach.net, which covers everything from community news to information on accommodation and tours. Jason Henzell at *Jake's* is also incredibly helpful, even if you're not a guest.

Accommodation

There is a wide variety of **accommodation** in Treasure Beach, and more guesthouses are springing up all the time. Seemingly every other house is a rentable **villa**; these vary from simple beach cottages to luxurious homes; ask at *Jake's*. In addition, **camping** is more feasible here than in other parts of Jamaica.

Caijan West of Billy's Bay ⓣ876/990-6641 or c/o *Jake's*. Camping sites and a couple of cottages in a fabulous mountainside setting about seven miles west of town on the coastal road to Black River. No electricity, but great views and atmosphere. You'll need a sturdy four-wheel-drive to get up here, or ask to be collected. ❷, camping ❶

Golden Sands Frenchman's Bay ⓣ876/965-0167. Longstanding and deservedly popular budget option on the beach, with twenty basic rooms and a communal kitchen. ❷

Ital Rest Great Bay ⓣ876/965-3231. Two cottages only at this gentle and beautifully landscaped place near the beach, each with separate rooms upstairs and down (ask for upstairs for the views and the breeze), and with kitchen and verandahs facing the sea. Small bar, restaurant and herbal steam room on site (US$50 for a steam and massage). Turn right just before the *Seacrab* restaurant and then take the first right. Rooms ❷, cottage ❸

Jake's Calabash Bay ⓣ876/965-0635, ⓕ965 0552, ⓦwww.islandoutpost.com. With an easy-going but cultured atmosphere, this delightful venue on its own tiny beach is the nicest, and liveliest, place to stay hereabouts. The gorgeous cottages are decorated in funky colours and have CD players and coffee makers. There's a pool and restaurant, and the bar draws a genial local crowd. ❺

Siwind Billy's Bay ⓣ & ⓕ876/965-0582, ⓔsiwind@cwjamaica.com. Small, tranquil and very friendly hotel with amazing views and steps down to a private beach. Rooms are simple, classy and clean, with screened windows and ceiling fans. You can prepare your own meals in the kitchen. ❸

Sunset Resort Hotel Calabash Bay ⓣ876/965-0143, ⓕ965-0555, ⓦwww.sunsetresort.com. Incongruously and fabulously kitsch resort in a lovely seaside setting. Huge comfortable rooms have A/C, fans, cable TV and coffeemaker; self-catering cottages are also available. There's a pool and a restaurant. Very friendly. ❹

Organized tours and activities

If you're interested in seeing the YS Falls, Gut River or other parts of the south from Treasure Beach, Treasure Tours (ⓣ876/965-0126, ⓔtreasuretours@info.com) offers good and reasonably priced **tours** (from US$35 per person). Red's Treasure Beach Tours (ⓣ876/965-0225 or 3101, ⓔsandyboy@yahoo.com) takes **cycling and walking trips** on off-road tracks to places such as the gorgeous Back Seaside (US$30 per person, snorkelling included); overnight trips and beach cookouts can also be arranged, and **bike rental** is available (J$500 per day). Dennis Abrahams (ⓣ876/965-3084) does excellent **boat tours** to Black River, Sunny Island, Alligators Pond and up and down the nearby coastline (US$35 per person for parties of four or more). **Fishing trips** with local fishermen can usually be arranged for around US$25 per person for a half-day – ask the people at your hotel to put the word out that you're interested. If you need to unwind, Shirley's **herbal steams** (US$30) and **massages** (US$60 for hour-long full body) are excellent. She's based next to *Ital Rest*, and will pick you up – call ⓣ876/965-3231 or 3111 to make an appointment.

Treasure Beach Hotel Frenchman's Bay ⓣ876/965-0110, ⓕ965-2544, ⓦwww.treasurebeachjamaica.com. Big, attractive resort on one of the best stretches of beach, with two pools, a restaurant and bar. Modern suites with oceanfront views all have A/C, ceiling fan and cable TV. ④

Wakiki Calabash Bay ⓣ876/965-0448. Rangy place set back from the road and overlooking the beach, with basic, clean rooms with fans and private bathrooms. Brilliant if you're on a budget. ①

The beach

If you're in the mood for sightseeing, there are a couple of places worth checking out just outside Treasure Beach (see below). Otherwise, it's just you and the **beach**. The swimming is excellent, though the undertow can get strong at times – ask at your hotel about present conditions. Although rocky headlands create occasional obstacles, you can stroll for miles on certain parts of the beach, particularly west of the *Treasure Beach Hotel*. The **Back Seaside** bluff, which protects the shore at Great Bay, is a lovely place to walk and watch for seabirds.

Eating and nightlife

Evenings are pretty low-key in Treasure Beach but there are a few good options for **food** and a couple of **bars** that keep late hours and get very full on the weekends.

Fishermen's Bar Frenchman's Bay. Easy-going local hangout up a lane off the main road with a small disco and a pool table out back. Very popular at the weekends with both locals and tourists, particularly Sunday nights. It stays open after every place else has closed.

Jake's Calabash Bay ⓣ876/965-0365. Good option for dinner and usually one of the busiest places in town. The blackboard menu changes daily but normally includes fish and lobster.

Natural Vibes Frenchman's Bay. Basic and tasty home cooking. There are some tables out on the main street. Open late.

Q-En's Coffee Shop Swaby's Plaza. Open from 7.30am daily for great ackee or omelette breakfasts (served till noon), and good Jamaican lunches and dinners. Pastries and coffee are available all day.

Seacrab Great Bay. Friendly local restaurant, near *Ital Rest*, serving good and inexpensive Jamaican staples like escovitched fish and curry goat.

South Jammin Frenchman's Bay. Unpretentious and popular bar serves up burgers, pizza and seafood. Pool table and cute pocket-sized garden.

Trans-Love Cafe Frenchman's Bay. This laid-back thatched patio is the essential stop for breakfast or brunch, offering fresh bread, cakes and fruit salads as well as ackee and saltfish and good jerk chicken.

Wild Onion Frenchman's Bay. The newest spot in town, this place draws a crowd for drinks at the open-air bar or for excellent seafood served in metal skillets.

Yabba *Treasure Beach Hotel* ⓣ876/965-0110. Good hotel food and enthusiastic service, though it's often quiet and consequently low on atmosphere.

Black River

Although it's St Elizabeth's largest town, **BLACK RIVER** is a quiet spot, and most travellers only nip in briefly to take a boat trip on the river. It wasn't always this way: in the mid-nineteenth century the town derived substantial wealth from exporting **logwood**, used to produce black and dark-blue dyes for the textiles industry. For a brief period the town was one of the most influential in Jamaica. But the introduction of synthetic dyes meant the end for the logwood trade, and today the only signs of those illustrious days are some wonderful but decrepit old gingerbread houses. **Buses** and **minibuses** stop behind the market, just off the High Street. Five minutes' walk away, the **Jamaica Tourist Board** (Mon–Fri 9.30am–4.30pm; ⓣ876/965-2074) has a small office on the upper floor of the Hendrick's building, 2 High St.

The nicest thing to do in Black River is to stroll along the **waterfront** and check out the old wooden buildings, many with gorgeous colonnaded verandahs and gingerbread trim and most in a perilous state of collapse. The **Waterloo Guesthouse**, built in 1819, is reputed to have been the first place in Jamaica to get electricity – installed to provide air conditioning for racehorses kept in the old stables – and to have boasted the island's first telephone. Nearby, the gleaming white **Invercauld Hotel**, built in 1889, reflects the confidence of the town during its heyday.

The main reason most people come to the town, however, is to take a **boat safari** on the **Black River**, which, at 44 miles, is Jamaica's longest. So named because the peat moss lining the river bottom makes the crystal-clear water appear inky black, the Black River is the main source for the **Great Morass** – a 125-square-mile area of wetland that spreads north and west of the river and provides a swampy home for most of Jamaica's surviving crocodiles as well as some diverse and spectacular birdlife. The boat tour is a very pretty trip into the Great Morass, although the term "safari" promises rather more excitement than it delivers. You are almost sure to see crocodiles (albeit fairly tame ones), and there are some marvellous **mangrove swamps** where you can normally spot flocks of roosting egrets as well as whistling ducks, herons and jacanas. To go on the ninety-minute tour (5 daily; US$15 per person), turn up at the dock by the bridge or contact St Elizabeth River Safari (☎876/965-2374) or Black River Safari Boat Tours (☎876/965-2513).

Middle Quarters and YS Falls

As you drive northeast from Black River, you'll reach an intersection directing you north for Montego Bay or east towards Santa Cruz and Mandeville. Head east and you'll soon pass **Middle Quarters**, a small crossroads where groups of women sell spicy, salty and delicious **pepper shrimp** from the Black River – perfect to add to your picnic if you're heading to the YS waterfall. Feel free to sample from the proffered bags before you buy, and reckon on around J$100 for a small bag (you're likely to get fresher fare from the roadside bar just beyond the crossroads). Shortly after Middle Quarters, a left turn takes you two and a half miles north to **YS**, an area dominated by the **YS farm**, home of the magnificent YS Falls. The name is thought to derive from the farm's original owners in 1684, John Yates and Richard Scott, whose initials were stamped on their cattle and the hogsheads of sugar that they exported. Today the 2300-acre farm raises pedigree red poll cattle – a Jamaican breed that you'll see all over the country – and grows papaya for export.

The **YS Falls**, a series of ten greater and lesser waterfalls, are great fun (Tues–Sun 9.50am–3.30pm; US$12). A jitney transports you across the farm's land and alongside the YS river to a grassy area at the base of the falls, where there's a changing room. You can climb up the lower falls or take the wooden stairway that leads to a platform beside the uppermost and most spectacular waterfall. There are ropes for aspiring Tarzans and pools for bathing at the foot of each fall. If water levels are low, you can also swim under the main falls and climb up into a cave behind them. Early morning is a good time to go, before the afternoon clouds set in and the tour buses arrive. Take a picnic and a book and you can comfortably spend a few hours loafing around on the grass and in the water. Cold beers and soft drinks are available nearby.

A **car** is extremely handy if you're heading for the falls, as they're a little off the beaten track, but if you're relying on public transport, **buses** run along the main A2 highway south of YS between Black River and Santa Cruz. Ask the driver to drop you at the junction, and you can usually find taxis waiting to run passengers up to the YS farm – make sure you negotiate a price before you get in (around J$150 is standard).

The Appleton rum estate

Some six miles east of YS Falls, the **Wray and Nephew rum estate** at **APPLETON** (Mon–Sat 9am–3.30pm; US$12; ⓣ876/963-9215, ⓦwww.appletonrum.com) has a great setting in the Black River valley among thousands of acres of sugarcane fields. At 250 years old, this is the oldest rum producer in the English-speaking Caribbean and the best-known of Jamaica's several brands.

You'll need a car to get here, or you can take a taxi from the nearby village of Maggotty. It's a good idea to call ahead to arrange a visit, if only to avoid arriving at the same time as a big tour party. The thirty-minute **tour** starts with a complimentary drink, followed by a whirlwind trip through the factory and warehouses and then outside to an old press, where donkeys used to walk in circles to turn a grinder that crushed juice out of the sugarcane. The tour concludes in a "saloon", where you can sample all seventeen kinds of rum and various rum-based liquors. The prices in the adjacent shop are far lower than supermarket prices.

Dominican Republic

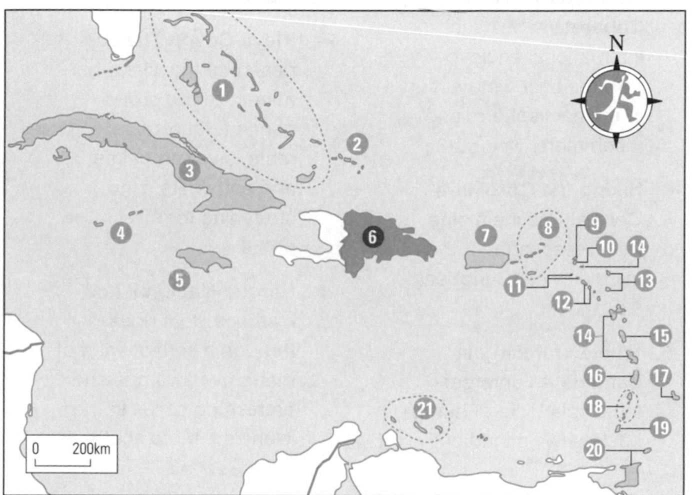

Dominican Republic Highlights

* **Colonial Santo Domingo** Chock-full of 500-year-old architecture – including the hemisphere's first cathedral, university, hospital and more. See p.309

* **Watersports in Cabarete** A bustling international enclave with the best windsurfing in the hemisphere, and much more. See p.335

* **Hiking the Cordillera Central** Pristine alpine wilderness, right in the middle of the Caribbean. See p.341

* **Whale-watching in Samaná** An unforgettable spectacle of humpback whale migration; catch it from December to February. See p.326

* **Old-style Cuban son at the Mauna Loa** Catch a Buena Vista-style Cuban *son* show in a plush Santo Domingo ballroom. See p.314

* **Playa Cosón** The best beach on the island bar none, with no crowds, gentle turquoise currents, swaying palms and soft white sand stretching for miles. See p.329

* **Parque Nacional Los Haitises** Boat rides through a surreal snarl of mangrove swamps and prehistoric caves in the island's remote southeast. See p.322

Introduction and Basics

Occupying the eastern half of the island of Hispaniola, the **Dominican Republic** (or the DR, as it's often known) is a hugely popular destination, thanks to the portion of the country that most resembles the image of a Caribbean playland: the crystal-clear waters and sandy beaches lined with palm trees, of which the DR has plenty. This vision of leisurely days spent by the sea and romantic nights filled with merengue and dark rum is supported by what turns out to be the largest all-inclusive resort industry in the world.

Set on the most geographically diverse Caribbean island, the DR also boasts virgin alpine wilderness, tropical rainforests and mangrove swamps, cultivated savannas, vast desert expanses and everything in between within its relatively small confines – slightly smaller than the US states of New Hampshire and Vermont combined – providing staggering opportunities for **ecotourism** and **adventure travelling**.

The DR also lays claim to some of the more intriguing culture and history in the area, dating back to its early cave-dwelling groups, the **Taínos**, who recorded much of their activities in the form of rock art – it's quite likely you'll find yourself clambering down a dark cave to view some of these preserved paintings during your stay. In addition, as Dominicans are often quick to point out, their land was the setting for Christopher Columbus's first colony, La Isabela, and Spain's first New World city, **Santo Domingo**, at the end of the fifteenth century. Though the island quickly lost this foothold, the events that took place during its brief heyday did much to define the Americas as we know them.

Where to go

The southeastern part of the country probably has the loveliest all-inclusive resort zones, **Bávaro** and **Punta Cana**, both holding pristine coastline stretching for kilometres on end. These are slightly overshadowed, if not in attractiveness then in sheer magnitude, by the complex at **Playa Dorada** along the north coast. Fortunately, this is close by **Puerto Plata**, an historic city worth examining for its wealth of Victorian architecture and proximity to developed stations like windsurfing capital Cabarete, to the east.

More great beaches are scattered about the **Samaná Peninsula**, poking out at the country's extreme northeast, from where you can also check out migrating humpback whales. In the mountainous interior, a few **national parks** make for good hiking terrain; while midway along the southern coast, **Santo Domingo** is an obvious draw, for its history and big urban feel.

When to go

The northern hemisphere's winter is high tourist season in the Dominican Republic; this is when the Dominican climate is at its optimum, having cooled down just a bit. You'll therefore save a bit of money – and have an easier time booking a hotel room on the spot – if you arrive during the spring or the fall, which is just fine, as the **temperature** doesn't really vary all that much from season to season. Keep in mind, though, that the Dominican Republic is right in the centre of the Caribbean **hurricane** belt, and gets hit with a major one every decade or so; August and September are prime hurricane season, though smaller ones can occur in the months preceding and following.

Getting there

The cheapest and most frequent **flights** depart from gateway cities such as Miami and New York. Flights from the latter average about US$450–550. As there are no non-stop scheduled flights to the Dominican Republic from the UK, many British and Irish visitors to the Dominican Republic arrive on a charter flight as part of a package holiday,

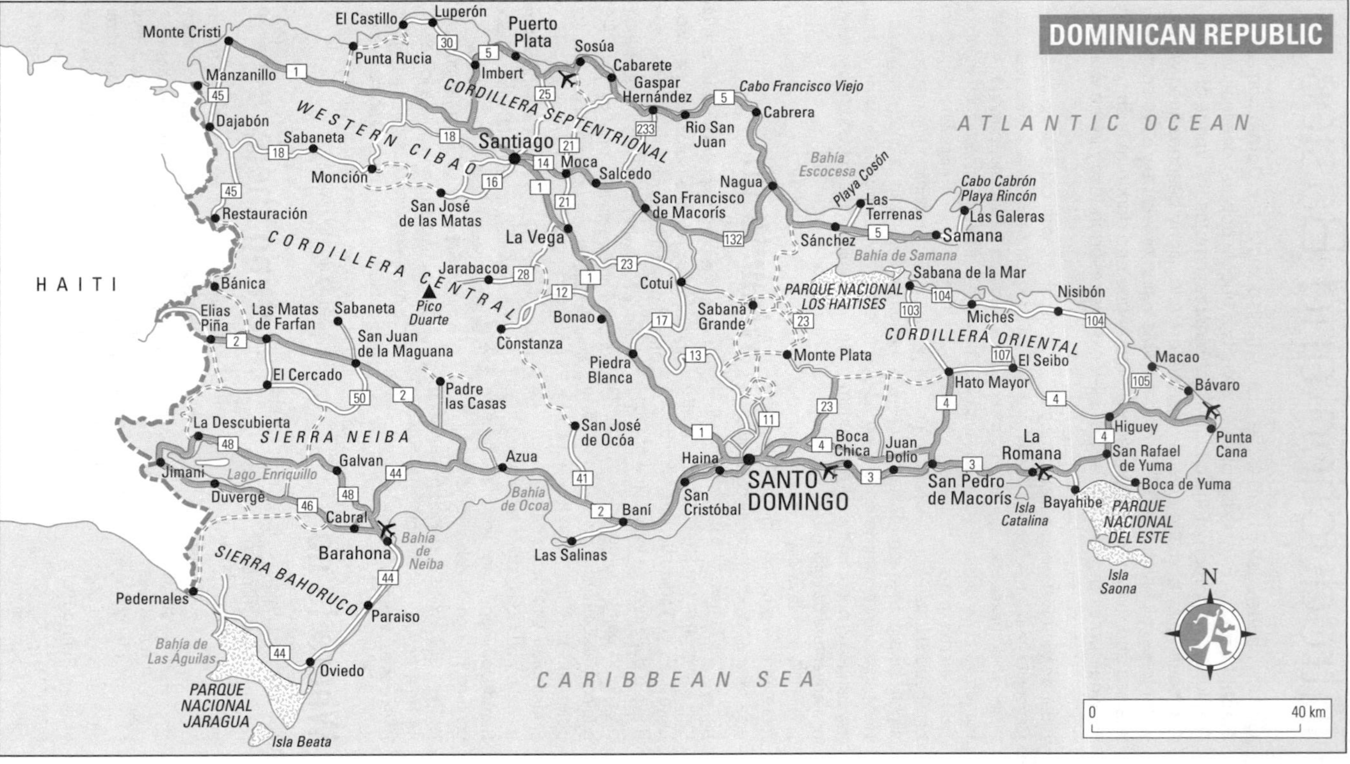
DOMINICAN REPUBLIC
ATLANTIC OCEAN
CARIBBEAN SEA
HAITI
Monte Cristi
El Castillo
Luperón
Puerto Plata
Sosúa
Cabarete
Gaspar Hernández
Cabo Francisco Viejo
Cabrera
Punta Rucia
Imbert
Manzanillo
Dajabón
Rio San Juan
CORDILLERA SEPTENTRIONAL
WESTERN CIBAO
Sabaneta
Santiago
Moca
Salcedo
Moncíon
Nagua
Bahía Escocesa
Playa Cosón
Cabo Cabrón
Playa Rincón
Las Terrenas
Las Galeras
San José de las Matas
San Francisco de Macorís
Restauración
La Vega
Sánchez
Samana
Bahía de Samana
CORDILLERA CENTRAL
Jarabacoa
Pico Duarte
Cotuí
Sabana de la Mar
Bánica
PARQUE NACIONAL LOS HAITISES
Nisibón
Elias Piña
Las Matas de Farfan
Sabaneta
Bonao
Sabana Grande
Miches
San Juan de la Maguana
Constanza
CORDILLERA ORIENTAL
Monte Plata
Macao
El Seibo
El Cercado
Piedra Blanca
Hato Mayor
Padre las Casas
Bávaro
La Descubierta
San José de Ocóa
Higuey
Punta Cana
SIERRA NEIBA
Boca Chica
Juan Dolio
La Romana
San Rafael de Yuma
Galvan
Azua
Haina
Jimaní
Lago Enriquillo
SANTO DOMINGO
Boca de Yuma
San Pedro de Macorís
Duvergé
Bahía de Ocoa
San Cristóbal
Baní
Isla Catalina
Bayahibe
PARQUE NACIONAL DEL ESTE
Cabral
Bahía de Neiba
Barahona
Las Salinas
SIERRA BAHORUCO
Isla Saona
N
Pedernales
Paraiso
Bahía de Las Águilas
Oviedo
PARQUE NACIONAL JARAGUA
Isla Beata
0
40 km

though you can also fly via the States or various stops in Europe; try Iberia Airlines for the least expensive deals. Visitors from Australia and New Zealand will need to travel first to the US or Europe and pick up onward connections from there. Most flights go into Santo Domingo, but some fly into Puerto Plata. For phone numbers of airlines see pp.12–18 and 36–38.

Options for arriving in the Dominican Republic **by boat** are mostly limited to hitting the country as one of the ports of call on a longer **Caribbean cruise**. For a list of cruise operators see pp.14 and 16.

Otherwise, it is possible to arrive via **ferry** from Mayaguez, Puerto Rico, on *Ferias del Caribe* (☎809/688-4400, Puerto Rico ☎787/832-4800), but it's a long, uncomfortable overnight trip. Ferries depart Mayaguez three times a week; the cost is US$144 one-way, plus the US$10 entry tax and US$60 for a private cabin.

Entry requirements

Citizens and permanent residents of the US, Canada, the UK, Ireland, Australia and all EU countries don't need a visa when visiting the Dominican Republic, but must obtain a ninety-day Dominican Republic **tourist card** for US$10 (US dollars only) at the airport on arrival. New Zealanders need to apply for an $A80 visa from the embassy as well.

Money and costs

The official Dominican currency is the **peso (RD$)**, which comes in notes of 5, 10, 20, 50, 100, 500, 1000 and 5000; there are also 0.10, 0.25, 0.50 and 1 peso coins, though only the last sees much use. The exchange rate varies from day to day, but typically hovers at around 16–17 pesos to the US dollar. It's impossible to find Dominican pesos outside the country, but visitors are well advised to come armed with a substantial amount of US dollars, as these are the most readily accepted (and exchangeable) foreign currency in the land. The best places to **change money** are the **banks**, which offer good exchange rates; keep your receipts, as this allows you to exchange 30 percent of the pesos back into hard currency (dollars or euros) on departure. In a pinch, smaller **casas de cambio** are fine, though you should avoid the **street moneychangers**.

The Dominican Republic is one of the last true budget destinations in the Caribbean. Package deals are relatively low-priced, and in many parts of the country shoestring travellers can spend as little as US$30/£19 per day. The savings are spread unevenly, though, and some things are pricier here than elsewhere: riding from town to town via public transport can cost as little as US$0.35/£0.20, but car rental will set you back at least US$45/£28 a day.

Information, websites and maps

The glossy **promotional material** handed out by Dominican Consuls and Tourist Agencies are pretty to look at but seriously lacking in hard facts. With the emphasis on the package vacations that have earned the country so much money, they hold little value for independent travellers. Their **maps** are likewise relatively useless, though there are several excellent ones of the country available, including the 1:600,000 Dominican Republic map published by Berndtson & Berndtson.

Getting around

The Dominican Republic's **bus** companies provide an excellent, inexpensive service over much of the country. Lines at the stations move quickly, there's plenty of room for luggage on the vehicles and trips are relatively pleasant. Even more extensive, and cheaper, is the informal network of **guaguas** – ranging from fairly decent minibuses to battered, overcrowded vans – that cover every inch of the DR; in most cases, you should be prepared for some discomfort – and you'll have a hard time fitting in much luggage. **Taxis** are another option for getting around the cities, and by foreign standards are relatively cheap; reputable operators are listed throughout the chapter.

Car rental is common as well, but the

Websites

The Dominican Republic maintains a large presence on the **web**, though, as ever, ferreting out a specific piece of information can take some time. The following are a few tried and tested sites.

www.computan.on.ca/~pdowney.travel.html A dizzying array of links to hundreds of Dominican-related sites and a deep archive of travellers' personal accounts of all-inclusive vacations.

www.dominican-mirror.com Hourly updated satellite photographs of the DR, and current windsurfing weather conditions for Cabarete.

www.dr1.com The most heavily trafficked tourist message board, and a useful daily news bulletin on the country.

www.hispaniola.com A good site dedicated to Dominican tourism, with a Dominican Spanish phrasebook, daily weather and an interactive map of Cabarete.

www.popreport.com An exhaustive news bulletin and comprehensive roundup of tourist attractions and businesses in the Puerto Plata area.

cost is generally high. **Domestic airlines**, on the other hand, are reasonably economical, and can make sense if you're not exploring much beyond the main centres. Finally, a number of **tour operators** in Santo Domingo, Puerto Plata and the all-inclusive resorts organize individual itineraries and packages with transport included.

By bus

Caribe Tours (in Santo Domingo ☎809/221-4422) boasts by far the most extensive bus network, while **Metro** (in Santo Domingo ☎809/566-7126) can get you from the capital to the Cibao, Puerto Plata and the Samaná Peninsula. Both have comprehensive brochures available in their stations, listing destinations and departure times. In addition, you'll find several regional bus companies, though vehicles and drivers tend to vary more in quality. Unless it's a public holiday, you won't need **advance reservations**, but you should arrive at least an hour before the bus leaves to be sure of getting a seat. As the bus companies strive to stay in competition with *guaguas*, rates are extremely cheap. Even a cross-country trip from Santo Domingo to Samaná or Monte Cristi will set you back no more than RD$70, while shorter trips fall in the RD$40–50 range.

By guaguas, públicos and motoconchos

The informal system of *guaguas*, an unregulated network of private operators, is a distinctive Dominican experience that you should try at least once. Aside from the local colour, they're worth using because they're incredibly cheap and cover far more of the country than the bus companies. To catch a *guagua*, either ask for the location of the local station or simply stand by the side of the road and wave your arms at one as it passes. For longer trips, you'll often have to transfer *guaguas* at major towns, but even the longest leg of the trip will cost no more than RD$40; more often, you'll be paying RD$5–10.

Santo Domingo to the southeast and the Barahona region are often served by far more comfortable, air-conditioned **minibuses**; along the Silver Coast, the vans are augmented by private cars called *públicos*, which charge RD$5 and only go to the next nearest town and wait to fill up before heading off. *Públicos* also make up part of the **city transport** system in Santo Domingo, and dominate it in Santiago. City routes rarely cost more than RD$2. In Puerto Plata and other smaller towns, city transit is instead in the form of *motoconchos*, inexpensive, small-engined motorbikes that ferry you from place to place; they're faster than the *públicos* but can be dangerous.

By car

Car rental is expensive in the DR, though you can cut your costs a bit – and avoid a lot of hassle – by booking in advance with an international operator. Rates start around US$45–50 per day, with unlimited mileage but no discount for longer rental periods; you should also get full collision insurance, an extra US$10–12 per day. Even with collision, though, you're contractually responsible for any damage up to RD$25,000. You should therefore take special care to note *all* dents, scratches and missing parts before signing off. Dominicans drive on the **right-hand side of the road**, often at a breakneck pace. You'll have to keep a careful eye out along the highways, as large commercial buses and cargo trucks constantly veer into the opposite lane to pass slower vehicles.

By plane

If you're travelling across the country, say from Santo Domingo to Samaná, and aren't especially interested in what lies in between, it's worth considering a **domestic flight**. Air Santo Domingo (℡809/683-8006, ⓦwww.airsantodomingo.com) is a good local carrier, affiliated with Air Europa, offering fast, fairly priced connections between Puerto Plata, Punta Cana, El Portillo (near Las Terrenas), La Romana, Santiago and Santo Domingo. Flights cost RD$500–1000 and last no more than an hour.

Accommodation

The Dominican Republic has become the most popular destination in the Caribbean thanks to its preponderance of **all-inclusive hotels**, which make package vacations here far cheaper than elsewhere in the region. The all-inclusives do, though, have their downside: the food is usually not that great, and you'll be stuck in a walled-off complex for the whole of your trip, which can get a bit claustrophobic. There are, however, plenty of other options for travellers wanting to get out and see the country: luxury high-rise resorts along the capital's Malecón, independently operated beach hotels, rooms for rent in Dominican family homes, and an assortment of bearable budget hotels, many with private bath, hot water and a/c. Away from the main tourist spots expect to pay around RD$150–300 for the night; in resort towns prices rise to RD$250–500. **Reservations** are essential for the all-inclusives, where you'll get up to 75 percent off the price by booking with a travel agent before you arrive as part of a package.

There are **no youth hostels** in the DR, but a good way to cut expenses are the traditional *pensiones* still found in many towns, though over the past two decades they've begun to die out. There are also no **campgrounds**, and few travellers choose to camp here because of the lack of regulation.

Food and drink

If you take all your meals at an all-inclusive hotel, you'll get little sense of how Dominicans **eat** and **drink**; the "international" buffet fare on offer at these resorts can't compete with the delicious, no-nonsense cooking at the many mom-and-pop restaurants just outside their walls. Dominicans call their cuisine "comida criolla", and it's a delicious – if often a bit greasy – blend of Spanish, African and Taíno elements, with interesting regional variants across the island. Dishes usually include rice and beans – referred to locally as *la bandera dominicana* (the Dominican flag) – using either *habichuelas* (red beans) or the tiny black peas known as *morros*. Most often the rice is supplemented with chicken, either fried, grilled or served *asopao* (in a rich, soupy sauce). Invariably main courses come with *plátanos* (deep-fried green plantains, which locals often inundate with ketchup), and a small coleslaw salad. Outside of the major cities, **vegetarians** will often have to stick to rice and beans.

Local **breakfasts** are traditionally starchy and huge, and typically include *huevos revueltos* (scrambled eggs), sometimes *con jamón* (with bits of ham mixed in); *mangú*, mashed plantains mixed with oil and bits of fried onion; and *queso frito*, a deep-fried cheese. Dominican **lunches** are the day's main meal. Aside from the omnipresent chicken, popular main courses include *mondongo*, a tripe stew strictly for the strong of stomach; *mofongo*, a tasty blend of plantains, pork rinds and garlic; and *bistec encebollado*, grilled steak topped with onions and peppers. **Special occasions**, particularly in rural areas, call for either *chivo* (roast goat) with *cassava*, a crispy, flat bread inherited from the Taínos; or *sancocho*, a hearty stew with five different kinds of meat. For the very best in Dominican eating, go for the **seafood**, which is traditionally prepared one of five ways: *criolla*, in a flavourful, slightly spicy tomato sauce; *al ajillo*, doused in a rich garlic sauce; *al horno*, roasted with lemon; *al orégano*, in a tangy sauce with fresh oregano and heavy cream; and *con coco*, in a tomato, garlic and coconut milk blend especially prevalent on the Samaná Peninsula. The best local fish are the *mero* (sea bass), *chillo* (red snapper) and *carite* (kingfish). Other popular seafoods include *langosta* (clawless lobster), *lambí* (conch), *camarones* (shrimp), *pulpo* (octopus) and *cangrejo* (crab).

As far as drinks go, Dominican **coffee** is among the best in the world. Most Dominicans take it *solo*, with a great deal of sugar added, which is the way it's sold for RD$1 by morning street vendors, and handed out for free in the petrol stations. Dominican *café con leche* is made with steamed milk and is extremely good. **Jugo de naranja**, fresh orange juice squeezed as you order it, is another omnipresent Dominican morning drink; be sure to ask for it *sin azúcar* (without sugar). Later in the day you should sample the fresh **coconut milk** sold by street vendors, and the many Dominican **batidas**, popular fruit shakes made with ice, milk and either papaya, mango, pineapple or banana.

There are several Dominican **beer** brands, but by far the best and most popular is **Presidente**, served in both normal-sized and surreally large bottles, and comparing favourably with beers from across the world. Also popular are the very good, inexpensive local **rums**, Brugal, Barceló and Bermúdez.

Phones, post and email

It's not hard to keep in touch with home by **phone** or **fax** while you're in the DR because storefront phone centres are scattered about the country, though the price can be a bit steep. These phone centres are run by DR's many **private telephone companies**. The oldest, most venerated and by far the most omnipresent company is **Codetel**, which charges RD$5 per minute to North America; RD$18 per minute to Europe; and RD$26 per minute to Australia and New Zealand. The rates are a couple of pesos cheaper if you use a Codetel **calling card**, sold at Codetel phone centres in denominations of RD$25, 45, 95, 145, 245 and 500. You also have the option of going to one of Codetel's competitors that have sprung up over the past decade, the most popular of which is **Tricom;** they charge RD$5 per minute to North America; RD$15 to Europe and RD$24 to Australia and New Zealand. **Local calls** cost RD$1 per minute, but it's important to note that a telephone call between towns in the DR is considered long-distance, and charged at the same rate as North American calls; all areas of the DR, however, are under one area code, ⓣ809. If at all possible avoid calling collect with any of these companies.

> The **country code** for the Dominican Republic is ⓣ809.

Dominican **correos**, or post offices, are notoriously slow; even if you use **special delivery** (highly recommended) you'll still have to allow at least three weeks for your postcard or letter to reach North America, and at least a month for it to reach Europe or Australasia. Postage costs RD$3 to North America, RD$4 elsewhere.

Email, on the other hand, is steadily growing in importance, with many phone centres in the larger cities offering internet and email access, and a few private cybercafés cropping up in the resort areas.

Outdoor activities

Opportunities for **sea sports** are naturally tremendous, ranging from swimming, snorkelling and scuba diving, windsurfing and surfing, to deep-sea fishing and whale-watching. Though many beaches are protected from powerful ocean currents by natural barriers, others have dangerous **riptides** along them, and should be avoided by all but the strongest of swimmers.

The vast majority of **Dominican reefs**

have been damaged beyond repair by careless local fishing practices, notably the daily dropping of anchors by thousands of small vessels. The only place you'll still find a large system of intact reefs is the stretch west of Puerto Plata, between La Isabela and Monte Cristi. By no coincidence, this is also by far the most remote coastal region in the country, and devilishly difficult to access for **scuba diving and snorkelling**. A number of tour operators and most all-inclusive hotels in the resort towns can take you to the more modest reefs around the island.

The north coast resort of Cabarete is known internationally as the **windsurfing** capital of the Americas. Learning here is a challenge due to the strength of the waves and wind, though a dozen different windsurfing clubs offer equipment rental and tutoring. **Surfing** is less organized and done mostly by locals. Though you won't find any schools for surfing, popular venues include Playa Encuentra near Cabarete, Playas Grande and Preciosa just east of Río San Juan and Playa Boba north of Nagua.

The country's five separate mountain ranges provide several options for **mountain sports**; most popular are mountain biking, horseback riding and several-day mountain treks. Cabarete's Iguana Mama (see p.336) is the one major mountain-bike tour outfit in the country, offering challenging daytrips into the Cordillera Septentrional and week-long mountain-bike and camping excursions from one side of the country to the other. The best **hiking** can be found along the trails leading from disparate parts of the Cordillera Central to Pico Duarte, the highest peak in the Caribbean; see p.343 for details. **Horseback-riding** excursions are also quite popular. In addition to the plethora of outfits that offer day rides along the country's many beaches, you'll find quality mountain-riding operators in Cabarete, Punta Cana, Las Terrenas and Jarabacoa. Also in the mountains, Jarabacoa is the centre for **white-water rafting and kayaking**; see p.342 for more information.

Finally, though there are several small, nondescript **golf courses** spread across the island, three of them stand head and shoulders above the pack: the Pete Dye-designed Teeth of the Dog course at *Casa de Campo* in La Romana, and the excellent Robert Trent Jones courses at Playa Dorada and Playa Grande on the Silver Coast. All three have the majority of their holes set on spectacular open oceanfront and are occasionally used as tournament venues.

Opening hours, festivals and holidays

Business hours in the Dominican Republic are normally 8.30am–6pm Monday through Friday, and 8.30am–12.30pm on Saturday. About half of the stores still close for the midday siesta. Banks are generally open Monday through Friday 8.30am–noon and 2–5pm, with a few open on Saturday.

The Dominican Republic has a bewildering barrage of **festivals**. On every day of the year, there seems to be some kind of celebration somewhere, the majority of which are regional *fiestas patronales*, held in honour of the city's or town's patron saint. These traditional fiestas are one of the great pleasures of a trip to the DR; the list overleaf covers only a few of the top events.

Crime and safety

Aside from the poorest neighbourhoods in Santo Domingo and Santiago, the Dominican Republic is a relatively safe place – though women travelling solo need to stay on their guard even here. In cities, take the same precautions that you would anywhere else: don't flaunt your wealth with fat rolls of pesos, leave your expensive jewellery at home and avoid walking alone late at night.

Corruption is rife throughout the **police force**; many officers do little besides collecting small bribes. Nevertheless, you shouldn't give an officer a bribe unless he first asks, albeit rather obliquely; if he does ask, you're probably best off complying, provided he doesn't ask for more than RD$20 or RD$30. The good news for you is that police are routinely instructed not to ask bribes of foreigners, and their only other focus is **crime**

Major holidays and festivals

January

Virgen de Altagracia

January 21, the most important religious day in the Dominican calendar, including a several-day pilgrimage to Higuey.

Duarte Day

Holiday in honour of the Father of the Country, with public fiestas in all major towns on January 26.

February

Carnival

The pre-eminent celebration of the year, held on every Sunday in February and culminating on February 27. The biggest festival is in La Vega, with Santo Domingo a close second.

Independence Day

Celebration of independence from Haiti and the culmination of the Dominican Carnival (Feb 27). The place to be is Santo Domingo.

April

Semana Santa

The Christian Holy Week (variable, usually early to mid-April) is also the most important week of Haitian and Dominican *vodú*. Festivals take place in the Haitian bateyes and in Haina.

May

Espiritu Santo

Huge celebrations in the capital's barrio Villa Mella, pueblo Santa María near San Cristóbal and the El Pomier caves, and San Juan de la Maguana – held seven weeks after Semana Santa.

June

San Pedro Apostol

A magnificent *Cocolo* festival in San Pedro de Macorís on June 29, with roving bands of *guloyas* performing dance dramas on the street.

August

Festival of the Bulls

Higuey's *fiesta patronal* (Aug 14), with processions coming into the city from all sides – some from as far as 30km – with cowboys on horseback and large herds of cattle.

December

Christmas

Guloya festivals in San Pedro de Macorís, Haitian Voodoo celebrations in the Haitian bateyes and rural groups of Caribbean-style Navidad carollers in the campos (Dec 25).

Festival of the Bulls

Traditional cattle festival in Bayaguana (Dec 28).

against tourists, which they are adamant about quashing; dial ⓣ911 in case of an emergency.

Penalties for **drug use and possession** are extraordinarily stiff, and Dominican prisons are notorious. Drug possession is the one crime you won't be able to bribe your way out of; whatever you do, don't carry any with you into the country.

Though violent attacks against **women travellers** are rare, many women find that the constant barrage of hisses, hoots and comments comes close to spoiling their vacation. Whatever you do, don't be afraid to seem rude; even the mildest polite response will be considered an indication of serious interest. Chances of trouble depend to an extent on where you are. Avoid walking alone on city streets late at night and you'll circumvent much of the risk; it's also a good idea to opt for private taxis over *motoconchos* and *guaguas* after dark.

History

Before Columbus, Hispaniola was inhabited by the **Taínos**, an Arawak group that had migrated up from the Amazon basin and maintained an advance culture on the island for centuries. This all came to an end in 1492, when **Christopher Columbus** "discovered" the New World. After stopping off at the Bahamian island of San Salvador, Columbus landed in what is today the Dominican Republic, where he encountered the Taínos. Attempting to circle around the island, his ship the *Santa Maria* grounded against a coral reef on December 25, 1492, forcing him to set up a small fort there – which he named La Navidad, leaving 25 men there before heading back with his remaining ships.

Upon returning in late 1493, Columbus found his fort burned and the settlers killed. He established his first small colony further east – **La Isabela**, today the village of El Castillo – where he set up a trading settlement to trade cheap European goods in return for large quantities of gold. La Isabela soon fell apart. Settlers died in the hundreds from malaria and yellow fever, and one disgruntled colonist hijacked a ship and headed back to Spain to complain. Columbus followed him back in 1496, and during his absence the colony was abandoned, with most Spaniards re-settling at Santo Domingo along the mouth of the Ozama River. When Columbus returned in 1498, the colonists refused to obey his orders, and in 1500 he was sent back to Spain in chains.

Spain's King Ferdinand replaced Columbus with **Nicolás de Ovando**, with instructions to impose order on the unruly outpost. Ovando instigated the monumental construction in today's Zona Colonial and engaged in the systematic destruction of Taíno society, apportioning all Taínos to Spanish settlers as slaves and forcing their conversion to Christianity. Lacking resistance to Old World diseases and subjected to countless acts of random violence, the Taínos were quickly exterminated through overwork, suicide and disease.

To make up for the steep decline of forced labour, the Spaniards began embarking on **slaving expeditions** throughout the Caribbean and Central America in 1505, laying the foundation for future Spanish colonies. By 1515 the Spaniards had wiped out enough Native Americans that they began looking to slave labour from Africa, setting in motion the African slave trade. Santo Domingo's power slowly eroded as Spain branched out across the Americas, and by the end of the sixteenth century was little more than a colonial backwater. The **French** began encroaching in 1629, settling the island of Tortuga and branching out from there onto the western side of Hispaniola. When the French colony's slaves revolted in the early nineteenth century, they had little trouble invading and occupying Spanish Hispaniola, ruling it for 21 years. Only in 1843 were the Spanish colonists able to boot the invaders out, and for the first time establish the Dominican Republic as an independent country.

But this independence did not last long. A series of warlords known as **caudillos** tore the country apart in their quest for money and power, and in 1861 strongman Pedro Santana sold the island back to Spain. The Spaniards didn't last long, though; almost immediately a new revolutionary movement was formed, and the occupiers were forced to withdraw in 1865. A renewed period of extended civil warfare between *caudillos* ensued until the **United States** intervened in 1914. The Americans stayed for over eight years, successfully reorganizing the nation's financing but instituting a repressive national police. When the US left, this new police force took control, and its leader **Rafael Leonidas Trujillo** maintained absolute totalitarian control over the Dominican Republic for three decades. In the late 1950s, though, Cuba's Fidel Castro took an interest in overthrowing the dictator, and concerns about a possible Communist takeover prompted the CIA to train a group of Dominican dissidents, who **assassinated** Trujillo in a dramatic car chase on May 30, 1961.

Upon Trujillo's death, Vice President **Joaquín Balaguer** rose to power, and continued his totalitarian practices. Balaguer was deposed in a popular 1965 uprising, but the US military again intervened and soon placed him back in control. Only in 1978 was he forced to hold free and fair elections – and was promptly thrown out of office, only to win it back in 1986 after an extended economic crisis. Balaguer managed to edge out his rivals again in 1990, but left the presidential race in 1994 when it was obvious that he would not beat **Leonel Fernández**, who ran a slick, centrist American-style campaign and edged the competition out by a few thousand votes. 1998 saw the first back-to-back free and fair elections in the Dominican Republic's history, as Fernández gave way to political opponent and current Dominican President **Hipolito Mejia**. The Dominican Republic has also enjoyed the highest economic growth rate in the entire hemisphere (though this has slackened of late), and the outlook today for the nation is better than it has been in centuries.

6.1

Santo Domingo and around

Santo Domingo isn't the tropical paradise most travellers come to the Caribbean in search of, but at the core of the rather bewildering sprawl the old Spanish colonial capital – the very first European city of the New World – lies magically intact along the western bank of the Río Ozama. This was the domain of **Christopher Columbus**: founded by his brother Bartolomé, ruled by him for a time and claimed a decade later by his son Diego. After five centuries, the Columbus palace can still be found alongside the cobblestone streets and monumental architecture of the walled, limestone city the family built.

Far more than just history makes Santo Domingo an integral part of any trip to the Dominican Republic; it is, after all, the modern face of the country, and as such has a non-stop liveliness not seen in many other places. The vitality extends, though in a slightly more disappointing manner, to the very reachable beaches east of the city, at **Boca Chica** and **Juan Dolio**, both fairly built-up resorts.

Santo Domingo

Most visitors to **SANTO DOMINGO** understandably make a beeline for the **Zona Colonial**, Santo Domingo's large, substantially intact colonial district, home to dozens of wonderful old buildings and a dramatic setting right on the river. Many never bother to venture outside of this expansive, historic neighbourhood, but while it rates the most attention you should also make the effort to check out at least a few other diversions – especially around the barrios of the **Gazcue** and **Malecón** – throughout the city.

Arrival and getting around

The majority of visitors arrive at **Aeropuerto Internacional Las Américas** (℡809/549-0858), the country's largest, located 13km east of the city proper. The airport is far enough away from the city centre to make a **taxi** the most efficient way into town if you're not renting a car; you shouldn't pay more than RD$300.

A fairly sophisticated bus system links Santo Domingo to the rest of the country. If arriving by **bus**, you'll have no trouble finding a taxi or public transport from your terminal, including Caribe Tours at Av 27 de Febrero and Navarro (℡809/221-4422); Metro at Máximo Gómez 61 and Av 27 de Febrero (℡809/566-7126); and Terrabus at Guarocuya 4 (℡809/531-0383).

There is no official **public transit** system in Santo Domingo, but the informal network of *públicos* and *guaguas* manage to cover every inch of the city and can get you pretty much anywhere for under RD$10. Just stand on the corner of a major street and wave your arms at the first car with a taxi sign. More comfortable are private **taxis**; reputable operators include Atupal (℡809/554-0922), Cristiano (℡809/594-2049) and El Refugio (℡809/687-1572).

Accommodation

There's a wide variety of **accommodation** in the city, but budget rooms in decent neighbourhoods are hard to come by. Most expensive are the high-rises along the **Malecón**, which have great rooms and service. If you've got this kind of money, though, consider one of the smaller pensions tucked away in the **Zona Colonial**. For peace and quiet at a more reasonable rate, head to one of the small hotels in residential **Gazcue**.

Zona Colonial

Aida El Conde 474 and Espaillat ⓣ809/685-7692. The only hotel with balcony rooms on El Conde and a good bargain for clean, simple accommodation. ②

Nicolás Nader Luperón 151 and Duarte, ⓣ809/687-6674, ⓕ565-6204, ⓔhostal@naders.com. A well-regarded, small luxury hotel with spacious, tastefully decorated rooms in a colonial-era mansion. ③

Palacio Duarte 106 and Ureña ⓣ809/682-4730, ⓕ687-5535, ⓦwww.dominican-rep.com/Hotel-Palacio.html. Perhaps the best place in the old city for the money, featuring large rooms, attentive service and all the amenities in a 1628 mansion. ③

Malecón and around

Duque du Wellington Independencia 304 ⓣ809/682-4525. Small hotel a block from the water with friendly service and clean, spacious rooms. Hot water, A/C, telephone and cable TV. ②

Maison Gatreaux Llúberes 8 ⓣ809/687-4856. Great value. Large rooms with A/C, comfortable beds and especially strong hot showers. US$2 extra for cable TV. ②

El Napolitano Malecón 101 ⓣ809/687-1131, ⓕ687-6814, ⓦwww.hotelnapolitano.com. Good value compared to the other large seaside establishments, with spacious, modern rooms, ocean-view swimming pool, casino, two restaurants and beauty parlour. ③

Renaissance Jaragua Malecón 367 ⓣ809/221-2222, ⓕ686-0528, ⓔh.jaragua@codetel.net.do. Massive luxury resort with big rooms, great service, swimming pool, hot tub, four restaurants, bar, disco, casino and a tropical garden. ⑥

Gazcue

Felicidad Aristides Cabrar 58 ⓣ809/221-6615. Clean rooms in a small *pensión* with hot water. Not particularly attractive but the neighbourhood is quiet and pretty. ①

La Grand Mansión Danae 26 ⓣ809/689-8758. Unpretentious and functional on a quiet residential street, with private hot-water bath and nice rooms. ❶

The Zona Colonial

Though the **Zona Colonial** – straddling the western mouth of the Río Ozama – is crammed with monumental architecture, it's very much a living neighbourhood thanks to the many cafés and clapboard row-houses where thousands of people live and work. The most important monuments can be seen in a single day; thorough exploration requires two or three.

The town gates east to Parque Colón

A good place to begin exploring is the massive **Puerta de la Misericordia** (Gate of Mercy) on Hincado and the Malecón, a sixteenth-century fortified city entrance. On February 27, 1844, Ramón Mella fired off the first shot of the revolution against Haiti here. Follow Mella's torchlit route up Hincado to Calle El Conde and the **Puerta El Conde**, an imposing stone structure where Mella first raised the new national flag. The gate leads into beautiful **Parque Independencia**, a popular meeting place encircled by a traffic-choked ring road.

Stretching east from Parque Independencia is **Calle El Conde**, once Santo Domingo's main thoroughfare but closed off to motorized traffic in the 1970s and now a broad promenade lined with cafés, restaurants and stores. Follow it eight blocks to **Parque Colón**, a pleasant open space surrounded by beautiful colonial and Victorian buildings. At the west end of the park is the nineteenth-century town hall, while to the north you'll find a series of cigar and souvenir shops.

The cathedral and around

Most imposing of the buildings along Parque Colón is the **Catedral Santa María de la Encarnación** (daily 8am–6pm), originally intended to be the religious centre of the West Indies. Built between 1521 and 1540, the cathedral's **western facade** is a prime example of Plateresque architecture, a style that features an overabundance of fanciful ornamentation. The gold Hapsburg seal and statuary that once surrounded the main portals were stolen by Sir Francis Drake – the current ones are modest reproductions. Inside, under a Gothic-styled ribbed vault, and just to the right of the pulpit, **Santa Ana Chapel** bears the tomb of colonial administrator Rodrigo de Bastidas and the only surviving original stained-glass window, an angel hovering over Virgin and Child. Beside it, the **Chapel of Life and Death** has a Rincón Mora window – reminiscent of Chagall – showing a decidedly deranged John the Baptist baptizing a clean-shaven Christ.

Pass through the cathedral's southern door and you'll enter the enclosed **Plaza of the Priests**, once the city cemetery. Across the plaza, the **Alley of the Priests**, an attractive walkway lined with bougainvillea, leads past the old priests' quarters. Exiting onto the street from here, it's a block north to **Iglesia Santa Clara**, the New World's first nunnery. Built in 1552, it was severely damaged by Drake and renovated by a blustery local businessman named Rodrigo Pimentel.

From the entrance to the Alley of the Priests you can also walk a half-block west to **Plaza Padre Billini**, at Billini and Meriño, a small public plaza backed by a row of expensive antique, jewellery and clothing shops. If you're in no mood to shop, cross to **Casa Tostado**, on the plaza's southeast corner, built in 1503. Inside you'll find the **Museum of the Nineteenth-Century Dominican Family** (Mon–Sat 9am–4pm; RD$5), featuring a number of antique furnishings.

Calle de las Damas

Calle de las Damas (Street of the Ladies), the first road laid out by Nicólas de Ovando when he moved the town to the river's west side, received its name in

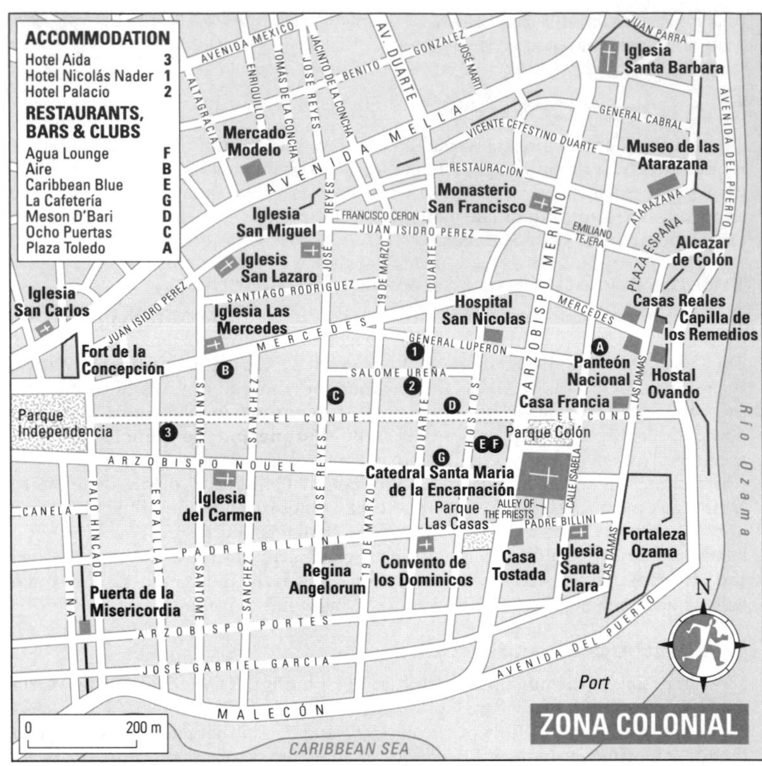

1509, thanks to the retinue of women who would accompany Diego Columbus' wife María de Toledo down the street to church. On the street's southern end **Fortaleza Ozama** (daily 9am–7pm; RD$10) was long Santo Domingo's most strategic site. Built in 1502 and enlarged over the centuries, it's set on a steep bank over the mouth of the Ozama and was the departure point for the Spanish conquests across the Americas. The largest structure is the medieval **Tower of Homage**, the most impenetrable part of the fortress and long used as a prison. Also on the grounds are the old arsenal and the excavated remains of the provisional fort from 1502.

Across the street you'll pass two more restored colonial buildings before arriving at **Casa Francia**, originally the home of conquistador Hernán Cortes. It was here that he plotted his conquest of Mexico; you'll find his family's coat of arms in the second gallery. Across the street, **Hostal Nicólas de Ovando** incorporates the homes of the Ovando and Davila families, both prominent in the early colony. Attached to the hotel's north wall is **Capilla de los Remedios**, the Davilas' private chapel, with an especially pretty triple-arched belfry.

Casa Davila looks directly across at **Plaza María Toledo** – a broad walkway with a sixteenth-century fountain – and the **Panteón Nacional** (Mon–Sat 9am–7pm; free), built from 1714 to 1745 as a Jesuit convent. In 1955 Trujillo renovated it and reinterred most of the major military and political figures from Dominican history. The building's Neoclassical, martial facade seems particularly suited for its sober task, topped with a prominent cupola flanked by statues of Loyola and Jesus. The interior has been completely redone, with Italian marble floors and an enormous central chandelier. Beside the Panteón is **Casa de las Gárgolas**, named for the prominent row of five grimacing gargoyles above the door.

Plaza España

Calle de las Damas ends at **Plaza España**, an attractive, tiled open space surrounded on all sides by monuments and with terrific views across the river, thus explaining the outdoor cafés that proliferate. An intact section of the old town wall still skirts the eastern plaza, extending to **Puerta San Diego**, the colonial-era entrance from the port.

At the southern end of the plaza, **Museo de las Casas Reales** (Tues–Sun 9am–6pm; RD$15; ⓣ809/682-4202), built between 1503 and 1520, was the administrative centre of the West Indies, housing the Royal Court, Treasury and Office of the Governor. Inside, the museum's rather hodgepodge collection includes a few Taíno artefacts, Spanish navigational instruments, and an armoury donated by Trujillo with examples of weaponry used here since Columbus. Opposite the Casas Reales is the **Alcazar de Colón** (daily 9am–5pm; RD$20; ⓣ809/689-5946), the fortified palace of the Columbus family, built by Diego from 1511 to 1515. This building is the finest local example of the late Gothic style called **Isabelline**, characterized by plain, linear surfaces adorned only with Islamic portals and delicate vine ornaments. The museum itself holds an array of sixteenth-century ornaments, including religious tapestries, a display case of period silverware and a sixteenth-century harp and clavichord.

Bordering the Alcazar to the north is a winding row of colonial storefronts known as **Las Atarazanas**. Follow it to the end where the Reales Atarazanas, once the colonial port authority, contains the **Museo de las Atarazanas**, Colón 4 (daily 9am–6pm; RD$15; ⓣ809/682-5834). Inside you'll find the recovered booty from the wreck of the sixteenth-century Spanish galleon *Concepción*, sunk during a hurricane in the Bahía de Samaná.

El Convento de los Dominicos and around

Back to the south of El Conde, towards the Malecón, stand three ancient churches worth a detour. The oldest, the 1510 **Convento de los Dominicos**, Billini and Hostos (Mon–Fri 7–9am, 5.30–7pm, Sun 7.30am–12pm, 7–8pm), held the New World's first university, San Tomé de Aquino. Its striking stone facade is framed by decorative two-dimensional pillars; blue *Mudéjar* tiling runs along the top of the portal, and a profusion of red Isabelline vine ornamentation surrounds the circular window in the centre. A block east on Billini/José Reyes is nunnery **Regina Angelorum** (Queen of the Angels), with huge external buttressing, decaying gargoyles and a sombre stone facade. Knock on the caretaker's door in the back to have a peek inside, where you'll find an eighteenth-century Baroque altar with a stunning silver retable. Smaller but prettier is **Iglesia del Carmen**, erected at Arz Nouel and San Tomé in 1590. Its facade boasts a decorative Isabelline red-brick portal topped by a fanciful Islamic peak.

The Malecón

The **Malecón**, the capital's oceanfront boardwalk, commences within the Zona Colonial. An intact section of the old city wall follows it for 100m to **Fort San José**, built on a strategic oceanfront promontory after an attempted invasion by the British in 1655. The cannons that remain appear to point across the street at a fifty-metre high statue of **Fray Montesino**, a sixteenth-century priest who preached against the Taíno genocide. Further on you'll find **La Obelisca**, placed by Trujillo in 1941 to honour repayment of long-outstanding debt to the US. A kilometre west is another obelisk, **El Obelisco**, built in 1936 to commemorate Santo

Domingo's temporary re-christening as Ciudad Trujillo. Informal **party zones** abound along the capital's boardwalk, with especially lively scenes occuring nightly at the municipal port at Calle del Puerto, La Parillada along the San Jose fort, and at the intersection with Av Máximo Gómez.

Gazcue and Mirador del Sur

West of the Zona Colonial and north of the Malecón is rambling, tree-shaded **Gazcue**, a middle-class neighbourhood highlighted by the **Plaza de la Cultura**, Máximo Gómez and Ureña, a complex of museums alongside the National Theatre.

The first stop should be the **Museo de Arte Moderno** (Tues–Sun 9am–5pm; RD$10; ⓣ809/685-2153), four storeys dedicated to twentieth-century Dominican art, with a magnificent permanent collection on the second and third. Watch in particular for the paintings of **Candido Bidó**, whose stylized idealizations of campesino life have won international acclaim. The museum owns six Bidós, all of them on the second floor, including his most famous, *El Paseo a las 10am*, a stylized painting of a Dominican woman in a sunhat with a handful of flowers.

The plaza's other main attraction is the **Museo del Hombre Dominicano** (Tues–Sun 10am–5pm; RD$20; ⓣ809/687-3622), which holds an extraordinary collection of Taíno artefacts, and a good anthropological exhibit on Dominican *fiestas patronales*. Less enticing is the **Museo de Historia y Geografía** (Tues–Sun 9.30am–5pm; free; ⓣ809/686-6668), which takes you through an uneven collection of historical memorabilia from the past two centuries.

East of the Ozama

Though most attractions lie west of the Río Ozama, there are a few scattered points of interest along the eastern bank and beyond. The best-known of these is the controversial **Columbus Lighthouse** (daily 9.30am–5.30pm; RD$15; ⓣ809/592-1492) – known locally as **El Faro** ("the lighthouse"), a monument completed in 1992, the 500th anniversary of Columbus' "discovery". Within this bombastic eyesore stands the baroque **mausoleum of Christopher Columbus**, with dozens of flowery angels hovering above the marble casket alongside a 24-hour honour guard.

El Faro towers over the western end of **Parque Mirador del Este**, a pleasant stretch of manicured woodlands spanning the length of the barrios east of the Ozama. At the park's far eastern tip are a series of large caves dotted with freshwater lagoons. Known as **Los Tres Ojos**, "The Three Eyes" (daily 9am–5pm; RD$10), the Taínos used them for religious ceremonies; more recently they've been the setting for some half-dozen Tarzan movies.

Dominican syncretism

The syncretic religion **vodú dominicana** – the mixing of European and African religions in South America and the Caribbean – is very much a part of Dominican culture, though Eurocentrism and official disfavour make it an object of shame. Cousin to Haitian Voodoo, it came about during the colonial era, when European Christianity was imposed on African slaves from the Congo and West Africa. The Africans mixed Catholicism with their own belief system, and over time various Christian saints came to be linked to deities imported from Africa.

Vodú involves ceremonies using altars covered with depictions of saints, offertory candles, plastic cups of rum and crosses honouring the **Guedes**, bawdy cemetery spirits known to spout lascivious songs when they possess humans. **Possession** is an integral part of *vodú* ceremonies, both by saints and the spirits of dead Taíno warriors. You'll see *vodú* paraphernalia, including love potions, spray cans that impart good luck in the lottery and Catholic icons at the many *botánicas* in towns throughout the country.

Eating

Dining options range from the omnipresent *comedores* and *pica pollos* to gourmet restaurants with speciality cuisines from around the world. At the more expensive restaurants, expect to spend RD$300–400.

Zona Colonial

Caribbean Blue Hostos and El Conde ☎809/682-1238. Best restaurant in the city, set in a sixteenth-century mansion but with very modern décor; all food is cooked in the restored 1520 brick oven. Try the sushi, the shrimp risotto, the great Caesar's salad and a *trufa mágica* for dessert.

La Cafetería El Conde 253. Best of the cafés along El Conde and a hangout for local artists. Delicious breakfasts with fresh orange juice and *café con leche*.

Plaza Toledo Isabela la Católica and Luperón. Beautiful outdoor courtyard featuring linguini with shrimp or criolla sauce and delicious dessert crepes.

Malecón

Fogarate Malecón 517. Some of the best Dominican food in the city, doled out in a fun atmosphere full of multi-coloured thatched roofs. Try the traditional *asopao* rice with chicken dish served in a battered tin bowl.

Vesuvio Malecón 521. Most renowned restaurant in the city, deservedly so for its vast array of delicious, if expensive, pastas. Next door they have a more downscale dining room for pizza, sandwiches and crepes.

Gazcue

Don Pepe Pasteur 41 and Santiago ☎809/686-8481. This is the place to go if you've budgeted for one big splurge. The menu is a display of fresh seafood on ice, including lobster and an assortment of fish.

La Mezquita Independencia 407. Outstanding little seafood restaurant with a cozy dining room and a loyal local following. Specialities include mero (*criolla* or *al orégano*), octopus, and *lambí*.

El Provocón 4to Santiago and José Pérez, with other locations throughout the city. Outdoor patio offering heaping portions of grilled chicken, rice-and-beans and salad. Open 24 hours.

Outer districts

Lumi's Park Av Lincoln 809 just north of 27 de Febrero. Fun outdoor, tropical garden atmosphere in which you can enjoy home-style Dominican *mofongo* and grilled steaks.

Tacos del Sol Av Lincoln 609 and Locutores. Popular outdoor Mexican joint with tacos, burritos and fajitas, though the frozen daiquiris and pleasant outdoor plaza are what attract the crowds.

Drinking, nightlife and entertainment

The Malecón is the traditional focus of **nightlife**; along with some of the city's finest dance halls, the boardwalk is crowded with outdoor restaurants that start getting crowded around 10pm and stay open into the early morning. There are also clubs across the city that specialize in **Cuban son**. Weekends see plenty of activity, but the busiest night for local clubs is Monday, when most are booked with big-name acts.

The Zona Colonial is a great place to go **bar-hopping**. At night the ruins are especially atmospheric, and dotted around them are a variety of neighbourhood joints, jazz bars and slick New York-style clubs. The other major centre is the Plaza Central, where most wealthy young Dominicans hang out. The Malecón also has a number of informal set-ups with a liquor shack surrounded by tables and chairs; most popular of these is *Plaza D'Frank*, two blocks west of the *Centenario Hotel*.

Bars

Agua Lounge Hostos and El Conde, Zona Colonial. Super-hip, tremendously popular small club on the second floor of *Caribbean Blue*. The crowds show around 1am.

Meson D'Bari Hostos and Ureña, Zona Colonial. Atmospheric after-work gathering place notable for its soundtrack of traditional *bachatas*, *merengue périco ripao* and old-style Cuban *son*.

Ocho Puertas José Reyes 107, Zona Colonial. Trendy techno bar set in a gorgeously restored colonial warehouse, with lounge rooms and a young, wealthy scene.

Discos and live music

Zona Colonial

Aire Mercedes 313 ⓦwww.aireclub.com. Home to the beautiful-people set in the city, this is a pretty remarkable, high-end rave joint with a mixed straight and gay crowd. Check out Wednesdays, which is "Foam Night", when the entire club is filled with four-feet-high, thick bubble foam.

Malecón

Jet Set Independencia 2253 ⓣ809/535-4145. Very nice seventh-floor disco with great views of the city. RD$50 cover.

Jubilee Malecón 367, *Renaissance Jaragua Hotel* ⓣ809/688-8026. Luxurious hotel disco featuring great sound and light systems, though serving expensive drinks. RD$100 cover.

Mauna Loa Calle Héroes de Luperón at Malecón, Centro de los Héroes ⓣ809/533-2151. Super-suave nightclub and casino with tables looking out onto a big-band stage reminiscent of the Roaring Twenties. If you love Buena Vista Social Club, this place is a must. RD$25 cover.

Outer barrios

La Guácara Taina Av Mirador del Sur ⓣ809/530-2666. The most famous club in the city, set in a huge natural cave.

Vieja Havana Av Máximo Gómez, Villa Mella. Great outdoor *son* hall best on Thursday and Sunday nights, when they hold old-style dance contests.

East of the Ozama

Monumento del Son Av Charles de Gaulle and Los Restauradores, Barrio Sabana Perdida. Famous outdoor *son* hall 5km north of the Las Américas highway.

Listings

Airlines Air Santo Domingo (ⓣ809/683-8006); Air Canada, Ricart 54 (ⓣ809/567-2236); American, El Conde 401 (ⓣ809/542-5151).

Banks Banco Popular (24-hour ATM machines), Calle Isabela la Católica and Tajeras; Calle Duarte and Mella. Scotiabank (24-hour ATM machines), Av Duarte and Mella; Calle Isabela la Católica and Mercedes.

Embassies Canada, Máximo Gómez 30 (ⓣ809/685-1136); United Kingdom, Av Lincoln 552 (ⓣ809/540-3132); United States, Calle Nicolás Pensión (ⓣ809/221-2171).

Hospitals Centro Médico Semma, Perdomo and Joaquín Peres (ⓣ809/686-1705); Clínica Abreu, Beller 42 (ⓣ809/688-4411).

Internet Deremate, Mercedes and Meriño (daily 9am–10pm, RD$35/hr).

Pharmacies Carol, Ricart 24 (ⓣ809/562-6767); San Judas Tadeo, Independencia 33 (ⓣ809/685-8165).

Police Dial ⓣ911.

Post office Av Héroes de Luperón just off the Malecón (ⓣ809/534-5838).

Telephone Codetel, El Conde 137; Tricom, Hermanas Mirabal 127.

Wiring Money Western Union, Av Lincoln 306 (Mon–Sat 9.30am–noon, 2–5pm).

Around Santo Domingo

Those looking for a bit of Caribbean beach should head to **Boca Chica**, a festive, though overrun resort town 10km east of the airport; further along is **Juan Dolio**, a strip of resort-heavy beachfront.

Baseball

Baseball is the most exciting spectator sport in Santo Domingo; two separate professional teams, **Licey** and **Escogido**, play in the winter professional league from mid-November through early February; games are at Estadio Quisqueya, Máximo Gómez and Kennedy (tickets RD$50–150; ⓣ809/565-5565, ⓦwww.beisboldominicano.com).

Boca Chica

Once one of the island's prime swimming spots, **BOCA CHICA** curves along a small protected bay, with transparent Caribbean water paralleling a long line of beach shacks. Sadly, the town has become so overwhelmed with tourism – and an accompanying plethora of shysters and informal "guides" – that it's no longer the best spot along the coast to spend some time, and a major draw these days is prostitution. Sitting on the **beach** is the main daytime activity, and the waters are low and calm enough for a good swim. Expect a big crowd on weekends.

Accommodation

There are plenty of **hotels** in Boca Chica, including three **all-inclusives** (only two are on the beach) and a sprinkling of small **hostels** all across town.

Boca Chica Vicini and 20 de Diciembre ⓣ809/523-4521, ⓕ523-4438, ⓔb.resort@codetel.net.do. Best local all-inclusive resort, with beautiful grounds, modern rooms and good food. ❸

Europa Calle Dominguez and Duarte ⓣ809/523-5721, ⓔhtleuropa@codetel.net.do. Highly recommended little French-run hotel with 33 ocean-view rooms and outstanding service. ❷

Tropic Lost Paradise Vicini and Del Sur ⓣ809/523-4424. Check here first if you're on a rock-bottom budget. ❶

Eating and drinking

There are several quality **restaurants** in Boca Chica, but the very best places to eat are the beachside food shacks serving fresh seafood. The **bars** are all along the main strip, Calle Duarte.

D'Lucien Duarte 69. Pricey patio restaurant with views of the promenade and fresh seafood displayed on ice.

Portofino Duarte 44. Beachfront pizzeria with great atmosphere.

Romagna Mia Duarte 74. Solid Italian fare in a pleasant little courtyard restaurant a block from the beach. The pastas are excellent, but you should treat yourself to the great fresh seafood.

Juan Dolio

Just east of Boca Chica begins a 25-kilometre-long line of rocky coast dotted with all-inclusive resorts, collectively known as **JUAN DOLIO**. This resort area has never quite matched Boca Chica, its northern rival, but a couple of its new resorts are the equal of any all-inclusives in the country – if it weren't for the beach. Though the sand is perfectly acceptable, dead coral under the water makes swimming and walking in the water uncomfortable, and the beaches are no match for what you'll find at Punta Cana. Nonetheless, you can have a good time here, primarily because of a couple of great independent hotels and the plethora of local nightlife.

Accommodation

Barceló Talanquera Carretera Las Américas Km 13 ⓣ809/541-1166, ⓕ541-1292. The tops of the Juan Dolio resorts, with palatial grounds, great rooms and suites, plus shopping gallery, three swimming pools and sports facilities. ❻

Fior di Loto Calle Central 517 ⓣ809/526-1146, ⓕ526-3332, ⓔhfdiloto@codetel.net.do. Highly recommended independent hotel decorated in the style of a Rajasthan palace, with twenty well-appointed rooms of varying sizes. The restaurant here is outstanding as well, and it's a great place to meet other travellers. ❷

△ A fort

Eating and drinking

For **dining**, stick to the two excellent Italian restaurants along Juan Dolio's main strip. The best place for **nightlife** depends on which night of the week it is. The entire Juan Dolio crowd heads to *Café Giulia* (Vila del Mar 288) on Mondays, *Chocolate Bar* (Calle Central 127) on Fridays and *El Batey* disco (Calle Central 84) on Saturdays.

Fior di Loto Calle Central 517. Tremendous pastas, traditional Dominican seafood dishes and some really excellent Indian curries set amid a pleasantly off-beat dining room of Far Eastern artefacts and private couches shielded by billowing curtains.

Restaurante El Sueño Calle Central 486. Formal Italian fare in a relatively swank outdoor patio and with outstanding service. In addition to the pastas, which are excellent, try the chicken scallopini in white wine sauce or bass filet in mushroom sauce.

6.2

The Southeast

The Santo Domingo valley stretches east along the coast from the capital, encompassing vast tracts of sugarcane. North of these fields roll the verdant hills of the Cordillera Oriental, which terminate at the bowl-shaped swamp basin of Parque Nacional Los Haitises. This is the Dominican Republic's **SOUTHEAST**, known primarily for its popular resort zones **Bávaro** and **Punta Cana**, bookends of a thirty-kilometre strip of uninterrupted sand lined with all-inclusives.

Past these attractions, the Southeast is fairly poor, rural and bereft of must-see sights – with the exception of two national parks. **Parque Nacional del Este**, poking into the Caribbean at the southeastern tip of the Dominican Republic, continues the theme of great beachfront, especially along **Isla Saona**, while the mangrove swamps of **Parque Nacional Los Haitises** hide several Taíno caves visited by boat.

San Pedro de Macorís

Crowded **SAN PEDRO DE MACORÍS**, seventy kilometres east of Santo Domingo, owes its uneven development to the boom-and-bust fortunes of the sugar industry. Victorian civic monuments built during the crop's glory years stand along the eastern bank of the Higuamo River, a far cry from the squalor of the surrounding neighbourhoods. Many of the 125,000 people of San Pedro are descendants of *Cocolos* – "The English", as many of them prefer to be called – imported during the early twentieth century as seasonal field labour. Their presence is most obvious during the **Cocolo festivals** held at Christmas and the Feast of San Pedro (June 24–30), when competing troupes of masked dancers known as **mummers** wander door to door along the major thoroughfares in elaborate costumes, and perform dance dramas depicting folktales and biblical stories.

Continuous urban migration has made the bulk of San Pedro a pretty miserable place, and the first view of its smokestacks and sprawling slums is a bit off-putting. What redeems it is its **Malecón**, a bustling seaside boardwalk with public beaches at either end. Head north from the Malecón onto Avenida Charro at the *Hotel Macoríx* to get a quick glimpse of the Victorian architecture built during the city's heyday. Foremost is the 1911 **Iglesia San Pedro Apostol**, Av Charro and Independencia, a three-aisled whitewash church with a prominent bell-tower. Time has been less kind to the old **town hall** a block south of the church, partially in ruins and occupied by a metalwork factory.

Far more than for architecture, though, San Pedro is famous for its baseball players, including Pedro Guerrero, George Bell and Sammy Sosa, and a pilgrimage to **Estadio Tetelo Vargas**, Av Circunvalación and Carretera Mella, a spacious, tattered concrete temple to the sport, is compelling for serious fans. Look in Santo Domingo newspapers for schedules; tickets are available during the winter baseball season on the night of the game for RD$85–115.

Practicalities

Though San Pedro is fairly large, there's not much in the way of **accommodation**; the top hotel in town is the amenity-laden *Howard Johnson Hotel Macoríx*,

Malecón/Deligne (Ⓣ809/529-2100, Ⓕ529-9239, Ⓔhj.macorix@codetel.net.do; ❷), which has impeccable service and a patio/swimming pool area that thrums with live merengue on weekends.

For **food** head straight to *Rubi Mar* (Av Charro across from Iglesia San Pedro), a romantic little riverside restaurant hidden behind the clapboard stalls where local fishers sell the day's catch; specialities include garlic shrimp and melt-in-your-mouth grilled dorado. San Pedro's **nightlife** is clustered along the ocean boardwalk; the current hot spot is the high-tech disco *Lexus*, and there are outdoor beer halls with ocean views and dancing all along the Malecón.

La Romana and Casa de Campo

LA ROMANA, 37km east of San Pedro, has been a one-company town since the South Porto Rico Sugar Company built the mammoth Central Romana mill in 1917; it was the only sugar operation not taken over by Trujillo during his reign. The mill was sold to Gulf & Western in 1967, who used the profits to diversify their holdings in the area, constructing the lavish *Casa de Campo* resort. The town itself is not especially interesting, though **nightlife** is good and a walk along the rambling barrio that borders the river's western bank makes for a pleasant hour. Also worth a visit in winter is **Michelin baseball stadium** on Abreu and Luperón at the city's west end, home of the La Romana Azucareros (check Santo Domingo newspapers for schedules; RD$50–150 for tickets) – perhaps not as exciting as the games in San Pedro, but good play nevertheless.

The **Casa de Campo** resort just east of La Romana, accessible via a marked Highway 4 turn-off, is a massive complex. It costs a bit more than the all-inclusives along Bávaro Beach, but you'll be spared the security paranoia, compulsory plastic wristbands and terminally bland buffet fare of most deluxe Dominican accommodations. The complex encompasses seven thousand manicured acres set along the sea and boasts two golf courses, a 24-hour tennis centre, fourteen swimming pools, equestrian stables, a sporting clay course and so forth. In addition to the spacious, comfortable rooms, there are 150 luxury private villas with butler, private chef and maid. The crowning pleasure is **Playa Minitas**, a gorgeous strand of beach protected by a shallow coral reef – nice enough that some spend their whole vacation on it.

Flanking the resort to the east is another Gulf & Western brainchild, **Altos de Chavón**, a high-concept shopping mall perched atop a cliff looking out over the Chavón River. Constructed to the specifications of a sixteenth-century Italian village with artificially aged limestone, it exudes dreary kitsch like few places in the country, its cobblestone streets littered with double-parked tour buses and its "Tuscan" villas crammed to the gills with dime-store souvenirs.

Practicalities

Acommodation at *Casa de Campo* (Ⓣ809/523-3333, Ⓕ523-8548, Ⓦwww.casadcampo.com; ❼–❽) won't disappoint, as rooms are large, well appointed and include all the amenities one would expect for the price. Décor is more in line with top-flight corporate hotels, as opposed to the dreary motel rooms you'll find in most Dominican all-inclusives. Within town, the solid but somewhat drab *Olimpo*, Abreu and Llúberes (Ⓣ809/550-7646, Ⓕ550-7647; ❷), qualifies as best overnight option, with good service, A/C, telephone and cable TV.

Casa de Campo used to have far better **food** than the other Dominican all-inclusives, but quality has deteriorated sharply over the past few years. Nevertheless, they do offer meal plans costing US$12 for breakfast, US$50 for breakfast and dinner and US$65 for all three meals. The best restaurants in La Romana are around the town's parque central, including *Shish Kebab* (Calle Reales a block south of the park), a decent little Lebanese joint, and the more formal *La Casita*, Richiez 57 and Doucuday (Ⓣ809/223-0568), whose Italian menu includes seafood pastas and lobster in cognac. La Romana's **nightlife** nets few tourists but can be a lot of fun. Head first to *Fava* disco on Gonzalvo just off the park.

Bayahibe and Parque Nacional del Este

The former fishing village of **BAYAHIBE** was once the most beautiful and remote spot along the entire coast, but due to over-building by the big all-inclusive hoteliers, the place has been ruined and retains little intrinsic beauty or interest. The only reason to stop here is to use it as base camp from which to visit **PARQUE NACIONAL DEL ESTE**, a park just east of Bayahibe on a peninsula jutting south into the Caribbean. The national park maintains a maze of forests, trails, caves and cliffs, home to an impressive array of birdlife and signs of early Taíno activity. Not much of the park, however, is conveniently accessible; no roads lead directly into its interior, and the best method of approach is to hire boats from Bayahibe to hit specific points along the rim.

The most popular part of the park – and rightfully so – is **Isla Saona**, an island off the southern coast lined with alternating stretches of idyllic, coconut tree-backed beachfront and mangrove swamp, unpopulated except for two tiny fishing villages. The larger ships stop off at **Mano Juan**, a strip of pastel shacks with a hiking trail that leads inland, an expensive restaurant and a couple of modest beachfront eateries; or **Piscina Natural**, a sand bar with a clear lagoon behind it good for swimming.

Another good option is to **hike** into the interior of the park to the Cuevas José María, a set of stunningly beautiful caves 10km from Bayahibe. Inside them is a treasure-trove of Taíno rock art, including 1200 pictographs depicting the major events of Taíno mythology and some historical events, including a 1501 peace treaty that the Taínos established with the Spaniards.

Practicalities

The road that leads into town ends at a car park crowded with tour buses that shuttle package-resort patrons to the larger catamarans docked a few metres further on. If you're on your own, you can sign on for a trip to Saona at **Scubafun** (Ⓣ809/301-6999; US$75), a local tour operator located right in the village centre.

Budget **accommodation** in Bayahibe is plentiful but somewhat dreary. The most pleasant of the dozen local *cabañas* are *Trip Town*, Malecón (Ⓣ809/707-3640; ❶) and *Nina*, Calle Segunda (Ⓣ809/224-5431; ❶, ❷ with breakfast), both on the waterfront. Of the **all-inclusives**, *Club Dominicus* is best (Ⓣ809/686-5658, Ⓕ687-8583; ❻), a lavish compound frequented mostly by Italian tourists that offers good food, a great beach, numerous watersports, tennis, aerobics and a dive centre. You can choose between a standard A/C hotel room and a more primitive but private bungalow.

For **lunch** go to the small unmarked *comedor* across from the police station, which has good fresh fish dishes daily. At night you can try *Kettly Berard* on Calle Segundo, a small Haitian-run establishment with good Creole cuisine – though you'll be subjected to a bit of harassment from the family salesman trying to sell you cheap souvenirs.

Boca de Yuma

On the northeastern tip of Parque Nacional del Este sits pueblo **BOCA DE YUMA**, for the most part passed over by tourism because of its lack of appealing beaches, though its setting along squat, ocean-pounded bluffs is undeniably impressive. Since Bayahibe has been so badly mangled by ill-conceived hotel construction, this has become the prime spot for independent travellers, with one great little hotel/restaurant and a nice enough beach across the river which you can reach via a RD$10 ferry.

The other major nearby attraction is fortified **Casa Ponce de León** (Mon–Sat 9am–5pm; RD$10), the home of conquistador Ponce de León located northwest of town in pueblo San Rafael de Yuma. He settled here after land was cleared and the locals slaughtered in the Higuey war of 1502–1504, and established an extremely profitable farm that provided Santo Domingo and the gold mines of San Cristóbal with cassava bread and salt pork. It's now maintained by the parks department, who have renovated the two-storey house into a museum meant to evoke de León's life and times. San Rafael is about 9km north of Boca de Yuma, so if you don't have a car use one of the hourly *guaguas* that ply the route between the two towns.

If looking for a **place to stay**, try *El 28* (Calle Principe two blocks north of the waterfront, ⓣ809/476-8660; ❷), an Italian-run set of bungalows with hot showers and a swimming pool. The chef at the hotel's restaurant is the proprietor's 74-year-old mother, who makes home-made gnocchi and other traditional Italian dishes, plus melt-in-your-mouth fresh fish.

Punta Cana and Bávaro

From Higuey, an unpleasant dusty town 50km or so north of Boca de Yuma known throughout the country as a holy city, a paved road winds 35km east to the tropical playlands of **PUNTA CANA** and **BÁVARO**, two resort areas on either end of a long curve of coconut tree-lined beach. Go elsewhere if you want to explore the country, as these resorts tend to be cities unto themselves: most encompass vast swaths of beachside territory, expansive tropical gardens and several separate hotels. Fortunately, the beach is big enough that it doesn't get overly crowded despite the 700,000 visitors each year; with enough fortitude you could walk some thirty kilometres without seeing the sand interrupted once.

Arrival and accommodation

If you're not flying to the resorts via charter at **Aeropuerto Punta Cana** (ⓣ809/688-4749), from where you'll be ferreted to your hotel by bus, you'll have to get here by private car or *guagua* from Higuey. **Taxis** are usually waiting at the airport and the entrance to the resorts; otherwise, call ⓣ809/552-0617 for pickup.

Most people staying in the **all-inclusives** are on package tours, so it's rare to actually call up such a hotel and request a room for the night. You'll get much better deals in any case if you book at home through a travel agent.

Bávaro Beach Resort ⓣ809/686-5797, ⓕ686-5859. Lovely grounds and spacious rooms, though the buffet food is lacklustre. Book a room in the Beach or Garden complexes, closer to the water, or the Palace, which is not all-inclusive and slightly more expensive, allowing you to eat outside the resort. ❺

Cortecito Inn Calle Playa Cortecito ⓣ809/552-0639, ⓕ552-0641. This is the place if you don't want to go all-inclusive. It's right by the beach, some rooms have private balconies, and there's a swimming pool and restaurant too. Breakfast included. ❸

Melía Bávaro ⓣ809/221-2311, ⓕ686-5427, ⓔhotelmelia@codetel.net.do. The very best of the resorts, slightly more expensive but well worth it, with opulent contemporary architecture, sculpted tropical gardens, and a choice of suites or bungalows. Luxurious amenities include bathrobes, a daily newspaper of your choice and a glass of champagne. ❺–❼

La Posada de Pleda Calle Playa Cortecito ⓣ809/221-0754. One of the few budget options, located in the large beachfront home of a local family. ❷

Ríu Resort ⓣ809/221-7515 ⓕ682-1645. Classy Julio Iglesias brainchild with swimming pools punctuated by artificial palm islands, great food and service. Some rooms come with a private hot tub. Casino, tennis courts, dive school, windsurfing and deep-sea fishing. ❼–❽

The beaches and inland

If you're not staying at one of the resorts, head to the public-access beach at **Cortecito**, a kilometre north of the first Bávaro turn-off from the highway – the only village left along the entire stretch – an agreeably laid-back hangout populated by backpackers, independent European vacationers and a slew of Dominican vendors with souvenir stalls set up along the sand. If even this is too much, head 6km south from Punta Cana to pueblo **Juanillo**, a fishing village with no amenities that sits on equally superb waterfront.

Eating and drinking

In the unlikely event you'll be **eating** outside of the resorts, go to *White Sands*, 1.5km north of Melía Bávaro, with a beachfront patio where you can feast on barbecue and great paellas. The budget-minded can also try *Tropical Bávaro Restaurant* in Cortecito, which offers fresh fish dinners nightly for RD$150. **Nightlife**, too, is concentrated in the resorts, but *Disco Mangú* is a dance hall/sports bar near the *Flamenco Bávaro* resort that stays pretty crowded all night.

Hato Mayor and Sabana de la Mar

Despite its lush surroundings, in the pretty rolling hills and orange groves of the Cordillera Oriental, overcrowded **Hato Mayor**, 40km north of San Pedro de Macorís on Highway 4, is one of the poorest towns in the region and has little of interest for visitors. Most get only a passing glance anyway while taking Highway 103, the only paved road to Sabana de la Mar and Parque Nacional Los Haitises. You're unlikely to want to **spend the night** in Hato Mayor, but in a pinch you can head to *Centenario*, Mercedes/Hincado (☎809/553-2800; ❶), the only formal hotel in town, with clean rooms and private bath but no hot water.

Sabana de la Mar is a dusty little port unremarkable but for its use as a setting-off point for the highly recommended boat tours of Parque Nacional los Haitises (see below). It also happens to be fairly convenient to the Samaná Peninsula (see p.324); ferries depart regularly from the wharf at the northern end of town (daily 11am & 5pm; RD$50). You won't really want to use Sabana de la Mar as a base for anything – the hotels are pretty substandard – but just east of the town (and close to the entrance of Los Haitises) is *Paraiso de Caña Hondo* (☎809/556-7483; ❷), which has a small restaurant and a very nice set of rooms, plus a natural pool with cascades.

Parque Nacional Los Haitises

PARQUE NACIONAL LOS HAITISES, a massive expanse of mangrove swamp that protects several Taíno caves, 92 plant species, 112 bird species and a wide variety of marine life, spreads west of Sabana de la Mar around the coastal curve of Bahía de Samaná. Though twelve hundred square kilometres in total, only a small portion of that is open to the public, accessible by organized tours.

The **Ruta Litoral** – the standard 2.5-hour boat tour – hits three main areas of interest within the park. First up is **Cueva Arena**, a large grotto that has numerous Taíno drawings of families, men hunting, supernatural beings, whales and sharks. You can stop for a half-hour at the beach cove here if you'd like, from which you get a good look at **Cayo Willy Simons** – once a hideout for the infamous pirate – recognizable by the dozens of birds circling around: pelicans, herons, terns, frigates, even an occasional falcon. The next stop is to grottoes **San Gabriel** and **Remington**, both with Taíno faces carved into their walls. From here you'll pass the ruins of a 100-year-old banana wharf, with pelicans perching on the remaining wooden supports, to reach **Cueva de la Linea**, which was once intended to hold a railroad station for the sugarcane that was grown in the area.

Practicalities

You'll need to hire a guide from Sabana de la Mar for the trip, which runs around RD$700 for up to four people. They can be picked up at the national park office at the town pier. The port of entry to the park is a tiny pier called **Caña Hondo**, entered via a signposted turn-off on the road to Hato Mayor at the village's southern end. From there you'll travel 12km along a bumpy dirt road to the pier before you set off along a mangrove-lined canal and into the bay.

6.3

The Samaná Peninsula

It's not hard to appreciate the beauty of **THE SAMANÁ PENINSULA**, a thin strip of land poking from the Dominican Republic's northeast. Perhaps the most appealing part of the whole country, the region boasts a coast lined with beaches that conform strictly to the Caribbean archetype of powdery white sand and transparent green-blue sea.

Besides bumming on the beach, visitors come to see the thousands of **humpback whales** that migrate to the Bahía de Samaná during the winter. Whale-watching has become a thriving local industry, peaking between mid-January and mid-March. Most whaleboats depart from **Santa Bárbara de Samaná** (generally shortened to Samaná), the largest town on the peninsula and a welcome break from the more typical beach-oriented tourist resorts. If the hustle and bustle of more typical Dominican towns becomes too much for you, head east to **Las Galeras**, a pristine horseshoe of sand that, despite considerable development in recent years, still maintains an air of tranquillity. Along the peninsula's north coast you'll find the beautiful beaches of the remote expat colony of **Las Terrenas**, a burgeoning hang-out for independent travellers.

The **Carretera 5 (C-5)** that skirts the Dominican north coast leads all the way from Puerto Plata to Santa Bárbara de Samaná. At Sánchez, which nestles in the northwestern corner of the rectangular bay, another good road with spectacular views crosses the mountains to Las Terrenas. Travellers heading this way can catch the half-hourly pick-up trucks from the Texaco station on the C5. Recently paved roads now link Samaná with Las Galeras and Las Terrenas although the road to the latter gets a little rougher after El Limón.

Samaná

Protected on its southern side by an elongated strip of land that breaks apart into a series of small islands, **SANTA BÁRBARA DE SAMANÁ** possesses a remarkably safe harbour, giving the city a tremendous strategic potential that's never been fully realized. The town is now more of a focus for travellers wishing to get away from the all-inclusives and the main embarkation point for whale-watching and other boat trips.

Arrival, orientation and accommodation

The C-5 that stretches along the country's north coast leads directly onto the Malecón – a pretty concrete boardwalk that divides the shops and restaurants from the ocean. Together, the C-5 (known locally as Avenida Rosario Sánchez) and the Malecón are the only major thoroughfares in the city. Incoming buses stop in the centre of the Malecón, easy walking distance from most hotels, while *guaguas* stop and set off from the large city market (El Mercado), right on the C-5, close to a few budget accommodations but a half-kilometre north of the seafront.

Samaná has an array of **accommodations**, from luxury resorts to dirt-cheap options, but the latter are not quite as comfortable as those you'll find in Las Terrenas to the north.

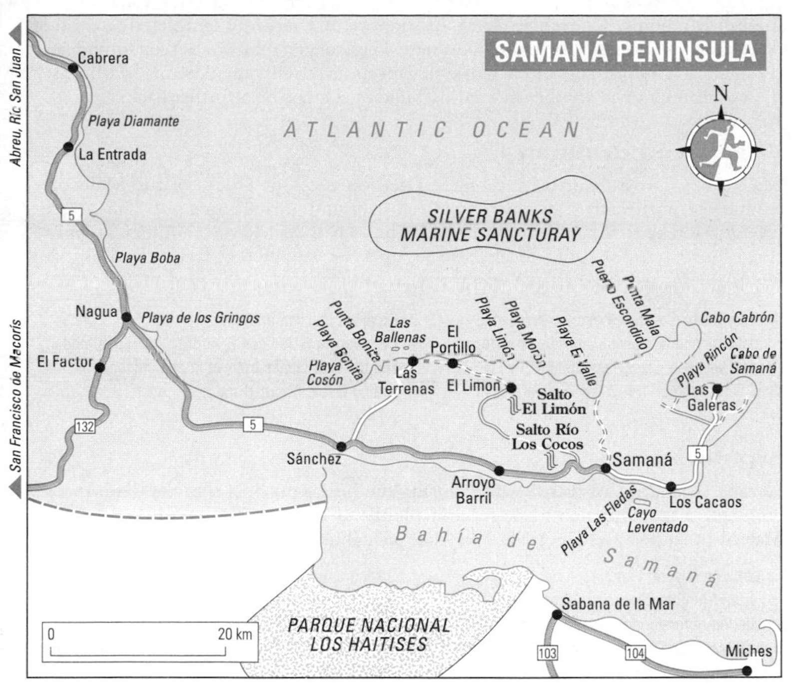

Bahia View Av Circunvalación ☎809/538-2186. Exceptionally clean budget hotel with a friendly proprietor and better than average rooms with private showers. ❶

Casa de Huespedes Mildania Calle Fco. Del Rosario Sánchez 41 ☎809/538-2151. Clean and tidy rooms with private showers in an immaculate Dominican house. ❶

Hotel Doria Duarte 1 ☎809/538-2041. Wildly popular small hotel off the Malecón. Clean, basic and well placed. ❶

Gran Bahía Las Galeras road ☎809/538-3111, Ⓕ538-2764, Ⓦwww.occidental-hoteles.com. One of the great gems of Caribbean resorts, with a majestic oceanfront setting east of town, immaculate grounds, and well-maintained rooms. ❹

Tropical Lodge Malecón ☎809/538-2480, Ⓕ538-2068, Ⓦwww.tropical-lodge.com. One of the best hotels on the peninsula, with modern rooms, hot showers, bay views, a superbly placed hot tub and attentive service. ❸

The Town

Samaná is undeniably charming, with pretty, spacious neighbourhoods, winding streets that amble up the hills and a warm sense of community intact. The centre of activity is the city's **Malecón**, a broad, concrete boardwalk across the street from numerous outdoor cafés, storefront shops and patches of park. At night the Malecón's restaurants and bars buzz with activity and music, a fairly mixed scene of Dominicans, expats and foreign visitors.

A few blocks back from the waterfront, the old First African Wesleyan Methodist Church of Samaná popularly known as **La Churcha**, Santa Bárbara and Duarte (daily 9am–6pm), tangibly maintains what African-American culture is left in Samaná. The prefabricated, tin-roofed structure was originally shipped over by the

English Methodist Church in 1823, in support of a recently emigrated African-American community that still remains here. These days it's known as the Dominican Evangelical Church and often works harmoniously with the African Methodist Episcopalian Church, another interesting building a few blocks further back.

Eating and drinking

Samaná's best **restaurants** are concentrated on the four blocks of the Malecón around the port, with waterside expat joints serving great French and Italian and several good spots for Dominican food. The expats also have a number of **bars** along the waterfront, while locals have set up a festive clutch of beach shacks serving beer, rum and fried chicken on the Malecón just west of the port.

Café de Paris Malecón 6. French-run expat hangout serving up delicious pizzas and crepes.
Camilo Malecón. Classy, reasonably priced Dominican restaurant right on the waterfront. Excellent chicken and rice.
L'Hacienda E De León 6. Affordable French food and the best steaks in town in an outdoor café setting below *Naomi* disco.

Nightlife

Samaná has a great **nightlife** scene during the busier times of the year, with three crowded discos open until dawn and plenty of outdoor restaurants along the Malecón that become especially lively late at night.

La Loba Av Rosario Sánchez. A fun, massive rough-and-tumble Dominican dance floor with a smattering of foreigners. RD$20 cover.
Naomi Malecón. Slick, dark and bustling meat market with great light shows and sound system, playing a mix of merengue and European techno. RD$40 cover.
Rancho Allegre Malecón. Traditional outdoor dance floor, with the familiar sounds of merengue and *bachata*.

Whale-watching

Humpback whales have used the Dominican Republic's Samaná Bay and Silver Bank coral reef sanctuary as a **nursery and breeding ground** for untold millennia. They return each winter after spending nine months fanning out across the North Atlantic and by mid-January more than twelve thousand of them move around the waters of the country's northeast coast. They're at their liveliest in Samaná's tepid depths, as males track females, compete for attention and engage in courting displays, while mothers teach their calves basic survival skills.

Adult humpbacks grow to 15m long, weigh up to forty metric tons, and are black with distinctive white patches. Among the behaviours that you may see while whale-watching are **breaching** – hurtling the entire body above the surface before landing back down in a spectacular crash – and the **trumpet blow** – a tremendous, low blast that can be heard from several kilometres away. Humpbacks also engage in the **whale songs**, an eerie combination of moans and chirps formed into short phrases that are shuffled and put together in a basic form of communication. All of this is done to advance the serious business of **mating and birthing**. The female gestation period is a full year, so calves that are conceived in the bay one year are given birth here the next; there's a good chance you'll see at least one of the babies, which can weigh a ton and are light grey.

Whale-watching as a local tourist industry was begun in the 1980s by Kim Beddall, then an itinerant scuba instructor with no formal training as a marine biologist although she's since been instrumental in the implementation of a code of conduct for whale-watch boats. Beddall still runs excellent **whale tours** through her Whale Samaná/Victoria Marine operation, Malecón (Ⓣ & Ⓕ809/538-2494; US$38), and if you're here during the season, you won't find a more enthralling excursion.

Around Samaná

Samaná's best attribute is its convenience as an inexpensive base from which to explore some of the peninsula's more compelling sights. Ferries leave three times daily to nearby **CAYO LEVANTADO**, the original Bacardi Island photographed in the 1970s rum campaign. Although it's undisputedly beautiful, the huge tourist infrastructure that's been set up around it somewhat destroys its desert island charm and unless you're visiting as part of a whale-watching tour, there are better places on the peninsula to spend a day on the beach. Along the eastern tip of the peninsula, and easily reachable by *guagua*, a series of attractive beaches lead toward **Las Galeras**, as pretty a spot as any along the coast, and the even better beach at **Playa Rincón**.

Las Galeras

A horseshoe-shaped beach cove sheltering a modest village at the far eastern end of the peninsula, **LAS GALERAS** has seen considerable changes over the last few years. Despite the construction of *Casa Marina Bay*, a large all-inclusive, and numerous other hotels near the main beach entrance, it still maintains a peaceful, timeless ambience. The solitude that Las Galeras was once famous for has now gone but it's been replaced with some tasteful amenities that should make most visitors' stays more comfortable. The beaches, however, are still as stunning as always.

Accommodation

Most of Las Galeras's **hotels** are found along the main road or spread out to the north and south behind the beach.

Casa Por Que Non Calle Las Galeras ⓣ809/538-0011 or 514/661-9013 (Montreal). Two light and airy rooms attached to a private house with a lovely garden. Excellent breakfasts every day and home-cooked dinners by arrangement. Open during winter only. ❷

Club Bonito Beach Road South ⓣ809/538-0203, ⓕ538-0061, ⓦwww.club-bonito.com. A beautifully designed and fabulously decorated establishment littered with odd maritime artefacts, with large rooms, a colourful garden, and a nice pool. The restaurant is well worth a try too. ❹

Paradiso Bungalows Calle Las Galeras ⓣ809/538-0210. The best of the several private bungalows on offer, right off the beach with a cosy, tropical communal garden. ❷

Todo Blanco Beach Road South ⓣ809/538-0201, ⓕ538-0064, ⓔtodoblanco@hotmail.com. Tasteful to the extreme and a genuine haven of tranquillity, with huge rooms, a pretty garden and a superb authentic Italian restaurant. ❹

Villa Serena northern beach road ⓣ809/538-0000, ⓕ538-0009, ⓦwww.villaserena.com. Housed in a beautiful faux-Victorian mansion with a large, manicured tropical garden on the beach, facing a small desert island. Perfect for honeymooners. Their restaurant is one of the best in town. ❻

Eating

There are plenty of **eating** options scattered along the main road on the way into town and also a good selection of restaurants in the main hotels.

Chez Denise Calle Las Galeras. Traditional French food and creperie on a terrace near the beach.

Dominican Kitchen beach entrance. Not so much a restaurant as a collection of shacks serving excellent seafood dishes. Prices can vary for tourists so check before ordering.

L'adventure Calle Las Galeras. French-run pizza joint with good-value specials.

Playa Rincón

Hidden from the rest of the peninsula by the upper prong at its easternmost end, **PLAYA RINCÓN** boasts the top Samaná beach bar none. Follow the signposted paved road north for approximately 8km from the Samaná–Las Galeras road, and then turn right, in a tiny pueblo, onto a rocky dirt road that leads onto the beach

(4x4 recommended). Alternatively take a boat from Las Galeras, departing at 9am from Dive Samaná, *Casa Marina Bay Resort*; US$10. Of all the warm, clear waters on the island, Rincón has the very finest – moderately deep with manageable waves and a bright turquoise transparency that can't be matched – combined with a three-kilometre stretch of whiter-than-white sand and a sprawling coconut forest behind it. For now the only buildings are a couple of Dominican fish shacks serving fresh seafood at both ends of the beach; check prices before eating but expect to pay around RD$100 per person. This is an eminently more enjoyable day out than Cayo Levantado.

Las Terrenas and around

Set midway along the peninsula's remote northern coast, the former fishing village of **LAS TERRENAS** has grown over the past twenty years from backwater to an expat-dominated resort town renowned for its buoyant nightlife. Though development has led to a new paved road from Sánchez and a town centre which, along with the beach, is lined with restaurants, bars and shops, the inland Dominican barrio remains much the same as it was.

Las Terrenas makes for a pleasant base camp from which to explore the northern part of the Samaná Peninsula; on either side are less developed beaches such as **Playa Bonita**; a day trip to the **El Limón waterfall** is also highly recommended.

Arrival, information and getting around

The only way to get to Las Terrenas **by road** if you don't have your own car is a RD$40 pick-up truck leaving every half-hour from the Texaco station at Sánchez. Alternately, you can **fly** into El Portillo Airport, 6km east of town, on Air Santo Domingo (ⓣ809/240-6094), which has daily flights from Puerto Plata, Punta Cana, La Romana and Santo Domingo.

You probably won't have too much trouble just walking where you want to go – the town's layout is exceedingly straightforward, with just one main thoroughfare, the Carretera Las Terrenas – but if you need a lift anywhere, **motoconcho** rides within town are RD$10 during the day, double that at night.

Accommodation

Development in Las Terrenas has meant the loss of most of its rock-bottom **accommodation** options. What remains are pricier inns and *cabañas*, though none that should be too much of a strain on anyone's budget. Note that nearby Playa Bonita (see opposite) also has a collection of more secluded hotels.

Cacao Beach Calle Playa Cacao ⓣ809/240-6000, ⓕ240-6020, ⓦwww.samana.net/cacao-beach. Tasteful all-inclusive with a stunning reception area and peaceful grounds. Comfortable, quality rooms in small *cabañas* scattered around the gardens. ④

Casas del Mar Calle El Portillo ⓣ809/360-2748. Clean *cabañas* with welcoming proprietors, access to the beach and a scenic location slightly away from the main part of town. ②

Diny Calle Playa Cacao ⓣ809/240-6113. Recommended budget hotel directly on the water, though it can be very noisy in the early morning. ①

Kanesh Beach Hotel Calle Playa Cacao ⓣ809/240-6187, ⓕ240-6233, ⓦwww.samana-lasterrenas.com/kanesh. Excellent-value beachfront hotel with better than average rooms and sea views. Wicked Indian food. ②

Las Cayenas Calle Playa Cacao ⓣ809/240-6080, ⓕ240-6070. A popular American hangout, *Las Cayenas* is a little inn in an old beachfront manor with a palm-shaded patio area. ②

Tropic Banana Calle Playa Cacao ⓣ809/240-6110, ⓕ240-6112, ⓔhoteltropic@codetel.net.do. The oldest hotel in Las Terrenas, and still one of the very best. The well-kept rooms are large, with private balconies, and the extensive palm-covered grounds include a swimming pool and tennis court. ②

The Town

Aside from spectacular day trips to the surrounding countryside, the beach, which stretches uninterrupted 2km in either direction from town, is the focus of daytime entertainment. Just west of the Carretera is the less lively beach area, which stretches a full 2km to **Playa Las Ballenas** – a section of the beach named for three oblong islands in the waters just beyond it that resemble breaching humpback whales – before ending in a patch of swamp. The beach east of the intersection has just recently been built up, and has a slightly funkier feel, dominated by low-end *cabañas* and bars until the construction peters out entirely.

Eating and drinking

In keeping with its expat-dominated culture, Las Terrenas's **restaurants** have a fully international flavour with Italian, Spanish, French, Mexican and even Indian options available. Most of the hotels along the beach have their own restaurants and bars and these tend to cater as much for passing trade as they do for residents. The social scene, too, tends to be based around the beachfront joints, with most of the action close to the main road.

Baro Latino Calle Playa Cacao. Bustling café with a huge menu including good breakfasts and pizzas. Good for people-watching too.
Casa Azul Calle Playa Cacao. Part of the redeveloped fishing shacks, serving terrific, if pricey, seafood.
Casa Boga Calle Playa Cacao. Another of the beachside shacks that serves the best fish in town.
Casa Coco Calle El Portillo. Reasonably priced pizzeria with a candlelit outdoor seating area.
Comedor Jahaira The only place to go for *comida criolla* in Las Terrenas, and incredibly inexpensive. From the town centre, head up the Carretera Las Terrenas and take the second dirt track on the right after the Centro Commercial.
Kanesh Beach Hotel Calle Playa Cacao ⓣ809/240-6187. Excellent Indian food that needs to be ordered at least one day in advance.
Nuevo Mundo Carretera Las Terrenas. This is the place to party in Las Terrenas, an insanely popular disco a few metres south of the main crossroads.

West of Las Terrenas: Playa Bonita and Playa Cosón

Playa Bonita, 13km of uninterrupted beach that begins just west of Playa Las Ballenas, boasts the kind of powdery white sand you might expect to see only in tourist brochures. There's been a fair bit of development in recent years but this has been done carefully and the **hotels** do little to detract from the beauty and serenity of the heavenly beaches. Indeed, if you're looking for natural beauty, peace and quiet, you're far better off staying here than in Las Terrenas. The best of the bunch is *Atlantis Hotel & Restaurant* (ⓣ809/240-6111, ⓕ240-6205, ⓔhotelatlantis@codetel.net.do; ❷), whose rooms are palatial and pretty; try to book either the Jamaica or the Grenada room, both with panoramic views of the beach. Also nice is the *Acaya* (ⓣ809/240-6161, ⓕ240-6166, ⓦacaya.free.fr; ❷), a modern hotel with A/C and all the amenities, including swimming pool, free snorkelling gear and a thatch-roofed beachside restaurant. The cheapest rooms on the beach and excellent value are *Casa Grande* (ⓣ & ⓕ809/240-6349, ⓦwww.casa-grande.de; ❷), five good-sized rooms in a large house.

From Playa Bonita's entrance, a sand road provides access for four-wheel-drives and motorbikes, past a beachfront populated at most by a few small groups of people taking advantage of the isolation to swim or sunbathe naked, until, after 6km, you reach **Playa Cosón** a small fishing village holding two gourmet beach shacks with tables and chairs on the sand, serving grilled, fresh-caught fish for a few pesos.

East of Las Terrenas: El Limón

Eleven kilometres east of town, and little more than a crossroads with a few shacks attached, dusty **El Limón** seems unpromising at first, but does make an ideal base for excursions to the magnificent El Limón waterfall to the south. Upon arrival you'll be beset by several local *buscones* trying to steer you to one of the excursion outfits; the best is Casa Santi, just south of the crossroad on the road to Samaná. The **waterfall** is accessible by horse from the town and takes 2.5 hours round-trip, well worth it to see the 50m of torrential white water dropping from a cliff in the middle of the wilderness. Expect to pay around RD$350 for the round-trip with a good lunch included.

From Las Terrenas, a **motoconcho** here costs RD$30, and during the day *guaguas* ply the El Limón route once an hour during the day for RD$20. Getting back is more of a problem if you're depending on public transport – it's standard practice (and safe) to hitchhike from here. Every hour or so, a *guagua* will pass by.

6.4

The Silver Coast

The Dominican Republic's **SILVER COAST**, 300km of prime waterfront property on the country's northern edge, is the most popular tourist destination in the Caribbean. With a seemingly unending supply of great beaches around the booming towns of **Puerto Plata** and **Cabarete**, such a designation is no surprise. The Carretera 5 skirts the coast all the way east from Samaná to just past Puerto Plata, making **getting around** this part of the region a breeze. The country's two major bus companies ply the highway, along with the *guaguas* and plentiful *público* taxis. Heading west of Puerto Plata is more of a challenge (but not impossible) if you don't have a four-wheel-drive.

Puerto Plata and Playa Dorada

PUERTO PLATA and **PLAYA DORADA** comprise the mass tourism capital of the Caribbean. The city of Puerto Plata is a vibrant Dominican town of 200,000 that's well worth exploring for its historic architecture and nightlife. Its core, the **Old City**, borders the port to the east, a narrow grid of streets that was once the swankiest neighbourhood in the country. Around the original town sprawls a patchwork maze of industrial zones and concrete barrios known as the **New City**, formed over the past century with the growth of the town's industry. Most visitors, though, are here for package tours to Playa Dorada – located a kilometre east of the city limits – a walled-off vacation factory that pulls in over a half-million tourists each year.

Arrival and getting around

Six kilometres east of town, **Aeropuerto Internacional Luperón** (☎809/586-1992), usually referred to as Puerto Plata Airport, is the main northern entry point into the country. There is a Banco de Reservas **currency exchange** (Mon–Fri 8.30am–6.30pm) within the strip of shops lining the front of the airport, alongside a number of **car rental** offices. While most of the more expensive hotels have shuttle buses, any of the *motoconchos* can take you into town for RD$20, and there are plenty of taxis to take you to points further out. Arriving by **bus** is another option; the city is a major junction point for Caribe Tours (☎809/586-4544) and Metro (☎809/586-6062), whose vehicles arrive here from the south (via Santo Domingo and Santiago) and the east (via Samaná).

Central Puerto Plata is compact enough to make **walking** your best option. If you want to go to Playa Dorada or Costambar, you may want to take one of the ubiquitous *motoconchos*, which should cost RD$20 (RD$10 within town). Cheaper but far slower are the **public buses** shuttling between Playa Dorada and the parque central. The price is RD$3 but it can take up to 45 minutes to get from one side of town to the other. **Taxis** are relatively expensive (RD$60 to Playa Dorada), but are the fastest mode of transport and far safer than *motoconchos*.

Accommodation

The best luxury **hotels** are east of town within Playa Dorada, but as **all-inclusives** your freedom is limited some. If you want to explore the city itself there are plenty of moderately priced options in and around the old town and the Malecón.

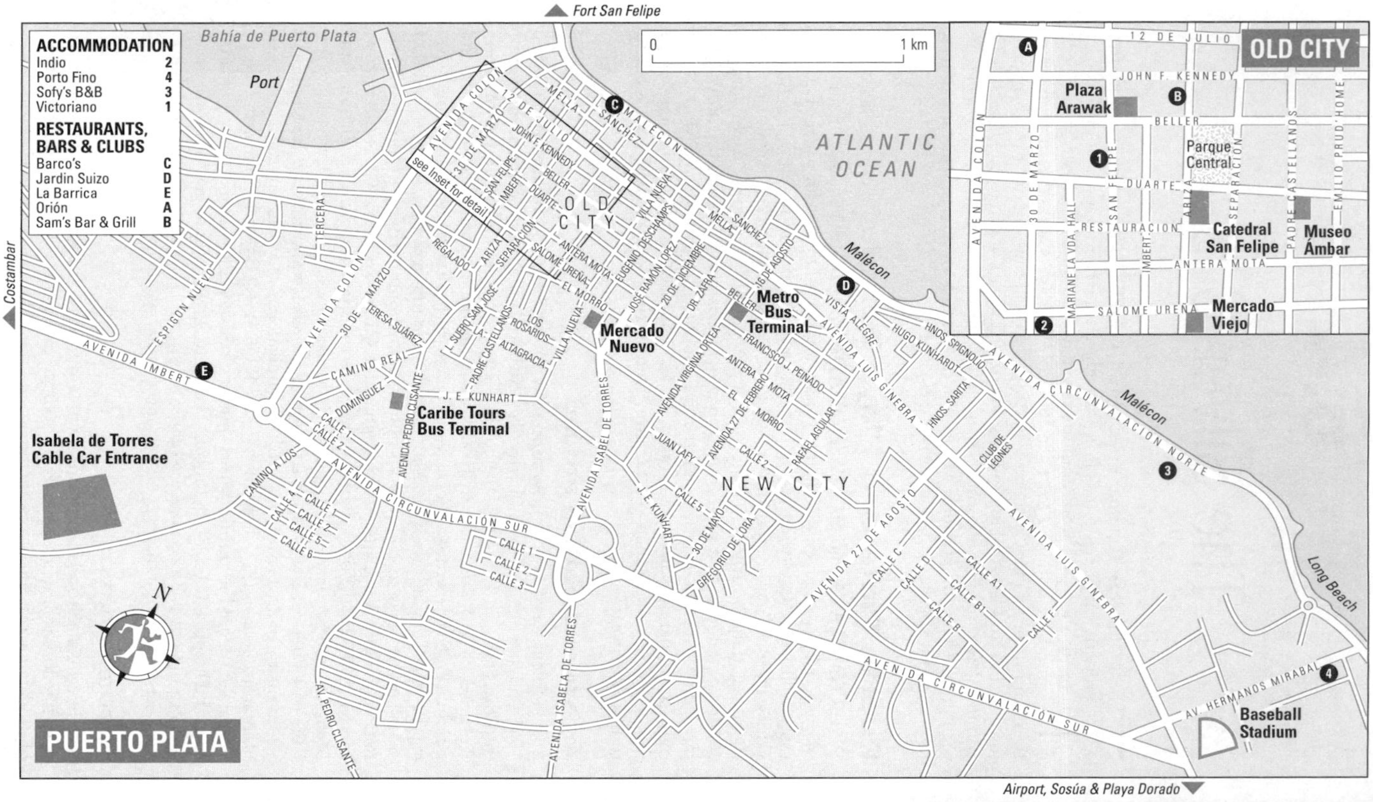

PUERTO PLATA
ACCOMMODATION
Indio 2
Porto Fino 4
Sofy's B&B 3
Victoriano 1
RESTAURANTS, BARS & CLUBS
Barco's C
Jardin Suizo D
La Barrica E
Orión A
Sam's Bar & Grill B
Fort San Felipe
Costambar
Airport, Sosúa & Playa Dorado
Bahía de Puerto Plata
Port
ATLANTIC OCEAN
0
1 km
Malécon
Long Beach
OLD CITY
NEW CITY
see Inset for detail
Metro Bus Terminal
Mercado Nuevo
Caribe Tours Bus Terminal
Isabela de Torres Cable Car Entrance
Baseball Stadium
AVENIDA CIRCUNVALACION NORTE
AVENIDA CIRCUNVALACIÓN SUR
AVENIDA LUIS GINEBRA
AVENIDA 27 DE AGOSTO
AVENIDA ISABEL DE TORRES
AVENIDA PEDRO CLISANTE
AV. PEDRO CLISANTE
AVENIDA IMBERT
AVENIDA COLON
AV. HERMANOS MIRABAL
ESPIGON NUEVO
TERCERA
CAMINO REAL
CAMINO A LOS
DOMINGUEZ
J. E. KUNHART
AVENIDA VIRGINIA ORTEA
AVENIDA 27 DE FEBRERO
JUAN LAFY
30 DE MAYO
GREGORIO DE LORA
FRANCISCO J. PEINADO
RAFAEL AGUILAR
VISTA ALEGRE
HUGO KUNHARDT
HNOS. SPIGNOLIO
HNOS. SARITA
CLUB DE LEONES
16 DE AGOSTO
12 DE JULIO
JOHN F. KENNEDY
MELLA
SANCHEZ
MALECON
BELLER
DUARTE
SAN FELIPE
IMBERT
SEPARACIÓN
ARIZA
REGALADO
SALOME UREÑA
ANTERA MOTA
EL MORRO
VILLA NUEVA
EUGENIO DESCHAMPS
JOSÉ RAMÓN LOPEZ
20 DE DICIEMBRE
DR. ZAFRA
LOS ROSARIOS
ALTAGRACIA
PADRE CASTELLANOS
L. SUERO SAN JOSÉ
TERESA SUÁREZ
30 DE MARZO
CALLE 1
CALLE 2
CALLE 3
CALLE 4
CALLE 5
CALLE 6
CALLE A1
CALLE B1
CALLE B
CALLE C
CALLE D
CALLE F
OLD CITY
Plaza Arawak
Parque Central
Catedral San Felipe
Museo Ámbar
Mercado Viejo
AVENIDA COLON
30 DE MARZO
MARIANE LA VDA. HALL
RESTAURACION
PADRE CASTELLANOS
EMILIO PRUD'HOME

Puerto Plata

Indio 30 de Marzo 94 ⓣ809/586-1201. A good mid-range accommodation with private baths, hot showers, mosquito nets and communal courtyard in a fairly quiet location. ③

Porto Fino Ave Hermanas Mirabal ⓣ809/586-2858, ⓕ586-5050. Clean and comfortable air-conditioned rooms, way nicer and quieter than the *Victoriano* for only a few bucks more. A long way from town and the action though. ①

Sofy's Bed and Breakfast Las Rosas 3 and Ginebra ⓣ & ⓕ809/586-6411, ⓔgillin.n@codetel.net.do. A cozy private home with a hibiscus-filled courtyard patio and two large rooms rented to travellers. Price includes free laundry service and a terrific cooked breakfast. ②

Victoriano San Felipe 33 ⓣ809/586-9752. A true budget option with clean but depressingly plain rooms and warm water. Can be very noisy at night. ①

Playa Dorada

Gran Ventana ⓣ809/320-2111, ⓕ320-2112, ⓦwww.victoriahoteles.com.do. The newest and the very best of the resorts in Playa Dorada. Extensive sports facilities and better-than-acceptable service. ⑥

Jack Tar Village ⓣ809/320-3800, ⓕ320-4161, ⓦwww.allegroresorts.com. The oldest of the Playa Dorada resorts and long highly regarded but don't expect the same kind of four-star service you'd get back home. Two large swimming pools and a popular user friendly casino. Adults only. ⑥

Paradise Resort ⓣ809/320-3663, ⓕ320-4864, ⓦwww.amshamarina.com. Known for its excellent restaurants, sports facilities and children's programme. Rooms and grounds well maintained, and ethnic "theme nights" keep the buffet food varied. Popular with the British. ⑥

Puerto Plata: The Old City

The once-exclusive **Old City**, a compact area bounded by Avenida Colón, the Malecón and Calle López, visually retains much of the Victorian splendour of its past, when it was populated by wealthy landowners, dock workers and European merchants. A good place to begin wandering is the colonial-era **San Felipe** fort (9am–noon & 2–5pm; closed Wed; RD$30), a limestone edifice perched atop a rocky point at the seaside Malecón off Avenida Colón. The Spaniards constructed it in 1540 as a defence against corsairs and a prison for smugglers. Once past the unnecessary freelance tour guides that surround it, you can climb up several of the towers and gun turrets, or down into the old prison cells.

The heart of the Victorian city is the **Parque Central**, at the corner of Separación and Beller, a fast-paced focal point for transportation and tourism. Shaded benches and the central **gazebo** supply a much needed dose of tranquillity. South of the park looms the large **Catedral San Felipe**, which blends Spanish Colonial and Art Deco influences. The remaining three sides are surrounded by some of the best **Victorian architecture** in the city, notably a colossal white gingerbread mansion on the northwest corner.

One block east of the Parque Central on Duarte and Castellanos, the popular **Museo Ámbar** (Mon–Sat 9am–6pm; RD$30) comprises two floors of amber-related exhibits in a renovated mansion called Villa Berz, built by one of the town's wealthiest German tobacco families a century ago. The museum's collection, culled from the amber mines in the Cordillera Septentrional south of Puerto Plata, consists of Jurassic and Triassic leaves, flowers, spiders, termites, wasps, ants and other insects trapped in amber, along with one small lizard several million years old.

Puerto Plata: The New City

Puerto Plata's **New City** spreads outward in three directions from the Old, roughly bounded by the port, Circunvalación Sur and Avenida Hermanas Mirabal, though additional, less developed barrios exist beyond this convenient circumscription. The centre of the city's social life is the two-kilometre-long **Malecón**, a sunny, spacious boardwalk lined with hotels and all manner of commerce. During the day it's a popular place to hang out or lie on the beach, while at night a strip of bars open up along with numerous restaurants and outdoor shacks selling Dominican fast food.

The Malecón begins at **Long Beach**, on the town's far eastern end, not the most picturesque beach by any stretch, but with a convivial mood, peopled largely by merengue-blaring teens. A row of **outdoor bars** extends for several hundred metres from here down the adjoining Avenida Hermanas Mirabal.

Puerto Plata's crowning attraction is the suspended **cable car ride** (Mon–Sat 8.30am–3.30pm; RD$50) that goes to the top of Mount Isabela. The entrance is at the far western end of town past the port, just off the Circunvalación Sur on Avenida Teleférico. It's not to be missed; the views of the city on this 25-minute trip are stupendous. At the summit a statue of **Christ the Redeemer**, a slightly downsized version of the Río de Janeiro landmark with its arms spread out over the city, crowns a manicured lawn.

Playa Dorada

Playa Dorada, just 1km east of Puerto Plata on the C-5 but truly a world away, is walled off from the outside universe; inside its confines are fourteen separate massive resorts, and meandering between them is one of the best golf courses in the country, designed by Robert Trent Jones. Frequented by a half-million package tourists per year (the majority from Canada and Europe), the main draw is obviously the **beach**, 2km of impeccably white sand dominated by a variety of hotel-run activities, including beach volleyball, merengue lessons and parasailing, along with numerous local souvenir vendors and hair braiders. Even if you're not a guest, getting through the front gate is not a problem. Either sneak onto the beach via entries beside the *Dorado Naco* complex or just east of the *Playa Dorada Hotel*, or buy a **day-pass,** available from each resort, costing from US$35 to US$50, and entitling you to five hours on the grounds, including meals and drinks.

Eating

Most of Puerto Plata's **restaurants** are scattered within the Old City and along the Malecón, the latter also lined with cheap food shacks.

Barco's Malecón 6. A great people-watching spot on the Malecón with a sidewalk patio and a second-floor terrace. They serve good pizzas, lamb and goat dishes.

Cafe Cito Sosúa Highway, km4 ☎809/586-7923. The best restaurant in town has recently moved and is now situated 500m west of Playa Dorada. Great food – try the filet mignon – and jazz music make for a memorable night out.

Jardin Suizo Malecón. Top-end international fare in a smart but relaxed building close to the water's edge. Seafood specials including excellent tuna steaks.

Sam's Bar & Grill Ariza 34. Established meeting place for fellow travellers, with good-value daily specials. The American breakfasts and philly cheesesteak are highly recommended.

Drinking and nightlife

Fed by a metropolis full of dance-crazy Dominicans and vacationing foreign hordes, Puerto Plata's **nightlife** establishments are crammed with dancers until dawn. While Playa Dorada resorts and their restaurants are off limits to non-guests, the discos are open to all.

Puerto Plata

La Barrica Circunvalación Sur and Av Colón. Hip, strictly Dominican music disco catering mostly to city-dwellers cutting vicious moves. There are no lights in the entire club – the waiters use flashlights.

Orión 30 de Marzo and 12 de Julio. Slightly intimidating, but the most popular dance spot in town, featuring strictly merengue and *bachata*.

Playa Dorada

Andromeda *Heavens Hotel.* Large, modern dance floor with mostly Dominican music despite the foreign clientele.

Hemingway's Cafe *Playa Dorada Plaza.* Haven for crazed drunken tourists intent on having a good time. Friday's ear-splitting karaoke night is the most popular; Thursdays and Saturdays feature good rock 'n' roll.

East of Puerto Plata

The resort development that began around Puerto Plata has over the past two decades gobbled up most of the prime beachfront east of the city. As such, you'll have to keep going all the way east, for approximately 70km, to the small, friendly fishing village of Río San Juan to find anything approaching unspoiled coastline. Even closer, though, and easier for those with limited time, is the bustling resort town of **Cabarete**, a windsurfing enclave that's quickly being swallowed by tourism construction.

Cabarete

Stretched along the C-5 between the beach and lagoon that bear its name, **CABARETE** is a crowded international enclave that owes its existence almost entirely to **windsurfing**. The main beach, Playa Cabarete, has ideal conditions for the sport, and the multicultural cross-section of its aficionados attracts a growing community from across the globe.

Arrival and accommodation

Virtually all of Cabarete is on the **Carretera 5**. Buses, *guaguas* and *motoconchos* will all drop you off along the main strip, a crowded patchwork of restaurants and bars, tour operators and souvenir shops.

Bahía Arena Carretera 5 ⓣ809/571-0370, ⓕ571-0523, ⓦwww.cabaretevillas.com. The best high-end value, especially if you're with a large group: a selection of individually designed condominiums right by a quieter stretch of beach with a pool and tennis court as well. ④

Banana Boat Carretera 5 ⓣ & ⓕ809/571-0690, ⓔmaribeldelcarmen54@yahoo.com The oldest and best of the budget accommodations, located just off the Tricom plaza. Very busy, so book in advance. ①

El Magnifico Carretera 5 ⓣ & ⓕ809/571-0868, ⓦwww.hotelmagnifico.com. Three different buildings with eye-catching architecture and wild ethnic-style interiors set around a tranquil pool area. This place is a real haven yet it's just a five-minute stroll from the town centre. ④

Residencia Dominicana Calle Las Orquideas ⓣ & ⓕ809/571-0890, ⓔresdom@hipaniola.com. Small hotel with good, clean rooms and a peaceful garden and pool. Located on the Orquideas road, south of the C-5, at the eastern end of town. The place usually fills up, so it's a good idea to reserve in advance. ②

Villa Taina Carretera 5 ⓣ809/571-0722, ⓕ571-0883, ⓦwww.villataina.com. Classy hotel with top-notch service and a selection of stunning individually designed rooms, some with sea views. ④

Exploring Cabarete

What there is of a town consists of the hectic strip of restaurants and hotels along the C-5, just behind the water. The real action here is centred nearly completely on the **beach**. During the day it's full of windsurfers – calm water and light breezes during the morning make it a perfect place for beginners, but as the day wears on, and the trade winds kick in with full force, the experts take over. Further out from the centre, both east and west, you can have the beach to yourself. At night, the bars and restaurants spill out onto the sand, helping create a superb atmosphere.

Two kilometres further west, on a white-sand beach hidden behind Punta Goleta, Cabarete is playing its part in the birth and infancy of a new sport – **kitesurfing**. In many ways similar to windsurfing, kitesurfing needs less wind to really get moving and the best riders perform huge jumps and tricks that would be impossible with a sail.

Eating and drinking

Cabarete has an array of good **dining** options, most of them opened by European expats, and hence with some unusual cuisines for this part of the country. The entire town is packed with **bars**, but a select few garner the majority of the business.

Cabarete adventure sports outfitters

Dare2fly ⓣ809/571-0805, ⓕ571-0856, ⓦwww.dare2fly.com. Part of the Vela/Spinout windsurf centre (see below), this dedicated kitesurfing outfitter offers rentals and gives lessons at the Kite Beach daily.
Iguana Mama ⓣ809/571-0908, ⓕ571-0734, ⓦwww.iguanamama.com. Offers US$30 mountain-bike day trips and week long bike tours of the island, hikes up Mount Isabela (see p.334) and several-day treks through the Cordillera Central to Pico Duarte (see p.343). They also do whale-watching in Samaná Bay for US$125/day, horseback riding for US$25/half-day and a whole stack of cultural tours.
Vela/Spinout ⓣ809/571-0805, ⓕ571-0856, ⓦwww.velacabarete.com. German-owned and the best-equipped of Cabarete's windsurf centres with free daily clinics and a lively social scene. US$160 for ten hours equipment rental; US$100 for three-hour classes; US$25 equipment insurance.

Casa del Pescador Carretera 5. The best seafood in town in an idyllic candlelit atmosphere right on the beach.
El Tiguerre Road to the Lagoon/Caves. Excellent, inexpensive Dominican food served by friendly proprietors and set in a rustic barrio on the outskirts of town. A real Dominican experience.
Las Brisas Carretera 5. The town's loudest and most popular disco bar, featuring a mix of merengue and techno.
Lax Carretera 5. Popular bar that's more relaxed than most of the beachside spots, with live music on Sundays.
Miro's The best of Cabarete's beach restaurants with fantastic fish dishes and a good selection of wine. The Moroccan tuna is out of this world.
Onno's Carretera 5. Lively bar/restaurant which really gets going in the small hours – plays mainly European and American hits.
Panadería Repositera Dick Carretera 5. Various gourmet breads for a few pesos, great Danishes and croissants. Excellent breakfasts with fresh-squeezed orange juice and cappuccino.

West of Puerto Plata

The contrast east and **west of Puerto Plata** couldn't be more striking. In place of the paved highways and resort complexes, you'll find vast stretches of untrammelled wilderness along rough dirt tracks, though some are slowly being converted into freeways. One thing that doesn't change, however, is the proliferation of lovely beaches.

El Castillo and La Isabela

From Puerto Plata, the Carretera de las Américas heads 50km west to **El Castillo**, a seaside village located on the site of Columbus's first permanent settlement. It's easy to see why he picked it, since the town is set on a splendid bay of tranquil, blue water and a solid wall of imposing, Olympian peaks.

Just off the main highway, before you make town, is the entrance to **Parque Nacional La Isabela** (9am–5.30pm, closed Sun; RD$30), which preserves the ruins of La Isabela, the first European town in the New World. Centred on the private home of Columbus himself, which is perched atop a prominent ocean bluff, the park also encompasses the excavated stone foundations of the town and a small museum.

A few kilometres further on, you enter the village, draped over a steep hillside above Playa Isabela, which attracts few beach-goers and is instead marked mainly by small wooden boats. A kilometre offshore is an intact **coral reef** where there's a healthy, multicoloured reef bed that's home to thousands of tropical fish and sea creatures. The *Rancho del Sol* hotel (see below) can arrange **diving and snorkelling trips**.

If looking to **spend the night**, check out *Rancho del Sol* (Ⓣ809/543-8172; ②), located off the Carretera de las Américas at the town entrance, which rents simple but well-maintained duplexes with kitchen and bath. They also have a great seafood restaurant – the menu varies with the day's catch. *Miamar*, Calle Vista Mar (Ⓣ809/471-9157, Ⓕ471-8052; ②, breakfast included), is a modern hotel with a swimming pool and enormous rooms with lovely ocean views. For good Dominican cuisine try *Milagro*, near the entrance to *Rancho del Sol*, a small and friendly *comedor* with a good selection of local dishes.

Punta Rucia and Playa Ensenata

From El Castillo a dirt road extends west and heads to a series of beaches that relatively few foreign visitors make it to. There are two rivers to be crossed en route, and a 4x4 is recommended. After 14km, a turn-off heads north to **Playa Ensanata**, where many Dominican families come to take advantage of the shallow waters. The beach is lined with shacks where you can eat grilled, freshly caught fish extremely cheaply. Just around the point from Playa Ensanata, **Punta Rucia** is yet another beautiful beach, featuring bone-white sand and more great mountain views. It attracts fewer people than Ensanata and is dotted with fishing boats, but has several good places to stop for lunch or a beer. At Punta Rucia's western edge is *Punta Rucia Sol* (Ⓣ809/471-0173; ①), a German-owned hotel with a few simple but pleasant rooms with private cold-water baths. It has a decent restaurant and a very laid-back, tranquil ambience. There are a few down-home Dominican seafood **restaurants** on Punta Rucia as well.

Monte Cristi

West from Punta Rucia, the roads deteriorate even further and the only sensible way to make for the Haiti border is to turn south back onto the C-1 at **Villa Elisa**. The further west you go, the more the landscape transforms itself – gone are the swaying palms and grassy pastures, replaced by scrubby cactus plants and dusty dry soil inhabited mainly by goats. The carretera terminates at the westernmost outpost of the Silver Coast, **Monte Cristi**, founded in 1501 and at one point one of the country's most important ports. These days it resembles a dusty frontier town bearing only the occasional tarnished remnant of its opulent past along wide, American-style boulevards. Most visitors are here to use the town as a base from which to explore the local **beaches** and the **Parque Nacional Monte Cristi**, an expanse that protects a towering mesa named El Morro and an enormous river delta. To reach the park, take the beach road north of the city towards **Playa Juan de Bolaños**, the area's most popular beach but quite disappointing in comparison to others on this coast. Once past the restaurants that clutter the beach's entrance, the road arrives at the entrance to the eastern half of the park, which is divided in two by Monte Cristi's beaches. Its eastern section is often referred to as Parque El Morro, after the flat-topped mesa **El Morro** that takes up a good chunk of it. Climbing the mesa is a lot easier these days as the park office has built a set of steps up from the road's highest point (RD$50 entrance fee). At the foot of El Morro's eastern slope is a lovely and unpopulated **beach** accessible by parking at the end of the road and continuing down on foot. The western half of the national park encompasses a dense mangrove coast dotted with small lagoons; informal tours are led from the *Los Jardines* hotel (from RD$300 per person; see overleaf), on which you'll see several river deltas thick with mangroves and perhaps even a couple of crocodiles.

Practicalities

The best **accommodation** option in Monte Cristi is *Cayo Arena*, Playa Juan de Bolaños, 250m west of the beach entrance (Ⓣ809/579-3145, Ⓕ579-2096; ③), a set of large, full-service apartments right on the beach with ocean-view balconies, A/C, kitchenettes, swimming pool, bar and 24-hour security. Also on the beach, a little more basic but definitely better value if there are only two of you is *Los Jardines*, Playa Juan de Bolaños (ⓣ809/579-2091, ⓦwww.elbistrot.com; ❷), which has simple rooms with cold-water showers. Note that these hotels get busy over the weekend and the rates go up accordingly. The best **restaurant** in town is *El Bistrot*, Calle Bolaños (ⓣ809/579-2091), which serves great seafood dishes in an atmospheric courtyard.

6.5

The Cibao

CIBAO (rocky land) is the word Taínos used to describe the **Cordillera Central** mountain range that takes up much of the Dominican Republic's central interior. These mountains are the highest peaks in the Caribbean, including Pico Duarte, the Caribbean's tallest at 3087m. The heart of the range is protected as **Parques Nacionales Bermúdez and Ramírez**.

Today, though, Dominicans use the term Cibao more to describe the fertile Cibao Valley, a triangle of alluvial plain that contains some of the deepest topsoil in the world. In the valley sits vibrant **Santiago**, the country's second largest city after Santo Domingo, well positioned for short excursions into the neighbouring farmland.

The region is penetrated by the **C-1**, also known as the Autopista Duarte, that links the northwest with the southeast, via Santiago and Santo Domingo. But, with most of interest gathered in the northern reaches, many vistors also take advantage of the good roads that hurdle the Cordillera Septentrional from the north. Once in the mountains, the best progress is made by following the biggest and best roads between towns, even when the distance travelled is far greater, which is often the case. Buses link most of the towns and *guaguas* make up for any shortfall.

Santiago

Founded in 1504 as a mining town and demolished by an earthquake in 1562, **SANTIAGO** has been associated with tobacco since it was introduced for export to the French in 1697, and is also the home of *merengue périco ripao* – the classic Dominican music using accordion, tambora and güira.

Today, there's a good club scene based mostly around this indigenous music, so you won't lack for fun at nights. During the day, **downtown Santiago** supplies enough diversions to merit a full day or two of ambling about.

Arrival and getting around

All three highway entrances to town – the Autopista Duarte, the Carretera Duarte and the Carretera Turística – lead directly to the city centre. If you're arriving by **bus**, your station will likely be on the north or east side of town, from where you can get a RD$40 taxi closer to the heart of downtown. There are also **guagua stations** on the corner of 30 de Marzo and Cucurullo (*guaguas* to Mao and Monciòn), and on Calle Valerio a block west of Parque Valerio (to San José de Las Matas). Another arrival option is the **Cibao International Airport** (☎809/226-0664), a twenty- minute drive from the centre.

A complex system of battered public taxis – referred to locally as **motoconchos** – should cover most **city transport** needs; a one-way ride runs RD$5. **Private taxis** wait at the city parks, though you can call directly for pickup: reliable operators include Camino (☎809/971-7788). As always, you're best off sticking with an established international firm for **car rental**. Options include Budget, 27 de Febrero (☎809/566-6666); Honda, Estrella Sadhalá and 27 de Febrero (☎809/575-6077); Metro, Carr Jacagua 42 (☎809/570-5911); and Nelly, Av Salvador E. Sadhalá 204 (☎809/583-6695).

Accommodation

Santiago is pretty well set up for **accommodation**, from budget options up to the *Gran Almirante*, the one five-star hotel in town.

Centro Plaza Mella 54 ⓣ809/581-7000, ⓕ582-4566, ⓦwww.hodelpa.com. Large Western-style hotel with large comfortable rooms, a gym and a worthwhile restaurant. ❷

Colonial Cucurullo and 30 de Marzo ⓣ809/247-3122, ⓕ582-0811. Great little budget hotel with excellent service, clean rooms, A/C and TV. ❶

Dorado Cucurullo 88 ⓣ809/582-7563. Good-value cheapie with fan and hot water. Not quite as nice as *Colonial*, but comfortable enough. ❶

Gran Almirante Estrella Sadhalá and Calle 10 ⓣ809/580-1992, ⓕ241-1492, ⓦwww.hodelpa.com. Luxury hotel in a wealthy northeastern suburb with all the amenities. ❸

The City

Most places of interest are **downtown** and within walking distance of one another. In fact, many visitors spend their whole stay in the area bounded by the main city park and the **Monumento a los Héroes de la Restauración** (Mon–Sat 9am–noon & 2–5pm; free), Santiago's distinctive symbol and most impressive sight. Built by Trujillo in honour of himself, it was quickly rededicated upon his death to the War of Independence with Spain. It's possible to climb the stairs up the monument – a statue of Victory personified as a woman tops its seventy-metre pillar – to take in the breathtaking panorama of Santiago and the surrounding valley and mountains.

Calle del Sol, which borders the monument to the west, is the city's major shopping district and the heart of downtown activity, lined with department stores, banks and sidewalk stalls selling clothing, household wares and fast food. Follow Del Sol north to 30 de Marzo and the **Parque Duarte**, a bit overcrowded but covered by a tree canopy and lined with horse-and-carriage drivers. At the park's southern end stands the **Catedral Santiago** (1895), a concrete building with intricate carvings on its mahogany portals. Just across the street the excellent **Museo del Tabaco**, on 16 de Agosto and 30 de Marzo (Tues–Fri 9am–noon & 2–5pm, Sat 9am–noon; free), housed in a old Victorian tobacco warehouse, presents a history of the crop's use dating back to Taíno times. Three blocks south of the park **La Habanera Tabaclera**, 16 de Agosto and San Luis (Mon–Fri 8.30am–4.30pm; free), is the oldest working Dominican cigar factory and one of the few in the city that offers tours, though free samples are not included.

In the opposite direction, a few blocks northwest of the park, sits the fascinating **Museo Folklórico de Tomas Morel**, Restauración 174 (Mon–Fri 8.30am–1.30pm & 3.30–5.30pm; free). Inside is a remarkable collection of papier-mâché Carnival masks, alongside various Taíno artefacts and early Spanish household items. The masks, though, are the main focus, with an array of spectacularly baroque and evil-looking demons.

Eating

You'll have no problem finding plenty to **eat** in Santiago, whether it's at fine dining establishments, low-key *comedores* or American fast-food chains.

El Café Texas and Calle 5, Los Jardines ⓣ809/587-4247. Swanky, white-linen restaurant specializing in sea bass and racks of lamb.

Daiqui Loco JP Duarte and Oueste. Festive outdoor bar with the best grilled sandwiches and burritos in town. Frozen daiquiris are also a speciality.

Olé JP Duarte and Independencia. Creole restaurant with Dominican standards and American-style pizzas in a thatch-sheltered terrace.

Rancho Luna Carretera Turística km 7, ⓣ809/736-7176. Top-quality steakhouse and piano bar with excellent service, a huge wine list and great views over the city.

Drinking and nightlife

Santiago **nightlife** is rowdy, diverse and seemingly non-stop; most clubs are completely empty until midnight and don't close until dawn.

Alcazar *Gran Almirante Hotel*, Estrella Sadhalá and Calle 10. The best disco in town: it doesn't get hopping until 1am, but stays full until 7am. Dress sharply. RD$50 cover.

Bar Code Cuba 25. Popular courtyard bar with live Caribbean music. Definitely one of *the* places to hang out.

Francifol Del Sol at Parque Duarte. Classy pub with the coldest beer in town. A good place for drinks and conversation.

Tin Marín Estrella Sadhalá and Argentina. Frenetic and fun outdoor bar for the wealthy twenty-something crowd.

San José de las Matas

The easiest excursion into the mountains from Santiago is **San José de las Matas**, a sleepy hill station looking out over the northern Cordillera Central. There's little to do within town but take a leisurely walk and admire the views; for one such lookout, take the dirt path behind the post office, on 30 de Marzo, to a **cliff-top park** with a good vantage over the neighbouring mountains. Most points of interest lie a bit outside San José, such as the **Balneario Vidal Pichardo Trail**, 10km north at the confluence of the rivers Anima and Bao, which is ideal for a day's hike.

If you're arriving from Santiago, it will likely either be by *guagua* (hourly; RD$20), or by car – simply head west on Calle 30 de Marzo, cross the Hermanos Patiño bridge and continue west for 28km. Most visitors choose to make a day trip of the town, but those looking to **stay the night** will find a couple of good hotels, including *Hotel Restaurant San José,* 30 de Marzo 37 (☎809/578-8566; ❶) with basic rooms, ceiling fans and hot water. *Los Samenes* is as good a place to eat as any, with a great little **restaurant** serving typical Dominican platters.

The Cordillera Central

The **Cordillera Central** contains the Carribean's tallest, most beautiful mountains. For the most part, the roads are horrific, and so getting from place to place often requires a convoluted route, leaving the mountains via one paved road and then re-entering them via another. To head deeper into the range you'll need a donkey; blazed trails lead to **Pico Duarte** from several points.

La Vega

LA VEGA, just 30km south of Santiago, started out as one of Columbus's gold-mining towns. Aside from the ruins of this old settlement, **La Vega Vieja**, there's little in today's noisy, concrete city to hold your attention. However, La Vega's **Carnival** celebrations in February are generally acknowledged to be among the most boisterous and authentic in the nation. A twenty-block promenade is set up between the two main parks, along which parade platoons of demons in impressively horrific **masks**, the making of which is somewhat of a local specialty craft.

There are no good in-town **hotels**; most lack even the most basic amenities like toilet seat, mosquito net or hot water. *San Pedro*, Cáceres 87 (☎809/573-2844; ❶), is the least seedy and cleanest, but is still not especially comfortable. You'll fare slightly better with local **restaurants**, notably the second-floor *Salón Dorado* above Engini Car Wash, Cáceres and Restauración, which has a hip décor, fun crowd and pool tables. The **bus** stations, Caribe Tours (☎809/573-3488), Metro (☎809/573-7099) and Vegano Express (☎809/573-7079), are all on the Carretera La Vega, just off the Autopista Duarte. **Guaguas** to Jarabacoa set off from the corner of 27 de Febrero and Restauración.

Jarabacoa

JARABACOA, a mountain resort peppered with coffee plantations, is popular with wealthy Dominicans for its cool summers. The pine-dominated mountains immediately surrounding the town hold three large waterfalls, several rugged trails fit for day hikes, three rivers used for white-water rafting and the busiest starting-point for treks up Pico Duarte; see the box below for local outfitters.

Arrival and accommodation

Located some 30km southwest of La Vega, the town's well served by **public transport**; Caribe Tours, at the main crossroad, across from the Esso station, runs four buses daily to La Vega, Bonao and Santo Domingo. *Guaguas* pick up and drop off at Esso in the centre and by the Shell station on the Constanza road.

With the recent increase in visitor numbers, Jarabacoa's **accommodation** options have improved radically. In addition to the possibilities listed below, **camping** is an option around Manabao or at Balneario la Confluencia; if you want to get further away from civilization, most farmers will let you camp on their land, provided you ask first.

Brisas del Yaque Luperón ⓣ809/574 4490. Clean, modern hotel just off the town centre. The rooms come with A/C, TV and a fridge. ❷

Gran Jimenoa Av La Confluencia, Los Corralitos ⓣ809/574-6304, ⓕ574-4345, ⓦwww.granjimenoa.com. Best hotel in town with large A/C rooms in a new building overlooking a pleasant pool area. ❷

Hogar Mella 34 ⓣ809/574-2739. The best budget hotel in town, with private showers, clean rooms and a pleasant courtyard. ❶

Pinar Dorado road to Constanza km 1 ⓣ809/574-2820, ⓕ574-2237, ⓔpinardorado@codetel.net.do. Pleasant hotel with TV, A/C, hot water, private balconies, restaurant and bar. ❷

The Town

Most of the action in town is centred on its major crossroads, a few blocks north of the small **parque central**. The point at which the Río Yaque del Norte and Río Jimenoa meet is a popular spot for swimming, a half-kilometre north of the main crossroads.

The most popular local attractions are the three **waterfalls** (*saltos*), which are all enough of a trek that you'll want either your own transport or a ride on a *motoconcho* (RD$50–100 one-way). Most popular is the crashing **Lower Salto Jimenoa** (daily 8.30am–7pm; RD$5), which boasts a deep pool good for swimming. It's 3km east of town off the Carretera Jarabacoa. **Salto Baiguate**, 1km south of town on the road to Constanza (daily 8.30am–7pm; free), is a bit taller, plus it has a large cave and a swimming hole at its base. The steepest Jarabacoa waterfall is the **Higher Salto Jimenoa**, or Salto Jimenoa Uno, as it's often called. This isn't so easy to find

Jarabacoa tour operators

Franz's Aventuras del Caribe Hato Viejo 21 ⓣ809/574-2669 ⓕ574-2669, ⓦwww.hispaniola.com/whitewater. Top of the bunch when it comes to white-water adrenaline rushes, offering basic rafting, kayaking and canyoning. They also arrange early morning pick-ups from the hotels along the north coast.

Rancho Baiguate road to Constanza km 5 ⓣ809/574-6890, ⓕ574-4940, ⓦwww.ranchobaiguate.com.do. One of the island's biggest tour operators, with most of their clients coming on excursions from the all-inclusives on the north coast. As well as culture tours they also run adventure trips including white-water rafting, canyoning, paragliding, mountain trekking, mountain biking, jeep safaris and horseback riding. Longer trips include a guided hike to Pico Duarte.

but if you head out on the road to Constanza for 7km, you'll pass through a small pueblo before coming to a few shacks on the right. Almost directly opposite these is a jeep-size driveway that quickly deteriorates into a narrow and steep footpath. Continue down to the bottom and scramble over some huge slabs to the pool at the waterfall's base. It's a pretty awesome sight: the water drops 75m from a hidden lake above, and thunders into a huge pool at its base. The spray at the bottom creates its own rainbows and it's easy to see why this was chosen as a setting for a scene in *Jurassic Park*.

Eating

Don Luis Colón and Duarte at parque central. Good mid-range restaurant facing the park, with steak, seafood and the usual Dominican staples.

El Rancho Main crossroad at town entrance. Excellent high-end restaurant serving good pizza plus specialities like baked chicken stuffed with banana.

Pico Duarte and the Cordillera Central's national parks

Two national parks, **Bermúdez and Ramírez**, protect much of the mountains, cloud forests and pines present in the Cordillera Central, each encompassing over seven hundred square kilometres. By far the best way to explore the region is on an organized trek up **Pico Duarte**, at 3087m the tallest mountain in the Caribbean, which is actually located between the two parks but generally approached via Bermúdez.

A number of strenuous treks lead up the peak, which towers over the centre of the range alongside its sister mountain La Pelona. The most popular one starts from the tiny pueblo of La Ciénega, 25km southwet of Jarabacoa, where you'll need to register for the 46km round-trip at the park's entrance office on the far side of the village. Here, you'll need to pay the RD$100 **park entrance** and hire at least one **guide** for every five people (RD$100/day plus meals). It's also a good idea to rent at least one **mule** (RD$125/day) – chances are the guide will insist upon it – to carry water and food as well as to get you down safely if things go wrong.

The best bet is to arrive in the afternoon, sort out the formalities and then camp down in the village with a view to starting out early the next morning. The first leg is a comfortable 4km riverside stroll to a bridge across the river at **Los Tablones**. Once over the river, however, the climbing starts for real and you'll gain over 2000m in the next 14km, mostly on a badly eroded track that wends its way through some wonderfully wild woodland. Regular stops at official picnic sights allow you to get your breath back and to peep out through the canopy for a glimpse of the totally pristine wilderness that surrounds you. You'll spend the night in a ramshackle cabin at **La Comparticíon** and then scramble up the last 5km at around 4.30am to be on the bare rocky summit for sunrise. It's quite a stirring sight to watch the sun creep over the horizon, casting a bright-red hue on the banks of cloud beneath your feet.

Treks can be made any time of the year, but hikes should never be attempted without a waterproof coat, winter clothing, a sleeping bag and hiking boots. You'll also need to bring enough food for yourself and the guide (this is best bought in Jarabacoa). It's definitely worth considering the two **tour operators** who operate trips up this trail: Iguana Mama, in Cabarete (see p.336); or Rancho Baiguate, in Jarabacoa (see opposite), as they'll take care of all the logistics for you.

6.6

Barahona

Occupying the coast west of Santo Domingo and taking its name from the major city at its centre, the **BARAHONA REGION** was once the focus of Trujillo's personal sugar empire; vast tracts of cane still take up much of the land north of **Barahona** city, but today this is one of the country's poorest regions. As a result, the stunning Barahona **coastline** is almost completely undeveloped, making it perfect for independent travellers willing to rough it a bit in exchange for unblemished natural beauty.

Barahona and around

BARAHONA city isn't an especially pleasant place. Founded in 1802 and once the informal capital of Trujillo's multimillion-dollar sugar industry, the city has fallen on hard times due to the closing of the local sugar mill. That said, the locals are friendly and it does have a couple of good hotels, making it a useful base to explore the undeveloped coastline that stretches west of the city. If sticking around, head either to the Malecón, which is quite beautiful, or the parque central, a major hangout at night.

Most visitors arrive **via guagua or car**; coastal Highway 44 connects the city with Azua, Baní and Santo Domingo to the east before continuing west all the way to the border. If spending the night, most **accommodations** are within a couple of blocks of the seaside Malecón. The best of the lot is the *Gran Barahona*, Mota 5 (Ⓣ809/524-3442; ❷), with comfortable rooms that have A/C, TV and hot water. There's a decent array of **places to eat**; *Melo's Café*, Anacaona 12 (Ⓣ809/524-5437), is the best of the lot, an unpretentious diner with delicious American breakfasts and nightly dinner specials. Also worth checking out is *Brisas del Caribe*, a seafood restaurant on the far eastern end of the Malecón; the creole shrimp and broiled kingfish are house specialities.

West of Barahona

The gorgeous coastline west of Barahona is the region's premier attraction, yet it remains virtually undiscovered by outsiders. The first major beach spot is Baoruco, 15km west of Barahona along Highway 44, a tiny fishing village with the best hotel in the Barahona region, *Casa Bonita* (Ⓣ809/696-0215, Ⓕ223-0548; ❸), with great views, a patio with a swimming pool and an elegant restaurant.

Five kilometres beyond Baoruco, pueblo **San Rafael** holds an enticing beach, if one with a strong, crashing surf. Fortunately, a **waterfall** thrums down the nearby mountains and forms a natural swimming pool at the entrance. **Paraiso**, another 5km to the west, is the biggest town along this stretch, but still doesn't boast much in the way of facilities. It does have a long strand of superb sandy beach, along which stands *Hotel Paraiso* (Ⓣ809/243-1080; ❶), a decent place to stay for the night.

A better beach lies yet 5km further west, in **Los Patos**, where the ocean is joined again by a river descending from the mountains to form a freshwater swimming pool. The beach, surrounded with dense mangroves, stays pretty active throughout the week, and beach vendors are set up to take care of most visitors' needs. The one

hotel, *Virginia*, Calle Peatonal (no phone; ❶), is pretty basic with private cold-water bath and no toilet seats.

East of Barahona

Heading east of Barahona toward San Cristóbal and the capital stand a string of colonial-era towns that appear congested and unappealing at first sight, but hide beaches that make stopovers worthwhile. First up is **Azua**, 60km east of Barahona on Highway-2. Though there's nothing left of the original city, Azua is one of the oldest European cities in the New World, founded by future conqueror of Cuba Diego Velázquez in 1504. What is still here, though, is the five-kilometre-long **Playa Monte Río** a short drive south of town, which offers beautiful views of the rolling El Número mountains. There's very little development around the beach; rather, the calm waters are lined with fishing boats and a few locally run outdoor restaurants.

Another 40km east on the Carretera Sánchez, less than 20km east of the turn-off to the mountain town of San José (see box below), coastal **Baní** has in recent years turned relatively prosperous, an upswing that has spurred much population growth, if not exactly prettified the place. There are few diversions within the town, but the nearby beaches are the main draw. Best of the bunch is **Las Salinas**, a small town consisting of little more than a few dozen houses scattered about a white-sand beach, 16km southwest at the end of the Carretera Las Calderas. Sand dunes, salt-pans and rolling hills surround the village, which makes for a fine place to do some **windsurfing**; taking advantage of these conditions is the *Salinas High Wind Center*, Puerto Hermosa 7 (☎809/310-8141 or 471-9463; ❷), a small but extremely nice resort catering mostly to wealthy Dominicans.

San Cristóbal and around

SAN CRISTÓBAL, Trujillo's hometown, enjoyed its heyday during his rule; today the cramped, asphalt city qualifies as one of the country's least appealing. That said, it is well situated for exploring the unforgettable **El Pomier** caves to the north.

From the town it's 20km due north to the caves; if you don't have your own transport, pick-up truck *guaguas* leave every thirty minutes from the north end of

Barahona's mountain hamlet

Tucked away in the mountains along the Río Ocóa, **San José de Ocóa**, 27km north of the Carretera Sánchez along Highway 41, attracts weekenders from across the country, most of whom are eager to beat the valley heat, visit the local river *balneario* and take advantage of the lovely, sometimes rugged, mountain landscape. The town itself is an easy-going and fairly modest hamlet, unremarkable but for its majestic setting. Just south of town, though, is **El Manantiel**, the local river *balneario*, a kilometre down a dirt road off the highway, where you'll find several good spots for swimming among the boulders and ice-cold cascades. Plenty of other people – particularly families – opt for the outfits that siphon off fresh water from the river into large swimming pools, such as **Las Yessicas** (daily 8.30am–2am), visible from the highway and with a large pool, a restaurant and a popular dance floor.

Accommodation options in town are plentiful but decidedly no-frills, intended as they are to serve families who don't mind shacking up several to a room. Options include *Sagrato de Jesús*, Cañada/San José (☎809/558-2432; ❶), and *Pensión San Francisco*, 37 Pimentel (☎809/558-2741; ❶), both not especially luxurious but acceptable. *Baco*, a half-block west of the parque central, serves quality **meals** like *chivo guisado* (goat stew) or chicken with rice, beans and plantains.

San Cristóbal's public market. **Reserva Arqueológica El Pomier** (daily 9.30am–5pm; RD$50) protects the most extensive collection of cave paintings in the Caribbean, though this claim to fame draws strangely few visitors. Upon arrival, you'll be assigned a park guide who expects a RD$40 tip and will take you to the first of three enormous, easily accessible chambers; the first alone holds 600 pictographs. Alternately, you can head north on a *guagua* from the parque central in San Cristóbal to **La Toma** (daily 8.30am–7.30pm; RD$5, parking RD$20), a series of large cemented pools supplied with fresh water from the Haina River.

The only **hotel** in San Cristóbal is basic but clean *Aparta-Hotel Ayala*, Padre Ayala 110 (☎809/528-3040; ❶). **Dining** choices are also limited; try *Plaza Carolina*, General Cabral one block south of Constitución, an outdoor *comida criolla* spot.

7

Puerto Rico

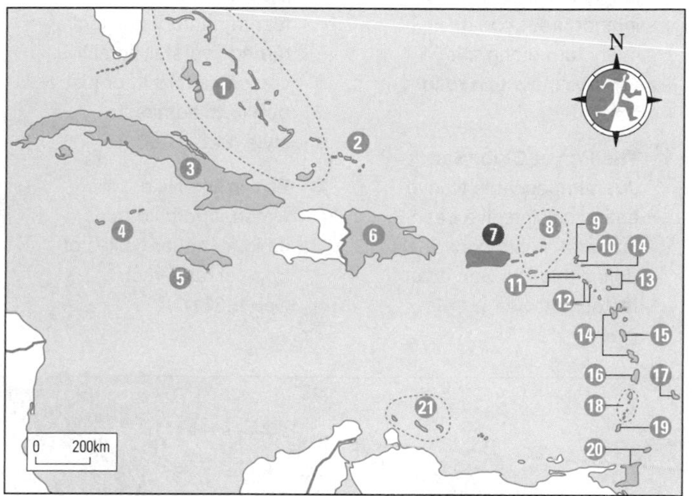

Puerto Rico Highlights

* **Old San Juan** Watch the sea crash around this enclave of colourful Spanish colonial architecture. See p.363
* **La Ruta Panoramica** Stunning views of the jungle-like Puerto Rican interior greet you at every turn along this winding mountain road. See p.382
* **The Parrot Club, San Juan** Impeccable Nuevo Latino cuisine, live Latin jazz and a chic crowd define this Old San Juan restaurant. See p.367
* **Vieques and Culebra** These laid-back yet ravishing islands off Puerto Rico's east coast hold the country's best beaches. See p.384
* **El Convento, San Juan** Stay a night at this fifteenth-century convent turned five-star hotel if you can afford it, or just pop in to admire its style. See p.360
* **El Yunque** Hike, birdwatch, or orchid hunt amid 43 square miles of tropical rainforest. See p.371

Introduction and Basics

Geographically, **Puerto Rico** is a Caribbean hub, presiding squarely over the waters between Hispaniola and the Virgin Islands. As a commonwealth of the US, however, it remains a world apart from its island neighbours, over a distance that can be measured not just in kilometres, but in dollars. It's island life with infrastructure, the likes of which the Tropic of Cancer seldom sees: excellent interstate highways, for example, allow travellers to zip from coral reef to five-star restaurant, and hikers can traipse through the spectacular El Yunque rainforest on well-paved trails maintained by the US National Forest Service. American influence is strongest in **San Juan**, where even the ramparts of El Morro – which staved off European aggressors for 500 years – haven't managed to prevent the influx of big- name American fast-food and retail chains. But the capital retains a distinctly Latin character at its core, with **Old San Juan** hosting a treasure-trove of pastel Spanish colonial architecture on exquisitely restored cobblestoned streets.

Despite the threat of overdevelopment from US dollars, most of the 35-by-100-mile island has managed to elude despoilment. Even in the crowded capital, it's hard to find a sullied beach, and outside the major cities nature is largely untouched – especially in the jungly, mountainous interior; on the relatively hidden beaches along the southwest coast; and on the offshore islands. In fact, the rich natural resources and wide range of **hiking**, **birding**, **diving** and **caving** opportunities make Puerto Rico as much a magnet for eco-tourists as for sun-worshippers.

Where to go

No matter where you are in Puerto Rico, you're never more than a couple of hours by car from **San Juan**, whose colonial architecture in its old town is a must-see. More historic vestiges can be found in the southern city of **Ponce**.

Hikers won't want to miss **El Yunque,** the only tropical rainforest in the US park system, with miles of trails, and flora and fauna galore. **Birdwatching** is also excellent in the arid landscape of **Guánica State Forest**, a World Biosphere Reserve in the southwest.

Puerto Rico is also home to pretty beaches and coral reefs; for **diving** and **snorkelling** check out the beautiful offshore islets of **Vieques** and **Culebra**.

If you prefer going underground, rather than underwater, spelunkers from all over the globe are drawn to the **Río Camuy Cave Park** in the northwest, known as **karst country** — where limestone has eroded over the centuries to form sinkholes and a vast network of caves that can be explored.

When to go

Puerto Rico's pleasant **tropical climate** is virtually seasonless, though temperatures are slightly higher from June to September; note it may be considerably cooler in the mountains. Rainfall varies around the island – heaviest in El Yunque, which receives up to 200 inches a year, and lightest in the southwest desert region, getting only 37 inches a year.

Hurricanes are so common in Puerto Rico that they got their name here; the English word for these storms with winds of over 75mph comes from the name of the Taíno god of malevolence, Jurakán (pronounced hu-ra-kan). Hurricane season runs June through November, when the weather is hottest and wettest, with the risk highest in September.

Getting there

San Juan's **Luis Muñoz Marín International Airport** is serviced by almost

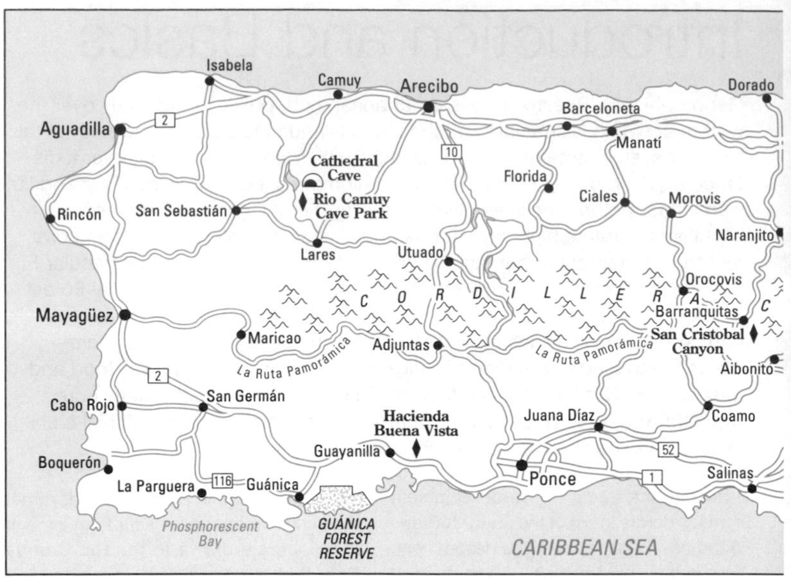

thirty US and international carriers, with half the Caribbean's flight traffic passing through it. The main US gateways are New York and Miami. A hub for **American Airlines /American Eagle**, San Juan is also serviced by major airlines such as British Airways, Air Canada, Air France, Iberia and Air Jamaica (see pp.12–18 for contact details). Jet Blue (☎800/538-2583) flies direct from New York for as little as US$250 round-trip. A typical high-season return ticket from London runs about £450.

There are no flights to San Juan from Australasia.

International and domestic flights also travel through two smaller airports: **Mercedita** in Ponce (☎787/842-6292) and Eugenio Maria de Hostos in **Mayagüez** (☎787/833-0148).

Puerto Rico is one of the world's top **cruise ship** destinations. For a list of carriers, see pp.14 and 16.

Money and costs

Puerto Rico uses **US currency**, which generally comes in bills of US$1, $5, $10, $20, $50 and $100; the dollar (sometimes referred to as a peso) is made up of 100 cents in coins of 1¢ (penny), 5¢ (nickel), 10¢ (dime), 25¢ (quarter) and 50¢ (half-dollar). Major credit cards are widely accepted at hotels and restaurants.

Although Puerto Rico's GNP is lower than that of any of the fifty states, **prices** are not drastically cheaper than on the mainland. In San Juan, the least you can expect to pay for accommodation, without sharing a bath, is US$65 for a double room; an average lunch at a modest establishment runs US$5 to $12, with comparable dinners from US$10 to $20.

ATMs – called ATHs ("a todas horas", or "at any hour") – are abundant in cities; you'll find them in banks, supermarkets, casinos and most of the larger hotels. In smaller towns and rural areas, you'll have to look a little harder. If you're at a loss, ask for directions to the local Banco Popular. Regular banking hours are Monday to Friday from 8.30am to 2.30pm.

Expect to pay eleven percent **tax** on rooms with casinos, nine percent on hotels without, and nine percent on country inns. There is no tax on food and merchandise.

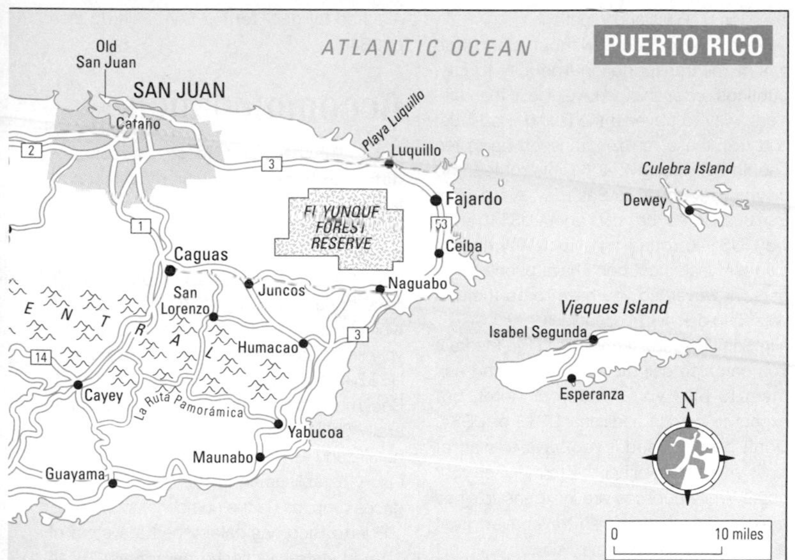

Information, websites and maps

The Puerto Rican Tourism Company, or PRTC (℡800/866-5829 or 787/721-2400; Ⓦwww.prtourism.com), has offices in San Juan at the Luis Muñoz Marín International Airport (℡787/791-1014) and Old San Juan, in Ponce (℡787/284-4913), Vieques (℡787/741-5000), Aguadilla (℡787/890-3315) and Cabo Rojo (℡787/851-7015). The helpful multi-lingual staff is more than eager to suggest and book hotels and restaurants, arrange activities and even intervene in case of theft or illness. Be sure to grab a copy of their 40-page *Puerto Rico Travel and Sports Planner*, which has lists of accommodation and phone numbers for many transportation and recreation services.

The PRTC also publishes *Que Pasa?*, a bimonthly glossy with a calendar of events, feature-length stories on various attractions and regions, and helpful listings. Another publication, *Places to Go,* distributed by CP Management, can also be useful and is free at hotels and tourist offices.

Maps are available at PRTC offices, and are included in the *Puerto Rico Travel and Sports Planner* and *Que Pasa?*. Street and road maps are also sold in bookstores.

Getting around

If you **rent a car,** you'll make the most efficient use of your time. While you may get a cheaper deal from a local rental company, national chains such as Avis (℡800/874-3556), Hertz (℡800/654-3131) and Budget (℡800/468-5822) are very likely to be more reliable, and offer 24-hour emergency service. Weekly rates for an economy car in San Juan start at around US$280. AAA (℡800/222-4357 or 787/764-4913) also operates emergency roadside assistance for members. Driver's licences from the UK, US, Canada, Australia and New Zealand are valid for up to three months.

Highways are fast and fairly well maintained. As in the US, motorists drive on the right side and speed limits are posted in miles per hour. Unlike the US, distances are posted in kilometres and road signs are in Spanish. In the cities, be aware that drivers are often reckless and impatient.

While Puerto Rico is without islandwide bus or rail transportation from city to city, **públicos** are an inexpensive, if less than efficient, way to traverse the island. Part-bus, part-taxi, these vehicles transport up to ten people over somewhat flexible routes and distances Monday to Saturday. A trip from San Juan to Ponce costs about US$10 one-way, US$20 round-trip. Each city has its own terminal; most don't have phone numbers, however, so you have to go there in person to ask about schedules.

In San Juan, the terminal is in Rio Piedras. You can also call the *público* line and ask them to pick you up at your hotel, but expect to pay an additional US$3 or US$4. Don't be surprised if you have to wait at least an hour, at either the terminal or your hotel. While *públicos* are inexpensive, they make frequent stops, so travel over great distances can be extremely slow.

Daily domestic **flights** depart from San Juan's international airport for Aguadilla, Fajardo, Mayagüez and Ponce. Frequent commuter flights for Vieques and Culebra depart from the **Fernando L. Rivas Dominici Airport** (☎787/729-8711) in Isla Grande, near the San Juan neighbourhood of Miramar, and from Fajardo (see p.384 for details). Vieques and Culebra can also be reached by daily **ferries** from Fajardo (see p. 384).

Major público lines

The following services all originate in San Juan:

Blue Line ☎787/765-7733 (to Rio Piedras, Aguadilla, Aguada, Moca, Isabele and other destinations)
Chóferes Unidos de Ponce ☎787/764-0540 (to Ponce and other destinations)
Línea Boricúa ☎787/765-1908 (to Lares, Ponce, Jayuya, Utuado, San Sebastian and other destinations)
Línea Caborrojena ☎787/723-9155 (to Cabo Rojo, San Germán and other destinations)
Línea Sultana ☎787/765-9377 (to Mayagüez and other destinations)
Terminal de Transportación Pública ☎787/250-0717 (to Fajardo and other destinations)

Accommodation

Puerto Rico has a wide range of **accommodation options**, from rustic mountain cottages to fancy beachfront high-rises. For a room endorsed by the PRTC, with air conditioning and TV, you'll spend anywhere from US$50 to US$450. For lower prices, you'll have to suffer the heat and share a bath in typically basic and dingy surroundings. The very finest hotels and inns cost a minimum of US$200 a night. During high season, mid-December through mid-April, prices are generally US$20–30 higher at small inns and hotels, and as much as US$50–100 higher at luxury establishments. The rest of the year, prices drop, as do the number of tourists.

Puerto Rico has established a system of 20-odd state-sanctioned **paradores**. These so-called country inns are intended to be convenient for accessing the island's beaches, mountains and towns, and most are located in picturesque settings west of San Juan. For a complete list, contact one of the PRTC offices. Don't assume these places will be first-rate; always ask to see a room before you book.

If you're looking for cheap above all else, ask the PRTC for the list of guesthouses they do not endorse; most of these have shared baths in very basic settings without air conditioning; PRTC agents will tell you which ones inspire the most complaints or compliments.

For those wishing to pitch a tent, there are many legal **campgrounds**, the majority on beaches and in national parks and forests. To camp on these public lands you'll need a **permit**, and cost varies according to site. Contact the Department of Natural Resources (☎787/724-3724) no later than two weeks before your trip.

Food and drink

In recent years, Puerto Rico – and San Juan in particular – has commanded a growing reputation as the culinary hot spot of the Caribbean. World-renowned chefs at vanguard restaurants prepare dynamic **Nuevo**

Latino cuisine – a twist on traditional criollo cooking, with an emphasis on fish, fruits, tubers and dark rum sauces or marinades with tropical ingredients. You'll also find every manner of ethnic food in the capital, including Indian, Thai, French and even Romanian.

Criollo fare, however, is still the staple of the Puerto Rican diet. Meats are mostly served with rice and red beans *(habichuelas)* or *tostones* – medallions of mashed, fried plantains. *Sofrito* – a sauce made from cilantro, onions, garlic and peppers – is used to season many dishes, as is *adobo*, a mixture of garlic, oregano, paprika, vinegar and oil. The food is typically tasty but much of it is starchy and fried in animal fat, and pork is far more popular than fish outside of the major cities.

The system of state-sanctioned **restaurants**, called *mesones gastronómicos*, presumably ensures a standard of decency among participating restaurants (most of which serve traditional criollo food), but the quality can vary widely. For a list of these establishments, contact the **Country Inns Central Information Office** (☎800/866-7827) or pick up a copy of *Que Pasa?*.

Budget travellers can fill up at cheap rice-and-beans joints all over the island or seek out savory criollo staples like *asopao de pollo* (stewed chicken) and *plátanos* (plantains) or *lechón asado* (roast pork) and *mofongo* (a ball of crushed, fried plantains and seasonings), sold from trailers or the backs of pickup trucks. *Reposterías* are also a good bet. Found in San Juan and in strip malls islandwide, they have some of the island's best coffee, along with breakfast *postres* – slightly sweet pastries filled with meat or cheese; they also sell soups, tortillas, seafood salads and fresh bread. Note that in all but the best restaurants, fresh vegetables are hard to come by, but supermarkets like Pueblo usually carry a good supply.

Coffee in Puerto Rico is strong, served black or with heated milk (*café con leche*), and very sweet. Look out for signs for refreshing *coco frío* – chilled coconuts punctured with drinking straws. While not as common, **fresh-fruit drinks** made from mangos, papayas and oranges (known as *jugo de china*) are also available. Not surprisingly, **rum** (*ron*) is the national drink, as Puerto Rico is the world's largest producer of this sugarcane-based liquor; more than twenty brands are distilled here. The locally brewed beer is Medalla; Presidente, from the Dominican Republic, is also popular.

For the most part, **tap water** is safe to drink. However, it's wise to avoid it after storms and instead stick with bottled water, which is widely available. If in doubt, ask the locals.

Phones, post and email

Outside Puerto Rico, dial ☎787/555-1212 for **directory information**. Attendants usually answer in Spanish but will switch to English at your request; within Puerto Rico, dial ☎411. All telephone numbers are seven digits long and preceded by ☎787, which must be used for both local and long-distance calls; for long-distance, dial a "1" first.

Post offices, located in most major and small towns, are open from 8am to 5pm weekdays, though some have Saturday morning hours.

Decent **internet** service is hard to come by, except at major hotels, and the rare cybercafé.

The **country code** for Puerto Rico is ☎787.

Opening hours, holidays and festivals

In general, **business hours** are 8.30am to 5.30pm Monday to Friday. On the **public holidays** listed below, government offices, banks and schools are closed, and museum hours and transportation schedules may change.

Festivals

The following festivals are the most popular organized events in Puerto Rico. In addition to these, each town celebrates its **patron saint's day** (*fiesta patronale*) and the ten days leading up to it. The PRTC has details.

February/March

Carnaval Ponce

Celebration during the six days preceding Lent,

featuring parades of traditional *vejigantes,* or masked revelers.

May/June

Casals Music Festival San Juan

Two weeks of orchestral music with world-renowned musicians.

Heineken Jazzfest San Juan

Four days of Latin jazz, performed by Puerto Rican and international musicians, at the Sixto Escobar Park in Condado.

San Juan Bautista Day/Noche de San Juan (June 24/23)

San Juan's *fiesta patronal.* Parties and festivities in Old San Juan culminate with crowds walking backward into the sea three times, in honour of St John the Baptist.

July

Santiago Apostol Festival Loiza

Good place to experience the customs of *santería.* Very African in flavor, with costumed parades and *bomba* drumming. Not to be missed.

November

National Bomba y Plena Festival Ponce

African-based drumming and singing, by performers from all over the island.

Public holidays

January 1 New Year's Day
January 6 Three Kings' Day
January 10 Eugenio María de Hostos's Birthday
Third Monday in January Martin Luther King, Jr., Day
Third Monday in February Presidents' Day
March 22 Abolition Day
March/April Palm Sunday, Good Friday, Easter Sunday
April 21 Jose de Diego Day
Last Monday in May Memorial Day
July 4 Independence Day
July 17 Luís Muñoz Rivera's Birthday
July 25 Constitution Day
July 27 Jose Celso Barbosa's Birthday
First Monday in September Labour Day
Second Monday in October Columbus Day
November 11 Veterans' Day
Fourth Thursday in November Thanksgiving Day
December 25, Christmas Day

Crime and safety

Puerto Rico is hardly crime-free, but most violent crime is confined to poor urban areas. Tourist spots are, for the most part, safe, and conspicuously guarded by police. Nevertheless, **pickpocketing** occurs; guard your cash and valuables in a safe place and be alert. Try to avoid walking alone on deserted beaches, hiking alone and travelling around alone at night.

If you ask a Puerto Rican for directions, more often than not you'll be told, "Follow me." Most people have only the best intentions, but be aware that **carjackings** occur with some regularity. Avoid asking complete strangers for directions if you can, especially at night, and particularly if you're a woman travelling solo. Be sure to park in well-lit areas and don't leave valuables exposed in your vehicle, even during the day.

In case of **emergency**, dial ⓣ911.

Health

Cases of **dengue fever**, transmitted by mosquitoes, have been reported in Puerto Rico in recent years. Early symptoms include sudden fever and aching joints, after which a rash sets in. The disease itself, which typically lasts several days, isn't treatable, but symptoms are. The best medicine is prevention, through the use of liberal amounts of mosquito repellent. Mosquitoes are most rampant in July.

History

As far back as 100 AD several indigenous groups occupied Puerto Rico – first the Arcáicos, then the Igneris, and finally the Taíno who arrived in 600 AD and dubbed the island "Borinquén". This last group had a long-lasting effect on Puerto Rican culture and bloodlines; many Puerto Rican words come from the Arawak language spoken by the Taíno, and it is estimated that sixty percent of Puerto Ricans today have Taíno ancestry.

Full-blooded Taíno were driven off the island almost entirely by the mid-sixteenth century, 150 years after Spanish occupation. When Christopher Columbus landed on Puerto Rico, which he called San Juan Bautista, in 1493, it was the Taíno who guided his troops there from Hispaniola, where the Spanish had taken the Indians as guides and slaves. And it was the Taíno who safeguarded Ponce de León's passage through Puerto Rico in search of gold when the Spanish government granted him authority to colonize the island in 1508.

Upon entering office as Puerto Rico's first governor, Ponce de León quickly began converting the Taíno to Christianity and subjecting them to forced labour. The church also began sanctioning intermarriage, rendering permissible the longstanding Spanish tradition of keeping Taíno mistresses. Their offspring, called *mestizos*, sustained Taíno heritage after the Indians fled the island to escape subjugation, save for the remnant who took refuge in the Central Mountain region.

In 1511, the Spanish began migrating to a headland on the northern shore that naturally protected a large bay. Ponce de León named the settlement Puerto Rico, or rich port. Through a cartographic error, however, the name of the city and the island were eventually switched, and San Juan became the capital of the island of Puerto Rico. The colonists' second settlement, after Caparra across the bay, San Juan afforded the best natural fortification against invaders.

The colonists grew sugarcane, plantains and bananas, citrus fruits and ginger. Once the Taíno fled, the Spanish saw the need for new slave labourers and began importing West Africans in 1518; by 1530 they constituted half the population.

With its peerless vantage in the Caribbean, Puerto Rico was soon caught between European rivals grappling to lay claim to its strategic position and rich natural resources. By 1521, *sanjuañeros* recognized the value and vulnerability of their port, and began building a massive stone wall around the perimeter of the settlement. Less than 20 years later, the Dutch raided San Germán, a settlement on the western coast, inspiring *sanjuañeros* to begin constructing the formidable stone fortification called Fuerte San Felipe del Morro, which still stands at the headland of Old San Juan. After a few failed attacks, the British managed to seize and burn San Juan in 1598, but they were done in by dysentery. The Dutch attacked successfully in 1625, again burning the city, but were also overcome by disease soon thereafter.

Puerto Rico was left vulnerable, and islanders were impoverished and resentful that they were seeing so little return on their labour for the Spanish. They were not allowed to participate in government, trade with other nations, or move around the island. In rebellion, they began trading sugar and rum illegally.

The Spanish empire, though weakening, sent General Alejandro O'Reilly to establish order in the latter half of the eighteenth century. He built roads and schools and encouraged literate Spaniards to immigrate to the island, while dropping trade restrictions and lowering taxes. From 1765 to 1800, the economy boomed and the population tripled, to 155,000.

By the turn of the century, Puerto Rico was thriving. In the wake of the French Revolution, slaves began revolting in the French Caribbean colonies, driving white planters to Puerto Rico, and stepping up sugar and rum production on the island. Puerto Rico began a lucrative exchange with the US, exporting sugar, rum and coffee. Slavery wouldn't be abolished in Puerto Rico until 1873.

From 1810 to 1822 Simón Bolívar, the "Liberator", began freeing Spanish colonies, leaving Spain with nothing but Puerto Rico and Cuba by the mid-1820s. To keep the islanders happy and nurture their loyalty, the Spanish further lowered taxes and opened up more ports for trade. And to *guarantee* their loyalty, they established a military government that lasted 42 years.

The first move toward independence came in 1838, in a liberation movement led by Buenaventura Quiñones. Spain quashed the effort, and a few subsequent ones, but by 1897 Puerto Rico finally got what it wanted – independence from Spain as an autonomous state. However, in the concluding battle of the Spanish-American War the next year, American forces took Ponce and gained another US territory.

Islanders became US citizens in 1917, but revolutionary movements continued to brew, and led to several bloody altercations between radicals and police, such as the 1937 Ponce Massacre in which twenty protesters died. Soon, steered by Luis Muños Marín, head of the Popular Democratic Party and the island's first governor under US jurisdiction, Puerto Rico began making strides as an industrially developed entity; the island drafted its first constitution and elected Marín as governor in 1947.

In 1967, in the first referendum addressing the issue of sovereignty, Puerto Ricans voted to remain a commonwealth, rather than become a full US state or independent nation. Two more referenda followed in 1993 and 1998, and both were voted down in favour of the status quo.

The move for independence remains strong, fuelled in no small part by opposition to the US Navy's occupation of Vieques since World War II, and its use of this island for bombing practice (which the current administration says will cease in 2003). But thus far the voices of protest haven't been strong enough to outweigh the hefty subsidies that Puerto Rico receives from the US government each year.

7.1

San Juan

Founded in 1521 by Ponce de León, the capital of Puerto Rico, **SAN JUAN**, is the oldest city in US territory. Home to 1.6 million (more than a third of the island's citizens), it is also the heart of Puerto Rican tourism. What draws travellers here year-round are miles of smooth, clean beaches, a wide range of accommodation, fabulous restaurants and, of course, Old San Juan, whose beautifully restored historic sights surrounded by crashing turquoise surf are reason enough to make a trip to Puerto Rico.

Along with Old San Juan, resort-filled Condado is the most popular neighbourhood for visitors thanks to its excellent beachfront and fine boutiques, and these two sections of the capital share the highest concentration of restaurants and lodging options. There's also much to explore as the city extends to the south and east, including the beachfront neighbourhoods of Ocean Park and Isla Verde; up-and-coming Santurce with its numerous art galleries; the financial district of Hato Rey; and the college-town vibe in Rio Piedras.

Within just a couple hours' drive from San Juan are Puerto Rico's rarest natural resources and some of the best beaches and coral reefs in the Caribbean. The El Yunque rainforest, Luquillo Beach and the Rio Camuy Cave Park all make excellent day trips.

Arrival and information

You'll most likely arrive at the **Luis Muñoz Marín International Airport** (☎787/791-4670), 14km east of San Juan in the suburb of Carolina. The **Puerto Rican Tourism Company** (PRTC) has three offices here; the main one is outside terminal C on the first level. Friendly staff will assist you in arranging transportation and lodging, going so far as to call around for the best deals.

San Juan is about twenty to thirty minutes' drive from the airport along Rte 26 W (Avenida Baldorioty de Castro). Major **car rental** agencies operate airport offices. By **taxi**, the cost is US$8 to Isla Verde, US$12 to Condado and US$16 to Old San Juan. The **public bus** (#C45) is air-conditioned and cheap – just 25 or 50 cents – but it takes about an hour to get to the city and requires a transfer to the #A5 in Isla Verde if you're staying in Condado, and another change to the #B21 in Condado if you're staying in Old San Juan.

If you arrive by **público** from another part of the island, you'll arrive via the bus terminal at the base of Old San Juan, on the bay side, not far from the **cruise ship** port; buses and taxis are plentiful from here.

The **PRTC** also has offices in Old San Juan, both housed in restored colonial structures: **La Casita**, the pink building on Calle Comercio near the docks (Mon–Wed 8.30am–8pm, Thurs & Fri until 5.30pm, Sat & Sun 9am–8pm; ☎787/722-1709), and **La Princesa** on Paseo de la Princesa (Mon–Fri 9am–4pm; ☎787/721-2400).

Getting around

While the city is fairly easy to navigate by car, it is large enough to make bus travel tedious at best and the use of taxis prohibitively expensive; renting a car (see p.351)

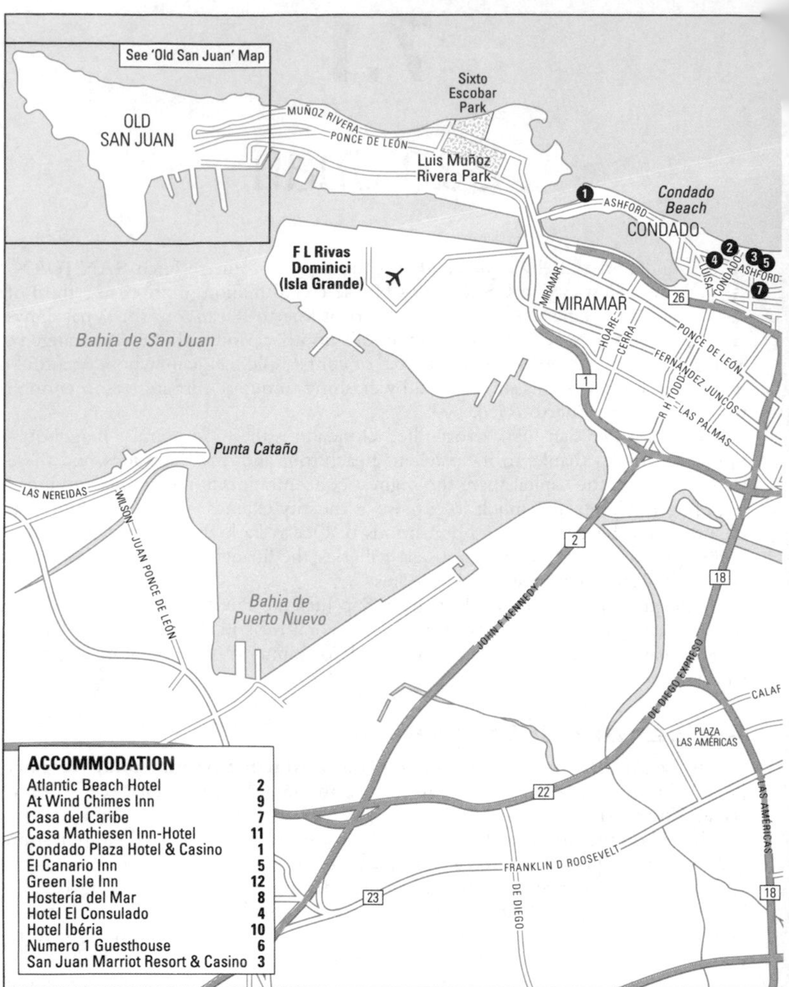

is the way to go. If you're staying in Old San Juan or Condado for just a few days, however, you may choose to travel by foot; both neighbourhoods are compact enough for strolling.

By car

If you rent a car, you may want to consider spending a little extra on insurance, particularly if you intend to drive in the capital: Puerto Rican drivers can be very unpredictable. You'll need to **drive defensively** and stay alert at all times. Don't be caught off guard, for instance, if a car suddenly passes you on the sidewalk or shoulder. Rubbernecking is great sport – mostly on the part of men checking out the pretty girls, a phenomenon that's almost comically exaggerated in San Juan. It's also not uncommon to encounter cars turning without signalling, barrelling down the

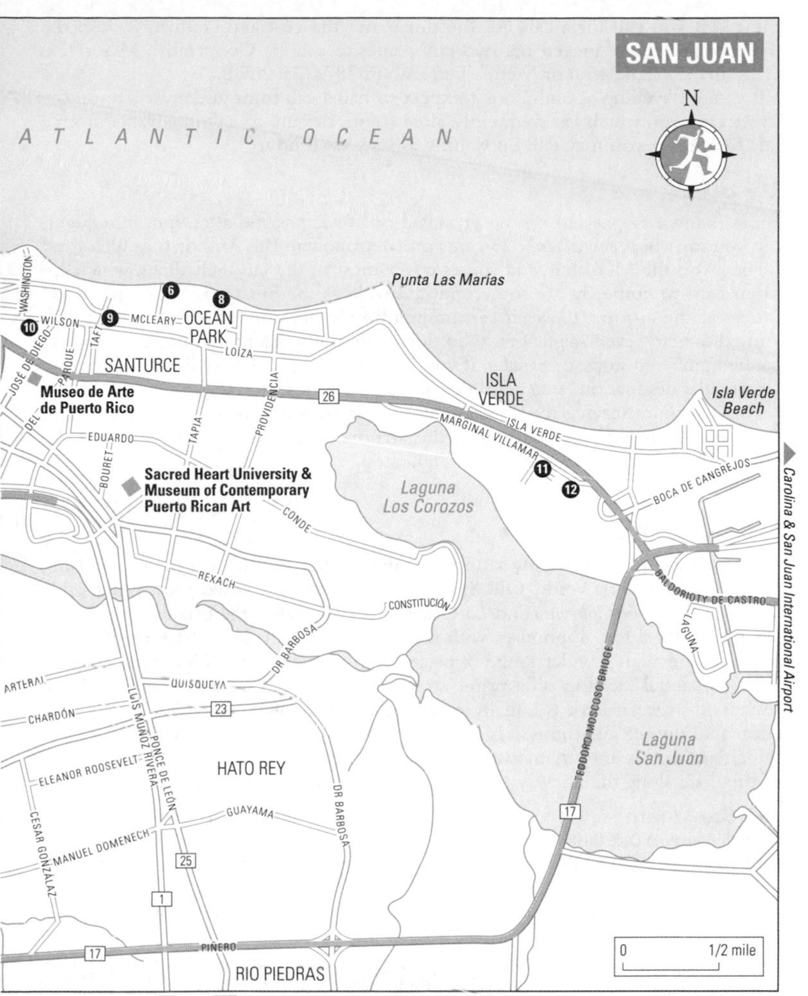

centre of the road, or not using headlights at night.

Prepare yourself for many narrow **one-way streets** indicated (or not, in some cases) by *tránsito* signs with arrows pointing in the direction of traffic. When in doubt, go slow and note the direction of parked cars.

Parking can be a nightmare. Many businesses don't have car parks, so vehicles line up on the sidewalk, and many drivers think nothing of straddling two spaces.

By taxi

Plenty of **taxis turísticos** cruise the streets during the day in Condado and Old San Juan; in other neighbourhoods, you may have to call first. Taxis are supposed to charge US$1 to start and 10 cents for each 1/13 of a mile, but in practice drivers never turn on their meters, so you'll need to agree on a price before you set foot in the car. If you call for a cab, ask the dispatcher the cost and confirm it with the driver when you're picked up. Two companies to call are Cooperative Major Taxi Cabs (☎787/723-2460) or Metro-Taxi Cab (☎787/725-2870).

If you're travelling at night, don't expect to hail a cab from just anywhere on the street; taxis run much less frequently after 10pm. Be sure to call in advance from a safe location as you may end up waiting as long as an hour.

By bus

Buses (known as *guaguas*) can be slow, and on weekends and after 9pm infrequent, but you can't beat the price – 25 cents on Metropolitan Bus Authority vehicles and 50 cents on the Metrobus, and routes cover most of the city. Schedules, which are often hard to come by, are sometimes available at the bus terminal, or at PRTC offices at the airport. *Guaguas* can be helpful for newcomers learning their way around the city; even *sanjuaneros* who don't ride them orient themselves according to the numbered stops, or *paradas*. If you ask for directions, you're likely to hear that a particular destination "está cerca de parada 23" (is near stop 23).

Most bus lines service rough neighbourhoods en route to popular tourist areas, particularly those that depart from the airport. Watch your valuables amid the crowd, and take care to get off at the right stop.

Accommodation

Most of San Juan's accommodation is concentrated in Old San Juan, Condado, Ocean Park and Isla Verde. Old San Juan boasts the city's two most remarkable places to stay – *El Convento* and *La Galería* – and overall is the priciest neighbourhood, save for a few flophouses with shared baths. Condado is a deservedly more popular base, with a wider range of price options (including several excellent bargains), a central location on a prime stretch of beach and some of the city's finest restaurants. Ocean Park is equally nice, and much quieter, and has a selection of affordable, unique guesthouses. Isla Verde hosts some all-inclusive beachfront resorts, which are worlds unto themselves, as well as some of San Juan's best bargains; most of these are along the freeway, but are just few a blocks from the beach.

Old San Juan

Hotel El Convento Calle Cristo 100 ☎787/723-9020. Gorgeously restored seventeenth-century Carmelite nunnery – worth seeing, even if cost prohibits staying. It features a four-storey quadrangle with long breezy arcades, high vaulted ceilings and balconies overlooking an interior garden. There's a small pool, jacuzzi and gym, several restaurants, a casino and designer shops. Rooms with mahogany beams and rich colour

Useful San Juan bus routes

All of the following buses, with the exception of #45 from the airport, originate at the bus terminal.

Bus	Destination
Metrobus 1	Rio Piedras, Hato Rey, Santurce, Old San Juan
Metrobus Express	Rio Piedras, Hato Rey, Old San Juan
#A5	Old San Juan, Stop 18 (*parada* 18) in Santurce, Loiza St, Isla Verde, Los Angeles, Iturregui
#C10	*AcuaExpreso* ferry, Hato Rey, Borinquen Ave, Eduardo Conde, Loiza St, Condado, Isla Grande, Stop 18
#B21	Old San Juan, Condado, Stop 18, Fernandez Juncos, Plaza Las Américas
#C45	Airport to Isla Verde

schemes have A/C, TV/VCR, stereo systems, refrigerators, phones and bathrobes. 8

Hotel Milano Calle Fortaleza 307 ☎787/729-9050. Nineteenth-century building with rooftop bar and restaurant overlooking San Juan Bay has restored rooms with A/C, cable TV, phone and mini-fridges; some have harbour views. Ask to see room before booking; some are very small. 4

La Galería Calle Norzagaray 204–206 at San Justo ☎787/722-1808. Restored, museum like seventeenth-century captain's quarters with balconies, winding stairs, Spanish tiles, high beamed ceilings and dark woods. Antiques and art by owner are all for sale. Twenty-four plush rooms – each one unique – have A/C and phone; Continental breakfast is served in an indoor garden. 5

Condado

Atlantic Beach Hotel Calle Vendig 1 ☎787/721-6900. This Condado hotel has been a gay landmark for decades. Boisterous indoor/outdoor bar on wide swath of beach showcases live drag shows and DJs almost daily, and there's also a rooftop deck and jacuzzi. 4

At Wind Chimes Inn 1750 Calle McLeary on Taft ☎787/727-4153. This intimate restored Spanish villa a few blocks from the beach is enclosed by a stucco wall with arched entryways, interior patios and gardens, and has a pool with fountain and an outdoor bar. Rooms have private bath, A/C, ceiling fan, cable TV and phone with jack for internet access. Best bargain in Condado. 3

Casa del Caribe Calle Caribe 57 ☎787/722-7139. Walled-in escape with interior garden and patio located one block from restaurants and the beach; same owners as *At Wind Chimes*. Nine rooms have private bath, A/C, ceiling fan, cable TV and phone with jack. Continental breakfast is included. 3

Condado Plaza Hotel & Casino Avda Ashford 999 ☎800/624-0420. Located in the far west end of Condado, this enormous fancy hotel has a private beach, seven restaurants, several pools, the largest casino in Puerto Rico and great live salsa. Richly coloured, elegant rooms are bright and spacious, and have private terraces – most of which overlook the ocean or lagoon – and 24-hour room service. 8

El Canario Inn Avda Ashford 1317 ☎787/722-3861. The most pleasantly located of the clean, modest budget hotels. Small, basic rooms with cable TV, phones and A/C; Continental breakfast included. Interior garden and patio are home to resident *coquís*. 5

Hotel El Consulado Avda Ashford 1110 ☎787/289-9191. Distinguished-looking former Spanish consulate with tile floors, balconies and terracotta roofs. Clean, spacious rooms have A/C, cable TV, internet access and safe boxes; some with balconies. 4

Hotel Ibéria Avda Wilson 1464 ☎787/722-5380. Small, Spanish-style hotel in a residential section of Condado. Very simple accommodations with a restaurant, solarium and terrace. Rooms have A/C, cable TV and phone. 4

San Juan Marriot Resort and Casino Avda Ashford 1309 ☎787/722-7000. Looming 21 storeys over Condado, this major resort is popular with business travellers and convention-goers. It hosts two restaurants, 24-hour business centre, two tennis courts, health club and spa, game room, casino, two oceanside pools, a whirlpool and lounge with live Latin jazz and salsa. Spacious, generic rooms have TV/VCR, phone, safety box and hairdryer. 9

Ocean Park and Isla Verde

Casa Mathiesen Inn-Hotel Calle Uno 14, Isla Verde ☎787/726-8662. Safe, no-frills option off freeway in Isla Verde, with same owners as *Green Isle*. One block from beach, with swimming pool. Clean, unexciting rooms have cable TV, A/C, phone and safe box; some with kitchenette. Ask for a room away from street. 3

Green Isle Inn 36 Calle Uno, Isla Verde ☎787/726-4330. Great bargain in safe but charmless area, one block from the beach, with a pool on premises. Spacious rooms with cooking facilities, private bath, A/C, cable TV and phone. Meagre Continental breakfast included. 3

Hostería del Mar Calle Tapia 1, Ocean Park ☎787/727-3302. Simple but appealing, and directly on the beach. Rooms with A/C, phone and cable TV; some have ocean views and kitchenette. On-site restaurant in gazebo overlooking the ocean serves vegetarian and macrobiotic fare, steaks and seafood. 3

Numero 1 Guest House 1 Santa Ana, Ocean Park ☎787/726-5010. Lives up to its name, attracting many repeat customers, many of whom are gay. Features an interior garden, swimming pool, terrace with ocean views and an excellent bar and restaurant (*Pamela's*). Twelve elegant rooms have A/C, ceiling fan and phone. Continental breakfast included. 5

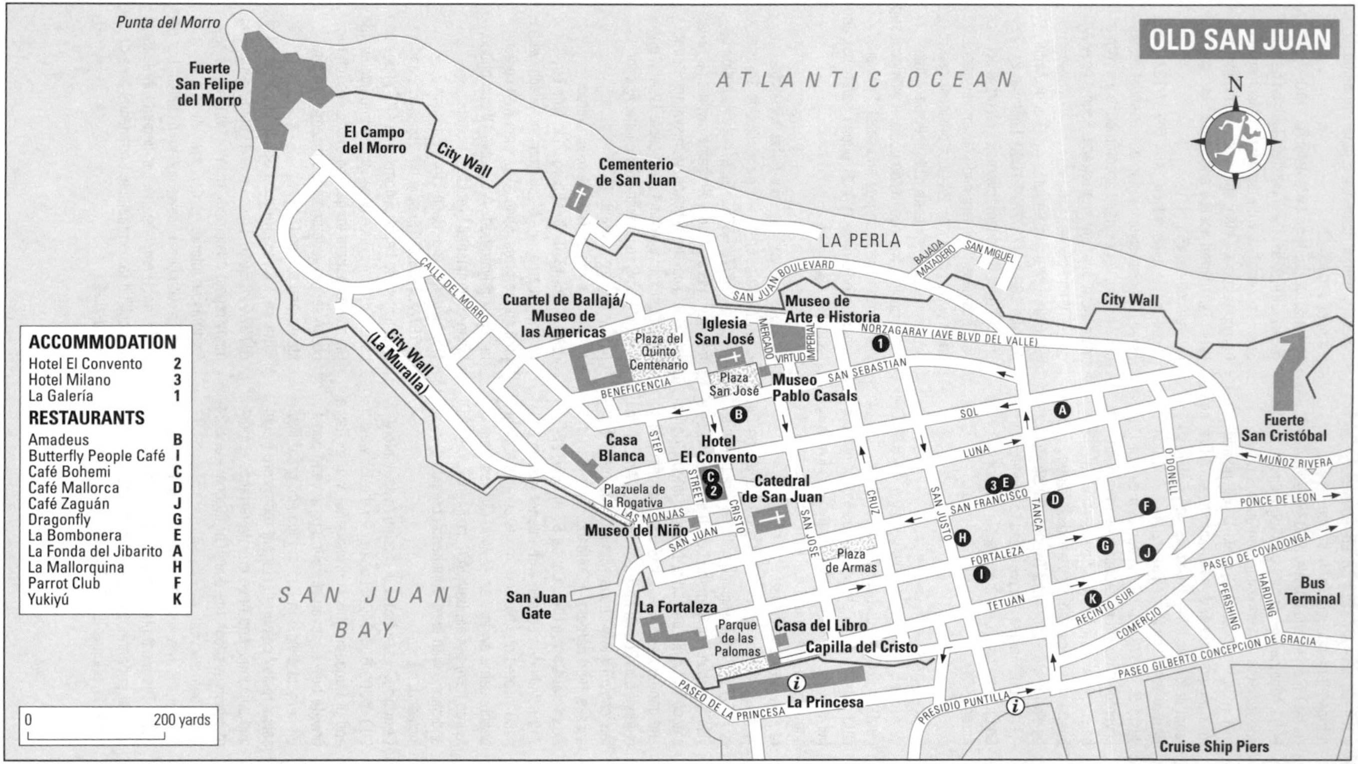

OLD SAN JUAN

ATLANTIC OCEAN

SAN JUAN BAY

N

Punta del Morro

Fuerte San Felipe del Morro

El Campo del Morro

City Wall

Cementerio de San Juan

LA PERLA

City Wall

City Wall (La Muralla)

Cuartel de Ballajá/ Museo de las Americas

Plaza del Quinto Centenario

Iglesia San José

Plaza San José

Museo de Arte e Historia

Museo Pablo Casals

Casa Blanca

Hotel El Convento

Catedral de San Juan

Plazuela de la Rogativa

Museo del Niño

Plaza de Armas

San Juan Gate

La Fortaleza

Parque de las Palomas

Casa del Libro

Capilla del Cristo

La Princesa

Fuerte San Cristóbal

Bus Terminal

Cruise Ship Piers

CALLE DEL MORRO

SAN JUAN BOULEVARD

BAJADA MATADERO

SAN MIGUEL

NORZAGARAY (AVE BLVD DEL VALLE)

MERCADO

IMPERIAL

VIRTUD

SAN SEBASTIAN

BENEFICENCIA

SOL

LUNA

STEP STREET

CRISTO

SAN JOSE

CRUZ

SAN JUSTO

SAN FRANCISCO

TANCA

O'DONELL

LAS MONJAS

SAN JUAN

FORTALEZA

TETUAN

RECINTO SUR

COMERCIO

PASEO DE COVADONGA

PERSHING

HARDING

PASEO GILBERTO CONCEPCION DE GRACIA

MUÑOZ RIVERA

PONCE DE LEON

PASEO DE LA PRINCESA

PRESIDIO PUNTILLA

ACCOMMODATION

Hotel El Convento	2
Hotel Milano	3
La Galería	1

RESTAURANTS

Amadeus	B
Butterfly People Café	I
Café Bohemi	C
Café Mallorca	D
Café Zaguán	J
Dragonfly	G
La Bombonera	E
La Fonda del Jibarito	A
La Mallorquina	H
Parrot Club	F
Yukiyú	K

0 200 yards

Old San Juan

As recently as the 1970s, **Old San Juan** (Viejo San Juan) was a reminder of better times, a dingy assemblage of Spanish colonial relics that seemed to have crumbled in tandem with the empire that constructed them. In a mere thirty years, however, enough restoration has taken place that this seven-block square is today considered the best-kept trove of Spanish colonial architecture in the western hemisphere and has been named a World Heritage Site. Steep, narrow streets are cobbled with smooth, iridescent bricks known as *adequines*, and feature buildings – the oldest of which were constructed in the sixteenth century – with bright pastel facades and wrought-iron balconies abloom with plants and flowers.

The old town occupies the headland of a two-and-half-mile-long island (connected by bridge to the mainland) that shelters the Bay of San Juan, for centuries Spain's most important port in the New World. When Ponce de León moved the first settlement of Caparra here in 1511, he named the city Puerto Rico, or "rich port", because its position made for such a fine stop for shipping. (The island itself, at this time, was still named San Juan.) Soon the bay became the central hub for exports of New World riches, and the small island that sheltered it became the most coveted piece of real estate in the western hemisphere. At one time, the entire city was enclosed by stone walls to ward off the British, Dutch and French troops competing for this supreme location in the Caribbean. Now, only a portion of the wall, known as **La Muralla**, and the ramparts of **El Morro** and **San Cristóbal** remain, no less imposing 500 years later.

Today the port is busy with cruise ships – rather than the boats of old transporting sugar, coffee, slaves and rum – and the old town hosts a polyglot of foreigners on holiday who help to make tourism Puerto Rico's biggest industry. If you have only a day here, you're best off losing yourself among the streets to soak in some of the history, or joining an organized walking tour of the most important buildings – the PRTC has information. If the heat and steep, crowded streets get to be a bit much, you might want to consider riding the **free trolley** that leaves from the bus terminal on Calle La Marina (Mon–Fri 6am–8pm, Sat & Sun 8am–8pm, departures every 15min). You can get on or off anywhere along the route.

La Muralla and La Fortaleza

Begin your wanderings along **Paseo de la Princesa**, a busy cobblestoned promenade, and head west along the southern city wall. The prim, grey and white Neoclassical building you'll see before you come to Calle Presidio is known as **La Princesa**. Built as a prison in 1837, it is today home to the main PRTC office (see p.351) as well as a gallery showcasing the work of Puerto Rican artists.

Known as **La Muralla**, the city wall, which is up to twenty feet thick in some places, is a sight in itself. Until the late nineteenth century, it encircled all of Old San Juan with 3900 metres of sandstone, culminating in the fortress of El Morro (see p. 364) at the headland. Construction began in 1539 and wasn't finished until 1782. Until 1897, when part of the wall was destroyed to facilitate urban development, the city was accessible only through five huge, heavily guarded wooden doors that closed at nightfall. One such door, **La Puerta de San Juan**, stands at the end of Paseo de la Princesa near the port. Completed in 1635, this imposing red door was the first of the entrances to be built and was the check-in point for Spaniards delivering colonists and goods; today it is one of only three doors that remain.

Once inside the wall, follow Calle Recinto Oeste to **La Fortaleza** (Mon–Fri 9am–3.30pm; free; ⓣ787/721-7000 ext 2358), the oldest executive residence of its kind in the western hemisphere. Built in 1540, this palatial mansion overlooking the bay has served as the governor's home since the seventeenth century, and was originally the island's first fortress. While there is no access to the government offices, visitors may take a free guided tour through the dungeon and lush Moorish gardens; dress appropriately.

Head back down Calle Recinto Oeste until it takes an uphill turn. On your left, at the intersection of Caleta Las Monjas, you'll come upon a plaza with a tall sculpture known as **La Rogativa.** This striking Giacometti-like bronze, set dramatically against the bay, commemorates the city's salvation from the British in 1797.

Fuerte San Felipe and around

Continue walking up Recinto Oeste until you come upon the unmistakable **Fuerte San Felipe del Morro** (daily 9am–5pm; tours in English depart at 11am & 3pm; US$2; ☎787/729-6960), known simply as **El Morro**. A bulwark if ever there was one, it covers the headland of San Juan Bay with a sprawling fortress that rises 140 feet above the Atlantic. Built between 1540 and 1783, the thick walls are so old and weathered they have begun to look like outcroppings of bedrock, as though six levels of towers, barracks, secret passageways, dungeons and ramps were carved from a natural cliff. Even if military history isn't your thing, the views of the ocean, El Yunque and the Cordillera Central are superlative.

Heading back into town along Calle del Morro, you'll reach the **Museo de las Américas**, at Calle Norzagaray (Tues–Fri 10am–4pm, Sat & Sun 11am–5pm, free; ☎787/724-5052). Housed in the former military barracks of the Cuartel de Ballajá, it showcases North and South American folk art. Just south of the museum, follow Calle Beneficencia to the 500-year-old **Plaza San Jose** and the **Iglesia San José** (weekdays except Thurs 7am–3pm; Sat 8am–1pm; Sun Mass at noon). The church's pristine facade belies the fact that it's the second oldest church in the western hemisphere. Built by Dominican friars in 1523, the family of Juan Ponce de León worshipped under its vaulted Spanish Gothic ceilings. The adjacent **Convento los Dominicos** (Mon–Sat 9am–5pm) was also built in 1523, to accommodate the Dominican monks. Nearby, the **Museo Pablo Casals**, 101 Calle Sebastian (Tues–Sat 9.30am–5.30pm; US$1; ☎787/723-9185) houses manuscripts, photographs and instruments of the famed Spanish cellist who lived in Puerto Rico from 1956 until 1973. A museum of a different sort, the **Museo de Arte e Historia de San Juan**, is on Calle Norzagaray at Calle MacArthur (Tues–Sun 10am–4pm; free; ☎787/724-1875). Something of a cultural centre, it showcases Puerto Rican art and music, and hosts a number of concerts and festivals.

Along Calle de Cristo

Along Calle de Cristo, heading back towards Paseo de la Princesa, you'll find plenty of restaurants and cafés, several of them in *El Convento*, a gorgeous hotel that was once a nunnery, before you reach the **Catedral de San Juan** on the corner of Caleta de San Juan (daily 8am–5pm; Mass Mon–Fri 12.15pm, Sat 7pm, Sun 9am & 11am). Built around 1535 and restored in the nineteenth century, this Spanish colonial cathedral includes pieces of its original Gothic-style balustrades, archways, ceiling and stairwell. While it's not especially beautiful, it houses the remains of Ponce de León, as well as an eerie vestige of the Roman era – a mummy of the early Christian martyr San Pío.

Across from the cathedral, the **Museo del Niño**, 150 Calle de Cristo (Tues–Thurs 9am–3.30pm, Fri 9am–5pm, Sat & Sun 12.30–5pm; US$2.50; ☎787/722-3791), offers hands-on fun for kids, who can play dress up or pretend to work at a barbershop, construction site and more. A few blocks south, the **Casa del Libro**, 255 Calle de Cristo (Tues–Sat 11am–4.30pm; US$2; ☎787/723-0354), is dedicated to the art of bookmaking, and boasts a collection of 6000 books – including 200 that predate the sixteenth century.

The **Capilla de Cristo** lies at the end of Calle de Cristo (Mon, Wed & Fri 10.30am–3.30pm), a dainty stone chapel erected in 1753 at the foot of a precipice overlooking San Juan Bay. The reason for its construction is the subject of much dispute. Some believe it was built to celebrate a miracle after a young man raced up the hill on horseback, plummeted over the city wall into the sea, and survived.

Others maintain that both horse and rider died, and the chapel was erected to ward off future mishaps.

Next door is **La Parque de las Palomas**, home to flocks of what must be the Caribbean's best-loved pigeons, and regarded by Puerto Ricans as some sort of magical place. Locals not only feed the pigeons (a vendor sells bird feed on site), but they allow the normally bothersome birds to land on them, which they regard as a good omen. Even if birds are not your cup of tea, the park affords wonderful views of the bay and port.

Fuerte San Cristóbal and the north end

Over on the northeastern edge of Old San Juan, stretching along Avenida Muñoz Rivera (Route 25) and Calle Norzagaray, **Fuerte San Cristóbal** (daily 9am–5pm; tours in English at 10am & 2pm; US$2; ☎787/729-6960) was San Juan's second stronghold. Where El Morro was the prime defence against attacks by sea, San Cristóbal, built from 1634 to 1785 and originally covering 27 acres, prevented land-based assaults. Today, the maze-like fortress is maintained by the National Park Service, and visitors can explore its secret tunnels, moats, dungeons and 150-foot walls. The entrance is on Calle Norzagaray.

La Perla, the slum outside the northern city wall as you walk west on Calle Norzagaray away from the fort, is a deceptively quaint-looking neighbourhood that is best avoided. Trenchantly impoverished, it gained notoriety with Oscar Lewis's 1966 grim novel, *La Vida*, and has been an enclave of crime for centuries. Many of San Juan's early colonizers are buried nearby, in the **Cementerio de San Juan**, which can also be dangerous. Like La Perla, it's best viewed from a safe distance – from La Muralla, or La Plaza del Quinto Centenario on Norzagaray and Beneficencia streets.

Condado

Set on a peninsula straddling the Atlantic and the Laguna Condado, **CONDADO** was built in the 1950s as the island's first resort area, and after a decline in the 1980s it has again bloomed in popularity. Today its wide, tiled sidewalks lined with palms, fancy boutiques, trendy restaurants and high-rise resort hotels and casinos make it San Juan's slickest neighbourhood. Next to Old San Juan, it's the best area to explore on foot, particularly the main drag, **Avenida Ashford**.

Just a block from Avenida Ashford is two-mile **Condado Beach**, the best stretch of sand in town, though far from the best on the island. It's certainly the most accessible beach for the great number of tourists who stay in the luxury hotels here, and its smooth sand and good swimming make it pleasant enough. There are lots of watersports available, and plenty of outdoor bars and restaurants are to be found on the beach itself, or within walking distance.

Condado also has the city's liveliest **nightlife**. Many of the top dance clubs are here, and some of the hotels book fantastic live salsa. **Gay travellers** will also find the area to be very gay-friendly.

Ocean Park and Isla Verde

East from Condado along the coast, a couple of other beachfront neighbourhoods attract their fair share of visitors. When Avenida Ashford becomes Calle McLeary, you'll find yourself in **Ocean Park**, an affluent residential district on a wide swath of pretty, palm-lined sand. Thanks to a city code barring the construction of buildings taller than three storeys, it is more intimate than Condado, and while there isn't much of interest here for the sightseer, there are several lovely inns and guesthouses and a handful of good restaurants.

The next major beachfront area, further east and just before the airport, is **ISLA VERDE**. This is the place to base yourself if you want ultra-cheap digs and don't mind strip malls, or if you opt for luxury accommodations of the all-inclusive sort that give you no need to leave the premises. Like all the waterfronts in San Juan, the beach is good for sunbathing and swimming, though its location – two blocks from the freeway (Rte 26) and its service roads – leaves something to be desired.

Santurce

Slightly inland and south of Ocean Park, **SANTURCE** is a neighbourhood in transition with a growing art scene that's outstripping its dodgy reputation. Once a fashionable business and residential neighbourhood, it had its share of social problems in the latter half of the twentieth century. While Santurce still has some undesirable sections, the city's best art museums are here, along with some fine restaurants and funky cafés. There are also a growing number of galleries that have relocated here from Hato Rey (see below), bringing young artists with them. It's worth a visit, but try to come with a companion, stay on well-travelled streets and walk with caution after dark.

The new **Museo de Arte de Puerto Rico** is at 300 Av Jose de Diego (Tues–Sat 10am–5pm, Sun 11am–6pm; US$5, US$3 students; ⓣ787/977-6277, ⓦwww.mapr.org). Its permanent collection, occupying the Neoclassical west wing, traces the evolution of Puerto Rican art from the sixteenth century to the present. The east wing showcases a five-storey stained-glass window by local artist Eric Tabales, which overlooks an extraordinary five-acre sculpture garden and lily pond. Don't miss the collection of *santos*, saints carved in wood. The museum also houses chef Wilo Benet's masterpiece restaurant *Pikayo* (see p. 368).

Another museum of note is located on the campus of Universidad del Sagrado Corazón, just off Avenida Ponce de León on Calle Rosale. The **Museo del Arte Contemporáneo Puertorriqueño** (Mon–Fri 8am–5pm; Sat 9am–5pm; free; ⓣ787/728-1515, ext 2408) is the island's best showcase for paintings, sculpture, photography and new-media works by young internationally known Puerto Rican artists, such as Rosa Irigoyen and Pepón Osorio.

On Calle Canals, with an entrance marked by large, metallic avocados, the open-air **Plaza Mercado** is packed with stalls selling fresh produce, sandwiches, flowers, meats, cheese and the like, and is always crowded with locals doing their daily shopping. On Friday evenings, it makes for an interesting happy hour - all types, from suits to young artists, come here to hang out on into the night.

Hato Rey

San Juan's financial district, **HATO REY** is located just south of Santurce. Its main stretch, Avenida Ponce de León, is lined for a mile with high-rise office buildings and hotels and restaurants catering to the business trade. Amidst the pricey shops, there are a few good contemporary art galleries. The best of the lot, **Galería Botello** at Avenida F.D. Roosevelt 314 (Mon–Sat 10am–6pm; ⓣ787/754-7430) – not to be confused with the knockoff in Old San Juan – sells the work of some of the island's most acclaimed younger artists, like Mari Mater O'Neill, whose reputations extend as far as New York and Europe. The work is reasonably priced, by London or LA standards, and is worth a look.

For shopaholics, the Caribbean's largest mall – with more than 200 stores – the **Plaza Las Américas** (Mon–Sat 9am–9pm, Sun 11am–5pm; ⓣ787/767-5202) is on Avenida F.D. Roosevelt, off Route 26.

Rio Piedras

With palms and terracotta in lieu of ivy and bricks, **RIO PIEDRAS**, at the southern end of the city, is San Juan's equivalent of a college town, home to the main campus of the **University of Puerto Rico** (ⓣ787/763-4408). Located on Avenida Luis Muñoz Rivera, the university hosts cultural events throughout the year, and the campus itself is a lovely place for a stroll, with a youthful vibe and cheap bars and restaurants nearby.

A five-minute walk away is the not-to-be-missed **Mercado de Rio Piedras** (Mon–Sat during daylight hours), four blocks of indoor-outdoor shopping along the Paseo de Diego, with everything from rare fruits to high heels. It's "bien puertorriqueño" (very Puerto Rican), and full of bargains, especially if you know how to haggle.

If you fancy packing a picnic with some goodies from the market, the 75-acre **Jardín Botánico** (daily 9am–4.30pm; free; ⓣ787/250-0000 ext 6580) is a pretty spot. Tucked away at the junction of highways 1 and 847, about a mile from UPR quad, you'll find cinnamon and nutmeg trees, 125 types of palms, more than 30,000 orchids (call ahead to arrange a viewing) and a lotus lagoon.

Eating

San Juan is garnering a reputation as the **culinary capital of the Caribbean** – a smorgasbord of both international cuisines and endless variations on Puerto Rican staples. Condado and Old San Juan have the highest concentration of good restaurants, but fine food can be found in most areas of the city which draw visitors, and Miramar, the residential district south of Condado, also has its fair share of eateries.

Old San Juan

Amadeus Calle San Sebastian 106 ⓣ787/722-8635. Excellent nouvelle Caribbean cuisine served until 2am to a hip crowd in a handsome, eighteenth-century brick and stone building; try the dumplings with guava sauce and arrowroot fritters or the smoked salmon and caviar pizza. Entrees US$10–26.

Butterfly People Café Calle Fortaleza 152 ⓣ787/723-2432. Inexpensive quiches, salads and sandwiches with a tropical twist, and fresh fruit juices; walls covered with framed butterflies.

Café Bohemio *Hotel El Convento*, Calle de Cristo 100 ⓣ787/723-9200. Cheap way to experience *El Convento* – seventeenth-century nunnery turned five-star hotel. Good spinach and ricotta crepes or ceviche in tequila sauce. Live music Tuesday through Friday after 9.30pm. Entrees US$9.50–14.50

Café Mallorca Calle San Francisco 400 ⓣ787/724-4607. People line up at this eatery for its famous pastries and hot chocolate; also on offer is good *café con leche*, fruit salads, pancakes and eggs for breakfast, and criollo staples for lunch and dinner. You can eat well for US$5–10. Closes at 7pm.

Café Zaguán Calle Tetuan 359 ⓣ787/724-3359. Cosy, attractive expat hangout, with indoor and outdoor seating, offering tasty ceviche, soups and wraps, and excellent pulled pork quesadillas with papaya salsa. Open until midnight Tues–Sat. Entrees US$15–32.

Dragonfly Calle Fortaleza 364 ⓣ787/977-3886. Spinoff of the *Parrot Club* (same owner), offering Nuevo Latino with an Asian twist. Wonderful halibut ceviche with ginger, coconut milk and scallions, and Moo-shoo Mongolian beef wraps. Live music Tues, Thurs & Sat until midnight. Entrees US$12–25.

La Bombonera Calle San Francisco 259 ⓣ787/722-0658. Century-old institution for morning pastries, excellent coffee, sandwiches and criollo classics like rice with squid or marinated roast pork and fried plantains. Open daily 7.30am–8pm.

La Fonda del Jibarito Calle Sol 280 ⓣ787/725-8375. This reasonable bistro-style restaurant is as popular with local bohemians as with tourists, and the lamb stew and goat fricassee are excellent.

La Mallorquina Calle San Justo 207 ⓣ787/722-3261. Expensive for criollo fare, but the atmosphere fits the bill. Established in 1848 and run by the Rojos family for about a hundred years, it is reputedly San Juan's oldest restaurant. Try the garlic soup and lobster asopao.

Parrot Club Calle Fortaleza 363 ⓣ787/725-7370. This requisite Old San Juan experience is pure Nuevo Latino, and the inspiration for many other restaurants. A chic crowd dines on impeccable dishes, while listening to mellow live Latin jazz. The house special: rare tuna broiled with dark rum and orange essence with yucca and cassava mash. Entrees US$18–29.

Yukiyú Calle Recinto Sur 311 ⓣ787/721-0653 or ⓣ787/722-1423. Chef Igarashi's sushi is reputed to be Puerto Rico's best. Pricey cooked dishes – seared on a teppanyaki grill – are also plentiful and very good.

Condado

Ajili-Mojili Avda Ashford 1052 ☎787/725-9195. Superb classic criollo cuisine prepared by chef Mariano Ortiz attracts a loyal following of upscale sanjuaneros. The menu features the likes of savoury pork loin sautéed with onions, and plantain-encrusted shrimp in white-wine herb sauce. Entrees US$18–30.

La Patisserie Francés 1504 Avda Ashford ☎787/728-5508. This cheery spot with Spanish tiles and wrought-iron furniture is a nice spot for a breakfast of stuffed croissants, or lunching on fresh fish or vegetable salad topped off by gorgeous pastries.

Marisquería Miró Avda Condado 76 ☎787/722-9583. Award-winning Catalán chef Jose La Villa prepares intensely memorable fish dishes like baked halibut in cabrales cheese sauce and seafood with black rice. Entrees US$15–20.

Metropol 105 Avda de Diego ☎787/268-3045. Generous portions of hearty Cuban dishes like stuffed Cornish game hen and smoked pork hocks are served by an attentive waitstaff in this handsome, Old World bistro. Very good value. Alternate locations in Isla Verde ☎787/791-4046 and Hato Rey ☎787/751-4022.

Zabó Creative Cuisine Calle Candina 14 ☎787/725-9494. Elegant setting with a distinct gay vibe in an early twentieth-century mansion; dining on the verandah. Chef Paul Carroll's masterpieces include a smoked cheddar, chicken and mango chutney appetizer in a fried shell, and fresh fish over yellow raisin couscous in a mango-rosemary curry. Entrees US$18–28.

Ocean Park and Isla Verde

Che's Calle Caoba 35, Ocean Park/Isla Verde ☎787/726-7202. Argentine-style grill with reputedly the most tender, flavourful *parrillada* (grilled, marinated meat) and good Chilean and Argentinian wines. Entrees US$15–25.

Dunbars Calle McLeary 1954, Ocean Park ☎787/728-2920. This sprawling, collegiate dive with upscale bar food is boisterous even during mid-week. Live music on Fridays.

Panadería España Avda Baldorioty de Castro, Calle Marginal, Isla Verde ☎787/727-3860. Good place to stock up for a picnic, a block from the beach. Excellent sandwiches, *café con leche*, tortillas and thick chicken soup with vegetables.

Repostería Kasalta 1966 Calle McLeary, Ocean Park ☎787/727-7340. This stainless-steel emporium of cured meats and cheeses, breads, wines and fine imported goods is a requisite stop. The *café con leche* is superb.

Miramar and Santurce

Augusto's Cuisine *Hotel Excelsior*, Avda Ponce de León 801, Miramar ☎787/725-7700. Somewhat stuffy hotel restaurant offering serious French and Continental cuisine. Chef Augusto Schreiner delivers the likes of veal brains au beurre noir with capers and a hot chocolate soufflé to die for. Entrees US$24–36.

Chayote *Hotel Olimpo Court*, Av Miramar 603, Miramar ☎787/722-9385. International cuisine by chef/owner Mario Pagan features unlikely blends of fresh tropical ingredients. Menu items include ceviche in rosewater essence with sweet yam croquettes or halibut with yam gnocchi in fresh corn cream sauce. Entrees US$23–26.

Pikayo Museo de Arte de Puerto Rico, Avda de Diego 300, Santurce ☎787/721-6194. Changing menus by celebrated chef Wilo Benet and views of a gorgeous five-acre garden have earned this ultra-chic spot inside the new museum the distinction of being "one of the world's 100 most exciting restaurants". The lamb chops with ripe plantain *salpicón* and conch spring rolls with orange *sofrito* sauce are extraordinary. Entrees US$29–35.

Drinking and nightlife

San Juan has a very healthy nightlife, to say the least. In addition to the lively **bars** at restaurants like the *Parrot Club*, *Dragonfly* and *Amadeus* (see above), there are numerous venues around the city where you can grab a **drink** or **dance** the night away to Puerto Rico's famous **salsa** (see box opposite) or merengue – delivered live or by a DJ – or perhaps a little hip-hop or underground.

Asylum 1320 Avda Ponce de León, Santurce ☎787/723-3258. San Juan's most progressive club pumps underground dance music to a hipster crowd.

Bar Rumba 152 Calle San Sebastian, Old San Juan ☎787/725-4407. Live salsa Thursday to Sunday. Young crowd, compared to most salsa joints. You can get a quick lesson in salsa or rumba.

Borinquén 4800 Avda De Isla Verde ☎787/268-1900. The atmosphere and location – along a service road – are unremarkable, but the beer is

Music in Puerto Rico

Salsa is unquestionably the sound of the island. You hear it on the radio and on the beach, in cafés and live in the best hotels. This upbeat and very danceable Latin sound is set to complex African rhythms and has a strong foundation in jazz. Developed in the nightclubs of New York in the 1940s, and made most popular by the late Tito Puente, salsa is experiencing a surge of renewed popularity on the island. Though it's hard to find salsa played live anywhere but in the best nightclubs these days, every town seems to have a spot where locals – young and old alike – gather to listen and dance to the likes of Celia Cruz and Afro-Cuban All-Stars.

The folk music and dance tradition called **bomba** still has a presence in Puerto Rico. Much like Cuban rumba, it is based on intricate West African percussion. The drummer's objective is usually to provoke a response from a dancer, which incites a sort of competition, with musician and dancer performing in response to the other's lead. **Plena** is often performed along with *bomba,* although the two folk music styles have very different roots. *Plena* is believed to derive from Taíno and Spanish traditions and involves a ten-string guitar, called a *cuatro*, and a hollowed gourd, like a maraca, called a *guiro.* Interestingly, *plena* was once a means of reporting the news; singers effectively recited the day's events.

home-made here in San Juan's only brew pub.

Café ? (Café Pregunta) 157 Calle San Jose, Old San Juan ⓣ787/723-5467. Things get pretty rowdy here with merengue and salsa most nights. Also live *bomba* on Wednesdays.

Club Laser 251 Calle Cruz, Old San Juan ⓣ787/725-7581. A good mix of locals and tourists gather to dance into the night at this hip-hop club near the port.

Cups 1708 Calle San Mateo, Santurce ⓣ787/268-3570. This lesbian bar has a low-key atmosphere and a good mix of types and nationalities.

El Batey across from *El Convento*, Old San Juan. This dark, grungy fixture, open until 6am, is usually mobbed. Has a very "local bar" feel, despite the number of outsiders.

Eros 1257 Avda Ponce de León, Santurce/Miramar ⓣ787/722-1131. Basically a gay club, but all persuasions come here to dance on Saturday nights. Music is salsa and New York-style house. Also dance, drag and strip acts. Open to 4am on weekends.

△ Fording a deep puddle en route to Guajataca

7.2

Around San Juan

It's worth reserving a day for exploring outside the city limits; in fact, a trip to **El Yunque** national rainforest, 25 miles southeast of the capital, is a must. From there it's easy to get to **Playa Luquillo**, a palm-lined *balneario* (public beach) on the northeast shore. **Rio Camuy Cave Park**, set in an eerie, lunar-like landscape an hour west of San Juan boasts world-class spelunking, and makes for another good escape from the noise and haste of the city. All three places are serviced regularly by hotel shuttles.

Piñones State Forest, just east of Isla Verde, is on the farthest reaches of city bus routes. Here, you can bike, surf, picnic, party and sample food from the kiosks along the wild beaches. As a local gathering spot, it's a world apart culturally – far more Afro-Caribbean than the capital proper.

El Yunque

The Caribbean National Forest, commonly known as **EL YUNQUE** (daily 7.30am–6pm; free), looms, shrouded in mist, over eastern Puerto Rico. The 28,000-acre forest is visible from San Juan rooftops, 25 miles away, rising 3500 feet above sea level on the easternmost stretch of the Cordillera Central. The only rainforest in the US Forest System, it is deluged with more than 100 billion gallons of rainfall a year, and is home to more than 240 tree species and a panoply of rare flora and fauna, most notable of which is the endangered *cotorro,* or Puerto Rican parrot, in the oldest stand of the forest; only thirty are in existence, all of them here.

Some of the trees in the **palo colorado**, the section of forest that grows above 2000 feet, have stood for more than a thousand years. In fact, the only remaining virgin forest on the once tree-covered island is here. Below 2000 feet is the driest section of El Yunque, with **tabonuco**, **palm**, and **ausubo** trees, and more than fifty types of **orchids**. The region above 2500 feet is dominated by mountain palms, ferns and mosses. The highest level of growth is **cloud forest**, also known as dwarf forest, where trees, stunted by strong trade winds, rarely grow higher than twelve feet tall.

To explore the forest, you can choose from among 23 miles of pathways, many of them paved. The trails with the finest views depart from the **Palo Colorado Information Centre** (daily 9.30am–5pm) at km 11.8, about half a mile from the summit. The most popular, **El Yunque Trail**, ascends through cloud forest to El Yunque peak; for **waterfalls**, take the **Coca** or **La Mina** trail. More experienced hikers may want to tackle the almost four-mile **Tradewinds Trail** which climbs **El Toro**, the **highest peak** in the forest, at 3522 feet. It's a good idea to wear good walking shoes with rubber soles, and light, loose clothing; also bring a poncho in case of rain. There are no concession stands, only vending machines; so bring snacks.

Practicalities

While El Yunque is not served by public transportation, organized tour buses do pick-ups at San Juan hotels most days of the week. Alternatively, you can also hire a private guide through the forest's **Rent-a-Ranger** programme; call ☎787/888-1880 for details. To reach El Yunque by car from San Juan, take 26 east toward Carolina, which becomes 3 east to Carolina/Fajardo. In the town of Rio Grande, turn right onto 191. Follow 191 for about three miles until you reach the forest. You'll see a sign on your right indicating the entrance to the **El Portal Tropical Forest Centre** (daily 9am–5pm; US$3; ☎787/888-1810), which has hands-on exhibits, a twelve-minute film and an elevated canopy walkway. It makes a good starting-point if you want to learn about the forest, and visitor information, maps and brochures are also available.

Camping is legal with a permit in many sections of the forest, including El Toro. You can obtain one near the entrance at the Catalina Work Centre on Route 191.

Luqillo

Many day-trippers from San Juan round out a morning trip to El Yunque with an afternoon at **PLAYA LUQUILLO**'s *balneario* or public beach (daily 8.30am–5pm; parking US$2; ☎787/889-5871), 45 minutes from the capital on Highway 3. The crowds, especially on weekends, are no surprise, as the calm waters here are perfect for swimming. Kiosks sell fun beach fare, from piña coladas and beers to grilled meats and *empanadillas.* Visitors who prefer starry nights to city lights may camp here on the beach (30 campsites with bathhouse; US$13 a night or US$16 with hookup).

If privacy is what you seek, walk along the rock jetty at the eastern end of the *balneario* until you reach **Playa Azul**, which is wild, equally pretty, and often devoid of people. Farther east still, **La Pared** is the local surfer beach, where waves pound the shore and numerous surfing competitions are held throughout the year.

Rio Camuy Cave Park

An hour west of San Juan, on Route 129 at km 18.9, **RIO CAMUY CAVE PARK** (Wed–Sun 8am–5pm; US$10; ☎787/898-3100) is one of the largest cave systems in the world, with some seventeen entrances into its 268 acres of tunnels, sinkholes, stalagmites, stalactites and underground rivers. Known as "karst country", the strange landscape in this region was formed as rivers originating from the rainforest of the Cordillera Central carved their way to the ocean through porous limestone, creating vast networks of sinkholes and tunnels.

The standard tour of Rio Camuy, which lasts about two hours, begins at the visitor centre. A trolley from here runs through palm and banana trees into Clear Cave Junction, a 200-foot-deep sinkhole. You then proceed on foot past enormous boulder-like stalagmites, rocks that fold like drapery or drip like candles, and bats that flit overhead, under ceilings as tall as 170 feet. In places, the River Camuy is visible rushing past, far below. The second part of the tour takes you by trolley to the Tres Pueblos sinkhole, a vast chasm that measures 650 feet wide and 400 feet deep – large enough to accommodate El Morro.

Adventurous visitors can rappel down a rock wall to view the newly opened Cathedral Cave featuring 42 Taíno petroglyphs, or descend hundreds of feet into sinkholes and body-raft through an underground river; contact Aventuras Tierra Adentro in San Juan for details (☎787/766-0470). At US$85 to US$100 per person the trips aren't cheap, but the experts who lead them have the highest regard for safety.

The park can be reached easily by car, or on an organized tour from San Juan; ask at your hotel.

Piñones State Forest

Just east of the San Juan city limits on Highway 187, **Piñones State Forest** is where locals go to let loose on weekends, when a winding road along five miles of wild beaches becomes the site of an ongoing party, and **roadside kiosks** sell the likes of raw oysters, seasoned pork and *coco frío*. At any time, you can also take advantage of an excellent **bike path** along the shore and good **surfing**.

Festivities and activities aside, the forest, thick with almond and palm groves, is an important **wildlife refuge**, home to more than 45 bird species, including pelicans and several types of heron, and sheltering the island's largest mangrove lagoon.

A few words of caution: keep an eye out for yourself and your vehicle (thefts are common), and don't eat anything raw, particularly the oysters.

7.3

The southwest

The drive along the **southwest coast** of Puerto Rico is almost reason enough to visit the area: the extreme contrast of sea and mountainside can be arresting, with surf pounding alongside the road to the south, and a surge of rock-face to the north. At times, the light gets very clear and bright here, both ethereal and spooky when a faint mist hovers over the mountains.

Besides the staggering views, the southwest of Puerto Rico is known for two significant troves of historic architecture, in **Ponce** and **San Germán**. It also has some of the island's prettiest beaches and the **Bosque Estatal de Guánica**, a vast subtropical dry forest. Not to be outdone, the bay at **La Parguera** boasts excellent **diving** at **The Wall** along with Puerto Rico's second highest concentration of bioluminescence in **La Bahía Fosforescente.**

Positioned mid-way between Ponce and San Germán, **Guánica**, and nearby La Parguera, make the best hubs for exploring the southwest, offering the more appealing accommodation options in the region.

Ponce

An hour and a half from San Juan via Highway 52, **PONCE** is best known for its art museum and its beautifully restored historic district, a showcase of nineteenth century Creole architecture. The city is liveliest during **Carnaval** when the streets fill with parades of musicians, floats, dancers and *vejigantes* – revellers in devilish-looking painted masks. Things also heat up here in November, during the **Fiesta Nacional de Bomba y Plena** when drummers and dancers gather to compete. There are also a number of interesting sights on the outskirts of town, including **Tibes Indian Ceremonial Park** and **Hacienda Buena Vista.**

While the historic centre is indeed worth seeing, the city still feels like it lacks energy, and the architecture may fail to impress, especially if you come here after a few days in San Juan. Note that on Mondays and Tuesdays Ponce's cultural and historical institutions are closed.

Some history

Known as La Perla del Sur ("the pearl of the south"), the settlement of Ponce was recognized by the Spanish in 1692, and named after Loíza Ponce de León, the great grandson of Juan Ponce de León. It developed over the next four centuries into an important cultural and commercial centre – essentially a southern capital of the island – largely due to its proximity to the sea. By 1831, it was designated a harbour, but trade was permitted only with Spanish ships. However, with the northern capital a good distance away, over the Cordillera Central, it was hard for the governor to keep tabs on the southern city.

Contraband flourished for the better part of the nineteenth century, as did the arts under the auspices of the Serrallés family, the makers of Don Q rum. The family commissioned European architects to construct mansions downtown, and imported European paintings, music and books. The city became known as a haven for liberal ideas, safe from San Juan's allegiance to Spain, and eventually became a breeding ground for the nationalist movement. As a means of throwing off Spanish sovereignty, the city was glad to surrender to American troops when they entered Puerto Rico via Ponce in 1898, bringing the Spanish-American war to an end and ceding Puerto Rico to the US. What they didn't realize, however, was that the Americans would put a stop to illegal trade and herald a precipitous downturn in Ponce's good fortune (see box p.377).

In 1995, after a difficult period in the city's history, US$500 million was invested in the restoration of the historic centre as a means of jump-starting tourism.

Arrival, information and getting around

The **Mercedita Airport** (☎787/842-6292) is located about four miles east of Ponce on Highway 5506, off Highway 1. American Eagle makes daily trips from San Juan which take around half an hour. A taxi ride into the city centre costs about US$10.

Públicos leave from Calle Union, north of the Plaza de Las Delicias in the historic part of town. See the list of *público* lines on p.352. Ponce has several **taxi** companies; most reliable is Ponce Taxi (☎787/642-3370). A free sightseeing **trolley** tour leaves from the cathedral (see p.376) and runs through the historic district to Castillo Serrallés.

The **PRTC**'s Ponce office (☎787/284-4913) is in the Paseo del Sur plaza on

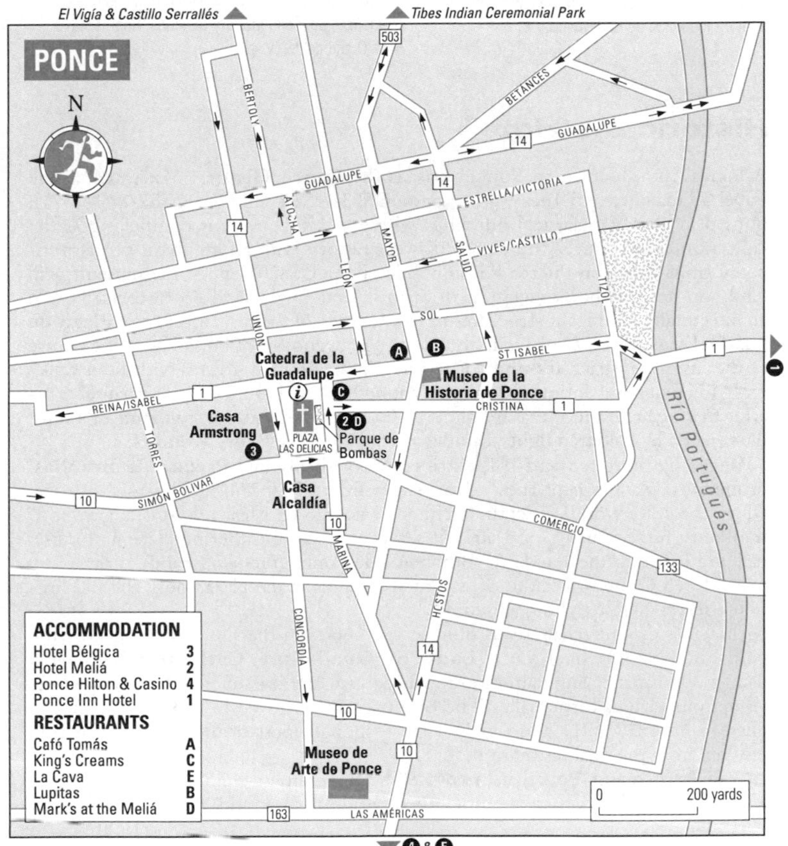

Route 1. Information is also available at the **Ponce Municipal Tourist Office** (☎787/843-0465) which has a small branch on the second floor of the Citibank Building on the Plaza de Las Delicias, as well as a conveniently located kiosk in the Parque de Bombas building across the street.

Accommodation

The old hotels in downtown Ponce have more character than the chains outside the historic district, but while they're inexpensive, they're also faded to the point of being a bit depressing. If you're spending more than a night here, you may want to consider staying in Guánica or La Parguera (see pp.378 and 379), within a half-hour's drive of Ponce.

Hotel Belgica Calle Villa 122 ☎787/844-3255, Ⓕ844-6149. More charming than the *Melía* (below), with a super-affable innkeeper, but still a rather dismal old hotel in the heart of the historic district. Ask for a high-ceilinged room. ③

Hotel Melía Plaza de Las Delicias ☎787/842-0260. Faded grand hotel with an excellent restaurant, *Marks* (see p.378). If you're in town to see the historic district, the *Melía* has the best location, with musty-smelling, spacious rooms right on the Plaza de Las Delicas. ④

Ponce Hilton and Casino Avda Caribe 1150 ☎787/259-7676, Ⓕ259-7674. Expensive, glittery compound outside of town, facing a small, rocky Caribbean beach, with two restaurants, three bars, a pool, tennis courts, fitness area, spa and full business centre. ⑧

Ponce Inn Hotel Rte 1, km 123.5 ☎787/841-1000, Ⓕ841-2560. Ten minutes from town in Mercedita. What the medium-sized rooms lack in character is made up for with amenities like a jacuzzi, pool and laundry facilities. Rooms have A/C and cable TV. ④

Historic district

A logical introduction to Ponce's past is the **Ponce History Museum**, Calle Isabel 53 (daily except Tues 9am to 5pm; US$3, US$1 children; ☎787/844-7071), housed in two Neoclassical buildings whose architecture is as compelling as the collection, which traces the city's 300-year history, with an emphasis on its non-comformist stance on Puerto Rican politics. For a US$20 deposit, the museum will lend you its guidebook (written in Spanish and English) to 45 historically and architecturally significant structures in town. Some of them surround the **Plaza de Las Delicias,** or Plaza of Delights, a lovely hodgepodge of buildings at the centre of the historic district. It's unified by carefully landscaped greens, with tiled walkways, fountains and antique lamplights dating back to 1916. The Indian laurel topiaries that encircle the plaza are almost 100 years old, and the Fountain of Lions, illuminated by coloured lights, came from the 1939 New York World's Fair.

Ponce's signature red-and-black striped Moorish-inspired **Parque de Bombas**, or firehouse (daily except Tues 9.30am–6pm; free; ☎787/284-3338), was constructed for the 1883 World's Fair; the architect, Máximo de Meana y Guridi, gave it to the Ponce fire company soon after. It served as a social gathering place and music hall and home to the Banda de Bomberos de Ponce (firemen's band), directed by Juan Morell Campos, a statue of whom also stands in the plaza; today the old firehouse serves as a firefighter museum.

The city's original chapel was built in the 1660s on the site of what is now the pale blue Neoclassical **Our Lady of Guadalupe Cathedral** (Mon–Fri 6am–3.30pm; Sat & Sun 6am–noon), whose structure has suffered damage over the years from various earthquakes. The original was destroyed in 1835 and rebuilt in phases – in 1839, 1911 and finally 1930 – though most of the existing structure resulted from the final restoration.

Casa Armstrong-Poventud may well be the prettiest building on the Plaza de Las Delicias, with its ornately embellished facade and caryatids flanking the heavily

The Ponce Massacre in the Plaza de Las Delicias

The early twentieth century was a rough time for Ponce. Profits stalled, hurricanes destroyed coffee production, the price of sugar bottomed out and the US favoured San Juan for development over its uppity nationalist rival to the south. By the time the Great Depression took hold, Ponce had had it. Revolution fomented more fervently than ever, leading to one of the US's most egregious injustices toward the territory of Puerto Rico: the Ponce Massacre.

With the influx of European art and culture in Ponce had come a substantial number of students and intellectuals. On March 21, 1937, protesters in favour of Puerto Rican independence gathered in the Plaza de Las Delicias to stage a march. They had secured a parade permit, but the then governor, Blanton Winship, revoked it at the last minute. Nevertheless, about one hundred unarmed protesters marched, eventually finding themselves face to face with 150 police officers with pistols. When the marchers began to sing the national anthem, *La Borinqueña*, a shot rang out, culminating in a blaze of gunfire. Twenty people died (seventeen of them protesters who were shot in the back), and many more were wounded. Governor Winship blamed the protesters, and the US government left it at that. Eventually, however, an investigation by the American Civil Liberties Union determined that it was the police who were to blame.

carved wooden front doors. Built by a Scottish banker as a private home in 1900, the French Neoclassical structure now houses the Instituto de Cultura Puertorriqueña Sur (Mon–Fri 9am–5pm; ☎787/844-2540).

Outside the historic district

If you have the time, a few sights outside Ponce's historic district warrant a visit – in particular, the **Museo del Arte de Ponce**, just south of the centre at 2325 Avda Las Américas (daily 10am–5pm; US$4, children US$2, students US$1; ☎787/848-0505), held to be the best in the Caribbean. With about 850 paintings and 800 sculptures, the collection is strong on Pre-Raphaelite and Italian Baroque work and includes pieces by Velázquez, Lord Leighton, Rubens, Delacroix, Benjamin West and Puerto Rico's two most esteemed masters – Jose Campeche and Francisco Oller.

Just northwest of town, sharing a hill with the 100-foot-tall, 70-foot-wide cross of **El Vigía**, from which the Spanish kept watch over the waters around the port of Ponce, is the **Museo Castillo Serrallés** (daily except Mon 9.30am–5pm; US$3; ☎787/259-1774;). It's hard to believe that this 14,000-square-foot, Spanish Revival mansion was built during the Great Depression. Home to the Serallés family, the manufacturers of Don Q rum, the estate is an exercise in excess, now worth about US$25 million. It took four years to build and passed through several generations of the family until the mid-1980s. Details were so carefully preserved it looks as though the house was occupied just yesterday.

About two miles north of Ponce, at km 2.2 on Highway 503, **Tibes Indian Ceremonial Park** (daily except Mon 9am–4pm; US$2; ☎787/840-2255) was uncovered in 1975, when floodwaters from Hurricane Eloise retreated from the area. Excavation teams found 186 graves from 300 AD, pre-Taíno *bateys* (courts used for ceremonial ball games), tools, pottery and a star-shaped stone formation with points facing the direction of sunrise and sunset during the solstice and equinox. Much of what was discovered can be viewed by the public, along with a re-created Indian village.

Visitors to the accurately restored **Hacienda Buena Vista** (by appointment; US$5; ☎787/722-5882), about ten miles north of town, at km 16.8 on Highway

123, can get a glimpse of what life was like on a nineteenth-century coffee plantation. In its heyday, the hacienda used slave labour to grow cacao, plantains, pineapple, yams and corn in addition to coffee, and was one of the first on the island to use industrial machinery, such as the corn mill, cotton gin and coffee de-pulper.

Eating and drinking

For a metropolis of its size, the quality of the food in Ponce is wanting, especially if you've been spoiled by San Juan's impressive range of options. A few places will tide you over, however, and *Mark's at the Melía* is excellent.

Café Tomás Calle Isabel ☎787/840-1965. Good *café con leche*, hearty criollo cooking and sandwiches are available at this neighbourhood hangout.

King's Creams Plaza de Las Delicias. Delicious ice creams with unusual tropical flavours; perfect for a stroll around the plaza.

La Cava *Ponce Hilton and Casino*, Avda Caribe 1150 ☎787/259-7676. Continental menu changes every six weeks; past offerings include duck foie gras with toasted brioche and an excellent black and white soufflé. There's also a champagne and cigar bar. Entrees US$25–28.

Lupitas Calle Isabel ☎787/848-8808. Filling, reasonably priced Mexican food in a courtyard setting, with live music on weekends.

Mark's at the Melía *Hotel Melía*, Plaza de Las Delicias ☎787/842-0260. Renowned chef Mark French prepares inventive variations on criollo staples, like *mofongo* with barbecue tamarind duck or corn-crusted red snapper with yucca puree. Entrees US$18–28.

Guánica

Home to **Bosque Estatal de Guánica**, the world's best example of subtropical dry forest, the landscape in **GUÁNICA** jumps from scrubby and ordinary to eerily lunar, with blanched trees curling like arthritic old bones and the roots of mangrove trees at water's edge ensnaring the land and anything else in the way. The town of Guánica itself is rather dismal, but makes an excellent hub from which to explore the southwest, with everything of interest within a thirty-minute drive.

Bosque Estatal de Guánica

Scientists surmise that a mere one percent of the world's subtropical dry forest still exists; 9900 acres of it survive on the internationally protected lands of **Bosque Estatal de Guánica**, or Guánica State Forest, located a few miles south of town (daily 9am to 5pm; free, guide to trails US$1; ☎787/821-5706). This United Nations World Biosphere Reserve is home to 700 plant species, notably a thousand-year-old **lignum vitae tree**, as well as 100 bird species. Often called the best **bird-watching** spot in Puerto Rico, it boasts several rare species including the Puerto Rican emerald-breasted hummingbird, the yellow-shouldered blackbird and, rarest of all, the endangered **Puerto Rican nightjar.** The forest is also home to bullfinches, the Puerto Rican woodpecker, the lizard cuckoo, and crested toads and leatherback turtles.

The park features 28 isolated beaches and offshore cays, and twelve **hiking** trails of varying lengths and degrees of difficulty, most of which are marked. All but a few trails depart from the **ranger station** at the end of Highway 334. The best way to spend your time here is to hike to the beach along the Cueva trail and take a different route back; ask for suggestions at the ranger station. Detailed (albeit somewhat confusing) maps and descriptions of the various trails are available. The hikes can be hot and buggy, so bring plenty of sunscreen and insect repellent. You'll also want to wear light clothing that will also protect you from brambles and cacti.

Practicalities

Conveniently located approximately midway between Ponce and San Germán, Guánica has a better selection of **accommodation** than either of its neighbours. In fact, **Mary Lee's by the Sea**, Rte 333, at km 6.7 (☎787/821-3600; ④) is one of Puerto Rico's most charming places to stay. Situated by a mangrove swamp, with kayaks and motor boats to take guests to beaches across the water, it has cheerful, sprawling apartments with a very tropical feel, some with sea views. Nearby **Copamarina Beach Resort,** Rte 333, km 6.5 (☎787/821-0505, ℱ821-0070; ⑥), offers rustic elegance at an affordable price on a private beach with two pools, jacuzzi, boat launch, beachside bar, boat rentals, gym and two excellent restaurants (see below). Well-equipped rooms even have internet access. For campsites, you'll have to travel into the **Bosque Estatal de Susúa**, above Guánica on Highway 368, km 2.1. **Almacigo I and II** (☎787/833-3700) have space for 165 people, campfire areas, running water and bathrooms. Permits required from Department of Natural Resources (☎787/724-3724).

Guánica also boasts some good **eateries**. *Café San Jacinto*, Rte 333, km 66 (☎787/821-4149), is a lively locals' favourite near the Gilligan's Island ferry dock. Criollo staples, many with fresh fish and seafood, cost around US$7–12. Also popular with locals is the plain but inexpensive *Vista Bahía*, 83 Av Esperanza Idrach (☎787/821-4402), located in town. If you're looking for something a bit more upscale, *Copamarina Coastal Cuisine* at the *Copamarina Beach Resort* is expensive but well worth the price for its grilled fish and meat dishes with inventive tropical marinades and sauces; the grilled lamb is out of this world. *Copamarina*'s more casual option is the reasonably priced *Las Palmas Café*, which is open until 6pm. Criollo staples, burgers and sandwiches will run you less than US$12.

La Parguera

West of Guánica via Route 116 then 304 south, the fishing village of **LA PARGUERA** is best known for its bioluminescent bay, or **La Bahía Fosforescente**. It also affords some of the best diving in Puerto Rico at **The Wall**, about five miles offshore. Around La Parguera you could lose yourself amid the maze of mangrove swamps, channels, canals and offshore islands and cays. The village itself makes a pleasant hub from which to explore the region, with a good sampling of pleasant accommodations, decent restaurants and a lively bar culture.

Like Mosquito Bay on Vieques (see p.385), **La Bahía Fosforescente** is a mangrove swamp illuminated at night by millions of organisms called dinoflagellates, which light up when disturbed. Years of tourist infestation, and resultant environmental abuses, however, have diminished the luminosity here, compared to Mosquito Bay, but boats (charging US$5) still leave every night from La Parguera pier at 7.30pm and 12.30am. Unlike others tours, **Alelí Tours** (☎787/899-6086) will let you swim for a while in the water, an experience which makes you feel as if you're gliding through the Milky Way.

Divers are drawn to La Parguera's innumerable coral reefs offshore, many of them still unexplored. The Wall runs from Guánica to Cabo Rojo and drops to depths of 2000 feet, with visibility up to 120 feet. Snorkelling, too, is excellent; barracudas, morays, manatees, nurse sharks and sea turtles abound. Contact Paradise Scuba (Rte 304 in town, ☎787/899-7611) or Parguera Divers at *Parador Posada Porlamar* (☎787/899-4171) for equipment and details on expeditions.

Kayak rentals are available from Alelí (see above) for US$10–15 an hour and US$50–60 a day. In case you're not up for a workout, you can also rent Boston whalers with slow engines for about the same price from Cancel Boats at the town docks (☎787/899-5891).

Practicalities

There are a number of interesting **places to stay** in La Parguera. *Parador Posada Porlamar*, Rte 304, km 3.3 (Ⓣ787/899-4015 Ⓕ899-5558; ③), offers 24 comfortable and well-equipped A/C units styled like the area's "floating houses" on stilts in the water. Surrounded by mangroves and hillsides, they're very private, and charter boats leave from the dock here for La Bahía Fosforescente. A stone's throw away, state-approved *Parador Villa Parguera* (Ⓣ787/899-7777, Ⓕ899-6040; ④) has luxurious units with private balconies and views of La Bahía Fosforescente, and a pool, restaurant (see below) and dance club on site with weekend cabaret acts.

The cheapest **eats** in town are at the pier, where vendors grill a variety of fresh fish for less than US$4. Many of the village's restaurants are also here. There is an abundance of good, inexpensive grub and, in general, the atmosphere is very young and lively, thanks to the college crowd La Parguera draws on weekends and in summer. On Friday and Saturday nights live music accompanies good pub food at *Parguera Blues Café*, Centro Comercial El Muelle, Avda Los Pescadores (Ⓣ787/899-4742). Worth trying away from the pier, on Route 304, are the restaurant at *Parador Villa Parguera*, which offers an excellent sampling of native cuisine and buffets on Friday and Saturday; and *Los Balcones* (Ⓣ787/899-2145), where you can dine on seafood and criollo specialties on a terrace overlooking the main street.

Cabo Rojo Peninsula

Not to be confused with the town by the same name, twelve miles away, the Cabo Rojo Peninsula culminates in a red-hued limestone **promontory**, also known as Punta Jagüey, which extends into the Caribbean at the island's southwest tip. A fifteen-minute hike to the **Faro de Cabo Rojo** (lighthouse), built in 1881, affords one of Puerto Rico's most dazzling vistas – a three-sided view of the Caribbean from a jagged cliff, with raptors circling overhead and red boulders below rising like stalagmites from the crashing turquoise surf. Several desolate, white-sand coves are visible from the top, and you can further reward your efforts by hiking to one of them and spending the afternoon there undisturbed by other humans.

The drive here on Highway 301 is also remarkable, past salt flats, mangrove swamps and gnarled trees. From La Parguera, drive west on highways 304, 305 and 303 to 301 south. Follow 301 until the road ends; the huge white mountains are salt piles awaiting shipment owned by Las Salinas de Cabo Rojo. When the road becomes unpassable, park and begin to hike up the cliffs to the lighthouse. The walk is only mildly challenging – and profoundly rewarding, but note that this area can be desolate and is best avoided by women travelling alone.

San Germán

The second oldest settlement in Puerto Rico, **SAN GERMÁN** is 16 km from the Cabo Rojo Peninsula, and an hour's drive from Ponce. Founded in 1512, the city is home to the oldest church under US jurisdiction, and an array of period architecture – 36 acres of San Germán's historic centre are on the National Register of Historic Places.

Despite this distinction, a sense of neglect and indifference to history pervades the town. Its architecture seems very much in disrepair, and the nearly 39,000 residents don't seem particularly proud of the heritage. The greatest signs of life on the ancient stone and brick streets and plazas are skater kids, and locals seem far more interested in the strip of fast-food joints, shops and bars on Calle Luna, a block off the main squares. San Germán is so easy to reach from Ponce, however, that if you're in the southwest it's worth a trip here just to see the churches and dine on some of the island's best food at *Café Cilantro* (see below).

Maps and architectural tours are available at the mayor's office (☎787/892-3500) outside the historic centre on Calle Luna. You can also tour the town by **trolley**, which departs from La Casa Alcaldía Antigua, at the eastern end of Plaza Francisco Mariano Quiñones in the historic centre, from Thursday to Sunday.

The Iglesia de Porta Coeli on the Plazuela de Santo Domingo (Wed–Sun 9am–4.15pm; ☎787/892-5845) is the city's chief attraction and the oldest standing church on US turf. Originally built as the chapel for a Dominican monastery, the simple structure was completed in 1607; an adjacent convent was destroyed in 1868, save for the front wall, which still remains. Today, the site functions as a museum of *santos* and other religious artefacts. Set on top of a hill, it is accessed via steep pyramidal brick steps.

Far more ornate than Porta Coeli is the yellow Spanish Baroque **Catedral de San Germán de Auxerre**, on the Plaza Francisco Mariano Quiñones. Still an active parish, it was built in 1739 on the site of an older chapel dating from 1573, and is famed for the trompe l'oeil fresco on its ceiling in the main nave, lit by a brilliant crystal chandelier. Visit during Mass or call ☎787/892-1027 to see if the chaplain will unlock the doors.

Practicalities

While there are no decent places to stay in San Germán, there are a couple of **eating** establishments worth mentioning. **Café Cilantro**, Calle Luna 85 (☎787/264-2735), has superb Nuevo Latino cuisine in a gorgeously restored nineteenth-century Spanish colonial home with terraced gardens, columns and Portuguese tiles. Chef Carlos Rosario is touted as one of island's best, and his lobster and fresh fruit salad with coconut vinaigrette is a must. If you're starving and *Cilantro* is closed, the seafood and traditional criollo dishes at *The Oasis*, a government-sanctioned *mesón gastronómico* in a musty old hotel at Calle Luna 72, will do.

7.4

La Ruta Panoramica

The interior of Puerto Rico – in the Cordillera Central, which runs like a mountainous rudder, east to west, along the length of the island – is best explored along **LA RUTA PANORAMICA**. A 165-mile assemblage of about forty roads, the Panoramic Route can be heartstopping – not just dazzlingly beautiful, but twisting through mist-shrouded, folded peaks, often without dividers, and sometimes with precipitous drops on either side of the narrow road.

In the mountains, the temperature is much cooler, the air heavy and wet, and the vegetation lush and jungle-like. You'll hear sounds of roosters and *coquís* and see houses built on stilts and towns wrapped in fog, seemingly lost in time. You'll catch glimpses of both the Atlantic and the Caribbean at various points along the route, which bypasses canyons and forests.

The road begins in **Yabucoa**, a beach town on the east coast, and ends at Mayagüez; to do the entire length without stopping would take a whole day. Plan on at least two days and take your time on the often harrowing roads. Unless otherwise indicated, all the stops described below lie directly on the route, so follow the Ruta Panoramica signs carefully as you drive, as the route numbers change often.

The first major stop is the town of **Guavate**, legendary for its *lechón*, juicy roast suckling pig cooked on an outdoor spit. For the best *lechón*, turn south off La Ruta Panoramica onto Route 184; at km 27, half a dozen restaurants specialize in selling the tasty meat, most notably *Lechonera El Rancho Original* and *El Monte*. Customers are charged by the weight of their plate (about US$6 a pound). Locals come in droves on the weekend, when live music fills the outdoor seating area.

Many *sanjuaneros* come to this area for the 6000-acre **Reserva Forestal Carite** (☎787/745-4545) in what is known as the "Guavate region", less than an hour south of San Juan, where you can hike, camp, fish, bird-watch, swim and escape the heat. Three **rivers** originate here – the Rio Grande de Loíza, the Rio Grande de Patillas and the Rio de la Plata; the reserve, which stretches over the Sierra Cayey, was established in 1935 to protect this important watershed from erosion caused by development. It is home to two campsites and 25 **hiking trails**, the most popular one starting from **Charco Azul**, a bluish freshwater **swimming hole** within walking distance of Route 184. You will see signs for Carite on 184 between La Ruta Panoramica and the *lechonerías* farther south on 184.

Turn back on 184 and continue west on 179, 7741, 7737, 7722 and 7718 to **San Cristóbal Canyon**, a stunning, 500-foot-deep gorge that stretches for five miles and is home to Puerto Rico's highest **waterfall**, on the Río Usabón. The gorge, visible from the intersection of routes 725 and 162, is hard to access on foot without trespassing on private land, and the slopes can be very dangerous. You can **hike** it, but it's best to go with an organized tour. Groups leave from *La Piedra* restaurant (☎787/735-1034) on Carreterra 7710, km 0.8, next to the Parque Mirador, at 8.30am on Saturdays; call ahead to make a reservation or to arrange a private hike. Bring water and sturdy hiking shoes.

On Route 162 the charming little mountain town of **Barranquitas** is best known as the 1859 birthplace of **Luis Muñoz Rivera**, champion of Puerto Rican independence before Spain ceded rule to the US. Rivera is remembered at the **Casa Natal Luis Muñoz Rivera** on Calle Luis Muñoz Rivera (daily except Mon

& Thurs; 1–4.30pm; free; ⓣ787/857-0230), a museum in the very simple criollo home where Rivera was born. Meanwhile, the **Mausoleo Familia Muñoz Rivera**, 7 Calle Padre Berrios (same hours as Casa Natal; free), contains the remains of Rivera and his son, Luis Muñoz Marín, another extremely important political shaper of modern Puerto Rico and founder of the Popular Democratic Party. If you get hungry, **Bar Plaza**, Calle Barcello (ⓣ787/857-4909), on the plaza, is an inexpensive *repostería* dishing up excellent roast chicken with rice and beans for US$4.

From Barranquitas, head south on Route 162 to Route 143 west, an uphill drive which will take you to the 7000-acre **Toro Negro Forest Reserve**. Three thousand feet above sea level, this ten-mile stretch of La Ruta Panoramica takes you far from civilization and over the **highest peak in Puerto Rico**, the Cerro de Punta, at 4389 feet. This is easily the most tortuous, narrow stretch of the route; landslides are common, and fog can be thick. The views, however, are stunning when the mist clears, and at km 40, a rare vista of both coasts awaits the intrepid traveller.

You'll find a **ranger station** at km 32.4 on Route 143 at the Area Recreativa Doña Juana, but their maps are virtually useless. If you want to **camp**, you can pitch a tent not far from here at Los Viveros at km 3.2. Apply for a permit fifteen days in advance at the Department of Natural Resources in San Juan (ⓣ787/724-3724).

Maricao, near the western end of the La Ruta Panoramica, hosts a **coffee harvest festival** in mid-February, but its natural setting alone makes it worth a visit any time of year. The town is snug in the mountains, with some steeply inclined streets, and gorges and streams just on the outskirts. Don't think about finding the perfect cup of coffee during your stay here; even the most authentic-looking joints in town sell imported stuff.

7.5

Vieques and Culebra

Even if you're staying in Puerto Rico for just a week, it's worthwhile to catch a ferry or hop a puddle-jumper to **VIEQUES** or **CULEBRA**, the two relatively undeveloped islets off the eastern coast known as the Spanish Virgin Islands – and geologically a part of the Virgin Islands. Snorkelling, diving, fishing and swimming are superlative here, and ravishingly beautiful, often isolated, beaches abound on both islands. A laid-back atmosphere prevails, despite Vieques's added fame as the site of controversial bombing practices conducted by the US – a history that Culebra shares, though it's not part of that island's present.

Vieques

Just seven miles off the eastern shore of Puerto Rico, 21-mile-long **VIEQUES** feels a world away. Despite the controversial construction in 2000 of Martineau Bay, a five-star resort near the airport, its countryside remains untrammelled. Many locals still get around on horseback and chickens still stop cars in the roads, which are devoid of traffic or traffic lights.

Since 1948, the western and eastern thirds of the island have been occupied by the US Navy, which uses these portions for **bombing practice**. The military occupation of Vieques is undoubtedly the most substantive complaint about life under the US flag, protested widely on the Puerto Rico mainland and even by celebrities and politicians stateside.

It is indeed disturbing to be sipping coconut juice on an abandoned beach, with the sounds of shelling audible, though of course it's not constant. In 1999, after a local civilian was killed by a stray bomb, President Bill Clinton demanded that military training on Vieques be phased out in five years; nevertheless, bombing has continued, despite suits and protest against it.

Arrival, information and getting around

You'll land on Vieques, by air or by sea, in **Isabela Segunda**, the rather plain town

Travelling to the offshore islands

The Spanish Virgins are easily reached by **plane** from San Juan or the port city of **Fajardo** on the eastern coast, via Vieques Air Link (☎1-888/901-9247) or Isla Nena (☎1-888/263-6213). Flights from San Juan leave for Vieques from the international airport (US$69 one-way) and to both islands from Isla Grande airport, which is somewhat cheaper (US$43 one-way to Vieques; US$50 to Culebra). Flights are much cheaper from Fajardo, within an hour's drive from San Juan (US$19 one-way to Vieques; US$25 one-way to Culebra). Either flight takes just around a half-hour.

The **Puerto Rican Port Authority** (☎1-800/981-2005 or 787/863-0705 in Fajardo; ☎787/741-4761 in Vieques; ☎787/742-3161 in Culebra) also runs **ferries** to the Spanish Virgins. The trip takes about an hour and is dirt-cheap: US$2 to Vieques and US$2.25 to Culebra. You may even bring your car aboard, but you have to reserve a space at least two weeks in advance. Call for schedules and to make reservations.

on the north side (referred to around the rest of the island as "the far side"). It has the island's only **post office** and **ATM**, but that's no reason to stay; indeed, best to press right on to the south side of the island.

Públicos on the island generally run from 8am to 6pm, though Ana Luz Rubles runs 24 hours (☎787/313-0599). For **information**, contact the tourism office (☎787/741-0800), or rely on any of the resorts listed below.

Around the Island

Just a fifteen-minute ride south from Isabela Segunda takes you to **Esperanza**, the main town on the Caribbean coast. Without question, the beaches on this side of the island are superior (the Atlantic beaches tend to be rocky) and the landscape more attractive.

The Strip, a waterside drag in Esperanza, has a lovely white seaside promenade and a picturesque collection of indoor/outdoor restaurants and guesthouses. Heading east from town are Vieques's three most popular beaches. About a thirty-minute walk down Route 997 leads to the *balneario* **Sombé** (Sun Bay), a two-mile crescent of bone-coloured sand lined with trees and coconut palms where wild horses graze. The turquoise, deep-blue and jade-green waters are mildly rough, and the beach can be busy on weekends, but on weekdays or off season, it's easy to feel as though you have it to yourself.

East along the dirt road from Sombé is **Media Luna,** a tidy, half-moon cove with baby-bath water. The beach is very narrow with lots of seaweed and almond trees, and the water is incomparably calm and warm. Further on, **Navío** is another attractive stretch, and the most popular with locals, enclosed by rock walls with stark white sands and impossibly translucent turquoise waters. However, the surf is quite rough, and the wind can stir up the sand to the extent that it's uncomfortable to lie on the beach.

One of the highlights of a visit to Vieques is a night-time boat ride around **Mosquito Bay**, said to contain the highest degree of bioluminescence in the world. This shallow-water mangrove swamp is home to trillions of dinoflagellates, which light up in self-defence when disturbed. The boat trundles through them, leaving glittery contrails in its wake, with fish darting past like shooting stars, and stops mid-swamp to let passengers take a dip. Captain Sharon Grasso runs tours through **Island Adventure** (☎787/741-0720). Wear a swimsuit under your clothes, and bring goggles if you have them.

Accommodation

At Waters Edge & the Villa North Shore Road, Isabela Segunda ☎787/741-1128. The island's only beachfront resort is a great deal for the money. Rooms are spacious and minimally elegant, and there are two pools and a restaurant on the premises. ④

Bananas The Strip ☎787/741-8700. Pioneer guesthouse established in mid-1980s. Eight rustic, airy rooms off breezeway open onto jungle and have A/C and refrigerators. Lively bar. ②

The Crow's Nest Road 201, km 1.5 ☎787/741-0033. Located ten minutes from the beach by car on a forested hill overlooking the Atlantic. Spacious rooms with private bath, A/C, and kitchenette. There's a pool and excellent restaurant. ④

Inn on the Blue Horizon Rte 996, km 4.2 ☎787/741-3318, ℱ741-0522. Vieques's most beautiful place to stay, in a seafront, Mediterranean-style structure on a cliff, attracts a very fashionable crowd. Three cabins have private balconies and sea views. No phones or TVs; only two rooms have A/C (breezes amply compensate). The island's best restaurant and bar are on the premises. ⑦

La Finca Caribe Hwy 995 ☎787/741-0495. Rustic, eco-sensitive mountain lodging offering run-down but charming and spacious cottages with hammocks everywhere, open-air showers, and beautiful gardens. Rooms also available in the Great House. Staff-led bike tours of island are available. ③

Posada Vista Mar Calle Almendro ☎787/741-8716. Hacienda-style inn slightly off The Strip in Esperanza. Five clean rooms seem cosy rather than small – like you're entering a stranger's well-kept home for the night. Excellent criollo cuisine on offer at the restaurant. ❷

Sombé Beach (☎787/741-8198). Legal camping on *balneario* with outdoor showers, toilets and changing rooms. ❶

Trade Winds The Strip ☎787/741-8666. Spacious, tidy A/C rooms, four with terraces facing the Caribbean. Friendly innkeeper and good seaside open-air restaurant. ❸

Eating, drinking and nightlife

Bananas (see previous page). Pizza, wings, sandwiches and other bar grub are on offer at this lively, sometimes raucous, open-air pub. Dinner US$8–15.

Café Blu and the Blue Bar *Inn on the Blue Horizon* (see above) ☎787/741-3318. Locals mingle with New York and LA fashion types in an elegant, open-air setting with sea views, offering Continental cuisine with a sometimes tropical twist. The bar with is well known among the jet-set and travel writers. Entrees US$19–24.

Chez Shack Hwy 995 ☎787/741-2175. Six miles northwest of Esperanza in forest surroundings, the *Shack* offers excellent grilled foods, including lobster, plus a live steel band on Mon nights. Entrees US$14–18.

La Dulce Esperanza Calle Almendro ☎787/741-0085. This place is basically a tiny bakery (with a significant number of mosquitoes), but you can sit at indoor picnic tables and snack on healthy versions of standard Puerto Rican pastries, as well as sandwiches (US$5), calzones and pizza.

Posada Vista Mar (see above). Local favourite serving excellent *asopao*, *tostones*, and other criollo favourites on a screened-in porch. Feels like grandma's kitchen. Entrees US$7–14.

Trade Winds (see above). Rustic porch with ceiling fans overlooking the Caribbean. Menu features savoury fresh grilled fish and steaks in tropical marinades and sauces. Entrees US$12–18.

Trapper John *The Crow's Nest* (see above) ☎787/741-0033 The specialty here is lobster, prepared various ways; steak and fresh fish with a tropical twist are also popular. The second-floor deck has a view of El Yunque. Entrees US$14–21.

Culebra

North of Vieques, and not quite twenty miles east of Fajardo, tiny **CULEBRA** is surrounded by two dozen islets and cays that afford snorkelling and dive sites touted as some of the Caribbean's best. Just as spectacular are the island's miles and miles of stunning **beaches**, many of them uninhabited. As with Vieques, the US Navy used Culebra for bombing practice, though this ended in 1975. Since 1909, the entire coastline and large portions of the 7000-acre interior have been designated wildlife preserves to protect the rare seabirds and sea turtles that nest here.

You'll definitely want to concern yourself with that natural environment while you're here; home to about 2000 inhabitants, the island has no nightclubs or resorts, and only one sleepy town, called **Dewey**, a ragtag assemblage of two-storey wooden lean-tos, bars and restaurants whose streets are full of drifters hanging about.

Arrival, information and getting around

The lone **airport** is north of Dewey, and right by the main roads that run across the island. The **ferry** arrives right by Dewey's main strip, if you can call it that. That same strip, Calle Pedro Marquez, is also home to Banco Popular, which has an ATM machine; a branch of Citibank; and a branch of the **US Post Office**. **Town Hall**, on Calle Pedro Marquez (☎787/742-3288), is home to a small tourist information office, but the information you'll get here is extremely limited.

For **públicos** try Willy's (☎787/742-3537). It might be best in most cases to leave the driving to others; most roads pitch headlong into precipitous slopes, with crater-sized potholes, and if you want to rent a car, make sure it's a four-wheel-drive. Otherwise **bikes** may well be the way to go, available for US$15 a day, or US$80 a week, from Culebra Bike Shop (☎787/742-2209). To get out to the outer cays, rent a **kayak** from your guesthouse or boats from Ocean Safari (☎787/379-1973), which offers pick-up and delivery, Culebra Dive Shop (☎787/742-0566), or Casa Ensenada and Culebra Boat Rental (☎787/742-3559). Rentals cost about US$40 a day.

Around the island

In 1909, President Theodore Roosevelt learned of the migratory bird colonies here and further curtailed human exposure by establishing the **Culebra National Wildlife Refuge**, which encompasses one third of the island's 7000 acres. Overseen by the US Fish and Wildlife Service (☎787/742-0115), these protected lands are the domain of endangered sea turtles, including the seven foot long leatherback turtle, which can weigh up to 1400 pounds; and 50,000 seabirds, of thirteen species, including terns, boobies, white-tailed and red-billed tropic birds, and laughing gulls.

Between March and April, travellers can aid in **leatherback turtle breeding**, an extraordinary experience to behold. For more information, contact Roberto Matos (☎787/724-2816 or 3640) or the Caribbean Fish and Wildlife Service in Boquerón (☎787/851-7297).

On the north coast, west of the Refuge and about two miles north of Dewey, is **Flamenco Beach,** a *balneario* with showers and legal campsites. The arcing white sand is fine like baking flour, and the beach is very level and smooth into the water, without rocks or lots of shells. As with most other island beaches, it's deserted and paradisiacal during the week, much busier at weekends.

Playa Zoni, way over on the island's eastern side, and **Playa Brava**, on its northern side, east of the refuge, are remote but also excellent for sunbathing, though the latter is a bit rough and you'll need to take care. Neither is all that easy to get to. Zoni is up and over a steep hill off Highway 250 from the airport. The road gets extremely rugged, so it's best to park and walk the rest of the way when it does. Brava can be reached heading on Highway 250 to km 4, left past the cemetery and down to a gate, where a trail heads to the beach.

Diving on Culebra is excellent. Protected by the US Fish and Wildlife Service, the reefs are in near-perfect condition. Various sections are host to barracuda, stingray, blue tang, brain corals, lavender sea fans, trumpet fish, parrot fish, blue tang, and hawksbill turtles. For the best locations, contact Culebra Dive Shop (☎787/742-0566), Culebra Divers (☎787/742-0803), or Reef Link Divers (☎787/742-0581) for snorkelling; the first in this list is also the place for information on **kayak rental, fly fishing** for bonefish, **snorkelling,** and **underwater photography**.

Accommodation

Club Seabourne Fulladoza Road, km 1.5 ☎787/742-3169. Excellent, clean cottages, villas and rooms, some with furnished balconies overlooking the water. Pool and excellent restaurant and bar on premises. Rather upscale for Culebra. ❹

Culebra Beach Villas Flamenco Beach ☎787/767-7575. Attractive beachfront villas and apartments with full kitchens; very popular, so book early. ❹

Flamenco Beach ☎787/742-0600. This legal campground on the *balneario* is a mob scene on weekends and in summer. ❶

Mamacitas Calle Castelar, Dewey ☎787/742-0090. Handful of apartments and rooms above one of Dewey's most popular restaurants. ❸

Posada La Hamaca Calle Castelar, Dewey ☎787/742-3516. Clean, inexpensive, basic rooms in the heart of "town" near canal. Terrace overlooking water. ❸

Villa Boheme Fulladoza Road ☎787/742-3508. Very pleasant rooms, some with sea views, balconies or sun decks. Those that don't have a room with kitchenettes can use the communal kitchen and barbecue. Beach gear rentals are available. ❹

Eating, drinking and nightlife

Club Seabourne (see overleaf). Fish and chips, seafood stroganoff, lobster, and steaks, all a bit upscale for Culebra. Entrees US$12–20.

Dinghy Dock south of drawbridge on Carreterra Fulladoza ☎787/742-0581. Gourmet breakfasts – smoked salmon, eggs benedict, etc – and grilled foods and pasta dishes for dinner. Produce for sale every Tues night. Entrees US$12–20.

El Batey Calle Escudero toward airport from Dewey ☎787/742-3828. Great grilled burgers, criollo food, and hot, hot salsa at night. Worth visiting Saturday night for *salsa* and serious Boricúa vibe. Entrees US$3–6.

Mamacitas (see overleaf). Waterside dining under a tin-roof gazebo, where you can enjoy criollo food, burgers and burritos, accompanied by calypso and reggae music. The bar is popular with locals. Entrees US$12–20.

Oasis Calle Pedro Marquez, Dewey ☎787/742-3175. Superb pizzas with gourmet toppings, tasty salads and the "coldest beer on Culebra" attract a hip but unpretentious crowd. Entrees US$5–9.

8

The Virgin Islands

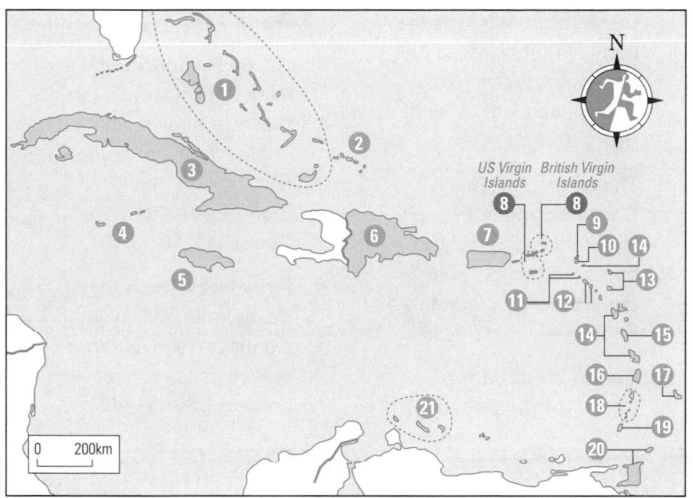

The Virgin Islands Highlights

* **Magens Bay Beach, St Thomas** This half-mile-long stretch of powder on St Thomas is consistently voted one of the best beaches in the world. See p.404

* **Jump-Up, St Croix** Catch this monthly street party in Christiansted for live music, dancing, stilt walkers and lots of food. See p.415

* **The Baths, Virgin Gorda** Scramble through the grottoes, caves and pools created by these out-size volcanic rocks. See p.440

* **Bomba's Full-Moon Party, Tortola** Decadent bash presided over by the self-proclaimed king of Tortola. See p.435

* **Wreck of the RMS Rhone** View the haunting remains of *Rhone* at the bottom of Sir Francis Drake Channel. See p.437

* **Gorda Peak National Park, Virgin Gorda** Lush preserve strewn with unique flora and fauna and capped by the island's 1370-foot peak. See p.440

* **Painkillers** The *Soggy Dollar* in White Bay is said to have invented these intense rum concoctions. See p.446

Introduction and Basics

Chill Caribbean culture, idyllic beaches, wild mountainous interiors and balmy temperatures make the **Virgin Islands** one of the most popular destinations in the Caribbean. Made up of over one hundred islands, cays, islets, reefs and rocks, the islands attract in excess of two million visitors a year for the **fishing**, **sailing**, and spectacular **snorkelling** and **diving**. Natural attractions aside, the colonial legacy, which has seen many flags flying over the islands in the past three hundred years (Dutch, French, Danish, British and Spanish to name a few), has left some charming historic architecture, particularly in the towns of the United States Virgin Islands, together with atmospheric ruins of sugar plantations and a culture that is something of a melting pot.

A territory of the USA, the **United States Virgin Islands (USVI)** can, with their international cuisine, mini-shopping malls and American-style amenities, initially seem rather too much like its big brother with the added advantage of duty-free shopping. But further exploration reveals the strong roots of West Indian culture, no more so than at Carnival time when the streets of St Thomas are overtaken with colourful costume-parades, bands and food stalls selling delicious creole food. The **British Virgin Islands (BVI)** are less touched by tourism and the majority of visitors are yachters – the calm waters, gentle breezes, deep bays and short distances between anchorages have long made the BVI a **sailing** paradise.

The mainstay of the **economy** in the Virgin Islands is tourism, though the USVI have a lucrative sideline in the Hess Oil Refinery and a reasonable manufacturing industry, while the BVI receive significant income from licence fees paid by foreign companies taking advantage of the BVI's tax exemptions.

Where to go

Most visitors to the Virgin Islands head straight for St Thomas, though it can feel overcrowded and familiar; more serene surroundings await on St Croix and St John, especially the latter, which offers excellent **hiking.**

In the BVI, the main draws are the wondrous **reefs** and sandy **beaches**, along with myriad watersports and boating activities; **Brewer's Bay Beach** in particular has excellent snorkelling, while the well-preserved wreck of the **RMS Rhone** off Salt Island is the highlight of any visit. To the northwest, peaceful Virgin Gorda is home to the unusual natural attraction known as **The Baths**, colossal boulders surrounded by pools teeming with marine life.

When to go

The Virgin Islands' **climate** is subtropical, with temperatures ranging from 26°C to 31°C (79–89°F) in summer to 22°C to 28°C (72–82°C) in winter. Easterly trade winds keep the humidity low, with May and June the stickiest months. Heavy rain is rare except during **hurricane season** (June–Nov) when most of the annual rainfall of 100mm arrives, though most of it is in the form of brief showers. The last major hurricanes to hit the Virgins, Hurricane Luis and Hurricane Marilyn, occurred within two weeks of each other in September 1995 and caused several billion dollars of damage. Unsurprisingly, there are good deals to be had in hurricane season – November is the best because off-season prices are still in effect, yet the weather is often just as good as in December.

Getting there

The main gateway to the Virgin Islands is the **Cyril E. King International Airport** on St Thomas, which handles direct flights from the US (American, Continental, US Air and United among others) and flights from San Juan, Puerto Rico. There are also direct flights from the US to the Henry E. Rohlsen

Airport on St Croix. Cape Air (☎508/771/6944 or 1/800-352-0714, ⓦwww.capeair.com) and American Eagle fly daily from San Juan to St Thomas. There are no direct flights to the BVI; you have to go via St Thomas or San Juan – American Eagle, LIAT and Air Sunshine all operate daily flights from San Juan to Tortola and Air St Thomas flies from San Juan to Virgin Gorda.

For contact numbers of airlines see pp.12–17 and 36–37.

Getting around

Hopping **from island to island** is easy either by air or, more popularly, using the network of inter-island ferries. **On the islands** themselves you can do much of your exploring on foot using taxis, rental cars, bikes or boats for longer distances.

By air

Getting between the islands **by air** is relatively easy. Between **St Thomas and St Croix** there are a couple of options: American Eagle and Cape Air fly this route (about US$100–125 round-trip) or there's Seaborne Airlines' seaplanes (several daily; 15min; ☎340/773-6442) – cheaper and more of a thrill. There's no airport on **St John** so you need to take a ferry either from Charlotte Amalie (nearest to the airport; US$7 one-way; 40min), or Red Hook (US$3 one-way; 20min). The car ferry (same ports) costs US$40 round-trip.

To get **from the USVI to BVI** there are scheduled flights from St Thomas to: Tortola (daily with LIAT, CaribAir, Air Sunshine; Mon, Wed & Fri with Clair Aero (☎284/495-2271); Virgin Gorda (Mon–Sat with Air St Thomas); and Anegada (Mon, Wed & Fri with Clair Aero). From St Croix there are daily flights to Tortola with Air Sunshine. Charter flights to Tortola, Virgin Gorda and Anegada are always available with Fly BVI. Within the BVI, there are regular flights by Fly BVI and Clair Aero.

By bus and car

On the main islands of the USVI there's a government-operated **bus** service, **VITRAN** (☎340/774-5678), which makes designated stops (look for rainbow-coloured buses on signposts). While buses are cheap (generally US$1 per trip and 25¢ per transfer), bus stops aren't always conveniently located and trips, especially in and around Charlotte Amalie, can be a slow process. Apart from the irregular Scato Bus Service on Tortola there is no public transport on the BVI. In most cases you'll find it easier on both the USVI and BVI to get a taxi or, better still, rent a **car**, which is easily done on most of the major islands. Book your car in advance if you're coming during peak season and expect to pay upwards of US$40–50 per day (weekly rates are lower). Note that in the USVI and BVI cars **drive on the left** side of the road. On the BVI you'll need a **BVI driving licence** (US$10) that can be issued by the car rental company. **Taxis** in the Virgin Islands charge by the destination so it pays to pack in as many people as you can. Rates are set by the government and taxi drivers are required to carry a rate card; ask to see it if you're unsure of the fare and always agree on your price before you set off.

By sea

There is an excellent network of **inter-island ferries**, though it's advisable to call ahead for times as they often change. As a rough guide to prices, a round-trip fare between Tortola and St. John is US$40; between Tortola and Virgin Gorda US$20. Between St Thomas and St Croix there is a high-speed catamaran (75min; US$60 round-trip).

Between BVI

Jost Van Dyke Ferry Service ☎284/494-2997, and **When** ☎284/494-2997. Between Tortola and Jost Van Dyke.
Marina Cay Ferry ☎284/494-2174. Free ferry connecting Beef Island to Marina Cay.
North Sound Express ☎284/495-2138. Between Beef Island and Virgin Gorda.
Peter Island Ferry ☎284/495-2000. Between Tortola and Peter Island.
Saba Rock Ferry ☎284/495-9966. Between the North Sound and Saba Rock.
Smith's Ferry Services ☎284/495-4495. Between Tortola and Virgin Gorda.

Between USVI and BVI

Inter-Island ☎340/776-6597. Between Red Hook, St John, Tortola, Virgin Gorda and Jost Van Dyke.

Native Son ☎1888/273-3284 or 284/495-4617. Between Tortola & St Thomas (Charlotte Amalie & Red Hook).
Smith's Ferry Services ☎284/495-4495. Between Tortola (Road Town and West End), St Thomas and Virgin Gorda.
Speedy's ☎284/495-5240. Between Tortola, Virgin Gorda and St Thomas.

Between USVI

Inter-Island ☎340/776-6597. Between Red Hook and St John.
Transportation Services ☎340/776-6282. Between Charlotte Amalie, Red Hook and St John.
Virgin Islands Fast Ferry ☎340/719-0099. Between Charlotte Amalie and St Croix.

Alternatively you may prefer to **charter a yacht**, either with a crew or by yourself (bareboat). Either way you're looking at upwards of US$2000 per week for a boat in high season, and if you're going **bareboat** you'll have to demonstrate that you have sufficient sailing experience. You'll also need accurate maps and charts to navigate the many reefs surrounding the islands. You must clear **customs** on entry to the USVI (unless you are coming from a US port) at Charlotte Amalie, Cruz Bay, Christiansted or Frederiksted. In the BVI customs points are at Great Harbour, Jost Van Dyke, Spanish Town on Virgin Gorda, and Road Town and Soper's Hole on Tortola.

Money and costs

The **currency** for the US and British Virgin Islands is the **US dollar**. Branches of major **banks**, most with **ATMs**, are located in most towns. Major **credit cards** are accepted widely on the islands at hotels, restaurants and car rental agencies. However, there's always a risk that some small out-of-the-way place won't take them, so it pays to travel with some cash if you plan to go off the beaten track. **Travellers' cheques** are also widely accepted and most hotels allow guests to cash personal cheques. Be warned that there's a government **room tax** (8 percent in the USVI; 7 percent in the BVI) on all accommodation and an 8–15 percent service charge on everything else in hotels, so check bills before **tipping**. The standard tip for good service is 15 percent in restaurants and bars; around 10 percent for taxis.

Information

All main towns in the Virgin Islands have **tourist offices**. The official agencies are the **US Virgin Islands Department of Tourism** (Ⓦwww.usvi.net) and the **BVI Tourist Board** (Ⓦwww.bviwelcome.com). Your lodgings may also be an excellent source of local information – resorts and large hotels in particular will often help guests (and sometimes non-guests) set up trips, car rental and activities, especially on the smaller islands without official tourist offices.

Accommodation

Accommodation in the Virgin Islands covers the entire scale from campsites with bare sites to super luxury-resorts on private islands. There aren't any youth hostels in the Virgin Islands but you'll still be able to find some budget accommodation in most places. **Campsites** start at around US$20 for a bare site. The next rung up, **guesthouses**, vary widely in quality, price and size from basic rooms above a bar to cosy beachside Inns, but you can expect to pay around US$50–100 for a double room per night. **Hotels** range from small places (mainly in towns and villages) with a pool and bar (for around US$75–150) to resorts with beachfront accommodation and all facilities (upwards of US$150). Bear in mind the **room tax** (see above). If you're planning on a lengthy stay it might be worth checking out renting a **private villa or home**.

Depending on the **season**, rates can vary widely. Depending on the room you choose, it's generally 20–40 percent cheaper during low season (May 1 to Dec 14). If you are visiting in high season you should book a few months in advance to be sure of getting the place you want.

Food and drink

Because the Virgin Islands have flown several flags during their history there is a rich culinary heritage combining **Dutch, English, French, African, West Indian and other**

influences. And while there's plenty of fine international cuisine to be had, particularly on the larger USVI like St Thomas and St Croix, you should definitely try out the many wonderful West Indian dishes showcasing the best of **creole cuisine**. Generally speaking, you'll pay around US$6–15 for a meal at a café or standard restaurant; US$18–30 for an entrée at more upmarket places. The USVI has the full range of international cuisine; eating on the BVI you're more likely to have to stick to West Indian food, with international dishes confined mainly to upmarket places or snack-style places serving sandwiches, burgers and pizzas.

Restaurants often close for several hours between meals, generally 3–5pm and many places close before 10.30pm. As always you should reserve in popular places and call ahead for those in out-of-the-way spots to make sure they're open. When it comes to dress, the BVI are a little more formal than most other islands. For any sit-down meal in a smart restaurant men are advised to wear long trousers and a collared shirt.

In the Virgin Islands, **West Indian** fare is the food of choice for locals. An average dish consists of spiced meats, lots of starches and very few vegetables. **Conch**, a shellfish that has a similar texture and taste to squid, and **goat**, which is very similar to pork, are served almost any way you can imagine. A popular dish that often sells out quickly is conch in butter sauce. Common side dishes include fried **plantains and fungi**, which is very similar to American stuffing. Many fish and chicken dishes are served with fruit salsa, or a coconut milk sauce. Spicy foods, such as foods rubbed with Caribbean curries or Jamaican jerk spices, are also popular. For a quick and inexpensive meal, locals grab a **roti** – meat, potatoes, carrots and onions simmered in a creamy curry sauce and folded between warm flatbread, occasionally with some chutney on the side. Be careful when you eat a chicken roti, because locals eat them with the bones.

Rum – in particular Cruzan rum made on St Croix – is definitely the spirit of choice and rum punch is the most popular rum drink. Locals drink a mixture of two shots of dark rum, a teaspoon of sugar and a splash of water. Virgin Island **beers** include Caribe (very similar to Corona), Foxey's Lager and Blackbeard Ale, but you can also get foreign beers like Red Stripe, Heineken and Guinness.

Phones, post and email

Local calls on public payphones cost 25 cents for five minutes. To call the islands **from overseas** dial the international dialling code + 1+ area code + number (instructions on **calling overseas** from the Virgin Islands are on p.40). For **international calls** you are best off using a prepaid phone card, such as the Virgin Island Traveler's Card, which is available in US$10 increments from shops, post offices and most hotels. If you carry a **mobile phone**, try dialing ⓣ6611 to enquire about use on the island, though it's best to inquire with your carrier well in advance of making your trip.

Post offices (open generally Mon–Fri 7.30am–4.30pm & Sat 7.30am–noon) can be found in most main towns. However, many hotels will sell you stamps and mail letters for you.

Some hotels offer free **internet access** to guests; otherwise you'll have to log on at one of the cybercafés – they're not widespread but most major towns will have one. The two main USVI **newspapers** are *The V.I. Daily News* and *The Independent* – both on St Thomas. In the BVI it's the *BVI Beacon* (Thurs) and *The Island Sun* (Sat), plus the free weekly, *Limin' Times*, which carries **listings** of upcoming events.

The **country code** for the BVI is ⓣ284; for the USVI it's ⓣ340.

Opening hours, holidays and festivals

For the most part in the USVI and BVI **businesses** are open Monday to Saturday

Public holidays

USVI

January 1 New Year's Day
January 6 Three Kings' Day
January Martin Luther King Jr's Birthday (third Mon)
Third Monday in February Presidents' Day
March 31 Transfer Day
March/April Maundy Thursday, Good Friday, Easter Monday
Last Monday in May Memorial Day
July 3 Emancipation Day
July 4 Independence Day
July Supplication Day (date varies)
First Monday in September Labour Day
Second Monday in October Columbus Day
November 1 Liberty Day
November 11 Veteran's Day
Fourth Thursday in November Thanksgiving Day
December 25 Christmas Day
December 26 Boxing Day

BVI

January 1 New Year's Day
March 11 Commonwealth Day
March/April Good Friday, Easter Monday
May/June Whit Monday
June 11 Queen's Birthday
July 1 Territory Day
August BVI August Festival Days
October 22 St Ursula's Day
November 12 Birthday of Heir to the Throne
December 25 Christmas Day
December 26 Boxing Day

8am–5pm, and **shops,** museums and historic sights Monday to Saturday 9am–5pm. On the USVI **bank opening hours** are Mon–Fri 9am–3pm, and some open Saturday morning; BVI banks close slightly earlier at around 2.30pm. Government buildings are open 9am–5pm weekdays. Always **call ahead** to make sure your destination is open, especially in the off-season. Both the USVI and the BVI celebrate local **public holidays** as well as many of the holidays celebrated in their mother countries. The government and banks close for major holidays, but stores, restaurants and tourist attractions generally stay open. The main cultural event to look out for in the Virgin Islands is **Carnival** – a couple of weeks of costumed street parades including mocko jumbies (stilt walkers), calypso and steelpan bands, street stalls and all-night partying and dancing. St Thomas Carnival – the second largest in the Caribbean after Trinidad – takes place the last two weeks in April (see p.405). Some other Virgin Islands have mini-carnivals – Virgin Gorda's is in mid-February and St John's the first few days of July – and if you happen to be in the BVI the last two weeks of July you'll be swept along in the nightly entertainment and music of the **BVI Summer Festival**.

Crime and personal safety

For the most part the Virgin Islands are low in **crime** and much of what there is is drug-related, with theft and occasional muggings the main problems. The poorer areas of main towns and villages are, as you'd expect, the crime hot spots, so you should stick to well-lit, busy main roads after dark in all towns in the Virgin Islands. Furthermore, don't pick up hitchhikers, even if it's common for locals to do this – they probably know who they're picking up.

Health

You're far more likely to leave the Virgin Islands feeling healthier than you have in ages, but it pays to be cautious about certain fish – you're best off avoiding reef fish such as snapper, grouper and barracuda while in the BVI as the marine toxin, **ciguatera**, which affects only these reef fish, is prevalent here (see also p.24).

Emergency phone numbers

For **emergencies**, you can dial ⓣ911 in the USVI on any telephone for fire, police or medical assistance. In the BVI the number is ⓣ911, or 999 on some islands. For **marine emergencies**, call Virgin Islands Search and Rescue (VISAR) by dialling ⓣ999 or via VHF Ch.16.

Watersports and outdoor activities

The Virgin Islands are a paradise for almost any **watersports** you can imagine – diving, snorkelling, windsurfing, parasailing – as well as fishing, sailing and hiking. See the individual island accounts for details of companies offering anything from snorkelling day trips to weeklong sailing courses. **Fishing** is a popular pastime on the islands – wahoo are hot from August to February, marlin September to January, mahi mahi from February to May and tuna November to January. However, note that the removal of any marine organism from BVI waters is illegal for non-British Virgin Islanders without a recreational **fishing permit**. Call the Fisheries Division at ⓣ284/494-3429 for information.

History

Although there is some evidence that the Virgin Islands were populated by Amerindian tribes as far back as 1500 BC, the earliest tribe known to have settled here was the Igneri, the first wave of **Arawaks**, who arrived from South America in huge canoes, landing on St Croix sometime between 50 and 650 AD. The next wave of Arawaks – the Taíno – arrived around 1300; skilled in agriculture they set about farming the islands of St Croix, St John and St Thomas only to be displaced in the early part of the fifteenth century by the aggressive warrior tribe known as the **Caribs**. By the time Columbus set foot on the islands in 1493 during his second voyage, the Caribs were well established and the indigenous Arawak tribes had dwindled to a fraction of their original number. Columbus named the islands **Las Virgenes**, "the virgins" – their sheer number and pristine condition reminding him of the legend of St Ursula, a feisty fourth-century European princess, and her "army" of 11,000 virgins, who were raped and killed by a Hun prince and his henchmen. After the Spaniards pretty much wiped out the entire population of native peoples, the islands were safe for colonization and ripe for mass planting of sugarcane.

The first half of the seventeenth century witnessed a period of intense **colonial squabbling** with the British, Dutch, Spanish and French establishing proto-colonies on various islands until the **Danes** interceded in 1666 and began their period of domination over the islands west of St John, while the **English** gained control of the eastern section of islands. The Danes are credited with developing their islands into some of the busiest ports in the West Indies; the **slave trade** boomed, **pirates** were a common (and often welcome) sight, but more importantly, **sugarcane** flowered into a major cash crop. However, owing to many factors, including natural disasters and the **emancipation of the islands' slaves** (1834 in the British West Indies, 1848 in the Danish West

Indies), the economy of the islands soured in the early to mid-1800s.

The **US** didn't get their hands on the Danish West Indies until the twentieth century. Worried that the Germans would use the islands as submarine bases in **World War I**, the US government purchased them from the Danes in 1917 for US$25 million – to the approval of much of the population who anticipated American investment in education and health. Meanwhile in the BVI, a "crown colony" since the 1870s, rumblings of dissatisfaction were beginning over their negligent and distant ruling power. The effect was catching and by the **Thirties** most citizens of the USVI were feeling similarly let down by the US: their expected improvements in living conditions hadn't materialized and the islands had become little more than a US naval base with the attendant problem of unruly sailors. A visit by President Roosevelt in 1934 revitalized the US attitude to the USVI and before long huge improvements to the islands' infrastructure were in full swing. But by the end of the **Forties** both territories were actively seeking more **independence** and the right to elect their own government – the BVI got theirs in 1967 when they were permitted a ministerial system of government headed by an elected Chief Minister. The following year, the USVI gained the right to elect their own governor.

Today, the USVI are considered a territory of the United States and have one seat in Congress. Islanders are US citizens and pay taxes, but they cannot vote for the President of the United States. The BVI are a dependent territory of Britain and are overseen by a governor appointed by the British monarch, though they are more or less self-governing. The governor presides over the five-member Executive Council, while the Legislative Council consists of a twelve-member elected body with a ministerial system.

8.1

The United States Virgin Islands

With its sea-swept landscapes, historic towns, duty-free shopping and luxurious resorts, the **UNITED STATES VIRGIN ISLANDS** bask in the combination of familiar yet exotic that makes them one of the most popular cruise-ship destinations in the Caribbean. America aside, it's the Danes who have had the most influence on the islands. Successful sugarcane exporters and slave dealers, they built most of the major towns, and there are plentiful reminders of their presence in the **colonial architecture** of the historic cities of Charlotte Amalie and Christiansted and in the ruins of sugar plantations scattered across the green mountainous slopes.

Of the sixty islands, islets and cays (most of which are uninhabited) that make up the USVI, the biggest and busiest are St Thomas, St Croix and St John. Each has a distinctive mood and culture, and you haven't really seen the USVI until you've checked out all three. **St Thomas**, with its picturesque capital, Charlotte Amalie, is the most American of the islands – hip and stylish (at least compared to the rest of the Caribbean) with upmarket shops and restaurants and a history born of trade rather than sugar. **St Croix**, the largest of the islands, is the most distant so sees little

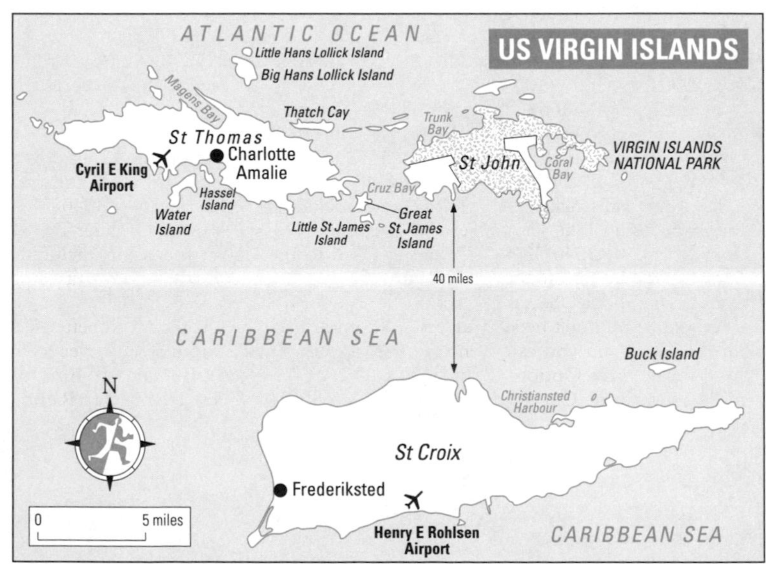

of the hordes that flock to St Thomas and St John, though the cruise-ship ports of Christiansted and Frederiksted still attract visitors with their mix of historic sights and good shopping and restaurants. **St John**, the smallest of the islands is virtually all wilderness, its National Park, part on land, part underwater, the major attraction for its miles of hiking trails and quiet beaches.

St Thomas

The most accessible and Americanized of the Virgins, **ST THOMAS** is the capital of cool – the couture, accommodation and cuisine hub of the Caribbean. Its mercantile roots – the port at **Charlotte Amalie** has been an important merchant centre since the 1700s – still prevail and Charlotte Amalie's renovated old warehouses now house a wealth of galleries, restaurants and shops. It can all seem a bit too sanitized, but if you look deeper – a trip to the western side of the island or *Ashley's Mobile Restaurant* is a good start – you can still find Caribbean culture alive and kicking. The small town of **Red Hook** offers all the amenities of Charlotte Amalie on a smaller scale. It doesn't have much in the way of historical buildings, but the harbour is hopping with yachters and those seeking ferries for St John and beyond. The north and east of the island have the best **beaches**, including **Magens Bay**, consistently voted one of the world's best.

Arrival, information and getting around

St Thomas's **Cyril E. King Airport** is three miles west of Charlotte Amalie. VITRAN **buses** run from the airport to Charlotte Amalie; the first leaves at 6am and the last at 9.30pm. **Taxis** (for 2 persons) to Charlotte Amalie cost around US$5; for resorts on the eastern end of the island it's US$10–20. Most major **car rental** companies have offices at the airport and in Havensight Mall (see also below).

Information booths at the airport offer free brochures and maps, including helpful publications such as *St Thomas This Week* and the *West Indies Visitor's Guide*. In downtown Charlotte Amalie, there is a USVI Division of Tourism office at the Old Customs House (ⓣ340/774-8784). There's also a National Park Service visitor centre across the street from the ferry dock in Red Hook. **Post offices** are located in Emancipation Garden, Charlotte Amalie (ⓣ340/774-3750); on Veteran's Drive, Charlotte Amalie (ⓣ340/774-6980); and at the Havensight Mall (ⓣ340/776-9897). Charlotte Amalie has a few **internet cafés**: Beans, Bytes & Websites in the Royal Dane Mall (ⓣ340/777-7089); Kings Caribbean Coffee Café at the Waterfront, and the Royal Dane and Havensight malls (ⓣ340/774-0677); and Little Switzerland Internet Café, Main Street (ⓣ340/776-2010).

Getting around the island, VITRAN **buses** operate services to Red Hook (hourly 5.30am–8.30pm) and to the west as well. **Taxis** come in all shapes and sizes – vans, cars and trucks; reputable operators include Allie's Taxi Stand (ⓣ340/777-8007); East End Taxi Service Ferry Dock (ⓣ340/775-6974); and Islander Taxi & Tour Services (ⓣ340/774-4077). From town to the east of the island, including Red Hook, the fare for two people is US$10–15. General two-hour sightseeing tours go for about US$30.

Although you don't need a **car** on St Thomas, it will give you a much better feel for the island and you can even take the car ferry (US$27 round-trip) over to St John for the day. Options include Avis (ⓣ340/774-1468); Budget (ⓣ340/776-5774); Discount Car Rental (ⓣ340/776-4858); and Tri Island Car Rental (ⓣ340/776-2879).

Charlotte Amalie and around

CHARLOTTE AMALIE sweeps around St Thomas Harbour in a striking combination of red-roofed whitewashed buildings backed by lush green villa-dotted hills. At any one time there can be up to eleven cruise ships scattered around the harbour. Add to that the hundreds of ferries and yachts that pass through and you get a feel for this vibrant, cosmopolitan, often congested port town whose 12,500 population is swelled daily by bargain-hunting tourists. Many of them head straight for the famous **shopping district** whose renovated merchant warehouses contain shops selling everything from cut-rate diamonds, perfume and fine textiles to monstrous Cuban cigars. But there's much more to Charlotte Amalie than shopping – the town is full of historic sites like the **99 Steps**, **Fort Christian** and the **St Thomas Synagogue**, the world's second oldest Jewish house of worship. Named Charlotte Amalie in honour of the wife of Danish King Christian V, the Danish influence here is strong – much of the historic **colonial architecture** is still standing and streets are commonly referred to by the Danish word *gades*. On the peninsula due west of Charlotte Amalie, the smaller, quieter neighbourhood of **FRENCHTOWN** has been home to most of St Thomas's French descendants for centuries, and some fantastic restaurants.

Accommodation

Charlotte Amalie and Frenchtown contain the majority of the island's small **hotels**, **historic inns** and **cosy B&Bs**. While they generally have pools, easy beach access is not an option and this is reflected in the price. There are only a few resorts nearby. For groups, the many **villas and private homes** tucked in the hills are a better option. Try: *Blazing Villas* (ⓣ340/776-0760 or 1-800/392-2002); *Calypso Realty* (ⓣ340/774-1602 or 1-800/747-4858); *McLaughlin-Anderson Villas* (ⓣ340/776-

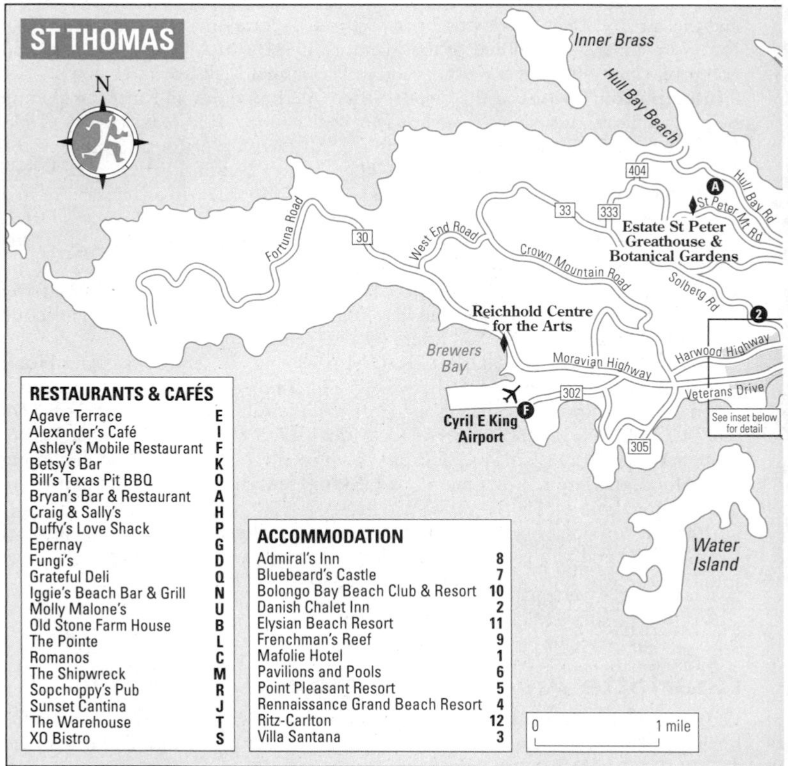

0635 or 1-800/537-6246); and *Paradise Properties* (☎340/779-1540 or 1-800/524-2038).

Hotels and inns

Admiral's Inn Villa Olga, Frenchtown ☎340/774-1376 or 1-800/544-0493 ℱ340/774-8010. The only lodging of note in Frenchtown, half a mile away from the hustle and bustle of town. Of the twelve rooms, the four with the ocean views (and balconies) are more expensive. There is no restaurant on premises, but just downstairs is *The Pointe* (see p.405). ❺

Crystal Palace Bed and Breakfast Charlotte Amalie ☎340/777-2277. This classy mansion with wrought-iron gates, is located in the heart of the historic district. The décor is a bit stuffy (Victorian antiques and furniture), but there's a great view of the harbour. Rooms with private bath and shared bathrooms are available. ❹

Danish Chalet Inn Solberg Road, Charlotte Amalie ☎340/774-5764 or 1-800/635-1531, ℱ340/777-4886. Located in the hills above downtown, this West Indian-inspired B&B feels a little too much like grandma's house, but at US$89 a night it's a good deal. The fifteen rooms are basic and only a few have private baths and A/C. There's no pool but there is a hot tub, sundeck and honour bar. ❹

Hotel 1829 Government Hill, Charlotte Amalie ☎340/776-1829 or 1-800/524-2002, ℱ340/776-4313. This bright orange building with huge mahogany shutters and a cool brick, fieldstone and natural wood interior is the most atmospheric small hotel on the island. The front porch, complete with bamboo furniture and cooled by overhead fans, is the perfect place to read a novel by Graham Greene, for whom, it is rumoured, the hotel was a favourite haunt. Rooms vary in size but all are good value, with prices starting at US$100 for a single, and the restaurant is excellent (see p.405). ❻

Mafolie Hotel 7091 Estate Mafolie, Charlotte Amalie ☎340/774-2790 or 1-800/225-7035,

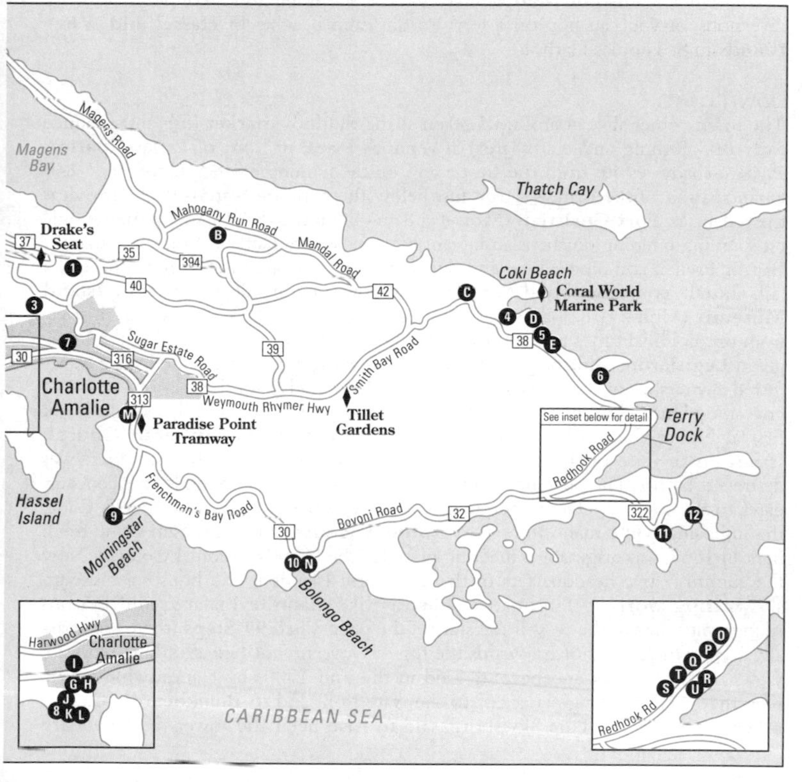

Ⓕ340/774-4091. The rooms in this hillside retreat are clean, the view of the harbour is stunning and free shuttles are provided to Magen's Beach, but you'll need a car or taxi to get back and forth to town. ❺

Villa Santana 2D Denmark Hill, Charlotte Amalie Ⓣ340/776-1311. Built in the mid-1850s by exiled Mexican general Santa Anna (remember the Alamo?) from stolen money, this six-unit inn is located at the crown of Denmark Hill (easy walking distance to downtown). Units have been created out of the general's library, wine cellar, kitchen and so on, and are a steal at around US$125 per night. ❺

Resorts and condos

Bluebeard's Castle Bluebeard's Hill, Charlotte Amalie Ⓣ340/774-1600 or 1-800/524-6599, Ⓕ340/774-5134. Originally a fort built in 1735, this 170-room hotel overlooks the harbour and has a pool, fitness centre and tennis courts. There's no beach but a free shuttle to Magens Bay is available. Standard rooms, starting at US$195, have most amenities and all suites, US$395, have kitchenettes. ❽

Frenchman's Reef 5 Estate Bakkeroe, South Shore Ⓣ340/776-8500 or 1-800/524-2000, Ⓕ340/776-3054. From the outside, this palatial hotel seems like a dream come true – the lavishly landscaped grounds offer two private beaches, oceanfront tennis courts, four restaurants and three bars. But although most rooms have sea or harbour views they're rather small, and the furniture and linen is more motel than hotel. ❾

The Town

Most of Charlotte Amalie's sights are within the same square mile and can easily be explored on foot – the bustling **downtown** shopping area occupies the numerous narrow streets linking Waterfront Drive and Main Street (Dronningens Gade) while historic sights cluster on the slopes just east on **Government Hill**. Further east of downtown **Havensight Mall** offers yet more shopping and a couple of touristy diversions, or you can hop on a ferry to the calm beaches of **Hassel and Water Islands** in St Thomas Harbour.

Downtown

The town comes alive at around 5.30am at the outdoor **market** (fish and produce early on, clothing and crafts later) at Vendor's Plaza, in front of **Emancipation Park**, a shady respite from the hustle and bustle, which commemorates the 1848 emancipation of the island's slaves. Just below the park, on Waterfront Highway, is the red-brick **Fort Christian** (Mon–Fri 8am–4.30pm & Sat 10am–3pm), the oldest standing building on the island. Danish troops resisted attacks from the Spanish, British, French and pirates here and during its 300-year life the fort has also been a jail, church, courthouse, and home for the governor. Inside, the **Virgin Island Museum** (Mon–Fri 8.30am–4.30pm; free) evocatively charts the islands' history from pre-colonial times to the present day. Due south, on Veteran's Drive, the lime-green **Legislature Building** (daily 8am–5pm) is the place where the Danes transferred ownership of the islands to the US in 1917; today it's the seat of the USVI governing body. Head north on a steady climb up Government Hill, taking a break first at Norre Gade, where the Georgian-style **Frederick Lutheran Church** stands on the site of the first Danish church in the Virgin Islands, which was destroyed by fire. The current structure, built by black parishioner, Jean Reeneaus, dates to the early nineteenth century. Northeast of the church, on Kongens Gade, the imposing white mansion of **Government House** (Mon–Fri 8am–5pm; free), built in 1867, was originally a meeting place for the Danish Colonial Council. Now the administrative headquarters of the US Virgin Islands it also houses a museum showcasing work by famous local artists like Camille Pissarro and Pepino Mangravatti. Just to the west is the start of the palm-lined **99 Steps** (there are actually 103), which lead north towards the top of Government Hill affording exquisite views of the harbour and beyond. Laid in the mid-1700s by Danes living in the hills, they were the original access to the waterfront and to **Blackbeard's Castle**, otherwise known as Fort Skytsborg, said to have been the tower the legendary

The legend of Blackbeard

Blackbeard, made infamous in Robert Louis Stevenson's novel *Treasure Island*, is said to have walked the streets of Charlotte Amalie when the island was a legal refuge for pirates, who sold their contraband freely – wild days when anything and everything was legal and the town was affectionately known as Beer Hall. Born Edward Teach in Bristol, England, Blackbeard was the meanest man the seas have ever seen – a heavy drinker (rum mixed with gunpowder) and a notorious lady-killer (he murdered all fourteen of his wives).

pirate Blackbeard (see box above) used for an unobstructed view of the ocean.

Heading back to the main shopping area, stop off at Crystal Gade to see the charming **St Thomas Synagogue** (Mon–Fri 9am–4pm) with its white pillars, stone walls, mahogany pews and sand floor (symbolizing the exodus from Egypt). The building dates to 1833 and is the western hemisphere's second oldest synagogue, not to mention the longest continually in service in America. Next door, the **Weibel Museum** (same hours) is an interesting exhibition of the three hundred years of Jewish history in the islands. Just before you hit the shops check out the **Camille Pissarro Gallery**, 14 Main St, where the artist was born in 1830. One of the founders of the French Impressionist school, Pissarro grew up on this street, working for his father; his experiences here would become the subjects of some of his later paintings.

Havensight Mall

At the eastern end of the bay, Havensight has a few malls, the cruise-ship dock and a couple of interesting but expensive attractions. For US$72, **Atlantis Submarines**, Havensight Cruise Ship Dock (☎340/776-5650), will take you 90ft below the surface of the water where you can peer through portholes at stingrays, sharks and whatever else happens to swim by. Going to the other extreme, **Paradise Point Tramway**, 9617 Estate St, across the street from the Havensight Mall (☎340/774-9809; US$15), operates gondolas that whisk you 700ft above sea level up the side of Slag Hill for stunning views of downtown, the harbour, Water and Hassel islands. Overpriced food and drinks await you at the top.

Water and Hassel islands

Hop on a ferry (US$3 one-way) for a relaxing day trip across the harbour to Hassel Island and Water Island. Uninhabited **HASSEL ISLAND** is part of the Virgin Islands National Park system. Relaxed exploration can be fun but there's not much to see here, apart from the relics of an old British military garrison from their occupation during the 1800s and the shell of a failed hotel (the hotel from Herman Wouk's novel *Don't Stop the Carnival*). **WATER ISLAND** (ferry from Crown Bay Marina; US$3 each way) has a small population but is slowly developing into the fourth USVI – bring a picnic and spend the day lazing on its glorious sandy beaches or cycling round the island. **Water Island Bike Tours** at Crown Bay Marina (☎340/714-2186) do three- to four-hour bike tours of the island, mostly on paved roads (US$49).

Around Charlotte Amalie

With a car or by taxi it's worth seeking out some of the attractions just outside Charlotte Amalie. On Route 40 north of town, **Drake's Seat**, crowded with tour buses, is a popular lookout point where it is said Sir Francis Drake himself sat to look out for his fleet and watch for enemy ships. On the same road, roughly two miles west, the mountainside perch of **Estate St Peter Greathouse and**

Botanical Gardens (daily 9am–4pm; ☎340/774-4999) is worth a trip for the breathtaking views alone. Once you've got your breath back, grab a complimentary rum punch, shop for local art and take a tour of the luscious gardens which boast over two hundred species of plants and trees. Two and a half miles east of town on Route 38 at Tutu, **Tillet Gardens** (☎340/775-1929) was once a Danish farm; it's now St Thomas's answer to an artists' colony, where you'll find all sorts of artisans at work and a shop to buy their wares. Call ahead to time your visit with one of the many jazz and classical concerts. Nearby, *Polli's Mexican Restaurant* is a great place to stop off for a bite before heading back to town.

Beaches

There are several good beaches within striking (if not walking) distance of Charlotte Amalie. On the **north side** of the island, the mile-long sandy stretch of **Magens Bay Beach** (US$3 per car) on Route 35 is the island's longest beach and is almost always included in lists of the world's best beaches. Protected by two dramatic peninsulas (the one to the east is the upmarket area of Peterborg where the rich and famous like Michael Jordan own homes), it's the perfect beach for swimming and sunbathing, though the snorkelling isn't up to much. There's a grill serving sandwiches, pizza and burgers, and waitresses in bikinis walk the beach taking drink orders. On your way out, hit *Udder Delights* for one of their famous milkshakes. Round the peninsula to the west, **Hull Bay Beach**, also on Route 37, is a favourite with the locals, especially surfers who ride the choppy waves rolling in from the Atlantic. In the distance you can see Inner and Outer Brass, two cays that are part of the US Virgin Islands. *Larry's Hideaway* on the road in provides hot grub, drinks and the occasional live band.

Beaches on the **south side** of the island aren't as good but are easy to get to. **Brewers Bay Beach**, on Route 30, three miles west of town, is fairly unpopulated, except for students from the nearby University and has a few snack trucks, while **Morningstar Beach** at *Marriott Frenchman's Reef*, on Route 315 one mile south of Havensight, is the closest and easiest to access from Charlotte Amalie. On the waterfront at Charlotte Amalie, look for the small ferry called *The Reefer*, which provides access throughout the day (make sure to ask time of last return trip) for US$3 each way. Back on Route 30 and two miles east, **Bolongo Beach**, surrounded by the *Bolongo Bay Beach Club and Resort*, offers grill grub, frozen drinks and pick-up volleyball games.

Eating and drinking

St Thomas's **restaurants** can afford to bring great chefs to the island – in fact, the restaurant scene is so hot here that it's not too far-fetched to expect Bobby Flay, Drew Neiporent or even Mario Batali to set up shop soon. Throw a stone in **Frenchtown** and you'll hit any number of intimate places popular with locals and out-of-towners. While the finest spots abound with entrees approaching Manhattan prices, there are options for all budgets, from roadside stands to burger joints to ethnic cuisine.

Charlotte Amalie

Ashley's Mobile Restaurant Cyril E. King Airport ☎340/774-1533. If you're looking for a quick and authentic West Indian meal, this is the place. Some swear the stewed chicken served with rice is the best on the island. Daily 8am–9pm.

Beni Iguana's *Grand Hotel* Court ☎340/777-8744. This sushi bar with outdoor courtyard is located in the historic district, part of the Grand Galleria. Start with "our Famous Mussels" drenched in the house's mouthwatering Iguana Sauce. Sushi pieces cost US$2.50–3. Lunch Mon–Sat 11am–5pm, dinner Tues– Sat 5–10.30pm.

Bill's Texas Pit BBQ Veteran's Drive ☎340/776-9579. This mobile outdoor pit serves slow-smoked barbecue with a thick, tangy sauce. The most expensive item on the menu is a rib plate with a side and a roll, which goes for US$9. There are two other locations, in the Sub Base and Red Hook areas.

Cuzzin's Caribbean Restaurant and Bar 7 Back St

☎340/777-4711. Located in an eighteenth-century stone building in the heart of the downtown shopping district, *Cuzzin's* serves up everything from stewed goat to burgers. But it's the West Indian dishes like conch in butter sauce, sides like fungi and juices like *maubi* (a root) that top the bill. Lunch Mon–Sat 11am–5pm, dinner Tues–Sat 5–9.30pm.

Glady's Café Waterfront at Royal Dane Mall ☎340/774-6604. Bacon, eggs and French toast for breakfast, or well-priced West Indian fare for lunch, including the hard-to-find local favourite saltfish and dumplings.

Herve Government Hill ☎340/777-9703. An eclectic mix of contemporary American, French and Caribbean fare (lunch around US$10; dinner US$25) on a hilltop location with amazing views just minutes from Main Street.

Hotel 1829 Government Hill ☎340/776-1829. A fine upmarket restaurant in one of the island's most historic hotels. Have a cocktail over a game of backgammon before dining by candlelight on one of the many signature dishes like barbecue duck breast in *hoisin* sauce.

Pita Express 6 Wimmelskafts Gade ☎340/777-4072. Quick and cheap hummus wraps, gyros and more in the heart of downtown.

The Roti Shop 38 Princesse Gade ☎340/714-1741. As the crowds testify, this is the best roti on the island, packed with curried potatoes, a few vegetables and your choice of chicken, goat, conch or other types of meat or seafood.

Shipwreck Tavern Al Cohen Plaza across from Havensight Mall ☎340/777-1293. If you just want a burger and a beer, this is the place—three-quarters of a pound of beautiful beef and US$2 drafts.

Virgilio's 18 Dronningens Gade ☎340/776-4920. Beyond the fountain and huge mahogany front doors is a cosy, elegant Italian restaurant. Pasta is the popular choice but the veal is a close runner-up.

Zorba's Government Hill ☎340/776-0444. The island's only Greek and Mediterranean restaurant, located in a fine example of eighteenth-century Danish architecture. Meals are reasonably priced and run the gamut from spanakopita to brick-oven pizzas.

Frenchtown

Alexander's Café 24A Honduras ☎340/776-4211. Small comfortable bistro serving moderately priced entrees (pastas US$10–12) with Austrian and Italian influences. *Alexander's Bar and Grill*, next door, serves food from the same kitchen but has a more relaxed, bar feel. Mon–Sat 11.30am–5pm & 5.30–10pm.

Betsy's Bar 59 Honduras ☎340/774-9347. Betsy just might be the coolest bartender on the island, and her bar is a local favourite. There's bar food (burgers and munchies) and occasional live music.

Craig and Sally's 22 Honduras ☎340/777-9949. Hands down the most intimate and consistently delicious restaurant on St Thomas. It's expensive (around US$25 per entree) but the creative, ever-changing menu is worth it and there's an exquisite wine list with over 200 vintages. Lunch and dinner Tues–Sun.

Epernay Champagne Bar and Night Club 24A Honduras ☎340/774-5348. A small, hip, intimate bistro with an extensive menu serving everything from pizza to sushi to oriental shrimp bok choy (US$18) plus twenty wines by the glass. The bar is a great place for early evening cocktails and there's a nightclub upstairs.

The Pointe Villa Olga ☎340/774-4262. Set on the terrace of an old stone house with views off the point of the Frenchtown peninsula, this place is heaven for steak lovers – cuts like the dry-aged rib-eye are grilled perfectly. The salad bar (US$16.95) offers everything from freshly grilled vegetables to artisan breads. Mon–Sat 5.30–10pm, Sun 10am–2.30pm.

Sunset Cantina Gregorie East Channel ☎340/777-4014. Located right on the water, the *Cantina* serves Mexican food with an emphasis on seafood, such as *chile rellenos* stuffed with crab meat and served with rice and beans (US$16).

Nightlife and entertainment

Nightlife in Charlotte Amalie revolves around **bars**, particularly on Main Street, with live music and the occasional DJ. There's also more cultured entertainment – art shows, community theatre and eclectic music ensembles; pick up a copy of *St Thomas This Week* for what's on when. The most anticipated (and drunken) event of the year, though, is **Carnival** (☎340/776-3112, Ⓦwww.vicarnival.com) – St Thomas's is one of the oldest and largest celebrations in the Caribbean and really kicks into gear the last two weeks of April. The revels take place all around downtown Charlotte Amalie with elaborate costumed street parades, a dancing till dawn frenzy called J'ouvert, music competitions like the famous Panorama and a final blowout when fireworks light up St Thomas harbour. For a little primer, read Herman Wouk's novel *Don't Stop the Carnival.*

Bars and clubs

Betsy's Bar (see p.405). Live entertainment, ranging from rock 'n' roll to reggae on Friday and Saturday nights (no cover charge).
Epernay Upstairs (see p.405). This loungey, late-night dance club is popular with the island's professional set. DJs spin disco, house, hip-hop, jazz and much more until 2am.
Fat Tuesday 25B Dronningens Gade ⓣ340/777-8676. Nightly themes such as "toga" and an ever-flowing supply of strong, fruity cocktails make this place popular with the college crowd.
The Green House Bar and Restaurant Veteran's Drive ⓣ340/774-7998. After the dinner crowd has left, the music starts pumping with DJs or live reggae bands.
Inn at Blackbeard's Castle Lounge Government Hill ⓣ340/776-1234. Mellow music ranging from piano to guitar seven nights a week starting at 7pm.
Shipwreck Tavern (see p.405). Two-dollar Coronas, big screen TVs and heavy-duty burgers make this place a favourite among sports fans.

Entertainment venues

Pistarkle Theatre ⓣ340/775-7877. Located at Tillet Gardens, this 200-seat air-conditioned venue is one of the island's main outlets for theatre and dance.
Reichhold Center for the Arts Rte 30, west of the airport ⓣ340/693-1559. Located at the University of the Virgin Islands, this is the island's largest performance space showcasing local and international music, theatre, dance and ballet.

Red Hook and around

Most of St Thomas's resorts are found on the east side of the island whose main settlement, **RED HOOK**, surrounding the bay of the same name, is the other town of note on St Thomas. Though much smaller, not nearly as cultured as Charlotte Amalie and easily done in a day, it's a fun little place to shop, eat and grab a drink or two. With its few malls, it caters mostly to the hundreds of folks who get on and off ferries leading to and from St John, Tortola and other Caribbean islands, and to the high-end resorts nearby. The main tourist attractions on this side of the island are the **beaches** and the **Coral World Marine Park**, on Route 38 at Coki Point (daily 9am–5.30pm; US$18, US$9 children; ⓣ340/775-1555). This 4.5-acre park boasts an imaginative array of marine and non-marine attractions including the Undersea Observatory, Sea Trekkin' (separate fee US$68) – an air helmet that enables you to walk along an underwater trail – Caribbean Reef Encounter (an 80,000-gallon tank teeming with reef life), Turtle Pool, and Iguana Feeding Area. **Coki Beach** on Smith Bay right next to Coral World Marine Park is probably the best beach for **snorkelling** on the island, though it can get really crowded. Come early to avoid the throngs of cruise-ship snorkellers. There's a great natural reef, plus all the amenities you could want: snack trucks, drinks, rental equipment and much more.

Accommodation

Staying on the east side of the island you'll be limited to upmarket resort **accommodation**, all of which has easy access to a beach.

Bolongo Bay Beach Club and Resort 50 Estate Bolongo, South Shore ⓣ340/775-1800 or 1-800/524-4746, ⓕ340/775-3208, ⓦwww.bolongobay.com. This half-baked resort is on the wrong end of town, but it does have its merits: quiet beachfront location, three pools, a hopping nightlife and beer volleyball tournaments. The all-inclusive plan is a good deal. If you want to take advantage of the amenities at less than half the price, ask about rooms at the *Bayside Inn* on the premises. ❽
Elysian Beach Resort 6800 Estate Nazareth, Eastside ⓣ340/775-1000 or 1-800/753-2554, ⓕ340/776-0910. This large resort with 180 rooms has tennis courts, health club, pool, a palm-lined beach and several restaurants (most notably *Palm Court*), all set on 8.5 acres of waterfront. Grounds are well manicured and the rooms are clean and

roomy if a little dull. ⑧

Pavilions and Pools 6400 Estate Smith Bay, Eastside ⓣ340/775-6110 or 1-800/524-2001, ⓕ340/775-6130. Lacking a beach and restaurant, this is not your typical resort, rather a 25-villa complex, spaced enough apart to ensure privacy. Each villa has a bedroom (some have two), kitchen (maids do the dishes), living room and large bathroom, and the rooms are spacious and well decorated. Each villa has its own four-foot pool and patio. It's not a bad deal at US$275 a night for a high-season two-bedroom. ⑦

Point Pleasant Resort 6600 Estate Smith Bay, Eastside ⓣ340/775-7200 or 1-800/524-2300, ⓕ340/776-5694, ⓦwww.pointpleasantstthomas.com. This mountainside resort offers some of the best deals on the island. The suites are pleasant (bedroom, living area, small bathroom and balcony), the pool is right on the ocean and there are several great restaurants and bars on the premises. You also get free access to a rental car for up to four hours per day. The Junior Suite goes for about US$155 per night, but you have to stay at least three days (rates get lower the longer you stay). Watersports, beach access and tennis courts available. ⑦

Renaissance Grand Beach Resort Smith Bay Road, Eastside ⓣ340/775-1510 or 1-800/468-3571, ⓕ340/775-3757. The rooms aren't much to write home about, but the grounds, the huge pool, the beach and the bay are everything a resort should be. There are also several restaurants, bars and cocktail lounges, a full spa, exercise room, tennis courts and jet skis available for rent on the beach. Within walking distance of Coral World Marine Park and Coki Point. ⑨

Ritz-Carlton 6900 Great Bay Estate, Eastside ⓣ340/775-3333 or 1-800/241-3333, ⓕ340/775-4444. If you've got the money and can put up with the attitudes of regular Ritz guests, then you can't get much better than this. Set on fifteen acres of beautifully landscaped beachfront land, the resort blends European architecture with Caribbean charm. For the price the rooms are small but here you are paying top-dollar for the friendly staff who cater to your every need. Resort staples like multiple restaurants, beach, watersports options, tennis courts and fitness centre are also on site. ⑨

Eating, drinking and nightlife

There's great waterfront **food** and a hopping **nightlife** to be had in Red Hook or, for a more local experience, head off to one of the several restaurants in the hills on the north side of the island. At the more upmarket restaurants you'll need to look smart casual. If you want to make up a beach picnic or stock up your kitchenette head for Marina Market across from Ferry Dock.

Restaurants and cafés

Agave Terrace 4 Estate Smith Bay, *Point Pleasant Resort* ⓣ340/775-4142. One of the better resort restaurants and one of the better fine-dining choices on this side of the island. Great views and lobster cooked a variety of ways.

Bill's Texas Pit BBQ Across from Ferry Dock, Red Hook ⓣ340/776-9579. Best barbecue on the island be it chicken, ribs, brisket and so on.

Bryan's Bar and Restaurant Hull Bay Road, Northside ⓣ340/777-1262. Attracting a largely expat American crowd, this place does good food, specializing in grilled seafood, is moderately priced and there are great sunset views. The bar also serves food and there's live music on weekends plus billiards and darts.

Grateful Deli Red Hook Plaza, Red Hook ⓣ340/775-5160. The veggie choice on this side of the island. Does great bagels, sweets and a great cup of joe.

Molly Malone's American Yacht Harbor, Red Hook ⓣ340/775-1270. This open-air, garden-setting Irish pub serves great shepherd's pie and corned beef and cabbage, plus a great breakfast menu. Perfect for just having drinks too – or watching sporting events on the TV.

The Old Stone Farm House Northside ⓣ340/777-6277. The combination of setting (in a 200-year-old farm house) and creative cuisine like three-day Asian duck make this a fantastic experience every time. Right by the golf course, this makes for a perfect post-eighteen meal.

Romanos 97 Smith Bay, Smith Bay ⓣ340/775-0045. This is a swanky Italian restaurant off the beaten path but worth it for the delicious food and excellent service. While there are pastas on the menu, this is northern Italian, so meatier, fare. If you're adventurous, go for the veal tongue or the classic osso bucco. Always crowded, but it's worth waiting at the bar.

Schnitzel Haus Frydenhoj, Red Hook ⓣ340/776-7198. Authentic German restaurant specializing in veal – the weiner schnitzel is fantastic.

Sib's Mountain Bar Restaurant 33-5 Estate Elizabeth, Northside ⓣ340/774-8967. Like *Bryan's*, this place serves mostly locals, who come to the bar to catch up on gossip, play pool or watch football over beer and burgers. The other half is a great restaurant. Take a table outside in the garden, where the owner grows vegetables for the restaurant. Does a great brunch too.

Sopchoppy's Pub American Yacht Harbor, Red Hook ☎340/774-2929. Basic salads, subs, Mexican muchies and decent pizzas. Good for takeout or when drinking is more important than eating (bar overlooks the harbour).

XO Bistro Red Hook Plaza, Red Hook ☎340/779-2069. From the outside it doesn't look like much, but the inside is cosy and great for cocktails or aperitifs, with snacks.

Bars and clubs

Caribbean Saloon American Yacht Harbor, Red Hook ☎340/775-7060. The great thing about this place is not just that they have live music on select nights, but that the kitchen stays open until 4am, just like the bar. It's on the second floor overlooking the harbour.

Duffy's Love Shack Red Hook Plaza, Red Hook ☎340/779-2080. During high season, this place is so crowded and the music so loud it's a sight to behold. Shots and special potent cocktails are the favourites here.

Fungi's 4 Estate Smith Bay, *Point Pleasant Resort* ☎340/775-4142. Located on the beach below the resort (park above and walk down), this is a very informal place to eat, drink and dance from 7pm until the party ends.

Iggie's Beach Bar and Grill 50 Bolongo Bay, Bolongo Bay Beach Resort ☎340/775-1800. Live music on select nights at this open-air beach bar.

Puzzle's River Boat Lounge 109 Frydenhoj, Red Hook ☎340/775-9671. Newly purchased from original owner Jack Rosen, who recycled an old glass-bottom boat and turned it into a bar, *Puzzle's* is still a bar, but now caters to jazz lovers and the backgammon set.

The Warehouse 18A Smith Bay, Red Hook ☎340/775-1507. Located across from the ferry dock, this upstairs dive bar is a pour-your-own affair – meaning you make your drink as strong as you please.

Watersports and outdoor activities

Whether you are going **sport fishing** for the big boy-blue marlin or just looking to catch some tuna to throw on the grill, there are plenty of boats out of St Thomas. The following will be able to hook you up: American Yacht Harbor at Red Hook (☎340/775-6454); Charter Boat Center, Red Hook (☎340/775-7990) or Sapphire Beach Marina, Eastside (☎340/775-6100). For **golf** lovers the Mahogany Run Golf Course, Route 42 near Magens Bay (☎340/777-6006), is St Thomas's only golf course – an eighteen-holer that skirts the coastline. You can rent clubs and shoes – greens fees plus cart are around US$100. If you'd rather get up in the hills the Half Moon Stables at Rosendahl on Magans Bay Road (☎340/777-6088) offers two-hour **horse rides** into the hills for US$45. Most resorts have **tennis** courts open to non-guests for a nominal fee – try *Bluebeard's Castle Hotel* (☎340/774-1600); *Marriott Frenchman's Reef* (☎340/776-8500); *Rennaissance Grand Beach Resort* (☎340/775-1510); or *Wyndham Sugar Bay* (☎340/777-7100). There are also two public courts at Sub Base and Lindberg Bay. St Thomas has the full gamut of **watersports** from snorkelling and diving to parasailing – check out the following places.

Watersports

Aqua Action Red Hook Plaza, Red Hook ☎340/775-6285. Sales, rentals and bookings available but training is done at *Secret Harbour Beach Resort*.

Caribbean Parasail Adventures Frydenhoj ☎340/775-9360. Strap yourself in and be pulled high up in the air. This outfit will pick you up and drop you off at your resort.

Chartering the World ☎340/775-6972 or 1877/775-9834. Just give them a call, tell them what kind of sailing, sport fishing or powerboat adventure you're looking for and they'll do the rest.

Chris Sawyer Diving American Yacht Harbor, Red Hook ☎340/777-7804. This PADI five-star underwater centre can help you with all your diving needs. Their dive specialty is the wreck of the *Rhone* in the BVI (see p.437). Certification also available.

Fanfare Charters Across from Ferry Dock, Red Hook ☎340/715-1326. Whether daily or weekly, you can rent sailboats of all sizes, either captained or bareboat.

Limnos Charters American Yacht Harbor, Red Hook ☎340/775-3203. Limnos offers all kinds of package sails to the US and British Virgin Islands with crews knowledgeable on the history and folklore of the islands and surrounding seas.

Nauti Nymph Powerboat Rental American Yacht Harbor, Red Hook ☎340/775-5066. Choose the way you want your boat outfitted (snorkelling, water-skiing) and set out on your own adventure under your own control. Boats (25–29-footers) are pricey (up to US$300 per day), but it's the best way to go.

Snuba of St Thomas Coki Beach ☎340/693-8063. Want an intro to scuba, then Snuba – part snorkelling and part scuba – is for you.

Virgin Islands Eco-Tours 2 Estate Nadir, Red Hook ☎340/779-2155. Learn about Mangrove Lagoon while touring the Virgin Islands Marine Sanctuary by kayak.

West Indies Windsurfing Vessup Beach ☎340/775-6530. If your resort doesn't offer windsurfing lessons, give these guys a call and they'll have you flying across the seas in no time.

Shopping

St Thomas, and Charlotte Amalie in particular, is the shopping capital of the USVI. A **duty-free** port with low taxes on luxury goods, there are big savings to be made on jewellery, clothes, perfumes, cosmetics, alcohol and electronics. The heart of the **shopping district** is the six-block grid between Tolbod Gade to the east and Trom Peter Gade to the west. The Vendor's Plaza, a daily outdoor **market** (9am–5pm), just south of Emancipation Garden, offers better deals than the shops along Main Street. The following are a taster of some of the best places to bargain hunt around the island. All, with the exception of *Elizabeth Jane's*, are in Charlotte Amalie.

Club Cigar Main Street ☎340/774-8100. The best selection of cigars on the island for less than you would pay in the US.

The Crystal Shoppe 14 Dronningens Gade ☎340/777-9835. A large selection of fine crystal from Waterford, Hernd, Bellek, Lladro among others.

Diamond's International Main Street ☎340/774-1516. If you're in the market for an amazing diamond, these guys have the largest selection of loose rocks in the Caribbean, though better deals can be found. There are two other locations: along the waterfront and at Havensight Mall.

Elegant Illusions Copy Jewels Port of Sale ☎340/777-4670. If shopping for jewellery downtown has your wallet screaming, then do your buying here.

Elizabeth Jane's American Yacht Harbor, Red Hook ☎340/779-1595. The best selection of sterling silver jewellery at the best prices.

Island Newsstand Tolbod Gade and Norre Gade ☎340/774-0043. If you can't do without your daily newspaper from back home, bets are this stand will have it.

Local Color Hibiscus Alley ☎340/774-3727. Local artists like Sloop Jones display their utilitarian art: painted clothes ranging from dresses to shirts to hats.

Native Arts and Crafts Cooperative Tolbod Gade ☎340/777-1153. Every kind of art you could imagine made by local artists at rock-bottom prices.

Parrot Fish Music 2 Store Tvaer Gade ☎340/776-4514. This place has a great selection ranging from reggae to calypso to pan bands.

Tropical Memories Royal Dane Mall ☎340/776-7536. Paintings, textiles, pottery, blown glass and carved masks – all by USVI artists.

Tropicana Perfume Shop 2 Main Street ☎340/774-0010. Has the largest selection of perfumes in the Virgin Islands at prices lower than US prices.

St Croix

ST CROIX, the largest of the USVI, measuring 28 miles by 7 miles, is also the most remote, lying forty miles south of St Thomas. For many years this peaceful gem has been accessible only by air or cruise ship but now that a fast ferry connects the island to St Thomas, it's a must-see for all visitors to the USVI. The landscape, more gentle than its neighbours, is a mixture of rocky sierras, fertile coastal plain and rainforest and, of course, St Croix has its fair share of picturesque beaches. Architecturally the island is a few steps ahead of the other Virgins – the towns

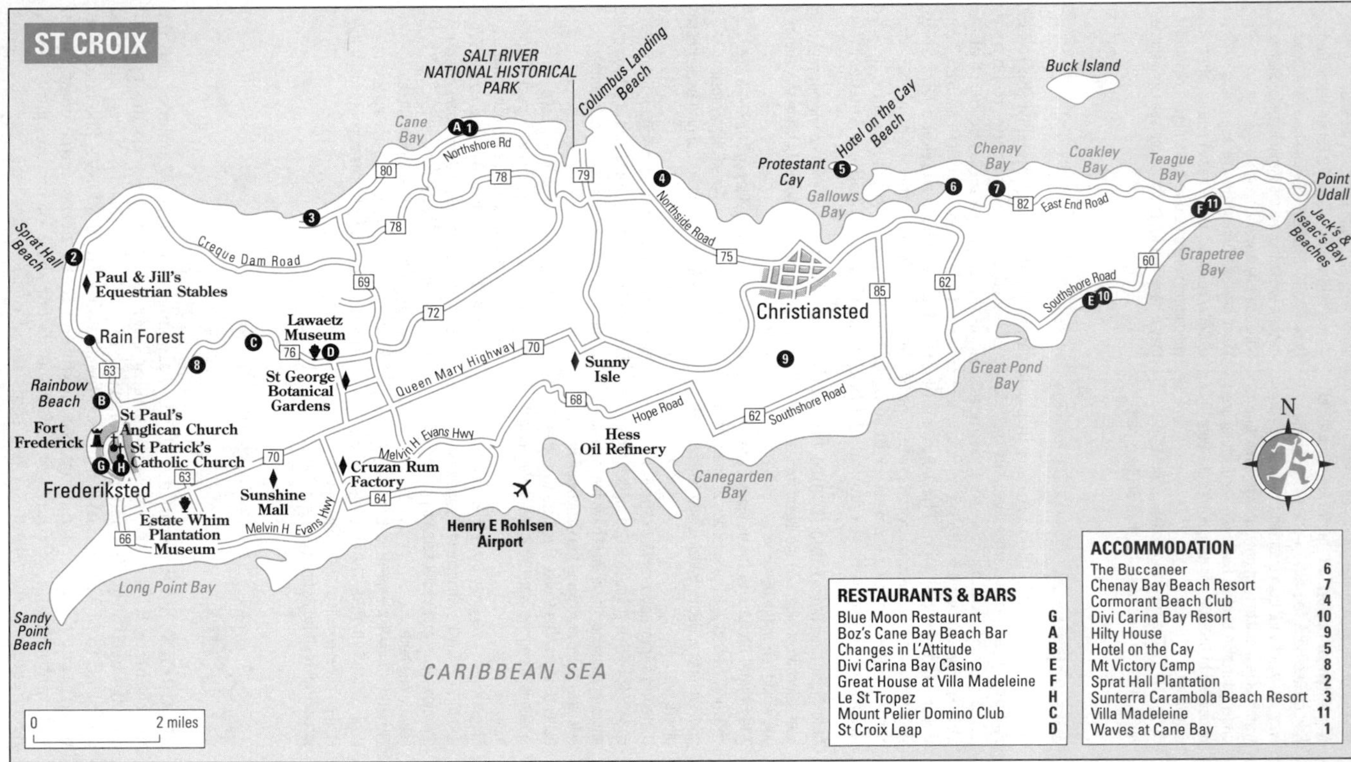
ST CROIX
SALT RIVER NATIONAL HISTORICAL PARK
Columbus Landing Beach
Buck Island
Hotel on the Cay Beach
Protestant Cay
Gallows Bay
Cane Bay
Northshore Rd
Chenay Bay
Coakley Bay
Teague Bay
Point Udall
Jack's & Isaac's Bay Beaches
East End Road
Northside Road
Grapetree Bay
Sprat Hall Beach
Creque Dam Road
Paul & Jill's Equestrian Stables
Christiansted
Southshore Road
Rain Forest
Lawaetz Museum
Queen Mary Highway
Sunny Isle
Great Pond Bay
Rainbow Beach
St George Botanical Gardens
St Paul's Anglican Church
Fort Frederick
St Patrick's Catholic Church
Hope Road
Hess Oil Refinery
Melvin H Evans Hwy
Cruzan Rum Factory
Canegarden Bay
Frederiksted
Sunshine Mall
Estate Whim Plantation Museum
Henry E Rohlsen Airport
Long Point Bay
Sandy Point Beach
CARIBBEAN SEA
0 2 miles
N
RESTAURANTS & BARS
Blue Moon Restaurant G
Boz's Cane Bay Beach Bar A
Changes in L'Attitude B
Divi Carina Bay Casino E
Great House at Villa Madeleine F
Le St Tropez H
Mount Pelier Domino Club C
St Croix Leap D
ACCOMMODATION
The Buccaneer 6
Chenay Bay Beach Resort 7
Cormorant Beach Club 4
Divi Carina Bay Resort 10
Hilty House 9
Hotel on the Cay 5
Mt Victory Camp 8
Sprat Hall Plantation 2
Sunterra Carambola Beach Resort 3
Villa Madeleine 11
Waves at Cane Bay 1

The St Croix Heritage Trail

One way to see the best of the island is to take the **St Croix Heritage Trail**, a 72-mile driving route that offers close-up glimpses and detailed information about over 200 sites and attractions around St Croix. The route weaves through the hills between Frederiksted and Christiansted, mostly on Centerline Road. All you have to do is look for and follow the small historic road signs displaying an old sugar mill. You can also pick up a map at their website (Ⓦwww.stcroixheritagetrail.com), or at any tourism office, and many hotels also have information and maps. If you don't have your own car, ask taxis for their special Heritage Trail Tour rates.

contain plentiful and beautiful examples of Danish colonial architecture and the landscape has many ruins of plantations and stone windmills from the island's days as king of the Caribbean sugarcane industry. Culturally, the island is a fusion of cuisines, ideas and customs, its employment opportunities (the Hess Oil refinery and tourism) and proximity to the US (and potential for US citizenship) attracting people from all over the Caribbean. The two major towns are historic **Christiansted**, on the northeast coast and **Frederiksted**, on the west coast. The latter only really comes to life when cruise ships dock but Christiansted is almost always lively. Don't leave without a visit to the tiny but spectacular **Buck Island**, off the northeast coast. The island has been administered by the National Park Service since 1948 and is a paradise of beaches, reefs and hiking trails.

Arrival and information

The **Henry E. Rohlsen Airport** is located on the southern side of the island. VITRAN **buses** run between the airport and Christiansted every hour (ask at the airport for a route map and schedule); a **taxi** from the airport will cost about US$10 to Christiansted and US$5 to Frederiksted. **Tourist offices** – at the airport, in Frederiksted (at the pier; Ⓣ340/772-0357) and in downtown Christiansted (Ⓣ340/773-0495) – will load you up with maps, brochures and advice. There are **post offices** in Christiansted, Gallows Bay, Richmond, Sunny Isle, Kings Hill, Frederiksted and Mars Hill. You can access the **internet** in Christiansted at A Better Copy, 52 Company St (Ⓣ340/692-5303); The Emporium, *The Tamarind Reef Hotel* (Ⓣ340/773-3266); or Strand Street Station, Pan Am Pavillion (Ⓣ340/719-6245).

Opening hours on St Croix tend to coincide with the arrival of cruise ships. In Frederiksted, for example, while most of the restaurants remain open daily, shops remain closed until a cruise pulls into port (about twice a week during the high season and once every two weeks in low season). Outside of Christiansted, you should always call ahead to make sure your destination is open, especially in the off-season.

Accommodation

There are all kinds of **accommodation** on St Croix – camping, eco-cabins, hostel-like options, private boarding rooms, hotels and beachfront resorts – and because the island is less touristed than the other USVI, prices are usually cheaper. For those on a **budget**, the cheapest hotels can be found in Frederiksted and Christiansted. Those seeking luxury should bear in mind that resorts on St Croix are less swanky than their St Thomas or St John counterparts and none has five stars.

If you're looking for a more natural experience and a way to save a little dough, **eco-tourism** is a great option. The rainforest provides a great setting for wilderness camping, whether you set out on your own or go on a guided trip. Whatever your pleasure, the **Nature Conservancy**, which offers two-hour hikes for US$10, and the **St Croix Environmental Association** (see p.418), which also offers two-hour hikes but for US$20, are great places to start. **Mt Victory Camp** is the only eco-camping option on the island. Located north of Frederiksted on Mahogany Road (☎340/772-1651), the grounds were built entirely by owner Bruce Wilson. There are four deluxe open-air cabins with futons, linens, coolers, propane stoves, cookware, utensils and communal toilets with running water. While you have to provide and cook your own food, Wilson offers information and help in booking every sort of outdoor adventure you can imagine from mountain biking to tours of ruins by a local historian to recommended eco-hikes led by local herbalist **Ras Lumumba Corriette** (see p.417)

Getting around

There aren't many bus stops on St Croix and they're not very conveniently located. **VITRAN** runs between Christiansted and Frederiksted (Mon–Sat every 30min; Sun every hour) but **private taxis**, running along Queen Mary Highway, are just as good an option. They stop on demand, which can be time-consuming, but they're cheap and are widely used by commuting locals (around US$2 before 6pm and US$2.50 after). If you need to call ahead for one, try St Croix Taxi Association (at the airport, ☎340/778-1088); Antilles Taxi Service, Christiansted (☎340/773-5020); Caribbean Taxi Service Tours (☎340/773-9799); or Frederiksted Taxi Tours (☎340/772-4775).

Alternatively, most hotels and resorts have cut-rate shuttles that will take you back and forth from Christiansted and Frederiksted at prearranged times (ask ahead). From the East End, taxis – generally station wagons, trucks or minivans – to Christiansted will cost between US$15 and US$25 for a round-trip, double that for Frederiksted. St Croix is a great island for driving around, especially along the **St Croix Heritage Trail** (see box on p.411).

Should you find the need for a car, several car rental firms have offices in and around Christiansted: Budget (☎340/773-2285); Caribbean Jeep and Car Rental (☎340/773-4399); Centerline Car Rentals (☎340/778-0450); Hertz (☎340/778-1402); and Thrifty (☎340/773-7200).

Christiansted and around

CHRISTIANSTED was established in 1735 by the Danes, who named the town after Christian VI of Denmark. Located on the north central coastline, it is the capital of St Croix and its most historic and developed city. Because of a building code installed by the forward-thinking Danes, much of Christiansted's original architecture still exists. In some cases, you can still see original street signs written in Danish. The streets are laid out so simply that it's almost impossible to get lost, and because of this it's a great walking city. It has a pleasant, aged feel, its handful of historic sights mingling with small courtyard restaurants and a vivacious bar scene down on the Wharf, on the city centre's northern edge. And once you've tired of the town's low-key attractions, you can indulge in plentiful watersports and beach activities nearby, or go on nature excursions to nearby **Buck Island**.

Accommodation

There are no official hostels on St Croix but there are some very cheap options in Christiansted for travellers on the skimp; however, nothing's that expensive on the island.

Christiansted

Breakfast Club 18 Queen Cross St ☎340/773-7383, ℱ773-8642. Basic hostel-style accommodation, with nine rooms, a hot tub, a busy bar, and much camaraderie among the guests. ❸

The Danish Manor Hotel 2 Company St ☎340/773-1377 or 1-800/524-2069, ℱ340/773-1913, ⓦwww.danishmanor.com. A three-storey hotel washed in pink paint surrounding a fairly private courtyard and sort-of seedy pool. Budget rooms, meaning no views and no amenities, are as low as US$49 a night and the seventh night is free. ❷

Hotel Caravelle 44A King Cross St ⓣ340/773-0687 or 1-800/524-0410, ⓕ340/778-7004, ⓦwww.hotelcaravelle.com. A 43-room, European-style hotel located just off the Wharf downtown, this is a favourite among those who want nice digs but would rather spend their money enjoying the island than on their accommodation. ⑤

Hotel on the Cay Protestant Cay ⓣ340/773-2035 or 1-800/524-2035, ⓕ340/773-7046, ⓦwww.hotelonthecay.com. This seven-acre island, located in Christiansted's harbour, gives you the best of both worlds – city life (just a ninety-second ferry ride) and your own private paradise. All rooms are spacious, have kitchenettes and fantastic balconies. ⑥

King's Alley Hotel 57 King St ⓣ340/773-0103 or 1-800/843-3574, ⓕ340/773-4431, ⓦwww.kingsalley.com. This 35-room boutique hotel in the heart of the King's Alley shopping district, is housed in a beautiful nineteenth-century building. The rooms, which go for US$99–168, complement the old-world feel with rich mahogany wood panelling. Recommended. ④

Pink Fancy 27 Prince St ⓣ340/773-8460 or 1-800/524-2045, ⓕ340/773-6448, ⓦwww.pinkfancy.com. An extremely cute and well-kept, gay-friendly historic inn (the oldest part of the four-building complex is a Danish townhouse from 1780) that in the 1950s was a favourite hangout of stage stars like Noel Coward. Rooms have names like "Sweet Bottom" and "Upper Love" and are the best bet for your money downtown. ⑤

Around Christiansted

The Buccaneer 25200 Gallows Bay ⓣ340/773-2100 or 1-800/255-3881 ⓕ340/778-8215, ⓦwww.thebuccaneer.com. Situated on 340 pristine acres, with three beaches, an eighteen-hole golf course and huge rooms with four-poster beds, this is perhaps the island's finest resort. ⑧–⑨

Chenay Bay Beach Resort Rte 82 ⓣ340/773-2918 or 1-800/548-4457, ⓕ340/773-6665, ⓦwww.chenaybay.com. Located on sedate Chenay Bay, east of Christiansted, this three-star resort offers fifty, tightly situated West Indian-style cottages, all with kitchenettes, located on a former sugar plantation. Ask about the monthly specials (with two days' free car rental and the fourth night free) that they run May–December. ⑧

Cormorant Beach Club 4126 La Grande Princesse ⓣ340/778-8920 or 1-800/548-4460, ⓕ340/778-9218, ⓦwww.cormorantbeachclub.com. West of Christiansted, this gay-owned, straight-friendly resort is located on a white-sand peninsula surrounded by the ocean. Rooms are nice, but old-fashioned. Package deals and meal plans (including drinks) make this a cheap higher-end option. ⑥

Divi Carina Bay Resort 25 Estate Turner Hole ⓣ340/773-9700 or 1-800/823-9352, ⓕ340/773-6808, ⓦwww.divicarina.com. Located across the street from the US Virgin Islands' only casino, all 126 funky, modern rooms overlook the sea and have kitchenettes. You'll need to rent a car, though, because it's so remote. ⑧

Hilty House Queste Verde Road ⓣ340/773-2594. Situated east of Christiansted, this is the island's only real bed and breakfast, an Italian-inspired hilltop house whose six rooms are located on the ruins of an eighteenth-century sugar plantation. No real restaurant, but dinner is served Monday night. ⑤

Sunterra Carambola Beach Resort ⓣ340/773-4455 or 1-800/619-0014, ⓕ340/778-1682. Designed in the Tahitian Rockefeller style of Caneel Bay, with rattan chairs, mahogany beds and terra-cotta floors. The golf course here is the best on the island. ⑧

Villa Madeleine Off Rte 82/Grapetree Bay ⓣ340/778-8782 or 1-800/496-7379, ⓕ340/773-2150. A West Indian plantation mansion is the centrepiece of this beautiful hotel, which also has arguably the best restaurant in the area east of town. Each villa has a kitchen and a pool. Prices are up there, but they're worth every penny. ⑨

Waves at Cane Bay Rte 80 ⓣ340/778-1805 or 1-800/545-0603, ⓕ340/778-4945. Situated west of Christiansted on Cane Bay, this is the place to stay if you want to literally roll out of bed, don your scuba gear and hit the water. ⑥

The Town

Christiansted has its fair share of historic public buildings and churches for you to sink your teeth into. There are also great options east and west of town and even Buck Island, off the northern coast. Perhaps the best place to start a tour of the town's sights is the **Scale House** at the top of King Street by the Wharf (daily 8.30am–4.45pm; ⓣ340/773-1460), which was built in 1856 as the weigh house for all the goods that passed through the harbour and nowadays houses the Christansted visitor's centre. Close by, the **Customs House** currently serves as the headquarters for the National Park Service (Mon–Fri 9am–5pm). **Fort Christianvaern**, off Hospital Street (daily 8am–5pm; US$2), constructed in 1749, is St Croix's finest example of Danish military architecture: its cannons still point out to sea, and inside you can take a self-guided tour through the dungeon's torture chambers, visit the officers' kitchen and the barrack rooms, and take in the building's history by way of text and well-displayed weapons, documents and other artefacts. The same ticket grants admission to the **Steeple Building** across the road (daily 8.30am–4.30pm), the island's first Danish Lutheran church, built in 1753 and now housing the national park museum, which offers exhibits on the history of the church, St Croix's indigenous tribes, sugar plantations, rum factories and slavery. The **West Indies Guinea Warehouse**, on the same street, is currently the post office but used to house the trading company that basically built the town of Christiansted. A short walk north, **Government House**, on King Street, was originally the mansion of a Danish merchant, built in 1747, but today this long, bright-yellow building (one of the prettiest in town) houses the local government. If it's open, slip into the courtyard, where you'll be met by a flowing fountain and lush greenery. Afterwards, take in the **Lutheran Church of Lord God of Sabaoth**, further down King Street, built by the original Danish settlers in 1734, but later renamed the Dutch Reformed Church. Nearby, Company Street is the home of a regular Wednesday and Saturday **market** at which local farmers, fishermen and local craftsmen sell their goods on the site of the original 1735 slave market.

Around town

There are one or two sights beyond the town's limits that are worth seeking out. Around three miles west of Christiansted, the **Salt River National Historical Park and Ecological Preserve** is nowadays a freshwater channel by which lavish yachts enter the marina. But it was also the place where Columbus first sent sailors ashore here in 1493. This is also the site of many successful excavations, which have rendered artefacts from some of the indigenous peoples, and guided hikes are available. In the opposite direction from Christiansted, east, **Point Udall** is worth the trip – the easternmost point of the United States, and one of the most peaceful spots on the island. It's a windblown spot, but ideal for escaping the crowds, and hiking down one of many trails to the beach for a secluded afternoon of sun. Opposite, **Buck Island Reef National Monument** (☎340/773-1460), a mile out to sea, is St Croix's crown jewel, with picture-perfect deserted beaches, great hiking and an underwater trail for snorkellers. It was proclaimed a National Monument in 1962 by President John F. Kennedy, and consists of 700 acres of Caribbean reef and sea and 180 acres of land. Most hotels can set up an excursion for you, which will leave from the Christiansted wharf or Green Cay Marina. The only way to visit is on one of these guided tours, but you can get dropped off on your own secluded beach with a picnic lunch and a bottle of wine.

Beaches

The beach at the *Hotel on the Cay*, across the harbour from Christiansted, is the closest **beach** to town. It's accessible only by the regular US$3 ferry, and offers watersports rentals, a restaurant and bar. Further away, the beach at **Cane Bay**, six miles or so west of Christiansted off Route 80, has great snorkelling, plus a dive shop that offers trips, a beach bar and restaurant. Closer to town, **Columbus Landing Beach** is the beach off the Salt River where Columbus's men first came ashore.

Eating and drinking

Despite being the least touristed of the USVI, St Croix has not only a wide selection of cuisine at all price levels, but some of the best high-end dining spots in the Caribbean. While there are a few great **places to eat** in Frederiksted (see p.417),

Christiansted is the culinary capital of St Croix and it's a mostly casual experience with no need to dress up.

Bachus 52 Queen Cross St ☎340/692-9922. Expensive, but without a doubt one of the best dining experiences you'll have in the Virgin Islands. Request a table overlooking the street and choose something special from the largest wine list on the island. Open Tues– Sun 6–10pm. Recommended.
Boz's Cane Bay Beach Bar Rte 80 ☎340/778-5669. Burgers and beer on the beach at Cane Bay, west of town. Cash only.
Cheeseburgers in Paradise East End Road ☎340/773-1119. Though lacking any sort of ambience, some argue this place serves the best cheeseburger-and-beer combo on the island. Daily 11am–10.30pm.
Company Street Bar and Grill 2110 Company St ☎340/773-6880. Cheap sandwiches and salads served daily 11.30am–4am (closed for lunch during summer).
Fort. Christian Brew Pub 55 King's Alley ☎340/713-9820. Hot sandwiches, pastas, jambalayas and other Cajun favourites. While the food is always a safe bet, the local-brewed beer is a must-try. On Monday night, if you order a steak, all the beer you can drink is free. Located on the boardwalk overlooking the water.
Great House at Villa Madeleine South Side Road ☎340/778-7377. Situated east of Christiansted, this historic West Indian plantation, with great views of Teague Bay to the north and Grapetree Bay to the south, has decent French-accented adventurous food. Dinner Mon–Sat 6–10pm. Recommended.
Harvey's 11B Company St ☎340/773-3433. Reasonably priced fare, specializing in creole dishes and barbecue. Generally open Friday and Saturday nights only, but call ahead as days and hours vary.
Indies 55–66 Company St ☎340/692-9440. Upscale fish and meat dishes served with a Caribbean flair for US$15–30 served in a rustic eighteenth-century courtyard. Open for lunch and dinner.
Kim's 45 King St ☎340/773-3377. Dine among locals at this dirt-cheap West Indian eatery. The conch in butter sauce melts in your mouth. Daily 11am–9pm.
Luncheria 6 Company St ☎340/773-4247. Cheap and savoury Tex-Mex food with killer margaritas for just a buck. Open Mon–Sat 11am–9pm.
Marina Bar King's Landing Yacht Club ☎340/773-0103. Have a Bloody Mary and a hearty egg breakfast while watching seaplanes land on the water. Or chomp on a veggie burger at lunch. All meals US$5–12. Daily 7am–9pm.
Morning Glory Coffee and Tea Off East End Road ☎340/773-6620. Owner and third-generation coffee roaster Margo Loe ensures you get a top-notch cup of joe at this Gallows Bay café. She also has a full breakfast menu and wraps and salads for lunch. Mon–Sat 7am–3pm.
Savant Hospital Street ☎340/713-8666. Upscale restaurant that serves a fusion of Thai, Mexican and Caribbean cuisine in a stylish atmosphere on the eastern edge of town. Mon–Sat 5.30–10pm.
Shenanigan's 1102 Strand St/Pan Am Pavilion ☎340/713-8110. Fast and friendly Southern cooking for travellers on a budget. A great bet for breakfast and lunch.
Tuto Bene 2 Company Street ☎340/773-5229. A small favourite since 1991, serving northern Italian fare with a Caribbean twist, with prices ranging between US$16 and US$29 per entree. No reservations accepted, but there's a small bar where you can wait. Daily 5–10pm.
Zeny's Bar and Restaurant 39–40 King Cross St ☎340/773-4393. Cheap and authentic Puerto Rican fare located next to Market Square. Go for simple fried pork chops and curried stews or try local favourites such as saltfish and dumplings or sautéed pig feet. Daily 8am–11pm.

Nightlife and entertainment

While nowhere on St Croix is known for its crazy **nightlife**, Christiansted is your best bet. During high season, take a moonlit stroll along the waterfront and you're bound to find a party of clinking beer mugs and live music. Cover charges almost don't exist on the island, so you can poke into any place and have a pop while you check out the scene. Most restaurants have bars, which offer live music (mostly on weekend nights), ranging from jazz to rock to reggae to calypso to acoustic. If you want to get a great taste of Caribbean **steel panning**, find out where local Bill Bass (Ⓦwww.billbasssteelpans.com) is playing. Look out also for the **Jump-Up** (☎340/713-8012), a Carnival-like street party that takes place in downtown

Christiansted regularly during tourist season between 6pm and 10pm. Expect live music, dancing, mocko jumbies (stilt walkers), crafts and lots of food.

Bars, clubs and nightlife

Boz's Cane Bay Beach Bar (see overleaf). Live reggae Thursday and Saturday nights, plus steel band music during Sunday brunch 10am–2pm.
Cheeseburgers in Paradise (see overleaf). This small informal eatery offers live music ranging from piano to acoustic guitar to calypso Thursday through Sunday nights, generally beginning at about 7pm.
Club 54 54B Company St ☎340/773-8002. Christiansted's hottest nightclub: DJs every weeknight and live music every weekend. Cheap food and drink specials. Open Wed–Mon until 3am.
The Deep End Bar *Cormorant Resort and Beach Club*. Live jazz every Friday at 7pm.
Divi Carina Bay Casino 54 Estate Turner Hole ☎340/773-9700. East of Christiansted, this is the island's only casino, open Mon–Fri 10am–4am; weekends and holidays 10am–6am.
Indies (see overleaf). Live jazz Thursday and Friday night, starting about 7pm.
The Marina Bar *King's Alley Hotel* ☎340/773-0103. Very lively once the sun goes down, especially during the Monday night crab races.
The New Wreck Bar 5A-B Hospital St ☎340/773-6092. St Croix's only real rock venue. Live music Wednesday through Saturday nights. Dance floor, island décor.
Off the Wall Bar and Grill Blues, jazz and acoustic music Friday through Sunday 6–9pm.
The Terrace Lounge *Buccaneer Hotel*. Calypso bands every Friday and Saturday 8–11pm. Cover charge is usually US$5 for those not staying at the hotel.

Shopping

Christiansted is the **shopping** capital of the island, its speciality being jewellery of all ilks, and the usual array of local arts and crafts – on which, of course, no tax is payable. The Caribbean Bracelet Company, King's Alley Walk, is good for jewellery; the Iona Skye Gallery, 2220 Queen Cross St, is the outlet of a husband-and-wife team of jewellery-makers; Many Hands, in the Pan Am Pavillion, has a great range of local arts and crafts, pottery, jewellery and music; while Mark Austin, 3AB Queen Cross St, handpaints beach pails, garden watering pails, calabash bowls, frames, and more. Finally, the Mitchell-Larsen Studio, 58 Company St, sells all types of hand-blown glassware made by its resident artisans.

Frederiksted and around

FREDERIKSTED, seventeen miles away on the west coast of the island, is smaller than Christiansted, though it is closer to the airport and its harbour attracts weekly cruise ships. Frederiksted fell victim to a huge fire in 1879, which means many of its clapboard buildings date from the turn of the century but sit on original stone foundations that date back to the mid-1700s. The main strip of Strand Street, which skirts the waterfront, offers shopping and restaurants, but overall Frederiksted is a fairly sleepy place until the cruise ships pull into port. In town, be sure to visit **Fort Frederik**, a large rust-coloured building next to the pier that was built in 1760: it was the site of the slave emancipation of 1848. Inside, there's an art gallery and museum (Mon–Fri 8.30am–4pm). Other architectural highlights include **St Paul's Anglican Church**, built in 1812, and **St Patrick's Catholic Church**, built in the 1840s, both on Prince Street. Frederiksted isn't as safe as Christiansted, and anywhere off the main strip should be avoided altogether during the evening. For example, don't walk to Rainbow beach after dinner and drinks in town.

Around town

Outside Frederiksted, there are a few places to take in on a leisurely day trip. The **St George Village Botanical Garden** is perhaps the highlight, a few miles inland at 127 Estate St in Kingshill (Mon–Sat 8am–4pm; US$5; ☎340/692-2874), with beautiful botanical gardens flourishing amid the ruined buildings of an old estate. Just south, across the Queen Mary Highway, the **Cruzan Rum Factory** offers tours (Mon–Fri 9–11.30am & 1–4.15pm; ☎340/692-2280), and the **Estate Whim Plantation Museum**, back towards Frederiksted on Route 76 (Mon–Sat 10am–4pm; ☎340/772-0598), has been restored as it was during Danish times, with a period museum of agricultural tools and other exhibits. If you like this, try also the **Karl and Marie Lawaetz Museum** on Route 76, which also devotes itself to mid-eighteenth century life on the farm; don't miss the nearby **St Croix Leap** on Mahogany Road, a wood-working studio that sells jewellery, furniture and other crafts by local craftspeople.

Practicalities

The *Frederiksted*, 442 Strand St (☎340/772 0500; ④), is a decent modern option if you want to **stay** in town, with a pool, bar and restaurant, and TVs and phones in most rooms. The best **meal** to be had in Frederiksted is served at the *Blue Moon*, 17 Strand St (☎340/772-2222), a small bistro that offers a mixture of Asian, Cajun and Caribbean cuisine along with live jazz. A close second is *Le St Tropez*, 67 King St (☎340/772-3000), which serves primarily French cuisine. For late-night drinks, occasional dancing, bar games and live music try *The Saloon*, 6 Market St (☎340/772-BEER), and Pier 69, 69 King St (☎340/772-0069). For a unique experience, you must make a happy-hour trip to the **Mount Pellier Domino Club**, east of town on Route 76 (☎340/772-9914). Go for the beer-drinking pigs – yes, you throw them a can of beer, they crush it between their jaws, drink it dry and then spit out the can – and stay for the ambience (dirt floor and thatched roof) or a mean game of dominoes.

There are several **beaches** around Frederiksted that offer great amenities. **Rainbow Beach**, half a mile north on Route 63, has good snorkelling and several beach bars and restaurants, such as *Changes in L'Attitude* (☎340/772-3090), which offers Tex-Mex and general American fare, plus darts, billiards and watersports rentals. *Sandcastle on the Beach*, on Route 71 (☎340/772-1205), is located on a beautiful stretch of white sand and has rooms of various size and price aimed mainly at the gay and lesbian community. At **Sprat Hall Beach**, a mile north on Route 63, there is the *Sunset Grill* (☎340/772-5855), which serves grilled food and drinks for beachcombers. There's also **Sprat Hall Plantation** (☎340/772-0305; ⑤), a guesthouse filled with antiques located on twenty acres of virgin land. Next door is Paul and Jill's Equestrian Stables (☎340/772-2880), where a two-hour ride into the nearby rainforest costs US$50. The largest beach in the entire Virgin Islands is **Sandy Point**, directly south of Frederiksted, which can be reached by following Melvin Evans Highway (Route 66).

Watersports and outdoor activities

St Croix Bike and Tours, Pier 69 Courtyard, Frederiksted (☎340/772-2343) hires out **bikes** (US$7.50 for first hour, US$2.50 each hour thereafter) or you can join a guided tour of rainforest and beaches on the western end of the island (US$35). Multi-day rentals cost US$25 for the first day and US$10 for each additional day. There are two types of **fishing** offered on the island – fishing the flats for tarpon, bonefish and permit fish or deep-sea fishing along the edge of the island. Catch-22 (☎340/778-6987) does full and half days on a Bertram 38; Lisa Ann Charters (☎340/773-3712) runs a 42-footer out of Green Cay Marina; *Louie Louie* (☎340/773-1902) is a 32-foot custom boat that also offers island hopping and snorkelling trips; and Fantasy Charters (☎340/773-0917) operates a 30-foot powerboat out of the Gallows Bay St Croix Marina. For **golfers**, Carambola Golf Club, a par-70 course at *Sunterra Carambola Beach Resort* (see p.413), is the best on the island and has a four-star rating by *Golf Digest*. A round of eighteen holes with a cart will generally cost you US$50–70, depending on the season. St Croix offers great **hiking**: Ay-Ay, Kingshill (☎340/772-4079), does personalized eco-hiking and tours at any price range by herbalist, naturalist and son of a long line of bush women, Ras Lumumba Corriette. For a special treat, ask him to show you where he lives. **Nature Conservancy**, 52 Estate Little

Princess, Christiansted (☎340/773-5575) offers hikes to Jack's Bay, Isaac's Bay and others for around US$10. St Croix Environmental Association, Arawak Building, Suite 3, Gallows Bay (☎340/773-1989), runs hikes to Estate Mt Washington, Estate Caledonia, the rainforest and Salt River.

Like all Caribbean islands, St Croix is **watersports** crazy. While most activities and trips can be booked along the waterfront in Christiansted, remember that many outfits offer hotel pick-ups and can help booking entire vacations. Also, most hotels and public beaches offer kayak, jet ski and snorkel rentals.

Watersports

Big Beard's Adventure Tours Pan Am Pavillion, Christiansted ☎340/773-4482. This outfit specializes in snorkelling trips to Buck Island on one of two catamarans. They also do beach barbecues and sunset trips.

Buck Island Charters ☎340/773-3161. Full- and half-day sails on a trimaran leaving from Green Cay Marina.

Cane Bay Dive Shop Pan Am Pavillion in Christiansted ☎340/773-4663; Strand Street, Frederiksted ☎340/773-0715; and Cane Bay, North Shore ☎340/773-9913. They offer all levels of instruction, rentals and sales and will even customize dive packages.

Caribbean Adventure Tours ☎340/773-4599. Whether you embark on an island sightseeing excursion, a sunset trip or an eco-photo tour, this is the place to call for kayaking.

Llewellyn's Charter, Inc St Croix Yacht Club/Teague Bay ☎340/773-9027. One of the most respected sailing charters, which has been in service for over twenty years.

Mile Mark Charters ☎340/773-2628. Located on the Christiansted waterfront, these guys offer everything from sailing charters to powerboat rentals to glass-bottom boat tours, and they are the only company authorized to take dive trips to Buck Island.

St Croix Ultimate Bluewater Adventures ☎340/773-5994. Located in the Caravelle Arcade in downtown Christiansted, this dive shop offers everything from wreck dives to rental and sales to introductory dives for kids aged 8 and above.

St Croix Water Sports *Hotel on the Cay* ☎340/773-7060. This is the place to go for a parasailing adventure or to rent wave-runners and windsurfers.

St John

Located just three miles east of St Thomas and only accessible by boat, **ST JOHN**, the smallest and most pristine of the USVI, is the perfect hideaway and a paradise for nature lovers. Twenty square miles of lush mountains rise from perfect white-sand beaches, and with two-thirds of the island designated a **National Park** – one of the largest areas of wilderness in the whole of the Caribbean – there's an abundance of flora and fauna, including wild cats and burros, hummingbirds and iguanas to look out for. You really need to come for longer than a day trip to get the most out of the scenery, miles of hiking trails, numerous secluded beaches, and many reefs to snorkel. A hike into the mountains will also take you past man-made sights – ruins dating from the eighteenth century when the island had over one hundred successful sugar plantations and a population of two hundred whites and one thousand slaves. The main town on St John is **Cruz Bay**, home to half of the island's four thousand inhabitants and the best of the island's shopping, eating and nightlife.

Arrival and information

You'll find maps and brochures on the **ferry dock** in Cruz Bay (next to the ticket booth); grab a free copy of the *St John Guidebook*, which has a great map of Cruz Bay. The **tourist office** is located in town next to the post office. There is also a **National Park Visitor Centre** (daily 8am–4.30pm; ☎340/776-6201), at the creek in Cruz Bay, on the other side of the car ferry dock, north of the town centre. The exhibits will give you a taste of what you can expect to encounter on your hike and the centre will provide maps of the park for self-guided walks, help you plan your trip or book you onto guided hikes with park rangers. There is a post office in

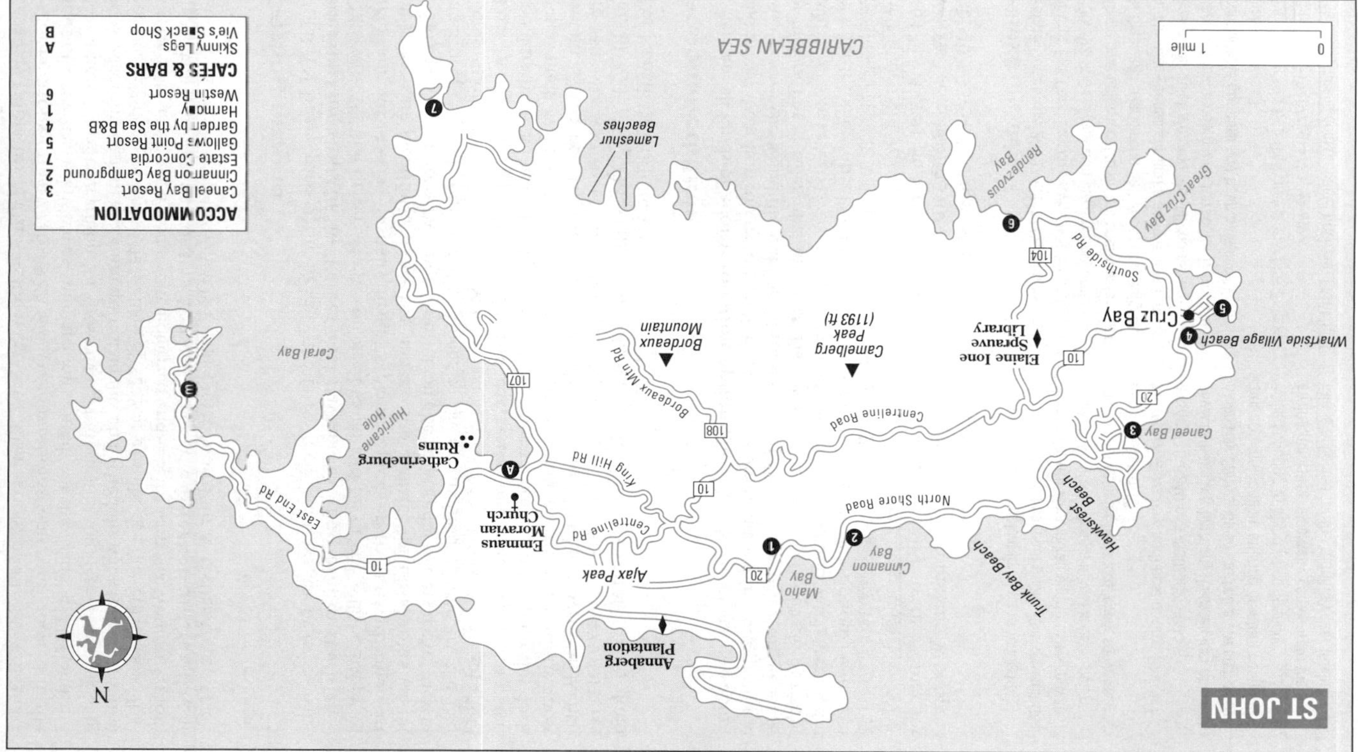

ST JOHN
N
ACCOMMODATION
Caneel Bay Resort 3
Cinnamon Bay Campground 2
Estate Concordia 7
Gallows Point Resort 5
Garden by the Sea B&B 4
Harmony 1
Westin Resort 6
CAFÉS & BARS
Skinny Legs A
Vie's Snack Shop B
CARIBBEAN SEA
0 1 mile
Annaberg Plantation
Ajax Peak
Maho Bay
Cinnamon Bay
Trunk Bay Beach
Hawksrest Beach
Caneel Bay
Wharfside Village Beach
Cruz Bay
Great Cruz Bay
Southside Rd
Rendezvous Bay
Elaine Ione Sprauve Library
Camelberg Peak (1193 ft)
Bordeaux Mountain
Bordeaux Mtn Rd
Centreline Road
Centreline Rd
North Shore Road
King Hill Rd
Emmaus Moravian Church
Catherineburg Ruins
Hurricane Hole
Coral Bay
East End Rd
Lameshur Beaches
10
20
104
107
108

Cruz Bay (Mon–Fri 7.30am–4.30pm and Sat 7.30am–noon; ⓣ340/779-4227).

Connections (ⓣ340/776-6922, ⓦwww.connectionsstjohn.com), located in the heart of Cruz Bay, is known as "information central" for the island and beyond and does a little bit of everything for those living and vacationing here. They can help book accommodation, recommend restaurants and schedule watersports activities. For boaters, they monitor VHF channel 72. You can check your email, as well as receive snail mail, get a document notarized and receive cash via Western Union; they even issue money orders. You can access the **internet** in Cruz Bay at Computer World (ⓣ340/693-9393) and Quiet Mon Pub & Cyber Celtic Café, (ⓣ340/779-4799).

Getting around

VITRAN **buses** park at the head of the ferry dock and leave about every half-hour, making stops in the Park, Coral Bay and the East End of the island. Otherwise, tell the driver where you need to go and he or she will be happy to help you out. **Taxis** – usually brightly painted pick-up trucks with open-air canopies – are plentiful in Cruz Bay and are also available for island tours (about US$12 per person for a two-hour tour). Don't be surprised if drivers try to pack in other people going your way. If you need to call a taxi ahead of time, try the Taxi Commission (ⓣ340/776-8294); St John Taxi Services (ⓣ340/693-7530); and C&C Taxi Tours (ⓣ340/693-8164). **Bike and car rental** outfits are available; in fact, you'll probably be hounded by agents of the latter as soon as you step off the dock but a quick walk around Cruz Bay will present you with many options, most around US$55 per day. You can also call Avis (ⓣ340/776-6374); Best Car Rental (ⓣ340/693-8177); Conrad Sutton Car Rentals (ⓣ340/776-6479); Hertz (ⓣ340/693-7580); Hospitality Car & Jeep Rentals (ⓣ340/693-9160); and St John Car Rental (ⓣ340/776-6103).

Accommodation

There are all kinds of **acommodation options**, from beach camping, eco-cabins, and private boarding rooms to beachfront resorts and mountain villas, but given the small size of the island the number of rooms is more limited and prices are generally higher. The smaller inns in **Cruz Bay** and the campgrounds outside of town, which also have eco-accommodations complete with A/C and kitchenettes, are best for travellers on a budget. For groups a villa may be the best option. Here are a few great places to start your search: Caribbean Villas and Resorts (ⓣ340/776-6152 or 1-800/338-0987, ⓦwww.caribbeanvilla.com); Destination St John (ⓣ340/F779-4647 or 1-800/562-1901, ⓦwww.destinationstjohn.com); Private Homes for Private Vacations (ⓣ340/776-6876, ⓦwww.privatehomesvi.com); and Windspree (ⓣ340/693-5423, ⓕ693-5623, ⓦwww.windspree.com).

Hotels and inns

Estate Concordia 20–27 Estate Concordia, east of Cruz Bay/Coral Bay ⓣ340/693-5855 or 1-800/392-9004, ⓦwww.maho.org/Concordia. These nine units, located on the southeastern end of the island overlooking Salt Pond, are really out of the way – rental car and a serious need for peace and quiet are required. All rooms are spacious and modern with terracotta floors and comfortable furniture and have balconies with water views. ❺

Garden by the Sea Bed and Breakfast Enighed, Cruz Bay ⓣ340/779-4731, ⓦwww.gardenbythesea.com. Located between Frank and Turner bays in a tropical jungle surrounded by banana trees and coconut palms, this tranquil B&B offers colourful West Indian charm with a private snorkelling beach. Rooms have exposed-beam ceilings, four-poster beds and lovely showers. Recommended. ❺

Harmony Maho Bay, northeast of Cruz Bay ⓣ340/776-6240 or 1-800/392-9004, ⓦwww.maho.org/harmony. Located just above the *Maho Bay Camps*, these studios are a step above tent accommodation, offering creature comforts while adhering to Maho's eco-friendly environment. The electricity comes from the sun, rain is collected for the running water in your kitchenette and private bath, and wind scoops help pull breezes through lofted rooms that have laptops monitoring your energy consumption. Recommended. 7

Inn at Tamarind Court Cruz Bay ⓣ340/776-6378 or 1-800/221-1637, ⓕ340/776-6722, ⓦwww.tamarindcourt.com. This pink, twenty-room, B&B-style inn offers all the amenities and solitude you'll need while keeping you close to all the action in Cruz Bay. Accommodation ranges from simple rooms with shared baths (US$38–48) to more spacious apartments with full kitchens and private baths for as little as US$98. There are no phones, no TV and no pool. If you are a light sleeper, make sure to ask for a room far away from the courtyard bar and restaurant. 4

St John Inn Off Rte 104, Cruz Bay ⓣ340/693-8688 or 1-800/666-7688, ⓕ340/693-9900, ⓦwww.stjohninn.com. On the outskirts of Cruz Bay, this little hideaway offers thirteen rooms (some shared baths), all of which are individually decorated. Some have wooden armoires, wrought-iron beds or four-poster mahogany beds, kitchens and ocean views. 5

Resorts

Caneel Bay Resort Rte 20, north of Cruz Bay ⓣ340/776-6111 or 1-888/767-3966, ⓕ340/693-8280, ⓦwww.caneelbay.com. Opened in 1955 and set on a peninsula bordered by the Atlantic and the Caribbean, this early eco-resort was the brainchild of Laurence Rockefeller (health permitting, he still visits every Christmas). While there are no phones (they offer wake-up knocks rather than calls) or TVs, who needs them with so much to do (or rather not to do) on this lush estate? Rooms are beautifully decorated with dark woods and rose-coloured tiles and most offer views of one of the seven beaches and the sea beyond. There are six restaurants and a new wine bar/cigar room. Best deals are the garden rooms, which have the largest showers. Recommended. 9

Gallows Point Resort Gallows Point, just south of Cruz Bay ⓣ340/776-6434 or 1-800/323-7229, ⓕ340/776-6520, ⓦwww.gallowspoint.com. The only resort within walking distance of Cruz Bay, set on a four-acre peninsula overlooking the Caribbean. The suites accommodate up to four people and all have fully equipped kitchens, spacious living rooms and water views. While the property doesn't really have a beach, the digs are relatively cheap; garden rooms with harbour views go as low as US$175 per night during the low season. 9

Westin Resort Rte 104, southeast of Cruz Bay ⓣ340/693-8000 or 1-800/937-8461, ⓕ340/693-8888, ⓦwww.westinresortstjohn.com. Sitting on a 47-acre compound overlooking Rendezvous Bay, this small self-serving community means that you never have to leave the premises, though Cruz Bay is just a US$6 taxi ride away. Convenient golf cart shuttles carry guests back and forth between the beach, restaurants, bars, shopping centre, deli, spa, tennis courts and gym. The concierge desk helps you book all sorts of off-premise activities. 9

Campgrounds

Cinnamon Bay Campground Rte 20, northeast of Cruz Bay ⓣ340/776-6330 or 1-800/539-9998, ⓕ340/776-6458, ⓦwww.cinnamonbay.com. Forty smallish cottages (5) with patios, cooking equipment and utensils, charcoal grill, propane stoves and communal bathrooms. Or you can go for one of the sixty canvas tents (US$58–80) with solid floors (10ft by 14ft). The tents don't have electricity but lanterns are provided. For those really wanting to rough it, there are 26 bare campsites (US$25) with a picnic table and charcoal grill. There is a restaurant and weekly activities, some for a nominal fee.

Concordia Eco-Tents Coral Bay ⓣ340/776-6240 or 1-800/392-9004, ⓦwww.maho.org. One of *Maho*'s sister eco-complexes on the eastern side of the island, these digs offer a few more modern amenities. Prices are similar (about US$10 higher), though the tents offer wind power and solar power, kitchenettes with running water, private toilets and solar-heated showers. A work exchange programme is also available.

Maho Bay Camps Maho Bay, northeast of Cruz Bay ⓣ340/776-6240 or 1-800/392-9004, ⓦwww.maho.org. Stanley Selengut started these camps in 1976 before the term eco-tourism even existed. Now Maho has 114 units tucked in the hills above Maho Bay connected by above-ground wooden walkways that leave the earth below relatively unscathed. The tent cottages have cots, linens, towels, cooking and eating utensils and propane stoves are included. Bath houses are communal and they recycle water to irrigate the vegetation. There's a restaurant that offers healthy fare and veggie options and the store sells most foodstuffs and sundries you'll need. They also offer a four-hour per day work programme in exchange for lodging. Recommended. 5

Cruz Bay and around

CRUZ BAY didn't become a port until the mid-1800s, when Danish soldiers from St Thomas used it as an outpost. Unlike towns on the other main USVI there's not much in the way of architecture, but it's a great place to spend a leisurely day shopping, eating and drinking. As you get off the ferry, in front of you, beyond the collection of taxis, there's a municipal park and pavilion – a great place to sit with a smoothie or a beer and take a load off. Keeping the water on your left, if you walk down Northshore Road, you'll see on your right **Mongoose Junction**, an upmarket outdoor mall, which is worth a look. **Wharfside Village Beach**, to your right as you exit the ferry dock, is the only beach in Cruz Bay, and while technically you can swim it's not recommended as this is a busy harbour. You're better off using the beach for powerboat rentals, sea-kayak tours and booking dive trips. Surrounding the beach is the outdoor mall, Wharfside Village. Apart from Cruz Bay the only other commercial area on the island is **Coral Bay**, the site of St John's first Danish colony, which now hosts a growing number of restaurants and shops catering mostly to the locals. It's also home to the **Emmaus Moravian Church**, the oldest church on St John. Dating to 1733, this was the original place of worship for the Danes who settled a colony here.

The rest of the island and the beaches

There are a few low-key attractions around the island. A five-minute drive out of the town centre, the **Elaine Ione Sprauve Library**, Enighed Estate, Rte 104 (Mon–Fri 9am–5pm; free; ⑦340/776-6359), is an eighteenth-century house containing an extensive collection of Caribbean reference materials unavailable anywhere else in the world and a display of photographs and artefacts. Four miles northeast of town, above Leinster Bay, a walk around the ruins of the well-preserved 1733 **Annaberg Plantation** (US$4) will give you your best impression of what a sugar plantation was like, plus some amazing views of the British Virgin Islands. If this whets your appetite for more ruins, visit the **Catherineberg Sugar Mill Ruins** (Rte 10), once a sugar plantation and rum factory, which, after the revolt of the 1730s served as the headquarters for the slave uprising. On the east side of the island the hills rise to a peak at **Bordeaux Mountain** (1277ft), the highest spot on St John. Stop for a scoop of ice cream or have some lunch or dinner on patios overlooking Lameshur Bay.

The Virgin Islands National Park

This spectacular and varied **National Park** encompasses about 7200 acres above ground and 5600 acres of marine sanctuary. The land was donated – with the stipulation it would be used for a National Park – to the federal government in 1956 by the then owner Laurence Rockefeller. Before you head off into the wilderness get some information from the **National Park Visitor Centre** at Cruz Creek (see p.48), which has an exhibition and free literature, and get hold of a copy of the Park Service's monthly schedule of ranger-led activities, such as adventure hikes, snorkelling trips, history programmes and nature walks. For some easy self-guided **beach hikes** that leave from Cruz Bay, ask the park ranger about trailhead locations for Lind Point, Salomon and Honeymoon (the nude beach). You'll need to drive or get a taxi to the start of the self-guided trails to the Annaberg Sugar Mill Ruins (see above), Cinnamon Bay Loop and the Francis Bay Trail. All of these trails are a half-mile over easy terrain. For the more adventurous, there's the **Reef Bay Trail**, on Centerline Road, accessible by bus. This three-mile hike takes you downhill through rainforest (look for the kapok trees, with their cloaked roots), cactus woodland, past petroglyphs and sugar mill ruins before bringing you out at a beach. You can either hike back up or arrange, for a small fee, for a boat to take you back to Cruz Bay (individuals arrange through the Park Service; groups call Sadie Sea ⑦340/776-6421).

Beaches

St John has its fair share of white-sand **beaches** and stunning azure bays where you can sunbathe, nap in a hammock, float in tranquil waters and snorkel the reefs. Most offer dressing facilities and restrooms and some have amenities such as beach bars, snack huts, T-shirt shops and watersports rentals. No beaches charge admission, and by law all beaches (up to 15ft) are public, even those that skirt private resort property. For smaller, more out-of-the-way beaches, such as those on the eastern part of the island like Lameshur and Salt Pond, get a map from the National Park's Contact Station in Cruz Bay. Northeast of Cruz Bay there's a fine selection of beaches, including **Trunk Bay**, St John's best and most popular beach. The **snorkel trail** here (marked by red, white and blue buoys) is stunning and has underwater plaques to help you identify the coral and fish you see. There's also food and facilities though you'll need to bring your own snorkel equipment. Further east, at **Cinnamon Bay**, part of the National Park's campground, you can rent kayaks, snorkel equipment, bicycles and even get a windsurfing lesson. For a break from the beach, head out on the Cinnamon Bay Nature Trail, which loops through ruins and returns you to the beach. **Hawksnest Beach**, on the other side of the peninsula from the *Caneel Bay Resort* (see p.421), is a favourite with locals because it's not tourist-heavy. There's snorkelling, changing facilities and picnic tables here.

Eating and drinking

St John has great dining options for people on all budgets. If you're self-catering, St John has several grocery stores, though don't be surprised by the prices and the limited supply of perishables. Although most restaurants and bars are located in **Cruz Bay** (or very close), some are now starting to spring up in Coral Bay.

Asolare Rte 20, Caneel Hill ☎340/779-4747. One of St John's oldest estates and a romantic spot for dinner – come early for drinks and the sunset over Cruz Bay before tucking into the Asian-inspired dishes.

Bamboo Grill Wharfside Village ☎340/774-4112. Quick and cheap Thai, Japanese and Asian food. As there are only two outdoor tables, you might have to sit on the curb.

Café Wahoo Wharfside Village ☎340/776-6600. This second-floor eatery offers both indoor and patio dining for lunch and dinner. The coconut-fried spinach ravioli (US$7.50) is a must. Otherwise, the fare is succulent seafood and steaks ranging from US$16 to US$25. There's a good American wine list to boot.

Dockside Pub Ferry Dock, Cruz Bay (no phone). A great place to grab breakfast sandwiches, freshly made cold-cut subs for the beach or a cold Carib beer to quench your thirst.

J.J.'s Texas Coast On the municipal park, Cruz Bay ☎340/776-6908. Eat great breakfast burritos (US$4.95; weekends only), lunch or dinner outside or at tables around the indoor bar. Always a cheap, reliable option.

The Lime Inn Cruz Bay ☎340/776-6425. A mainstay since 1984, this open-air restaurant with full bar serves good seafood, steaks and an all-you-can-eat shrimp feast on Wednesday night. Owner Rich Meyer's hook hand adds to the seafaring ambience.

Morgan's Mango Wharfside Village ☎340/693-8141. Open only for dinner, this Caribbean-inspired eatery offers a cornucopia of flavours to tempt your taste buds. The flash-fried flying fish is tasty, the ceviche is refreshing and the citrus chicken is gorgeous. Veggie dishes also available.

Paradiso Cruz Bay ☎340/693-8899. One of St John's standouts, this comfortable Mongoose Junction restaurant should be one of your first stops for dinner. Ask for a table on the wraparound, second-floor terrace and watch the world pass below. While pricey, you can't go wrong with the grilled garlic and herb sirloin with a rock lobster and roasted corn relish (US$30).

The Stone Terrace Cruz Bay ☎340/693-9370. Overlooking the bay, you can feast on interesting light dishes like lobster, garlic and chive wontons (US$9) and a seared tuna spinach salad with ginger potato cakes and cellophane noodles (US$12), or opt for more hearty fare such as the macadamia and tamarind encrusted pork tenderloin (US$25).

Sun Dog Café Cruz Bay ☎340/693-8340. Tucked away on the second floor of Mongoose Junction, this is a great place to take a load off after hours of shopping. The chicken philly steak is a good bet, even at a pricey US$8.25. Open Mon–Sat 11am–6pm.

Uncle Joe's BBQ Cruz Bay ☎340/693-8806.

Served hot off an outside grill on picnic tables under a tarp stretched between two cars, hands down, this is the best barbecue on the island.

Vie's Snack Shop Hansen Bay ⓣ340/693-5033. More like a snack shack, there's not much here for your eyes to feast on. But the conch fritters, some swear, are the best in the Caribbean. Other snacks include meat pies and Johnny cakes. For dessert, grab a home-made coconut tart.

ZoZo's Cruz Bay ⓣ340/693-9200. A favourite among locals who want to splurge on some killer Italian food that never misses. The handmade lobster ravioli is out of this world.

Nightlife and entertainment

While there are no discos, clubs or theatres on the island, there are lots of great **bars** and festivals that give you a chance to tilt a few back and party. For those with more refined tastes, the bar at *Caneel Bay* offers nightly calypso, pan bands and fine wines from 8.30pm to 11pm.

The Beach Bar Wharfside Village ⓣ340/714-0516. Located just outside Low Key Watersports, this is the perfect spot for a burger and a beer after a tough day on the water. For appetizers, try the flying shrimp. Always hopping around happy hour. Live music Thursday, Friday and Saturday nights.

Duffy's Love Shack Behind the municipal park,Cruz Bay ⓣ340/693-8886. The better half of the Duffy's party empire that started in St Thomas, this place is still known more for its drinks than for its burritos, tacos and burgers. But once you've had a Bikini-tini, Shark Tank or a Tiki God Rum Punch, who cares?

Fred's Restaurant, Bar and Cut-Rate Store, Cruz Bay ⓣ340/776-6363. The food is missable but the dancing and live calypso music on Wednesday night and live reggae on Friday night really hit the spot. Hailed as the biggest Friday night party around. On other nights, don't be surprised if someone starts off some all-night karaoke party.

The Inn at Tamarind Court 34E Enighed ⓣ340/776-6378. Bar and restaurant with country rock on Wednesday night and reggae on Saturday night.

Larry's Landing Wharfside Village ⓣ340/693-8802. A pour-your-own bar facing the beach that offers pool and video games. There are also TVs here for you to watch the big game.

Skinny Legs Coral Bay ⓣ340/779-4982. You'll know you've made it when you see a parking lot full of rusted-out beaters and ratty dogs scratching their fleas. This local shack bar, adorned with old flip-flop and broken-sandal mobiles and smashed windsurfing boards, is a fun drinking spot popular among the boating crowd and locals. There's occasional live music. Sandwiches and burgers only for US$5–7.

Woody's Seafood Saloon Cruz Bay ⓣ340/779-4625. Look for all the people spilling onto the street and you'll know you've found *Woody's* – a hole in the wall serving fried seafood and a party of booze and beautiful waitresses. Open until 2am most nights. It's popular with the college crowd who woof down shots with names like Surfing on Acid.

Watersports and outdoor activities

Arawak Expeditions (ⓣ340/693-8312) runs half- and full-day **mountain-bike tours** for US$45–80 per person. If you want to try some **fishing**, Bite Me Charters (ⓣ340/779-4585) does full, three-quarter and half-day trips aboard one of two boats, *Gone Ketchin'*, a 31ft cabin boat and *See Bee*, a 28ft Bertram, for US$400–850 for up to six people. Dorado Sport Fishing (ⓣ340/693-5664) has a 32ft catamaran, which leaves from Coral Bay for trips to catch wahoo, tuna, dolphin, marlin and sailfish off the South Drop of St John. Fishing, drinks, bait and tackle are all included at a price of US$60–80 per hour. For the ultimate fishing experience arrange a trip on *The Marlin Prince* (ⓣ340/693-5929), a custom 45ft Viking with an air-conditioned gallery, shower, and even a washer/dryer. They provide all types of fishing, even flyfishing for marlin, but their specialty is tournament fishing. Expect to pay US$1200 for a boat of six for a full day of marlin mania. You can go **horse riding** with Carolina Corral, Coral Bay (ⓣ340/693-5778) on an hour-long ride that climbs the Johnny Horn Trail to the top of Hurricane Hole (US$35). Half-day and night-time rides are also available. There are public **tennis** courts on the outskirts of Cruz Bay (open till 10pm; free) or courts at *The Westin* (ⓣ340/693-8000; non-guests US$15 an hour).

Watersports

St John offers a little of everything for **watersports** enthusiasts. It's best to buy your own mask before you come or at a dive shop in Cruz Bay – rentals are often shabby and if they don't fit right water will seep into your mask and ruin the experience. Divers will not find much on their own, but PADI training and excursions for certified divers can be booked to shipwrecks, larger reefs and underwater caves. All kinds of chartered **sailing** excursions are available – most leave Cruz Bay at about 10am, returning at 4pm and include lunch. You can go through one of the services mentioned below, inquire inside Connections (see p.420) or just look at advertisements tacked on telephone posts.

Adventures in Paradise Cruz Bay ⓣ340/779-4527. Offers sport fishing, sailing charters, snorkel trips and parasailing.

Arawak Expeditions ⓣ340/693-8312. This adventure outfitter offers kayak expeditions (US$40 for half-day, US$75 for full-day) around St John and surrounding islands. Longer trips include camping on deserted beaches and inn-to-inn multi-island packages.

Cinnamon Bay Watersports Center ⓣ340/776-6330 or 1-800/539-9398. This campground facility rents snorkel equipment, offers windsurfing lessons and can help book other watersports activities.

Cruz Bay Watersports Palm Plaza, Cruz Bay ⓣ340/776-6234, ⓦwww.cbw-stjohn.com. This ultimate dive shop offers PADI and NAUI training and daily two-tank/two-site dives that leave at 8.30am and return by 12.30pm (US$85). Packages are available. Ask about the popular Jost Van Dyke trip, which is equal parts snorkelling and drinking.

Low Key Watersports Wharfside Village, Cruz Bay ⓣ340/693-8999, ⓦwww.divelowkey.com. Life's a party at this PADI five-star training facility that offers great night dives and wreck dives to the *Major General Rogers*, a Coast Guard vessel that went down off St Thomas about 25 years ago, and the *RMS Rhone*, a mail vessel that sunk in 1867 just off the BVI's Salt Island (see p.437). General two-tank/two-site dives go for US$80.

Noah's Little Arks Wharfside Village, Cruz Bay ⓣ340/693-9030. Rent an 11ft dinghy and motor yourself around the island for exploring and snorkelling. Make sure to ask for a map of the reefs; if you break the motor you pay for it.

Ocean Runner ⓣ340/693-8809. Offers 20, 22 and 25ft powerboat rentals. You must have experience with boats, but basic lessons and day captains are available. Prices vary by season and size of boat, but be ready to pay at least US$225 for a full day.

Proper Yachts Mongoose Junction ⓣ340/776-6256. This outfit has been serving watersports enthusiasts since 1970. They charter bareboats and captained yachts for snorkel and scuba trips or sightseeing sails.

8.2

The British Virgin Islands

Forming roughly two chains separated by the Sir Francis Drake Channel, the **BRITISH VIRGIN ISLANDS** are a haven for snorkelling, fishing and diving enthusiasts. The BVI also offers some of the best **sailing** in the world and the towns and bays bustle with the constant comings and goings of yachts and cruise ships mooring up at the many marinas and anchorages. Less developed than the USVI, the islands maintain their identity – Caribbean influences still dominate in food, music and culture, the English connection is only really evident in the language, and the resorts are modest and in keeping with their surroundings. What the BVI lack in glitz and historical sites they make up for in unspoilt beauty – stunning tree-covered peaks, secluded coves, long palm-fringed sandy **beaches** and spectacular **reefs** whose breathtaking marine life and numerous shipwrecks make for some of the best diving and snorkelling in the Caribbean.

A minority of the islands, all but one of which are covered in steep green hills, contain the majority of the 20,000 population. The largest and most developed, **Tortola**, is the main resort centre and home to the capital, Road Town. Quieter **Virgin Gorda** offers largely upmarket accommodation centred on its own mini-archipelago and watersports playground, the North Sound. Yachters flock to little

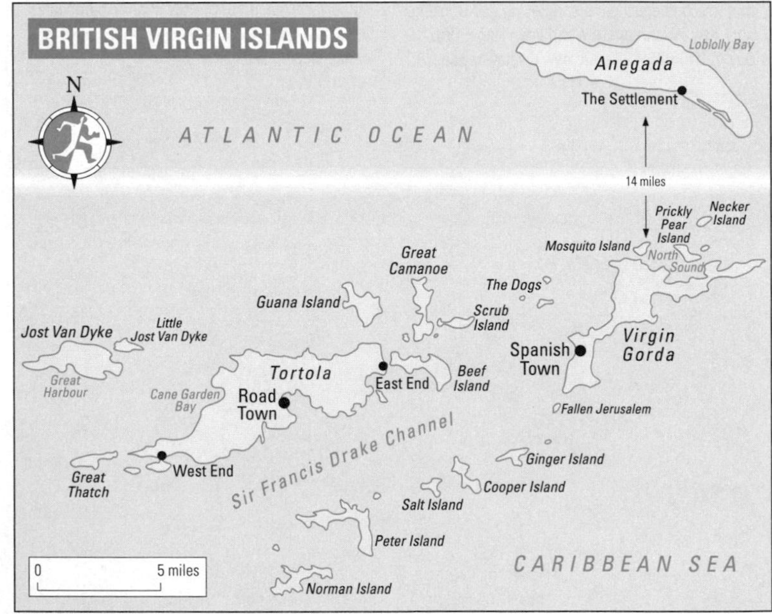

Jost Van Dyke to clear customs and hit its infamous bars, while **Anegada**, the non-hilly Virgin, is a coral atoll teeming with wildlife whose endless beaches, maze of reefs and bonefishing pull in day-trippers. The **outlying islands**, several of which are privately owned, see transient populations of guests at exclusive resorts or yachters who swim ashore.

Tortola

TORTOLA ("land of turtle doves" in Spanish), with a population of around 15,000, is the commercial and cosmopolitan centre of the BVI. Also the largest of the BVI, Tortola's twenty square miles of stunning mountain scenery rise to a peak of 1780ft, the highest in the BVI, at **Sage Mountain** on the west of the island. **Road Town**, roughly halfway along the more developed southern coast of the island, is home to the governor's residence, and most of Tortola's few historic sights. The **west of the island, especially the north coast, has some of the best beaches** and resorts and the liveliest nightlife – the **eastern end** is less well established on the tourist track but has some fine, often deserted beaches, including the island's best beach for surfing.

The island is best explored by car; **Ridge Road**, running east–west along the mountains' backbone, offers stunning views across the Francis Drake Channel. It gives access to the Belle View Overlook, **Mount Healthy National Park**, the touristy restaurant/bar *Skyworld*, which offers the island's only 360-degree view, and Sage Mountain National Park (just off Ridge Road).

Arrival, information and getting around

From **Beef Island International Airport** it's a short hop across the Queen Elizabeth II Bridge to East End on Tortola. Taxis cost US$12–15 for the six miles to Road Town; US$20–25 for destinations in West End. Local regulations prevent car rental agencies from having offices at the airport but some offer a free pick-up and drop-off service (see below). The inter-island **ferries** dock at either West End or Road Town.

Banks, **information** and post offices are all found in Road Town, though you will be able to get hold of maps at the airport and most hotels. Some hotels and resorts offer free internet access to guests; otherwise, the best deals are at CaribWave Internet Café, Waterfront Drive, Road Town (☎284/494-7549; US$8 for 15min, US$12 for 30min or US$20 for an hour) and Cyber Café, Trellis Bay (☎284/495-2447).

Public **transport** is limited to Scato's **bus** service – a fleet of pick-up trucks running to no particular schedule and no particular stops, you just flag them down as they approach. **Taxis** are easy to come by unless there's several cruise ships in town. There are stands at the ferry docks in Road Town and West End (look out for the brightly coloured stands with men chatting and playing checkers). If you need to arrange for one ahead of time, try BVI Taxi Association (☎284/494-7519); Wickham's Cay (☎284/494-2322); and Beef Island Taxi Association (☎284/495-1982). **Car rental companies** on the island include Dede's Car Rental, Fat Hog's Bay (☎284/495-2041); Del's Jeep & Car Rental, Cane Garden Bay (☎284/495-9356); Dollar Rent-a-Car, Prospect Reef and Long Bay Beach (☎284/494-6093); Hertz, West End (☎284/495-4405); ITGO Car Rental, Wickham's Cay (☎284/494-5150); and Tola Car Rentals, Fish Bay (☎284/494-8652). If you'd rather be out on the water, you can hire a small **dinghy** or even a large **powerboat** to get around – prices range between US$50–300 per day.

Road Town

Three-quarters of the island's inhabitants live in **ROAD TOWN**, either downtown, along its environs or in the hills above. The **harbour** has over the centuries provided

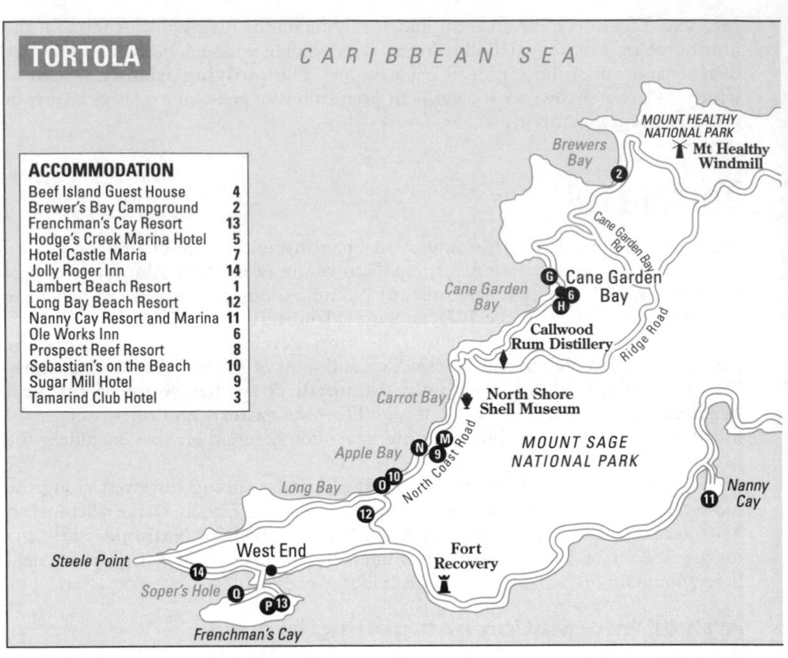

shelter for fleets of Dutch, French, Spanish and English ships. Today, cruise ships, yachts and ferries fill the bay, unloading their cargo of tourists into the town's bustling and traffic-packed maze of streets. Road Town's sights are all low-key but they're fairly close together and the streets and waterfront have a buzz all of their own with fishing boats unloading their haul and cruise ships docking. Most sights of interest, including the **Folk Museum** and **Botanic Garden**, together with the majority of shops and restaurants can be found on the two principal thoroughfares – historic **Main Street** and the more touristy **Waterfront Drive** – which run parallel to the water.

Maps and brochures are available at the **BVI Tourist Board office** on the second floor of the AKARA Building, Wickhams Cay I (Mon–Fri 8.30am–4.30pm; ⓣ284/494-3134, ⓔbvitour@surfbvi.com), at the ferry terminal and in most hotels.

Accommodation

Apart from *Prospect Reef Resort*, there is no beachfront **accommodation** in Road Town, but the hotels perched on the surrounding hills offer spectacular views of the harbour and the Sir Francis Drake Channel beyond, while those around marinas will have you falling asleep to the tinkling sound of halyards in the wind. If you'd prefer to rent a **villa** or private house try My Private Paradise (ⓣ202/554-8880 or 1-800/862-7863, ⓦwww.myprivateparadise.com); *Areana Villas* (ⓣ284/494-5864, ⓦwww.areanavillas.com); Best Vacations Imagineable (ⓣ284/494-6186); or Mount Sage Villas (ⓣ284/495-9567). If you'd prefer to be a few steps from the beach head for the west of the island – lovely resorts and small hotels skirt Long Bay, Carrot Bay and Cane Garden Bay.

Hotel Castle Maria Waterfront Drive ⓣ284/494-2553, ⓕ494-2111. The rooms are nothing special, but the place is very clean and the staff friendly. There's a restaurant, bar and pool. Excellent value, with prices ranging from US$70 for a single room to US$140 for four people per night. ❻

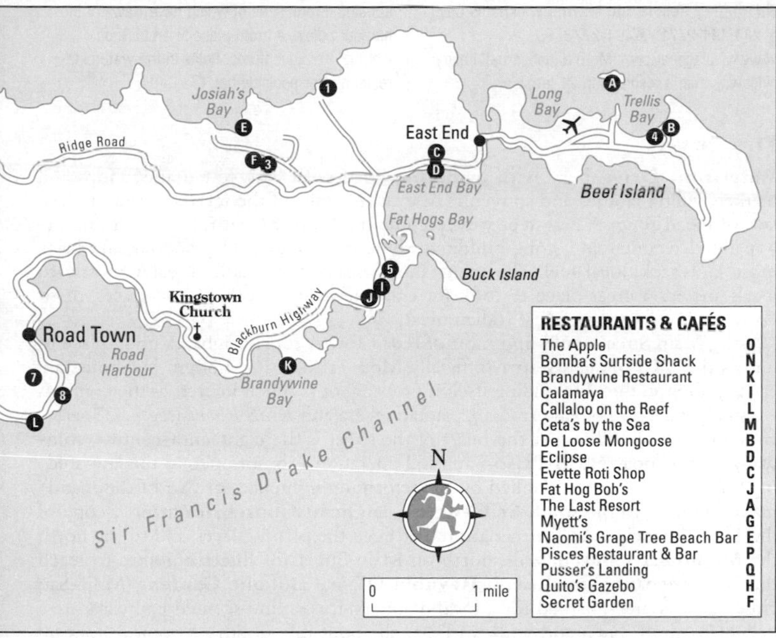

Maria's Hotel by the Sea Waterfront Drive ⓣ 284/494-2595, ⓕ 494-2420. A clean and moderately priced choice located along the waterfront. Rooms are decorated in typical Caribbean flavour with floral fabrics and wicker furniture, and each has a balcony and kitchenette. *Maria's Restaurant*, on the premises, is great for local cuisine. Special deals are available for stays of seven days or longer. ⑤

Moorings-Mariner Inn Waterfront Drive, Wickhams Cay II ⓣ 284/494-2332 or 1-800/535-7289, ⓕ 284/494-2226. Next to the docks for the Caribbean's yacht charter giant, Moorings. The hotel, situated around the marina, is in a relaxing spot within walking distance of town and caters mostly to yachters. All rooms are a decent size and come with kitchenettes. Has all the usual facilities including a swimming pool. ⑦

Nanny Cay Resort and Marina Nanny Cay ⓣ 284/494-4895 or 1-866/284-4683, ⓕ 284/494-0555, ⓦ www.nannycay.com. Almost a little city in itself, this resort overlooking a quaint marina has all you could need – restaurants, two swimming pools, a watersports centre, tennis, volleyball, spa, an internet café, small supermarket and charter services. For US$80–185 (depending on the season) for a standard studio room, it's a steal. ⑥

Prospect Reef Resort Waterfront Drive ⓣ 284/494-3311 or 1-800/356-8937, ⓕ 284/494-5595, ⓦ www.prospectreef.com. The only mega-resort in Road Town, set on a prime piece of land with a beach, spa and fitness centre. There's a wide variety of rooms but many are worn, dirty and have unexpected guests (you might find yourself sharing your bed with a lizard). However, the all-inclusive room prices and amenities make up for the below-average lodging. ⑥

Pusser's Fort Burt Hotel Waterfront Drive ⓣ 284/494-2587 or 1-888/873-5226, ⓕ 284/494-2002. The commanding harbour views from this hillside retreat, built on the remains of a seventeenth-century fort, make this one of the top options in town. The outdoor patio is perfect for a drink at sunset. Rooms vary in size, but most are large, and several multi-bedroom suites, complete with private pools, are also available. All have balconies, A/C, TV and refrigerators. The restaurant here is one of the best in town. ⑥

Sea View Hotel Waterfront Drive ⓣ 284/494-2483, ⓕ 494-4952. If you shun the resorts, preferring to spend the bulk of your money on food, drinks and adventure, this is the best budget deal around. Basic but clean rooms for about US$50 a night. ③–④

Village Cay Resort and Marina Wickhams Cay I ⓣ284/494-2771, ⓕ494-2773, ⓦwww.villagecay.com. More a lush, small luxury hideaway than a resort, with 21 large, well-appointed rooms, all of which have views of the harbour below. A great place to embark on watersports adventures. Relax in the waterside restaurant or poolside bar. ❺

The Town

Waterfront Drive, busy with traffic and lined with bars, restaurants, shops and markets selling clothes and souvenirs to tourists fresh off the ferries, is the modern face of Road Town. A few steps west, picturesque **Main Street** is lined with brightly painted wooden and stone buildings, some more than 200 years old, and has a more laid-back, local feel. The many shops and restaurants here cater mostly to locals and it's a great place to look for crafts, jewellery, clothing and spices, or sit down to an inexpensive West Indian meal.

Along Main Street you'll find most of Road Town's tourist sights. A good place to start is the **VI Folk Museum** (officially Mon–Fri 8.30am–4.30pm but hours are erratic), though the old building itself is probably of as much interest as the contents – a small collection of Amerindian, plantation-era and *RMS Rhone* (see p.437) artefacts. The white building at the heart of the street is the eighteenth-century colonial prison – today **HMS Prison** and still operational so not open to the law-abiding public. The prison is flanked by the reforming influences of two of the island's main religions, to the south **St George's Anglican Church**, featuring a copy of the 1834 Emancipation Proclamation that freed the islands' slaves, and to the north the **Methodist Church**. Walk north on Main Street for fifteen minutes to reach the four-acre oasis of the **Joseph Reynold O'Neal Botanic Gardens** (Mon–Sat; closes at dusk; free), named for a local dignitary. Its jasmine-scented pathways are a delight to stroll down and you can learn all about the wealth of tropical flora on display – orchids, banana trees and cactus among others – through self-guided walks. Finish off your exploration of Road Town with a visit to **Fort Burt**, set on a hillside above Waterfront Drive at the southern end of town, which offers wonderful views of the harbour. Only the foundation and mezzanine remain of this seventeenth-century fort built by the Dutch to guard Road Harbour, so once you've glanced at the ruins, drop in at the *Pusser's Fort Burt Hotel*, grab a drink and watch the sun set over the bay.

Eating and drinking

Conjuring up delicious dishes with seafood such as conch, mahi mahi and Anegada spiny lobsters, Tortolan cuisine is something to be savoured. Meats are often grilled and Tortolans are famed for their barbecue. In Road Town, you'll find superb local cuisine at bargain prices, including a wide selection of well-priced **West Indian and barbecue restaurants**, grilled seafood, simple sandwiches and plenty of vegetarian options. If you're self-catering or just putting together a beach **picnic**, *Riteway Food Market*, next door to the *Prospect Reef Resort* and *Ample Hamper*, a gourmet deli next to the Village Cay Marina are good places to hit.

C&F Restaurant Purcell Estate ⓣ284/494-4941. Located just east of town, this lively local favourite is difficult to find so call ahead for directions or take a taxi. It's worth it, though; the barbecued fish and seafood is hands down the best on the island. It's open evenings only and always busy so be prepared to wait. Main courses cost upwards of US$12.

Callaloo on the Reef Waterfront Drive ⓣ284/494-3311. This breezy restaurant in the grounds of the *Prospect Reef Resort* is run by culinary institute students who hone their skills on dishes like ravioli in a pumpkin cream gratin and citrus-and-ginger pork in a pineapple sauce.

Capriccio di Mare 196 Waterfront Drive ⓣ284/494-5369. An Italian restaurant whose outdoor patio is a great place to sip espresso or enjoy a light meal. The menu includes an array of pizzas, sandwiches and salads, but the tasty bowls of pasta for under US$13 are the main draw. The mango bellini is also a highlight. Open for breakfast, lunch and dinner. Closed Sun.

Courtyard Coffee Shop Main Street ☎284/499-2194. A good place to take a break from sightseeing and shopping in the area. Specialty coffees, teas and pastries served from 7.30am.

Crandall's Pastry Plus Fishers Estate south of town, near *Moorings-Mariner Inn* and *Prospect Reef Resort* ☎284/494-5156. This bakery does the best pastries on the island, though the coffee leaves something to be desired. Also sells cakes and West Indian food to go. Open till 5pm.

Healthy Choices Wickhams Cay I ☎284/494-4733. A good choice if you're vegetarian or just fancy a break from seafood and grilled chicken. Does low-salt and low-fat soups, salads and veggie meals. The baked patties are highly recommended.

La Dolce Vita 200 Waterfront Drive ☎284/494-8770. Choose from 24 flavours of delicious ice cream served in waffle cones, both of which are home-made.

Le Cabanon Main Street ☎284/494-8660. An airy and relaxed French bistro good for lunch – try the cured ham and goat cheese tartine – or dinner. A light lunch costs around US$7; dinners can go as high as US$30. Late at night, the restaurant turns into a disco of sorts.

Midtown Restaurant Main Street ☎284/494-2764. Almost always open (7am–11pm daily) and a favourite among locals. Cheap and delicious local cuisine – the curried whelk is excellent, while less adventurous souls can't go wrong with the baked chicken.

The Pub Waterfront Drive, near Fort Burt ☎284/494-2608. Long-time Road Town favourite serving up everything from burgers to steaks to fresh fish, with nightly specials, such as prime rib on Thursday and all-you-can-eat mussels on Wednesday. Has a great waterfront location to enjoy the happy hour and live music at weekends.

Pusser's Road Town Pub Waterfront Drive ☎284/494-3897. Road Town's nautical take on the English pub is a popular tourist choice. If you're hankering for some English fare, you can sup a pint and down a plate of bangers and mash (US$12.95). For something a little more Caribbean, try one of the many rums on offer followed by the jerk chicken or pineapple quesadilla (US$8.95).

Rita's Bar and Restaurant Wickhams Cay I/Omar Hodge Bldg ☎284/494-6165. Delicious soups, ribs and seafood, all cooked West Indian-style.

Roti Palace Abbott Hill, just off the southern end of Main Street ☎284/494-4196. The place may be crowded and hard to find, but once you try one of the mouthwatering rotis packed with seafood, meat or veggie options and served with a side of rice and plantains, all seems right with the world. Prices are hefty, though, ranging between US$8 and US$16.

Nightlife and entertainment

While Road Town might be the place to find most everything else, its **nightlife** is more mellow than that on the west side of the island. You won't find many clubs or discos with DJs here, but if you're content with some **live music** (check the *Limin' Times* for what's on), **drinking** and **dancing** there's plenty on offer, especially on weekends.

Cafesito Romasco Building ☎284/494-7412. Often has live music on Saturday and Wednesday nights, plus a daily happy hour (or two) from 4.30pm to 6.30pm.

Le Cabanon (see also above). A restaurant by day and disco by night, this popular hot spot is the current favourite with young expats in Tortola. Saturday sees the place overrun for the biggest party on the island. The atmosphere is chic wine bar so dress is smarter than the average bar in Road Town.

Moorings-Mariner Inn (see also above). Popular with visiting yachters, this is only really an option if you fancy a quiet drink and the latest yachting gossip and mariners' tales.

The Pub Waterfront Drive. *The Pub* (see also review in "Eating and drinking" above) may no longer be the hippest place to hang out but the all-day "happy hour" on Friday sets the weekend off to a good start. During regular daily happy hour, free wings are served 6–7.30pm. Has live music most weekends.

Pusser's Pub Waterfront Drive. Lively Road Town institution popular with tourists and yachters. Crowds gather here for nickel-beer night on Thursday 8–11pm, while ladies roll in to drink for free Tuesday 8–11pm.

Scuttlebutt Located at the *Prospect Reef Resort* (see p.429), this waterside pub offers simple bar food, strong drinks and live entertainment every Friday night. On other nights you might find entertainment as diverse as karaoke and domino competitions.

Village Cay Marina Wickhams' Cay I. Happy hour

4.30–7pm daily with free nachos and wings, and live pan music every Saturday at 6pm.

Virgin Queen Fleming Street ⓣ284/494-2310. While food is served here – the pizza is great – you're best off planting yourself at the bar and joining in any number of conversations, which will usually lead to a game or two of darts.

West End and around

The west side of the island, with its main area of settlement, **WEST END**, is home to Tortola's resort scene, more relaxed than Road Town and with an abundance of excellent **beaches**, seafront accommodation and nightlife. Popular with yachters and landlubbers alike, the anchorage of **Soper's Hole**, a quaint collection of shops, restaurants and lodgings, is located just across the bay from the West End ferry docks. However, most of the resorts, hotels and small inns are clustered either around **Steele Point**, at the very western tip of the island, or along the stunning beaches and in the hills above **Long Bay**, **Apple Bay**, **Carrot Bay** and especially **Cane Garden Bay**. The western end is also the party side of Tortola; aside from the entertainment laid on by hotels, there are local favourites ranging from *Bomba's* wild full-moon parties to BVI reggae great Quito Rhymer. Tourist sights are few and far between but the **Callwood Rum Distillery** (officially Mon–Sat 8.30am–6pm but hours are erratic; US$1 for a short tour) at the west end of Cane Garden Bay provides an interesting behind-the-scenes look at one of the BVI's most popular products. It still makes rum in copper vats the same way islanders did centuries ago and there's a chance to buy some of the tipple in the shop.

Accommodation

Almost all of the **accommodation** – from resorts to cosy inns – on the western end of the island has ocean views. Don't automatically expect air conditioning; many rooms are simply cooled by overhead fans or the sea breezes. This side of the island is also home to Tortola's only **campsite**, at Brewer's Bay. The hills around the western side of the island are clustered with **villas and private homes** (see the *BVI Welcome Tourist Guide* for a detailed list). The following companies offer some of the best places: Villas of Fort Recovery (ⓣ284/495-4354 or 1-800/367-8455); Icis Vacation Villas (ⓣ284/494-6979); Heritage Villas (ⓣ284/494-5842); Grape Tree Vacation Rentals (ⓣ284/495-4229); and Purple Pineapple Rental Management (ⓣ284/495-3100).

Hotels and resorts

Frenchman's Cay Resort West End ⓣ284/495-4844 or 1-800/235-4077, ⓕ495-4056, ⓦwww.frenchmans.com. This small, luxury resort offers self-contained beachside villas with one or two bedrooms, though you pay by the person. A one-bedroom villa during May is US$160 for one person, plus US$10 per additional person up to four total. The resort has a beach, freshwater pool, balconies, great views, kitchenettes, but no TV or A/C, though a refreshing breeze permeates the place. Closed Sept. ⑦

Jolly Roger Inn West End ⓣ284/495-4559, ⓦwww.jollyrogerbvi.com. At the entrance of Soper's Hole, just down the shore from the West End ferry dock, this five-room inn is definitely for the rough-and-ready traveller. Sailors hang around as there are US$15 per night moorings and a dinghy dock offering access to a restaurant and live-music bar. Basic rooms, some with shared baths. ④

Long Bay Beach Resort Long Bay ⓣ284/495-4252 or 1-800/729-9599, ⓕ495-4677, ⓦwww.longbay.com. Located on a 52-acre estate, this is the largest and most well-rounded resort on Tortola, offering rooms, beachfront cabanas and family villas. The deluxe beachfront rooms are the way to go here though they can be pricey (US$170–375), depending on the season). The *Beach Café*, an old stone plantation renovated into a restaurant and bar, adds to the well-prepared meals. Other amenities include watersports, tennis courts, a swim-up poolside bar, small shopping complex and fitness centre. Package deals help cut down the cost. ⑨

Ole Works Inn Cane Garden Bay ⓣ284/495-4837, ⓕ495-96180. Built on the remains of a 300-year-old sugar plantation, this eighteen-room

△ Emancipation Garden, St Thomas, USVI

inn is owned by renowned reggae performer Quito Rhymer, whose band plays across the street at *Quito's Gazebo* (see opposite). Rooms are basic but have A/C. ❺

Rhymer's Beach Hotel Cane Garden Bay Ⓣ284/495-4639, Ⓕ495-4820. This brightly coloured hotel (it's more like a motel) is right on the beach and offers very simple rooms, all with A/C, kitchettes and balconies offering views of the beach. ❸–❹

Sebastian's on the Beach Little Apple Bay Ⓣ284/495-4212 or 1-800/336-4870, Ⓕ495-4466, Ⓦwww.sebastiansbvi.com. The best rooms are the beachfront or the villa rooms, though the beachfront rooms are better value, ranging from US$130–230 a night, and they literally open right on the beach. The on-site restaurant, *The Seaside Grill*, serves breakfast, lunch and dinner (see below). ❻

Sugar Mill Hotel Little Apple Bay Ⓣ284/495-4355 or 1-800/462-8834, Ⓕ284/495-4696, Ⓦwww.sugarmillhotel.com. Located in the ruins of a seventeenth-century sugar mill, this elegant, well-managed boutique hotel has 24 guest cottages, all tastefully decorated in colourful West Indian style with rattan furniture. The on-site restaurant is one of the best on the island (see below). ❼

Camping

Brewer's Bay Campground Brewer's Bay Ⓣ284/494-3463. Choose from bare campsites (you provide tents and so on) for US$15 upwards and prepared campsites for around US$30 that include canvas tents, beds, linens, propane lamps and stoves, plus other cooking and eating utensils. A beach bar, restaurant and commissary are also on-site. ❶

Beaches

CANE GARDEN BAY, a mile-long stretch of sand backed by lush green hills, is the most popular and most accessible of Tortola's beaches – a drawback when the cruise ships are in town as the crowds can get unbearable. It's also Tortola's party beach attracting a mix of locals, tourists and yachters. You can hire all kinds of **watersports** gear here, and there are plenty of restaurants, bars and hotels. The bay is a popular anchorage for yachters who come in for a day of sun or a night of fun. The surf may not be nearly as good as at Josiah's Bay Beach (see opposite), but **APPLE BAY**, south along the coast from Cane Garden Bay, still pulls the surfers in (especially during January and February when the waves are at their best), as much for the fun atmosphere as the surfing scene. There are restaurants, bars and several hotels on the beach and alongside the road skirting the western side of the island. North along the coast from Cane Garden Bay, palm-fringed **BREWER'S BAY BEACH** is the most secluded beach on the western side of the island; you won't find any crowds even during the height of the season. The abundant coral also makes it the best beach in the area for **snorkelling**. The island's only **campsite** (see above) is located here, along with several beach bars and grills.

Eating and drinking

Some of the best **food** can be found on this side of the island. Many of the places listed below have **outdoor decks**, perfect for sipping a cocktail while the sun sets before tucking into a delightful spread of huge Anegada lobster. Always call to check places are open as schedules can vary, especially in the off-season.

The Apple Little Apple Bay Ⓣ284/495-4437. This moderately expensive West Indian restaurant inside a local home serves excellent fish steamed in lime butter.

Ceta's by the Sea Cappoon's Bay Ⓣ284/495-4263. Great fried chicken and johnny cakes, along with occasional live music in the evenings. Serving lunch and dinner.

Myett's Cane Garden Bay Ⓣ284/495-9543. A large open-air bar that hops with live music late at night, as well as a restaurant. Start with the tasty conch chowder, and no matter what meal you order –whether it's the Anegada lobster or the veggie pasta – be sure to ask for a side of the locally renowned peas and rice.

Pisces Restaurant and Bar Frenchman's Cay Ⓣ284/495-3154. Serves up home-style West Indian breakfasts, lunches and dinners. Open daily 7am–10pm.

Pusser's Landing Soper's Hole Ⓣ284/495-4554. Both a dockside bar with informal outdoor eating and formal indoor dining. The extensive menu ranges from English pub food to seafood cooked in various styles (macadamia encrusted, char-grilled, creole blackened or herb braised).

Quito's Gazebo Cane Garden Bay ☎284/495-4837. The restaurant in the back half of this oceanfront spot offers basic meat, fish and pasta dishes, while the front half has a bar, dance floor and stage where owner and local favourite Quito Rhymer plays his killer reggae. Every Friday night a fish fry draws a large, fun crowd.

Sebastian's Seaside Grill Little Apple Bay ☎284/495-4212. Look right out over the ocean as you eat breakfast (banana pancakes), lunch (grilled pork tenderloin sandwich) or dinner (surf and turf). No matter what time of day, try one of Sebastian's superb rum coffees.

Sugar Mill Restaurant Little Apple Bay ☎284/495-4355. This hotel restaurant, by far one of the best dining experiences on the island, is located in an old stone rum distillery and has a changing menu that's consistently good, including peanut pumpkin soup, scallops in puff pastry with a roasted red pepper sauce and almond-crusted lamb loin.

Nightlife and entertainment

Much of the scene on the western side of the island revolves around the monthly **full-moon parties** at *Bomba's Surfside Shack* – or **live reggae music** and dancing. If your tastes area are more low-key, you won't have to look too hard to find relaxing pan music or the simple sounds of an acoustic guitarist.

Bomba's Surfside Shack Cappoon's Bay ☎284/495-4148. Bomba and his driftwood shack are legendary in the BVI for their monthly full-moon parties, when hundreds of people pack the streets in a bacchanalian frenzy of dancing and drinking, while Bomba himself reigns over the party like a Carnival King from a huge throne. On a more mundane note, Wednesday and Sunday nights feature live reggae music.

Da Wedding Cane Garden Bay ☎284/495-4236. Local calypso stars the Lashing Dogs frequently play here; otherwise, come Wednesday night for fungi music by the Lover Boys as well as the fish fry.

Elm Beach Bar Cane Garden Bay ☎284/494-2888. Lively and friendly place with Pan music every Friday 5–8pm.

Jolly Roger West End ☎284/495-4559. Rock 'n' roll is the music of choice here every Friday and Saturday night, with dancing on the outdoor patio overlooking Soper's Hole. Near the West End ferry dock.

Myett's Cane Garden Bay ☎284/495-9543. Live music – reggae cover versions, rock, steel pan – Friday through Monday nights and a daily sunset happy hour and barbecue 5–7pm.

Pusser's Landing Soper's Hole ☎284/495-4554. They do a little bit of everything here: happy hour deals (5–7pm), 25¢ chicken wings, daytime pig roasts, live music on weekend evenings and steel drums during Sunday brunch. Call ahead for details on upcoming events.

Quito's Gazebo Cane Garden Bay ☎284/495-4837. Reggae performer Quito Rhymer plays at his own restaurant and bar, singing Marley-esque songs with his band, The Edge, on Friday and Saturday nights and putting out a more mellow, acoustic set on Tuesday and Thursday. One of the few places on the island where everyone from yachters and tourists to locals and the hardcore reggae crowd get together and pack the dance floor. Arrive early (before 9pm) to bag a spot and avoid the cover charge.

Sebastian's Little Apple Bay ☎284/495-4212. Live entertainment Friday and Saturday; Sunday night is fungi by local band, The Spark Plugs.

East End and around

For many years, the **eastern side** of the island had nothing to offer visitors. Now, you'll find several good bars and restaurants on Beef Island's **Trellis Bay**, which has a decent beach whose breezes make it a good place to learn to windsurf, in **East End** itself and in the rising star of the area, **Fat Hog's Bay**. The **beaches** on the east of the island are among its most secluded and peaceful. **Josiah's Bay Beach** is the surfers' favourite but even if you don't hang ten, it's worth a day trip. Start early with a great beachside breakfast at *Naomi's* (see p.437), before exploring the dramatic beach and body-surfing the killer waves. On your way back, stop at **Josiah's Bay Plantation** to walk through the ruins, check out the artwork in the gallery and enjoy a late lunch on the patio of the *Secret Garden* (see p.437).

Accommodation

The east of the island hasn't got the **accommodation** clout of the west or Road Town, but a few places deserve consideration, especially if you want to avoid the crowds, be near the airport or close to ferries to nearby islands.

Beef Island Guest House Trellis Bay ⓣ284/495-2303, ⓕ495-1611. This B&B is the closest lodging to the airport and to the North Sound Express ferry docks. The four beachfront rooms are simple and fairly well maintained, but only have fans. Each room has its own bathroom, and there's also a common room. ⑤

Hodge's Creek Marina Hotel Hodges Creek ⓣ284/494-5000, ⓕ494-7676, ⓦwww.hodgescreek.com. Moderately priced hotel, anchorage and mini-mall overlooking a busy marina and the Sir Francis Drake Channel. There are 28 rooms and five suites (with kitchenettes), all brightly though blandly decorated, and there's also a pool and a great restaurant on site (see below). Make sure you ask for a room with a balcony view of the marina. ⑦

Lambert Beach Resort Lambert Bay ⓣ284/495-2877, ⓕ495-2876, ⓦwww.lambertbeachresort.com. Not as good as the *Long Bay Beach Resort*, but it comes close. The major downfall is that you're out in the middle of nowhere, though the resort does rent cars. The upsides are that the rooms are pleasant, the complex is peaceful, the beach is long and the pool is a stunner. The beachfront and garden rooms have tile flooring, colourful wood furniture and large bathrooms; the hillside rooms are two-bedroom villas with full-size kitchens. Rooms range from mid-level to fairly pricey. ⑥

Tamarind Club Hotel Josiah's Bay ⓣ284/495-2477, ⓕ495-2795, ⓦwww.tamarindclub.com. Located on the northeast side of the island, this intimate hotel is off the beaten track, but what it lacks in location it makes up for with charm, good prices, and peace and quiet. Each of the nine rooms is individually decorated and all have basic amenities, including A/C and a mini-fridge. The on-site restaurant is very good (see opposite). ⑤

Eating and drinking

Restaurants on this side of the island are not only varied, but plentiful. On the other hand, **nightlife**, with the exception of live music in some restaurants and the odd bar, is practically non-existent.

Bing's Drop-In Bar East End ⓣ284/495-2627. Primarily a local after-hours dance spot, and a plain old bar the rest of the time. A fun and safe experience for non-locals.

Brandywine Restaurant Brandywine Bay ⓣ284/495-2301. The gourmet menu at this small estate, which offers fine dining in a peaceful scenic setting, features an array of duck, lamb and seafood dishes in Florentine style. While you may wince at the prices (around US$35 for a three-course meal), it's worth every penny.

Hodges Creek Marina *Calamaya* ⓣ284/495-2126. This funkily designed terrace restaurant overlooking Hodge's Creek Marina fuses Italian and West Indian fare. You can't go wrong with the Cubana grilled sandwich (shrimp, ham, pineapple and cheese), the West Indian roast pork (suckling pig roasted on a spit) or the banana ravioli dessert.

De Loose Mongoose Trellis Bay ⓣ284/495-2303. Located on the water's edge next to the *Beef Island Guest House* (see above), this bar and restaurant serves breakfast, lunch and dinner. Prices are good and the food's decent if unexceptional. There's live music every weekend and Sunday night is beach barbecue night.

Eclipse Fat Hog's Bay ⓣ284/495-1646. Dishes at this small, homey spot, overlooking Penn's Landing Marina, range from Spanish paella to Thai green curry to Indian biryani. Open for dinner only. Tues–Sat.

Evette Roti Shop Fat Hog's Bay. Right across the street from Penn's Landing Marina, this hole in the wall is a good place to stop for inexpensive roti.

Fat Hog Bob's Fat Hog's Bay ⓣ284/495-1010. This large, fun-loving place has a spirited ambience that's part Tahitian club room and part American bar and grill. Eat on the patio overlooking the bay or drink at the bar or in the large cocktail lounge. There's a big-screen TV for the major sports events plus live music on the weekends. Open for lunch and dinner. Main "Bob-B-Q" courses start at US$15.

The Last Resort Trellis Bay ⓣ284/495-2520. Located on an islet in the middle of Trellis Bay (take the two-minute ferry). While dinner is nothing special and not particularly cheap – usually a fish or meat buffet that starts at 7.30pm – the setting and owner Tony Snell's post-dinner cabaret act are worth the trip. Prices start at US$20.

Naomi's Grape Tree Beach Bar Josiah's Bay ⓣ284/495-2818. This little shack on the beach offers great West Indian breakfast, lunch and dinner at dirt-cheap prices. Plates are colourfully presented and portions are hearty – the juicy cheeseburgers are a highlight.

Secret Garden Josiah's Bay ⓣ284/495-1834. Part of the Josiah's Bay Plantation Art Gallery, this outdoor café set among the ruins of the original plantation buildings is about as peaceful as you can imagine. The menu includes home-made soups, falafel sandwiches and grilled scallops. Main courses start at US$10.

Tamarind Club (see review in "Accommodation" above). If you're staying on the eastern side of the island this cosy hotel restaurant tucked away in the hills above Josiah's Bay is worth a visit. You can't beat the "Grilled Coeurs of Soya Ginger Glazed Swordfish with Mango Salsa and Wasabi".

Watersports and outdoor activities

Tortola has the full range of watersports and boating activities – **snorkelling**, **diving**, **windsurfing**, **powerboating**, **fishing** and **sailing** (from scenic day charters to full-moon booze cruises). The only place to play **tennis** is at resorts and hotels with courts. These include *Frenchman's Cay Resort* (see p.432), *Long Bay Beach Resort* (see p.432), *Moorings-Mariner Inn* (see p.429), and the *Prospect Reef Resort* (see p.429). All charge about US$7 an hour for non-guests, except *Moorings*, which is free of charge on a first-come first-served basis. **Horse riding** is a great way to explore the mountains. Shadow's Stables, on Ridge Road (US$25 per hour; ⓣ284/494-2262), offers rides through Sage Mountain National Park. The owner, Elton "Shadow" Parsons, is descended from a long line of local farmers who tilled the land where the stables now stand; his knowledge of local history and funny stories makes him the perfect guide. If you prefer to use your own legs, there are three excellent **hiking trails** in Mount Sage National Park.

Snorkelling, diving, surfing and windsurfing

Baskin in the Sun *Prospect Reef Resort*, Road Town and Soper's Hole ⓣ284/494-2858 or 1-800/650-2084, ⓦwww.baskininthesun.com. For diving and snorkelling, you can't get much better than this outfit, which has thirty years' experience. They offer daily morning and afternoon dives, plus regular night dives. Instruction courses for all levels and hotel/dive packages are available. Their website gives full details of the sites visited and their rates. Snorkel trips cost around US$25; dives range from US$85 for a half-day to US$456 for a seven-day package.

Boardsailing BVI Trellis Bay and Nanny Cay ⓣ284/495-2447. One of the best options for windsurfing whatever your level. Also does sea-kayaking lessons, tours, rentals and sales.

High Sea Adventures Fat Hog's Bay ⓣ284/495-1300. Hit the Indians, the Baths, Peter Island or any of the other snorkelling hot spots with Captain Roy. Half-day trips (US$60) include two snorkel sites and full-day trips (US$85) take in four. He also does fishing trips – a one-day trip for four

The wreck of the RMS Rhone

The wreck of the **RMS Rhone** has been voted the Caribbean's number one **wreck dive** by several diving magazines. The 310-foot British mail steamer and passenger ship was torn in two by a devastating hurricane in 1867 and sank to the bottom of Sir Francis Drake Channel, near Salt Island, together with her cargo of cotton and copper and 124 passengers. The bow sits about 80 feet underwater and the stern in about 15 to 50 foot of water. The dive makes for an eerie experience as both parts are very well preserved – the crow's nest is fully intact, not to mention the engine room and the battered propeller. Colourful coral, large schools of fish and other marine creatures live on and around the ship. Most of the dive shops run trips to the wreck – see listings above.

guests costs US$300.

HIHO *Prospect Reef Resort*, Road Town ☎284/494-0337. Your one-stop option for windsurfing or regular hang-ten surfing – does sales, rentals, lessons and directions to the best beaches.

Underwater Safaris Moorings Dock, Road Town ☎284/494-3235. Dives to all the usual spots. Single-tank dives are US$55 and two-tank dives are US$80.

Sailing and powerboating

Jolly Mon Boat Rentals Fat Hog's Bay ☎284/495-9916. Captained half- and full-day powerboat trips ranging US$275–850.

King Charters Nanny Cay Marina ☎284/494-5820, ⓦwww.kingcharters.com. Day trips or powerboat and motor yachts rentals (with or without captain). Day trips are on the 50ft luxury motoryacht *Antillean* and include lunch ashore.

M&M Powerboat Rentals Village Cay Marina ☎284/495-9993, ⓦwww.powerboatrentalbvi.com. Half- or full-day and weekly rentals of 20, 22 and 25ft boats. The 22ft *Contender* with 150hp motor rents for US$275 per day.

The Moorings, Ltd *Moorings-Mariner Inn*, Road Town ☎284/494-2331, ⓦwww.moorings.com. Moorings is the largest charter boat company in the Caribbean. Whether you want to skipper your own boat or sail with a captain and crew they will help you plan your entire vacation.

Offshore Sailing School *Prospect Reef Resort*, Road Town ☎1-800/221-4326, ⓦwww.offshore-sailing.com. This experienced company operating out of *Prospect Reef Resort* offers six-day learn-to-sail courses, including a live-aboard option, and ten-day fast-track to cruising courses. Prices start at US$1645 including accommodation and all course materials. Their website has full details of all courses and prices.

Sunsail Charters Hodge's Creek Marina ☎284/495-4740, ⓦwww.sunsail.com. While not as large as Moorings, Sunsail is a serious rival with its immaculate fleet of boats and friendly service.

Fishing

Blue Ocean Adventures ☎284/499-1134. Half-day, full-day and overnight charters available for fishing tuna, wahoo or Atlantic blue marlin. Price covers everything, including lunch.

Caribbean Fly-Fishing Outfitters ☎284/494-4797. For a unique Caribbean fishing experience, go for tarpon, bonefish and permit on a fly rod.

Fort Burt Marina ☎284/494-4200. Many different fishing outfits work out of this marina. Just give them a call and they'll help you find a charter to suit your needs.

Persistence Charters Ltd ☎284/495-4122. Sail out of Soper's Hole with six friends on a 31-footer (all bait, tackle, drinks and snacks included) for US$400 for a half-day or US$700 for a full day.

Virgin Gorda

VIRGIN GORDA, twelve miles east of Tortola, might just be the perfect Virgin Island – peaceful, blessed with abundant natural assets, and sometimes gloriously deserted. Ten miles long and two miles wide (at its widest), the island got its name – "fat virgin" – from Columbus in 1493 during his second voyage through the area. The name refers to the landscape – mountainous in the middle and thin at each end. Most visitors to the island stay on the luxury resorts (some accessible only by water) at **North Sound**. Skirted on one side by Virgin Gorda and on the other by several major reefs and a series of small islands **– Mosquito**, **Prickly Pear**, **Saba Rock**, **Eustacia** and **Necker** – the North Sound provides excellent watersports, hiking trails, deserted beaches and some of the best diving and snorkelling in the BVI.

The tourist dollar has yet to make much of an impact on **SPANISH TOWN**, Virgin Gorda's main settlement located at its southern end and home to most of the 2500-plus islanders. Unprepossessing and very poor, it consists mainly of a jumble of run-down, windowless houses with chickens running through the yards. The town's only nod to tourism is **Virgin Gorda Yacht Harbour**, the island's main marina, where you'll find most of the handful of restaurants and shops, as well as the banks and tourist information centre. The North Sound Road leading from Spanish Town to the small village of **Gun Creek** is the starting-point (well signposted or

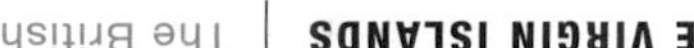

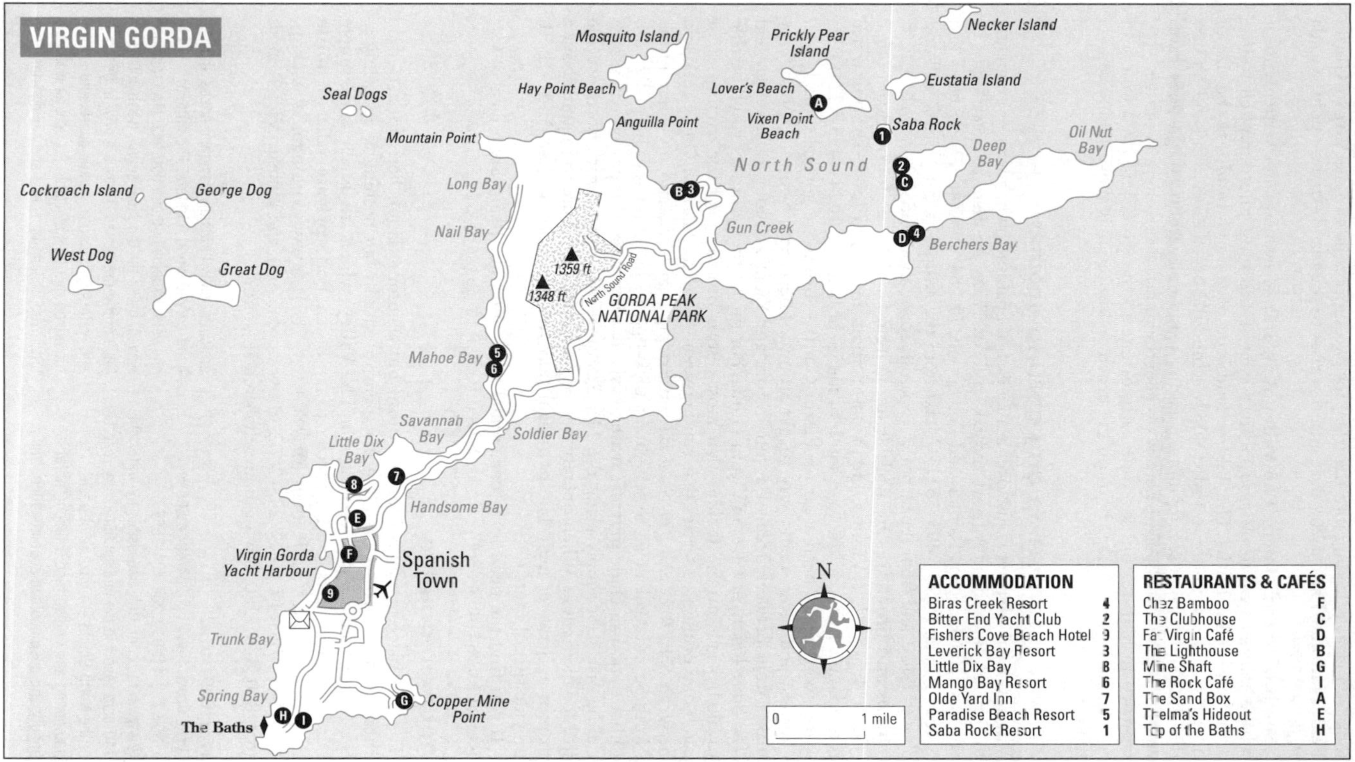
VIRGIN GORDA
Mosquito Island
Prickly Pear Island
Necker Island
Eustatia Island
Seal Dogs
Hay Point Beach
Lover's Beach
Vixen Point Beach
Saba Rock
Anguilla Point
Mountain Point
North Sound
Deep Bay
Oil Nut Bay
Cockroach Island
George Dog
Long Bay
Gun Creek
Berchers Bay
Nail Bay
West Dog
Great Dog
1359 ft
1348 ft
North Sound Road
GORDA PEAK NATIONAL PARK
Mahoe Bay
Savannah Bay
Soldier Bay
Little Dix Bay
Handsome Bay
Virgin Gorda Yacht Harbour
Spanish Town
Trunk Bay
Spring Bay
The Baths
Copper Mine Point
N
0
1 mile
ACCOMMODATION
Biras Creek Resort 4
Bitter End Yacht Club 2
Fishers Cove Beach Hotel 9
Leverick Bay Resort 3
Little Dix Bay 8
Mango Bay Resort 6
Olde Yard Inn 7
Paradise Beach Resort 5
Saba Rock Resort 1
RESTAURANTS & CAFÉS
Chez Bamboo F
The Clubhouse C
Fat Virgin Café D
The Lighthouse B
Mine Shaft G
The Rock Café I
The Sand Box A
Thelma's Hideout E
Top of the Baths H

look for the stairs leading into the trees) for two short trails into the **Virgin Gorda Peak National Park**, a 260-acre area that rises to the island's highest point, Gorda Peak, at 1359ft.

South of Spanish Town, **The Valley** is an area of even smaller settlements at whose southern tip lies Virgin Gorda's biggest and most photographed tourist attraction – **The Baths**. This bizarre landscape of volcanic **boulders** the size of houses stretches from the wooded slopes behind the beach to the sand and on into the clear aquamarine sea, forming a natural seaside playground of grottoes, caves and pools. The **snorkelling** here is excellent and, not surprisingly, it can get very crowded in high season, so come early or late in the day. There are also lots of restaurants, bars and shops both on the beach and in the hills above, connected via trails.

Arrival, information and getting around

Virgin Gorda's **airport** is just over a mile east of Spanish Town, but most people fly to Tortola's Beef Island Airport and take a ferry. **Taxis** are there to meet flights or you can call Mahogany Rentals and Taxi Service (ⓣ284/495-5469) and Andy's Taxi & Jeep Rental (ⓣ284/495-5511). A taxi from the airport to Gun Creek will cost about US$20, and from the airport to Spanish Town about US$5.

Maps and brochures are available from Virgin Gorda's BVI Tourist Board office (ⓣ284/495-5181) at Virgin Gorda Yacht Harbour in Spanish Town. The post office is in Spanish Town, on the road south of the yacht harbour (ⓣ284/495-5224).

You won't really need a car on Virgin Gorda – **boats** are generally the fastest, cheapest and most scenic way to get around. The North Sound Express ferry makes stops between Trellis Bay on Tortola, and Yacht Harbour, *Leverick Bay* and *The Bitter End Yacht Club* on Virgin Gorda. For most other journeys you'll be able to hitch a ride on the **ferries** that most resorts provide for their employees, or catch one of the free ferries that run between *The Bitter End* and Gun Creek and between *Saba Rock* and *The Sand Box* on Prickly Pear Island and anywhere in the North Sound. Call ahead to schedule a pick-up (see list of ferries on pp.392–93). Other options include **private water taxis**, renting your own powerboat, which can be pricey, or simply using the 11ft Boston Whalers that most resorts provide free for their guests. When operating your own boat, make sure to inquire about a map of underwater reefs. The two main **taxi firms**, Mahogany and Andy's, both provide special tours.

If you find the need for a **car**, rental companies are Island Style Jeep & Car Rental (ⓣ284/495-6300) and L&S Jeep Rental (ⓣ284/495-5297).

Accommodation

The best place to stay is **North Sound** but accommodation here doesn't come cheap. **Spanish Town** has a few inexpensive options but nothing as appealing as the North Sound resorts or rooms in **The Valley**, which are usually fairly simple but have great views and easy access to the beach. For a **private villa or home** try: Virgin Gorda Villa Rentals (ⓣ1-800/848-7081, ⓦwww.virgingordabvi.com), Caribbean Villas (ⓣ1-877/248-2862, ⓦwww.cvoa.com), and Unusual Villa Rentals (ⓣ1-800/846-7280, ⓦwww.unusualvillarentals.com).

North Sound

Biras Creek Resort ⓣ284/494-3555 or 1-800/223-1108, ⓕ284/494-3557, ⓦwww.biras.com. Only accessible by water, this 140-acre resort is the undisputed luxury resort of the North Sound – a mixture of posh pampering and undisturbed freedom, natural beauty and cosmopolitan sophistication. Units are cottages with locally designed linens and hand-carved wood furniture. The outdoor showers, especially those that face the crashing waves, make for the most scenic wash you'll have in the Caribbean. There's a private beach and watersports centre, tennis courts and motorized dinghies available for use, as well as organized helicopter, scuba and sailing trips. But the *pièce de résistance* at *Biras* is the food (see p.442). 9

Bitter End Yacht Club and Marina ⓣ284/494-2746 or 1-800/872-2393, ⓕ284/494-4756, ⓦwww.beyc.com. *The Bitter End* is a huge, lush waterfront resort (reachable only by water), whose superb amenities include several restaurants, a great English pub, a decked-out commissary, several boutiques and even an outdoor movie theatre. The beachfront villas that climb the steep hills like treehouses are of Tahitian design and are cooled by the wind; their outdoor patios have hammocks. There are lots of activities for the whole family, not to mention good-value packages. 9

Leverick Bay Resort ⓣ284/495-7421 or 1-800/848-7081, ⓕ284/495-7367, ⓦwww.virgingordabvi.com. The cheapest accommodation in the North Sound, this resort is more a hotel, marina and collection of shops. The rooms, which at publication time were being renovated, are simple and offer great views of the bay. Amenities include a laundry, grocery store, charter services, scuba shop, salon and spa, several restaurants and bars, a pool, tennis court and gasoline. The North Sound Express ferry offers dockside access. An enormous selection of private villas are also available. 6

Saba Rock Resort ⓣ284/495-9966, ⓕ495-7373, ⓦwww.sabarock.com. This unusual eight-room hotel, marina, restaurant and bar is perched on a huge rock in the middle of the North Sound. The one- and two-bedroom villas are the nicest on the property (US$350–500); the beach units are the cheapest (US$150). 6

Spanish Town and The Valley

Fishers Cove Beach Hotel The Valley ⓣ284/495-5252 or 1-800/621-1270, ⓕ284/495-5820, ⓦwww.fischerscove.com. Located half a mile south of the Virgin Gorda Yacht Harbour, this small beachside complex offers individual cottages and hotel rooms – all with views of Sir Francis Drake Channel. The Garden View rooms have private patios and are the only rooms with air conditioners. During high season these rooms go for US$165 a night and there are special deals for stays of seven days or more. 6

Little Dix Bay Little Dix Bay ⓣ284/495-5555 or 1-800/928-3000, ⓕ284/495-5661, ⓦwww.littledixbay.com. A mile north of Spanish Town, this relaxed though very refined resort is set among rolling, flower-filled grounds near a crescent-shaped white-sand beach. The luxurious rooms come with comfortable rattan furniture and terracotta floors, and above all else, the service reigns: fresh ice is brought to your room several times a day. This is the sister resort to the highly successful *Caneel Bay* on St John, just a ninety-minute ferry ride away, and a package deal is offered for the pair. There are hiking trails, a fitness centre, floodlit tennis courts and even a tennis pro on hand for lessons. 9

Mango Bay Resort Mahoe Bay ⓣ284/495-5672, ⓕ495-5674, ⓦwww.mangobayresort.com. A small beachfront resort heavily influenced by Italian architecture and cuisine, and comprising nine duplex villas and two private homes), located on seven blooming acres. Three of the duplex villas are just thirty feet from the water. There are no tennis courts or gym, but the exquisite beach offers plenty of watersports. Nevertheless, it's rather pricey for what you get. 9

Olde Yard Inn North Sound Road, Spanish Town ⓣ284/495-5544 or 1-800/653-9273, ⓕ284/495-5986, ⓦwww.oldeyardinn.com. This fourteen-room inn is set on a hill overlooking Handsome Bay, amid a manicured garden with shady trees. The moderately priced rooms are simply designed, with cedar walls and balconies. It's not the most salubrious of locations, hence the huge wall surrounding the property. The inn has a pool and provides transportation to the beach in nearby Savannah Bay. 6

Paradise Beach Resort Mahoe Bay ⓣ284/495-5871, ⓕ495-5872. A small luxury resort tucked between steep hills and a beautiful beach protected by an offshore reef. Studios, one- and two-bedroom villas with ceramic tile roofs are available, all with a balcony and full kitchen and use of a jeep. There is no restaurant on site, but a private chef is provided (for an extra fee). Studios with garden views are the best deal here – US$125–185, but between US$250 and US$300 is average. 6

Beaches

The Baths may be more like your local swimming pool on the hottest day of the year, but Virgin Gorda has plenty of quiet **beaches** offering ample opportunity for long walks on endless white sand, quiet picnics, excellent snorkelling and wonderful sunsets. The best are accessible only by water so you'll need to hire a boat. **Prickly Pear Island** has a collection of secluded beaches including long, sandy Vixen Point,

Sand Box Beach and idyllic Lover's Beach – as you'd expect, the smallest and most private of them all. **Hay Point Beach** on the now-deserted island of Mosquito, is another good option.

If you feel like having some facilities nearby, **Deep Bay Beach** is a good bet; it's the official beach for *Biras Creek Resort* but you don't have to be a guest to frolic in the ocean or plant yourself on a beach chair. You can reach Deep Bay by hiking from *The Bitter End* or by hiring your own boat. The best beach for snorkelling, **Long Bay Beach**, just south of Mountain Point, can be reached by road or sea; if you're coming by car take Plum Tree Bay Road, a dirt road that winds due north away from North Sound Road about two miles out of Spanish Town. If you're staying in Spanish Town, **Savannah Bay Beach**, one mile of deserted beautiful white sand, is your closest option. When the beach at The Baths is too crowded, swim (or walk) north around the last outcropping of rocks to **Spring Bay Beach**, which offers more great boulders, snorkelling and sand without the crowds.

Eating

You can get anything from local food in the villages around Gun Creek to gourmet dining at lavish *Biras Creek Resort*. **Gun Creek** can be reached by ferry (the staff ferries from resorts to Gun Creek are free, but beware, they don't run late) or road. From the ferry dock, it's a short taxi ride or a steep uphill walk to the strip at the top for some cheap and delicious local food. Try *The Twin House* (Ⓣ284/495-7469) for large curried and boiled fish meals, *Gunney's* for simple fried chicken or *Angie's* Friday night barbecue. **Spanish Town** has plenty of moderately priced restaurants, most of which also double as bars and dance clubs (see opposite) later in the evening. If you want to make up a **picnic**, *The Wine Cellar and Bakery* (Virgin Gorda Yacht Harbour) is the best place to get a good bottle of wine, plus cookies and sandwiches to go.

North Sound

Biras Creek *Biras Creek Resort* Ⓣ284/494-3555. This elegant resort restaurant and bar on a hillside overlooking the North Sound welcomes non-guests for breakfast, lunch and dinner. Though pricey, the food is delicious; the halibut covered in an olive compote, lobster and chocolate fondant will leave you begging for more. Smart dress is required. Call for reservations.

The Clubhouse *Bitter End Yacht Club* Ⓣ284/494-2746. The resort's main restaurant serves steaks, seafood, pasta and a selection of fusion foods in an open-air dining room, just steps from the beach. Reservations are required.

Fat Virgin Café *Biras Creek Resort* Ⓣ284/495-7052. A small, inexpensive, outdoor restaurant, located at the resort's Marina Village, on the dock just east of the main *Biras* landing, serving everything from baby back ribs to flying fish sandwiches to burgers. Friday night is Chinese night. If you're staying at another North Sound resort, come by dinghy.

The Lighthouse Leverick Bay Ⓣ284/495-7154. Located on the waterfront, *The Lighthouse* is two restaurants in one: a refined upper level serving expensive grilled steak and seafood entrees, and a more casual, less expensive lower level offering great pizzas, burgers and conch fritters. Drinks also available from the bar. There's a happy hour every day 5–7pm (including 30¢ chicken wings), karaoke on Thursday night, and live music on Monday, Friday and Saturday nights during high season.

Saba Rock Restaurant North Sound Ⓣ284/495-7711. A unique dining experience on a small rock between Virgin Gorda and Prickly Pear. The changing nightly buffet (often with prime rib) costs US$25, while the Sunday West Indian buffet includes live pan music in the US$20 price. An à la carte menu offers burgers and sandwiches as well. Open for lunch and dinner. Also offers a free ferry for guests to and from any location in the North Sound.

The Sand Box Prickly Pear Ⓣ284/495-9122. This relaxed beach bar on the island of Prickly Pear is accessible only by water. Anchor your boat and swim ashore for the day – or arrange for your hotel to drop you off. Grab a sandwich for lunch, laze on the beach and then go back for a fish supper. Main courses start at around US$18.

Spanish Town

The Bath and Turtle Lee Road, Virgin Gorda Yacht Harbour Ⓣ284/495-5239. Tamarind ginger chicken wings (US$6.75), West Indian chicken sandwiches (US$9.75) or barbecue ribs (US$14.95) are just a few of the options for lunch or dinner (breakfast also served).

Chez Bamboo Spanish Town ☎284/495-5752. Located on the town's main strip, *Chez Bamboo* serves great New Orleans-style food and some of the strongest drinks you'll find on the island. Tucked away behind a sea of trees and vine-covered latticework, you can dine on dishes like bouillabaisse and desserts like the pumpkin pecan pie. Main courses are upwards of US$20.

The Crab Hole The Valley ☎284/495-5307. If you're hankering for some genuine local food, like callaloo soup, salt fish and stewed goat, this inexpensive spot is the place to go.

Mad Dog's The Valley ☎284/495-5830. By the entrance to The Baths, this is a great place for a burger, hot dog and beer – or the excellent piña coladas.

Mine Shaft Copper Mine Road, The Baths ☎284/495-5260. A lively restaurant, near the old copper mine, offering simple grilled items, sandwiches and salads. Monday is lobster night and Tuesday is West Indian barbecue night.

Olde Yard Inn (see also overleaf). While this hotel restaurant serves good food every night, Sunday night features an all-you-can-eat barbecue.

The Rock Café Tower Road ☎284/495-5472. The café, near The Baths, is a locals' favourite for dining, drinks and dancing. You can eat outside, at tables nestled between boulders, or inside under the A/C. The menu ranges from Italian to Mexican to Caribbean, and includes the café's specialty – the delicious Anegada lobster (US$27).

Top of the Baths The Baths ☎284/495-5497. Located as the name suggests on the hills above The Baths, this place serves breakfast, lunch and dinner, and is worth a visit for the views and sunsets alone. A piña colada completes the mood. The food is really good too – and not too expensive (around $10 for lunch; US$20 for dinner). Try the seafood ceviche appetizer followed by the succulent Cornish hen.

Drinking and nightlife

Nightlife on Virgin Gorda takes the form of hopping from bar to bar by boat for a mellow drink and live music – many of the **bars** have their own ferries connecting them to anywhere in the North Sound. **Gun Creek** is a good place to start. When you step off the ferry, grab a cold one at *The Last Stop Bar*, then, once up the hill, try the *Butterfly* for beer and dominoes or *Gunney's Cool Corner*, where you can drink cheaply, eat fresh-fried chicken wings, play pool or sing some serious karaoke. The party epicentre of the North Sound is *Saba Rock Resort*, with nightly **live music**, drink specials and dancing.

In Spanish Town a few of the restaurants (see opposite for details) liven up later in the evening. *The Bath and Turtle* has two happy hours daily (10.30–11.30am and 4–6pm) as well as live music, usually pan, calypso or reggae, every Wednesday night. *Chez Bamboo* hops on Friday nights when locals and tourists come to dance and party and *La Tequila* above *The Rock Café* heats up after the last meal is served downstairs. The *Mine Shaft* is the location for Virgin Gorda's monthly **full-moon party**, inspired by *Bomba's Shack* on Tortola (see p.435); try their signature drink – The Cave-In. *Thelma's Hideout* (☎284/495-5636), at the edge of *Little Dix Bay*, might be difficult to find, but it's unmissable. Thelma is a character, who will drink beer and play darts with you all night long. There's also a pool table and the occasional live band or DJ.

Watersports and outdoor activities

Many **fishing** boats from Tortola (see p.438) will also pick up guests on Virgin Gorda for a day of deep-sea or sport fishing. At **BVI Watersports** (☎284/495-7558), Captain Bennu offers various packages around the sound, or try **Captain Kevin Gray** (☎284/495-6666), who has two boats, one for inshore light tackle and one for offshore deep-sea fishing. Rates range from US$350 for a half-day to US$950 for a full day.

Virgin Gorda isn't especially known for its **hiking**, but a few simple nature trails thread the hills connecting *Biras Creek* to *The Bitter End*; both resorts provide free maps to guests and non-guests alike. You can also hike to the top of **Virgin Gorda Peak National Park** (see p.440). Most of the resorts have **tennis** facilities, free to guests but also open to non-guests for around US$6–10 per hour. *Biras Creek*, *Leverick Bay* and *Little Dix Bay* have the most courts.

Watersports

The North Sound in particular offers excellent **watersports** opportunities – the companies below are recommended. Many outfits operating out of Tortola (see p.437–38) also provide watersports for travellers on Virgin Gorda.

Bitter End Yacht Club ⓣ284/494-2746. The club offers equipment rentals, lessons and charters: kayaks, Lasers, Hobies, Rhodes19s, J24s and Freedom 30s. Also located here is the Nick Trotter Sailing School (ⓣ284/494-2745).

Dive BVI ⓣ284/495-5513, ⓦwww.divebvi.com. This dive shop in Leverick Bay (with a branch at Yacht Harbour) has been in business since 1975 and offers rentals, sales, dive trips and five-star PADI training. Trips hit all the hot spots – a two-tanker is US$85. Beach and snorkel trips to Anegada depart twice daily.

Kilbrides Sunchaser Scuba ⓣ284/495-9638. Located at the *Bitter End*, this is the most established dive outfit in the BVI and Kilbride is a legend in the area. Daily trips include The Dogs, Salt, Ginger and Cooper islands as private charters or groups. Lessons range from beginner to dive-master.

Leverick Bay Watersports ⓣ284/495-7376. You can rent boats ranging from ten-foot dinghies to a 28-foot Parrotfish powerboat here. They also rent out small sailboats, kayaks and offer water-skiing, wake boarding and parasailing.

North Sound Watersports For boat charters, day trips and deep-sea fishing. Glass-bottom boat reef tours cost US$20 per hour and jet ski rentals US$70 an hour.

Spice ⓣ284/495-7044. Half-, full- and multi-day trips for sightseers and snorkellers. Prices range from US$35 per person for sunset boat trips up to US$600 for full-day private charter for up to eight people.

Spirit of Anegada ⓣ284/495-5937. Book a day of sailing and snorkelling aboard this old-fashioned 44-foot gaff schooner with its wooden helm and authentic details. Group charters for a full day are US$85 per person, while a full-day private charter for up to six people costs US$550.

Jost Van Dyke

JOST VAN DYKE, named after the seventeenth-century Dutch pirate who made it his hideaway, is a tiny, undeveloped, mountainous island three miles off the north-west coast of Tortola. This idyll of wooded hills and secluded bays has changed little since a Quaker colony settled here in the 1700s to farm sugarcane – in fact most of the island's 160 inhabitants (all either Chinnerys or Callwoods) are descended from Quaker slaves. The island has only had electricity for ten years, not everywhere has running water, there's only one paved road and the low-key tourist scene owes much to the yachts that stop here to clear **customs** in Great Harbour. Yet sailors and tourists alike flock here to enjoy the magical combination of friendly locals, unspoilt beauty and party atmosphere: two of its **bars** are famous and have helped earn Jost Van Dyke the title of party capital of BVI.

The three main areas of activity are all on the south side of the island and accessible by car or boat. The focal point is the palm-fringed beach and settlement of **Great Harbour**. The beach isn't the best on the island for swimming but has the advantage of being close to the amenities along sandy laid-back Main Street, where you'll find rooms for rent, a handful of bars, boutiques, a provision store and even an ice cream shop. *Foxy's* (see opposite), tucked in the corner, is the major draw. **White Bay**, half a mile to the west beyond Pull and Be Damm Point, has the island's best beach and is home to its other famous drinking hole, the *Soggy Dollar Bar* (see p.446), as well as a hotel and a few bars and shops. Just over a mile to the east of Great Harbour, **Little Harbour** is a good place to eat – the spiny lobster here will be the biggest you've seen in your life. Although no scuba **diving** or sailing outfits operate on Jost Van Dyke, many on Tortola will pick you up if you're staying on the island. You can rent dinghies from Sharkies Dinghy Rental at Little Harbour (ⓣ284/495-9487).

Getting around

Taxis in Great Harbour Bay will take you to White Bay for about US$5 and to Little Harbour for around a dollar more (or call George's Land Taxi ⓣ284/495-9253 or White Stone Taxi Service ⓣ284/495-9487). There's also Bun's Tequila **Water Taxi** (ⓣ284/495-9281). Jost Van Dyke's only paved road runs along the eastern and southern shore of the island – there are two **rentals cars** on the entire island, assuming both are working. The company that owns them, Paradise Jeep Rentals (ⓣ284/495-9477), has its offices in a gas station within walking distance of Great Harbour. Note that there are no banks on Jost Van Dyke.

Accommodation

Despite persistent rumours of imminent major development on Jost Van Dyke, the island still has only one hotel among its limited **accommodation** options, which also include private villas, guesthouses and a **campsite** at White Bay, *White Bay Campground* (ⓣ284/495-9312), which offers bare sites for US$15 a night, sites equipped with tents for US$35, plus small and large screen-windowed cabins for US$50–60. Special barbecue, chicken and fish buffets are offered throughout the week, but there's also a shared kitchen for cooking and storing refrigerated foods.

Wherever you choose, though, it pays to call ahead and reserve. Rooms can be rustic and the lack of flush toilets and air conditioning will be inconvenient for some.

Christine's Guest House ⓣ284/495-9281. Located upstairs from *Christine's Bakery* and within walking distance of Great Harbour, this small bed and breakfast with basic rooms for two to three people is popular with sailors in need of a break from cramped and often hot sailboat sleeping. 3–4

Rudy's Mariners Inn ⓣ284/495-9282. Five simple rooms that aren't good for much more than crashing, thanks to the noisy bar downstairs. 4

Sandcastle White Bay ⓣ284/495-9888, ⓕ495-9999, ⓦwww.sandcastle-bvi.com. The best lodging on the island, although this hotel only updated to electricity in 1996. Six large beachfront cottages (with outdoor showers) are cooled by fans, while the newer, more hotel-like cottages have A/C. There is also a restaurant, bar and beach to enjoy. Day sails, scuba diving and fishing can be scheduled through KC the bartender. 7

Sandy Ground Estates Little Harbour ⓣ284/494-3391 or 1-800/284-8300, ⓦwww.sandyground.com. Eight secluded villas with a private beach and featuring stunning ocean views from tiled terraces. Most are two-bedroom and are available by the week only. It's out of the way so bring enough food and drink for your stay or ring ahead and ask the staff to stock your villa with provisions. 9

White Bay Villas White Bay ⓣ410/571-6692, ⓦwww.jostvandyke.com. Six lovely villas perched above this idyllic bay and moments from the beach. The villas range in size from a huge plantation with three bedrooms and three bathrooms to a one-bedroom unit. Stays are usually arranged by the week, but the owners try to accommodate shorter stays. 8

Eating and drinking

Despite its small size Jost Van Dyke has a surprisingly vibrant **eating and drinking** scene and, with the famous *Foxy* at the helm, it's the party island of the BVI. Most of the fun takes place during the day, particularly on weekends, in a variety of places in Great Harbour Bay, Little Bay and White Bay, some of which are no more than beachside shacks with no running water.

Christine's Bakery Great Harbour ⓣ284/495-9281. This quiet little place is great for breakfast or an afternoon sandwich – the banana bread is a treat.

Club Paradise Great Harbour ⓣ284/405-9267. Great West Indian food like conch stew and curried chicken. Every Wednesday night there's a pig roast, and there's occasional live music and limbo.

Foxy's Great Harbour ⓣ284/495-9258. This is the bar that put Jost Van Dyke firmly on the yachters' map. When you think about waterfront bars, island music and beach barbecues, *Foxy's* is the standard by which everything else should be compared. Sit at picnic tables under the thatched roof or stretch out on the beach, drinking and eating (lobster, grilled fish, rotis and sandwiches). A legend throughout the BVI, larger-than-life Foxy Callwood himself does twice daily shows (Mon–Sat) – playing calypso and telling stories and jokes (but call ahead to see if Foxy feels like playing that day). Barbecue nights are Friday and Saturday.

Ivan's Stress Free Bar White Bay Campground ☎284/495-9358. *Ivan's* has a barbecue (US$20) and live music Thursday and Friday nights. The bar operates on an honour system, so be sure to keep your own tab and pay when you leave.

Sandcastle Restaurant White Bay ☎284/495-9888. Non-guests can make reservations (and should, by 4pm) to eat with guests of the hotel at the large communal table. Jost Van Dyke's only fine-dining option, with a set menu of lamb, duck, crab cakes and the like for around US$35. (No dinner on Friday.)

Sidney's Peace and Love Little Harbour ☎284/495-9271. A more reserved *Foxy's*, this is a Jost Van Dyke institution that's been serving up food and fun for over 25 years. Choose from steak, shrimp, ribs, chicken and conch stew, plus hearty helpings of rice and peas, coleslaw, potato salad, steamed vegetables and corn for US$18–25. However, the highlight here is lobster, bigger than anywhere else on the islands. Sidney still catches them himself and cooks them over an open fire the island way. Thursday night has all-you-can-eat lobster and live music for US$39.

Soggy Dollar Bar *Sandcastle Hotel*, White Bay ☎284/495-9888. Named for the wet bills brought by patrons who swim to the bar, *The Soggy Dollar*, located right on the beach, is perhaps best known as the inventor of the Painkiller, a potent mix of dark rum, pineapple and orange juices, coco lopez and fresh nutmeg. Saturday and Sunday are especially fun but can get very crowded. Local musician, Ruben Chinnery, plays a mixture of blues and Jimmy Buffet-esque island tunes every Sunday afternoon. Sandwiches are available at lunch.

Anegada

Lying fourteen miles north of Virgin Gorda, remote **ANEGADA** is the odd Virgin out – a flat coral and limestone atoll almost completely surrounded by the **Horseshoe Reef**, one of the world's largest. The waters are treacherous to shipping – a plethora of wrecked crafts litter the reef – but this only adds to the already excellent **snorkelling** and **diving** that draws day-trippers by the boatloads. Anegada is also famed for its **lobster**, miles of undeveloped **beaches** and some of the best **bonefishing** in the world.

The best of the beaches, miles of pristine white sand, and snorkelling are on the north coast. At **LOBLOLLY BAY**, a picture-postcard Caribbean paradise with a bar and restaurant, the waters teem with schools of mojarra, needlefish and mantis shrimp. On the western side of the beach, the dark reef area in middle of the lagoon contains three small caves and a wreck, among which you'll spot elkhorn and brain coral, angelfish, snapper and huge grouper. **Cow Wreck Beach**, six miles to the west, is another good snorkelling spot; it has a changing room, plus food and drinks. Anegada's natural assets aren't limited to its reefs; the whole island is a **wildlife sanctuary**, home to turtles, birdlife, including flamingo and osprey, and the endangered rock iguanas, which are bred and protected in its carefully monitored reserves.

Anegada Harbour, on the southwest coast, is nothing much to speak of – just a long, thin dock with lobster traps tied to its side – but it's a good place to base yourself for exploring the island. The area, which includes Pomato Point and Setting Point, has plenty of lodging, restaurants, bars and gift-shops. The little **Pomato Point Museum** (☎284/495-8038) is worth a visit for its small but evocative display of items recovered from shipwrecks around the island, ranging from cannons to gin bottles. Around four miles east of here (southeast of the airport) is **The Settlement**, where most of the island's 150 inhabitants live. You'll find diners, bakeries, a post office and a police station here.

Arrival and getting around

Most hotels offer guests a free shuttle from the island's **airport**. Getting around the island is fairly easy – the main road loops round to most of the main places of interest – and, for once, given the flat terrain, **cycling** is a realistic option, for short distances anyway. It gets very hot and dusty on the shadeless roads so always carry plenty of water and a hat. *The Anegada Reef Hotel* (see below), on the front of the harbour dock, can help you schedule everything from bike rental to car rental to a shuttle ride to beaches on the north side of the island (US$6). Alternatively, call Anegada Taxi (Ⓣ284/495-0228) or rent a vehicle (around US$40 per day) through ABC Car Rentals (Ⓣ284/495-9466) or DW Jeep Rentals (Ⓣ284/495-8018).

Accommodation

Most of the **accommodation** on the island is located on the **south shore** and is fairly basic, though there is something to suit all budgets, including a great **campsite** at Loblolly Bay. With surroundings like these, though, you can't really do better than go back to nature by staying in one of the simple **beachfront cabins** that will make you feel like Robinson Crusoe.

Anegada Beach Cottages Pomato Point Ⓣ916/683-3352, Ⓦwww.anegadabeachcottages.com. Three fully furnished cottages with modern kitchen and bathroom set on a private beach (no A/C but plenty of cooling sea breezes). There are two one-bedroom cottages and one double cottage linked by connecting door. ⑥

Anegada Reef Hotel Setting Point, Anegada Harbour Ⓣ284/495-8002, Ⓕ495-9362, Ⓦwww.anegadareef.com. This lovely hotel, located at the head of the harbour, is pretty much the focal point of the island acting as a de facto tour operator arranging beach shuttles, rental cars and fishing trips. Stay in one of its twenty rooms or three cottages and eat a fantastic lobster meal in its restaurant. ⑦

Mac's Campground Loblolly Bay Ⓣ284/495-8020. Set just back from the beach under shady trees, this is a great little campground in the middle of Loblolly Bay with ten tent platforms (bare sites are around US$15, with a tent US$35). The site has basic facilities – showers and a kitchen – and a bar.

Neptune's Treasure Anegada Harbour Ⓣ284/495-9439. Primarily a restaurant and bar, but there are also four comfortable guesthouse double and single rooms, all with private baths. ④

Ocean Range Hotel The Settlement Ⓣ284/495-9522. If you'd rather stay this side of the island, you're best off here – six simple units with private outdoor balconies, all with A/C, TV, private baths and kitchenettes. ③–④

Pomato Point Cottages Anegada Harbour Ⓣ284/495-9466. Simple beachfront cottages that rent for US$100 per day. Perhaps the best deal on the island – and a very good location. ④

Eating and drinking

Most **restaurants** catch their own **seafood** and will be happy to tell you where and how it was caught. The local specialty, the spindly but huge **Anegada lobster**, is delicious and worth ordering at least once. For dinner at any of the following it's advisable to call ahead and make a reservation.

Anegada Reef Hotel (see also above). Popular dining spot where hotel guests dine alongside leather-faced boaters for cocktails and a candlelit dinner of grilled fish, chicken, steak and lobster (don't worry, you can still wear your shorts). Main courses start at US$20.

The Big Bamboo The North Side Ⓣ284/495-2019. This huge restaurant in Loblolly Bay caters to the beach crowd, with a good lunch and dinner menu – crab cakes, fish and shrimp, ribs, lobster and burgers too. All meals come with rice and fried plantains, while the drink of choice is the Rum Teaser.

Cow Wreck Beach Bar and Grill Ⓣ284/495-8047. Wash down conch fritters, lobster salad or Belle's famous lobster with the bar's own Wreck Punch. Serves lunch and dinner.

Dotsy's Bakery The Settlement Ⓣ284/495-9667. Dotsy's delicious home-made tarts, breads and cakes are a great way to start the day; or stop by for lunch or dinner – she also serves up sandwiches, pizza, chicken and burgers.

Neptune's Treasure Anegada Harbour T284/495-9439. The owners catch, cook and serve their own grilled fish and lobster – main courses for around US$20.

Pomato Point Restaurant Anegada Harbour ⓣ284/495-8038. Located at Pomato Point, this hot spot serves lunches and dinners of chicken, ribs, fish and lobster. The daily happy hour is from 5pm to 6pm and there's live music every Wednesday.

Watersports

Anegada doesn't have much in the way of organized **watersports** but the *Anegada Reef Hotel* (see overleaf) can help you book fishing trips and also rents out dive equipment, snorkelling gear and sea kayaks. Alternatively, both Virgin Gorda (see pp.443–44) and Tortola (see pp.437–38) have charter operators that run snorkelling and fishing trips to Anegada. Boardsailing BVI (see p.437) arranges windsurfing trips to Anegada. If you want to try your hand at **bonefishing**, your best and cheapest bet is simply to walk around The Settlement inquiring about guides.

Outlying islands

There are a few islands accessible from Tortola that are worth a visit. **PETER ISLAND**, three miles across the Francis Drake Channel from Tortola, is home to the luxurious *Peter Island Resort and Yacht Harbour* (ⓣ284/495-2000 or 1-800/346-4457, ⓕ284/495-2500, ⓦwww.peterisland.com; ⑨), which offers sea-view rooms, an all-inclusive range of watersports, tennis, bikes, hiking and sailing activities, and extremely elegant dining at its *Tradewinds Restaurant* (also open to non-guests). Non-guests can visit the island and use the secluded, palm-fringed beaches – the Peter Island Ferry (ⓣ284/494-9647) connects the island with Road Town on Tortola (US$14 one-way; free if you have a reservation at *Tradewinds*). There's more casual fare – wood-oven pizzas and salads – available at *Deadman's Beach Bar and Grill*. Peaceful, unpretentious and good value, **COOPER ISLAND**, four miles east of Peter Island, has a lone hotel and a few vacation homes. *The Cooper Island Beach Club* (ⓣ413/863-3162 or 1-800/542-4624, ⓕ413/863-3662, ⓦwww.cooper-island.com) offers twelve doubles (⑦) and two beach houses (ⓣ513/232-4126; ⑨) set on beautiful **Manchioneel Bay** with its long beach and fantastic snorkelling – the thick, sea grass attracts a dazzling assortment of green turtles, eagle rays and huge queen conch. There are no roads and no cars on the island – the ferry (ⓣ284/494-3311) that carts guests and non-guests (US$10) back and forth from the *Prospect Reef Resort* on Tortola is the only access.

Eight-acre **MARINA CAY**, which offers great snorkelling, was made famous by author Robb White and his wife, Rodie, who moved here in 1936, built a home and lived without running water or electricity. His book about the experience, *Two on an Isle*, was made into a movie in the 1950s, starring Sidney Poitier. The only place to stay on the island is *Marina Cay Resort* (ⓣ284/494-2174, ⓕ494-4775, ⓦwww.pussers.com; ⑦), connected to Trellis Bay by a short ferry ride (8 daily; free), which has basic rooms or two-bedroom villas. The old White residence is still here, recently restored by Pusser's (owners of the resort) into *The Hilltop Bar*; it hosts barbecues, and has live music. A more extensive menu is available at the *Pusser's* beachside restaurant, whose bar has a happy hour daily from 4pm to 7pm.

Uninhabited and largely untamed **NORMAN ISLAND**, the westernmost BVI, is only accessible by hired boat and there are no places to stay, yet thousands of people in high season flock here every day to snorkel and soak up the party atmosphere – and look for gold. Rumours are that there is hidden **treasure** all over the island – three chests of gold have reportedly been discovered since the mid-1700s, and it's stories such as these that have led some to suggest that Norman Island was the model for Robert Louis Stevenson's *Treasure Island*.

The party scene revolves around two **bars** (both of which also serve food). *Billy Bones* (ⓣ284/494-4770, ⓦwww.billybones.net), with its own private stretch of beach, draws crowds with its strong drinks and loud music. The other hot spot, the bar/restaurant *The Willy T* (Ⓣ284/494-0183, Ⓦwww.williamthornton.com), is a converted schooner permanently moored in the Bight, a large bay and a popular anchorage for yachters. It's one of the most raucous and unusual drinking spots in the BVI and the top deck often sees inebriated patrons removing their clothes and diving into the water.

Anguilla

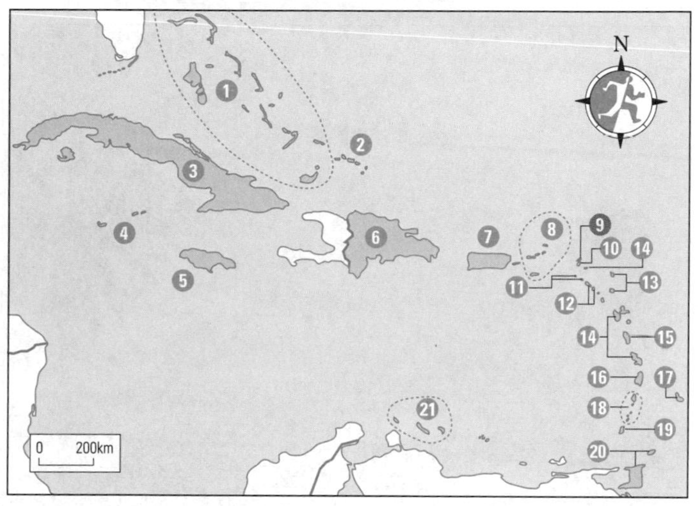

Anguilla Highlights

✱ **Shoal Bay** One of the region's greatest beaches, big enough that you'll find your own quiet spot away from the crowds, and dotted with several good restaurants. See p.458

✱ **Scilly Cay** Take the ferry out to this tiny island and snack on tasty fresh lobster, grilled for you right by the beach. See p.459

Introduction and Basics

Barely 35 square miles in size, and rising to a highest point of just over two hundred feet, Anguilla has an interior that is dry, dusty and covered in scrubby vegetation. However, this fact is largely ignored by an increasing stream of visitors who beat their way here for the glorious turquoise waters and truly stunning beaches. Some of these, particularly Rendezvous Bay in the southwest and Shoal Bay in the northeast, are among the finest in the Caribbean.

Long ignored by tourists, tiny Anguilla has benefited from careful study of the planning mistakes that have badly damaged neighbours like **St Martin/St Maarten**, where runaway development has led to rising crime and serious social problems. By contrast, Anguilla has eschewed large-scale tourist complexes, successfully aiming for top-quality, high-end development with relatively limited impact on the island's scarce resources. As a result, the island feels very safe, welcoming and relaxed. If you're happy with beach wandering, watersports and plenty of good restaurants, Anguilla is hard to beat.

Like other Caribbean islands Anguilla is a year-round destination; however, the best time to visit is between mid-December and mid-April when rainfall is low and the heat is tempered by cooling trade winds.

Getting there

Visitors arrive by plane at **Wallblake Airport** in the very centre of the island and by ferry at Blowing Point on the south coast. There are no direct **flights** from Europe or North America, but American Eagle, Winair and LIAT provide daily connecting services from Puerto Rico, St St Martin and Antigua respectively. Daily **ferries** run from Marigot Bay in St Martin to Blowing Point in Anguilla every thirty minutes from 8am to 7pm, the journey taking 25 minutes and costing US$10 each way.

For phone numbers of airlines, see pp.12–18 and 36–37.

Getting around

There is no public transportation system, so you'll need to **rent a car** if you want to explore the island. Options include Carib (☎264/497-6020), Connor's (☎264/497-6433) or Triple K (☎264/497-2934) and you can expect to pay US$45–50 a day. Most of the rental companies are based in The Valley, but will normally either deliver to your hotel or pick you up and bring you to their offices. **Temporary licences** cost US$20 and are supplied by the car rental company. Vehicles drive on the left.

Taxis are available on ☎264/497-5054 and 497-6089.

Consulates

The **UK** is represented in Anguilla by a governor (☎264/497-2621, ℗264/497-2292). There are no US, Canadian, Australian or New Zealand embassies or commissions in Anguilla.

Departure tax

The **departure tax** is US$10 at the airport, US$2 for ferry departure.

Phones, post and email

Telephone kiosks are scattered around the island; most take phonecards, sold at many shops and hotels or at the Cable and Wireless office in The Valley.

The **post office** is in The Valley and open Monday to Friday 8.30am–3.30pm.

Most hotels will let you hook up to their **internet** connection for minimal or no charge, and there's an internet café at *Ripples* restaurant in Sandy Ground.

The **country code** for Anguilla is ☎264.

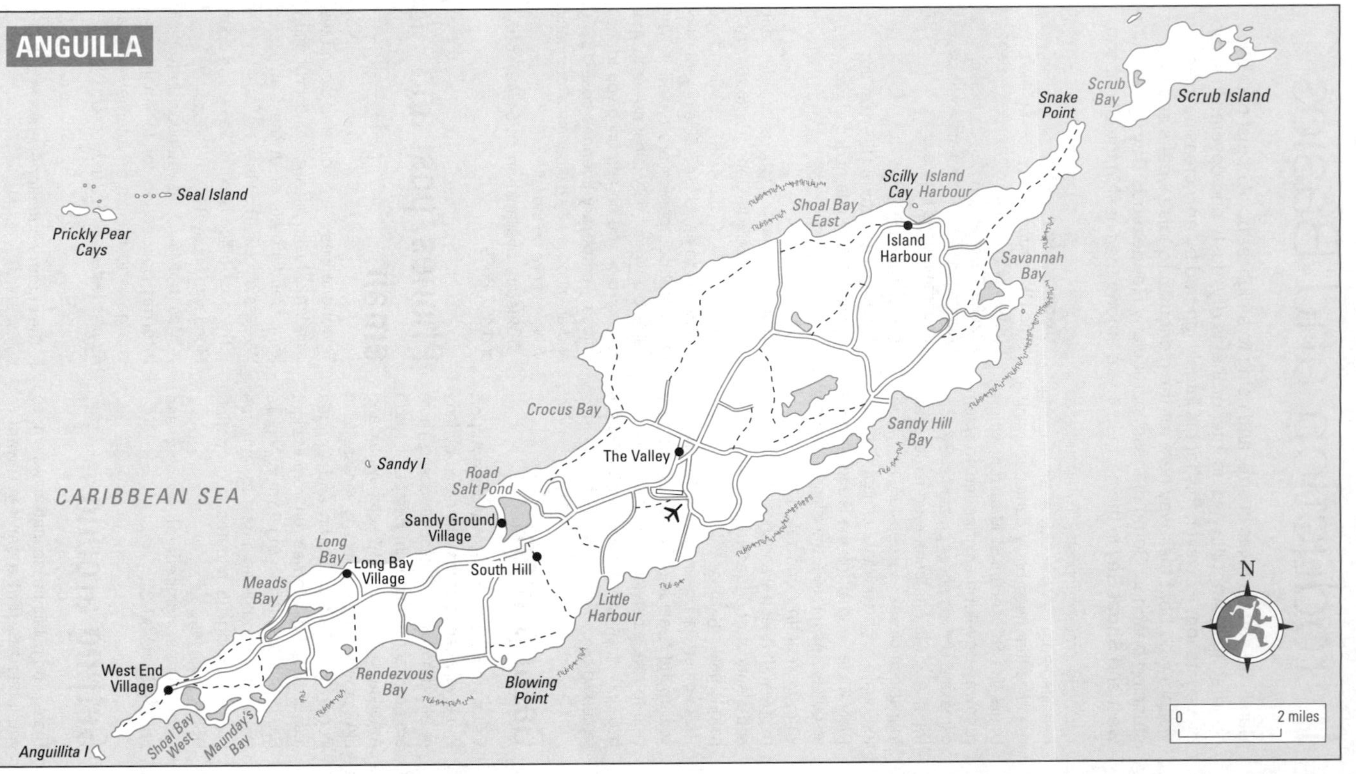
ANGUILLA
Dog Island & The Cays
Seal Island
Prickly Pear Cays
Scrub Island
Scrub Bay
Snake Point
Scilly Cay
Island Harbour
Island Harbour
Shoal Bay East
Savannah Bay
Sandy Hill Bay
Crocus Bay
The Valley
Sandy I
Road Salt Pond
CARIBBEAN SEA
Sandy Ground Village
Long Bay
Long Bay Village
South Hill
Meads Bay
Little Harbour
Rendezvous Bay
Blowing Point
West End Village
Shoal Bay West
Maunday's Bay
Anguillita I
N
0
2 miles

Information and maps

The helpful **tourist office** is just across from Wallblake House (☎264/497-2944, ®www.ahta.ai) and open Monday to Friday 8.30am–5pm. They have a free map of the island (which you'll also find at many of the hotels). You'll also find useful information at ®www.anguilla-vacation.com

Money and costs

The official currency of Anguilla is the **Eastern Caribbean dollar (EC$)**, although US dollars are widely accepted. The EC$ is divided into 100 cents. Bills come in denominations of 5, 10, 20, 50 and 100 EC dollars; coins in 1, 2, 5, 10 and 25 cents. At the time of writing, the **rate of exchange** was roughly EC$2.70 to US$1.

Credit cards are taken at most hotels and restaurants.

Most of the **banks** are in The Valley and include Barclays, Scotia and National Bank of Anguilla, normally open from Monday to Thursday 8am–2pm and Friday 8am–4pm.

Seafood aside, almost everything is imported, so prices are relatively high. To compound matters, a 15 percent **service charge** is added to your bill at many restaurants, and 18 percent in **tax** and service charges at most hotels.

For ambulance, fire and police dial ☎911.

Holidays and festivals

As well as the public holidays listed on p.45, Anguilla celebrates **Anguilla Day** on May 30, **Constitution Day** on August 6 and **Separation Day** on December 19.

There's a fun but fairly low-key summer **carnival**, normally during the first week of August, with boat races, live bands, a Miss Anguilla pageant and a calypso show. Boat races are also held over Easter weekend and during the run-up to the carnival – keep an eye out in the newspapers and free tourist magazines for locations and times.

Language

Much as in other former British colonies, the official language of Anguilla is **English**.

History

Amerindians are thought to have settled in Anguilla around 1500 BC, living in small settlements dotted around the island. Major remains have been found at twenty sites including the Fountain (see p.458), the island's only natural spring, near Shoal Bay. Columbus missed the island on his trips to the New World in the 1490s, but Spanish explorers who passed by shortly afterwards named the island Anguilla (Spanish for eel) for its long thin shape.

The first Europeans to establish a permanent base here were the **British**, who arrived in 1650 and began growing tobacco and cotton, and raising livestock with a small number of imported slaves. Short on rainfall, and without the size or the quality of soil to enable its plantations to compete with nearby islands, Anguilla never really flourished. Those who could afford to leave made off for more prosperous islands.

For centuries the islanders who remained managed on little more than **subsistence farming** and **fishing**. Furthermore, they developed a reputation for boat building and seamanship, running boats that exported salt and fish and carried local men off for seasonal work in the sugar fields of Santo Domingo (present-day Dominican Republic) and the oil refineries of Aruba and Curaçao.

After World War II, with its major Caribbean colonies pressing for independence, Britain showed little interest in continuing to maintain Anguilla. For convenience, it was decided in the 1960s that the island should be administered alongside nearby **St Kitts** and **Nevis**, and a union of the islands was put in place. Anguillans, who regarded the politicians on St Kitts as arrogant and bullying, were outraged and demonstrated against the union. They declared independence, sending home the policemen installed by St Kitts and calling in a Harvard law professor to draft a national constitution.

Showing a wholly disproportionate reaction, British troops decided to invade and crush **"The Rebellion"**. In March 1969 a crack battalion of over three hundred stormed ashore, only to be met by local citizens waving flags and demanding to be put back directly under British rule. Not a shot was fired, and the event was dubbed Britain's Bay of Piglets.

Shame-faced, Britain resumed direct responsibility for Anguilla, which it has maintained to this day, with the island run by an elected government but the British-appointed Governor in charge of matters of defence and foreign policy. **Tourism** took off in the 1980s, when day-trippers from nearby St Martin/St Maarten began to arrive in droves. Today the industry drives the local economy, leaving fewer and fewer of its nearly 10,000 inhabitants dependent on the trade in lobster and fish that sustained previous generations.

9.1

The island

Anguilla is centred around its modest capital, **The Valley**, from which roads head both east and west to the island's fine beaches and natural attractions, chief among them shimmering **Shoal Bay East** and **Rendezvous Bay**. There are no towns or villages as such on the island, and the closest thing you'll find are the small clusters of houses found in areas such as **Sandy Ground** and **Island Harbour**.

Accommodation

Most **accommodation options** on Anguilla are at the expensive/luxury end of the scale, many of them on their own superb stretch of beach (open to guests and non-guests alike), but there are a few good options in other price ranges, though they may be harder to find at peak times such as Christmas and Easter. Conversely, during the slow season, including most of the summer, prices at the top hotels can fall dramatically.

Anguilla Great House Beach Resort Rendezvous Bay ⓣ264/497-6061, ⓕ497-6019, ⓦhttp://66.197.138.54/index.html. Attractive and quiet spot, with 27 rooms in a series of cottages spread over a large resort beside Rendezvous Bay, with a good pool and restaurant and watersports equipment. 8

Arawak Beach Inn Island Harbour ⓣ264/497-4888, ⓕ497-4889, ⓦwww.arawakbeach.com. Seventeen colourful and spacious rooms, all with patios or balconies, furnished with Caribbean art and a stone's throw from the harbour. There's a freshwater pool and the restaurant offers up good food all day. 7

Cap Juluca Maunday's Bay ⓣ264/497-6666, ⓕ497-6617, ⓦwww.capjuluca.com. Fabulous resort with accommodation strung out along one of the island's best beaches in tasteful and ultra-comfortable villas. The whole place is designed for maximum relaxation with minimal effort and distraction, right down to the shaded sun loungers discreetly placed at a good distance from your neighbour and periodically called on by staff offering a cooling drink or sorbet. Rooms start at US$735 in winter.

Casa Nadine The Valley ⓣ264/497-2358. The simplest accommodation option on the island. Eleven no-nonsense rooms, perfectly adequate if all you're looking for is a cheap place to crash in between days on the beach. 2 year-round.

Easy Corner Villas South Hill ⓣ264/497-6433, ⓕ497-6410. Twenty-two reasonable, self-catering apartments just back from the main road in South Hill and a short drive from the nearest beach. All have rattan furniture, cable TV, A/C, decent-sized bedrooms and a fully equipped kitchen. Single bed villas 7 (though you can often negotiate at quiet times).

Rendezvous Bay Hotel Rendezvous Bay ⓣ264/497-6549, ⓕ497-6026, ⓦwww.rendezvousbay.com. Friendly, longstanding hotel on superb Rendezvous Beach and offering some of the best value on the island. Rooms are a good size and well furnished, and many have balconies or patios, the best with great sea views. There's an excellent outdoor restaurant on site. 5

Seaview Sandy Ground ⓣ264/497-2427. Just two one-bedroom apartments at *Seaview* but probably the best value in the area (3). Clean and comfortable, and close to good inexpensive places to eat and drink. If they're full, there are similar places nearby in Sandy Ground – try *Syd-An's* (ⓣ264/497-3180, ⓕ497-5381; 3) or *La Palma* (ⓣ264/497-3260, ⓕ497-5381; 4).

Shoal Bay Villas Shoal Bay East ⓣ264/497-2051, ⓕ497-3631. Choice location on the white sands at Shoal Bay East and fifteen comfortable and good-sized rooms ranging from studios (9) and one-bedroom apartments (US$295) to three-bedroom villas (US$445). All have their own kitchen and there's a restaurant, a pool and watersports equipment.

The Valley

A couple of minutes' drive from the airport and pretty much in the dead centre of the island, **THE VALLEY** is Anguilla's only town but not a place where you'll want to spend a great deal of time. It's a functional rather than inspiring place, home to government, banks and the main shops, and with little of historic or architectural interest.

The main sight of note is **Wallblake House** (Tues–Fri 10am–noon; US$5), built in 1787 by a local sugar planter and one of the oldest buildings on Anguilla. The house and its outbuildings of stables and kitchens are not on the scale of plantation houses to be found elsewhere in the Caribbean – a sign that planters here were less successful – but the combination of thick-cut stone and intricately carved timber is undeniably attractive. Donated to the Catholic Church in 1959, the house proved too small for holding services and the adjoining St Gerard's Catholic Church with its peculiar cobbled stone frontage was therefore built in 1966.

West of The Valley

A mile west of The Valley, **Sandy Ground** is the island's main low-budget hangout area, with a number of inexpensive places to stay and eat and a friendly and relaxed atmosphere. There's a nice beach, and the tiny village backs onto a large salt pond popular with local birdlife; islanders used to rake salt here for export to the Americas until the costs became prohibitive. Offshore, visible from Sandy Ground, **Sandy Island** is a tiny deserted isle with a handful of palm trees, just six hundred feet long and a great place for snorkelling and swimming. If you go in the early morning, before any of the day-trippers from St Martin arrive, you may well have the island to yourself. Boats (US$10 round-trip) leave from the pier between about 9.30am and 4pm whenever there's demand and there's a beach bar on the island that sells lunch and drinks.

South of Sandy Ground the road leads down through the residential area of South Hill to Blowing Point, where the ferries from St Martin dock (see p.453 for ferry details). There's little to see in either of these places, but just east of Blowing Point, the sparkling white sand that fringes **Rendezvous Bay** offers one of the island's most spectacular beaches – the two-mile crescent is a great place to find shells. Head past the *Anguilla Great House Beach Resort* for public access to the beach.

Further west still, there's more blindingly white sand at **Maunday's Bay**, home to exclusive *Cap Juluca*, one of the island's top-notch resorts (see overleaf), while west of here Shoal Bay West is another curve of lovely white sand that's worth a visit if you're touring the island.

East of The Valley

Wherever you're staying on Anguilla, it's worth making the journey out to **Shoal Bay East** on the island's northeastern coast, where you'll find one of the finest beaches in the Eastern Caribbean, backed by coconut palms and sea grape. The pristine white sand shelves gently down to the turquoise waters and, though it's often busy, you can always find your own patch of beach and water. Snorkelling gear, lounge chairs and towels can be rented from outlets around the *Shoal Bay Villas* resort where you'll also find a series of laid-back bars and cafés (see overleaf).

At the west end of Shoal Bay, a dirt track leads to **The Fountain** – a cave that is the island's most important archeological site, where many Amerindian petroglyphs were found in 1979. The petroglyphs include rare depictions of deities – including a 2000-year-old carving of Jocahu, their supreme God – and the site may well have been a religious or ceremonial centre and even a place for pilgrimage from other islands. Sadly, although the government has long had plans to develop the area as a national park, the Fountain remains closed in order to preserve the petroglyphs.

Further east, **Island Harbour** is home to much of Anguilla's fishing fleet, along with a touch of tourist development. While it's not especially pretty, it's one of the most engaging parts of the island with its brightly painted boats and fishermen laying out their catch for sale. It's also worth making the trip to the harbour to catch a boat out to tiny **Scilly Cay** (see review below), where you can have an excellent lunch at the restaurant and swim and snorkel in the clear waters.

At the extreme east end of the island, the appealingly named **Scrub Island** is also only accessible by boat (don't try to swim it as the currents will drag you off to St Martin). Home to a colony of goats, a garden of frangipani trees and an abandoned hotel and airstrip, it offers a couple of good snorkelling patches but no food or drink so bring your own. Boats make the trip when needed for around US$60 round-trip; ask at one of the bars in Island Harbour for details.

Eating, drinking and nightlife

There are many good **restaurants** in Anguilla, many focusing on local seafood such as snapper, grouper, conch and lobster. Island specialities include pumpkin soup, conch salad and goat stew, though you'll rarely find these at the more upmarket joints. **Nightlife** is pretty quiet, with the occasional live band at one of the bars in Sandy Ground or Shoal Bay East. To see what's on, pick up the free monthly *What We Do in Anguilla*, available from the tourist office, airport and most hotels.

Cedar Grove *Rendezvous Bay Hotel* ☎264/497-6549. Excellent hotel restaurant on the southwest coast, where you can eat on the terrace or in the garden overlooking the magnificent bay. Evenings sees the chef serving up a more formal menu of gumbo soup, interesting salads and fresh, tasty seafood. There's live music every Sunday from 7pm. Open daily for lunch and dinner.

Covecastles Shoal Bay West ☎264/497-6801. Top-quality French- and Caribbean-style food, from starters such as sautéed snails with garlic butter, through mains of lobster laced with fresh truffle cream sauce to unforgettable black-and-white chocolate mousse cake with raspberry sauce. Expect to pay for the privilege, around US$60 for three courses. Dinner only, closed Tues.

Johnno's, Sandy Ground ☎264/497-2728. Easy-going open-plan bar and restaurant on the beach at Sandy Ground, dishing up tasty and inexpensive meals of pumpkin soup, grouper, snapper, curried goat and burgers for US$8–12 per person. Occasional live music on Saturday and Sunday. Open daily for lunch and dinner.

Koal Keel The Valley ☎264/497-2930. Probably *the* place to go if you're feeling in the money, with a fine hand in the kitchen behind exquisite dishes like crayfish ravioli, seared foie gras with truffles and lightly curried lobster. Starters run US$10–20, main courses US$25–40, and there's a seven-course tasting menu for US$100. Open Friday to Monday, dinner only.

Le Beach Bar Shoal Bay Villas ☎264/497-5598. One of a series of beachfront bars along glorious Shoal Bay, all fairly similar in price and quality, *Le Beach* offers simple meals all day, ranging from sandwiches, burgers and pizza for lunch (US$5–10 per person) to fish and chicken meals in the evening at double those prices. There's also a West Indian buffet on Wednesday from 6.30pm for US$20 per person, with live music. A good place, too, to just chill out after exerting yourself in the sea (you can rent snorkels nearby). Open daily for lunch and dinner.

Old Cotton Gin Ice Cream Parlour The Valley ☎264/497-3328. Fantastic variety of delicious ice creams (coconut, mango, ginger and the like) as well as soft drinks, coffee and home-made cakes. Open daily except Tues, 10am–8pm.

Ripples Sandy Ground ☎264/497-3380. Delicious food dished up all day, specializing in local seafood dishes like creole snapper or coconut shrimp as well as pasta and burgers. There's a half-price happy hour every evening 5–7pm and you can expect to pay US$25–40 for three courses (drinks not included). Open daily noon–midnight.

Roy's Crocus Bay ☎264/497-2470. English-style pub on the beach, offering good and reasonably priced sandwiches and fish and chips at lunch, a more formal menu including seafood, sirloin steaks and prime rib in the evening, with starters from US$5 and main courses from US$20. Daily happy hour with half-price drinks and cheap food 5–7pm and live music on Saturday evening. Open daily for lunch and dinner.

Scilly Cay opposite Island Harbour ☎264/497-5123. Flag down the boat that crosses between the harbour and the cay just offshore, and settle down for tasty food in a great beachside location. Grilled chicken and lobster are the main ingredients on the menu (expect to pay US$25–35 per person) and there's live music on Wednesday, Friday and Sunday. Worth phoning ahead to reserve a table. Open noon–4pm, closed Mon.

Smitty's Island Harbour ⓣ264/497-4300. Friendly little bar and restaurant on the beach, with fish and lobster fresh off the boats as well as barbecued chicken, ribs and burgers. Main courses start at around US$6. Open daily for lunch and dinner.

Watersports and excursions

Diving on Anguilla is good and focuses around a number of wrecks that have been deliberately sunk and now attract schools of colourful reef fish and interesting coral formations. Shoal Bay Scuba and Watersports (ⓣ264/497-4371, ⓦwww.shoalbayscuba.ai) and Anguillan Divers at Island Harbour (ⓣ264/497-4636) both offer resort dives and full training; expect to pay US$450 for PADI certification, US$80 for a two-tank dive.

A number of operators offer **sport fishing** trips. Try Blues Ltd (ⓣ264/497-6164) or Anguilla Angling Adventures (ⓣ264/497-5907), who charge around US$500 for a full day's charter in pursuit of tuna, wahoo and mackerel or for bottom-fishing trips for reef fish.

Sailing trips from Sandy Ground to points around the island include those on *Sail Chocolat*, a 35-foot catamaran that makes lunch and snorkelling trips to the nearby cays (US$80 per person) and sunset cruises (US$50), both with complimentary drinks. Book on ⓣ264/497-3394. Other boat tours, including snorkelling and fishing trips and visits to offshore islands are organized by Checkers Fun Tours (ⓣ264/497-4071) and Shoal Bay Scuba (see above).

10

St Martin/St Maarten

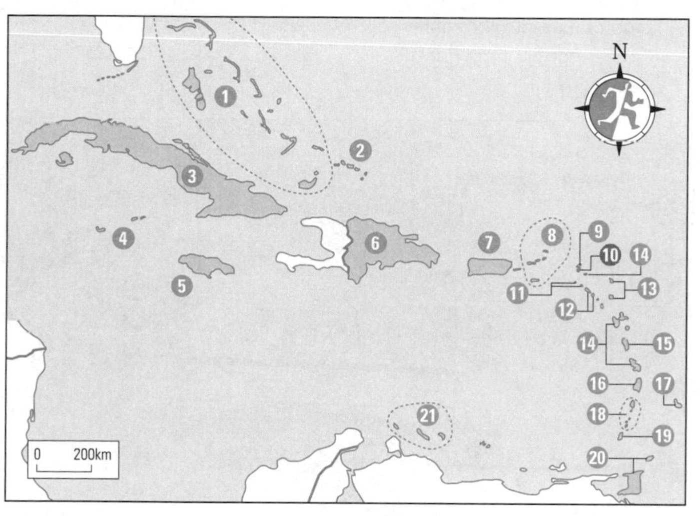

St Martin/St Maarten Highlights

* **Orient Beach** Simply one of the best you'll see, appealing for its inviting sands, warm sea and ample watersports. See p.470

* **Pic Paradis** Escape the crowds and hike to the top or just into the rainforest from Loterie Farm. See p.471

* **Grand Case** Run the gauntlet of gourmet restaurants offering everything from delectable local seafood to fine French cuisine. See p.470

Introduction and Basics

Shared between the French and the Dutch since the mid-seventeenth century, the tiny island of **St Martin/St Maarten** is one of the most touristed islands in this part of the Caribbean and a huge duty-free shopping area. Opinions about the island are as divided as the island itself. Ask the streams of repeat visitors, and they'll tell you that this tiny island is paradise on earth, with fabulous beaches and every type of tourist facility imaginable. Ask others, and you may hear how rapid and barely controlled development has turned a once-beautiful place into "a graceless monument to vulgarian greed", as one disgruntled writer put it.

The truth lies somewhere in between. The island does boast some of the finest beaches in the Eastern Caribbean, particularly at **Orient Beach** on the French side, as well as some stunning scenery, most notably in the interior around **Pic Paradis**, and many excellent restaurants and hotels on both sides of the border. On the other hand, the hunt for the tourist dollar can feel unrelenting and, at times, it is hard to discern the real country under the veneer of concrete development, souvenir shops and the waves of tourists (all particularly acute on the Dutch side in the capital Philipsburg).

If all you want to do is lie on the beach and play in the sea, both St Martin and St Maarten are not bad options. Travelling between the French and Dutch sides (as many visitors do) is hassle-free, since the border is marked only in one spot (by a small obelisk) and there are **no border crossing formalities**. Ultimately, if the crowds get too much for you, bear in mind that it's a very short flight or ferry ride to some of the quietest and most undeveloped islands in the entire Caribbean – particularly delightful are Saba and St Eustatius (see p.479).

As in much of the Caribbean, the island is a year-round destination; however, the best time to visit is between mid-December and mid-April when rainfall is low and the heat is tempered by cooling trade winds.

Getting there

Visitors pour onto the island by **plane**, with virtually all of the international flights landing at Juliana Airport on the Dutch side of the island. American Airlines offers daily flights from New York and Miami in the US as well as from Puerto Rico, while Air France provides several flights a week from Paris. Within the wider Caribbean, LIAT is the main service provider, with connections to and from almost all of the islands.

St Martin is also a convenient base for visitors to other islands. Windward Islands Airways (known as Winair; ☎599/545-4237) flies frequently to Saba (US$120 round-trip), St Eustatius (US$120 round-trip) and Anguilla (US$60 round-trip), while Air Caraibes flies to St Barts (US$100 round-trip). Special deals are regularly offered on all of these flights (day return trips, for example, can be dramatically lower than the advertised price) and it's worth calling to enquire. (For phone numbers of airlines, see pp.12–18 and 36–37.)

Ferry services are also frequent: ferries run from Marigot Bay to Anguilla every thirty minutes from 8am to 7pm, the journey taking 25 minutes and costing US$10 each way. In good weather, the *Voyager* ferry (☎599/542-4096 or 590/87 10 68) travels daily between Marigot and St Barts (45min) and twice a week between Philipsburg and Saba (1hr); the *Edge* ferry (☎599/544-2640) makes the same trips.

Information and maps

There are tourist offices in Philipsburg (see p.475) and in Marigot (see p.469), each crammed with maps and brochures.

The **departure tax** is US$20 at the airport, US$6 for flights within the Netherlands Antilles.

Money and costs

On the French side of the island, the **euro (€)** is the local currency; some, but certainly not all, establishments will quote or accept US dollars. Euro notes are issued in **denominations** of 5, 10, 20, 50, 100, 200 and 500 euros, and coins in denominations of 1, 2, 5, 10, 20 and 50 cents and 1 and 2 euros. At the time of writing, the **rate of exchange** was US$1 to €1.10. On the Dutch side, the currency is the **Netherlands Antilles guilder (NAf)** (with a rate of exchange of US$1 to NAf1.78), though prices are always quoted in US dollars. For consistency, all prices in this chapter are quoted in US dollars.

There are plenty of **banks** on both sides of the island with 24-hour cashpoint facilities in the main towns.

Most hotels and restaurants on the Dutch side add 15 percent **service charge** and 5 percent **government tax**. On the French side, they add 10–15 percent for service and a 5 percent **occupancy tax**.

Given the scale of tourist development, it's pretty easy to get by on whatever **budget** you're on. Accommodation will be your main expenditure, but there are moderately priced places to stay in on both sides of the border. The French side in particular has some top-class and top-priced places to eat, but both sides have plenty of good, inexpensive options.

Getting around

The local **bus** service is efficient and cheap. Buses run frequently from 7am to midnight between Philipsburg and Marigot and usual-

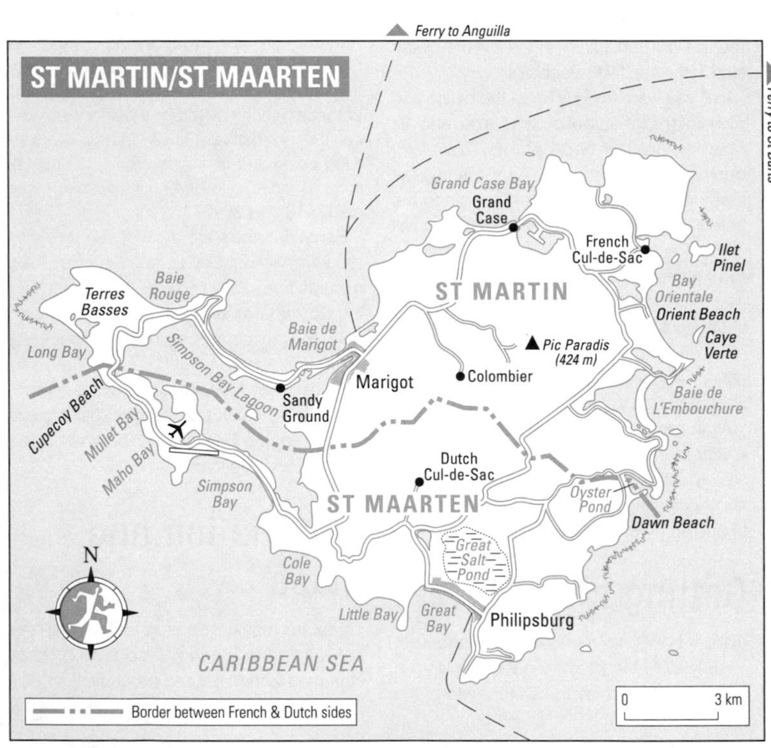

ly continue up to Grand Case. The flat fare is US$1.50 and drivers will accept dollars or euros (though not always florins if you're on the French side). Minibuses run all over the island, depending on the driver's whim, and charge between US$1.50 and US$3 depending on distance. Both buses and minibuses can be taken from bus stops in Philipsburg and Marigot; elsewhere, flag them down as they pass.

If you want to explore the island (and you should certainly do some touring) consider hiring a **car** for a few days. Driving is easy (on the right-hand side of the road), and there are plenty of car rental outlets at the airport; competition keeps prices reasonable, starting at around US$40 per day. Try Paradise (☎599/545-3737), Safari (☎599/545-3186), St Louis (☎599/545-3244), or Budget (☎599/545-4030). Most will deliver to your hotel. Scooters can also be rented for around US$30 per day; try Rent a Scoot (☎590/87 20 59) in Nettle Bay.

Finally, **taxis** are easy to come by in Philipsburg and Marigot, less so elsewhere. Rates are fixed both from the airport and from the ferry dock in Marigot; ask before you hop in. Guided taxi tours cost around US$35 for one to two people for a two- to three-hour tour. In Marigot, try ☎590/87 56 54, in Grand Case ☎590/87 75 79 and in Philipsburg ☎599/542-2359.

Phones, post and email

Calls between the two sides of the island count as long-distance, with each side having its own **phone code**. To the Dutch side, dial ☎00 plus 599 before the seven-digit number; to the French side, dial ☎00 plus 590 before the six-digit number.

There are post offices in Marigot and Philipsburg.

Most hotels will let you hook up to their **internet connection** for a nominal charge. In Philipsburg, Parcel Post on Front Street (Mon–Sat 9am–4pm) offers internet access, as does Cyberzone in Marigot, opposite the tourist office and museum (daily 10am–8pm; around US$3 for fifteen minutes).

Holidays and festivals

The biggest parties on the island are the two **carnivals**, held on French St Martin over Lent and on the Dutch side in late April and early May, with the main bash normally on April 30, Queen Juliana's birthday. The Dutch affair is easily the bigger of the two, with plenty of colourful and noisy parades and live music every night, from local calypsonians to international stars like Trinidad's Mighty Sparrow and Antigua's David Rudder, as carnival gears up to its grand finale.

As well as the public holidays listed on p.45, each island celebrates its own distinct holidays.

Public holidays

St Martin

May 25 Ascension Day
July 14 Bastille Day
July 21 Schoelcher Day
November 1 All Saints Day
November 11 Feast of St Martin

St Maarten

April 30 Queen's Day
October 21 Antillean Day
November 11 St Maarten Day

Health and safety

Crime has increased significantly on the island over the last decade. Car crime is particularly prevalent, so don't leave valuables in your hire car when you park it at the beach or in town. Muggings are also on the increase, and it's advisable not to walk on unlit areas of the beach or the main towns at night.

Emergency numbers

Ambulance ☎87 86 25 (French side), ☎130 (Dutch side)

Police ☎911 (French side), ☎111 (Dutch side); non-emergency ☎590/87 50 06 or 87 88 33 (French side); ☎599/542-2222 (Dutch side).

Language

Dutch and **French** are the native languages. **English** is spoken almost everywhere on the Dutch side and in most places on the French side. Many people on both sides speak a creole language known as Papiamento.

Watersports and excursions

Watersports are excellent across the island. Orient Beach in the northeast is the watersports centre of the island, with a host of outlets along the bay renting jet skis, windsurfers, hobie cats and snorkelling gear as well as parasailing and boat trips out to nearby Green Cay and Ilet Pinel. On the Dutch side of the island, Simpson Bay also has plenty of operators hiring out the same equipment.

Diving on the island is good, though not in the top league, with four main schools. The Scuba Shop (☎590/87 48 01 or 599/545-3213, ⓦwww.thescubashop.net) has outlets on both sides of the island, Dive Safaris (☎599/542-9001) and Ocean Explorers (☎599/544-5252) are on the Dutch side while Scuba Fun Caraibes (☎590/87 36 13) is on the French side. Among the highlights are the dive to *HMS Proselyte*, a shipwreck from 1801 now home to an artificial reef teeming with marine life, including nurse sharks and schools of fish, and a series of fabulous coral reefs at The Maze.

There are some fine **windsurfing** spots on the island, with the calm waters of Coconut Grove on the northeast coast providing the main centre for beginners. You can rent boards there at Le Galion Watersports (☎590/87 37 09) and at Windy Reef (☎590/87 08 37). Orient Beach is also good for windsurfing, and you'll see operators renting boards along the beach.

Sailing trips are offered by a number of operators. The 75ft *Scoobidoo* catamaran (☎590/87 20 28) takes daily sailing, snorkelling and beach tours from Anse Marcel, charging US$30 for a sunset cruise, US$45 for a half-day cruise and US$75–85 for a whole day, which might be to Anguilla or the deserted Prickly Pear island. The huge catamaran *Golden Eagle* (☎599/530-0068) takes daily trips from Philipsburg to St Barts and various offshore islands, stopping for snorkelling and shelling en route. Tahuna Charters (☎590/27 33 43 or 599/544-4354) offers private charters by catamaran from Marigot to Anguilla, St Barts and offshore islands.

History

Amerindian remains dating from as early as 2000 BC have been found near the village of Grand Case on the French side of the island, though little is known about the island's first visitors. **Columbus** sailed past on November 11, 1493, naming the island after St Martin of Tours whose holy day it was. Few navigators took much interest for the next century.

During the 1620s **French** and **Dutch** colonists began to settle, forerunners of the division of the island later in the century, with the Dutch building the first fort at Philipsburg in 1631. The **Spanish**, however, were keen on the island for strategic reasons and claimed it, subsequently fighting off a lengthy siege by Dutch troops led by **Peter Stuyvesant**, later to become governor of the Dutch colony of New Amsterdam (today's New York City).

By 1648, the Spanish had lost interest in the island, and the French and Dutch governments agreed to divide it in two, populating it with settlers from home. The land was given over to the production of sugar, cotton, tobacco and salt, with slaves imported from Africa to work on the plantations. However, the soil was poor and the island never prospered, largely sinking into obscurity as the centuries passed.

Despite frequent disagreements between the French and the Dutch, including border skirmishes and wholesale invasions and deportations, the boundaries remain pretty much the same today as were agreed on in 1648. The Dutch side, known as **Sint Maarten**, is part of the Netherlands Antilles; the French side part of a department of Franco, with representation in the French parliament. As throughout the region, tourism drives the modern economy, bringing floods of visitors and attendant social difficulties, particularly rising crime and problems with immigration from other islands and from South America.

10.1

St Martin

French **ST MARTIN**, spread over 52 square kilometres, is less touristed than the Dutch side, despite having some of the finest beaches and restaurants and the most attractive scenery. **Marigot** is the pleasant and likeable capital, worth at least a couple of hours of your time, while the delightful long stretch of white sand at **Orient Beach** is the pick of the beaches, with a great choice of watersports to keep you busy. The island's gourmet capital **Grand Case** has a string of excellent restaurants, while **Loterie Farm** offers great hiking away from the crowds into an unspoiled area of rainforest and up to **Pic Paradis**, the island's highest point.

Accommodation

Most of the visitors to the French side of the island stay either in the Orient Bay area on the northeast coast or in Grand Case on the west coast. On the whole, **accommodation** in Grand Case is on a smaller scale, while Orient Bay has more of a range, from small boutique places to 400-room resorts. During the low season, rates can fall by as much as forty percent (though this is rare at the smaller places).

Marigot

Le Royale Louisiana ⓣ590/87 86 51, ⓕ87 96 49. Seventy rooms at this longstanding Marigot hotel, scattered around and above a central courtyard, not worth going out of your way for but perfectly adequate if you have to stay in the town. ❹

Orient Bay and Cul-de-Sac

Alizea Cul-de-Sac ⓣ590/87 33 42, ⓕ87 41 15. Fabulously landscaped and overlooking gorgeous Orient Bay, a ten-minute walk away, the hotel is one of the best options on this side of the island. All rooms have kitchens and are tastefully decorated and furnished, the restaurant is good and the relative isolation means that it's very peaceful at night. ❻

Blue Bay Orient Bay ⓣ590/87 62 00, ⓕ87 37 27. Giant, 400-room hotel at the quieter, northern end of the beach, with a big pool, several restaurants and excellent amenities. All rooms have balconies, with the best and largest rooms overlooking the sea. Popular with European tour groups. ❻

Orient Bay Hotel Orient Bay ⓣ590/87 31 10, ⓕ87 37 66, ⓦwww.orientbayhotel.com. A series of cosy pastel-coloured villas arranged around two swimming pools, each with a kitchen, living room and TV. Rates start at ❼ for the smaller villas (two to three people), ❾ for the larger ones (four to five people).

St Tropez Caribe Orient Bay ⓣ590/87 42 01, ⓕ87 41 69. Large but reasonably attractive development, just a short walk from the beach and with all rooms enjoying their own terrace or balcony. ❼

Sunrise Hotel Cul-de-Sac ⓣ590/29 57 00, ⓕ87 39 28. Small, friendly and good-value hotel with twenty rooms organized around a swimming pool, each with a terrace overlooking the nearby hills and out to Ilet Pinel (accessible by the hotel shuttle boat). There's a decent restaurant and rooms have kitchen facilities. Small studios ❺, the larger ones ❻

Grand Case

Grand Case Beach Club ⓣ590/87 51 87, ⓕ87 59 93. Seventy-five well-equipped and colourfully decorated condos, all with kitchens and A/C, on the beach in Grand Case. Popular with families, the place also has tennis courts and a restaurant. ❽

Hevea ⓣ590/87 56 85, ⓕ87 83 88. Small guesthouse with six small but cute colonial-style rooms with beamed ceilings, wooden beds and air-conditioning. Guests are entitled to discounted food at the hotel's restaurant. ❹

L'Esplanade ⓣ590/87 06 55, ⓕ87 29 15.

Welcoming place on the hillside overlooking Grand Case, decorated with curved stone staircases and colourful tiles. All rooms are very comfortable; the standard rooms are large and the duplexes are vast. There's a quiet pool and a very relaxed feel to the place. ⑧

Le Petit Hotel ⓣ590/29 09 65, ⓕ87 09 19, ⓦwww.lepetithotel.com. Small Mediterranean-style hotel on the beach in Grand Case, with nine studios and a single one-bedroom suite. Each room has a fully equipped kitchen and dining area, tiled floors, rattan furniture, cable TV, plus A/C and ceiling fans. There's no pool, but you get to use one at sister hotel *L'Esplanade*, a short walk away. Studio ⑨

Oyster Pond

Captain Oliver's ⓣ590/87 40 26, ⓕ87 40 84, ⓦwww.captainolivers.com. Attractive resort overlooking the lovely sheltered anchorage of Oyster Pond, half in French and half in Dutch territory. There's a big pool, and the fifty large rooms (ask for one with a sea view) are comfortably furnished and air-conditioned. Delightful Dawn Beach is a short drive away ⑤

Marigot

Likeable **Marigot** is the main town on St Martin and well worth a short visit. At first sight, the place seems too cluttered with traffic, shops and people to be enjoyable, but make your way down to the water and Marigot grows on you, distinctly both French and Caribbean in style. The town has spread along Marigot Bay, with a selection of interesting restaurants and stores and a sparkling new marina at its western end.

The main focus of the **harbour** is at the bottom of Rue de la République, the location of the booking and departure points for ferries to Anguilla and other islands (see p.463), and you'll normally see the ferries lined up alongside a fleet of fishing boats. Just west of here, beyond the taxi rank, are a group of bars and "lolos" or food shacks, where you can get excellent and inexpensive island fare. Continuing west brings you to the main **public market** (Tues–Sat 6am–3pm), where you'll find plenty of souvenir stands selling T-shirts, wooden carvings and the like, as well as a host of fruit and vegetable vendors hawking their colourful produce. It's a lively place, though there are few great bargains for shoppers.

Further west still, the grand development of the **Port La Royale marina** is also worth making for, with a number of classy shops selling designer gear and jewellery, outlets offering boat and fishing trips and loads of bars and restaurants overlooking the water.

Beyond the marina, the main **tourist office** (Mon–Fri 9am–1pm and 2.30–5pm) has plenty of information and brochures. You should certainly make a point of stopping at the nearby **archeological museum** (Mon–Sat 9am–1pm and 3–6pm; US$5), for its detailed and highly informative exhibits on the Amerindians who lived on the island in the pre-Columbus era as well as more recent history. Evocative black and white photographs of quiet streets populated with a handful of children and donkeys, and of labourers toiling in the salt industry, provide images of what the island looked like before tourism took hold. The museum is a welcome antidote to the all-pervading tourism and helps you appreciate that St Martin is more than just an attraction.

Finally, on the other side of the ferry points, a fifteen-minute climb from the harbour, **Fort Louis** (always open; free) has the scant remains of a 1789 fort built to protect the town from the raids of British sailors and offers fine views across the bay.

Sandy Ground and Baie Rouge

Less than a kilometre west of Marigot, the main road curves around to the long spit of land known as **Sandy Ground** that separates the huge Simpson Bay Lagoon from the sea at Nettle Bay. The isthmus is lined with hotels, restaurants (including the very popular *Mario's* – see p.472) and small shopping malls, though if you're not staying there, the area holds little of interest. The beaches are not particularly impressive and you're better off heading a couple of kilometres further west to the lovely and normally quiet white sandy stretch at **Baie Rouge**. Here you'll find a handful of vendors selling food and drink on the beach and you can rent snorkelling gear from a shack.

If you are looking for even more privacy on the beach, continue past Baie Rouge and take the right-hand turn-off signposted for **Baie aux Prunes** or make your way round the headland to **Baie Longue** where you'll find a vast expanse of white sand, perfect for strolling and shell collecting.

Grand Case

Grand Case has built itself a deserved reputation as one of the finest dining centres of the Eastern Caribbean and, as you walk down the main drag which makes up a large part of this tiny town, it's easy to see why. A series of fairly expensive restaurants lines the otherwise unremarkable street, with daily specials chalked up outside and classy wine lists displayed in the windows.

It's far from obvious why the great restaurateurs decided to set up shop in Grand Case since – food aside – there's nothing spectacular about the town. There are a handful of very good places to stay but there's little else specific in the town to bring you here. The sandy beach that lines the wide, sweeping bay is nice but modest compared to others on the coast and, outside the restaurants, there's little in the way of nightlife.

Anse Marcel, French Cul-de-Sac and Ilet Pinel

Heading east of Grand Case for 1.5km, past the salinas and the local airport, the road forks, heading south towards fabulous Orient Bay or north for the tiny settlements of Anse Marcel and Cul-de-Sac, from where you can hop on a boat to Ilet Pinel just offshore. **Anse Marcel** is a mini-resort, with a couple of large hotels, a marina and a pleasant long sandy beach. **Cul-de-Sac** – home to St Martin's mayor and characterized by its cute little red-roofed houses – is even smaller, but popular for trips to the pristine and uninhabited **Ilet Pinel**, where there is excellent snorkelling (rent gear from the shack for US$10 per person) and lovely, calm waters for swimming. Boats regularly make the two-minute trip (no set schedule), from the pier in Cul-de-Sac (US$5 per person round-trip) and there are barbecue stalls and drink vendors on the island, and even a small gift-shop.

Orient Beach

The area around **Orient Beach**, at the northeast end of the island, is one of massive commercial development, with hotels, villas and condominiums springing up along a two-kilometre strip. The beach itself, too, is an incredible hive of activity, with restaurants, bars, watersports outlets and most of all hordes of people strung out along its length. Don't be put off by the crowds, though, because this is one of the great beaches in the Eastern Caribbean, a fabulous swathe of white sand bordering an inviting, turquoise sea.

Whether you want to rent a jet ski or a windsurfer, take a snorkelling trip or visit an offshore cay, or even if you just want to splash or wander in the shallows, this is a great place to do it. The southern end of the beach, protected from the surf by nearby Green Cay, is the best area for watersports and where the main crowds congregate. Beach chairs and umbrellas can be rented for US$5 a day, while boat trips to Green Cay or Ilet Pinel will set you back around US$10–15. If you're strolling on the beach, watch out for the sudden onset of nudism at the very end, which is largely given over to the "clothing optional" crowd.

Butterfly Farm

No prizes for guessing what's on display at the **Butterfly Farm** just south of Orient Bay (daily 9am–4pm; US$10, US$5 for children), with numerous varieties imported from Indonesia and South America taking it easy on a cabbage leaf or fluttering around under a giant net. It's informative as well as colourful, and a reasonable distraction when you've had enough of the beach.

Oyster Pond

Divided in half by the border, **Oyster Pond** on the coast southeast of Orient Bay is an oyster-shaped and almost completely landlocked anchorage, popular with yachters. The marina and most of the hotel/condominium development is on the French side of the border, though the best beach in the area is Dawn Beach on the Dutch side, and certainly worth a visit if you're passing by. There is good snorkelling offshore and, when the waves are rolling in, it's a good place for body surfing though a little rough for small children. There are great views across to St Barts and, when you need sustenance, there are a couple of good food shacks too.

The interior

While most of the tourist development in St Martin is along the coast, the interior remains delightfully unspoiled, its peaceful countryside making for an appealing side-trip if you have a car. Just north of Marigot, you can turn right onto a road signposted to **Colombier**, where a scattered settlement of old wooden houses, small farms and picturesque meadows strewn with munching cattle gives a picture of island life that has changed little over the last fifty years.

A little further north still lies **Loterie Farm**, a nature-lover's delight and one of the highlights of a visit to St Martin. The farm, once a sugar estate, is now a 150-acre working farm where the owners have carved eco-trails that you are free to wander in either alone or as part of a guided tour (US$5, US$25 per group; call ahead to book on ⓣ590/87 86 16). The trails head into the "hidden forest", where you'll find giant silk cotton trees as well as groves of mango and palm trees fed by quiet streams. Those with the energy can make their way up to **Pic Paradis**, at 390 metres the island's highest point and a three-hour round-trip. Take good footwear, as the trails can be rocky. To get there, follow the main road from Marigot signposted to Pic Paradis. Five hundred metres up a steep hill a right turn is signposted to the farm, taking you through fields of papayas, melons, bananas and vegetables. If you continue up the hill instead, it's another 2km to the **peak**, past some of the island's most expensive homes, many set back from the road with flamboyant vegetation to guard them from prying eyes. Unless you've got a four-wheel-drive vehicle, you'll need to park at the top and walk for a further ten minutes to get fantastic views out over the island.

Eating and drinking

As you'd expect with a French island, St Martin is **a place for food lovers**, and the great news is that you don't have to break the bank to eat well.

Marigot and Sandy Ground

Claude Mini-Club Marigot ⓣ590/87 50 69. Colourful, lively and popular Marigot spot, with a daily specials menu for around US$25 and a huge dinner buffet on Wednesday and Saturday laden with roast pork and beef, lobster and a mountain of side dishes for US$40. Delicious dessert soufflés are worth the US$9. Daily for lunch and dinner, closed Sun lunch.

La Plaisance La Marina Port La Royale, Marigot ⓣ590/87 85 00. One of several lively open-air eateries in the marina, with a good range of reasonably priced salads, pasta dishes and local seafood. Daily for all meals.

Le Bar de la Mer Marigot ⓣ590/87 81 79. Grilled fish, sandwiches, pizza and salads make up the main part of the menu in this easy-going and reasonably priced place near the harbour. Daily for lunch and dinner.

Lolos Marigot. A collection of tiny bars and restaurants around the central market, highly recommended for inexpensive and authentic island food, such as curried goat or chicken with peas and rice for US$8, bullfoot soup for US$4 or fresh grilled fish and johnny cake for US$9. A live band plays on Wednesday evenings. Mon–Sat 7am–8pm.

Mario's Bistro Sandy Ground ☎590/87 06 36. A favourite with locals, the waterside location at *Mario's* makes it one of the most romantic places for dinner, and booking is essential. Seafood is the specialty, with delicious starters of scallops and mussels (US$6–10), while well-prepared main courses (US$15–30) include pan-fried snapper, succulent roast duck and a selection of steaks. Daily for dinner.

Orient Bay and Cul-de-Sac

Kontiki Orient Bay ☎590/87 43 27. Good if pricey place on the beach, with fresh and tasty grilled fish and chips for US$18, wholesome salads for US$10, pasta dishes from US$12 and specials like iced mango and honey soup for US$8. Daily for breakfast and lunch.

Le Piccolo Cul-de-Sac ☎590/87 32 47. Delicious food at this brightly painted chattel house beside the main road, where starters of seared tuna and crab ravioli (US$6–9) will set your taste buds tingling in time for main dishes such as tandoori snapper (US$15) and exquisite desserts. Sun–Mon, dinner only.

Pedros Orient Bay ☎590/57 78 25. One of the better of the beach cafés on this very popular beach, with friendly waiters dishing up tasty barbecued chicken and fish dishes served with peas and rice for US$8–10. The place is often crowded with those taking a break from the sun with a cooling beer. Daily for all meals.

Grand Case

Le Tastevin ☎590/87 55 45. Elegant French-owned place overlooking the water and offering a fine selection of French food, from foie gras and snails to fresh local seafood and steaks, all prepared with skill and imagination. One of the best places to eat in town, with prices to match. Daily lunch and dinner.

L'Hibiscus ☎590/29 17 91. Another of the excellent Grand Case options in a typical creole house (though there is no sea view), with carpaccio of tuna and lobster flamed in rum among the signature dishes. Expensive. Daily 6.30–10.30pm.

Lolos A great range of shacks and barbecue pits around an open courtyard offering up tasty fish, barbecued chicken, spare ribs and the occasional lobster, together with side dishes such as potato salad, peas and rice, macaroni cheese and coleslaw, a whole plate costing around US$10.

Nightlife

For **nightly entertainment**, *Club One* is the main **nightclub** in Marigot, a lively and welcoming place popular with locals and tourists alike. Based at the Marina Port La Royale, it's open from around 10pm Friday through Sunday. *Pasha*, at the waterfront in Marigot, is also a local favourite, decked in velvet and animal-skin prints and with a cool open-air terrace. West of Marigot in Sandy Ground is *Heaven's Disco*, a good spot for traditional Caribbean sounds, including zouk, merengue and salsa.

10.2

St Maarten

Other than the language and some of the names, there is little you could describe as characteristically Dutch about Dutch **ST MAARTEN**. This side of the island, measuring a mere 37 square kilometres, has seen a huge tourist boom since the 1960s, both in overnight and cruise-ship visitors, making it one of the most heavily touristed areas in the region. On the whole, St Maarten seems to be geared towards servicing its international visitors and it can be hard to discern much of an individual identity.

The heavily commercialized town of **Philipsburg** is the main draw for shoppers and cruise-ship passengers and has the best restaurants, sandwiched in between casinos, T-shirt and duty-free shops and fast-food joints. The town is built right on Great Bay, and has its own large beach.

Relatively few visitors stay in Philipsburg, however, and much of the recent development has been along the western end of the island, south of the giant Simpson Bay Lagoon, where a series of attractive bays indent the coast. Particularly worth making for are **Cupecoy Beach** and **Mullet Beach** in the southwest. Despite the fact that this side of the island can feel crowded, there's plenty of fun to be had on the good-quality beaches and at the multitude of lively bars and restaurants.

Accommodation

In contrast to the French side, **resorts** here tend to be large and can feel somewhat impersonal. As you're probably on the Dutch side for the beach, there's no real reason to stay in Philipsburg; you'll find a variety of beachfront places scattered along the south coast.

Joshua Rose Guest House Backstreet 7, Philipsburg ⓣ599/542-4317. Simple guesthouse on the east side of town, a short walk from Bobby's Marina, with fairly basic facilities but decent rooms. ❹

Maho Beach Hotel Maho Bay ⓣ599/545-2115, ⓕ545-3180, ⓔMahobeach@ssholidays.com. Recently subject to a complete overhaul, the *Maho Beach* is a huge resort with six hundred rooms, nine restaurants, its own disco and casino, and excellent facilities. Despite the numbers, the beach is big enough that you can normally find a quiet spot of your own. ❽

Oyster Bay Beach Resort Oyster Pond ⓣ599/543-6040, ⓕ543-6695, ⓦwww.oysterbaybeachresort.com. Large and rather impersonal resort spread over eight acres on the east coast of the island, a short distance from superb Dawn Beach. Rooms are spacious and pleasant and there's a large pool. Rates are high, but you can find good package deals. ❽

Passangrahan Philipsburg ⓣ599/542-3588, ⓕ542-2743. Colonial in feel and once a guesthouse for royal visitors, *Passangrahan* overlooks the sea on the south side of Front Street and makes a good base for exploring if you want to stay in town. Its former grandeur has faded but it's comfortable enough and there's a welcoming bar and good restaurant. ❺

Summit Resort Simpson's Bay Lagoon ⓣ599/545-2150, ⓕ545-2615, ⓦwww.thesummitresort.com. Popular spot on a bluff overlooking the lagoon, with forty cottages offering appealing accommodation in studios and duplexes. The hotel has a restaurant, bar and tennis courts and offers free shuttle service to Mullet and Cupecoy beaches. ❼

△ View from Fort Louis, Marigot

Philipsburg

Packed with cruise-ship visitors during the day, the lively hustle and bustle of **Philipsburg** – the main town of St Maarten – makes it an entertaining place to spend a couple of hours, even if shopping is not high on your holiday agenda. If it is, you're in heaven.

Although the town is unrepentantly in search of the tourist dollar and most of the development is fairly modern, there are a handful of attractive eighteenth- and nineteenth-century buildings dotted along the heaving main drag of Front Street and in the grid of quieter streets behind it, and there are some good places to put your feet up and get a tasty bite to eat. In the evening, when the crowds have gone, the place takes on a different, slightly seedy, feel, and can even feel a little threatening if you move away from the main well-lit areas on Front Street or around Bobby's Marina in the east.

The small town was founded in 1733 on a sand bar that separated the sea from a series of inland salt ponds, and named for Scotsman John Philips, one of the island's early pioneers. All four of its main roads run east–west along the thin strip of land that still divides Great Bay from the Great Salt Pond, with busy **Front Street** facing south onto the blue expanse of the ocean and bursting with duty-free shops selling liquor, jewellery and T-shirts.

Towards the eastern end of the street, **Wathey Square** is effectively the town centre and the main focus for visitors, housing the **tourist information kiosk**, a couple of banks and a handful of bars and restaurants. The square is less than a minute's walk from long semi-circular Great Bay Beach, not one of the most impressive on the island but normally strewn with a few swimmers and sun-seekers.

If you're on the north side of the square, check out the graceful architecture of the grand old **courthouse**, built in 1793 and serving in its time as a fire station and a jail. Today it's the post office. Just 200m west of the square, the cute little wooden **Methodist church** was built in 1851 and makes for a welcome sanctuary from the lunacy of the vendors outside.

In the opposite direction, the eastern end of Front Street has the more attractive of Philipsburg's historic buildings, lined with a group of elegant **colonial houses** distinctive for their downstairs store or warehouse with steps leading up from the street to a verandah for the living quarters above. Almost at the end of Front Street, the small **St Maarten museum** (Mon–Fri 10am–4pm, Sat 10am–1pm; US$1) is worth a look for its exhibits on island history from Amerindian times and articles salvaged from local shipwrecks. Just around the corner from here, heading south around the edge of the bay, there's always plenty of boating activity at Great Marina and Bobby's Marina, as well as a couple of good places to eat.

Inland from Front Street you'll find a labyrinth of small streets and alleys leading back towards the huge **Great Salt Pond** where salt-rakers once scraped a living collecting the "white gold". There's nothing particular to head for, with the pond now devoid of activity since the demise of the salt industry after World War II, but amidst the modern concrete buildings are pretty gingerbread cottages and courtyards draped with bougainvillea and hibiscus and, of course, plenty more shopping and eating opportunities.

The southwest

The headland at the western end of **Great Bay** divides it from Little Bay and a series of smaller sandy bays that lead around to the great spread of Simpson Bay. The attractive but secluded beach at **Cay Bay**, where Dutchman Peter Stuyvesant was injured in battle against the Spanish, can only be reached by unpaved roads or by following an equestrian trail from Cole Bay.

Continuing west towards Juliana International Airport, the road leads for several kilometres along a narrow strip of land that divides the beach at Simpson Bay from the vast Simpson Bay Lagoon that dominates this side of the island. There's not much of note here, other than a number of hotels and a host of other, rather unsightly developments, but the lagoon is a popular spot for watersports.

Heading west beyond the airport brings you to further resort development and a series of good white-sand beaches at Maho Bay, Mullet Bay, Cupecoy Beach and Long Bay (Baie Longue), before you round the headland to Pointe du Plum. **Maho Beach** is often drowned out with noise as planes roar into the airport, particularly at the busiest time between noon and 3pm, but is nonetheless busy; the *Sunset Beach Bar* (see below) is invariably packed when the sun goes down.

Mullet Bay tends to be the most crowded of the local beaches, visitors pouring in for gentle surf and white sugary sand as well as the ample shade provided by a lovely stretch of palm trees. There is plenty of parking space near the beach but surprisingly few facilities, so bring a towel and some drinks. **Cupecoy** has long been the main beach in the area for nude bathing, a dramatic place with sandstone cliffs and caves, though the once-beautiful beach has been spoiled in recent years by tide erosion. Here you can rent beach chairs and buy food and drinks. Beyond Cupecoy, the turquoise waters of **Long Bay**, actually in St Martin, make it a delightful place to swim.

Eating and drinking

Philipsburg is an excellent place for **eating out**, with a range of places from classy French and Indonesian to simple places for a snack during a shopping expedition. Consider making a trip in for dinner at least one night during your stay. Elsewhere, there are few great options, though *Spartaco* in Cole Bay is a highly impressive Italian place.

Antoine 103 Front St, Philipsburg ☎599/542-2964. Elegant French restaurant overlooking Great Bay and offering up tasty and interesting food: look for starters of snails or coquilles St Jacques for US$9–11 and mains of grouper in almonds, snapper in garlic or steak au poivre for US$20–25. Dinner Mon–Sat.

Barefoot Terrace Philipsburg ☎599/542-0360. Inexpensive food and beer mean that this waterside place in Wathey Square is always packed during the day, with visitors munching on sandwiches, salads and burgers as well as local seafood specials. Mon–Sat 8am–7pm.

Kangaroo Court 6 Hendrickstraat, Philipsburg ☎599/542-4278. A good stopping-off point as you tour the town, offering an excellent range of coffees as well as tasty muffins, pastries, bagels and sandwiches to replenish flagging energy levels. Daily breakfast and lunch.

L'Escargot 84 Front St, Philipsburg ☎599/542-2483. Colourfully tiled and brightly painted, *L'Escargot* is one of the town's longest-running restaurants. French specialities include frog's legs and caviar as well as a variety of snail options, while the trademark dish of grilled red snapper in pineapple and banana sauce will set you back US$23. Thursday is cabaret night, when US$50 includes dinner and the show. Daily lunch and dinner.

Spartaco Almond Grove, Cole Bay ☎599/544-5379. Superb Italian food served in a lovely old mansion, where everything is claimed to be home-made or imported from Italy. There's a wide range of pasta specialties and the freshest of local seafood. A classy selection of Italian wine adds to the aura of authenticity. Tues–Sun dinner only.

Sunset Beach Bar Beacon Hill Road, Maho Bay ☎599/545-3998. Lively bar on Maho Beach that makes for a great place to catch the sunset, with cheap beer and a variety of sandwiches, burgers and pizza. There's live music on Wednesday, Friday and Saturday. Daily all meals.

Turtle Pier Airport Road, Simpson Bay ☎599/545-2562. Right on the lagoon and within walking distance of the airport, making this a good place to grab a meal or a beer before you fly. The food is described as "creative Caribbean", so expect to find fish and lobster in a variety of local styles (creole or pan-fried, for example) and there's a small menagerie of monkeys and parrots to distract the kids. Daily for all meals.

Wajang Doll 167 Front St, Philipsburg ☎599/542-2687. Excellent and popular Indonesian restaurant, with typical main dishes of snapper fried in chillis and tamarind or chicken in coconut milk for US$15–20, plus good-value and substantial rijstaffels (literally "rice-tables") comprising 14–19 different dishes for US$20–25 per person. Mon–Sat 6.45–10pm.

Nightlife

Keep an eye out in the papers (particularly the *Daily Herald*) and tourist publications for what's happening on the island; there's regular **live music** but the locations tend to vary from week to week. Some of the best places include the *Boathouse* in Simpson Bay (☎599/544-8256), particularly on Friday nights with local bands playing a mixture of blues, reggae and rock; the *Greenhouse*, at the east end of Philipsburg by Bobby's Marina (☎599/542-2941), which brings in the crowds with canned and live music and a regular two-for-one drink special; *Footsteps* in Cole Bay (☎599/544-2156), good for reggae music on a Saturday evening; and the *Axum Jazz Café* at 7 Front St in Philipsburg (no phone), which occasionally pulls in big international stars. There are also a dozen casinos that will be happy to relieve you of your holiday money.

Saba and St Eustatius

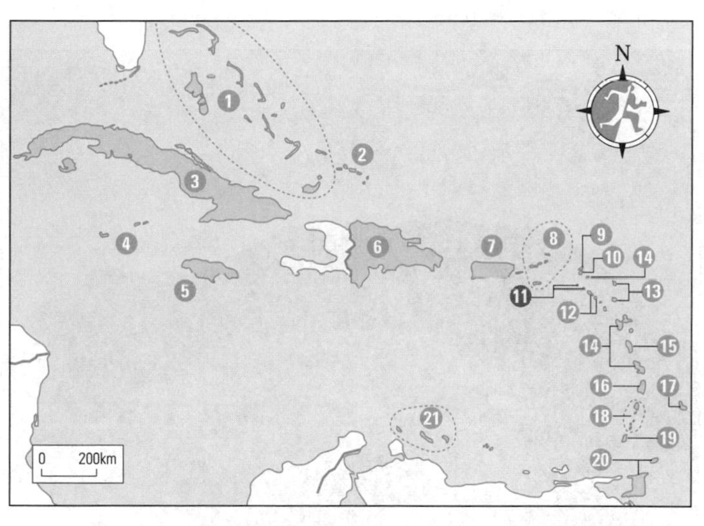

Saba and St Eustatius Highlights

✱ Mount Scenery, Saba
The hike to the top may not be easy, but the magnificent island views repay the effort.
See p.487

✱ Saba's island fringes
Pristine reefs and multi-coloured fish abound in the island's superb marine park. See p.488

✱ Oranjestadt, St Eustatius
Take in the island's colonial past on a gentle wander through town.
See p.491.

✱ The Quill, St Eustatius
Explore the spectacular rainforest inside the crater of this dormant volcano. See p.493.

Introduction and Basics

The unspoiled Caribbean endures in an overlooked corner of the region occupied by the tiny Netherlands Antilles isles of Saba and St Eustatius.

Home to just 600 people and little known even to seasoned travellers to the area, Saba is a true pleasure to visit. Priding itself on showcasing the "Caribbean as it used to be", **Saba's** superb **diving** and great **hiking** more than compensate for the absence of a decent beach. Most refreshing of all – particularly after St Martin, from where nearly all visitors come – is the lack of tourist development that has kept the island "the unspoiled queen" that the tourist authorities avow.

Similarly, **St Eustatius** (or Statia), 27km to the northwest, moves to the slow pace of island life, with good diving and hiking to be had, the latter especially the case inside the crater of **the Quill**, the island's dormant volcano.

As in much of the Caribbean, the islands are year-round destinations; however, the best time to visit is between mid-December and mid-April when rainfall is low and the heat is tempered by cooling trade winds.

Getting there

The great majority of visitors arrive by plane. Windward Islands Airways (known as Winair; ☎599/416-2255 in Saba; ☎599/318-2735 in St Eustatius) make the fifteen-minute flight to Saba from St Martin/St Maarten three times a day, usually en route from or to St Eustatius. It's a short flight that ends with the plane dropping onto one of the world's shortest runways at Juancho E. Yrausquin Airport. The round-trip costs US$120.

Statia is also served by Winair, which flies six times a day from St Martin/St Maarten, usually en route from or to Saba. It's a short flight and the round-trip costs US$90.

Except in rough weather, *The Edge* (☎599/514-2640 in St Maarten), a high-speed ferry popular with day-trippers, makes the one-hour crossing to Saba's Fort Bay from the marina at Simpson Bay, St Maarten, leaving at 9am and around 4pm.

For phone numbers of airlines, see pp.12–17 and 36–37.

> On both islands the **departure tax** is US$10, or US$5 if you're headed onward to another of the islands of the Netherlands Antilles.

Getting around

There is no public transportation on either Saba or St Eustatius. You can hire a **car** (although it normally works out cheaper to use taxis as there's not much driving needed). On Saba try Johnson's (☎599/416-2269) or Scouts (☎599/416-2205) and expect to pay around US$50 a day. On Statia try Fasha's (☎599/318-2543) or Mansion (☎599/318-2764) and expect to pay around US$40 a day for a car and US$30 for a scooter. Drive on the right and bear in mind that the only gas station on Statia is at Fort Bay (Mon–Sat 8am–3pm).

There are always taxis at the airport, though you may be asked to share the ride. On both islands rates are fixed; expect to pay US$10 from the airport to Windwardside (Saba), and US$6 from the airport to Oranjestad (Statia). A two-hour guided island tour on either Saba or Statia will cost US$40–45. If you need to arrange a taxi ahead of time on Statia call ☎599/318-2620.

Money and costs

The official currency is the **Netherlands Antilles guilder (NAf)**, but the US dollar is quoted and accepted everywhere. The guilder is divided into 100 cents. Notes come in denominations of 5, 10, 25, 50, 100, 250 and 500 guilders; coins in 1, 2.5, 5, 10, 25 and 50 cents. The guilder is tied to the US dollar at a rate of US$1 to NAf1.80.

Credit cards are accepted at most hotels

and restaurants. On Saba there are several banks in Windwardside including a Barclays (Mon–Fri 8.30am–3pm). St Eustatius has several banks in Oranjestad including a Barclays (Mon–Thurs 8.30am–3.30pm, Fri 8.30am–12.30pm and 2–4.30pm). Neither of the islands has ATMs.

Costs are fairly high as the great majority of food, drink and other items is imported. On Saba there is a government room tax of 5 percent, and most hotels and restaurants add a 10 to 15 percent service charge. Tipping is up to you. On St Eustatius a 7 percent service charge for hotels and 15 percent for restaurants will normally be added to your bill.

Phones, post and email

There are **telephone** booths on Saba in The Bottom and Windwardside that you can use for international and local calls. On Statia, there are booths at the airport and around town; all take phonecards, sold at the airport and in stores.

Saba has **post offices** in The Bottom and in Windwardside, while Statia's only post office is on Cottageweg in Oranjestad and is open Monday to Friday 7.30am–4pm.

Most hotels will let you hook up to their **internet** connection for a minimal or no charge. On Saba, the *Breadline* internet café in Windwardside is open Monday to Saturday 10am–7pm and charges US$3 for ten minutes online.

The **country code** for both Saba and St Eustatius is ⓣ599.

Public holidays and festivals

As well as the public holidays listed on p.45 each island observes **Queen's Day** on April 30 and **Ascension Thursday** on the second Thursday in May.

Late July sees the **Saba Summer Festival**, a thoroughly enjoyable week of noisy parades, steel bands and colourful street parties, while **Carnival** is Statia's biggest party, taking place over ten days from late July to early August and finishing with a jump-up party at dawn on the last day and the crowning of the calypso king.

Language

Although Dutch is the official language of Saba and St Eustatius, **English** is spoken everywhere and taught as the first language at school.

For **histories** of Saba and St Eustatius see pp.483 and 489.

11.1

Saba

At the top of the Eastern Caribbean chain, and despite covering just thirteen square kilometres, **SABA** has plenty of small delights. Its quaint villages are neat and attractive places, its main road swept clean daily and largely free of the traffic that plagues nearby islands. Even more appealing, the island's volcanic origins and limited development mean that spectacular vegetation and scenery is within easy reach of the main villages, and an even more spectacular world of coral and fish just yards offshore.

Unless you're visiting St Martin, in which case you should at the very least make a day trip here, the main drawback of visiting Saba is the difficulty and cost involved in getting there. If that doesn't put you off, and you aren't looking for an island with busy action and nightlife, Saba's a great choice.

Some history

Saba is the peak of a volcano that last erupted some five thousand years ago, leaving a steep-sided and now luxuriously vegetated island. **Amerindians** were the first visitors, coming to the island in long dug-out canoes as they made their way from the river deltas of Venezuela up the chain of eastern Caribbean islands. The first Amerindian settlers probably arrived around 700 AD and lived in small communities based around fishing and simple farming. A handful of their artefacts are displayed in the museum in Windwardside (see p.485).

Columbus passed by the island in 1493 but didn't stop, and the island was largely ignored by European travellers until the Dutch laid claim to it in 1632, despatching a team from nearby St Eustatius (see p.489) to take up residence near Fort Bay in 1640. Unlike many islands in the area, the steep terrain meant that large sugar, tobacco or cotton plantations were not feasible, so development remained limited to a handful of small farms. Stone steps were carved down to Fort Bay to allow supplies to be brought in by ship, and remnants of the old trails and the stone walls built to enclose the farms can still be seen around the island.

Today, the island remains part of the **Kingdom of the Netherlands**, one of five Dutch islands in the Caribbean with their central administration in Curaçao (see p.804). Its tiny population is divided fairly equally between the descendants of the black slaves brought in to work the fields and the white farm-owners who ran them, although Sabans are often outnumbered by a combination of students at the US-owned medical school, expatriates and day-tripping tourists.

Accommodation

Though the **accommodation** options on Saba have been depleted by a recent bout of hurricanes, there's still a good mix of the elegant and the simple to cater for most budgets. Places to stay are scattered across the island, but Windwardside makes the most convenient base for hikers and has the best eating options.

Cranston's Antique Inn The Bottom ⓣ599/416-3203, ⓕ416-3443. Just five rather simple rooms at this longstanding and recently renovated guesthouse, all with four-poster beds, TV and A/C; there's also a small pool. ⑤

El Momo Cottages Windwardside ⓣ &

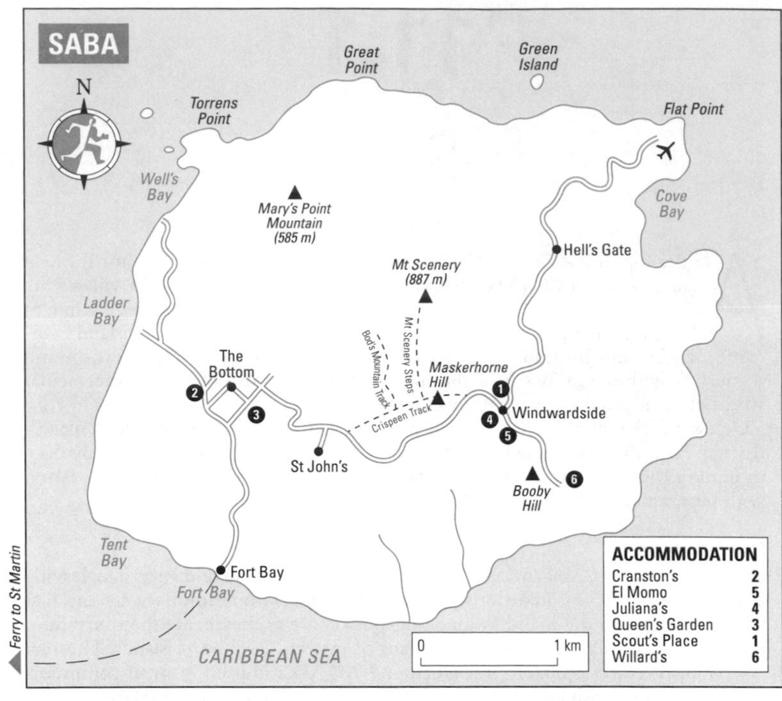

Ⓕ599/416-2265, Ⓦwww.elmomo.com. Five gingerbread cottages are dotted around the tropical gardens at this basic but easy-going place high on Booby Hill, and at US$40/50 a double room in summer/winter, it's the cheapest option on the island. Bathrooms are shared and there are hammocks to crash out in. ③

Juliana's Windwardside Ⓣ599/416-2269, Ⓕ416-2389, Ⓦwww.julianas-hotel.com. Bright and cheerful small hotel, with nine decent rooms as well as a separate apartment and two cottages, all with cable TV, private bathrooms and balconies. There's a small pool with sun loungers, and great views up to Mount Scenery and over the ocean. Expect to pay around US$70 for a single room in summer, US$100 in winter, and around US$30 more for a double room. The cottages and apartment go for US$115/135 in summer/winter.

Queen's Garden Resort The Bottom Ⓣ599/416-3494, Ⓕ416-3496, Ⓦwww.queensaba.com. Attractive and classy resort, set out in an isolated location nearly a kilometre east of town. There's a good-sized pool and jacuzzis, while the rooms are well equipped with antique furniture, kitchens, TV and fans or A/C. Superb private villas are also available (from US$400). ⑧

Scout's Place Windwardside Ⓣ599/416-2740, Ⓕ416-2741, Ⓔ Sabadivers@unspoiledqueen.com. German-owned, the largest of Saba's hotels has just fourteen simple but clean rooms, plus pool and restaurant, in a quiet location just off the centre of the village. This well-equipped place caters largely to divers, but it also makes a good base for walking and hiking if you haven't got your own transport. Ask for a room with an ocean view. ④

Willard's Windwardside Ⓣ599/416-2498, Ⓕ416-2482, ⒺWillard@sintmaarten.net. Saba's most luxurious hotel, with a handful of rooms perched away from it all on a cliff on Booby Hill overlooking Windwardside and the ocean. There's a large heated pool, a tennis court and a fancy restaurant, and the rooms and shared areas are fitted with attractive furniture. Double US$400.

The island

Saba's tiny **airstrip** is at the island's northern end. From here, the dramatic road – known as the Road – rises sharply towards the small village of Hell's Gate. Just outside the airport, a left turn off the Road takes you along Cove Bay Road towards a sign pointing to **Flat Point**, where you can see the remains of an abandoned boiling house, used during the eighteenth century to produce molasses from sugarcane grown on the island. Today Flat Point is a desolate place, with cacti and sea grape scattered around the coastal bluffs and plenty of good tide pools for hunting crabs and sea urchins.

Back on the Road, after a dozen or more switchbacks you reach **Hell's Gate**. Souvenir-hunting apart, there's no great reason to stop here. The main landmark is the Holy Rosary Church, which was built in the 1960s; behind it, Saban women at the community centre (weekdays 9am–noon & 2.30–5pm) sell traditional Saban lace, woven into handkerchiefs, napkins and tablecloths.

Windwardside

Beyond Hell's Gate, the Road cuts through rainforest-covered cliffs, offering spectacular views across the island as it winds towards **WINDWARDSIDE**, the main base for hiking trips (see p.487) and home to the tiny but worthy Saba Museum. It's a charming, relaxed and welcoming village with little traffic, and it makes the best place to stay and eat on the island. Bougainvillea, banana and palm trees line the road, lending colour to village gardens.

At the far end of the village, the **tourist office** (Mon–Fri 8am–5pm; ⓦwww.sabatourism.com), a small café and several art galleries are housed in **Lambee's Place**, once home to Josephus Lambert Hassell, a Saban who took a correspondence course in engineering and – despite official and learned protests that it was impossible – designed and oversaw the construction of "the road that couldn't be built", running from the airport in the north to Fort Bay in the south. A plaque outside the tourist office recalls Hassell's exploits; just beyond here you can start the hike to Mount Scenery (see p.487).

The **Saba Museum** (Mon–Fri 10am–noon & 1–4pm; US$2), housed in a 150-year-old cottage, recreates with a touch of nostalgia the traditional home of a nineteenth-century Saban sea captain, with a four-poster bed draped with Saban lace, a piano, maps and sextants in the study, and an old rock oven in the kitchen. Scattered around the house are artefacts from the island's past, among them pre-Columbian Amerindian finds such as a large cooking pot, polishing stones, tools and a cassava griddle. Much of the island's history is told through magazine articles from around the world that recount visits to Saba over the last century (particularly hair-raising are the descriptions of arriving by sea), as well as letters to and from Saban residents written in the eighteenth century. Pride of place goes to a letter from George Bush senior, thanking a Mr and Mrs Stewart for their (unspecified) support during the Gulf War. The bust in the

Saban lace and spice

Once an important export, **Saban lace** is now the traditional souvenir of a trip to the island. The history of local lace-making started in the 1870s, when Mary Gertrude Johnson returned to Saba from Venezuela, where she had learned the art in a Caracas convent. She passed her knowledge on to local women and the skills have been passed down through the generations. It's pretty stuff, if pricey. Saba Artisan Foundation has an outlet in The Bottom selling home-made crafts including lace and linen products.

If you're after something a bit stronger, **Saba Spice** is a potent rum-based herby liqueur made locally.

pretty grounds is of revolutionary Simón Bolívar, a gift from the government of Venezuela.

Southeast of Windwardside, **Booby Hill** has a couple of small hotels as well as some of the island's most expensive houses, which command magnificent views out to sea.

The Bottom

Having crossed through Windwardside the Road passes through tiny **St John's** – home to the island's only school – en route to Saba's main village The Bottom, the seat of government and the island's administrative centre. Beyond the town there's a wonderful view of the village, ranks of little white houses with traditional red roofs and green-trimmed shutters, nestled in among the surrounding peaks.

As you drop down the hill to **THE BOTTOM**, the first two buildings on the outskirts comprise the Saba University School of Medicine, whose students you'll see around the island, almost all of them from North America. Further down is the department of public works in a white-stone old school building and, on your right, the oldest Anglican church on the island, thought to date from the mid-1700s. Beyond here, the tidy streets are lined with old stone walls and white picket fences.

In the centre of the main square, a patch of grass holds the bust of **Samuel Charles**, a policeman gunned down here in 1989 in a rare drugs-related incident that shocked the island. Around the square, a series of neat buildings house the fire and police stations and the courthouse, while a handful of munching goats and immaculately dressed schoolchildren are likely to be roaming the nearby streets. At the western edge of the town, the grand **governor's house** (not open to the public) has particularly intricate wooden fretwork and splendid galleries.

Beyond the Bottom

West of The Bottom, a road ploughs through to Saba's only beach of note at **Wells Bay**, where you'll find a rather uninspiring patch of sand, though it makes a good spot to snorkel (bring your own gear). Heading south the Road winds down through dry, cactus-strewn terrain to the port at **Fort Bay**, home to the main dive operations and the arrival point for passengers coming to the island by boat (see p.481).

Eating and drinking

For a tiny island, Saba has a surprising variety of **places to eat**, with restaurants in most of the hotels and a good series of other places in Windwardside. As you'd expect, the local cuisine is heavily geared towards seafood.

Brigadoon Windwardside ☎599/416-2380. Set in an attractive old Saban house on the edge of the village, this friendly little place offers creole fish dishes featuring grouper and snapper, as well as more typical chicken, steak and lobster options. Reckon on around US$30 for three courses without wine. Open daily for dinner.

Cranston's The Bottom ☎599/416-3202. Tasty food served all day among the tropical flowers in the garden of Saba's oldest hotel, with local fish specials running around US$10 for lunch and US$15 in the evenings. Open daily for breakfast, lunch and dinner.

Guido's Windwardside ☎599/416-2230. The main island nightspot and pool hall, offering perfunctory food including burgers and pizzas for US$6–10. Open Monday to Friday for dinner only.

In Two Deep Fort Bay ☎599/416-3438. A good place to catch up on some lunch after a dive trip, *In Two Deep* offers inexpensive sandwiches, burgers and pizza, and fine views across the ocean and the tiny harbour. Open daily for breakfast and lunch.

Scout's Windwardside ☎599/416-2205. One of the busiest places during mealtimes, particularly in the evening when the diving crowd stops in. The rotis and burgers are good and cheap, while dinner often includes a fixed price three-course menu for under US$20. Open daily for breakfast, lunch and dinner.

Swinging Doors Windwardside ☎599/416-2506. Daily specials are chalked up outside this lively and pub-like saloon, with staples like chicken, burgers and ribs and moderately priced barbecues on Tuesday and Friday nights. Open daily for lunch and dinner.

Tropics Café Windwardside ☎599/416-2469. Friendly and inexpensive café offering large muffins and croissants to dunk in your coffee for breakfast and perfectly adequate sandwiches, burgers and omelettes at lunchtime, plus pitta pockets for US$6 and salads from US$7. Dinner options are more sophisticated – contemplate sweet pea and basil soup for US$6 and a seafood "pillow" with a variety of fish for US$14. Closed Sun.

Y11K Windwardside ☎599/416-2539. Probably the pick of the island's eateries. Eat inside or (better) out on the wooden deck overlooking Mount Scenery. There are good chicken and shrimp salads to graze on for around US$10, inexpensive sandwiches for snacking or, for dinner or to celebrate the end of a great hike, surf and turf for US$18 and pasta dishes running US$8–15. Open Monday to Saturday for lunch and dinner.

Hiking

The most popular **hike** on the island is from Windwardside up **Mount Scenery**, up 1064 concrete steps. The path is easy to follow, starting just west of the tourist office (see p.485), but it's a tough climb, taking an hour to ninety minutes to reach the top. Don't be put off; it's well worth the effort for the fantastic views and gorgeous tropical and quasi-Alpine vegetation. Much of the hike goes through secondary rainforest, with elephant ear ferns and mountain palms among some of the dramatic plants.

At the summit is an undisturbed and beautiful elfin forest of large mountain mahogany trees, their trunks and branches often covered in mosses, bromeliads and ferns. As for wildlife, you're sure to see colourful butterflies and birds as you climb, among them hummingbirds, bananaquits and tremblers if you're lucky, and you may spot a harmless racer snake slithering through the undergrowth.

There are several shelters en route to the summit, but there's nowhere to get refreshments so take **water** with you. As it can get very hot, particularly between noon and 2pm, plan to start your climb early in the morning, preferably on a relatively cloudless day, and take the best-grip footwear you've got. Once at the top (which can get rather chilly) don't miss the grand **lookout** over the neighbouring islands; to reach it head left of the communications tower and continue 100m along the pathway.

There are a couple of interesting side trails to the Mount Scenery climb. The round-trip **Maskehorne Hill Track**, veering off to the left near a small farmer's hut about fifteen minutes into your climb, adds another twenty minutes to your journey. It's a stiff clamber over large boulders and thick tree roots into the heart of the rainforest, ending on an outcrop of rocks that offers a dramatic view over Booby Hill and out to sea, before you retrace your path to the steps.

Further up the mountain, the delightful **Crispeen Track** cuts off to the west, passing through pastureland and farming plots before reaching the isolated Mountain Cottage, from where another lovely walk (**Bod's Mountain Track**) heads off to the right and then sharply right again to lead up the southwestern side of Mount Scenery. Alternatively, continue ahead at Mountain Cottage and follow the track down through a steep valley, flanked by abundant rainforest for about twenty minutes and you'll reach the deserted hamlet of **Crispeen**. The place was originally named for St Crispin – the patron saint of shoemakers; Dominican priest Père Labat, who visited Saba in 1701, wrote that "the Sabans ply trade in no other business except shoemaking". Beyond Crispeen the track descends along a rather less interesting stone path down to The Bottom, from where it's easy to hitch a ride back to Windwardside.

For **other hiking options** on Saba, get hold of a copy of the *Trail Guide* pamphlet and the Saba Conservation Foundation's booklet *Saban Trails* from the tourist office in Windwardside or the trail office across the road from the tourist office.

Diving

Superb **diving** is the reason most tourists make it to Saba. A marine park was designated in 1987, and carefully controlled operation of the dive sites scattered throughout the park (which surrounds the entire island) has kept the reefs in pristine condition. Visibility is excellent and, as well as fine coralheads near the surface for snorkelling, there are sheer walls dropping to over 300m just offshore. Most of the best dive sites are on the calmer, western side of the island, where you'll find great pinnacle dives as well as ridges and beautiful coral gardens.

Operators include Saba Deep (ⓣ599/416-3347, ⓦwww.sabadeep.com), Saba Reef (ⓣ599/416-2541, ⓦwww.sabareef.com) and Sea Saba (ⓣ599/416-2246, ⓦwww.seasaba.com). Rates are normally US$50/90 for a one-/two-tank dive, US$65 for a night dive and US$30 for a snorkelling trip, with an extra charge for equipment. A resort course for first-time divers costs around US$80 and (if there are three or more takers) a full certification course taught over four or five days runs about US$350. Bear in mind that prices normally come down significantly if you visit the island as part of a package that includes diving. For example, seven nights' accommodation and ten dives cost US$992/1138 per person at *Juliana's* (US$822/889 if two divers are sharing a room) and US$680 year-round at *El Momo*, booked through Sea Saba. Check the websites of the dive operators and the hotels (see p.483) for the latest deals, which change frequently.

11.2

St Eustatius

Despite a fascinating colonial history, Statia, as everyone knows the little island of **ST EUSTATIUS**, is now a tropical but slightly forlorn outpost of the Kingdom of the Netherlands. Once a proud and wealthy "entrepôt" or trading post between South America and Europe, the money and people have slipped away, leaving a historical curiosity that makes for an interesting day trip from St Maarten.

As with nearby **Saba**, the main drawback for those contemplating a trip is the expense and awkwardness of getting there. Those who make the effort will find that they have left the tourists behind for a tranquil and friendly spot, with good diving and hiking opportunities.

Some history

Statia was settled by **Amerindians** from Venezuela and Guyana, with evidence of their occupation dating to at least 300 AD. It is likely that some Amerindians were still here when Columbus passed by in 1493, but there were none when the first European settlers arrived, beginning with the French, who stopped here briefly in 1629 and were followed by Dutch settlers from Holland in 1636. Crops including tobacco and sugar were planted and, despite title regularly swapping between European nations, the island flourished.

The eighteenth century was Statia's heyday, with over eight thousand residents and more than 3500 ships visiting every year during its peak to **trade** both in local crops and in slaves. Janet Schaw, a Scot visiting the island in the 1770s, described the main town as "a place of vast traffic from every corner of the globe. The ships of various nations which rode before it were very fine…from one end of the town to the other is a continued mart, where goods of the most different uses and qualities are displayed…rich embroideries, painted silks, flowered muslins…exquisite silver plate, the most beautiful I ever saw."

At the time of Ms Schaw's visit, local entrepreneurs were making great profits running arms and supplies to the troops of George Washington's revolutionary army, and the island's most famous moment came in 1776 when Fort Oranje fired its cannons to salute an American ship. Needless to say the British, who largely controlled the eastern Caribbean, were not amused. In 1781 **Admiral Rodney** led an assault on the island in which many ships and supplies were seized and buildings along the harbour in Lower Town were torched and destroyed.

The period after Rodney's invasion saw a gradual decline in the island's fortunes. The abolition of slavery in the mid-nineteenth century was the death knell of the plantation system and, with the relentless exodus of residents, the island returned largely to **fishing** and **subsistence farming**. Today Statia is home to a little over two thousand people, dependent on government jobs and the steady trickle of tourists to keep the economy ticking.

Accommodation

You'll almost certainly want to stay in **Oranjestad**, the island's main town, which has a few simple guesthouses and a couple of hotels. There is a 7 percent service

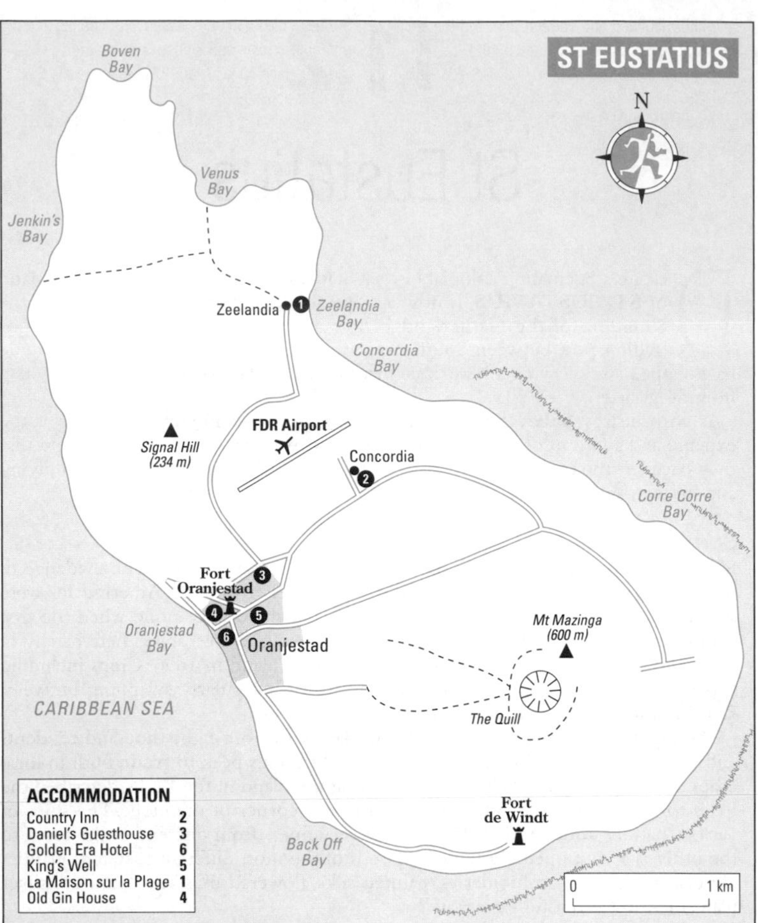

charge on room rates. The prices below are for the lowest-price double in high season unless otherwise specified.

Country Inn Concordia, southeast of Zeelandia ⓣ & ⓕ 599/318-2484. Just six rather simple rooms at this longstanding and popular guesthouse ten minutes east of the airport, all with cable TV and A/C. The friendly owners attract repeat visitors and they're happy to cook meals on demand. ③

Daniel's Guest House Oranjestad ⓣ & ⓕ 599/416 -2265. Five minutes' walk south of town, this small and very easy-going guesthouse has a couple of cosy rooms. ②

Golden Era Hotel Oranjestad ⓣ 599/318-2345, ⓕ 318-2445. Twenty clean and tidy rooms in this pleasant if slightly faded little hotel on the shoreline in Lower Town, just below Fort Oranje. All rooms have TV, A/C and private bathrooms. There's a small saltwater pool and a reasonable restaurant by the water. ④

King's Well Oranjestad ⓣ & ⓕ 599/318-2538. On the northwest edge of town, *King's Well* has ten rooms just above Oranje Bay, a short walk from the beach. Rates include a full breakfast and cost US$55 single, US$65–90 double depending on the size. Ask for a room with a view of the ocean.

La Maison sur la plage Zeelandia ⓣ 599/318-2256, ⓕ 318-2831. Although the beach here isn't great for swimming (see p.492), *La Maison* itself is splendidly isolated and comfortable, and there's an excellent restaurant on site (see p.492). ④

Old Gin House Oranjestad ⓣ599/318-2319, ⓕ 318-2135, ⓦwww.oldginhouse.com. The most luxurious of the island's hotels, an old colonial-style building with all modern conveniences. There's a pleasant pool, shaded with palms and with comfortable sun loungers and hammocks, and the place is handy for town. Choose from fourteen poolside rooms (⑥), plus a couple of ocean-view rooms (⑦). There's an excellent restaurant too (see p.492).

The Island

Virtually everyone arriving in Statia lands at the **Franklin Delano Roosevelt Airport**, which sits in the centre of the roughly pear-shaped island. A short drive to the southwest is Oranjestad, the capital and only town, while the Quill – a dormant volcano that offers the most dramatic scenery and best hiking on the island – can be seen off to the southeast.

Oranjestad

You'll almost certainly be staying in likeable, laid-back **Oranjestad** if you stop overnight on Statia. If you're just here on a day trip, it'll take you at least a couple of hours to have a good look around, and there are several places where you can get a splendid lunch.

While the town is rather sprawling, you'll want to confine your exploring to the main points of interest in the centre. **Upper Town** is where most of the (leisurely) action is, and makes for a pleasant place to wander and visit the island's museum and main colonial buildings. Linked by a footpath to Upper Town, **Lower Town** is the area of the old port, now home to the best beach locally and further ruins of the island's once-great past.

Upper Town

Fort Oranje (always open; free) is Oranjestad's dominant building, strategically situated on the cliffside overlooking Lower Town and Oranjestad Bay. The first fortifications were put up by the French settlers who came in 1629 but later abandoned the island. The Dutch who followed shortly after enlarged the fort in 1636, leaving it pretty much in its present state. The fort is also the site of the island's friendly and accommodating **tourist office** (Mon–Fri 8am–noon & 1–5pm; ⓣ599/318-2433, ⓦwww.statiatourism.com), which has maps and brochures.

The fort was restored in 1976, partly to celebrate the American Bicentennial, and with its cannon and old stone and brick walls it makes an evocative place, commanding fine views across the town and out to sea. Memorials in the cobbled courtyard include a plaque commemorating the momentous salute to the American ship *Andrew Doria* in 1776 (see p.489) and one to Dutch Admiral de Ruyter, who was stationed here in 1665.

Just outside the fort, the expertly restored **Government Guesthouse** is now home to the local governor and the courthouse, while a couple of minutes' walk away to the northeast the little **St Eustatius Museum** (Mon–Fri 9am–5pm, Sat 9am–noon; US$2), housed in one of the town's eighteenth-century houses, is one of the finest of its era and well worth stopping by. Historical finds ranging from Amerindian pottery and tools to colonial glassware and furniture are dotted around the first floor and basement, and there are exhibits that explain the importance of the sea trade to the island during its heyday. As you wander around, you'll get a feel of the high quality of life that the island's merchants enjoyed during their brief period of dominance. Admiral Rodney liked the lifestyle so much that he set up his base here after ransacking the island in 1781.

Among the colonial ruins in the centre of town are the remains of **one of the oldest synagogues** in the Caribbean. Drawn to the island's growing reputation as a trading post, Jewish settlers came here in the early eighteenth century from

Europe and Brazil, establishing successful shops and businesses around the port. The synagogue – down an alley across the road from the library – was built in 1739 (to the east, the oldest graves in the Jewish cemetery date back to the same period), though with the gradual Jewish emigration over the twentieth century the yellow-brick building has fallen into sad ruin, its roof gone.

A final relic of St Eustatius's golden era, the once-splendid mid-eighteenth century **Dutch Reformed Church** on Kerkweg, half a kilometre south of the Government Guesthouse, is also largely abandoned, though the tower was restored in 1981 and you can climb it for good views over the Upper and Lower Town free of charge.

Lower Town

Lower Town, the harbour area, carries little sign of its former glory, though you can see the ruins of old warehouses and stores that have collapsed into the sea, either through the deliberate action of the British navy in 1781 or through hurricane damage and crumbling neglect over the two centuries since. A short stroll along the waterfront and under the cliffs is enough to get a feel for the place's history, after which you'll want to make your way to **Oranje Beach** to the north for a snooze on the beige and black sand and a spot of snorkelling along the old seawall.

The rest of the island

There's not a great deal to see outside Oranjestad. Heading south the normally deserted main road leads past pretty little Key Bay to the sparse remains of eighteenth-century **Fort de Windt**, from where you'll share some great views across the ocean to St Kitts (see p.502) with a handful of roaming goats. It takes about 45 minutes to walk from the centre of town as far as the fort.

North of town the road winds past the airport up to **Zeelandia**, named for the southern province of Holland from where the island's first settlers came. The decent two-mile-long dark sand beach here makes a good spot for beachcombing and hiking though not for swimming, as the water is rough and known for dangerous undertows. West of the beach, a dirt track leads north through the scrubland along which you can hike down to another beach at Venus Bay or into the interior (see "Hiking" opposite).

Eating and drinking

Whether you're here for the day, or spending a couple of nights, there's enough variety of **restaurants** to keep you well fed throughout your stay.

Blue Bead Bar and Restaurant Gallows Bay ⓣ599/318-2873. Attractive little place just above the water in Lower Town that makes a good and inexpensive place for lunch if you're wandering around, with tasty salads, sandwiches, and fish and chips. Evenings dinner gets pricier, but you'll find good local grouper and snapper as well as meat dishes and lobster. Open daily for lunch and dinner.

Cool Corner Oranjestad ⓣ599/318-2523. Chinese and West Indian food on offer all day at this popular if unspectacular spot, featuring curries, sweet and sour dishes, fish sandwiches and other staples at US$8–12 a dish. Open daily.

La Maison sur la plage Zeelandia Beach ⓣ599/318 2256. Excellent restaurant, a ten-minute drive from Oranjestad, offering classy local seafood dishes such as creole snapper, lobster thermidor and an array of meat specialities that might include rack of lamb and beef tenderloin. Expect to pay US$15–25 for a main course. Open daily for lunch and dinner.

Old Gin House Oranjestad ⓣ599/318-2319. One of the best eating options on the island, with a Belgian chef serving a variety of French and Caribbean-influenced dishes. Lunch is normally served on the patio and features fresh fish as well as lighter meals; dinner at the elegant terrace restaurant normally includes lobster, steaks and curried dishes. A simple lunch will come to around US$12, and a three-course dinner US$30-40. Open daily.

Super Burger Oranjestad ⓣ599/318-2609. A good place to stop for a quick bite as you explore. Locals pop in and out all day for their sandwiches, chicken, burgers and ice cream. Open daily.

Hiking

By far the most popular hiking on St Eustatius is up the slopes and into the crater of **the Quill**, a dormant volcano that dominates the landscape of the southern end of the island, rising 2000ft to a crater that is itself nearly 1000ft across. You can follow good and well-signposted trails up and around the slopes of the volcano and into the crater itself, where a spectacular **rainforest** teems with wild orchids and anthuriums, hummingbirds and lizards.

To reach the Quill, take the road southeast out of Oranjestad and follow the signs leading to the trailhead. The footpath begins in low-level scrub, climbing through dry woodland and taller vegetation to the crater, a 45-minute walk away. From the crater rim, you can climb down into the crater itself, though you'll need to take a little care as the path is not always easy to follow. Walking through the thick vegetation to the crater bottom, you may spot coffee, cocoa and cinnamon trees, remains of the once-cultivated crops, as well as masses of bananas. Look out, too, for the huge silk cotton or kapok trees that can grow up to 150ft tall.

Alternatively, turn right along the crater rim, following the often slippery **Mazinga track** which offers fabulous views into the crater and across to neighbouring islands as you make your way through dense and humid rainforest and elfin woodland forest to the highest point on the island, often shrouded in clouds.

Besides the Quill, the island has a number of other **trails** worth exploring. At the northern end of the island are a couple of walks that lead to isolated bays and remote dry areas (once farmed, but now abandoned to the goats) dotted with Turk's-head cacti, century plants and sea grapes. Follow the dirt track that starts to the west of Zeelandia's only hotel and drop down through thorny scrub to a rocky area at Venus Bay, or turn right at the highest point and follow the path to the cliffside for fine views across the island and its neighbours.

A brochure detailing the island's hikes is available from the tourist office (see p.491).

Diving

Diving on Statia is excellent. Over two hundred shipwrecks are thought to litter the water off the west coast of the island, now crusted with coral and teeming with fish, though only a handful of these are accessible to divers. Some of the top dive sites (including "the Supermarket", where two coral-covered shipwrecks lie 60ft down and just 150ft apart) are just minutes from shore, and divers can expect to see turtles, stingrays and puffer fish, and perhaps even the rare flying gurnard. **Snorkelling** is good, too, with many ruined buildings and some of the wrecks lying in shallow turquoise waters just offshore.

Operators include Dive Statia (Ⓣ599/318-2435, Ⓦwww.divestatia.com) and Golden Rock Dive Centre (Ⓣ599/416-2541, Ⓦwww.goldenrockdive.com). Rates are normally US$50/80 for a one-/two-tank dive and US$25–30 for a snorkelling trip, with equipment being extra. A resort course for first-time divers costs around US$85 and (if there are three or more takers) a full certification course taking four or five days for US$350. Bear in mind that prices normally drop significantly if you visit the island as part of a **package** that includes diving. For example, seven nights' accommodation and ten dives can cost as little as US$500 per person based on double occupancy. Check the websites of the dive operators and hotels for the latest deals.

12

St Kitts and Nevis

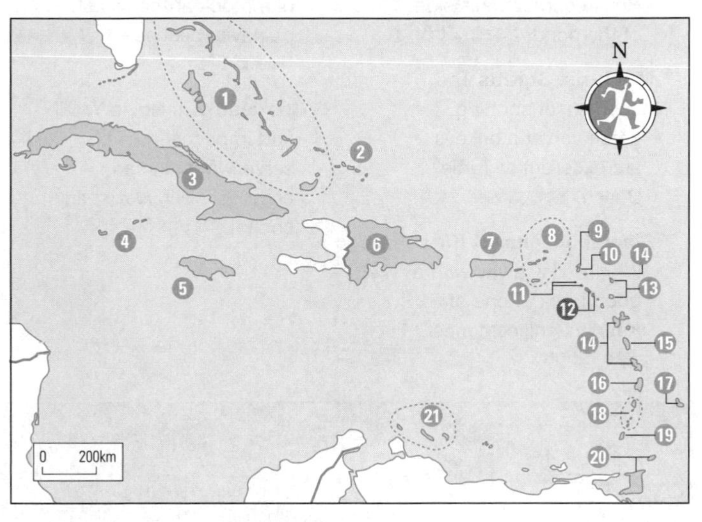

St Kitts and Nevis Highlights

* **Pete's BBQ, St Kitts** Follow the locals to this popular shack for delicious grilled lobster. See p.503.
* **Brimstone Hill, St Kitts** The most impressive British garrison this side of the pond. See p.505.
* **Monkeys, St Kitts** The chances of spotting green vervet monkeys are excellent at Turtle Beach. See p.504.
* **Plantation inns, St Kitts** Idle the day away with a good book at one of St Kitts' magnificent inns. See p.506
* **Sunshine's, Nevis** Nevis' best bar, known for its powerful rum-laced "Killer Bee". See p.508
* **Nisbet Beach, Nevis** Arrive early to grab a hammock at the nicest of Nevis' beaches. See p.508
* **Charlestown, Nevis** You'll find impeccably preserved West Indian architecture in Nevis' tiny capital. See p.507

Introduction and Basics

The islands of St Kitts and Nevis, which together comprise the smallest nation in the western hemisphere, are unique in the Eastern Caribbean for their remarkable preservation of West Indian culture and attitudes. Nowhere else in the region will you find such pristine examples of colonial architecture, gorgeous plantation inns, ramshackle sugar mills and genuine hospitality.

While there are ample opportunities for excellent diving and snorkelling, hiking and horse riding, kicking-back is the order of the day on both islands, their low-key ambience stemming, in large part, from the lack of massive resorts common elsewhere in the region. St Kitts' popular **Frigate Bay area** is currently undergoing expansion, however, which may herald a new era.

Where to go

For sheer atmosphere, St Kitts and Nevis' rambling **plantation inns** offer, bar none, the islands' most captivating getaways. If you want to spend your days relaxing on a verandah with a good book, surrounded by old-world charm, head for St Kitts' northern section, and Nevis **Gingerland** region, where you'll find the largest concentration of inns.

With the exception of Nevis' **Pinney's** and **Nisbet**, the islands' **beaches** are nowhere near as grand as the sandy stretches found in other parts of the Caribbean, and many of St Kitts' are black volcanic sand. Still, there are a good number to choose from, especially in St Kitts' **Frigate Bay** area, and the marvellously undeveloped **South-East Peninsula**. Nevis' options are fewer, but less crowded, and ideal if **privacy** ranks high on your list – the island is popular with celebrities for exactly this reason.

Brilliant marine life and submerged shipwrecks provide excellent **diving** conditions off the islands, particularly on the Caribbean side. Exhilarating **hiking** trails head into inland **rainforests** and up to the summits of Mount Liamuiga and Mount Nevis.

Basseterre and **Charlestown**, St Kitts' and Nevis' respective capitals, hold some interesting Caribbean heritage, including charming traditional skirt-and-blouse style houses, as well as British and French influences.

When to go

St Kitts and Nevis are both great year-round tropical destinations, with **temperatures** averaging 81°F (27°C). Sunny days are tempered by refreshing breezes, nights are cool, and there is no rainy season to speak of (though rainshowers can occur throughout the year).

Getting there

Most visitors arrive by **air**. Travellers from the US, Canada and Europe can fly with numerous airlines that service St Kitts and Nevis, including American Airlines, British Airways, Air Canada, Carib Aviation, LIAT, Nevis Express (☎869/469-9755) and Winair (☎869/465-2186). Flights to both islands connect in Antigua, St Croix, St Martin and San Juan, the most common stopover from the US and Canada. There are no flights from Australasia. For phone numbers of airlines, see pp.12–18 and 36–37.

Cruise liners (see p.14 and 16–17 in Basics) regularly berth in Basseterre. For information about **ferry** services, see "Getting around" on p.499.

When leaving St Kitts and Nevis, you'll need to pay a **departure tax** of US$16.50.

Money and costs

The **Eastern Caribbean dollar (EC$)** is the official currency on both islands. Notes are in denominations of EC$100, 50, 25, 10 and 5; the EC$1 coin equals 100 cents. Hotels tend to post their rates in US dollars, which are also widely accepted. Unless noted otherwise, prices in this chapter are quoted in US dollars. Most **banks** have **ATMs** that dispense the local currency; the

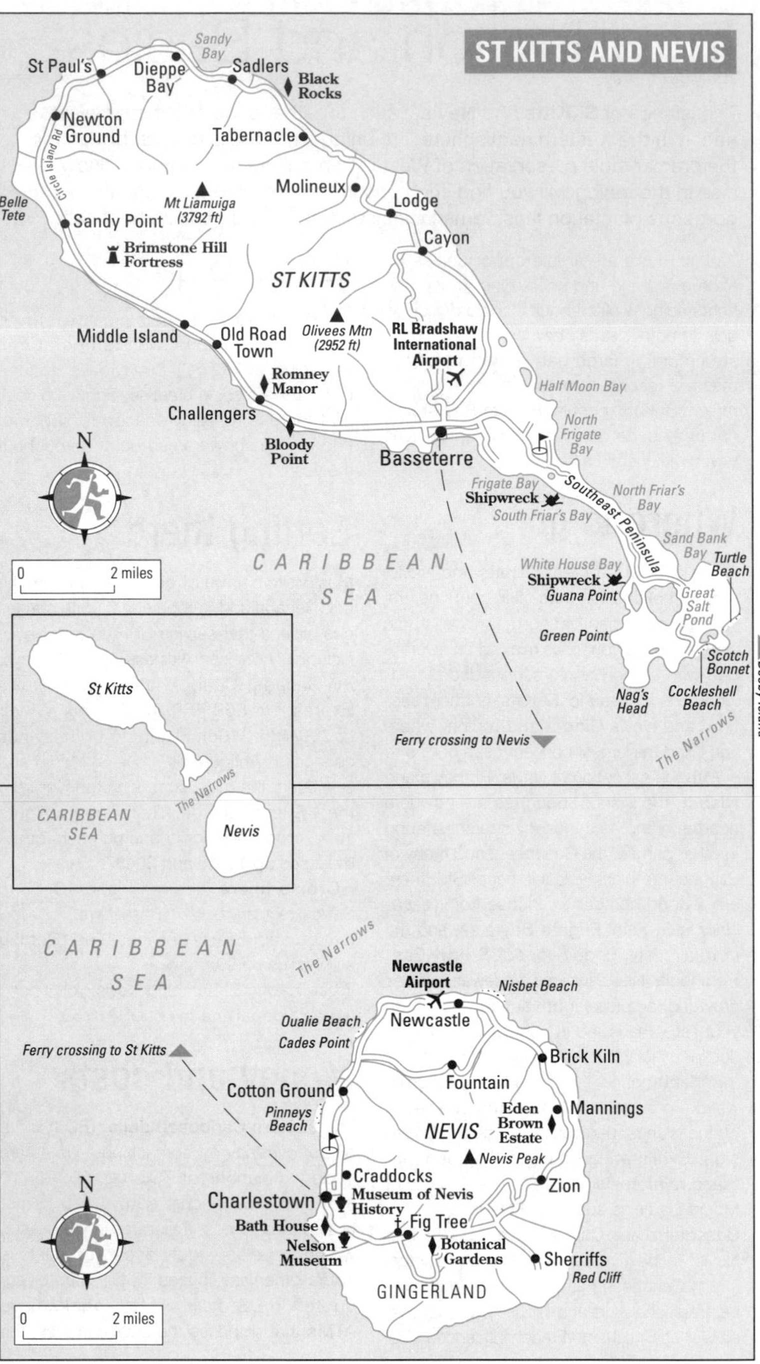

12 ST KITTS AND NEVIS

Royal Bank's ATM in Basseterre dispenses US dollars as well. Tellers here will also **change money** (Mon–Thurs 8am–3pm, Fri 8am–5pm); the exchange rate is fixed at EC$2.70/US$1. When paying for goods using US cash, the rate is usually lower, at US$1/EC$2.60.

While Nevis is significantly more expensive than St Kitts, with two people sharing a room you can get by on under US$50/day in either place, though you'll be relegated to their scarce and hardly spectacular budget hotels.

Note that most hotels and restaurants automatically charge 7 per cent **tax** plus 10 per cent service charge; in Nevis, the hotel tax is 8 per cent.

Information

Each island has its own tourism office and official **website** with links to hotels and services that you can book yourself (see p.502 and 507). Other sources to try are the website of the St Kitts and Nevis Hotel and Tourism Association (Ⓦwww.stkittsnevishta.org), covering accommodation and tour operators, and the government's website (Ⓦwww.stkittsnevis.net), which provides general background.

Getting around

Driving is on the left on narrow but fairly good roads with the odd pothole. These are nothing to the **bus** drivers who career around at alarming speeds. If you don't have your own wheels, and aren't up for a bus ride, you can get around by **taxi**. Island-hopping is most convenient by **ferry**, or you can take a ten-minute **flight**.

By bus

Public **buses** traverse northern St Kitts and all of Nevis from 6am until around 7pm on weekdays and Saturdays. Emblazoned with names like "Reggae Master" and blaring music from open windows, these minivans are easy to spot; you can catch them in the capitals or flag them down on the main roads outside of town; keep in mind that they don't follow any particular schedule. Fares are based on distance, with the most expensive trip, on both islands, being EC$3.50.

Note that in St Kitts, buses service the Circle Island Road, but not the resort areas south of Basseterre.

By taxi

Taxis congregate at both island airports and by the piers downtown in their respective capitals. By day, the most expensive trip will cost close to US$20; double that for complete island tours, night trips (Mon–Fri 10pm–6am), all day Sunday and holidays. To call for a taxi in St Kitts, dial Ⓣ869/465-8487 or 4253; in Nevis, call Ⓣ869/469-9790 (airport taxi stand) or 869/469-1483 or 5631 (Charlestown). You can also arrange for one at your hotel.

By car

There are no **car rental** offices at either of the islands' airports, but most agencies in Basseterre and Charlestown provide airport, ferry and hotel pick-up if you reserve in advance; they'll also arrange your mandatory **visitor's driver's licence** (EC$50). Rental companies include Avis (Ⓣ869/465-6507), TDC (Ⓣ869/465-2991; Ⓦwww.tdcltd.com) and Delisle Walwyn (Ⓣ869/465-8449; Ⓦwww.delisleco.com). Rates start at around US$30/day. As a general rule, to rent a car you must be 25, have had your licence for at least two years, and possess a major credit card that can be swiped for a US$500 deposit.

Note that if you intend to split your time between Nevis and St Kitts, some agencies, including the above, arrange dual-island rental packages, which is useful since only one island ferry allows you to take a car (see below).

By boat

Two to three **ferry** crossings a day embark from Basseterre and Charlestown. *Caribe Queen* (Ⓣ869/466-6119) and *Sea Hustler* (Ⓣ869/469-0403) both charge EC$20 round-trip for **passengers** only. If you want to take a **car** across, go with *Carib Breeze* (Ⓣ869/466-6734; EC$30–$40 round-trip). Tickets, sold on the day of travel only, usually go on sale about an hour before the scheduled departure time; it's best to arrive early. Crossings are about an hour, depending on conditions.

Leeward Island Charters (☎869/465-7474) offers daylong **sails** between Nevis and St Kitts; Sea Nevis Charter Boat (☎869/469-9239) has half-day, full-day and sunset sails.

By plane

There are several flights a day between St Kitts and Nevis with Nevis Express (see p.37 for contact info). The nine-seater two-prop planes fly for US$50 round-trip.

Accommodation

While St Kitts' Frigate Bay has a couple of large resorts, the rest of the island's **accommodation** is in small, cosy hotels and former-plantation **inns**. Similar smaller-scale lodgings are found on Nevis, with the exception of the *Four Season's Resort*. If you're booking your trip yourself, be sure to ask about **package deals** at island hotels.

While **camping** is legal and free on both islands' beaches, there are no facilities.

Food and drink

In addition to extravagant dining on both islands, there are plenty of inexpensive spots in the capitals to grab a bite. Fresh **seafood** is the fare of choice, with the most expensive offering being the spiny lobster. Another speciality is flying fish, served grilled and in sandwiches. Plantation inns tend to favour **West Indian** curries and seasoned vegetables, while a touch of **Jamaican**, like jerk chicken and rotis, is quite common at smaller restaurants and some beach grills.

The most popular **drink** is CSR (Cane Spirit Rothschild), a clear sugarcane liqueur, mixed with Ting, a tangy, grapefruit soda. Carib is the local **beer**; St Kitts also brews Guinness.

Phones, post and email

Many public **telephones** take coins; those that don't take **phonecards**, available in EC$10, EC$20 and EC$50 denominations from the post office, Cable and Wireless outlets, and convenience stores.

> The **country code** for St Kitts and Nevis is ☎869.

The regional prefix for both islands is ☎869. For directory assistance when you're there, dial ☎411.

The **postal** service has offices in Basseterre and Charlestown (Mon–Wed & Fri 8am–3pm, Thurs & Sat 8am–12noon). Sending a postcard costs EC$0.80 to the US, EC$1 to the UK and Europe, and EC$1.20 to Australia; add 10–40¢ for letters.

The **internet** is only starting to catch on here and checking **email** is expensive. St Kitts' only internet café, *Leyton's*, is on Basseterre's Fort Street. Nevis' sole web source, *Connextions*, is on Main Street in Charlestown, south of the pier.

> In case of emergency, dial ☎911.

Opening hours, holidays and festivals

As a general rule, **opening hours** are Monday through Friday 8am–noon and 1–4.30pm, with some banks closing around 3pm earlier in the week. Shops and services tend to stay open later when there's a cruise ship in town, but essentially close up altogether on Sunday, when the only places operating are hotel restaurants.

As well as the **public holidays** listed on p.45, St Kitts and Nevis celebrate **the Queen's Birthday** on the second Saturday in June, **August Monday** on the first Monday in August, and **Independence Day** on September 19.

In addition to closures on holidays, businesses on St Kitts often shut down during festivals, the biggest of these being **Carnival**, which runs from December 24 to January 3, with calypso performances and costumed street dancing. June brings the four-day **Music Festival**, a showcase of headlining calypso, soca, reggae, salsa and gospel acts. Nevis' main festival, the weeklong **Culturama** takes place in early August, with music performances and beauty pageants; the end of the month is **Carifiesta** time, a ten-day affair attracting artists from around the Caribbean.

History

First sighted by Christopher Columbus on his second New World voyage in 1493, St Kitts was originally known as Liamuiga, or Fertile Land, by resident Caribs. Designated "St Christopher" by Columbus, the island wasn't settled until over a century later, when an Englishman named Sir Thomas Warner came ashore in 1623, and established **Old Road Town**. A small posse sailed for Nevis five years later and set up a camp near **Cotton Ground** that later fell to a 1680 earthquake.

St Kitts didn't remain entirely British for long, as the threat posed by oppressed native **Caribs** prompted Warner to form a union with the French the following year. Their combined legions decimated the lot in a bloody battle in 1627.

The ensuing liaison was tenuous as the island was split between the two colonial superpowers. The French lorded over the northern and southern coasts and established the modern-day capital, **Basseterre**; the British controlled the leftover areas in between. These were occasionally wrested from the British by the French as well, culminating in a one-month siege at **Brimstone Hill** in 1782. The **Treaty of Paris**, signed the following year, officially returned St Kitts to the British and put an end to the squabbles.

Nevis, meanwhile, had no part in the struggle, and instead became the region's most profitable sugarcane producer and destination of choice for Britain's rich and famous thanks to its **natural spas**. Indeed, **Lord Nelson** made his mark here by marrying local **Fanny Nisbet** in 1787.

The two islands were only joined as a federated state in 1983, following failed geopolitical associations like the West Indian Federation and the Associated States that included neighbouring Anguilla. The one condition for their union, that Nevis be allowed to separate at a later date, may ultimately prove their undoing, as the latter continues to strive for independence.

12.1

St Kitts

Paddle-shaped **ST KITTS** lies a few miles northwest of Nevis, just across The Narrows. Lush rainforest covers the central mountain range that forms the island's spine, while the surrounding lowlands are largely given over to sugarcane fields. Most visitors tend to head directly to the resort area of **Frigate Bay**, focusing their time in the southern region where all of the island's beaches are found. The best of these fringe the **South-East Peninsula**, an undulating spit skirted by the island's only white sand. Nearer to St Kitts' centre, the capital, **Basseterre**, is worth a visit for its concentration of traditional **skirt-and-blouse** style houses, while traces of the island's imperial past lie closer to its north end, where the star attraction, **Brimstone Hill Fortress**, presides over the Caribbean. The northern coast has its own quiet appeal, with fields of overgrown sugarcane sheltering gracious **former-plantation inns**, while the Atlantic side offers dramatic vistas and little else.

Arrival and information

The **Robert L. Bradshaw International Airport** (Ⓣ869/465-8121), located two miles from Basseterre, is well served by **taxis** costing US$7 to the capital, US$11 to Frigate Bay and US$15 to Sandy Point. There is no bus service from here, but some resort hotels pick their guests up on request. For details on **car rental**, see p.499.

Ferries from Nevis dock at Basseterre's central pier.

For **information**, visit the friendly tourism office in Basseterre's Pelican Mall (Mon–Fri 8am–4.30pm; Ⓣ869/465-4040 or 1-800/582-6208, Ⓦwww.stkitts-tourism.com).

Basseterre

Settled by the French following the partition of St Kitts in 1628, the island capital, **BASSETERRE**, on the Caribbean coast, is French in name only today. Its centre, **The Circus**, reflects the town's later British dominion; the roundabout circling the green **Berkeley Memorial Clock** is allegedly modelled after London's Piccadilly, though the only obvious similarity is the traffic. Traces of British rule also dominate due east, in the historical town centre, **Independence Square**, where walkways imitating the spokes of a Union Jack are inlaid with red stones. A maiden-topped fountain at its nexus, a gift from Queen Elizabeth to commemorate St Kitts' independence in 1983, marks the spot that once hosted the Lesser Antilles' largest **slave market**; slaves were bathed at the small red fountain on the square's south side prior to mounting the stage. The square looks onto the staid 1927 **Immaculate Conception** cathedral, its substantial twin-towered facade devoid of the drama associated with Anglican **St George's**, a few blocks northwest of the Circus. The French parish that originally stood here was incinerated in 1706 by the British, who rebuilt their own church in 1856–59, complete with menacing spearheads on the ground-floor Gothic windows.

English–French distinctions aside, Basseterre's most remarkable aspect is its preservation of traditional Caribbean **skirt-and-blouse homes** built with stone ground floors topped by wooden levels – the stone prevented flooding, the wood allowed a breeze – and trimmed with dainty gingerbread fretwork. Many demonstrate a certain cultural ingenuity, most obvious along **Fort Street**, where old sentinel walls have been incorporated in their construction. Others are deceptively ancient, having been rebuilt using stones from Brimstone Hill Fortress (see p.505), following an 1867 fire that ravaged most of the town. (Note that if you want to take pictures of private homes, you should get the owner's permission first.) A decent collection of photographs pre-dating the fire is displayed at the **St Christopher Heritage Society** (Mon–Fri 9am–5pm, Sat 9am–noon; free), at the foot of the Circus.

Accommodation

There are only a few in-town **hotel** options, and most cater to business travellers or visiting dignitaries. The exception is the island's lone **budget** option, *Glimbaro*.

Bird Rock Beach ⓣ869/465-8914 or 1-800/621-1270, ⓕ869/465-1675, ⓦwww.birdrockbeach.com. This hotel, with the only real beach around, has 46 standard doubles and a swim-up pool bar. 5

Glimbaro on Cayon Street ⓣ869/465-2935, ⓕ869/465-9832, ⓔglimbaro@caribsurf.com. Despite a reception that doubles as an exterminator's office, the ten twin-bedded rooms here are decent enough. 2

Ocean Terrace Inn ⓣ869/465-2754 or 1-800/524-0512, ⓕ869/465-1057, ⓦwww.oceanterraceinn.net. Basseterre's best hotel has three freshwater pools and well-equipped rooms and suites with kitchens. 6

The Palms ⓣ869/465-0800, ⓕ869/465-5889, ⓦwww.palmshotel.com. Though the doubles and suites here are just average, their location, on a second-storey right on the Circus, can't be beat. 4

Eating and drinking

Some of the cheapest **food** in St Kitts can be found at Basseterre's ferry docks, where roadside shacks grill up great seafood for a fraction of the price you'd pay elsewhere. A number of other eateries in town also offer tasty meals.

American Bakery Fort Sreet. A good selection of inexpensive pastries, cakes and sweets, and one of the only spots open on Sundays. Mon–Sat 6am–7pm, Sun 2–7pm.

Ballahoo The Circus ⓣ869/465-4197. Boasting a prime location on an airy verandah, this popular moderately priced restaurant has a fine seafood menu, including superb lobster thermidor. Mon–Sat 8am–11pm.

Bambu's Bank Street. A trendy joint with an affordable pub-style menu ranging from jerk chicken wings and burgers to nachos and conch fritters.

Chef's Church Street. A verandah with a low-key ambience and inexpensive sandwiches and burgers.

Fisherman's Wharf Below *Ocean Terrace Inn*. Moderately priced tasty seafood served at picnic tables on a breezy pier; head to the buffet to pile on extra fixings like creole rice and mac-and-cheese.

Pete's BBQ Ferry docks. This inexpensive rustic roadside BBQ shack serves, hands down, the best lobster you'll eat on St Kitts and, quite possibly, in the entire Eastern Caribbean; the heaping orders of spare ribs are pretty mouthwatering too. Open Fri & Sat night only.

Frigate Bay

St Kitts' only beach resort area, **FRIGATE BAY** is three miles southeast of the capital, on flatlands sandwiched by the Atlantic and Caribbean Sea. On the Atlantic side lies **North Frigate Bay** beach, a deep golden band fronting unswimmable waters thanks to a strong undertow. The narrow **South Frigate Bay** (also known as Timothy Beach), on the calmer Caribbean side, has a **watersports** shack with snorkelling gear, windsurfers and kayaks; staff also organize three-hour snorkelling trips to nearby reefs and shipwrecks (US$25). Between the two beaches is St Kitts' expansive, 27-hole **golf course**, and a **casino**.

Despite the dearth of beachfront in the immediate vicinity, Frigate Bay is currently the focus of major expansion efforts; the sprawling 1000-room *Royal St Kitts* (ⓣ869/465-1290 or 1-888/217-5645), slated to open in late 2002, will rank as the Eastern Caribbean's biggest resort.

Accommodation

Frigate Bay ⓣ869/465-8935 or 1-800/266-2185, ⓕ869/465-7050, ⓦwww.frigatebay.com. Located within walking distance of South Frigate Bay, the nicest of the area's small resorts has forty airy rooms in sunny yellow and blue-trimmed units. Use of golf course and pool with swim-up bar are included. ⑦

Horizon Villa ⓣ869/465-0584 or 1-800/830-9069, ⓕ869/465-0785, ⓔtrafalga@caribsurf.com. Perched above the Caribbean, this resort of one- to four-bedroom ivy-covered villas looks like it belongs in the English countryside. Spacious units include kitchens, terraces and superb views; rates include greens fees. ⑧

Timothy Beach ⓣ869/465-8597 or 1-800/288-7991, ⓕ869/466-7085, ⓦwww.timothybeach.com. A pleasant, laid-back hotel on South Frigate Bay beach; the sixty rooms, with king-size beds and wicker furniture, aren't fancy, but they're good value. One- to two-bedroom apartments with kitchens also available. ⑤

Eating and drinking

Since Frigate Bay lacks a town centre, most area **restaurants** are located inside hotels.

Cisco's Oriental Bistro Behind *Island Paradise*. Low-frills bistro serving up typical Chinese dishes and a tasty lobster with bamboo concoction. Dinner only; closed Tues.

Marshall's At *Horizon Villa* (ⓣ869/466-8245). The most upscale option in the area, this restaurant has a swanky poolside setting and expensive seafood.

Monkey Bar On South Frigate Bay beach. The best spot around to drink and mingle with the locals, this small thatched beach hut gets especially rowdy on Fridays after work.

PJ's Pizza Bar and Restaurant Facing the golf course. The only non-hotel-affiliated eatery around is an excellent source of super-cheap pizzas, sandwiches, chili and lasagna. It also encourages liberal imbibing during the daily happy hour from 6pm to 7pm. Dinner only; closed Mon.

Sunset Café At *Timothy Beach*. You can people-watch from a beachside terrace at this popular spot while noshing on a wide range of beach fare or the chef's signature pasta carbonara.

South-East Peninsula

The **SOUTH-EAST PENINSULA**, which extends towards Nevis from Frigate Bay, boasts grassy peaks and St Kitts' finest **beaches**. These only became publicly accessible in 1990, with the opening of the twisting road that cuts through the peninsula's centre. Despite the development potential heralded by the road, hotel construction has been slow and the area remains almost as remote as ever. You're likely to spot one of the island's numerous **vervet monkeys** as you head south to the peninsula's most happening pocket, **Turtle Beach**, home to a lively beach bar and restaurant, the *Purple Turtle*. The shores around **Booby Island**, an islet facing the beach, abound with marine life, providing good **snorkelling** and **diving**; contact Pro Divers for details (ⓣ869/466-DIVE, www.prodiversstkitts.com). The one downside is the beach's popularity with cruise-ship day-trippers; if things get too busy, nearby **Cockleshell Beach**, around a hill to the west, is a good alternative.

Halfway down the western coast, **White House Bay** fronts a modest stretch of sand with some of the best **snorkelling** on the island, thanks to a shallow-lying **shipwreck** just offshore. The two bays at the neck of the peninsula, **North Friar's Bay** and **South Friar's Bay**, get more visitors because of their proximity to Frigate Bay.

Currently the only place to **stay** on the peninsula is the *Turtle Nest*, a spacious one-bedroom apartment over the restaurant at Turtle Beach, with expansive living room, full kitchen and great views (Ⓣ869/465-9086, Ⓔgary@caribsurf.com; ❺).

Along the Circle Island Road

The northern part of St Kitts, traversed by the **CIRCLE ISLAND ROAD**, is an easy half-day excursion, though if you have the time, you should break up the drive with lunch at St Kitts' best West Indian restaurant, *Rawlins Plantation Inn* (see overleaf). Better yet, base yourself at one of St Kitts' charming **plantation inns** that are concentrated in this part of the island. The topography here is typical West Indies, with scores of sugarcane fields, windmills and ramshackle churches.

Bloody Point to Middle Island

The first stop of note, four miles north of Basseterre, is **Bloody Point**, a hillock on the outskirts of Challengers village that witnessed a brutal Carib massacre in 1626. A one-hour hike affords glimpses of cartoon-like petroglyphs engraved into the rocky hillside.

After the point, the road heads down to the seaside village of **Old Road Town**, the island's first settlement under Sir Thomas Warner's tenure (see p.501); the only vestige is a derelict redbrick building that once served as Government House. Better maintained are the **petroglyphs** that pre-date Warner's arrival, etched on a boulder along the nearby road signposted to Romney Manor; the pregnant-looking character is a fertility idol. The onetime estate of Thomas Jefferson's great grandfather, **Romney Manor** lies at the end of the road, its smart yellow cottages now home to Caribelle Batik (Mon–Fri 8.30am–4pm; closed Sat & Sun), a popular **handicraft** boutique. The surrounding grounds feature a **botanical garden** (free) with a 350-year-old saman tree as its centrepiece. The derelict ruins of Jefferson's brother William's sugar plantation lie below, notable for the extensive aqueduct that's used today as the departure point for **rainforest hikes**. Greg's Safaris (Ⓣ869/465-4121, Ⓦwww.skbee.com/safaris) offers half-day treks in the area for US$40, as well as more strenuous full-day climbs up Liamuiga (see p.506) for US$60. Back on the main road, another mile north along the Caribbean coast, lies **Middle Island** village, where an unkempt cemetery contains Sir Thomas Warner's extravagant marble **tomb**.

Brimstone Hill Fortress National Park

A few miles north of Middle Island, the conical 800ft **Brimstone Hill** hulks over the flatlands, its name derived from the sulphuric odours exuding from nearby underwater vents. The British mustn't have minded the smell since they chose the hill's flanks to support a **fortress** (daily 9.30am–5.30pm; US$5) so grand it was nicknamed the "Gibraltar of the West Indies". Started in 1690 and expanded over the course of the following century, the sprawling garrison ultimately proved insufficient defence – it was captured by the French in 1782 after a one-month siege. The Paris Treaty forced its return a year later, but the fortress fell into disuse as relations eased between the warring nations and the dwindling economics of sugarcane production meant island resources no longer needed protection. Abandoned in 1853 and left to deteriorate until 1965, an ambitious restoration project has returned the fortress to its former splendour, and earned it UNESCO World Heritage Site recognition in 2000.

The prominent hilltop compound, the **Citadel**, provides spectacular views from its parapets. The fortifications themselves surround a water catchment system. The enclosing barracks house an eclectic **museum** showcasing military paraphernalia, Carib tools and decorative *adornos* (small clay figurines) and a rubbing of the petroglyphs at Old Road Town (see p.505). On the grassy parade, stairs access the lower bastions on a promontory with a tiny **military cemetery** outside the rampart walls. A **canteen** near the steps serves snacks, or you can picnic.

Note that the **bus** to Brimstone Hill drops you off on the main island road, after which it's another 2km on foot up a very steep hill.

Sandy Point to Black Rocks

Beyond the fortress, the road passes the remains of **Fort Charles**, a 1672 military outpost used as a leper colony from 1890 to 1995, before arriving in **Sandy Point**, St Kitts' second largest town. Not much happens here, except for **diving** at the offshore reef; contact Dive St Kitts for more information (Ⓣ869/465-1189 or 1-800/621-1270, Ⓦwww.divestkitts.com). The point itself is a rather grubby black-sand beach.

Lying in the flatlands below the crater-capped **Mount Liamuiga** (see p.505 for hiking information), the island's highest point at 3792ft, the northern coast is set to change dramatically in upcoming years as high-rolling developers transform it into St Kitts' secondary resort area. For now, the coastal stretch between **Newton Ground** and **Sandy Bay** retains an evocative old-world aura, with windswept ocean vistas, fields of untamed sugarcane and the ruins of abandoned plantations; what few estates remain now house **inns** (see below) that make for excellent lodging or lunch stops. The main settlement this far north, **Dieppe Bay**, is a former French village that marks the start of the Atlantic coast. Midway down the Atlantic side lies St Kitts' jaw-dropping natural wonder, **Black Rocks**, a jumble of solidified black lava formations that tumble into the sea. A viewing area is signposted to the left of the main road.

Practicalities

Even if you don't stay at one of St Kitts' **plantation inns**, you should make a point of experiencing some of their old-world ambience by stopping in for a **meal** (reservations recommended for dinner). By far the most authentic, situated inland from the northern coast, *Rawlins Plantation* (Ⓣ869/465-6221, Ⓕ465-4954, Ⓦwww.rawlinsplantation.com; US$430 includes full board), has ten distinctive stone cottages furnished with antiques, a library sitting room and 25 acres of land infused with the scent of sugarcane. A glossier option just outside of Dieppe Bay, *Golden Lemon* (Ⓣ869/465-7260, Ⓕ465-4019, Ⓦwww.goldenlemon.com; breakfast included; ⑨), has a splendid location on a black-sand beach, eight spacious Main House rooms with gabled roofs and eighteen newer villas with full kitchens and private plunge pools. *Ottley's* (Ⓣ869/465-7234 or 1-800/729-0709, Ⓕ869/465-4760, Ⓦwww.ottleys.com; ⑨), a few miles south of Black Rocks, offers 24 expansive rooms with flounces befitting a princess – Anne, for one, has stayed here – and beautifully manicured grounds.

12.2

Nevis

Inundated with sugarcane, gorged with wild bougainvillaea and hibiscus, and sprinkled with overgrown windmills, tiny **NEVIS'** rural beauty and backwater charm make it unique in the Caribbean, and are the keys to its appeal. Most of the sightseeing consists of poking around the enchanting capital, **Charlestown**, where well-preserved **skirt-and-blouse** houses and a couple of excellent history **museums** provide an easy afternoon's distraction. Outside the capital, you're left to wander about the odd country church, go **horse riding** in the hinterlands, **hike** up **Mount Nevis**, explore unspoiled **dive** sites off the coast, or – as many visitors do – spend most of your time on one of the four white-sand beaches.

The island is small enough that it can be experienced on a day trip from St Kitts – a good option if you're watching your budget, as Nevis is a good deal pricier.

Arrival and information

Those arriving by **air** at Nevis' miniscule Newcastle Airport land on the north coast, miles away from the capital and most lodging. Hotels typically pick up guests on request; otherwise, **taxis** charge US$10 to Pinney's Beach and the capital, and US$17 to Gingerland inns. There is no bus service from the airport. **Ferries** drop passengers in the centre of Charlestown, a hop and a skip from Pinney's Beach. For information, the helpful **tourism office** is a two-minute walk northeast of Charlestown's pier, on the east side of Main Street (Mon–Fri 8am–5pm; ⓣ869/469-1042, ⓦwww.nevisisland.com).

Charlestown and around

Nevis' small capital, captivating **CHARLESTOWN**, boasts an impeccable assemblage of gingerbread-trimmed **skirt-and-blouse houses**, in keeping with residents' resolutely old-fashioned attitudes. These traditional attitudes can also be seen in the 1825 **courthouse** on a day that someone's being tried for swearing in public; you'll see the cusser in question sitting in a draconian crib-like prisoner's box. The upstairs **library**, with its heavy-set ceiling braced by mahogany gunwales, is equally devoid of modernity. Indeed, it seems the only thing that's changed about Charlestown in its near four-hundred-year history is that the 1778 **Bath House** – once the Caribbean's most happening spa – closed its shutters for good in the 1950s. The **hot springs**, however, at the south end of town, remain as invigorating as ever, and Nevisians and visitors alike are still fond of immersion. To partake of them yourself, you'll have to bring a towel and don your suit in advance, as there are no facilities.

The best place to garner some island background is at the quaint **Museum of Nevis History** on Main Street (Mon–Fri 9am–4pm, Sat 9am–noon; US$2). Its informative collection of odds and sods occupies the main floor of a Georgian-style building on the grounds where Alexander Hamilton was born in 1757. While the Hamilton house was devastated by a mid-1800 earthquake, sovereign state-making is still being discussed above the museum in chambers used by Nevis' pro-independence House of Assembly. Near the hot springs at the opposite end of town, the **Horatio Nelson Museum**, on Building Hill Road (Mon–Fri 9am–4pm, Sat 9am–noon; US$2), focuses on Lord Nelson, who came ashore in 1785 and wound up marrying the governor's niece, Fanny Nisbet. While the collection consists mainly of kitsch and some pilaster copies of Nelson's Column, it gives a captivating overview of Nelson's Caribbean adventures.

Along Government Road lies a remnant of another chapter in Nevisian history, a **Jewish cemetery** whose oldest stone dates from 1684. It's thought that a nearby grey-stone building served as a **synagogue**.

Practicalities

With the exception of a couple of rather downtrodden hotels, Charlestown is utterly lacking in **accommodation** options. If you're on a budget, though, the *Sea Spawn Guest House* on Main Street (ⓣ869/469-5239; ❷), near Pinney's Beach, will suffice, with eighteen small rooms equipped with private bath and portable fan. **Restaurants** are more numerous. *Café des Arts* is a delightful place serving up sandwiches, quiches and strong coffees on the ground floor and gardens of Hamilton House, across from the Museum of Nevis History. *Eddy's*, south of the pier, on Main Street, dishes out fish and chips and the like on a second-floor verandah; it turns into a **karaoke** bar on Wednesday nights and a 1970s **disco** on Fridays. Closer to the pier, the seaside terrace at *Unella's* is an appropriate backdrop for the fine seafood on offer; red snapper and lobster make star appearances, but don't come cheap. Set back from the main road, on Chapel Street, *Le Bistro* is a cosy place with daily fish specials that's also popular for its Friday **happy hour**. For beach picnics, stock up at *The Nevis Bakery* on Happy Hill Alley.

Around Charlestown: Pinney's Beach

By far the most popular beach on Nevis, **Pinney's Beach** is not the island's finest, but, being just a fifteen-minute-walk from the Charlestown pier, is the most convenient for day-trippers from Nevis and cruise passengers. The four-mile-long stretch has a smattering of rusty cannons and crumbling bastions belonging to **Fort Ashby** – one of eight fortifications that defended the coast in the 1700s – at its northern end.

You can **stay** right on the beach at the ultra-swanky *Four Seasons* (ⓣ869/469-1111, ⓕ469-1040, ⓦwww.fourseasons.com; US$495). A less pretentious option lies a couple of miles further up the coast, at the amiable *Inn at Cades Bay* (ⓣ869/469-8139, ⓕ469-8129, ⓦwww.cadesbayinn.com; ❼) where sixteen spacious waterfront bungalows are fronted by hammock-strung porches. You can **eat** home-cooked beach fare and hearty Sunday brunches at the inn's restaurant, *Tequila Sheila's*; or blackened fish and conch dishes at *Seafood Madness*, on Pinney's Road; and grilled seafood and lobster at Nevis' best **bar**, *Sunshine's*, on Pinney's Beach – famous for its Killer Bee, a potent rum and passion fruit concoction.

Oualie and Nisbet beaches

Further up the west coast, **Oualie Beach** graces a calm cove with the island's greatest concentration of **watersports** outfits right on the sand. You can rent snorkelling gear from Nevis Watersports (ⓣ869/469-9060) and Scuba Safaris (ⓣ869/469-9518, ⓔscubanevis@caribsurf.com); both organize half-day outings, and the latter is also the island's only **dive** outfit. One of the island's most popular diving excursions visits the **Monkey Shoals**, a grotto-filled stretch of reefs five miles offshore, halfway between Nevis and St Kitts.

After Oualie Beach, the island road wraps around the northern slopes of **Mount Nevis** and passes the airport before reaching **Nisbet Beach**, Nevis' nicest. Its deep white sand, facing the Atlantic, is scattered with elegant coconut trees strung with hammocks.

Practicalities

Of the three places to **stay** on the northern coast, *Oualie Beach* (ⓣ869/469-9735 or 1-800/682-5431, ⓕ869/469-9176, ⓦwww.oualie.com; ❼) is the most casual; its pretty gingerbread cottages are all well appointed and have screened-in verandahs. The sprawling *Mount Nevis* (ⓣ869/469-9373 or 1-800/756-3847, ⓕ869/469-9375, ⓦwww.mountnevishotel.com; ❽), perched on a plateau, is blessed with awesome panoramic views, but its 32 rooms lack panache. The poshest of the bunch, *Nisbet Plantation* (ⓣ869/469-9325 or 1-800/742-6008, ⓕ869/469 9864, ⓦwww.nisbetplantation.com; US$475, includes full board), occupies thirty acres backing Nevis' finest beach; options range from small cottage rooms to one-bedroom suites. Nearby, Garner's Estate (ⓣ869/469-5528) offers **horse riding** for US$45.

Nevis' best **restaurant** is just south of Oualie Beach. Thirty different Caribbean dishes are served dinner-party-style at the magnificent *Miss June's* (ⓣ869/469-5330; dinner only; reservations required), allowing you to meet fellow visitors and locals alike. A bit further south, *Bananas* (Thurs–Sun; dinner only) is also good, set in a garden with jazz in the air and a light bistro menu of tasty Caribbean flavours. To dine right over the water, head to *Pizza Beach* (open daily for dinner) behind the airport, for decadent pizzas like the Nevisian Surprise.

Should you want to climb Mount Nevis, it's a good idea to go with a guide. **Top to Bottom** (ⓣ869/469-9080; US$10–30) has numerous trekking options, and local herbologist Michael Herbert (ⓣ869/469-3512; US$20-35) also makes the ascent.

The Atlantic Coast to Gingerland

Nevis' **ATLANTIC COAST**, a scenic haven of rustic settlements with evocative names like Brick Kiln, is completely devoid of resorts and beachfront but nonetheless worth the detour for its historic remnants. Centuries-old stone ovens still line the road and some houses rest on piled rocks, holdouts from the days when landless squatters had to move from plantation to plantation.

Rambling **GINGERLAND** begins south of the crumbling ruins of the reputedly haunted Eden Brown Estate and stretches along the southern coast to the outskirts of Charlestown. Known for the island's largest concentration of sugar plantations, which have since been transformed into inviting **inns**, the region's otherworldy charm and lush vegetation make it idyllic. Lord Nelson and Fanny Nisbet obviously thought so – they opted to hold their nuptials in Fig Tree village's picturesque 1680 **St John's Anglican church**. The only other sight is a **botanical garden** (Mon–Sat 9am–4.30pm; closed Sun; US$9) near *Montpelier Inn* (see below) where stepped terraces burgeon with violet orchids and Spanish-moss-draped trees. Be sure to visit the rainforest conservatory showcasing inland Nevis' inland flora; the resident speaking parrots are a lark.

Practicalities

While there are no beaches to speak of in Gingerland, the region's plantation **inns** provide shuttle services to and from Pinney's Beach (see opposite). The inns are all located east of Fig Tree within a few miles of one another, and accessed off the main road. All include breakfast in their rates and serve delicious West Indian curries and Nevisian seafood in their **restaurants** (reserve for dinner). The most characterful of the inns, *Hermitage* (ⓣ869/469-3477, ⓕ469-2481, ⓦwww.hermitagenevis.com; US$325), is also the island's oldest, a 1740 estate with antique-furnished cottages around a colonial Great House; it also offers horse-riding trips (US$45). *Montpelier* (Ⓣ869/469-3462, Ⓕ469-2932, Ⓦwww.montpeliernevis.com; ⑧) does justice to the phrase "royal treatment" – the late Princess Diana chose the well-appointed cottages for a pre-divorce announcement retreat, and the stunning grounds hosted Nelson and Nesbit's wedding reception. The relaxed *Golden Rock* (Ⓣ869/469-3346, Ⓕ469-2113, Ⓦwww.golden-rock.com; ⑦) has homey rooms scattered about an 1815 plantation, cosy communal areas and a tropical courtyard. The panoramic views at *Old Manor* (Ⓣ869/469-3445 or 1-800/892-7093, Ⓕ869/469-3388, Ⓦwww.oldmanornevis.com; ⑨), a handsome cut-stone house on a plateau, are matched by well-appointed and comfortable rooms with four-poster beds.

13

Antigua

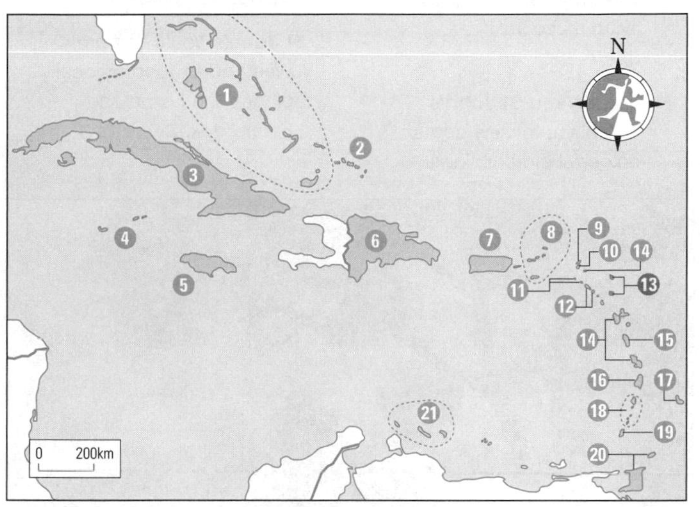

Antigua Highlights

✱ **Long Bay** An appealing stretch of white sand with good snorkelling around the reef just offshore. See p.526

✱ **Nelson's Dockyard** Once a busy Georgian dockyard, now an intriguing living museum. See p.530

✱ **Long Street, St John's** The place to view some colourful old buildings and catch an entertaining game of cricket too. See p.521

✱ **Barbuda** Spectacular Palm Beach is just one of the highlights of this delightfully secluded island. See p.536

✱ **St John's** You'll find great West Indian food at local places like *Home* and *Papa Zouk*. See p.523

Introduction and Basics

Famous for its beaches and its cricket players, tiny Antigua is now one of the Caribbean's most popular destinations. The country has taken full advantage of the publicity gained from its independence in 1981 – and the remarkable success of its cricketers since then – to push its name into the big league of West Indian tourism alongside Barbados and Jamaica.

After the **British** settled the island in the 1600s, it was for centuries little more than a giant sugar factory that produced sugar and rum to send home. Around Antigua, the tall brick chimneys of a hundred deserted and decaying sugar mills bear witness to that long colonial era. Today, though, it is tourism that drives the country's economy; dozens of hotels and restaurants have sprung up around the coastline, there's a smart airport, and a number of outfits run boat and catamaran cruises and scuba-diving and snorkelling trips to the island's fabulous coral reefs.

Where to go

If all you want to do is crash out on a **beach** for a week or two, you'll find Antigua hard to beat. The island is dotted with superb patches of sand – look out for **Dickenson Bay** in the northwest, **Half Moon Bay** in the east and **Rendezvous Beach** in the south – and, while the nightlife is generally pretty quiet, there are plenty of great places to eat and drink. But however lazy you're feeling, it's worth making the effort to get out and see some of the country. The superbly restored naval dockyard and the crumbling forts around **English Harbour** and **Shirley Heights** are as impressive as any historic site in the West Indies, and there are lots of other little nuggets to explore, including the capital, **St John's**, with its tiny museum and colourful quayside, and the old sugar estate at **Betty's Hope**. And, if you're prepared to do a bit of walking, you'll find some superb **hikes** that will take you out to completely deserted parts of the island.

Antigua's sister island **Barbuda** feels a world apart from its increasingly developed neighbour, even though it's just fifteen minutes away by plane. Despite its spectacular beaches and coral reefs, tourism is very low-key. Even if you can only manage a day trip, you'll find it thoroughly repays the effort involved in organizing a tour.

When to go

Antigua's tropical climate makes it a year-round destination. The weather is at its best during the high season, from mid-December to mid-April, with rainfall low and the heat tempered by cooling trade winds. As you'd expect, prices and crowds are at their peak during high season.

Things can get noticeably hotter during the summer and, particularly in September and October, the humidity can be oppressive. September is also the most threatening month for the annual hurricane season, which runs officially from June 1 to October 31.

Getting there

There are plenty of **flights** from the US and Canada. American Airlines generally offers the best fares and has the most comprehensive schedule from the US to Antigua; all of its flights connect either through Miami or San Juan, Puerto Rico. BWIA flies nonstop to Antigua from New York City, Miami and Toronto, while Continental has nonstop flights from Miami and Newark, New Jersey. Air Canada offers the best fares out of Toronto.

Most **British and Irish visitors** to Antigua are on some form of package tour that includes a charter flight direct to the island. Alternatively British Airways, Virgin and BWIA fly from London, and you can find similar fares with other carriers that require a stopover in the US. There are no direct flights from Ireland to Antigua, but there are

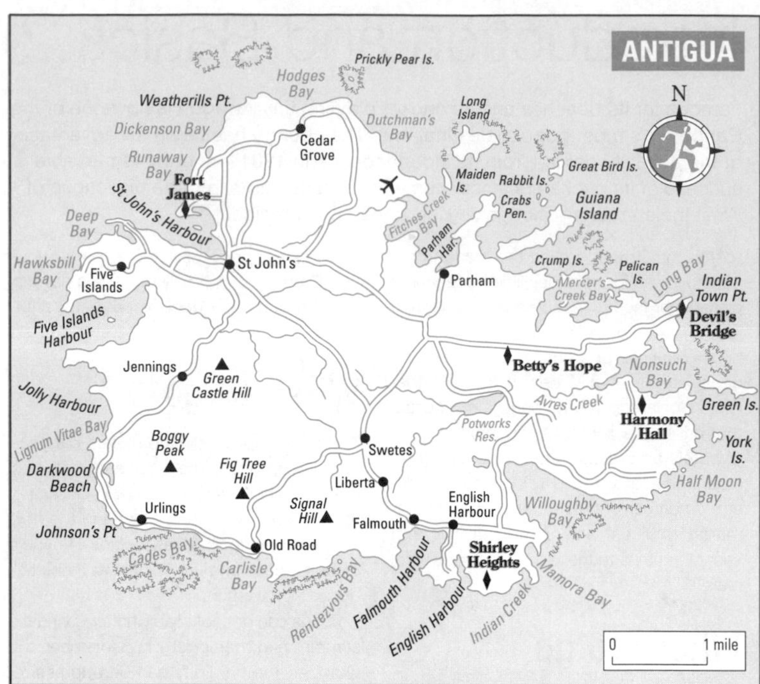

For international flights the **departure tax** is US$20 (EC$50), payable at the airport when you leave.

good connections via London or via New York and Miami.

Visitors from **Australia and New Zealand** will need to take a flight to one of the main US gateway airports and pick up onward connections from there. Generally the least expensive and most straightforward routes are via Miami, from where there are regular flights to St John's.

For phone numbers of airlines, see pp.12–18 and 36–37.

Money and costs

The island's unit of currency is the **Eastern Caribbean dollar (EC$)**, divided into 100 cents. It comes in bills of US$100, $50, $20, $10 and $5 and coins of US$1, $0.50, $0.25, $0.10, $0.05 and $0.01. The rate of exchange is fixed at EC$2.70 to US$1.

In tourist-related business, the **US dollar** is often used as an unofficial parallel currency, and you'll often find prices for hotels, restaurants and car rental quoted in US dollars (a policy we have adopted in this guide). Bear in mind, though, that you can always insist on paying in EC$ (and the exchange rate usually works out slightly in your favour).

If you are using US dollars or travellers' cheques to pay a bill, check in advance whether your change will be given in the same currency (it usually won't).

Banking hours are generally Monday to Thursday 8am–2pm and Friday 8am–4pm. Most of the banks are in St John's and include Antigua Commercial Bank, Barclays, ABIB and Bank of Antigua. (The latter has a branch in Nelson's Dockyard.) Bank of Antigua and ABIB in St John's are also open on Saturday morning.

Most hotels and restaurants automatically add a **service charge** of 10 percent and

government tax of 7 percent. It's always worth asking if it's included in the quoted price or will be added on later.

Information and maps

The government **tourist office**, at the western end of Nevis Street (☎268/462-0480), has a smattering of brochures and maps.

The internet is a good source of information. The following are a few of the more helpful general sites.

Websites

ⓦ**www.antigua-barbuda.org** The official site of the national tourism authority has info on forthcoming events, places to stay, car rental outfits and more.

ⓦ**www.antiguacarnival.com** The summer schedule is set out in detail, and there's a "scrapbook" of last year's Carnival and details of this year's bands.

ⓦ**www.antiguanice.com** Masses of information, from hotels and restaurant reviews to details of travel agents and links to the island's news.

Getting around

Speedy and inexpensive **buses** and minibuses run to certain parts of the island, particularly between St John's and English Harbour on the south coast and along the west coast between St John's and Old Road, although none goes to the big tourist area of Dickenson Bay and Runaway Bay.

By car

If you want to tour around, you're invariably better off renting a **car** for a couple of days, though rental prices are fairly high, starting at around US$40 per day, US$250 per week. You'll have to buy a local driving licence for US$20 (valid for three months and sold by all of the car hire firms). Reliable firms include: Avis (☎268/462-2840), Budget (☎268/462-3009), Dollar (☎268/462-0362), Hertz (☎268/462-4114), Oakland (☎268/462-3021) and Thrifty (☎268/462-9532).

By taxi

If you just want to make the odd excursion or short trip, it can be cheaper to hire **taxis**, identifiable by the H on their number plates and easy to find in St John's, Nelson's Dockyard or at the airport. Elsewhere you'll often need to call or ask your hotel to arrange for one. Try West Bus Station Taxis (☎268/462-5190) or Antigua Reliable (☎268/460-5353). Fares are regulated but there are no meters, so be sure to agree on a price before you get into the car.

By bike and motorcycle

Since Antigua is so small, and there are few steep inclines, it is ideal **cycling** territory, and bikes can be rented for around US$15 per day, US$70 a week. Hiring a scooter or **motorcycle** is just as much fun – prices normally start at around US$30 per day, US$150 a week (plus US$20 for the local driving permit) – and can be a fantastic way of touring around, though you'll need to watch out for madcap drivers on the main roads. Rental agents for both bikes and motorcycles include Cycle Krazy, St Mary's Street in St John's (☎268/462-9253), Paradise Boat Sales at Jolly Harbour (☎268/460-7125) and Shipwreck in Parham (☎268/464-7771; they deliver to your hotel, so cost a little more).

Accommodation

While most visitors stay on the **northwest coast**, there are a handful of good places on the much more isolated east coast and around Falmouth and English Harbour (where the beaches are less impressive), and a wider range of options on the west coast. Accommodations on the quiet and undeveloped island of **Barbuda** range from the rustic to the luxurious, but all of them, whatever the price bracket, offer decent value. Always call ahead to book, and remember to bring mosquito repellent.

During the low season, rates are liable to fall by as much as forty percent (though this is rare at the cheapest places), and proprietors are far more amenable to bargaining. Many of the all-inclusive hotels have a minimum-stay requirement, and rates are quoted per person per night based on double occupancy.

Keep in mind that every place adds **government tax** of 8.5 percent to the bill and almost all add a **service charge** of 10 percent. With some those extras are included in the quoted price; always ask. All places listed are on the beach unless mentioned otherwise.

Food and drink

There are plenty of good **eating** options on Antigua and, though prices are generally on the high side, there's usually something to suit most budgets. Around most of the island, hotel and restaurant menus aimed at tourists tend to offer familiar variations on Euro-American style food, shunning local specialities – a real shame, as the latter are invariably excellent and well worth trying if you get the chance.

Antiguan specialities include the fabulous **ducana** (a solid hunk of grated sweet potato mixed with coconut and spices and steamed in a banana leaf), **pepperpot stew** with salt beef, pumpkin and okra, often served with a cornmeal pudding known as **fungi**, various types of **curry**, **salted codfish**, and **souse** – cuts of pork marinated in lime juice, onions, hot and sweet peppers and spices.

During the winter season (Dec–April) it's best to make reservations at many of the places recommended – and, if you've got your heart set on a special place, arrange it a couple of days in advance if you can. As for **prices**, some restaurants quote their prices in EC$, others in US$, others in both. We've followed their practice, using whichever currency a particular restaurant quotes. Government tax of 8.5 percent is always added to the bill and, particularly at the pricier places, a 10 percent service charge is also automatic.

On **Barbuda**, restaurants are low-key places with quiet trade. If you're coming on a day-trip package your meal will normally be arranged for you, but if you're making your own arrangements give as much advance notice as you can so that they can get the ingredients in.

Phones and post

Most hotels provide a **telephone** in each room and local calls are normally inexpensive. You'll also see phone booths all over the island, and these can be used for local and international calls. Most of the booths take phonecards only, available at hotels, post offices and some shops and supermarkets.

The **country code** for Antigua is ⓣ268.

Post offices are located in English Harbour (Mon–Fri 8.30am–4pm), St John's on Long Street (Mon–Fri 8.15am–4pm) and in Woods Centre (Mon–Thurs 8.30am–4pm, Fri 8.30am–5pm).

For fire, ambulance or police emergencies, dial ⓣ911 or 999.

Public holidays and festivals

The main events in Antigua are the summertime **Carnival** and the **April Sailling Week**, but there are other events to distract you from the beach, including international cricket and windsurfing tournaments, and a jazz festival. The tourist boards have full details of all activities.

As well as the public holidays listed on p.45, Antigua celebrates **Caricom Day** in early July, **Carnival** on the first Monday and Tuesday of August, **Independence Day** on November 1 and **United Nations Day** in October.

Festivals and events

January

Red Stripe Cricket Competition ⓣ268/462-9090

February

Valentine's Day Regatta, Jolly Harbour ⓣ268/461-6324

March–April

Test cricket ⓣ268/462-9090

April

Classic Regatta ⓣ268/460-1799

Sailing Week ⓣ268/460-8872

May

Pro-Am Tennis Classic, *Curtain Bluff Hotel* ⓣ268/462-8400

July/August
Carnival (see p.524) ⓣ268/462-4707
September
Bridge Championship ⓣ268/462-1459
October
National Warri Championship ⓣ268/462-6317
November
Antiguan Craft Fair, Harmony Hall ⓣ268/460-4120
December
Nicholson's Annual Charter Yacht Show ⓣ268/460-1530

Tours

If you don't fancy driving, there are a couple of local companies who offer islandwide **sightseeing tours**, either to a set itinerary or customized to your needs. Remember to check whether the price includes entrance fees to the various attractions. If you can't get a good price from any of the companies below, check the taxi operators listed on p.515 about guided taxi tours.

Tropikelly Trails (ⓣ268/461-0383) offer five- to six-hour tours from US$65, including a picnic lunch, with trips to Great George Fort, Boggy Peak and a pineapple farm, or a half-day tour for US$35. Estate Safari Jeep Tours (ⓣ268/463-4713) organizes similar tours, including Betty's Hope sugar plantation, Great George Fort and lunch on the beach, while Antours (ⓣ268/462-4788) and Bo Tours (ⓣ268/462-6632) also take in the island's main sights, including English Harbour and Betty's Hope at a similar cost.

Diving and snorkelling

Diving is excellent on the coral reefs around Antigua and Barbuda, with most of the good sites – places like Sunken Rock and Cape Shirley – on the south side of the larger island and many of them very close to shore, rarely more than a fifteen-minute boat ride away. Expect to see a wealth of fabulously colourful reef fish, including parrot fish, angelfish, wrasse and barracuda, as well as the occasional harmless nurse shark and, if you're lucky, dolphins and turtles. The reefs for the most part are still in pristine, unspoiled condition, and, though there is no wall diving and most dives are fairly shallow, there are some good cliffs and canyons, and a handful of wrecks.

Antigua has plenty of reputable dive operators scattered conveniently around the island, so you should always be able to find a boat going out from near where you're staying. Rates are pretty uniform: reckon on around US$50 for a single-tank dive, US$70 for a two-tank dive and US$60 for a night dive. Beginners can get a feel for diving by taking a half-day **resort course** for around US$80–100. Full **open-water certification** ranges from US$300 to US$500. Call around for the best deal.

Serious divers should consider a **package deal**, either involving a simple package with three or five two-tank dives (roughly US$180–200 and US$265–300 respectively) or a deal that includes accommodation and diving. Prices for these can be pretty good value, particularly outside the winter season, and it's worth contacting the dive operators direct to find out the latest offers.

Barbuda's diving is at least as good as Antigua's, with countless wrecks dotted around the nearby reefs, but, sadly, there is no established dive outfit on the island. At the time of writing, the *Palmetto Beach Hotel* (see p.538) was planning to offer diving for guests but not (yet) for visitors, so if you're interested it's worth asking some of the Antiguan dive operators for the latest information.

Snorkelling around the islands is excellent, too, and several of the dive operators take snorkellers on their dive trips, mooring near some good, relatively shallow coral-heads. Reckon on around US$15–20 for an outing, including equipment.

Dive operators

Dive Antigua *Rex Halcyon Cove Hotel*, Dickenson Bay ⓣ268/462-3483, ⓕ462-7787. The longest-established and best-known dive operation on the island, based on the northwest coast, though prices are normally a little higher than most of the others. They offer a glass-bottom boat to take snorkellers out to the reef.
Dockyard Divers Nelson's Dockyard ⓣ268/460-1178, ⓕ460-1179. Decent-sized dive shop (and the only outfit in the English Harbour area offering snorkelling tours) that lays on diving trips around the south and west coasts.

Jolly Dive Jolly Harbour Marina ⓣ268/462-8305. Second-oldest dive shop in Antigua and very popular with guests at the big, local hotels; look elsewhere if you want to go out in a small group.
Octopus Divers English Harbour ⓣ268/460-6286, ⓕ463-8528, ⓦwww.octopusdivers.com. Reputable outfit with one of the most comfortable dive boats on the south coast, and some good-value hotel/diving package deals from time to time – check their website for details.

Boats and catamarans

There is no shortage of **boat and catamaran trips** to be made around Antigua, with the emphasis – not, it must be said, everyone's cup of tea – normally on being part of a big crowd all having a fun time together. Most of the cruises charge a single price, including a meal and all the drinks you want, and the two main cruise companies, Kokomo and Wadadli Cats, offer virtually identical trips, travelling on large and comfortable catamarans. A more interesting and unusual **eco-tour** is offered by Adventure Antigua.

The most popular **cruise** sails right round Antigua, taking in some snorkelling and lunch at Green Island off the east coast. There is also a superb snorkelling trip to Cades Reef on the south coast, stopping off for lunch on one of the west coast beaches, and another to uninhabited Great Bird Island – where there's plenty of birdlife – off the northeast. Finally, there's a "triple destination" cruise on Sundays to English Harbour via Green Island, ending with a taxi ride up to the steel-band party on Shirley Heights and another taxi home.

Each of the trips is offered by Kokomo and Wadadli, and both will pick up passengers from a number of locations on the west coast. All are out from around 9am until 4pm, apart from the triple-destination tour (roughly 10am–sunset). The circumnavigation cruise costs US$75 per person, Cades Reef US$60 and the triple-destination cruise US$90, all prices including snorkelling gear, a buffet lunch and an open bar. Children under 12 are half-price.

Boat operators

Adventure Antigua ⓣ268/727-3261 or 560-4672, ⓦwww.adventureantigua.com. Owner Eli Fuller takes passengers by motorboat on a seven-hour ecotour of the northeast coast of the island, showing where the endangered hawksbill turtles lay their eggs, and through the mangrove swamps, to spot rays, frigate birds, osprey and turtles. There are several snorkelling opportunities, and lunch is served on a deserted beach. Cost is US$90 per person, and the trip goes out between two and five times a week, depending on demand.
Jolly Roger Pirate Cruises ⓣ268/462-2064, ⓦwww.jollyrogercruises.com. Hearty party cruises, with rope-swinging and walking the plank for would-be pirates and limbo competitions and calypso dance classes for the rest. Around US$50 per person.
Kokomo Cats ⓣ268/462-7245, ⓦwww.kokomocat.com. Round the island trips (Tues, Thurs, Sat), Cades Reef (Fri), Great Bird Island (Wed) and a triple-destination cruise (Sun) on fast and comfortable catamarans. Kokomo also offers sunset cruises (Tues, Thurs, Sat) from Jolly Harbour on the west coast, out from 6.30pm to 9pm (US$40).
Wadadli Cats ⓣ268/462-4792. Offers circumnavigation cruises (Thurs, Sat), a sunset cruise (Sat US$40), a triple-destination cruise (Sun) and a trip to Cades Reef (Tues).

History

Antigua's first people were the nomadic Ciboney, originally from present-day Venezuela, whose earliest traces on the island date from around 3100 BC. By the early years AD the Ciboney had been replaced by Arawak-speaking Amerindians from the same region.

The first European sighting of Antigua came in 1493 when **Columbus** sailed close by, naming the island Santa Maria la Antigua. The island remained uninhabited for over a century until, in 1624, the first **British settlement** in the West Indies was established on the island of St Kitts (see p.502), and the British laid claim to nearby Antigua and Barbuda. Within a decade, settlers at Falmouth on the south coast had experimented with a number of crops before settling on **sugar**, which was to guarantee the island its future wealth. For the next two hundred years, sugar was to remain the country's dominant industry, bringing enormous wealth to the **planters**.

Unlike most of Britain's West Indian colonies, Antigua remained British throughout the colonial era. This was due, in large part, to the massive fortifications built around it, the major ones at places like Shirley Heights (see p.531) on the south coast.

As the centuries passed, conditions for the slaves who worked the plantations improved very slowly. Even after the abolition of slavery in 1834, many were obliged to continue to labour at the sugar estates, for wages that were insufficient to provide even the miserly levels of food, housing and care formerly offered under slavery.

Gradually, though, **free villages** began to emerge at places like Liberta, Jennings and Bendals, often based around Moravian or Methodist churches or on land reluctantly sold by the planters to a group of former slaves. Slowly a few Antiguans scratched together sufficient money to set up their own businesses – shops, taverns and tiny cottage industries. An embryonic black middle class was in the making. Nonetheless, economic progress on the island was extremely slow. By World War II, life for the vast majority of Antiguans was still extremely tough, with widespread poverty across the island.

After the war, Antigua continued to be administered by Britain, but gradually the island's politicians were given authority for the running of their country. Slowly, the national economy began to take strides forward, assisted by the development of tourism. By the elections of 1980 all parties considered that, politically and economically, the country was sufficiently mature for full independence and the flag of an **independent Antigua and Barbuda** was finally raised in November 1981.

13.1

St John's and around

With a population of around 30,000 – nearly half the island's total – bustling **ST JOHN'S** is Antigua's capital and only city. No one could accuse it of being the prettiest city in the West Indies, but it does have a certain immediate charm and, in the centre, there are plenty of attractive old wooden and stone buildings – some of them superbly renovated, others in a perilous state of near-collapse – among the less appealing modern development. It'll only take you a couple of hours to see everything, but you'll probably want to come back for at least one evening to take advantage of some excellent **restaurants** and **bars**.

Arrival and getting around

Flights touch down at **V.C. Bird International Airport** on the northeast coast. There is no bus service to and from the airport. You'll find numerous **car rental outlets** at the airport, as well as **taxis**: from the airport, expect to pay US$7 to St John's, US$6 to Dickenson Bay or Runaway Bay and US$25 to English Harbour. Renting a taxi for a day's sightseeing comes to around US$60–70.

There's little reason **to stay** in St John's as it's a fair distance from a decent beach, but if you need to spend the night here, *Joe Mike's Hotel* on Nevis Street (Ⓣ268/462-1142, Ⓕ462-6056; ③) is a friendly place with just a dozen rooms, right in the centre of town.

The City

As all of the main places of interest in St John's are close together, the easiest way to see the place is **on foot**. You should certainly make your way to **Redcliffe Quay** – where the waterfront and its colonial buildings have been attractively restored – as well as the tiny **National Museum**, which offers a well-presented rundown on the country's history and culture. If you've got time, take a stroll through some of the old streets, and check out the city's twin-towered **cathedral** perched on top of Newgate Street. Redcliffe Quay and nearby **Heritage Quay** are the best places to eat, drink and shop for souvenirs, though you'll probably want to avoid them if the cruise ships are in, when the steel drums come out to play "Hot, Hot, Hot" and the area almost disappears beneath a scrum of duty-free shoppers.

Around Redcliffe Quay

Spread over several acres by the waterside, **Redcliffe Quay** is probably the best place to start your tour of the city. Named in honour of the church of St Mary Redcliffe in the English port city of Bristol, this is one of the oldest parts of St John's, and incorporates many old warehouses – now attractively restored as small boutiques, restaurants and bars – and a wooden boardwalk that runs alongside the water. There's not a huge amount to see, but it's a pleasant place to wander and soak up some of the city's history.

Many of the waterfront warehouses once housed supplies – barrels of sugar and rum, lumber for ship repairs, cotton and sheepskins – for the British navy and local merchant ships that traded between Antigua and the mother country during the eighteenth century. Behind the quay around the western end of Nevis Street there

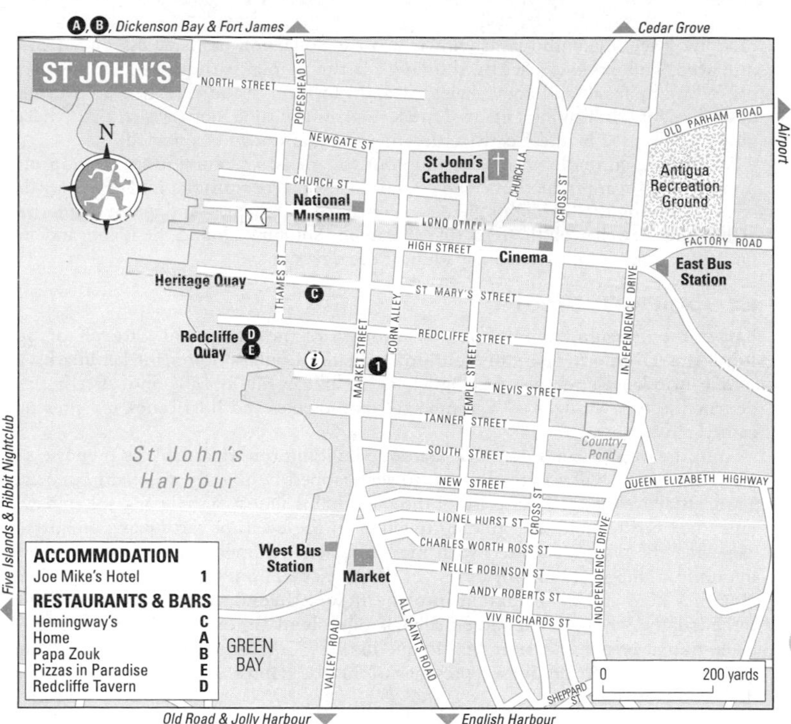

once stood a number of barracoons, compounds where slaves were held upon their arrival in the island, before they were sent to the plantations or shipped to other Caribbean islands.

Back at the front of the quay, a short stroll north takes you up to **Heritage Quay** at the foot of High Street. This modern concrete quay is given over to cruise-ship arrivals and dozens of duty-free shops designed to catch their tourist dollars, along with a few roadside stalls where local vendors flog T-shirts and distinctive Haitian art. Take a quick look at the **cenotaph**, which is a memorial to Antiguans who died during World War I, a **monument to V.C. Bird**, first prime minister of the independent country, and the **Westerby Memorial**, which commemorates a Moravian missionary who dedicated his life to helping Antiguans in the decades after emancipation from slavery in 1834.

Long Street and around

From the water, Long Street runs east as far as the **Antigua Recreation Ground**, the country's main cricket venue and home to most of the action during the ten-day Carnival each July and August (see p.524). Many of St John's finest old buildings line this street, including a couple of fabulously colourful liquor stores, still in operation more than a century after first opening.

The National Museum

Housed in a 1747 Neoclassical courthouse on the corner of Long and Market streets, the **National Museum of Antigua and Barbuda** (Mon–Fri 8.30am–4pm, Sat 10am–2pm; free) occupies just one large room, but it's indisputably worth thirty minutes of your time while you're exploring the capital – you can almost feel the enthusiasm with which the collection has been assembled and displayed. The exhibits start by showing off the islands' early geological history, backed up by fossils and coral skeletons, and move on to more extensive coverage of its first, Amerindian inhabitants. Jewellery, primitive tools, pottery shards and religious figures used by these early settlers are well laid out and explained.

Continuing chronologically, the museum touches on Columbus, the European invasion and sugar production – the country's *raison d'être* from the mid-seventeenth century. Among the highlights are an interesting 1750 map of Antigua showing the plantations, as well as all the reefs that threatened shipping around the island, and an intriguing exhibit on the emancipation of the slaves.

St John's Cathedral

East of the museum, the imposing twin towers of the **Cathedral Church of St John the Divine** (daily 9am–5pm; free) are the capital's dominant landmark. A simple wooden church was first built on this hilltop site in 1681 and, after heavy destruction was wrought by a number of earthquakes and hurricanes, the present cathedral was put up in 1847.

From the outside, the grey-stone Baroque building is not particularly prepossessing – squat and bulky with the two towers capped by slightly awkward cupolas. More attractively, the airy interior of the cathedral is almost entirely encased in dark pine, designed to hold the building together in the event of earthquake or hurricane, and the walls are dotted with marble tablets commemorating distinguished figures from the island's history, some of them rescued from the wreckage of earlier churches here and incorporated into the new cathedral. In the grounds of the cathedral, the whitewashed and equally Baroque **lead figures** on the south gate – taken from a French ship near Martinique in the 1750s during the Seven Years' War between France and Britain – represent St John the Baptist and St John the Divine, draped in flowing robes.

Fort Bay

A short drive or taxi ride from town, heading north from St John's on Fort Road, a left turn at the old pink *Barrymore Hotel* (just north of the Texaco station) takes you out to the capital city's most popular beach and some of the best-preserved **military ruins** on the island. The road winds its way around to the coast at **Fort Bay**, where a long, wide strand of grainy white sand – packed with city-dwellers on weekends and holidays – offers the nearest quality beach to town. At its northern end, you can hire beach chairs from *Millers* (see opposite), and there's a vendors' mall nearby if you want to hunt for souvenirs.

At the other end of the strip, 550ft further on, a host of food and drink stalls open up at busy times, when a crowd descends from town, transforming the place into a lively outdoor venue. If you want to swim, there's a protected, marked area at the top of the beach; elsewhere, the water is normally fine but you'll need to watch out for occasional undercurrents.

Fort James

At the far end of Fort Bay stands eighteenth-century **Fort James** (always open; free), built above the cliffs that overlook the entrance to St John's harbour. You can walk or drive around to the south side of the fort, where the main gate is still in place. Together with Fort Barrington, on the opposite side of the channel (see p.534) and St John's Fort on Rat Island – still visible down the channel – this fort was designed to deter ships from attacking the capital, which had been sacked by French raiders in 1668. Earthworks were first raised in the 1680s, but the bulk of the fort was put up in 1739, when the long enclosing wall was added.

Today, the fort is pretty dilapidated but offers plenty of atmosphere: unkempt, often windswept and providing great views across the channel and back down to

St John's harbour. Rusting British cannons from the early 1800s point out to sea and down the channel, their threat long gone but still a dramatic symbol of their era. Elsewhere, the old powder magazine is still intact, though leaning precariously, and the stone buildings on the fort's upper level – the oldest part of the structure, dating from 1705 – include the master gunner's house, the canteen and the barracks.

Eating and drinking

Hemingway's St Mary's Street ☎268/462-2763. Atmospheric, early nineteenth-century green and white wooden building with a balcony overlooking the street and Heritage Quay. Can be overwhelmingly popular when the cruise ships are in; at other times it's a great place to be, serving a range of excellent food from sandwiches and burgers to fish and steak dinners, with prices for a main course between US$12 and US$25. Mon–Sat 8.30am–11pm; closed Sun.

Home Restaurant Lower Gambles ☎268/461-7651. Attractive restaurant in a converted home, a little way from the centre of town, serving great, adventurous West Indian food. Look for starters of roast peppers and beets in balsamic vinegar and garlic (EC$18), main courses of mahimahi with plantain mousse (EC$60) or blackened redfish (EC$55). Mon–Sat dinner only; also lunch on Sat; closed Sun.

Papa Zouk Hilda Davis Drive, Gambles ☎268/562-1284. Imaginative Antiguan food served on a tiny patio festooned with flowers. The menu is small but interesting, with local produce thrown into dishes like creole bouillabaisse or a seafood medley. Wed–Sat 6–11pm, Nov–April Mon–Sat.

Pizzas in Paradise Redcliffe Quay ☎268/480-6985. Pub-like restaurant, popular with tourists for lunch and dinner, serving reasonable-quality food inside or outdoors under the trees at decent prices – pizzas, salads and baked potatoes as well as more typical Antiguan fish and chicken meals at EC$15–35. Closed Sun.

The Redcliffe Tavern Redcliffe Quay ☎268/461-4557. Housed in one of the renovated quayside warehouses, the atmospheric tavern serves good American/Caribbean food all day, with options such as flying fish in beer batter, jerk chicken, creole shrimp and pan-fried mahimahi fish all for around US$15. Mon–Sat 8am–9pm.

Entertainment and nightlife

King's Casino Heritage Quay ☎268/462-1727. The city's main casino, packed with slot machines and offering blackjack, roulette and Caribbean stud poker tables for the more serious players. Live bands and karaoke give the place a bit of atmosphere after 10pm. The casino will normally lay on one-way shuttle services to St John's for those coming to gamble for the night. It'll pick you up anywhere, but you're stuck with the taxi fare home. Mon–Sat 10am–4am, Sun 6pm–4am.

Millers by the Sea Fort James ☎268/462-9414. One of the best venues on the island, this large and often lively restaurant and bar has live music every night varying from local jazz and soca bands to guitarists and karaoke. Look out, too, for special events here on the big outdoor sets, which normally charge a cover between EC$30 and EC$50.

Ribbit Green Bay ☎268/462-7996. *Ribbit* is the island's main nightclub, popular with Antiguans and tourists alike. Fri & Sat 10.30pm–5am; EC$20.

Listings

All services listed are in **St John's** unless otherwise stated.

Airlines American Airlines (☎268/462-0952); British Airways (☎268/462-0876); BWIA (☎268/480-2942); Carib Aviation (☎268/462-3147); LIAT (☎268/480-5600 or 5610); and Virgin (☎268/560-2079).

American Express At the corner of Long and Thames streets (Mon–Thurs 8.30am–4.30pm, Fri 8.30am–5pm; ☎268/462-4788).

Bookshops First Edition, Woods Centre (Mon–Sat 9am–9pm). Excellent place, with the best range of books – including fiction and local interest – in Antigua.

Carnival

The highlight of Antigua's entertainment calendar is its **Carnival**, a colourful, exuberant party held for ten days, from late July until the first Tuesday in August. Warm-ups start in early July, with steel bands, calypsonians and DJ's in action across the island, and Carnival proper gets cracking with the opening of Carnival City at the Antigua Recreation Ground in St John's. This is where all of the scheduled events take place, though you'll often find spontaneous outbreaks of partying across the city, and a festival village is set up nearby to provide space for the masses of food and drink vendors who emerge out of nowhere.

The major Carnival events take place over the last weekend and you'll have to cancel sleep for a few days of frantic action. The **Panorama** steel-band contest (Fri night) and the Calypso Monarch competition (Sun night) are both packed and definitely worth catching, while on the Monday morning – the day on which the islands celebrate slave emancipation in 1834 – **Jouvert** (pronounced "jouvay", and meaning daybreak) is a huge jump-up party starting at 4am. The Judging of the Troupes and Groups competition in the afternoon sees ranks of brightly costumed marching bands and floats parading through the city streets, being marked for colour, sound and general party attitude.

Tuesday has a final costumed parade through the streets, finishing with the announcement of all of the winners and a roughly 6pm–midnight last lap from Carnival City – "the bacchanal" – as the exhausted partygoers stream through St John's, led by the steel bands. All in all, it's a great event – certainly one of the best of the Caribbean's summer carnivals – and a great chance to catch the Antiguans in a non-stop party mood.

Embassies British High Commission, 11 Old Parham Rd (☎268/462-0008); US Consular Agent, Pigeon Point, English Harbour (☎268/463-6531).
Film Island Photo, Redcliffe and Market streets, sells film and does one-hour photo development; Benjie's, Heritage Quay, offers the same service and has various camera accessories at duty-free prices.

Pharmacies Full-service pharmacies in St John's: Benjies, Redcliffe and Market streets (Mon–Wed 8.30am–5pm, Thurs & Sat 8.30am–4pm, Fri 8.30am–5.30pm; ☎268/462-0733); and Woods, Woods Centre (Mon–Sat 9am–10pm, Sun 11am–6pm; ☎268/462-9287).
Police The main police station is on Newgate Street ☎268/462-0045. Emergency ☎268/462-0125 or ☎999 or 911.

13.2

From Runaway Bay to Half Moon Bay

North of St John's, **Runaway Bay** and adjoining **Dickenson Bay** constitute the island's main tourist strip, with a couple of excellent beaches, a host of good hotels and restaurants, and plenty of action. Continuing clockwise round the island brings you to its Atlantic side, where the jagged coastline offers plenty of inlets, bays and swamps but, with a couple of noteworthy exceptions, rather less impressive beaches. Tourist facilities on this side of the island are much less developed, but there are several places of interest. **Betty's Hope** is a restored sugar plantation; **Devil's Bridge** offers one of the most dramatic landscapes on the island; at picturesque **Half Moon Bay** you can scramble along a vertiginous clifftop path above the pounding Atlantic; and at the delightful **Harmony Hall** you can relax from your exertions with an excellent lunch and a boat ride to Green Island.

Accommodation

Antigua's **northwest coast** is the most popular destination for visitors, with a series of large and small hotels dotted along the lovely beaches, and plenty of restaurants, watersports and beach life.

Dickenson Bay Cottages Dickenson Bay ⓣ268/462-4940, ⓕ462-4941, ⓦwww.nikegroup.co.uk/antigua/cottages.htm. Thirteen spacious, airy and attractively furnished cottages strewn around a well-landscaped garden and medium-sized pool, up on a hillside overlooking the bay. Just a short walk from the beach and from the much busier *Rex Halcyon Cove*, where guests have subsidized use of the facilities, including tennis courts and sun loungers. One-bedroom cottages ⑧ for two people, two-bedroom cottages US$325 for up to four.

Harmony Hall Brown's Bay ⓣ268/460-4120, ⓕ460-4406, ⓦwww.harmonyhall.com. A delightful place in the middle of nowhere. The six simple but stylish rooms have large bathrooms, comfortable beds and small patios. The beach isn't up to much, but a small free boat regularly ferries guests out to the clean, white sand at Green Island (see p.527). The classy restaurant is normally busy; when it's closed (as it is most evenings) the hotel lays on separate food for guests. Nov to mid-May only. ⑥

Lashings Runaway Bay ⓣ268/462-4438, ⓕ462-4491, ⓦwww.lashings.com. Good, low-cost option, with a wide stretch of clean, white beach and decent snorkelling just offshore. All fourteen rooms, rustic and perfectly adequate, face out to sea, and there's also a good restaurant on site (see p.528). The place is a long walk (or a US$6 taxi ride) from tourist facilities, and the ocean view is marred a bit by the oil-pumping station 3km offshore. The 24-hour outdoor bar, which has live entertainment most nights, can be noisy. ④

Rex Halcyon Cove Dickenson Bay ⓣ268/462-0256, ⓕ462-0271, ⓦwww.rexcaribbean.com. Sprawling low-rise resort, rather faded but with good-sized rooms, a decent pool and tennis courts and a delightful restaurant on the Warri pier. ⑥

Long Bay Hotel Long Bay ⓣ268/463-2005, ⓕ463-2439, ⓦwww.longbay-antigua.com. Small, friendly and secluded all-inclusive choice located by a tiny turquoise bay, with twenty cosy rooms and cottages. Guests enjoy use of a few sailboats and windsurfers, plus there's a good tennis court, a big library and a game room. The chef is excellent and the bartender makes the best rum punch on the island. Closed September and

October. Rooms start at US$355 for two, including breakfast and dinner.

Sandals Antigua Dickenson Bay ⓣ268/462-0267, ⓕ462-4135, ⓦwww.sandals.com. Part of the popular, all-inclusive Caribbean chain, this resort has 189 luxury rooms cleverly spread throughout the resort to reduce the sense of being part of a crowd. Four restaurants offer excellent Italian, Japanese, southern US and international food, and all watersports are included in the daily rate. ⑧ per person per day, though (heterosexual) couples only are allowed.

Sunset Cove Resort Runaway Bay ⓣ268/462-3762, ⓕ462-2684. This hotel has lost its beach entirely in heavy sea swells, and you have to walk five minutes around the headland to swim comfortably. That aside, it's a very pleasant place and great value. There's a small freshwater pool, and the rooms are sizeable and all have kitchen facilities and cable TV. Standard room ④, one-bedroom villas (four to six people) ⑥

Runaway Bay and Dickenson Bay

A few miles north of St John's, a series of attractive white-sand beaches runs around the island's northwest coast. Most of the tourist development is concentrated along Runaway Bay and Dickenson Bay, where the gleaming beaches slope gently down into the turquoise sea, offering calm swimming and, at the northern end of Dickenson Bay, a host of watersports. **Runaway Bay** is the quieter of the two and, because there are fewer hotels to tidy up their "patch", is strewn with more seaweed and rocks. It's still a great place to wander in the gentle surf, despite the northern end's erosion by heavy swells.

Trapped between two imposing sandstone bluffs, **Dickenson Bay** is fringed by another wide, white-sand beach, which stretches for almost a mile between Corbison Point and the more thickly vegetated woodland of Weatherill's Hill at its northern end. It's a lovely bay, shelving gently into the sea and with a protected swimming zone dividing swimmers from the jet skiers, windsurfers, waterskiers and parasailers offshore. The northern half of the beach fronts some of the largest of Antigua's hotels, thus the area can get pretty busy, with a string of bars, hair braiders and T-shirt sellers doing a brisk trade, but it's still an easy-going place, with minimal hassle.

Island Arts Gallery

There are few points of interest worth stopping for on the northeast coast, but Nick Maley's **Island Arts Gallery** in Hodges Bay (Mon–Fri 9am–5pm) is certainly one of them. Maley, originally a film make-up artist for movies like *Star Wars* and *Krull*, is a British painter who has worked on Antigua for over a decade and shown his striking and original works at exhibitions across the Caribbean and North America. Maley's small gallery and studio – resounding with the squawks of the parrots he and his wife breed in their lush garden – are crammed with his paintings and prints, as well as those of Antiguan, Haitian and other West Indian artists. There is plenty of exuberant colour and some captivating local portraits beside the more predictable landscapes and seascapes. The gallery is signposted up a side street, off the main road that skirts the northeast coast. If you want to meet Maley, call ahead on ⓣ268/461-6324 as he's sometimes at his Heritage Quay store in St John's.

Betty's Hope to Long Bay

The partly restored **Betty's Hope** (Tues–Sat 10am–4pm; EC$5) is the island's very first sugar estate. Built in 1650, the place was owned by the Codrington family for nearly two centuries until the end of World War II; by that time its lack of profitability had brought it to the edge of closure, which followed soon after. Although most of the estate still lies in ruins, one of the windmills has been restored to working condition, and a small and interesting museum at the visitor centre traces the history of sugar on Antigua as well as the development and restoration of the estate.

East of Betty's Hope and approaching Long Bay, a track signposted off to the right takes you out for half a mile to **Devil's Bridge**, on a rocky outcrop edged by patches of grassy land, tall century plants and sunbathing cattle. Wander round the promontory to the "bridge", a narrow piece of rock whose underside has been washed away by thousands of years of relentless surf action. The hot, windswept spot offers some of the most fetching views on the island, back across a quiet cove and out over the lashing ocean and dark reefs to a series of small islands just offshore. En route back to the main road, a dirt track on your right after 30 yards leads down to a tiny but gorgeous bay – the perfect place for a picnic.

Past the turn-off for Devil's Bridge, at the end of the main road, **Long Bay** is home to a couple of rather exclusive all-inclusives, which doesn't stop you from getting access to a great, wide bay, enormously popular with local schoolkids, who are often splashing around or playing cricket at one end of the beach. The lengthy spread of white sand is protected by an extensive reef a few hundred yards offshore (bring your snorkelling gear) and there's a great little beach bar for shelter and refreshment.

Harmony Hall and Green Island

Tucked away on the east coast overlooking Nonsuch Bay, the restored plantation house at **Harmony Hall** (closed May to Oct) is now home to a tiny, chic hotel and one of the island's best restaurants (see below), as well as a free art gallery that showcases monthly exhibitions of local and Caribbean art from November to April.

From the jetty, boats regularly make the five-minute run out to deserted **Green Island**, where the beaches are powdery and the snorkelling excellent. If you're not a guest, there's a small charge for the boat service – ask at the bar of the hotel.

Half Moon Bay

One of the prettiest spots on Antigua, **Half Moon Bay** has a half-mile semicircle of white-sand beach partially enclosing a deep-blue bay, where the Atlantic surf normally offers top-class body-surfing opportunities. Since the closure in 1995 of the hurricane-damaged hotel at the southern end, the beach is often pretty empty.

Eating, drinking and nightlife

With a wide range of hotels scattered about the **north coast**, there is a steady stream of punters looking for good places to eat, and plenty of decent **restaurants** have popped up as a result, though there are few options in the low-budget range. **Dickenson Bay** has the widest choice.

Bay House *Trade Winds Hotel*, Dickenson Bay ☎268/462-1223. Smart restaurant overlooking Dickenson Bay, and a romantic place for a drink at sunset followed by top-class food. Tasty and creative starters, plus main courses that might include pan-fried kingfish with a pepper salsa (US$20) or fillet of beef marinated in soy sauce with Chinese cabbage (US$26). Save room for dessert – the chocolate *millefeuille* with raspberry sauce (US$9) is beyond superlatives. Daily 7am–10pm.

The Beach Dickenson Bay ☎268/480-6940. Newly refurbished and brightly painted restaurant on the beach serving good food all day. Lunches include sushi, satay, burgers and salads for US$8–10; dinner specials might be sesame-crusted tuna, meaty pasta or seafood stew for US$20–30. Daily 8.30am–midnight.

Coconut Grove *Siboney Beach Club*, Dickenson Bay ☎268/462-1538. One of the top food choices on the island for the great cooking, friendly service and delightful open-air beachside location. Mouthwatering starters include deep-fried jumbo shrimp in a coconut dip (US$12.50), while main courses feature dishes like mahimahi in a mango salsa (US$23) and rock lobster in creole sauce (US$23). The coconut cream pie is magnificent (US$9.25). Daily for lunch and dinner.

Lashings Runaway Bay ☎268/462-4438. Busy, beachside place at *Lashings Hotel*, with a massive menu, 24-hour bar and pizzas until 4am. Pizzas start at EC$16, while dishes of blackened swordfish, barbecued chicken or cottage pie range from EC$25 to EC$45. Daily for breakfast, lunch and dinner. The 24-hour bar rocks with live local bands on Friday and Saturday evenings and, during holidays, test matches and Carnival, pretty much every night. There's a small cover charge. Open nightly.

The Lobster Pot Runaway Bay ☎268/462-2855. Good food served all day on a large beachfront covered verandah at the back of the old *Runaway Bay Hotel*, devastated by Hurricane Luis, but still overlooking a lovely beach. For lunches there's blackened fish, shrimp and chicken linguine (US$12–15) and sandwiches and salads (US$7–10), while dinners range from thick soups (US$5–7.50) to various lobster options (US$30 and up). Daily 7.30am–midnight.

13.3

Falmouth and English Harbour

An essential stop on any visit to Antigua, the picturesque area around **Falmouth** and **English Harbour** on the island's south coast holds some of the most important and interesting historical remains in the Caribbean and is now the region's leading yachting centre. The chief attraction is the eighteenth-century **Nelson's Dockyard**, which was the key facility for the British navy that once ruled the waves in the area. Today it's a living museum where visiting yachts are still cleaned, supplied and chartered. Nearby are several ruined forts as well as an abundance of attractive colonial buildings on the waterfront, several converted into hotels and restaurants.

Across the harbour from the dockyard, there is further evidence of the colonial past at **Shirley Heights**, where more ruined forts, gun batteries and an old cemetery hold a commanding position over the water.

The area also has a handful of spots off the beaten path that repay a trip, including the massive military complex at **Great Fort George**, high in the hills above **Falmouth**, and the wonderful **Rendezvous Bay** – outstanding in an area with a paucity of good beaches – a short boat ride or less than an hour's hike from Falmouth.

A car is invaluable for touring around this area of the south coast. There are frequent **buses** between St John's and English Harbour, handy if you just want to explore Nelson's Dockyard, but to get up to Shirley Heights you'll certainly need your own transport or a taxi.

Accommodation

Plenty of good restaurants and nightlife and the proximity to **Nelson's Dockyard** make this an attractive area in which to stay, though if you're after serious beaches you'll want to look elsewhere on the island.

Admiral's Inn Nelson's Dockyard, English Harbour ⓣ268/460-1153, ⓕ460-1534. Built in 1788 as the dockyard's supply store and now attractively restored, this is one of the best accommodation options in Antigua, with a great colonial atmosphere, welcoming staff, a romantic setting by the harbour and sensible prices. An occasional free boat ferries guests to a nearby beach. ⑤

Catamaran Hotel Falmouth ⓣ268/460-1036, ⓕ460-1506. Friendly little place on the north side of the harbour in Falmouth, adjacent to a small marina. The beach is not great for swimming and it's a bit of a hike to the action at the dockyard, but the rooms are comfortable and good value. ④

The Inn at English Harbour English Harbour ⓣ268/460-1014, ⓕ460-1603, ⓦwww.theinn.ag. Attractive old hotel, popular with repeat guests and spread over a large site beside the harbour next to a pleasant white-sand beach. There are 22 rooms in a two-storey building bedecked in bougainvillea; prices start at US$320/190 in high/low season. ⑨

Falmouth and around

The main road south from St John's, cutting through the very centre of Antigua, first hits the coast at **Falmouth Harbour**. This large and beautiful natural harbour has been used as a safe anchorage since the days of the earliest colonists, and the town that sprang up beside it was the first major settlement on the island. Today, though the harbour is still often busy with yachts, Falmouth itself is a quiet place, most of the activity in the area having moved east to **English Harbour** and Nelson's Dockyard, divided from Falmouth Harbour by a small peninsula known as the **Middle Ground**.

Great Fort George

High above Falmouth, and offering terrific panoramic views over the harbour and surrounding countryside, are the ruins of **Great Fort George** (also known as **Monk's Hill**), one of Antigua's oldest defences, built in the 1690s as a secure retreat for Antigua's tiny population.

These days the fort is in a very dilapidated state, but it's well worth the effort to get there for the fabulous views and a quiet but evocative sense of the island's past. Much of the enormous stone perimeter wall is intact while, inside the main gate and to the right, the west gunpowder magazine (built in 1731) has been well restored.

To get to the fort you'll need a four-wheel-drive vehicle; the alternative is a thirty-minute hike. A precipitous but passable track leads up from the village of Cobbs Cross, east of Falmouth; alternatively, from Liberta (north of Falmouth) take the inland road to Table Hill Gordon, from where another track winds up to the fort.

English Harbour and around

The road east from Falmouth leads to the tiny village of Cobb's Cross, where a right turn takes you down to the small village of **ENGLISH HARBOUR**, which today consists of little more than a handful of homes, shops and restaurants. Another right turn leads down to **Nelson's Dockyard**, to the excellent **Pigeon Beach** and to the Middle Ground peninsula. Alternatively, head straight on for the road that climbs up into the hills to the military ruins at **Shirley Heights**.

Nelson's Dockyard

One of Antigua's definite highlights, the eighteenth-century **Nelson's Dockyard** (daily 8am–6pm; EC$13, includes admission to Shirley Heights) is the only surviving Georgian dockyard in the world. Adjacent to a fine natural harbour, the place developed primarily as a careening station – where British ships had barnacles scraped from their bottoms and were generally put back into shape. It also provided the military with a local base to repair, water and supply the navy that patrolled the West Indies and protected Britain's prized colonies against enemy incursion.

The dockyard was begun in 1743, and most of the present buildings date from 1785 and 1792, many of them built from the ballast of bricks and stones brought to the island by British trading ships, which sailed empty from home en route to loading up with sugar and rum.

During the nineteenth century, however, the advent of steam-powered ships which needed less attention coincided with a decline in British interest in the region, and the dockyard fell into disuse, finally closing in 1889. The 1950s saw a major restoration project, and in 1961 the dockyard was officially reopened as both a working harbour and a tourist attraction.

Entering the dockyard, the first building on your left is the **Admiral's Inn**, built in 1788 and originally used as a store for pitch, lead and turpentine. Today the place houses a hotel and restaurant, and is one of the most atmospheric spots on the south coast. Adjoining the hotel, a dozen thick, capped **stone pillars** – looking like the relics of an ancient Greek temple – are all that is left of a large boathouse, where ships were pulled in along a narrow channel to have their sails repaired in the sail-loft on the upper floor.

From the hotel, a lane leads down to the harbour, passing various restored colonial buildings, including the remains of a guardhouse, a blacksmith's workshop and an old canvas and clothing store that provided supplies for the ships. Just beyond, the Admiral's House (a local residence that never actually housed an admiral) was built in 1855 and today serves as the dockyard's **museum** (daily 8am–6pm; free), good for a quick tour for its small but diverse collection, which focuses on the dockyard's history and the island's shipping tradition, aided by models and photographs of old schooners and battleships.

Fort Berkeley

The narrow path that leads from behind the *Copper and Lumber Store Hotel* to **Fort Berkeley** is easily overlooked, but a stroll around these dramatic military ruins should be an integral part of your visit. Perched above the crashing surf on a narrow spit of land that commands the entrance to English Harbour, the fort was the harbour's earliest defensive point and retains essentially the same long, thin shape today that it had in 1745.

Pigeon Beach

There's not much in the way of beach around Nelson's Dockyard but a good place to head for after some sightseeing is **Pigeon Beach**, five minutes' drive or twenty minutes' walk west of the dockyard. As you head out of the dockyard, turn left just before the harbour and follow the road past a series of restaurants and the Antigua yacht club. Keep going past the *Falmouth Harbour Apartments*, take the uphill track that goes sharply left and follow the road down to the right, where you'll find a wide expanse of white sand and a welcoming **beach bar** (though the bar is sometimes closed during the summer).

Shirley Heights

Spread over an extensive area of the hills to the east of English Harbour, numerous military ruins offer further evidence of the strategic importance of this part of southern Antigua. Collectively known as **Shirley Heights** (although technically this is only the name for the area around Fort Shirley), it's an interesting area to explore, with a couple of hiking opportunities for the adventurous who want to escape the crowds completely (daily; from 9am to 5pm there's an EC$13 entry charge which includes admission to Nelson's Dockyard).

Follow the road uphill from the tiny village of English Harbour and you'll pass the late eighteenth-century **Clarence House**, an attractive Georgian home built in 1787 for Prince William, Duke of Clarence (later King William IV), who was then serving in the Royal Navy. (At publication time, the house was undergoing renovation.) Past here, a right-hand turn-off leads down to the *Inn at English Harbour* (see p.529) and the attractive crescent of Galleon Beach, where numerous yachts are normally moored just offshore.

Ignoring the turn-off and carrying straight on you'll pass the free **Dow's Hill Interpretation Centre** which, frankly, has virtually nothing to do with the history of the area and is pretty missable. Beyond the centre, the road runs along the top of a ridge before dividing where a large cannon has been upended in the centre of the road. Fork left for the cliff known as **Cape Shirley**, where you'll find a cluster of ruined stone buildings – including barracks, officers' quarters and an arms storeroom – known collectively as the **Blockhouse**. On the eastern side a wide gun platform looks downhill to a narrow inlet at **Indian Creek**, beyond that to the **Standfast Point** peninsula and Eric Clapton's enormous house and gatehouse, and beyond that over the vast sweep of Willoughby Bay. Every year, stories leak out about Clapton and friends like Elton John and Keith Richard turning up for a jam at one of the island's nightclubs.

If you take the right-hand fork at the half-buried cannon, the road will lead you up to the ruins of **Fort Shirley**. On the right as you approach are the still grandly arcaded though now roofless officers' quarters, overgrown with grass and grazed by the ubiquitous goats; opposite, across a bare patch of ground, are the remains of the military hospital and, in a small valley just below the surgeon's quarters, the **military cemetery** with its barely legible tombstones dating mostly from the 1850s and reflecting the prevalence of disease, particularly yellow fever..

The road ends at the fort itself, where a restored guardhouse now serves as an excellent little bar and restaurant, *The Lookout* (see below). The courtyard – where a battery of cannons once pointed out across the sea – now sees a battery of cameras snapping up the fabulous views over English Harbour, particularly on Sundays when the tourists descend in droves for the reggae and steel bands.

Eating, drinking and nightlife

Most of the good south coast **restaurants** are concentrated around Nelson's Dockyard and nearby Falmouth Harbour. Two others to look out for are *Alberto's* – a five-minute drive or taxi ride away– and the *Lookout*, high up on Shirley Heights.

Alberto's Willoughby Bay ☎268/460-3007. Probably the best food on the south coast, hosted by the eponymous long-time proprietor in an out-of-the-way spot. Recurring evening meals include thin slices of breadfruit roasted in a garlic and parsley sauce (EC$25) and pan-fried tuna or wahoo with wasabi and ginger (EC$60). Top desserts send you happily on your way. Tues–Sun dinner only; closed July–Oct.

HQ Nelson's Dockyard, English Harbour ☎268/562-2563. Excellent place in the heart of the dockyard serving imaginative Asian/Caribbean fusion food. Starters at US$7–10 include Thai squid salad and sashimi; main dishes of hot and sweet fish (US$17), chilli lamb (US$23) or lobster that you choose from the tank (US$27). The similar lunch menu offers cheaper snacks. Daily for lunch and dinner.

Hype English Harbour ☎268/562-2354. Loud nightclub and bar on a pier over the water, with DJs during the week and bands at the weekends. Popular with both the sailing crowd and locals. Wed–Sun 7pm–1am. No cover charge.

The Last Lemming Falmouth Harbour ☎268/460-6910. Tasty food at this frequently crowded harbourside spot, though the service can be dreadfully slow. Pan-fried catch of the day (US$12–16) and grilled steaks (US$15–22) are typical of the daily offerings. Daily for lunch and dinner.

The Lookout Shirley Heights ☎268/460-1785. The only place for a refreshment break while you're up on the Heights, offering up simple meals from US$5 on a large patio with superb views over the harbour and the dockyard (daily for lunch and dinner). The Sunday (and, to a lesser extent, Thursday) barbecues have a great party atmosphere, pulling a huge crowd for the reggae and steel-band performances (from 4pm, no cover charge).

13.4

The west coast

Tourism makes a firm impression on Antigua's **west coast**, with hotels dotted at regular intervals between the little fishing village of **Old Road** in the south and the capital, St John's. Two features dominate the area: a series of lovely beaches, with **Darkwood** probably the pick of the bunch for swimming, snorkelling and beachcombing, and a glowering range of hills known as the **Shekerley Mountains** in the southwest, offering the chance for a climb and some panoramic views. The lush and thickly wooded **Fig Tree Hill** on the edge of the range is as scenic a spot as you'll find, and you can take a variety of **hikes** inland to see a side of Antigua overlooked by the vast majority of tourists. Due west of St John's, the **Five Islands** peninsula holds several hotels, some good beaches and the substantial ruins of the eighteenth-century **Fort Barrington**.

Accommodation

Antigua's **west coast** has more rooms than any other part of the island, covering a wide range. The Five Islands peninsula, just north of here, has a handful of good hotels, though these feel a little more isolated.

Hawksbill Beach Five Islands ⓣ268/462-0301, ⓕ462-1515, ⓦwww.hawksbill.com. Attractive, sprawling hotel on the Five Islands peninsula, overlooking the bay and the jagged rock – shaped like the beak of a hawksbill turtle – that pokes up from the sea and gives the place its name. Four beaches, dramatic views, lovely landscaped gardens and a restored sugar mill converted into a store all add to the atmosphere. 9

Jolly Harbour Villas Jolly Harbour ⓣ268/462-6166, ⓕ462-6167, ⓦwww.jollyharbourantigua.com. Fifty waterfront villas, mostly two-bedroom with a full kitchen and a balcony overlooking the harbour. Plenty of shops, restaurants and sports facilities (including a golf course and large, communal swimming pool) are nearby, but the place feels somewhat bland and unimaginative. 7

Rex Blue Heron Johnson's Point ⓣ268/462-8564, ⓦwww.rexcaribbean.com. Medium-sized and very popular all-inclusive on one of the best west coast beaches, with 64 comfortable and brightly decorated rooms and a small pool a stone's throw from the sea. All-inclusive rates start at US$280/260 per room per night. 9

Fig Tree Hill

Heading west at the town of Swetes, you can follow the main road through the most densely forested part of the island, **Fig Tree Hill**. You won't actually see any fig trees – the road is lined with bananas (known locally as figs) and mango trees as it carves its way through some gorgeous scenery down to the south coast at Old Road. About halfway along the drive, you can stop at a small roadside shack which calls itself the **Cultural Centre**, where you can get a drink and some fruit from local farms.

A dirt track leads south from the shack to a **reservoir** – the island's first – where you'll find picnic tables set up around the edge of the water. Those interested in a more serious hike can take the **Rendezvous Trail**, which crosses the **Wallings Woodlands** to the nearly always empty beach a two-hour walk away at Rendezvous Bay. Even a short stroll repays the effort; the woodlands are the best remaining example of the evergreen secondary forest that covered the island before the British settlers arrived, and are home to more than thirty species of shrubs and trees, including giant mahogany trees, and masses of noisy birdlife. The trail starts on your left just before you reach the steps of the reservoir – bear in mind that, though it's pretty hard to get lost, the main path is little used and in places can quickly become overgrown and hard to make out.

Boggy Peak

Beyond Fig Tree Hill, and through the small town of Old Road, the road follows the coast past a series of banana groves and pineapple plantations, and around **Cades Bay**, with delightful views out to sea over Cades Reef. On the right, half a mile from Old Road, a track leads up into the Shekerley Mountains to **Boggy Peak**, at 1312m the highest point on the island. The panoramic view from the top – in good visibility you can even make out St Kitts, Guadeloupe and Montserrat – repays the effort of making the steep drive or the one-hour climb. Unfortunately, the peak is now occupied by a communication station, safely tucked away behind a high-security fence, so you'll need to make arrangements to visit with Cable & Wireless in St John's (☎268/462-0840). If you haven't the time or the inclination, the views from outside the perimeter fence are almost as good.

Darkwood Beach and around

Continuing west through the village of **Urlings**, the road runs alongside a number of excellent beaches. First up is **Turner's Beach** and **Johnson's Point**, where the sand shelves down to the sea beside a couple of good beach bars, including *Turner's* (see opposite), which rents snorkelling gear. The snorkelling is better just north of here at **Darkwood Beach**, a wide stretch of beach running right alongside the main road and a great spot for a swim. Look out for small underwater canyons just offshore, and schools of squid and colourful reef fish. Beachcombers will find this one of the best places on the island to look for shells and driftwood.

Just north of Darkwood Beach lies **Jolly Harbour**, where a marina complex includes rental apartments, a golf course, restaurants (see opposite) and a small shopping mall. It's a world apart from the "real Antigua" – like a small piece of America transplanted in the Caribbean.

Five Islands

To the west of St John's the highway leads out through a narrow isthmus onto the large **Five Islands** peninsula, named for five small rocks that jut from the sea just offshore. There are several hotels on the peninsula's northern coast, a few more on its west coast, though the interior is largely barren and scrubby, and there's not a huge amount to see. A half-mile offshore from **Hawksbill Bay**, a large rock in the shape of the head of a hawksbill turtle gives the place its name. To reach the bay, and some excellent beaches, follow the main road straight through the peninsula.

On Goat Hill, at the northern point of the peninsula close to the *Royal Antiguan* hotel, the circular stone ruins of **Fort Barrington** overlook gorgeous Deep Bay. The British first built a simple fort here in the 1650s, to protect the southern entrance to St John's Harbour, though it was captured by the French when they took the city in 1666. Take the twenty-minute walk around the beach to the fort for the dramatic sense of isolation as you look out to sea or back over the tourists sunning themselves far below on the bay.

Eating and drinking

As well as a series of eateries lined up along the marina at **Jolly Harbour**, this side of the island offers a handful of places dotted along the coast.

Dogwatch Tavern Jolly Harbour ☎268/462-6550. English-style pub, right beside the marina, with pool tables and dartboards, and an inexpensive outdoor snack bar and grill that sells burgers (EC$20), hot dogs (EC$10), red snapper with peas and rice (EC$28) and steak with fries (EC$45). Bar open Mon–Fri 11am–10pm, Sat & Sun 5–10pm, restaurant daily from 6pm.

Steely Bar Jolly Harbour ☎268/462-6260. This lively place, overlooking the marina in the heart of the Jolly Harbour complex serves food all day. A full breakfast will set you back EC$23, while an extensive lunch menu features salads (EC$19–27), hot dogs and burgers, and dinner might include pan-fried duck breast (EC$52) or Cajun snapper with rice (EC$43). There's also entertainment every night. Daily 8am–late.

Turner's Beach Bar and Grill Johnson's Point ☎268/462-9133. Delightful little restaurant on another of the best west coast beaches. It's an unpretentious place, with plastic furniture right on the sand, but the cooking is good and the atmosphere mellow. The evening menu includes chicken curry (US$11), grilled red snapper (US$14) and grilled lobster (US$22), as well as rotis (US$7). The lunch menu is the same but slightly pricier. Call ahead for a reservation at night. Daily 11am–9pm.

13.5

Barbuda

With its magnificent and often deserted beaches, its spectacular coral reefs and its rare colony of frigate birds, the nation's other inhabited island, **Barbuda** – 48km to the north of Antigua – is a definite highlight of any visit to Antigua. Don't expect the same facilities as on Antigua; **accommodation** options are limited, you'll need to bring your own snorkelling or diving gear, and you'll find that schedules – whether for taxis, boats or meals – tend to drift. This is all, of course, very much part of the island's attraction.

Half the size of its better-known neighbour, **Barbuda** developed quite separately from Antigua and was only reluctantly coerced into joining the nation during the run-up to independence in 1981. The island is very much the poor neighbour in terms of financial resources, and its development has been slow; tourism has had only a minor impact, and fishing and farming remain the principal occupations of the tiny population of 1500, most of whom live in the small capital, **Codrington**.

Away from the beaches, the island is less fetching, mostly low-level scrub of cacti, bush, small trees and the distinctive century plants; for most of the year it is extremely arid and unwelcoming. There are a couple of exceptions: in the **southwest** the island suddenly bursts to life, with a fabulous grove of coconut palms springing out of the sandy soil (and providing a useful source of export revenue), while in parts of the interior, government projects are reclaiming land from the bush to grow peanuts and sweet potatoes, also for the export market. For the most part, though, the island is left to the scrub, the elusive wild boar and deer and a multitude of birds – 170 species at last count.

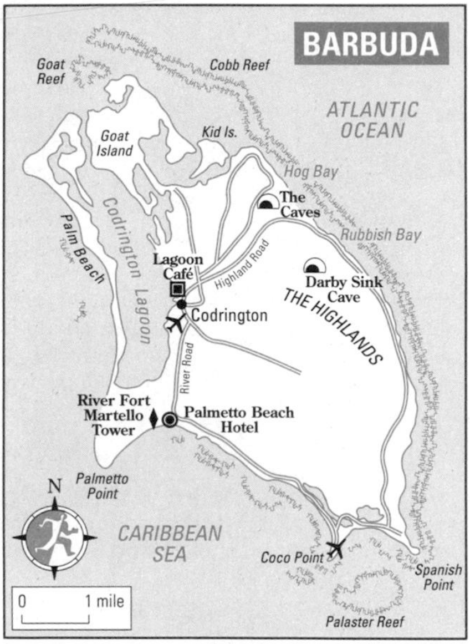

Getting there

The only scheduled **flights** to Barbuda are from Antigua on Carib Aviation (☎268/462-3147 or 3452; UK ☎01895/450710, US ☎646/336-7600). They offer four flights a day from the main airport in Antigua (leaving at 7am, 8am, 9am and 5pm, returning thirty minutes later in each case) and charge US$50 round-trip. The planes take twenty minutes. More excitingly, the journey can be made by **boat**, although the cost of the four-hour crossing from St John's to River Landing on Barbuda's south coast tends to be pretty exorbitant at around US$150 one-way. A handful of

The tiny and now uninhabited volcanic rock known as **Redonda**, some 56km to the southwest of Barbuda, is occasionally visited by yachters – though with no sheltered anchorage, the landing is a difficult one. There is no regular service to the island, nor anywhere to stay save for a few ruined mining buildings.

local boat operators run occasional trips (try Foster Hopkins on ☎268/460-0212 or Byron Askie on ☎268/460-0065).

Taking a **day tour** to the island is the best way to guarantee getting both a driver and a boat operator to take you to the bird sanctuary. Both D&J Forwarders (☎268/464-3228 or 773-9766) and Jenny's Tours (☎268/461-9361) will organize a carefully packaged day tour for US$150, including flights, pick-up at Barbuda airport, a jeep tour of the island, lunch and a boat visit to the bird sanctuary. Your driver will also leave you on the beach for as long as you want – just remember to take a bottle of water. Occasional day tours by boat are run by Ecoseatours (☎268/463-0275) and Adventure Antigua (☎268/560-4672 or 727-3261), both of which run fast boats to the Barbudan beaches in an hour and a half for snorkelling and beach cruising. Costs are around US$120 per person.

Codrington

CODRINGTON, the island's capital and only settlement, holds almost the entire population within its grid of narrow streets. It's a well-spread-out place, with plenty of brightly painted single-storey clapboard or concrete buildings. There are a couple of guesthouses, a handful of restaurants, bars and supermarkets, but, for the most part, people keep to themselves, and there is little sign of life apart from a few curious schoolchildren, dogs and the occasional goat. On Sundays the capital livens up with a cricket match at the Holy Trinity School.

Codrington Lagoon

To the west of town, **Codrington Lagoon** is an expansive area of green, brackish water, fringed by mangroves. The lagoon is completely enclosed on its western side by the narrow but magnificent strip of **Palm Beach**, over 13 miles long, but there is a narrow cut to the north where fishing boats can get out to the ocean. Lobsters breed in the lagoon and you'll probably see them at the pier being loaded for export to Antigua – an important contribution to the local economy. Equally significant – for this is what is starting to bring in the tourists – a series of mangrove clumps to the northwest of the lagoon, known as **Man of War Island**, is the home and breeding ground for the largest group of **frigate birds** anywhere in the Caribbean. The sight as you approach them by boat (see overleaf) is quite spectacular – the mothers will take to the skies as you draw near, joining the multitude of birds wheeling above you, and leaving their babies standing imperiously on the nest but watching you closely out of the corner of their eyes. The display gets even more dramatic during the mating season, from late August to December, when hundreds of the males put on a grand show – puffing up their bright-red throat pouches as they soar through the air just a few yards above the females, watching admiringly from the bushes.

Practicalities

If you need **to stay** in Codrington, *Nedd's Guesthouse* (☎268/460-0059; ③), offers a handful of comfortable and airy rooms, with a kitchen and grocery store downstairs. If it's full, the owner should be able to direct you to someone who'll rent you a room, or try Byron Askie (☎268/460-0065).

Dining and nightlife is limited in Codrington. The easy-going *Green Door Tavern* (daily 11am–9pm; no phone) has tasty inexpensive local food and a barbecue on Friday and Saturday evenings, while the island's main nightly hangout, the *Lagoon Café* (☎268/460-0439; daily lunch and dinner), is a dimly lit place offering simple, inexpensive meals like steamed grouper or curried chicken with peas and rice, guys playing dominoes and the (very) occasional live band.

To see the frigate birds, you'll need to hire one of the small **boats** (for around US$50) that leave for the sanctuary from the main pier just outside Codrington. It's advisable to visit as part of a tour or to make arrangements through your hotel or car rental.

The rest of the island

Apart from any beach or snorkelling stops, a tour of the island is a pretty brief affair. Away from the lagoon, there are few sights and they're all pretty missable unless you're determined to get your money's worth.

North of Codrington a series of dirt roads fans out across the upper part of the island. One of these leads into the heart of the island, to the scant remains of **Highlands House**, the castle the first Codringtons built on the island in the seventeenth century. The views across the island from here are as panoramic as you'll find. Another dirt road leads up to the northeastern side of the island, where a series of **caves** has been naturally carved into the low cliffs. These are thought to have sheltered Taíno and possibly Carib Indians in the centuries preceding the arrival of Europeans in the island. Scant evidence of their presence has been found here, however, except for some unusual **petroglyphs**. The entrance to the main cave is opposite a large boulder, with the ruins of an old **watchtower** built up alongside. You'll need to scramble up the rocks for five minutes, then make a short, stooped walk inside the cave to reach the petroglyphs – a couple of barely distinguishable and very amateurish faces carved into the rockface.

River Fort

You can clamber around some more substantial remains at the **River Fort** in the southwest of the island, just beyond the coconut grove. The fort provides a surprisingly large defence for an island of Barbuda's size and importance. The island was attacked by Carib Indians in the 1680s and by the French navy in 1710, but there was too little valuable property here to tempt any further assailants into braving the dangerous surrounding reefs. As a result, the fort never saw any action, and its main role has been as a lookout and a landmark for ships approaching the island from the south.

The remains are dominated by a **Martello tower**, one of the many built throughout the British Empire during the Napoleonic Wars. Right below the tower, the **River Landing** is the main point for access to Barbuda by boat and is always busy with trucks stockpiling and loading sand onto barges to be taken to replenish beaches in Antigua – a controversial but lucrative industry for the Barbudans.

Practicalities

If you need a **place to stay**, the *Palmetto Beach Hotel* (☎268/460-0440, Ⓕ462-0742, Ⓦwww.palmettohotel.com; ⑧, all-inclusive, excluding drinks), west of the fort, is on a fantastic stretch of beach, with 24 beachfront suites all with A/C and a private verandah. The rooms are big, comfortable and stylishly decorated. The food, mostly Italian, is excellent.

The French West Indies

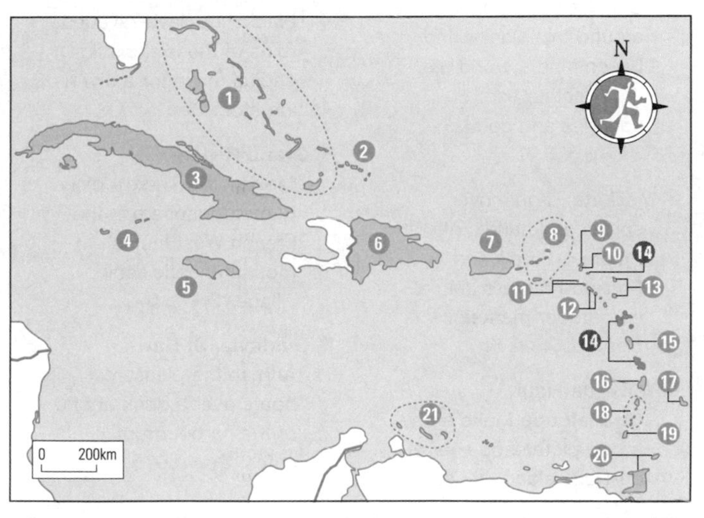

14 THE FRENCH WEST INDIES

The French West Indies Highlights

* **Parc National de Guadeloupe** Hike to thundering waterfalls, ascend cloud-capped mountain peaks, and go deep into humid jungle at this outstanding reserve. See p.553

* **Plage Malendure, Guadeloupe** The Caribbean depths around this black-sand beach hold a world of technicolour fish, sponges and coral. See p.555

* **Markets** Haggle over spices and handicrafts at Pointe-à-Pitre's and Fort-de-France's animated outdoor markets. See pp.548 & 566

* **Terre-de-Haut, Guadeloupe** Make a day trip to picturesque Terre-de-Haut island, full of attractive Breton architecture and fringed by lovely white-sand beaches. See p.557

* **Les Salines, Martinique** This stunning crystalline bay in the island's southern region is perfect at sunset. See p.570

* **St-Pierre, Martinique** The blackened, lava-ravaged ruins of the island's first capital make for a diverting stop. See p.571

* **Grand'Rivière, Martinique** There's plenty of atmosphere in the French West Indies' most authentic fishing village. See p.572

* **Gustavia, St Barts** Admire the pleasure boats over a drink at one of the harbourfront cafés. See p.575

Introduction and Basics

Beaten by the Atlantic on one side and caressed by the Caribbean on the other, the four volcanic islands that comprise the **French West Indies** boast some of the Caribbean's most varied scenery between their coasts. Extending almost 650km across the Eastern Caribbean, the islands of **Guadeloupe**, **Martinique**, **St Barthélemy** (St Barts) and French **St Martin** (covered in its own chapter, p.461), are a heady blend of long sandy beaches, humid rainforests, craggy mountain peaks, dazzling turquoise waters and dramatic limestone coasts.

The larger islands are crowned by dormant **volcanoes**, including the Eastern Caribbean's highest summit, Guadeloupe's **La Soufrière**, and its most devastating, Martinique's **Mont-Pelée.** The thundering **waterfalls** that course their flanks feed dense interior **rainforests** before flowing out to sea, where gorgeous **beaches** in hues ranging from white to gold and midnight black drop off to a brilliant technicolour world of fish and coral that delight **divers** and **snorkellers** alike. The smallest island, St Barts, lacks the lush greenery common to its southern siblings, but amply compensates with spectacular and often **secluded** beaches, and an unparalleled ambience of exclusivity.

Despite their setting amidst predominantly English islands, the French West Indies have remained remarkably, even obstinately, French, especially so St Barts, a veritable Mediterranean holdout cast away on the Caribbean Sea. In contrast, Guadeloupe and Martinique have merged the hallmarks of **French** culture – vices like wine, sweets, coffee and cigarettes abound – with the best **Creole** traditions – spicy food, atmospheric architecture and languid attitudes. The two meet head-on most noticeably in the major cities, like Guadeloupe's **Pointe-à-Pitre** and Martinique's **Fort-de-France**, where Caribbean marketplaces join smoke-filled cafés, narrow streets jammed with honking cars, and fading wood colonial houses.

Where to go

Guadeloupe has the most to offer one-stop island visitors, from a massive **Parc National** with impressive **rainforest** flora and **hiking** trails and ample **beaches**, to a phenomenal **dive** site and four remarkable **offshore islands**, including the charming **Terre-de-Haut**.

Martinique, in contrast, suffers somewhat from overdeveloped package-tour-oriented resort towns, like flashy **Pointe-du-Bout**, but less developed areas, like the **Presqu'Île Caravelle** still exist. Resort-bound visitors can also explore more authentically Martiniquan pockets like the charred ruins at **St-Pierre** and the superb **Habitation Clément** rum distillery, both of which evoke something of Martinique's past, and escape the sun-worshipping throngs by **hiking** on Mont-Pelée.

For those who can afford it, tiny **St-Barthélemy** (St Barts) is the ultimate get-away – a decadent beach-trimmed isle with a luxurious, self-pampering mindset, and nothing to do but lie on the sand by day and eat sumptuously at night. While you may go home broke, you'll be completely rejuvenated.

When to go

Most of the year, puffy white clouds parade through a clear blue sky, and warm balmy breezes gently ruffle hair and sway palm fronds: T-shirt, shorts and sandals kind of weather, interrupted now and then by a **tropical shower**.

From July to November, however, this halcyon state of affairs may be interrupted by the **hurricane season**. the wettest time of the year and also the most humid. The best time to visit is between mid-December and mid-April, when the weather is dry and the heat is tempered by cooling trade winds.

Getting there

Both Guadeloupe and Martinique are served by numerous airlines, including Air Canada, Air Caraïbes, Air France, Air Guadeloupe (☎0590/21 12 90), Air Martinique (☎0590/21 13 40), Air St-Martin (☎0590/21 12 88), American Airlines and LIAT. In addition, Guadeloupe is served by Air La Liberté (☎0590/21 14 68), Air Calypso (☎0590/89 27 77) and Corsair (☎0590/21 12 50), and Martinique by Cubana. Flights to Guadeloupe arrive daily from Antigua, Dominica, Paris, San Juan and St Martin. Martinique has flights arriving daily from Paris, San Juan and St Lucia. Both islands are served by weekly flights from Montreal.

Airlines that fly to **St Barts** are Air Caraïbes, Air St Thomas, St Barth Commuter and Winward. St Martin is the major hub; flights also arrive daily from San Juan and St Thomas. (For phone numbers of airlines, see pp.12–18 and 36–37.)

Ferries run daily between St Barts and both French St Martin and Dutch St Maarten. They also link Guadeloupe and Martinique with Dominica and St Lucia. For information about travelling by boat between Guadeloupe, Martinique and St Barts see "Ferries", p.38.

Money and costs

Since the French West Indies are overseas extensions of France, the prices for food and lodging are considerably more expensive than elsewhere in the Caribbean. Thanks to its celeb status, St Barts is in a class all its own when it comes to budgetary considerations.

In 2002, the **euro** (€) became the official currency on all three islands. Euro notes are issued in denominations of 5, 10, 20, 50, 100, 200 and 500 euros and coin denominations of 1, 2, 5, 10, 20 and 50 cents and 1 and 2 euros. The **US dollar** is also widely used on St Barts. Unless otherwise noted, prices in this chapter are given in US dollars.

You'll find major **banks** in all island capitals and resort areas, usually equipped with **ATMs**. Tellers exchange travellers' cheques and cash, for a small commission, Monday through Friday 8am–noon and 2.30–5pm. **Moneychangers**, found near the main island tourist offices don't charge commission.

Even at two people sharing a room, it will be difficult to get by on less than US$50/day. The most simple double room costs around US$50; the same room near a beach **costs** $60–$70. Rates include all tax and service charges, and many also include breakfast. The cheapest option around is **camping** – Guadeloupe and Martinique both have sites for around $15/night. Otherwise, consider going in low season, when rates go down by almost half (May to Nov).

The best restaurant deals are the three-course **prix-fixe** menus. On Guadeloupe and Martinique they're commonly priced around $15 for dinner, while St Barts charges around $20 a head; they're usually modestly cheaper at lunchtime. The best lunch bargains are hefty ham and cheese baguettes and sodas from the beachside trucks that cost about $3. **Wine** can actually be less expensive than soda, at $1-$1.50 a glass in some bars.

Getting around

You'll be hard-pressed to make it to all French islands in one trip, as travelling between them is far from straightforward. Certainly, checking out two islands per visit is feasible – Guadeloupe and Martinique both have regular **ferry** crossings between them, as do St Martin and St Barts.

The best way to get around each island is with your own wheels; what **public transportation** exists in Martinique and Guadeloupe is far from efficient, while St Barts – which happens to have the worst **roads** of the lot – has none whatsoever.

By bus

While getting around Martinique and Guadeloupe by **bus** is the most reasonably priced mode of transportation (€1–€3.50), the service is not for those in a hurry. Known as *taxis collectifs* (or "TC"), they're actually cramped minivans which generally run from 6am to 6pm weekdays, with scant service after 2pm on Saturdays and none on Sundays. There's no real schedule to speak of

– they leave from the capitals when they're full. To board one outside the capitals, simply flag it down along the road; keep in mind, however, that TCs are often packed in the hinterlands. Tell the driver where you're going when you board and pay him when you get off.

By taxi

Taxis in the French West Indies are expensive, charging a minimum of €5 even if you're just going down the street, and doubling their rates Monday through Friday 8pm–6am and all day Sundays and holidays. Fortunately, the only time you're really likely to need one is to get yourself to and from your hotel and the respective islands' ferry docks or airport.

By car and hitching

Driving requires a good dose of fearlessness. The French drive like maniacs – especially in Martinique. Guadeloupe is slightly less harried but still necessitates that you be alert at all times, especially when driving in the busy capitals. St Barts has grown increasingly dangerous in recent years as the cars plying its narrow, mottled-cement roads have become both bigger and faster. Most **car rentals** start around $50/day. See individual islands for details.

Hitchhiking is very common on Martinique and Guadeloupe due to the irregular bus service. The usual precautions apply.

By boat

The most common passenger **boats** are twin-hulled catamarans with a covered upper deck and an enclosed, air-conditioned lower one. Note that the trip from Guadeloupe to Martinique can be choppy. Unlike the buses here, ferries do attempt to follow a schedule of sorts, especially those making the 40min–1hr 30min crossings to Guadeloupe's offshore islands (see p.558). The boats making the 1.5–3hr trips between Guadeloupe, Dominica and Martinique (see "Ferries", p.38), however, rarely leave on time as passengers must acquire a boarding pass and go through customs beforehand, a badly managed process that requires a 45-minute minimum lead-time. Even if you've bought your ticket in advance – which is recommended for all sea passages – you'll still have to join the crowd in front of the quayside ticket wicket to procure your boarding pass.

By plane

There are several flights daily between the three islands, but don't expect efficient service. Much of the **air traffic** consists of twenty-passenger airplanes that rarely leave on time and have low cargo weight restrictions – you'll likely arrive without your luggage in high season. The fifteen-minute island hops between mainland Guadeloupe and its offshore isles are done by nine-seater planes with similar weight restrictions; more importantly, they may not take off at all if they're under-booked.

Information

Each island has its own tourism office and official website with links to **information** and hotels and services that you can book yourself (see pp.548, 566 and 575). Martinique also has offices abroad (see p.30).

Accommodation

While Guadeloupe and St Barts have a wide range of independent hotel options, Martinique is heavily geared to **package-tour** travellers, with the result that most hotels are chains – to get the best rates consult a travel agent.

Bungalow-style lodging is extremely popular on Guadeloupe and Martinique – basically a fully equipped studio or one-bedroom apartment with your own kitchen. If you're concerned about costs, they're an effective way to save money since you're not paying for hotel services, and you can make your own meals. A growing **bed and breakfast** industry is also starting to make a dent in the hotel scene thanks to lower prices and familial service; the best are part of the *Gîtes de France* network (Ⓣ01 49 70 75 75, Ⓕ01 42 81 28 53, Ⓦwww.gites-de-france.fr). There are no B&Bs on St Barts, though you can rent a luxurious **villa**.

While **camping** is forbidden on St Barts, Martinique has a couple of maintained campsites in Anse-à-l'Âne and Ste-Anne, and visitors are allowed to pitch their tents for free on the island's beaches during French school holidays (July–August and the March break). On Guadeloupe camping is only allowed at the established campsite in Pointe-Noir.

Food and drink

Unlike St Barts, where restaurants are predominantly **French**, most of Guadeloupe and Martinique's sit-down **meals** are **creole** in origin and **seafood**-based. The exceptions are **breakfast**, which usually consists of a short espresso, croissant and fruit juice, and **beachfare**, mostly filling ham and cheese baguettes, crepes and pastries.

Lunch is the meal of the day – and the lengthy shop closures around the noon hour reflect this custom. The only French traces you'll see here are the common use of the **prix-fixe menu** that usually includes at least a starter and a main course and good selection of French wines to wash down the **spicy** creole food. Dishes like *crabes farçi* (stuffed land crabs), *boudin* (blood pudding), *accras* (cod fritters) and the various *colombos*, a curry using *cabri* (goat), *poulet* (chicken), *lambi* (conch) and *ouassous* (crayfish), are the spiciest of all, though some resort areas tend to tone them down. Most main courses come with rice or beans.

The most expensive item on any menu is *langoustine*. Other dishes, like *féroce d'avocat* (a zesty avocado and cod purée), *calalou* (a spinach-like soup), and grilled fish like *vivanneau* (red snapper), marlin and *requin* (shark) tend to be less filling.

Individual islands have their specialities too. Guadeloupe's offshore **Marie-Galante** is known for a hearty *bébélé*, a thick "everything in the pot" soup of African origin made only on Saturdays, while Martiniquan chefs make *coq colombo*, a rich rooster curry.

French wine availability notwithstanding, the most popular **drink** on Martinique and Guadeloupe is **ti-punch**, a boozy rum, sugar and lime concoction. A diluted version, **Planter's Punch**, mixes the booze with fruit juice. Both islands also produce their own local **beers**: Guadeloupe's Corsair is a light brew that goes down nicely with rich creole fare, ditto for Martinique's Lorraine.

The **tap water** on Martinique and Guadeloupe is safe to drink; St Barts is more touch-and-go, as the island lacks a freshwater source. The finer hotels all provide potable water, but the budget places may get theirs from unreliable rain-catchment systems; if you're staying at the latter, you're better off buying bottled water, which is widely available on all islands.

Phones, post and email

There are public **telephones** on every square and many street corners, all of which accept only plastic ***télécartes*** (phone cards). You can buy them in units of 50/€6,72 and 100/€13,40 from any post office and most *tabacs* (tobacco shops). For the best rates, call after 7pm. Many payphones also list a 1-800 AT&T phone number to dial for **collect** calls.

Telephone numbers on all three islands are ten digits long, starting with 0. To make local calls on any of the islands, dial the ten-digit number. International calls to Martinique and Guadeloupe do not require the 0 – simply dial the international access code of the country you're calling from (see below), followed by the digits after the 0. To make an international call to St Barts, however, dial the international access code, followed by ☎590, then ten-digit number.

Sending letters home using the French **postal system** is straightforward – postcards and airmail letters cost €1.34 to North America, €1.04 to Europe and €1.80 to Australia.

The **internet** is still relatively new here, available mostly in the more resorty areas. Consequently, checking your **email** can be expensive. Until the islands catch up with the wired world, **fax** remains the preferred mode of written communication.

> The **country codes** for Martinique (☎596) and for Guadeloupe and St Barts (☎590) are now part of their ten-digit telephone numbers.

Opening hours, holidays and festivals

As a general rule, **opening hours** run 8am–noon and 2.30–7pm during the week and 8am–noon on Saturdays. On Sundays little is open, and some shops take Wednesday afternoons off, too. In addition to closures on national **holidays** (see box on this page) the islands also shut down to celebrate local holidays, the most notable being the abolition of slavery, celebrated on May 22 (Martinique) and May 27 (Guadeloupe); the man responsible for this feat, Victor Schoelcher, is honoured on July 21.

Holidays aside, some big festivals add spice to the region, the largest of all being **Carnival**, which runs yearly from January to Ash Wednesday in both Guadeloupe and Martinique, with dancing and music performances culminating in the election of the year's beauty queen. The **Christmas** season dovetails with the bi-annual **Jazz Fest** in Martinique, a weeklong music festival in Fort-de-France at the beginning of December showcasing acts from France and former French colonies. The only other notable event is a spiritual one, **La Toussaint** (All Souls Day), when red votive candles are lit throughout the cemeteries.

The major annual event in St Barts is its own celebration on August 24, complete with watersports and music. Earlier in the year, the Cinéma Caraïbes **film festival** in late April showcases Caribbean films over five days, and a two-week international **music festival** takes place in January, which includes ballet and other dance performances.

For **histories** of Guadeloupe, Martinique and St Barts, see individual island accounts.

Public holidays

January 1 New Year's Day
March/ April Easter Sunday, Easter Monday
May 1 Labour Day
Fortieth day after Easter Ascension Thursday
Seventh Monday after Easter Pentecost Monday
July 14 Bastille Day
August 15 Assumption
November 1 All Saints Day
November 2 All Souls Day
November 11 Armistice Day
December 25 Christmas Day

Crime and safety

St Barts has so little crime that people still leave their car doors unlocked. The same isn't true of Martinique, where **break-ins** at the parking lot near Mont-Pelée's hiking trails have been reported. Even so, the most common **crime** in Martinique and Guadeloupe is pick-pocketing – as long as you don't flash your money around, you're unlikely to have problems. Their major cities, however, are rather sketchy at night, with **prostitutes** and **drug dealers** hanging out in squares; they're significantly less trouble, however, than the Creole men who commonly **harass** white **women travellers**. While most is harmless catcalling, the worst offenders will grope you in the street. You can avoid harassment by covering up in town and avoiding eye contact.

Emergency numbers

Guadeloupe ⓣ0590/82 00 89 (gendarmerie); ⓣ0590/89 77 17 (police).
Martinique ⓣ0596/60 60 44 (medical); ⓣ17 or ⓣ59 40 00 (police).
St Barts ⓣ0590/27 60 35 (medical); ⓣ0590/27 66 66 (police).

14.1

Guadeloupe

The largest French West Indian island, **GUADELOUPE** encompasses a massive 1704 square kilometres, the majority of which is taken up by its two adjoining mainland islands, Basse-Terre and Grande-Terre, whose outline resembles a greenbacked butterfly in flight. Its two "wings" have entirely different personas and equally misrepresentative names: the western **Basse-Terre**, or "low-land", is anything but, given its central core is dominated by mountain ranges, including the Lesser Antilles' highest peak, **La Soufrière**. These surround the island's bountiful **rainforest** and descend to meet twinkling black-sand beaches like **Plage Malendure** that extend to protected underwater **dive** sites abounding with aqualife.

The eastern "wing", the furled **Grande-Terre**, or "large-land", is slightly smaller than Basse-Terre, utterly flat by contrast, and predominantly rural. Most of the action happens along its southern coast, where one white-sand beach after another seems to merge endlessly along the coast, with the stunning **Plage Caravelle** forming the centrepiece. Its outer reaches are pounded by the savage **Atlantic Ocean** to produce jagged limestone outcroppings like the windswept **Pointe-des-Châteaux**, and the exquisite **Lagon de la Porte d'Enfer** natural swimming pool.

Guadeloupe's offshore islands are equally diverse. **Marie-Galante**, with its rural landscape of sugarcane, hearkens back to a Guadeloupe of thirty years ago, while **La Désirade**, the most desolate of the lot, is quite possibly the Caribbean's least developed island. The most visited-offshore isle, tiny **Terre-de-Haut**, is the prettiest of all, with quaint architecture and fabulous bays and beaches.

Some history

Unlike the other islands in the French crown, the **Spanish** actually attempted to colonize Guadeloupe – twice – in the 1500s, after Columbus discovered its fertile soil during his second New World voyage. They were assailed both times by menacing Caribs, and it took the **French**, who arrived in 1635, to establish the French West Indies' first capital a few years later, at **Basse-Terre**. Their successful implementation of slavery by the 1670s caught British attention, who strove to overtake the island several times in the mid-1700s, and succeeded in occupying it from 1759 to 1763, when they built up the harbour at Pointe-à-Pitre and expanded sugarcane trade markets to North America. The 1763 **Paris Treaty** returned Guadeloupe to France but the British invaded again in 1794. The French responded by sending in troops led by black nationalist **Victor Hugues**, who launched a reign of terror by freeing and arming local slaves, killing hundreds of royalists and attacking American ships; not surprisingly, the US declared war on France.

Napoleon reinstituted order by appointing a governing general who restored slavery in 1802. Peace was not to endure for long, however, as the British were still keen on controlling the fiefdom, and they continued to manage parts of the island between 1810 and 1816, when the **Vienna Treaty** ended their attempts for good.

Slavery wasn't actually abolished in the French West Indies until 1848, after a dogged anti-slavery campaign mounted by French cabinet minister **Victor Schoelcher**. Since then, the only real issue has been Guadeloupe's status within the French government. The promise of political decentralization in the late 1900s gave

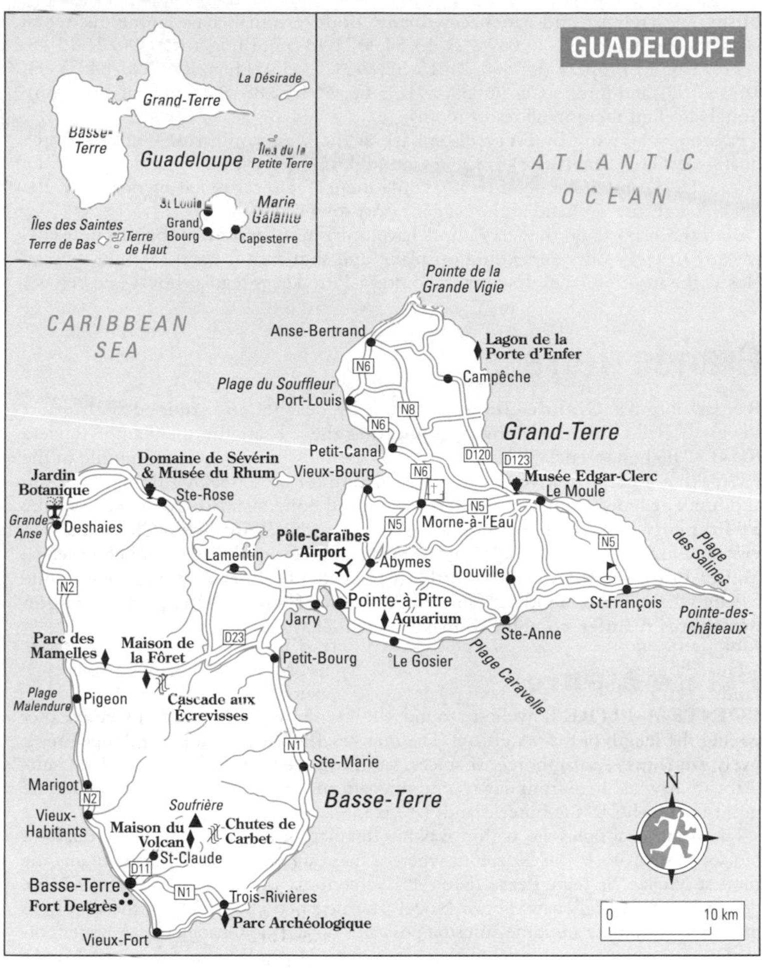

birth to **pro-independence** uprisings, some occurring as recently as 1999, when Guadeloupe, Martinique and Guyana (in South America) joined forces to sign the **Basse-Terre Declaration** seeking greater autonomy from the French government.

Arrival, information and getting around

Passengers arriving by **plane** land at one of mainland Guadeloupe's two airports: modern **Pôle-Caraïbes** or, less frequently, **Le Raizet**, a run-down nearby terminal used by **charter** flights. Both lie about 6km outside of Pointe-à-Pitre and are well served by metered **taxis** that cost between €20 and €60 to southern points (SOS ⊕0590/83 63 94; Taxigua ⊕0590/83 90 00).

If you're planning exploring the island, it's recommended that you rent a **car** at the airport and head out on your own, since the only other island transport, **mini-**

buses, are irregular and patience-wearing. Both terminals have numerous rental agencies, including Avis (Ⓣ0590/21 13 54, Ⓕ21 13 55); Budget (Ⓣ0590/21 13 48, Ⓕ21 13 63); Europcar (Ⓣ0590/21 13 52, Ⓕ21 13 53); Hertz (Ⓣ0590/84 57 94, Ⓕ84 57 90); and Jumbo Car (Ⓣ0590/91 55 66, Ⓕ91 22 88, Ⓦwww.jumbocar.com). You'll also find them in all resort towns.

Passengers arriving by **ferry** disembark at the westernmost of Pointe-à-Pitre's quays, the **Gare Maritime** (or Quai Gatine).From here, you can catch a taxi to Le Gosier (€15) and St-François (€50); while there are no car rental agencies near the docks, plenty are on hand at the bigger resort towns.

Both the airport and the ferry docks have tourism **information** booths near customs with flex-hours depending on plane and ship arrival times. Should they be closed, the main office in downtown Pointe-à-Pitre keeps regular hours (see below).

Grande-Terre

Remarkably flat **Grande-Terre** is skirted by beaches and studded with resort towns so glossy that the highway connecting them bears the nickname "Riviera Road". The busiest enclave, **Le Gosier**, has the most amenities and nightlife of the lot, making it the definitive one-stop destination for those seeking nothing but sun and fun. The crowds thin out further east, around bohemian **Ste-Anne** and swanky **St-François**, and are almost non-existent along the **Pointe-des-Châteaux**. No visit to Guadeloupe would be complete without a visit to the colourful commercial hub of **Pointe-à-Pitre**, while northern pockets like **Port-Louis**, a picturesque fishing village at the mouth of calm **Plage du Souffleur**, and the dramatic **Lagon des Portes d'Enfer**, combine to make a terrific day out.

Pointe-à-Pitre

POINTE-À-PITRE is liveliest around the **Quai de la Darse**, an extensive pier edging the length of the waterfront. The quay itself is lined with Guadeloupe's most lively **markets** – a jamboree of spices, fruit, fish, T-shirts and various island sundries are hawked here from dawn until mid-afternoon – and serves as the departure point for **ferries** to the outer islands (see p.558).

The scant local sights are within walking distance of the quay, starting a couple of blocks west, at no. 9 rue Nozières, where a handsome colonial house contains the modest **Musée St-Jean Perse** (Mon–Fri 9am–5pm, Sat 8.30am–12.30pm; €2.28), devoted to the island's native-born Nobel laureate poet. The quality of the displays is patchy, though there are some amusing postcards of bygone Guadeloupe. A better collection is situated a few blocks further west, at no.24 rue Peynier, where the **Musée Schoelcher** (Mon–Fri 9am–5pm; €1.52) showcases abolitionist Victor Schoelcher's (see p.546) assorted bric-a-brac – his own copy of the Venus de Milo among them.

A couple of blocks north of the Quai, behind the charmless **Place de la Victoire** that commemorates Victor Hugues' (see p.546) victory over the British, is Pointe-à-Pitre's major landmark, the Gustav Eiffel-designed steel **Cathédrale de St-Pierre-et-St-Paul**. Look for screws and bolts protruding from the columns in the apse.

The **Aquarium de la Guadeloupe** (daily 9am–7pm; €6.40, €3.51 under-12's), five kilometres east of Pointe-à-Pitre, will appeal to kids, especially its open turtle and shark aquariums. The nearby remains of **Fort Fleur-d'Épée** (daily 9am–5pm; free), a seventeenth-century Vauban-style military base, have commanding views of Grande-Terre and the sea, but little remaining infrastructure.

Practicalities

Information on Guadeloupe and its outer islands, including free, detailed Chemin Bleu road **maps**, is available from the main tourism office, 5 square de la Banque, across from la Darse's markets (Mon–Fri 8am–5pm, Sat 8am–noon; ⓣ0590/82 09 30, ⓕ83 89 22; ⓦwww.antilles-info-tourisme.com). You can check **email** at *Rapido*, 42 Centre John-Perse (daily 9am–1pm & 2–5pm; €3.05/15min) and send regular mail from the **post office** on place de l'Hôtel de Ville (Mon–Fri 7am–6pm, Sat 7am–noon).

There's no good reason to **stay** in Pointe-à-Pitre, but for those getting on or off boats in the dead of night, the small but appealing rooms at the portside *Hôtel St John Perse*, 10 Centre John-Perse (ⓣ0590/82 51 57, ⓕ82 52 61, ⓦwww.saint-john-perse.com; ④ with breakfast) are your best option. Otherwise, the spartan *Maison de la Marie-Galante*, 12 place de la Victoire (ⓣ0590/83 87 83; ②), will only do if you need a transit stay; the cheapest rooms are fan-only.

The city's few **restaurants** are equally lacklustre, but *Le Petit Palais*, 4 place de l'Église (Mon–Fri 6.30am–4.30pm), has pastries and coffee; *Maharaja Monty*, 43 rue Achille René-Boisneuf, serves up quality Indian curries in a French colonial-meets-Taj Mahal setting; and nearby, *La Fougère*, 34 rue Peynier, is the most attractive eatery in town, with tasty and affordable creole specials.

Le Gosier

Guadeloupe's premier resort area, **LE GOSIER**, lies 7km east of Pointe-à-Pitre, its proximity to the city spurring major resort development that has given the small town a dual personality. The area known as **Pointe de la Verdure** resembles a gated community, with slick resort hotels enclosed by electric gates, and has private, man-made white-sand beaches dotted with canopied chairs and watersports huts that rent **snorkelling** gear, **windsurfers** and **body-boards**. Further east along the main road, **boulevard Général-de-Gaulle**, you'll find an authentic Caribbean village of rustic colonial houses and tight-knit streets perched above a small public **beach**.

Le Gosier's best beach is actually 100m offshore, on the sweet **Îlet du Gosier**, a minuscule, undeveloped isle. There's good **snorkelling** to be had in its surrounding waters, as a capsized tug lies near the landing dock and there's an active coral reef to the rear – bring a mask and flippers with you, as you won't be able to rent them on site. Most resort hotels will **ferry** you over by speedboat for a hefty €7.62; local fishermen at a pier east of the town beach will go the five-minute distance by outboard for €2.29. Be sure, in both cases, to arrange a return time before disembarking. Bring a picnic lunch, or grab a bite from the dockside **snack** shacks.

Accomodation

Arawak Pointe de la Verdure ⓣ0590/84 24 24 or 1-800/742-4276, ⓕ0590/84 38 45, ⓦwww.fram.fr. Family hotel popular with tour groups. Comfortable A/C doubles on the beach, heaps of activities for the under-12 set, and tennis courts and a fitness centre for adults. ⑤

Créole Beach Pointe de la Verdure ⓣ0590/90 46 46, ⓕ90 46 66, ⓦwww.leader-hotels.gp. Le Gosier's classiest resort hotel, the 156 stylish, well-equipped doubles have sea or garden views; there's also a private beach and three-tiered swimming pool. ⑧

Flamboyants Chemin des Phares et des Balises ⓣ0590/84 14 11, ⓕ84 53 56. Colourful doubles and bungalows with views of Îlet du Gosier from a tranquil hilltop location about 1km east of town. ③

Formule Économique 112–120 Lot Gisors ⓣ0590/84 54 91, ⓕ84 29 42, ⓦwww.formuleeconomique.com. Friendly, bargain basement lodging down a badly lit residential street north of the town beach; while rates increase with bathtubs, terraces, kitchenettes and more space, the cheapest rooms are tiny. ②

Îlet de la Plage Plage Gosier ⓣ0590/84 20 73, ⓕ84 25 71. Pleasant and spacious fan-only or A/C studios overlooking the town beach with balconies and kitchenettes; book well ahead in high season. ②

Vieille Tour Gosier 5 Montauban ⓣ0590/84 23 23, ⓕ84 33 43, ⓦwww.accorhotels.com. The old windmill incorporated into the reception area gives this Sofitel chain hotel character; the 180 spacious rooms lack atmosphere, but are polished and well appointed. ⑨

Eating, drinking and nightlife

L'Affirmatif II 17 blvd Général-de-Gaulle. A cosy haunt serving up reasonably priced massive wood-oven pizzas and the odd creole dish; popular with locals.

Au P'ti Paris Périnet. A gorgeous creole house east of town with delicious thin-crust pizzas and light salads, and entertaining theme nights like café-theatre (Wed), magic (Fri) and live music (Sat).

Loolapaloosa 122 rue Montauban. Gimmicky Cuban-style nightspot where bartenders dressed like Che Guevara periodically set the bar on fire – mind your fingers – while the clientele sweats to salsa 'til the wee hours.

Lotus D'Or 38 blvd Général-de-Gaulle. Good Vietnamese establishment whose house speciality, Mi Xao Don, is loaded with pork, shrimp, chicken, squid and crispy noodles and is big enough for two.

Tex-Mex 115 rue Montauban. Over-the-top Mexican restaurant-bar with bullfight videos and a neon-lit wagonwheel; the tacos are cheap and the Dos Equis flows until late.

Plage Caravelle and Ste-Anne

Le Gosier's beaches are but sandboxes when compared with **PLAGE CARAVELLE**, a sensational swath of sand 13km eastward, whose picture-postcard turquoise bay has been colonized by Club Med. If you're not a paying guest, you can still hit the beach by following the signs to *Le Rotabas* hotel (see below), where a dirt path ends at a turnstyle. You won't be allowed to play with Club Med's water toys – for those, head to casual **STE-ANNE**, a small village another kilometre eastward, with its own adequate stretch of sand. A beachfront **watersports** centre here rents kayaks, body-boards, windsurfers and canoes daily except Sunday.

Practicalities

Aside from Club Med there are only a few places to **stay** in the immediate vicinity. The closest to Plage Caravelle, *Le Rotabas* (ⓣ0590/88 25 60, ⓦwww.lerotobas.com; ❺ including breakfast), offers appealing, if cramped, garden-view bungalows steps from the sand. In Ste-Anne, *Auberge du Grand Large* (ⓣ0590/85 48 28 ⓕ88 16 69, ⓦwww.aubergelegrandlarge.com; ❷) has several small, faded bungalows 50m from the beach and standard doubles. Nearby, at the bohemian *Mini Beach* (ⓣ0590/88 21 13, ⓕ88 19 29, ⓦwww.travel.to/minibeach; ❷) there are three eclectic bungalows and some basic terraced doubles. A handful of simple, open-air creole **restaurants** line Ste-Anne's beach. An exception to the rule, *Kon-Tiki*, serves pastas and steak from covered picnic tables. Beach trucks also dish out merguez-stuffed **baguettes**, burgers and fries. *Américano*, a western-styled **bar** popular with locals and tourists alike, features live acts on Friday.

St-François

What glamorous **ST-FRANÇOIS**, a posh harbour town another 20km due east of Ste-Anne, lacks in beachfront, it makes up for with its mast-filled **marina**, where a boardwalk lined with chic boutiques, cafés and restaurants draws attractive mainlanders for people-watching over drinks. Often used as a convenient departure point for **ferries** to Guadeloupe's offshore islands (see p.558), some boats here also take **divers** out to nearby waters. The major land activity happens next door to the marina, at the eighteen-hole **golf course**, Guadeloupe's only greens; the closest **beaches** are a few kilometres east of town, along the Pointe-des-Châteaux (see opposite).

The town centre has none of the marina's polish, but is a fun place to wander about. Radiating from the **Place du Marché**, a roundabout circled by an active covered **market**, the tapered one-way streets are so disjointed it's easy to get lost here. You'll find some atmospheric, albeit downtrodden, **wooden colonial houses**; there used to be more before the town was hit by hurricane Hugo. You can pick up an excellent **map** marked with addresses and information at the Office du

Tourisme (Mon, Tue, Thurs & Fri 8am–noon & 2–5pm, Wed 8am–12.30pm, Sat 8am–noon; ⓣ0590/88 48 74) on the right-hand side of avenue de l'Europe as you head towards the marina.

Practicalities

The only **budget** hotels are located in the town centre, across from the market – expect to wake up early. *Le Kali* (ⓣ0590/88 40 10; ➋) has simple doubles, most with fans and shared baths. **Resorts** are clustered around the marina. *Kayé La* (ⓣ0590/88 10 10, ⓕ88 74 67; ➍) has standard doubles with A/C, TV and full bath. If they're booked, as they often are with tour groups, try the **studios** next door at *Hôtel Résidence Fort Marina* (same numbers; ➍). The classiest option, *Méridien*, is on the north side (ⓣ0590/48 05 00 or 1-800/543-4300, ⓕ0590/88 51 00, ⓦwww.lemeridien-saintfrancois.com; ➑), with balconied rooms, pool, tennis court and private **beach**.

Most of St-François' **dining** options frame the marina; the exception, *Jerco Chez Nise*, on rue Paul-Tilby, is a local favourite, with a nine-course menu that makes a great island sampler. *Le Navy*, on the marina's south side, has heaping bowls of mussels, while next door's *Quai 17* serves pizzas. On the north side, *La Terrasse* has an excellent creole prix-fixe menu.

Towards Pointe-des-Châteaux

Guadeloupe's outermost tip, a needle-shaped isthmus that pokes into the Atlantic, culminates 11km east of St-François at the majestic **POINTE-DES-CHÂTEAUX**, where a trio of barren limestone rock formations leap from the ocean, the tallest crowned by a wooden **cross**. You can't swim here due to the strong tides, but there's a colourful **café** on site with reasonable prix-fixe creole menus. If you fancy a dip, the nearby **Plage des Salines**, with its natural breakwater, is sufficiently sheltered; shacks serve drinks and grilled fish on picnic tables perched above the water on stilts. Back towards St-François, **Plage Tartare**, a small cove popular with nudists, is Guadeloupe's only bona fide "naturalist's paradise".

Le Moule

Guadeloupe's original capital, **LE MOULE**, a short drive north of St-François on the N5, is hardly scintillating, though it does have a couple of decent beaches. You'll pass one of them, the sea-grape shaded **L'Autre Bord**, on your way in; the other, **Plage des Baies**, about 1km north of town, fronts a shallow bay ideal for young swimmers. The only other attraction is the underwhelming Amerindian archeology displays at the **Musée Edgar-Clerc** (Tues–Sun: April–Aug 10am–6pm; Sept–March 9am–5pm; €1.52), located past Plage des Baies on the right of the D123 towards Gros-Cap.

North to Anse Bertrand

North from Le Moule on the D120 is Guadeloupe's most enchanting swimming hole, the **LAGON DE LA PORTE D'ENFER** (Gates of Hell). Despite the ominous name, the two salt-ravaged bluffs create a heavenly setting by funnelling the raging Atlantic into a calm, fallopian lagoon. A ten-minute hike reaches the top of the eastern barrier cliff for stupendous coastal **views**. A terrific **restaurant**, *Chez Coco*, cooks up tasty barbecued fish and chicken at the water's edge.

Another 2km further on, **POINTE-DE-LA-GRANDE-VIGIE** is Grande-Terre's northernmost point and a **lookout** onto nearby islands. When you leave the Pointe, the road switches to the southern D122, passing **ANSE LABORDE**, a slim Atlantic-facing beach subject to large swells, before hitting sleepy **ANSE BERTRAND**, with its ramshackle wooden houses and aluminium shacks.

△ Picnic table near Point-de-la-Grande-Vigie, Guadeloupe

Port-Louis and south to Morne-à-l'Eau

Grande-Terre's standout village, **PORT-LOUIS**, is a fishing hamlet with mint-condition **wooden colonial houses**. The ambience alone is sufficient cause to stop here, but most people come for its magnificent beach, **PLAGE DU SOUFFLEUR**, a long golden band with a boardwalk hustled by locals churning divine coconut sorbet. At the southern end, *Siwo Evasion*, on rue de la Liberté (☎0590/58 83 25 or 0650/55 19 10, ⓦwww.actipages.com/siwo), rents **jet skis** and arranges guided outings to hard-to-reach beaches. Be sure to save some euros for *La Paillote*, a crumbling hacienda-style **café** nearby.

Heading south from Port-Louis, the N6 courses through unremarkable **Petit Canal** on its way to the **cemetery** at **MORNE-À-L'EAU**, 7km south. Hundreds of black-and-white-tiled mausoleums cover a hillside at the entrance of town with a recurring diamond motif that lends the impression of walking through a human-scale card game. From here, the N6 meets up with the N5 to reach Pointe-à-Pitre (see p.548) 15km later.

Basse-Terre

Undulating with mountain ranges, gushing with waterfalls and packed with rainforests, **BASSE-TERRE** provides a rugged antidote to Grande-Terre's glossy resorts. Scenic **hikes** in the inland **Parc National de la Guadeloupe** descend to the base of the **Chutes de Carbet** and ascend the slopes of **La Soufrière**. Outlying **beaches**, ranging from golden pockets like **Grande Anse** to sparkling black stretches like **Plage Malendure**, extend underwater to one of the world's top **dive** sites.

Despite everything it has to offer, Basse-Terre is bereft of resort centres; instead you'll find bungalows and small hotels. Even if Grande-Terre is your base, you should still make time for a day trip here. You can easily explore some of the rainforest in the morning, hit Grande Anse for lunch and go diving in the afternoon.

Parc National de la Guadeloupe

The most accessible parts of the **PARC NATIONAL DE LA GUADELOUPE**, a tremendous 17,300ha rainforest that encompasses the volcanic La Soufrière (see p.556) and the thundering Chutes de Carbet (see p.557), branch off from the Route de la Traversée (D23), Basse-Terre's cross-island road. Recently designated a UNESCO Biosphere Reserve, the park has numerous **hiking** trails, the easiest of which, the stroll to the **Cascade aux Écrevisses** and the meandering **Bras David**, can be done in a morning. The former is signposted to the left about 7km inland on the Route de la Traversée and is a straightforward 100m walk along a jungly pathway that culminates at a modest teal cascade. The latter begins another two kilometres westward along the same route, behind the **Maison de la Fôret** (Wed–Mon 9am–1.15pm & 2–4.30pm; closed Tues), which has free English trail **maps** for three nearby walks. The **Découverte de Bras David** is the shortest of these, consisting of a dark twenty-minute loop that gives a good introduction to the flora common to the interior, like moss-covered white gum trees and hardy acomat-boucan with enormous buttressed trunks. The park's fauna is showcased 3km further west, at the **Parc des Mamelles** (daily 9am–5pm; €5.34), where local endangered species are bred, the wily racoon chief among them. From here, the Route de la Traversée makes a steep descent to end at the southern outskirts of Pointe-Noir and the coastal N2 (see overleaf).

Practicalities

A couple of mountain **lodges** are situated near the park. Facing the Parc des Mamelles, *Couleur Caraïbes* (ⓣ & ⓕ0590/98 89 59; closed Sat in low season & June 15–30 annually; ❸) has six basic garden bungalows. At the park's eastern end, in Petit-Bourg, the welcoming *Auberge de la Distillerie* (ⓣ0590/94 25 91, ⓕ94 11 91, ⓔauberge.distillerie@wanadoo.fr; ❸ with breakfast) has A/C rooms with hammock-strung balconies and a pool. The lone park **restaurant**, midway along the Route de la Traversée, *Gîte des Mamelles*, serves good local dishes for lunch only.

Northern Basse-Terre

The N2 north of the Route de la Traversée makes a roller coaster drive up the Caribbean coast with picture-postcard scenes at every descent. Though this coast is rocky in spots, there are a couple of soft sand beaches, including Basse-Terre's finest, **Grande Anse**. The scenery changes dramatically the further northeast you go, as fields of sugarcane dominate the landscape around **Ste-Rose**. A couple of **rum distilleries** and a phenomenal **botanical garden** are the main draws this far north.

Pointe-Noir

The first settlement north of La Traversée, quiet **POINTE-NOIR** owes its name to the dark volcanic highlands that encircle – and shade – its tangled streets. Some rays filter through to **Plage Caraïbe**, a gritty beach just south of town where a friendly **dive** outfit (ⓣ0590/99 90 95, ⓕ99 92 69) organizes outings to the depths around Îlets Pigeon (see opposite) and rents snorkelling gear.

The locals – known as Ponti-Néris – are renowned for their Arabica coffee beans; some perfume the grounds of the magnificently restored **Caféière Beauséjour** (Mon–Sat 10am–5pm, Sun 10am–6pm; closed Mon in Sept & Mon–Thurs in Oct; ⓦwww.cafeierebeausejour.com; €6.10), a plantation house with stunning sea views. Ponti-Néris are equally adept carpenters, and you can check out the tools of their trade and mahogany furnishings at the **Maison du Bois** (Mon–Sat 9.30am–4.30pm; €0.76), near the southern outskirts. Opposite is Guadeloupe's only **campsite**, the hospitable *Camping de la Traversée* (ⓣ0590/98 21 23, ⓕ98 25 23; ❶), with pleasant grounds, access to a pebble beach, and some casual, fan-only double bungalows with balconies and kitchenettes .

Deshaies and Grande Anse

Quaint **DESHAIES**, Basse-Terre's most inviting village, lies a few kilometres up the coast, its wooden creole houses clasped around a deep harbour. The tempo here is so relaxed that the toughest part of your day may well involve deciding from which waterfront terrace to watch the sunset after lounging on **GRANDE ANSE**, Basse-Terre's longest beach, 2km north of town. To get there, follow the signs to *Le Karacoli* (see opposite); do not take the road signposted to Grande Anse – it's a rocky, unpaved mess.

Practicalities

You can **stay** steps from the sand at the *Fleurs des Îles* (ⓣ0590/28 54 44, ⓕ28 54 45, ⓦwww.fleursdesiles.com; ❸), which rents out comfortable poolside bungalows by the week only. Nearby, *Habitation Grande-Anse* (ⓣ0590/28 45 36, ⓕ28 51 17, ⓦwww.grande-anse.com; ❺) has spacious kitchen-equipped doubles, studios and apartments, 300m from the beach. In town, the *Fort Royal* (ⓣ0590/25 50 00, ⓕ25 50 01; ❻) is a big swanky resort with two beaches, one of which is clothing-optional.

Beachside **restaurants** range from shacks frying up inexpensive crispy chicken *boucané* and fresh red snapper, to terraced affairs with three-course creole menus.

By far the best of the lot is *Le Karacoli*, an atmospheric place serving spicy *crabe farçi* and delicious *conch fricassé* on a tree-shaded beach terrace. Deshaies's rue Principale has several fine options for eating and sunset-watching, including *Piano Piano* (dinner only; closed Wed), on the back terrace of a restored colonial house, and *Le Kaz* (dinner only; closed Wed) across the street.

North to Ste-Rose

The one spot not to miss along Basse-Terre's north coast is the **Jardin Botanique de Deshaies** (daily 9am–5pm; €8.84; Ⓦwww.jardin-botanique.com), about 1km past Grande Anse. The gardens feature waterfalls, orchid-covered trellises, and lily ponds, and are home to pink flamingos and loriquets and parrots.

Past the gardens, the N2 heads into a region dominated by sugarcane and bamboo with little worth stopping for until you hit the east coast **STE-ROSE**, an important agricultural town near two inland **rum** establishments. Closest is the **Domaine de Sévérin** (Mon–Sat 8.30am–1pm & 2–5.30pm; free; Ⓦ www.rhumagricole.com/severin), Guadeloupe's last waterwheel-operated distillery; to see the 200-year-old wheel in motion, you'll have to get there before 12.30pm.

Further inland, the multi-faceted **Musée du Rhum** (Mon–Sat 9am–5pm; €6; Ⓦwww.rhumagricole.com/musee) counts an impressive scythe collection among its rum-related equipment, and a spectacular insect collection upstairs, donated by a local writer; another chamber houses forty-odd model ships.

Southern Basse-Terre

Southern Basse-Terre is significantly more developed than the north, with sizeable coastal towns merging into one other along the N2, culminating with Guadeloupe's capital, also named **Basse-Terre**. Dominated by the island's highest point, the sulphuric **La Soufrière**, the region's other draws are the **Chutes de Carbet** waterfalls and the abundant underwater marine life around **Îlets Pigeon**.

Plage Malendure and Îlets Pigeon

The French West Indies' top dive site lies 4km south of La Traversée on the N2, off **PLAGE MALENDURE**, a sliver of dark volcanic sand that can get brutally crowded in high season as busloads arrive for the thrice-daily **diving** outings offered by numerous beachside outfits. Dives take place around two uninhabited offshore islands, **Îlets Pigeon**, in a 400ha reserve brought to international acclaim in the 1960s when Jacques Cousteau declared it one of the best dive sites he'd ever visited. Since then, upwards of 60,000 dives have taken place here yearly; even so, the marine life still thrives with coral and multicoloured fish. Visit in the late morning, when the sun hits the water directly and the colours are most vibrant.

Practicalities

For **information**, hit the tourism bureau right on the beach (Mon–Fri 8am–7pm, Sat & Sun 8.30am–4.30pm). Local hotels (see below) usually have partnerships with dive outfits that give their guests a **discount**; day-trippers can try the top-notch *Guy et Christian* (Ⓣ0590/98 82 43, Ⓕ98 82 84, Ⓦwww.plaisir-plongee-caraibes.com), across from the beach car park. You can also explore the underwater action aboard *Nautilus*, a boat with a glass hull that makes hour-plus voyages with snorkelling pit-stops (€18.29; 10.30am; noon; 2.30pm & 4pm; Ⓣ0590/98 89 08, Ⓕ98 85 66).

Despite its popularity, the area is a low-key place with scarce accommodation and restaurant options. The poshest **lodging**, the *Domaine de la Malendure* (Ⓣ0590/98 92 12, Ⓕ98 92 10, Ⓦwww.leader-hotels.gp; ❺), has Caribbean views, well-appointed doubles and villas and a pool. The appealing *Rocher de la Malendure* (Ⓣ0590/98 70 84, Ⓕ98 89 92, Ⓔlerocher@outremer.com; ❸) is right on the water, and has

A/C bungalows with balconies and kitchenettes. While beach trucks sell sandwiches and crepes by day, your best night-time **dining** options are the terraces at the *Rocher de la Malendure*, which serves generous prix-fixe menus, and *La Touna*, on the N2, with decent creole and French meals. Should you simply fancy a pint, *Le Ranch*, 2km south of the beach, has a good **bar** as well as pizzas, salads and fish.

South to Basse-Terre

The N2 hugs the coastline as it makes its way south, passing a slew of charming fishing villages with deep bays. The only diversion of note before Basse-Terre, the **Musée du Café** (daily 9am–5pm; €5.34), on the outskirts of Vieux-Habitants, is a working coffee mill that produces some seriously strong Arabica beans – you can get a buzz on a complimentary cup at the end of the visit.

You'll know you've reached the outskirts of the French West Indies' first settlement, **BASSE-TERRE**, when traffic comes to a halt. There's not much pay-off once you reach the centre, as Guadeloupe's administrative capital is a hot, downtrodden place with little to recommend it. The main public square, **Place du Champs d'Arbaud**, is a concrete eyesore, and many of the surrounding buildings are modern structures more suitable to a busy French suburb than a Caribbean island.

While the town core is pretty unappealing, two sights at Basse-Terre's southern outskirts are worth checking out if you've come this far. **Notre-Dame-du-Mont-Carmel**, a church fronted by Art Nouveau lamps, is reputed for its curative powers – look for marble thank-you plaques along the apse. Nearby loom the commanding ruins of the 1643 **Fort Delgrès** (daily 8am–5.30pm; free). The fort never saw battle, but its military cemetery contains the tomb of one of Guadeloupe's first governors, Admiral Gourbeyre. To get there, follow the signs for Fort St-Charles – the fort has gone through several name changes and the latest has yet to make it on signage.

While there's little point staying in town, if you get **hungry**, *La Taverne*, on avenue du Général Félix-Éboué, across from the town square, has inexpensive wheat pizzas and wine.

La Soufrière

The easiest way to reach the Lesser Antilles' highest peak, the 1467-metre **LA SOUFRIÈRE**, is by heading north on Basse-Terre's main north–south artery, avenue du Général Félix-Éboué. North of town, it changes to the D11 and cuts a steep path to **St-Claude** – the last place en-route for water and food supplies.

You'll need good walking shoes to make the 1.5hr ascent to La Soufrière's often cloud-covered summit, as the path that winds up its western flank gets rockier, tighter and more slippery as it nears the top. The trailhead starts about 8km past St-Claude, at **Savane à Mulets**, a car park at an elevation of 1142m. You'll pass deep gorges and panoramic vistas of the surrounding countryside before arriving on a moonscape plateau of boiling sulphuric cauldrons. Though you're officially not allowed to hike to the very top nowadays, most people ignore the sign and continue the ascent at their own risk. The adventurous can commit to a four-hour hike from Savane à Mulets to the Chutes du Carbet (see opposite).

Trois-Rivières

Lying at the confluence of three rivers a few kilometres east of the capital, **TROIS-RIVIÈRES** was a significant Amerindian settlement before French colonizers arrived and ousted the natives. What traces remain of its original tenants can be seen at the exceptional **Parc Archéologique des Roches Gravées** (daily 8.30am–5pm; €1.52), a park scattered with blackened boulders engraved with cartoonish human **petroglyphs** dating from circa 300 AD. A helpful pamphlet detailing the location of the markings is available at the entrance.

While the park is the star attraction here, Trois-Rivières also acts as a **ferry** departure point for Les Saintes (see below), which lie a short 10km offshore, making for a shorter voyage than from Pointe-à-Pitre (see box overleaf for times). The pier is at the end of a well-marked spur road 2km south of the town centre and has a couple of decent **cafés** alongside; a nearby car park charges €1.83/day.

Les Chutes de Carbet

Praised by Christopher Columbus in 1493, and ogled by thousands of tourists since, the magnificent **CHUTES DE CARBET** originate 1300m up La Soufrière's flanks and plummet down 10km inland from the N1 north of Trois-Rivières. While Columbus only referred to one chute in his diary, there are in fact three **waterfalls** here, the middle one, a mighty 110-metre cascade, getting the greatest attention as it's the trio's most accessible. To reach it, follow the signs (and the crowds); a stairwell descends to a dirt path that hits the fall's basin in twenty minutes.

The secondary trails for the **first** and **third falls** branch off from the same path – the former is the highest, at 115m, and reached by a 4.5hr round-trip hike along an occasionally muddy, but otherwise decent, trail. The third waterfall, a mere 20m high, is the least dramatic, and the hardest to reach; the 5.5hr circuit cuts through some narrow and slippery patches. An easier way to get to it is via Capesterre, a couple of kilometres north on the N1; a well-signposted turn-off in the centre of town ends at the start of a 2hr round-trip trail.

North to La Traversée and Pointe-à-Pitre

Little happens along the stretch of N1 that connects the falls with the Route de la Traversée and Pointe-à-Pitre. The only commendable stop, the botanical gardens of the **Domaine de Valombreuse** (daily 9am–6pm; ⓦwww.valombreuse.com; €6.86), are in the hinterlands of Petit-Bourg. Here, red alpinia, porcelain roses, and heliconia bloom in the shade of papyrus and oleander trees. Another twenty minutes along the N1 lands you back in Pointe-à-Pitre (see p.548).

Offshore islands

Guadeloupe's four **OFFSHORE ISLANDS** make for delightful day or overnight trips from the mainland. The closest, Mediterranean-like **Terre-de-Haut**, is one of two inhabited islands that form **Les Saintes**. Its much drier and rockier sibling, **Terre-de-Bas**, makes a good escape from the crowds next door. Further out lies **Marie-Galante**, a laid-back island with graceful beaches that are only starting to get touristy. In the far distance, sparsely populated **La Désirade** looms like a capsized rowboat, its shores so undeveloped that visitors may feel like castaways.

Terre-de-Haut

Terrific beaches and attractive architecture make tiny **TERRE-DE-HAUT** the most striking of Guadeloupe's outer islands. Since its dry climate prevented the introduction of sugarcane, it was instead settled by white Breton and Poitevin fishermen whose ancestors are today touted as the Antilles' best – their unique fishing boats, light and rapid wooden outboards called **Saintoises**, are famous in the trade.

Measuring a mere 5km from end to end, the craggy spit is capped by the 309-metre **Chameau** and anchored by a darling village simply called **Le Bourg** – The Town – which borders the **Baie des Saintes**, a glorious harbour enclosed by hilly outcroppings.

Ferries to the offshore islands

Several **ferries** make crossings to Guadeloupe's outer islands from Pointe-à-Pitre, St-François and Trois-Rivières, and a couple of companies run passengers between the outer islands as well. The largest operators – Brudey Frères and Express des Îles – are more reliable than the smaller outfits and tend to leave on time.

Keep in mind that schedules are subject to change, and that boats often leave late.

Ferry operators

Brudey Frères (Guadeloupe ⓣ0590/90 04 48, ⓕ93 00 79; Martinique ⓣ0596/70 08 50; ⓦwww.brudey-freres.fr)
Express des Îles (Martinique ⓣ0596/63 12 11, ⓕ63 34 47; Guadeloupe ⓣ0590/83 12 45, ⓕ91 11 05; ⓦwww.express-des-iles.com)
Comatril (Guadeloupe ⓣ0590/91 02 45, ⓕ82 57 73)
Iguana (Guadeloupe ⓣ0590/50 05 09, ⓕ22 26 31)
Deher (Guadeloupe ⓣ0590/99 50 68, ⓕ99 56 83)

Travel details

Pointe-à-Pitre to: **Grand-Bourg**, Marie-Galante (3 daily; 45min; €30 round-trip); **St-Louis**, Marie-Galante (1–3 daily; 45min; €30 round-trip); **Terre-de-Haut** (1 daily; 1hr; €28.20 round-trip).

St-François to: **La Désirade** (1 daily; 45min; €19.82 round-trip); **St-Louis**, Marie-Galante (1–2 daily, except Sat; 45min; €22.87 round-trip); **Terre-de-Haut** (1–2 daily, except Sat; 1h 30min; €25.92 round-trip).

Trois-Rivières to **Terre-de-Haut** (2 daily; 20min; €16.77 round-trip).

Terre-de-Haut to: **Pointe-à-Pitre** (1 daily; 1hr; €28.20 round-trip); **St-François** (1 daily, except Sat; 1h 30min; €25.92 round-trip); **St-Louis**, Marie-Galante (1 daily, except Sat; 45min; €16.77 round-trip).

Terre-de-Bas to **Terre-de-Haut** (3–5 daily; 20min; €5.34 round-trip).

St-Louis, Marie-Galante to: **Pointe-à-Pitre** (1–2 daily; 45min; €30 round-trip); **St-François** (1 daily, except Sun; 45min; €22.87 round-trip); **Terre-de-Haut** (1 daily, except Sat; 45min; €16.77 round-trip); **Terre-de-Bas** (4–5 daily; 20min; €5.34 round-trip); **Trois-Rivières** (2 daily; 20min; €16.77 round-trip).

Grand-Bourg, Marie-Galante to: **Pointe-à-Pitre** (3 daily; 45min; €30 round-trip).

La Désirade to **St-François** (2 daily; 45min; €19.82 round-trip).

Arrival and information

Ferries to Les Saintes depart from Pointe-à-Pitre, St-François, Marie-Galante and Trois-Rivières; you can also **fly** with Air Caraïbes (ⓣ0590/82 47 00, ⓕ82 47 48; 4 flights Mon–Fri; 2 flights Sat & Sun; €80.50). Most hotels will arrange to pick you up from the airport, ten minutes outside the town centre, or the pier; you can get around on **foot**, though **scooter** is the favoured means for island-roaming. Several pier-side outfits rent them for €22.87–€30.49/day. The only island **bank**, the Crédit Agricole (Tues, Thurs & Fri 9.15am–2.30pm), is on rue Jean-Calot, left of the pier; its **ATM**, beside the *mairie* (town hall), a couple of blocks right of the pier, has been known to be empty, so bring some cash just in case. For island **information**, including **maps**, head to the helpful Office du Tourisme, rue de la Grande Anse, behind the *mairie* (Mon–Sat 8am–noon & 2–5pm, Sun 8–11am; ⓣ0590/99 58 60, ⓕ99 58 48; ⓦwww.les-saintes-tourisme.com).

The island

Most of the action happens around the **pier**, which drops arriving boat passengers off onto a miniature square where elderly women sell bittersweet coconut and guava *tourment d'amour* (agony of love) cakes, a tradition started by fishwives mourning their husbands' absence at sea.

East of the pier, atop a steep incline, you can get a bird's-eye **view** of Les Saintes from the 1867 **Fort Napoléon** (Mon–Fri 9am–12.30pm; €3.05; www.fort-napoleon.com), an outpost that got more use as a penitentiary than a defensive camp. The restored barracks now host the small **Musée d'histoire et traditions populaires**, showcasing traditional *Saintoise* crafts and full-scale fishing boats. Outside, sections of the parapets have been transformed into a prickly, iguana-inhabited **cactus garden**.

The island's best beach, **Plage de Pompierre**, lies southeast of the fort, along an almost perfectly enclosed bay. Free-roaming goats and roosters lie right down beside you here; they usually want some of your **food**, acquired from women selling baguettes and sodas near the entrance. To get to the beach, turn left when you reach the T-junction at the base of the hill from the fort, or take the road behind Le Bourg's church. Terre-de-Haut's other good beaches are on the southwest coast. **Pain du Sucre** – a modest nod to Rio's Sugar Loaf – wades into a deep cove, while nearby **Anse Crawen** is foregrounded by a sign proclaiming "Attention: Nudisme"; its waters, not surprisingly, are busy with stripped-down snorkellers.

Hundreds of white sand crabs scuttle the headland of the island's longest beach, **Grande Anse**. Unfortunately, its location, on Terre-de-Haut's Atlantic-facing coast, makes swimming impossible due to strong currents. Still, it's the best spot for sunrise, and you can take a plunge a few minutes east, off narrow **Anse Rodriguez**.

Accomodation

Auberge les Petits Saints ⓣ0590/99 50 99, ⓕ99 54 55, ⓦwww.petitssaints.com. This inn near Grande Anse is chock-full of antiques – all of which are for sale – and its dozen tastefully decorated doubles have balconies with views of the pool and sea. ⑤ including breakfast.

Bois Jolie ⓣ0590/99 50 39, ⓕ99 55 05, ⓦwww.ifrance.com/boisjolie. The only hotel near Anse Crawen and Pain du Sucre; bungalow-style doubles have A/C, porches and private beach and pool access. ④

Coco Playa Rue B-Cassin ⓣ0590/92 40 00, ⓕ99 50 41, ⓦwww.im-caraibes.com/cocoplaya. Refurbished hotel on Le Bourg's western outskirts; some rooms have terrific harbour views. ④ including breakfast.

La Saintoise Rue B-Cassin ⓣ0590/99 52 50. Ten straightforward budget doubles with private bath and A/C right in the centre of Le Bourg. ③

Eating and drinking

Auberge les Petits Saints (ⓣ0590/99 50 99; see above). The place to splurge; the decadent seafood prix-fixe menu is served on an antique-furnished terrace.

Jardin Créole Ferry dock. Wave goodbye to all the day-trippers from this funky, chummy second-floor pier-side bar; there's plenty of cheap beer, email access, pizzas and other items to distract you.

La Paillote Plage Marigot (closed mid-Sept–mid-Oct; lunch only). Wood-oven-fired fish and chicken are the hallmarks of this popular seaside terrace eatery; zouk nights (Wed & Sat) get their share of raves too.

Terre-de-Bas

TERRE-DE-BAS, twenty minutes west of Terre-de-Haut by **ferry** (see opposite), needn't rank high on your must-see list, unless you're looking for isolation. There's only one easily accessible beach at **Grande Anse**, a small community ten-minutes' walk from the pier, and a handful of rugged **hiking** circuits through the arid inland foothills. Few forge on to quaint **Petite-Anse**, at the island's western end, only really of note for its pretty conch-decorated **cemetery**.

Marie-Galante

Although Columbus baptized round **Marie-Galante** after his ship, Guadeloupe's largest offshore island is colloquially known nowadays as Grande-Galette, after its flat-stone shape. Overgrown with **sugarcane** and scattered with crumbling **windmills**, the 158-square-kilometre island 25km south of Pointe-à-Pitre has remained a rural and unhurried place that produces Guadeloupe's best and strongest **rum** – a woozy 59 percent alcohol – by adhering to customs that have altogether disappeared elsewhere. You'll likely see sugarcane cut by **scythe** and hauled on oxen-pulled **cabrouets** – the wooden chariots typically found in museums nowadays. Sights like these surpass the island's **beaches** which, mind you, are nothing to sniff at.

Marie-Galante's 12,400 inhabitants divvy up between three towns: the capital, **Grand-Bourg**, and smaller **St-Louis** and **Capesterre**. The island's flatness – its highest point is a mere 150m – makes it ideal **walking and biking** terrain. There's also some decent **diving** off the south coast.

Arrival, information and getting around

While you can **fly** to Marie-Galante with Air Caraïbes (Ⓣ0590/82 47 00, Ⓕ82 47 48; 3 flights daily; €80.50), most visitors arrive by boat (see p.558 for details). Depending on where you've caught the **ferry** – Pointe-à-Pitre, St-François or Les Saintes – you'll arrive either at Grand-Bourg or St-Louis. Both quays have nearby **car** rental booths with rates around €45.73/day; if you're day-tripping, ask for a "tarif-touristique" to shave €10 off the price. For **automatic** cars, head to the reliable Aïchi Location (Ⓣ0590/97 88 02) or Hertz (Ⓣ & Ⓕ0590/97 59 80), though booking ahead is always advisable. **Minibuses**, or TCs, also service the island.

For **information**, the highly competent Office du Tourisme, on rue du Fort in Grand-Bourg (Mon–Fri 8am–4pm; Sat 9am–noon; Ⓣ0590/97 56 51, Ⓕ97 56 54; Ⓦwww.ot-mariegalante.com), has activity brochures and an excellent **map**. The hiking **trail guide** – *Les sentiers de randonnée pédestre* (€3.81) – is in French only.

Grand-Bourg

Largely destroyed by fire in the early 1900s, and hit by a brutal hurricane in 1928, the island capital of **GRAND-BOURG** was rebuilt with a lot of two-storey cement structures, but has enough surviving wooden creole houses to remind visitors of its roots. It's a compact place, with a few narrow streets heading north of the harbour, where the peeling **Notre-Dame-de-Marie-Galante** church overlooks the town **market** (6am–mid-afternoon). There's little to do here by day except wander about and peruse the market goods, and even less to do by night. The main attraction is the ruins of the island's one-time richest sugar plantation, **Château Murat** (free), 1.5km east of town. At its acme, in 1839, over 300 slaves worked the surrounding fields; three examples of the shacks they lived in are behind the former kitchen.

Practicalities

There's not much in the way of **lodging** in Grand-Bourg and little reason to stay here anyway. If you're catching an early-morning ferry, the fan-only rooms at *Arbre à Pain*, on rue Dr-Etzol (Ⓣ0590/97 73 69; ❷), will suffice. For **food**, there's a pleasant bakery, *Le Soleil Levant*, on Petit Place du Marché. More substantial fare can be had at *Le Papaye Club*, on rue Beaurenon, with delicious home-cooked creole options. For quick eats, *Le Moana* on rue du Dr-Selbonne serves up good pizza.

St-Louis

Marie-Galante's oldest hamlet, quiet **ST-LOUIS**, is mostly visited as a debarkation point from inter-island ferries (see p.558) and for its nearby **beaches**. Starting 3km north of town, the fine crescent moons of **Plage Moustique**, **Anse Canot** and **Anse de Vieux-Fort** are rarely crowded. None has facilities, leaving you to rely on St-Louis for **food**. A bakery with pastries and sandwiches occupies a corner facing the pier. *Katimini Pub*, a hole-in-the-wall restaurant and bar to the left of the pier, has filling *boudin*, *accras*, and *crabe farçi*, and is popular with young locals, especially on weekends when the tables often get pushed aside for zouk-style **dancing**. *Le Refuge*, another good spot 2km south of town via the N9, is strong on seafood and doubles as a *gîte* (B&B) with comfortable A/C **rooms** and individual apartments (ⓣ0590/97 02 95, ⓕ97 11 36; ❸). The island's only resort, *Cohoba* (ⓣ0590/97 50 50, ⓕ97 97 96, ⓦwww.leaderhotels.gp; ❻), is nearby, offering fully equipped doubles or bungalow-style chambers by a small, private beach.

Capesterre

Popular with scuba divers, laid-back **CAPESTERRE** occupies scenic lowlands near Marie-Galante's best beach, **Plage de la Feuillère**. Another good beach in the vicinity, **Petite Anse**, also gets its share of sunbathers, while between the two, the excellent Scubaguad **diving** centre (€38.11; ⓣ & ⓕ0590/97 20 59, ⓔpaul.villevieille@wanadoo.fr), runs thrice-daily trips to the island's pristine underwater sites. The best overview of the local flora and fauna is at **Marée Sucré**, a shallow bay busy with rays, tiny baby fish, angelfish and trumpetfish.

Back on land, Capesterre's other draw is the mint-condition **Moulin de Bézard** (daily 10am–2pm; €1.52), a functioning windmill 6km north of town, located behind some superbly restored slave shacks.

Practicalities

Capesterre's **lodging** options aren't fancy but do have more character than those elsewhere in Marie-Galante. The hacienda-styled *Hôtel Hajo* (ⓣ0590/97 32 76; ❸) is between the two beaches on the N9; its appealing fan-only rooms have ocean views and most have private bath. In town, there are mosquito-netted doubles, studios and bungalows with peaked roofs at the intimate *Le Zagaya* (ⓣ0590/97 37 84, ⓕ97 22 47, ⓦwww.le-zagaya.com; ❸). On a hillside over town, *Le Soleil Levant* (ⓣ0590/97 31 55, ⓕ97 41 65; ⓦwww.multimania.com/residsoleill; ❷) has impeccable A/C rooms, some of which open onto a communal terrace. Other than the beach kiosks selling snackish fare, **dining** options are scarce in Capesterre – you're better off heading to Grand-Bourg (see opposite).

La Désirade

Sighted by Columbus during his second New World voyage in 1493, **LA DÉSIRADE** appeared an oasis to his sailors, whose yearning for land earned the whalebacked isle its name – "the desired one". It ultimately proved anything but, as it's the most arid and rocky of Guadeloupe's outer islands. The lack of agricultural

Getting drunk before noon

Marie-Galante's major "sights" – if they can be called that – are the **distilleries** that ferment some of the region's strongest rum, which you can taste-test, liberally and free of charge, before lunch. Indeed, all three, Capesterre's Bellevue (Mon–Sat 7.30–11.30am), Grand Bourg's Bielle (Mon–Sat 9.45am–1pm, Sun 10.30–11.30am) and Père Labat (Mon–Sat 7am–noon), maintain morning hours only. Just be sure to eat something for breakfast first.

options gave it only one use to later French colonizers – ironically as a dumping ground for their "undesirables". From the early 1700s to the late 1950s, it served as a leper colony, a legacy it's only beginning to shed, as travellers are drawn by its off-the-beaten-track persona.

Lying 11km off Guadeloupe's Pointe-des-Châteaux (see p.551), and measuring the same distance from end to end, the two-kilometre-wide island is cut by several mountain peaks topped with wind turbines. While the north coast is marked by rough seas, the south side has some decent beaches within easy access of the ferry dock and the main settlement, **Beauséjour**, a wee village with a miniature church, fading wooden houses and a conch-shell-decorated sailor's cemetery. Two smaller communities, **Le Souffleur** and **Baie-Mahault**, are a few kilometres eastward along the only island road; the latter hosted the leprosarium, whose only vestiges, the chapel walls, lie in ruins on the outskirts of town. Both villages front the island's nicest beaches, the better of which, the two-kilometre long **Le Souffleur**, is shaded by coconut trees.

Practicalities

The island's small size makes it an easy day trip. **Ferries** make the forty-minute crossing from St-François, or you can **fly** with Air Caraïbes (ⓣ0590/82 47 00, ⓕ82 47 48; 2 flights Mon–Fri; 1 flight Sat & Sun; €80.50). Regular **mini-buses** are the most convenient and inexpensive way to get around – €1.52 will get you from one end of the island to the other. If you prefer your own wheels, you can rent **bikes** and **scooters** from a handful of outfits facing the pier for €7.52–€22.87/day.

Accommodation options are limited; you can stop in at the town hall in Beauséjour (Mon, Tue, Thurs & Fri 8am–noon & 2–5pm; Wed & Sat 8am–noon) for a list of boarding houses. The two island hotels, *L'Oasis* (ⓣ0590/20 02 12; ❷) and *Le Mirage* (ⓣ0590/20 01 08; ❷), are 300m from the pier, in a brutally arid section, with ultra-basic fan-only rooms with shared or private bath. Note that, unlike the rest of Guadeloupe (and indeed, the Caribbean), La Désirade's high season runs from July to September, when the rain actually enhances the countryside. The few **restaurants** that serve the island are mostly concentrated near the pier, with creole dishes like *lambi fricassée* and *poulet colombo* dominating the menu. There is no island **bank**.

14.2

Martinique

Visitors to **MARTINIQUE** will have to do some legwork to discover the island Columbus once lauded as the "...most charming country there is in the world". Aggressive development has resulted in resort towns complete with artificial beaches and pastel-hued cement hotels more appropriate to a Florida landscape than the French West Indies. That said, Martinique's resort emphasis makes the island ideal for all-inclusive travel, and most resorts organize optional day trips to the spots that give an idea of what brought the developers here in the first place.

The second largest holding in the French West Indian empire, Martinique's 1100-square-kilometre terrain is topped by a series of mountain peaks. The most imposing, the dormant **Mont-Pelée** volcano, wreaked devastation on **St-Pierre** in 1902; traipsing about the fabled city's charred ruins nowadays is an eerie experience. **Botanical gardens** teeming with indigenous flora evoke Martinique's original designation as Madinina (island of flowers), while the stupendous **Habitation Clément** distillery hosts a fascinating anti-Columbus exhibit. In between these sights, villages like isolated **Grand'Rivière** and Atlantic-facing **Tartane** steadfastly retain the customs emblematic of traditional Caribbean fishing villages; the latter, on the **Presqu'Île Caravelle**, is also the island's most laid-back destination, a wonderfully underdeveloped stretch that boasts some of Martinique's finest beaches.

Most **package tours** head straight to Martinique's southern edges, where the island's spectacular **Les Salines** beach is located, along with a host of smaller white-sand stretches, and hamlets like **Ste-Anne** and **Diamant** that have escaped the build-up elsewhere. The island's beaches get increasingly black as you head north, culminating in the breathtaking **Anse Couleuvre** at the island's furthest reaches – *the* place to go for total isolation.

Some history

Though discovered by Columbus on his last New World voyage in 1502, the Lesser Antilles' third largest island wound up being settled in 1635 by French colonizers instead. Starting from a small encampment on the northwest side that would later become **St-Pierre**, the French made their way to **Fort-de-France** and completed their island take-over eight years later by massacring the remaining Caribs.

By this time, the French had begun importing slaves and sugarcane, and their efforts drew British interest near the end of the 1700s. An almost two-century power struggle ensued, with the French losing Martinique to the British over a century later, then getting it back as part of the **Paris Treaty** in 1763, only to lose it again 1794. The tug-o'-war ended for good in 1815, when the British returned the island on **Vienna Treaty** orders.

Martinique's return to the motherland was bittersweet, as France continued to endorse slavery well after neighbouring British islands had abolished the practice in 1833. It didn't help matters that Emperor Napoleon had married the daughter of a local plantation-owner, **Joséphine Beauharnais** (see p.567)– it's said he continued to endorse slavery as a favour to his in-laws. A dogged anti-slavery campaign by French cabinet minister **Victor Schoelcher** saw the practice's end in 1848.

The twentieth century started off with a bang, on May 8, 1902, when a sudden

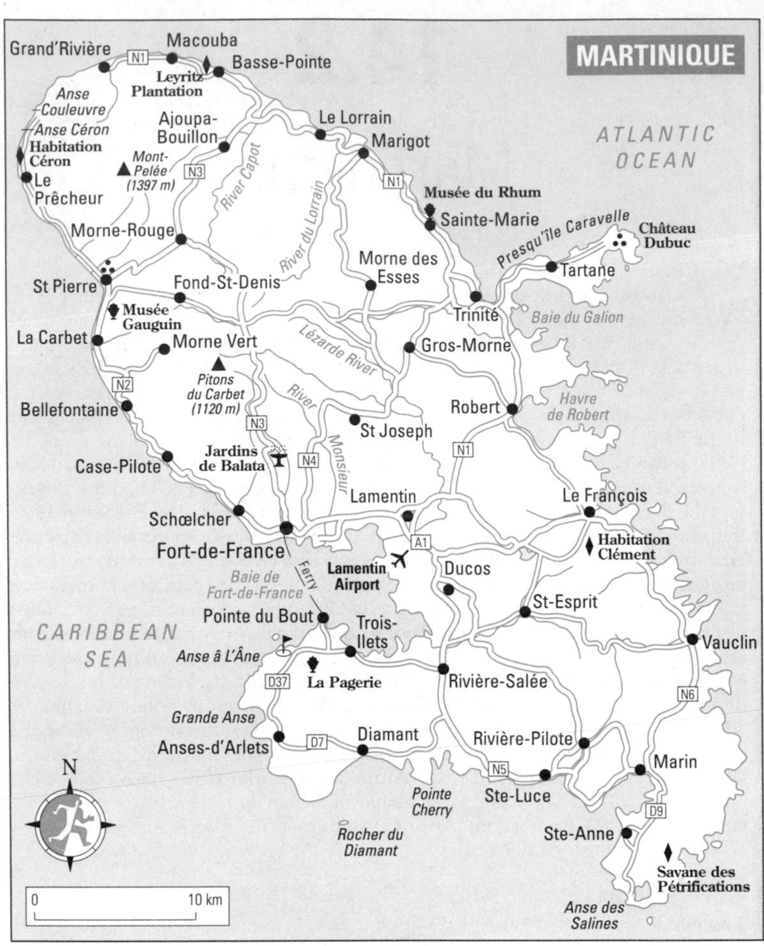

eruption of **Mont-Pelée**, the volcano at its northern reaches, destroyed St-Pierre and all its inhabitants. The latter part of the century was marked by social unrest caused by pro-independence factions seeking **sovereignty** from France that turned violent more than once; in an effort to quell the movement, Martinique received greater overseas department status and powers in 1982–83.

Arrival, information and getting around

Passengers arriving by **plane** land at Martinique's **Aéroport du Lamentin**, a snazzy terminal about 9km from Fort-de-France and 11km from the nearest southern resort town. Taxis from the airport charge €15.25 to the capital and €20 and up to the southern coast; there are no public buses from the airport. If you intend to do any additional island exploring, you'd be wise to rent a **car** on the spot; several agencies (see overleaf) are located to the left of the airport exit, with rates starting around €50/day. The airport's tourism counter stocks **information**, and staff can make on-the-spot reservations for you; the main tourism office is in downtown Fort-de-France (see overleaf). You can also check out ⓦwww.martinique.org.

Passengers arriving by **ferry** disembark at the **terminal inter-îles** on the southern outskirts of Fort-de-France. The fastest way to reach resort areas south of the capital is by taking a **taxi** (Radio Taxi-Service ⓣ0596/63 10 10 or Martinique Taxi ⓣ0596/63 63 62) straight to the **débarcadère** in downtown Fort-de-France, and hopping aboard a cross-bay **vedette** (see p.567), to avoid the brutal traffic jams on the southern highways. You can still rent a car in southern resorts, and most agencies will let you drop it off at the airport when you leave. Agencies with outlets at the airport and most resort towns are: Avis (ⓣ0596/42 11 00); Budget (ⓣ0596/42 16 79); Europcar (ⓣ0596/42 42 42); Hertz (ⓣ0596/42 16 90); and Jumbo Car (ⓣ0596/42 22 22, ⓕ 42 22 32, ⓦwww.jumbocar.com). Rent-a-Car (ⓣ0596/51 51 32, ⓦwww.rentacar-caraibes.com) has rates as low as €30.34/day.

Fort-de-France

Often likened to a miniature Paris, **FORT-DE-FRANCE** is stunning to behold when arriving by sea, with its panorama of colonial houses and multiple church steeples wrapping around the **Baie des Flamands** and ascending into the surrounding moutainside. The capital city is, unfortunately, much better seen from afar than up close – its main streets, even high-fashion **rue Victor-Hugo**, are pretty grubby, with peeling paint and sagging frames. The town is also much better by day; at night, it's sketchy, with public squares plied by vagrants and prostitutes. The best day to visit is Saturday before lunch, when the streets fill with locals and tourists alike, and the sounds of tam tam and steel drums resonate throughout the main core.

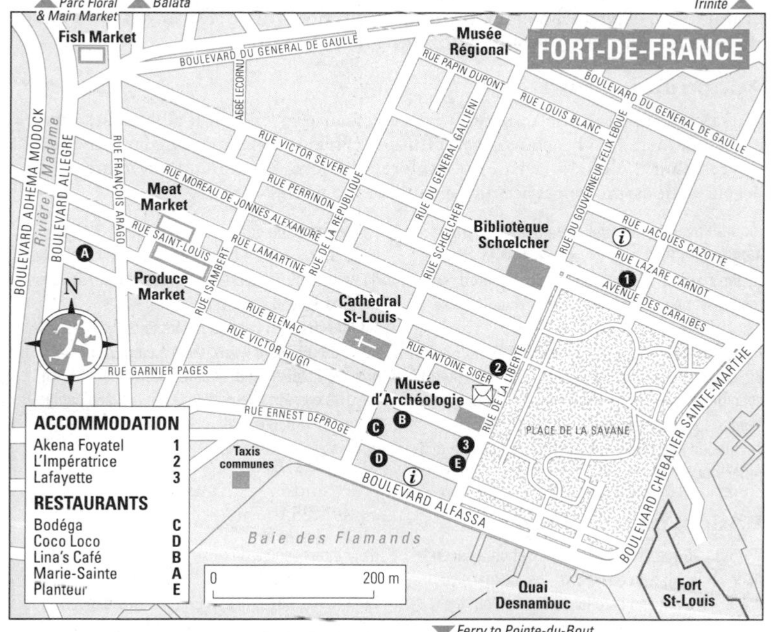

The Town

Fort-de-France-specific **information** can be obtained at the small Office de Tourisme, 76 rue Lazare Carnot (Mon–Fri 8am–5pm, Sat 8.30am–12.30pm; ⓣ0596/60 27 73, ⓕ60 27 95, ⓔotv.fort.de.france@wanadoo.fr). Most of the city's activity happens around **La Savane**, a park planted with royal palms and bamboo along the harbourfront facing **Fort St-Louis**, an imposing 1640 Vauban-style military base set on a promontory above the bay. The fort is still in use today – the only way to gain access is by 45-minute guided tour (daily on the hour 10am–3pm; €3.81).

The city's most striking landmark, the unusual Byzantine and Beaux-Arts styled **Bibliothèque Schoelcher**, overlooks La Savane from the west, on rue de la Liberté (Mon 1–5pm, Tues–Fri 8am–5pm, Sat 8.30am–12pm). Designed to house abolitionist Victor Schoelcher's (see p.546) personal book collection, the library was shown at the Paris 1889 World Fair before being dismantled and shipped piecemeal to Martinique's capital. Just down the street, at 9 rue de la Liberté, the engaging **Musée Départemental d'Archéologie** (Mon–Fri 8am–5pm, Sat 9am–noon, closed Sun; €3.05; ⓦwww.cg972.fr/mdap) has a two-storey exhibit devoted to Amerindian artefacts from Martinique and the surrounding islands. Best are the 100-odd *adornos*, the miniature clay figureheads used by Arawaks to decorate bowls and vases. The **post office** is nearby on rue de la Liberté, across from La Savane (Mon–Fri 7am–6pm, Sat 7am–noon), while a short walk up rue Blénac, away from the park, brings you to the *Cyber Web Café*, upstairs at no. 4, where you can check your email (Mon–Fri 11am–2pm, Sat 6pm–2am).

North of La Savane, at 10 blvd Général-de-Gaulle, the **Musée Régional d'Histoire et d'Éthnographie** (Mon, Wed–Fri 8am–5pm, Tues 2–5pm, Sat 8am–12.30pm, closed Sun; €3.05) occupies a splendid Neoclassical 1887 villa. The main interest is upstairs, where four rooms are decorated with mahogany furniture, gold candelabra and fine latticework to evoke a late 1800s bourgeois home.

Fort-de-France's other discernible landmark, the rust-coloured **Cathédrale St-Louis,** on rue Schoelcher, boasts a 57-metre steeple and an apse inset with Martiniquan-themed stained-glass windows. On the northwest outskirts, the **Parc Floral** (Mon–Thurs 9am–3pm, Fri 9am–noon; €0.30) is a pleasant place to relax after strolling the busy **markets** across the street.

Accommodation

There's not much reason to **stay** in Fort-de-France given that it all but dies out at night and there's no beach to speak of nearby. Still, if you're catching an early flight or are using the city as a base to explore northern Martinique, there are a few decent options; the best is actually outside of the town centre.

Akena Foyatel 68 av des Caraïbes, ⓣ0596/72 46 46, ⓕ73 28 23, ⓦ www.hotels-akena.com. By far the town's best lodging; 38 standard rooms overlook La Savane, and include A/C, TV and breakfast. ❹

L'Impératrice 15 rue de la Liberté ⓣ0596/63 06 82, ⓕ72 06 30. This *grande dame* has definitely seen better days, but its location, smack dab in front of La Savane, and the odd room with four-poster bed and balcony, make it a reasonable mid-range option. ❸

Lafayette 5 rue de la Liberté ⓣ0596/73 80 50, ⓕ60 97 75. The 24 budget rooms aren't fancy, but do come with TV and A/C, and are steps from the ferry docks and La Savane. ❷

Squash Hotel 3 blvd de la Marne ⓣ0596/72 80 80 ⓕ63 00 74, ⓦwww.karibea.com. The most upscale hotel around, situated 1km west of town; the 108 comfortable doubles with A/C and cable TV are on grounds with a pool, fitness centre and three squash courts. ❹

Eating and drinking

Bodega 28 rue Ernest d'Eproge. Set on a second-floor verandah with bay views, the inexpensive Italian-creole menu here lacks pizzazz, but the daily three-course prix-fixe offerings are hearty and well priced.

Coco Loco Rue Ernest d'Eproge. This happening

waterfront restaurant-bar serves up reasonably priced *magret de canard* and maxi-brochettes, but its huge and creative drinks list eclipses the food menu.

Lina's Café 15 rue Victor Hugo (closed Sun–Mon nights). A smart two-storey gourmet café with inexpensive, delicious sandwiches, pâtés, quiches, and the best coffee in town.

Le Marie-Sainte 160 rue Victor Hugo (Mon–Sat 8am–3pm). This uninspired dining room serves, hands down, the town's best creole food, with spicy concoctions like *accras* and rich *coq fricassée*.

Le Planteur 1 rue de la Liberté (closed afternoons Sat & Sun). This second-floor eatery has good views and moderately priced creole and French dishes like tasty seafood stew and *langouste cassolette*.

Southern Martinique

Most sun-worshippers head directly to **SOUTHERN MARTINIQUE**, where the Caribbean is bordered by the island's only white-sand **beaches**, including **Les Salines**, at the southernmost tip. Successively built up in recent years, many of the towns have lost much of their Martiniquan character; the most generic, **Pointe-du-Bout**, is nonetheless the most touristed, thanks to its proximity to Fort-de-France. Further south, **Diamant** and **Ste-Anne** are more authentic and less crowded.

Trois-Îlets to Pointe-du-Bout

You won't have much reason to stop at **TROIS-ÎLETS**, the first hamlet along the southern coast, unless you want **information** on nearby Pointe-du-Bout, which falls under its jurisdiction; the tourism office is on place de l'Église (Mon–Sat 9am-5pm, Sun 9am–noon). On the town's outskirts, the **Poterie des Trois-Îlets** hosts a handful of potters that sell their wares at the end of a red-clay road. Another kilometre westward is the engaging **Maison de la Canne** (Tues–Sun 9am–5.30pm; €3.05), a sugarcane museum that's especially thorough on the history of slavery.

Past Trois-Îlets in the direction of Anse-à-l'Âne, the main road branches off to the right and left around Martinique's **golf course**. The right leads to Pointe-du-Bout (see below), the left to **La Pagerie**, Empress Joséphine's homestead until the age of 16. While the main house was destroyed by a hurricane in 1766, the stone kitchen now hosts an engaging **museum** (Tues–Fri 9am–5.30pm, Sat & Sun 9am–1pm & 2.30–5.30pm; €3.05) dedicated to the empress's torrid relationship with Napoleon. You'll find some intriguing pieces, like the doctored wedding certificate stating their mutual ages as 28, and a falsified coronation scene depicting Napoleon's mother among the guests – if fact, she didn't attend because she disliked Joséphine.

Pointe-du-Bout

Anchored around an almost perfectly square harbour, **POINTE-DU-BOUT** gets most of its traffic from upper-class French hedonists with money to burn; the costs

Moving on from Fort-de-France

From Fort-de-France, the fastest and easiest way to reach Martinique's southern beaches is by **vedette** (ferry boat) run by Madinina (☎0596/63 06 46) or Somatour (☎0596/73 05 53, ®www.somatour.com). A regular ferry service connects the capital to Pointe-du-Bout, with service on the half-hour from the **quai Desnambuc** near the main tourism office (6.30am–8pm; €5.79 return) and a couple of late night crossings at 11.15pm and 12.10am. Ferries for Anse Mitan and Anse-à-l'Âne have a similar schedule between 6.20am and 6.45pm, but are unreliable afterwards. For points elsewhere in Martinique, you can catch one of the **minibuses** that cover the island, from **Pointe-Simon**, southwest of the tourism office.

of staying in this ersatz area – even the beaches are artificial – are the highest on Martinique. Still, the polished veneer may appeal to some, especially those in need of a good urban fix after staying in a less-equipped community further south along the coast. You can always escape the scene with *Lychee Plongée* (ⓣ0596/66 05 26 ⓕ66 14 98, ⓔlycheeplongee@wanadoo.fr €45.74), a **diving** outfit on the Pointe's outskirts that hits the grottoes around the Rocher du Diamant (see opposite).

Accommodation

There are at least a dozen places to **stay** but you can save significant euros by checking into one of the hotels clustered to the west of Anse Mitan, the natural white-sand beach at the mouth of the Pointe.

Auberge de l'Anse Mitan ⓣ0596/66 01 12, ⓕ66 01 05. Secluded at Anse Mitan's western-most edge, this welcoming family-run inn has twenty lacklustre but affordable rooms with sea or garden views. ③ with breakfast.

L'Impératrice Village ⓣ0596/66 08 09, ⓕ66 07 10, ⓦwww.caribin.com/impvillage. Furthest from Anse Mitan, these comfortable kitchenette- and A/C- equipped studios share pleasant grounds with a pool and private beach. ⑤ with breakfast.

Novotel Carayou ⓣ0596/66 04 04, ⓕ66 00 57, ⓦwww.accor-hotels.com. This secluded Pointe-du-Bout option has a private beach, ample water toys and 200 comfortable rooms, many with sea views. ⑦

Village Créole ⓣ0596/66 03 19, ⓕ66 07 06, ⓦwww.villagecreole.com. Upscale studios and one- to two-bedroom apartments in the hub of Pointe-du-Bout with full kitchen, TV, A/C and parking. ⑤

Eating and drinking

Scads of **restaurants** on the Pointe serve international cuisine ranging from Chinese to Cuban; what "local" restaurants there are can be found near Anse-Mitan.

Au Poisson d'Or Anse Mitan (closed Mon). Generous portions of creole fare are served up both à la carte and prix-fixe for lunch and dinner at this relaxed spot on the road leading to the beach.

Au Regal de la Mer Anse Mitan. Decadent fish tartar and ostrich steak are just part of the stellar menu at this expensive French-creole eatery-cum-piano bar by the pier.

Chez Fanny Anse Mitan (closed Wed & mid-Aug–Sept). This cheap canteen-style restaurant facing the beach has an agreeable daily prix-fixe menu with an accent on simple home-cooked meals.

Anse-à-l'Âne

The crescent-shaped **ANSE-À-L'ÂNE**, just 2km east of Pointe-du-Bout, fell within developers' viewfinders recently, and earned its very own resort, the *Club des Trois-Îlets* (ⓣ0596/68 31 67, ⓕ68 37 65, ⓦwww.accor-hotels.com; ⑥ with breakfast). The *Club* runs a popular **dive** shop (ⓣ0596/68 36 36; €30.50–46), and clients can use the hotel's pool. The other side of the grey sand here is still pretty laid-back, with a campsite and restaurant dominating the waterfront property instead of canopied beach chairs. There are minimal places to **stay** otherwise; one, *Le Courbaril* (ⓣ0596/68 32 30, ⓕ68 32 21, ⓔloc.courbaril@wanadoo.fr; ②), offers forty cheerful fan-only bungalows with kitchenettes and terraces right on the beach. *Le Nid Tropical* (ⓣ0596/68 31 30, ⓕ68 47 43; ①), one of Martinique's rare maintained **campsites**, is due east of the *Courbaril*; the dozen-odd sites are complemented by simple fan-only beach bungalows. The ferry from Fort-de-France docks at the pier facing the campsite.

South to Diamant

The D37 south of Anse-à-l'Âne skirts Grande Anse, a gorgeous harbour packed with colourful fishing boats, followed by Anse d'Arlets and Petit Anse, both quiet seaside villages with their own agreeable sandy stretches, before climbing 477-metre Morne Larcher, southern Martinique's highest point. The road here can get pretty tight, with a number of hairpin turns, but it's worth the grinding gear-shifting to reach the south side, where the road plunges down to the sea and the rocky outcropping known as **Rocher du Diamant** leaps into view. This volcanic islet 3km off the coast of Martinique is popular with scuba divers, as its depths are loaded with violet coral, multicoloured sponges and finely carved grottoes. Above sea level, its surface commands attention for its bizarre history. In 1804, the British claimed the rough-cut-diamond outcropping as a battleship, the HMS Diamond Rock, and established unsinkable barracks on her cliffs. After using it to fend off French vessels for seventeen months, the British were outsmarted by the French, who sent over a rum-loaded ship – the isolated mariners drank the hooch, weakening their defences, and enabling the French to recapture the island.

The town of **DIAMANT** itself, which lies a few kilometres east of the eponymous Rocher, is a picturesque place, with pretty blue and coral houses overlooking a fine bay bounded to the east by the cloistered Pointe de la Cherry. The four-kilometre beach here is one of Martinique's nicest, but the swell can be rough; even so, it's still worth checking out for the awesome vista of the Rocher huddled below Morne Larcher.

Practicalities

Diamant's hotels are located outside of the town centre. About five kilometres west, *L'Anse Bleue* (Ⓣ0596/76 21 91, Ⓕ76 47 50; ③ including breakfast) has attractive wooden cottages and a handful of balconied doubles. If you've got the cash, though, stay at the *Relais Caraïbes* on Pointe de la Cherry; its picturesque bungalows have sitting rooms with exposed-wood ceilings near a pool overlooking the Rocher and Morne Larcher (Ⓣ0596/76 44 65, Ⓕ76 21 20, Ⓔrelais.caraibes@wanadoo.fr; ⑦ with breakfast).

Diamant's best **restaurants** have terraces right over the sand. *Snack 82*, behind the town pharmacy, has affordable lunch and dinner prix-fixe Creole menus as well as beachfare. Further east, *Diamant Plage* (closed Mon & June–Oct), serves up fine grilled fish and an excellent house *langoustine*. Next door, *Chez Lucie* has a wide-ranging choice of creole dishes on their prix-fixe menu, including delicious *fricassée d'ouassous* and *lambi colombo*.

Ste-Anne

Delightful **STE-ANNE**, Martinique's southernmost village, seems almost blissfully unaware of the *Club Med* and hopping beaches nearby. The town itself revolves around two miniature squares: place Abbé Morland, at the north end, fronts a charming sandstone church, while place 22-Mé to the south hosts the bus depot. The two narrow roads that run between them are lined with comely two-storey houses that overlook a deep emerald-blue bay.

The friendly **tourism office** on the left side of the road as you head into town (Mon–Fri 8.30am–5pm, Sat until 3.30pm, Sun 9am–12.30pm) has heaps of information on what's doing in the area. There's a quality **dive** outfit, *Kalinago* (Ⓣ0596/76 92 98, Ⓕ76 95 38, Ⓔkalinago@wanadoo.fr), across the street with English-speaking instructors on hand. You can also check out the underwater action on the glass-bottomed *Aquabulle* that leaves the pier facing the town church in the morning and afternoon; the latter makes time for snorkelling (1–1.5hrs; €21.34–25.92).

Accommodation

Domaine de l'Anse Caritan Route des Caraïbes Ⓣ0596/76 74 12 Ⓕ76 72 59, Ⓦwww.anse-caritan.com. A swanky hotel with an exceptional beachfront location and 228 well-appointed and spacious rooms; there's also a gorgeous pool and landscaped grounds. ⑥

La Dunette Rue JM Tjibaou Ⓣ0596/76 73 90, Ⓕ76 76 05. Right on the main drag with eighteen straightforward A/C and TV-equipped rooms. Ask for one overlooking the water – there's no extra charge. ④ with breakfast.

Manoir de Beauregard Av Nelson Mandela ⓣ0596/76 73 40 ⓕ76 93 24. The eleven A/C rooms at this former plantation estate are a bit tired, but the main house encloses a grand salon outfitted with Louis XV armoires. ⑤ with breakfast.

Vivre & Camper Pointe Marin ⓣ0596/76 72 79, ⓕ76 97 82. Reservations are a must at this beachfront campsite, where you can either bring your own gear or rent the whole kit and kaboodle – a six-man tent with table, chair, mattresses, stove and dishes. ①

Eating and drinking

Coco Nèg 4 rue Abbé Huard (dinner only). A cosy restaurant run by a young Martiniquan couple who emphasize simple but flavourful local dishes like *calalou* soup, *conch colombo* and pig stew. Prices are moderate.

L'Épi Soleil Rue JM Tjibaou. Small pastry and sandwich counter; the place to pack a beach picnic.

Les Tamariniers Place de L'Église. A wonderful diner with superlative service and delicious creole dishes like red snapper, avocado and lobster, and grouper. Prices are moderate to expensive.

La Terrace Place du 22-Mé. Alfresco restaurant with rustic furnishings, good people-watching from its covered terrace and straightforward, inexpensive home-cooked creole meals.

Les Salines

The stupendous **LES SALINES**, 5km south of Ste-Anne, is considered Martinique's best beach with good reason: its pristine white sand trims an azure bay framed by swaying palm trees. The one danger is the poisonous manchineel trees, especially common at the southernmost end; they're marked with splashes of red paint (see p.25). Should you get bored with sun-worshipping, the sand is backed by a natural **salt pond**, for which the beach is named, and borders a desolate petrified forest, **La Savane des Petrifications**; both make good side-explorations.

While the beach has countless **snack** trucks selling baguettes, crepes and drinks, its **facilities** aren't spectacular – if possible, don your suit in advance. **Camping** (free; see p.543) is permitted on the beach during school holidays. If you don't have your own wheels, you can catch a *taxi-commune* to Les Salines from the **bus** station in Ste-Anne; make sure to confirm return times.

Northern Martinique

The blend of ruins, botanical gardens, rainforests and mountainous areas common to **NORTHERN MARTINIQUE** offers a sharp counterpoint to its southern resort towns. One route here, the roller-coaster Route de la Trace, cuts through the lush valleys of **Mont-Pelée** and **Morne-Rouge**, while the Caribbean-hugging N2 is lined by silvery-blue-tinted black beaches. The most remarkable sight in this region is **St-Pierre**, the town destroyed by Mont-Pelée in 1902, while **Anse Couleuvre**, at the northernmost tip, is Martinique's most secluded beach.

Up the Caribbean coast

Once past the suburban communities outlying the capital, the N2 passes through a series of fishing villages before reaching **Carbet**, the spot Columbus claimed for Spain in 1502. North of here, two roadside black-sand beaches blend into one another, the first of which, **Anse Turin**, appeared in some of Paul Gauguin's works. He and his friend Charles Laval stayed in a nearby slave cottage during a brief stint in Martinique in 1887, when the two were recovering from malaria. While the shack is long gone, the bizarre **Musée Paul Gauguin** (daily 9am–5.30pm; €3.05), off to the right before the tunnel to St-Pierre, commemorates Gauguin's short residency with reproductions of his works by local artists and copies of bitter letters to his wife.

Immediately north on the N2 are the superb ruins and grounds of the pre-1643 **Habitation Anse Latouche** (Mon–Sat 10am–4.30pm; €2.52, €1.75 children), the island's largest sugar plantation in its heyday. The grounds and buildings were destroyed by Mont-Pelée's 1902 eruption, but vestiges of a 1716 aqueduct and dam are still visible – the only examples of their kind on Martinique.

St-Pierre

Little Pompeii, as Martinique's former capital, **ST-PIERRE**, is now known, begins due north of the Habitation Anse Latouche. On May 8, 1902, a sudden eruption of Mont-Pelée devastated the then 250-year-old town along with its 30,000 inhabitants in a mere ninety seconds. The lone survivor, **Louis Cyparis**, only made it out alive because the prison cell in which he was locked up was sufficiently ballasted to withstand the heat. The grim effects of the lava's path are evident throughout the compact town, where blackened **ruins** dominate the landscape.

The best place to start your explorations is the must-visit **Musée Vulcanologique** on rue Victor Hugo (daily 9am–5pm; €1.53), a small museum containing contorted glass and soot-streaked porcelain salvaged from the rubble; the staggering centrepiece is a squashed church bell that once sounded Mass.

Facing the museum are St-Pierre's most impressive ruins, those belonging to the 1831-32 Bordeaux-inspired **theatre**: all that remain are the twin entrance staircases and the archway-encircled oval auditorium, but they capture something of its former splendour. Connected one level below the theatre's northeast corner is what's left of the town jail – Cyparis's life-saving thick-walled cell is among the foundations. South towards the waterfront finds the **Quartier du Figuier**, the extensive ruins of several eighteenth-century portside storehouses.

Practicalities

While St-Pierre is easily walkable, the rubber-wheeled Cyparis Express train covers the town with a narrated tour (French only) starting opposite the Quartier du Figuier (Mon–Fri 9.30am–1pm & 2.30pm; €7.62). For **information**, drop into the helpful Office de Tourisme on Victor Hugo facing the theatre ruins (daily 9am–5pm; ⓣ0596/78 15 41). They share space with the Bureau de la Randonnée (ⓣ0596/78 30 77), an outfit that arranges **canyoning** trips – combination whitewater and rainforest expeditions – and gives out **hiking** information. Tropicasub, on the southern outskirts (ⓣ0596/78 38 03, ⓦwww.multimania.com/tropicasub), takes **divers** out to explore shipwrecks off the coast.

There are only a handful of places to **stay** in the area. Above town, *Le Fromager*, Route des Fonds, St-Denis (ⓣ0596/78 19 07; ❷), has sea views from its four mountain-edge bungalows. North of the centre, the dive-package-oriented *Résidence Surcouf* (ⓣ0596/78 32 73, ⓕ78 13 82, ⓦwww.residencesurcou f.com; ❸) offers basic bungalows and a pool. Back in Carbet, the fancier *Marouba Club* (ⓣ0596/78 00 21, ⓕ78 05 65; ❺) is on a private black-sand beach. **Dining** options are equally limited to a handful of bakeries; *Le Fromager*'s restaurant (see above, lunch only), which serves up quality creole food on an open-air terrace; and *Habitation Joséphine*, a waterfront restaurant with good-value three-course Creole menus and fishermen's specials.

Beyond St-Pierre

North of St-Pierre, the coastal road rims the Caribbean after passing the **Tombeau des Caraïbes**, the limestone cliff from which the last of the Carib chieftains committed suicide in 1658 – after swallowing poison – rather than submit to colonialization. The villages along this quiet northern stretch, **Le Prêcheur** and **Anse**

Belleville, are among the island's oldest, and their harbours make a picturesque prelude to the **Habitation Céron** (daily 9.30am–5pm; €6), a secluded seventeenth-century sugar plantation that now cultivates bananas, cocoa and crayfish.

As you leave the plantation, turn right to reach **Anse Céron**, a relatively secluded black-sand beach equipped with changing facilities and a snack bar. For total isolation, forge onwards on the N2 as it ascends a jungly mountain road before descending to **Anse Couleuvre**, a magnificent emerald bay with a volcanic sand beach. A path to the left of the car park hits the sand in short order; a longer one to the right passes the ruins of a chocolate plantation, the aroma of which still pervades the air. The latter trail is also the start of a grinding eighteen-kilometre (6hr), walk to Grand'Rivière (see below).

Route de la Trace

Opened by the Jesuits in the early 1700s, the snaking **ROUTE DE LA TRACE**, or N3, rises into the foggy altitudes of **Mont-Pelée** and the **Pitons du Carbet** northwest of Fort-de-France before heading to the Atlantic coast.

The major stop along this route is the botanical **Jardins Balata** (daily 9am–5pm; €6.48; ⓦwww.jardindebalata.com), 10km northwest of Fort-de-France. The landscaped gardens contain lily ponds and hundreds of palms and fruit trees, and afford awesome vistas of the Pitons de Carbet. Three kilometres back, the Byzantine **Sacré-Coeur-de-Balata** overlooks the capital from a hillside plateau; the 1928 domed church is a miniature replica of Montmartre's.

Heading another 10km inland from the gardens, the N3 reaches the **Site de l'Alma**, a cascading river with shallow pools in a dark rainforest, then moves onward to Martinique's highest settlement, **Morne-Rouge**, located 450m above sea level. The town's proximity to **Mont-Pelée**, the 1397-metre-high volcano that dominates northern Martinique, is the main reason to stop here; the **Maison du Volcan** (ⓣ0596/52 45 45, ⓕ52 33 02), signposted off the rue Principale, organizes hikes to the summit. Nearby, the island's **youth hostel**, *Auberge de Jeunesse*, on rue Jean-Jaurès (ⓣ0596/52 39 81, ⓕ52 39 64; ❶ with breakfast), has beds in dormitory, single or double rooms.

A junction at the northern outskirts of Morne-Rouge marks the end of the Route de la Trace; the eastern N2 hits St-Pierre (see p.571) in 8km while the westward N3 carries on past the access road to Mont-Pelée, signposted to Aileron 2km after the turn-off.

Onward to the Atlantic coast

The one stop of note along the stretch of N3 that heads towards the Atlantic is the **Gorges de la Falaise** (daily 8am–5pm; €6.86), on the southern outskirts of Ajoupa-Bouillon. With the help of a guide, visitors cross rainforest scenery before descending into rushing cascades with some invigorating swimming. While the one-hour hike is not difficult, the stone pathways can be slippery, so bring good shoes.

Most people who come this far usually finish with a visit to the circa-1700 **Leyritz Plantation** in Basse-Pointe, the coastal town north of the N3 where it meets the N1; if you have the time, continue to Grand'Rivière (see below) instead. The touristy sugar-plantation-turned-**hotel** (ⓣ0596/78 53 92, ⓕ78 92 44; ❻) is among Martinique's best-preserved colonial holdovers, with handsome grounds and a water mill; guests sleep in attractive terracotta roofed cottages once home to married slaves.

North to Grand'Rivière

Nowhere evokes old Martinique better than secluded **GRAND'RIVIÈRE**, a jewel of a fishing village huddled on lowlands framed by Mont-Pelée's dramatic flanks. The drive from Basse-Pointe alone makes a visit worthwhile – the thirty-minute route is the island's most thrilling, with tight hairpin turns, overgrown hillsides and bridges suspended over gorges. The roller coaster ends at the village's black-sand beach, and the only way to go forward from here is by foot or sea. A **syndicat d'initiative** facing the town church (Mon–Fri 8am–5pm, Sat & Sun 9am–1pm or in high season 4pm; ⓣ0596/55 72 74), organizes outings for around €30. You can dig into crayfish and coconut sorbet at *Chez Tante Arlette*, a creole **restaurant** near the *syndicat d'initiative*, with generous three-course prix-fixe menus. There's also a handful of simple **rooms** upstairs (ⓣ0596/55 75 75; ③ with breakfast).

Central Martinique

CENTRAL MARTINIQUE, the region that extends south from the capital to Trois-Îlets and north to Ste-Marie, consists of little more than suburban outposts. That said, the **Presqu'Île Caravelle** that protrudes into the mighty Atlantic, is definitely worth a side-trip, as is the **Habitation Clément**, a remote rum distillery that came to international fame when it hosted the 1991 Gulf War summit between the then French President François Mitterand and US President George Bush Sr.

Presqu'Île Caravelle and around

Despite boasting some of Martinique's top beaches, the twelve-kilometre long **PRESQU'ÎLE CARAVELLE** has remained delightfully underdeveloped. Sweeps of sugarcane and bamboo crush up against the access road before opening onto dramatic ocean vistas and arriving at the peninsula's solitary village, quaint **Tartane**, where a glorious Atlantic-facing beach is busy with fishing boats and red-throated pelicans angling for dinner.

Aside from Anse Tartane, there are five other Atlantic-facing **beaches** nearby, the best of which, **Anse l'Étang**, is 1km east of town. Double that distance is windswept **Anse Bonneville**, with prime windsurfing conditions. The peninsula's other draw, the protected **nature reserve** at its tip, has several **hiking** trails and contains what's left of the 1740 **Château Dubuc** (daily 8am–6pm; €2.29), a homestead with ruins of several slave *cachots*, small solitary-confinement units.

A couple of sights within easy driving distance combine to make a good half-day outing. The vicinity of Ste-Marie finds the engaging **Musée du Rhum** (Mon–Fri 9am–5pm, Sat 9am–1pm; free entry and tasting), where a mint collection of rum-related paraphernalia is complemented by hilariously outdated advertising campaigns. The area's main attraction, however, is the stellar **Habitation Clément**, 10km south of the peninsula, at the western outskirts of Le François (daily 9am–6pm; closed Sept; €7, rum-tasting included; ⓦwww.rhum-clement.com). The graceful property sits on eighteen hectares of grounds but the highlight is its unusual anti-Christopher Columbus exhibit in the rum-ageing room.

Practicalities

To **stay** near Anse l'Étang, try the bungalows with kitchenettes and A/C at *Village de Tartane* (ⓣ0596/58 06 33 or 60 31 61, ⓕ63 53 32, ④ with breakfast). Further east, on a commanding hillside perch, are the kitchen-equipped bungalows at *La Caravelle* (ⓣ0596/58 07 32, ⓕ58 07 90, ⓦperso.wanadoo.fr/hotelcaravelle; ④). The peninsula's most upscale hotel, *La Goelette* (ⓣ0596/58 76 10 ⓕ58 76 20, ⓦwww.hotellagoelette.com; ⑤), has spacious balconied suites with kitchenettes.

Most of the **restaurants** are inexpensive spots located near Anse Tartane, typically offering daily fish specials or spicy creole fare. The best is at *La Caravelle* (see above), with tasty twists on local dishes like *shark colombo* and *crab calalou*. For something other than creole or fish, the *Mini-Golf Beach Club* by Anse l'Étang serves pizzas until 1am most nights, and transforms into a disco on Saturdays.

14.3

St Barthélemy

The Caribbean playground of the rich and famous, the diminutive 25-square-kilometre **ST BARTHÉLEMY (St Barts)** looks like it's been plucked from the Côte d'Azur and dropped into the Antilles. Situated 25km south of St Martin (see p.461) and 175km north of Guadeloupe (see p.546), the boomerang-shaped island is sprinkled with picturesque red-roofed **villas** and edged by some of the Caribbean's loveliest **beaches** and **bays**. Many of the beaches are only accessible by sea, giving the island a rare sense of **seclusion**. Even the most beautiful stretches – **Grande Saline**, **Anse Colombier** and **Anse Gouverneur** – never get crowded and, thanks to building laws forbidding big resort developments, everything is small-scale, including the capital, **Gustavia**, whose tallest buildings are shorter than the highest palm trees.

St Barts' privacy doesn't come cheaply, but considering the throngs that crowd the island's neighbours in high season, paying a little more for some personal space can make all the difference.

Some history

St Barthélemy was spotted by Columbus in 1493 and named for his younger brother, Bartolomeo. The first French delegation to settle the island, in 1648, came

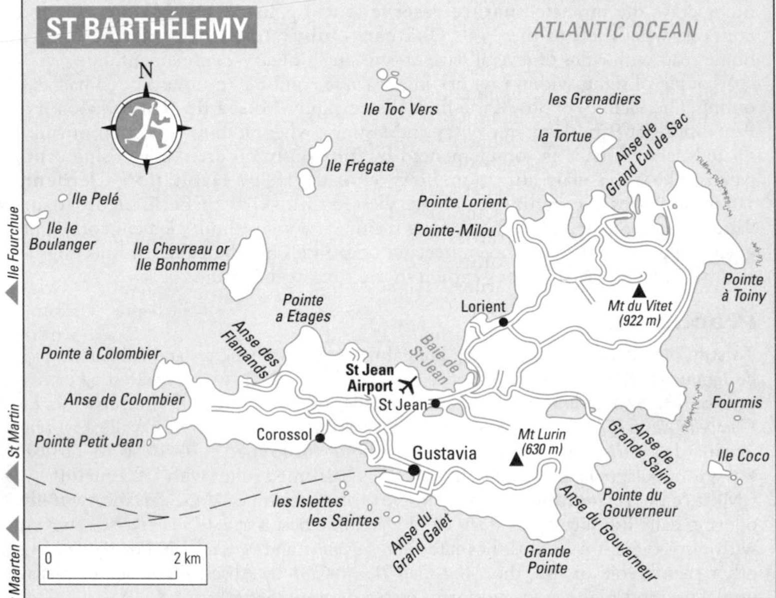

from nearby St Kitts (see p.495). Their effort was disastrous, however, as native Caribs massacred the lot in 1665. It was almost a decade later before a second attempt, this one by Norman and Breton Huguenots, was made. Under their reign, Gustavia's hurricane-proof harbour became a popular mooring port for buccaneers, who carried plunder from Spanish galleons in their holds; one legendary pirate, Montbars the Exterminator, even set up headquarters here.

Over a century later, in 1784, France's Marie-Antoinette ceded ownership to Sweden's King Gustaf II in exchange for free-port rights in Gothenburg. But after serving as an American-friendly port during the Revolution and, later, the War of 1812, Gustavia suffered a devastating fire in 1852 that proved too costly for the Swedes. They sold it back to France in 1878, for 320,000FF (US$45,700 today), and the French condition that it remain a duty-free port. The island's administrative status changed in 1974 it, when came under neighbouring Guadeloupe's jurisdiction.

Arrival, information and island transport

Most overnight visitors arrive by twenty-seater **planes**, on a miniature runway that essentially ends in the water – making for a spectacular, if occasionally daunting, arrival. The terminal is also a modest affair. There's an **ATM** on the ground floor, or, to **exchange** currency, head across the street to the St-Jean Centre Commercial.

Day-trippers from St Martin (see p.468) usually come by **ferry**, on a one-hour trip that docks in the centre of Gustavia, at the Quai Général-de-Gaulle.

Many hotels meet flights or ferries on request. While there are two **taxi** stands – one at the airport, the other at Gustavia's Quai Général-de-Gaulle – there are no public **buses**. (Call ahead for a taxi on ⓣ0590/27 66 31.) Consequently, most visitors rent a **car** – several agencies are located a few metres past the airport exit; reservations are a must in high season. Outfits include Budget (ⓣ0590/27 66 30 or 27 67 43); Caraïbes Welcome (ⓣ0590/27 82 54); Europcar (ⓣ0590/27 74 34); Islander Car (ⓣ0590/27 70 01 or 27 60 61); Soleil Caraïbe (ⓣ0590/27 67 18); Thrifty (ⓣ0590/27 73 22 or 27 64 05); Turbé (ⓣ0590/27 60 70). Tropic'all Rent, on Gustavia's rue du Roi Oscar II (ⓣ0590/27 64 76), also rents scooters. If you don't rent a car, consider staying in St-Jean; it has the highest concentration of restaurants and shops outside the capital, and two beaches.

For **information**, head to the extremely helpful Office Municipal de Tourisme (Mon–Thurs 8.30am–12.30pm & 2–5.30pm; Fri until 5pm; ⓣ0590/27 87 27, ⓕ27 74 47, ⓔodtsb@wanadoo.fr) on Quai Général-de-Gaulle. Advance island web surfing and reservations can be done through ⓦwww.st-barths.com. The **post office** is in Gustavia on rue du Centenaire (Mon, Tue, Thurs & Fri 8am–3pm, Wed & Sat 8am–12.30pm). **Internet access** is essentially limited to ANT Informatique, on rue Jeanne-d'Arc and Centre Alizés, on rue de la République.

Of the **watersports operators** around here, the highly recommended Sailing Marine Service, on La Pointe (ⓣ0590/27 70 34, ⓕ27 70 36, ⓦwww.st-barths.com/marine.service), runs half- and full-day sails (US$50–72) on a twin-hulled catamaran. Ocean Must (ⓣ0590/27 62 25, ⓦwww.saintbarth-prestige.com), on La Pointe, has water-skiing (US$52/30min) and Sea-Doo rentals (US$60/30min).

Gustavia

St Barts' capital, dollhouse-size **GUSTAVIA**, is an appealing blend of red-roofed villas and heavy-set grey-stone buildings that plays second fiddle to its deep U-shaped harbour, where yacht-watching over a bottle of wine at a waterfront **café** ranks as the unofficial town sport. A close runner-up for that title is **shopping**, as dozens of duty-free boutiques line the main drag, **Rue de la République.**

The town's few historical sights can all be seen in under an hour. The architectural highlight, the chunky circa-1800 Swedish **Wall House**, anchors the west side of the harbour from **Place Vanadis**, named for the last Swedish military vessel to leave the island after the 1878 French repossession ceremony. The former storehouse now hosts the mundane **Musée de St Barthélemy** (Mon 2.30–6pm, Tues –Fri 8.30am–12.30pm & 2.30–6pm, Sat 9am–1pm; €2), a modest collection of tools, maps and other oddities. On the south side of the port, the cheerful 1855 **St Bartholomew** Anglican church, with its sandstone facade topped by a minute wood-shingled belfry, contrasts sharply with the sombre, Hispanic-influenced **Notre-Dame de l'Assomption** nearby. A short walk west from both churches is Gustavia's small beach, the pinkish seashell-covered **Anse du Grand Galet**, not surprisingly a boon for beachcombers. At the other end of town, a red-topped lighthouse graces a promontory once home to **Fort Gustaf**, though scant evidence of its military origins remains save the odd cannon and sentinel; the main attraction today is the magnificent **view** of Gustavia and surrounding islands.

Accommodation

Most of St Barts' **hotels** are located outside the capital, where the better beaches are found. Still, a couple of in-town options are the island's best **bargains**.

Carl Gustaf Rue des Normands ⓣ0590/29 79 00, ⓕ27 82 37, ⓦwww.carlgustaf.com. A decadent fourteen-suite hideout with perks like private "plunge" pools and prime sunset views. Suites US$800.

Presqu'Île La Pointe ⓣ0590/27 64 60, ⓕ27 72 30, ⓔapa@wanadoo.fr. The cheapest lodgings around; the ten rooms aren't much, but do have A/C and private baths, and some have balconies. ❸

Sunset Rue de la République ⓣ0590/27 77 21, ⓕ27 81 59, ⓔsunset-hotel@wanadoo.fr. A cosy option with eight comfortable rooms right on the waterfront and a sunny verandah. ❹

Eating and drinking

Bar de l'Oublie Rue de la France. Open-air brasserie with a snackish menu of sandwiches and salads.

Chez Maya Public Beach ⓣ0590/27 75 73. Quite possibly the island's favourite, the daily menu at this nondescript beachfront restaurant lists tasty dishes like tomato and mango salad and duck à l'orange. Reservations required; prices are moderate to expensive. Dinner only; closed Sun.

L'Iguane Carré D'Or; closed Sun. Outdoor, teak-furnished café, with moderately priced sandwiches and salads by day and sushi and sashimi by night.

Le Sapotillier Rue du Centenaire ⓣ0590/27 60 28 (dinner only). A superlative setting in a handsome waterfront house with an expensive but delicious menu including frogs' legs fricassee and snail lasagne. Reservations advised.

Le Select Rue de la France. That this inexpensive outdoor pub inspired Jimmy Buffett's classic "Cheeseburger in Paradise" says it all.

St-Jean

St Barts' busiest enclave, the twin-beached **ST-JEAN**, lies so close to the airport that incoming planes practically land on the longer of the two white-sand crescents. This technicality hasn't prevented the area becoming the island's premier resort though; its first hotel, the spectacular *Eden Rock* (see below), was established here in the 1950s atop the quartzite promontory that divides the two stretches. Since then, St-Jean has become the most happening spot on the island after the capital, with plenty of shops, restaurants and bars, both on and off the sand. The bay itself, protected by coral reefs, has decent **snorkelling** and **windsurfing** conditions.

Accommodation

Eden Rock ⓣ0590/29 79 89 or 1-877/563-7105, ⓕ0590/27 88 37, ⓦwww.edenrockhotel.com. Cushy palace with fourteen rooms, cabins and suites decked out in mahogany furnishings, a spa and gym. Prices start at US$340.

Emeraude Plage ⓣ0590/27 64 78, ⓕ27 83 08,

Ⓔemeraudeplage@wanadoo.fr. This low-frill beachfront hotel has whitewashed cottages with terraces, kitchenettes, A/C and TV, but no pool. 6

Tom Beach Ⓣ0590/27 53 13, Ⓕ27 53 15, Ⓦwww.tombeach.com. The twelve characterful beachfront creole cottages come with appealing touches like four-poster beds, VCR and stereo, and hammocks; there's internet access at reception. 9

Tropical Ⓣ0590/27 64 87, Ⓕ27 81 74, Ⓦwww.tropical-hotel.com. This smart hotel has pleasant garden- and bay-view rooms up a steep hill from the beach. Closed June–mid-July. 8 with breakfast.

Village St-Jean Ⓣ0590/27 61 39, Ⓕ27 77 96, Ⓦwww.villagestjean.com. Popular family-run hotel near the beach offering standard rooms and cottages with kitchens. 7 including breakfast.

Eating and drinking

Chez Annick A popular roadside café with a sizeable selection of inexpensive, tasty sandwiches.

KiKi-é Mo Next door to *Annick*'s, this busy roadside hut dishes out paninis, pastas and antipasto.

Le Pélican Huge, mouthwatering portions of moderate to expensive fresh fish and steak are served on a beachside terrace and lounge chairs.

La Plage At *Tom Beach* (see above). The "Woodstock 3685km" signpost indicates its pretensions, but even post-Woodstockians will wax poetic about *La Plage*'s deep sofas, comfy armchairs, and impressive servings of fresh grilled fish and creole fare; moderate to expensive.

Village Créole Brasserie offering pizza, *moules frites* and beer on tap.

Lorient

From St-Jean, the road makes a short climb before descending into quiet **LORIENT**, the site of the first French settlement in 1648. Today, its smallish bay is popular with **windsurfing** aficionados. Otherwise, the town's main appeal is its proximity to St-Jean. The best **accommodation**, the recently reopened *La Banane* on the way into the village (Ⓣ0590/27 68 25, Ⓕ27 68 44, Ⓦwww.labanane.com; US$420 including breakfast), has eight ultra-stylish creole cottages and two Zen-retreat-like pools. *La Normandie*, on route des Salines (Ⓣ0590/27 61 66, Ⓕ27 98 83; 3), is a good-value option with a pool and simple but agreeable A/C rooms. Lorient's **restaurant** scene is confined to *K'Fé Massaï* (Ⓣ0590/29 76 78; dinner only; closed Tues), a sophisticated French-creole eatery at the entrance to town, and *Jojo Burger*, with inexpensive fried chicken and delicious burgers near the beach. The organic *Vitolive*, on route des Salines (Mon–Sat 10am–7pm), offers tasty tapas, sandwiches and free olive-tastings daily.

Anse de Grande Saline and Anse Gouverneur

Two of St Barts' best undeveloped beaches are approached from well-marked secondary roads south of St-Jean and Lorient. The local favourite is the white-sanded **Grande Saline** that backs a salt pond at the island's core. The other, the facility-less **Anse Gouverneur**, lies around another headland, at the end of a steep descent that passes hidden villas and marvellous views of St-Jean. You can **eat** near Grande Saline at *Le Grain du Sel*, a chilled-out place serving burgers and sandwiches; *Le Tamarin* (closed June–Oct) a hammock-strung eatery offering fine salmon and *langoustine*; and *Le Gommier*, a creole joint serving good local fare.

Pointe-Milou to Grand Cul-de-Sac

A couple of kilometres past Lorient, the main road passes the island's swankiest neighbourhood, **POINTE-MILOU**, a collection of stunning villas on a rocky cliff. The lone **hotel** here, *Christopher* (Ⓣ0590/27 63 63 or 1-800/763-4835, Ⓕ0590/27 92 92, Ⓦwww.st-barths.com/christopher-hotel; US$460 with breakfast), is tucked along the base of the point, with 42 well-appointed rooms and a terrific free-form pool. **Dining**-wise, the cosy *Ti St-Barth* (ⓣ0590/27 97 71; dinner only) is recommended for its blend of creole and French fare.

Grand Cul-de-Sac

From Pointe-Milou, the road slopes down to reach the golden beach at **GRAND CUL-DE-SAC**, a tranquil lagoon ideal for families with children in tow. There's not much privacy to be had here since virtually every grain of sand has been colonized by major **hotels**. Of these, the most appealing may be the *Sereno Beach* (ⓣ0590/27 64 80 or 29 83 30, ⓕ27 75 47, ⓦwww.serenobeach.com; closed Sept–Oct; ⑧), with smallish but attractive garden-view rooms, and sea-view suites with private solariums. More upscale is the *Guanahani* (ⓣ0590/27 66 60, ⓕ27 70 70, ⓦwww.leguanahani.com; US$500), St Barts' largest hotel; the 76 well-appointed rooms have high-pitched roofs and terraces.

You need never leave the enclave to **eat**, given each hotel hosts up to three restaurants. *Le Rivage*, at *St Barth's Beach*, has a fine selection of creole dishes. Nearby *La Gloriette*, between *St Barth's Beach* and *Sereno Beach*, serves moderately priced prix-fixe French and creole menus on its rustic seaside terrace; the *crab farçi* is superb. The haven's standout, *Bou Bou's* (ⓣ0590/29 83 01), is a sumptuous affair at *Sereno Beach*, with Moroccan touches like throw pillows and wood carvings, and upscale Mediterranean cuisine.

West of Gustavia

Tiny **COROSSOL**, a fisherman's village 4km west of Gustavia, evokes an Antillian flavour altogether absent elsewhere on St Barts. The local women wear white, shoulder-length sunbonnets, and weave *latanier* leaves into baskets and hats, which they sell from their front porches. The main sight here, the quaint **Inter-Oceans Museum** (Tues–Sun 9am–12.30pm & 2–5pm; closed Mon; €3) along the waterfront, showcases over 9000 seashells from around the world.

On the opposite coast, **FLAMANDS** village tumbles down quietly onto a long stretch of golden sand at Anse des Flamands, a broad bay backed by *latanier* and banana trees. Close by is another secluded beach, **Anse Colombier**, reached by a twenty-minute hike around a headland at the island's westernmost tip. The beach has no facilities, though, so bring water and food with you. Places to **stay** on this side of the island are limited. *Baie des Anges* (ⓣ0590/27 63 61, ⓕ27 83 44, ⓦwww.st-barths.com/baie-des-anges; US$345) has spacious rooms with terrace-kitchenettes right on Anse des Flamands. Nearby, the deluxe *Isle de France* (ⓣ0590/27 61 81 or 1-800/810-4691, ⓕ0590/27 86 83, ⓦwww.isle-de-france.com; US$545) has well-appointed doubles and suites and a squash court.

Dominica

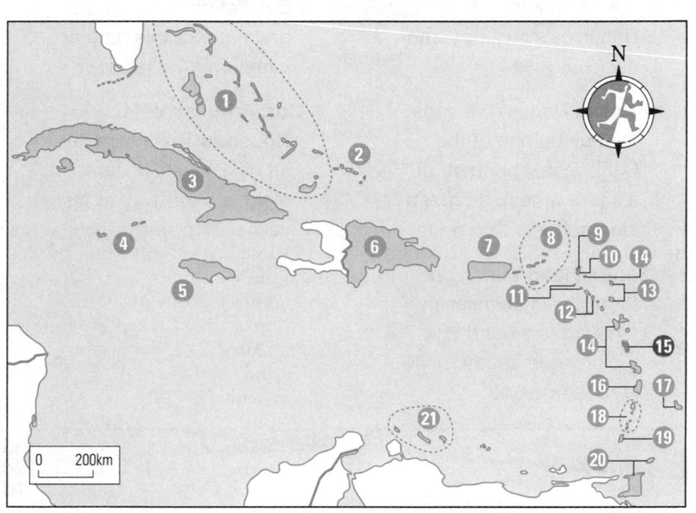

Dominica Highlights

* **Titou Gorge** Swim against the cold current to reach the warm waters of the hidden waterfall. See p.591

* **Indian River** Take a colourful slow boat ride upstream into Dominica's swampy interior. See p.593

* **Roseau** Dominica's capital may be one of the Caribbean's poorest, but it's also among its most atmospheric. See p.586

* **Scotts Head** Watch out for migrating whales in the waters around this picturesque southern village. See p.588

* **Carib Territory** Carib traditions survive in the homeland of the region's remaining Carib Indians. See p.594

* **Boiling Lake** Hike inland past the eerie Valley of Desolation to reach the perimeter of this natural cauldron. See p.591

* **Cornerhouse café, Rouseau** This characterful café's weekly quiz night is a fun way to test your brainpower. See p.587

Introduction and Basics

The first thing you'll notice about **Dominica** (pronounced Dah-min-EE-ka) is how intensely green the island is. Lush, steep-sided peaks rear up 4700 feet to meet cloud-capped summits that receive enough heavy rainfall to feed hundreds of mountain streams. These in turn nourish the majestic **rainforest** vegetation that covers over sixty percent of Dominica's centre.

Lying halfway between Guadeloupe and Martinique (see Chapter 14, p.546), Dominica's appeal has nothing to do with fabulous beaches – what few exist are paltry – or idle days spent under a palm tree. Rather, its abundant nature invites rigorous **hiking** to deep emerald pools, waterfalls and bubbling lakes. Offshore are superb drop-offs, volcanic arches and caves busy with stingrays, barracuda and parrotfish, making for some of the Caribbean's best **diving**, while **whales** and **dolphins** often play off the southern coast, near **Champagne**, a unique effervescent bay.

Despite all that Dominica has to offer for **eco-tourism**, however, it's still vastly under-visited, in no small part because it's not easy to reach. There are no direct flights from the US or Europe, and ferries from surrounding islands don't stop daily.

Where to go

Most **hikers** head directly to Dominica's **Morne Trois Pitons National Park**, the expansive rainforest that covers most of the island's southern reaches. Its centrepiece, **Boiling Lake**, requires a full-day trek, but hitting the park's numerous waterfalls, like **Emerald Pool**, is easily achieved, even by novice hikers. **Divers**, in contrast, head to the waterfront south of Roseau where several outfits run trips to impressive underwater craters around **Scotts Head** and the northern **Cabrits National Park**'s drop-offs.

A somewhat livelier pace is felt in the island capital, **Roseau**, which can be also be a good base camp for island activities, as most guesthouses here also organize rainforest treks and sea dives. It's also the only place with any real **nightlife** to speak of.

When to go

The best time to visit is between January and June, when the weather is at its driest; during August and October, the wettest months, rainfall ranges from thirty inches in Roseau to ten times that in the interior. As elsewhere in the Caribbean, **hurricane season** lasts from June 1 to November 30.

Getting there

To reach Dominica you must first **fly** to Antigua, Barbados, Guadeloupe, Martinique, Puerto Rico, St Lucia or St Martin/St Maarten and catch a connecting flight from there. Airlines that fly to the island include American Eagle, Air Guadeloupe, Caribbean Star and LIAT. **Flights** arrive from Antigua four times daily, and from Guadeloupe and St Lucia twice daily. (For phone numbers of airlines, see pp.12–18 and 36–37.)

Express des Îles is a high-speed catamaran operator that connects Dominica with Guadeloupe, Martinique and St Lucia. Boats run to Roseau from Fort-de-France in Martinique five times a week (1.5hr); from Pointe-à-Pitre five times a week (1hr 45min); and from Castries in St Lucia twice a week (3hr 35min). Tickets are around EC$190–220 one-way.

Getting around

The easiest way to **get around**, especially for first-time visitors, is to have someone else do the driving – the roads are challenging for even the most adept drivers (see p.583). You can arrange a **guide** either through your guesthouse or hotel, or one of the better island tour companies (see p.588).

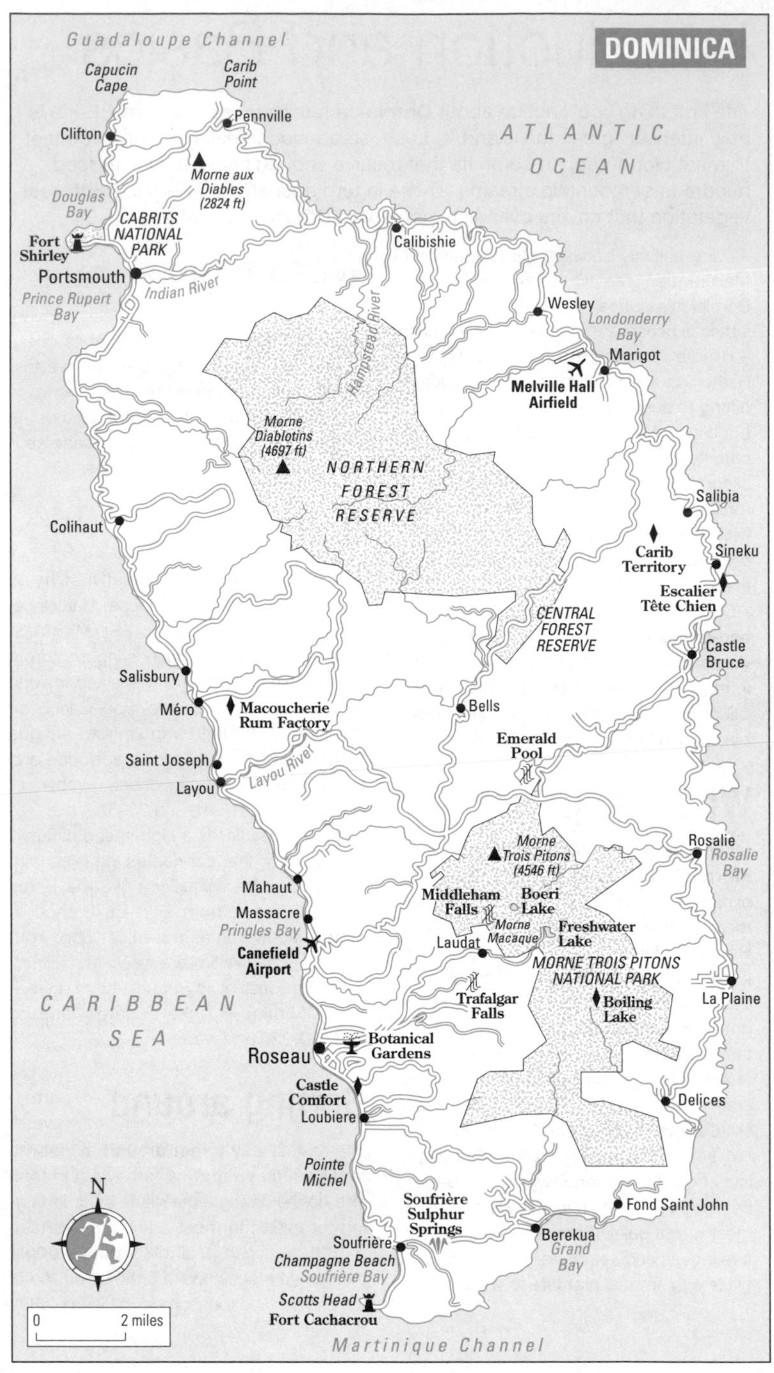
DOMINICA
Guadaloupe Channel
Capucin Cape
Carib Point
Pennville
Clifton
Morne aux Diables (2824 ft)
ATLANTIC OCEAN
Douglas Bay
CABRITS NATIONAL PARK
Fort Shirley
Portsmouth
Calibishie
Indian River
Prince Rupert Bay
Hampstead River
Wesley
Londonderry Bay
Marigot
Melville Hall Airfield
Morne Diablotins (4697 ft)
NORTHERN FOREST RESERVE
Salibia
Colihaut
Carib Territory
Sineku
Escalier Tête Chien
CENTRAL FOREST RESERVE
Castle Bruce
Salisbury
Méro
Macoucherie Rum Factory
Bells
Saint Joseph
Layou River
Layou
Emerald Pool
Rosalie
Rosalie Bay
Morne Trois Pitons (4546 ft)
Mahaut
Middleham Falls
Boeri Lake
Massacre
Pringles Bay
Morne Macaque
Freshwater Lake
Canefield Airport
Laudat
MORNE TROIS PITONS NATIONAL PARK
Trafalgar Falls
Boiling Lake
La Plaine
CARIBBEAN SEA
Botanical Gardens
Roseau
Castle Comfort
Loubiere
Delices
Pointe Michel
N
Soufrière Sulphur Springs
Fond Saint John
Berekua
Soufrière
Grand Bay
Champagne Beach
Soufrière Bay
Scotts Head
Fort Cachacrou
0
2 miles
Martinique Channel

By bus

Dominica's public **bus** system is reliable, with regular service along the Caribbean coast and less regular service to traffic-congested rainforest destinations like the Emerald Pool (see p.592), Trafalgar Falls (see p.591) and the town of Laudat (see p.591). The fifteen-seater minivans run from 6am to 7pm, Monday through Saturday, with service iffy at best on Sundays. Flag them down on the road, tell the driver your destination and pay when you get off. The most you'll have to pay is EC$3.50.

By car

Driving is on the left on narrow, badly paved roads. You'll be hard-pressed to exceed the 20mph speed limit as certain spots have no guardrails whatsoever, even on deadly mountain switchbacks, and many have deep rain gutters alongside. Other routes are nothing more than mud-covered rock (be aware that local car insurance does not cover damage to tyres). None of the roads are lit at night, making it unwise for first-time visitors to cruise around after dark.

If you intend to do a lot of island driving, renting a four-wheel-drive vehicle is your best option, even though they cost more (from US$55/day). Aside from a Budget rental office near Canefield Airport), and a courtesy phone inside the terminal that rings to Valley Car Rentals), Dominica's **car rental agencies** are based in Roseau); they'll meet you at the airport if you've made advance reservations. See p.588 for car rental details. To drive on the island, you'll need to buy a one-month **local driver's licence** (US$10) from airport immigration.

By taxi

Taxis congregate at both island airports and are much more expensive than buses. You're unlikely to use one except to get to and from the airports (see p.586).

By boat

The Express des Îles **ferry** that connects Dominica and neighbouring Guadeloupe and Martinique bypasses the island altogether on Tuesdays and Thursdays – something to keep in mind if you're planning incoming or onward travel by sea. A similar ferry also connects the island with St Lucia twice a week.

By plane

Dominica has two modest **airports**, Canefield and Melville, the former being much closer to Roseau, the National Park and the dive centres south of the capital. When booking your ticket, you can request Canefield as your destination – LIAT's tickets denote the respective airports with C (Canefield) and M (Melville) after the arrival/departure times.

The main carrier, LIAT, is hardly reliable, however. Locals refer to it as "Leave Island Any Time", since it's often up to two hours behind schedule. You should definitely reconfirm your onward flight to ensure that it's still scheduled.

Money and costs

The official currency of Dominica is the **Eastern Caribbean dollar (EC$)**, although US dollars are widely accepted and used to quote hotel and service rates. The EC$ is divided into 100 cents. Bills come in denominations of 5, 10, 20, 50 and 100 EC dollars; coins in 1, 2, 5, 10 and 25 cents. At the time of writing, the **rate of exchange** was EC$2.70 to US$1.

Most Roseau **banks** have ATMs dispensing local currency. Tellers here will also change money for transactions (Mon–Thurs 8am–3pm, Fri 8am–5pm). When paying for goods with US dollars in cash, the rate is usually lower, at $EC2.60/US$1.

Even though Dominica is poor by Caribbean standards, it's not the cheapest place to visit. Additional costs for guides and activities have a way of increasing your bill, as do incidentals like the US$15 **departure tax** levied at the airport when you leave. A **whale-watching** outing will be your biggest one-time expenditure, at US$50/four-hour trip; **diving** is only slightly less expensive, at US$45/single-tank dive.

At the bottom of the scale, you could manage on a **daily budget** of US$30, if you split the cost of a fan-only, shared-bathroom double in a Roseau guesthouse, travel by bus, hike without a guide, and skip diving and whale-watching altogether. A budget of US$70/day will allow you to stay in a rainforest guesthouse and hire a guide.

Information

In addition to representation abroad (see p.29), Dominica has **information** kiosks at both airports, the ferry docks and on the Bay Front (see p.586). The island's official website, ⓦwww.dominica.dm, has links to hotels and services that you can book yourself, though the glossier, corporate-sponsored ⓦwww.delphis.dm is more user-friendly.

Accommodation

Dominica's **accommodation** options are nowhere near as fancy as elsewhere in the Caribbean, but that's a large part of the island's appeal. Hikers will find a clutch of **rainforest guesthouses** nestled amidst the greenery offering terrific packages that include guides, hearty food, and casual lodging in a convivial atmosphere. What modern **hotels** exist are mostly concentrated in Roseau and the Castle Comfort area and cater predominantly to divers with thorough packages and well-equipped, if impersonal, rooms. Note that some hotels apply a 15 percent **tax** to the bill, so you should always ask whether it's included when booking. In the interest of preserving the sanctity of the rainforest, **camping** is forbidden.

Food and drink

Dominica's **cuisine** is simple. You'll find basic fried chicken and fish and chips, **creole** cuisine like goat columbo and callaloo soup (a creamed spinach type soup), and Caribbean staples like roti (curry-filled flat bread).

The national dish is the ubiquitous **mountain chicken**, actually giant legs of a mountain crapaud (toad) endemic to Dominica and Montserrat that is caught only between September and March to keep its numbers from dwindling. Prepared in a variety of ways, it does taste like chicken, and goes down nicely with the light local beer, **Kubuli**.

Due to the countless fresh-water sources, the **tap water** here is superb. Bottled water is also readily available for hikes.

Opening hours, public holidays and festivals

Generally, **opening hours** are Monday to Friday 8am–1pm and 2–4pm. Banks tend to keep shorter hours (Mon–Thurs 8am–3pm, Fri until 5pm). Shops and services close altogether on Sunday, when the only things open are hotel restaurants. In addition to closures on **holidays** (see box below), Dominica often shuts down during lively festivals, the biggest of which, **Carnival**, takes place during the last two weeks of Lent, with calypso performances, costumed street dancing to lapo kabwit (goat-skin drum) bands, beauty pageants and such. The first week of June is the **Dive Fest**, with waterfront parties and cruises, while October showcases the three-day **Creole Music Festival**, a jamboree of Caribbean rock, African soukous and Louisiana zydeco. One of the biggest parties around happens the week prior to **Independence Day** (Nov 3), with colourful celebrations and traditional creole food and music.

Phones and post

There are public **telephones** at every square and many street corners, many of which

Public holidays

January 1 New Year's Day
First Monday in March Carnival Monday
March/April Good Friday, Easter Monday
May 1 May Day
Eighth Monday after Easter Whit Monday
First Monday in August August Monday
November 3 Independence Day
November 4 Community Service Day
December 25 Christmas Day
December 26 Boxing Day

take coins; those that don't take **phone cards**, which you can buy from the post office, Cable & Wireless outlets and some convenience stores. For the best rates, call after 7pm. There are only a couple of places to check your **email** in Roseau (see p.588), with surprisingly reasonable rates.

The sluggish Dominican **postal** service is headquartered at the corner of Roseau's Hillsborough and Bay streets (Mon–Wed & Fri 8am–3pm, Thurs & Sat 8am–noon). Sending a postcard anywhere in the world costs EC$0.55 – add EC$0.35 for letters to North America and Europe and EC$0.65 for those to Australia, Africa and the Middle East.

The **country code** for Dominica is ☎767.

Language

The official language is **English**, supplemented by a French-based Creole.

History

In a rare imaginative lapse, Columbus simply named **Dominica** for the day he discovered it in 1493: Sunday. He didn't stick around long and, for over two centuries, interest in Dominica was virtually non-existent, so much so that a 1660 treaty between the British and French left it to the resident **Caribs**. The French rescinded the deal when they colonized Dominica in the 1720s, starting a near-century-long tug-of-war with the British, who finally trumped them in 1805. Even so, French influence has remained strong, abetted by Dominica's position between **Martinique** and **Guadeloupe**.

Little of note happened in the ensuing century, until Dominica received its **independence** in 1978, introducing a period of political instability that continues to this day. The island's first prime minister, Patrick John, was forced to resign in 1979 after making a questionable land deal with US developers. That same year, **Hurricane David** devastated much of the island's meagre infrastructure, and rebuilding was left to John's successor, Eugenia Charles, the Caribbean's **first woman prime minister**, who did so while surviving two coups against her. Subsequent leadership has been dogged by embezzlement and corruption charges, and though a beloved politician, Roosevelt "Rosie" Douglas, was elected prime minister in 2000, his sudden death just eight months later left the country under a coalition government, one that has inspired frequent political protests.

Roseau

The only trace of modernity in Dominica's capital, **ROSEAU** (pronounced rose-oh), is its lengthy, tidy waterfront promenade, **Bay Front**. Otherwise, the compact town is a colourful assortment of ramshackle West Indian **colonial houses** with louvred windows, intricate fretwork, and sagging second-floor balconies held up over narrow streets by stilts. Despite the town's obvious poverty, it's a remarkably atmospheric place to stomp about: the roads get narrower as you head in from the harbourside area, passing covered **markets** and distinctive **cornerhouses**.

Arrival, information and getting around

Flights touch down at either **Canefield Airport**, just outside Roseau, or **Melville Airport**, much farther away on the northeast coast. Taxi rates from Canefield Airport to Roseau are fixed at EC$20. You can also walk out to the main road and flag down a minibus that will cost you about EC$2 to go the two miles to the town centre. Getting into the capital from Melville Airport is much more expensive: your best bet is to share a taxi (EC$42 per person) since doing it alone costs EC$130, and what bus service exists is unreliable at best.

Ferries arrive at the northern edge of Roseau, within walking distance of most guesthouses and hotels. If you're staying in the Castle Comfort area, a mile south of Roseau, grabbing a taxi or a bus (EC$1) are inexpensive options.

Both the airports and the ferry docks have modest **information** counters (daily 6.30am–6pm); the main island **tourist office** is in Roseau, on the Bay Front (Mon–Fri 8am–4pm, Sat 9am–2pm; ⓣ767/448-2401). All have detailed island **maps**.

Accommodation

Aside from a couple of snazzy options near the Bay Front, most of Roseau's **accommodation** is in low-key guesthouses. The Castle Comfort area, one mile south, has a handful of modern waterfront hotels that cater largely to divers, but there's no town centre whatsoever.

Roseau

Continental Inn 37 Independence St ⓣ767/448-2214 or 2215, ⓕ448-7022, ⓔcontinental@cwdom.dm. A good budget option with a communal balcony and a night security guard; the nine basic rooms have fans and cable TV (make sure yours actually works); some have private bath. ❷

Fort Young Victoria Street ⓣ767/448-5000 or 1-800/766-6016, ⓕ448-8065, ⓦwww.fortyounghotel.com. An attractive waterfront hotel incorporating the walls of the eighteenth-century fort, and offering cushy doubles, a seaside pool and jacuzzis. ❹

Garraway 1 Dame Eugenia Charles Blvd ⓣ767/449-8800, ⓕ449-8807, ⓦwww.garrawayhotel.com. A glossy option with 31 commodious doubles, picture windows overlooking the sea or the town, but no balconies. ❺

Ma Bass Central Guesthouse 44 Fields Lane ⓣ767/448-2999. An appealing guesthouse with eight spotless fan-only rooms, shared or private bath, and a shared balcony with pleasant views. US$35–50.

Sutton Place 25 Old St ⓣ767/449-8700 or 4313,

Ⓕ448-3045, Ⓦwww.delphis.dm/sutton. Recommended eight-room boutique hotel with appealing touches like wrought-iron gates, antique-furnished rooms trimmed with damask and chintz flounces, and a courtyard. ❹

Vena's Guesthouse 48 Cork St Ⓣ767/448-3286 or 449-2001, Ⓕ448-0539. Known as the birthplace of author Jean Rhys, the rooms here are dim, basic affairs with ceiling fans and mostly shared bath. ❷

Castle Comfort

Anchorage Ⓣ767/448-2638, Ⓕ448-5680, Ⓦwww.anchoragehotel.dm. A motel-style option with 32 large, well-equipped doubles and quads; the superior rooms have ocean views and some have balconies. ❹

Castle Comfort Lodge Ⓣ767/448-2188, Ⓕ448-6088, Ⓦwww.castlecomfortdivelodge.com. The place to stay if you plan to spend most of your Dominican vacation underwater. Its fifteen modest air-conditioned rooms are priced by the number of dives per stay. There's a hot tub in the garden for post-diving relaxation; breakfast, dinner and kayak use are included in rates. ❻

Sea World Guesthouse Ⓣ767/448-5068, Ⓕ448-5168. Eight clean rooms with fan, TV and telephone in a cheery yellow building with a ground-floor grocery store. ❷

The Town

The best place to start your explorations is the engaging **Dominica Museum** on the Bay Front (Mon–Fri 9am–4pm, Sat 9am–noon; EC$2), where you can trace the island's history and culture through Amerindian artefacts, a full-scale replica of a thatched Carib house, and King George III's silver mace, given to Dominica in 1770.

In the cobblestoned square behind the museum, and filling the alleyway alongside, is the **Old Market**, formerly the site of the island's slave market, now filled with vendors selling handicrafts. (Fresh produce is sold at the **New Market**, at the end of Mary E. Charles Boulevard past the ferry docks.)

The rest of Roseau's noteworthy sights lie to the southeast and northeast of the square. Those in the southeast are located around the *Fort Young Hotel* (see opposite). Due south from the hotel on Victoria Street is the 1905 **Free Library**, paid for, oddly enough, by American philanthropist Andrew Carnegie. Across from the library sits the **New Parliament Building**, a whitewashed two-storey mansion surrounded by landscaped grounds (closed to the public).

Alternatively, heading northeast on Church Street away from the Old Market and taking a left turn onto Virgin Lane leads to the colourful **Methodist Church**, and the staid Gothic **Roman Catholic Church**, worth a quick look if you're passing by.

Past the churches, a right turn on Queen Mary Street leads to the entrance to the fanciful forty-acre **Botanical Gardens** (daily 6am–10pm; free), below Morne Bruce hill, home to a variety of local flora, as well as an old yellow school bus crushed by a massive baobab commemorating Hurricane David's destructive powers. A few steps away, behind a parrot aviary, a fifteen-minute trail ascends **Morne Bruce** for stellar summit views.

Eating, drinking and nightlife

Dining out in Roseau is a casual affair, with meals primarily consisting of hearty local dishes served in cosy rather than classy surroundings. What **nightlife** exists is moderately dressier.

Balas Bar and Lounge *Fort Young Hotel*, Victoria Street. This hotel bar backed by the fort's original wall offers a lively cocktail hour on Friday nights from 6pm to 8pm.

Cartwheel Café Dame Eugenia Charles Blvd. Light, inexpensive tropical breakfasts and flavourful curry lunch fare in a handsome stone house on the waterfront.

Cornerhouse 6 King George V St. Atmospheric café on a second-floor verandah with comfy indoor sofas, a small book exchange, and internet access for EC$3/15min. The menu has a range of sandwiches and creole specials, and there's a popular quiz night on Wednesday (7–10pm).

La Robe Creole 3 Victoria St. An intimate masonry-walled pub with an extensive wine list and good, moderately priced creole dishes like chicken columbo and spicy seafood. Downstairs is *Mousehole*, a takeout joint offering inexpensive rotis, meat pies, sandwiches and pastries.

Sutton Grill *Sutton Place Hotel*, 25 Old St ⓣ767/449-8700. One of Dominica's few expensive restaurants does grilled chicken and tuna filet sandwiches at lunch, and juicy steak for dinner, in an outdoor courtyard. On Wednesday night, there's live music at *The Cellar* bar downstairs.

World of Food 48 Cork St. Popular, casual eatery in the courtyard of *Vena's Guesthouse* (see p.587), good for cheap sandwiches, fish dishes and dessert. One of the only places you'll find open on Sundays.

Listings

Airlines American Airlines (ⓣ767/445-7204 or 7477); Air Guadeloupe (ⓣ767/448-2181); EC Express (ⓣ1-800/523-5585); LIAT (ⓣ767/448-2421 or 2422).

Banks Royal Bank, Bay Front; Scotiabank, 28 Hillsborough.

Car rental Budget, Canefield Airport (ⓣ767/449-2080, ⓕ449-2694, ⓦwww.delphis.dm/budget); Best Deal, 15 Hanover St (ⓣ767/449-9204, ⓕ449-9207, ⓦwww.bestdeal-rent-a-car.com); Courtesy, 10 Winston Lane (ⓣ767/448-7763, ⓕ448-7733, ⓦwww.delphis.dm/courtesycarrental); Valley Rent-a-Car, Goodwill Road (ⓣ767/448-3233, ⓕ448-6009, ⓦwww.valleycarrentals.com).

Dialling codes The island prefix is ⓣ767. For directory assistance once there, dial ⓣ411.

Diving Anchorage Dive Centre (ⓣ767/448-2638, ⓕ448-5650, ⓦwww.anchoragehotel.dm); Dive Castaways (ⓣ767/449-7812 or 1-888/Castaways, ⓕ767/449-6246, ⓦwww.divecastaways.dm); Dive Dominica (ⓣ767/448-2188 or 1-888/262-6611, ⓕ767/448-6088, ⓦwww.divedominica.com); East Carib Dive (ⓣ & ⓕ767/449-6575 or 1-800/867-4764); Nature Island Dive (ⓣ767/449-8181, ⓕ449-8182, ⓦwww.natureislanddive.dm).

Emergencies ⓣ999

Internet Cable & Wireless, corner Hanover Street and Long Lane (Mon–Fri 8am–7pm, Sun 8am–4pm; EC$5/30min); *Cornerhouse Café*, 6 King George V St (closed Sun; EC$7/30min).

Sailing Arica (ⓣ767/440-0777 or 245-3418, ⓔarica66@hotmail.com), does three-hour sails to the southwestern coast, with snorkelling at Champagne and some whale-watching in season.

Taxis ⓣ767/449-8533 or ⓣ235-8648.

Tours Dominica Tours (ⓣ767/448-0990, ⓕ448-0989, ⓦwww.dominicatours.com); Ras Tours (ⓣ767/448-0412, ⓦwww.delphis.dm/ras); Whitchurch Tours (ⓣ767/448-2181, ⓕ448-5787, ⓦwww.whitchurch.com).

Whale-watching Anchorage Dive Centre (ⓣ767/448-2638, ⓕ448-5650, ⓦwww.anchoragehotel.dm); Nature Island Dive (ⓣ767/449-8181, ⓕ449-8182, ⓦwww.natureislanddive.dm).

Southward to Scotts Head

Heading south from Roseau, the coastal road winds past green hillsides on the way to the pretty fishing village of **SOUFRIÈRE**. The main attraction here is **Champagne Beach**, named for the bubbles in the offshore waters, created by hot springs in the depths of nearby **Soufrière Bay**, a protected marine park. The bay itself has a calm cove, good snorkelling, and you can rent diving, kayaking and snorkelling gear on the village outskirts at top-quality Nature Island Dive (ⓣ767/449-8181, ⓕ449-8182, ⓦwww.natureislanddive.dm). You can check out the source of the hot springs one mile inland from Soufrière, at **Sulphur Springs** (daily 9am–5pm; EC$2).

Beyond Soufrière, an unpaved road curves around the bay to delightful **SCOTTS HEAD**, a village of brightly painted tin shacks and equally colourful fishing boats moored below a teardrop-shaped peninsula. A stroll to the tip of the headland reveals vestiges of **Fort Cachacrou**, a defence post dating from the early 1700s, and awesome coastal views. The surrounding waters shelter Dominica's best **diving** (see box opposite), and are visited by migrating **whales** from November through April, often visible from land.

Diving

Of Dominica's over forty **dive sites**, the most impressive are found around **Scotts Head**, where submerged volcanic craters are covered with seafans and busy with schools of fish and lobster. Seahorse sightings are common at nearby **Soufrière**, while squid and stoplight parrotfish swim around **Champagne Reef**, site of a sub-aquatic hot spring.

The best diving sites northward on the Caribbean coast are around **Cabrits National Park** where reefs drop off to sandy bottoms over 100ft below the surface. Nearby **Douglas Point** has three sites worth exploring, including a coral-and-sponge-covered canyon and a 50ft wall with ample lobster, barracuda and mackerels. For **wreck** diving, Pringles Bay near Canefield Airport holds the remains of a tug and barge.

Back in the village, fresh bread is sold from porch-side baskets, and coffee and hard drinks poured at roadside shacks – that's pretty much the only **food** around apart from the expensive waterfront *Sundowner Café*, which cooks up fresh fish, lobster and crab, and mixes a potent rum punch. The café's owners run a small **hotel**, opposite, *Herche's Place* (Ⓣ767/448-7749, Ⓦwww.delphis.dm/herches; ④), whose clean rooms come with fan and TV. The only other lodging nearby is the exquisite *Petit Coulibri* (Ⓣ767/Ⓣ446-3150, Ⓦwww.delphis.dm/petit; ⑧); its secluded, upscale cottages have fabulous ocean views and are set to reopen in 2003 after renovations.

15.2

Morne Trois Pitons National Park

Dominica's best hiking trails are found in the magnificent, 16,000-acre **MORNE TROIS PITONS NATIONAL PARK**, which spreads over the island's southern region and rises to the 4550ft **Morne Trois Pitons**. Packed with primordial rainforest and sparse elfin woodland, and broken up by volcanic fumeroles and piping hot springs, the UNESCO World Heritage Site is an astonishing wilderness, likely to surpass any you'll find in the Caribbean.

Hikes run from the easy five- to ten-minute walks to beautiful **Emerald Pool** and stunning **Trafalgar Falls**, to the more arduous treks to **Freshwater** and **Boeri lakes**. The latter two start from the town of **Laudat**, 3.5 miles northeast of Roseau, also the location of the trailhead to **Boiling Lake**, a fascinating geological wonder buried deep inside the forest.

Around Laudat

The park's major hikes begin at **LAUDAT**, a village 1970ft above sea level with stupendous views of the undulating countryside (for details on how to get here, see opposite). The trail to one of Dominica's tallest waterfalls, the refreshing 275ft **Middleham Falls**, begins just south of town off the road into Laudat, and is a straightforward 45-minute walk through yanga palms, wild anthurium and leafy bromeliads. Thirty minutes past the falls lies **Tou Santi**, a collapsed lava tube emitting warm, smelly gases, and whose crevices shelter bats and the occasional boa constrictor.

At the entrance to Laudat proper, a well-marked and groomed path heads off to the largest of Dominica's four lakes, **Freshwater Lake**, 2500ft above sea level at the end of a gradual 2.5-mile trail north of the town centre. There's not much to see here, aside from sulphurous jets that leave rust marks on nearby rocks and greenery; more interesting is **Boeri Lake**, a crater lake enclosed by jagged boulders, 1.25 miles further along the same trail.

Park practicalities

Trail **maps** are available (EC$0.50–1) at the **Forestry Division** offices in Roseau's Botanical Gardens (☎767/448-2401, ext 417; see p.587). Of all the treks, only those for Boiling Lake and parts of Trafalgar Falls definitely require a **guide**; conveniently, all of Dominica's guesthouses can arrange one as part of your package. Otherwise, unaffiliated guides charge EC$20–50 depending on the hike's length and difficulty. You'll find these guides hanging out at the trailheads, where **park fees** must be paid (individual hikes EC$2, day-pass EC$5, multiple weeklong access EC$10). All of the trails can be done in a day: the longest, the hike to Boiling Lake (see opposite), is a seven-hour round-trip affair. In all cases, bring sturdy shoes and raingear; for longer hikes, make sure you have enough water and food.

At Laudat's eastern outskirts, an unsightly centipede-like contraption funnels a forceful mountain current into the island's main hydroelectric plant. Before reaching the plant, the water rushes below the unusual **Titou Gorge**, a dark passageway sheltered by solidified lava formations, about ten minutes' walk from the plant alongside the centipede. If the current isn't too rough, you can swim beneath the formations to a small waterfall at the back; if you see brown water sputtering in the access pool it means that the current is strong and you should not go in. You can warm up afterwards by leaning against a hot spring that feeds the pool.

Invigorating swimming aside, Titou Gorge is also visited as the last stop before the trailhead to Dominica's ultimate hike, a full-day outing to **Boiling Lake**, an eerie 207ft-wide cauldron of bubbling greyish-blue water shrouded in vaporous cloud. Thought to be a flooded fumerole through which gases escape from molten lava below, Boiling Lake is the second largest of its kind in the world. The hike takes in vistas of canopied Chatannyé and Bwa Bandé trees, rainbow-coloured hot springs, and the petrified **Valley of Desolation** – a richly forested area that was reduced to a moonscape of mosses and lichens after an 1880 volcanic eruption. The six-mile, seven-hour round-trip should only be attempted by experienced hikers and with the help of a guide.

Practicalities

The main **guesthouse** is the very accommodating *Roxy's Mountain Lodge* (Ⓣ & Ⓕ767/448-4845, Ⓦwww.delphis.dm/eiroxys; ❸), where spacious doubles feature attractive woodwork. Its small **restaurant** packs hearty picnic lunches and serves organic creole cuisine at night.

To reach Laudat, take King George V Street 2.5 miles inland from Roseau, until you reach a fork with signs pointing left. From here the road has brutally tight hairpin turns, some potholes and no guardrails – honk to signal your presence. There is also a sporadic **bus** (EC$3) which departs across from the Botanical Gardens on Trafalgar Road, every two hours after 6.30am; buses leave Laudat for the return trip about 45 minutes later. **Taxis** cost EC$70.

Trafalgar Falls

At the park's southwestern edges, the twin waterfalls known as **Trafalgar Falls** crash down a sheer 200ft rockface. The upper falls flow from the roiling currents at Titou Gorge (see above) while the lower are fed by the Trois Pitons River, which itself originates in the Boiling Lake region (see above). The falls are easily accessible along a short trail, shaded by flowering bowers and canopied trees, that starts from *Papillote Wilderness Retreat* (see below). While most visitors are content to enjoy the falls from a raised viewing platform at the end of an easy walk, the more adventurous can forge ahead, with the help of a guide, down to the lower falls' base for a dip in the sizeable pool.

You can **stay** near the falls at the upscale *Papillote Wilderness Retreat* (Ⓣ767/448-2287, Ⓕ448-2285, Ⓦwww.papillote.dm; ❹), a lovely inn with eight simply decorated doubles and a botanical garden with hot spa pools that work wonders on sore muscles. Nearby, the bohemian *Cocoa Cottages* (Ⓣ767/448-0412, Ⓦwww.delphis.dm/ras; ❹) has cheerful hammock-strung and mosquito-netted rooms, and intimate dining and living areas.

The terrific *River Rock Café* below the falls serves local **food** like mountain chicken on a splendid terrace overlooking the rainforest. Lunch is served à la carte, but dinner must be ordered in advance. The *Papillote Wilderness Retreat* (see above; dinner reservations required) also serves divine flying fish, tuna, prawns and chicken dishes, along with fresh juices, on an open-air terrace.

To reach the falls **by car**, take the road heading east from Roseau, taking a right fork 2.5 miles inland and following the signs to the village of Trafalgar. The trailhead is on the right, about a mile onwards, facing the *Papillote Wilderness Retreat* (see above). **Buses** are fairly regular; look for ones marked "Trafalgar" at the stop facing the Botanical Gardens on Trafalgar Road (EC$2.50). **Taxis** from Roseau cost EC$50.

Emerald Pool

Dominica's most-visited natural wonder, the deep **Emerald Pool** at the base of a 40ft waterfall, is midway between Canefield and Castle Bruce and reached by an easy five-minute walk along a well-maintained jungly pathway whose paved sections date from its original use as a Carib trail. The pool itself is a wonderful spot for a swim, though it can get overly crowded on Tuesdays with cruise-ship passengers.

The Emerald Pool is a 45-minute drive northeast of Canefield Airport along a steep road with hairpin turns. You can also hop aboard one of the frequent **buses** beside Roseau's New Market (EC$2.50). **Taxis** from Roseau cost EC$50.

15.3

The rest of the island

Dotted with impoverished fishing villages and graced with a couple of hiking trails around the island's highest peak, rocky northern Dominica isn't nearly as compelling as the rest of the island and needn't be a priority if you're on a short visit. While the Caribbean coast has some decent black-sand **beaches** around the towns of **Mero** and **Portsmouth**, they're secondary to the north's main points of interest. The extensive ruins of Fort Shirley in **Cabrits National Park**, and the Caribbean's only modern-day Carib homeland, the Atlantic-facing **Carib Territory**, can both be visited as a daytrip from Roseau.

North to Portsmouth

North of Roseau, the coastal road passes the Layou River, then climbs through **St Joseph**, a rickety fishing hamlet perched on extremely steep roads, before hitting the village of **Mero**. There's little of interest here, save for the black-sand beach, where there's good **snorkelling** to be found in front of *Castaways Beach Hotel*. Heading inland immediately north of Mero you'll arrive at Dominica's finest rum distillery, **Macoucherie** (Mon–Fri 7am–3pm), which produces rum from sugarcane grown on its estate.

Still further up the coast is the **Northern Forest Reserve**, a 22,000-acre parkland and home to the island's highest peak, the 4747ft **Morne Diablotin**. Despite the reserve's gargantuan size, only two **hiking** trails have been created here, both of which begin four miles inland along a well-signposted access road hedged by banana and pineapple plantations. The easier **Syndicate Nature Trail** is a straightforward 1.6km loop past a couple of **parrot**-viewing platforms; two endangered species – the imperial (or Sisserou) parrot and the red-necked parrot make their home here, and sightings often occur during early morning and late afternoon. The second of the hikes, a rugged day-long outing to the summit of Morne Diablotin, should only be attempted with a guide, which can be arranged through your hotel for about EC$50.

Portsmouth

Dominica's second largest town, down-at-the-heels **PORTSMOUTH**, has a picturesque location along Prince Rupert's Bay but functions mostly as a university centre. Originally envisioned as the island's capital, plans went awry when the swampy, mosquito-infested environs couldn't be tamed. While there's not much to keep you in town, the **Indian River** on the southern outskirts is worth a visit for the boat trips upriver through the marshy backwaters that stymied developers. Sightings of blue herons and crabs are common, and you'll stop for drinks at an alfresco jungle bar. Park Service representatives take visitors upstream from the river's mouth – the best guide goes by the name of Macaroni (1.5hr; EC$25).

Portsmouth's other noteworthy attraction is the twin-peaked **Cabrits National Park** (daily 9am–5pm; ECS$2), a grassy headland jutting out into the Caribbean Sea 1.5 miles north of town. While the park encompasses the island's largest swamp and the shoals and coral reefs of nearby **Douglas Bay** (see Diving box p.589), the main point of interest is the ruins of **Fort Shirley**. Built between 1770 and 1815 mostly by the British to defend against the French, and completed by the latter when they took control of the island, the fort became a mammoth complex that ultimately was abandoned in 1854. The ruins closest to the entrance have since been restored, while those further afield remain cloaked in jungle overgrowth. Stop by the visitor centre at the entrance for maps.

Practicalities

A mile south of Portsmouth, the decent **doubles** and bungalows at *Coconut Beach Hotel* (ⓣ767/445-5393 or 5415, ⓦwww.coconutbeachhotel.com; ❹) face a long golden beach. More upmarket is the beachfront *Picard Beach* (ⓣ767/445-5131, ⓕ445-5599, ⓦwww.delphis.dm/picard; ❻); its picturesque creole cottages come with verandahs and kitchenettes. Portsmouth's limited **dining** options include the pink-roofed *Cabin*, on Bay Road, the main drag, for fish and chips; *Big Mama's*, in the town centre two blocks inland, with fried chicken and curry shark; and the slightly more refined beachfront *Blue Bay* (ⓣ767/445-4985), for tasty mountain chicken and columbos.

Carib Territory

From Portsmouth, a road heads east across the island, passing towering royal palms and seemingly endless banana plantations, to the Atlantic coast where you'll encounter dramatic vistas of the ocean pounding against unusual **red rock** outcroppings, and roadsides bursting with red-hued hibiscus, poinsettia and malvina.

There's little to keep you in the string of villages clinging precariously to the rugged cliffs here, though they do offer some picture-postcard views before reaching **Bataka**, the northernmost village of the **CARIB TERRITORY**. This 3700-acre reserve is home to the only remaining tribe of Carib Indians in the Caribbean; a modern community, its traditions are nonetheless still evident in the intricate, handcrafted woodcarvings and baskets sold in huts along the 7.5-mile coastal road south of Bataka. The community's centre, the longhouse-shaped **Ste Marie of the Caribs Church**, overlooks the sea from **Salybia**, the main settlement, its dug-out canoe altar framed by colourful frescoes of Carib life. It's not obviously marked from town, though, so you're best to ask a local for directions.

Southward, at the village of **Sineku**, a sign points seaward to the serpentine **Escalier Tête Chien** (or "dog's head stairs"), a peculiar lava formation that resembles steps climbing out of the sea. Despite its name, according to Carib legend the lava outcrop is thought to be the embodiment of a boa constrictor.

The friendly *Carib Territory Guesthouse* at Crayfish River (ⓣ767/445-7255, ⓦwww.delphis.dm/ctgh; ❷) has basic **doubles** and a communal verandah with ocean views and can arrange diving, snorkelling and birdwatching tours.

△ Gommier tree canoe, Carib Territory

16

St Lucia

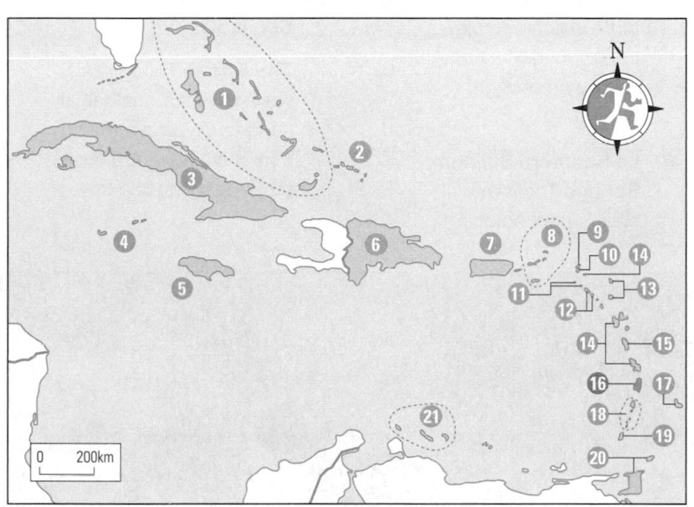

St Lucia Highlights

* **Eastern Nature Trail** Hike along St Lucia's wild and underexplored Atlantic coast. See p.629

* **Marine Turtle Watch, Grande Anse** Stay up all night on an eco-friendly turtle watch and view these wonderful creatures by moonlight. See p.630

* **La Soufrière Sulphur Springs** The island's boiling pool holds a bizarre tourist appeal. See p.623

* **Jungle Biking, Anse Mamin** Take a top-notch mountain bike through acres of trails in a private rainforest, just minutes from Soufrière. See p.605

* **The Pitons** Though best viewed with a cocktail at sunset, St Lucia's magic peaks are a feast at any time. See p.623

Introduction and Basics

St Lucia more than lives up to the paradisal Caribbean stereotype: a glorious mix of honey sand beaches, translucent waters sheltering reefs swarming with tropical fish, lush interior rainforests, and a thriving culture that encompasses literature and theatre as well as music and dance. However, in contrast to other islands in the region, where the tourism infrastructure has been steadily expanding since the 1960s, St Lucia has only recently begun to attract visitors in any number. As a result, tourism has a much lower profile here, and this low-key feel is one of the island's biggest assets.

Despite the lack of hype, St Lucia's tourist facilities are top notch, and, unusually, cater to all budgets – you can stay at luxury hotels or inexpensive guesthouses, dine in world-class restaurants or at roadside kiosks, and shop in large duty-free malls or at open-air village markets. With little of the jaded hustle that can mar more established Caribbean destinations, St Lucia makes for a relaxed, informal and incredibly friendly place to visit.

Where to go

If it's **beaches** you prefer, then you'll probably head first to the tourism strongholds of the **northwest coast**, the "Golden Mile" of St Lucia's resorts towns. Hard to miss and worthwhile all the same is St Lucia's most famous sight – the monolithic twin peaks of the **Pitons** to the south. In the interior, the rainforest-smothered mountains of the **forest reserves** are strikingly beautiful and rich in flora and fauna, while the wild and windswept beach of Grande Anse on the east coast is where you'll catch the moving sight of **leatherback turtles** nesting in the sands.

When to go

For many visitors St Lucia's biggest attraction is its tropical climate. During **high season** (December to April), the island is pleasantly hot, with little rain and constant northeasterly trade winds keeping the nights cool. Temperatures rise even further during the **summer months**, which can also be wet: the rainy season lasts from June to October. The rainy months coincide with the **hurricane season**, which runs roughly from late August to October.

Getting there

In testament to the island's growing popularity as a holiday destination, international airlines have consistently increased their flight schedules from **North America** over the years. During the high season, flights are on a daily basis, with services only slightly reduced in the low season. Air Canada flies once a week from Toronto and US Airways now flies direct from Philadelphia to St Lucia; from JFK, Air Jamaica goes via Grenada or Antigua, BWIA via Port of Spain and AA via San Juan, and all have domestic connections; Jet Blue and United also fly to San Juan from JFK and Continental flies there from Washington – it's easy to pick up an American Eagle connecting flight from San Juan to St Lucia.

The great majority of British and Irish visitors to St Lucia arrive on a **direct charter flight** as part of a package holiday – and even if you plan to travel independently this is still the cheapest way to get here. Charters do have limitations, however, notably a fixed return date of one, two or a maximum three weeks. When it comes to direct **scheduled flights**, the choice is limited: Virgin flies once a week direct from London Gatwick and once via Antigua; BWIA departs twice weekly from London Heathrow; and BA has three flights a week via Antigua.

Visitors from **Australia and New Zealand** will need to take a flight to one of the main US gateway airports and pick up onward connections from there. Generally, the least expensive and most straightforward routes are via New York or Miami.

For phone numbers of airlines, see pp.12–18 and 36–37.

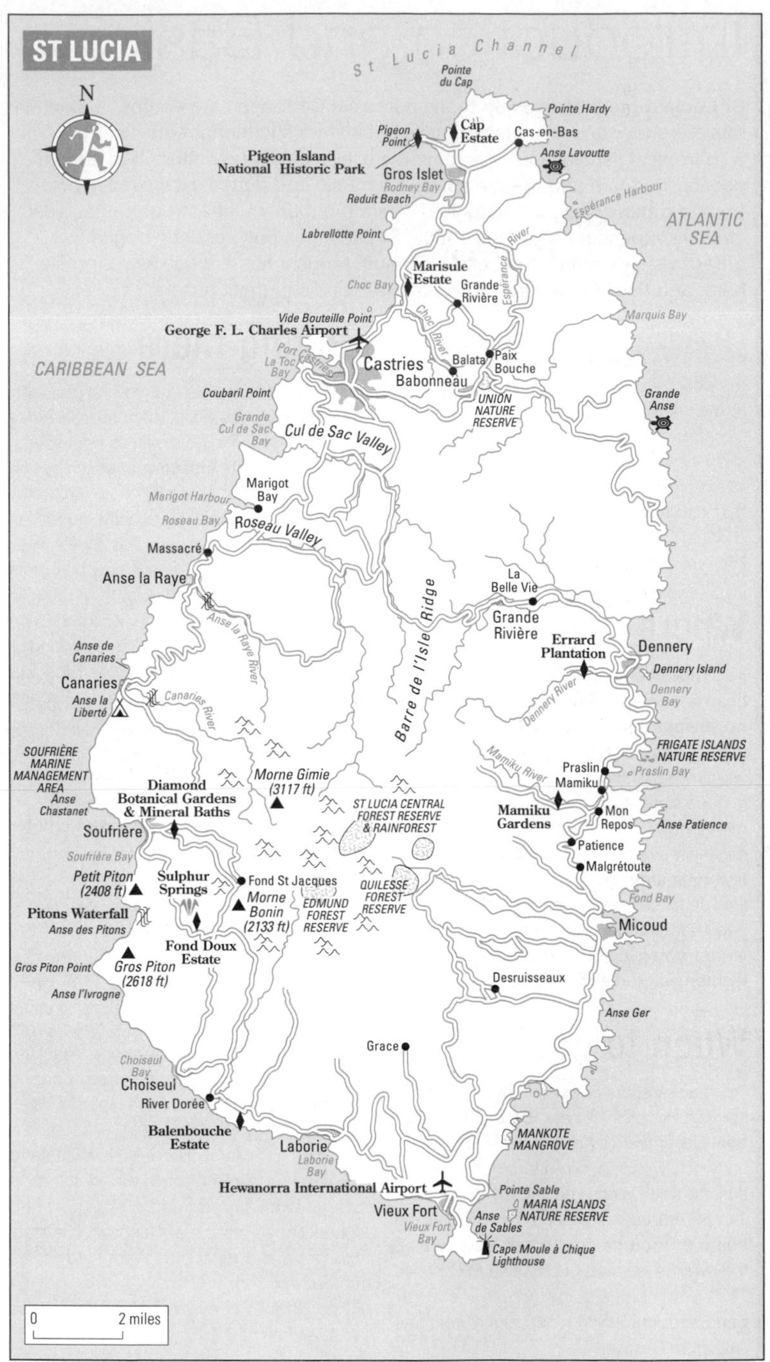
ST LUCIA
N
St Lucia Channel
Pointe du Cap
Pointe Hardy
Pigeon Point
Cap Estate
Cas-en-Bas
Anse Lavoutte
Pigeon Island National Historic Park
Gros Islet
Rodney Bay
Reduit Beach
Espérance Harbour
ATLANTIC SEA
Labrellotte Point
Esperance River
Marisule Estate
Choc Bay
Grande Rivière
Choc River
Vide Bouteille Point
Marquis Bay
George F. L. Charles Airport
Port Castries
La Toc Bay
CARIBBEAN SEA
Castries
Balata
Paix Bouche
Babonneau
Coubaril Point
UNION NATURE RESERVE
Grande Anse
Grande Cul de Sac Bay
Cul de Sac Valley
Marigot Bay
Marigot Harbour
Roseau Bay
Roseau Valley
Massacré
Anse la Raye
La Belle Vie
Anse la Raye River
Barre de l'Isle Ridge
Grande Rivière
Errard Plantation
Dennery
Dennery Island
Anse de Canaries
Canaries
Anse la Liberté
Canaries River
Dennery River
Dennery Bay
FRIGATE ISLANDS NATURE RESERVE
SOUFRIÈRE MARINE MANAGEMENT AREA
Anse Chastanet
Diamond Botanical Gardens & Mineral Baths
Morne Gimie (3117 ft)
Mamiku River
Praslin
Praslin Bay
Mamiku
ST LUCIA CENTRAL FOREST RESERVE & RAINFOREST
Mamiku Gardens
Mon Repos
Anse Patience
Soufrière
Soufrière Bay
Patience
Malgrétoute
Petit Piton (2408 ft)
Sulphur Springs
Fond St Jacques
Morne Bonin (2133 ft)
EDMUND FOREST RESERVE
QUILESSE FOREST RESERVE
Fond Bay
Pitons Waterfall
Anse des Pitons
Micoud
Fond Doux Estate
Gros Piton Point
Gros Piton (2618 ft)
Anse l'Ivrogne
Desruisseaux
Anse Ger
Grace
Choiseul Bay
Choiseul
River Dorée
Balenbouche Estate
MANKOTE MANGROVE
Laborie
Laborie Bay
Hewanorra International Airport
Pointe Sable
Vieux Fort
Anse de Sables
MARIA ISLANDS NATURE RESERVE
Vieux Fort Bay
Cape Moule à Chique Lighthouse
0 2 miles

Embassies and consulates

Office of the British High Commission, NIS Building, Waterfront, PO Box 227, Castries ⓣ758/452-2484 or 2485, ⓕ453-1543, ⓔbritish@candw.lc

Money and costs

St Lucia is not cheap, and you'll pay US and European prices for restaurants and accommodation. St Lucia's official currency is the **Eastern Caribbean dollar** (EC$), which trades against the US dollar at an official rate of EC$2.70 to US$1 for travellers' cheque exchanges, slightly less for cash conversions. In the case of hotels, car rental, restaurants and practically everything related to tourism, most **prices** in St Lucia are quoted in both EC and US dollars, and occasionally only in the latter. Note that ATM machines only dispense EC dollars.

Major **credit cards** such as Visa, American Express and MasterCard are widely accepted for payment. The island's Royal Bank of Canada **ATM**s accept Cirrus and Plus cards, as well as Visa and MasterCard. Cash machines are located on William Peter Boulevard in Castries, at the Rodney Bay Marina, and on New Dock Road in Vieux Fort. The Caribbean Banking Corporation ATMs at Micoud Street in downtown Castries and Gablewoods Mall, north of town, take the same cards. US dollar **travellers' cheques** are accepted by many businesses, but it's wise to always carry some cash with you, as taxi drivers, market stalls and many smaller restaurants or guesthouses won't accept credit cards or travellers' cheques.

Banks hours are Monday to Thursday 8am–3pm, and Friday 8am–5pm. The National Commercial Bank exchange bureau at Hewanorra airport in Vieux Fort has extended hours (Mon & Tues 12.30–9pm, Wed 4.30–9pm, Thurs 2–9pm, Fri 12.30–9pm, Sat 2.30–9pm, Sun 1–9pm), and the Royal Bank of Canada branch at the Rodney Bay Marina is open 8am–noon each Saturday. Banks always offer the most favourable **exchange rate**.

Taxes and tipping

Hotels in St Lucia will almost always add two extra charges to their bills that may not be included in quoted room rates: a 10 percent **service charge** and an 8 percent government **accommodation tax**. These can bring your bill up an alarming 18 percent – a hefty addition for a week's stay even at a medium-priced hotel – so it's well worth checking whether taxes are included in the price before you book. Restaurants often add a 10 percent **service charge** onto the bill as well, and cab drivers should be tipped the same percentage.

You must pay a EC$54 **departure tax** when leaving St Lucia by air, and an EC$20 tax if you depart by ferry.

Information and maps

The **St Lucia Tourist Board** maintains several offices abroad (see p.30), and it's worth contacting them to pick up general information and free maps before you leave. For the best **on-island information**, contact the main office of the St Lucia Tourist Board in the Sureline Building, just after the roundabout on your way north from Castries (PO Box 221, Castries, St Lucia, WI; ⓣ758/452-4094 or 5968, ⓕ453-1121, ⓦwww.stlucia.org). There are also **tourist board kiosks** at George F.L. Charles Airport (see p.608), the La Place Carenage and Pointe Seraphine (see p.611) shopping complexes in Castries, at Hewanorra airport (see p.625) in Vieux Fort, and at the waterfront in Soufrière (see p.622).

Getting around

How easy you'll find it to **get around** St Lucia depends very much on where you want to go. While the more populated parts of the island are well connected by buses, parts of the east and northwest coasts are only accessible to those with their own transport. If you're laid-back enough to cope with both waiting to be picked up and frequent stops along the route, travelling by **bus** is probably the most convenient and economical way to get around. **Taxis** are a more expensive alternative, though the ideal way to get around is, of course, to rent a **car**. If a car is beyond your budget, renting a **motorbike** is worth considering, though this isn't exactly the safest way of getting around. To drive a car or ride a motorbike on the island, visitors must purchase a temporary St Lucian **licence**. Valid for three months, these cost EC$54 (US$21) and are issued by rental companies, the immigration departments at the airports and any island police department on production of a valid licence (or an international permit) from your own country of origin. Remember that in St Lucia drivers stick to the **left side** of the road. In and around Castries, Soufrière and Marigot Bay, it's also possible to take advantage of the convenient **water-taxi** system, mostly used by tourists and especially handy for getting to nearby beaches.

By bus

Identifiable by an "H" on the licence plate, St Lucia's **buses** are small vans with customized windscreens emblazoned with colourful names such as "Tempt Me" or "Redemption". Though all of the island's buses are privately owned, the inexpensive **fares** are set by the government: you'll pay no more than EC$10 to travel between any two points on the island. From Castries, a ride to the north should cost EC$2.50, while a trip to Vieux Fort runs around EC$8.50. Schedules are less predictable, with most drivers waiting until the bus is full before setting off; still, as a general rule, services between major towns run every thirty to sixty minutes from about 6am until 10pm on weekdays, with an extended timetable on Fridays for the Gros Islet Jump-Up and a reduced timetable on Saturdays – practically no buses run on Sundays. Small cement pavilions serve as **bus stops**, but if you flag a bus down anywhere along a route, it will probably stop if it isn't jammed full.

By taxi

Taxis are also identifiable by an "H" on the licence plate and are in plentiful supply. You'll see them cruising for fares on the streets of the main towns, and at obvious locations such as airports and tourist spots like Pigeon Island and Reduit Beach. Though all taxis are unmetered, **fares** are expensive and also set by the government, and drivers are required to carry a rate sheet in their car. While most drivers stick to the already overblown set rates, it's always best to confirm the fare before getting in. Taxis also offer **guided tours** for around US$20 per hour (for as many as four people), or US$140 for a full day, but unlike standard fares, this rate is often negotiable.

By car and motorbike

Car rental **rates** start at US$45 per day for a compact, manual-shift vehicle without air conditioning, and go as high as US$90 for a luxury model. Jeeps and other 4WD vehicles, which you'll need to explore some parts of the island, range from US$65 to US$100. You'll generally pay less during low season, or if you rent for three or more days. While mileage is unlimited, rates don't include **petrol**, which at the time of writing costs around EC$6.75 per imperial gallon. Wayne's Motorcycle Centre, just north of Castries (ⓣ758/452-2059), is the island's only **motorbike** rental outlet.

Car rental companies

Avis Castries ⓣ758/452-4554, Hewanorra Airport ⓣ758/454-6325, George F.L. Charles Airport ⓣ758/452-2046; ⓔavisslu@candw.lc
Budget/Sunset Motors Castries ⓣ758/452-0233, Hewanorra Airport ⓣ758/454-5311; ⓦwww.budgetslucia.com
Cool Breeze Soufrière ⓣ758/459-7729 and four other airport locations
Courtesy Gros Islet ⓣ758/452-8140, ⓔcourtesycar@candw.lc
Guy's Gablewoods Mall, Castries ⓣ758/451-7147
Hertz Hewanorra Airport ⓣ758/454-9636, George F.L. Charles Airport ⓣ758/451-7351; ⓔhertz@candw.lc
Vacation and Corporate Car Rentals Castries ⓣ758/452-9404, ⓕ450-2272; ⓔvcrental@hotmail.com

Tours

Several local companies offer conventional **guided tours** of St Lucia's east coast and central mountains aboard 4WD trucks. Most are all-day, all-inclusive expeditions averaging a hefty US$90 per person, with stops at waterfalls, high mountain viewing areas and beaches; some involve rainforest hikes of up to three hours. For more information, contact Jungle Tours in Castries (Ⓣ758/450-0434, Ⓕ450-9154, Ⓦwww.jungletoursstlucia.com) or Sunlink Jeep Safaris in Rodney Bay (Ⓣ758/452-8232). A more adventurous option is the inland and coastal **guided walks** offered by the St Lucia National Trust (Ⓣ758/452-5005, Ⓦwww.slunatrust.org) and the Forest and Lands Department (Ⓣ758/450-2231 or 2078, Ⓦwww.slumaffe.org). Helicopter tours and airport transfers (Ⓣ758/453-6950, Ⓕ452-1553) are also available, costing around US$100 for a transfer from Vieux Fort to Vigie – not so bad when you consider the cost and time of a regular taxi – and from US$45 per person for a ten–minute jaunt round the north.

Accommodation

While thankfully not as all-inclusive-ridden as many Caribbean islands, tourist facilities on St Lucia have much improved over the last two decades, and **accommodation** runs the full range, from spa and sushi all-inclusives and medium-sized family hotels to inexpensive local bed and breakfasts and guesthouses and even a campsite. The majority of establishments are moderately sized and priced, but large resorts and luxury exclusionist locales are becoming increasingly common, causing some local contention and dismay. When booking accommodation, it's important to bear in mind that St Lucian hotels generally levy a total of 18 percent in **taxes** to the bill (see p.601); the prices quoted in this chapter are exclusive of that 18 percent tax.

Another accommodation option is renting a **villa**, available even in the most remote parts of the island. Rates often include maid and cooking services, rental cars and other amenities; count on spending US$700–4000 per week in high season. For rentals, contact Tropical Villas (PO Box 189, Castries Ⓣ758/452-8240, Ⓦwww.tropicalvillas.net) or Top O' The Morne (PO Box 376, Castries Ⓣ758/452-3603, Ⓕ453-1433).

Food and drink

Though St Lucia's **restaurant scene** is dominated by small, reasonably priced eateries with few pretensions, there are a few upmarket restaurants offering haute cuisine, and you're unlikely to be disappointed by them. The stalls in the Castries Central Market (see p.611) are excellent value, as are many of the local restaurants in Soufrière; the majority of St Lucia's restaurants, though, are clustered around the tourist areas. For a truly local experience, don't miss one of the island's weekend fish fries – Anse La Raye on Friday nights and Dennery on Saturdays are the most rewarding.

Like most of St Lucia's shops and businesses, many of the island's smaller restaurants are closed on Sundays, and opening hours may change during the off-season, with some restaurants closing for up to a month at a time. It's best to also call ahead for **reservations**, particularly in the high season – if you do so, some restaurants will even transport you to and from your hotel at no extra cost.

Phones and post

St Lucia's **phone system** is reliable. Public phone booths are located all around the island and take either **coins** (EC$1 or EC$0.25) or the **phone cards** available from Cable Wireless offices, post offices, pharmacies and convenience shops.

All major towns and villages have a **post office**; and the major ones in Anse La Raye, Castries, Dennery, Gros Islet, Micoud, Soufrière and Vieux Fort are open Monday through Friday 8.15am–4.30pm; sub-offices are open 1–5pm. The General Post Office on Bridge Street in Castries (Ⓣ758/452-5157)

> The **country code** for St Lucia is Ⓣ758.

is the island's largest and has a philatelic bureau. Sending postcards and packages to the US, Canada or Europe costs less than EC$1, but as they can take up to two weeks to reach their destination, you might want to send urgent items home via the **courier services** in Castries: FedEx are on Derek Walcott Square (ⓣ758/452-1320), DHL are on Manoel Street (ⓣ758/453-1538), and UPS on Bridge Street (ⓣ758/452-7211).

Entertainment, nightlife and festivals

Though St Lucia isn't exactly the **nightlife** capital of the Caribbean, there's plenty to do after dark. Many hotels and restaurants in the west coast resort areas offer some sort of **live music** or **dancing** most nights of the week, and between Castries and Cap Estate, and particularly at Rodney Bay, there are numerous bars and restaurants where you can have a drink or a meal while listening to anything from a traditional chak-chak group to the hotter licks of a reggae, calypso or steel-pan band. The best source of current entertainment **information** is local newspapers and the tourist publication *Tropical Traveller* (ⓦwww.tropicaltravellers.com).

In early or mid-May, the island plays host to the **St Lucia Jazz Festival** (ⓦwww.stluciajazz.org), which has attracted some of the jazz and R&B worlds' biggest names – including Herbie Hancock, Wynton Marsalis and George Benson. The four-day event takes place at several venues, the main ones being Pigeon Island, the Cultural Centre on the outskirts of Castries and Great House in Cap Estate. Some shows are free, but for most you'll need to pay an entrance fee (US$38–50), or you can buy a **pass** giving entry to all of the events for around US$230.

A round of dancing, street masquerading and general partying, St Lucia's July **Carnival** (called *Jounen Kweyol* in Patois) is one of the true showcases of the island's culture, with storytelling, folk dancing and traditional music afforded as much prominence as the more contemporary Carnival melee of sequinned bikinis and thumping soca music. Carnival **information** is available from the tourist board in St Lucia (ⓣ758/452-4094 or 5968, ⓕ453-1121, ⓦwww.stlucia.org), and from offices abroad (see p.30).

Sport

With miles of easily accessible sandy beaches, St Lucia is perfect for **watersports**. Larger resort hotels often have their own watersports facilities, usually **snorkelling**, **scuba diving**, **sea kayaking**, **windsurfing** and **sailing** on small, single-sail one- or two-person Sunfish boats. Some places also have their own **yachts**, often catamarans, for sunset and snorkelling excursions, as well as fishing trips. Except at all-inclusives, non-guests can usually use in-hotel facilities – for a fee, of course.

Diving

St Lucia's **diving** is not as highly regarded as the region's more pristine scuba environments, such as Saba or Bonaire. Visibility is generally fair, but rivers spilling into the ocean at places such as Soufrière and Vieux Fort bays can muddy the vistas. Still, many of the reefs – particularly in the south around the base of the Pitons – are excellent dive sites, and there are several submerged wrecks to explore. The island also offers up plenty of good certification programmes. If you're a serious enthusiast, it might be worth looking into packages offered by hotels such as *Anse Chastanet* (see p.758), which bundle flights, accommodation and a specified number of dives at ostensibly discounted rates.

Snorkelling

Snorkelling is particularly good around the island's southwestern fringes, where the Soufrière Marine Management Area (ⓣ758/459-5500, ⓦwww.smma.org.lc) hugs the shoreline for nearly seven miles. The reefs here are pristine by most standards, and the area is set aside as a protected area for fishing and recreational use; the nominal dive fee (US$4 per day or US$12 per year) goes toward the park's upkeep.

Watersports operators

Buddies Scuba Vigie Marina, Castries ⓣ758/452-5288 or 450-8406. Scuba and snorkelling.
Club Mistral Anse de Sable, Vieux Fort ⓣ49/881-909601-1 in Germany, ⓦwww.club–mistral.com. Windsurfing.
Dive Fair Helen Choc Bay, Vigie Marina and Anse Cochon ⓣ758/451-7716 or 451-7710, ⓦwww.divefairhelen.com. Scuba.
Dolphin Divers Rodney Bay ⓣ758/452-9485. Scuba and snorkelling.
Frog's Diving *The Still Plantation and Beach Resort*, Soufrière ⓣ758/450-8831, ⓦwww.frogsdiving.com; *Windjammer Landing*, Labrellotte Bay ⓣ758/452-0913. Scuba, snorkelling, water-skiing, banana boat rides, windsurfing, kayaking and sailing.
Marigot Dive Resort Marigot Bay ⓣ758/451-4974, ⓦwww.marigotdiveresort.com. Scuba, sailing, windsurfing, snorkelling, kayaking.
Rosemond Trench Divers Marigot Bay ⓣ758/451-4761. Scuba, snorkelling, paddle-boating and Sunfish sailing boats.
Scuba St Lucia *Anse Chastanet*, Soufrière ⓣ758/459-7755, ⓦwww.scubastlucia.com. Scuba and snorkelling.

Boat trips

Gliding up and down St Lucia's accessible and calm west coast, **sightseeing** and **party boats** (usually customized catamarans) offer an alternative way to see the bays and interior mountain peaks. Most excursions include stops for snorkelling and swimming, or a visit to a coastal village (probably Soufrière or Marigot Bay) as well as lunch and drinks. Just bear in mind that as the boats are often crowded with rowdy revellers taking advantage of the free-flowing rum, the trip may not be the quiet cruise you might anticipate; if you're looking for a more sedate excursion, say so when you book. One of the best **cruise operators** is Endless Summer Cruises (ⓣ758/450-8651), which runs full- and half-day tours out of Rodney Bay to Soufrière's sulphur springs and Diamond Falls, or to the Pitons, with stops at beaches around Anse Cochon for swimming and snorkelling, as well as sightseeing at Marigot Bay.

Jungle biking

Jungle biking is one of St Lucia's most recent adventure sports, accessible only by boat from the beach at Anse Chastanet. Set in an old sugar plantation just inland from Anse Mamin, Bike St Lucia (ⓣ758/459-7755, ⓦwww.bikestlucia.com) has cut trails suitable for all abilities, and you can expect to see anything from eighteenth century colonial ruins and swimming holes to hundreds of fruit trees along your chosen trail.

Hiking

Hiking through St Lucia's central rainforests and preserves is the best way to experience the island's fabulously beautiful **interior**; despite being laced by walkable trails, the mountains often go unexplored by beach devotees. You don't necessarily need guides for many of the hikes (though hiring one will help to identify local flora and fauna), but you do need advance permission and an inexpensive permit from the **Forestry and Lands Department** to enter protected areas such as the Edmund Forest Reserve and the Barre de L'Isle area (see p.619 for more information).

Local culture and language

In typical Caribbean fashion, the heart and soul of St Lucian **culture** is a syncretic amalgamation of the customs, languages, religions and societal norms of the island's French and British colonizers, and of the Africans that they brought with them. Today's population of 158,000 is of predominantly African origin, and some ninety percent of St Lucians are Roman Catholic, with the remainder made up of Protestant, Anglican and a small number of Rastafarian believers. However, though Christian hymns are sung lustily enough to raise the church roofs each Sunday, St Lucia is also a society in which esoteric African traditions of magic and spiritualism survive. Carnival is the best example of this fusion of Christianity and ancient belief: one of the stock characters of costume parades is the moko jumbie, a wildly attired figure on stilts representing the spirit world.

Language is another aspect of St Lucian culture that shows African influence. Though African languages were suppressed as soon as slaves arrived on the island, French planters still needed to communicate with their workers, and gradually, the common language of **St Lucian Creole** (*Kweyol*) – also called Patois, although this is seen as somewhat derogatory – evolved, heavily laced with French as well as African and English grammar and vocabulary. Though St Lucia's official language is **English**, Creole is spoken widely throughout the island, on the radio, in parliament, and despite the fact that it has only recently appeared in written form, there is already a St Lucian Creole translation of the Bible.

History

Unlike most other Caribbean islands, the European "**discovery**" of St Lucia is an ambiguous matter, though it's most likely that the first European to sight the island was a **Spaniard**. Juan de la Cosa had sailed with Christopher Columbus on his first two voyages, and during an independent expedition of 1504, he sighted St Lucia and named it El Falcón on the maps he prepared. In 1511, the island appeared on a Spanish Royal Cedula of Population as St Lucia, and was included on a Vatican map of 1520.

As they did with many other islands in the region, the Spanish claimed St Lucia *in absentia* soon after de la Cosa's visit, but their attempts to establish settlements were swiftly repelled by the native Caribs, and they made no great effort to colonize the island. In 1600, the **Dutch** made an abortive attempt to develop St Lucia, and the next Europeans to arrive did so by accident. In 1605, a **British** ship called the *Olive Branch* was blown off course on its way to Guyana, and its 67 settlers were forced to land on the island's south coast. Soon after negotiating with the Caribs for shelter, the settlers were attacked. A prolonged battle followed, and five weeks later the nineteen surviving settlers escaped in Carib canoes. Similar clashes between Caribs and small bands of settlers continued for another dozen years, during which time the **French** were busy building up their Caribbean presence, and were able to claim St Lucia alongside several neighbouring islands with little opposition.

In 1651, St Lucia was **sold** to Governor du Parquet of neighbouring Martinique, who built a bastion on the peninsula to the north of Castries now called Vigie. The French continued to battle with the Caribs until a **peace agreement** was signed in 1660. Over the next 150 years, prolonged and bloody Anglo-French **hostilities** saw the "Helen of the West Indies" change hands fourteen times. In spite of the fighting, the French made the first concerted efforts to turn St Lucia into a money-making colony, settling along the fertile southeast coast and establishing a **town** that they called Soufrière in 1743, and officially designating it the capital in 1746. By 1765, they had introduced **sugarcane**, setting up vast plantations and bringing in **slaves** from West Africa to tend the crops that they hoped would earn them huge profits.

In retaliation for French support of the fledgling colonies in America's war of independence, the British initiated a prolonged attack against the French in 1778. After four years of fighting, Britain's **Admiral George Rodney** had established a bastion and a regional base for British ships at Pigeon Island, and from here he launched an attack on French naval forces stationed at the nearby Les Saintes archipelago off the coast of Guadeloupe. The French navy was decimated, and British victory in what became known as the **Battle of the Saints** signified that French domination of the Caribbean was soon to end.

However, French control of St Lucia was not immediately relinquished. The 1783 Treaty of Paris put St Lucia into French hands once again, and during the 1789-99 French Revolution all the towns were renamed, French nobles were executed by guillotine, and, in a radical move of solidarity, the Republicans **freed the slaves**. Sensing that the British would soon regain power, the Africans justly feared for their new-found freedom. While many stayed on the plantations, others formed a loosely knit freedom-fighting group known as the **Brigands**, who proceeded to launch attacks against the British, levelling plantations and terrorizing the island.

In 1814, the **Treaty of Paris** brought Anglo-French conflicts in the Caribbean to a long-overdue conclusion, with France ceding St Lucia to the British. Once the island was firmly established as a **crown colony**, St Lucian economics mirrored the pattern of slave-holding islands throughout the Caribbean. A brief period of prosperity followed the cessation of war, but this lasted only until the **abolition of slavery** in 1834. Though freed Africans were contracted to the plantations as indentured workers for a further four years, St Lucia's estates soon ceased to be profitable, and the economy crumbled.

Over the next several decades, the question of independence from Britain grew, and in 1958 St Lucia joined other British colonies in the **West Indies Federation**, a political grouping formed with the aim of winning self-rule. By the time St Lucia was granted full self-government in 1967, a two-party system had developed, with the conservative, business-friendly United Workers Party (UWP) consolidating support and vying for power with the more liberal St Lucia Labour Party (SLP). After years of lobbying, Britain finally acceded to the successive autonomy movements throughout the Caribbean and granted the new state of St Lucia **independence** on February 22, 1979. However, the island remains a Commonwealth country and a constitutional monarchy, with the British sovereign as the titular head of state, represented on the island by a governor general.

16.1

Castries and around

Home to some 60,000 people (more than a third of the island's total population), St Lucia's capital of **CASTRIES**, on the northwest coast, is a metaphor for contemporary West Indian urban culture: at times busy and congested, at times somnolent and peaceful, the town feels somewhat stuck between a centuries-old West Indian lifestyle and a desperate push to modernize. Though Castries is easy to navigate on foot, the town is not particularly blessed with museums, theatres or historical sights, and you'll find that it's primarily a place where people go to conduct business or do some shopping rather than take sightseeing trips.

Despite its contemporary feel, Castries retains a certain unaffected charm, due more to its setting than anything else. The town is wrapped around the deep harbour of **Port Castries**, where hundreds of cruise ships dock each year to unload tourists for a day of duty-free shopping at the city's malls. Spreading back from the harbour is **downtown** Castries, a dozen or so blocks of noisy streets, shops, bus stands and general congestion. North of downtown and across the harbour is **Vigie Peninsula**, a flat spit of partially reclaimed land that hosts the island's largest duty-free complex, as well as the small **George F.L. Charles Airport**, several hotels and waterfront restaurants.

The country's capital is surrounded by hills to the east and south: the southern Morne Fortune range once provided a natural defence for the island's various occupiers, and the remains of several **forts** and **batteries** scattered throughout the area are worth a quick look.

Arrival and information

St Lucia's regional airport lies just over half a mile from downtown Castries, the public transport hub for the island: several informal bus depots are scattered around town. Formerly known as Vigie Airport, Castries' small **George F.L. Charles Airport** (Ⓣ758/452-1156) on Vigie Peninsula mostly handles small aircraft arriving from neighbouring Caribbean islands and South America. There's a **tourist information** booth (Ⓣ758/452-2596) as well as a row of **car rental** kiosks inside, while just outside the arrival area is a **taxi** stand. If you've arrived from Guadeloupe, Dominica or Martinique via the high-speed **L'Express des Iles** ferry (see "Ferries", p.38), you'll disembark at the North Wharf docks, from where it's a short walk southeast along Jeremie Street to the rest of town.

The administrative office of the **St Lucia Tourist Board** is on the second floor of the Sureline Building complex (Ⓣ758/452-4094 or 5968, Ⓕ453-1121, Ⓦwww.stlucia.org) in Vide Bouteille, north of Castries. However, visitors may find themselves better served by the knowledgeable and helpful staff of the **tourist information kiosk** in Pointe Seraphine (Mon-Fri 8am–4.30pm; Ⓣ758/452-7577), which often remains open to accommodate cruise-ship visitors who arrive outside regular opening hours.

Castries is not an easy city to navigate by **car**. On weekdays in particular, the narrow streets are congested and choked with randomly parked cars and trucks. However, **parking** – once a nightmare – is now a dream, thanks to the new municipal multi-storey garage (EC$1.50/hr) opposite Castries market, on the John

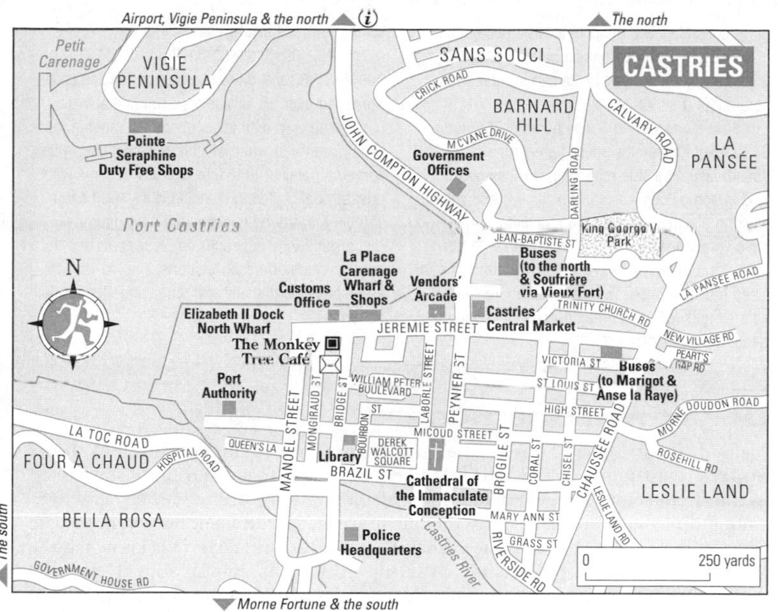

Compton Highway as you come into town. If you don't want to pay, you might find a place at the **car park** outside the Marketing Board building behind the market on Jeremie Street.

If heading out of town by **bus**, all the terminals and main stops are located in the downtown area. Services **north** to Gros Islet and Cap Estate (route 1A) leave from the Anglican School on Darling Road. For Vieux Fort and the **south** via the east coast (route 2H), head to the terminal at the junction of Jean Baptiste Road and Darling Road, while **Soufrière** buses (route 3D) leave from Carl's Crescent. Anse la Raye and **Marigot** buses (route 3C) depart from Victoria Road between Chausée Road and Chisel Street, and to **Dennery**, **Praslin** and **Mon Repos** (route 2D) head out from the Micoud Street junction.

Accommodation

Unless you have a yearning for busy streets and traffic, there's no compelling reason to stay in **downtown Castries**, and you'll find that most of the more pleasant hotels are located on the harbour or bays around town.

East Winds Inn Labrellotte Bay ⓣ758/452-8212, ⓕ452-9941, ⓦwww.eastwinds.com. Homey meets palatial in this understated, peaceful all inclusive. Rooms are spacious and well appointed, the beach is private and the pool generous. There are no staff variety shows here, nor group activities; what sets *East Winds* above the rest are the quality rooms and restaurant and the handsome gardens. 9

Green Parrot The Morne ⓣ758/452-3399 or 3167, ⓕ453-2272. Slightly tatty and infused with the air of a former hot spot, this 55-room inn in the hills south of Castries offers a chance to wallow in the coolish breezes drifting up the hills. The restaurant's West Indian cuisine is a real draw, as is its alfresco seating with views of Castries below. There's a pool, and the hotel provides complimentary transport to local beaches. 5

Seascape Bon Air, Marisule ⓣ758/452- 1645, ⓕ452-7967, ⓦwww.seascape-stlucia.com. Three wonderful, if basic, self-contained wooden cottages with balconies, set in acres of beautiful gardens sweeping down to a secluded beach below. The well-ventilated rooms are homey with great coastal views; the pool is large and deep and often watched over by myriad bathing pets. Only the sound of extensive birdlife can intrude on the serenity of it all. ❸

Sundale Guesthouse Sunny Acres ⓣ758/452-4120. Paul Kingshott's small, tightly run guesthouse on a side road near the Gablewoods Mall is scrupulously clean, inexpensive and within walking distance of Choc Bay's beaches. Rooms have verandahs, fans and private bath with hot water, and the three one-bedroom apartments can sleep four at a push. There's a communal lounge with TV and VCR, and breakfast is included in the rates. No credit cards. ❷

Windjammer Landing Labrellotte Bay ⓣ758/452-0913, ⓕ452-0907; in US ⓣ1-800/743-9609, ⓦwww.windjammerlanding.com. Sprawled over 55 hillside acres on and above Labrellotte Bay, with accommodation ranging from luxury rooms to white-stucco, self-contained villas, some containing up to four bedrooms, some with private pools, all with stunning views. Golf carts shuttle you around between the site's four restaurants (one is beachside), four pools and the beach, which offers watersports. The kid-friendly atmosphere is unusual and refreshing. Rooms ❽, cottages ❾

Downtown Castries

Named for St Lucia's famous poet and Nobel Prize-winner, **Derek Walcott Square** is just southeast of Castries Market between Micoud and Brazil streets, and its fine architecture and central location make it an ideal place to start any city tour. Though it's a peaceful place today, the square has had a turbulent history. In the late eighteenth century following the French Revolution, the square was known as the Place d'Armes, and a **guillotine** was set up by Republicans anxious to do away with selected members of the nobility. It was then labelled Promenade Square, and later still Columbus Square (1892), before being given its current name in 1993. Bordered by Brazil, Micoud, Bourbon and Laborie streets, this small city centre-piece is a landscaped oasis in an otherwise congested town. The east side of the square is shaded by an immense **saman tree**, thought to be more than 400 years old.

Bordering the south side of the square, **Brazil Street** is the city's congested and busy architectural showcase. Miraculously, many of its structures escaped the hurricanes and fires of the early colonial days and the mid-twentieth century. Excellent examples of colonial West Indian architecture stand toward the centre of the street, directly across from Derek Walcott Square. Nearly ninety percent of St Lucians are **Roman Catholic** – a legacy of years of French colonial rule – and the cornerstone of the island's faith is the imposing brick-and-mortar **Cathedral of the Immaculate Conception** dominating the square's east side. With room to seat two thousand communicants, the foundation of the current structure dates to 1894, but today's building was not completed until 1931. In 1957, the former church was granted the status of a cathedral, and was visited by **Pope John Paul II** in 1986. Recently, though, the cathedral has been home to much less illustrious visitors. On December 31, 2000, several members of a local cult claiming to align itself with the Rastafarian faith barged into the cathedral, setting fire to the members of the congregation and killing both a priest and a nun. Rastafarians throughout the island condemned the attack, denying any link to their religion. Since then, there have been two further attempts at such antics made by this cult, but security is now greatly improved and both proved unsuccessful.

Unless Mass is in progress, you're allowed inside to have a look around the ornate **interior**, bathed in rich red and diffused yellow light from ceiling portals, and busy with detailed carved wood inlay, wood benches, iron ceiling supports and stately pillars. Note the ceiling paintings of Catholic saints and apostles, with St Lucie in the centre and the vivid murals painted by island artist Dunstan St. Omer, who also designed St Lucia's flag.

The Central Market and around

Vividly colourful and often loud, **Central Market** on Jeremie Street at the northern perimeter of downtown is one of the busiest parts of Castries. Newly built and rambling, the structure houses several markets, all of which are busiest on Saturday mornings. Inside are rows of **craft booths**, with vendors selling baskets, spices, carvings, T-shirts, straw hats and tacky souvenirs. Under an orange roof to the left of the Jeremie Street entrance is the colourful and busy **fruit and vegetable market**, where you can find a wealth of fresh produce. Across from the Central Market on **Peynier Street**, and easily identifiable by the rust-coloured roof, is the **Vendor's Arcade**, another set of craft stalls selling the same rather tacky wares at slightly higher prices.

Vigie Peninsula

Framing the northern half of Port Castries, the heavily developed **Vigie Peninsula** is partially made up of land recovered from the sea by successive government reclamation projects. At the peninsula's southern end, overlooking the bay, is the **Pointe Seraphine shopping complex** (Mon–Fri 9am–5pm, Sat 9am–2pm), which advertises itself as the Caribbean's biggest duty-free shopping complex. It's not (the honour goes to the Charlotte Amalie mall in the US Virgin Islands), but it is certainly the largest that St Lucia has to offer, and it's still growing. Two adjacent cruise-ship berths deliver disembarking tourists directly to the stores, while the **taxi stand** (Ⓣ758/452-1733) and the **water taxi** to downtown Castries (every 30–45min, more frequent when cruise ships are docked; US$1) stand by to cater for the day-trippers.

From Pointe Seraphine the main highway runs north to Rodney Bay. Parallel to it, between the airport runway and the sea, is the more picturesque **Peninsular Road** – to reach it, follow the well-marked signs to Vigie Airport. Flanking the road is **Vigie Beach**'s two-kilometre stretch of smooth if rather dirty sand. It's not much to look at, but the water is usually calm and inviting. Once clear of the airport, Peninsular Road winds uphill towards Vigie Lighthouse at the apex. The entire peninsula was once a fortification, and many buildings here are restored military quarters, built from red brick in the late nineteenth century. At the western end of the peninsula, St Lucia's **National Archives** (Mon–Thurs 9am–4pm, Fri 9am–2pm; Ⓣ758/452-1654, Ⓦwww.geocities.com/sluarchives/index.html) are housed in a circa-1890 building: inside, you can browse through hundreds of old photos, lithographs, postcards and maps, which provide a good historical perspective of the island.

North and east of Castries

With beaches, forts and forest-smothered hills, the area **around Castries** is well worth exploring, and most sites, thanks to good public transport links, are reachable without a car. The busy Castries–Gros Islet Highway runs north, passing Vigie Peninsula and a string of unappealing industrial sites, shops, restaurants, hotels and schools before swinging to the coast to run parallel to sweeping **Choc Bay**. Fringed to the north by Labrellotte Point, a sheltered bay hosting a couple of luxury resorts, and to the south by **Vide Bouteille Point**, site of St Lucia's long-destroyed first **fort**, built by the French in 1660, Choc Bay is a handsome 1.2-mile stretch of often secluded sand.

From Choc Bay the Castries–Gros Islet Highway swings into the suburban **Sunny Acres** area, home to one of the island's larger shopping complexes, **Gablewoods Mall**, particularly good for groceries. Just past the mall, the winding but relatively smooth **Allan Bousquet Highway** strikes into the interior. Ten minutes' drive from the coast is the village of **Babonneau**, a small farming community huddled into the central hills of the island's northern half and worth visiting for both the sweeping hill views and for a taste of rural St Lucia. Several rivers flow through the hills around the settlement, and some say that Babonneau is a Patois version of the old French phrase *barre bon eau*, meaning, roughly, "mountain ridge, good water".

Set high in the hills east of Castries at Morne Pleasant, the **Folk Research Centre** (or *Plas Wichès Foklò*, to give it its Patois name) is a museum and cultural centre set in an old estate house originally owned by the eminent Deveaux family (Mon–Fri 8.30am–4.30pm; donations accepted; ⓣ758/453-1477). Dedicated to preserving the culture and language of St Lucian Creole, the centre houses a small but comprehensive **museum**: exhibits include a reproduction of a traditional *ti-kay* hut, and examples of indigenous musical instruments. The diminutive **research library** upstairs, accessible during opening hours, holds one of the island's best collections of books, research papers and photographs relating to St Lucia's folklore and history.

South of Castries

The La Toc Road leads west from downtown Castries along the south side of the harbour. Toward the western outskirts of town, as the road begins to climb, is the sizeable **Victoria Hospital**, the island's largest; a mile or so beyond, still on La Toc Road, is **La Toc Battery** (Dec–April daily 9am–3pm; May–Nov by appointment only; EC$6; ⓣ758/451-6300), one of the island's best-preserved examples of British military bastions. The 2.5-acre, nineteenth-century cement fortification features mounted cannons and dim underground bunkers, tunnels and cartridge storage rooms; one of the bunkers holds a large exhibit of antique bottles. Also in the grounds is a small **botanical garden**, where guides will answer questions and conduct tours at no extra cost.

In order to pass from Castries to the south of the island, winding through the loosely demarcated suburb of **Morne Fortune** is inevitable. Comprising a series of hills that flank the capital to the south, the area's high elevation provides striking views of the city and the north coast – on a clear day you can see the island of Martinique – and to the south, glimpses of the conical Pitons at Soufrière. The area is reachable via Manoel Street in downtown Castries, which becomes Government House Road as it begins its snakelike ascent towards **Government House** (open by appointment only Tues & Thurs 10am–noon & 2–4pm; ⓣ758/452-2481, ⓦwww.stluciagovernmenthouse.com), an imposing, white Victorian two-storey structure dating from 1895. The building houses the small Le Pavillon Royal Museum (ⓦwww.lepavillonroyal.com), where you can see a collection of artefacts and documents relating to the history of the house as well as modern St Lucian pieces of significance,

A few winds and turns beyond Government House, Morne Road takes you into the heart of the neighbourhood to the top of the 260-metre Morne Fortune itself, named "Good Luck Hill" by the French. The hills were first fortified by the French in 1768, then recaptured (and renamed **Fort Charlotte**) by the British in 1803. Several of the existing military encampments, cemeteries, barracks and batteries are slated to be restored and opened to the public; however, the process is incomplete and many are still in a state of disrepair. The best-preserved remnants are now part of a multipurpose government complex as well as the **Sir Arthur Lewis Community College**, named for St Lucian Nobel Prize-winner who is buried in the grounds. The college itself comprises several larger, nineteenth-century yellow-brick structures with gleaming white columns, all of military origin. You're free to amble about and visit the buildings and **Inniskilling monument**, honouring British soldiers who battled the French here in 1796, which is on the south side of the college complex behind the Combermere Barracks.

Eating and drinking

There are a few places to **eat** downtown, good for grabbing a quick bite while shopping or sightseeing – by far the best of these are the stalls at Castries Central Market. For a more formal meal, head into the surrounding hills, where stunning views accentuate the experience.

Castries

Castries Central Market Jeremie Street ☎758/453-6580. Daily 6am–5pm. Market vendors, shoppers and local business people flock to eat breakfast or lunch at these dozen or so restaurant stalls in a small, crowded alleyway behind the market. Taken at unadorned plastic tables, the servings of seafood, rotis, rice and beans or meat and dumplings are hearty and delicious. Most stalls don't accept credit cards.

The Monkey Tree Café Corner of Cadet and Jeremie streets ☎758/451-3004. Mon–Fri 7am–5pm, Sat 7am–3pm, Sun cruise ship days only. Feels like a mini-canteen but serves better food: local dishes, plated salads and the unusual 'hot plate cooking' system, where you choose a little from a variety of main and side dishes, thereby designing your own meal. Cheap and filling, at least.

Around Castries

Big Chef Steakhouse Rodney Bay Marina ☎758/450-0210, Mon–Sat from 6pm. Popular local TV chef caters for those who like their meal meaty. From an 8oz tenderloin to "as big as you can handle", these meats are not for the faint at heart – or the gourmet. Pasta and seafood is available, if you must.

Bon Appétit Morne Road, Morne Fortune ☎758/452-2757. Mon–Fri 11am–2pm & 6.30–9.30pm, Sat & Sun 6.30–9.30pm. Reservations are essential at this popular, rather expensive five-table restaurant in the Castries hills. House specialities are steaks and seafood, the cuisine is international and French nouveau – smallish servings tastefully arranged and embellished with minimal amounts of heavy sauces – and the wine selection is as impressive as the views of the harbour below.

Coal Pot Vigie Marina, Vigie ☎758/452-5566. Mon–Fri lunch & dinner, Sat dinner. One of the island's busiest and best restaurants – dinner reservations are essential. The New World cuisine is French-influenced, decorative and pricey, but the seafood is fresh and the salads are recommended. Directly on the water's edge, the dark interior is embellished with local artwork; this is a perfect place for a special night out.

Froggie Jack's Vigie Marina, Vigie ☎758/458-1900. Daily lunch & dinner. A warm, personal bar and restaurant that's big on excellent food and small on overdressed pomp. The restaurant sits above the marina, and the fare is prepared to order by an experienced Frenchman, and emphasis is on seafood and home-smoked meats.

Green Parrot The Morne ☎758/452-3399 or 3167. Daily 7am–late. Irascible chef Harry Edwards trained at the illustrious *Claridge's* hotel in London, but now he's content with presiding over Wednesday and Saturday night floorshows and cooking up creole, West Indian and international food with flair. Great seafood and views down onto Castries Harbour. Ladies wearing flowers in their hair, accompanied by well-dressed gents, eat for free on Mondays; otherwise the prix-fixe (call for days) is EC$90 and the restaurant will pay round-trip taxi fares for groups of four or more, or the one-way fare for parties of two.

The Wharf Castries–Gros Islet Highway, Choc Bay ☎758/450-4844. Daily 9am–midnight. This beachside restaurant lays on occasional live music – look out for family nights and other theme evenings, as well as the regular Tuesday night karaoke songfest.

16.2 | ST LUCIA | Gros Islet and the north

16.2

Gros Islet and the north

St Lucia's compact northern tip encompasses the "Golden Mile" of coastal resort towns as well as the remote and arid northern shoreline between Pointe du Cap and Pointe Hardy, and quiet Cas-en-Bas on the rugged northeast coast. On the west coast, the sweeping, two-mile horseshoe of **Rodney Bay** contains the majority of the region's tourist trappings. The town here is the most popular resort area, with a deep-water yacht harbour and a marina complex housing several rather shabby shops and restaurants, as well as the restaurant-and-hotel-lined **Reduit Beach**, one of St Lucia's most popular, and least local, strips of sand. Across the harbour channel is the quiet fishing village of **Gros Islet**, a place to soak up some local flavour at small, unpretentious creole restaurants. Just about the entire village is overtaken each Friday night for the raucous **street party**, or Jump-Up, when the streets are blocked off and revellers pour in for a rowdy night of roadside foodstuffs, music and alcohol.

Rodney Bay's northern half is framed by the heavily visited **Pigeon Island National Historic Park**, an outcrop attached to the mainland by a causeway in the 1970s. Heavily fortified by the British in the eighteenth century, the island has been transformed into a recreation park enjoyed by visitors and St Lucians alike, who come to tour the restored remains of military buildings or enjoy the string of beaches and walking trails.

16

Arrival and getting around

Getting around St Lucia's northern point is relatively easy, since frequent **buses** run the length of the coast between Castries, Gros Islet and Cap Estate near the island's northern tip. Marked Route 1A, they leave from the Marketing Board behind the Central Market on Jeremie Street. Schedules are theoretical, for buses tend to leave when they are full or ready, but count on at least one departure every hour from 6.30am until 10pm, with more services for the Jump-Up on Friday night. You'll pay EC$2.50 to travel from Castries to Reduit Beach, Rodney Bay Marina or Gros Islet. If you're travelling from farther afield, you'll have to change buses at Castries. If you don't have a car and would rather avoid public transport, the most hassle-free mode of transport is to hire a **taxi**. From downtown Castries to any of the resorts along the northeast coast, expect to pay around EC$40–50.

Accommodation

As St Lucia's main tourist heartland, the island's northern tip is plentifully supplied with large resorts, medium-sized hotels and inexpensive guesthouses, the majority located in the "Golden Mile" between **Rodney Bay** and **Gros Islet**.

Capri Smuggler's Cove, Cap Estate ⓣ758/450-0009, ⓕ450-0002, ⓦwww.capristlucia.com. An adorable ten-room guesthouse nestled in the hills above Smuggler's Cove, this is the perfect getaway for independent travellers and those who like a touch of home and camaraderie. The well-appointed rooms all have stunning views of the bay, there's an open-air honour bar, a reasonable restaurant and rates include breakfast. All guests have free access to the Oasis spa facilities at neighbouring *Le Sport* and there are yoga, t'ai chi and meditation classes on an outdoor wooden deck overlooking the pool and herb garden below. ⑤

Candyo Inn Rodney Bay ⓣ758/452-0712, ⓕ 452-0774. Close to some of the island's best swimming spots and restaurants (it's 5min on foot to Reduit Beach) yet surprisingly quiet. Decorated with florals, pinks and potted plants, standard rooms and apartment suites are sizeable; the latter come with kitchenettes and separate sitting rooms. There's a small pool and snack bar. 4

La Panache Guesthouse Cas-en-Bas Road, Gros Islet ⓣ758/450-0765, ⓕ450-0453, ⓦwww.lapanache.com. Scattered on a hill with views west to Gros Islet, the seven colourful rooms all have private baths, mosquito nets and fans. There's a photograph-festooned restaurant, a gazebo-style lounge with TV and books to borrow, and Cas-en-Bas beach is only around 1500m to the east. 2

Le Sport Cap Estate ⓣ758/450-8551, ⓕ450-0368; in US ⓣ1-800/544-2883; ⓦwww.thebodyholiday.com.

One of the island's few all-inclusive resorts that manages to make non-predatory singles feel comfortable. Usually full of stressed-out city types indulging in the all-inclusive spa treatments, exercise classes, hikes, watersports, golf lessons and t'ai chi, who perhaps don't notice the cold and barren rooms and just adequate beach. The food is plentiful, healthful and well prepared, though, especially at the superlative *Tao* (see p.619). 9

Rainbow Hotel Reduit Beach ⓣ758/452-0148, ⓕ452-0158, ⓦwww.rainbowstlucia.com. The soon-to-be-refurbished *Rainbow* has 76 spacious and comfortable rooms, most of which overlook the pool. The atmosphere is cosy for a place so big; there's a restaurant, bar and fitness centre on site and Reduit Beach is right across the street. 6

Villa Zandoli Reduit Beach ⓣ758/552-8898, ⓕ452-0093, ⓦwww.stluciahotels-guesthouse.com. A special, brightly painted guesthouse with a single, two twins and two doubles; the owner also has three one-bedroom apartments across the way. The guesthouse rooms are cheery and large, there's also a communal area, a barbecue, free internet access and a well-equipped kitchen. No private bathrooms though. Single 2, double 3

Rodney Bay and Reduit Beach

Named **RODNEY BAY** after eighteenth-century British commander George Brydges Rodney, the current incarnation of this former American army base is a compact but fully fledged tourist resort, sandwiched between the glorious if over-crowded Reduit Beach and the shops and yachting facilities of Rodney Bay Marina. The mangrove swamp that once separated the villages of Rodney Bay and Gros Islet has been replaced by a man-made harbour channel, which opens out into a deep-water lagoon dotted with bobbing yachts. From the Castries–Gros Islet Highway, the main road into town (look for the sign to Rodney Bay) is on the left side, just before JQ's shopping mall, thwe harbour and marina.

The settlement itself is quite small, and most of the activity is split between the beach and the **Rodney Bay Marina**. The marina is considered by many to be among the finest in the Caribbean, with plenty of slips and full services for boaters as well as a few somewhat grotty and unappealing restaurants, banks and gift-shops. The complex is also a good spot for booking **watersports**: numerous operators are based here, and activities range from scuba diving, deep-sea fishing and pleasure boat cruises, to windboard, sailboat, car and motor-craft rentals. At the south end of the marina, just after you turn into Rodney Bay from the highway, you can hop on the rather touristy **ferry** to Pigeon Island (ⓣ758/452-8816; US$10).

Behind the marina lies the original reason for Rodney Bay's growth into a tourism epicentre: the inviting, easily accessible **Reduit Beach**, around 1km long and among the prettiest on the island, with a wide swath of fine white sand, a generally calm surf, and views of Pigeon Island to the north and the coastal hills to the south. Don't be fooled into thinking you've found a Caribbean haven though: the beach is generally packed with the well-oiled bodies of the area's visiting sun-worshippers and is not exactly a secluded hideaway. Unsurprisingly, it's also lined with places to stay, many of them large-scale but low-lying concrete blocks sitting directly, and intrusively, on the beach, and their proximity adds to the general crowded feel. The beach hotels provide chairs and umbrellas for their guests, and many will rent them out to visitors staying elsewhere for a daily rate of around US$10.

Gros Islet

Just across the channel from Rodney Bay lies **GROS ISLET**, a small fishing village of rickety, rust-roofed wooden homes and narrow streets lined with fruit and vegetable vendors. The beach is somewhat dirty, and generally the town holds little of interest for the visitor. Come Friday nights, though, Lucians and visitors alike pour in for the **Friday night street party** or **jump-up**, when everyone lets loose and parties. Much of the town is blocked off, and armies of snack vendors peddling barbecue, fried fish, hot cakes and cold beers arrive to feed the hungry masses. Bars open their doors onto the street, street corners are festooned with speakers and the music is loud. Things get going around 10pm and last till late, and despite the distinctly sexual undertones, it's generally a good-natured affair. Yet, despite an unobtrusive police presence, a slightly seedy side has developed of late, consolidated by the presence of several drunks and hustlers in the crowd, including those selling (illegal) drugs. Women should be prepared for unwarranted attention and really shouldn't attend alone – instead, considering hiring a taxi driver as your guide. Common sense advice applies here as it does anywhere: leave your valuables in your accommodation and refuse anything that seems suspect.

Cas-en-Bas

Just past Gros Islet at the Shell petrol station, a dirt track known as the Cas-en-Bas Road strikes east off the coastal highway toward a small settlement on the remote east coast called **CAS-EN-BAS**, worth visiting for its string of secluded **beaches**. You can walk the track in an hour, much more appealing than negotiating the endless mucky potholes by 4WD – don't even attempt it after rain, or in a normal car. Alternatively, you could approach the beaches via the road behind the golf course in Cap Estate, a much less exhausting, albeit less interesting, option. The ocean marks the end of the Cas-en-bas Road, and here you'll find a wonderful, secluded beach with some shady spots and an outlying reef taming the rougher waters of the Atlantic. There's an even more isolated spot – **Secret Beach** – ten minutes' walk north, along a trail that hugs the rocky, cactus-strewn coastline – look out for a track that goes back down to the water.

Thirty minutes' walk **south** of Cas-en-Bas along the unmarked coastal path brings you to the beach at **Anse Lavoutte**, favoured by **leatherback turtles** as a secluded spot for egg-laying between March and July. If you want to witness this spectacle for yourself, you must join a turtle watch (see p.630). Visitors to these shores should take the utmost care in the water here, for these unmarked and unmanned beaches have seen many people – locals and tourists alike – drown, victims of powerful Atlantic undercurrents. The area is deserted, so tell someone where you are going before you set off.

Pigeon Island National Historic Park

The 45-acre **Pigeon Island National Historic Park** (daily 9am–5pm; EC$10 or US$4) is a handsome promontory of land striking into the ocean just north of Gros Islet. It's no longer an island though, despite its name, having been linked to the mainland via a causeway during the 1970s. Today, it's one of St Lucia's most popular relaxation spots, a combination of easy hiking trail, concert venue, historic site and pleasant lunch stop with the added bonus of several excellent beaches and a fine pub. In the hotter months, it's best to visit Pigeon Island early in the day, as the hills provide excellent views and are well worth the climb, which is more than pleasant before it gets too hot.

The island has served as a base for several notable inhabitants, from the Arawaks, who are alleged to have left behind clay pottery, to the infamous pirate François Leclerc, also known as Jambe de Bois or Wooden Leg. In 1778, Pigeon Island was fortified by the newly arrived British colonials, and it was from here that Admiral Rodney launched the attack against the French that effectively ended their domination of the Caribbean. When African slaves were given their freedom following the French Revolution, imminent British repossession caused them to fear re-enslavement and spurred them into action. Tagged as the "**Brigands**", the Africans banded together to create a minor rebellion, razing plantations and even taking brief possession of Pigeon Island, before signing a peace treaty in 1798. Since then, the island has been a camp for indentured East Indian labourers, a quarantine station for patients afflicted with tropical disease, and a whaling station. Declared a national landmark in the 1970s, and afforded the protection of the St Lucia National Trust, the island's buildings were restored, the causeway was constructed, and Britain's Princess Alexandra opened the park to the public on February 23, 1979, the day St Lucia gained its independence.

Visiting the park

To get to the park, turn west at the sign from the Castries–Gros Islet Highway. Ignore the monstrous blue hotel on the left of the causeway if you can, instead focusing on the handsome public **beach** on your right. Once you've passed the main gate, paid your entrance fee and collected a free map, the **Pigeon Island Museum and Interpretive Centre** is on your right, located in an old officers' mess. A mini-museum of the island's chequered past, the one-room centre is worth a brief look for its displays of Amerindian axes, clay bowls, flint and shell tools and antique colonial furniture; there's also a twenty-minute video presentation describing the history of St Lucia in brief. Just below the centre is the wonderfully cavernous *Captain's Cellar Pub*, housed in an old barracks and well worth visiting for an ice-cold Piton after tackling the park's hills.

Past the Interpretive Centre, the south side of the island is peppered with the remains of the **military barracks** and **encampments** built by the British, including gun batteries, a powder magazine, a lime kiln and the ruins of the British Admiral's Fort Rodney. Some structures are more intact than others, such as the thick-walled powder magazine to the left of the entrance and the old cooperage near the beach on the south side of the island – now home to the park's toilets. On the waterfront south of the fortifications, there's a small dock where you can catch the rather expensive tourist **ferries** (EC$25 one-way) to Rodney Bay Marina. Nearby is the *Snooty Agouti*, sufficient for sandwiches, snacks and cold drinks.

Several prominent hillocks dominate the island north of the military buildings; of these, 110-metre **Signal Hill** is the highest. A marked trail leads right to its base, from which it takes about fifteen minutes to reach the peak, affording panoramic views south to Gros Islet and the outskirts of Castries, and north over the expanse of the St Lucia Channel to the island of Martinique.

Eating and drinking

Back-to-back restaurants in the busy "Golden Mile" north of Castries provide a staggering number of choices. Beachside eateries along Reduit Beach offer dining with sea breezes, and Rodney Bay as a whole seems to have more restaurants per square mile than anywhere else on the island. During the Friday night **street party** in Gros Islet, restaurateurs and vendors set up roadside barbecues and sell roasted chicken, fish or meats, as well as cold beers to wash it down. North of Gros Islet, the restaurants thin out a bit, but a number of vendors set up in front of the entrance to Pigeon Point and at the causeway beach.

Restaurants

The Cat's Whiskers Rodney Bay ☎758/452-8880. Tues–Sun 8am–late. Unassuming pub-restaurant once known as *Mel & H's Old English Pub*, serving hearty traditional English fare from full breakfast to Ploughman's Lunches and kidney pies, hand-cut chips and boiled meat as well as reasonable brews on tap (EC$8). The popular Sunday brunch is a feast: roast beef, Yorkshire pudding and all the trimmings.

Charthouse Rodney Bay Marina ☎758/452-8115. Mon–Sat 5–11pm. Steaks, ribs and lobster are the specialities, and as they're cooked better here than anywhere on the island reservations are necessary. Vegetarians take note: there's little to nothing of interest on offer here. The dark-wood, marina-side restaurant (reserve seats on the waterside deck) also serves seafood and creole dishes. Top it off with a Cuban cigar, on sale at the restaurant.

Great House Castries–Gros Islet Highway, Cap Estate ☎758/450-0450. Tues–Sun 4.30–10pm. Fine dining (afternoon tea and dinner only) in a 235-year-old stone plantation house overlooking Bécune Bay, with seating inside or on the stone patio. The cuisine is West Indian and French – try the lamb with garlic and rosemary – and the four-course set menu (around US$40) offers excellent value. Adjacent is the Derek Walcott amphitheatre, where you can see occasional works by the man himself before or after dinner, depending upon schedules.

Key Largo Castries–Gros Islet Highway ☎758/452-0282. Daily 9am–11pm. Casual pizza place on the east side of the Castries–Gros Islet Highway, across from the marina, serving by far the best pizza on the island, freshly cooked in a wood-fired brick oven. Excellent pasta dishes and freshly squeezed juices also available.

The Lime Rodney Bay ☎758/452-0761. Daily breakfast, lunch & dinner. "Liming" is West Indian slang for "hanging out", and this is one of Rodney Bay's more popular spots to do just that. The eclectic menu is a mix of palatable steaks and seafood done "Lucian style", with indoor and alfresco (on the patio next to the road) dining, and live music weekly – Sunday is karaoke night. Also

Exploring St Lucia's interior forest reserves

Stretching across the island's central and north-central interior, the vast, uninhabited and irregularly shaped **St Lucia Forest Reserve** comprises the 19,000 acres of rainforest and dry forest which are maintained by the government's forestry department. Though many of the trails within the reserve were used as transportation routes in the early colonial days, today most people who venture in do so for pleasure rather than necessity. Arrestingly beautiful and teeming with exotic flora and wildlife, the forests offer an absorbing alternative to the sun-and-beach culture of coastal resorts.

St Lucia's protected forest reserves (and all of the hiking trails within them) are maintained by the **Forestry and Lands Department** (☎758/450-2231 or 2078, ⓦwww.slumaffe.org). The department also determines public access (some parts of the interior are restricted) and provides trained **hiking guides**. A flat fee of EC$25 covers access to a single trail as well as the services of a guide. At extra cost, the forestry department can sometimes arrange **transport** to the trails. As the forestry department is understaffed, you should always call a few days in advance to arrange guides or transport.

Unless you elect to arrange your transport with the forestry department or take a tour with Castries-based commercial companies such as Jungle Tours (☎758/450-0434) or Sunlink Jeep Safaris (☎758/452-9678), **getting to the trails** is not an easy proposition. Public transport is limited, but you can reach some trails by taking an inland **bus**, which will cost EC$5 or less. Services run directly to the start of Union and Barre de L'Isle walks, but for most of the hikes listed below, you'll have to take a bus to the nearest town and walk to the start of the trail, often a few miles away. If you decide to opt for a **taxi**, make arrangements to be collected at an appointed hour, as you're unlikely to find drivers cruising for fares in the mountains. If you can afford it, renting a **car** is the easiest option.

Union Nature Trail

The short, easy **Union Nature trail** (daily 8am–4.30pm; EC$25) starts about twenty minutes' drive from Castries, in the forestry department's headquarters, which also contains a medicinal herb garden, a depressing **mini-zoo** and an interpretive centre where you can learn about endangered species. The easy 1.6km **trail** loops through open late on Wed, Fri and Sat for dancing to a wide range of live music, making for one of the island's hottest nightlife venues.

Razmataz Reduit Beach Road, Rodney Bay ☎758/452-0800. 4pm–late, closed Thurs. If you've come to St Lucia for tandoori, then this popular Reduit Beach restaurant is your best bet. Specialities are spicy vindaloo, korma and tikka masala, all prepared with tandoori (grilled) chicken, lamb or beef – there are plenty of non-meat options as well, plus occasional live music.

Spinnakers Reduit Beach, Rodney Bay ☎758/452-8491. Daily 9am–11pm. Appealing beach bar and restaurant serving an international mix of steaks, grilled seafood, and lobster that's more upscale than you'd expect for a beach bar. The setting is hard to beat, especially at sunset.

Tao *Le Sport*, Cap Estate ☎758/450-8551. Dinner daily. Superlative East/West fusion cuisine, impeccable service and a gorgeous setting overlooking the bay make this one of the island's finest dining experiences. Booking is essential: request a table on the edge of the balcony, choose from sushi, tofu dishes and wonderful seafood and don't forget to leave room for dessert.

Bars and clubs

Indies Rodney Bay ☎758/458-0509. Upscale in its own way – proper dress is required, meaning no beach wear – but full of a pretty young crowd, *Indies* puts on busy theme nights; the popular Wednesday nights are 'all inclusive' (entry/drinks) for US$10. Friday and Saturday nights entry alone costs EC$10.

Shamrock's Pub Rodney Bay ☎758/452-8725. On the Rodney Bay waterfront, *Shamrock's* is a rocking place with something going on every night of the week – from beer pitcher offers to ladies' night and theme nights, live music to karaoke; it always draws a crowd. Also on hand are pool tables and table football games.

Triangle Pub Rodney Bay ☎758/452-0334. Small barbecue next to *The Lime* (see p.618) which puts on live music every night, from reggae and steel bands to jazz. Great fun, great mix of people and great cheap food, too.

dry forest that was once planted as a tree nursery, returning after about an hour of walking if you don't make too many stops. To get there, turn off the Castries–Gros Islet Highway along the signposted Allan Bousquet Highway; after a winding 2.5km, you'll see a large fence to the right; turn right at its end to reach the centre.

Barre de L'Isle Trail

The "island ridge" **Barre de L'Isle trail** (weekdays 8.30am–4pm; EC$25) bisects the Central Forest Reserve and the island itself. It's a worthwhile, mildly challenging adventure that provides a good look at St Lucia's richly diverse topography and mountain flora and fauna: throughout, the trail alternates between a thick overhead cover of trees and wide-open areas with expansive vistas in all directions. The two-hour hike – four if you extend the trek and climb the ridge of Mt La Combe – is well enough marked to go it alone, though a guide will be able to identify bird, tree and plant species along the way.

The signposted start of the Barre de L'Isle trail strikes into the forest directly from the central Castries–Dennery highway, opposite the rangers' hut and a twenty- to thirty-minute drive or bus journey from downtown Castries. Buses leave from Manoel Street in Castries – tell the driver where you're heading, as he'll know where to drop you.

Edmund Forest Reserve

Spreading over the southwestern interior, the **Edmund Forest Reserve** (daily 8am–4pm; EC$25 per trail) offers a ten-kilometre (3.5hr), guided hike through the heart of the island to the open western plains, with wonderful views along the way, including a spectacular sighting of Morne Gimie. The eight-kilometre drive to the Edmund Reserve takes about an hour from the west coast. From Soufrière take the inland road to Fond St Jacques, bypassing the turn-off to Morne Coubaril Estate and the south. The road to the trails is signposted off the main road, and after a twenty- to thirty-minute drive, depending on the condition of the road, a wooden forestry department **ranger station** is the first indication that you're in the reserve itself. Relying on public transport to get here is not really a viable option.

16.3

Soufrière and the west coast

The **west coast** of St Lucia is incredibly beautiful, rich and varied in its attractions and notable for its pretty beaches and, in parts, its decided lack of tourist traffic. You can search out isolated waterfalls, hike through astounding rainforest, swim, snorkel and scuba dive in secluded bays and visit peaceful fishing villages, all without the commercial feel of the northwest coast. However, the area is not without its more blatant tourist draws, and these are centred around **Soufrière**, which dwells in the shadows of the imposing **Pitons**, and where attractions, upmarket hotels and restaurants lend a bustling air of activity and touristic progress.

Getting around

A treacherously steep and twisted – if well-paved – road snakes along the southwest coast, making the trip from Castries to Soufrière an entertaining drive, but **bus** schedules between the two towns are a labyrinthine affair. If you're based in Soufrière and want to travel to the capital, infrequent services along the west coast (particularly in the afternoon) mean it's often easiest to first travel south to Vieux Fort, and switch buses there for the final leg of the trip; you should allow the better part of a day for the journey.

Accommodation

Staying along the west coast between Castries and Soufrière is ideal if you want to get away from heavily trafficked tourist areas and relax in some of the finest resorts and guesthouses on the island. The beaches are inviting and uncrowded, and the limited number of accommodation choices (the vast majority in **Marigot Bay** or **Soufrière)** tend to be less resort-like than those further north.

Anse Chastanet Anse Chastanet Ⓣ758/459-7000, Ⓕ459-7700; in US 1-800/223-1108, in UK 0800/894057; Ⓦwww.ansechastenet.com. Genteel, old-style and expensive, this resort is aesthetically planned over a hill above Soufrière's nicest beach. The larger rooms are extortionate, but are spacious and airy, like very luxurious treehouses with lovely ocean or mountain views; basic rooms are still incredibly pricey but much less distinctive. Reception and one restaurant are on an upper level, the beach and another eatery are 100 steps below and there's a great in-house jungle biking outfit (see p.605). ⑨

Anse La Liberté Campsite One mile south of Canaries off West Coast Highway Ⓣ758/459-4540, 453-7656 or 454-5014 Ⓕ453-2791, Ⓦwww.slunatrust.org/all. Maintained by the National Trust, this campsite is set around four miles of hiking trails, a fifteen minute walk from the beach or half-hour from the main road. Bare sites, tents and elevated tents are available, with picnic tables, fireplaces, shower blocks, kayaks, and a communal solar-powered pavilion. Site only ①, tent or elevated platform tent ②

Le Mirage Guesthouse 14 Church St, Soufrière Ⓣ & Ⓕ758/459-7010. Owner John Lamontagne worked as a chef in London for nearly forty years before returning home and opening the *La Mirage* guesthouse and restaurant in 1998. The four suites sleep three and are clean and basic but comfortable with en-suite bathrooms, ceiling fans, a mini-fridge and a balcony overlooking Church Street. No credit cards. ②

Ladera Resort Soufrière–Vieux Fort Road ⓣ758/459-7323, ⓕ459-5156; in US ⓣ1-800/841-4145, ⓦwww.ladera-resort.com. Views are key in this unusual hillside resort, which looks down 300m over the Pitons and the bay. Deliberately open to the elements, rooms are without a back wall in order to maximize both the vista and the sense of being at one with nature; night-time tree frogs, mosquitoes and the sulphurous smell from the springs below rather increase the sensation. Most rooms have plunge pools where the "fourth wall" should be and the restaurant has an excellent reputation, though overall something doesn't quite seem to gel. ⑨

Marigot Beach Club Marigot Bay ⓣ758/451-4974, ⓕ451-4973. Ensconced on the north side of the bay and a couple of minutes from the road's end by water taxi, the location has long been the main draw; the open-air restaurant is named *Doolittle's* after the Rex Harrison movie filmed here in the 1960s. Villas and studios are brimming with amenities and come with kitchen/ettes, and the pool, beach, watersports and shops manage to keep guests plenty busy. Studios ③, villas ⑤

Sea Horse Inn Marigot Bay ⓣ758/451-4436, ⓕ451-4872, ⓦwww.seahorse-inn.com. Reached via water taxi from the docks, this elegant but simple getaway on the north side of the bay is set in a 1920s stone house and run by an accommodating, if very protective, Canadian couple and their two lovely dogs. The five rooms have mosquito nets, overhead fans and en-suite bathrooms, and there's a small pool and a pleasant public room with bar overlooking the bay. Rates include breakfast and ferry passes. Generally there's a seven-night minimum stay. ⑤

Still Plantation Fond St Jacques Road ⓣ758/459-5179 or 7261, ⓕ 459-7301, ⓦwww.thestillresort.com. Out on the road to Fond St Jacques, near the turn-off for the Diamond Waterfall, is a peaceful escapist's guesthouse set on a 400-acre working cocoa plantation. The modern studios and apartments are incredibly spacious and quiet, the latter have kitchens, all have fans and some A/C. There's a restaurant, large pool, and bar on site, the owner offers plantation tours on horseback and beach/town shuttles are complimentary. ②–③, ③–④ with kitchen and A/C.

Stonefield Estate Soufrière ⓣ758/459-5648, ⓕ 459-5550, ⓦww.stonefieldvillas.com. These ten spacious villas on the well-manicured grounds of an old plantation may be Soufrière's best-kept secret; designed and decorated with nature in mind, they rival the aesthetic of any of the area's luxury hotels at a fraction of the cost. Each airy villa has separate kitchen and sleeping areas, hammocked wooden balconies affording glorious views of the Pitons, slatted wooden windows and wonderfully spacious and private open-air showers, with flowers trailing all around. A pool, restaurant and bar are situated to maximize the mountain views and beach shuttles are free. ⑦

Marigot Bay

From Castries, the West Coast Highway scoots through winding, hilly terrain and passes the signposted turn-off for **MARIGOT BAY** some 5km south; if travelling by bus, it's worth asking the driver if he'll make the two-kilometre detour down to the bay. There's no real town here, but there is a fistful of reclusive hotels and peaceful guesthouses strung along the north and south sides of the bay. These, along with a couple of good restaurants and waterside bars and a few local shops on the road down make up the village. While it's not the busiest spot, the sheltered inner lagoon is one of the island's best-protected natural yacht harbours, and Marigot's waters are permanently dotted with boats and their crews.

At the end of the steep access road from the highway is the compact waterfront village. To the right is the ever-crowded jetty of **The Moorings Yacht Charters**, and clustered around the complex are a small **police station, customs and immigration** office (ⓣ758/452-3487, VHF 16) for incoming yachts, and a **taxi stand** (ⓣ758/453-4406). Set a few metres back from the waterfront are entrances to the brace of small hotels set high in the hills overlooking the bay, and a small path to your left leads to *The Shack* (see p.624), one of the most enjoyable restaurants in the bay.

The *Marigot Beach Club* and its **beach** (the bay's best swimming spot) are – despite the sign – actually a few hundred yards across the water, accessible 24 hours a day via a small ferry boat (EC$3 round-trip). The beach is spacious but compact, with calm surf, plenty of shade and good snorkelling to its west side; unfortunately, several drug dealers hang around here, and will inevitably try to sell you some of their wares. Legal refreshments are available from *Doolittle's*, and the hotel also runs a watersports concession.

South of Marigot Bay, the highway dips through the sharp west coast hills to the next settled area, **ROSEAU**, a valley extensively planted with fields of bananas, dotted with small settlements and home to the St Lucia rum distillery. Also of note here is the community of Roseau's church, which features some fine *omeros* murals of the black madonna by local artist Dunstan St. Omer.

Soufrière and around

Officially established in 1746, **Soufrière** is the oldest town in St Lucia and was the island's capital under French rule. Naturally framed by hills and dominated by the looming, conical **Pitons** – twin volcanic peaks thrusting straight out of the sea to the south of the town – Soufrière's deep **bay** is extremely picturesque, particularly when viewed from the hilly coastal roads as you enter town from the north or south. This unspoiled allure has often drawn the attention of film producers: scenes from *Superman II*, *Water*, and the more recent *White Squall* were shot in and around town.

Taxis and **buses** heading north to Castries and south to Vieux Fort and for the east coast cluster around the town square and the waterfront; the latter is also the place to hop aboard convenient **water taxis**, which traverse the area servicing all of the nearby bays, many of which are difficult to access from the land without your own car. Water taxis (☎758/454-5420) also offer **sightseeing trips** to Castries and back. At US$350 for four, the trips are expensively exotic. One-way trips (no sightseeing) for four or more people cost around US$90-100 for four.

Downtown Soufrière

The largest settlement of the southwest coast, **SOUFRIÈRE** is still a quiet place, charming in its lack of polish and filled with a melange of architectural styles ranging from slapped-together wooden fishing huts to modern cement blocks. Some buildings, particularly those around the town square, recall the ornate facades of French colonial days. Most visitors just come for the day and do a quick tour of the beaches, the Sulphur Springs and the mineral baths, all fine attractions in themselves, but very touristy and devoid of local presence or a true taste of St Lucia's southwest coast. Save time to explore the town itself so you don't make the same mistake.

Soufrière's **tourist office** (Mon–Fri 8am–4pm, Sat 8am–noon), on the waterfront and across from the main pier, is a handy source of local information – staff can also direct you to members of the tourism department's helpful guide corps who give walking tours of the town. The town is small enough to explore on foot, and the abundance of jammed one-way streets and the lack of parking render vehicles inadvisable. You can park at the pretty **waterfront**, a jumble of piers and boat slips where local fishing craft and tourist party boats dock, and where you'll find a small **fish market** in the blue building behind the *Old Courthouse Restaurant*. A well-maintained walkway edges the northern waterfront, where ornate streetlamps, benches and poinciana trees make for a pleasant evening stroll. At its southern end lies a small **crafts centre** (Mon–Sat 9am–4pm), where local artisans sell anything from carvings to straw hats at a reasonable price.

A block inland, hemmed in by Bridge and Church streets is the big and grassy **town square**, laid out by Soufrière's settlers in the eighteenth century and, during the French Revolution, the scene of numerous **executions** by guillotine. It's a peaceful and shady space today, bordered by businesses and homes built in the classic French colonial style with second-floor balconies and intricate decorative woodwork. Dominating the east end of the square is the **Lady of Assumption Church**, built in 1953 on the site of several older churches destroyed by earthquakes and fire. Soufrière has what might be viewed as bad weather karma: the town was pummelled by hurricanes in 1780, 1817, 1831, 1898 and 1980, and by an earthquake in 1839, while in 1955 half the town was razed to the ground by a huge fire.

Anse Chastanet Beach

To the immediate north of Soufrière is the popular **Anse Chastanet Beach**, long, wide and presided over by the resort of the same name (see p.620). It's one of the island's finest beaches, and a great place for scuba excursions, with several good **dive sites** nearby and – due to the proximity of the reef to the shore – remarkably good snorkelling right off the beach. Scuba St Lucia (see box on p.605 for details) is an excellent dive operation by the water, renting snorkelling as well as scuba gear. Anse Chastanet is reachable via a deplorably bad, pothole-filled road, jutting right from the main road just before you enter Soufrière from the north. The two-kilometre track takes about fifteen minutes by car or 45 minutes on foot, or you can catch a water taxi from Soufrière (US$10 one-way).

Diamond Botanical Gardens

The **Diamond Botanical Gardens** (Mon–Sat 10am–5pm, Sun 10am–3pm; EC$7; ☎758/459-7565), situated 2km east of Soufrière, are the main attraction at Soufrière Estate, a former sugar plantation dating from 1713 that formed part of a 2000-acre land grant bestowed by Louis IV to the Devaux family. Heavily frequented tours include trips to the gardens themselves, some overly modernized **mineral baths**, a pleasant nature trail, an ornate waterwheel, old mill and the **waterfall**. Though you can't swim by the waterfall, you can splash about in the slightly pungent depths of the baths in an outdoor pool or in several smaller tubs inside; the water is cooler than you might expect, but still manages to reach 41° (106°F) in certain tubs. In addition to the main entry fee to the complex, you'll pay EC$6.50 to use the pool and EC$10 for a private bath. The gardens' lure is somewhat marred by the high volume of tourist traffic, but come very early or in late afternoon and its well worth your time.

La Soufrière Sulphur Springs

Misleadingly billed as the world's only drive-in volcano, **La Soufrière Sulphur Springs** (daily 9am–5pm; EC$3), a short drive south of town off the road to Vieux Fort, was a **volcano** some 13km in diameter before it erupted and collapsed into itself around 40,000 years ago. La Soufrière remains active to this day – theoretically, it could erupt any time – but as it is now classified as a **solfatara**, meaning it emits gases and vapours rather than lava and hot ash, a molten shower is extremely unlikely. Turn into the springs at the signed road and it's quickly apparent that you're in the midst of a volcano – killed off by sulphuric emissions, the vegetation becomes sparse and an eggy odour hangs in the air. The services of an official (and very informative) **guide** are included in the entrance fee, and they will walk you up from the car park lot to the viewing platforms that overlook sections of the crater, seven barren acres of steaming, bubbling pools of sulphur-dense water and rocks tinged green and yellow. Some years ago, visitors were allowed to walk across the crater, but this practice was stopped when one of the guides fell through a fissure – though sustaining severe burns, he lived to tell the tale. Now only goats occasionally hop across the pools and rocks, cheerfully oblivious of how close they are to becoming stew.

The Pitons

Towering more than half a mile above sea level, the anomalous and majestic peaks of the **Pitons** dominate the southwest coast. Visible on a clear day from as far north as the hills of Castries, these breathtaking cones are undoubtedly St Lucia's most photographed feature. Overlooking the south side of Soufrière's harbour, the northern peak is Petit Piton; south of Petit is Gros Piton, wider at the base but similar in height. Maps give various elevations for each of the peaks, some even claiming that Petit is taller than Gros Piton, but the St Lucian government figures of 734m (2460ft) and 798m (2620ft) respectively are generally accepted.

Beyond their aesthetic appeal, the Pitons offer an opportunity – literally – for high adventure. Though climbing up **Petit Piton** is discouraged by local authorities – there are fragile ecosystems to take into account, as well as the inherent difficulty and danger of climbing a near-vertical slab of rock – some still seem willing to clamber up. This is not, however, to be advised. **Gros Piton**, while it's still a challenge, is much more manageable. It's a long and hot half-day ascent, one best tackled early in the day, and the path branches off in several places, making a guide necessary. The Soufrière Regional Development Foundation (☎758/459-5500) in town will usually be able to find a good guide, and you'll pay about US$50 per person.

Eating and drinking

The coast road south of Castries hosts a small number of good-value **eateries**, and Soufrière holds its own against the tourism strongholds of the northwest, with a wealth of eating places ranging from small cafés to more elegant restaurants for relaxed evening dining. Some of the hotels also offer wide-ranging evening menus and comfortable beachside restaurants for lunching during the day.

Captain Hook's Castries Road, Soufrière ☎758/459-7365. Tiny, with plastic outdoor tables and a less than inspired interior, this very local joint at the southern end of Soufrière serves great prix-fixe seafood dinners for EC$40 and huge portions of delicious fish or chicken and chips for EC$25.

Dasheene *Ladera Resort*, Soufrière ☎758/459-7323. Daily 8–10am, 11am–2.30pm & 6.30pm–late. An eclectic mix of West Indian, oriental, Italian and vegetarian cuisine, the majority of it traditional but artful. Dinner is expensive, and usually delicious, but the buffets can be mediocre and lunch hit-and-miss. The views of the Pitons and bay below are astonishing – come up for drinks before sunset .

JJ's Marigot Bay Road ☎758/451-4076. On the road to the bay, *JJ's* runs a popular seafood night on Wednesday, with dancing to all sorts of music afterward, and a popular Saturday night BBQ. It used to be much rowdier here in the past, but complaints from bay residents have led to a toning down of the entertainment here: a godsend if you are trying to sleep at 3am.

La Haut Plantation Soufrière ☎758/459-7008. Great, friendly service and excellent fresh seafood make this charming poolside restaurant just south of Soufrière a great place to stop for lunch or evening cocktails – the view of the Pitons is perfect.

La Mirage 14 Church St, Soufrière ☎758/459-7010. Mon–Sat lunch & dinner. An informal, local ground-floor restaurant serving vegetarian specialities such as pasta and creative salads, as well as fish and chips, roasted chicken and pizza, all of which are substantial and sensibly priced.

Old Courthouse Restaurant Soufrière waterfront ☎758/459-5002. Daily 8am–midnight. This bright lavender-painted building just north of the fish market building is indeed an old courthouse, dating back to 1898 – the thick-doored bathrooms were the former cells. The moderately priced cuisine – West Indian with Asian twists – is solid and recommendable, but with just nine tables, five overlooking the water, reservations are essential.

The Shack Marigot Bay ☎758/451-4145. Daily lunch & dinner. Cheap, filling and tasty American-style fare (think burgers, salads and sandwiches) with a Caribbean twist – the Kingfish burger is excellent – and plentiful seafood in a lovely floating café-restaurant on the bay. Happy hour is 5–7pm; come for the sunset.

16.4

The south coast

St Lucia's **southern coast** boasts some striking scenery: south of Soufrière, the thin mountain road whirls and dips inland before swinging toward the ocean to reveal a string of coastal villages and, ultimately, the island's second largest town, **Vieux Fort**, all framed by the towering ranges of the Central Forest Reserve. This southwest corner was once an **Amerindian** stronghold, and petroglyphs have been found throughout the area, suggesting a long and fruitful habitation by the Arawaks and Caribs. After Europeans arrived, the area was home to large **plantations** producing bananas, coconuts, cocoa and sugarcane, though these have been replaced by smaller farms and fishing enterprises.

Arrival, information and getting around

Most visitors arrive in St Lucia at **Hewanorra International Airport** in Vieux Fort, and onward transportation throughout the island is readily available – if somewhat slow – from here. Your first stop should be the **tourist office** (Mon–Fri 7am–last flight, Sat & Sun 10am–last flight; ⓣ758/454-6644) just outside the arrival area, where you can pick up brochures and maps and get the lowdown on the latest official taxi rates. There are half a dozen **car rental** booths at the airport, open daily from 8am until the last flight, which can arrive as late as 10pm. Also on the concourse, and directly outside the arrival area, is a **taxi** stand. Taxis to Castries from the airport or anywhere in Vieux Fort travel the wide and slick East Coast Highway and turn inland toward the capital at Dennery. The **fare** to Castries is EC$140 and the 58-kilometre trip takes a bit more than an hour. Vieux Fort to Soufrière is EC$150, and the 42-kilometre ride takes forty minutes to an hour, depending upon your driver's tolerance level for pothole-filled roads.

In Vieux Fort, **buses** to Castries (route 4B) leave from New Dock Road on the south side of the airport, while the stand for west coast buses to Soufrière (route 4A) is also south of the airport at Clarke Street, next to a traffic light and a Shell service station.

Accommodation

The area **south of Soufrière**, through the fishing villages of Choiseul and Laborie to Vieux Fort, is more residential than tourist-oriented and offers a relaxed alternative to the relentless activity of the northwest coast.

Balenbouche Estate Balenbouche Bay ⓣ758/455-1244, ⓕ455-1342, ⓦwww.balenbouche.com. Scattered with fruit trees, old plantation building remains and even a few Amerindian rock carvings, this charming, slightly dilapidated eighty-acre plantation just south of Choiseul is most welcoming. Anse Touloulou beach is a brief walk away, the rooms – some in the estate house and others in adjacent cottages with kitchens – are clean and cosy; some share baths, some have cold water only. ②, ③ with kitchen.

Juliette's Lodge Beanfield, Vieux Fort ⓣ758/454-5300, ⓕ454-5305, ⓦwww.julietteslodge.com. Conveniently close to Hewanorra International Airport and popular amongst airline crews. The 27 rooms are comfortable and clean with A/C, the three apartments spacious and there's a lively restaurant serving basic but hearty fare. There's also a pool and mountain bikes available for hire, and the beach is a few hundred yards down the road. Rooms ④, apartment ⑤

Mirage Beach Resort Laborie Bay, Laborie ⓣ758/455-9763, ⓕ455-9237, ⓦwww.cavip.com/mirage. Right on the bay in the calm, beautiful fishing village of Laborie, this divine spot offers five well-appointed rooms by the water, some with kitchenette and terrace; the friendly owners also operate a French/creole open-air restaurant and bar on site. ❸, ❹ with kitchenette.

Choiseul

South of Soufrière, the west coast road meanders through hilly inland terrain, passing several small settlements before descending abruptly toward the coast and the community of Choiseul, named for the compact village of **Choiseul** itself: the turn-off is on the right, just past a white Anglican church. This is a quiet place, with little to do save swimming by the beach or river and exploring the pretty waterfront. About half a mile south of the village, though, is the small satellite settlement of **La Fargue**, best known for the **Choiseul Arts and Craft Development Centre** (open Mon–Sat, call for hours; ⓣ758/459-3226), the best place on the south coast to buy locally produced crafts.

Vieux Fort and around

Jammed with traffic, **VIEUX FORT** is St Lucia's second largest town and its most southerly settlement, a busy commercial centre and the base for businesses which service sprawling **Hewanorra International Airport**, just north of downtown. Both the town and the airport lie on a relatively flat plain that slopes gently toward the north and the south-central mountains, and as the southern tip of St Lucia comes to a point around Vieux Fort, the runway stretches – literally – from the east to the west coast of the island.

Just south of Vieux Fort – in fact, it's St Lucia's most southerly point – lies **Cape Moule à Chique Lighthouse**, reached by bearing left onto New Dock Road at the town roundabout and then left again into the hills, and one of the finest viewpoints on the island. The **Anse de Sables beach** stretches some 2km from the foot of the cliffs here to Pointe Sable, and is the only place to swim near Vieux Fort. A favoured spot for windsurfers thanks to mild surf and the presence of the Club Mistral (Nov–June 8.30am–5pm; ⓦwww.club-mistral.com) at its southern end, the expansive seashore is usually windy, with virtually no trees for shade; nor are there toilet facilities except for those at the oceanside bars and restaurants. Also at the south end of the beach is the **Maria Islands Interpretive Centre** (Mon–Fri 9am–4.30pm; ⓣ758/454-5014), a small natural history centre as well as the place to arrange a trip to the Maria Islands, which lie about half a mile offshore (see below). The one-room **museum** provides an interesting insight into local ecosystems and history, with displays on Amerindian culture (including skeletal remains and a skull found in the area), as well as on mangroves and marine life.

Maria Islands Nature Reserve

Just over half a mile off the Anse de Sables shore are the two scrubby, windswept cays that comprise the **Maria Islands Nature Reserve**. Both islands are breeding areas for numerous **sea birds**, including the booby and frigate, and are home to two rare reptiles, one of which – the **kouwés snake** – is found nowhere else in the world. About a metre long with dark green and brown markings, the harmless *kouwés* ("couresse") once thrived on the mainland but was eradicated by the mongooses introduced by sugarcane planters; today, they number a mere one hundred or so. The other reptile is St Lucia's *zandoli tè*, or ground lizard, found only on the Maria Islands and nearby Praslin Island on the east coast, were some of their number were transferred due to the extreme aridity of the Marias in the dry season. At around 35cm long with a bright blue tail and a yellow belly, the male is easily recognized; females are brown with darker vertical stripes, and therefore less ostentatious.

There's a short but comely **beach** of golden sand on the larger of the two islands, Maria Major, with a **reef** a few metres offshore. Several unmarked and unchallenging **trails** loop around the islands, and though it's difficult to get lost on such tiny pieces of land, no one is allowed on the Marias without an **authorized guide** from the St Lucia National Trust. To arrange one, phone or call in at the Maria Islands Interpretive Centre (see opposite). Costing EC$94 for one person and EC$80 per person for groups of two or more, the trips begin at the centre and consist of walking tours of the islands as well as stops for swimming and snorkelling (bring your own gear). Though you can arrange Saturday or Sunday trips, the centre is open only on weekdays, and its hours can be erratic – it's always best to call ahead.

Eating and drinking

Though there's less choice than along the north and west coasts, the south has its share of good places to **eat** nonetheless. There are some reliable hotel restaurants near Hewanorra airport, and for snacks, try the beach bars along the Anse de Sables shoreline. If you fancy some western-style fast food, there's a branch of *KFC* at JQ's Plaza in Vieux Fort.

Il Pirata Vieux Fort ⓣ758/454-6610. Tues–Sun 7am–9.30pm. Dark Italian restaurant that isn't enhanced by a drab beachside setting near to the crumbling remnants of an old dock. The food, though, is a happy contrast; specialities include deep-oven pizza, home-made pastas and a decent fish Milanese.

Mirage Beach Resort Laborie Bay, Laborie ⓣ758/455-9763, ⓕ455-9237, ⓦwww.cavip.com/mirage. Good, local food in a relaxing alfresco restaurant; the waves lap gently just below you as you eat.

The Reef Beach Café Anse de Sables ⓣ758/454-3418. Tues–Sat 10am–late. A basic beachside restaurant and bar serving standard fare of beers, burgers, pizza and some West Indian dishes. On weekends during the high season, there's typically a lot of live music and dancing on the beach, with a predominantly young crowd of tourists, windsurfers from *Club Mistral*, locals and students from a nearby medical school. During the off-season, call to find out if there's anything happening.

16.5

The east coast

Churned up by the Caribbean trade winds, the pounding waters of the Atlantic have carved out a rough and jagged **east coast** on St Lucia, one that's mainly ignored by visitors – to their loss. Characterized by lively surf smashing against rocky and cliff-lined shores and a verdant blanket of banana plants, the area provides a visual as well as an atmospheric contrast to the north and west. Less suited to farming and fishing, the region is also sparsely inhabited in comparison to other island regions.

St Lucia's **coastal highway** parallels the eastern shoreline from Vieux Fort to Dennery, where it cuts inland, heading northwest across the island to Castries. It's by far the fastest way to travel the 58km between Vieux Fort and the capital; it's also the preferred route for buses and taxis between the two towns. Along the way, east-coast **bus** stops include Micoud, Desruisseaux (in the hills south of Micoud), Mon Repose, Praslin and Dennery, but due to erratic scheduling, exploring the coastline by bus is not particularly efficient.

The southeast coast

Named in honour of the French Governor de Micoud, who ruled St Lucia from 1768 to 1771, the relatively sizeable town of **MICOUD** spreads back from the sheltered bay of Port Micoud. The suitability of the harbour to fishing, and the ready availability of fresh water from the **Troumassé River**, which borders the town to the south, are the principal factors cited by archeologists as evidence of intense **Amerindian** presence in the area. Some nine settlements are believed to have existed in the Micoud Quarter, and to have been rapidly abandoned after the arrival of European settlers in the eighteenth century.

Aside from the pretty bay, dotted with fishing boats and churches, Micoud is best known as the birthplace of the island's first prime minister, **John Compton**, though there's nothing to commemorate the connection. The town is also renowned as a particularly enthusiastic focal point for two island-wide carnivalesque religious **festivals**: **La Rose** in August and **La Marguerite** in October.

The Mamiku Gardens and Fox Grove Inn

Just a few minutes north of Micoud by car lies one of the most serene places in St Lucia, the beautifully landscaped fifteen-acre **Mamiku Gardens** (daily 9am–5pm; EC$15, or $20 with guide; ⓣ758/455-3729, ⓦwww.mamiku.com). The gardens are teeming with brightly coloured exotic blooms such as hibiscus, ginger and heliconia, and you can explore the former plantation site via a simple network of short **walking trails**, each with resting spots at suitably beautiful points.

Within walking distance of the gardens is the east coast's finest dining and accommodation option, the **Fox Grove Inn** (ⓣ758/455-3271, ⓕ455-3800, ⓦwww.foxgroveinn.com; ❸). The charming, basic rooms here have lovely views, and there's both a swimming pool and pool table on site. The **restaurant**, open to non-guests as well, features delicately prepared fresh seafood and lobster, when in season, from the village of Dennery to the north. Portions are generous, the salads excellent (try the smoked king fish) and, like the rooms, the views over acres of banana plantation to Praslin Bay and the Fregates are second to none.

Fregate Islands Nature Reserve

Occupying the northern section of Praslin Bay some 10km north of Micoud is the **Fregate Islands Nature Reserve** (daily Aug–April 9am–5pm, tours only). The reserve is centred around the two tiny **cays** just metres offshore and named for the seagoing **frigate bird** that nests here between May and July, when the reserve is completely off limits. Glossy jet-black birds with forked tail feathers, male frigates have distinctive red or bright orange throat pouches which are expanded during mating time to attract females. As you're not allowed onto the islands themselves, the reserve is best explored on the mainland section via an easy, 1.5km **walking trail** that loops through a changing scenery of thick vegetation to dry spots of low-lying bushes and cacti, passing a **waterfall** that flows in the rainy season, a mangrove swamp and an observation point overlooking the Fregate Islands before returning to base.

The reserve is marked by a sign in front of a small car park on the ocean side of the highway; however, when you get there, you'll probably find the entrance gated and locked. The Fregates are maintained by the **St Lucia National Trust** (Ⓣ758/452-5005 or 453-1495, Ⓦwww.sluna.org), and no one is allowed in without one of their authorized guides, who will conduct **tours** for groups of two or more; these are best booked in advance and cost EC$55 per person. A pleasant alternative – or addition – to touring the reserves is the **Eastern Nature Trail** (same contact details; US$12), a pleasant two-mile guided stroll along the Atlantic Coast. Again, call and book in advance.

Dennery and Grande Anse

Once known as Anse Canot, and later as Le Grand Mouyaba, **DENNERY** was given its current name by the French, following a 1768 visit to the town by the then Windward Islands governor, Count D'Ennery. The village extends back from a deep and protected **bay**, with uninhabited **Dennery Island** at its northern tip. A major export centre for agricultural produce throughout the nineteenth century, Dennery is a farming community today, and – since the addition of the large, Japanese-funded Daito Complex and Pier processing facility – it's also one of St Lucia's busiest **fishing** centres. The **town** itself is a jumble of compact streets with a few bars but nothing much of interest save the Saturday night **fish fry** on the seafront. A pleasant, low-key and mainly local affair, it's much less developed than the overpriced affairs at Anse La Raye and Gros Islet, and much less touristy too.

Around 10km north of Dennery, the wide, windswept **Grande Anse beach** boasts more than a mile of blonde sand set against a backdrop of cliffs and hills covered with dry vegetation. Once part of a plantation estate, the bay sits in the middle of an area slated to become a new **national park** comprising several other nearby beaches, including Anse Lavoutte to the north (see p.616). As with Anse Lavoutte, the beach here is a favoured nesting spot of the giant **leatherback turtles**, and turtle-watching tours are given throughout the egg-laying season (see box overleaf). National park or not, most of the roads to Grande Anse remain dirt and gravel tracks that become impassable after rains. A sedan car might make it, but a 4WD is a safer bet, and it's a good idea to ask locals about current conditions. Access is most often easiest from the west coast at Choc Bay (see p.611), via the paved Allan Bousquet Highway. At Babonneau, turn off onto the gravel and dirt track that leads to the village of Desbarra, from where a single track leads down to Grande Anse. The seven-mile ride from Choc Bay can take up to ninety minutes.

Turtle watching

In conjunction with the Department of Fisheries, Heritage Tours organizes an annual programme of **turtle watches**, allowing around 1000 visitors each season to experience the stirring spectacle of leatherback turtles laying their eggs. The watches take place daily in leatherback season (mid-March to mid-July) and cost US$65, which covers transport from your hotel and tent expenses, dinner, breakfast, sleeping mats and a T–shirt; you'll have to bring your own flashlight, toilet paper, and warm clothing, as nights can be cool and breezy. Once at the beach, you settle into a rustic tent village and take turns at patrolling the beach. Whenever a turtle is spotted, you'll be called to have a look. The watches are becoming very popular, and to ensure a place, it's best to contact Heritage Tours well in advance (PO Box GM868, Sans Souci, Castries, St Lucia, WI; ⓣ758/451-6058, 458-1587 or 452-506, ⓔheritagetours@candw.lc).

Barbados

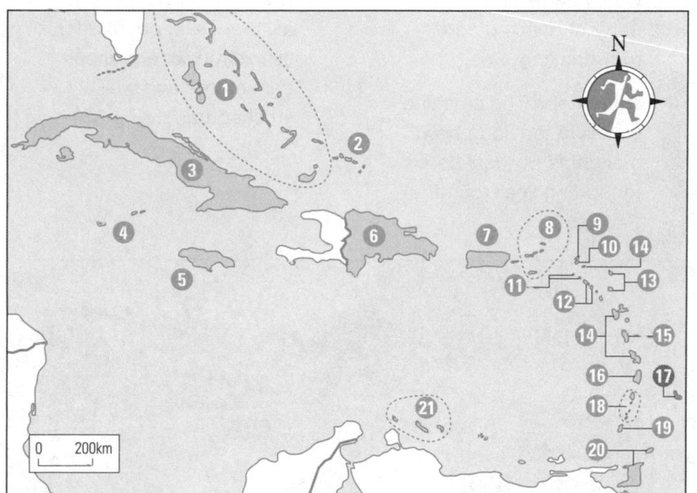

Barbados Highlights

* **Welchman Hall Gully** Stroll through some of the island's most wild and beautiful scenery. See p.660

* **Crop Over** One of the most fun festivals in the Caribbean – an extended party of dancing and rum-drinking. See p.644

* **Bathsheba** The crashing waves in the soup bowl make this an ideal spot for surfing year-round. See p.665

* **Holetown** Sample from the town's fabulous selection of restaurants, including a few good-value options. See p.656

* **After Dark, St Lawrence Gap** Dress up for a night out at *After Dark*, popular for its live music, enormous dance floor and well-stocked bar. See p.651

Introduction and Basics

Tourists pour into **Barbados** from all over the world, drawn by the delightful climate, the big blue sea and brilliant white sandy beaches. Many of them rarely stray far from their hotels and guesthouses, but those who make an effort find a proud island scattered with an impressive range of historic sites and, away from the mostly gently rolling landscape, dramatic scenery in hidden caves, cliffs and gullies.

For more than three centuries Barbados was a **British colony** and retains something of a British feel: the place names, the cricket, horse-racing and polo, Anglican parish churches, and even a hilly district known as Scotland. But the Britishness is often exaggerated, for this is a distinctly **West Indian country**, covered by a patchwork of sugar-cane fields and dotted with rum shops, where calypso is the music of choice and flying fish the favoured food.

The people of Barbados, known as **Bajans**, take great pride in their tiny island of 430 square kilometres and 250,000 people, which has produced writers like George Lamming, calypsonians like the Mighty Gabby and cricket players including the great Sir Gary Sobers, who have for decades had an influence way out of proportion to the size of their home country.

Tourism plays a major part in the country's economy and revenues have been put to good use. The infrastructure and public transport are first-rate and there is no sign of the poverty that continues to bedevil some Caribbean islands. Development has mostly been pretty discreet, many of the facilities are Bajan-owned, there are no private beaches and no sign of American fast-food franchises.

Where to go

Chief among the island's attractions are its old plantation houses – places like **St Nicholas Abbey** and **Francia**, superb botanical gardens at Andromeda and the **Flower Forest**, and the military forts and signal stations at **Gun Hill** and **Grenade Hall**. The capital, **Bridgetown**, is a lively place to visit, with an excellent national museum and great nightlife in its bars and clubs. Small and largely untouristed **Speightstown** – once a thriving and wealthy port – is a good place to wander for a couple of hours then grab a drink on a terrace overlooking the sea. And, of course, there are the beaches, from the often crowded strips such as **Accra Beach** and **Mullins Bay** to tiny but superb patches of palm-fringed sand in the southeast.

Diving is excellent on the coral reefs around Barbados, with the good sites all off the calm west and southwest coasts, from Maycocks Bay in the north right round to Castle Bank near St Lawrence Gap.

When to go

For many visitors, Barbados's tropical climate is its leading attraction – hot and sunny year-round. The weather is best, however, during the high season, from mid-December to mid-April, with rainfall low and the heat tempered by cooling trade winds. The peak season also brings the biggest crowds and the highest prices.

Things can get a good bit hotter in the summer, and, particularly in September and October, the humidity can become oppressive. September is also the most threatening month for hurricanes. The season officially runs from early June to late October, but big blows only hit about once a decade.

Getting there

By far the easiest and cheapest way to get to Barbados is by **air**.

The majority of British and Irish visitors travel on some sort of two-week **package tour** that includes a charter flight to the island. Alternatively a few airlines offer direct scheduled flights from London, while some

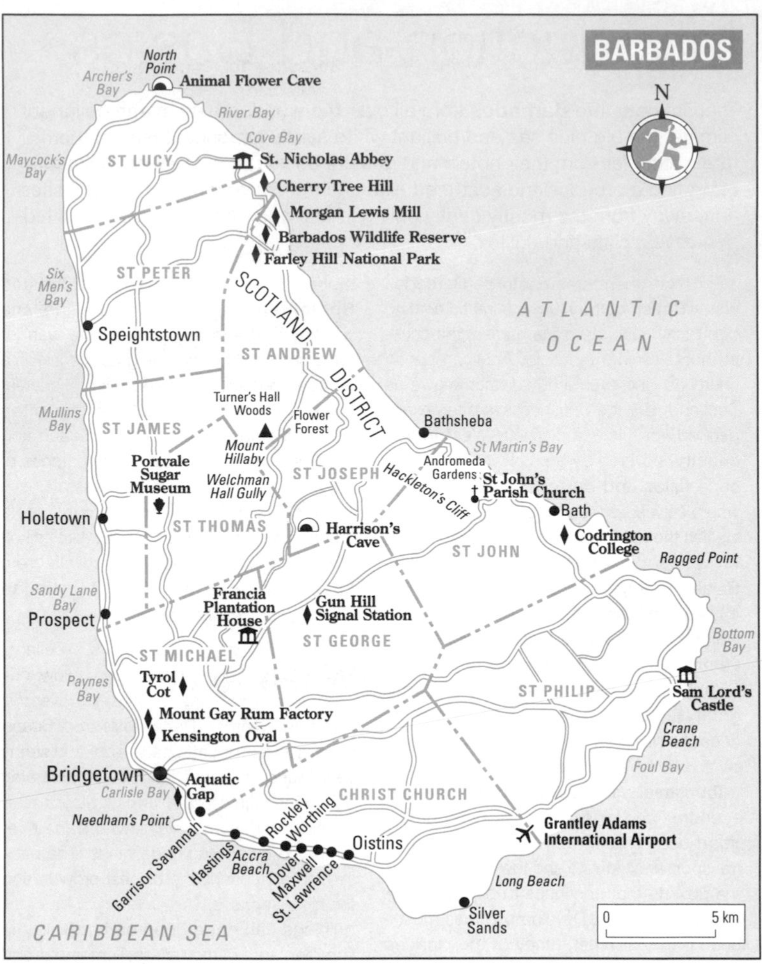

require stopovers in the US. There are no direct flights from Ireland, but there are connections via London or via New York and Miami. British Airways, Virgin and BWIA all fly from London.

Visitors from the US have a good number of options. BWIA flies non-stop out of New York, Miami and Dallas; American Airlines flies non-stop from NY and Miami, while Air Jamaica flies out of LA, NY, Chicago, Miami and several other major US cities. **Vacation packages**, including airfare, accommodation and sometimes meals, can be very good value.

BWIA flies to Barbados from Toronto, and Air Canada serves Toronto and Montreal.

There are no direct flights from New Zealand or Australia, and package deals are few and far between. Travellers from these countries will need to fly to one of the major US gateways and pick up onward connections from there.

The occasional **cruise ship** typically only docks in Barbados for a day or two at most.

Airport departure tax is presently B$25, payable at the airport when you leave, in local currency only.

Money and costs

Barbados is not a particularly cheap place to visit, and prices for many items are at least what you'd expect to pay at home. Bargaining is usually frowned upon, but during the off-season, it's worth asking for reduced rates.

The island's unit of **currency** is the **Barbados dollar** (B$), divided into 100 cents. It comes in bills of B$100, B$50, B$20, B$10, B$5 and B$2 and coins of B$1, B$0.25, B$0.10, B$0.05 and B$0.01. The rate of exchange is fixed roughly at B$2 to US$1; the US dollar is also widely accepted. Prices are normally quoted in B$, with the exception of accommodation which is almost universally quoted in US$, and we have followed this practice in this chapter.

Banking hours are generally Monday to Thursday 8am–3pm and Friday 8am–5pm. Bridgetown, Holetown and Speightstown have numerous banks, and there are branches at most of the south coast resorts; most have ATMs. Many **hotels** will also exchange money. Major **credit cards** are widely accepted, though not always at the smaller establishments.

Many hotels and restaurants automatically add a **service charge** of 10 percent.

Information, websites and maps

Brochures on the main attractions and events, and a good road map, are available from the **Barbados Tourism Authority** (BTA), which has an office at Harbour Road in Bridgetown (Ⓣ246/427-2623, Ⓕ426-4080) and a desk at the airport. While there is no detailed listings publication, the free fortnightly magazine *Sunseeker* – available from the tourist office and some hotels – carries information on many of the events. Keep an eye also on the daily papers and flyers posted up around the island.

Websites

Barbados Tourism Authority
Ⓦwww.barbados.org.
Up-to-date info on events, places to stay and eat, guided tours and car rental outfits, many of which you can book through the site.

Dive Barbados
Ⓦwww.divebarbados.net.
Useful for its descriptions of the island's main dive opportunities and its links to dive/accommodation deals.

Fun Barbados
Ⓦwww.funbarbados.com.
Informative island guide offering some excellent deals on accommodation and car rental.

Getting around

The bus system in Barbados is excellent, with blue government **buses** and yellow, privately owned **minibuses** running all over the island. Fares are a flat rate of B$1.50. Buses run roughly every half-hour between Grantley Adams International Airport and Bridgetown, stopping at or near most of the south coast resorts en route. Services to the resorts on the west coast are less frequent.

White minivans known as **route taxis** also operate like minibuses, packing in passengers and stopping anywhere en route. They're particularly numerous on the south coast and the fare is B$1.50.

Finding a **taxi** – identifiable by the Z on their numberplates – is rarely a problem. Fares are regulated but there are no meters, so agree on the fare beforehand. From the airport, expect to pay around B$40 to the hotels in St James on the west coast, B$50 to Speightstown, B$20 to Crane Bay and B$25 to the resorts in the southwest.

Driving is on the left. While the roads in Barbados are mostly good and the distances small, car rental prices are fairly high, starting at around B$90 per day, B$500 per week, for the mini mokes (open-sided buggies) that you'll see all over the island (you'll pay a little more for a regular car). As car rental companies here are all local, it can be easier to arrange rentals once you've arrived. Reliable firms include: Coconut (☎246/437-0297), Hill's (☎246/426-5280), Premier (☎246/424-2277) and Sunny Isle (☎246/435-7979).

Prices for **scooters** and **motorbikes** normally start at around B$80 per day; try Caribbean Scooters, Waterfront Marina, Bridgetown (☎246/436-8522).

Tours

Various local companies offer island-wide **sightseeing tours**. The following are just a selection of what's available.

Chalene Tours ☎246/228-2550. Daytrips to Speightstown, Farley Hill Park, Bathsheba and Sunbury Plantation House.

EL Scenic Tours ☎246/424-9108. Daily tours taking in one or more of the following: Harrison's Cave, the Flower Forest, Bathsheba and St John's Parish Church.

Island Safari ☎246/429-5337. Informative off-the-beaten-track LandRover trips.

Accommodation

With hotels stringing out virtually back-to-back both north and east of Bridgetown, there is no shortage of **accommodation** in Barbados. Heading up the **west coast** you'll find most of the pricier (and swankier) options, many of them concentrated around the lovely Paynes Bay or on either side of Holetown, but thinning out considerably as you continue north towards Speightstown. On the **south coast**, where the beaches are just as good (or better), accommodation is much more reasonably priced, with plenty of good-value guesthouses, particularly around Worthing and St Lawrence Gap. There are very few options elsewhere on the island. A handful of small, long-established hotels still do a light trade on the wild **east coast**, around Bathsheba and Cattlewash.

Food and drink

Despite the island's small size, the tourist market has produced a staggering variety of **places to eat**. Although most of Barbados's restaurants have a vague international flavour, it's well worth sampling traditional Bajan cuisine.

Fresh **seafood** is the island's speciality: snapper, barracuda and dolphin fish, as well as fresh prawns and lobster. Most popular of all is the **flying fish** – virtually a Bajan national emblem.

Look out, too, for other traditional Bajan dishes: the national dish is **cou-cou** (a corn-meal and okra pudding) and saltfish, and you'll occasionally find the fabulous **pudding and souse** – steamed sweet potato served with cuts of pork pickled in onion, lime and hot peppers. **Cohobblopot** (also known as pepperpot) is a spicy meat and okra stew.

For **snacks**, you'll find **cutters** (bread rolls with a meat or cheese filling), coconut bread, and more substantial **rotis** (flat, unleavened bread wrapped around a filling of curried meat or vegetables); all are widely available.

Rum is the liquor of choice for many Bajans. Hundreds of tiny rum bars dot the island, which are an integral part of Bajan social life. On the coast, you'll find fewer places that cater specifically to drinkers but, all-inclusives apart, most hotels and restaurants will welcome you for a drink even if you're not staying or eating.

Phones, post and email

Barbados's **postal service** is extremely efficient. The GPO is located in Bridgetown and there are branches across the island, in the larger towns and villages and at the airport.

Calling within Barbados is simple – most hotels provide a **telephone** in each room and local calls are usually free. You'll also see Bartel **phone booths** all over the island, and these can be used for local and international calls. Most of the booths take phone

The **country code** for Barbados is ☎246.

Emergency numbers

Police ☎211
Fire ☎311
Ambulance ☎511

cards only, available from hotels, post offices and shops.

If you want to access the **internet**, many hotels will let you use their computers for free or for a nominal charge. Alternatively, in St Lawrence Gap, *Bean & Bagel* (see p.651) offers internet access, as does Global Business Centre, a stall in the West Coast Mall in Holetown.

Holidays and festivals

The main **festival** in Barbados is the summertime Crop Over (see p.644), which reaches its climax on Kadooment Day when the festival monarchs are crowned. This is a great time to catch some of the island's famous calypso. There are plenty of other events to distract you from the beach as well (see box below). The tourist boards have full details.

The usual **public holidays** (see p.40) are celebrated, along with Errol Barrow Day (January 21), National Heroes Day (April 28), Labour Day (May 1), Emancipation Day (August 1), Kadooment Day (first Mon in Aug) and Independence Day (November 30).

Sports and outdoor activities

Alongside Jamaica and Trinidad, Barbados is one of the Big Three Caribbean **cricketing** nations, but while success in other sports has diverted attention from the game in the other two countries, Bajans remain largely focused on cricket. More perhaps than anywhere else on earth, the game is *the* national passion. If you get the chance, go and catch a day of international cricket at the Kensington Oval in Bridgetown.

The island also has a lively **equestrian** tradition, with races every other Saturday (except during April) at the Garrison Savannah **racecourse**, and at Sandy Lane in March. There are several **polo** fields as well, the most famous at Holder's House (see p.654).

For golfers, there are two eighteen-hole public **golf courses**: at the Barbados Golf Club (☎246/428-8463) and Sandy Lane (☎246/432-4563). Greens fees are around B$150. There is also a decent nine-hole course at the *Club Rockley* resort (☎246/435-7873) on the south coast.

Some of the best and most scenic **hiking** on Barbados is along the beaches, particularly between Martin's Bay and Bath and between Bathsheba and Cattlewash. Organized hikes are arranged by the Barbados National Trust (☎246/436-9033).

Festivals and events

January
Barbados Jazz Festival ☎246/429-2084
Barbados Windsurfing Championships ☎246/426-5837
Busta Cup Cricket Competition ☎246/426-5128

February
Holetown Festival ☎246/430-7300

March
Holder's classical music festival
Test cricket ☎246/426-5128
Oistins Fish Festival ☎246/428-6738

April
Congaline Street festival ☎246/424-0909

July–August
Crop Over festival (see p.644)

October
Barbados International Triathlon ☎246/435-7000

November
Caribbean Surfing Championship ☎246/435-6377
Festival of Creative Arts ☎246/424-0909

December
Barbados Road Race Series

Watersports

With excellent diving opportunities, the island has plenty of reputable **dive** operators (see box on this page), most of whom will provide transport to and from your hotel. Prices can vary dramatically between dive shops – but expect around B$100 for a single-tank dive, B$150 for a two-tank dive and B$120 for a night dive, including use of equipment. For full **open-water certification**, budget around B$750. Serious divers should consider a **package deal**; these may simply cover three or five two-tank dives (roughly B$400 and B$700 respectively), or may also include accommodation.

There's good **snorkelling**, too, again especially off the west coast, where there are plenty of good coralheads just offshore and sea turtles in the turtle grass near the *Lone Star*. Several of the dive operators also take snorkellers out on their dive trips for around B$20–30, including equipment. Many top hotels provide guests with free snorkelling gear.

A number of the hotels in the southeast cater mainly or exclusively for **windsurfers**; boards can be rented beside the *Silver Rock Hotel* (☎246/428-2866) or at the *Silver Sands Hotel* (☎246/428-6001), and cost around B$40 per hour, B$70 for half a day, or from the windsurfing schools, whose prices for coaching border on the extortionate. **Surfing** is also superb, particularly on the east coast at the Bathsheba "soupbowl", and boards can be rented from the *Round House Inn* in Bathsheba (see p.666).

If you're after **water-skiing**, **jet-ski rides** or a speedy tow on an inflatable banana, most hotels can find a reputable operator for you; Hightide Watersports (☎246/432-0931), in Sandy Lane Bay, is one of the most trustworthy. **Kayaks** can be rented from Kayaker's Point (☎246/428-6747) near Oistins.

Watersports operators

CoralIsleDivers Cavans Lane, Bridgetown ☎246/434-8377.
DiveBlueReef Mount Standfast, St James ☎246/422-3133, Ⓦwww.divebluereef.com.
Exploresub Barbados StLawrenceGap ☎246/435-6542.
Hightide Watersports *Sandy Lane Hotel*, St James ☎246/432-0931, Ⓔhightide@sunbeach.net.

Boat trips

There is no shortage of **boat trips** around Barbados, with the emphasis normally on being part of a big crowd. Most of the **cruise boats** charge a single price, which will depend on whether the trip includes a meal and/or "free" drinks, and live or canned music. The **catamarans** offer similar trips, though usually with a smaller number of passengers and less in the way of entertainment. All these boats sail out of Bridgetown's Shallow Harbour, but most will pick up guests from any of the major resorts.

Boat operators

Atlantis Submarine ☎246/436-8929. A boat takes you out of the Bridgetown harbour to board the sub, which then submerges to 30–45m, cruising slowly above the seabed for the thirty-minute trip. Everyone has a seat by a porthole, and there's a commentary from the co-pilot. B$150 per person.
Harbour Master ☎246/430-0900. Four-decker boat runs day tours, taking you up the coast to a beach, with a buffet lunch and free drinks (Tues & Thurs 11am–4pm; B$95). It also runs evening trips (Tues & Thurs 6–10pm), with a floor show, live band, dinner and drinks all included in the price, and a cheaper option (Sun 5–9pm; B$35), where you pay for your food and drinks and there's a DJ.
Jolly Roger ☎246/427-7245. Sleek, two-sailed "pirate ship" running west coast lunch cruises (Tues, Thurs & Sat 10am–2pm; B$123), with the emphasis on drinking and dancing up on the top deck, walking the plank and swinging from the yardarm into the sea.

History

The earliest settlers in Barbados were Amerindians, who came to the island in dug-out canoes from the Guianas in South America. Christopher Columbus, the first European visitor to the West Indies, never stopped at Barbados, but in the early sixteenth century, Spanish slave-traders arrived to collect Amerindians to labour in the gold and silver mines of New Spain.

In 1625 a party of British sailors landed in Barbados, claiming the island for their king, and in February 1627 eighty colonists landed at present-day Holetown. They quickly found that **sugar** grew well in the island soil, and the industry brought almost instantaneous prosperity. By the 1650s, Barbados was reckoned to be the wealthiest place in the New World.

As Barbados developed, a workforce was needed for the sugar plantations. At first, the main source of workers was **indentured labourers**, escaping poverty in England and Scotland. In return for their passage to Barbados, these men and women signed contracts to work on the plantations without wages for up to seven years. Later, large numbers of **West African slaves** were brought to Barbados, and the island slowly began to take on its present-day ethnic composition.

By 1700, the wonder days of Barbados sugar had passed. Huge fortunes had been made, but increased competition from Jamaica and the Leeward Islands had reduced profits. Many of the small planters were squeezed out of business, handing even more economic power to the large plantation owners.

In 1807 the British government abolished the slave trade. Far more threatening to the planters, though, was the movement for the abolition of slavery itself. Barbadian slave-owners made some small improvements in the slaves' working conditions, but the slaves realized that these were little more than a reluctant sop to the abolitionists. Rumours spread, claiming that emancipation was being blocked on the island. Frustration grew, and in April 1816 Barbados faced its only serious slave uprising.

Bussa's Rebellion – named for its alleged leader, an African slave from a plantation in St Philip – began in the southeast with attacks on property and widespread burning of the sugar fields, and quickly spread to all of the island's southern and central parishes. Within three days, however, the rebellion was crushed; just a handful of whites were killed, but over a thousand slaves were either killed in battle or executed afterwards.

Nonetheless, by the early 1830s the reformers in London had won the argument for the **abolition of slavery** and **full emancipation** took place on August 1, 1838. The planters remained confident that the new situation would work to their advantage; no longer responsible for the upkeep of their workers, they would have a large pool of cheap, unorganized labour desperate for work.

Some former slaves headed to the towns, particularly Bridgetown, but most had little choice but to continue work on the sugar estates. The white planters still ran Barbados; they owned almost all of the farmland, and controlled the Assembly that made the island's laws.

A significant influence on the island's development was the decision by the United States in 1904 to build the **Panama Canal**. By the outbreak of World War I Barbados had provided at least 20,000 workers – virtually all black and a huge percentage of the local workforce. Many returned with sizeable savings, which they were able to invest in new businesses and in land. The white planters, who had previously refused to sell land to blacks, were now obliged to do so by economic circumstances. Even if much of the land bought by blacks was marginal, by the 1930s the pattern of land ownership had changed dramatically.

Alongside economic change, the island saw significant political development. Black political parties were formed in the 1930s and 1940s to fight elections and, although executive power remained with the British-appointed governor, black politicians were appointed to the highly influential Executive Committee.

During the 1960s, **foreign investment** and tourism were actively encouraged to reduce the island's dependence on sugar. The British government finally recognized the capability of the Bajans to govern themselves and, in 1966, Barbados became an **independent country**.

Development has been fast since independence and the economy has boomed. Tourism remains the main money-earner, but success in manufacturing and other service industries means that not all of the island's eggs are in the tourism basket.

17.1

Bridgetown and around

With a gorgeous location beside the white-sand beaches of Carlisle Bay, busy **Bridgetown** is the capital and only city of Barbados. One of the oldest cities in the Caribbean, the architecture of Bridgetown today is largely a blend of attractive, balconied colonial buildings, warehouses and brash modern office blocks. The centre of activity is the Careenage, parking place for numerous sleek yachts overlooked by the **Barbadian parliament**. A number of the island's main religious buildings are within five minutes' walk of here, including **St Michael's Cathedral** and the **synagogue**, both erected on the sites of their mid-seventeenth-century originals.

Just north of the city there are a couple of **rum factories** that you can tour, while **Tyrol Cot** is an unusual nineteenth-century house that was home to two of the island's leading post-war politicians, Sir Grantley Adams and his son Tom Adams.

Southeast is the historic **Garrison area**, where the British empire maintained its Caribbean military headquarters from 1780 to 1905. It's an evocative place; the huge grassy savannah, today a racecourse and public park, was once the army's parade ground. The ranks of brightly coloured military buildings around its edge include the worthwhile **Barbados Museum** and the **Barbados Gallery of Art**.

Bridgetown is an extremely **safe** city, even at night, though you may want to avoid the seedy area southeast of the Fairchild Street bus station, particularly around Nelson Street and Jordan's Lane where the red-light district is located.

Getting there and getting around

Efficient **buses** and **minibuses** run to the city from all over the island. If you're driving here, you'll have to negotiate a slightly tricky one-way system, but there are many safe areas to park in the centre. Seeing the central sights is easiest **on foot**.

There is little reason to **stay** in Bridgetown, and the city has only one hotel of note: the *Grand Barbados Beach Resort* at Aquatic Gap (Ⓣ 246/426-4000, Ⓕ 429-2400, Ⓔ grandhtl@caribsurf.com; ⑥), which caters mainly to visitors on business.

The City

A good place to start your tour of Bridgetown is beside the **Careenage**, a long, thin finger of water that pushes right into the city centre. There are always plenty of expensive yachts and fishing boats moored at its western end. The **parliament buildings** (open to visitors during parliamentary debates), as well as bustling shops and a couple of smart restaurants can all be found in the immediate vicinity, some of the latter two housed in restored warehouses.

National Heroes Square and St Michael's Cathedral

On the north side of the Careenage is the tiny **National Heroes Square**, formerly known for over a century as Trafalgar Square. In 1999 the square was renamed,

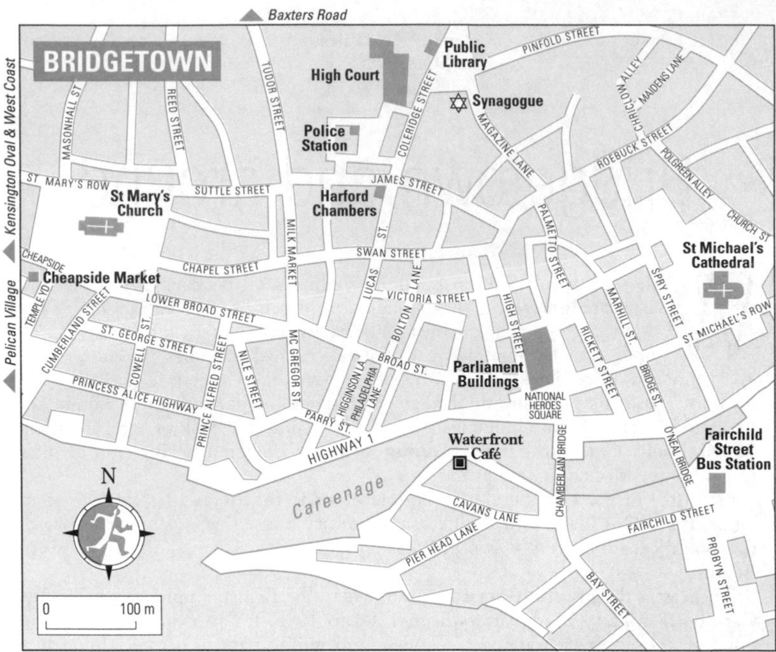

though at present a bronze statue of the British Admiral Horatio Nelson, surrounded by the whirlwind of Bridgetown traffic, still stands.

About 200m east of the square and parliament buildings, along St Michael's Row, the large, red-roofed **St Michael's Cathedral** (daily 9am–4pm; free) is the country's principal Anglican place of worship. A stone church was first erected here in 1665, although the present building mostly dates from 1786. It's a spacious, airy place, with a large barrel roof, and incorporates some fine mahogany carving in the pulpit and choir. The cathedral's sprawling churchyard is the resting place for many of the island's most prominent figures, including Sir Grantley Adams and his son Tom.

The old city

Back in the town centre, a network of narrow lanes links the main roads above the parliament buildings, marking the parts of the city that were first developed. Bridgetown's oldest surviving building is probably the attorney's office, **Harford Chambers**, on the corner of Lucas and James streets, with its irregular brickwork and classic Dutch gables.

Heading north up Coleridge Street, and across the road from the public library, you find the elaborate **drinking fountain** that was a gift to the city from John Montefiore, one of its leading Jewish traders, in 1865. Though not as jauntily painted as in its heyday, the fountain still has stone reliefs of Prudence, Justice, Fortitude and Temperance and exhortations to the thirsty citizens of Bridgetown to "Be sober minded" and "Look to the end".

Just south of the fountain, the pink and white **synagogue** (daily 10am–4pm; free) was first built in 1655 and rebuilt after hurricane damage in 1833. Jews were among the earliest settlers in Barbados; many of them arrived in the 1650s to escape the Inquisition in Brazil, bringing a knowledge of sugarcane cultivation that was to prove crucial in boosting the island's fledgling agriculture.

Although the country's Jewish population declined over the centuries, a revitalized Jewish community – boosted during the 1930s and 1940s by refugees from Europe – persuaded the government to let them take the building back after World War II. Extensive restoration has returned it to something like its original shape. The interior has been attractively restored, and newspaper articles displayed on the walls describe the restoration work and recount some of the history. Outside, the Jewish cemetery is one of the oldest in the western hemisphere.

Broad Street and the Pelican Craft Centre

Much of central Bridgetown is given over to shopping, with dozens of duty-free stores competing for the cruise-ship dollar. The main drag is **Broad Street**, which runs northwest from National Heroes Square. This has been the city's market centre since the mid-seventeenth century, and still retains some splendid colonial buildings amid the modern chaos of clothes and jewellery shops, fast-food joints and fruit vendors. It's worth a stroll, even if you're not planning to shop.

Beyond St Mary's Church, Broad Street runs into **Cheapside**, where you'll find the station for buses and minibuses heading north, as well as the **GPO** and one of the city's larger **public markets**. On your left, Temple Street runs down to the waterfront past a row of wooden stalls that mark the edge of **Temple Yard**, where many of the city's Rastas have set up small businesses selling sandals and other handcrafted leather goods, as well as their distinctive red, gold and green jewellery and headgear.

At the bottom end of Temple Yard, the main artery running east–west is the Princess Alice Highway. Five minutes' walk along the highway to the west, the **Pelican Craft Centre** is an excellent shopping complex built on reclaimed land, with a small art gallery, a dozen or so stores selling batiks, T-shirts, paintings and other souvenirs, and a couple of snack bars.

Eating, drinking and nightlife

Although few people make the trip into Bridgetown specifically to **eat**, there are a couple of excellent restaurants that open in the evening, and the city has some of the island's best venues for **nightlife** – several of them with stages right on the beach. If you're in town at night drinking or clubbing, you might want to check out the late-opening local joints on busy **Baxters Road**, just north of the town centre, where you can get a plate of food for around B$10.

1627 and All That ✆246/428-1627. Held in the central courtyard of the Barbados Museum (and including a tour of it), *1627 and All That* is a slick show that relates, through storytelling and traditional music and dance, the history of the island since the British first landed here. Thurs and Sun 6.30–10pm.

The Boatyard Bay Street ✆246/436-2622. Live bands play by the beach on Tues, Fri and Sun (B$10–25), there's canned music, limbo and fire-eating on Thurs, and, with the DJs spinning records on Sat, a B$35 cover gets you in and all you can drink. 8.30pm–1am.

Brown Sugar Aquatic Gap ✆246/426-7684. Attractive building with iron fretwork and an interior draped with greenery, serving the best seafood in the Garrison area; prices start around B$25. Daily 6–9.30pm.

Harbour Lights ✆246/436-7225. Another nightclub right on the beach that's open nightly but most crowded for the all-you-can-drink beach parties on Mon, Wed and Fri (B$25 entry). 8.30pm–1am.

The Waterfront Café Careenage ✆246/427-0093. Some of the best food in town, with an authentic Caribbean flavour, served indoors or out beside the

Crop Over and Carnival

The **Crop Over** festival, held every summer, traditionally celebrated the completion of the sugar harvest and the end of months of exhausting work for the field-labourers on the sugar estates. As with carnival in many countries (which immediately precedes a period of fasting), Crop Over carried a frenzied sense of "enjoy-yourself-while-you-may", as workers knew that earnings would now be minimal until the next crop. Alongside the flags, dances and rum-drinking, the symbol of the festival was "Mr Harding" – a scarecrow-like figure stuffed with the dried leaves of the sugarcane – who was paraded around and introduced to the manager of the sugar plantation.

Though Crop Over has lost some of its significance since the 1960s, with tourism replacing sugar as the country's main industry, it's still the island's main festival and an excuse for an extended party. Things start slowly in early July, with craft exhibitions and band rehearsals, heating up in late July and early August with street parades, concerts and competitions between the tuk bands, steel bands and – most importantly – the battle for the title of **calypso monarch**, dominated in recent decades by the Mighty Gabby and Red Plastic Bag.

The **Congaline Carnival** is held during the last week in April, with a varied package of mostly local music that includes soca, reggae, steelpan and calypso. Daily shows are held from mid-afternoon to late evening, usually at Dover pasture near St Lawrence Gap, and other events around the island conclude with a May Day parade through Bridgetown from the Garrison savannah to the Spring Garden Highway.

water. Try the creole snapper (B$35), or, if you're just after a snack, you can get soups and salads. Live music most evenings, normally steel pans (Tues & Wed) and jazz (Fri & Sat), and a buffet dinner on Tues. Mon–Sat noon–3pm & 6–10pm, Sun 6–10pm.

Listings

Airlines Air Canada (☎246/428-1635); Air Jamaica (☎246/228-6625); American Airlines (☎246/428-4170); British Airways (☎246/436-6413); BWIA (☎246/426-2111); LIAT (☎246/434-5428 and 428-0986); Virgin (☎246/228-4886).

Embassies Australian High Commission, Bishop's Court Hill, St Michael (☎246/435-2834); British High Commission, Lower Collymore Rock Street, St Michael (☎246/430-7800); Canadian High Commission, Bishop's Court Hill, St Michael (☎246/429-3550); United States Embassy, Broad Street, Bridgetown (☎246/436-4950).

Pharmacies Cheapside Pharmacy, Cheapside (Mon–Fri 7.30am–5.30pm, Sat 7.30am–1.30pm; ☎246/437-2004), Knight's, Lower Broad Street (daily 8am–1pm; ☎246/426-5196).

Post office Bridgetown's main post office is on Cheapside (Mon 7.30am–noon & 1–3pm, Tues–Fri 8am–noon & 1–3.15pm; ☎246/43-4800).

Taxis Nelson's (☎246/429-4421); Independence (☎246/426-0090).

North of the city

North of the city, and just above the Kensington Oval cricket ground, the Spring Garden Highway heads up along the west coast, skirting the beach almost all the way to historic Speightstown in the far northwest. Much of the area immediately north of Bridgetown is given over to industrial production, including a couple of **rum factories** that are open for tours. To the northeast is **Tyrol Cot**, the former home of Sir Grantley Adams.

Mount Gay Rum Factory

The **Mount Gay Rum Factory**, a five-minute drive north of town on the Spring Garden Highway (Mon–Fri 9am–4pm, 45min tours every half-hour; B$10; ⊕246/425-8757), offers marginally the better of the rum tours. It starts with a short film giving the history of the company, which first distilled rum on the island in 1703 and is reckoned to be the world's oldest surviving producer of the spirit. The tour covers all stages of production, including refining, ageing, blending and bottling. Afterwards, head to the bar, where the bartender demonstrates how to be a rum-taster, and you're given a complimentary cocktail.

Tyrol Cot

Five minutes' northeast of Bridgetown's city centre, the exquisite little house at **Tyrol Cot** (Mon–Fri 9am–5pm; B$11.50) was the launch pad for two of the island's most illustrious political careers. From 1929 it served as the home of Sir Grantley Adams, the first elected leader of pre-independence Barbados, and it was the birthplace of his son, Tom Adams, the nation's prime minister from 1976 until his death in 1985. The building itself has some unusual architectural features, while the family's memorabilia is scattered about.

Outside the house, a tiny **heritage village** has been built, featuring half a dozen old-fashioned chattel houses built to various designs; several showcase traditional handicrafts, with local artists selling (and occasionally demonstrating) their crafts, and there's a typical rum-shop where you can get a drink and a bite to eat.

The Garrison area

By the late seventeenth century, sugar-rich Barbados had become one of the most important of Britain's overseas possessions. To protect against possible invasion, defensive forts were erected along the calm south and west coasts, with the biggest of them protecting Carlisle Bay and the capital, Bridgetown. In 1705, work was begun on a major land fort near the capital, known as St Ann's Fort and designed to offer back-up protection. By 1780, as Barbados developed, the British decided to make the island the regional centre for their West Indian troops, and more and more army buildings were put up around the fort. Today, this part of the city's outer zone, just a couple of kilometres south of the centre, is known as the **Garrison area**. Chock-full of superb Georgian architecture, it remains one of Bridgetown's most evocative districts. It retains the most attractive of the island's colonial **military buildings** including, in a restored jail, the **Barbados Museum**. A short walk from the museum, the **Barbados Gallery of Art** merits a quick visit.

The savannah

The centre of the Garrison area is the **savannah**, a huge grassy space that served as the army's parade ground. The military buildings – barracks, quartermaster's store and hospitals, as well as the fort itself – stand in a rough square around its outer edges, flanked by coconut palms and large mango trees. The savannah is still active, with sports grounds and play areas bounded by the city's **race track**.

To the south, you can still see the thick eighteenth-century walls of **St Ann's Fort** (now used by the Barbadian defence force and closed to visitors) while, just north of here, the spectacular **Main Guard** – with its tall, bright-red tower and green cupola – is the area's most striking construction. This was the guardhouse, built in 1803, where court-martials and subsequent punishments were carried out; you're normally free to wander around the building, though there's little to see. Outside, ranks of cannons point menacingly across the savannah towards some superbly restored **barrack buildings**, which now serve as government offices.

The Barbados Museum and the Barbados Gallery of Art

Housed in the Garrison's old military prison on the east side of the savannah, the **Barbados Museum** (Mon–Sat 9am–5pm, Sun 2–6pm; B$11.50) is a treat. A series of galleries run clockwise around an airy central courtyard that once rang with the sound of prisoners breaking stones. Don't try to rush through – the place is stuffed with interesting and informative exhibits on the island's history, culture, flora and fauna, and also showcases **prints and paintings** of old Barbados, **African crafts**, and **decorative arts** from around the world. **Period rooms** show what a typical bedroom, living-room and dining room would have looked like in one of the plantation houses.

If you need a break, head for the on-site **café**. Twice a week the courtyard is also the venue for *1627 and All That*, an evening of dance and story-telling (see p.643).

Directly across the Garrison savannah, the tiny **Barbados Gallery of Art** (Tues–Sat 10am–5pm; B$5), is devoted to the art of the island and the wider Caribbean as well. Around three hundred paintings, prints and sculptures form the permanent collection and there are periodic exhibitions of **local and international art**.

17.2

The south coast

The southwestern parish known as **Christ Church**, the birthplace of tourism in Barbados, is dominated by the trappings of the holiday industry. The main highway here hugs the coast, linking a string of small resorts; each consists of a fringe of white-sand beach backed by a cluster of hotels, restaurants and tourist facilities. On the whole, the area is not as beautiful as the west coast, nor as lorded over by the staggering palaces of the mega-rich, but the beaches are just as fine, there are plenty of good eateries, and prices are much more reasonable.

As you head east from Bridgetown towards the airport, several of the coastal towns bear the names (and some of the atmosphere) of British seaside resorts. Each has its speciality, however: you'll find the best beaches at **Rockley** and **Worthing**, the liveliest restaurants and nightlife at **St Lawrence Gap**, and a bustling local scene at **Oistins**, while the quieter beaches at **Silver Sands** attract windsurfers and those who want to spend their holiday strolling on relatively deserted stretches of sand.

On the other side of the airport, in the southeast of the island, you enter the far less developed parish of **St Philip**. There's just a handful of hotels here, but the scenery is spectacular, with the Atlantic waves lashing the rocky coast.

Getting there and getting around

Getting around the south coast is a breeze. Buses and minibuses run from Bridgetown as far as *Sam Lord's Castle* (see p.649), passing through most of the tourist zones on the coast, while route taxis go as far as Silver Sands. Service stops around midnight, so you'll need a car or a private taxi after that. Getting here from the west coast is a little harder – buses run between Speightstown and Oistins, usually bypassing Bridgetown, though they're less frequent than the ones that ply the south coast. If you're driving, Highway 7 runs along the coast between Bridgetown and Oistins, from where it doglegs up past the airport and on to Crane Bay and *Sam Lord's Castle*.

Accommodation

Rockley and Worthing

Abbeville Hotel Rockley ⓣ246/435-7924, ⓕ435-8502, ⓔabbeville@sunbeach.net. Friendly and relaxed little place, motel-like in design, with a small pool. The rooms are simple and somewhat tired, but the setting, around a courtyard and huge bar, gives the place a welcoming feel. ❷

Accra Beach Hotel Rockley ⓣ246/435-8920, ⓕ435-6794, ⓔaccrareservations@yahoo.com. Attractive hotel with fifty elegantly furnished rooms right on the island's busiest beach, balconies overlooking the sea, palm trees strewn around the gardens and a giant swimming pool. For the evenings there's a Polynesian restaurant and an outdoor dance floor. ❻

Cleverdale Guesthouse Worthing ⓣ246/428-1035, ⓕ428-3172, ⓔkaribik@sunbeach.net. German-managed guesthouse with a communal kitchen, breakfast room, living room and spacious verandah. ❷

Shells Guesthouse Worthing ⓣ246/435-7253, ⓔguest@sunbeach.net. Eight simple rooms in this friendly, colourful place, with a TV lounge and pleasant bar/dining area. It's a quiet, low-key operation, and an ideal place to chill out for a few days. ❷

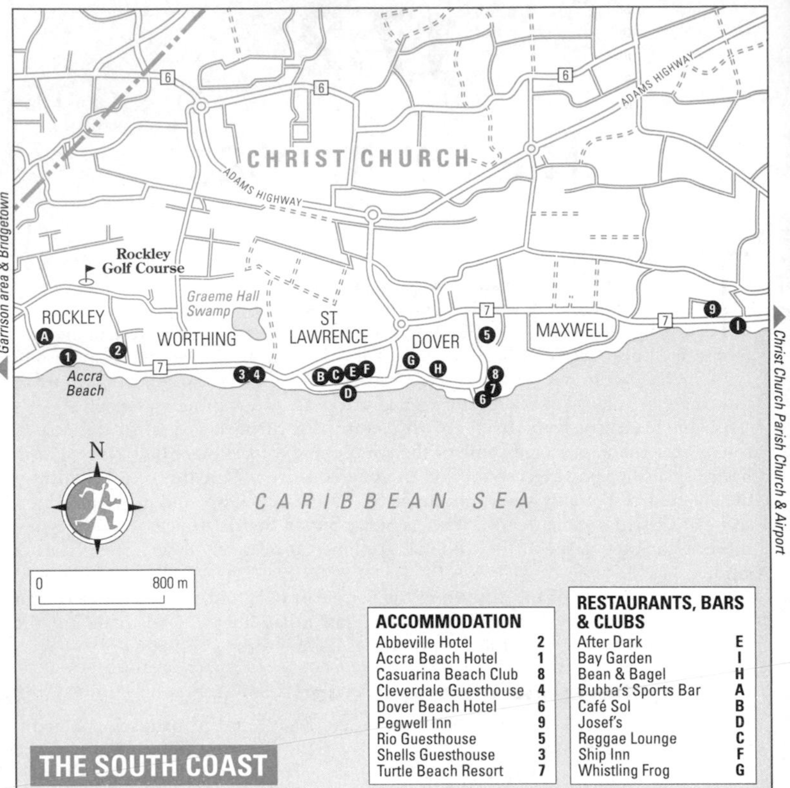

St Lawrence Gap and Dover

Casuarina Beach Club Dover ⓣ246/428-3600, ⓕ428-2122, ⓔcasbeach@bajan.com.
Big, popular and beautifully landscaped hotel on an excellent beach, with tennis courts, pool, lots of activities, and one of the finest collections of local art in the country. All rooms have self-catering facilities, and the front desk arranges tours, including cycle tours with the hotel's enthusiastic owner. ⑦

Dover Beach Hotel Dover ⓣ246/428-8076, ⓕ428-2122, ⓦwww.doverbeach.com.
Comfortable, laid-back place located beside a superb beach. All rooms have A/C, some have kitchenettes, and there's a good-size pool. Ask for a room with a beach or pool view. ④

Rio Guesthouse St Lawrence Gap ⓣ & ⓕ246/428-1546. The seven rooms at this Swiss-German guesthouse – popular with European budget travellers – are a decent size and very reasonably priced. ②

Turtle Beach Resort Dover ⓣ246/428-7131, ⓕ428-6089, ⓦwww.eleganthotels.com. Top-notch all-inclusive, with 160 rooms, fine restaurants, good watersports facilities and a kids' club . Delightful beach outside can get a bit crowded with the hotel's guests, but it's a short walk to find a quiet space. ⑦

Oistins and Silver Sands

Pegwell Inn Welchs (just west of Oistins) ⓣ246/428-6150. This tiny guesthouse is the cheapest place to stay in Barbados, and though it's beside the main road and can be a little noisy, it's only a five-minute walk to the beach. The four rooms all have fans and private bath. ②

Silver Sands Resort Silver Sands ⓣ246/428-6001, ⓕ428-3758, ⓔsilvsnd@sunbeach.net. The only full-blown resort in the area, elegantly furnished with two restaurants, tennis courts, a large swimming pool and over a hundred air-conditioned rooms spread across a large area of landscaped grounds. 5

The southeast

Crane Beach Hotel ⓣ246/423-6220, ⓕ423-5343, ⓔreservations@thecrane.com. Small, beautifully designed hotel, in a stunning setting high above Crane Bay marred somewhat by the adjoining timeshare apartment blocks. The beach is lovely, and there's a terrific restaurant (see p.652). 6

Sam Lord's Castle ⓣ246/423-7350, ⓕ423-5918, ⓦwww.samlordscastle.com. More mansion house than castle, with a handful (and the best) of the 280 rooms in the main house and the rest scattered around attractive gardens. There are three swimming pools, tennis courts and an exercise room, and some form of entertainment – from a steel band to karaoke – is laid on nightly. All-inclusive. 7

Christ Church

Most of the island's "lower end" tourism is concentrated in the southwest of Barbados, between Bridgetown and the airport, with several small villages offering a variety of lodgings and places to eat. There are excellent white-sand beaches all along this stretch of coast, and the sea is calm pretty much all year round.

Hastings and Rockley

A short ride east of Bridgetown, **HASTINGS** first developed in the eighteenth century as a by-product of Britain's military development of the nearby Garrison area (see p.645); soldiers from St Ann's Fort were quartered here. More than a century later, its proximity to the capital led to Hastings being developed as Barbados's first tourist resort, and a handful of grand old hotels still stand on the seafront to mark those glory days. Sadly, the once attractive beach has been heavily eroded, and the whole place now wears a somewhat forlorn expression.

A couple of miles further along Highway 7, **ROCKLEY**'s main attraction is its magnificent beach, known locally as **Accra Beach** – a great white swathe of sand, popular with tourists and local families, that can get pretty crowded at peak season and weekends. The people-watching is top-notch as hair-braiders, T-shirt and craft vendors and the odd hustler mingle with windsurfers and sun-worshippers, creating one of the liveliest beach scenes on the island.

Worthing

Like the Victorian seaside resort in England for which it is named, the once elegant village of **WORTHING** is now tatty and faded, but its relaxed feel and handful of decent, inexpensive guesthouses make it a popular target for budget travellers. There's a gleaming white beach, less crowded than Accra Beach further west but just as enjoyable, with a couple of laid-back bars and local guys offering boat-trips and waverunner rentals.

St Lawrence Gap

Just past Worthing, a right-hand turn takes you off Highway 7 to run along the coast for a kilometre or so, passing through the heavily touristed **ST LAWRENCE GAP** and **Dover** before rejoining the main road near Maxwell. As the most developed area of the south coast – with hotels, restaurants, tourist shops and vendors strung out along virtually the entire road – this is something of a tourist enclave; you'll see few Bajans here, other than those who work in the industry. Still, it's a laid-back place with more great beaches, particularly towards the eastern end of

St. Lawrence Gap, although erosion has taken its toll in a few spots. Most south coast buses and minibuses run through the area.

As perhaps expected for such a busy dining and nightlife strip, there are a few hustlers – mostly selling drugs – around St Lawrence Gap, but they're rarely over-pushy, and undercover cops are often on hand to nab the most persistent.

Oistins

Continuing east brings you into **OISTINS**, the main town along the south coast and one of its less touristed parts. A couple of **buses** run here from Bridgetown, as does **route taxi** 11, which continues to Silver Sands. The unusual name is a corruption of Austin, one of the first landowners in the area, described by an early historian as "a wild, mad drunken fellow, whose lewd and extravagant carriage made him infamous in the island". Austin is long gone, but it's still a busy little town, dominated by a fish market, that retains an authentic sense of Barbados before the tourist boom. The best time to visit is in the evening, when a dozen shacks in the central Bay Garden sell fried fish straight from the boats, and on Friday nights hundreds of people descend for a "lime", the local term for a social gathering.

Silver Sands and Long Beach

Silver Sands is famous for windsurfing, and attracts enthusiasts from all over the world, though non-surfers come here too for the quiet, easy-going vibe. Fantastic waves roll in for most of the year and there are a handful of (pretty expensive) places where you can rent a windsurfer if you haven't brought your own. The beaches are less busy than further west – mainly because of the often choppy seas – but equally attractive; true to its name, **Long Beach**, just beyond the *Ocean Spray Apartments*, is the longest beach on the island – a huge stretch of crunchy white sand strewn with driftwood – and is often completely deserted.

St Philip

The largest parish on the island, but with less than half the population of busy Christ Church, **St Philip** has a different feel from its more touristed neighbour, with no crowds, far less development and a general sense of isolation. The coastline here is rugged, with only a handful of white-sand beaches divided from each other by long cliffs and rocky outcrops. The sea is rough, too, with pounding Atlantic waves.

If you're relying on **public transport**, buses run along the south coast road as far as the hotel known as *Sam Lord's Castle*, passing the *Crane Beach Hotel* (see below), though if you're heading for any of the beaches, you'll need to walk down to them from the main road – usually around 500m.

Foul Bay and Crane Beach

Three or four kilometres beyond the airport, **FOUL BAY** is the largest beach on this section of the coast. Access isn't signposted; look out for the large Methodist Church beside the road in the small village of Rice and a right turn 100m further on takes you right down to the beach. It's a long, wide white-sand beach with a handful of fishing boats normally pulled up on its eastern side and few tourists (and no food and drink facilities). The long cliffs give the place a rugged feel but it's not particularly pretty.

Back on the main road, the **Crane Beach Hotel** lies half a kilometre beyond Foul Bay, commanding a superb site above Crane Bay. A house was first erected here in 1790 and today forms the east wing; during the 1880s the place was converted into a hotel, whose early guests included "Wild Bill" Hickock. More recently, developers have decided that a timeshare development is the best way of reaping tourist dollars from the site, and the hotel is now backed by a couple of large and brightly coloured apartment blocks. In spite of the development it's a fetching place and worth a look even if you're not staying. A long Roman-style swimming pool runs alongside the main hotel building at the top of the cliff and, beside the panoramic restaurant, two hundred steps lead down to a pretty beach.

Eating, drinking and nightlife

You'll find the widest variety of **places to eat** on the south coast, particularly at the crowded **St Lawrence Gap**, where street vendors flogging jerk chicken jostle with punters heading for the classy oceanfront restaurants.

St Lawrence Gap is also the heart of south coast **nightlife**, with plenty of options, whether you want to see a band or hit the dance floor.

Rockley and Worthing

Bubba's Sports Bar Across from the *Accra Beach Hotel* ☎246/435-6217. The food is secondary to the entertainment here, with large and small TV screens dotted around the place showing sport from around the world, but burgers, chicken and sandwiches are decent and well priced. Daily10am–10pm.

Carib Beach Bar next to the *Crystal Waters* guesthouse. A lively place for a drink, especially during happy hour from 5pm to 6pm, when you'll also get reasonably priced snacks including spicy chicken wings, shrimp kebabs and fish cakes. Daily 11.30am–10pm.

St Lawrence Gap and Dover

After Dark St Lawrence Gap ☎246/435-6547. The late-night zone – a huge and cleverly laid-out place with a dark disco and a massive stage and dance floor out the back for the live bands who play a couple of times a week. The bar – nearly 30m long – claims to stock every liquor you can name, and the crowd is a good mix of Bajans and tourists, all dressed to the nines. Cover charge varies. 10pm–3am.

Bean & Bagel Dover ☎246/420-4604. Great coffee, all-day breakfasts of bagels, pancakes and omelettes, muffins and tasty lunch options (lasagne, crab backs and the like) have made this internet café something of an institution for those staying at the eastern end of the Gap. Daily 7am–5.30pm.

Café Sol St Lawrence Gap ☎246/435-9531. Lively, often crowded Mexican place doing a roaring trade in margaritas and Mexican beers, particularly during the 6–7pm and 10–11pm happy hours; decent and sensibly priced burritos, tacos and enchiladas are available. Daily 6–11pm.

Josef's St Lawrence Gap ☎246/435-6541. Both the food and the service at this elegant coral-stone restaurant are as good as you'll find on the south coast, with candelit tables both indoors and (more romantically) down by the water's edge. Starters run B$8–22 and include soups, char-grilled shrimp and beef carpaccio; main courses of blackened dolphin, roast chicken or rack of lamb start at B$35. Daily 6–10pm, Dec–April also noon–2pm.

Reggae Lounge St Lawrence Gap ☎246/435-6462. Intimate, unpretentious club with a small bar up top and steps down to the open-air dance floor under the palm trees. The DJs love to play the latest Jamaican dancehall, but you'll also get "oldies" nights – Bob Marley, Jimmy Cliff, Peter Tosh – and live bands several times a week, usually Thurs and Sun. Cover charge varies. 9pm–late.

Ship Inn St Lawrence Gap ☎246/435-6961. English pub in style, with several bars and a small, sweaty dance floor, with the most tourist-friendly bands – reggae meets rap meets Marvin Gaye. There's music every night around 10.30pm–12.30am and bands, and a big crowd, on Tues and Sat 9pm–1am.

Whistling Frog Sports Pub Dover ☎246/420-5021. Great new bar/bistro serving food all day, from a buffet breakfast to lunch and supper of pepperpot stew or seafood caesar salad (all around B$15), though many here simply hang out with a drink watching sport on the TVs. Daily 7am–very late.

Oistins

The Bay Garden Oistins Market. One of the most atmospheric places on the island, with a dozen stalls offering a variety of seafood from conch fritters to fried kingfish to dolphin. Prices are low: you'll be hard-pressed to pay more than B$12 a head, and if you go into the covered *Fish Net* area you'll find plenty of Bajans tucking into equally good barbecued fish straight off the grill. Daily 5.30–10pm.

The southeast

Crane Beach Hotel ☏246/423-6220. The best food in the southeast, with a restaurant that overlooks the bay and serves excellent and innovative seafood dishes. A good lunch stop if you're making a day-trip to the area. Bear in mind, though, that prices are on the high side, and that the place tends to lack atmosphere out of season. Daily 11.30am–2pm & 5.30–9.30pm.

17.3

The west coast

Barbados's **west coast** (also known as the "platinum coast") is a fringe of bays and coves along the sheltered, Caribbean side of the island. Its sandy beaches and warm blue waters have made it the island's prime resort area. As a result, the coastline has been heavily built up; it holds the island's top golf courses and priciest hotels, and its sought-after private homes change hands at formidable prices.

You don't, however, need to win the lottery to visit. There's a smattering of reasonably priced places to stay and, as everywhere on Barbados, all of the beaches are public. Admittedly, it's a bit of a tramp to reach a few of them, but there are many that are well worth a visit, particularly those at **Prospect**, **Sandy Lane** and **Mullins Bay**. If you're into some serious exercise it's even possible to walk most of the way along the coast at low tide.

If you can drag yourself away from the beach, the region has other attractions. Lively, modern **Holetown** has a fine old church and a legion of shopping opportunities, while further north, **Speightstown** repays a visit for the colonial relics and picturesque old streets that recall its vanished heyday as a major port. A short detour inland, through fields of sugarcane and tiny farming villages, will take you to the sugar museum at **Portvale**.

Getting there and getting around

It could hardly be easier to **get around** on the west coast. North of Bridgetown, Highway 1 runs up the coast, rarely straying more than 100m from the shoreline. Highway 2A runs parallel to it, some way inland, and offers a speedier way of getting to the north of the island.

Buses and **minibuses** ply the coast road between Bridgetown and Speightstown all day, and there are bus stops every couple of hundred metres. Services normally stop at around midnight, after which you'll need a car or private taxi. If you're coming from the south coast, look for buses marked "Speightstown" – these usually bypass Bridgetown and save you having to change buses (and terminals) in the city.

Accommodation

Although the west coast of Barbados is renowned for its luxury hotels, several of which are ranked among the best in the Caribbean, there are a handful of cheaper places sandwiched in between.

From Prospect to Paynes Bay

Angler Apartments Derricks ⓣ & ⓕ246/432-0817, ⓔgostain@sunbeach.net. A dozen self-catering apartments in three small blocks shaded by mango and breadfruit trees and set back 200m from the highway. The fan-cooled rooms are comfortable, the atmosphere relaxed and friendly, and you're five minutes' walk from a good beach. The restaurant is excellent. ❹

Beachcomber Apartments Paynes Bay ⓣ246/432-0489, ⓕ432-2824, ⓔhassell@caribsurf.com. Small apartment block popular with families, offering large, luxurious balconied apartments or studios with smaller balconies. All rooms have kitchen facilities. ❼

Crystal Cove ⓣ246/424-2683, ⓦwww.eleganthotels.com. One of the best of the island's all-inclusives, with comfortable rooms, excellent food, good watersports and several pools, one with a swim-up bar under a waterfall. It's one of four west coast hotels owned by Elegant Hotels (all connected by a free boat taxi), and you're welcome to use the facilities at the sister hotels. ⑦

Smugglers' Cove ⓣ246/432-1741, ⓕ432-1749. Small, friendly but slightly cramped hotel complete with gardens colourfully decked out with crotons. The rooms all have tiny kitchenettes, and there's a bar/restaurant and small swimming pool, ten metres from the beach. Good value. ⑤

Around Holetown

Lone Star Mount Standfast ⓣ246/422-1617, ⓕ419-0597, ⓦwww.thelonestar.com. Fabulous little boutique hotel in an old house converted into four spectacular rooms right over the beach. Also home to one of the island's trendiest restaurants (see p.657). ⑦

Sandy Lane ⓣ246/432-1311, ⓕ432-2954, ⓦwww.sandylane.com. The jewel of the west coast, a magnificent place in every way (particularly since its massive rebuilding project). ⑦

Sunset Crest Resort ⓣ246/432-6750, ⓕ432-7229. Located ten minutes' walk from the beach, with several swimming pools, restaurants and bars, and over a hundred one-, two- and three-bedroom apartments scattered around the complex. ④

Around Speightstown

Cobblers Cove Hotel ⓣ246/422-2291, ⓕ422-1460, ⓦwww.cobblerscove.com. Spacious rooms are hidden around a beautifully landscaped garden. The main building – bright pink in colour but very English country-house in design – holds a splendid bar and restaurant (as well as two spectacular suites) and fronts onto a relatively empty beach. Overall, one of the most delightful hotels on the island. ⑦

Mango Lane Apartments ⓣ246/422-3146, ⓔclemlau@sunbeach.net. An assortment of colourful and lightly furnished chattel houses and apartments dotted around the local area, rented out by the friendly owners of the *Fisherman's Pub* in Speightstown (see p.658). ②

Sandridge Hotel ⓣ246/422-2361, ⓕ422-1965, ⓔbernmar@caribsurf.com. This three-storey hotel on a lovely strip of beach is as good value as you'll find on the west coast. It's not fancy, but the sizeable rooms are brightly decorated, there are two restaurants, a large pool, and great snorkelling offshore. ⑤

North to Prospect

There is little sign of the hotel extravaganza to come as Highway 1 begins to carve its way up the west coast through the tiny village of **PROSPECT**. Most of the area here is residential and the beaches – largely bereft of tourists – are popular at weekends and holidays with families up from Bridgetown. A good bet, if you want to swim, is **Prospect Beach** – a narrow crescent of sand, backed by manchineel trees and palms, and a calm turquoise bay. Public access is via a path just north of the all-inclusive *Escape Hotel*, and at busy times the beach can get crowded with the hotel's guests.

Continuing north, there isn't much to distinguish this area of coast other than a series of superlative bays and beaches, many of them tucked away behind an increasingly grand row of hotels and private mansions, themselves often hidden by security fences. A right turn opposite the *Tamarind Cove Hotel* winds upward into the island's interior, past the grand polo field at **Holder's House** – an old Great House and the venue for a prestigious classical music festival every March.

Sandy Lane

Back on the coast, the road through the area of Sandy Lane Bay is overhung with lush vegetation and reeks of wealth. In Barbados, the name **Sandy Lane** is synonymous with the grandest of the island's hotels, whose list of repeat celebrity guests is impressive. The place guards its guests jealously behind high walls and security guards. Nevertheless, as part of its deal with the government to get permission for the hotel (and the re-routing of the coastal road that it involved), the owners promised to provide a ten-metre right of way to the south of the property, giving public access to the shore. Today that access is still there and, if you've got the energy, you can wander down to the bay past the tall casuarinas and manchineel trees. The

△ Fisherman near Bridgetown at dusk

sweep of gently shelving sand, backed by the elegant hotel (completely rebuilt by its new Irish owners between 1998 and 2001), is magnificent.

Holetown and around

HOLETOWN is the third-largest town in Barbados – a busy, modern hub for the local tourist industry, if somewhat lacking in character. All west coast buses run through it, and the main highway is lined with fast-food restaurants, souvenir shops, banks and grocery stores. Just before you reach the centre, **Sunset Crest** shopping centre on the east side of the highway has plenty of places where you can pick up souvenirs. There are more shopping options once you reach Holetown itself, with a dozen reproduction chattel houses in the **chattel house village** (also alongside the highway) selling gifts and the like, and the nearby **West Coast Mall** offering equally good spending opportunities. On the northern edge of town, 1st and 2nd streets, lined with trendy restaurants, lead down to the sea.

Ten minutes' walk north of the centre of Holetown is **St James's Parish Church**, one of the most attractive on the island. It is also the oldest religious site in Barbados – the original wooden church was built here in 1628. The present church is a small, graceful building, with thick stone walls, and two columns supporting the stone chancel arch that divides the nave from the choir. There are the usual marble funerary monuments on the walls, while more modern works of art include a colourful biblical triptych by Ethiopian painter Alemayehu Bizumeh and bronze bas-reliefs of St James and St Mary by Czech sculptor George Kveton.

A couple of miles inland from Holetown is the informative **Portvale Sugar Museum**, signposted off Highway 2A just north of the main roundabout (Mon–Sat 9am–5pm; B$15). The small museum is the brainchild of Frank Hutson, a former sugar worker who rescued a load of rusting sugar-mill machinery, cleaned it up and incorporated it into the museum, adding captions, maps and photos explaining the role of sugar on the island since its introduction in the 1640s. Between February and June you can tour the adjacent sugar factory and view the full production process, from the loading and grinding of the cane to the crystallization of the brown sugar.

North to Mullins Bay

Once you've passed Holetown there is little of particular interest to hold you en route north to Speightstown. A series of exclusive hotels and grand private houses, fenced in behind security gates, is interspersed with small villages of shops, fishing shacks and chattel houses, keeping a typically Bajan toehold on the increasingly developed west coast. Access to many of the small bays along the coast is difficult, but **Mullins Bay** – a strip of sugary sand with a lively beach bar – is a good place to stop for a swim. Buses stop here and there's a car park across from the bay.

Speightstown

Small, run-down and utterly charming, **SPEIGHTSTOWN** (pronounced "Spikestown") is the second town of Barbados, though it remains largely untouched by tourist development. It was once a thriving port, famous for its tough-talking, uncompromising inhabitants – "Speightstown flattery" is an old Bajan term for a back-handed compliment. Over the last century, however, the place has declined precipitately, and there is little to do today but stroll around and soak up the remnants of the local fishing industry, a few stylish old buildings and a handful of excellent restaurants that cater for day visitors and the guests of nearby hotels.

Buses running up the west coast normally terminate at Speightstown, stopping at the eastern end of Church Street – from here, head down towards the sea, passing the parish church on your right. Queen Street has an unofficial tourist information office in the *Fisherman's Pub* (see p.658).

The Town

A mark of Speightstown's former importance is that three major forts were erected to protect it, with several additional gun emplacements scattered along the coast to add to the barrage of any enemy ships (though the only invasion was by the British in 1651). Little remains of the military hardware, but some of the old iron cannons from Fort Orange point out to sea from **the Esplanade**, to the north of town.

Across from the Esplanade, **St Peter's Parish Church**, on Church Street, was first built in the 1630s, making it one of the oldest churches in Barbados. Destroyed by the 1831 hurricane, the Georgian building was rebuilt in a graceful Greek Revival style – though with the standard tower tacked on for good measure – and the present incarnation is the result of superb restoration after the place was gutted by fire in 1980.

Back on the main road, head south across the bridge and past the fish market, always humming with vendors in the early morning. **Queen Street** is the main drag and has several grand old buildings that have survived the town's decline. Opposite *Mango*'s restaurant, **Arlington**, almost medieval in design, is a classic example of the island's early townhouses – narrow, tall and gabled, with a sharply sloping roof. While you're here, cross the road and check out the **art gallery** of the self-styled Gang of Four – of interest for the local paintings of Gordon Webster, Sarah Venables and Azziza, and the sculpture of Ras Bongo Congo.

Eating and drinking

Plenty of top-notch **restaurants** line the "platinum coast", some as good as anything you'll find anywhere in the Caribbean, though prices tend to be high. You'll have to look a bit harder to find interesting low-priced options, but they do exist, and several – including the *Fisherman's Pub* in Speightstown and the *Garden Bar* at *Angler Apartments* – are worth checking out, whatever your budget.

Prospect to Paynes Bay

The Cliff Fitts ☎246/432-1922. This long-standing west coast favourite is located in a pillared coral-stone building on a clifftop, with a small army of waiters and exquisite food. Expect some of the island's most innovative cooking and prices of B$75–90 for two courses before drinks. Daily 6–10.30pm.

Crocodile's Den Paynes Bay ☎246/432-7625. Funky bar, with pool table, darts and board games, canned and occasional live music, satellite sports and a great late-night atmosphere. Daily from 5pm.

Garden Bar Angler Apartments ☎246/432-0817. Small, laid-back, no-frills place offering traditional inexpensive West Indian meals like pepperpot, cook-up rice (rice and peas with salt beef and lamb, cooked in coconut milk) and Guyanese specialities like metagee (a root vegetable stew of plantains). Worth calling ahead, as some of the specialities take a while to prepare. Daily 6–8.30pm.

Marshalls Holders Hill. One-and-a-half kilometres inland, this relaxed local bar serves a wide selection of dishes for around B$15 – try the flying fish or stewed beef. An essential stop for cricket fans: the owner is cricket-mad and the walls are papered with cricket memorabilia. Head uphill, past Holder's Great House, and the restaurant is on your left, opposite the playing field. Daily noon–2pm & 5–9pm.

Holetown

Angry Annies 1st Street ☎246/432-2119. Brightly painted building just off the main highway, with a decent selection of local food – starters of fisherman's soup or flying fish fillets for around B$13, main courses of multicoloured Rasta pasta for B$30 or limbo lamb for B$55. Mon–Sat 6–10pm.

La Terra ☎246/432-1099. This Italian/Caribbean restaurant at Baku Beach has an expensive and ever-changing menu including starters like grilled baby calamari from around B$20, and main courses of pan-fried dolphin fillets from B$45. Save room for the chocolate mousse. Mon–Sat 11.30am–10pm.

Lone Star at the *Lone Star* hotel ☎246/419-0598. Spectacular seaside location, and the trendiest place on the west coast. Expect to find fish soup, sushi or crab cakes as starters (B$20–40). Main courses range from *moules marinieres* to pork tenderloin with polenta (B$50–70). There's also a first-class chilled seafood selection – a platter for two costs B$220. Daily 11.30am–5.30pm & 6.30–10.30pm.

The Mews ☎246/432-1122. Top-notch food is served at this Holetown townhouse – ask for a table on one of the terraces. The seafood is imaginative – try the baked snapper in a parmesan crust – and the place is often packed with local bigwigs. B$15–25 for starters, B$45–65 for mains. Daily 5.30–11pm.
Olive's Bar and Bistro ☎246/432-2112. Popular Holetown eatery, simple in design with its wooden floor and white tablecloths, but offering a wide choice of excellent meals. Starters include beef carpaccio or warm shrimp salad for B$19–22, with main courses like jerk pork with roasted garlic mash (B$40) or seared sea scallops (B$56). The relaxed upstairs bar is one of the best places for a drink. Daily 6–10pm.

Mullins Bay to Speightstown

Chattel House at *Sandridge Hotel* (see p.654). Slightly sanitized but hugely engaging version of a typical Bajan rum-shop with enthusiastic service and good, inexpensive cutters, burgers and pies. Don't miss the delicious weekend special of pudding and souse – an absolute steal at B$8. Daily 11am–9pm.
Fisherman's Pub Queen Street ☎246/422-2703. Delightful place, with a large verandah jutting out over the ocean, and the best-value food in town. You can munch on a sizeable roti or flying fish cutters at lunch for around B$5; at night, typical Bajan dinners cost around B$20. Daily 11am–10pm.

Entertainment and nightlife

Nightlife on the west coast is generally pretty quiet, mostly limited to steel bands and floor shows put on by the more exclusive hotels. There's not much in the way of local entertainment, but a couple of places occasionally feature a Bajan band.

Casbah Holetown ☎246/432-2258. Upmarket, attractive nightclub in the Baku/La Terra building, pulling a good crowd of Bajans and tourists for DJ sounds on Fri and Sat nights. Cover charge varies. 9pm–2am.
The Coach House Paynes Bay ☎246/432-1163. Live music most nights, with the island's top soca and steel bands as well as a Latin Fiesta night on Fri and the occasional karaoke evening. 8pm–2am.
Crocodile's Den Paynes Bay ☎246/432-7625. Bar with pool tables and darts that usually features live music on Fri and Sat with local bands, DJs and occasional Latin nights. 8pm–3am; happy hour 9–10pm.
Fisherman's Pub Speightstown ☎246/422-2703. Often the liveliest place in town, with a steel band on Wed nights, and occasional floor shows on the oceanfront verandah. 6–11pm.

17.4

Central Barbados

Don't expect dramatic topographical change as you head into the **interior of Barbados**; the landscape of the central parishes of **St George** and **St Thomas** is almost uniformly flat or gently rolling – perfect for the sugar crop that's been under cultivation here for almost four centuries. As you head north towards the parish of **St Andrew**, however, the land rises in a short series of peaks to the island's highest point, **Mount Hillaby**.

Despite its small area, central Barbados offers a considerable number of attractions to lure you away from the beach. The parish of St George has some rewarding historic sights, including the military signal station at **Gun Hill** and the beautiful plantation house at **Francia**. To the north in St Thomas – slap-bang in the middle of the island – is **Harrison's Cave**, a series of weirdly beautiful subterranean chambers. The narrow strip of jungle at nearby **Welchman Hall Gully**, hemmed in by cliffs and densely covered with the island's most attractive plants and trees, offers a unique glimpse of the island in its primal state, while the gardens at **Flower Forest** offer a more carefully managed look at local flora.

Getting there and getting around

Getting to and around the interior of Barbados is straightforward – buses from Bridgetown run to the main attractions, though services are less frequent than on the coasts. You'll save a lot of time if you rent a car for a day or two – a network of country lanes criss-cross the centre, offering easy access from the coast.

Gun Hill Signal Station

Gun Hill Signal Station (Mon–Sat 9am–5pm; B$9.20) sits among pretty landscaped gardens that belie its turbulent origins. Built in 1818 and restored by the Barbados National Trust, the watchtower offers fabulous panoramic views across the green, gently rolling hills of central Barbados and out to the ocean beyond Bridgetown. Guides give an expert introduction to the local history, and there is a small but immaculate display of military memorabilia, including flags of the various army regiments that were stationed here, maps of the island's many forts – 23 of them had been built as early as 1728 – and the cannons (never fired) that would have alerted the population to enemy invasion. Below the station, and visible from the tower, is a giant **white lion** – a British military emblem carved from a single block of limestone by soldiers stationed here in 1868.

Francia

Just south of Gun Hill, signposted off to the west, is **Francia** (Mon–Fri 10am–4pm; B$10), a working plantation growing sweet potatoes and yams for export. The plantation house is one of the most attractive in Barbados; it was also one of the last of the island's great houses, built at the end of the nineteenth century when the plantations were already in decline as the value of sugar fell on world markets. The sweeping stone staircase, triple-arched entrance and enclosed upper balcony are unusual features, reflecting the influence of the original French owner. The double-jalousied windows are also rare on Barbados, though they are also found at the nineteenth-century Tyrol Cot in Bridgetown (see p.645).

The pride of the house – and what really distinguishes it from the other great houses you can tour – is its superb collection of **antique maps** of Barbados and the Caribbean, collected from dusty bookshops and grand auction rooms around the world and dating back to the early sixteenth century, only decades after Columbus first "discovered" the region. Outside, the huge terraced garden feels very English in style, despite the abundance of tropical flora, including a gigantic mammee apple tree, mangoes, frangipani, hibiscus and the ubiquitous bougainvillea.

Harrison's Cave

Fifteen minutes' drive north of the Francia plantation, **Harrison's Cave** (40min tours daily 9am–4pm; B$25) is an enormous subterranean labyrinth, where underground streams and dripping water have carved huge limestone caverns with stalactites hanging like teeth from the ceilings and weirdly shaped stalagmites pushing up from the cave floor. The existence of caves here has been known for over two hundred years, though it was only by accident that the caves you'll see on your tour were discovered in 1970, and subsequently opened up to the public.

No serious potholing is expected of you – you're taken underground and around the various chambers on an electric tram, which, with the guide's mechanized voice-over, rather spoils the eerie, otherwise soundless atmosphere of the place. However, it can't completely detract from the beauty – you'll be hard put to find more spectacular cave scenery anywhere in the world.

Welchman Hall Gully

Signposted off Highway 2, a kilometre or so north of Harrison's Cave, the dramatic **Welchman Hall Gully** (Mon–Sat 9am–5pm; B$11.50) is a long, deep corridor of jungle, hemmed in by steep cliffs and abounding with local flora and fauna. Though a handful of non-indigenous plants have been planted here over the years, the vegetation is not dissimilar to that which covered the whole island when the British first arrived here. The gully itself was created aeons ago by a fissure in the limestone cap that covers this part of Barbados, and is named for a Welshman, General Williams, an early settler on the island and the first owner of the surrounding land. There are two entrances – one at either end of the gully and both with parking spaces – and buses from Bridgetown stop outside each one, where a National Trust represent-ative will take your money and give you a brochure describing the walk and the plants and trees.

A footpath leads down into the gully, and it's a short walk from one end of the marked trail to the other, along which prolific fruit and spice trees dangling with lianas offer protection from the sun. Keep your eyes out for green monkeys cavorting in the undergrowth.

Flower Forest

As you head across the parish boundary into St Joseph, the meticulously landscaped **Flower Forest** (daily 9am–5pm; B$13.80) is signposted just south of Highway 2. There is a great variety of indigenous and imported plants and trees here, all labelled with their Latin and English names and country of origin, and some fabulous views over the hills of the Scotland district, but overall the place feels just a little bit too neat and ordered. If you only have time to visit one of the island's botanical gardens, you're probably better off making for the more rugged Andromeda Botanical Gardens on the east coast (see p.665), but the Flower Forest is certainly worth a look if you're in the area.

The almost endless variety of trees include breadfruit, coffee, Barbados cherry, avocado and a single African baobab tree, and there is a fine collection of orchids, hibiscus and the "lobster claw" heliconias. Other highlights include Palm Walk, where dozens of different types of palm are scattered around.

17.5

The north

The **north of Barbados** is the most rugged and least visited part of the island, but nonetheless offers an excellent variety of places to explore. The most popular target is the **Barbados Wildlife Reserve**, home to hundreds of green monkeys and a host of other animals; nearby, there's an old signal station and a nature trail through the forest at **Grenade Hall**, while the lovely park and desolate ruins at **Farley Hill** make a good place to stop for a picnic. Just north of here there is a working **sugar mill** at Morgan Lewis and a superb Jacobean Great House, **St Nicholas Abbey**.

Getting there and getting around

Buses run through the northern parishes from both Speightstown and Bridgetown, though services are less regular than along the south and west coasts. If you're planning on visiting more than one of the main attractions – and you could comfortably see all of them in a day – renting a car will make getting around a lot less hassle.

Barbados Wildlife Reserve

Green **monkeys** are the chief attraction at the **Barbados Wildlife Reserve** (daily 10am–5pm; B$23, including access to Grenade Hall), just off Highway 1 in the parish of St Peter and directly accessible by bus from Speightstown or Bridgetown. The non-profit reserve was first established as the island's leading centre for conservation of the monkeys, and – more controversially – to look at the possibility of exporting them for medical research, particularly the production and testing of vaccines. As the idea of making it into a tourist attraction developed, other creatures were gradually introduced, including brocket deer, otters, armadillos, racoons and caiman alligators, as well as plenty of caged parrots, macaws and other fabulously coloured tropical birds.

Paths meander through the lush mahogany woods and, in a thirty-minute stroll, you'll see pretty much everything on offer, including the aviary, fishponds and birdcages. Monkeys swarm freely around the reserve in playful mood. The **information centre**, at the reserve's northeast corner, has excellent displays on the monkeys.

Grenade Hall Signal Station and forest

The **Grenade Hall Signal Station** (daily 10am–5pm; B$23, including access to Barbados Wildlife Reserve), was one of the chain of communication stations built in the years immediately after Barbados faced its first and only major slave revolt in 1816. The stations, which communicated by semaphore flags and lanterns, were designed to get news of any trouble afoot rapidly to the garrison in Bridgetown.

Grenade Hall is not as attractively located as Gun Hill (see p.659), though the watchtower offers great views of the surrounding countryside, and the place is certainly worth a quick tour if you're in the area. Prints of the British military hang downstairs, alongside various bits and pieces belonging to the signalmen – medallions, clay pipes, coins and pottery shards. Upstairs, the old semaphore signals are on display – though most of them post-date the era of possible slave revolts, and relate to shipping movements.

Below Grenade Hall, a large tract of **native forest** (same hours and ticket) has been preserved, and several kilometres of pathways loop down through the woods and under whitewood, dogwood, mahogany and magnificent silk cotton trees. Walking down from the signal station you can feel yourself entering a different ecosystem – shaded, damp, humid and sticky.

Farley Hill National Park

Just south of the wildlife reserve, **Farley Hill National Park** (daily 8am–6pm; free; car B$3.50) is a small, pleasant park at the top of a 300-metre cliff, with commanding views over the Scotland district (see p.665). It's a good place to retreat with a picnic once you've finished looking around Grenade Hall. The park is the site of what was once a spectacular Great House, built for a sugar baron in 1857 but destroyed in a fire a century later. Today, the charred coral-block walls of the rather ghostly mansion form the park's focus, surrounded by landscaped lawns and masses of fruit trees.

Morgan Lewis Sugar Mill

Set in the midst of the crumbling ruins of an old sugar factory, a short drive north-east of Farley Hill, with a tall chimney poking defiantly from the overgrown grass, **Morgan Lewis Sugar Mill** (Mon–Sat 9am–5pm; B$10) is the only windmill in Barbados still in operation. The island once boasted more than five hundred mills, all grinding juice from the sugarcane that covered the island like a blanket, but twentieth-century mechanization has all but eliminated them from the countryside. The Morgan Lewis mill, if not an essential object of pilgrimage during your stay on Barbados, provides an attractive and atmospheric testament to this part of the island's history.

Though it's no longer in commercial use, the mill – first built in the nineteenth century – is still in perfect working order. The sails, wheelhouse and British-made machinery have been thoroughly restored over the last few years, and you'll get a demonstration of how the thick bamboo-like stems were pushed through mechanical grinders to extract cane juice, subsequently used for making sugar.

Cherry Tree Hill

Heading north uphill from the sugar mill the main road sweeps past sugar fields before reaching a magnificent canopy of mahogany trees at **Cherry Tree Hill**. It's worth stopping to look behind you across the east coast and out to the Atlantic Ocean – one of the most spectacular views on the island. There is actually no record of cherry trees having existed here; the local legend that they were all chopped down because passers-by kept stealing the fruit sounds a little unlikely.

St Nicholas Abbey

Over the brow of the hill, a signposted right turn takes you to the Great House of **St Nicholas Abbey** (Mon–Fri 10am–3.30pm; B$10) – the oldest house on Barbados. Built during the 1650s, the white-painted structure was originally owned by two of the largest sugar-growers in the north of the island. How the place came to be called an abbey is unclear. So too is the reason for the fireplaces – completely unnecessary in view of the island's tropical weather – in the upstairs bedrooms. Presumably they are the result of the builders slavishly following the drawings of a British architect, regardless of the Caribbean climate.

Your entrance fee gets you a rather lacklustre guided tour of the ground floor of the house (the upstairs is still used, and closed to visitors), crammed with eighteenth-century furniture, Wedgwood porcelain and other traditional accoutrements of the old Barbadian aristocracy. The outbuildings at the back of the house are rather more rustic, and include the original bathhouse and a four-seater toilet.

While the tour of the house may be a little unexciting, there is an evocative twenty-minute black and white **film** that is shown on request. Made in 1934 by a previous owner of the abbey, it shows the family making a visit by sea from England to their West Indian home. There is some great footage of the boats arriving at Bridgetown harbour and of the pre-war city, followed by loving shots of the sugar plantation in action. After the film you can take a short stroll through the woods behind the house or grab a drink in the small café.

17.6

The east coast

For many, the rugged, little-explored **east coast** is the most beautiful part of Barbados. Almost all year round, the Atlantic waves crash in against this wild coastline, making for superb surfing but difficult and sometimes dangerous swimming. It's certainly worth making the effort to explore since this is a very different side of the island from the heavily touristed south and west; if possible, try to spend a night or two up here. If you can't stay, do at least check out one of the excellent restaurants around the laid-back old resort of **Bathsheba** for lunch.

Although the coastal scenery is the main attraction, there are a few specific places that merit a visit, most notably the delightful **Andromeda Botanical Gardens**. Specific sightseeing apart, this is a lovely area to drive through, particularly under the steep-sided **Hackleton's Cliff** that runs parallel to the coast, where the road weaves through lush tropical forest, offering stunning views over the ocean. You can also walk along the beaches at **Bath** and **Martin's Bay**, watching the surf ride in.

Codrington College

Signposted on your right as you head up the east coast, Skeete Bay and Consett Bay are a couple of quiet, pretty coves, each with a strip of sand backed by palm trees and with fishing boats pulled up on the beach as they have been for centuries. Just north of Consett Bay, on the clifftop, stand the handsome buildings of **Codrington College** (daily 10am-4pm; B$5). The first degree-level institution in the English-speaking West Indies, it continues to teach theology to budding Anglican vicars, and is now affiliated to the University of the West Indies.

The approach to the college is dramatic, along a long avenue lined on either side with a graceful row of tall cabbage palms and ending beside a large ornamental lake covered in waterlilies. The buildings are arranged around an unfinished quadrangle, with an arched central portico that opens onto large, elegant gardens offering panoramic views over the coast.

St John's Parish Church

From Martin's Bay, a steep road climbs dramatically up through Hackleton's Cliff. Turn left at the top of the hill, past more sweeping fields of sugarcane, for the Gothic **St John's Parish Church** (daily 9am-5pm; free), probably the most elegant of the island's churches. Like many of the parish churches, St John's – typically English with its arched doors and windows and graceful tower – was first built in the mid-seventeenth century but, following severe hurricane damage in the great storm of 1831, now dates from around 1836.

The floor of the church is paved with ancient memorial tablets, rescued from earlier versions of the building, and a Madonna and Child sculpture by Richard Westmacott stands to the left of the main entrance. Most attractive of all is the reddish-brown pulpit, superbly hand-carved from four local woods and imported oak and pine. Outside, the expansive graveyard is perched on top of the cliff, looking down over miles of jagged coastline and crammed with moss-covered tombs, family vaults and a wide array of tropical flora.

Hackleton's Cliff and Scotland

From the church, follow the road north where, after a kilometre or so, a sign diverts you to **Hackleton's Cliff**. This steep 300-metre limestone escarpment marks the edge of the **Scotland** district to the west and, to the east, the rugged east coast whose limestone cap was eroded by sea action many centuries ago. At the end of a short track, you can park right by the edge of the cliff for fabulous views across the craggy hills of Scotland, nostalgically named by early settlers for its supposed resemblance to the land of Robert Burns, and up the sandy northeast coastline.

Andromeda Botanical Gardens

Back on the main highway, a bit further north, the colourful, sprawling **Andromeda Botanical Gardens** (daily 9am–5pm; B$12) make up one of the most attractive spots on the island, spread over a hillside strewn with coral boulders and with vistas over the Bathsheba coastline. Created by local botanist Iris Bannochie, the gardens feature masses of local and imported shrubs and plants, landscaped around a trail that incorporates several ponds and a giant, ancient bearded fig tree.

The colourful hibiscus garden, on your left as you enter, is the best place to see the tiny hummingbirds that frequent the place. The trail then takes you past some old traveller's trees and a small clump of papyrus before turning uphill past a series of heliconia – including the bizarrely shaped "beefsteak" heliconia – and a Panama hat tree. The bearded fig tree is the real star of the gardens, but there are plenty of other highlights, including a bank of frangipani, rose of Sharon trees, superb cycads and a *Bombax ellipticum*, also known as the shaving brush tree for the large pink-bristled flower it produces. At the lower end of the trail is the Queen Ingrid Palm Garden.

Beyond the gardens the road continues to the seafront and the *Atlantis Hotel* (see below), a slightly faded and very easy-going place overlooking **Tent Bay**. Built in the 1880s, this was one of the first hotels to be put up outside Bridgetown and, though there's not a great deal to do, the place offers an excellent buffet lunch.

Bathsheba

A kilometre or so north of Andromeda you'll reach a crossroads; the east coast road continues straight on, a left takes you towards Hackleton's Cliff (see above), while a right drops you down into **Bathsheba**. Picturesque, easy-going and washed by Atlantic breezes, this has long been a favoured resort for Bajans, though surprisingly few tourists make it up here. Small holiday homes and the odd rum-shop line the roadside as it runs along beside the sea.

If the bay here looks familiar, it's because this is one of the most painted landscapes in Barbados. Also known as the soup bowl, because of the crashing surf that comes racing in here pretty much all year round, the area is popular with surfers who stage annual tournaments. Unfortunately, the currents mean that it's not a good place to swim, but the wide brown beach is attractive here and an old pathway runs north and south if you fancy a walk.

Practicalities

A handful of small but characterful accommodation on the **east coast** offers a change from the built-up south and west of the island. It's a great, quiet area to unwind for a couple of days, away from the crowds. In Bathsheba try the *Atlantis Hotel* ⓣ246/433-9445; ❸), an ancient, faded and extremely welcoming place overlooking Tent Bay with good food and eight modest rooms – ask for one with a balcony. Just above the *Atlantis* and surrounded by an acre of tropical garden is *Sea-U Guest House* (ⓣ246/433-9030, ⓔsea-u@caribsurf.com; ❹), a friendly little

German-managed guesthouse offering four studios with kitchenettes and one guest room, and food is laid on if you don't want to cook.

For lunch or dinner, you can't go wrong at the *Round House Inn* (daily 11.30am–2.30pm & 6–10pm; ⓣ246/433-9678), which offers **top-quality cooking** and a casual, family atmosphere, halfway down the steep hill that plunges to Bathsheba Bay. The lunch and dinner menus are similar – offering dishes like blackened snapper for around B$35 – but you can also get sandwiches and salads at lunchtime for B$14 and up. There's an ocean view and you can sit indoors or on the verandah. It's also pretty much the only place to find regular live music in the area, with a decent jazz or reggae band on Tuesday and Saturday nights.

St Vincent and the Grenadines

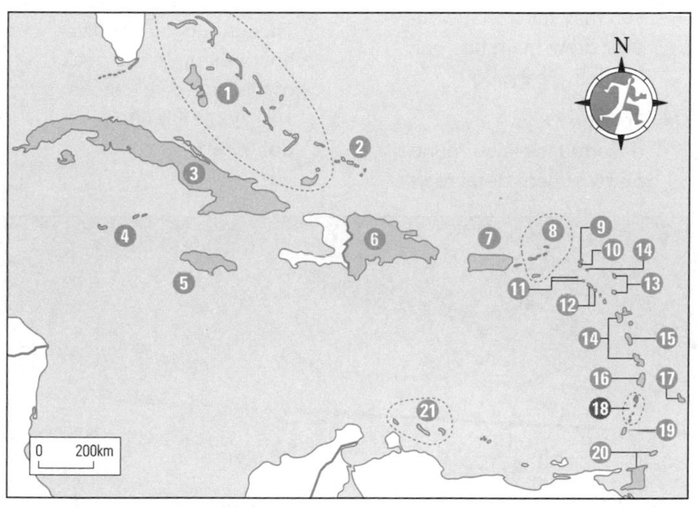

St Vincent and the Grenadines Highlights

- **MV Barracuda ferry** A great way to see Union Island and St Vincent and to enjoy the surrounding seas. See p.672
- **St Vincent's petroglyphs** Peering at these striking ancient images, you may think that whoever drew them has only just left. See p.680
- **Tobago Cays** Tiny deserted islets surrounded by superb coral reefs and sparkling turquoise waters. See p.689
- **Bequia** Besides glorious beaches, this laid-back island preserves its rich seafaring history through its boat building and whaling. See p.683
- **La Soufrière, St Vincent** Though rugged, the five-hour trek up to the peak of this active volcano is well worth the effort. See p.681

Introduction and Basics

Situated about one hundred miles west of Barbados, and nestled between St Lucia to the north and Grenada to the south, the string of islands known collectively as St Vincent and the Grenadines may be physically close together, but vary enormously in character, terrain and appeal.

The main centre of activity is **St Vincent**, the largest and northernmost of the Islands. As well as exploring St Vincent's two distinct coastlines – the rugged windward side and the gentle leeward side – and lush, interior hiking trails, don't miss the opportunity to spend time on the tiny isle of Bequia, just a short ferry ride away, a yachters' haven that also boasts shimmering beaches and a fascinating seafaring history. The less developed and less populated islands of **Canouan**, **Mayreau** and **Union** are all easily reachable by ferry and offer a taste of the unspoiled Caribbean, while **Mustique,** an island hideaway of the rich and famous, makes for an affordable day trip of swimming and snorkelling, though don't expect to find a cheap place to stay.

The uninhabited national park of the **Tobago Cays**, a cluster of islets which form the eastern point of a triangle between Union Island and Mayreau, are surrounded by coral reefs and unbelievably aquamarine waters and make an excellent excursion from nearby islands.

Where to go

No doubt the highlight of any trip to St Vincent and the Grenadines is making the strenuous trek through St Vincent's lush rainforest and volcanic ridges to the rim of **La Soufrière**, St Vincent's active volcano in the north of the island. Beyond St Vincent, the more than thirty islands that make up St Vincent and the Grenadines have largely not been affected by tourism, and this fact makes them a superb destination for adventurous sun-seekers, snorkellers, divers and yachters. Especially worthwhile destinations include the turquoise waters of the **Tobago Cays**, offering superb diving, snorkelling and windsurfing, and the delightful island of **Bequia**, whose relaxed pace of life and seafaring ways warrant a longer stay than the size of the island might suggest.

When to go

As in much of the Caribbean the best time to visit St Vincent and the Grenadines is during the **winter** – roughly January to May – when the tropical heat is tempered by cooling trade winds and rainfall is minimal. Between August and October is **hurricane season**, also the island's wettest season, though hurricanes needn't be a major concern when planning to visit.

Getting there

Flights touch down on St Vincent at **E.T. Joshua Airport** in Arnos Vale, roughly 1.5 miles southeast of the capital of Kingstown. The airport does not receive international flights from outside the Caribbean, so you'll need to fly first to Barbados, Grenada, Martinique, St Lucia, Puerto Rico or Trinidad and make a connection there. American Eagle, BWIA, Caribbean Star, LIAT, SVG Airways and Mustique Airways fly to St Vincent, Bequia, Mustique, Canouan or Union Island. It's also possible to travel to Union Island from Carriacou (one of Grenada's islands) by boat – see box on p.671 for details.

Embassies and consulates

Office of the British High Commission, PO Box 132, Granby Street, Kingstown ⓣ784/457-1701, ⓕ456-2570, ⓔbhcsvg@caribsurf.com

Money and costs

The official currency of St Vincent and the Grenadines is the **Eastern Caribbean dollar (EC$)**, although the US dollar is also widely accepted, as are major credit cards, at hotels and restaurants, and by car rental agencies and dive and tour companies. The EC$ is divided into 100 cents. Bills come in denominations of 5, 10, 20, 50 and 100 EC dollars; coins in 1, 2, 5, 10 and 25 cents. At the time of writing, the **rate of exchange** was roughly EC$2.70 to US$1.

There are plenty of **banks** on St Vincent, including Barclays Bank and Scotiabank on Halifax Street in Kingstown, both of which have ATMs. E.T. Joshua Airport has an **exchange bureau** which is open 8am–noon and 3–5pm on weekdays. There are also two banks on Bequia and a branch of the National Commercial Bank on Union Island; all have ATMs. **Banking hours** are generally Monday to Thursday 9am–3pm and Friday 9am–5pm; however, some banks close at 1pm.

The Jasper

The tiny passenger and cargo boat **The Jasper** runs between Union Island and Grenada's Carriacou on Monday and Thursday, leaving from the jetty at Ashton village on Union Island for Carriacou at 6.30am and departing Hillsborough on Carriacou for the return journey to Union Island at 12.30pm. The trip takes approximately **one hour** and the **fare** is EC$15 one-way. To travel between the two islands you must go through **immigration**, either on Carriacou at the end of the Hillsborough jetty or on Union Island at the airport.

The **bus fare** from Ashton to the airport is EC$3 and a bus will be waiting when *The Jasper* docks to transfer passengers. If you're arriving on Union Island from Carriacou, you must board this bus as you'll need to pass through immigration at the airport.

Be aware that *The Jasper* is a small, wooden motor-powered boat that has seen better days and which sometimes runs under sail, so expect a rough ride even when the sea looks calm. As well, departure can be delayed if the boat is waiting for cargo. If you're adventurous and have good sea legs, *The Jasper* can be fun – if not take a plane.

Hotels and restaurants will automatically add a 7 percent government tax and 10 percent service charge to your bill. Tipping is at your discretion, but not expected.

In St Vincent and the Grenadines a **departure tax** of EC$30 applies to stays longer than 24 hours.

Information, websites and maps

There are four **tourist information centres** in the area. The main one is on Bay Street in Kingstown, St Vincent; there is also an information desk inside E.T. Joshua Airport and tourist centres on Bequia (see p.683) and Union Island (see p.688).

You can pick up **maps** of St Vincent and most of the Grenadines at the main tourist information centre in Kingstown. A detailed Ordnance Survey map of St Vincent is also available from tourist information and some tourist-oriented shops.

Phones, post and email

The main **post office** is on Halifax Street in Kingstown (Mon–Fri 8.30am–3pm, Sat 8.30–11.30am). There are also branches in smaller communities on St Vincent, as well as on the other islands.

Coin- and card-operated **phones** can be found on all the islands, and you can buy cards from Cable & Wireless on Halifax Street in St Vincent, as well as tourist

Websites

Ⓦ www.grenadines.net
This regularly updated, comprehensive site features summaries of each island, articles, travel tips and promotions.

Ⓦ www.heraldsvg.com
Check this site for the online version of St Vincent and the Grenadine's daily newspaper, *The Herald*.

Ⓦ www.nbcsvg.com
Listen to local news and sports programmes on the website of the National Broadcasting Corporation for St Vincent and the Grenadines.

Ⓦ www.vincy.com
A business-oriented site with information on the country and its people, there are also news items and a telephone directory.

information centres and shops.

Kingstown has a couple of **internet cafés**, and others can be found on Bequia and Union Island.

The **country code** for St Vincent and the Grenadines is ☎784.

Getting around

Details on **transport** to specific islands is covered in the individual island sections. Islands without bus services however are small enough to walk around.

By bus

Buses are small minivans that operate on the larger islands. On St Vincent, buses run from the bus terminal in Kingstown, next to the Little Tokyo Fishmarket, from 6am to 8pm, although service is much less frequent on Sundays than during the rest of the week. The terminal is organized into three lanes marked **Leeward**, **Windward** or **Kingstown**. Ask any driver if you're not sure which one you want.

Although buses pack in as many people as possible, play loud music and drive very fast around the steep mountain roads, they are very safe, fun and heavily used by locals. Though there are frequent **bus stops**, buses can be flagged down anywhere along the route – you'll always know when one is around by their incessant use of the horn. Let the conductor know when you want to get off and pay as you leave. Fares from Kingstown work out to around EC$1 to the airport, EC$1.50 to Villa Beach, EC$3 to Argyle and EC$2 to Buccament. Similar bus services run on Bequia (see p.683) and Union Island (see p.688).

By car

To rent a car you'll need a local driving permit, available for EC$50 in Kingstown, either from the police station on Bay Street or from the Licensing Authority on Halifax Street (Mon–Fri 9am–3pm).

Avis (☎784/457-2847) is the only international car rental company on the islands and has offices at E.T. Joshua Airport and on Paul's Avenue in Kingstown, but there are plenty of local agencies, including Slim's and Baba's (☎784/457-0458); Ben's Auto Rentals (☎784/457-2321), which rents jeeps; and Terry's Rental and Taxi Service (☎784/457-9430). Remember that **driving** is on the left-hand side.

Prices range from US$50 to US$65 per day and there is little difference between local and international firms.

By scooter and bike

Scooters can be rented from Speedway Bike and Scooter Rental (☎784/456-4894) for US$30 per day or US$180 per week. Sailor Cycles on Middle Street in Kingstown (☎784/457-1274) rents **bikes** for around EC$20 per day.

By taxi

Taxis are plentiful on St Vincent and tout aggressively for business around the jetty and waterfront area of Kingstown. Fares are regulated but there are no meters, so be sure to agree on a price before you get into the car.

The **central taxi rank** is next to the *Heron Hotel* (see p.677) on Upper Bay Street and main taxi companies include Belford Taxis (☎784/457-9190) or Terry's Rental and Taxi Service (☎784/457-9430). Fares from Kingstown to the airport run about EC$20 and from the airport to Villa Beach EC$15.

By boat

The **ferry** is a wonderful way to see the islands – especially if you don't want to stay at them all – and makes for the cheapest "cruise" by far. The MV *Barracuda* plies the glorious waters of the Caribean between St Vincent, Bequia, Canouan, Mayreau and Union Island. (Be sure to keep your eyes peeled for flying fish, whales and dolphins.) From St Vincent expect to pay EC$15 to Bequia, EC$20 to Canouan, EC$25 to Mayreau and EC$30 to Union Island. Ferries also run frequently between Kingstown and Bequia – see box opposite for details.

To reach some of the smaller, uninhabited islands, **yacht charters** are the only option – see individual island sections for details.

MV Barracuda ferry schedule

The following scheduled times are approximate.

St Vincent to Union Island
Monday, Thursday and Saturday
Departs St Vincent at 10.30am
Bequia 11.45am (not on Saturdays)
Canouan 2pm
Mayreau 3.25pm
Arrives at Union Island at 3.45pm.

From Union Island to St Vincent
Tuesdays and Fridays
Departs Union Island 6.30am
Mayreau 7.30am
Canouan 8.45am
Bequia 11am
Arrives at St Vincent at noon.

By plane

Planes are a fast, convenient and relatively inexpensive option for travelling between islands. Sample one-way fares from St Vincent are US$25 to Mustique, US$30 to Canouan, and US$33 to Union Island. Caribbean Star, LIAT, SVG Airways, Trans Island Air and Mustique Airways all provide frequent service, and Universal Travel on Upper Bay Street, Kingstown (☎784/457-2779), is efficient in at organizing inter-island flights.

Accommodation

St Vincent and the Grenadines offer a wide range of **accommodation**, from small hotels, guesthouses and self-catering apartments to large and at times luxurious beach resorts. **Prices** vary almost as much as the type of accomodation. Most hotels, especially those that cater for business travellers – have year-round rates, while others drop their prices during summer months (mid-April to mid-December), though not by a lot. Finding a place to stay usually isn't hard, but during the winter months it's wise to **book ahead**.

Camping isn't an option here as there are no campsites in St Vincent and the Grenadines and camping itself is not encouraged.

Food and drink

St Vincent grows a variety of fruit and vegetables, among them oranges, breadfruit and avocado. The island also produces 90 percent of the world's supply of **arrowroot**, a plant whose starch is used in cooking and in making glossy computer paper. Fresh **seafood** is abundant on the islands, ranging from lobster to flying fish, with conch being particularly abundant.

While larger restaurants generally serve a mix of West Indian and international cuisine, you will almost always find **rotis**, curries and **jerk chicken** on offer. Vegetarians will find that most large cafés and restaurants cater for them, although smaller towns and islands may not be as amenable.

The beer of choice is **Hairoun** (the Carib name for St Vincent), brewed at the St Vincent Brewery in Kingstown, along with Guinness and a selection of popular **soft drinks**, such as ginger beer, tonic and soda water.

When dining out, bear in mind that prices generally increase after 7pm when most establishments switch to their more expensive dinner menus, and the number of inexpensive dining options dwindles significantly.

Opening hours and holidays

Business hours are generally Monday to Friday 8am–noon and 1–4pm and Saturday 8am–noon, although times can vary from store to store.

Aside from the public holidays listed on p.40, St Vincent and the Grenadines celebrate **National Heroes' Day** on March 14, **Caricom Day** on the second Monday in July, **August Monday** on the first Monday in August and **Independence Day** on October 27.

The following are a selection of the major festivals on the islands. St Vincent's **Carnival**, known as Vincy Mas, is usually held on the second Tuesday of July, although festivities begin at the end of June. Like other carnivals, Vincy Mas brings the whole island onto the streets to party with

parades, vibrant costumes and calypso and steel-band music. At the end of January there is also a **Blues Festival** that attracts international entertainers. Bequia hosts an **Easter Regatta,** while Union Island annually celebrates **Easterval**, a three-day festival of boat races, sports games and calypso music. Canouan's **Regatta** occurs at the end of May. The annual **Mustique Blues Festival**, which confusingly hosts events on both Bequia and St Vincent as well as Mustique, attracts top-name international acts during the end of January and beginning of February.

Outdoor activities

St Vincent and the Grenadines' **volcanic features** and **coral reefs** make their underwater topography ideal for diving. Breathtaking walls and spectacular drop-offs combined with large reefs and shallow coral gardens provide first-class day and night dives. Top sites include those around the coastlines of the larger islands, or the spectacular coral reefs of the Tobago Cays, reached on daytrips.

A large network of **hiking trails** weaves through St Vincent's rugged, mountainous interior; though you can follow them on your own, you'll be better off hiring a guide. The other islands are so small that walking is the easiest way to get around, but be wary of walking in the midday sun and take plenty of water.

Language

The official language is **English**, and French patois is also widely spoken.

Emergency numbers

Police, fire and **coast guard** ⓣ999
Police stations Kingstown ⓣ784/457-1211, Bequia ⓣ784/458-3350

History

Prior to European contact, the history of St Vincent and the Grenadines is hard to distinguish from that of the rest of the Eastern Caribbean. The first known inhabitants, the **Ciboneys**, were displaced by the **Arawaks** about 2000 years ago, who were in turn were swept out of the territory by the **Caribs** a thousand years later. It is only when the history of the Caribs collides with that of the later arrivals (both European and African) that the history becomes distinct.

St Vincent was a densely populated island, especially after it became a refuge for Caribs fleeing European control of other islands. Their numbers, combined with their ferocity, helped to repulse all European attempts to establish a foothold on the island. While all Europeans were resisted, the most virulent hatred was saved for the British who were presumptuous enough to grant the rights to St Vincent lands to their subjects. In the end, it was Britain's rival, France, who was allowed to form the first settlement in the early eighteenth century. By this time, the Grenadines (called Los Pajaros, or The Birds, by early Spanish sailors) had all been colonized and converted into plantation economies worked by slaves, while the native populations was eliminated, removed or marginalized.

In 1675, some years before the French settlement was established, a Dutch slave ship sank in the channel between Bequia and St Vincent. The crew and a large number of slaves perished, but many slaves managed to swim ashore and were accepted by the Caribs, forming one large community. However, within a couple generations, division emerged and the Caribs divided along racial lines: the **Black Caribs**, descendants of the slave-ship survivors, and **Yellow Caribs**, who were of strictly native heritage. European influence increased and plantations flourished, and in 1783 Britain was granted sole control of St Vincent as part of the Treaty of Paris, which officially ended the American Revolutionary War.

In 1795 French radical **Victor Hugues** instigated a revolt that resulted in the Yellow Caribs, led by Chief Duvallier, and the Black Caribs, led by Chatoyer, sweeping across the island, burning plantations and killing settlers in their wake. Chatoyer, convinced he could not be killed by another mortal, challenged the British commander, Alexander Leith, to a duel and was killed (though under mysterious circumstances).

A year later, Carib resistance was crushed. Most of the surviving Caribs, some 5000, were shipped to the island of Roaton, off the coast of Honduras, and the few that were allowed to remain were settled in the northeast tip of the island at Sandy Bay. The British soon set up a plantation economy and imported 18,000 African slaves to support it. When slavery was abolished in 1834, the freed slaves turned to small-plot farming, and European immigrant labour was brought in to replace them on the plantations.

However, this more expensive workforce, combined with the fact that cane was being replaced by **beet** as a main source of the raw materials for sugar, led to the decline of the plantation system throughout the region. What economy and politics had started, nature finished. In 1812, La Soufrière, a volcano in the north of St Vincent, erupted and destroyed coffee and cotton crops, and again in 1902, the final death knell of the island's plantation economy. Nature has played its part ever since. An eruption in 1979 (the year St Vincent and the Grenadines gained independence) led to the evacuation of 20,000 people and destroyed crops and land, and hurricanes in 1980 and 1986 damaged the agricultural industry even further.

St Vincent and the Grenadines, one of the poorest nations in the region, is still recovering. Perhaps surprisingly, given its strife and the political turmoil of its neighbours, the country has had a stable democracy since independence, and a government under James Mitchell's New Democratic Party since 1984.

18.1

St Vincent

ST VINCENT is famous for its black beaches of volcanic sand, found along its entire coastline. The Leeward (west) side of the island is characterized by secluded coastal valleys and fishing villages, while the dramatic Windward (east) side, lined with windswept beaches, is pounded by the waves of the Atlantic Ocean.

Despite these impressive assets, the main reason to visit lies more in the mountainous interior, which rises to an impressive 4000ft at **La Soufrière,** an active volcano that last erupted in 1979. Running through the region is a network of hiking trails that are tranquil and rich with wildlife.

Whether you choose to lie on the beach, engage in outdoor exertion, or a mixture of both, the island is small enough to take in the full range of activities over just a few days; the best place to start is **Kingstown**, the charming capital, which also makes a good base if you plan to hop around St Vincent's offshore islands or don't want to stay in expensive resort accommodation. The main tourist areas of **Villa Beach** and **Indian Bay** and the luxury resort of **Young Island** have the most popular beaches, though more appealing beaches lie in the more remote parts of the island.

Kingstown and the beach resorts

Situated in a sheltered bay on the southwest tip of St Vincent, the hardworking harbour town of **Kingstown** is the island's commercial hub. On weekdays the town moves at a frantic pace, especially around the bustling jetty, bus station and fish market. The heat here can be fierce as sea breezes barely penetrate the compact, one-way streets, lined with warehouses and dense with human and commercial traffic. Though breathtaking from a distance, Kingstown's harbour reveals the grubbiness of an active port city when you get closer to it. There's little to see along the industrial waterfront, but this matters little as the town's main appeal lies in its entertaining **streets**. Dressed in pristine white shirts and gloves, the traffic officers directing vehicles through the narrow roads lend an unexpected air of formality to this energetic, but laid-back town where locals are so preoccupied that they hardly glance at tourists. Things slow down considerably in the evenings when Kingstown is a shadow of its busy weekday self, and on Saturday afternoons and Sundays the town is very quiet.

Not far away are the major beach resort options on the island, **Villa Beach** and **Indian Bay**, both with some build-up, though neither as good a choice as the **offshore islands** within easy reach of the town.

Accommodation

Kingstown and the Villa Beach area hold St Vincent's highest concentration of places to stay, and may well be where you stay regardless of what area on the island you decide to visit – the options are better here than anywhere else. If you're looking for a real splurge, you can try the lone resort on **Young Island**, just offshore.

Kingstown

The Cobblestone Inn Upper Bay Street ⓣ784/456-1937, ⓕ456-1938, ⓦwww.thecobblestoneinn.com. Housed in a restored sugar warehouse, this gem of a hotel, with its cobblestone walkways and arches, is a tranquil haven. The rooms are comfortable and individually decorated, and come with all the amenities. ③. Weekend specials for two nights (US$100) and three nights (US$140).

Heron Hotel Upper Bay Street ⓣ784/457-1631, ⓕ457 1180, ⓔinncvg@caribsurf.com. Inexpensive place to stay, if a little noisy and shabby around the edges, but all rooms are air conditioned and en suite. ③

The New Montrose Hotel New Montrose ⓣ784/457-0172, ⓕ457-0213, ⓦwww.newmontrosehotel.com. Modern apartment-hotel on the Leeward Highway bus route, near the botanical gardens. All rooms have cable TV, private balcony and kitchenette; there is also a bar and restaurant on site. ③

Phoenix Apartments New Montrose ⓣ784/457-9481, ⓕ457-9859, ⓦwww.phoenixsvg.com. High on the hillside overlooking Kingstown and the harbour, this modern hotel has double rooms and spacious apartments with kitchen, lounge and private balcony. Breakfast at the hotel is US$5, and there's also a food store nearby. Doubles ②, apartments ②

Villa Beach and around

Beachcombers Villa Beach ⓣ784/458-4283, ⓕ458-4385, ⓦwww.beachcombershotel.com. Lovely, family-run place set in attractive gardens on the edge of Villa Beach and made up of colourfully decorated, little villas with en-suite bathrooms and patios. There's a health and beauty spa on site, as well as a pool, and a bar and restaurant over looking the beach. Rates include Continental breakfast. ③

Lagoon Marina and Hotel Ratho Mill ⓣ & ⓕ784/458-4308, ⓦwww.lagoonmarina.com. Situated on the south shore of St Vincent, this waterfront hotel has two pools, a restaurant and bar with ocean views, and brightly decorated rooms – all with direct internet and email access through cable TV. ④

Paradise Inn Villa Beach ⓣ784/457-4795, ⓕ457-4221, ⓦwww.paradiseinnsvg.com. Attractive, budget hotel near Villa and Indian beaches with self-catering apartments or rooms with private, ocean-facing balconies and air conditioning. ③

Young Island

Young Island Resort ⓣ784/458-4826, ⓕ457-4567, ⓦwww.youngisland.com. The most romantic and expensive place to stay on the island, consisting of luxury cottages each with ocean view, private terrace and fresh fruit and flowers. There's also a pool, tennis courts and a white-sand beach outfitted with sun loungers and hammocks. Meals at the on-site restaurant are inventive and elegantly served. Rates include breakfast and dinner (US$325–710).

The Town

Starting on Upper Bay Street, which runs parallel to the sea, you'll find the **tourist information centre** (Mon–Fri 8am–4.15pm; ⓣ784/457-1502, ⓦwww.svg-tourism.com) in an imposing government complex across the street from the vibrant two-storey **market**, crammed with stalls selling everything from fresh produce and local arts and crafts to toiletries and souvenirs. Just as busy, but twice as smelly, is the **Little Tokyo Fish Market** on the waterfront side of the road next to the bus station.

Heading west from the market's north end, Grenville Street turns into Tyrrel Street, which offers the **St George's Anglican Cathedral**, a traditional Georgian design with airy vaulted ceilings and exquisite stained glass. A window depicting an angel dressed in red robes was originally commissioned by Queen Victoria for London's St Paul's Cathedral; it was later bestowed as a gift to the church's bishop after the Queen deemed it inappropriate for angels to wear anything but white. Across the street stands the otherworldy **St Mary's Roman Catholic Cathedral** – one of the most striking cathedrals you're likely to see anywhere. Built in 1823 and designed by local Belgian Benedictine priest Dom Charles Verbeke, the church is constructed from dark volcanic sand bricks in an eclectic mix of architectural styles, Romanesque, Moorish and Georgian among them.

A ten-minute walk or a short bus ride northwest along the main road towards the Leeward Highway brings you to Kingstown's superb **Botanical Gardens** (daily;

free), an immaculately kept twenty-acre oasis that makes for a delightful place to wander or simply relax on a bench. Founded in 1765, the gardens are the oldest of their kind in the western hemisphere; there's even a 50ft breadfruit tree grown from one the original plants introduced here by Captain Bligh in 1793. Signs posted along an educational trail near the entrance explain how to identify various species of plant, and along the trail you'll spy the usual palm, bamboo, coconut and cashew trees, as well as more unusual flora such as custard apple and miraculous trees. There's also a small aviary on the grounds where St Vincent parrots are bred to keep them from extinction. Though the gardens are free, expect to be stopped by a "guide" at the entrance who will ask you to pay an EC$3 entrance fee, plus a tip, for showing you around.

If you fancy a panoramic view of Kingstown and the south Grenadines, head for eighteenth-century **Fort Charlotte**, situated on a 600ft-high ridge to the north of the town. Otherwise the collection of Lindsay Prescott paintings in the small museum inside the old barracks is reason enough to visit for their colourful depiction of Black Carib history. Fort Charlotte is about an hour's walk from Kingstown, slightly less for the energetic, and a short walk from the bus route that connects it with Kingstown – ask the bus conductor for directions.

Villa Beach and Indian Bay

Situated about four miles east of Kingstown is St Vincent's main resort area, a two-mile stretch of coast encompassing Village Beach and Indian Bay and frequented by yachters and tourists alike.

As Caribbean beaches go, **Villa Beach** is disappointing as it is shabby, dominated by a handful of average resorts and punctuated by the jetty that serves the far more attractive **Young Island** which sits just offshore. Although well used, the beach is not up to the quality of other, more remote beaches on the island; its thin strip of sand is ruined by two storm drains that continuously pour water into the sea. Equally unsightly are the graffiti-covered rocks separating the beach from adjacent **Indian Bay**; the latter is cleaner, more popular with locals and excellent for snorkelling.

Buses from Kingstown drop passengers off at the end of the short road leading down to the jetty on Villa Beach.

Eating and drinking

Eating options on the island are surprisingly limited, with again the most variety around Kingstown and Villa Beach. Prices tend to be lower in Kingstown than in

Young and Fort Duvernette islands

The two islands off Villa Beach – **Young Island** and **Fort Duvernette Island** – are more attractive than the mainland resorts, but in distinctive ways. The private, 35-acre Young Island is an exclusive resort (see p.677) and its gardens are a national wildlife reserve. The long golden beach offers a stark contrast to the rest of the island's lush, green foliage, and the whole place seems to float above the waters of the bay. If you want to visit the island without staying overnight, you will need to phone the resort for permission. Water taxis to Young Island leave from the jetty on Villa Beach and cost EC$2 one-way.

Tiny Fort Duvernette Island, whose steep cliffs rise to 250ft above sea level, offers splendid views of the Grenadines, as well as a crumbling fort, complete with original 24-pound guns and an eight-inch mortar. Built at the beginning of the nineteenth century to defend Calliaqua Bay from European rivals, the fort is unsafe and caution is advised when exploring its remains. Catch a water taxi from Young Island to Fort Duvernette Island and arrange a pick-up time with the driver for the return trip. The round-trip fare is approximately EC$20.

Villa Beach, where you can expect to pay at least twice as much for food and drink than anywhere else on the island. In addition, many Villa Beach establishments add a 15 percent service charge, instead of the usual 10 percent. Bear in mind that most restaurants in Kingstown close on Sunday. Bars in Kingstown are mainly stalls frequented by locals.

Kingstown

Basil's Bar and Restaurant Upper Bay Street ⓣ784/457-2713. Popular with the guests of the *Cobblestone Inn* upstairs, *Basil's* has a tasty menu featuring conch chowder (US$4) for lunch and chicken in tomato ginger sauce (US$14) and lobster in mornay sauce (US$25) for dinner. Closed Sun.

Bounty Restaurant Egmont Street ⓣ784/456-1776. This pleasant café doubles as a small art gallery and second-hand bookshop. It serves numerous breakfast options (from US$3), and there are various rotis and curries for lunch.

Diner's Delight Long Lane Upper ⓣ784/437-1105. Diners can either sit inside and look out over the busy street or sit on a shady terrace at the back of the restaurant. The food, basic but good, includes rotis for US$3–4, and chicken and fish with rice for not much more. Take-away is available.

Perkey's Pizza Grenville Street ⓣ784/456-2020. Average pizza and burger restaurant (with take-away) serving up pizza slices from US$2 and whole pizzas from US$10. One of the few eating options on a Sunday evening.

Tony's Original Pizza Halifax Street ⓣ784/457-2430. A pizza and burger joint with bar, located in a courtyard off the street. The staff are very friendly and the music upbeat, and this is one of the few places for cheap food in the evening as its menu and prices remain the same all day (pizzas start from US$11, burgers US$2). Open daily though hours vary.

Villa Beach

Lime Restaurant and Pub Villa Harbor ⓣ784/458-4227. With a wall made up of lobster traps, fishing nets draped around the ceiling and even a mechanical singing fish in the ladies' toilet, the feel of the sea permeates this waterfront restaurant. The food is excellent and the pub menu at lunch features curries from US$15. Reservations are required for dinner, when prices range from US$23 for dolphin fillet to US$32 for African black pepper steak. There is also a long cocktail and cigar menu.

Slick's Bar and Restaurant Villa Harbor ⓣ784/457-5783. Serving international dishes such as lamb chops, stuffed chicken breast and creole cuisine, the lunch menu includes soups (from US$5) and burgers (from US$6), while a typical dinner dish is grilled kingfish (US$17). Limited accommodation available. Open 10am–midnight.

The airport

Pizza Party Opposite the airport, Arnos Vale ⓣ784/456-4939. Located between Kingstown and Villa Beach, this popular fast-food restaurant has a menu of pizza, barbecued chicken and local dishes from US$7. Credit cards not accepted. Open daily 9am–11pm.

Nightlife and entertainment

Kingstown is the centre for island **nightlife**, such as it is, though often that's limited to people hanging out in the streets, with car stereos usually providing the music. For official establishments, try *The Attic*, at Melville and Grenville streets (11am until late; EC$10–15 cover charge; ⓣ784/457-2559), which has **live music** – usually jazz or soca – most nights, and is a decent and popular place to watch sports on the multi-screen TVs (though their Hairnoun Calendar Girls Nights won't be to everyone's tastes). The limited, pub menu is available throughout the day. You'll also find live music in many of the bars and restaurants at Villa Beach, among them *Slick's* (see above), which is a good choice for local music.

Diving and sailing tours

Due to its volcanic origins, the underwater topography of St Vincent is breathtaking, and there are no shortage of dive operators on the island to help you explore it. Dive St Vincent, next to the Young Island jetty at Villa Beach (ⓣ784/457-4928, ⓕ457-4948, ⓦwww.divestvincent.com), offers numerous dives, courses and packages, some of which include accommodation. Packages for seven days' accommodation and diving range from US$719 to US$1820 (the latter covers a stay at Young Island), depending on where you stay and the number of dives you make. They also organize an excellent snorkelling trip to the stunning 60ft Falls of Baleine (see p.682). Dive Fantasea, also based in Villa Beach (☎784/457-5560, Ⓦwww.divefantasea.com), runs day and night dives for both beginners and experienced divers; they also operate Fantasea Tours, arranging one-day sailing trips to some of the Grenadine Islands, including Mustique and the Tobago Cays, for prices starting from US$70.

The rest of the island

Most of the island's sights outside Kingstown and the main resort areas are accessible from the coastal highway that runs up both the island's **Leeward** and **Windward** coasts. However, except for St Vincent's southwest corner, where a few roads penetrate inland, St Vincent's mountainous **interior** can be reached only via walking trails, and in one case only by boat.

The Leeward coast

On the Leeward coast the road clings to the mountainside, with little to protect you from the steep drops, and runs as far as **Richmond Beach**. The drive will take you past lush valleys, formerly the site of vast plantations, but now farmed by smallholder farmers, and black-sand beaches, ideal for swimming and snorkelling.

Less than a mile north of the pretty village of **Barrouallie**, with its quaint, ornately trimmed houses, is the tranquil, black-sand beach of **Wallilabou Bay**. There are no facilities here, so bring your own food, but the idyllic surrounds are perfect for a quiet bit of sunbathing and a dip in the ocean. While you are in the area, continue north for a mile on the inland side of the road to reach **Wallilabou Falls**, an attractive 13ft cascade of water where you can escape the heat by taking a refreshing swim.

Well worth a visit is **Buccament Bay**, a half-hour drive or bus ride from Kingstown. Reached by a short walk from the main road down a dirt track – marked by a signpost to *Buccama on the Bay* restaurant (see opposite) – this small, secluded horseshoe beach is used more by local villagers than tourists. Gazing inland from the beach, past the fishing nets hung out to dry, you'll find the view of the rugged mountain peaks stunning. The valley here is the site of a former sugar plantation; the cliffs that frame it feature some of St Vincent's ancient **petroglyphs**. As you walk along the dirt track towards the beach, you'll come across a sign on the

Petroglyphs

The word **petroglyph** literally means drawings on stone, and although these striking white inscriptions on St Vincent have been attributed to the Ciboneys, Arawaks and Caribs, the identity of the people who created them is still disputed. Most petroglyphs, such as those at Layou, are deeply cut into hard andesite rock, but some are carved onto agglomerate, rock made from a mass of volcanic fragments such as those near Argyle and Buccament.

Although efforts are being made to make access easier, petroglyphs take a bit of hunting out. The most popular sites are at Buccament (see above), Layou, and Barrouallie on the Leeward coast. At Layou a cluster of them can be found near the river by the Bible Camp, on the main road to the north of the town; however, they are on private land and you'll need permission from the owner to see them (EC$5 per person; ☎784/458-7243). At Barrouallie, petroglyphs can be found in the yard of the local secondary school.

left-hand side announcing the "Petroglyphs of Buccament". Although some of the fields in the area are fenced off and look like private land, visitors can walk up to the cliff face (watch out for the grazing cows along the way) to view a collection of evocative white etchings in the rock.

Practicalities

If you're not staying in the main beach resorts or Kingstown, the Leeward coast offers really the only other major facilities around. Try the *Emerald Valley Resort and Casino*, Penniston Valley (Ⓣ784/456-7824, Ⓕ456-7145, Ⓔeemvcasino@caribsurf; ❹), a collection of tropical lodges in a peaceful Leeward valley, all with kitchenettes and balconies overlooking a mountain stream. The beach is an energetic one-mile walk away, but the resort has its own pool and tennis courts, and even a casino, which offers all the typical gaming options.

Buccament Bay is where you'll find the best **place to eat** in all of St Vincent, *Buccama on the Bay* (Ⓣ784/456-7855). Reservations are required for dinner, when a three-course meal – fresh and delicious, prepared with produce from local farms – costs just US$26–30. The restaurant can be reached by bus from Kingstown; just ask to be dropped off at Buccament's main road and follow the signposted dirt track for about ten minutes down to the sea. A return taxi to Kingstown costs about EC$40.

The Windward coast

The highway on the Windward coast leads all the way up to the village of **Fancy**, at St Vincent's northern tip, and offers startling views of rugged coastline and sweeping beaches. A noteworthy stop along the Windward side is the windswept beach of **Argyle**, a bleak and rocky stretch more reminiscent of northern Scotland than the Caribbean – no swimming is allowed here. Situated to the west of Argyle is the rich fertile valley of **Mesopotamia**, where bananas, nutmeg, cocoa, coconuts and breadfruit all grow in abundance. Here and further north in the colourful **Montreal Gardens** (Dec–Aug Mon-Fri 9am–5pm; EC$5), the views of the river valleys and ocean are, some say, hard to match anywhere in the Caribbean.

Most buses travel only as far as **Georgetown**, halfway up the coast; check at the bus station in Kingstown if you want to travel further up. To get to Georgetown you'll have to pass through the **Black Point Tunnel**, which was drilled by slave labour in 1815 to create a direct route for transporting sugar from the northern plantations to Kingstown. The 350ft tunnel was considered an engineering feat in its time and remains impressive today, especially as you can still see the old blast holes in the volcanic rock. The only other point of interest on this highway is the **Owia Salt Pond**, a short distance south of Fancy, near the village of Owia – home to the remaining descendants of the Black Caribs. The tidal pools are sheltered from the roiling Atlantic by a huge wall of rock, and the cool, clean salt waters here are used by locals and visitors alike.

The interior

St Vincent's **interior** can only be explored by walking trails, which are not always well marked. The **Vermont Nature Trails** on the Leeward side, about five miles from Kingstown, are one of the few places where you are likely to spot the endangered St Vincent parrot, a colourful bird recognizable by its pale head, blue tail and wing-tip feathers, and russet wings. Here the **Parrot Lookout trail** threads its way through lush rainforest, rising approximately 500ft, and you also stand a good chance of seeing hummingbirds, black hawks and green heron along the way. The trails begin near the top of Buccament Valley and pass picnic areas along the way.

Hiking is also excellent in the north of the island around the stunning peak of **La Soufrière**. The trail to the summit leads through fertile rainforest, banana plantations and volcanic ridges and is a rigorous one: the ascent to the crater is approximately three miles and takes around five hours. The best way to explore this area is on an organized tour as the trail is not clearly marked and guides can also point out features along the way.

In the remote northwest tip, beyond the reach of the coastal highway, lie the breathtaking 60ft **Falls of Baleine**, where a swim in the large rock-lined pool is unforgettable and time spent in this stunning spot is well worth the trip. The falls are only reachable by organized tour (see p.680).

18.2

The Grenadines

THE GRENADINES consist of 32 islands and cays, some of which are reachable by plane, but most only by boat. Each island has its own distinct character and appeals to a particular crowd, whether it's the exclusive decadence of **Mustique** or the rustic appeal of **Union**, or the yachters and sun seekers who flock to **Bequia** or those who wish to get away from it all in tiny **Mayreau**. All, however, tend to share superb diving and snorkelling opportunities, as well as pristine white-sand beaches and a relaxed atmosphere.

Bequia

Though separated from St Vincent by a mere nine miles, **BEQUIA** (pronounced "beck-way"), with its aura of tranquillity and relaxed pace, feels light years away from frantic Kingstown. No visit to St Vincent and the Grenadines is complete without a stop on Bequia's seven square miles, where the beaches are breathtaking and the inhabitants friendly. However, don't be fooled into thinking that there's little here to experience except a laid-back attitude and stunning scenery. Bequia may have these in abundance, but the island also has a rich seafaring history from which time-honoured traditions, such as whaling and boat building, are still practised; it was the island's proximity to the migration path of the **humpback whale** that made it the most important whaling station in the area during the nineteenth and twentieth centuries.

Arrival, information and getting around

James F. Mitchell Airport, near the village of Paget Farm, is situated in the southwest of the island, approximately three miles from the capital of Port Elizabeth. (See p.673 for flight details.) **Ferries** run frequently, often three to four times daily, from Kingstown on St Vincent to Port Elizabeth, operated by *The Admiral* and *The Bequia Express*. Journey time is an hour; cost is EC$15.

Brochures, leaflets and maps are available from the **tourist office** at the end of the ferry jetty in Port Elizabeth (Mon–Fri & Sun 9am–noon & 1.30–4pm, Sat 9am–12.30pm, closed on public holidays; Ⓣ784/458-3286, Ⓕ458-3964, Ⓦwww.bequiasweet.com).

Buses, or "dollar vans" as they are known, depart from the end of the ferry jetty in Port Elizabeth for points around the island. Service is frequent and efficient, but the island is so small and scenic that walking is the best way to explore most of it. Fares are EC$1–2 depending on how far you travel. **Taxis** are plentiful and wait under the almond trees of Port Elizabeth's waterfront. The fare from Port Elizabeth to the airport is EC$30 and to Friendship Bay EC$20. If you need to call for one ahead of time, try Bequia Car Rentals and Taxi Service (Ⓣ784/458-3349).

Accommodation

There is no shortage of **accommodation** on Bequia, where options vary from basic to luxury. The more expensive choices tend to be small hotels, full of character and very comfortable. That said, most of the accommodation here is of a high quality and even the more budget options are excellent value for money. Although you'll find much of the accommodation concentrated around Port Elizabeth and Friendship Bay, there's also plenty throughout the island.

Crescent Beach Inn Crescent Beach, near Industry Bay ⓣ784/458-3400. Situated in the northeast of the island near the Turtle Sanctuary, this secluded inn has pleasant rooms, and a bar and restaurant next door. Breakfast is included with the room rate and the beachside bar has table tennis and darts. No credit cards accepted. 3

The Frangipani Belmont Walkway, Port Elizabeth ⓣ784/458-3255, ⓕ458-3824, ⓦwww.frangipani.net. This old family home has been converted into a hotel and is a truly special place to stay, both for location and atmosphere. The five basic rooms in the main house have mosquito nets over the beds and shared showers, toilets and balcony, while the cottage-like units in the back come with king-size beds and private bathrooms. An excellent and popular waterfront bar and restaurant is on site, as well as a tennis court for guest use. 6

Gingerbread Hotel Belmont Walkway, Port Elizabeth ⓣ784/458-3800, ⓕ458-3907, ⓦwww.gingerbreadhotel.com. This hotel, with its ornate trimmings does look like it should be made out of gingerbread. Luxurious suites, some with four-poster beds, include kitchen, private bathroom, and a large porch overlooking Admiralty Bay. The hotel arranges tennis, kayaking, windsurfing and scuba diving for guests as well as excursions to nearby islands. 7

Julie and Isola's Guest House Port Elizabeth ⓣ784/458-3304, ⓕ458-3812, ⓔjulies@caribsurf.com. Situated on the main street near the jetty, an old wooden boarding house with simple, comfortable rooms with showers, toilets and fans. A bar, restaurant and laundry service is on the first floor. 3

Taylor's Apartments Friendship Bay ⓣ784/458-3458, ⓕ457-3420, ⓦwww.connix.com/~bequia. Located on the opposite side of the island from Port Elizabeth, near the little village of La Pompe, these airy, well-maintained apartments have wonderful panoramic views of Friendship Bay and nearby islands. The family that owns these apartments runs the *Port Hole* restaurant in Port Elizabeth (see p.686), and is involved in many other island activities, including car rental and sailing excursions. 3

Port Elizabeth

Port Elizabeth, Bequia's main town, is nestled deep inside **Admiralty Bay**, the island's large natural harbour and favourite stop for yachters from all over the world. This relaxed little town has lost none of its lively Caribbean character, despite cosmopolitan influences brought by settlers and sailors of many nationalities. While the few hours it takes to explore the town are time well spent, most will find it a pleasant distraction from Bequia's main attraction – its fabulous beaches.

The busy centre of the town is the jetty, where ferries from Kingstown dock and sailing boats depart for other Grenadine islands. At the end of the jetty is a small market selling fresh produce, spices and a plethora of tourist fare, including T-shirts, jewellery and locally made jams. Port Elizabeth's main drag, **Front Street**, with its collection of souvenir shops, yacht provisioners and restaurants, leads into **Belmont Walkway**, where most of the town's accommodation is to be found. Among the shops, top ones to check out are the Mauvin Model Boat Shop, which sells handmade model boats, Bequia Bookshop, for its large selection of Caribbean literature, maps and prints, and the Garden Boutique, with locally produced batik bags.

Across the road from the Garden Boutique, just before the main street becomes Belmont Walkway, you'll find the understated **St Mary's Church**. With its profusion of wood beams painted pale blue, its pristine white, wooden pews and tall doors letting in the salty sea breeze, the church feels very much a part of the ocean it faces. Two striking paintings hang on either side of the altar, one of St Vincent and the other of Our Lady of the Seas, both painted by English artist John Constable in 1953.

The beaches

While Bequia's beaches fulfil every expectation of a Caribbean paradise – with sparkling sands and crystal-clear waters – what makes them unforgettable is their appealing roughness. Expect to find rocky headlands, and dense palm woodland that extends to the edge of the beaches, and an aura of castaway isolation. Although the swimming is fantastic, the sea is not tame, at times unleashing large, wild waves which pound the beach to create a dramatic (though not dangerous) setting.

The crown jewel of Bequia's beaches is the stunning **Princess Margaret Beach**, a few minutes' walk over the Princess Point headland from the end of Belmont Walkway, or a quick jaunt by water taxi from Port Elizabeth. Here, the waves froth onto golden sands and the beautiful sunlight bouncing off the waters is perfectly framed by shady palm fronds and stark rocky outcrops. Swimming, sunbathing and snorkelling along this large horseshoe bay is excellent and the beach is never crowded. It has, however, few facilities, apart from the occasional vendor selling trinkets, beer or soft drinks.

To the south of Princess Margaret Beach, and a short walk from Port Elizabeth along the road to the interior, lies the busier **Lower Bay**, where you'll find another striking beach with more in the way of tourist amenities.

Friendship Bay in the southwest is still within easy walking distance and also served by frequent buses. Despite its clutch of hotels and restaurants, this broad sweep of Atlantic shoreline remains unspoiled. The picture-perfect beach is ideal for swimming, snorkelling and diving, and a climb up the steep hillside behind it may afford a rare glimpse of a breaching whale.

The rest of the island

On the northeast tip of the island at the end of Industry Bay is the **Oldhegg Turtle Sanctuary** (daily; EC$10; ☎784/458-3245), which endeavours to save the endangered Hawksbill turtle, distinguished by its pointed bill and sleek shell. In the winter months, baby turtles are collected from the beach soon after they are hatched and released two years later when they are fully capable of looking after themselves and have a vastly increased chance of survival.

On the southwest tip of the island near the village of La Pompe is the **Athneal Petit Museum** (open daily, no set hours; US$2; ☎784/458-3322), dedicated to local hero and whaler Athneal Ollivierre as well as the island's long history of whaling. The tiny, shrine-like collection is full of fascinating whaling artefacts as well as the odd inclusion like signed photos of Clint Eastwood and Tom Cruise, both said to have been inspired by Ollivierre's exploits.

The museum also holds various artworks by local professor Sam McDowell, whose home and **studio** in Page Farm is not far away (by appointment; (☎784/458-3865), if you can't get enough of it at the museum.

Eating and drinking

Bequia has a fine selection of character-filled **restaurants** and **bars** dotted around the island and concentrated along Port Elizabeth's waterfront. The Belmont Walkway has a particularly excellent selection, but it's worth trying options farther afield.

Crescent Beach Inn Crescent Beach, near Industry Bay ☎784/458-3400. This large shady bar by the ocean is a unique and unpretentious place, making for a perfect refreshment stop on the way to the Turtle Sanctuary, or a memorable night out, especially at full moon when the owners organize a beach barbecue. At lunchtime, sandwiches start from US$3 and starters at dinner include pumpkin soup (US$4) and curried shrimp (US$17) as a main course.

The Frangipani Belmont Walkway, Port Elizabeth ☎784/458-3255. The food and the view is first-class. This restaurant is popular with yachters, especially those crewing larger vessels, which makes for a friendly and lively atmosphere. Breakfast starts at 7am, the lunch menu features numerous sandwiches, burgers and omelettes from US$4 and seafood is a specialty in the evening, when main courses average US$15. Thursday night is barbecue night; reservations are required.

Green Boley Belmont Walkway, Port Elizabeth ⓣ784/458-3041. This laid-back, welcoming bar is one of the few places where prices stay the same all day. Here you'll find budget-conscious travellers and family groups munching on tasty rotis and substantial sandwiches (from US$3), fish and chips (US$6) and conch curry (US$8). There is often live music and always a good crowd.

Lina's Bayshore Mall, Port Elizabeth ⓣ784/457-3388. This small, but popular take-away bakery and delicatessen caters primarily for yachters, selling a selection of fresh-baked breads and pastries, great for beach picnics.

Mac's Pizzeria Belmont Walkway, Port Elizabeth ⓣ784/458-3474. It easy to see why dinner reservations are recommended at this bustling and trendy Italian restaurant. Diners eat on a large, sea-facing terrace, decorated with fairy lights and set to a funky sound system. Lobster pizza is a specialty, but many cheaper and unusual options are also available, as are pastas, salads and quiches. Pizzas US$9–30.

Port Hole Belmont Walkway, Port Elizabeth ⓣ784/458-3458. This basic but very popular restaurant has a reasonable lunch menu featuring tasty rotis from US$3 and sandwiches from US$2. The evening menu includes Caribbean and international dishes starting at US$10. There's also a small supermarket and a large book exchange on the premises.

Nightlife

Bequia's **nightlife** is limited, but there is always live music and a friendly ambience throughout the island. In Port Elizabeth most bars and restaurants along Belmont Walkway feature **live music** on alternate nights – *The Whaleboner* (ⓣ784/458-3233) is a popular option, while above Court's furniture shop near the jetty, *Rainbow's End* (ⓣ784/457-3688) is a lively restaurant with karaoke or live music most nights (no cover). In Lower Bay there's the beachfront *Keegan's Bar* (ⓣ784/458-3530), where the boisterous crowd is as entertaining as the live music. Drinks are reasonable, and the sunset from the little outdoor seating area is splendid.

Diving and sailing

All local **dive companies** offer similar packages. Try Bequia Dive Adventures (ⓣ784/458-3504, ⓦwww.dive-bequia.com) or Sunsports (ⓣ784/458-3577, ⓔsunsport@caribsurf.com). Given the island's long seafaring history, Bequia is the best place in the Grenadines to take a **sailing** excursion to one of the other nearby islands. Highly recommended is the romantic 80ft sailing schooner *The Friendship Rose* (call ⓣ784/456-4709 or ask for details at the tourist office, p.683). The ship makes frequent trips from Port Elizabeth's jetty to Mustique, the Tobago Cays and Canouan. Trips start at US$50 and lunch is included in the price. The *Passion* (ⓣ784/458-3884, ⓕ457-3015, ⓦwww.vincy.com/passion) offers day trips on a 60ft catamaran to Mustique (US$70).

Mustique

Situated just seven miles southeast of Bequia, beautiful **MUSTIQUE** is a fantasy island for the ultra-rich. Most visitors to the island are day-trippers drawn by the island resort's air of exclusivity, though their explorations are fairly restricted as much of place is privately owned and curious visitors are discouraged. Those who do spend some time here can enjoy the island's hilly terrain, its large plain to the north and seven lush valleys leading to the white-sand beaches along its coast.

Mustique's first inhabitants were European planters who arrived in the 1740s. The decline of the West Indian sugarcane industry in later years led to the closing of the plantations, and prospects for the island faded. Mustique didn't regain its footing until 1958 when Scottish landowner Colin Tennant bought the 1400-acre island for £45,000 and transformed it into a holiday hot-spot for the rich and famous. Now under the management of a private corporation, the island is a haven for pop stars and celebrities of the likes of Mick Jagger, David Bowie and Elton John, all of whom own properties on the island.

Practicalities

Mustique's **airport** is situated in the north of the island and receives daily flights from St Vincent and other Grenadine islands (see p.673). For details on sailing tour operators on other islands who organize day trips to Mustique, see Fantasea Tours on St Vincent (p.680), *The Friendship Rose* and *Passion* on Bequia (see opposite).

Accommodation and **eating** options are limited but luxurious and must be booked in advance. The two hotels, *Cotton House*, at Endeavour Bay (Ⓣ784/456-4777, Ⓦwww.cottonhouse.net; US$900), and *The Firefly*, overlooking Britannia Bay (Ⓣ784/456-3414, Ⓕ456-3514, Ⓦwww.mustiquefirefly.com; US$480), have every amenity imaginable; other than the two hotels, the only other way to stay on the island is to rent one of 57 decadent villas through the Mustique Company (Ⓣ784/458-4621, Ⓕ456-4565, Ⓦwww.mustique-island.com; US$3000–30,000 daily–weekly). To see who's who in town, head to *Basil's Bar and Restaurant* (Ⓣ784/458-4621, Ⓦwww.basilsmustique.com), a bamboo and thatch bar extending off the beach – and on stilts in the ocean. Main courses for dinner start at EC$70.

Canouan

In the middle of the Grenadine island chain, tiny, crescent-shaped **CANOUAN** – the Carib word for turtles – consists of three square miles of lush green hills and beautiful reef-protected white-sand beaches. It is these beaches that draw an increasing number of visitors and the island is largely set up to cater for their needs. The low, undulating hills are pleasant for walking, and you'll meet more goats than people along its peaceful pathways. However, there's no beating the beaches and the sunbathing, swimming, snorkelling and diving here are all first-class. The coral reefs are just offshore, which means the beaches are well protected and snorkellers needn't be daring to investigate them – though care should be taken to preserve these living organisms. The local dive company, Dive Canouan (Ⓣ784/458-8044, Ⓕ458-8875), can arrange dives for beginners and experienced divers.

Practicalities

There are no restaurants independent of **accommodation** on Canouan, but each hotel has its own facilities, with menus ranging from French cuisine and West Indian fare to pizza. The top choices include *Anchor Inn Guest House*, Grand Bay Ⓣ & Ⓕ784/458-8568; ❸), a tiny guesthouse in a two-storey home near the beach, with three simple rooms, and breakfast and dinner included in the room rate, and *Canouan Beach Hotel*, South Glossy Bay Ⓣ784/458-888, Ⓕ458-8875, Ⓦwww.canouan.com; ❾), which is built on a spectacular beach with views of the islands to the south. The cottage-style rooms give the feel of privacy and complimentary watersports are included in the rates, as are all meals, soft drinks, rum punch and wine in the evening.

Mayreau

With a population of a mere 250 occupants, **MAYREAU** is the smallest of the inhabited Grenadine islands. It almost goes without saying that the beaches, watersports and views are wonderful, but unless you want to splash out for a stay at one of the exclusive resorts, there is little to warrant anything more than a day's exploration.

As with most of the small Grenadines, visitors come for the immaculate beaches, of which Saline Bay and Salt Whistle Bay are justly popular. The sands of **Saline Bay** in the south are nearly a mile long and completely undeveloped, though when a cruise ship visits the island this beach can get very busy. With dazzling white sand and pale-blue waters **Salt Whistle Bay**, home of a small resort (see below), is both stunning and a favourite anchorage for yachts. Good hiking can be found on the island. A long trail winds its way from Salt Whistle Bay to Salt Whistle village, home to a striking, tiny stone Catholic Church whose windows and grounds provide incredible views. If you visit the church during a local wedding, you'll be fortunate, as these are very well celebrated on Mayreau; flags are flown from relatives' houses and rum is sprinkled over graves to encourage ancestors to bless the union. To get married on the island you'll need to stay more than 72 hours, and a more romantic setting would be hard to find.

Practicalities

If you're planning to stay over here, first stop might be *Dennis' Hideaway*, Saline Bay (Ⓣ & Ⓕ458-8594, Ⓦwww.dennis-hideaway.com; ❷), a peaceful guesthouse consisting of five rooms, each with a private bathroom and balcony facing the sea. Downstairs, the bar and restaurant opens at 7am for breakfast (included in the room rate). Lunches start at EC$10 and evening meals include locally caught sea food and mouthwatering spare ribs (US$16–26). More expensive is *Saltwhistle Bay Club* (Ⓣ784/458-8444, Ⓕ458-8944, Ⓔesaltwhistle@grenadines.net; ❾), a quiet beachside resort whose charming, airy bungalows made of local stone each have private patios. There's an open-air restaurant too, serving standard Caribbean dishes.

Other **eating** options include the beachside *Island Paradise* (Ⓣ784/458-8941), with local favourites like callaloo soup, conch stew and red snapper; expect to pay about US$15 for a main course at dinner. Similar dishes can be had at *J & C Restaurant and Bar* (Ⓣ784/458-8558), such as curried conch, snapper and West Indian cake. Transport by boat is included in their reasonable prices. Tucked away in the hills, *Righteous and de Youths* (Ⓣ784/458-8558) serves Caribbean fare along the lines of rotis, saltfish and rum punch. Prices are upwards of US$8, and free transport is available for diners from hotels.

Union Island

Rustic **UNION ISLAND**, the southernmost of the Grenadines, is primarily a stop-off for visitors to the Tobago Cays and a point of entry for yachters into St Vincent and the Grenadines. The terrain of this roughly three-mile-long and one-mile-wide island is less than spectacular, its low scrubby hills rising to a height of 1000ft at Mount Taboi, the tallest peak in the Grenadines, but the untamed scruffiness is much the point of it all. As such, it's a nice daytrip away from any resort pretension.

The commercial centre, **Clifton**, has whatever **tourist information** you might need (daily 9am–noon and 1–4pm), as well as the airport, ferry jetty and a local market. On the waterfront, east towards the airport, the complex at **Bougainville Centre** holds most of the local facilities, including Maggie: A Union Island Bus (Ⓣ784/45-8843), a tour operator that organizes trips around the island for EC$100.

Above the small village of **Ashton**, towards the centre of the island, a few hiking trails wend their way through the hills, offering good walking terrain and excellent views of the surrounding Grenadines, while the remote beaches of **Richmond** and **Big Sand Beach** on the northern end of the island can be reached by road from Clifton. The best snorkelling to be had is at **Lagoon Reef**, which protects the southern coast of the island. Teeming with colourful marine life and rarely visited, the reef provides excellent conditions, especially around **Frigate Island**.

If you want to venture beyond Union Island, Captain Yannis (T784/458-8513, F458-8976, Eyannis@caribsurf.co,), based at the *Clifton Beach Hotel* (see below), operates day trips on 60ft **catamarans** to the neighbouring islands of the Tobago Cays and Palm Island for EC$140; a filling lunch, drinks and the use of snorkelling equipment are included in the price. **Diving** can be arranged through Grenadines Dive (T784/458-8138, F458-8122, Wwww.grenadinesdive.com), which offers easy to adventurous dives; among the latter is a dive to a 90ft volcanic valley complete with a bubbling seabed.

Practicalities

Stay at *Anchorage Yacht Club*, Clifton (T784/458-8221, Wwww.ayc-hotel-grenadines.com; ⑤), right on the waterfront, with comfortable rooms that have good views from private patios. The hotel restaurant, with its own live shark pool, live music and wonderful sea views, serves tasty fish and pasta dinners (US$9–16). More unusual is *Castello's*, opposite the post office in Clifton (T784/458-8117; ②), its rambling garden holding a rustic little house with a couple of quaint rooms and access to the owner's kitchen; the bathrooms are outdoors. Artist/owner Castello sells her work in the gallery and serves the best rum punch and coconut cake on the island. Otherwise, the relaxed *Clifton Beach Hotel* (T & F784/458-8235, Wwww.cliftonbeachhotel.com; ②/④), has basic rooms and cottages, plus an excellent restaurant on the premises.

Tobago Cays

The numerous tiny deserted islets and coral reefs of the lovely **TOBAGO CAYS** are known for their superb snorkelling, diving and windsurfing opportunities. During high season their waters are busy with visiting yachts and local vendors touting everything from food to jewellery from their boats. The cays' popularity, however, is leading to their destruction as anchoring boats and over-fishing have caused considerable damage to the coral reefs. The islands are now a wildlife reserve, and fishing, jet skis and anchoring dinghies are all prohibited to preserve the endangered coral.

Sailing day trips to the Tobago Cays can be organized from other Grenadine islands; try Fantasea Tours on St Vincent (see p.680) and Captain Yannis on Union Island (see above). Resorts also offer packages that include trips like these.

Grenada

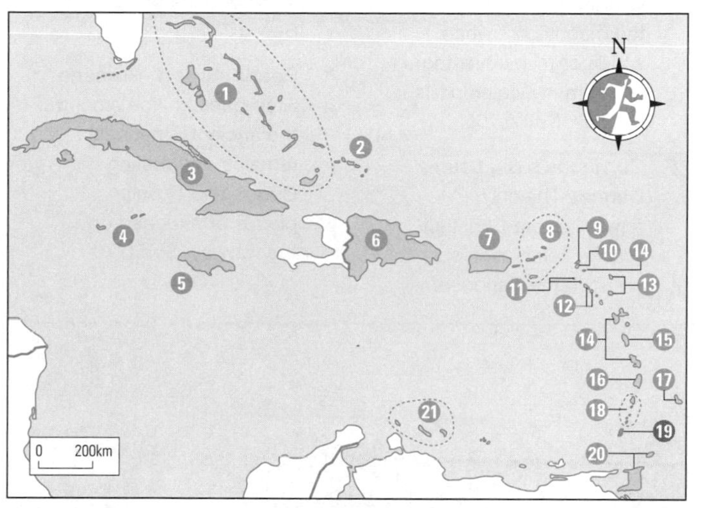

GRENADA

19

Grenada Highlights

* **Grand Etang National Park, Grenada** Hike the many trails that thread through the lush rainforest past waterfalls and crater lakes. See p.710
* **Grand Anse Beach, Grenada** Sunbathe on the magnificent white sands or take advantage of the many watersports options. See p.706
* **Carriacou's Big Drum Dances** The only remaining pre-Christian African celebration surviving in the Caribbean and a highlight of the island's regatta. See p.712
* **Petite Martinique** Savor the joys of doing nothing on this tranquil island, whose main attraction is its slow pace of life. See p.717
* **Pearls Airport, Grenada** Step back in time among the ancient Amerindian remains and rusting Cuban and Russian planes abandoned on the runway. See p.709

Introduction and Basics

The southernmost of the Windward Islands, Grenada is known as "The Isle of Spice", producing one third of the world's supply of nutmeg along with quantities of cinnamon, cloves, ginger, turmeric and mace. While largely dependent on agriculture, the tiny nation of Grenada – which includes neighbouring Carriacou and Petite Martinique as well as other smaller Grenadine islands – is steadily earning a reputation as a holiday destination, but it remains relatively unspoiled compared to other more popular Caribbean islands.

All three of the main islands offer excellent *watersports* opportunities, while Grenada in particular has its share of stunning black- and white-sand beaches, ranging from the resort-lined *Grand Anse Beach* on the southwest tip to the ruggedly spectacular *Bathway Beach* in the northeast. But what makes Grenada truly spectacular is the dense tropical *rainforest* of its mountainous interior, rich in birdlife and laced with a network of hiking trails that provide magnificent views of the surrounding peaks.

Ringing the island are a variety of communities, chief among them the elegant capital of *St George's*, as well as the charming fishing village of *Goyave* on the west coast and, on the east coast, *Grenville*, the country's agricultural heart. The country's inhabitants, 90 percent of whom live on the island of Grenada, are descended from British, French, African and West Indians settlers, and their inviting and friendly nature belies the country's turbulent history.

Much smaller and far less visited are the islands of *Carriacou* and *Petite Martinique*, appealing for their slow pace and a welcome respite from the tourist crowds on Grenada.

Where to go

Of Grenada's many attractions a few stand apart. The mountainous interior of the lush rainforest of *Grand Etang National Park* is a walker's paradise, with its network of trails leading to spectacular waterfalls, fascinating crater lakes and mist-shrouded mountain peaks. Among the country's numerous white-sand beaches, by far the most stunning is Grenada's *Grand Anse*, whose long horseshoe bay is the focus of the island's tourist trade. For a taste of laid-back island life, as well as smaller beaches and secluded sunbathing, there's the tiny island of *Petite Martinique* just a short ferry ride away.

When to go

Grenada's climate is warm and humid, with a *rainy season* from June to December – it rarely rains for more than an hour and lets up on some days. The coolest time of the year is November to February, also the island's high season, though average temperatures are only in the low twenties Celsius.

Getting there

Flights arrive at *Point Salines International Airport*, located on the southwest tip of Grenada, approximately five miles from the capital, St George's. American Airlines flies daily from the US while from the UK British Airways flies direct twice weekly and Monarch every Thursday. *Indirect flights* are offered by BWIA, via Trinidad and Air Jamaica via Montego Bay. Daily inter-island flights can be arranged with Caribbean Star and LIAT, both of which offer connections from Barbados, Trinidad and the rest of the Windward Islands.

Package tours can be an economical option as their combined airfares and accommodation prices are often cheaper than booking flights and hotels separately. Just Grenada (ⓣ01373/814214, ⓦwww.justgrenada.co.uk) offers flexible packages with accommodation ranging from luxury to self-catering.

Although flying is the quickest and easiest option for travelling between neighbouring islands, it is possible to travel by *boat* to Carriacou from Union Island, the most southerly of the Grenadine islands and under

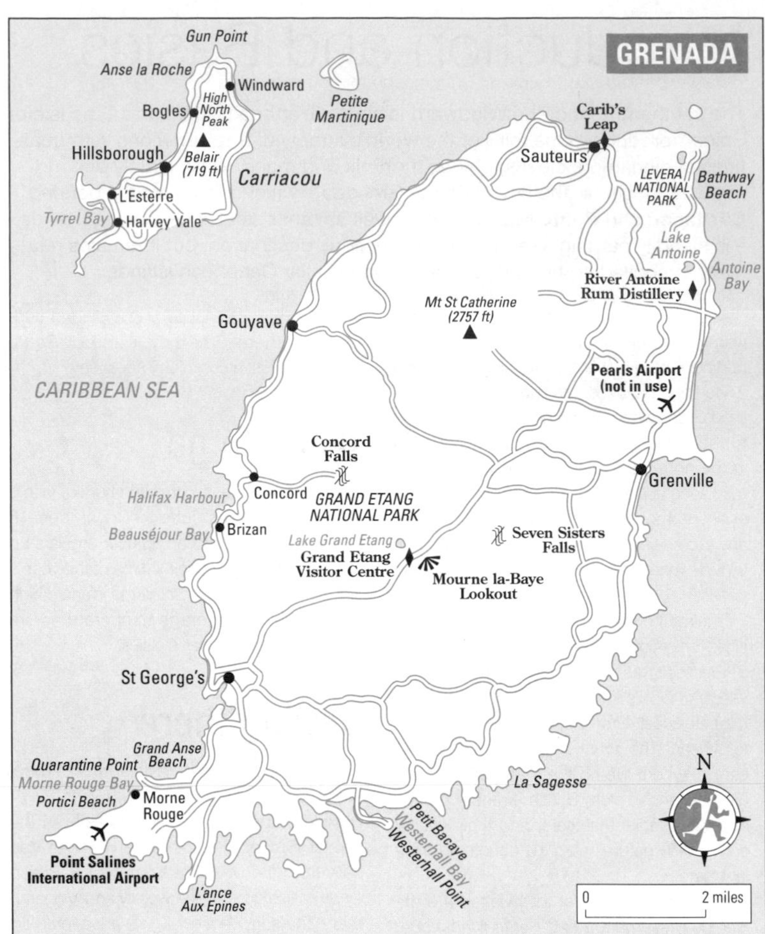

the jurisdiction of St Vincent (covered in Chapter 18, starting p.667). This journey, however, is only recommended for the adventurous as the one-hour trip can be quite rough.

Entry requirements

A valid passport and a return or onward ticket are required for *entry*, and immigration will stamp your passport with the exact number of days you plan to spend in the country. They will also ask where you intend to stay.

Embassies and consulates

UK British High Commission, Netherlands Building, Grand Anse, St George's ⓣ473/440-3222, ⓕ440-4939, ⓔbhcgrenada@caribsurf.com.
US American Embassy, Point Salines, St George's ⓣ809/444-1173.

When leaving, you'll be required to pay a **departure tax** of EC$50.

Websites

@www.grenadaexplorer.com From accommodation to eco-tourism this large site contains detailed travel information and features an excellent search option.

@www.grenadagrenadines.com An attractive and easy-to-navigate site, crammed with travel information. Brochures can also be ordered online.

@www.grenadaguide.com Comprehensive site covering accommodation, restaurants, airlines, car rentals, tours and dive operators. You can also send virtual postcards of the island, complete with a calypso soundtrack.

@www.grenadianvoice.com This online edition of the local weekly contains all the latest Grenadian news, weather and entertainment listings.

@www.letsgogrenada.com Another detailed travel information site with plenty of details on local festivals and cricket matches.

@www.travelgrenada.com Filled with travel information and tips, as well as maps, a currency calculator and even local recipes.

Information, websites and maps

The main visitor centre is the *Grenada Board of Tourism*, located on the cruise-ship dock in St George's (T473/440-2279, F440-6637, @www.grenada.org); you'll find it well-stocked with brochures and maps. There is also an *information booth* at the airport, just before immigration, and one at the Craft and Spice Market on Grand Anse Beach (see p.706). The Grenada Hotel and Tourism Association in St George's (PO Box 440, T473/444-1353, F444-4847, @www.grenadahotelsinfo.com) can help book accommodation. On *Carriacou* the main tourist office is in Hillsborough on Patterson Street.

Adequate, free *maps* – including one that details a historic walking tour of St George's – are available at tourist offices and many hotels. A detailed Ordnance Survey map can be purchased for EC$15 from hotels and tourist shops.

Money and costs

Grenada's official currency is the *Eastern Caribbean dollar (EC$)*, although the US dollar is widely accepted at hotels, restaurants and shops, and by car rental and taxi companies. The EC dollar is divided into 100 cents. Bills come in denominations of 5, 10, 20, 50 and 100 EC dollars; coins in 1, 2, 5, 10 and 25 cents. At the time of writing, the *rate of exchange* was roughly EC$2.70 to US$1.

Credit cards and major *travellers' cheques* are accepted at most hotels, restaurants and larger shops. In this chapter prices such as bus fares and admission fees have been quoted in EC$; all other prices are given in US$.

Banking hours are Monday to Thursday 8am–3pm, Friday 8am–5pm. Barclays Bank, Scotiabank, Grenada Bank of Commerce and National Commercial Bank all have branches in St George's and the Grand Anse area. Most have an *ATM*, and there's also one at Point Salines Airport.

An 8 percent *government tax* is added at hotels and restaurants on top of a 10 percent *service charge*. Tipping is at your discretion, but not necessary.

Phones and post

Pay phones can be found throughout the island. Some accept only phone cards, which you can buy from the main visitor centre, at the airport, in shops and from the Cable & Wireless office on the Carenage.

The general *post office* (Mon–Fri 8am–3.30pm) is on Lagoon Road in St George's and there are smaller offices in

The *country code* for Grenada is T473.

towns and villages on Grenada, Carriacou and Petite Martinique.

You'll find a couple of *internet cafés* in St George's and one on Carriacou. See individual island sections for specific details.

Emergency numbers

Police and fire ⓣ911

Ambulance in St George's ⓣ434, in St Andrewsⓣ724 and on Carriacou ⓣ399

Coast guard ⓣ399

Getting around

Getting around Grenada is fairly straightforward, though you'll end up travelling more miles than you expect due to the hilly terrain.

By bus

By far the cheapest way to get around is by *bus.* These privately owned but government-regulated minivans cram in as many people as possible, drive very fast and play loud reggae, ragga and soca. Don't be intimidated, however, as they're also great fun and safe.

Buses run 6am–8pm daily, with a less frequent service on Sundays and holidays, and routes run from the main terminal at the market in St George's to cover the entire island. Simply ask the driver which bus to get on. *Bus stops* punctuate all routes, you can also flag one down at any point along the way, and with their constant honking, you'll always know when they are around. *To get off* simply rap the side of the van and pay as you leave. From St George's, expect to pay EC$1.50 to Grand Anse, EC$3 to Grand Etang, EC$5 to Grenville, EC$5.50 to Sauteurs and EC$3.50 to Gouyave.

Although the *airport* is not on a main bus route, it is possible to take a bus there; stop any bus going to Grand Anse Beach and ask if it will take you to the airport, which is just a few miles further on. Expect to pay the *off-route fare* of EC$10 for this service. It's sometimes possible to pick up one of these off-route buses at the airport on its way back to the main route to St George's or Grand Anse.

By car

To *rent a car* you will need a valid driver's licence and a local permit, available from most car rental agencies and police stations for US$30. Dollar (ⓣ473/444-4786) and David's' Car Rental (ⓣ473/444-3399, ⓔcdavid@caribsurf.com) have offices at the Point Salines International Airport, while Avis (ⓣ473/440-3936) operates out of St George's. Cars and *jeeps* cost US$50–70 per day. *Driving* is on the left-hand side.

By scooter and bike

To drive a *scooter* you will need a local *licence* available from police stations for around US$30. Scooters can be rented from Eze Rentals (ⓣ473/444-3263) and cost US$21 a day or US$120 per week. *Bikes* can be hired from Trailblazers (ⓣ473/444-5337, ⓦwww.adventuregrenada.com), or Sunsation Tours (ⓣ473/444-1595); expect to pay US$15 per day or US$90 per week. Be warned – cycling can be tough going on Grenada as roads are mostly hilly and the smaller ones are not always well maintained.

By taxi

Taxis are plentiful and you will be constantly hassled by drivers seeking business. Fares from the airport to Grand Anse are around EC$25 and to St George's EC$30; expect to pay about EC$4 per mile for journeys from St George's to the rest of the island. A *surcharge* of EC$10 is added between 6pm and 6am. Taxi companies to try are Blue Moon Taxis (ⓣ473/444-6666) in Grand Anse and The Carenage Taxi Co-operative (ⓣ473/444-9223), which has a stand opposite the *Nutmeg Restaurant* (see p.703) on the Carenage.

By boat

The *Osprey passenger ferry* (ⓣ473/440-8126) is the most efficient and cheapest way to travel between Grenada, Carriacou and Petite Martinique. It departs from the Carenage in St George's (opposite the red fire station) for Carriacou Monday to Friday 9am and 5.30pm, Saturday 9am only and Sunday 8am and 5.30pm. It then departs Carriacou for Petite Martinique Monday to Friday 10.30am and 7pm and Sunday 9.30am and

7pm. The *return trip* leaves Petite Martinique for Carriacou Monday to Saturday 5.30am and 3pm and Sunday 3pm, and departs Carriacou to Grenada Monday to Saturday 6am and 3.30pm and Sunday 3.30pm only. The journey takes ninety minutes between Grenada and Carriacou and twenty minutes from Carriacou to Petite Martinique. The fare from Grenada to Carriacou and Petite Martinique is EC$40 one-way, EC$75 round-trip and from Carriacou to Petite Martinique EC$10 one-way, EC$20 round-trip.

By plane

St Vincent and the Grenadines Airways (ⓣ473/444-3549m, ⓦwww.svgair.com) *flies* daily from Grenada, Barbados, and St Vincent and the Grenadine Islands to *Lauriston Airport*, one mile south of Hillsborough on Carriacou (see p.712).

There is no airport on Petite Martinique, and the only way to get there is by boat or ferry (see above).

Tours

Most of the island can easily be explored by bus, but, if you're short on time, *organized tours* are an excellent way to see the island in a day and learn about its history and culture along the way. Local tour guide Mandoo (ⓣ473/440-1428, ⓦwww.grenadatours.com) has an encyclopedic knowledge of Grenada's history and politics and his selection of full- and half-day *bus and trekking tours* cost US$40–90 per person. His full-day bus tours covering Halifax Bay, Gouyave, Carib's Leap, Grenville and Grand Etang National Park cost US$55 (this includes entrance fees, lunch and even impromptu stops for fruit along the way); and half-day trekking tours at US$40 visit either Mt Qua Qua or Seven Sisters Falls.

Sunsation Tours (ⓣ473/444-1594, ⓔqkspice@caribsurf.com) also runs full- and part-day tours. At US$50 the "*Grenada in a nutshell*" tour passes through the island's major sites, while more specialized tours, such as a visit to the outstanding private gardens on the island, can also be organized for US$35.

Another option is Adventure Jeep Tours (ⓣ473/444-5337, ⓔadventure@caribsurf.com) whose all-terrain *jeeps* will take you deep into the rainforest, with some trips including a swim and snorkel. Full-day tours cost US$65.

If you fancy *biking* around the island, Trailblazers (ⓣ473/444-5337, ⓦwww.adventuregrenada.com) runs full-day off-road cycling tours for US$60, which will take you into the rainforest and include lunch and time on the beach.

Accommodation

Most *accommodation* on Grenada is clustered around the tourist-saturated southwest, but there are some interesting and unusual places to stay outside this area. A variety of lodging is available, ranging from self-catering apartments to modern resort complexes.

Prices are much lower during the summer months – April to December – which is also the rainy season. Furthermore, accommodation rates on Carriacou and Petite Martinique are significantly lower than on Grenada, ranging from US$25 to US$125 per night; on Grenada prices vary between US$30 and US$500.

There are no *youth hostels* on the island, but the numerous *guesthouses* are aimed at more budget-minded travellers and locals. *Camping*, though permitted in Grand Etang National Park, is not encouraged, and there are no facilities.

Food and drink

Grenada grows many kinds of fruits, vegetables and spices, all of which are for sale in the colourful market in St George's (see p.701). Seafood is plentiful, ranging from conch – known locally as *lambie* – to flying fish. Also widely available and unmissable are delicious *rotis*, thin layers of pastry folded around various fillings. Favourite starts include *callaloo* soup and *nutmeg ice cream* is an island specialty.

The beer of choice is *Carib*, brewed on the island and available in all bars. Likewise rum produced in Grenada's distilleries is used in a wide variety of punches and cocktails. Be sure to sample the locally produced *fruit juice*. Bursting with flavour, what's on offer depends on the season; those made from passion fruit and sorrel are both delicious and well worth trying.

All three islands have a good number of *places to eat*, ranging from Chinese to creole, though vegetarians will find generally that most restaurants do not cater for them. Outside of St George's on Grenada, however, dining options tend to be mainly *hotel restaurants and bars*. Most establishments serve a dinner menu after 7pm that is considerably more expensive than meals served during the day, and the choice of inexpensive restaurants dwindles after this time.

Opening hours, public holidays and festivals

Business hours are generally Monday to Friday 8am–4pm and Saturday 8am–1pm. When a cruise ship is in harbour some tourist shops in St George's will stay open later and on Sundays.

As well as the *public holidays* listed on p.40, Grenada celebrates Independence Day on February 7, Corpus Christi on the ninth Thursday after Easter, Emancipation Days on the first Monday and Tuesday in August and Thanksgiving on October 25.

The biggest event on Grenada's *festival* calendar is its lively and colourful *Carnival*, held every year on the second weekend in August. Although Carriacou's Carnival is in early March, the island's main event is the *Carriacou Regatta*, which takes place in late July/early August and brings boats of all kinds from all over the Caribbean. Petite Martinique also hosts an annual *regatta* over Easter. Jazz festivals are held on Grenada and Carriacou in May and mid-June respectively.

Outdoor activities

Grenada's underwater terrain is as beautiful as the lush green landscape rising above it, and there's no shortage of *dive operators* to help you explore it. Most dive shops operate from resorts on Grand Anse Beach in Grenada and out of Tyrrel Bay in Carriacou, and cater for all levels of experience. Though shallow reef, wall and drift dives are all on offer, the most popular site is the wreck of the *Bianca C* (see p.702) on Grenada, known locally as the "Titanic of the Caribbean".

For those who prefer to explore on dry land there are *hiking trails* throughout Grenada's lush Grand Etang National Park, where you can take a brief stroll or walk all day on these often fragrant trails, encountering local flora and fauna, dramatic waterfalls and stunning views. In many cases the best option is to hike with an experienced tour operator (see p.697).

Language

The official language is *English*, although French patois is also widely spoken.

History

Long before Columbus sighted Grenada and named it Concepción (the name Grenada was given by homesick Spanish sailors and adopted by the British) on his third voyage to the Americas in 1498, Grenada had been settled by a series of migrating Amerindian peoples. Its first known residents were the Ciboney, who populated much of the Eastern Caribbean and left little but a few artefacts and petroglyphs behind. The Ciboney were replaced or absorbed by Arawaks, who came to the island by way of Venezuela and the outflow of the Orinoco River. In turn, the Arawaks were invaded and enslaved by the Caribs, who were making their way up through the islands from Guyana.

The *British* were the first Europeans to attempt to settle the island in 1609, followed in 1650 by the *French*, whose first town sank into the mouth of St George's lagoon. These efforts were fiercely resisted by the Caribs. In 1651, the French took decisive action against the Caribs, pushing them north to *Sauteurs* where, rather than surrender to French control, they threw themselves off a cliff, now known as Caribs' Leap and, ironically, marked by a Catholic church.

Control of Grenada passed between France and Britain as part of the settlements of various treaties, while both countries established *plantations* of indigo, tobacco, coffee, cocoa and sugar, worked by African slaves, until the French ceded the island to Britain in the Treaty of Paris in 1783, the French-brokered agreement which formally ended the American War of Independence.

In 1795 *Julian Fedon*, a mulatto planter, led a peasant rebellion based on the principles of the French Revolution and controlled most of the island for fourteen months before the rebels were crushed by British reinforcements. British rule was stable throughout the nineteenth century, a peace that culminated in 1877 with Grenada being granted Crown colony status and a measure of independence.

In 1967, Grenada became a semi-independent state within the British Commonwealth and seven years later an independent country. By that time, control of the government was firmly in the hands of *Eric Gairy*, a union leader who had led the resistance to British rule since the 1950s. During the 1970s, Gairy's rule became increasingly dictatorial and his secret police (*the Mongoose Gang*) more notorious in their corruption and their suppression of the opposition. Gairy was ousted from power on March 13, 1979, by a bloodless coup led by Maurice Bishop, the charismatic leader of the left-wing New Jewell Movement whose father had been killed during demonstrations against Gairy's rule.

Bishop's *Revolutionary Government* became a pawn of the Cold War, supported by Cuba, Nicaragua and the Soviet Union but reviled by the United States. The period of Revolutionary Government came to an end in 1983 with Bishop's imprisonment by enemies within his own government and an American-led invasion – on the pretext of evacuating American medical students from the island, but having more to do with the fear of increased Soviet influence in the Caribbean.

Grenada's first post-revolution elections were held in 1985 and won by *Herbert Blaize*, Gairy's political opponent from the 1950s and 1960s. More recently, a shadow was cast over the country's leadership by the investigation of Dr Keith Mitchell, leader of the parliamentary government, and his alleged links to the collapse of a bank that supported him during his election campaign.

19.1

St George's

Grenada's capital, **ST GEORGE'S**, is an attractive colonial town nestled in the hillsides above a horseshoe-shaped harbour. Low, whitewashed and terracotta-roofed buildings follow the sweep of the bay, standing out against the rich green of the surrounding vegetation. During the eighteenth century, the town was partly gutted by three devastating fires, leading to legislation that restricted the height of buildings and banned the use timber. The result of all this is a town dominated by **British colonial architecture** but with a distinctly Mediterranean feel.

St George's won't take more than a day to explore, and it's worth taking time away from the beach to do so. Though the **market** is at its liveliest on Saturday morning, most shops close on Saturday afternoons, Sundays and public holidays, making the town a quiet place during those times – except when a **cruise ship** docks, in which case the town explodes into a frenzy of activity. Market stalls spring up on shore, restaurants and bars fill up, street vendors and local guides come out in force, and all visitors – whether they're cruise-ship passengers or not – become the focus of a barrage of offers from taxi drivers and spice sellers.

Bear in mind, though, that although St George's is a laid-back town, attitudes veer towards the conservative, and it is considered rude to wear **swimwear or high-cut shorts** in the streets and in shops and restaurants.

Accommodation

With few **accommodation** options in St George's itself most visitors choose to stay in the area around the Lagoon, just to the south of town. Don't expect to find any luxury hotels here, but its location between St George's and Grand Anse Beach makes this a convenient base from which to explore the island.

Bailey's Inn Springs, St George's ⓣ473/440-2912, ⓕ440-0532, ⓔotwaybailey@caribsurf.com. Situated on a hillside outside St George's, this charming inn has several attractive rooms with private bathrooms, and one self-contained apartment. Room ❷

Lazy Lagoon Lagoon Road ⓣ473/443-5209, ⓦwww.spiceisle.com/lazylagoon. One of the most laid-back places to stay on the island, its colourful tropical cottages feature large studio rooms, with cooking facilities, private bathrooms and verandahs. The owner will even stock the fridge with Carib beer for you. If you don't fancy drinking alone in the on-site bar, *The Hornibaboon Watering Hole* is friendly and hosts the occasional live band. ❷

Mamma's Lodge Lagoon Road ⓣ473/440-1623. Overlooking the Lagoon, this relatively new guesthouse offers simple accommodation and includes an enormous breakfast in the room rate. All rooms have fans and a radio, and there's a TV lounge and bar for guests. ❷

Mitchell's Guest House H.A. Blaize Street ⓣ473/440-2803. This simple guesthouse on the hillside behind the Carenage, in an older, but still central part of St George's, is a good budget option. The rooms are basic but clean and have a shared bathroom. ❷

Tropicana Inn Lagoon Road ⓣ473/440-1586, ⓕ440-9797, ⓦwww.tropicanainn.com. Popular with business travellers, this immaculate and friendly inn facing the Lagoon has a variety of rooms, all with private bathroom and cable TV, and a few with balconies. The bar and restaurant on site are excellent and the full Grenadian breakfast – a plateful of saltfish stir-fry, fish cakes, savoury bakes and seasonal fruits – will keep you going until dinner time. ❸

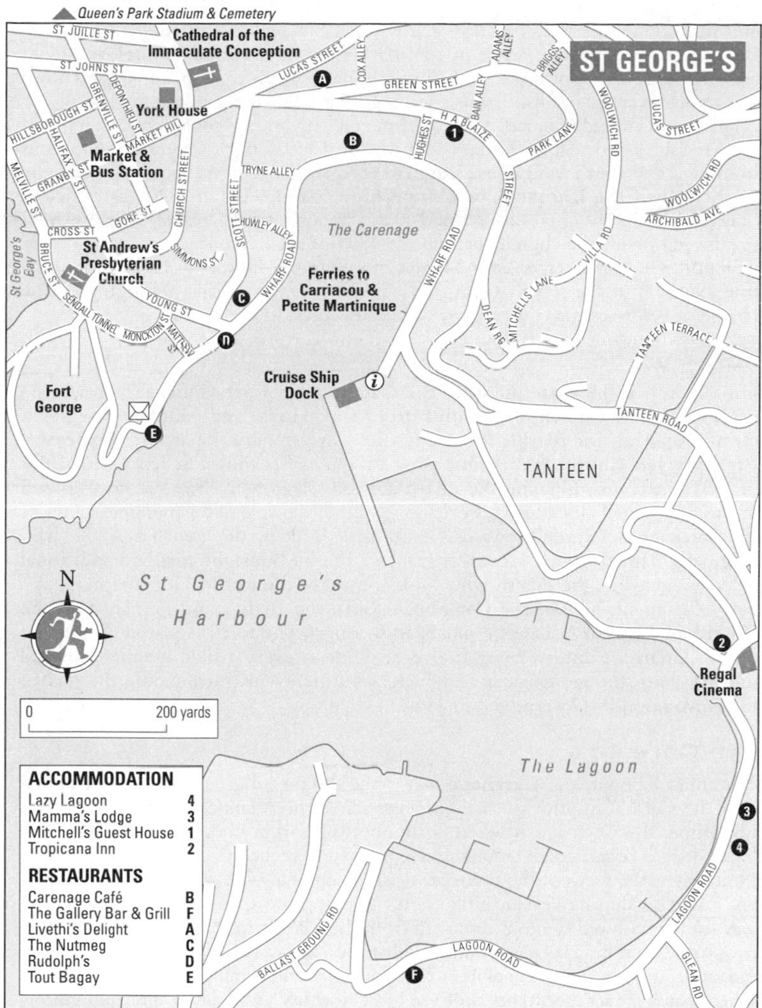

The Town

The core of the town is a maze of streets surrounding the harbour – the **Carenage** – and leading away to the west where they concentrate around the lively **market square**, the heart of town.

The market square and around

Once the site of the town's slave exchange until trading was made illegal in 1807, the colourful **market square** on Halifax Street is now the bustling and aromatic centre of St George's, where stalls crammed with local spices and fresh produce vie for your senses alongside vendors selling barbecued corn cobs. Clothes, shoes, music and much more are traded here and its sense of contained mayhem is further enhanced by the market's function as the main bus terminal for the entire island. Buses from the Carenage arrive at the market via the **Sendall Tunnel**, located a few blocks to the south; the tunnel was built in 1895 to stop horse carts from scrambling over the headland, thus allowing their safe passage to the market.

The streets around the market are worth exploring as they contain many architectural treasures and will give you a feel for local life – not to mention numerous stunning views. Just inland, above the market square on Upper Church Street is the **Cathedral of the Immaculate Conception**. Completed in 1820, the cathedral houses a number of impressive stained-glass windows, the beauty of which is overshadowed only by the church's panoramic view of the harbour.

Opposite the cathedral is **York House**, home to the Houses of Parliament and a fine example of the town's Georgian architecture. The mace belonging to the House of Representatives is reputed to be the largest in the world.

Fort George

On a hilltop at the western end of the Carenage sits **Fort George**. To reach the entrance, follow Church Street south from York House and continue along as it climbs up the hill to the fort. On the way up you'll pass **St Andrew's Presbyterian Church**, a dark, imposing structure also known as Scot's Kirk. Built in 1831, the church is famous for its bell, cast in Glasgow in 1833 and now housed in the four-spired clock tower. Fort George itself has splendid panoramic views of the Carenage and beyond towards Grand Anse. Built by the French in 1705 (who originally named it Fort Royal) to protect the harbour, the fort had additional defences added by the British who took control of the fort in 1763 and made it a part of their defence of the Caribbean (both the British and French used the Windward Islands as a base to raid Spanish ships). The fort has played an integral role in Grenada's history, being the focal point of every armed intervention and military coup, the most recent of which were the events surrounding the end of the Revolutionary Government in 1983.

The Carenage

The inner harbour, the **Carenage**, was once the meeting point for ships from all over the Caribbean prior to their journey across the Atlantic to Britain. A perfect horseshoe, the Carenage is where a number of working boats and smaller cruise liners dock – larger vessels requiring deeper waters anchor just offshore. The waterfront area is the focus of the town's tourism, complete with duty-free stores, high-end souvenir shops, cafés and restaurants. Ringing the Carenage is a paved walkway dotted with old cannons removed from the island's forts and now used as bollards to tie up ships. Halfway around the harbour, the walkway opens out to accommodate some sea-facing benches, a favourite meeting point for locals. This is also where you'll attract the attention of the local "**guides**", who often approach visitors by starting to chat about the history of the island. Be warned, they expect payment for their time (about EC$20 per hour), so if you don't want them to take you on a guided tour of the town, be firm and extract yourself as soon as you can.

It is also here that you will find the statue of the **Christ of the Deep** looking out to sea, arms outstretched to commemorate the events of October 22, 1961, when the Carenage was the scene of the largest shipwreck in the Caribbean. The **Bianca C**, a 600ft-long Italian ocean liner, was anchored in St George's when an explosion occurred in its engine room. The whole ship soon caught fire and a fleet of local boats, yachts and swimmers raced to the rescue, managing to save everyone aboard – except for a crewman who later died of severe burns. As the still-burning ship was being towed to the shallow waters around Point Saline, the towrope broke and the *Bianca C* sank a mile and a half offshore. The bronze statue was donated by the ship's owners in recognition of local rescue efforts.

Toward the western end of the Carenage, take a left turn on narrow Young Street to Monckton Street where Grenada's **National Museum** (Mon–Fri 9am–4.30pm, Sat 10am–4pm; EC$5) is housed in a building constructed by the French in 1704 as a prison and army barracks, and subsequently used by the British as the island's first hotel. Exhibits include Amerindian artefacts and information on the political events of 1979 that led to the US invasion in 1983.

The Lagoon

Not strictly part of St George's, the **Lagoon**, a ten-minute walk south of the town past the docks, is the site of the first town in Grenada. Fort Louis, established by the governor of Martinique in 1650, has since sunk into the Lagoon, and today this naturally protected inch of water is a popular anchorage for yachts. While the waterfront is largely parkland, the rest of the area is home to a clutch of hotels, restaurants and stores, and residential properties higher in the hills.

Eating and drinking

In St George's most **places to eat** are to be found around the Carenage, where options range from cafés to restaurants. Dining here is inexpensive, laid-back and a bit more authentic than at the beaches.

Carenage Café The Carenage ☎473/440-8701. The open terrace facing the water makes a great place for visitors to relax and watch the world go by. A basic menu features rotis, sandwiches, pizzas and great ice cream, and prices start from US$3. Internet access is also available.

The Gallery Bar and Grill Lagoon Road ☎473/435-3003. Roast beef, Yorkshire puddings and pasta dishes share space on the menu with local cuisine at this popular restaurant. The walls are lined with work by local artists and the friendly relaxed atmosphere makes this a favourite with visiting yachters. Internet access is also available. Open 7.30am–11pm.

Livethi's Delight H.A. Blaize Street (no phone). This small take-away serves an extensive range of basic vegetarian food, such as soya and vegetable rotis and sandwiches, as well as a selection of local fruit juices such as sorrel and passion fruit.

The Nutmeg The Carenage ☎473/440-2539. Famous for its Grenadian-style seafood dinners and nutmeg rum punch, this very popular restaurant also has sweeping views of the Carenage and beyond. Burgers and rotis (from US$3) make up the lunch menu, while typical dinner dishes include Caribbean shrimp cocktails (US$10) and a delicious seafood platter (US$20).

Rudolf's The Carenage ☎473/440-9946. Friendly, relaxed and full of character, this reasonably priced pub/restaurant serves a variety of local and international food, including fish burgers (US$4), lamb creole salad (US$11) and a range of steaks (US$12). Open 10am to midnight Mon–Fri.

Tout Bagay The Carenage ☎473/440-1500. Reservations are recommended for dinner at this colourfully decorated restaurant at the far west end of the Carenage, where the menu has everything from seafood, curried goat, steaks and vegetarian options. Main courses start at US$15.

The Tropicana Inn Lagoon Road ☎473/440-1586. Besides the mouthwatering full Grenadian breakfast (US$6), this restaurant serves consistently tasty and reasonably priced dishes. Order food to go at the take-away annex next door where large portions of fish with vegetables and rice cost US$4.

Shopping and entertainment

Throughout St George's you will find plenty of **arts and crafts shops**, many aimed at cruise-ship passengers and varying in price and quality. Among the better ones is Art Fabrick (☎473/440-0568) on Young Street, where local **batik** artists can usually be seen at work. Fedon Books (☎473/435-2665) on H.A. Blaize Street has an extensive range of Caribbean literature and history books, and Turbo Charge Record (☎473/440-0586) on St John's Street is recommended for recordings of local reggae, soca and ragga music.

The town has a smattering of entertainment options, including *Rudolf's Bar* (see above) and *Tropicana Inn* (see above), both of which offer **live steel-band and calypso music** in the evenings. St George's also has a cinema: the Regal Cinema on Lagoon Road (☎473/440-2403) screens current mainstream films and charges EC$7-15.

If you get the chance, go and catch a day of **cricket** at Queens Park National Stadium (Ⓔgrnoc@caribsurf.com), a five- to ten-minute walk north of St George's. Though ticket prices rise as high as EC$40 for an international game, for EC$5 you can watch it sitting among the graves atop Cemetery Hill.

19.2

The southwest

The southwest corner of the island is home to Grenada's most popular beaches. Only two miles from St George's is the king of them all, **Grand Anse**, whose long curve of immaculate white sands is frequented by locals and visitors alike. Further south and separated by the headland of Quarantine Point, formerly a leper colony, is the secluded **Morne Rouge Bay**. A favourite among wealthy tourists, the beach is excellent for swimming and it's also a popular place to snorkel. Continuing south beyond the airport are several smaller beaches and **Lance Aux Épines**, a peninsula at Grenada's southernmost point dotted with many luxury homes. **Prickly Bay** on the peninsula's west side is a popular anchorage for yachts and home to a good-sized palm-fringed beach where watersports are abundant. **Mount Hartman Bay** on the eastern side may lack beaches, but has no shortage of stunning views over the island's south coast. Be aware that, while some visitors to these beaches do sunbathe topless, this practice is not permitted anywhere on the island.

Accommodation

Blue Orchid Hotel Grand Anse ⓣ473/444-0999, ⓕ444-1846, ⓦwww.blueorchidhotel.com. A two-minute walk from Grand Anse Beach, this basic hotel has its own restaurant and is also close to tennis and basketball courts. All rooms have private bathrooms, a refrigerator and ocean-facing balconies. ❹

Coyaba Beach Resort Grand Anse ⓣ473/444-2011, ⓕ444-4808, ⓦwww.coyaba.com. An attractive beachfront resort surrounded by landscaped tropical gardens. The comfortable rooms all have hairdryers, cable TV and individual terraces, and amenities include a swimming pool, tennis and volleyball courts and Grenada's only swim-up bar. ❽

The Flamboyant Hotel Grand Anse ⓣ473/444-4247, ⓕ444-1234, ⓦwww.flamboyant.com. One of the island's most luxurious resorts where all rooms, from standard to deluxe, have ocean-facing terraces. If you get bored with the beach the hotel has its own swimming pool, table tennis, pool tennis and even board games to keep you occupied. ❽

Hummingbird Inn Grand Anse ⓣ473/444-4216, ⓕ444-5917, ⓔhumm@caribsurf.com. This small, colourful inn, located in Grand Anse, which has a communal verandah, is the perfect place to watch sunsets. All rooms have a refrigerator and ceiling fans. ❸

La Luna Portici Beach ⓣ473/439-0001, ⓕ439-0600, ⓦwww.laluna.com. The sixteen beach cottages of this hideaway resort are the most exclusive places to stay on the island. Each pastel-coloured cottage has a plunge pool, TV, video and CD player, and there's also a stunning beachfront swimming pool and free watersports, which is just as well as a night here can set you back as much as US$500.

Lexus Inn Belmont ⓣ473/444-4780, ⓕ444-4779, ⓔlexus@caribsurf.com. A short walk from Grand Anse Beach, this attractive complex of oceanfront one-bedroom apartments has a private swimming pool that's also good for snorkelling. ❹

Roydon's Guest House Grand Anse ⓣ&ⓕ473/444-4476, ⓔroydons@caribsurf.com. This popular guesthouse with both private rooms and apartments is within walking distance of Grand Anse Beach. However, it is situated on a main road and can be noisy at night. Room ❸, apartment ❻

Grand Anse Beach

Most people's experience of Grenada begins and ends with the stunning **Grand Anse Beach**, a 1.3-mile stretch of white sand with a stunning view of St George's and the surrounding hills. Even on busy days large pockets of peace and quiet can be found amidst the gaggles of tourists that congregate near to their hotels. The sea is exquisite and there is no shortage of opportunities to water-ski, windsurf or be pulled around the bay in an inflated inner tube by speedboat. The Craft and Spice Market selling jewellery, clothes and the ubiquitous spices (daily 8am–6pm) is situated at the north end of the beach, which also has a number of small refreshment bars, as well as showers and toilets. Lockers can be hired from the sea-damaged *Cot Bam* restaurant (see below) halfway along the beach. Many vendors wander the beach touting their wares and you're likely to get some hassle from them, though not much.

Just south of Grand Anse on the other side of Quarantine Point lies **Morne Rouge**. Having fewer resort complexes and being slightly harder to reach, this smaller and shadeless beach has an air of exclusivity and is excellent for swimming, snorkelling and private sunbathing.

The next beach along the coast, just past Petit Cabrits Point, is the even more isolated **Portici Beach**, which is accessible from the main road to the airport – just take the turn marked "Beach House Bar and Restaurant" and follow the dirt track down to the shore. The walk from the airport takes about twenty minutes, so if your plane is delayed you can while away your time on the sands rather than in the departure lounge. Here, if anywhere, you'll bump into the rich and famous who visit Grenada – the beach backs onto the exclusive resort of *La Luna* (see p.705).

Diving

Many of the island's **dive companies** operate out of Grand Anse Beach. Dive Grenada (Ⓣ473/444-1092, Ⓕ444-5875, Ⓦwww.divegrenada.com), based at *The Flamboyant Hotel* (see p.705), is a long-established outfit which organizes a variety of snorkelling and diving trips, including the challenging dive to the *Bianca C* shipwreck. Beginners can take a resort course (US$75) that includes a session in the hotel pool followed by a shallow reef dive, and additional courses are discounted US$75. Another reliable dive company on the island with an environmental focus is Ecodive and Trek (Ⓣ473/444-7777, Ⓕ444-4808, Ⓦwww.scubadivegrenada.com), based at the *Coyaba Beach Resort* (see p.705).

Eating and drinking

The southwest is where you'll find the island's more upmarket **restaurants**, most of which are connected to hotels and resorts.

Bamboo Village Spiceland Mall Ⓣ473/439-3939. Immaculate white cloths cover every table at this elegant restaurant whose floor-to-ceiling windows create a light, airy ambience. Freshly prepared by professional Chinese chefs, the food is delicious and the varied menu includes a number of vegetarian options. Lunch boxes start at US$5 and main courses at US$8. Open daily until 11pm.

Brown Sugar Restaurant Grand Anse Ⓣ473/444-2374, Ⓦwww.brownsugarrestaurant.com. With a panoramic view of Grand Anse Bay from the surrounding hills and an interior which replicates an old plantation house, this is a lovely place to eat. Main courses start at US$13 and include "oil down" – Grenada's national dish – a blend of fish, meat, local fruits, dumplings and callaloo leaves, and La-Ja-Bless – Caribbean shrimps covered in shredded coconut.

Cot Bam Grand Anse Ⓣ473/444-2050. Don't be put off by the dilapidated exterior that has been half-reclaimed by massive waves stirred up by Hurricane Lenny in 1999. *Cot Bam* serves the best rotis on the island, as well as large sandwiches, both starting at US$3 – about half what you'd pay anywhere else on the beach.

De Solei Grand Anse Ⓣ473/439-0555. Situated in the grounds of *the Allamanada Beach Resort*, the menu of this popular poolside restaurant features a range of Caribbean and American dishes. For lunch try the kosher hot dogs with fried mushrooms (US$4) and for dinner the Sunflower Quesadillas stuffed with shrimp and crisp vegetables, or else the Striplion of Beef smothered in Jack Daniel's-flavoured butter (US$22).

La Boulangerie Le Marquis Complex ☎473/444-1131. A cosy French bakery that offers the usual croissants, baguettes and quiches (from US$2), as well as made-to-order Italian pizza (US$2 a slice, US$8 for a whole pizza) and a selection of pasta dishes.

Nightlife

The island's **nightlife** is focused around the hotel bars and restaurants in the Grand Anse area, among them *The Flamboyant* amd *Coyaba Beach Resort*, both of which feature live steel and calypso music. In Grand Anse, above the National Commercial Bank, is the popular cocktail lounge and restaurant *Casablanca* (Mon–Sat 5pm–3am, Sun 7pm–3am; no cover; ☎473/444-1631), with a large screen TV and pool table, as well as a variety of board games including chess, backgammon and dominos. The island's best-known and busiest nightclub is *Fantazia 2001* in Mourne Rouge (☎473/444-2288). For a small cover charge you can bop until the small hours of the morning. "Blast from the Past" on Wednesdays is a favourite, while on Saturdays you're invited to "Dance the Night Away" to a blend of reggae, hip-hop and R&B.

19.3

The rest of the island

There is much more to Grenada than its tourist beaches and the bustle of St George's. Travelling around the island you will encounter the variety of its terrain – from the mountainous rainforest of the interior to the rugged shoreline of the northeast. There are three main areas to be explored: the sheltered and gentle **Leeward Coast**, the weather-beaten **Windward Coast**, and the rich greenery of the protected **interior**.

Accommodation

Grenada Rainbow Inn Grenville Ⓣ473/442-7714, Ⓕ 442-5332, Ⓦwww.grenadarainbowinn.com. The rooms at this delightful inn near Grand Etang National Park are clean and comfortable and come with private bathrooms, balconies and cable TV. Organic food is available at the hotel restaurant. ❷

La Sagesse Nature Centre La Sagesse Ⓣ & Ⓕ473/444-6458, Ⓔlsnature@caribsurf.com, Ⓦwww.lasagesse.com. Easily accessible by public transport, yet also one of the most secluded places to stay on the island, is this sedate old manor house on the edge of a quiet beach. The elegant rooms have retained their original grandeur and the food at the beachfront restaurant and bar is delicious. ❺

Petit Bacaye Cottages Westerhall Ⓣ & Ⓕ473/443-2902, Ⓦwww.petit-bacaye.com. These palm-thatched cottages on the edge of a small bay are the place to stay if you're seeking solitude. The rooms are simple and tastefully decorated, but don't expect to find a TV or radio. If you feel the need for company there is a small restaurant and bar on the premises, and buses to St George's pass close by. ❻

Plantation House Morne Fendue Ⓣ473/442-9330. Built from colourful stones from a nearby river, this authentic old plantation house has simple rooms, some with private bath. The restaurant serves a West Indian buffet in the evenings for which reservations are advised. ❷

Leeward Coast

Heading north from St George's the **Leeward Highway** is a scenic road that twists and turns in on itself until finally reaching Sauteurs and the famous Caribs' Leap. The drive is a rough ride, thanks to damage from **Hurricane Lenny** in 1999, which didn't come near the island but caused 20ft waves to smash into its Leeward side. Repair work is still under way, as is the construction of new sea defences.

As the highway winds along it passes through a number of colourful fishing and former plantation communities such as **Beauséjour Bay**, centre of radio communication for the Revolutionary Government from 1979, and the small town of **Brizan**, once a safe haven for escaped slaves and now home to a recording studio built by pop star Billy Ocean, a native Grenadian.

After passing through **Halifax Harbour**, where you'll find the Grenada Dove Sanctuary, a reserve for the national bird of Grenada (also known as the invisible bird because sightings are rare), the road leads through the tiny village of **Concord**, birthplace of calypso legend the "Mighty Sparrow" and on to **Gouyave**, a lovely old sea-weathered town, whose long main street overhung with balconies and strings of lights belongs more to the Wild West than the Caribbean. Famous for its fishing, the town celebrates Fisherman's Birthday (June 29), the Feast Day of SS Peter and Paul during which residents of Gouyave head down to the beaches in the morning to bless the fishing boats and then party the rest of the day away. Goyave is also one of the main centres of the **nutmeg industry**, and a worthwhile stop is the town's nutmeg processing station (Mon–Fri 8am–4pm), where employees lead tours through the various stages of nutmeg and mace production for US$1. You'll also see something of the island's working culture – a slice of Grenada that the resorts in the southwest gloss over.

Situated at the end of the road is the exposed and windswept village of **Sauteurs**, dominated by both a Roman Catholic and an Anglican church – symbols of the conflicts in Grenada's colonial past. The main attraction is **Caribs' Leap**, a steep cliff rising more than 100 feet out of the ocean, from which the last of the island's Carib Indians threw themselves in an effort to resist French rule. From up here you'll have a stunning view of the channel where the Atlantic Ocean and the Caribbean Sea meet, which is punctuated by an arch of rock known as London Bridge, and offshore islands, including Carriacou.

Windward Coast

Travelling south from St George's, veer left at the Spiceland Mall on Grand Anse Main Road. A sharp left at the next junction will put you on Grand Anse Valley Road, which heads east towards **Westerhall Bay**. The road clings to the island's east coast, passing the secluded and pretty beach of **Petit Bacaye**, before heading on to **La Sagesse Bay**. A dirt track opposite the La Sagesse Natural Works restaurant and bar leads down to the sheltered beach with its straggling palm trees and small mangrove swamp, and to **La Sagesse Nature Centre** (see also opposite), formerly the home of the late Lord Brownlow, Queen Elizabeth II's cousin, who in the early 1970s built the infamous Brownlow's Gate, which blocked public access to the beach until the Revolutionary Government nationalized the estate in 1979. A map of the walking trails in the area can be obtained from the Nature Centre, which also organizes special day packages (US$30) that cover transportation from your hotel, a guided nature walk, lunch and a little time on the beach.

Continuing north around the eastern side of the island, the endlessly twisting road in various states of repair leads on to Grenada's second largest town, **Grenville**. Established by the French in 1763, the town is the backbone of the country's agricultural sector and home to Grenada's largest nutmeg processing station. There is little of interest in the town, but the best day to visit is a Saturday when a large colourful market selling fresh fish, fruit, vegetables and spices becomes a lively attraction. The market square is also the focus of the **Rainbow City Festival** held every year in late July and early August. Celebrating emancipation, this vibrant festival features street dancing and calypso bands.

Regardless of the time of year, the eerie **Pearls Airport**, two miles north of Grenville, is reason enough to visit the area. With a duty-free store whose specials are still posted in the window and a café that looks as if it will open at any minute, it is as if time stopped the moment the airport was abandoned in 1984 after the opening of the Cuban-built Point Salines Airport in the southwest. Two rusting Cold War relics – a Russian Aeroflot plane and a Cubana aircraft – lie just off the runway, and are slowly being dismantled by weather and vandals. The area was once a large Amerindian settlement and burial ground, and a large number of artefacts have been recovered, and though it is illegal to remove artefacts, this doesn't stop local children from attempting to sell them to visitors.

About two and a half miles north is the **River Antoine Rum Distillery** (Mon–Fri 8am–4pm; US$2; ⓣ473/442-7109), the oldest functioning distillery in the Caribbean; the water wheel has been crushing juice from locally grown sugarcane since 1785. Tours led by workers take you through the fragrant factory, which still uses traditional distilling methods to produce its powerful 150-proof rum.

Lake Antoine is well worth the detour from the main road north. Surrounded by lush agricultural land, this spectacular sixteen-acre lake inside the crater of an extinct volcano has been known to bubble when eruptions have occurred in the region, prompting speculation that it is linked to a volcanic chain. Looking toward the coast from the lake's edge you can see rugged **Antoine Bay**, originally called Conception Bay as this was the name given by Columbus when he first sighted it in 1498.

From Antoine Bay the road leads to the far northeast and **Levera National Park**. It's not hard to understand why this remote part of the coastline attracts so many visitors; the undulating hills of this volcanic landscape are threaded with scenic hiking trails. On the easternmost tip of the island **Bathway Beach** is a striking, windswept beach shaded by palm trees and popular for picnics, although swimming past the reef is not permitted due to dangerous undercurrents. Visitors can buy refreshments at a roadside bar and learn more about the area at the visitor centre, which has small displays explaining the region's geology, and showers and rest rooms and even an outdoor amphitheatre.

The interior

Grenada may be famous for its beaches, but visitors who take time to explore the mountainous **interior** of the island will be rewarded with the experience of lush, tropical rainforest at its best. Reached by a fifteen-minute drive or bus ride from St George's, the 3860 acres of **Grand Etang National Park** make up a sizeable chunk of the island's interior. Here the dense, humid and often fragrant forest reveals another side of Grenada – far removed from its exclusive tourist beaches and the frenzy of St George's. At intervals the dense rainforest canopy opens out, revealing sweeping views of the mountain peaks – often shrouded in low cloud and mist. In addition to the diverse and colourful flora and fauna, the forest is also home to many species of birds, including hummingbirds, hawks and the elusive Grenada dove. Mona monkeys, identified by their white bellies and pointed ears, also live in the interior; however, your chances of seeing one are low. Forming a network throughout the park are **walking trails** covered with nutmeg shells, which crunch loudly underfoot and infuse the air with a spicy aroma. These trails vary from gentle fifteen-minute walks to full days of serious hiking for which the services of a guide are recommended (see p.697). Be sure to wear sturdy footwear, especially after rain when the trails are often muddy and slippery underfoot.

The **visitor centre** just inside the park's main entrance (Mon–Fri 8.30am–4pm; park entrance fee EC$5; ☎473/440-6160) provides maps of the forest trails and also houses displays illustrating the rainforest's ecosystems.

Surrounded by dense rainforest and often shrouded in mist is **Grand Etang Lake**, 1700ft above sea level, Grenada's water reservoir and an essential stop, while **Mourne La-Baye** lookout, the midpoint of the road between St George's and Grenville, provides a panoramic view of the rainforest, including the majestic 2757ft peak of **Mount St Catherine**, the highest point on the island.

No trip to Grenada is complete without a visit to at least one of many waterfalls that punctuate its interior. Among the most famous and accessible by road (just turn inland from the Leeward Highway at Concord) is the **Concord Falls**. These three waterfalls, one of which is 65ft high and has a freshwater pool large enough for swimming at its base, are one of the highlights of the Grand Etang National Park. Here you won't have to take a dip in the pool to get wet – the air is saturated with water and heavy with the scent of nutmeg and cinnamon, both of which grow close by. To the east of the park, and reached only by a pleasant hike through a private plantation of cocoa, nutmeg and banana trees, is the **Seven Sisters Falls**. This striking series of seven waterfalls is well worth the walk and its large pool at the base is perfect for a refreshing dip.

Eating, drinking and entertainment

There are a couple of superb places to eat in the south, including the restaurant of the *Plantation House* at Morne Fendue (see p.708). In Westerhall Point, there's *Chez Karin* (℡473/443-2300), a relaxed, open-air restaurant where the menu changes daily, depending on what's available at the market. Saturday is barbecue night and Wednesday is devoted to tapas. The places open every day except Thursday, from 6pm, with last food orders taken at 9.30pm. La Sagesse Natural Works restaurant and bar (℡473/443-1695), on the main road before the turning to La Sagesse Nature Centre (see p.709), is a lovely restaurant set in an old rum distillery, where the old water wheel and distilling vats are part of the décor, as are the chairs made from old rum barrels. Lunch dishes include fish and chips (US$5) and fish with rice (US$7), and there's a small shop inside selling locally made crafts.

If you need a break from beaches, Grenville's Deluxe Cinema (℡473/442-6200) screens current mainstream **films** and charges EC$7–15 admission.

19.4

Carriacou

The most southerly of the Grenadine islands, **CARRIACOU** (an Arawak name meaning "island of reefs") is at thirteen square miles the largest of the island chain that lies between Grenada and St Vincent. Although just a short ferry hop from Grenada, the seven thousand inhabitants of Carriacou, fondly nicknamed "Kayaks" by Grenadians, enjoy a more relaxed pace of life than their neighbours. The main town of **Hillsborough**, surrounded by low, forested hills, won't detain you for long, but the rest of the island, especially to the south and west, promises good walking, excellent watersports and unspoiled beaches. Diving is also good on the island, with a range of sites for all levels of experience, including the wreck of a small World War I gunboat. There's enough here to warrant more than a day trip if you want to escape the trappings of the tourist industry for a few days.

Carriacou also has no shortage of **culture**. Belief systems of the African slaves remain strong on Carriacou and are preserved in rituals such as the powerful **Big Drum Dance**, a pre-Christian ceremony in which ancestors communicate with their descendants (see box below). The Big Drum Dances, along with street parties and calypso, are the highlights of the **Carriacou Regatta** held every August, during which descendants of the island's Scottish boat builders show off their hand-built schooners. Other festive times to visit are **Carnival**, celebrated before the start of Lent, **May Day** and the **Parang festival** prior to Christmas – all are opportunities to hit the streets, dance and eat, and there is never any shortage of calypso.

Arrival and information

Carriacou is easily accessible by **air**, with daily connecting flights from Barbados, Grenada, St Vincent and other Grenadine islands; flights touch down at **Lauriston Airstrip** one mile south of Hillsborough. However, by far the most scenic and economical way to get here from Grenada is the regular *Osprey Express* **passenger ferry** (see p.696), which arrives and departs from the Hillsborough jetty. The ferry also runs between Carriacou and **Union Island** in St Vincent and the Grenadines; passengers from Union Island must pass through immigration at the small office across the main road, opposite the foot of the jetty. The **tourist office** (Mon–Fri 8am–noon & 1–4pm; ⓣ473/443-6014) on Patterson Street is where you can pick up accommodation information and a map of the island. Both Barclays Bank and

The Big Drum Dance

The **Big Drum Dance** is an integral part of all festivities in Carriacou. Rooted in ancestral worship and tribal identity, the tradition has survived the centuries since it came to the Caribbean with the West African slaves. The drums are made from old rum kegs and goatskin and, until independence, were banned by the British who saw them as a threat to Christianity and feared they would incite rebellion. The ritual has survived, thanks to absentee European landowners and the people's determination to preserve their culture. Once reserved for special occasions, such as the launching of a boat or a funeral ceremony, the vibrant drumming and dancing is now also performed for tourists.

Kick'em Jenny

Directly under the ferry route from Grenada to Carriacou lies a growing underwater volcano known as **Kick'em Jenny**, whose peak is now approximately 100 metres from the surface of the water, but creeping higher all the time. Kick'em Jenny's first known eruption, which lasted 24 hours, occurred on July 24, 1939. This produced a column of water and debris over 900ft high and tsunamis in Grenada and the south Grenadines. Ten smaller eruptions have occurred since, the most recent on March 26, 1990, when earthquakes triggered by them were felt in Grenada and the Grenadines.

Kick'em Jenny is continually monitored by the Seismic Research Unit at the University of the West Indies in Trinidad, which issues warnings if there are signs of over-activity.

For details and a sonar image of the volcano, visit Ⓦwww.uwiseismic.com/kejtitle.html

National Commercial Bank have branches in Hillsborough; the latter has an ATM. The lone post office (Mon–Fri 8am–noon & 1–4pm) is in front of the pier, while pay phones can be found in front of the Cable & Wireless office on Patterson Street (Mon–Fri 7.30am–6pm, Sat 7.30am–1pm). Phone cards can be bought inside.

Getting around

Buses operate from the jetty in Hillsborough and typical fares are EC$1.50 for trips up to one mile and EC$2.50 for those over one mile. A service also runs from Lauriston Airport, Tyrrel Bay and Belmont to south of Hillsborough and north to the town of Windward. **Taxis** run from the airport to Hillsborough for around EC$10 and to Belair for roughly EC$15. **Water taxis** from the jetty are the easiest way to get to the beaches. **Car rental agencies** include Sunkey's Auto Rentals in Hillsborough (Ⓣ473/443-8382); Martin Bullen (Ⓣ473/443-7204), who is based at the island's only petrol station on Patterson Street in Hillsborough; and John Gabriel (Ⓣ473/443-7454) in Tyrrel Bay. All charge around EC$110–135 per day. **Bikes** can be hired from Wild Track Cycles in Tyrrel Bay (Ⓣ473/443-6472), for EC$50 per day or EC$25 for a half-day.

Accommodation

Despite its small size Carriacou has a selection of good-value **accommodation** options.

Hillsborough

Ade's Dream Guest House Main Street Ⓣ473/443-7317, Ⓕ443-8435, Ⓔadesdea@caribsurf.com. Claiming that "your best dream awaits you", this charming guesthouse with its ornate balconies has a range of rooms from small with shared bathroom to larger, new rooms with kitchenettes and private bathrooms. A grocery store is on the ground floor and the well-reviewed seaside restaurant is right across the street. ❸

Gramma's Apartments Main Street Ⓣ473/443-7255, Ⓕ443-7256. Though this central hotel isn't much to look at from the outside, the rooms are well decorated and have kitchenettes and private patios. ❸

Green Roof Inn Seaview, Beausejour Bay Ⓣ & Ⓕ473/443-6399, Ⓦwww.greenroofinn.com. A ten-minute walk north of Hillsborough (or an EC$1.25 bus ride), this small family-run inn is a peaceful haven with breathtaking views. The rooms are simple but stylish and all have mosquito nets and fans. Bikes and snorkel equipment are available for rent and Continental breakfast and airport/jetty transfer are included in the rates. ❺

Millie's Guest House Main Street Ⓣ473/443-7310 Ⓕ443-810. On the beachfront side of Main Street, this rambling hotel with covered wooden balconies is good-value budget accommodation. One room has a private bathroom and the rest share bathrooms and kitchens. ❷

Silver Beach Hotel ⓣ473/443-7337, ⓕ443-7165, ⓔsilverbeach@ grenadines.net. Nestled by the water's edge in a secluded bay, this small resort has a range of one-bedroom suites, some of which are self-catering. Free transport is available from the airport and bus tours and sailing excursions can be arranged. One free night is offered for every seven-night stay. ④

The rest of the island

Carriacou Yacht and Beach Club Tyrrel Bay ⓣ473/443-6123, ⓕ443-6292, ⓔcarriyacht@caribsurf.com. Surrounded by palm trees, this self-contained complex at the water's edge is a popular haunt for yachters. The rooms are neat and comfortable and all have private bathrooms, refrigerators and coffeemakers. The resort also has its own bar and restaurant. ②

Kido Ecological Inn Prospect ⓣ & ⓕ473/443-7936, ⓔkidy-ywf@caribsurf.com. Eco-tourism is high on the inn's list of priorities due to its location on a forested ridge on the northwestern coast. The inn is also a research station and birdwatching, hiking, cycling, sailing and diving are all available, as is the chance to volunteer for one of their on-going ecological projects. Accommodation includes a two-bedroom villa and large pagoda, and there's a well-stocked library. ⑤

Mom and Dad Holiday Apartments Belmont ⓣ473/443-8056. Five minutes from lovely Harvey Vale Beach, the rooms at this gleaming white apartment block are fitted with mahogany furniture and all come with a well-equipped kitchen and verandah. ③

Paradise Inn L'Esterre Bay ⓣ473/443-8406, ⓕ443-8391, ⓦwww.paradise.cacounet.com. Right on the edge of the beach, this small, attractive inn has spacious rooms, each with private shower and toilet and ceiling fans. *Ali's* restaurant on site has a varied menu, and dive operator Tanki's has a base here offering PADI courses and snorkelling trips. ②

Scraper's Bay View Cottages Tyrrel Bay ⓣ473/443-7403. Appealing Caribbean-style apartments whose modest rooms all have private kitchens and bathrooms. The adjoining bar and restaurant serves a range of fish and pasta dishes as well as sandwiches and burgers. ③

Hillsborough

A small cluster of weather-worn buildings overlooking the sea, Hillsborough may be the main point of entry to the island, but has little to warrant a long stay and is easily explored in an hour or two. The town stretches along its at times tatty Main Street, which runs parallel to the beach. Here most of the town's **places to stay and eat** as well as banks and public services are to be found. The beach around the jetty is narrow and a heavily used part of the working harbour – though not for recreation.

The main focus of Hillsborough is its **jetty**, which punctuates the middle of the town and offers a view of nearby Union Island (see p.688). Throughout the town old stone merchant houses serve as a reminder of the island's colonial, sugar-producing past, as does its small but interesting **Historical Museum** on Patterson Street (Mon–Fri 9.30am–4pm, Sat 10am–4pm; EC$5). Housed in the restored ruins of an old gin distillery, the museum features a varied collection of Amerindian utensils and pottery, and has sections devoted to the island's European and African heritage. There are no other attractions for visitors to Hillsborough, though Monday is a lively day in town when local fruit and vegetable farmers bring their produce to the market – a small, haphazard collection of stalls gathered around the jetty. There is much more to Carriacou than Hillsborough and to make the most of a visit to the island you'd do best to venture farther afield.

The rest of the island

Approximately two miles southwest of Hillsborough past the airport, is the small village of **L'Esterre**, home of local artist Canute Calliste, who claims a mermaid visited him when he was a small boy and blessed him with the gift of painting and music. So productive is his gift that Canute, now in his nineties, has been known to finish sixteen paintings in one day. You can view his cheerful and vibrant paintings at the artist's shop and studio in the village.

The main road then leads south away from L'Esterre, and on to one of the most popular beaches in the area, **Tyrrel Bay**, also known as Hurricane Bay. The three-mile journey to this large horseshoe bay on Carriacou's western side is covered by a frequent bus service from Hillsborough. Here the waters are well protected and the beaches golden, and it is a favourite anchorage for yachts, especially during storms. Though hurricanes are not much cause for concern on Grenada, in 1955 Hurricane Janet broke the rules and stormed into the region with 150mph winds, causing extensive damage.

Tyrrel Bay is also famous for its oysters, and here protected tree oysters grow amongst mangrove roots which you can reach by boat. Just yards inland from the bay is the pretty village of **Harvey Vale**. There's not much here to explore, but do take time to visit an old Amerindian well, whose waters are thought to have therapeutic qualities.

Looming over Hillsborough about a mile to the north is **Belair**, a peak 719ft above sea level that commands sweeping views of the Grenadines – especially Sandy Island and Grenada. Here you will find scenic walking trails and the ruins of old French and British plantations nestled amongst white immortelle trees.

Anse La Roche, a peaceful beach where turtles swim ashore to lay their eggs at night, lies on the northwest coast of the island. The beach is only accessible by water from Hillsborough or by foot from the small village of **Bogles**, which is the terminus of a bus route from the capital. With its sea life-infested coral reefs lying just offshore, this crescent-shaped gem of a beach is one of the best places to snorkel in Grenada. It's also a pleasant spot to simply lie back and watch the yachts sail by, but make sure to bring food and drink as there are no facilities.

A short walk from Anse La Roche is the northernmost tip of the island known as **Gun Point**, named for the cannons that used to contribute to the region's defences and which falls under the jurisdiction of the island of St Vincent. On the east side of the headland is the 955ft **High North Peak**, the highest point on the island and a protected national park, and the tiny and picturesque fishing village of **Windward**. The windswept community's occupants are boat builders and descendants of Scottish immigrants who brought the craft here from Glasgow, back when the island was still under British colonial rule. Claiming to use plans passed down through the generations, many of these crafts people now work at Tyrrel Bay. **Petite Carenage Bay** is also nestled in the northeast corner of the island, between Gun Point and Windward, and is home to a mangrove restoration project managed by Kido Research Station (*Kido Ecological Inn*, see opposite). You can explore a unique and ancient eco-system whose dense vegetation and shallow waters are home to numerous fish, insects and birds. Kido organizes guided tours of the mangrove swamp, as well as whale and dolphin watching tours, both of which are recommended.

Ocean activities

Carriacou is especially good for **reef diving** and quieter than Grenada for practising other **watersports**. Diving, snorkelling, water-skiing and windsurfing are popular on the island and can be arranged through Carriacou Silver Diving Ltd (☎473/443-7882, Ⓦwww.scubamax.com), whose office is in Hillsborough. Offering a range of day and night dives, this company caters for all levels of experience and will also arrange accommodation, island tours and even barbecues. Single dives start at US$38 and day trips are US$130 per person. Arawak Divers in Tyrrel Bay (☎473/443-6906) offers a similar range of dives and runs day excursions to the Isle of Rhonde and the Tobago Cays. Diving and watersports can also be organized through Tanki's Watersports Paradise Ltd (☎473/443-8406), who are based at the *Paradise Inn* on Paradise Beach (see opposite). One of the most popular places to dive is **Sandy Island**, just off the coast from Hillsborough, whose stunning beaches and vibrant coral reefs have made it a popular location for television commercials. Sadly, its popularity has also been its undoing as damage from dropped anchors is damaging the coral and eroding the reef.

Eating, drinking and nightlife

When it comes to **dining** and **nightlife** on Carriacou the main options are hotel bars and restaurants. There are a few of independent establishments, but don't expect a lively nightlife or too much choice in places to eat.

Callaloo by the Sea Main Street, Hillsborough ☎473/443-8004. A quaint restaurant with fine views of Sandy Island and Hillsborough Bay. Seafood is a specialty and the menu also has a range of chicken dishes, as well as chips and a selection of salads. Open Mon–Sat 10am–10pm and the same time on Sundays in season. Prices range EC$16–50.

Caribbee Country House Bogles ☎473/443-7380. Located in a tiny village two miles from Hillsborough, this elegant restaurant specializes in French creole fare made from fresh local produce, herbs and spices. Fish dishes feature heavily on the menu, and for added romance you can dine under the stars in the tropical gardens. Prices start at US$25 and reservations are requested.

Scraper's Restaurant Tyrrel Bay (no phone). Reasonably priced burgers, sandwiches and pasta dishes, among others, are on the menu at this seaside spot. Prices start from EC$18 a head for dinner.

Sea Wave Restaurant Main Street, Hillsborough ☎473/443-7317. Across the road from *Ade's Dream Guest House* (see p.713), this no-frills restaurant cooks up a combination of Caribbean and international dishes starting from EC$18. Open daily 7am–9pm.

What's the Scoop Main Street, Hillsborough ☎473/443-7256. This bakery and ice cream parlour beneath *Gramma's Apartments* (see p.713) has reasonably priced sandwiches, rotis for less than EC$3 and of course ice cream, which you can enjoy at the tables outside. Open 7am–7pm.

19.5

Petite Martinique

Situated approximately three miles northeast of Carriacou, **PETITE MARTINIQUE** is in effect one large, mile-wide hill of unspoilt forestland whose 738ft peak provides a panoramic view of the other Grenadine islands. Petite Martinique's 486 acres were first settled by the French in the seventeenth century and its nearly one thousand inhabitants are mainly their descendants. The sea has long been the main source of income for locals, who continue the tradition of seafaring, fishing and boat building – and some say, smuggling – to this day.

As the island is tiny, don't expect to find a lot to do or see. This is in fact a great place to do nothing. Most people visit on a day trip from Grenada or Carriacou. If the ferry is too slow for you (see p.696), the **tourist office** in Carriacou can book a speedboat which will whiz you across the water in a matter of minutes for EC$120 round-trip. Once there, you can easily walk around Petite Martinique's one road, which runs along the west coast to where the best beaches are to be found.

Petit Martinique's **Carnival** is held in the two days before Lent, and at Easter the island holds its two-day **regatta**, which features the famous greasy-pole contest, in which competitors inch their way out over the water along a slippery pole to reach the prize hanging at the end.

Practicalities

As most visitors are here on a day trip **accommodation** and **dining options** tend to be limited, and many bars and restaurants are part of hotels. Try *Melodies Guest House* (Ⓣ473/443-9052, Ⓕ443-9093, Ⓔmelodies@caribsurf.com; ❷), a family-run guesthouse just three minutes' walk from the main jetty where rooms are luxurious. The restaurant and bar serves a variety of local food and you can choose to eat either inside or under shady trees on the edge of the sea. There's also *Miracle Mart Guest House* (Ⓣ473/443-9118, Ⓕ443-9022, Ⓔjhingram@caribsurf.com; ❷), a small but attractive guesthouse with three clean, comfortable rooms – all good value. The hotel has its own restaurant and superb views of the north Grenadine islands. Also overlooking the harbour is *Seaside View Holiday Cottages* (Ⓣ473/443-9007, Ⓕ443-9052; ❷), an attractive collection of one- and two-bedroom self-catering beachfront cottages, all of them well maintained. There's an on-site supermarket and gift- shop, and the owners will also arrange pick-up charters from Carriacou.

An **alternative** to the island's hotel restaurants is *Palm Beach Restaurant* (daily 10am–10pm; Ⓣ473/443-9103), whose specialty is seafood. The stunning harbour view also makes this a fine place to enjoy a cocktail or two. Main courses range from US$10 for jerk chicken to US$24 for grilled lobster.

20

Trinidad and Tobago

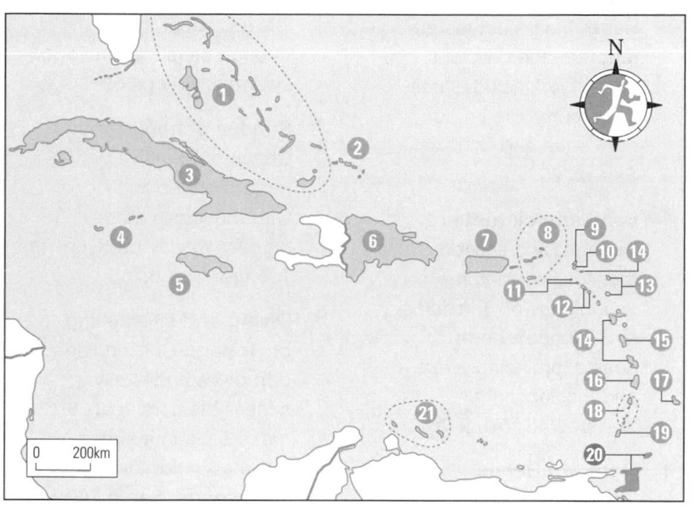

Trinidad and Tobago Highlights

* **Carnival, Trinidad** The original West Indian carnival – now exported worldwide – features spectacular costumes and fabulous music. See p.727

* **Trinidad street food** Better than most restaurant fare, the delicious street food includes delicious curry-filled rotis, corn soup and doubles. See p.726

* **Leatherback turtles** During laying season these huge creatures nest nightly on Trinidad's and Tobago's north coasts, providing a rare and moving sight. See pp.745, 748 & 767.

* **Northern Range, Trinidad** The densely forested peaks are home to over 100 species of mammal, 430 types of bird and stunning waterfalls. See p.742

* **Caroni Swamp, Trinidad** Visit the nesting grounds of the stunning scarlet ibis on a boat trip through eerie mangrove swamps. See p.750

* **Sunday School, Tobago** Check out the live pan performances and "lime" with the locals at the biggest weekly party on Tobago. See p.765

* **Diving and snorkelling on Tobago** Challenging drift dives and easily accessible coral reefs make Tobago a superb destination for these watersports. See p.760

Introduction and Basics

Just off the coast of the South American mainland they were once part of, **Trinidad and Tobago** (usually shortened to T&T) form the southernmost islands of the Lesser Antilles chain and the most influential republic in the Eastern Caribbean. They are the most exciting, underexplored and uncontrived of the Caribbean islands, rich in indigenous culture. A cultural pacemaker best known as the home and heart of West Indian **Carnival**, the nation can also boast having the most diverse and absorbing society in the region.

T&T remain relatively **inexpensive** as natural gas and oil reserves have ensured economic independence and freedom from the tourist trade. Regionally, they are the richest destinations for **eco-tourism**, combining the flora and fauna of the Caribbean with the wilder aspect of the South American mainland. In Trinidad, you can hike through undisturbed tropical **rainforest**, take a boat ride through mangrove swamps and watch **leatherback turtles** nest on remote beaches. **Birdwatching**, with more than 430 species in an area of 4830 square kilometres, is among the world's best. **Tobago** (300sq km) has glorious beaches and stunning coral reefs. Declared the "**Disneyland of diving**", Tobago has the largest brain coral in the world and sightings of manta rays are common.

Equally absorbing are T&T's dynamic towns and cities, showcases for the architectural, religious and **cultural traditions** of their cos-

mopolitan populations. The 1.3 million inhabitants hail from India, China, Portugal and Syria as well as Africa, England, France and Spain, and though racial tensions are inevitably present, Trinbagonians (as they're collectively known) co-exist with good humour, and are proud of their **multiculturalism**. The result is a highly creative culture with a lively music scene that rivals even Jamaica.

Unlike its Caribbean neighbours, Trinidad experienced full-scale slavery for a relatively short fifty years, while the Dutch, French and British were too busy fighting over Tobago to dedicate it to the demands of King Sugar. Consequently, the national psyche is characterized by a strong sense of identity and a laid-back enjoyment of the good things in life, best displayed in the local propensity for "**liming**" – meeting friends for a drink and a chat. With more than a dozen public holidays, local festivals and the pre-Lenten Carnival, a no-holds-barred two days of dancing in the street, the islands' reputation of knowing how to party is well deserved.

Where to go

A visit to **Trinidad** inevitably begins in the capital, **Port of Spain**, home to most of the island's accommodation and the centre of its transport system. The most accessible beaches are on the north coast, while the **Northern Range** offers excellent hiking and superb birdwatching. In contrast to the north, central Trinidad is dominated by flat agricultural plains with a population of primarily Indian descent. The island's greatest natural assets are located here: **Caroni swamp**, nesting area of the scarlet ibis, and the protected wetlands of **Nariva**, home of manatees and anacondas. The burgeoning city of **San Fernando** is a friendly base to explore Trinidad's "deep south", an area largely unvisited by tourists, where modern oil towns contrast with the picturesque fishing villages and deserted beaches.

In **Tobago**, the majority of visitors stay in the hotel-dominated western tip. A more genuine picture of local life can be seen in the capital, **Scarborough**, and along the northern coast in friendly **Castara** or at the fishing village of **Charlotteville**.

When to go

Most travellers come to T&T between January and March, during the **Carnival season** when the climate is at its most forgiving (25–30°C/72–87°F). By May, the dry season parches the lush landscape and bush fires often rage through the hills. The rainy season starts in June and lasts till December, but in September there's a dry spell known as the *petit carem*, an Indian summer of two to four weeks; it's an excellent time to visit, with flights at low-season rates. Tobago hoteliers hike rates during **high season** (mid-Dec to mid-April), as do Trinidad hotels during Carnival, but smaller hotels on both islands charge the same all year round.

Getting there

Cheap flights to Trinidad and Tobago from the **US** and **Canada** are scarce, although flights from the East Coast are considerably less expensive than from other areas. **American Airlines** runs daily flights from most US and Canadian cities connecting through Miami and San Juan to T&T. **Air Canada** flies direct to Trinidad from Toronto three times a week. You can also buy an Air Canada ticket from Toronto to Tobago, but you'll have to switch to LIAT in Barbados (weekends only). **BWIA** offers daily flights at competitive prices from New York and Miami.

The vast majority of **British** and **Irish** residents visiting Trinidad and Tobago are on a package tour. **Monarch Airlines'** (tickets available through tour operator Golden Caribbean ⓣ01293/881079) fares start at £357 for rainy June, escalating to £689 for the popular Christmas season. **British Airways** flies direct to Tobago from the UK once a week on Saturdays, departing from London, Gatwick. **BWIA** has daily flights from London Heathrow to Piarco, Trinidad. Transfers to Tobago on frequent daily BWIA flights can be arranged, and are included in the fare to the smaller isle.

There are no direct flights **from Australia** or **New Zealand**; you'll need to go through a gateway in the US or Canada.

Of the scores of shipping companies that peddle **all-inclusive cruises**, few include

Trinidad and Tobago on their itineraries, and each line routes only a couple of ships per year through the islands, so be prepared for inflexible dates of travel. Two companies that stop in T&T are Holland America and Windjammer (ⓣ1-800/327-2601, ⓦwww.windjammer.com).

For phone numbers of airlines and cruise ship operators, see pp.12–18 and 36–37.

Entry requirements

Citizens from the UK, Ireland, Canada and most EU countries do not require a **visa** for stays of less than three months, and US citizens may stay up to two months without a visa. Nationals of Australia, New Zealand and South Africa all require visas before entering the country.

When leaving T&T, you'll be required to pay a TT$100 (US$17) **departure tax** in local currency.

Money and costs

The local currency is the **Trinidad and Tobago dollar (TT$)**, divided into one hundred cents. Coins start at 1 cent and range up through 5, 10 and 25 cents. Notes start at 1 dollar and are in denominations of 5, 10, 20 and 100. Keep some in small denominations as supermarkets and bars may exchange TT$100 but taxis and street vendors often can't and should be paid with TT$20 or less.

Travellers' cheques and **credit cards** are accepted in most restaurants, high-class shops and hotels. In smaller establishments and rural areas they are unlikely to take anything but local currency. **Personal cheques** are not usually accepted in hotels, and most host homes do not have credit card facilities.

As the **exchange rate** is much more favourable on the islands it is best to buy local currency once you have arrived in T&T. At the time of publication it was around TT$6 to US$1. **Piarco Airport Exchange Bureau** (6am–10pm) has reasonable rates, although it is not as competitive as the banks in Port of Spain: Republic (Independence Square), Royal (Park Street) and Scotiabank (Frederick Street). In San Fernando try Republic (Coffee Street) and in Arima the Republic (Broadway) or the Royal (corner of Queen and Devenish streets).

Travellers flying into **Tobago** can change money at the Republic Bank (Mon–Thurs 8–11am & noon–2pm, Fri 8am–noon & 3–5pm) in the **Crown Point Airport**. Most banks on the island are located in Scarborough; Republic is on Carrington Street, while Scotiabank is on Milford Road and First Citizen on Lower Milford Road.

The TIDCO map of the islands marks the locations of **ATMs**, which provide cash advances on your accounts at home.

Banking hours vary slightly, but are usually Monday to Thursday 8am–2pm and Fridays 8am–noon and 3–5pm. Most banks in Trinidad's larger malls open and close later (9am–6pm) with no break. Outside banking hours money can be exchanged in the larger hotels in Port of Spain. Most shops and vendors will accept **American dollars** – pay in small denominations and be prepared to receive your change in local currency.

Trinidad and Tobago are undoubtedly one of the cheapest Caribbean destinations due to their low profile on the tourist market. It is possible to survive on £20/US$28 a day – if you're prepared to take the least expensive accommodation, eat at low-cost cafés and travel by public transport. If you stay at tourist accommodation and eat at finer restaurants, you will need at least £60/US$85 a day. A rental car will add around £30–40/US$45–60 per day.

During **Carnival season**, all accommodation rates in Port of Spain rise 10–70 percent, as do other prices, including entrance fees, drinks and taxi fares. If you want to enjoy yourself during Carnival, plan on budget at least £100/US$140 a day.

Information and websites

Offices of the T&T tourist board, **TIDCO** (Tourism and Industrial Development

Websites

There are hundreds of T&T-oriented **websites**, which differ hugely in style and content, The listings below are for sites with good general content, and lots of links to get you started.

ⓦwww.carnaval.com The best T&T Carnival site, with features on everything from *mas* camps and panyards to music, accommodation and restaurants. Pretty good for visits to Port of Spain, too.

ⓦwww.homeviewtnt.com Slick site with extensive content, from live feeds to radio stations, sports, news, music, Carnival, history, listings and loads of Trini titbits. A good place to start.

ⓦwww.lanic.utexas.edu/la/cb/tt Huge directory of T&T-related links, organized by category, from academic research and arts and culture to business and economy, and the environment.

ⓦwww.search.co.tt Exhaustive directory of T&T-related sites.

ⓦwww.visittnt.com Maintained by TIDCO, this is the best all-rounder, with country details, attraction listings, flight information and feature pages on Carnival, soca and calypso, with links to lots of other pertinent sites.

Company of Trinidad and Tobago, ⓦwww.visittnt.com), located in the US, Canada, UK and T&T, send out information packs on request, which include useful accommodation and calendar of events booklets, as well as glossy promotional pamphlets and sometimes a road map. On the islands their information booths at Crown Point and Piarco airports have friendly, helpful staff. Tobago's main tourist advice centre is at the **Tobago House of Assembly** (THA) in Scarborough (ⓣ868/639-2125 or 4636, ⓔtourbago@tstt.net.tt).

With some of the best writers of the Caribbean, the local media are an excellent introduction to T&T. The main **newspapers** include the broadsheet, *Trinidad Guardian* (ⓦwww.guardian.co.tt), the tabloid *Express* (ⓦwww.trinidadexpress.com) and *Newsday* (ⓦwww.newsday.co.tt); **Tobago** boasts only one paper, *Tobago News*, published on Fridays. Though the islands have two **terrestrial TV** stations – the main local news slot is at 7pm on TV6 – **cable TV** is predominant. **Radio** is hugely popular, with the best stations for conemporary local music being **Yes FM**, **POWER 102**, **The Vibe** (Comedy Tempo) and **WE FM**.

Getting around

Travelling around Trinidad and Tobago takes ingenuity and patience. Public transport is minimal, so an unofficial, private system of **route taxis**, **maxi taxis** and **private taxis** fills the gaps. If you wish to see more than the urban areas, however, it is advisable to **rent a car**.

By bus

Though the small network of **public buses** has improved in recent years through the introduction of rural buses in Trinidad and an expansion of Tobago's services, public transport remains erratic, with most buses clustered around peak hours. **Tickets** cost around TT$2–10 and must be bought in advance from the Port of Spain and Scarborough bus terminals or from small general stores around the country. All buses in Trinidad leave and terminate at **City Gate/South Quay** in Port of Spain. In **Tobago**, all buses depart from the terminal on Greenside Street in Scarborough.

By car

Tobago's roads are much quieter than Trinidad's; the main hazards are blind corners and cows by the roadside. Road signs are based on the **English system** (although distances and speed limits are in kilometres), and you must drive on the left. Petrol stations are scarce outside urban areas, it's wise to keep the tank full. **Car rental** starts at US$35 per day in Trinidad and US$50 in Tobago. Thrifty is the only major **internation-**

al chain on both islands, though there are many local firms. Econo Cars (191–193 Western Main Rd, Cocorite ⓣ868/669-1119, ⓔeconocar@trinidad.net) is the least expensive in Trinidad, while in Tobago, Sherman's (Lambeau ⓣ868/639-2292, ⓔshermans@trinidad.net) is the most reliable, and Baird's (Crown Point ⓣ868/639-2528) rents jeeps, motorbikes and scooters. All companies require you to be **25 or over** and to have held a driving licence for a minimum of two years, and require a credit card imprint.

By taxi

Maxi taxis are private minibuses taking ten to twenty people, with set routes and standardized fares ($TT2–10) but no set timetables. An entertaining experience, for the décor, the music and the conversation, maxis are organized by region and have **colour-coded** stripes relating to the area in which they work. **Yellow** (Port of Spain to the Western Tip), **red** (the east) and **green** (central and south) commute between Port of Spain and outlying towns, while **black** (Princes Town), **brown** (San Fernando to the southwest peninsula) and **blue** (Tobago) work within their own areas. **Routes** radiate from main centres; you can board anywhere – just stick out your hand to be picked up. **Route taxis** follow similar rules, but take a maximum of five passengers and are slightly more expensive. **Private taxis** take you directly to your destination alone, but are as expensive as a British or US cab; always agree on the price beforehand.

Inter-island transport

For those wishing to **travel between Trinidad and Tobago**, there are two options: by ferry, slow and on rough seas but inexpensive (TT$50–60; ⓣ868/625-4906 or 623-2901), and by plane, which is quick but pricier. The boat leaves once daily from Port of Spain and Scarborough and takes five to six hours. BWIA operates seven to ten flights per day, with the trip lasting thirty minutes (US$24/TT$150 one-way and US$48/TT$300 round-trip; ⓣ868/627-2942, ⓦwww.bwee.com).

Accommodation

Most **accommodation** in Trinidad is located in Port of Spain and the larger towns, while in tourist-oriented Tobago most hotels are found in the Crown Point area on the island's western tip. Expect to pay US$20–70 for a room in Port of Spain and slightly more in Tobago. There are no high and low seasons in Trinidad, but rates may rise by up to 70 percent during Carnival. In Tobago high-season rates (quoted throughout the guide) operate between December and mid-April, dropping by 25 percent in low season. We have taken **room tax** (10–15 percent) and **service charge** (10 percent) into account, but it's worth checking each time you rent a room whether these have been included.

One time of year you simply cannot count on getting a room in Trinidad is the three weeks before and after **Carnival**. Rooms must be booked months in advance. Most hotels, guesthouses and host homes (see below) offer special Carnival packages for the Friday before Carnival to Ash Wednesday; expect to pay US$70–90 per night for a basic room, and anything up to US$200 in the smarter hotels.

For those looking for an alternative to standard hotels, **guesthouses** are small-scale properties with less facilities (expect a shared bathroom and fan instead of A/C), while private **host homes** are an excellent and inexpensive option giving you greater insight into the local lifestyle. They normally cost around US$35 per person. For host homes in Trinidad contact the Bed and Breakfast Co-Operative Society (ⓣ & ⓕ868/663-4413); in Tobago contact Ms Miriam Edwards of the Tobago Bed and Breakfast Association (ⓣ & ⓕ868/639-3926, ⓔmaredwards@hotmail.com).

Those travelling in a group may prefer holiday **villas**: in Tobago prices range from US$150 to US$4000 per week. A useful go-between is the Tobago Villas Agency on Shirvan Road (PO Box 301, Scarborough ⓣ & ⓕ868/639-8737) while ⓦwww.seetobago.com is a good source of all types of Tobago accommodation.

Alternatively **beach houses** and **furnished apartments** are advertised in local newspapers.

Food and drink

One of the highlights of Trinidad and Tobago is the fantastic cuisine, a unique blend of African, Indian, Chinese and European influences. Although you may be offered insipid tourist-oriented fare in larger hotels, **local cooking** – meaning anything from **Indian curry** to **creole oil-down**, or **Spanish-style pastelles** – still reigns supreme.

The national dish is the **creole** staple, **callaloo** – dasheen leaves cooked with okra and coconut. Other creole favourites are **oil-down**, vegetables stewed in coconut milk, **cowheel soup** and **fish broth. Wild meat**, such as agouti, lappe, manicou and even iguana are a staple of Tobago's harvest festivals, while no trip to that island would be complete without tasting the delicious **coconut curried crab and dumpling**. **Indian** influences have created the unofficial national dish: invented in Trinidad, the **roti** is a stretchy flat bread (called a skin) containing curried meat, vegetables or fish.

In **Trinidad**, where tourism is minimal and most people prefer to eat at home, **restaurant culture** is only just developing. There are stylish places to eat but the majority are no-nonsense venues where the food is invariably inexpensive and delicious. The best option is **street food**; **doubles** (runny channa sandwiched between soft, fried **bara** bread), **oysters**, **corn soup** and a variety of **pies** – fish, vegetable and meat. The St James district of Port of Spain offers particularly rich pickings, and with food subject to stringent hygiene checks, eating on the hop rarely constitutes a health risk. The ubiquitous **bake and shark** is best consumed on Maracas beach, where vendors compete to produce the tastiest version of fried bread filled with shark meat. **Tobago** has more tourist-oriented restaurants with prices to match. Local seafood and creole dishes feature, but you'll encounter plenty of imported US steak and chips as well. Remember **tax** (up to 15 percent) and a **service charge** (usually 10 percent) will be added to your bill.

Carib and **Stag** are the light, locally produced lagers, while **Royal Extra** or **Mackeson** stouts are excellent local alternatives to **Guinness** – also brewed in Trinidad and used in the local Guinness-flavoured ice cream. The best rum is produced by the Trinidadian **Angostura/Fernandes** manufacturers, makers of the world-famous Angostura Bitters; their **Black Label** red rum is considered sublime.

The best non-alcoholic thirst quencher is the vitamin- and mineral-packed **coconut water**, fresh from street vendors. **Mauby**, made from tree bark, cloves and aniseed, is delicious but an acquired taste, while fuchsia **sorrel**, made from a flower of the hibiscus family, is a sweet drink enjoyed at Christmas.

Phones, post and email

Public **telephones** take 25¢ coins but if you're making **international calls**, it's easier to use the **Companion phone cards** (TT$10, TT$30, TT$60 and TT$100 + VAT) issued by Telecommunication Service of T&T (TSTT) and available in newsagents, pharmacies and supermarkets. You can **rent a cellular phone** from Caribel (Ⓣ868/652-4982, Ⓦwww.caribel.com) for around US$35 per week plus call charges. Only tri-band units work in T&T, and as TSTT has a monopoly your **mobile** phone will not work unless you register with them first. Phones must be TDMA and digital compatible.

The local **TT Post** is reliable if a little slow. A normal letter takes one to two weeks to Europe and the US, three to Australia. Most towns and villages have a **post office** (Mon–Fri 8am–4.15pm). Letters and postcards to anywhere in the world cost TT$4.50, and decorated aerogrammes can be sent worldwide for TT$2. **Post boxes** are small, red, rare and easily missed.

You'll find internet services mainly at cybercafés, computer shops and some hotels in Port of Spain, Crown Point and Scarborough. Prices are generally TT$10–15 for half an hour.

> The **country code** for Trinidad and Tobago is Ⓣ868.

Festivals and public holidays

Trinbagonians have a well-deserved reputation for partying. With thirteen public holidays embodying T&T's cultural and ethnic diversity, there are plenty of occasions to celebrate.

Carnival, held on the Monday and Tuesday before Ash Wednesday, is the most famous – a hedonistic two days of drinking and dancing in ornate and revealing costumes. In **Trinidad**, especially in Port of Spain, everything shuts down for two days, and increasingly three, as people use Ash Wednesday to recover. Other popular Trinidadian celebrations are the Islamic **Hosay** (see p.738) during May–June, and the Hindu **Phagwa** festival (see p.751). The festival of **Diwali**, celebrated nationwide in late October, honours the Hindu goddess of light. *Deyas* – small oil-wick candles – are lit in every house.

For music lovers October's **World Steel Band Festival**, known as "Pan is Beautiful", features music ranging from classical to the latest calypso tunes. In May, the month-long steel-band festival **Pan Ramajay** is held, and December is the season of **parang** – nativity songs sung in Spanish, sounding more Latin American than Caribbean.

In **Tobago** the eagerly awaited **Tobago Heritage Festival** occurs in the last two weeks of July and features traditional customs, storytelling and festivities. The **Charlotteville Fisherman's Fete**, held on Man O' War Bay in the middle of July, is a wild beach party. On the Tuesday after Easter in Buccoo, **crab and goat races** are held. These bizarre spectacles are entertaining to watch – though for those betting they're no laughing matter. For the latest information on events and a festival calendar, contact TIDCO at ☎868/623 6022.

Public holidays

January 1 New Year's Day
December/January Eid-ul-Fitr
March/April Good Friday, Easter Monday
March 30 Spiritual Baptist (Shouter) Liberation Day
May/June Corpus Christi
May 30 Indian Arrival Day
June 19 Labour Day
August 1 Emancipation Day
August 31 Independence Day
October Diwali
December 25 Christmas Day
December 26 Boxing Day

Crime and safety

Though Trinidad has a reputation in the region for violent crime, much of this is exaggerated and crime rarely affects tourists. In Tobago crime is rare – most locals leave their doors unlocked. Use your common sense and take the **precautions** you would in any strange environment. If you need the police, dial ☎999, and for emergency services (fire and ambulance) it's ☎990. **Harassment** hasn't reached anything like the proportions you'll encounter in more established destinations, but as independent travellers are still a novelty, **women** travelling solo should expect attention. This usually consists of verbal comments and is rarely threatening. Though you may be offered **marijuana**, and perhaps even **cocaine** in Tobago, it is illegal to sell or possess either and penalties are severe.

Emergency numbers

Police ☎999
Ambulance and fire brigade ☎990

Outdoor activities

Unique in the Caribbean for its environmental diversity, a visit to T&T would not be complete without seeing the wildlife in its natural habitat. The islands rank among the world's top ten birding sites, with more than **430 recorded bird species** per square kilometre. The most accessible places to see birdlife in **Trinidad** are the Asa Wright Nature Centre (see p.745) and the Caroni Bird Sanctuary (see p.750) – nesting place of the scarlet ibis. In **Tobago**, head for Little Tobago, also known as Bird of Paradise Island, and the protected Tobago Forest Reserve.

There is excellent **hiking** to be had in the

Trinidad forests of the Northern Range and the Chaguaramas hills; though make sure you go with a group as it is easy to get lost in the jungle. **Snorkelling** and **scuba diving** are extremely popular; both are best in **Tobago**, where the water is clear and the coral reef spectacular. The best dive spots are Speyside, Charlotteville and around the Sister's Rocks. If you prefer to stick to **swimming**, bear in mind that undertows and strong currents make many of Trinidad's (and some of Tobago's) **beaches** downright risky. If in doubt, check with a local. Maracas is Trinidad's most popular beach, though most agree that the best are in Tobago, where the water is cleaner and the facilities more developed. The increasingly commercial Pigeon Point is the queen here, though the undeveloped Castara, Parlatuvier, Englishman's Bay and Pirate's Bay are far more stunning. Lush **waterfalls** such as Argyll in Tobago and Blue Basin, Maracas and La Laja in Trinidad offer great **freshwater swimming**, while big breakers around Mount Irvine in Tobago and Toco in Trinidad make ideal conditions for **surfing**.

The main **yachting** centre is Chaguaramas, a haven especially during hurricane season. For more information contact the Trinidad and Tobago Yachting Association (ⓣ868/634-4519), or consult the *Boaters' Directory*, available from marinas and the tourist board.

There are hundreds of **tour companies** in T&T offering everything from **hiking**, **birdwatching** and **kayaking** to more conventional **driving tours**. The average cost is US$50–100 per day, though the **Chaguaramas Development Authority** (ⓣ868/634-4364 or 4349, ⓦwww.chagdev.com) provides excellent hiking from US$25. **Wildways** (ⓣ & ⓕ868/623-7332, ⓦwww.wildways.org) operates out of both Trinidad and Tobago and is one of the best, ploughing profits back into eco-educational programmes for local schools. **Island Experiences** (ⓣ868/625-2410, ⓕ627-6688, ⓔgunda@wow.net) provides tailor-made cultural tours including *mas* camps and panyards, and **Caribbean Discovery Tours** (ⓣ868/624-7281, ⓕ624-8596, ⓦwww.caribbeandiscoverytours.com) gives informative hikes and safaris with a birdwatching, animal-spotting slant.

Music

Trinbagonian music is some of the most exciting and thought-provoking in the Caribbean. The heart of T&T's music scene is **calypso**, which comments on shifting attitudes to love, gender, race and religion. It's most eloquent proponent is **David Rudder**, Trinidad's answer to Bob Marley. The best place to hear calypso is in the "tents" at Carnival, such as: **Calypso Revue**, **Kaiso House**, **Maljo Kaiso**, **Yangatang** and **Spektakula Forum**.

Equally popular nowadays is **soca**. Most attribute the birth of this musical style to the late calypsonian **Lord Shorty** (Ras Shorty I), whose souped-up rhythm created a more danceable form reflecting the then popular disco. Soca dominates Carnival, with more than 400 new songs released per year. The **Road March** title – the song played most often during Carnival – is now a soca domain, often taken by singers such as **Super Blue** and **Machel Montano**.

East Indians have given soca their own slant through **chutney**, mixing soca beats with sitars, dholak drums and Hindi and English lyrics. Vocalists to look out for include **Rikki Jai**, Sonny Mann and Drupatee Ramgoonai. Chutney has also influenced the conventional soca industry; white calypsonian Denise Plummer continues to flirt with the form, as does Machel Montano.

In the poor Port of Spain suburb of Laventille, **oil drums** brought by US troops in World War II were hammered into concave sections that produced rough notes, creating the **steel drum**, or **pan** as it's known locally. Though **panyards** were initially seen as dens of iniquity, the movement gained respectability as the music became more complex. These days, the panyard calendar revolves around **Panorama**, the nationwide competition held during Carnival. Other places to listen to the sweet pan music are local panyards and national events such as **Pan Ramajay** (see overleaf).

Carnival is the best time to hear local music. T&T's musical spectrum is wider than these styles: at Christmas, you'll hear the Spanish-sounding **parang**, while East Indian festivals such as Hosay (see box on p.738) and Phagwa (see box on p.751) take place to **tassa** drumming, and Jamaican dancehall reggae is popular all year round.

History of Trinidad

For a history of Tobago, see p.758.

Trinidad was the first inhabited island of the Caribbean, settled by **Amerindians** from South America as early as 5000 BC. They called it "Ieri", the land of the hummingbird. When **Christopher Columbus** "discovered" the island in 1498 – naming it **Trinidad** after the three peaks of the Trinity Hills – there was a population of 35,000, who had trade links to South America. Within three hundred years, the indigenous people were all but wiped out through exposure to European diseases and Spanish massacres. **Spanish settlers** arrived in 1592 but the Spanish empire had neither the desire nor the resources to develop the island. Governors of Trinidad did as they pleased and **pirate** attacks were commonplace. In 1783 Spain issued the **Cedula of Population**, to encourage fellow Catholics – **French planters** – to settle; the land allocated depended on the number of **slaves** they brought with them. Unusually for the region, immigrants of mixed European/African race could also receive land, thus opening the way for a property-owning coloured middle class.

Though Spanish-run, the island's culture became increasingly French: it was during this period that **Carnival** was introduced. Things heated up politically when the **British**, led by Sir Ralph Abercromby, invaded in 1797. The Spanish surrendered with hardly a shot fired and Thomas Picton became governor, ruling with a **reign of terror**. By 1802, Picton's activities had become an embarrassment even to the British government and he was demoted.

The island became a British experiment, a **Crown colony** ruled directly from London but governed by French and Spanish law. Planters, forced to look for alternative sources of labour after the **Act of Emancipation**, introduced **indentured Indian labourers** to the island in 1845. By 1917, when the system finally ended, some 145,000 Indians, mainly from Calcutta, had arrived. Though better regulated than slavery, the working and living conditions of the labourers were indistinguishable from those of slaves. Many never returned to India, accepting land in lieu of their passage home. Known still as "East Indians", they have contributed greatly to island's culture, especially with their food. Further adding to the ethnic mix in T&T were immigrants from other parts of the world, among them **Africans**, **Portuguese** labourers, **Chinese,** a handful of Jews, and **Syrians**.

Several components – including the oil industry, an anti-indentureship movement, and the establishment of the *Beacon* (1931–34), a stridently anti-colonial, anti-government magazine – meant Britain faced an increasingly unruly population. World War II brought economic improvements as large areas, such as the Chaguaramas peninsula, were leased to the **US military** to establish their Caribbean base. In return, the Americans improved Trinidad's infrastructure and brought oil drums to the island, inspiring the invention of the **steel drum**.

Though **universal suffrage** was granted in 1945, Britain did not hand over control until 1956, when the **People's National Movement** (PNM), under the leadership of the Oxford-educated historian **Dr Eric Williams**, took power. **Independence** was granted in 1962 but the colonial structure of society remained. Disillusionment led to the **Black Power** movement in the late Sixties, resulting in jobs being given to locals rather than expatriates. By 1970, Trinidad was bankrupt but vast **oil** reserves, discovered just as the world was sliding into the 1974 oil crisis, meant the country found itself swimming in money overnight. When oil prices fell in the 1980s, the economy went into recession. As the population became increasingly dissatisfied, the political opposition unified, and in 1986 PNM was ousted for the first

time in favour of the **National Alliance for Reconstruction** (NAR), led by the Tobagonian **A.N.R. Robinson**. Within a year the government was breaking up under the pressure of harsh economic measures imposed by the IMF. In 1990, the **Jamaat-al-Muslimeen** – a revolutionary Muslim organization – attempted to overthrow the government (see p.735) and though the coup was crushed, the government's authority was undermined, and the following year the PNM returned to power.

Over the next five years, the PNM stabilized the economy and paid off the IMF. The 1995 election, and every election since, has split the country down the middle along race lines, with the PNM and the Indo-Trinidadian **United National Congress** both winning an equal number of seats. The first Indo-Trinidadian prime minister, **Basdeo Panday**, took power in 1995 but despite winning the most votes in both the 2000 and 2001 elections, the president controversially appointed Patrick Manning (PNM) prime minister. Currently the country is being run without a parliament while the impasse continues, neither party willing to share power despite a hung parliament. Another election is planned for 2003.

Trinidad and Tobago can boast the most **stable economy** in the Caribbean, thanks mainly to oil's continuing source of revenue. In recent years, rising crime rates, drug trafficking, high rates of domestic violence and HIV infection, not to mention political corruption, have ensured that locals have more to worry about than what to wear to next year's Carnival.

20.1

Port of Spain and the Western Tip

PORT OF SPAIN is the hub of Trinidad's booming economy, and the main port of arrival for many immigrants from other Caribbean islands. It's also the centre of Trinidad's rich **cultural life**, with countless *mas* camps (see p.737), art galleries, panyards and theatres. The city is bordered by the Gulf of Paria on one side and the Northern Range on the other, providing its 51,000 inhabitants with both mountain and sea views. The mish-mash of the city's architectural styles can seem rather ugly at first sight, especially **downtown**, but look closely and you'll spot many fine nineteenth-century buildings along with quaint "gingerbread" houses, so named because of their intricate fretted woodwork.

Thanks in large part to its fine natural harbour, Port of Spain was made Trinidad's capital in 1757. The downtown area is the oldest section of the city, and despite its run-down appearance is the **shopping** and **finance centre** of the capital. Within the compact grid of streets surrounding broad Brian Lara Promenade/Independence Square and bustling Frederick Street, internationally known shops jostle for space with old Spanish warehouses, offices, shops and the paraphernalia of the docks, while the thoroughfares are jammed with traffic, pedestrians and pavement vendors. The discovery of offshore oil in the 1970s left the city with a sleek **financial district**, dominated by the imposing twin towers of the Central Bank on the western side of the promenade.

Tumbling down the hills to the east of the city are the poor suburbs of Laventille and Belmont, established by freed slaves after **emancipation** in 1834. West of the city centre lies Woodbrook, an elegant middle-class suburb settled in the early twentieth century. Established by Indian immigrants in the nineteenth century, the St James district further west still has streets named after the settlers' home towns. North of the city at the base of the Northern Range are the districts of St Ann's and Maraval, which have fast become the centre of the city's expanding hotel trade. In addition, settlers from China, Portugal, Venezuela and Syria all came to Trinidad to try their luck. Descendants of these groups, and those of the French, Spanish, British, African and Indian communities, ensure that Port of Spain retains its cosmopolitan mix of peoples and cultures.

Arrival and getting around

Port of Spain is about 20km northwest of **Piarco International Airport**. Official **airport taxis** will take you to the capital for US$20 (30min, 1hr during rush hour). Alternatively, take a shared **route taxi** (leaving from behind the wire fencing) to Arouca Junction on the Eastern Main Road (TT$2). From there, catch an eastbound **red-band maxi taxi** to **City Gate**, the main transport terminus downtown (TT$3.50). **Route taxis** to Arouca Junction are open to negotiation to take you directly to Port of Spain for TT$60–80, though you may share the car with others.

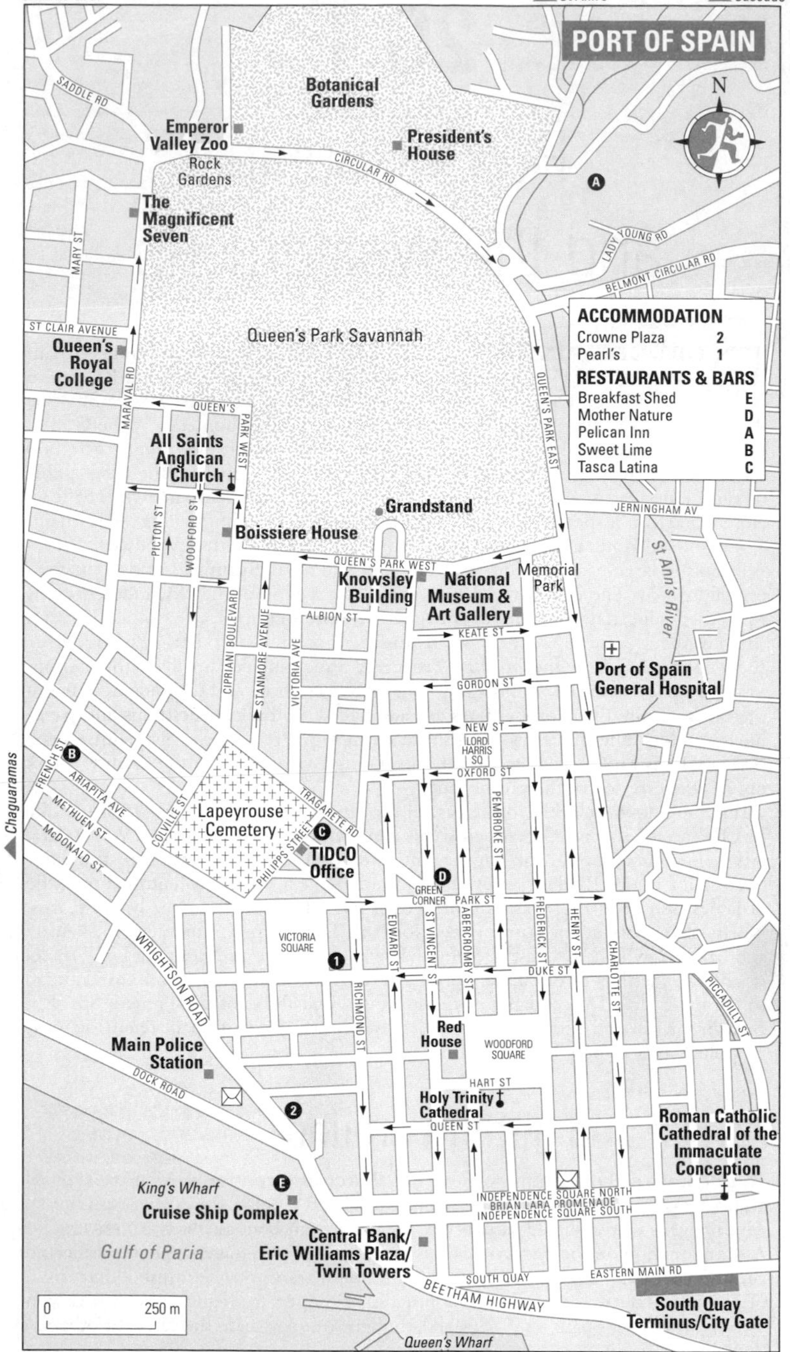
PORT OF SPAIN
Maraval
St Ann's
Cascade
Chaguaramas
Churchill Roosevelt Highway & Piarco Airport
N
ACCOMMODATION
Crowne Plaza 2
Pearl's 1
RESTAURANTS & BARS
Breakfast Shed E
Mother Nature D
Pelican Inn A
Sweet Lime B
Tasca Latina C
Botanical Gardens
Emperor Valley Zoo
President's House
Rock Gardens
The Magnificent Seven
Queen's Park Savannah
Queen's Royal College
All Saints Anglican Church
Grandstand
Boissiere House
Knowsley Building
National Museum & Art Gallery
Memorial Park
Port of Spain General Hospital
St Ann's River
Lapeyrouse Cemetery
TIDCO Office
VICTORIA SQUARE
GREEN CORNER
LORD HARRIS SQ
WOODFORD SQUARE
Red House
Holy Trinity Cathedral
Main Police Station
Roman Catholic Cathedral of the Immaculate Conception
King's Wharf
Cruise Ship Complex
Central Bank/ Eric Williams Plaza/ Twin Towers
Gulf of Paria
South Quay Terminus/City Gate
Queen's Wharf
0 250 m
SADDLE RD
CIRCULAR RD
LADY YOUNG RD
BELMONT CIRCULAR RD
MARY ST
ST CLAIR AVENUE
MARAVAL RD
QUEEN'S PARK WEST
QUEEN'S PARK EAST
JERNINGHAM AV
PICTON ST
WOODFORD ST
CIPRIANI BOULEVARD
STANMORE AVENUE
VICTORIA AVE
ALBION ST
KEATE ST
GORDON ST
NEW ST
OXFORD ST
PEMBROKE ST
FRENCH ST
ARIAPITA AVE
METHUEN ST
McDONALD ST
COLVILLE ST
TRAGARETE RD
PHILIPPS STREET
PARK ST
EDWARD ST
ST VINCENT ST
ABERCROMBY ST
FREDERICK ST
HENRY ST
CHARLOTTE ST
PICCADILLY ST
DUKE ST
WRIGHTSON ROAD
RICHMOND ST
DOCK ROAD
HART ST
QUEEN ST
INDEPENDENCE SQUARE NORTH
BRIAN LARA PROMENADE
INDEPENDENCE SQUARE SOUTH
SOUTH QUAY
EASTERN MAIN RD
BEETHAM HIGHWAY

If **arriving by ship**, you'll pull into Port of Spain's docks. Private taxis tout for passengers at the exit, but route and maxi taxis travel the same road and are far cheaper.

Port of Spain has a compact, grid-based city centre. **City Gate**, located east of the docks, is the main transport terminal, and many route taxi ranks are located in this area. Most of the sights are within walking distance of each other, but bear in mind that under the hot sun energy fades fast.

Maxi taxis operating in Port of Spain and the west – recognizable by their yellow stripes – can be caught in three locations. For **Diego Martin/Petit Valley**, the maxi rank is at the junction of South Quay and St Vincent Street. Maxis bound for **Maraval** (and sometimes **Diego Martin**) go via **St James** and start at the corner of Charlotte and Oxford streets. Maxis for **Carenage** and **Chaguaramas** go via **Ariapita Avenue** and **Woodbrook** and start at Green Corner (corner of St Vincent and Park streets).

Route taxis, which are usually old but functional cars, are distinguishable by the H numberplate. Starting points are dotted around Port of Spain, so it is best to ask a local to find the appropriate stand. From 7pm until 5am, many taxi stands relocate to Brian Lara Promenade/Independence Square. Private taxis can be ordered by phone (try Independence Square Taxi Service ⓣ868/625-3032 or Ice House Taxi Service ⓣ868/627-6984) or by going to their ranks at Brian Lara Promenade/Independence Square, but be warned they're as expensive as any in the US or Europe. There are a variety of **car rental firms** in Port of Spain if you prefer to have your own transport. Singh's, 7–9 Wrightson Road (ⓣ868/623-0150) and Econo Cars, 191–193 Western Main Road, Cocorite (ⓣ868/622-8072) are reputable.

Accommodation

The main areas for **accommodation** in Port of Spain are the city centre, **Woodbrook** and **St Ann's-Cascade**. The **city centre** is obviously convenient, though Woodbrook has the most inexpensive accommodation and the lion's share of the **guesthouses**. St Ann's-Cascade has more modern facilities but is slightly less accessible, though excellent for Carnival activities. Another alternative is the burgeoning **Maraval** on the north of the city. If you're planning to come for the festival, make sure you book well in advance; the higher codes relate to Carnival season.

Hotels

Crowne Plaza Wrightson Road, ⓣ868/625-3366, ⓕ625-4166, ⓦwww.crowneplaza.com. Glitzy corporate hotel with all mod cons; pool, three restaurants, bar and gym. Rooms are equipped with hairdryer, iron, coffeemaker, A/C, cable TV and great views over the Gulf of Paria and the capital. Breakfast is included in the rates. ❼–❾

Kapok 16–18 Cotton Hill, St Clair ⓣ868/622-5765, ⓕ622-9677, ⓦwww.kapok.co.tt. Stylish, spacious rooms decorated with rattan furniture and batik. All have A/C, satellite TV, dataport and an en-suite bathroom. There's a good restaurant and bar, along with a swimming pool, gym and sundeck on site, and breakfast is included in the Carnival rate. ❻–❼

Normandie 10 Nook Ave, St Ann's ⓣ868/624-1181, ⓦwww.normandie.com. One of the city's more atmospheric hotels, with an on-site theatre, art gallery and 21 excellent shops as well as a popular restaurant and café. All rooms have A/C, cable TV, phone with voicemail and en-suite bathroom, and there's a lovely pool. Breakfast included in the room rate. ❹–❼

Guesthouses

Fondes Amandes 9b Fondes Amandes Rd, St Ann's ⓣ868/624-7281, ⓕ624-8596, ⓔcaribdis@wow.net. Charming family home with a pool and flower-filled garden. Rooms are eclectic; some have a private bathroom, and one accommodates four to six people. Breakfast is included. ❷–❹.

Katsura 17a Hillside Ave, Cascade ⓣ868/625-6637, ⓕ622-9968, ⓦwww.katsuratrinidad.com. Radiating zen-like calm, this Japanese-style guesthouse has carp in the pond and gorgeous views over town. Rooms have A/C and en-suite

bathroom, and for a little extra TVs and fridges are available. Carnival rates include breakfast. ④–⑤

Par-May-La's Inn 53 Picton St, Newtown ⓣ868/628-2008, ⓕ628-4707, ⓦwww.parmaylas.com. On a quiet street (though very convenient for downtown), with helpful hosts and a communal verandah where breakfast – included in the rates – is served. Very spacious A/C rooms with phone, TV and en-suite bathroom. ③–⑥

Pavilion Inn 149 Tragarete Rd ⓣ868/633-8167 or 628-2547, ⓦwww.pavilioninn.com. Opposite the Queen's Park Oval, the *Pavilion* is convenient for matches and for Carnival. All rooms are appealing, with A/C, cable TV, private bathrooms, and rates include breakfast. ③–⑤

Pearl's 3–4 Victoria Square East ⓣ868/625-2158. This old colonial mansion, with a verandah overlooking picturesque Victoria Square, is the best bargain in Port of Spain. The basic rooms have fans, sinks and 1960s furniture. Perfectly situated for Carnival and downtown sightseeing. ①

Sundeck Suites 42–44 Picton St, Newtown ⓣ868/622-9560, ⓕ628-4707, ⓔpamelas@trinidad.net. Bright, modern self-catering apartments with kitchenette, ceiling fans, A/C, en-suite bathroom and TV; some have a small balcony. There's a sundeck on the roof, and facilities for the disabled. ③–⑤

Trinbago 37 Ariapita Ave, Woodbrook ⓣ & ⓕ868/627-7114, ⓔtourist@tstt.net.tt. This guesthouse has a tiny pool and a balcony overlooking Ariapita Avenue – perfect for watching Carnival. Rooms vary; some have A/C, some a fan, a few share bathrooms. ②–③

Ville de French 5 French St, Woodbrook ⓣ868/625-4776, ⓔschultzi2000@hotmail.com. Large rooms in a well-located colonial house, all with fans and sinks, some en-suite; there are a couple of self-contained units with kitchen as well. Excellent value, and breakfast is included in the Carnival rate. ②–④

Downtown Port of Spain

Dating back to the 1780s, Port of Spain's **downtown** area is the oldest part of the city as well as the capital's **shopping** and **financial centre**. With its busy docks, vast warehouses and jagged, industrialized skyline of cranes, gantries and containers, the first sight of the capital for anyone arriving by boat is also the city's most unattractive area, **King's Wharf** – the hub of Trinidad's booming import–export trade and also the place to catch a ferry to Tobago. Nearby, the **Cruise Ship Complex** caters to cruise passengers during their few hours on dry land with an overpriced craft market. Commonly referred to as **City Gate**, the grand Victorian stone building on South Quay – originally Port of Spain's **train station** – just east of the docks is the hub of Trinidad's transport system. This is the terminus for all buses and maxi taxis running to all parts of the island.

The heart of downtown, just north of the docks, is **Brian Lara Promenade/Independence Square**. Consisting of two parallel streets, divided by a paved area furnished with benches and chess tables, this promenade runs the width of the city centre. It is a popular after-work hangout; stalls are set up against closed offices and street food vendors do a brisk trade. During the festival season, the promenade hosts **free concerts** and performances, advertised in the local press and radio. The western end is dominated by the twin towers of the **Central Bank of Trinidad and Tobago** – the tallest buildings on the island – while the eastern end is marked by the imposing **Roman Catholic Cathedral**, completed in 1836 after sixteen years of construction. Near the cathedral on the southern side of the square, the **UCW Drag Brothers Mall** (Mon–Fri 8am–5.30pm, Sat 8am–2pm) is a great place to buy handmade leather sandals and local crafts.

Frederick Street, which bisects the promenade, is Port of Spain's main shopping drag, crammed with clothes and souvenir shops as well as street vendors selling home-made jewellery, belts, cassettes and arts and crafts. Halfway up, the pretty, tree-shaded **Woodford Square** provides a pleasant space to escape the crowds and listen to local orators at the equivalent of Hyde Park's Speakers' Corner. Anyone can join in – if they can get a word in edgeways. On the western side of the square is

The Red House and the 1990 coup

The imposing neo-Renaissance **Red House**, at the edge of Woodford Square, derives its name from an earlier building on the site which was painted bright red to celebrate Queen Victoria's diamond jubilee in 1897. The present structure, completed four years after its predecessor was destroyed in the 1903 water riots, was itself attacked in a **coup** in 1990, and bullet holes still scar the stonework.

The coup led by **Yasin Abu Bakr**, leader of the fundamentalist revolutionary group **Jamaat-al-Muslimeen**, occurred on July 27, 1990. The group stormed the Red House and took the prime minister and other government officials hostage. A **state of emergency** was declared.

Though many Trinidadians were discontented with the government at the time, due to harsh fiscal measures, few supported its violent overthrow. With little public support, the rebels surrendered, on condition of an amnesty, after a six-day siege. Bakr and 113 other Jamaat members were jailed for two years while the courts debated the amnesty's validity, and eventually set free after a ruling by the UK Privy Council.

Many Trinidadians found it hard to believe that such events could take place in stable, democratic, fun-loving Trinidad. With characteristic humour, the crisis was turned into amusing stories, such as those told of wild **"curfew parties"** and the explanations given to the police for the five TVs found in a neighbour's house.

the grand, though bullet-scarred **Red House**, seat of Trinidad and Tobago's parliament and site of the coup in 1990 (see box); on the square's southern side stands the city's **Anglican Cathedral**.

Uptown

Ranged around the broad, grassy expanse of the **Queen's Park Savannah** and framed by the foothills of the Northern Range, Port of Spain's **uptown** district oozes prosperity. Along the wide boulevards that ring the Savannah, the palatial mansions of the colonial plantocracy compete with the *Hilton* hotel, the residences of the republic's president and prime minister, and the glitzy modern headquarters of insurance companies. Away from this circuit of roads, the streets exude the sober opulence of embassy quarters, untouched by the urban razzmatazz of downtown Port of Spain.

The Queen's Park Savannah is Port of Spain's largest open space. Within the 3.7-kilometre circuit of its perimeter roads, its grassy expanse is crisscrossed by paths and shaded by the spreading branches of old samaan trees. Often deserted during the hot daylight hours, the Savannah comes to life after 4pm, with football games, joggers, and couples and families taking an early evening stroll. At this time, food stalls, serving tasty snacks such as roasted corn, bake and shark, pholouri and rotis are set up.

All Carnival competitions, including **Panorama**, **Dimanche Gras**, **Parade of the Bands** and **Champs in Concert**, are held in the grandstands on the southern side of the park. Many other events take place here, including performances by visiting international artists. Though the seats are numbingly hard, the setting is incomparably atmospheric, with performances taking place against a backdrop of the mountains and the starry Caribbean sky.

At the top end of Frederick Street, as the Savannah comes into view, stands the imposing, gabled **National Museum and Art Gallery** (Tues–Sat 10am–6pm, Sun 2–6pm; free) at the corner of Keate Street. The museum's collection is extensive and wide-ranging, covering everything from early **Amerindian history** and the technology of the **oil industry** to an excellent collection of works by **local**

artists. Worth a couple hours of browsing, the museum provides an essential overview of the history, economy and culture of Trinidad and Tobago.

One of the finest of the many mansions surrounding the Queen's Park Savannah is the ornately decorated **Knowsley Building**, on the corner of Queen's Park West and Chancery Lane. Resembling a fantasy doll's house, it's one of numerous examples of the work of Glaswegian architect George Brown, who introduced the mass production of fretted woodwork to the islands. **Boissiere House**, on the corner of Cipriani Boulevard and Queen's Park West, is perhaps the best example of the style, with a whimsical concoction of fretted wooden finials and bargeboards, stained glass depicting meandering strawberry vines and a small pagoda-like roof over one room.

North of Queen's Park West on Maraval Road stands a bizarre group of mansions affectionately known as the **Magnificent Seven**, a magical-realist parade of European architectural styles with a tropical slant. Constructed between 1904 and 1910, the remarkable buildings are the result of the competing egos of rival plantation owners, each of whom tried to outdo their neighbours in grandeur. Standouts among them are **Queen's Royal College**, first of the seven, built in Germanic Renaissance style, and now Trinidad's most prestigious school (former pupils include authors V.S. and Shiva Naipaul and the country's first prime minister, Eric Williams); **Whitehall,** a Venetian-style palazzo whose gleaming white paint gives it the air of a freshly iced birthday cake; and **Killarney**, or Stollmeyer, as it is sometimes known, which stands at the northern end. This fairy-tale castle, bristling with turrets and spires, was modelled on Queen Victoria's residence at Balmoral. Unfortunately none of these buildings is open to the public.

On the northern side of the Savannah is the **Emperor Valley Zoo** (daily 9.30am–6pm, last tickets sold at 5.30pm; TT$4, children 3–12 years TT$2). A magnet for local kids, it's worth a wander to get a close-up look at Trinidadian species that you're unlikely to see in the wild. Its collection of relatively well-kept animals is reputedly the most extensive in the Caribbean, including **brocket deer**, **quenk**, a large selection of **monkeys**, aquarium fish and snakes, as well as **ocelots**, **spectacled caiman** and numerous **birds**, including parrots, toucans and scarlet ibis.

Next door to the zoo, and spreading back from the Savannah toward the President's House, are the exquisite **Botanical Gardens** (daily 6am–6pm; free), home to one of the oldest collections of exotic plants and trees in the western hemisphere. There are no official guides, though for a small fee unofficial guides will take you round – a good idea as most of the labels have disappeared. A small **cemetery** within the gardens contains the crumbling gravestones of many of the island's governors. Behind the Botanical Gardens stands the **President's House**, a stately villa built in 1876. Behind it, hidden from view, is the **Prime Minister's Residence**. Both buildings are closed to the public.

The suburbs of Port of Spain

Behind the residential fretworked facades of the suburbs of Port of Spain lies the engine room of T&T's cultural life. The creative energy of **Carnival production** is concentrated in the western suburb of **Woodbrook**, while further west still, the streets of **St James** come alive with revellers at night throughout the year. In the east, **Laventille** is the home of the Caribbean's favourite instrument, **the steel drum**, while the suburb of **Belmont** is home to the fascinating Rada community. All the suburbs are a ten- to twenty-minute walk from the city centre, but as the heat can quickly sap your energy, it's wise to take a taxi to your destination.

Mas camps

Mas camps are the headquarters of the Carnival bands where the costumes are produced. Often converted private houses, the camps provide a focus for the whole Trinidadian art community, and you can usually watch costumes being made if you ring in advance – during the Carnival season they're regularly open 24 hours a day. All the bands display some ten to twenty designs in the run-up to Carnival, and costumes can even be purchased; prices start at about US$100. Contemporary costumes are increasingly revealing, catering to the mainly female participants' desire to show off their assets, though a few, such as those of the **Old Fashioned Sailors** camp and the designs of **Cito Velazquez**, still stick to traditional artistic creations. For an idea of traditional family-run camps visit the **Mas Factory** (15 Buller St, Woodbrook ⓣ868/628-1178) – known for their skilful wire-bending – and **D'Midas Associates** (15 17 Kitchener St, Woodbrook ⓣ868/622-8233) – famous for their feathers. Those interested in more modern factory-style production and minimal costumes should visit **Masquerade** (49–51 Cipriani Blvd, Newtown ⓣ868/623-2161).

For more information check the National Carnival Commission's website ⓦwww.trinbago.carnival.com

Woodbrook

The elegant middle-class district of **Woodbrook** – between Tragarete Road, Philipps Street and the Maraval River – was originally a sugarcane estate owned by the Siegert family, creators of Trinidad's famous Angostura Bitters, and many of the streets still bear their names. The suburb has traditionally been a middle-class residential area, and its streets are still graced by old houses with wonderful fretwork bargeboards, delicate balustrades and finials. Though it has become increasingly commercialized in recent decades, it is a safe and pleasant area to stay, with several good restaurants and a handful of lively nightspots. Woodbrook is also home to numerous **mas camps**, which burst into life during Carnival season, from November to February (see box).

At the edge of Woodbrook, on Philipps Street, is the entrance to the **Lapeyrouse Cemetery** (daily 6am–6pm), a walled burial ground dating back to 1813 and filled with Victorian – as well as more modern – tombs. At the western end of Tragarete Road is the **Queen's Park Oval** (ⓣ868/622-4325), Trinidad's premier **cricket ground**. Hosting national and international matches between February and April, you'll pay TT$35–80 for a seat in the stands, or TT$150–180 for an all-inclusive ticket to the Trini Posse stand (food and drink included).

St James

It was in the western suburb of **St James** that the British landed in 1797. Legend has it that they fortified themselves with rum punch that they found here, giving themselves the courage to capture Port of Spain. The area was settled by **Indian** indentured labourers after emancipation (see p.729), and local street names – Calcutta, Delhi and Madras – bear witness to their homesickness.

Today, St James is one of the capital's most cosmopolitan districts, with residents from all the country's ethnic groups. It's a bustling place, especially at night when it becomes the prime liming spot in Port of Spain. Music blasts from cars, bars and clubs; locals dressed in clubbing gear lime alongside old men in jeans and T-shirts; and street stalls sell roti, oysters, corn soup, halal sandwiches and jerk chicken. **Western Main Road**, which runs through the centre of St James, is a broad thoroughfare lined with shops, bars and take-aways. It's most known, though, as the scene of the annual Muslim **Hosay** processions (see box overleaf), which take place in May or June.

In the weeks running up to Hosay, it is possible to watch craftsmen build the ornate minareted tombs from bamboo and coloured paper (**tadjahs**); the houses

Hosay

The Islamic festival of **Hosay**, commemorating the martyrdom of Mohammed's grandsons Hussein and Hassan during the *jihad* (Holy War) in Persia, has been celebrated in Trinidad ever since the first Indian Muslims arrived in 1845. Its exposure to the island's other cultures has turned it into something carnivalesque, with lewd dancing and loud music, but local Shi'a Muslims have recently taken great pains to restore the occasion's solemnity.

Hosay is celebrated in Curepe, Tunapuna, Couva and Cedros, but the best place to see it is undoubtedly in St James. The celebrations take place over four days (occurring in May or June depending on the moon). All the parades start at 11pm and continue into the early hours of the morning. The third night is the most spectacular. Large *tadjahs* more than two metres high are paraded through the streets accompanied by loud tassa drumming, while dancers carry two large sickle moons representing the two brothers. At midnight there is the ritual "kissing of the moons", as the dancers symbolically enact a brotherly embrace. The following night the exquisite *tadjahs* are thrown into the sea, a sacrifice to ensure that prayers for recovery from sickness and adversity will be answered.

where they work have large flags planted in their yards. The task involves great financial, physical and spiritual sacrifice; the materials can cost up to TT$30,000, and the builders have to fast during daylight hours and refrain from alcohol and sexual activity for the duration. Understandably, perhaps, not many of the younger generation find the prospect appealing, and as the years pass fewer and fewer *tadjahs* are being built.

The eastern suburbs: Belmont and Laventille

Port of Spain's eastern suburbs are rarely visited by tourists but **Belmont** – the city's first suburb – has a close-knit community famous for its continuance of African traditions and the celebration of feasts and festivals of the Orisha religion, a Yoruban faith with a somewhat clandestine presence in Trinidad and Tobago. Neighbouring **Laventille**, with its steep alleys lined with ramshackle houses made from salvaged boards and galvanized roofing, perches on the hillside in defiance of gravity. The area has spawned many a great pan player and calypsonian, was the birthplace of the **steel drum** and was celebrated by the Nobel laureate **Derek Walcott** in his poem "The Hills of Laventille". Many visitors are put off the area by scare stories, but much of this is exaggerated. Exploring with a local resident will certainly help you to get more out of the area; Elwyn Francis (ⓣ868/627-3377), a trained tour guide with the Chaguaramas Development Authority, conducts excellent walking tours of the area for TT$50.

Panyards

The best way to hear **pan** is live, in the open air on a warm starry night. Though there are many official events organized, an often more enjoyable time can be had by going to a local **panyard** when they practice – you may even be given the chance to play yourself. The most accessible panyards to visit in Port of Spain are BWIA Invaders (Tragarete Road, opposite the Queen's Park Oval, Woodbrook), Phase II Pan Grove (13 Hamilton St, Woodbrook) and Amoco Renegades (138 Charlotte St, Port of Spain).

Eating

Port of Spain's **restaurant** scene has recently burgeoned. Ariapita Avenue is best for upscale establishments, and you'll most likely need to reserve a table here. For something more casual, there are scores of **cafés** in the downtown area, while the best **street food** is located in St James and, to a lesser extent, Independence Square.

Breakfast Shed Wrightson Road, Downtown Port of Spain, next to the Cruise Ship Complex. Hearty, inexpensive and excellent local food, served at long communal trestle tables mainly for local workers; expect to pay under TT$25. The traditional breakfast of bake and shark and cocoa is delicious. Daily 6.30am–3pm.

Chutney Rose 30 Fitt St, corner of Ariapita Ave, Woodbrook ⓣ868/628-8541. Elaborately decorated Indian restaurant serving Trini-style dishes for lunch – lamb koftas and fish with rice, peas, dhal and salad – and traditional Northern Indian cuisine in the evening. Meals from TT$70. There's also a take-away on site serving good rotis. Mon–Sat 11am–3pm & 6–11pm.

Indego 1 Carib Way, off Sydenham Avenue, St Ann's ⓣ868/624-6954. Located at the base of the Northern Range, this restaurant has wonderful city views, and the menu ranges from delicious bruschetta and ceviche as starters, to chicken and beef brochettes and imaginative seafood for mains. Meals from TT$150. Tues–Sat 7–11pm.

Irie Bites 68 Ariapita Ave, Woodbrook. Jamaican jerk shack painted red, gold and green that's the best of the cluster on this stretch of Ariapita Avenue. Seasoned with Jamaican spices and cooked over pimento wood, the jerk chicken, pork and fish are served with festival (a sweetish fried dumpling) for under TT$25. Mon–Thurs 11am–8pm, Fri & Sat 11am–9pm.

Mother Nature Vegetarian Restaurant St Vincent Street, Central Port of Spain. Creative vegetarian meals and wonderfully filling fruit punches – everything from beetroot to papaya for under TT$25. Mon–Fri 5am–5pm.

Sweet Lime Corner of Ariapita Avenue and French Street, Woodbrook. A great spot for people-watching and moderate prices (between TT$70–150). Satay chicken, crab backs, mussels and shrimp for starters, seafood, ribs and steaks for mains. Good kids' meals available as well. Mon–Thurs & Sun 4pm–midnight, Fri & Sat 5pm–1am.

Syps 3a Cipriani Blvd, Newtown. Intimate coffee bar and restaurant serving light lunches and dinners of crepes, quiche, crab backs, burritos and tacos. The coffees are delicious too. A great spot for an afternoon lime, a meal will set you back between TT$75–100. Mon–Thurs 10am–10pm, Fri & Sat 10am–midnight, Sun 10am–2pm & 6–10pm.

Drinking, nightlife and entertainment

Trinidadians seem to live to party, so it's no surprise that Port of Spain boasts excellent **nightclubs**, though **fetes** – large outdoor parties advertised by posters – are a better option if you want to immerse yourself in the local lifestyle. Most bars and nightclubs come alive after 10pm and are busiest from Thursday to Sunday. The capital also boasts a number of good **theatre** companies, including the **Trinidad Theatre Workshop** (TTW), which specializes in the work of Derek Walcott. During **Carnival** time a hectic schedule of fetes, competitions and calypso tents makes excellent entertainment. Check ⓦwww.carnivalondenet.com and ⓦwww.trinbagocarnival.com for an updated calendars of events.

Liquid Ground floor, Maritime Plaza, Barataria ⓣ868/675-9958. One of the newest clubs in Trinidad, where a bit of rock, pop and Latin is mixed in with the soca and reggae. Try and talk your way into the lavishly decorated VIP area and the Champagne Lounge with its black leather sofas. Entrance fee varies.

Pelican Inn 2–4 Coblentz Ave, St Ann's ⓣ868/624-7486. This Caribbean version of an English pub, popular with locals and tourists alike, is quiet on weekdays, but comes to life on weekends with a packed dance floor and DJs. Daily 11am–2am.

Smokey and Bunty's Corner of Dengue Street at 97 Western Main Rd, St James; no phone. This local institution draws a mixed crowd – young, old, arty, gay and straight. The bar clientele spills onto the pavement, making for some excellent people-watching. Mon–Thurs 10pm–3am, Fri–Sun 10pm–7am.

Tasca Latina 16 Philipps St, Woodbrook ☎868/625-3497. Spanish taverna-style bar and restaurant with a dance floor and friendly atmosphere. Live entertainment, popular at weekends, attracts a mature crowd. Entrance TT$30. Mon–Fri 11am–2am, Sat 6pm–2am. Closed Sun.

Upper Level West Mall, West Moorings. Pumping, friendly place playing soca, reggae and R&B to a sociable crowd of mostly local dancers. One of the most laid-back options in town, this is an essential part of your Port of Spain nightlife experience. Cover charge varies.

Listings

Embassies and high commissions British High Commission, 19 St Clair Ave, St Clair ☎868/622-2748, Ⓕ622-4555; US Embassy, 15 Queen's Park West ☎868/622-6371, Ⓕ628-5462.
Hospital The Community Hospital, 767 Western Main Rd, Cocorite (☎868/622-1191) and the St Clair Medical Centre, 18 Elizabeth St, St Clair (☎868/628-1451).
Internet In downtown Port of Spain, Multi Marketing Computers, upstairs at Town Centre Mall (Mon–Thurs 9am–5pm, Fri 9am–6pm, Sat 9am–3pm). In Woodbrook, *The Web Cafe*, 59 Carlos St (Mon–Sat 8am-7pm), has delicious food as well as computer terminals for TT$10–15 for half an hour.
Laundry Simply Clean Laundromat, 99 Saddle Rd, Maraval ☎868/628-1060. Costs TT$7–12 to do your own or TT$40 for a service wash.
Police Main Police Station, Wrightson Road ☎868/625-2684; in an emergency dial ☎868/999.
Post office TT Post, Tragarete Road, opposite Roxy roundabout, St James. Mon–Fri 8am–4.15pm.

The Western Tip

The **Western Tip** encompasses satellite suburbs of Port of Spain, friendly fishing villages, the island's largest national park and local playground and an extensive marina hosting international yachters escaping the hurricane belt. Easy and accessible to explore from Port of Spain, the furthest point is thirty minutes' drive from the city centre.

Travelling west from the capital you pass the ever-expanding middle-class suburbs of Diego Martin, Petit Valley, West Moorings, Goodwood Park and Glencoe. There's little of interest here for the visitor, apart from **River Estate** (daily 10am–6pm; free, but donations are appreciated) at the northern end of Diego Martin Main Road. Set amidst lush scenery is a restored wooden estate house, and the small **museum** of local history inside includes a rather bizarre but engaging diorama called "The River", depicting a random history of the estate with the help of floor-pad triggered sound effects. A ten-minute drive northeast of the estate is the **Blue Basin Waterfall,** one of the most accessible falls in Trinidad and also one of the smallest. The rainforest setting is beautiful, however, and blue emperor butterflies and exotic birds flutter through the undergrowth. The small pool at the base is good for bathing and is popular with children on weekends. To get there, stay on the main Diego Martin road past the River Estate, then turn right onto Blue Basin Road. Go up the steep hill till you reach a sign pointing to the waterfall and follow the track on foot for five minutes.

Back on the Western Main Road a few kilometres from the Diego Martin junction is the small fishing village of **Carenage**. On leaving the village you enter the area of **Chaguaramas** (pronounced Shag-ger-*rarm*-ms), with its wide expanses of grassland and virgin forests – much of which have been set aside to form the Chaguaramas National Park. More rainforest than park, the protected area spans the low-lying mountains of the western end of the Northern Range. Tracks into the forest take you along rivers to waterfalls and spectacular mountain views. On the flatlands opposite the Chagville beach are a series of buildings remaining from the US occupation of the area in World War II – the location of the **Callaloo** *mas* camp – the Carnival costume factory of one of Trinidad's most famous Carnival designers, Peter Minshall – and the **Chaguaramas Military History and Aviation Museum** (daily 9am–5pm; TT$10, children TT$7; ⓣ868/634-4391). The museum exhibits chronicle the military history of Trinidad and Tobago from 1498 to the present and though the presentation is somewhat haphazard, it is interesting in contrast to the typical beaches-and-palms image of the Caribbean.

Despite being the nation's playground, leisure development has, for the most part, been sensitive and unobtrusive. The protected Chaguaramas National Park is pristine rainforest, popular with hikers and birdwatchers, whilst the strip of flatland along the south coast is the only built-up area, shelter to a scattering of restaurants and nightclubs. On weekends the area becomes busy with locals going kayaking, hiking and cycling. There is a string of **beaches** along the south coast, though the sea can be dirty and polluted here; better swimming can be had on the north coast at **Macqueripe Beach**, a delightful cove that's easily accessible by road. To get there take the Tucker Valley Road from by *The Base* nightclub in the built-up stretch of Chaguaramas.

You can rent a kayak from the **Kayak Centre** (daily 6am–6pm; ⓣ868/633-7871 located immediately after the sign welcoming you to Chaguaramas), for TT$25 for a single and TT$35 for a double; both rates are per hour. Another energetic option is to rent a **mountain bike** from Bay Sports next door (Sat, Sun and public holidays 6am–6pm; ⓣ868/637-7281), costing TT$20 per hour, an extra TT$10 for a **guided ride** into the interior of the National Park. The **Chaguaramas Development Authority** (Mon–Fri 8am–4pm; ⓣ868/634-4227 or 4364, ⓕ634-4311), ⓦwww.chagdev.com) offers well-informed tours of the local area and the Bocas (see below) for anywhere between US$8 and US$25. The Chaguaramas **Golf** Course is open daily 7am–6pm; you'll pay TT$45 for nine holes, TT$5–50 to use the driving range and TT$30 to rent clubs.

Beyond the cluster of former military buildings and newly built restaurants, a plethora of **yachting** facilities draw some three thousand vessels each month. Past the **marinas** with their extensive facilities – supermarket, ATM, a doctor's service, shops, internet café and a bank – lies **the Cove** (daily 7.30am–6.30pm; TT$6), a beach with well-maintained facilities. From here you can go no further, unless you take a boat to the **Bocas**, or as locals refer to them "down de islands". These rocky islets are separated from the mainland by the **Bocas del Dragon** (**Dragon's Mouth**), a series of rocky channels connecting the Gulf of Paria with the Caribbean. Difficult to access, there is little tourist traffic to the islands. For those who do persevere, either by hiring a boat or booking a tour, **Gaspar Grande** is the most accessible, with caves – filled with bats and glittering stalactites and stalagmites – to visit and the **Bayview** resort – consisting of a restaurant, café, beach with facilities, swimming pool, hotel and self-catering apartments – making the trip most worthwhile. The fare to Gaspar Grande is TT$50 by boat from the Island Property Owners' Association marina (on Western Main Road, just before the Cove). Before disembarking, arrange a pick-up time to ensure that you're not stranded.

20.2

The north

The north of Trinidad is an eighty-odd-kilometre stretch dominated by the Northern Range, a rugged spine boasting the island's highest peaks, El Cerro del Aripo and El Tucuche. Trinidad's most splendid **beaches** line the coast to the north of the range, with the enduringly popular Maracas Bay melting into the quieter, undeveloped beaches of Blanchisseuse and beyond. The Arima–Blanchisseuse Road, the location of the Asa Wright Nature Centre – a bird-watcher's paradise – cuts across the mountainous spine, connecting the coast with the Eastern Main road: an amazing drive through lush **rainforest**,

Away from the jungle-smothered hills are some of Trinidad's most **densely populated** areas outside of Port of Spain – along the traffic-choked **Eastern Main Road** (EMR), known locally as the "East–West Corridor". Towns such as the historic **St Joseph** and **Arima** are home to the majority of the island's **African** population and Indian culture is far less visible here than in the south. Creole cooking reigns supreme and the soundtrack that blares from shops, bars and maxis is **soca** and Jamaican **dancehall**. Inland of the EMR, river valleys cut into the Northern Range to a host of interior attractions such as the island's two most spectacular

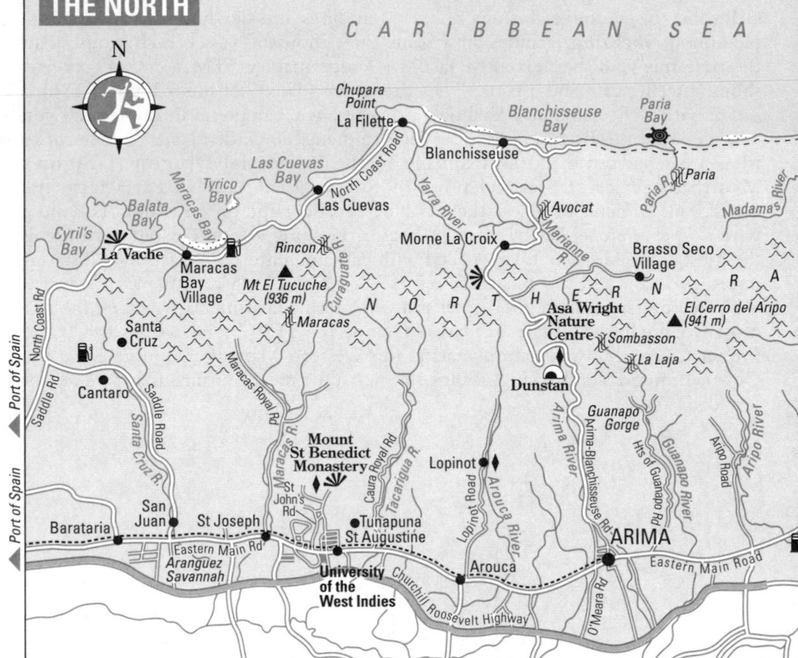

waterfalls, La Laja and Sombasson, and **river swimming** at Maracas Valley, Caura and Guanapo Gorge. The EMR ends abruptly just east of Arima, replaced by the winding minor roads spanning the weather-beaten northeast coast and tip. This wild and rugged peninsula, jutting some 20km into the Atlantic Ocean, is Trinidad's best-kept secret. The populace is overwhelmingly friendly, and along the **Toco coast** on its northern side, **leatherback turtles** clamber up the wave-battered sandy beaches to lay their eggs.

Though parts of the north are well served by **public transport** – especially the East–West Corridor – a **car** is useful to visit the more remote north coast. Surprisingly, there is not a huge amount of **accommodation** in the region, though there are clusters of guesthouses at Blanchisseuse and Grande Riviere. However, all the East–West Corridor is within an hour's drive from Port of Spain and there are a few excellent options for those wishing to stay in the interior. As the northwest tip is more than three hours' drive from the capital, it's better to arrange accommodation at one of the lovely guesthouses found in the region. Apart from unmissable bake and shark at Maracas beach and the hundreds of roti parlours, cafés and fast-food joints along the Eastern Main Road, there are few established **restaurants** in the area. Those that do exist are usually joined to hotels and welcome non-guests – recommended establishments are listed throughout the text.

The Saddle to Maracas Bay

Saddle Road (usually called "the Saddle") makes one of the island's best scenic journeys, climbing the Northern Range and joining the **North Coast Road**. Bordered by the glittering Caribbean sea on one side and cliffs smothered with tangled jungle on the other, its destination is Maracas, where predominantly local devotees soak up the sun. If you're going by **public transport**, route taxis to

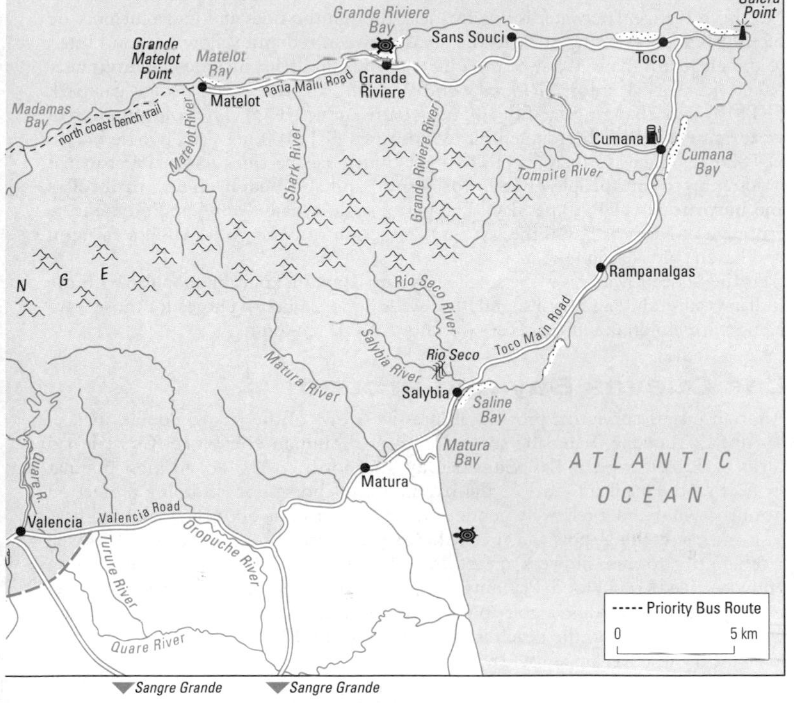

Maracas from Port of Spain leave from the corner of George and Prince streets (TT$8). The area hasn't yet succumbed to leisure development, and most villages here still rely on **fishing** or **farming**, and hotels are few and far between.

Gliding by St Andrew's Golf Course and the last of Maraval's grand residences, Saddle Road begins its serpentine ascent into the Northern Range. After a succession of hairpin bends, two four-metre-high stone pillars mark a **junction**. To the right, **Saddle Road** squeezes through a narrow gorge of rock (if driving through, beep your horn and approach with caution) before meandering downhill through the pastoral Santa Cruz valley, a half-hour scenic jaunt through cattle pastures and farmland to the urban bedlam of San Juan. Cricket supremo **Brian Lara** spent his childhood in Cantaro Village, the valley's largest community. The left of the junction is the North Coast Road, one of the smoothest on the island, built by US Army engineers in 1944 as a recompense for the American occupation of the Chaguaramas peninsula (see p.740). The brightly painted *Hot Bamboo Hut* (open for snacks and souvenirs, weekends only) is a sign you've nearly reached **La Vache Scenic Area**, where the coastal views are marvellous.

Maracas

MARACAS BAY, a 45-minute drive from Port of Spain, is more than a beach, it's an institution. Hundreds make the traditional Sunday pilgrimage from Port of Spain to see and be seen. It's also the island's main Ash Wednesday chill-out spot, where revellers come to relax after the mayhem of Carnival, and sound systems keep the prostrated bodies twitching to the beat. On weekdays it's much quieter – the sand is almost empty and the extensive facilities look a bit out of place.

A generous 1850-metre curve of fine off-white sand fringed with groves of palm trees is bordered by **Maracas Bay Village**, a fishing hamlet, on the west, and *Uncle Sam and Son's* bar – pumping out reggae and soca – on the east. Swimming out to sea, you'll get a sublime view of the beach and the cloud-tipped peaks of the Northern Range. The water is usually clear, though the tides and undercurrents are often dangerously strong; stick to the areas between red and yellow flags and listen to the lifeguards (daily 10am–6pm). The extensive **facilities** include numerous tasty bake and shark vendors (*Richard's* and *Natalie's* are the best), a huge car park (TT$10) and changing facilities (daily 10am–6pm; TT$1). The sole supplier of **watersports** is Blackbeard's, renting windsurfers (TT$100 per day), boogie boards (TT$20 per hour), surf kayaks (TT$30 per hour), banana rides – inflatable bananas holding up to four people (TT$25 for 10min) and also **beach chairs**, **umbrellas** and **hammocks** (TT$20 per day). The petrol station (daily 7am–7pm) on the eastern edge of Maracas Bay is the last on this section of coast, so it's wise to fill up if you haven't already done so.

Further east of Maracas is the smaller **Tyrico Bay**, inexplicably popular with the Indian community, and with slightly less wave action, a better choice for those travelling with children. Lifeguards are on duty daily 10am–6pm.

Las Cuevas Bay and around

After an inland curve that provides impressive views of the jagged double apex of Mount El Tucuche, Trinidad's second highest mountain, the North Coast Road turns back to the sea at **Las Cuevas Bay**, the north coast's second most popular strip of sand. Headlands enclose the bay in a tight horseshoe, affording protection from the wind and a relatively gentle surf – lifeguards put out yellow and red flags to mark safe bathing spots. Currently there's a car park above the bay (free), as well as changing rooms, showers and toilets (10am–6pm; TT$1) and a bar serving budget-priced creole food. Planning permission has been granted for a large hotel on the beach – including a golf course – so catch the sleepy village while you can. The only drawback to the beach is the legendary **sandfly** population – take repellent and try to cover up as the day wears on.

On the eastern outskirts of Las Cuevas, the secluded **One Thousand Steps Beach** is ideal for a secluded swim, but keep to a depth you can stand in – the tides can be strong even on apparently calm days. The beach is opposite Rincon Trace, which is the route to the spectacular **Rincon Waterfall**, a two-and-a-half-hour uphill walk through the bush. You'll need a guide to find this and the nearby **Angel Falls**; guides have to be arranged in advance as few tourists trek this way. Laurence Pierre (☎868/634-4284) is recommended. For those taking public transport, North Coast Road maxis and taxis from Port of Spain (corner of George and Prince streets, TT$15-16) travel this route to Blanchisseuse, as does the rural bus service from City Gate, but all tend to be clustered around peak hours.

Past the tiny villages of La Filette and Yarra is **Blanchisseuse** (pronounced "blaan-she-shers"), the last village before the road tails off into the bush. With a population of around three thousand and an attractive assortment of weather-beaten board houses wreathed by rambling bougainvillea, Blanchisseuse isn't exactly a hamlet, and the clutch of ever-growing flashy holiday homes on the western outskirts are testament to its growing popularity as a retreat. The atmosphere is relaxed and supremely friendly, and there are as many local holiday-makers as there are foreign. Tourists divide their time between enjoying the succession of marvellous sandy **beaches**, hiring a local guide and hiking through the rainforest, and river swimming in the nearby **Three Pools**, **Paria Beach** and **waterfall**, or the **Avocat Waterfall**. Local Eric Blackman, owner of *Northern Sea View Villa* (see opposite), is a good guide with tours including Three Pools with kayaking, hiking and swimming (TT$80 per person), Avocat Waterfall (TT$50) and a four-hour walk to Paria (TT$50). Take note that Blanchisseuse's three beaches have a reputation for rough and **treacherous waters**, particularly between November and February, so keep to a depth you can stand in, though the large waves are popular with local **surfers**. **Marianne** is the main beach stretching around 2km. At the eastern end the Marianne river **lagoon** is an inviting place to swim and you can also rent kayaks (TT$20 for 30min) from here. It's also an excellent place for birdwatching.

Beyond Blanchisseuse, the North Coast Road gives way to the only remaining piece of **undeveloped coastline** in Trinidad. The next piece of tarmac is some 30km away in Matelot (see p.747), leaving intact a sanctuary for bird and animal life, with gorgeous waterfalls and stunning beaches that are the favourite nesting sites for **leatherback turtles**. Through all this cuts the **north coast bench trail**, a two-day hike that requires camping in the bush along the way, though shorter options are available. If you prefer a solitary walk, go during the week; Saturdays, Sundays and public holidays are prime times for local hiking groups. A good local guide is Carl Fitz-James Jr (☎868/667-5968).

Practicalities

The best accommodation options for the north coast are located in Blanchisseuse, where there are a rash of guesthouses and host homes. *Laguna Mar*, c/o Zollna House, 12 Ramlogan Development, La Seiva, Maraval (☎868/669-2963; reservations also taken on ☎868/628-3731, Ⓕ628-3737, Ⓦwww.lagunamar.com; ❸), is the largest and most professional of the bunch. Tucked away at the end of the road, this comfy hotel has rooms housed in blocks of six with a communal balcony; each has two double beds, fans and bathroom. There is also a three-bedroom villa to rent. Marianne Beach is two minutes' walk away. The hotel restaurant, *Cocos Hut*, is in a converted cocoa-drying house and serves lunch and dinners consisting of tasty, local-style fish, chicken and meat. Expect to pay between TT$70–100 for a meal. Vegetarians are catered for – ask in advance. For those on a budget *Northern Sea View Villa*, North Coast Road and Wilson Trace (☎868/669-3995, Ⓦwww.ericblackman.com; ❷), is an excellent choice. These two basic apartments offer little in the way of luxury, but they are directly opposite Marianne beach and the owners are extremely friendly. Both apartments have two bedrooms with a fan, a kitchen, verandah and living room.

The Arima-Blanchisseuse Road

Inland from Blanchisseuse, the **Arima–Blanchisseuse Road** cuts south through the Northern Range, climbing high into misty peaks and through a tunnel-like road of green with overhanging canopies of mahogany, teak, poui, cedar and immortelle. There are impressive mountain views throughout the drive and you're more or less guaranteed to see **birdlife** wherever you stop; crested oropendola, hummingbirds and hawk-eagles are commonplace. For those wanting greater insight into the rainforest, naturalist Courtenay Rooks (Ⓣ868/622-8826, Ⓕ628-1525, Ⓦwww.pariasprings.com) does excellent **nature hikes** and **birdwatching trips** starting from US$45. He can also sort you out local accommodation if necessary.

Seven miles north of Arima lies a birdwatcher's paradise, the **Asa Wright Nature Centre** (PO Box 4710, Arima, Trinidad; Ⓣ868/667-4655; bookings in US via Caligo Ventures Ⓣ1-800/426-7781, Ⓦwww.asawright.org; ⑤–⑥). The 800,000-square-metre estate was established as a **conservation area** in 1967 and today the centre is Trinidad's most popular birdwatching retreat, with hummingbirds, honeycreepers, tanagers and manakins among the forty species making frequent visits to the verandah feeders. The centre offers luxurious accommodation, rates including three meals and afternoon tea. However, if you're not staying, it's a good idea to get there before 10am to avoid the rush – the centre's on many a tour-bus route and the excited squeals of an unusual sighting and the whirr and click of paparazzi-standard zoom lenses can spoil the peaceful setting. Open daily 9am–5pm, the entrance fee (US$10) includes an hour-and-a-half tour and access to the verandah. Residents of more than three nights get a tour of **Dunston Cave**, which houses the world's most accessible colony of **oilbirds**.

The East-West Corridor

Running along the southern flank of the Northern Range, the **East–West Corridor** is traversed by the **Eastern Main Road** (EMR), a driver's nightmare, the **Priority Bus Route**, a fast-track commuter thoroughfare that's accessible only to public transport, and the **Churchill Roosevelt Highway,** a quick route connecting Port of Spain with the northeast tip. Hot and dusty as it is, the slow pace of the EMR allows you to absorb the commercial chaos, passing through the old Spanish capital of **St Joseph** and ending at **Arima**, the corridor's largest town and home to what's left of Trinidad's **Carib** community. The road is also the gateway to many a day trip from Port of Spain, including the **Maracas waterfall** and the **Mount St Benedict Monastery**. Beyond Arima, the buildings let up, but a few country lanes lead to the two most impressive waterfalls on the island, **La Laja** and **Sombasson**.

St Joseph

The imposing **Mohammed Al Jinnah Memorial Mosque**, resplendent with a crescent- and star-topped main dome, signals your arrival into **ST JOSEPH**, Trinidad's oldest European town and first official **capital**. Lined with fretworked French and Spanish architecture, it's one of the better places along the EMR to get a flavour of the East–West Corridor. Striking uphill into Abercromby Street takes you through the town to the Maracas Royal Road, continuing north into the lush Maracas–St Joseph Valley. Eight kilometres from the EMR is the signposted Waterfall Road – the appropriately named route to **Maracas waterfall**. A spectacular ninety-metre fall best seen during the rainy season (June–Dec), it's an excellent place for a quick dip after the sweaty twenty-minute walk it takes to get there. Route taxis run from Curepe junction, a busy public transport exchange two kilometres east of St Joseph, to Maracas Valley between 7am and 6pm; the fare is around TT$4, though you'll pay more if you go off-route along Waterfall Road.

Mount St Benedict

Back on the EMR, past the busy town of Curepe, lies the crucifix-lined, serpentine St John's Road, the route to **Mount St Benedict Monastery**. Visible from the central plains, the white-walled, red-roofed buildings dominate the hillside. Established in 1912 by Benedictine monks fleeing religious persecution in Brazil, it's a great place to go for spectacular views, peace and quiet and a spot of afternoon tea at the neighbouring *Pax Guesthouse* (daily 3–6pm). Taxis for Mount St Benedict leave from the corner of St John's Road and the EMR (TT$3).

Past the junction with the Churchill Roosevelt Highway and the entrance to the **University of the West Indies St Augustine Campus** lies Caura Royal Road, the turn-off for **Caura Valley** – one of the most popular **picnic** and **hiking spots** in the East–West Corridor.

Practicalities

Though this area is within thirty minutes' drive of Port of Spain, if you wish to find accommodation outside the hustle of the capital, there are two excellent options for those seeking a more peaceful base from which to explore. **Pax Guesthouse**, Mount St Benedict (Ⓣ & Ⓕ868/662-4084, Ⓦwww.paxguesthouse.com; ❹), is perched adjacent to the monastary and commands magnificent views across central Trinidad. Along with an atmosphere of complete peace, the spacious rooms are furnished with antiques, some have private bathrooms and numbers 1 through 7 have great views across the central plains. The rates include breakfast and a delicious three-course evening meal (TT$100 plus for non-guests). Surrounded by rainforest, the guesthouse is a popular spot with bird lovers – hummingbirds are seen frequently on the verandah – and is an excellent, if not better alternative, to the Asa Wright Centre, for it is far less busy. The **Caribbean Lodge**, 32 St Augustine Circular Rd (Ⓣ868/645-2937, Ⓕ645-2937, Ⓔthecaribbeanlodge@hotmail.com; ❶), is a supremely friendly and attractive place adjacent to UWI campus. Their rooms are not fancy, catering mainly for visiting students, but they are functional and very clean, with shared or private shower; some have A/C and kitchenette. There's an area for washing clothes, and meals are available. It's the best bargain to be found in the East–West Corridor. Both accommodation options are convenient for the airport, which is just a ten- to fifteen-minute drive away.

Lopinot

Further east and easily missed is Arouca, notable only as the point where you turn off the EMR onto snaking Lopinot Road for an eight-kilometre drive to **Lopinot**. This pretty hamlet is best known for the **Lopinot complex**, a former cocoa estate that has been transformed into a beautiful, secluded picnic spot (daily 6am–6pm; free). Settled by the **Comte de Lopinot**, a planter who fled Haiti following the 1791 revolution, the estate house has been carefully restored, complete with a small **museum** dedicated to the culture of local residents. The community – mainly of Spanish, African and Amerindian descent – has spawned some of Trinidad's finest parang players; they can be heard at Christmas and the annual harvest festival on May 17. The route taxi fare from Arouca to Lopinot is TT$3; cars are fairly frequent (Mon–Sat 5am–6pm), but the service is reduced on Sundays.

Arima

Past Arouca, the EMR takes on a more rural aspect, wreathing through Cleaver Woods up to **Arima.** Named Naparima by the Amerindians who were the first to settle in the area, it has a far deeper history than its commercial facade would suggest. The town is home to what's left of Trinidad's **Carib** community – most of whom live around the crucifix-strewn **Calvary Hill**. The Santa Rosa Carib Community Association, formed in 1974 to look after their interests, has its headquarters on Paul Mitchell Street, behind the cemetery, and sells good-quality tradi-

tional Amerindian craft such as woven baskets or carved calabashes. Apart from the **Santa Rosa** festival – a combination of Catholic and Carib celebration, held during the last week in August – the only other compelling reason to stop in Arima is the fabulous open-air **market**, which is liveliest on Fridays and is a great opportunity to view local life and vegetables. As the region's **main transport hub**, maxis to Sangre Grande (TT$3), Manzanilla (TT$3), Toco (TT$7), Mayaro (TT$7) and Grande Riviere (TT$15) leave from Raglan Street and Broadway, whilst maxis to Port of Spain (TT$4) leave from the northern end of St Joseph Street. **Taxis** to Sangre Grande (TT$4) and Valencia (TT$2) leave from the roundabout, and taxis to Port of Spain ($TT5) can be caught on Broadway. Alternatively, catch the ECS **bus** to the capital outside the courthouse on Hollis Avenue ($TT4).

Once past the outskirts of Arima, a turn-off at the WASA Guanapo Waterworks sign leads to the **Heights of Guanapo Road**. This is a fantastic hiking area, but not a place to explore without a **guide**; Laurence Pierre is recommended (Ⓣ868/634-4284). The breathtaking **Guanapo Gorge**, the **La Laja** and **Sombasson waterfalls** are here – a vine-wreathed deep channel, a twenty-metre and a three-tiered fifty-metre cascade respectively – and you can see them all in a day, though you'll need to be pretty fit.

The Northeast Tip

Stretching from **Matura** in the east to **Matelot** in the north, the rugged coastline of Trinidad's **Northeast Tip** is a perfect escape from the bustle of the capital and the north–west corridor. At least a three-hour drive from Port of Spain to Matelot, the region seems suspended in a time warp; people and houses are few and far between and an air of hypnotic quiet pervades. The residents have the only community radio station on the island – Radio Toco 106.7 FM – which is great for giving you a taste of local life. **Farming** and **fishing** are the mainstays of the economy, and you'll lose count of the signs advertising shark oil, saltfish and sea moss for sale.

To explore the Northeast Tip easily you'll need your own car. Though there is a rural **bus** service (TT$8) – with buses concentrated at peak periods – and the occasional **maxi** and **taxi** (TT$6–20), service is somewhat sporadic; all leave from Sangre Grande – fifteen kilometres southeast of Valencia and accessible by public transport from Port of Spain and Arima. The quickest way by **car** from Port of Spain is to take the Churchill Roosevelt Highway, turn left when it ends, and then right onto the quiet portion of the EMR to Valencia, from where the Valencia Road swings north to the Toco coast.

After passing through the quiet town of Valencia and the one-street town of **Matura**, you reach the prime nesting sites of **leatherback turtles**. If you arrive during laying season (March–Aug), you'll need a permit to visit the beaches at night. Check with the offices of **Nature Seekers Incorporated** on the main road; they have trained guides. Past Matura, the Toco Road meets the east coast for the first time. The first safe place to swim is a beach just past the tiny village of **Salybia.** Opposite the entrance to the beach is the clearly signposted **Rio Seco waterfall trail** – a pleasant one-hour walk and the route to one of the area's more spectacular **waterfalls** (known locally as Salybia Waterfall), an eight-metre cascade surrounded by bathing pools. Approximately fifteen kilometres past Salybia is the village of Cumana, home to the last **petrol station** before Matelot (Mon–Sat 8.30am-6pm, Sun 8.30am–noon).

Toco and Galera Point

The largest town in the area, **TOCO**, is a proud, close-knit community with the highest concentration of Baptists in the Caribbean. Though there are often-mooted suggestions to build a ferry terminal to Tobago here, so far the village has been left in peace. As you enter the town, Galera Road strikes off to the right; this is where the **Toco Folk Museum** (open during school hours 8am–3.30pm, or ring ☎868/670-8261; TT$3, TT$2 children), located in the Toco Composite School, is based. A fascinating local project highlighting local history, the small museum houses Amerindian artefacts, snakeskins, butterflies and household items, including a gramophone and some rare 78rpm calypso records, which can be played if especially requested. The road continues to a good **beach** and **Galera Point**, the island's extreme eastern tip. Adjacent to the lighthouse is a windblown, rocky bluff, known as Fishing Rock, an atmospheric place where the Caribbean Sea and Atlantic collide in a swirl of aquamarine and shimmering slate froth. Standing on the rock you feel as if you are on the edge of the world, which is how a group of rebellious Amerindians must have felt in 1699 when they leapt to their deaths here rather than be killed by their Spanish slave-masters.

Past Toco, the road becomes **Paria Main Road**, running perilously close to the cliffs, where huge waves crash onto a wild and rugged coast. At the next village, **Sans Souci**, is a safe beach and the island's **surfing** capital – a regular venue for competitions.

Grande Riviere

One of the most appealing villages on the Toco coast, **Grande Riviere**, is also the only place in the area with any kind of tourist infrastructure. The beautiful beachside *Mount Plaisir Estate* **hotel** (see opposite) has spurred local residents to open up **guesthouses**, but development has remained low-key. Local people tend to be incredibly welcoming, often throwing parties for leaving guests.

The village boasts a superlative **beach**, famous for nesting **leatherback turtles** – it's common for 150 or more to lay simultaneously here in season. Local residents have formed the Grande Riviere Environmental Awareness Trust, to guard against poachers and provide guides (ask for Francisco or Carlos Chance at the *Mount Plaisir Estate* hotel; TT$18, children TT$10). As well as the beach there are hosts of **waterfalls** and **river walks**, and also excellent **birdwatching** – including the rare piping guan. Most guides work through the hotel; it's best to ask here for a reputable one. As for village life and entertainment, most of the action occurs at the *Mount Plaisir Estate* hotel, where the **bar** is everyone's favourite liming spot.

The road past Grande Riviere is passable, but only just. Apart from the popular swimming spot, Shark River, there's little reason to continue, and the road soon ends at the tiny fishing hamlet of Matelot.

Practicalities

Grande Riviere may be small but it has the best **hotel** in Trinidad. *Mount Plaisir Estate* (☎868/670-8381, Ⓕ670-0057, Ⓦwww.mtplaisir.com; ④) is by far the loveliest place to stay if you can afford it. The *Estate* overflows with easy style – the wooden rooms, decorated with handcrafted furniture, beautiful paintings and wall hangings, sleep four to six people – ask for one that opens directly onto the beach. There is an excellent restaurant on site that equals the best in Port of Spain. Food served includes home-made bread, local-style meat, fish and imaginative vegetarian options; expect to pay in excess of TT$150 for a three-course meal. They will also collect you from the airport. For those on a more limited budget, *McEachnie's Haven*, at Bristol and Thomas streets (☎868/670-1014 or 642-0477, Ⓔmchaven80@tstt.net.tt; ③), makes up in friendliness for what it lacks in style. A recent addition to the village, this yellow guesthouse has homely, though basic rooms sleeping up to four, with fans, mosquito nets and en-suite bathroom. The owner, Ingrid, cooks delicious meals on request for both guests and non-guests (TT$50–70), and as her children are tour guides and her husband, Eric, is a well-known local musician, a stay here makes for a great opportunity to get to know a local family, and the beach is just five minutes away.

20.3

Central and south Trinidad

Central and south Trinidad encompasses an astonishing variety of landscapes. The **west coast** is gritty and industrialized, punctuated by the odd oasis of calm such as the **Caroni Swamp** – home of the scarlet ibis – and Trinidad's busy second city, **San Fernando**. On the **east coast**, there are the stunning **Manzanilla** and **Mayaro beaches**, both lined with coconut palms and still undiscovered by the tourist trade, and inland sits the protected **Nariva Swamp**, home of endangered species such as the **manatee** (sea cows). In contrast to the northern east–west corridor, the central and southern regions of Trinidad are populated predominantly by people of Indian descent; watch out for Hindu temples, flags and Indian delicacies along the roadside.

Transport is no problem along the west coast; most towns are easily accessible from the **Uriah Butler–Solomon Hochoy Highway**, which runs from Port of Spain to San Fernando. Rural areas inland and the south and southwest coast can be more of a problem, however – **maxis** and **taxis** take long circular routes and the absence of road signs can make driving confusing.

Accommodation in the region is minimal, with most hotels geared more towards oil-industry personnel than to tourists. **Host homes** are your best bet, and an excellent way of meeting local people; contact the Bed and Breakfast Co-Operative Society (see p.725). Most of the region, however, can be reached from Port of Spain in a day trip, unless you plan to spend time on the south and south-eastern coast. **Restaurants** and **nightlife** are very limited in the region, though there are plenty of **fast-food places** serving cheap, filling meals, especially Indian and Chinese food, while the many small **bars** and **rum shops** provide friendly conversation and a good night out. In central Trinidad there are a few high-class **restaurants** at the **Grand Bazaar Mall** – at the junction of the Uriah Butler and Churchill Roosevelt Highways – *Apsara* is especially good, serving high-quality Indian food. An exclusive place, it lies opposite the Imperial Garden; expect to pay at least TT$150 for a meal (Mon–Sat 11am–11pm). In the south restaurants, hotels and entertainment are clustered in San Fernando. Recommended establishments are listed in the text.

Central Trinidad

The predominance of Indian culture is immediately noticeable upon joining the Uriah Butler–Solomon Hochoy Highway, as the twelve-metre statue of Swami Vivekananda presiding over the **National Council of Indian Culture** complex, looms into view on the eastern side of the road.

Caroni Swamp and Bird Sanctuary

Less than an hour's drive from Port of Spain is Trinidad's most heavily promoted environmental attraction, the **Caroni Swamp and Bird Sanctuary**. This is the only roosting place on the island of the **scarlet ibis**, the national bird sporting an amazingly bright red plumage. The swamp is home to 157 species of birds and caimans, snakes and silky anteaters; all can be observed in the water and the surrounding mangroves. It's a quiet, mysteriously beautiful place, and well worth a

Phagwa

A lighthearted celebration of the arrival of spring, the Hindu Holi festival – known in Trinidad as Phagwa (pronounced "pag-wah") – is held in March. Upbeat and carnivalesque, Phagwa celebrations are massive outdoor parties that represent a symbolic triumph of light over darkness. The festivities include the singing of devotional folk songs called **chowtals**, but the main focus is an intense fuchsia-pink dye known as **abir**, which is squirted from plastic bottles over participants wearing white. Games add to the fun; adults participate in **makhan chor**, where teams form a human pyramid in order to grab a suspended flag, while children compete in roti eating contests. **Chaguanas** hosts one of the largest celebrations in Trinidad, in an open space off Longdenville Old Road. There are other gatherings at Aranguez Savannah in San Juan and at Couva, but none is widely publicized – contact TIDCO for the exact dates (ⓣ868/623-6022).

visit. Tours, taken at dusk on small wooden boats, are available (TT$60/US$10), leaving daily 4–4.30pm and lasting two and a half hours; advance booking is advisable. Contact Nanan (ⓣ868/645-1305) or James (ⓣ868/662-7356) to book.

It is not possible to get close to the birds' roosting spot without disturbing them, so bring binoculars or a powerful zoom lens, or you'll see little more than red specks against the dark green foliage. Leave Port of Spain at 3pm if you're driving, and if catching public transport take **maxis** or **route taxis** bound for Chaguanas; ask them to drop you at the Caroni Swamp exit, from where it's a five-minute walk. Lashings of insect repellent are a must during the rainy season, when mosquitoes go on the offensive.

The Waterloo Temple

Past the sprawling settlement of **Chaguanas** – the birthplace of the Nobel Prize winner **V.S. Naipaul** and site of the annual Phagwa celebration (see box) – and onto the Southern Main Road, you'll pass a selection of small settlements and grandiose, crumbling estate houses. About a kilometre south of Chase Village, Orange Field Road cuts west off the Southern Main Road through the **Orange Valley Estate** to join the signposted Waterloo Road down to the sea. This superb drive through sugarcane plantations culminates half a kilometre down the road where, as you emerge at the sea, you'll be greeted by a remarkable scene. The gleaming white, onion-domed **Waterloo Temple** stands on a pier overlooking the waters of the Gulf of Paria at high tide, or extensive mudflats at low tide. The funeral pyres at the water's edge and the flags (*jhandes*) flapping in the breeze all contribute to the impression that you are standing by the River Ganges rather than on a Caribbean island.

Built in 1947 by **Seedas Sadhu**, an Indian labourer, the temple is a testament to one man's struggle against colonial bureaucracy; refused planning permission on land, he decided to build in the sea, using his bicycle to carry the foundation rocks into the water. Anyone can enter the temple, provided they remove their shoes first. Opening hours are Saturday and Sunday from 7am to 7pm, though the grounds are open daily between 7am and 7pm. To get to the temple by **public transport**, take a route taxi from Chaguanas to the start of Orange Field Road (TT$2–3), where you pick up another taxi (TT$3) to the temple.

Pointe-a-Pierre Wildfowl Trust

After Waterloo the Southern Main Road winds its way through Trinidad's economic heartland, an area of smoke-belching sugar and oil refineries. Past Claxton Bay, an industrial suburb cloaked in dust from the nearby cement factory, stands a stunning oasis of nature, located on the extensive grounds of the Petrotrin Oil Refinery. The **Pointe-a-Pierre Wildfowl Trust** consists of 250,000 square metres of attractively

landscaped grounds that are home to many **rare species of bird**, including the wild Muscovy duck, the red-billed whistling duck and white-cheeked pintail. Some of the rarer birds, including scarlet ibis, are caged to allow breeding programmes to continue. The Trust may be viewed **by appointment** only, to ensure that the birds are not scared away by overvisiting. To **drive** to the Trust from Port of Spain or San Fernando, leave the Uriah Butler–Solomon Hochoy Highway at the Gasparillo exit and follow the signs to the Petrotrin Oil Refinery. On **public transport**, take a Port of Spain–San Fernando maxi, route taxi or bus, and get out at the Gasparillo exit, from where the refinery is a two-minute walk. Once inside, it's another fifteen-minute walk to the Trust. The best time to visit is before 11am or after 3pm. Opening hours are Monday to Friday 8am–5pm, Saturday and Sunday 10am–4pm; contact Molly Gaskin (Ⓣ868/628-4145) or the office (Ⓣ868/658-4200 ext 2512, Ⓦwww.trinwetlands.org) forty-eight hours in advance for an appointment. Admission, including guided tour, is TT$5.

Manzanilla

In refreshing contrast to the smoggy, industrialized central west coast, central Trinidad's east coast features nothing more than miles of sand and endless coconut palms. South of Sangre Grande, the largest town in the east, the **coast** is dominated by the **Cocal**, 24km of unbroken sand, lined by grove upon grove of swaying coconut palms. The air is raucous with the calls of the **red-chested macaws**, and street vendors line the road selling crabs, cascadura, armoured catfish and watermelon, when in season. So far, the owners of the east coast coconut estates have declined to sell the property to hotel developers, and Manzanilla beach and the protected Nariva Swamp retain their idyllic seclusion. Deserted during the week, but popular at weekends, take care while swimming as the undercurrents can be dangerous. There are changing facilities at the northern end (daily 10am–6pm; TT$1). If you're planning to visit Manzanilla for the Ash Wednesday or Easter beach parties, try to get there early – it's not unknown for the traffic jams to start as far back as Valencia, some twenty kilometres to the northwest. The only hotel directly on the beach along this stretch of coast is the well-signposted **Calypso Inn** (Ⓣ868/668-5113, Ⓕ668-5116, Ⓔonthebeach@1funplace.com; ③). Beautifully located on the sands between Manzanilla and Matura, their smart double rooms have A/C, TV and a balcony overlooking the sea. There is also a bar and restaurant on site.

Nariva Swamp

The internationally recognized wetland of **Nariva Swamp** covers fifteen square kilometres behind the coconut estates along the east coast. The area is made up of agricultural land as well as reed-fringed marshes, mangroves and **Bush Bush Island**, bordered by palmiste and moriche palms and covered in hardwood forest. The swamp's unique freshwater ecosystem harbours large concentrations of rare **wildlife**, with some 58 species of mammals, 37 species of reptiles, and 171 species of birds. The swamp is also home to 92 species of mosquito, so remember to bring your insect repellent.

Nariva is the only place in Trinidad to see the threatened **manatee** or sea cow, a peculiar elephantine mammal that can grow up to three metres in length and weigh over 900 kilograms, and which feeds off water hyacinth, moss and waterlilies. The swamp is also an excellent place to view caimans, freshwater turtles, red howler monkeys, white-fronted capuchin monkeys, silky anteaters, opposums, porcupines and a wide variety of birds including savannah hawks, dicksissels, orange-winged parrots and the yellow-capped Amazon parrot. Its most alarming inhabitants must be the **anacondas**, capable of growing up to ten metres long; they're the heaviest reptiles in the world, and the largest in the Americas.

It's nigh impossible to visit the swamp independently, though you can take a peek by driving up Kernaham Trace – a small road at the southern end of Manzanilla beach leading to the tiny settlement of Kernaham village. To get a substantial look, you'll need a guide and permit to enter the swamp proper. South East Eco Tours (☎868/644-1072) offers excellent day trips (US$35–80) involving hikes, boat rides, lunch with local residents and trained guides from the local community. Caribbean Discovery Tours (☎868/624-7281) offers an equally good Nariva trip, with a walk through Bush Bush island (US$50–100). If you're a serious ornithologist, opt for the excellent birding tours offered by Rooks Tours that start at US$50 (☎868/622-8826).

The south

Geographically, Trinidad's **south** presents a mirror image of the north, with the low ridge of the forested Southern Range as its spine and a peninsula jutting out towards Venezuela. That's as far as the comparison goes, though, as apart from Trinidad's second city, **San Fernando**, the region is the most sparsely populated area of the island. Although many of the inhabitants still earn a living from agriculture, the economy is based around **oil**. Ironically, this is what has left the region so unspoilt; the petroleum business leases large expanses of forest from the government that remain largely undeveloped, providing homes for wildlife reserves and endangered species such as the ocelot. Tourists rarely venture this far south – those who do make a beeline for the **Pitch Lake**, the only potted attraction in these parts. Still, **Cedros** and **Erin** are picturesque areas, and **Mayaro** offers up a gorgeous swathe of sand on the southeast coast – a popular holiday resort with Trinidadians. Consequently there are few facilities for visitors and **transport** is tortuous, especially to the south coast. **Beaches** in the south are best visited during the dry season (Dec–May) as from June to November they are polluted by brackish water and litter swept downstream.

San Fernando

Nestled against the base of the bizarrely shaped **San Fernando Hill**, the city of **SAN FERNANDO** is the most striking in Trinidad. Usually referred to as the industrial capital of Trinidad and Tobago, it has an old-fashioned charm helped in large part by the old winding lanes studded with charming gingerbread buildings. It is also the best place in the region to find accommodation, good restaurants and lively entertainment. Far quieter than Port of Spain and with few tourists, you may be overwhelmed by local attention, although there is no need to feel intimidated: it is entirely well meant. There are no buses or maxis travelling within San Fernando, and **route taxis** charge a flat fare of TT$2 for most journeys, with an added dollar or two for off-route drops; you can hail one on any main street.

Most of the historical sights and shops are located on and around the **Harris Promenade**, a broad, elegant boulevard running west from the foot of the hill. At 200 metres high, San Fernando Hill – flattened with steep protruding points, the result of quarrying activity – overshadows the town centre and makes for a pleasant recreation area with picnic tables, a childrens' playground and panoramic views.

High Street is San Fernando's main shopping street, lined with clothes stores and street vendors. At its southern end is **Happy Corner**, location of a few renovated colonial buildings and **King's Wharf**, where you can buy fresh snapper, kingfish and shark at the local fish market. On **Carib Street** stands the city's oldest building, the **Carib House** – an eighteenth-century Spanish colonial building – while neighbouring **Coffee Street** is home to many of the south's **steel bands**, including the highly acclaimed **Fonclaire**. San Fernando is the hub of the south's transport system; from here you can catch maxis, buses and taxis to Port of Spain, La Brea, Princes Town and Point Fortin.

Accommodation

Most **accommodation** in the city caters for visiting oil-industry personnel, so expect a more business than holiday atmosphere.

Royal Hotel 46–54 Royal Rd ⓣ&ⓕ868/652-3924, ⓦwww.royalhoteltt.com. Comfortable and reasonably priced for facilities: bright rooms have A/C, cable TV, phone, fridge, jacks for internet access and en-suite bathrooms. There's a breezy open-air restaurant on site. ❹

Tradewinds Hotel 38 London St ⓣ & ⓕ868/652-9463, ⓦwww.tradewindshotel.net. Friendly place in a quiet suburb, though not as good value as the *Royal*. Smallish rooms have A/C, cable TV, fridge, minibar, kettle and en-suite bathrooms. There's a popular restaurant/bar on site, and breakfast is included in the rates. ❹

Eating and entertainment

San Fernando is definitely the centre of the region's **dining scene**: even if you're not staying in the city you'll inevitably end up eating at one of the city's fine restaurants and if you're looking for a little more entertainment than the local rum shop, the city is the only place to be.

Belle Bagai 20 Gransaul St. Simple menu of snacks – wontons, fish and chips, burgers – as well as more substantial steaks or fish dishes, average price per head TT$50–100. Good service and relaxed atmosphere in a pretty, old colonial house. Mon–Sat 3pm–late.

Club Celebs Top Level, Gulf City Shopping Complex ⓣ868/652-7641. The most popular nightspot in the south – a modern club and sports bar playing a wide variety of music to a young crowd. Entrance fee varies. Mon–Thurs & Sun 3.30–11pm, Fri & Sat 11am–4am.

Kolumbo Restaurant 34 Sutton St ⓣ868/653-7684. International cuisine with gourmet burgers and patés. Set in a restored colonial building, this stylish restaurant is very romantic at night, with live piano music on the upper level. Also serves afternoon tea. Price for a starter and main TT$70–100. Tues–Fri 4pm–midnight, Sat 6pm–midnight.

Nam Fong Lotus Restaurant 91–93 Cipero St ⓣ868/652-3356. Serves huge Chinese lunches and dinners for TT$25–70. A relaxing, comfy and more upmarket atmosphere than the usual plastic tables. Mon–Sat 10am–10pm.

Naparima Bowl 19 Paradise Pasture ⓣ868/657-8770. Comfy theatre and outdoor amphitheatre hosting plays, touring from Port of Spain, also big calypso and steel-band events. Ticket prices vary.

Tree House 38 London St ⓣ868/653-8733. Pleasant, friendly place inside the *Tradewinds Hotel* – a popular local haunt on a plant-decked balcony overlooking the city. Food is reliably good and the menu varied, from crab backs and shrimp bruschetta to seafood, steaks and Mexican and Cajun dishes; expect to pay TT$100 and upwards per person. Open very early for local and international breakfasts; reservations recommended for dinner. Mon–Thurs 5am–11pm, Fri–Sun 5am–11am.

Around San Fernando

Trinidad's **southwest peninsula**, known locally as the "deep south", offers a mix of gritty oil towns and marvellous drives through sleepy backwaters, forested hills, and teak and coconut plantations, down to beaches of soft brown sand backed by red-earth cliffs and lapped by calm seas. The larger towns, such as **Point Fortin** and the **Siparia-Fyzabad conurbation**, revolve around the oil industry and provide little interest to the passing visitor. The south coast, though, has a variety of excellent, deserted beaches at **Cedros** and **Erin,** while in the south east, **Guayaguayare** and **Mayaro** beaches are popular with Trinidadian holiday-makers – quiet during the week but busy on weekends and public holidays. If you're **driving** to Mayaro from Port of Spain, the quickest route is via the Churchill Roosevelt Highway to Valencia, through Sangre Grande and down the east coast via Manzanilla. This is also the quickest way by **public transport** – take a maxi to Arima, then one to Sangre Grande, and then one down to Mayaro. If you're coming from San Fernando and the west coast, drive east along the Manahambre, Naparima and Mayaro roads. Maxis go from San Fernando to Princes Town; change here for a maxi to Mayaro. There are few places to stay on the south coast – most are basic beach houses advertised in the local press. **Azee's Guest House**, 3.5-mile marker Guayaguayare Rd (ⓣ868/630-4619, ⓕ630-9140, ⓔazees@tstt.net.tt; ❷), is a small, friendly hotel just two minutes' walk from Guayaguayare beach. All rooms have A/C, cable TV, telephone, fridge and en-suite bathrooms, and there's a homey bar on site as well as a restaurant, good for meals even if you're not a guest. Popular with Trinidadian holiday-makers during school holidays, it is best to book ahead.

The Pitch Lake

Roughly 25km southwest of San Fernando lies the **Pitch Lake**, location of some of the world's finest-quality asphalt. The popular tourist attraction is well signposted 1.5km south of La Brea on the SMR. Locals may claim it as the eighth wonder of the world, but to the sightseer it bears a remarkable resemblance to the wrinkly hide of an elephant. It is a genuine curiosity, however, as there are only three such lakes in the world, the other two being in Los Angeles (Rancho La Brea) and Venezuela (Guanaco). Five to six million years ago, asphaltic oil flowed into a huge mud volcano, developing over time into the asphalt that is now extracted from the lake. The material is used to pave roads all over the world, including Pall Mall leading to Buckingham Palace in London, though the poor local village has yet to profit from this resource on their doorstep. Authorized guides operate from the main booth (TT$30), and if you plan on touring wear shoes with low heels and be careful not to let the pitch touch your clothes – it is a nightmare to clean.

20.4

Tobago

An elongated oval of just 41 by 14 kilometres, **TOBAGO** features astonishing riches including deserted beaches, pristine coral reefs and a wealth of lush rainforest – the island really does feel as if it's the last of the "unspoilt Caribbean". Though tourism has taken root with breathtaking speed – 40,000 people now visit the island each year – Tobago is hardly the typically jaded resort island. There are few all-inclusives, celebrations, such as the Easter **goat races**, are attended by more Tobagonians than tourists, and local culture is honoured at the annual **Heritage Festival** each August. Nevertheless, tourism *is* changing Tobago. Helping hands sharing the labour of pulling in seine fishing nets are still called by a resonant toot on a conch shell, but nowadays the fishermen often wait until they've captured an audience before hauling the catch onto the sand. And the African drumming that forms a major part of local **Orisha** and **Spiritual Baptist** ceremonies is now the soundtrack of many a hotel floorshow.

Physically, Tobago is breathtaking; heavy industry is confined to Trinidad, so the beaches are clean and the landscape left largely to its own devices. The flat coral and limestone plateau of the southwest – the **Lowlands** – is the island's most heavily developed region, with hotels clustered around powder-sand beaches such as **Pigeon Point** and **Mount Irvine**, home to excellent **surfing** (best during November to February). The tourist clamour is kept in check by the capital, **Scarborough**, a picturesque port town tumbling down a lighthouse-topped hillside.

The island's rugged **windward** (south) **coast** is lined with appealing fishing villages; **Speyside** and **Charlotteville** in the remote eastern reaches have some of the finest **coral reefs** in the southern Caribbean and **scuba diving** is a burgeoning industry. Tobago is an excellent and inexpensive place to learn to dive, and there's plenty of challenging drift diving for the more experienced, while the many reefs within swimming distance of the beaches make for fantastic **snorkelling**. The **leeward** (north) coast has Tobago's finest beaches; some, like **Englishman's Bay**, are regularly deserted, while at **Castara**, **Parlatuvier** and **Bloody Bay**, you'll share the sand with local fishermen.

The landscape of the eastern interior rises steeply forming the **Main Ridge** – the mountains sheltering the **Forest Reserve**, the oldest protected rainforest in the western hemisphere. Ornithologists and naturalists flock in for the **bird** and **animal** life that flourishes here; David Attenborough filmed parts of his celebrated *Trials of Life* series at **Little Tobago**, a solitary seabird sanctuary off the coast of Speyside. For more casual visitors, the squawking, chirruping forest offers plenty of opportunities for birdwatching or a splash in the icy **waterfalls**.

One point worth making is that Tobago's close-knit community keeps the island very safe – especially outside the Crown Point area. Ignore the warnings of all-inclusive hotels, which encourage tourists to stay on site claiming that Tobago is dangerous. The best food, entertainment and scenic areas are outside the hotel complexes, so be adventurous, explore and keep the locals in business.

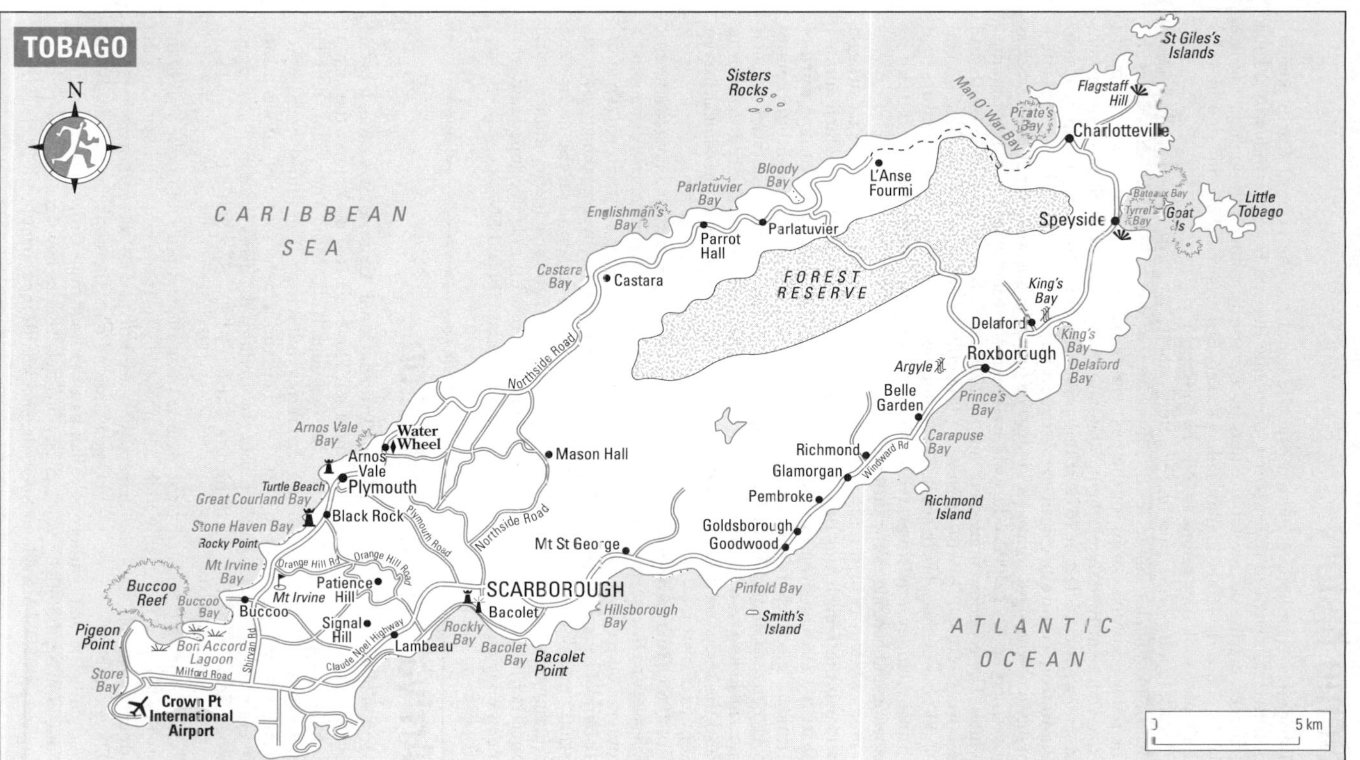
TOBAGO
N
CARIBBEAN SEA
ATLANTIC OCEAN
St Giles's Islands
Sisters Rocks
Flagstaff Hill
Man O' War Bay
Pirate's Bay
Charlotteville
Bloody Bay
Parlatuvier Bay
L'Anse Fourmi
Bateaux Bay
Little Tobago
Englishman's Bay
Parlatuvier
Speyside
Tyrrel's Bay
Goat Is
Parrot Hall
FOREST RESERVE
Castara Bay
Castara
King's Bay
Delaford
King's Bay
Delaford Bay
Roxborough
Argyle
Northside Road
Belle Garden
Prince's Bay
Arnos Vale Bay
Water Wheel
Arnos Vale
Mason Hall
Richmond
Windward Rd
Carapuse Bay
Turtle Beach
Plymouth
Glamorgan
Great Courland Bay
Pembroke
Richmond Island
Black Rock
Plymouth Road
Stone Haven Bay
Northside Road
Goldsborough
Rocky Point
Mt St George
Goodwood
Mt Irvine Bay
Orange Hill Rd
Orange Hill Road
Patience
Buccoo Reef
Buccoo Bay
Mt Irvine
Hill
SCARBOROUGH
Pinfold Bay
Buccoo
Bacolet
Hillsborough Bay
Smith's Island
Pigeon Point
Signal Hill
Rockly Bay
Bon Accord Lagoon
Shirvan Rd
Claude Noel Highway
Lambeau
Bacolet Bay
Bacolet Point
Store Bay
Milford Road
Crown Pt International Airport
5 km

Some history

Tobago has been hotly contested over the centuries. The original **Carib** population fiercely defended their *Tavaco* (the name derived from the Indian word for tobacco), driving off several attempts by European colonists throughout the late 1500s and early 1600s. English sailors staked Britain's claim in 1580, but in 1658 the Dutch took over, calling it "Nieuw Vlissingen".

Declared a no-man's-land in 1684 under the treaty of Aix La Chapelle, French, British and Dutch colonists lived fairly peaceably alongside free Africans, slaves and the remnants of the Caribs for the next eighty-odd years. But a French attempt to seize control in 1648 shook the neutral status and worried Britain enough for them to send a powerful fleet in 1672, taking possession of the island with swift precision. **Plantation culture** began in earnest soon after and the island rapidly became a highly efficient sugar, cotton and indigo factory. Africans were imported to work as slaves, and by 1772, 3000-odd were sweating it out under less than three hundred whites. The economy flourished, and by 1777, the island's eighty or so estates had exported 160,000 gallons of rum, 1,500,000lb of cotton, 5000lb of indigo and 24,000 hundredweights of sugar. The numerical might of the slave population led to many bloody **uprisings**, with planters doling out amputations and death by burning and hanging to the dissenters.

From 1781 to 1814, the island changed hands four times in a tit for tat struggle between the French and British, ending in British control, after which another phase of successful sugar production ensued. In 1899, Tobago was made a **ward** of Trinidad, effectively becoming the bigger island's poor relation with little control over her own destiny. With the collapse of the sugar industry, the black population, including **free Africans** who arrived in the mid-1800s, clubbed together to farm the land – the **"Len-Hand" system** – still celebrated in the annual harvest festivals.

In 1963, **Hurricane Flora** ravaged Tobago. In the restructuring programme that followed, attempts were made to diversify the economy, tentatively developing a tourist industry. By 1980, the island had her sovereignty partially restored when the **Tobago House of Assembly** (THA) was reconvened, with authority over the island's more mundane affairs. Nevertheless, with agriculture on the decline and tourism slowly becoming the main earner, the island's economic future is still uncertain; in 1998, Tobago was officially declared an underdeveloped and low-income region in order to qualify for aid from the UN and EU.

Arrival and information

Most people arrive via **Crown Point International Airport**, small enough to feel overwhelmed by the arrival of a single jet. There is a row of shops in the airport complex, among them a branch of the Republic Bank (Mon–Thurs 8am–3pm, Fri 8am–1pm & 3–5pm), useful for **currency exchange**. The tourist board office (daily 6am–9.30pm; ⓣ868/639-0509) is here too, a useful source of **information**. Internet access is also available, payable by credit card. There's also a small newsagent where local and Companion **phone cards** (TT$20, $30, $60, $100 + VAT) are sold.

Official **private taxis** advertise their rates on the taxi price list on the wall of the arrivals lounge. The rates are high, but not wildly so. If you're on a budget, cross the street and haggle with the drivers who are not part of the authorized system. There's an hourly shuttle bus between Crown Point (the stop's just outside the airport complex) and Scarborough (half past the hour from Crown Point and on the hour from Scarborough); you can buy bus tickets from newsagents. If you're heading towards Charlotteville or Speyside, check with the tourist board, as chartering a taxi is quite expensive and many hotels throw in free airport collection. Remember on your return journey all visitors must pay a TT$100 **departure tax**, in local currency.

If you're arriving by boat, you'll land in Scarborough docks; private and route taxi ranks are located at the docks entrance.

Getting around

Tobago's **public transport** system is slow and erractic, meaning **renting a car** is the best option if you're only on the island for a few days. Most of the international and local **car rental operators** are clustered around the airport; local operators tend to be cheaper but are less likely to offer 24-hour assistance. Sherman's (Ⓣ868/639-2292) is a recommended local operator, and amongst the internationals, Thrifty (Ⓣ868/639-8507) is reliable. Expect to leave a **deposit**, usually a credit card imprint; a notable exception is Auto Rentals (Ⓣ868/639-0644), which has one of the largest fleets in Tobago. **Scooters** are available from some beach outlets and cost approximately US$20 a day. **Motorbikes** are catching on fast and there are several places offering dirt bikes for about US$30 per day.

The blue-banded **maxi taxis** (see p.725) run only between Scarborough and Charlotteville. However, the **route taxi** network is extensive and convenient for short hops in the western portion of the island. If you're heading further afield, you'll need to travel into Scarborough, where the main taxi ranks are located by the docks.

Tobago's **buses** have greatly improved in recent years. From Scarborough, buses run along the windward coast to Charlotteville (6 daily; 4.30am–6.30pm, variable times). The leeward coast route extends from Scarborough to L'Anse Fourmi via Moriah, Castara, Englishman's Bay, Parlatuvier and Bloody Bay (6 daily, 4.30am–6.30pm, variable times). In the Lowlands, buses run from Scarborough to Mount Thomas via Les Coteaux and Golden Lane (8 daily, 5am–6pm, every two hours); they also go from Scarborough to Plymouth via Mount Irvine and Black Rock (5am–8pm, hourly). All tickets must be **pre-purchased** (fares range TT$2–8) and are available from shops in the airport complex and throughout the island.

For information on travel between Tobago and Trinidad, see p.725.

Organized tours

A multitude of tour companies offer rather sterile itineraries of Tobago's main sights costing US$55–70 per person; Classic Tours (Ⓣ868/639-9891, Ⓕ639-9892) and Sun Fun Tours (Ⓣ868/639-7461, Ⓕ639-7564, Ⓦwww.sunfuntour.com) are the best of the bunch. For custom-designed **hiking and wildlife tours**, Margaret Hinkson's Educatours (Ⓣ868/639-7422, Ⓔmagintob@hotmail.com) organizes excursions with local guides; prices start at US$65 for a guided trek through the rainforest and on to Argyll Waterfall (6hr), including lunch. Renowned naturalist David Rooks (Ⓣ868/639-4276, Ⓦwww.rooks-tobago.com) leads informed and professional tours to **Little Tobago** (US$65), Mark Puddy (Ⓣ868/639-4931) leads fabulous offbeat **hiking trips** to deserted beaches and waterfalls (US$25–40), and Tobago's only female taxi driver, Liz Lezama (Ⓣ868/639-2309 or 758-1748) offers an extensive island tour including lunch for US$60. Adventurous **sea safaris** aboard hobie cat mini-catamarans are available from Cool Runnings (Ⓣ868/639-6363, Ⓕ639-4755, Ⓦwww.outdoor-tobago.com; US$95–235), while popular boat **cruises** are offered by several operators; prices range from US$35 for a two-hour sunset trip to US$70 per person for a six- to eight-hour cruise.

Scuba diving and watersports

Tobago is one of the best **diving** spots in the southeastern Caribbean, internationally recognized for its exciting, though difficult, drift dives. The island's aquamarine seas are home to three hundred species of South Atlantic coral and a variety of spectacular multicoloured tropical fish. Tobago is best known for the enormous number of **manta rays** that are frequently encountered and the largest **brain coral** in the world. Speyside (see p.770) is known as "the Disneyland of diving", while Goat Island is popular for drift dives and Little Tobago is where many of the manta ray encounters occur. The island's **diving industry** was established in the 1980s and remains low-key, ensuring quiet dives, personal service and inexpensive rates. Prices for one to three dives are US$30–35 each; one-day resort courses US$55–65; five-day PADI open-water certification courses US$350–375; and advanced open water from US$225. Reliable operators include SubLime (ⓣ868/639-9642, ⓦwww.sublimescuba.com, ⓔsublime@tstt.net.tt), Proscuba (ⓣ868/639-7424, ⓦwww.diveguide.com/proscuba), Manta Dive Centre (ⓣ868/639-9969 or 9209, ⓔmantaray@tstt.net.tt, ⓦmantadive.com). Much of the exotic plant and fish life in Tobago's waters can also be seen **snorkelling**. Recommended sites include Pirate's Bay in Charlotteville, Arnos Vale, and Englishman's and Great Courland bays. Most dive operators rent out snorkelling equipment for US$10 a day, so note that if you plan to do plenty it's cheaper to bring your own.

Jetskis have yet to become a regular feature amid the surf (though you can rent them from R & Sea Divers Den on Pigeon Point, US$25 for 20min), while **kayaking** costs about US$10 an hour at Pigeon Point. Wild Turtle (ⓣ868/639-7936, ⓦwww.wildturtledive.com) and World of Watersports (ⓣ868/660-7234, ⓔinfo@worldofwatersports.com, ⓦwww.worldofwatersports.com) offer a variety of watersports including **water-skiing** and **inflatable bananas** (TT$80 for 15min), as well as **jet skiing** (TT$200 for 20min) and **windsurfing** (TT$200 for 60min). The most popular local **surfing** site is Mount Irvine beach – a well-kept secret, local surfers are trying to keep it that way; keen surfers should bring their own equipment as it's difficult to hire. Note that the water here is shallow and directly over coral reef, so surf fins can be badly damaged and no protective footwear is allowed to protect the reef from overeager surfers jumping in and damaging the coral.

Atmosphere varies from racy booze cruises to sedate sightseeing. Natural Mystic (ⓣ868/639-7245, ⓕ639-7888, ⓔmystic@tstt.net.tt) is the best boat operator. **Glass-bottom boat** tours of Buccoo Reef (US$20) leave from Store Bay, Pigeon Point and Buccoo.

Accommodation

Most of the island's **hotels** and **guesthouses** are concentrated in the tourist-oriented lowlands, meaning this is where you'll find the greatest choice and variety – from basic budget locally run rooms to lavish, luxurious hotel complexes. The upmarket hotels are clustered along the beaches between Buccoo and Plymouth, as are exclusive villas (costing US$110–600 per day, see p.725). There are a few excellent alternatives in the capital, while those wishing to spend time further afield – Castara, Speyside and Charlotteville – should book ahead as accommodation options are limited. The tourist board recommends a number of **host homes** in their standard accommodation listings booklet (available from offices worldwide; see p.725) – most rent at around US$35–55 per person, but you can often get a room for less than this, particularly in the off-season. The best way to find a good **B&B** is through Ms Miriam Edwards of the Tobago Bed and Breakfast Association (see p.725).

Blue Haven Bacolet Bay ⓣ868/660 7400, ⓕ660-7900, ⓦwww.bluehavenhotel.com. This recently restored historic hotel – former guests include Rita Hayworth – is the best luxury accommodation on the island. The lavish rooms have four-poster or sleigh beds, A/C, TV, minibar, phone and modern artwork, along with spacious bathrooms and a balcony overlooking stunning Bacolet Bay. There's a pool, mini-gym, spa and tennis court, and an excellent – though expensive – restaurant on site. Scarborough's a ten-minute walk away. 8–9

Blue Mango Second Bay Road, Castara ⓣ868/639-2060, ⓕ639-5414, ⓦwww.blue–mango.com. Simply furnished yet stylish one- and two-bedroom self-contained cottages with great bay views, cool breezes, well-equipped kitchens, mosquito nets and plenty of privacy. The owners also manage two cottages at nearby Little Bay and an old wooden house perched on a hill five minutes' walk from the beach. There's an excellent restaurant serving delicious local dishes on site as well. 4

Cholson Chalets Man O' War Bay, Charlotteville, Mount Pleasant ⓣ&ⓕ 639-8553. Completely charming green and white houses overlooking the beach at the Pirate's Bay end of town. The romantic, antiquated feel of the six simple rooms is supported by muslin curtains and wooden floors, fans, private bathroom, an optional maid service and a few kitchenettes; the upstairs flat is most appealing. Advance booking is recommended. 2–3

Hope Cottage Calder Hall Road, Fort George, Scarborough ⓣ868/639-2179. Set in a 100-year-old colonial building just before the hospital, this is one of the oldest guesthouses in Tobago and a great bargain. Rooms are plain with private bathroom and kitchenette, and there's also a three-bedroom cottage with shared kitchen on the two-acre grounds. 1

Indigo Pleasant Prospect, Stone Haven Bay ⓣ&ⓕ639-9635, ⓦhttp://homepage.eircom.net/~indigo. Nestled above the bar and restaurant of the same name, Caribbean colours and batiks decorate these basic but pleasant rooms which have A/C, mosquito nets, fridge, tea/coffee-making facilities and en- suite bathroom. Each has a balcony, some overlooking the beautiful Stone Haven Bay. A family room with TV is also available, and breakfast is included in the rates. 4

Kariwak Village Store Bay Local Road, PO Box 27, Scarborough ⓣ868/639-8442, ⓕ639-8441, ⓦwww.kariwak.co.tt. A jewel in the middle of bustling Crown Point. Accommodation is in thatched-roof cabanas furnished using local wood crafted on the premises; each has A/C and phone. Facilities include a pool, jacuzzi and fabulous restaurant/bar. The only downside is intermittent airport noise. 7

Man O' War Bay Cottages Man O' War Bay, c/o Pat Turpin, Charlotteville Estate ⓣ868/660-4327, ⓕ660-4328, ⓔpturpin@tstt.net.tt. Situated right on the bay in pretty landscaped gardens, the cottages are different shapes and sizes, with one to four bedrooms. All have fan, bathroom, hot water and kitchen, simple but attractive décor, books on the shelves, driftwood ornaments and an overwhelming feeling of peace. There's a small commissary on site and the maid/cook service is optional and costs extra. 4

Manta Lodge Main Road, PO Box 443, Scarborough ⓣ868/660-5268, ⓕ660-5030, in US ⓣ1-800/544-7631, ⓦwww.mantalodge.com. Located in Speyside opposite the bay, this hotel is colonial-style luxury catering for scuba enthusiasts. Standard rooms are small but stylish with ceiling fan and balcony; "superior" rooms provide more space and A/C, while the quirky attics have the lot plus a private sundeck on the roof. There's a good restaurant (breakfast included in the rates), pool and dive shop on site. 5–6

Mount Pelier Cottage Mount Pelier Crown Trace, Scarborough ⓣ868/639-4931, ⓔpuddy@tstt.net.tt. Unique and utterly fabulous home away from home in the host's self-built wooden house perched on Scarborough's hillside. These airy rooms (double, twin or single) have lattice windows, creative hand-carved décor and shared bathroom. Meals are served on a balcony overlooking the forest in the company of mot-mots, blue jays and bananaquits. Rates include excellent home-cooked breakfast, huge evening meals and the owner as personal guide and driver. 5–6

Richmond Great House Belle Garden ⓣ & ⓕ868/660-4467, ⓦwww.richmondgreathouse.com. An old plantation estate house with gorgeous colonial-style bedrooms with varnished wood floors and private bathrooms. There's a pool, tennis courts and restaurant on site. Rates include breakfast. 5

Speyside Inn Main Road, Speyside ⓣ & ⓕ868/660-4852, ⓦwww.caribinfo.com/speysideinn. Simple and beautifully styled inn with priceless bay views. The accommodation varies from a circular tower to octagonal corner rooms, but all have a bathroom, balcony and fan. There's an excellent restaurant on site (rates include breakfast) and good swimming is just a step away. 5–6

Sunshine Holiday Apartments Milford Road, Bon Accord ⓣ868/639-7482, ⓕ639-7495,

www.tobagointernet.com/sunshine. A ten-minute walk from Pigeon Point beach, these good-value rooms all have high ceilings, kitchenette, en-suite bathroom and porch, along with phones, A/C and cable TV. A pool is also available. 2

Two Seasons Shirvan Road, Pleasant Prospect, Stone Haven Bay 868/639-7713. Bargain accommodation set back from the road between Mount Irvine and Stone Haven beaches. Rooms are plain with wood floors, fan, mosquito net and a bed, but the atmosphere is friendly and meals are available from the restaurant downstairs. There's also a communal kitchen, lounge and bathroom. Guests must like animals as there are cats and dogs on the premises. 1

Eating and entertainment

Unlike Trinidad – where fetes and street food are a daily staple – Tobago is far more low-key. The best budget **food** options – including the sublime curry crab and dumpling – are available from the stalls on Store Bay. Most restaurants cater for the tourist trade, as most locals eat at home, and are therefore located in the Lowlands area, with pickings extremely slim further afield. If you're here in the slow season (April 15–Dec 15), bear in mind that many kitchens close at around 9pm. Apart from occasional concerts – look out for the posters – most **entertainment** on the island revolves around rum shops and the infamous Sunday School in Buccoo (see p.765).

Black Rock Cafe Grafton Road, Black Rock 868/639-7625. Popular open-air restaurant on the town's outskirts serving medium-priced soups, salads and fabulous fish dishes for lunch and daily dinner. Moderate prices, on average TT$70–100.

Blue Note Corner of Store Bay Local Road and Airport Road, by the police station, Crown Point. Appealing local-run and typically lively bar and restaurant serving up tasty fresh fish and a variety of local vegetables done with interesting twists. Average meal TT$70–100.

Café Petunia Old Milford Road, Little Rockly Bay, Lambeau. This delightful little café overlooking Little Rockly Bay has great atmosphere, excellent service and delicious home-made cakes, sandwiches, salads and cappuccinos. Expect to pay TT$10–50. Especially popular on Friday nights for happy hour (6–8.30pm) when the owner, Petunia, entertains her guests with soulful singing accompanied by a cuatro band. Open daily 10am–10pm.

Copra Tray Store Bay Local Road, Lowlands. Popular liming spots for locals and tourists with a dance floor, pool tables (TT$10 for 30min), an outdoor patio, a resident DJ and African drumming every Saturday night. International menu, good for a light lunch or a pre-drinking dinner of meatloaf, vegetable quiche, lasagne, calamari or pizza, served in a pleasant garden setting set back from the road. Prices $TT30–100. Watch out for the prowling menfolk. Closed Sun.

First Historical Café Windward Road, Studley Park. This eccentric, brightly painted café is a shrine to the island's history, every inch of wall being covered with handwritten accounts of Tobago's turbulent past alongside local anecdotes. The budget-priced food is good, though service painfully slow; breakfast is served from 9am, and you can have inexpensive salads, burgers and sandwiches for lunch.

Jemma's Treehouse Main Road, Speyside 868/660-4066. Popular with every island tour bus this place lurches crazily in the boughs of a tree, and the sea view is fantastic. Serves tasty creole-style food for reasonable prices; expect to pay $TT70–150. Breakfast (8.30–10am) is eggs, bacon or local fish dishes; lunch (available until 4pm) includes breadfruit or eggplant casserole, tannia fritters, fried plantain and salad; and dinner – fish, lobster and shrimp – is excellent, as are the puddings. No alcohol and closed Friday night and all day Saturday.

Kariwak Village Store Bay Local Road, Crown Point 868/639-8442. Fresh herbs and spices, inventive slants on local staples and genuine love in the kitchen makes this the best place to eat on the island. It's also one of the most expensive, with meals costing TT$150 plus. Breakfast and dinner menus are set – usually with a meat, fish or vegetarian option – and vegan food is available. Accompanied by live music, the Saturday night buffet is particularly good.

The Lush Shirvan Road, Mount Pleasant. Former site of Tobago's only horse-racing track, this popular pick-up joint is filled with locals and foreigners who come here for live music and DJs serving up ever-popular Jamaican and Trini tracks, alongside hip-hop, R&B and old-school soul. Tues–Sat 7pm–3am. Best night is Friday, when the crowd is at its biggest. Small cover charge.

Salsa Kitchen 8 Pumpmill Rd, Scarborough. Child-friendly, with an enticing menu of pizza, pasta, tapas and grilled food, along with fresh fruit juices and locally grown coffee for TT$70–150. At weekends the café livens up with nightly entertainment, music and dancing. Mon–Thurs 11am–10pm, Fri–Sun 11am–2pm & 6–10pm.

Shore Things Old Milford Road, Lambeau. A delightful café in a brightly painted old house with verandah overlooking the sea. Serves delicious light lunches, pizzas, pastelles, quiches and salads plus fresh pastries and fruit juices (TT$10–50). High-quality regional crafts and furniture are also on sale. Mon–Sat 10am–6pm.

Under the Mango Tree Black Rock. Lovely yellow-and-green café on the roadside serving sandwiches, pizza, salads and hot meals including coconut crusted chicken in peanut sauce, all freshly made, for under TT$70 and served inside or under the shady mango tree. Delicious fruit juices and amusing signs complete the atmosphere. Open 1–9.30pm for lunch and dinner. Closed Fri.

Lowlands: Crown Point to Arnos Vale

Tobago's flattest, most accessible portion is focused around a crowded five-kilometre stretch of **Milford Road** from the airport and Store Bay beach – a tiny area known as **Crown Point** – through Bon Accord, Canaan and Mount Pleasant, and 10km north along **Shirvan Road** to **Buccoo**, **Mount Irvine** and **Plymouth**. Usually lumped together as "the **Lowlands**", this is home to most of Tobago's residents as well as the vast majority of hotels, restaurants, nightclubs and the most popular beaches; you'll inevitably spend a lot of time here.

Tobago's most popular **beaches** are within shouting distance of the airport – **Store Bay** is a couple of minutes on foot, and **Pigeon Point** is about ten minutes further. **Buccoo** harbours two main attractions: an abundant **reef**, trawled by fleets of glass-bottom boats carrying snorkellers out to the coral, and the **Nylon Pool**, a metre-deep bathing spot on a sand bar in the middle of the bay. **Sunday School**, Tobago's biggest, brashest open-air party, is held in Buccoo as well. Potted attractions like the **Arnos Vale water wheel** complex and the **Kimme art exhibition**, as well as plenty of restaurants and the fabulous prospect of watching a **turtle** lay eggs metres from your hotel room, draw enthusiastic crowds of locals and tourists alike.

Store Bay to Pigeon Point

A two-minute walk from the airport brings you to the best and most popular place to swim in Crown Point, **Store Bay beach** (lifeguards 10am–6pm). Close to the main hotels and with excellent, inexpensive food and crafts available, the fine, off-white sand is a favourite with many people (including the notoriously unadventurous Trinidadian holiday-makers). Though the cove is fairly small, the crystal calm waters and family atmosphere make it excellent for children and for those with a keen interest in people-watching. Facilities include a car park, changing facilities (daily 10am–6pm; TT$1) with lockers (TT$10 per day), as well as a couple of bars blasting reggae and soca. Best of all are the row of stalls housing the famed cook-shops (8.30am–8.30pm) – *Miss Jean*'s and *Miss Esmie*'s are local institutions – a trip to Tobago would be incomplete without a plate of their **crab and dumplin'**. For a more expensive, though equally delicious meal, try *Kariwak Village* (see opposite), the best hotel and restaurant in the area. The purpose-built **craft shops** (8am–8pm)at Store Bay are one of the best places to buy souvenirs, including carved calabashes, leather sandals and batiks.

Running north from the airport past the entrance to Store Bay, Airport Road becomes Milford Road. Here, a left-hand turn (marked by the neon constellation of the *Golden Star* bar and restaurant) leads to **Pigeon Point beach** (daily 8am–7pm; TT$12), a picture-postcard Caribbean beach increasingly dominated by foreign sun-worshippers. The shoreline here – unlike the majority of Tobago's rugged beaches – is definitively Caribbean; powdery white sand and a turquoise sea lined with coconut palms. As an immensely popular strip that includes Tobago's most photographed pier – a weathered wooden boardwalk with a thatched roof hut at the end – it is one of the few places in the island to suffer from development. The shower blocks are shoddy, piles of beach chairs are rented at TT$5 a day and the fast-food chain *Pizza Boys* have ousted the local café (though it's sometimes possible to buy roti and the odd local dish on the beach). The groynes constructed to curtail beach erosion have reduced the water circulation, and this – along with general pollution – has allowed algae to flourish on the sea floor, making local people question the sagacity of swimming in what on a bad day resembles a rather milky soup. Though water quality is monitored by local environmental groups, and the chance of getting sick is pretty scant, try to shower off as soon as you leave the water and avoid immersing your head. During the rainy season, mosquitoes from the nearby marsh have a field day – insect repellent is essential. If you're driving into Pigeon Point, avoid parking under a coconut-laden palm – a single fallen nut can cause a lot of damage.

Bon Accord to Buccoo

Bisecting Tobago's low-lying southwest tip, ruler-straight Milford Road is the artery of the area, a busy main road traversing the Bon Accord, Tyson Hall, Canaan and Friendship communities. One community melts seamlessly into another, but as this is probably the most well-travelled thoroughfare on the island, the strip rapidly becomes familiar.

North of the road is **Bon Accord Lagoon**, a sweeping oval of mangrove swamp and reef-sheltered, shallow water which forms one of the most important fish nurseries on the island. The lagoon, despite suffering pollution in the past, is a sanctuary for conch, snails, shrimp, oysters, crab, urchins and sponges – though the thick sea grass makes them difficult to spot. The land is difficult to access, so it's best to go with a guide; Adolphus James (☎868/639-2231) is recommended. **No Man's Land** adjoining the lagoon is a beautiful deserted beach, often featured on boat cruises and an idyllic place to swim, a good place to escape the hotel-dominated area – for a budget place to stay check *Sunshine Holiday Apartments* (see p.761)

A kilometre or so before Milford Road widens into Claude Noel Highway, **Shirvan Road** strikes off to the left. This is the route to Buccoo Bay and its famous **reef** as well as several wide yellow-sand **beaches** and the neat coastal town of Plymouth. The first stretch is bordered to the left by a plantation of towering coconut palms and to the right by thick hedges masking what was once Shirvan Park **horse-racing track**, now *The Lush*, the place to "large it" (see p.762).

Studded with swanky restaurants, upmarket hotels, fruit stalls and simple board shacks, Shirvan Road continues north, passing turn-offs to quietly residential Mount Pleasant and Carnbee Village – the latter has a supermarket and petrol station.

Buccoo

There's a cluster of tourist-oriented signposts at the next crossroads, the intersection of Auchenskeoch (pronounced "or-kins-styor")/Buccoo Bay Road and Shirvan Road, known as Buccoo Junction. A right turn climbs into one of Tobago's smartest residential districts, where opulent villas nestle next to tiny villages, while the left takes you to **BUCCOO**, a small village haphazardly built around a calm and beautiful bay. Fishing remains a major industry here, but since the nearby reef has become a premier attraction, the community has embraced tourism. The annual **goat races**, established back in 1925, are held here each Easter and the event is

Sunday School

A Tobago institution, **Sunday School** is most definitely not for the pious. A massive beach party that the whole island seems to attend, Sunday School is the highlight of the week's nightlife. The action begins at 8pm, when the Buccooneers Steel Orchestra play pan for a couple of hours. The crowd begins to thicken at around 10–11pm, when the sound system at the covered beach facilities begins to play. Music policy is inevitably Jamaican dancehall with the most popular soca tunes thrown in alongside hip-hop and R&B. Experienced winers – "wining" being the locally practised art of gyrating hips in a provocative manner – display their skills, foreigners relax and the gigolos (and tourists) scout for a partner – it's a well-known pick-up joint. The largest Sunday School of the year takes place each Easter Monday, when several more sound systems add to the cacophony and parked cars back up all the way to the Mount Irvine golf course. To avoid car parking hassles it's a good idea to book a taxi to collect you at a prearranged time.

taken very seriously by competitors – jockeys train the belligerent animals, who continue to refuse to obey any orders, and the result is a joy to watch. **Crab races** also take place but are taken less seriously. The quiet village atmosphere disappears every Sunday when the masses descend for **Sunday School** (see box). The combined effect of a a muddy sea bed and its Sunday job as a urinal make Buccoo a terrible place to swim, though the palm-lined western fringe of the bay is more appealing with cleaner water and plenty of shells and coral fragments to collect.

Covering around twelve square kilometres of Caribbean sea bed, **Buccoo Reef** is the largest and most heavily visited reef in Tobago. Home to forty-odd species of hard and soft coral, the reef has taken around ten thousand years to grow. The corals make good feeding for the brilliantly coloured trigger, butterfly, surgeon and parrot fish. To the south of the reef is **Nylon Pool**, a gleaming coralline sand bar forming an appealing metre-deep swimming pool smack in the middle of the sea. It's said to have been named by Princess Margaret in the 1950s; she remarked that the water was as clear as her nylon stockings.

Sadly, carelessly placed anchors and removal of coral souvenirs mean many parts bear more resemblance to a coral graveyard than a living reef. Overfishing has reduced fish and crustacean populations, and misplaced spear guns have ripped chunks from the coral. Declared a protected national park in 1973, scant resources have failed to enforce the law and the damage continues unabated. Today, glass-bottom boat operators are more conscientious, anchoring only on dead reef and warning visitors that touching or removing reef matter and shells is illegal, but they still hand out the plastic shoes, making it possible for a single footstep to damage or kill hundreds of years' growth. Do your bit by standing on seabed only and refusing to buy any coral trinkets. **Glass-bottom boat** tours cost around US$20. The best leave from Buccoo and include snorkelling and a dip in Nylon Pool; the most reliable operators are Buccoo-based Johnson and Sons (☎868/639-8519). Trips taken at low tide are best for snorkelling.

Mount Irvine to Turtle Beach

The shaven greens of Tobago's first **golf course** herald the outskirts of **Mount Irvine**, the next coastal village past Buccoo. The challenging course plays host to the Tobago Pro-Am tournament every January, and greens fees are US$30 for nine holes, US$48 for eighteen – there's also a weekly rate of US$264 (☎868/639-8871). Around the next bend is **Mount Irvine Bay Beach**, a busy slip of fine yellow sand with just enough room for beach tennis and volleyball, surrounded by gazebos and the ubiquitous palms and sea grape trees. The facilities (daylight hours; TT$1) are adequate and there's a bar/restaurant on site doling out mountains of

△ Waterloo Temple, Trinidad

fried shark and bake. During summer months, the water is calm enough to make exploration of the ornate offshore **reef** a joy, but Mount Irvine becomes one of the island's best **surfing** beaches between December and March, when huge breakers crash against the sand all morning. Boards can be rented from Mt Irvine Watersports (☎868/639-9379), right next to the beach complex.

Past Mount Irvine is the sublime Stone Haven Bay, a good beach, though dominated by an all-inclusive hotel, expanding villa complexes and the inevitable beach vendors. Two friendly and less commercial options for accommodation are a few minutes' walk away, *Indigo* and *Two Seasons* (see pp.761 and 762).

Nestled in the hills behind the beach along Orange Hill Road (take the right turn just past the Mount Irvine golf course then follow the signposts) is the **Kimme Museum** (open Sun only, 10am–2pm, appointments taken for other days; TT$10; ☎868/639-0257, Ⓦwww.kimme.de). Here you'll find the private gallery of eccentric German sculptor Luise Kimme, who settled in Tobago in 1979. Her eerily beguiling wood and bronze sculptures are dotted around the artist's quirky, mural-decorated fretworked home, and a tour makes for a pleasant break from beach-related activities.

Back on the Shirvan Road, a few minutes' drive beyond a grating section of potholes marking the end of the small village of Black Rock, is another fine beach, **Turtle Beach**, a good kilometre of picturesque, coarse yellow sand. A two-storey uninspiring hotel dominates the sand – only its package tourist guests are allowed to use the purpose-built sun shelters – the constant presence of unadventurous guests has generated an ideal market for itinerant beach vendors. Though the beach is officially called **Great Courland Bay**, it acquired its colloquial title on account of the **turtles** that still lay eggs here in the dark of night. All of the hotels along this stretch organize a turtle watch during the laying and hatching seasons, but if you're not staying in the area, contact Nick Hardwicke at the small *Seahorse Inn* (☎868/639-0686) for turtle-watching expeditions.

Plymouth and Arnos Vale

A mile or so beyond Turtle Beach, Grafton Road meets a junction, where a left turn leads to **Plymouth**, Tobago's first European community, settled first by Latvians, then the Dutch and finally by the British. An attractive little town, its main attraction is **Fort James**, the oldest stockade in Tobago, built in 1811 by the British. The coral-stone structure and four cannons preside over an excellent view of Turtle Beach. If you're driving up the coast, it's wise to fill your tank at Plymouth's petrol station, as it's the only one for miles (Mon–Sat 6.30am–9pm, Sun 5.30am–9pm).

From the centre of Plymouth, a well-signposted but narrow road meanders through the greenery toward **Arnos Vale**, one of the few sugar estates to keep its land. The main point of access is at the old estate **water wheel**, now slickly packaged as a tourist attraction (daily 8am–11pm; TT$10). The wheel, pump and steam train that once transported sugar around the plantation have been restored, but the modest **museum** is disappointing, displaying a small selection of Amerindian pottery and colonial artefacts. Still, the estate is a pretty spot, lavish with flowering plants and lush foliage and nice for a relaxing drink. The local bay – overlooked by a hotel of faded grandeur – is great for snorkelling. Road improvements have finally linked Arnos Vale with the rest of the leeward coast. If you continue eastward along the coastal road for approximately ten kilometres you'll eventually hit **Moriah** and later **Castara**, covered in more detail overleaf.

The leeward coast and Tobago Forest Reserve

Beyond Arnos Vale, the leeward coast feels more remote than any other part of the island; tourist development is minimal, leaving the ravishing beaches at **Castara**, **Englishman's Bay**, **Parlatuvier** and **Bloody Bay** much the same as they were twenty years ago. **Fishing** is the main industry of the area, and you'll often see machete-wielding fellows trudging the route to small-scale plantations or meandering along with a pack of hunting dogs. Inland of Castara, the protected **forest reserve** is traversed by the Roxborough–Parlatuvier Road. Though the rainforest canopy looks impenetrable, even the most confirmed city-dweller should find the managed trails.

Though the area is accessible from Crown Point along the coast road via Plymouth, the twists and turns in the route make for a long drive. In fact, the quickest route to the leeward coast is along the **Northside Road**, which begins on the outskirts of Scarborough at Calder Hall, off the Claude Noel Highway. The road then works its way across the island to the leeward coast where it follows the coastline, passing through all of the settlements on this side.

Castara is an attractive fishing village that's slowly developing a nonchalant tourist-friendliness; low-key guesthouses are scattered on a hillside, while visitors dribble in to swim at the marvellous **beach** or splash in the nearby waterfall. Fishing remains the main earner at present, and the beach is one of the best places to participate in the pulling of a **seine net**, still in constant use by the supremely friendly posse of Rasta fishermen. The village abandons its languid air each August, when the beach is packed with revellers attending the **Castara Fishermen's Fete**, one of Tobago's biggest. It's also the only place along this stretch of coast that has accommodation for the foreign visitor. The *Blue Mango* cottages are the best option if you can afford them (see p.761).

Past Castara, houses and shops melt away and the road is flanked by enormous bamboo. The next worthy beach, **Englishman's Bay** (look out for the blue and white sign), is utterly beautiful and completely undeveloped save for a stall near the entrance serving hot meals (including roti on Sundays), soft drinks and bamboo craft.

East of Englishman's Bay, the coast road climbs upward and inland, passing through the diminutive community of **Parrot Hall** before descending to reveal one of the most arresting views on the island: **Parlatuvier Bay**, flanked by an absurdly pretty hillside scattered with palms, terraced provision grounds and the odd house. Another crescent of pearly sand, the bay makes **swimming** a vigorous experience: waves are usually quite strong and the water deepens sharply from the sand. The last accessible beach on the coast is **Bloody Bay**, another deserted shoreline; the right turn at the Bloody Bay junction takes you to the **Tobago Forest Reserve**.

Known as the Roxborough–Parlatuvier Road, the route to the reserve makes for a steep but beautifully quiet drive through the rainforest. The oldest protected rainforest in the western hemisphere is easily accessed at **Gilpin Trace**, marked by a huge slab of rock by the road in front of a forestry division hut. A trail strikes straight into the forest from here, but unless you only plan to go a few hundred yards, it's advisable to hire a **guide** (often waiting by the roadside; TT$100–200); you'll understand a lot more about forest dynamics, and you won't need to worry about getting lost.

Scarborough

SCARBOROUGH, Tobago's raucous, hot and dusty capital (population 18,000), spills higgledy-piggledy down the hillside. The island's administrative centre and its main **port**, the flourishing town is devoid of touristic pretensions. Don't expect a very cosmopolitan atmosphere, though; the docking of the **ferry** from Trinidad is spectacle enough to draw crowds of onlookers.

As the commercial centre of the island, one of the town's main attractions is the shopping. The town's **market**, located opposite the docks, with its fruit and vegetables display, bargain crafts and excellent fast food, is a must; main trading days are Friday and Saturday. And the **Fort King George** complex perched on the lighthouse-topped hill contains a local craft centre (Mon–Fri 9am–1pm)with more unusual items. This complex, at the top of the well-signposted Fort Street, is free to enter and contains a landscaped **park,** the largest fortification in Tobago, **Fort King George**, and at 140m above sea level, excellent views. It is also the site of the unmissable **Tobago Museum** (Mon–Fri 9am–5pm; TT$5, children TT$1). Collated by the Tobago Trust, the small but fascinating collection includes Amerindian artefacts, satirical colonial prints from slavery days, African drums and notes on local culture.

Away from the commercial clamour, the peaceful **botanical gardens** (daily, daylight hours; free), opposite the bus station on Gardenside Street, offer respite from the traffic and steep climbs that can make Scarborough a bit of an ordeal; visiting on an overcast day makes sightseeing more comfortable. The nearby **orchid house** displays most of T&T's indigenous orchids as well as a few imported species.

As Scarborough is so small, there are no bus services within the town, but you can easily see all the sights by foot. For **information**, head to the tourism offices of the Tobago House of Assembly, on the third floor of the NIB Mall, behind the market (8am–4pm; ⓣ868/639-2125 or 4636, ⓕ639-3566, ⓔtourbago@tstt.net.tt). Free **parking** is available at the wharf lot on the corner of Carrington and Castries streets. Scarborough is the departure point for **route taxis** serving the whole of the island; ask a local to find the appropriate stand. **Maxis** to Charlotteville leave two or three times a day from outside James Park on Burnett Street (TT$12). Three good accommodation options, for Scarborough as well as a base for the rest of the island, are: the *Blue Haven* hotel for the well-heeled, *Hope Cottage* for those on a budget and *Mount Pelier Cottage* for those who like the personal eccentric touch (see p.761).

The windward coast

Rugged and continually breathtaking, Tobago's southern shoreline is usually referred to as the **windward coast**. Narrow and peppered with blind corners and potholes, the Windward Road spans its length and sticks close to the sea, providing fantastic views of choppy Atlantic waters and tiny spray-shrouded islands. The parade of languid coastal villages is a complete contrast to the developed west. Though rip tides and strong undercurrents make some of the most attractive-looking beaches unsafe for swimming, there are plenty of sheltered bays to take a dip in the cool Atlantic. Some – such as **King's Bay** – have changing facilities, but at most you'll share the sand only with fishermen. Tour buses make regular rounds, but most of the windward traffic heads for the tiny village of **Speyside** and its smattering of guesthouses and small hotels. Fifteen minutes' drive from Speyside and directly opposite on the Caribbean coast, picturesque **Charlotteville** with its attractive hillside houses and perfect twin beaches, is the last point of call on the windward route. The tarmac ends here, replaced by a treacherous and often impassable stretch of coastal track that divides the town from the rest of the leeward coast.

The Windward Road

From Scarborough the Windward Road leads through numerous tiny villages, including **Mount St George** (the island's first British capital), Goodwood,

Goldsborough and Pembroke. Worth a stop en route is the *First Historical Café* at Studley Park, where local history and anecdotes make for a fascinating visit even if you're not hungry (see p.762).

Shortly after Glamorgan is a signposted left turn for the **Richmond Great House** (see p.761), a hotel, restaurant and essential point of call for almost all tour buses. Built of solid brick and whitewashed board in the eighteenth century, this was the estate house of the old Richmond sugar estate, and it offers fantastic views over the jungle-smothered interior hills. It also contains an extensive collection of African art and textiles; tours (daily 10am–4pm; TT$15) are available.

Past Richmond and the tiny village of Belle Garden is Argyll, the location of the **Argyll Waterfall** (daily 7.30am–5pm), signalled by the cache of guides waiting by the roadside. Official guides (carrying ID and wearing khaki; TT$15, plus tip) are located in the car park, the place to pay the entrance fee (TT$20). The falls, a pleasant fifteen-minute walk away, are the island's highest (54m) and are comprised of three main cascades – the different tiers are great for a dip.

Turning inland past the small village of Roxborough, the Windward Road swings through the hilltop village of **Delaford**, making one almighty bend at the outskirts to reveal a breathtaking view of the spiky coconut plantation surrounding beautiful, deep-blue **King's Bay** below. The **beach** (daylight hours; free) here is one of the few along the windward coast to provide changing facilities (TT$1) and is one of the few in the area.

Speyside

Past King's Bay, the coast swings out of view as the road turns inland. Constant hairpin bends and a steep incline make the going pretty treacherous, so if you're driving, don't let your surroundings become too much of a distraction. Luckily, a designated **lookout** point has been built before the descent into **SPEYSIDE** – be sure to stop, as there's an amazing view of the horseshoe **Tyrrel's Bay**, along with **Little Tobago** and **Goat Island** and an expanse of aquamarine coral-reef-strewn water.

Speyside feels as remote as it is; just over ten years ago the road was little more than a dirt track. Though the town is slowly adjusting to its latest role as a **scuba** destination, it still retains its fishing village atmosphere and small-town attitude. The main strip consists of several dive shops, a couple of restaurants, including the well-known *Jemma's* (see p.762), and a couple of hotels; *Speyside Inn* and the *Manta Lodge* are two of the better ones (see p.761).

As you descend into the village, a cluster of candy-floss-coloured grocery shops and snack bars surround a large playing field – the venue for local football matches – to the right. A dirt track running between the playing field and the sea takes you to the **beach** facilities, basic changing rooms and toilets (daylight hours; TT$1). The sand here is slightly wider than in the central part of the bay, and the famous **reefs**, Speyside's main attraction, are within swimming distance. Generally pristine with little sign of bleaching or human damage, the reefs boasts one of the world's largest **brain corals**, an awesome four metres high and six metres across. Apart from the regular shoals of small fish – butterfly, grunt, angel, parrot and damselfish – the currents also attract a number of deep-water dwellers, including **nurse sharks**, **dolphins** and, most notably, **manta rays**. For those who wish to see more than small fish and limited portions of reef, scuba diving is excellent in this area. The most popular Speyside dive sites include Japanese Gardens, Angel Reef, Bookends and Blackjack Hole, and most dives are of the drift variety (for reliable operators see p.760). **Glass-bottom boats** are a good way to see the reefs if you don't want to get wet, though you can always jump overboard for a spot of snorkelling as well. Frank's (☎868/660-5438), based at *Blue Waters Inn*, offers a basic tour with snorkelling at Angel Reef, as do local operators Fear Not (☎868/660-4654) for around US$15.

On leaving Speyside, just past the *Manta Lodge* hotel, the road forks; left takes you across the interior and into Charlotteville, while the right turn is the route to the astonishingly blue waters and rich reefs of **Bateaux Bay**, site of another luxurious hotel. Beyond Bateaux Bay are the picturesque Belmont and Starwood bays, but the road is often impassable; if so, ask a local fisherman to take you aboard a pirogue. Both bays offer great snorkelling and diving.

Little Tobago and Goat Island

Of the two misshapen islets sitting five kilometres or so out of Tyrrel's Bay, **Goat Island** is the closer, though it's privately owned and closed to the public. However, birdwatchers and hikers flock to the larger island, **Little Tobago**, a kilometre further out to sea. Known as "Bird of Paradise Island", it has been a bird sanctuary since 1924. Uninhabited, it's home to one of the largest seabird colonies in the Caribbean, including flocks of frigates, boobies, terns and the spectacular red-billed tropic bird, the latter especially prevalent between October and June. Make sure you take drinking water with you, as there are no refreshments available on the island. To get the most from your visit, hire an experienced guide such as David Rooks (Ⓣ868/639-4276, Ⓦwww.rooks-tobago.com; US$60), the man who persuaded David Attenborough to include Little Tobago in his famous BBC *Trials of Life* documentary. Local fishermen will be happy to take you to Little Tobago as well for around TT$75, though if you're interested in birdwatching, it's better to go in more expert company.

Charlotteville

From Speyside, the Windward Road strikes inland, climbing steeply upward through jungle-like mountain foliage before plummeting down to the opposite shoreline. Just before the descent, there's a stunning perspective of **Charlotteville**; houses tumble down a hillside to be met by calm Caribbean waters. Snugly situated under the protective cover of the two-kilometre-wide **Man O' War Bay**, Charlotteville is Tobago's foremost fishing community – more than 60 percent of the island's total catch is brought in by local fishermen. The town has an isolated feel, and though the tourist dollar is steadily encroaching upon this self-contained community, the atmosphere is so friendly that it's hard not to relax.

Charlotteville is actually one of Tobago's oldest communities, first settled by Caribs and then by the Dutch in 1633. Increasingly popular as a retreat, accommodation gets booked up quickly, *Cholson Chalets* and the *Man O' War Bay Cottages* are the best options (see p.761), though a number of locals will rent you a room in their house if the situation's desperate. There's little to do but arrange a **fishing** trip, while away the hours on the fine brown sand of **Man O' War Bay beach** (changing facilities, daylight hours; TT$1) or enjoy the excellent snorkelling in the sublime **Pirate's Bay**. Benches along the sea wall, the fishing pier and a covered pavilion are popular liming spots, great for soaking up the village scene. In July, Man O' War Bay is the site of Tobago's most popular fisherman's fete, held to celebrate **St Peter's Day**. Charlotteville's petrol station is open Monday to Saturday 6am–8pm and Sunday 6–11am & 8.15–8.30pm.

21

The ABC Islands

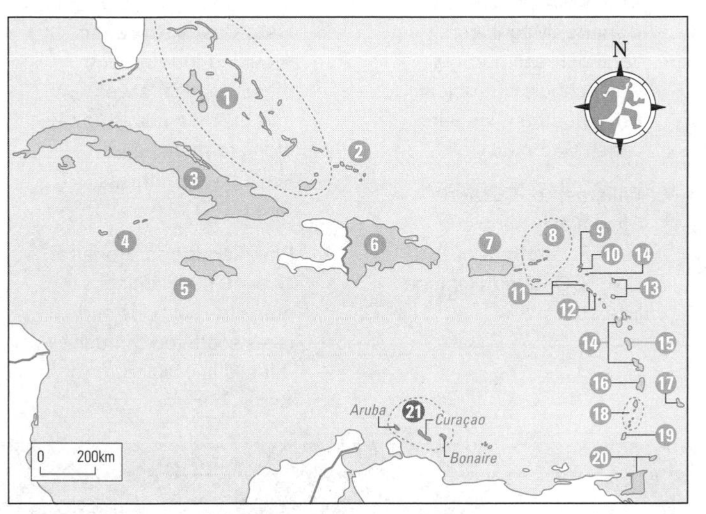

The ABC Islands Highlights

* **Aruba's beach strip** Seven kilometres of unspoilt white-sand beaches line the turquoise waters of the island's west coast. See p.786

* **Bonaire Marine Park, Bonaire** Magnificent coral gardens harbour vast schools of tropical fish just off the leeward coast. See p.801

* **Willemstad, Curaçao** Stroll along the picturesque waterfront of this UNESCO World Heritage Site. See p.807

* **Arikok National Park, Aruba** Explore the Martian-like interior, home to towering stands of cacti, divi divi trees, iguanas and herds of wandering goats. See p.789

* **Hato Caves, Curaçao** A guided tour through these mystical caves and their incredible flowstone formations will leave you breathless. See p.810

* **Pink flamingos, Bonaire** Over 10,000 flamingos grace the saltpans and lakes scattered throughout this tiny island. See p.799

Introduction and Basics

At the bottom of the Caribbean chain of islands, just north of Venezuela, lie Aruba, Bonaire and Curaçao, collectively known as the "ABC islands". Part of the Netherlands Antilles, these tiny islands have a similar heritage, all having been originally inhabited by the Caiquitíos Indians before the arrival of the Spanish, and later the Dutch, with whom they have been tied to ever since.

Over the centuries, however, each island has developed its own distinct identity. Aruba is the priciest and **most touristed** of the three islands, attracting mostly American holidaymakers on package vacations as well as cruise-ship passengers to its glamorous beachfront resort complexes, flashy casinos, upscale boutiques and duty-free shops. Laid-back Bonaire, renowned for its phenomenal **diving and snorkelling**, and also offering good hiking opportunities, draws visitors from around the world in search of an outdoors-oriented vacation. Much less known than its smaller neighbours – except in Holland, the Caribbean and South America – Curaçao lags behind Aruba and Bonaire in terms of tourism. But still it attracts its share of travellers who come for its beaches and to experience the charms of the capital city of Willemstad, home to some of the most attractive **colonial architecture** in all of the Caribbean.

Where to go

Most travellers to Aruba spend their time in the resort areas between Eagle and Palm beaches or in the capital of **Oranjestad**, where the casinos and shop-filled streets are the main diversions. Those interested in natural attractions head to **Arikok National Park** to explore its arid landscape and rugged coastline. West of the park finds interesting rock formations at **Casibari** and **Ayó** along with the nearby Bushiribana **Gold Ruins** and much-photographed **Natural Bridge**.

Divers and snorkellers flock to Bonaire to surround themselves with colourful marine life at the **Bonaire Marine Park** and **Klein Bonaire** on the western side of the island. Unique to the ABCs, the island is also home to a large number of **pink flamingos** that are mostly concentrated around the colourful **saltpans** in the south. In the far north, hiking enthusiasts should make for **Washington-Slagbaai National Park**.

Not to be missed on Curaçao is lively **Willemstad**, whose pristine Dutch colonial architecture has earned it the designation of a UNESCO World Heritage Site, and whose cultural and historical attractions hold much of interest. Most of the best **beaches** are in the northwest, not far from **Christoffel National Park**, which boasts a variety of flora and fauna and good hiking trails. For something different, take a guided tour of the limestone **Hato Caves** or visit the **plantation houses** scattered about the island.

When to go

The ABC islands are a year-round destination, though **peak** tourist season is mid-December to mid-April when the weather is at its best. Sitting outside of the **hurricane belt**, the islands generally enjoy warm weather year-round. The average daytime **temperature** is 28°C (82°F) and steady trade winds keep the humidity down.

All three islands receive very little **rainfall**, which usually comes in the form of gentle showers between October and March.

Getting there

Aruba's Oranjestad serves as a major Caribbean **gateway** for many international airlines serving the US, Holland and parts of the Caribbean and South America. Regularly scheduled **non-stop flights** depart from Miami, New York, Boston, Houston, Atlanta, Amsterdam, Bogotá, Caracas, San Juan and Curaçao. KLM is the only European airline flying directly to Aruba, while most of the major

American airline companies (see pp.12–18) operate from the US. Several **charter flights** depart from Canada and numerous US cities between December and April.

A few airlines provide relatively easy access to Bonaire from Europe, North America and the Caribbean: KLM flies **direct** from Amsterdam; American Eagle from San Juan. Air Jamaica has a flight from Miami with a brief stopover in Montego Bay. It's also possible to fly from other American **gateways** to Curaçao or Aruba and then hop on the short flight with Dutch Caribbean Express (formerly ALM) or Avia Air to Bonaire.

Travelling to Curaçao is relatively straightforward. Several international and regional airlines fly **direct** to Curaçao from the US, Holland and the Caribbean. KLM has daily direct flights from Amsterdam while American Airlines departs daily from Miami. It's also possible to fly direct from Aruba, Bonaire, St Martin, San Juan, Bogotá and Caracas with some of the **regional airlines** (see pp.36–37).

If you're travelling from Australia or New Zealand it's best to fly to Amsterdam or Miami and then make the necessary **connections** to Aruba or Curaçao, and from there to Bonaire.

A **ferry** service operated by Flamingo Fast Ferries shuttles passengers twice daily to and from Bonaire. The journey on the modern catamaran takes an hour and a half, and the crossing can be rough. Presently there is no ferry service between Aruba and Curaçao.

Many **cruise ships** dock in the capital cities for the day. For cruise-ship operators, see pp.14 and 16–17.

Entry requirements

Citizens from the US, Canada, New Zealand, Australia and most European countries must have a **valid passport** plus a round-trip or onward ticket in order to enter any of the ABC islands. Contact the nearest Dutch embassy or consulate for information regarding visas (see pp.21–22).

Departure tax

The following taxes may be included in your airline ticket.

Aruba	US$34.25
Bonaire	US$20
Curaçao	US$20

Money and costs

The official currency of Aruba, Bonaire and Curaçao **is the Netherlands Antillean Florin (NAf)**, also known as the guilder, which is divided into 100 cents. In Aruba it's known as the Aruban Florin and abbreviated as **AFl**. Florin **notes** come in denominations of 10, 25, 50, 100, 250 and 500, and **coins** come as 5, 10, 25 and 50 cents, one florin and five florins. The florin is fixed to the US dollar and is very stable, with the **rate of exchange** roughly US$1 to NAf1.77 at the time of publication. US dollars in cash are widely accepted at most hotels, restaurants and shops, as are most major credit cards. Banks are found throughout all three islands, with most **ATMs** located in the capital cities.

Aruba is an **expensive** destination, but it is possible to get by on US$125 a day if you're very conscientious. Bus travel is cheap, most beaches are free and there are a few rooms (mostly in the outskirts of Oranjestad) to be found for around US$70 a night. Lodging at the major beachside resorts starts at about US$175 per night, and many require a minimum stay of at least three nights. All-inclusive holiday packages from tour operators and charter companies usually offer the best value for your stay in Aruba.

Apart from your flight, accommodation is likely to be your greatest expense in Bonaire, particularly if you stay at one of the many **dive resorts** during peak season. If you want to do much exploring on and off the island, count on spending around US$150–200 a day, twice that if you're looking for a more luxurious vacation.

With a wide range of **accommodation** and eating options in and around Willemstad on Curaçao, it's possible to squeak by on a daily budget of less than US$60 a day, though you'll pay closer to double that if you want to take part in any tours or land- and water-based activities.

Information and maps

All three islands have **tourism information offices**, where friendly staff can provide maps, brochures and free magazines, as well as arrange tours or lodging.

The **Aruba Tourism Authority** (ATA) operates a tourist information office near Eagle Beach on L.G. Smith Blvd 172 (Mon–Fri 7.30am–noon & 1–4.30pm; ⓣ297/823777, ⓦwww.aruba.com). Grab a copy of *Aruba Nights* and *Aruba Experience*, both of which have maps and useful tips on accommodation, restaurants, activities, nightlife and beaches. A decent road map to the island (B&B Map to Aruba, 1:50,000) is available for US$4 at bookstores in Oranjestad.

Tourism Corporation Bonaire has a tourist information office in the centre of Kralendijk on Kaya Grandi 2 (Mon–Fri 7.30am–noon & 1.30–5pm; ⓣ599/717-8322, ⓦwww .InfoBonaire.com), where you can pick up *Bonaire Nights* and *Bonaire Affair*, two useful free magazines. A tiny visitors' information stand with a handful of brochures and maps is also at the airport.

The **Curaçao Tourism Development Bureau** (CTDB) operates a tourist information office just outside central Punda in Willemstad on Pietermaiiweg 19 (Mon–Fri 8am–5pm & Sat 9am–noon; ⓣ5999/616-0000, ⓦwww.curacao-tourism.com) and manages booths at the airport and at the cruise terminal in Otrobanda. They distribute *Curaçao Nights, Curaçao Explorer* and *Curaçao Holiday* as well as a free guide to the beaches and diving sites of Curaçao. The informative weekly dining and entertainment guide, *K-Pasa* (ⓦwww.k-pasa.com), can also be picked up at tourist offices and most hotels and cafés. The daily **newspaper** *Amigoe* and its online counterpart (ⓦwww.Amigoe.com) also has details on what's going around the island.

Accommodation

The vast majority of rooms in Aruba are in expensive resorts along the narrow beach strip between Eagle and Palm beaches. Expect to pay at least US$200 a night for a room, keeping in mind that many require a **minimum stay** of at least three nights during peak season. More reasonably priced apartment-style accommodation (less than US$100 per day) is available on the outskirts of downtown Oranjestad and away from the beaches. In addition, a 6 percent **tax** and 11 percent **service charge** will be added to your bill.

Bonaire is also pricey and offers very little in the way of budget accommodation. Most hotels and resorts are geared towards divers and as such have on-site dive centres that offer underwater certification courses, fill stations and gear rental, often as part of **package deals**. Most places are located a few minutes' drive outside of Kralendijk along the coast. Rooms typically start around US$150–200 per night during high season. There is a hotel **service charge** of 10–20 percent and a government room **tax** of US$6.50 per person per night.

Curaçao's options are more varied, and travellers can choose from budget-style apartments to exclusive hotels and dive resorts. Many of the more luxurious places are found along the coast just north and south of town, while most budget choices are in Punda and Otrobanda in downtown Willemstad. Be prepared to pay a **room service charge** of 6–15 percent.

While prohibited on Bonaire and Curaçao, **camping** is permitted in Aruba on parts of Eagle and Arashi **beaches** during Easter week and in early July when local schools are on holiday. Permits (US$15) must be obtained from local police officials who will tell you where you can set up camp.

Food and drink

You'll find ample **dining options** on all three islands, spanning a wide range of international and local cuisines and concentrated in the capitals and major tourist areas. On Aruba dining out tends to be an elegant and expensive affair, and you'll find a crop of top-class restaurants, though a number of good, reasonably priced options are also to be found. Dining on Bonaire and Curaçao is less expensive than on Aruba and caters to

all tastes and budgets. The best bargains on both islands are at snack stands and bars, busiest at lunchtime and serving scrumptious local meals (goat or conch stew, iguana soup, fried fish), cooked on an open grill, that can cost less than US$6.

You'll find imported brands of beer and wine at most restaurants and bars, as well as the locally produced beers – Aruba's **Balashi** and Curaçao's **Amstel Bright**. The islands' popular cocktails include the local liqueur **Curaçao Blue**, made from the peels of the Valencia orange. You'll also find delicious fruit drinks and smoothies sold at many snack stands.

Popular dishes on all three islands usually include **goat**, **chicken** and **beef**, as well as local **fish** such as red snapper, wahoo and barracuda. Not-to-be-missed **Aruban specialties** include *stoba*, goat stew with vegetables; *soppi di pisca*, a fish soup made with coconut milk; freshly caught red snapper or wahoo served with plantain or *funchi* (cornmeal); and *keshi yena*, a baked mixture of Gouda cheese stuffed with beef, fish or chicken and seasoned with spices, raisins, tomatoes and olives. For dessert or for a snack try the mildly sweet *pan bati*, which is similar to a thick pancake. You'll find similar local dishes on Bonaire and Curaçao, though slight local differences in their names.

Prices at dinner will on average set you back US$20–25, though you'll pay twice that at the finer restaurants on Aruba. On all three islands a 10–15 percent **service charge** is normally added to your bill; while the service is included it's not uncommon to add a little extra at your discretion (especially on Aruba where this is customary).

On all the islands **reservations** are recommended, especially during high season. Be aware that some restaurants open only for dinner, so it pays to check ahead if possible.

Names for local dishes

Aros bruin	brown rice
Funchi	cornmeal
Galina	chicken
Giambo	okra soup
Hobi duchi	cactus soup with pork, fish and/or shrimp
Kabritu	goat meat
Karni stoba	beef stew
Moro	rice and peas
Papaja stoba	papaya stew with pig's tail and corn beef
Piska kora	red snapper, usually deep-fried whole
Piska mula	wahoo, usually deep-fried
Snijboonchi	green beans
Sopi karni-piska	meat or fish soup

Getting around

Getting around on all of the islands is fairly straightforward, thanks to their small size. In most cases, however, you'll need to rent a car or taxi if you want to explore beyond the capitals and resort areas.

By bus

Aruba has an inexpensive and reliable daily **bus** service linking Oranjestad with all the major areas. The main **bus terminal** is located in town across from the Port of Call Shopping Centre, and buses depart frequently for the hotels; **route #10** services downtown Oranjestad and the hotel strip between Eagle Beach and Palm Beach. Tickets can be purchased directly from the driver (US$1.15 one-way; US$2 round-trip).

On Curaçao, buses run to all the major towns and districts, but the system is very slow and may require several **transfers** before you reach your destination. Bus terminals are located outside the post office in Punda and near the highway overpass in Otrobanda.

Bonaire has no public bus system.

By car

By far the easiest way to get around all three islands is with a **rented vehicle**, and all of the major rental agencies operate booths at the airports as well as at most hotel chains (see individual island sections for specific details).

While many of the major roads in Aruba are in excellent condition, you'd be wise to rent a **four-wheel-drive** vehicle (US$450/week) if you're planning to explore the interior or Arikok National Park, as the winding roads on this part of the island become rugged. Bear in mind that many of the **main highways** are labelled according to the direction you are travelling (you may be driving east on 7A, but as soon as you turn back the same road is referred to as 7B).

Most visitors to Bonaire rent **pick-up trucks** (US$40–60/day) to haul their bulky scuba equipment and tanks between their hotels and the dive sites. Rentals are handled at the airport (see p.795) and they will usually deliver the car to your hotel. For Washington-Slagbaai National Park you'll need a four-wheel-drive vehicle if you're not visiting on a tour.

By taxi

Taxis on the ABC islands are very safe and reliable, and can be hired from hotels, hailed from the street or requested by calling the central dispatch. **Rates** are fixed according to zones (there are no meters). Sightseeing tours around each island average US$30/hour on Aruba and Curaçao, and US$30 for a half-day on Bonaire; in all cases prices cover up to four passengers.

On Aruba, a ride from the capital to Eagle Beach costs US$5 and US$8 to Palm Beach for up to four people. Add an extra US$1 if you're travelling after midnight and US$3 on Sundays and holidays. For pick-up call the central dispatch (☎297/822116 or 821604).

On Bonaire, expect to pay anywhere from US$5 to US$12 to travel from downtown to most area hotels; US$16 to Lac Bay. A **surcharge** applies for more than four passengers and fares increase by 25 percent after 6pm and by another 50 percent after midnight. Call the central dispatch (☎599/717-8100) to arrange for pick-up from anywhere on the island.

On Curaçao a ride from most hotels to downtown costs US$8–12 and close to US$20 to the beaches south of Willemstad; fares increase by 25 percent after 11pm. Call the central dispatch (☎5999/869-0752) to arrange a pick-up.

By bike or scooter

Renting a **mountain bike** or **scooter** is a good option on islands like Bonaire, whose more than 300km of unpaved roads make this a pleasant way to see some of the island's unspoiled beauty. Bike and scooter rental agencies are found in Kralendijk (see "Listings", p.803). Plan on spending US$10–20 per day for a bike or US$18–25 per day for a scooter.

Phones, post and email

Payphones are located all over Aruba and Curaçao and many require **phone cards**, which can be purchased from shops or vendors throughout the islands. On Bonaire you're likely to be stuck calling from hotels – which charge exorbitant rates as they do on the other islands – unless you use the island's few payphones (see below).

On Aruba, international calls are best made from the **SETAR telephone office** in the Royal Plaza in downtown Oranjestad (daily 8am–10.30pm). There are also a few specially marked telephone **booths** where you can reach the international operator at the cruise terminal, airport and scattered throughout the downtown area.

On Bonaire local and international phone calls can be made from payphones outside the **TELBO office** near the tourist information office on Kaya Libertador S. Bolivar; phone cards can be purchased from a vending machine located near the front door of the office. There are also a few phones at the airport and in town where you can reach the international operator.

If you want to make an international call from Curaçao, it's best to call from the capital where there are a couple **of privately run businesses** that charge reasonable rates for international calls (see *C@fe Internet* under "Internet access" on p.812).

A few specially designated telephone **booths** in Willemstad and at the airport also have direct access to the international operator, allowing you to use your calling card or credit card.

Country codes

Aruba ☎297
Bonaire ☎599
Curaçao ☎5999

The **postal systems** in all three islands are relatively efficient, and **internet access** is available at hotels and a handful of locations in the capitals (see "Listings" sections for individual islands for details).

Opening hours, public holidays, and festivals

On all three islands, most shops and business are normally **open** Monday to Saturday 8am–noon and 2–6pm, with a few places on Curaçao opening on Sunday mornings if cruise ships are in port. **Banks** are generally open Monday to Friday 8am–3.30pm, and some close for lunch; the bank at Curaçao's airport is open Monday to Saturday 8am–8pm and on Sundays 9am–4pm.

Of the many festivals and celebrations on the islands, the one that all three share is **Carnival**, which on Aruba and Bonaire officially begins forty days before Lent, and is celebrated with parades, steel bands, costumes and colourful floats, though Bonaire's Carnival is smaller than those on the other islands. Curaçao has a month-long Carnival season, which kicks off on New Year's Day and culminates with a grand parade on the day before Ash Wednesday. Emotions run high during the four-day **Tumba festival**, a preamble to Carnival, when local musicians compete to have their piece (*tumba*) selected as the official road song.

During the rest of the year, Aruba's calendar includes **One Cool Summer**, a festival from May to October that features concerts, traditional food, and cultural and sporting events; the **Hi Winds Pro-Am Windsurfing competition** in June, which draws international competitors of all ages and skill levels; **Dera Gai** on June 24, a folkloric celebration commemorating the harvest; and the annual **Festival de las Americas** in October, a music celebration showcasing the unique rhythms of the Americas.

Outside Carnival, Bonaireans have a number of events to look forward to: the **Simadan harvest festival** in Rincon in April, when locals pay tribute to the farmers with traditional music and costumes; the week-long **Bonaire Dive Festival** in June, when activities and games focus on raising awareness of the importance of the coral reefs; and the **International Sailing Regatta** in October. The events of the preceding twelve months are recapped in song and dance during the colourful **Bari Festival** held in December.

Curaçao has a number of international events, including its **regatta** (late Jan or early Feb), when sailors from around the world compete in races near Willemstad; the **Jazz Festival** in May; and the **Salsa Festival** (dates vary in summer), which attracts popular international stars.

Public holidays

The following holidays are observed on all three islands, unless specified otherwise.

January 1 New Year's Day
January 25 G.F. Croes Day (Aruba)
Monday before Ash Wednesday Carnival Monday (Aruba)
March 18 National Anthem and Flag Day (Aruba)
March/April Good Friday and Easter Monday
April 30 Queen's Birthday and Rincon Day (Bonaire)
May 1 Labour Day
May 24 Ascension Day
July 2 Curaçao Flag Day
September 6 Bonaire Flag Day
December 25 and 26 Christmas
December 31 New Year's Eve

Language

The **official language** of the Netherlands Antilles is Dutch, although English and Spanish are also widely spoken, as is **Papiamentu**, a creole language that developed in Curaçao in the 1500s between the African slaves and their owners. The colourful language quickly spread to Aruba and Bonaire and evolved over time as Portuguese and Spanish missionaries,

Dutch merchants and South American traders each added their own vocabulary.

While you're more likely to hear English spoken in Aruba (due largely to the influx of US visitors) and Dutch in Curaçao, Papiamentu is the dominant language in **Bonaire**. The locals will be delighted if you attempt a few of the following phrases:

Useful phrases

Welcome	*Bon bini*
Good morning	*Bon dia*
Good afternoon	*Bon tardi*
Good evening	*Bon nochi*
How are you?	*Con ta bai?*
I am fine	*Mi ta bon*
Have a good day	*Pasa bon dia*
Thank you	*Masha danki*
Goodbye	*Ayo*
You're welcome	*Di nada*
Very good!	*Hopi bon*
See you later	*Te aworo*

Watersports

All of the ABC islands offer good **watersports** opportunities, though each has its own particular strengths. For diving, Bonaire is unmatched by its neighbours: pristine coral reefs dot the waters around the island, most of them on the sheltered western coast and around **Klein Bonaire**, a 1500-acre cay just offshore from Kralendijk. Diving is virtually nonexistent on the east coast due to rough waters and a rugged coastline. The majority of sites are so close at hand, all you need to do is park your truck, grab your gear and swim a few metres to the reef. There's also good windsurfing to be had at **Lac Bay** on the island's east coast.

Though Aruba is known more for its beaches than its diving, it does have some exciting **dives** at sites scattered along the northwestern coast of the island, including a few shipwrecks. Dive centres located at many of the hotels arrange charter boat tours to these spots. There are also excellent **windsurfing** conditions on the island just a few meters north at Hadicurari, while the best **snorkelling** is found still further north at Malmok and Arashi.

Curaçao has plenty of watersports to choose from. The island has some decent dive sites scattered on its leeward side along the southern coast in the twenty-kilometre **Curaçao Underwater Park** and around **Klein Curaçao**, a small deserted volcanic island to the southeast (an hour-and-a-half boat ride from Willemstad). Most sites are rich in coral formations while others have sunken ships and submerged artefacts. Some sites are easily accessible from shore but most require getting there by **boat**. Good snorkelling exists at most of these locations.

Emergency numbers

Aruba
Police Ⓣ100
Fire/ambulance Ⓣ115
Hospital Ⓣ87 4300

Bonaire
Police Ⓣ133
Fire Ⓣ191
Hospital/ambulance Ⓣ114

Curaçao
Police/fire Ⓣ911
Ambulance Ⓣ912
Hospital Ⓣ910

History

The first inhabitants of the ABC islands were the Caiquitíos Indians, an Arawak-speaking tribe from South America who established themselves on all three of the islands centuries before the arrival of the Spanish in 1499. In the years that followed, more Spaniards settled here in search of precious metals and drinking water. Not finding any gold or silver, they quickly dubbed the ABCs "las islas inutiles" or the "useless islands". (In fact, they should have looked harder on Aruba where over three million pounds of gold were discovered in the nineteenth century.)

Disappointed by the lack of natural resources, the Spanish **enslaved** many of the Amerindians and shipped them to Hispaniola to labour in the mines and plantations there. Returning in the mid-1520s to colonize the ABCs, the Spaniards introduced cattle and other livestock, and brought back many of the original slaves to work in agriculture.

During the early 1630s the **Dutch**, on a quest for a suitable Caribbean base from which to launch attacks against the Spanish, took control of Aruba, Bonaire and Curaçao, and the next century saw a drastic increase in commerce on all three islands.

Prized for its naturally deep harbour, its strategic location and its **saltpans** (salt was an important commodity for preserving fish and meat shipped back to Europe), Curaçao quickly developed into an important Dutch naval base. Bonaire was also valued for its vast quantities of salt and tracts of agricultural land left behind by the Spaniards. The **Dutch West India Company** began exporting large amounts of salt, along with sorghum, maize, divi divi pods (used in the tanning process) and meat to Europe and to the rest of the world. They also imported livestock to Aruba for the sole purpose of feeding the many slaves and colonists living on Curaçao.

More slaves from Africa and the Caribbean were brought in to work the salt fields and the **plantations**. Curaçao, in fact, became the Caribbean's busiest **slave depot** during the seventeenth century when the Dutch West India Company shipped tens of thousands of slaves to Curaçao and Brazil where they were sold to plantation owners from across the Caribbean and the Americas. Slavery wouldn't be abolished in the ABCs until 1863, after which the Dutch West India Company closed many of the plantations.

Economic prospects were bleak until the discovery of rich **oilfields** off the coast of Venezuela at the beginning of the twentieth century, which proved to be a boon for all three of the islands. Aruba and Curaçao both built refineries, attracting workers from Bonaire and around the world. These refineries flourished until they were forced to close in the mid-1980s. While the oil and salt industries remain important today, it was the **tourism initiatives** of the 1990s that revived the islands' economies, providing jobs for a substantial number of their populations and increasing the ABC islands' profile as a holiday destination, particularly for Aruba and Bonaire, the more well-known of the islands.

21.1

Aruba

With its seemingly endless supply of white sandy beaches and turquoise blue waters, **ARUBA** is one of the more popular Caribbean destinations for many sun-worshipers and cruise-ship passengers. The smallest of the ABC islands, Aruba is 25km north of Venezuela and only 30km wide. Over one million visitors a year come to this tiny island of 90,000 to indulge in the glitz associated with its luxurious beachside resorts, elegant restaurants, 24-hour casinos, shops and boutiques. The harbourside capital **Oranjestad** attracts many of the visitors, as do resort-filled **Eagle** and **Palm beaches** just north of town. In stark contrast to these glamorous areas, the rugged interior is dotted with stands of cacti, twisted divi divi trees and herds of wandering goats. In the Mars-like landscape of **Arikok National Park**, mysterious boulders painted with ancient petroglyphs and limestone caves are sights not to be missed.

Gold was discovered here in 1824, but the real economic boom began in the early 1900s when oil was discovered off the coast of Venezuela and a refinery was built here in **San Nicolas**. After its decline in the 1980s, the Aruban government launched a new initiative, focusing its attention on large-scale tourism. Seeking more independence and greater control of its finances, Aruba gained *status aparte* in 1986, thus allowing Arubans to have their own parliament, flag, currency and more freedom in their internal affairs than their counterparts in the Netherlands Antilles. Today more than half of the population is employed by the flourishing tourism industry and Arubans enjoy a higher standard of living than those living on many other islands in the Caribbean.

Arrival and getting around

The majority of visitors **fly** to Aruba's state-of-the-art Queen Beatrix International Airport (☎297/824800), a few kilometres south of Oranjestad. Numerous **taxis** wait for passengers outside the arrival terminal. If you are staying at one of the smaller hotels or guesthouses in town, the ride will set you back US$9; fares to the hotels along the beach are between US$16 and US$18. Alternatively, De Palm Tours (☎297/824400) operates an efficient network of air-conditioned **motor coaches** that take visitors to the major beachfront hotels. Round-trip tickets ($20; about 30 min) can be purchased from the booth at the terminal's baggage claim.

Cruise ships dock at the pier in downtown Oranjestad. Taxis are on hand to take you around the island.

For details on the **tourism information office**, located in the capital, see p.777.

Accommodation

The island is small enough that you can pretty much base yourself anywhere and be close to all activities and attractions. In downtown Oranjestad, there is really not much in the way of accommodation; most of the affordable guesthouses and apartments are

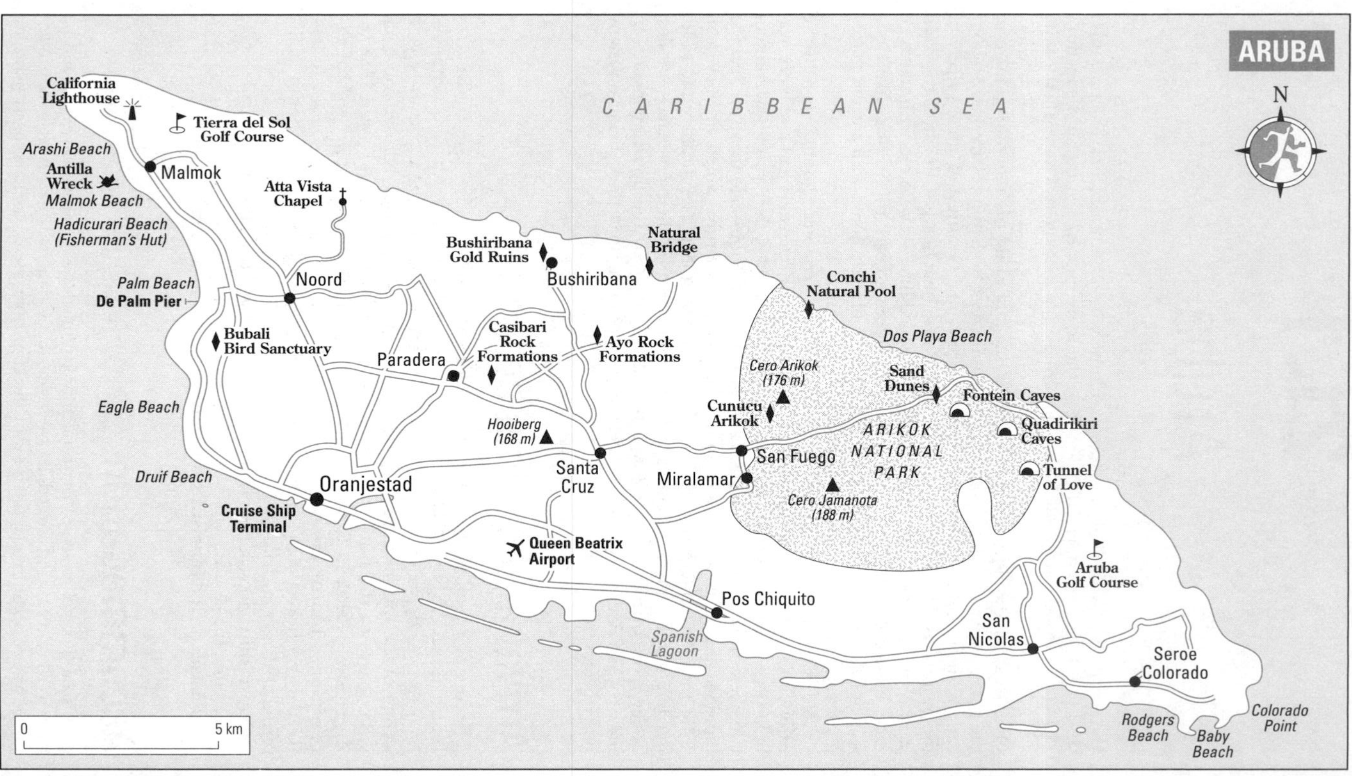
ARUBA
N
CARIBBEAN SEA
California Lighthouse
Tierra del Sol Golf Course
Arashi Beach
Malmok
Antilla Wreck
Malmok Beach
Hadicurari Beach (Fisherman's Hut)
Atta Vista Chapel
Palm Beach
De Palm Pier
Noord
Bubali Bird Sanctuary
Eagle Beach
Druif Beach
Cruise Ship Terminal
Oranjestad
Paradera
Bushiribana Gold Ruins
Bushiribana
Natural Bridge
Casibari Rock Formations
Ayo Rock Formations
Hooiberg (168 m)
Santa Cruz
Queen Beatrix Airport
Conchi Natural Pool
Dos Playa Beach
Cero Arikok (176 m)
Cunucu Arikok
Sand Dunes
Fontein Caves
Quadirikiri Caves
Tunnel of Love
ARIKOK NATIONAL PARK
San Fuego
Miralamar
Cero Jamanota (188 m)
Pos Chiquito
Spanish Lagoon
Aruba Golf Course
San Nicolas
Seroe Colorado
Rodgers Beach
Baby Beach
Colorado Point
0
5 km

located just outside the capital, while the majority of the more expensive resorts and hotels are along the main seafront strip between Eagle and Palm beaches.

Oranjestad

Aruba Sonesta Beach Resort L.G. Smith Blvd 82 ⓣ297/836000, ⓕ825317, ⓦwww.arubasonesta.com. There is no lack of activity at this enormous village-like resort in the heart of downtown. The complex contains fifteen restaurants, six bars, three pools, a number of boutiques, several fitness centres and a casino. Rooms are spacious and have balconies affording spectacular views of the coast or city. The real treat here is free access to a private island just a fifteen-minute boat ride away. ⑨

The beach strip and northwest tip

Allegro Resort and Casino Palm Beach ⓣ297/864500, ⓕ863191, ⓔbstanley@aruba.allegroresorts.com. Two high-rise towers offer over 400 one- or two-bedroom units or suites, all of which have the usual amenities, private bath and balconies. Guests can sign up for a wide variety of watersports activities or relax in one of several whirlpools. Live entertainment nightly. ⑨

Aruba Beach Villas Across from Hadicurari Beach on L.G. Smith Blvd 462 ⓣ297/861072, ⓕ861870, ⓦwww.arubabeachvillas.com. Rooms range from one- to two-bedroom apartments with kitchenettes to large private villas with ocean and sunset views. The location makes this hotel popular with windsurfers. ⑧

Bucuti Beach Resort Eagle Beach on L.G. Smith Blvd 55B ⓣ297/831100, ⓕ825272, ⓦwww.bucuti.com. The sixty comfortable one-bedroom units, popular with Europeans, are all furnished with A/C, phone, private bath, TV and a large terrace or balcony overlooking the water. There's a fitness centre on the premises, and meal plans are available. ⑧

Divi Aruba Beach Resort Druif Beach on J.E. Irausquin Blvd 45 ⓣ297/823300, ⓕ834002, ⓦwww.diviaruba.com. This all-inclusive mega-resort, popular with young families and couples, features two restaurants, beachside bars, a pool and 200 spacious one-bedroom units with Spanish décor. All rooms adjoin a small outside patio or balcony, and end-units offer stunning ocean views. Daily fitness activities and nightly entertainment are on offer, and guests can use restaurant or beach facilities at the neighbouring *Tamarijn Aruba Resort*. ⑨

The rest of the island

Aruba Blue Village Suites Cunucu Abao 37, Bubali ⓣ297/878618, ⓕ870081, ⓔaru.blue.v@setarnet.aw. Located ten minutes north of Oranjestad, right next to *Madame Janette's* restaurant (see p.793), this hotel has standard but comfortable suites furnished with kitchenettes. ⑤

Cactus Apartments Matadera 5, Noord ⓣ297/822903, ⓕ820433, ⓔcactus.apts@setarnet.aw. A basic hotel with thirteen apartments in the small town of Noord, just east of Palm Beach. Rooms have kitchenettes, A/C and TV. Laundry service, which is hard to come by and expensive on the island, is available here for a modest fee. ③

Turibana Plaza Apartments Noord 124, Noord ⓣ297/867292, ⓕ862658. This excellent-value small apartment complex with eighteen two-bedroom units has spacious, clean rooms with A/C, kitchenettes and daily service. It is located next to several restaurants, and is close to beaches and the capital. ③

Vistal Mar Apartments Bucutiweg 28 ⓣ297/828579, ⓕ822200. Located in a quiet neighbourhood behind the airport, this friendly hotel offers spacious one-bedroom apartments each with a kitchenette, living room and balcony overlooking the water. Owners Alby and Kathlyn Yarzagaray go out of their way to ensure your stay is a pleasant one. There's a swimming dock across the road. ④

Oranjestad

Named in honour of the Dutch Royal House of Orange, **Oranjestad** has been Aruba's capital since 1797 and has served as the island's main port ever since. Today, the small harbour continues to attract schooners, fishing boats and cruise ships from all over the world. The tiny capital on the southwest shore bustles with activity as thousands of visitors descend upon it each day to shop, dine or try their luck at one of the many casinos. The streets that make up the downtown core are lined with modern imitations of pastel-coloured Dutch colonial houses adorned with ornate gabled roofs; a good number of them have been renovated into shopping complexes, administrative buildings, museums and restaurants. A handful of older buildings, including Fort Zoutman and the lofty King Willem III Tower, offer reminders of Aruba's past. Just a hop and a skip away from the city is the island's main beach strip and resort area.

The City

For many tourists, the first glimpse of Oranjestad is along the busy palm-fringed thoroughfare of **L.G. Smith Boulevard**, the island's main artery connecting the capital with the hotel district and the northwest and with San Nicholas in the southeast. Running parallel to the harbour, the downtown stretch of the road is lined with shopping malls, boutiques, casinos, government offices and parliament buildings. Unless you plan to shop 'til you drop or while away the hours gambling, the city's sights won't occupy too much of your time. There are, however, a number of interesting cultural attractions, best explored, like the city itself, on foot, as everything you'll want to see is concentrated in a small area.

The picturesque harbour is a good place to begin your wanderings. Starting from the white **tourist information booth** adjacent to the Atlantis Pier, head east on L.G. Smith Boulevard. Turning left onto Oranjestraat, you'll reach the beautifully preserved **Fort Zoutman**, the oldest building on the island and perhaps the town's most important landmark. The fort was built in 1796 and played a vital role in securing Dutch interests on the island. Armed with four cannons, it was originally sited along the coast; centuries of shifting currents have changed the coastline so that today the fort now sits some 300m away from the water. The adjoining **Willem III Tower** was added in 1868 to serve as a lighthouse and the town's first public clock. The fort houses a small **historical museum** (Mon–Fri 9am–noon & 1.30–4.30pm; US$1.15) displaying an interesting collection of artefacts that trace Aruba's history. Its open-air courtyard also hosts the weekly folkloric **Bon Bini Festival** (Tues 6.30–8.30pm; US$3), which features traditional music and dance, and is the best place to try local dishes.

One block east of the fort, on Zuidstraat 27, is the fascinating **Numismatic Museum** (Mon–Fri 7.30am–noon & 1–4pm; free), home to over 30,000 historical coins from Aruba and around the world dating back to 220 BC. Some of the many highlights include a display of Aruban Indian shells used for barter, beads used as money by North American Indians and bills made of silk and linen.

At the north end of the city the tiny **Archeological Museum**, J.E. Irausquin Blvd 2-A (Mon–Fri 8am–noon & 1–4pm; free), has an impressive array of local artefacts and pottery. The most important exhibits include stone tools from 2000 BC, pottery from the ceramic period (500 AD) and the skeletal remains excavated from an Indian burial site.

Back near the harbour, around the corner from the Seaport Casino, is the quiet **Wilhelmina Park**, honouring the 1955 visit of Queen Juliana of the Netherlands, a white marble statue of whom dominates the plaza. The park is especially striking when tropical plants are in bloom between June and October. Benches set amongst the shady grove of trees makes this an ideal place to rest after sightseeing or a long day of shopping.

The beach strip and northwest tip

Easily reached from J.E. Irausquin Boulevard, which intersects the main L.G. Smith Boulevard, the **best beaches**, **watersports facilities** and hotels are found along the famous gold coast on the leeward side (northwest) of the island. Here, Aruba's best 7km of fine white sand stretches between Eagle Beach and Palm Beach and meets up with the turquoise waters of the Caribbean. Further northwest, good

Shopping

Duty-free shopping is an irresistible draw for many visitors to Aruba. Bargain-hunters crowd the heart of the shopping district in downtown Oranjestad, where shopping malls, duty-free stores, boutiques and craft shops line the main streets of L.G. Smith Boulevard, Havenstraat and Caya G.F. Betico Croes. Most stores are full of imported goods such as fragrances, linens, liquors, gold jewellery, watches, cameras, name-brand fashions and Dutch porcelain figurines. Malls of note are the large **Seaport Mall** within the luxurious *Sonesta Beach Resort and Casino* complex, the nearby two-storey **Royal Plaza Mall** at the corner of Weststraat and L.G. Smith Boulevard, and the open-air **Seaport Marketplace Mall** on the east side of the harbour and across L.G. Smith Boulevard. Shops are open Monday to Saturday 8am–6.30pm; many close for lunch between noon and 2pm. A small cluster of craft stalls selling typical souvenirs and wooden handicrafts can also be found at the Wharfside Market on L.G. Smith Boulevard.

conditions coupled with a handful of colourful coral reefs and sunken ships, attract windsurfers, divers and snorkellers.

Eagle Beach and Palm Beach

You can take bus #10 from the capital to **Eagle Beach**, the largest and most popular sandy stretch, offering plenty of shade and watersports activities. Several low-rise hotels nearby allow beach-goers to eat and drink at their restaurants and bars. Divi Winds (see box overleaf) offers windsurfing and sailing lessons, and rents boards, kayaks and snorkelling gear. A few kilometres north on J.E. Irausquin Boulevard is **Palm Beach**, known for its luxurious high-rise resorts and more superb watersports. De Palm Tours operates a pier here from which many of their water-based tours and activities originate (see box overleaf). The surrounding shallow waters and long stretches of clean sand are very popular with families. It gets crowded on weekends and holidays, during which time food stalls selling local dishes are set up.

There are a couple of diversions in the area if you're looking to take a break from the beach. Naturalists will delight in exploring the tropical enclosures of the nearby **Butterfly Farm** (daily 9am–4pm; US$10, US$5 children) located on J.E. Irausquin Boulevard across from the *Aruba Phoenix Beach Resort*. The small garden is home to many different types of plants and over forty species of butterflies, including the large-winged blue morpho. Interesting guided tours along the path provide insights into the life cycle and ecological importance of the butterfly. Around the corner, bird enthusiasts will enjoy the **Bubali Bird Sanctuary**, a small marshland sheltering hundreds of species of migratory waterfowl. A viewing platform atop a tower provides the only vantage point from which to observe the birds, which include terns, herons, troupials, cormorants and coots.

The northwest tip

Further north, along L.G. Smith Boulevard, is **Hadicurari**, locally referred to as Fisherman's Hut Beach, a popular **windsurfing** destination and host to the Hi Winds Pro-Am Windsurfing Challenge held each year in June. A couple of boardsailing companies offer windsurfing lessons and board rentals (see box overleaf).

Superb snorkelling, diving and swimming exist near the northern tip of the island at **Malmok** and **Arashi beaches**. Several coral reefs and offshore shipwrecks are worth checking out – you'll need a boat to get to them (see box overleaf).

Overlooking the northwestern tip of the island is the towering white **California Lighthouse**, a favourite place to enjoy sunsets. Built on top of a small hill and sandwiched between sand dunes, this 125-foot lighthouse was named in honour of a British steamship, the *California*, shipwrecked off the coast in 1891. Though nearly all of the ship's crew were able to make it safely to land, the Arubans were prompted to build the lighthouse in 1914 to warn other sailors of possible dangers off shore. Today the lighthouse is still operational and remains closed to the public. Nearby, in a building which once housed the lighthouse keeper, is an elegant Italian restaurant, *La Trattoria el Faro Blanco* (see p.793 for review).

The north coast and around

Leaving the beach district behind, Highway 4A heads east to Aruba's rugged north coast and its barren interior. Past the small community of Paradera, a series of road signs direct you to the mysterious **rock formations** of **Casibari** and nearby **Ayó**. Resembling something out of *The Flintstones*, nobody knows for sure how these smooth, monolithic diorite boulders came to be dropped here, particularly because their geology is so different from that of the rest of the island. Also a mystery is the

Watersports and activities

Aruba offers a wide selection of watersports and related activities, many of which are based on the stretch between Eagle Beach and Palm Beach.

Snorkelling excursions to nearby coral reefs and shipwrecks can be arranged with Fun Factory Sailing Adventure (☎297/862017), departing daily from the De Palm Pier behind the *Radisson Hotel* at 9.30am. The four-hour trip on board the catamaran ($55) includes an open bar, hot buffet lunch, snorkelling gear and visits to a couple of reefs and to the *Antilla*, a sunken World War II German freighter off the coast of Malmok. For an extra US$45 they offer the unique sport of snuba, which combines snorkelling and diving. **Diving** lessons and packages to area dive sites can be arranged with Pelican Watersports (☎297/872302), located next to De Palm Pier. They offer a variety of dive packages starting at US$160; a fully certified Open Water Certification course costs US$350. Red Sail Sports (☎297/861603), behind the *Hyatt Hotel* and *Allegro Resort* on Palm Beach, also has a series of dive courses, charter tours to area reefs and night dives.

Deep-sea fishing with Pair-a-dice Charters can be arranged by calling Captain Monty (☎297/929586). His crew usually fishes for marlin, wahoo, kingfish or barracuda. Half-day charters run US$280.

Aruba's only **kayak** company, Aruba Kayak Adventure (☎297/824400), offers a four-hour guided kayaking trip along the southern coast of the island near Spanish Lagoon, a legendary hiding place for pirates. The fee of US$65 includes hotel pick-up and delivery, use of kayak and brief instructions, lunch and snorkelling gear. They depart every morning at 9.30am.

A variety of **sailing** trips and sunset tours can be arranged with several agencies. Jolly Pirates (☎297/837355) operates a 70-ton schooner and organizes sailing and snorkelling trips departing from De Palm Pier (tours start at US$46). Mi Dushi Sailing Adventures (☎297/862010) sets sail Monday to Saturday on a sunset cruise ($25–28).

Divi Winds (☎297/837841), between the *Divi* and *Tamarijn* resorts on Druif Beach, offers **windsurfing** lessons ($45), sailing lessons ($50) and board rental ($15/hr). At Hadicurari Beach, Aruba Boardsailing Productions (☎297/860989) rents windsurfers at US$20 per hour or US$55 for the day; lessons start at US$135/day.

A different and exciting way to explore Aruba's underwater realm is on board the island's only passenger **submarine**. The *Atlantis Submarine* (☎297/886881) descends to 150ft and passengers can view schools of tropical fish, coral reefs and the remains of the *Mi Dushi* shipwreck. It leaves from the Atlantis Pier located across from the *Sonesta Resort* in downtown Oranjestad.

origin of the ancient **petroglyphs** found on the surface of a few of these boulders; the weathered vestiges of these paintings can be seen through protective steel bars. Both Casibari and Ayó offer well-groomed trails through the rock gardens lined with cacti, aloe and other species of plants, and steps carved into the boulders allow you to climb up for a panoramic view of the island and nearby **Hooiberg**, a 168-metre hill resembling a haystack.

Continuing north from Ayó, a gravel road leads to the **Bushiribana Gold Ruins**, the site of a gold smelter on the coast operational for most of the nineteenth century. Constructed with natural rock in 1825, a year after the discovery of gold triggered a mini economic boom, the smelter processed over three million tons of raw material from the nearby mines before it was abandoned some ninety years later. Today the crumbling ruins stand as a testament to Aruba's rich gold history. Unfortunately there are no guides on hand.

A short distance away, the road turns east and follows the coast for 2.5km until it ends at the **Natural Bridge**, perhaps the most photographed attraction on the island. Rising 25 feet above sea level and spanning a hundred feet across a small bay, this natural coral archway was carved by centuries of raging surf, strong winds and tectonic processes that continue to shape it today. A sandy beach, accessible by a set of stairs from the parking lot, allows visitors to take close-up pictures. The more adventurous can walk the entire length of the bridge and experience first-hand the powerful force of the pounding surf. A small "thirst-aid station" and café sells refreshments and snacks at the parking lot, which is often crowded with tour buses and hundreds of visitors.

Sitting on top of a hill overlooking the north coast, the charming **Alto Vista Chapel**, 5km west of the gold ruins, was the first Catholic chapel on the island. It was originally built by Spanish missionaries in 1750 and renovated two hundred years later. A necklace with a Spanish cross on display in the chapel dates back to the time of the original missionaries and is believed to be the oldest of its kind in the Netherlands Antilles. Getting there is relatively easy: head west along the coastal gravel road from the gold ruins or take Highway 2B north from the town of **Noord** for 0.5km and turn right at the narrow road which winds uphill to the chapel (3.3km).

Arikok National Park

The untamed beauty of Aruba is best experienced in **Arikok National Park**, a large protected area encompassing almost 20 percent of the island's landmass, stretching from the coast inland. Located on the eastern side of the island, the park preserves many of the natural, geological and cultural features that have shaped Aruba's past and present.

The park's desert landscape looks more like the Australian outback than a tropical Caribbean island, and is interspersed with bizarre patches of reddish-orange rock and soil formations. The hilly interior also reveals several abandoned gold mines and traditional country homes, while the park's rugged coastline is littered with sand dunes, grottoes and secluded bays. Growing throughout are groves of towering cacti, contorted divi divi trees and other thorny plants. Typical animals found here include burrowing owls, fruit-eating bats, lizards and herds of wandering goats.

A potholed dirt road and 34km of well-marked **hiking trails** allow visitors to see the park at their own pace. Access is via Highway 7A, which leads to the **park gate** near the town of San Fuego. Past the entrance, the highway turns into a very narrow dirt road and continues to the coast before it heads south toward San Nicolas. A sturdy 4x4 vehicle is highly recommended, as is sunscreen, drinking water and a hat. Guidebooks with trail maps can be purchased for US$15 at the gate.

Exploring the park

A sign posted shortly beyond the entrance will direct you to a **fork** in the road. Straight ahead leads to the coast, dunes and caves; heading right will bring you uphill to **Cunucu Arikok**, a small rocky garden surrounded by a stone and cactus-lined wall. Inside the enclosure a 1.5km trail guides visitors past several species of native and introduced plants as well as **rock formations** similar to those found in Ayó and Casibari. A **petroglyph** of an ancient bird is painted on one of these boulders. Close to the centre of the garden is a recently renovated **cas di torta**, a traditional nineteenth-century country home used by farmers who attempted to cultivate this relatively infertile land. This type of structure was typically constructed with rocks and dried cactus husks and held together with layers of mud and grass.

A short drive uphill from the garden will take you to the top of **Cero Arikok** (176m), where you'll be rewarded with a spectacular panoramic view of the park. From there the road continues for 3.6km to **Conchi**, a natural pool found close to the north coast. There is a good chance that in the near future the road to the natural pool will be closed to vehicular traffic – adventurous souls may wish to hike the hilly landscape to it; otherwise, the Desert Rose Equestrian Centre will continue to take visitors to the pool on guided horseback tours (☎297/947806; 2.5hr; US$40).

If you want to explore the coastline and its many caves, head back to the fork in the road at the main gate. Once there, take the road heading east for 5km. Along the way there is a four-kilometre hiking trail (watch for signs shortly after the fork) to the gold pits of **Miralamar** and the foot of **Cero Jamanota**, Aruba's highest peak (188m). Hiking conditions are relatively easy and involve navigating some small slopes.

Gently rolling white **sand dunes** mark the beginning of the coastline. The secluded **Dos Playa** beach can be reached by turning left at the dunes for 1.5km. Swimming is not recommended here – the surf is too dangerous, but it's an ideal place to stop for a picnic. Past the dunes the main road heads southeast along the coast; after 200m there's a small open-air **snack bar** (daily 10am–6pm) serving a good selection of burgers, chicken and seafood dishes for US$10–15. Film, drinks and a variety of munchies can also be purchased.

Turning right at the snack bar the road leads to the **Fontein Caves**, a collection of small grottoes that were once occupied by native peoples. Centuries of graffiti, brownish-red Indian rock paintings and beautiful flowstone formations adorn the walls and ceilings of these limestone caves. Fruit-eating bats roost during the day and fly out at night in search of food. Free tours are offered every fifteen minutes by the park rangers; flash photography is not permitted.

Adjacent to the caves is the **Fontein Garden** (Place Hofi Fontein), the site of a nineteenth-century **plantation** run by the Gravenhorst-Croes family. This was the only place on the north coast where permanent running fresh water was available throughout the year; this feature allowed for the plantation's development. The house has been restored and now houses a small **museum** displaying a scant collection of photos, tools and animal specimens.

San Nicolas and the southeast tip

Up until the late nineteenth century, **San Nicolas**, the oldest and largest city in Aruba, existed as a peaceful settlement of a few fishermen and their families living in small huts scattered along the southeast coast. All that changed in 1879 when the Aruba Phosphate Company began exporting locally mined **phosphate** in large quantities to the US. Subsequent demand, combined with the need for a larger workforce, prompted officials to build houses for their employees, and the makings of the town began. After vast oilfields were discovered off the coast of Venezuela during the early part of the twentieth century, the Largo Oil and Transport

△ Longsnout seahorse, Bonaire

Company announced plans to build an **oil refinery** near town. By 1951, the once-quiet village had a population of just over 20,000 residents, almost twice the size of Oranjestad – and twice the size of the town's current population. Social clubs, golf courses and luxurious homes in the new suburbs of Largo Heights and Cero Colorado were built for the hordes of workers – from the island and beyond – who flocked to this boomtown. When the refinery closed in 1985, the city was left in a shambles until it was reopened in 1991 by Coastal Aruba Refining.

The town hasn't got much to offer, other than a few abandoned ruins of old buildings that give a glimpse of the British-Caribbean charm of the town's former glory days. This will change, however, in the near future as plans for hotels and an exclusive shopping district are in the works. For now, restaurants, snack stalls and a handful of shops selling local crafts and souvenirs can be found alongside the picturesque promenade on Zeppenfeldstraat. A requisite stop is the legendary *Charlie's Bar and Restaurant* (see opposite for review), which dates back to 1941. Over sixty years' worth of mementos left by seamen, refinery workers, scuba divers and other visitors adorn the walls and ceilings.

Nearby, about 6km east of San Nicolas, are two small popular public **beaches**. To reach them, take Fortheuvelstraat out of town until you come to a huge cement anchor at the end of the road. Turn right on the main road and follow the signs to Rodger's Beach and Baby Beach. You'll first hit **Rodger's Beach**, which, despite a view of the nearby oil refinery, is a good spot with decent swimming conditions and the *Coco Bar and Grill Restaurant* (see opposite). Just east of here, the sheltered waters of **Baby Beach** offer ideal swimming conditions, especially for families with small children, as well as good snorkelling. Jads Beach Store (☎297/846070) rents beach and snorkelling gear.

Eating and drinking

The majority of the island's finer eateries are in the capital along Wilhelminastraat, serving everything from prime Argentine beef to local seafood dishes. Many are only open for lunch and dinner and some close on Sundays or Mondays; it's usually wise to make reservations. Most of the resorts also have their own restaurants.

Oranjestad

Captain Cooks Bakery Seaport Marketplace Mall. Serving delicious breakfast specials for US$5. Fresh bread, fruit shakes plus deli meats available daily from 7.30am until midnight (open 9.30am on Sun).

Cuba's Cookin' Wilhelminastraat 27 ☎297/880627. Genuine Cuban cuisine and lively entertainment are on offer at this traditional nineteenth-century country house. Try the lobster enchilada. Entrees US$20–30. Daily from 6pm until 10 or 11pm.

Don Carlos L.G. Smith Boulevard ☎297/836246. You can't get any closer to the water than this place serving reasonably priced authentic Italian cuisine directly on the waterfront in the heart of town. Very popular with young families, it can get rather busy. Daily 11.30am–4.30pm & 5pm–midnight.

El Gaucho Wilhelminastraat 80 ☎297/823677. Tender, juicy Argentine steaks grilled to perfection; for a real treat try the 16oz gaucho steak. Cosy atmosphere with an adjoining cocktail lounge and an extensive wine list. Mon–Sat 11.30am–11pm.

Iguana Joe's 2nd floor, Royal Plaza Mall ☎297/839373. Long one of Aruba's most popular restaurants. Delicious dishes include quesadillas and crispy calamari; vegetarian options also available. Don't miss out on their enormous tropical drinks like the famous Pink Iguana, a smooth, refreshing strawberry colada. Mains under US$20. Open Mon–Thurs 11am –11pm, Fri & Sat 11am–1am & Sun 4–11pm.

Qué Pasa? Wilhelminastraat 2 ☎297/834888. Popular dinnertime restaurant and bar with a small art gallery offering moderately priced Italian meals and other international dishes. Mains US$25. Daily 5pm–midnight.

Taj Mahal Wilhelminastraat 4A ☎297/884494. The only Indian restaurant in town. Delicious authentic dishes, averaging US$6, all prepared to order. Mon–Sat 11am–10pm & Sun 6–11pm.

Villa Germania Seaport Marketplace Mall ☎297/830078. One of the few places in town open for breakfast ($5–8), *Villa Germania* also has home-made European cuisine like schnitzel and sauerkraut and desserts for lunch and dinner (mains US$12–20). Open terrace faces the harbour. Daily 8am–10pm.
The Waterfront Seaport Marketplace Mall ☎297/835858. Specializing in seafood dishes as well as burgers and chicken dishes. Open for breakfast ($6–10), lunch and dinner (mains US$7–15). Daily 8.30am–11.30pm.

The beach strip and northwest tip

La Trattoria el Faro Blanco At the California Lighthouse ☎297/860786. Fine Italian dining in a small restaurant belonging to the former lighthouse keeper. The food is expensive but excellent, and the views off the ocean and sunset are stunning. Reservations recommended. Daily 11am–3pm & 6–10pm.
Madame Janette Near the mini-golf on Cunucu Abao 37 ☎297/870184. This very popular, friendly restaurant attracts both locals and tourists, and a varied menu features international and seafood dishes. Daily 6–10pm except Tues.

San Nicolas area

Charlie's Bar and Restaurant Downtown on Zeppenfeldstraat 56 ☎297/845086. This popular hangout has become something of a legend in Aruba. Over sixty years of mementos left here by seamen, refinery workers and scores of visitors cover the interior including everything from sport shirts to licence plates, business cards to photographs. Don't be turned off by all the "reserved" signs on the tables: the owners are keeping the table for you. Be sure to try the mouthwatering jumbo shrimp and *pasapalo* (delicious local-style tenderloin) served with their famous hot *honeymoon sauce*. Mon–Sat 11am–10pm.
Coco Bar and Grill Restaurant Rodger's Beach ☎297/843434. Decent Caribbean and local cuisine on a terrace overlooking the water. Open daily for lunch and dinner.

Nightlife

At night, the dazzling lights of Oranjestad attract party buses and scores of revellers who visit as many bars, nightclubs and casinos as possible before daybreak. Many of the restaurants and bars have live local bands on weekends, and most hotels and resorts offer theme nights and activities for their guests. If you're heart is set on spending an elegant evening, the glitzy Las Vegas style dance shows at the Crystal Theater in the *Sonesta Resort* are well worth the price of admission.

Café Bahia Weststraat 7 ☎297/889982. A staircase leads upstairs to an open-air dance floor. Local bands usually play on weekends, happy hour is on Fri 5–7pm and ladies night is Wed. Closes 3.30am on weekends and 2am on weekdays. No cover charge.
Carlos'n Charlie's Weststraat 3A ☎297/820355. A popular bar with tourists who dance to tunes from the 1960s to the 1980s. The music gets going after 11pm. US$3 cover charge.
Club E-Zone Bayside Mall on Weststraat 5. The largest indoor dance floor in town plays European music and attracts a fairly young crowd of tourists.
Crystal Theater Downtown at the *Aruba Sonesta Beach Resort* on L.G. Smith Boulevard ☎297/836000. An impressive heart-thumping "Let's Go Latin" dance show ($37) with live music and dancers. Show times are from Mon to Sat beginning at 9pm. The resort also has a 24-hour casino.
La Fiesta 2nd floor Adventura Mall on Klipstraat ☎297/889982. This trendy terrace bar attracts both locals and tourists. Latin beats are mixed with European and American tunes.
Mambo Jambos 2nd floor Royal Plaza ☎297/833632. Tables are removed on Fri and Sat for dancing; other nights this place is great for hanging out and listening to music. It's also a restaurant serving sandwiches and snacks. Latin tunes played throughout the day. Daily 10.30am–4am.
Radisson Aruba Caribbean Resort Casino *Radisson Caribbean Resort* on Palm Beach ☎297/864045. Casino surrounded by lavish drapery and Caribbean palms. The lounge and sports bar are also popular.
Stellaris Casino At the *Aruba Marriott* on Palm Beach ☎297/869000. One of the island's favourite casinos.

Listings

Airlines Aeropostal (☎297/837793); American Airlines (☎297/822700); Avianca (☎297/823388); Continental Airlines (☎297/880044); Delta (☎297/886619); Dutch Caribbean Express, formerly ALM (☎297/838080); KLM (☎297/823546).

Banks Many banks are located on Caya G.F. Betico Croes, including ABN/AMRO (☎297/821515); Aruba Bank (☎297/821550); Caribbean Mercantile Bank (☎297/823118); and Interbank Aruba (☎297/831080). Many ATMs are also found in shopping centres.

Car rental AC&E Jeep & Car Rental (☎297/830840); Alamo Car Rental (☎297/833244); Amigo Car Rental (☎297/860502); Bon Bini Rent a Car (☎297/834471); Budget Car Rental (☎297/828600); Caribbean Car Rental (☎297/822515); Econo Car Rental (☎297/887072); Hertz Car Rental (☎297/821845); Thrifty Car Rental (☎297/835335).

Internet access *Cyber Café*, 2nd floor Royal Plaza Mall (Mon–Sat 8.30am–9.30pm & Sun 10am–6pm; US$6 for 1hr); *Cyberzone Internet Café*, Seaport Marketplace Mall (Mon–Sat 9am–11pm & Sun 2–10pm; US$6 for 1hr).

Laundry Aruba Laundry & Cleaning, Hendrik Straat 30 (☎297/823627); Oranjestad Laundry, Arendstraat 107 (☎297/821638).

Pharmacies Pharmacies, called *boticas*, are open Mon–Sat 7.30am–7.30pm. Botica Eagle, near hospital (☎297/876103); Botica del Pueblo, Caya G.F. Betico Croes 48 (☎297/822154); Kibrahacha Botica, across from the SETAR telephone office on Havenstraat (☎297/834908).

Post office Main office is located across from the St Franciscus Church (Mon–Fri 7.30am–noon & 1–4.30pm). A small postal outlet is also located on the ground floor of the Royal Plaza Mall (Mon–Fri 8am–3.30pm).

21.2

Bonaire

Regarded as one of the world's premier sites for shore diving, the tiny boomerang-shaped island of **BONAIRE**, located 80km north of Venezuela, has much to offer those seeking an active tropical holiday. Beneath the clear blue waters, divers and snorkellers are treated to a stunning spectacle: schools of fish of every imaginable shape, size and colour swim with sea turtles and other marine creatures in and around the delicate coral and sponge gardens. All this and more can be found in the waters of the **Bonaire Marine Park**, which surrounds the entire island and its neighbouring offshore cay, the uninhabited **Klein Bonaire**.

As rugged and barren as the land may seem, the island has a different character to it depending on where you are. In the hilly north, the cactus-strewn landscape of **Washington-Slagbaai National Park** preserves remnants of the island's history along with a host of local flora and fauna. To the south, the land opens up and becomes flatter, and vast multicoloured **saltpans** attract the largest colony of **pink flamingos** in the Caribbean. If you're after more adventure, there's windsurfing at **Lac Cai**, on the island's east coast, and kayaking in the nearby mangrove swamps.

Outside of its natural attractions, Bonaire's appeal is low-key. In the evening you can enjoy the sunset while dining in one of the many restaurants found in **Kralendijk**, the island's tidy capital, also home to a few cultural attractions and numerous shops.

Arrival and getting around

Most visitors **fly** to Bonaire's **Flamingo International Airport**, located 5km south of Kralendijk. The easiest way to reach the capital or your hotel is to take a taxi from outside the terminal; expect to pay around US$8–12.

Several **cruise ships** also visit the island twice a week and usually spend most of the day in port, just long enough for passengers to take in some sightseeing and shopping.

It is also possible to take a **ferry** to and from Curaçao. The **Flamingo Fast Ferry** departs from the North Pier in Kralendijk twice daily at 6.30am and 3.30pm (US$55 round-trip; 1hr 30min each way; ⓣ599/717-7001). Tickets can be purchased by the pier or directly from the captain on board, and passengers are advised to arrive at least a half-hour before departure.

If you're planning to dive or wish to explore the interior, you'll be better off renting a car from the airport or your hotel. A pleasant alternative is seeing the island's unspoiled beauty by **scooter** (see "Listings" on p.803 for rental companies).

Accommodation

The largest concentration of Bonaire's **hotels** and **dive resorts** is along the coast just north and south of downtown Kralendijk. Most dive resorts will have a dive centre on the premises and many will have a house **reef** just offshore.

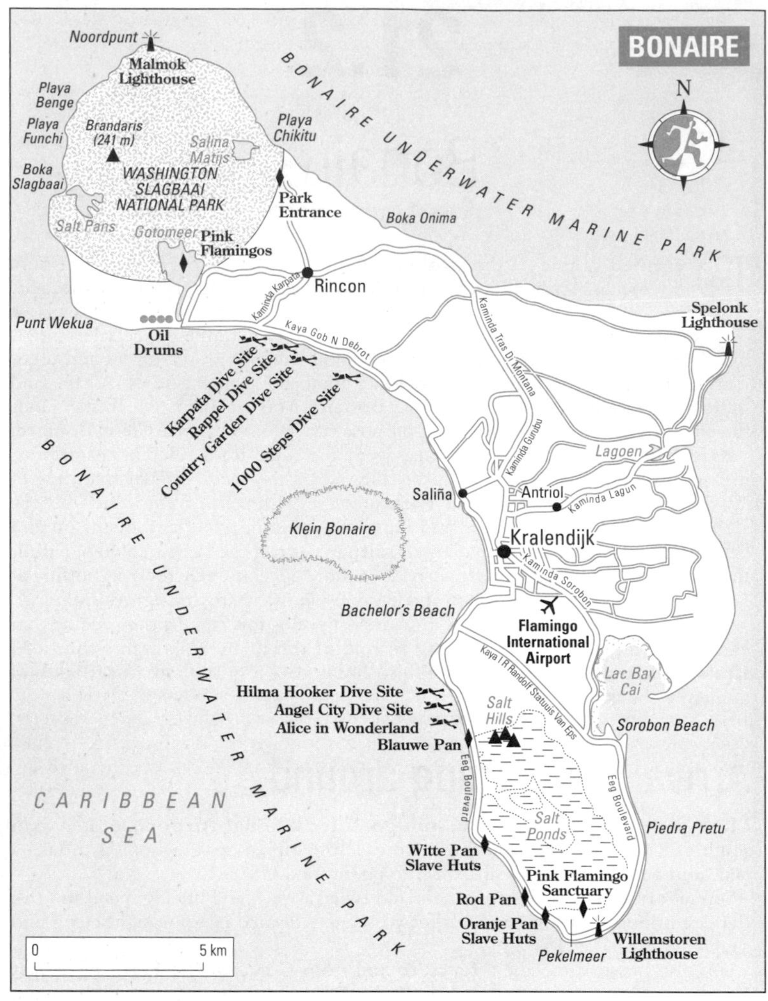

Kralendijk

Caribbean Court J.A. Abraham Boulevard ⓣ599/717-5353, ⓕ717-5363, ⓦwww.caribbeancourt.com. Located close to the airport and only five minutes from the beach. The hotel is built in the style of the charming houses that line the canals of Amsterdam; a small canal provides access to the oceanfront, perfect for those arriving by sailboat. Rooms are spacious with fully equipped kitchenettes, A/C and cable TV, and the small restaurant serves breakfast and light lunches. 7

Carib Inn J.A. Abraham Blvd 46 ⓣ599/717-8819, ⓕ717-5295, ⓦwww.caribinn.com. Centrally located and within walking distance of downtown, the inn has small apartments, many with kitchenettes. There's a dive centre, and the dockside gazebo is a great spot to enjoy evening sunsets. 4

Divi Flamingo Beach Resort J.A. Abraham Blvd 40 ⓣ599/717-8285, ⓕ717-8238, ⓦwww.divibonaire.com. This large resort, just minutes from downtown, has small standard rooms with terraces and a view of the pool, and spacious luxury rooms with private balcony and excellent ocean views. There's also a dive centre, tennis court, mini-mart, spa, casino, waterfront restaurant/bar, on-site tour operator and good snorkelling on the house reef. A slide show on the diversity of marine life is shown once a week. 6

Plaza Resort Bonaire J.A. Abraham Blvd 80 ⓣ599/717-2500, ⓕ717-7133, ⓦwww.plazaresortbonaire.com. The largest luxury resort on the island, located on the only stretch of beach downtown. Rooms tend to be very spacious with huge bathrooms; some have a decent view of the ocean. Excellent restaurants, a lively beachside bar, fitness centre, spa, pool, casino and dive centre are all on site. There's also decent snorkelling offshore, and gear (US$11/day) is available for rent to both guests and non-guests. 7

North of Kralendijk

Buddy Beach and Dive Resort Kaya Gobernardor N. Debrot 85 ⓣ599/717-5080, ⓕ717-8647, ⓦwww.buddydive.com. Oceanfront property just ten minutes north of town with spacious apartments furnished with kitchenettes, A/C, cable TV, private bath and patio or balcony; request an ocean view (upstairs, building #4). Popular dive-and-drive packages are available (see p.801), and there's also a pool and decent restaurant/bar on site. 5

Captain Don's Habitat Kaya Gobernardor N. Debrot 103 ⓣ599/717-8290, ⓕ717-8240, ⓦwww.habitatdiveresorts.com. One of the first dive resorts on the island, this laid-back place remains a favourite with divers. Simple but comfortable cottage-style rooms surround a pool and garden; many have kitchenettes, A/C and private bath. There's a fully equipped dive centre (see p.801); the gorgeous house reef is just offshore. 6

South of Kralendijk

Happy Holiday Homes Punt Vierkant 9 ⓣ599/717-8405, ⓕ717-8605, ⓦwww.happyholidayhomes.com. Reasonably priced bungalows south of the airport in a quiet residential neighbourhood, minutes from popular dive spots. Large rooms have kitchenettes, private bathrooms and cable TV. Very friendly staff; highly recommended for families. 3

Kralendijk

Set alongside a picturesque harbour on the west coast, the tiny capital of **KRALENDIJK** ("coral dike" in Dutch) is Bonaire's commercial centre and the first stop for anyone visiting the island. Marked by a few low-rise buildings painted in pretty pastel colours and a handful of narrow streets, the town holds most of the island's government buildings, shops, hotels, restaurants and bars. There's not much to do or see in town, other than shop or dine at the restaurants, many of which are on the waterfront. The town's couple of historical buildings and small cultural **museum** won't take more than an hour or two to explore.

The Town

KRALENDIJK can seem chaotic at times, especially when hordes of cruise-ship passengers crowd the small streets and zip around on mopeds or bicycles. The best time to see the town therefore is late afternoon when the cruise ships have departed. Due to the many one-way streets the town is easiest to explore on **foot**, and you won't need a map to see the few attractions, many of which are found close to the coast on the main roads of Kaya Charles E.B. Helimund and Kaya Grandi.

Perhaps the best place to get your bearings is follow the colourful **waterfront** thoroughfare known as Kaya Jan N.E Craane, which merges with Kaya Charles E.B. Helimund toward the south end of town. Along this route you'll find several government buildings, shops, restaurants and bars, as well as the occasional Dutch Caribbean-style building painted yellow and gold. Benches and a few palm trees en route make this stretch a popular place to take in the tropical surroundings or catch the sunset.

On the north end of the route, **Karel's Pier** is home to a favourite watering hole for locals and tourists, as well as Pirate Cruises (see p.801) and Seacow Watertaxi (see p.802). Across the way, you can also browse through the shops, boutiques and restaurants of the **Harbourside Mall**.

Further south and closer to the centre of Kralendijk is the Town Pier, often referred to as the **North Pier** and a superb spot for night diving. Its underwater pillars are encrusted with sponges, corals and other sea creatures, all of which come to life after sundown. The pier can be extremely busy at times with heavy cruise-ship and boat traffic, and you must obtain permission from the Harbourmaster if you wish to dive here. The Harbourmaster's office is located in Fort Oranje, a few metres to the south and across from the smaller Ro-Ro Pier.

Next door to the North Pier is a small open-air **market** where vendors peddle fresh produce and fish from Venezuela. Several souvenir stands selling locally made wooden handicrafts and artwork are usually set up inland across the avenue in **Wilhelminaplein**, a courtyard near the Protestant church. Here you'll find a monument honouring Eleanor Roosevelt's 1944 visit to American troops stationed on the island, as well as the **Van Walbeck Monument**, commemorating the landing in 1634 of the director of the Dutch West India Company.

At the southern end of the route sits the **South Pier**, which receives a fair amount of marine traffic. On the way you'll pass small, mustard-coloured **Fort Oranje** with its four cannons and stone lighthouse. The fort was built by the Dutch in 1817 to protect the island's flourishing salt industry, and has since served as a prison and a storage depot. Today, the fort is home to the city hall and a few government offices. There's really not much to see inside the buildings, and most people are content with taking a few snapshots and moving on.

Running parallel to the waterfront a block inland from Kaya Jan N.E. Craane is another main road, the short stretch of **Kaya Grandi**, where you'll find the **tourist information centre** (see p.577) and many of the island's shops, boutiques and restaurants.

The town's only other noteworthy sight is a ten-minute walk east of town. The quaint **Bonaire Museum**, Kaya J.v.d. Ree 7 (Mon–Fri 8am–noon & 1–5pm; US$1.50, children US$1), is worth a visit for its tiny but interesting collection of old photographs, artefacts and exhibits of folkloric costumes.

South of Kralendijk

You could easily spend a half-day exploring this scenic and flat part of the island, longer if you want to dive or snorkel the many sites found offshore. From Kralendijk head south along Boulevard L.A. Abraham for 5km until you reach the airport, where the coastal road Eeg Boulevard begins a 32km loop around the island's southern end, taking in numerous dive sites, glistening mountains of salt, slave huts dating back to Bonaire's darker days and a flamingo sanctuary hidden among the saltpans. Facilities are very limited in the area, so be sure to bring plenty of water and something to eat.

Shortly after the airport you'll see several dive and snorkelling sites just a stone's throw from the narrow beaches of washed-up coral; the most popular are the **shipwreck** at Hilma Hooker and the double **reef** at Angel City and Alice in Wonderland. Simply park your car near the site and swim the short distance to the site. Watch out too for the pink **Dive Bus**, which sells refreshments and has locker space for valuables. Stopping at different dive locations on this road, the bus has become a meeting place of sorts for divers. More importantly it serves as an emergency centre if divers run into trouble – it has a first aid kit and a cellular phone to call for medical help.

The road continues southwards alongside numerous dive sites as well as the expansive pink and turquoise **saltpans** belonging to Cargill Salt – one of largest businesses on Bonaire. Ocean water pumped into the pools gradually evaporates under the heat of the sun, leaving behind a briny solution from which salt crystals are eventually grown and harvested for export. The cement **obelisks** that remain standing today at Blauwe Pan and Rod Pan were used until 1863 as flagpoles signalling to trade boats that the salt was ready for export.

At Whitte Pan and 2km further south near Oranje Pan, you'll find clusters of small white and reddish-brown **slave huts** atop a bluff overlooking the exposed coastline. Built in 1850, these tiny cement buildings housed slaves from the nearby salt fields, each building just waist high with a steep roof and a tiny opening for a door and window. If you look carefully in the salt fields you can still see the trails once used by these slaves.

As the road winds its way to the southern tip keep your eyes peeled for the pink haze over the salt fields in the far distance. With binoculars it's possible to distinguish this haze as the thousands of **pink flamingos** that inhabit Pekelmeer sanctuary, the largest breeding ground of flamingos in the western hemisphere. These tall, graceful birds are shy by nature and easily disturbed by noise; to protect them the government has declared the entire area off limits – even the airspace overhead is closed to all air traffic. Each night many of these birds make their way to Venezuela and return to feed at dawn. Across from Pekelmeer stands the battered remains of the **Willemstoren lighthouse**, the first lighthouse built on the island in 1837.

From the lighthouse the road turns north and follows a more rugged coastline, passing **Piedra Pretu** (black stone), worth a brief stop for a wander among the large chunks of sun-bleached coral and piles of twisted driftwood, and to experience first-hand the awesome force of the waves that have shaped this side of the island.

At the north end of the road, just before it turns back towards Kralendijk, is **Lac Bay**, a shallow stretch of water on the east coast with the best **windsurfing** and **kayaking** conditions on the island. Shortly after *Sorobon Beach Resort* (clothing optional), you'll come upon a couple of locally run businesses renting boards and kayaks and offering windsurfing lessons, the most popular of which is Jibe City (daily 9am–5pm, closed Sept; ⓣ599/717-5233), whose lively snack bar is a hangout for surfers. You can also rent kayaks (from US$35/day) and windsurfing boards (US$60/day) and take windsurfing lessons (US$45 for beginners and advanced; board included for beginners only). The bay's sheltered waters and steady trade winds draw surfers of all levels and ages, and each October serve as the site of Bonaire's international windsurfing regatta.

Beyond Lac Bay the road heads inland for 500m before splitting into two roads. The right fork, Kaya I.R. Randolf Statuuis Van Eps, will take you to the hotels close to the airport, while the left, Kaminda Sorobon, leads back to downtown Kralendijk. Both roads pass through desert terrain littered with cacti and scrubby vegetation; watch out for the roaming wild donkeys and goats.

If you take Kaminda Sorobon, follow the signs to the dirt road leading east to **Cai**, a small point on the northern tip of Lac Bay. Every Sunday afternoon the place comes to life as scores of locals and surfers gather to listen to live music, dance, drink beer and eat local food. *Lac Suid*, a small restaurant at the end of the road (see p.803), is also a good place for a meal. You can also stop for snacks en route to the bay at *Maiky* (see p.803), which is signposted off Kaminda Sorobon.

The area is also the starting-point for **kayaking** trips to nearby mangrove swamps (Bonaire Boating organizes tours; see p.801).

Rincon and Washington-Slagbaai National Park

Bonaire's oldest settlement, **RINCON**, is nestled in a valley northwest of Kralendijk – a cluster of red-roofed houses, a gas station and one phone booth shared by all of its residents. Originally established as a Spanish settlement in the sixteenth century, Rincon eventually became home to many slave families who laboured in the nearby plantations and salt fields of the southern peninsula. The town is best visited during the annual **Rincon Day festival** (April 30), when visitors from all over the Caribbean come here for traditional music and dancing, and local food such as goat stew served with *funchi*. During the rest of the year Rincon is worth seeking out for its laid-back atmosphere and rural setting; before leaving be sure to stop at popular *Prisca's Ice Cream* on Kaya Komkomber for a taste of her famous concoctions.

Washington-Slagbaai National Park

From Rincon follow the main road northwest for 3.5km to **Washington-Slagbaai National Park** (8am–5pm, no entrance after 2.45pm; US$10), which occupies most of the island's northwestern tip. The land, which once belonged to two plantation owners who produced and exported vast quantities of aloe, goat meat and charcoal, is now a protected reserve for fascinating flora and fauna, including the towering cacti (known locally as *kadushi,* a staple of soups), pink flamingos and numerous species of parrot, bats, iguanas and lizards. Other highlights include salt ponds, rocky coves, plantation houses, snorkelling spots and **Brandaris Hill**, the highest point on the island (241m).

Once past the gate you can choose from two routes that will take you through the park: the shorter 24km **green route** (2hr) traversing the hilly interior or the longer 40km **yellow route** (4hr) that winds around the coast before venturing inland and joining up with the green route. Stick to the coloured trail markers and follow the map, keeping in mind that once you start your journey you cannot backtrack – all roads lead in one direction. Feel free to venture out of your car to explore the landscape at any of the stops marked on the map.

Both routes start by taking you past the saltpans of **Saliña Matijs**, which can be dry for most of the year, though between December and March hundreds of flamingos arrive here as soon as the saltpan fills with rainwater. From here the road forks into separate coloured routes. Taking the yellow route will bring you to **Playa Chikitu**, a popular sunbathing spot with a few umbrellas on the beach, though swimming is not advisable because of the strong outgoing current. Continuing along this route, you'll pass many rugged coves (*bokas*) and stunning vistas of the park; the green route, meanwhile, cuts west across the park, skipping the park's northern reaches.

At Brandaris Hill the yellow route joins the green route, and nearby you'll find decent snorkelling at playas Funchi and Bengé. The best place for swimming, however, is at **Boka Slagbaai**, 1.5km south of Playa Funchi. From there both routes make their way inland; the yellow route offers the option of seeing more flamingos at the larger saltpan of Gotomeer before joining the green route for the final stretch back to the park entrance.

Park practicalities

To navigate the park's bumpy and narrow dirt roads, a rugged **four-wheel-drive** vehicle is necessary, especially after a rainstorm; mountain bikes, scooters and camping are all strictly forbidden inside the park. The alternative is taking a **tour** led by Bonaire Boating, highly recommended for its coverage of the park's natural and cultural history (see opposite).

Before venturing in, stock up on refreshments and snacks at the small **plantation house** where you pay your fee, as there are no facilities past the park gate. You can also view a small collection of Arawak artefacts and tools at the nearby **museum**. Proper footwear and a pair of binoculars are recommended if you plan to leave your car for a bit of hiking.

Bonaire Marine Park and Klein Bonaire

Bonaire's pristine coral reefs and abundant marine life have been protected from development since 1979, when the government established the **Bonaire Marine Park** as a means of regulating diving and its impact on the marine environment. Comprising the entire coastline of the island, and that of the neighbouring uninhabited cay of **Klein Bonaire** – from the high-water mark down to 60m – the park is widely recognized as a model of marine conservation.

Bonaire has 86 **dive sites**, the majority of which are on the leeward side of the island. All sites are marked with yellow stone markers or a buoy and come with colourful names such as Country Garden, Forest, Yellow Man's Reef, Ol' Blue and Bloodlet. **Boats** are not permitted to drop anchor and must instead use the mooring site. The majority of sites can be reached directly from shore, while Klein Bonaire is accessible only by boat (many operators schedule charter trips to the island see box below). Popular dive and snorkelling spots include 1000 Steps, Karpata, Rappel, Country Garden, Pink Beach, and No Name on Klein Bonaire, and most sites harbour magnificent stands of elkhorn and brain coral as well as sponges surrounded by an array of tropical fish and marine invertebrates. Many resorts have an on-site house reef and offer a variety of underwater certification and photography courses.

The shallow and clear waters provide excellent visibility for **snorkelling**, and though a major storm in 1999 damaged many beaches and shallow-water corals, signs of recovery are already visible; snorkellers can still enjoy schools of parrotfish, trumpet fish, barracuda, moray eels and angel fish swimming around the sponges and numerous species of soft and hard coral.

Dive centres and tour operators

There's no shortage of **dive centres** on Bonaire, many of them located in hotels or resorts. All offer equipment repair and rental service and can organize boat tours to many of the dive sites, including those on Klein Bonaire. Expect to pay around US$20 for a shore dive, US$40 for a one-tank boat tour and around US$330 for a five-day underwater certification course, plus equipment rentals (US$8/day for regulators; US$10/day for snorkel, fin and mask; and US$11/day for tanks, including weights). Your best deal is to arrange a package deal with a resort, which usually covers accommodation, equipment rental and a specified number of dives. The following dive centres are recommended: *Buddy Beach and Dive Resort*, north of Kralendijk (see p.797), offers an eight-day drive-and-dive package for US$1100, including accommodation, a rental vehicle and unlimited airfills for shore diving, plus six boat dives. Also north of Kralendijk is *Captain Don's* (see p.797), which has a range of underwater certification and photography courses taught by highly qualified instructors. For **underwater camera** rentals (US$25–55/day), visit Photo Tours Divers, *Caribbean Court*, J.A. Abraham Boulevard (☎599/777-3460, ®www.bonphototours.com). Diving packages and instruction are also available here, as are inexpensive and unlimited airfills (US$99 for one week).

Bonaire also has many **tour operators** offering a range of land- and water-based activities; most will pick you up and deliver you back to your hotel. It's advisable to call ahead for reservations, especially when there's a cruise ship in town. Two worth trying are Pirate Cruises on Karel's Pier in Kralendijk (☎599/790-8330), which offers guided snorkelling trips to Klein Bonaire for US$25, departing at 9.30am and 1.30pm; and Bonaire Boating, based at *Divi Flamingo Beach Resort* (☎599/790-5353; for resort see review on p.796). The latter offers diving, snorkelling and sailing trips, in addition to activities like kayaking in the mangroves at Lac Bay (daily 9am; $42.50 for 3hr) and touring Washington-Slagbaai National Park (Tues & Fri 9am; US$65 for 6hr, including lunch).

Park practicalities

Rangers patrol the 6400-acre park to enforce the strict rules that govern the use of this facility. Divers and snorkellers will be asked to show their **Marine Park tag** (US$10, valid for one calendar year), available from island dive operators or from the Marine Park's office at Barcardera. They'll also need to attend a warm-up dive session with a qualified instructor, which can be arranged through any dive centre. Diving gloves and kneepads are not permitted, nor is disturbing or removing any coral, fish or marine invertebrate, whether dead or alive.

Besides the many dive centres that offer trips in the park, Seacow Watertaxi (☎599/780-7126) will also take you to Klein Bonaire for US$14 round-trip.

More information can be found on the park's website at Ⓦwww.bmp.org

Eating, drinking and nightlife

Surprisingly, for its small size there are plenty of good **eating opportunities** in and around Kralendijk, many of them within walking distance of downtown. It's possible to sample a variety of cuisines, among them Italian, Indonesian, Dutch and local fare. While **hotel restaurants** are generally more expensive than dining in town, Kralendijk also has a couple of grocery stores and bakeries offering a wide selection of fresh produce and imported goods (see opposite). The many **snack stands** scattered throughout the island are the best place to try delicious local fare, including goat, fish or conch stews. Most meals cost under US$8.

While Bonaire is not known for its nightlife, there are a few fun spots where you can unwind at the end of the day, and many of the bars at hotels and resorts have **live music** on weekends; check *Bonaire Update*, a free bimonthly publication for upcoming events and activities.

Kralendijk

City Café Kaya Grandi 7 ☎599/717-8286. A great place to grab a light snack and drink a pint or two as the sun goes down. Happy hour 5.30–6.30pm; live bands on weekends.

Cozzoli's Pizzeria Harbourside Mall ☎599/717-5195. One of the few places on the island open for breakfast, serving bacon and eggs as well as some fruit plates. For lunch and dinner they offer a variety of tasty pizzas and grill items starting at NAf20. The outdoor covered terrace has harbour views. Mon–Sat 8am–midnight, Sun 8am–10pm.

De Tuin Eetcafé Kaya L.D. Gerharts 9 ☎599/717-2999. A small, lively Dutch-owned café in the centre of town serving excellent meals starting at NAf25. Lunch and dinner usually include a good selection of seafood and curry dishes, as well as burgers and steaks. Internet access is also available (US$4/30min). Mon–Fri 11am–midnight, Sat & Sun 2pm–midnight.

Karel's Beach Bar On a small pier across from Harbourside Mall. A favourite watering hole for locals and tourists alike, with good views of the busy harbour. Happy hour 5.30–8pm. Local bands play on weekends.

Mona Lisa Bar and Restaurant Kaya Grandi 15 ☎599/717-8718. Located on the main street in town, this cosy Dutch-owned establishment serves scrumptious seafood and smoked chicken dishes. Expect to pay NAf35 for the catch of the day. Mon–Fri: restaurant 6–10pm, bar 4pm–2am.

Old Inn Opposite the *Plaza Resort* on Abraham Boulevard ☎599/717-6666. Affordable Indonesian restaurant serving up large portions of their famous rijsttafel (a feast of sweet and moderately spicy dishes). Can get crowded in the evenings. Open daily after 5pm except Wed.

North of Kralendijk

Bongos Beach *Eden Beach Resort* on Kaya Gobernardor N. Debrot 73 ☎599/717-7238. Popular beachside hangout offering tasty snacks and speciality drinks and especially lively on Friday nights. Happy hour 5.30–6.30pm. Mon–Fri 8am–11pm, Sat & Sun 8am–2am.

Giby's Terrace Kaya Andres A. Emerenciana ☎599/567-0655. Just minutes from downtown, *Giby's* is a well-known snack stand serving delicious conch and goat stews. Enjoy your meal outside on the small terrace or take it back to your hotel. Daily 10am–11pm, closed Tues.

It Rains Fishes Kaya Jan N.E. Craane 24 ☎599/717-8780. This popular, friendly restaurant on a covered outdoor terrace facing the water offers delicious and affordable local seafood dishes for NAf27.50. Also available are chicken, beef tenderloin and a selection of salads. Mon–Sat 5.30–10pm only.

Rendez-Vous Kaya L.D. Gerharts 3 ⓣ599/717-8454. One of Bonaire's oldest restaurants, with pictures of famous diners adorning its walls. Delicious home-made meals include catch of the day encased in puff pastry, and shrimp in a tropical sauce; lamb and beef dishes are also available. Entrees about NAf40. Daily 5.30–10.30pm, closed Thurs.

East of Kralendijk

Lac Suid Lac Bay. A small restaurant right on the coast, with an open-air dance patio, that serves a wonderful conch meal for less than US$10. Sun 11am–8pm.

Maiky ⓣ599/565-3804. Snack stand offering traditional Bonairean food; try the huge portions of chicken or goat served with rice or *funchi* (cornmeal). Daily 11am–3pm, closed Thurs.

Listings

Airlines Air Jamaica (ⓣ599/717-8500); American Eagle (ⓣ599/717-8500); Dutch Caribbean Express (ⓣ599/717-7880); KLM (ⓣ599/717-7447).

Banks Antilles Banking, Kaya P.L. Brion 12 (ⓣ599/717-4500); Banco di Caribe, Kaya Grandi 22 (ⓣ599/717-8295); Maduro & Curiel's Bank, Kaya L.D. Gerharts 1 (ⓣ599/717-5520).

Bicycle rental Cycle Bonaire, Kaya L.D. Gerharts 11D (ⓣ599/717-7558), and De Freewieler, Kaya Grandi 61 (ⓣ599/717- 8545), rent a mountain and touring bikes for about US$10–20 per day.

Bookshops Bonaire Boekhandel, Kaya Grandi 50 (ⓣ599/717-8499), has a small selection of paperback books, maps and stationery supplies.

Car and scooter rental AB Car Rental, located at the airport (ⓣ599/717-8980, ⓕ717-3880, ⓔinfo@Abcarrental.com); Hot Shot, Kaya Bonaire 4 (ⓣ599/717-7166, ⓔhotshot@bonairelive.com).

Internet access *De Tuin Eetcafé*, Kaya L.D. Gerharts 9 (Mon–Fri 11am–midnight, Sat & Sun 2pm–midnight); *Bonaire Live*, opposite *De Tuin*, upstairs in the Harbourside Mall on Kaya L.D. Gerharts 10 (Mon–Fri 9am–noon & 1.30–6pm; Sat 9am–noon & 2–5pm) offers access for around US$4 for 30min.

Pharmacies Botica Bonaire, Kaya Grandi 27 (ⓣ599/717-8905).

Post office Bonaire's main post office is located on Kaya Simon Bolivar near the tourist information office (Mon–Thurs 7.30am–noon & 1.30–5pm, Fri 7.30am–noon & 1.30–4.30pm).

Supermarkets Cultimara Supermarket, close to *De Tuin Eetcafé*, Kaya L.D. Gerharts 13 (ⓣ599/717-8278), has a large selection of fresh produce, meat and other grocery items.

21.3

Curaçao

CURAÇAO (population 170,000), the largest of the ABC islands, and the administrative centre of the Netherlands Antilles, remains relatively unknown outside of Holland and the Caribbean. Originally discovered by the Spaniards in 1499 and taken over by the Dutch in 1634, Curaçao has been slower to develop the kind of tourist industry its neighbours are famed for, though its capital city – and recently designated UNESCO World Heritage Site – **Willemstad**, rivals any in the Caribbean for picturesque charm. The island also offers decent diving and swimming possibilities, especially on the leeward side, with its secluded coves. More active pursuits can be had in the rugged and hilly interior: **Christoffel National Park**, in the north, is overgrown with towering cacti, scrubby vegetation and gnarled divi divi trees, well worthy of a hike around it. Besides such flora, island inhabitants include goats, bats, lizards, iguanas and countless species of colourful birds. The various **plantation houses** that dot the island are remnants from Curaçao's history as the Caribbean's busiest slave depot in the seventeenth century; the trade was finally abolished here in 1863.

Arrival and getting around

The majority of visitors fly to Curaçao's **Hato International Airport** (☎5999/868-1719), 12km northwest of Willemstad. Numerous car rental agencies, taxis and buses wait for passengers outside the arrival terminal. A **taxi** to downtown Willemstad usually costs US$8, while a ride to most hotels outside the city will set you back US$14 to US$20. Alternatively, many hotels provide a shuttle **bus** to and from the airport.

There are two **cruise terminals** in the capital, both of them in Willemstad's Otrobanda district. The mega-pier is located near the Riffort by the harbour entrance, a ten-minute walk from downtown. The smaller terminal is closer to downtown in Santa Anna Bay.

It's also possible to take a **ferry** to and from Bonaire. The *Flamingo Fast Ferry* departs Willemstad twice daily at 8.30am and 5.30pm (US$55 round-trip; 1hr 30min each way; ☎5999/461-7002). Catch the ferry at the dock across from the floating market in the Willemstad district of Scharloo. It's best to make reservations and arrive at least thirty minutes before departure.

For **guided tours** of the island: Atlantis Adventure (☎5999/461-0011) offers several sightseeing tours, jeep safaris and kayaking trips for reasonable prices; Taber Tours (☎5999/737-6637 or 6713) has a wide selection of city and island tours starting from US$20; Insulinde (☎5999/560-1340) offers sailing tours to Klein Bonaire for US$30; and Peter Trips (☎5999/465-2703 or 561-5368) has a variety of cultural and historical tours around the island starting at US$20.

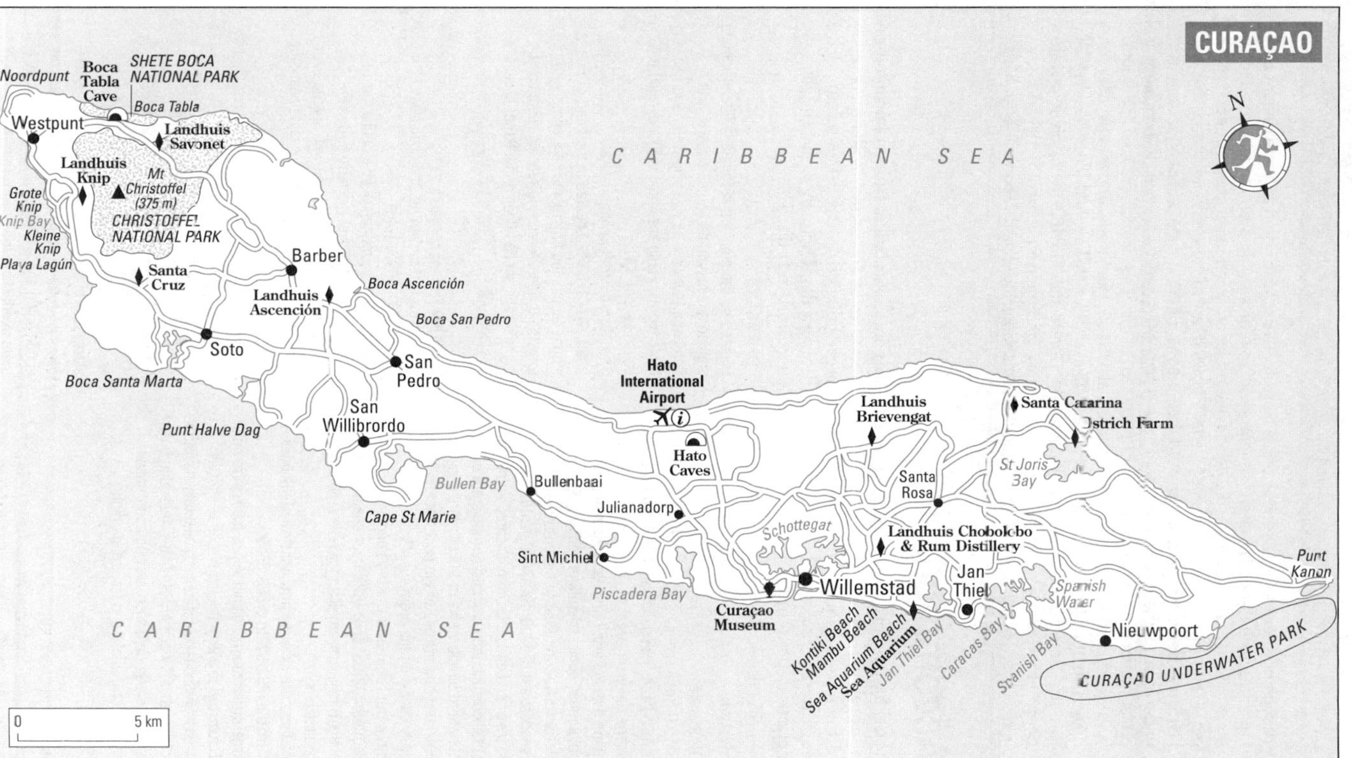
CURAÇAO
N
CARIBBEAN SEA
CARIBBEAN SEA
Noordpunt
Boca Tabla Cave
SHETE BOCA NATIONAL PARK
Boca Tabla
Westpunt
Landhuis Savonet
Landhuis Knip
Mt Christoffel (375 m)
CHRISTOFFEL NATIONAL PARK
Grote Knip
Knip Bay
Kleine Knip
Playa Lagún
Santa Cruz
Barber
Landhuis Ascención
Boca Ascención
Boca San Pedro
Soto
San Pedro
Boca Santa Marta
San Willibrordo
Punt Halve Dag
Hato International Airport
Hato Caves
Bullen Bay
Bullenbaai
Cape St Marie
Julianadorp
Sint Michiel
Piscadera Bay
Schottegat
Curaçao Museum
Willemstad
Landhuis Brievengat
Santa Rosa
Landhuis Chobolobo & Rum Distillery
Santa Catarina
Ostrich Farm
St Joris Bay
Jan Thiel
Spanish Water
Punt Kanon
Nieuwpoort
Kontiki Beach
Mambu Beach
Sea Aquarium Beach
Sea Aquarium
Jan Thiel Bay
Caracas Bay
Spanish Bay
CURAÇAO UNDERWATER PARK
0
5 km

Dive centres

Though nowhere near as renowned as Bonaire, Curaçao is home to some decent **diving** and **snorkelling**. There are several reputable dive centres on the island, most of them offering a variety of services including open-water dive courses, equipment rental and charter boat services. The following are highly recommended: *Habitat Curaçao Resort*, north of Willemstad (see below), offers a wide selection of courses, underwater camera rental, offshore diving and chartered boat dives to surrounding reefs; the friendly Dutch owners of Scuba Do, at Jan Thiel Beach (Ⓣ5999/767-9300), who have unlimited air fills and weights at US$85, numerous underwater courses beginning at US$200 and charters to Klein Curaçao for US$55; and the modern PADI five-star Seascapes Dive and Watersports Centre (Ⓣ5999/462-5905) on a private beach at the *Sheraton Curaçao* (see opposite), who offer equipment rental and storage, a host of courses and an introduction to snorkelling/diving programme for kids.

Accommodation

You'll have no problem finding a **place to stay** in Curaçao. The largest concentration of **hotels** and **dive resorts** is within fifteen minutes of downtown Willemstad, many of them to the south along the coast. The larger hotel chains are a five-minute drive northwest of the capital on the coast near Piscadera Bay. There are some budget-style options to be found in Willemstad's Punda and Otrobanda districts.

Hotels

Otrobanda

Estoril Hotel Breedestraat 181 Ⓣ5999/462-5244, Ⓕ462-2484, Ⓔedgar@banderaportuguesa.com. Set on the main street in Otrobanda, this hotel offers twenty basic but clean rooms with private bathrooms, public telephone and A/C. ❷

Hotel Otrobanda Next to the cruise terminal on Breedestraat Ⓣ5999/462-7400, Ⓕ462-7299, Ⓦwww.otrobandahotel.com. Located in the heart of Willemstad, the *Otrobanda*'s rooms are cramped but afford terrific views of the city; price includes breakfast and the use of the pool. There's also a lively casino on the premises. ❺

Pelikaan Hotel and Casino Langestraat 78 Ⓣ5999/462-3555, Ⓕ462-6063. Popular with budget travellers; small and simple rooms with air conditioning. ❷

Pietersz Guesthouse and Apartments Roodeweg 1 Ⓣ5999/462-5222, Ⓕ868-8519, Ⓔgermain@interneeds.net. A few metres from the *Estoril*, this is one of the top places to stay, its twelve gorgeous rooms coming with fully furnished kitchenettes, TV and private baths. Tucked in below is the *Pietersz Coffeshop*, serving home-made snacks, cold drinks and ice cream. Highly recommended. ❸

Punda

Hotel Buona-Sera Kaya Wilson Godett 104 Ⓣ5999/461-8286 and 465-8565, Ⓕ465-8344. Located on the outskirts of Punda, a fifteen-minute walk to downtown, this hotel, popular with European travellers, is near the water and has very basic rooms. Plans are in the works to build a beach on site. ❷

San Marco Hotel Columbusstraat 7 Ⓣ5999/461-2988, Ⓕ461-6570. Located in the heart of Punda atop a casino, the tiny rooms here come with private facilities. A relaxing reading room can be found on the second floor, and internet access is available. ❸

Scharloo

Hotel Mira Punda Van de Brandhofstraat 12 Ⓣ5999/461-3995, Ⓕ461-2392, Ⓔjoserosales@cura.net. Good location, next to Maritime Museum and the ferry to Bonaire. Ten simple rooms with fans, some with shared bath. Look for green building; entrance is on east-side gate. ❶

Out of Willemstad: diving resorts

Habitat Curaçao Located thirty minutes northwest of Willemstad near Rif. St. Marie Ⓣ5999/864-8800, Ⓕ864-8464, Ⓦwww.habitatdiveresorts.com. Attractive two-storey apartments set alongside a small beach. Spacious rooms complete with kitchenettes, air conditioning and a terrace or balcony – many of them overlooking the ocean. There's also a pool, restaurant and bar on site. Professionally run dive shop with boat excursions to nearby reefs. Friendly staff. Highly recommended. 6

Lions Dive Hotel South of Willemstad near the Sea Aquarium complex on Bapor Kibrá ⓣ5999/461-8100, ⓕ461-8200, ⓔinfo@lionsdive.com. Dutch-Caribbean style accommodation with ocean-facing rooms surrounded by a tropical garden. Clean rooms, many with balconies. Unlimited free access to Sea Aquarium and its private beach, plus free shuttle bus to downtown. 9

Sheraton Curaçao Resort J. F. Kennedy Boulevard ⓣ5999/462-5000, ⓕ462-5846, ⓦwww.ccresort.com. This deluxe beachfront resort with private beaches has it all. Besides the spacious rooms with balconies that afford beautiful views of the island or the ocean, there are two swimming pools (one for kids only), a spa and fitness centre, miniature golf, volleyball and tennis courts, two restaurants and snack bars, a beach-side bar, casino, watersports activities and on-site snorkelling and diving facilities. Ten minutes from the airport, five from downtown Willemstad, with free shuttle service to town. 8

Willemstad

The vibrant city of **WILLEMSTAD**, full of colourful colonial architecture, is the hub of activity in Curaçao. It's a cosmopolitan place, with enough cultural attractions, shopping and places to eat to satisfy those looking for an alternative to a typical beach vacation. Set alongside the southeastern coast and divided by a narrow, but deep channel, known as Santa Anna Bay, downtown Willemstad is split into two main districts – **Punda** on the east side and **Otrobanda** to the west. The former, with its gorgeous waterfront lined with elaborate eighteenth-century buildings and gingerbread mansions, is a distinctly Dutch settlement, home to boutiques, shops, museums and street-side cafés. Across the channel, Otrobanda, literally meaning "the other side" in Papiamentu (see p.780), is in the midst of having its core restored to its former glory, when business was thriving along its narrow streets.

Both sides are eminently walkable, and make for memorable wandering. They are linked by two bridges: the fifty-metre-high **Queen Juliana Bridge** – a four-lane highway towering above the harbour, and the **Queen Emma Pontoon Bridge** – a floating pedestrian bridge that swings open for passing ships and boats. Another district, the old Jewish neighbourhood of **Scharloo**, is north of Punda, as is **Schottegat**, a large inland body of water connected to Santa Anna Bay, where many of the oil refineries and dockyards are located.

The Dutch settled the city as a naval base in 1643, and built military strongholds to defend the naturally deep channel and harbour. As the economy flourished and attracted many Dutch and Jewish merchants, construction proceeded apace, with mansions built for the wealthy and new districts being created, though much fell into disrepair with Curaçao's economic downturn in the nineteenth century.

The City

The most remarkable and central of all landmarks in Willemstad is the **Queen Emma Pontoon Bridge**, which floats between the two central districts. Designed by US businessman Leonard B. Smith in 1888, it was designed to be able to swing open for boats entering the harbour – which it still does around thirty times a day. Back then, Smith charged 2¢ per person for anyone wearing shoes while allowing free access to those who walked across barefoot; no such restrictions apply today. Today crossing the bridge is free to all regardless of their footwear, or lack of it.

Across the pontoon bridge to the east, the scenic waterfront along the bustling street of **Handelskade** in Punda is the most photographed spot in all of Curaçao. Lined with centuries-old pastel-coloured buildings and a string of cafés, this is the best place in the city to start a walking tour. Many of the buildings found along here have been renovated into government offices, banks, shops and restaurants (the red tiles seen on the roofs of these buildings originally came from

Europe as ships' ballast). One of the best examples of traditional architecture is right across from the pontoon bridge at the multilevel **Penha & Sons**, a canary-yellow shop decorated with elaborate white gables, built in 1708. Close at hand is Punda's main **shopping district**, bounded by Handelskade, Madurostraat and Breedestraat.

Just south of the busy main street of Breedestraat is the large **Fort Amsterdam** complex, one of the first military strongholds built on the island in 1635 by the Dutch West Indies Company. Today, the restored fort seats the government of the Netherlands Antilles and other government offices. If you look closely you can still see a British cannonball embedded in one of its walls (the result of a brief skirmish between the Dutch and British in the early 1800s). Around the corner is the renovated Protestant **Fort Church**, the oldest church in Curaçao (built in 1769). Inside, a **museum** (Mon–Fri 9am–noon & 2–5pm; US$2) holds an interesting collection of historical artefacts, documents and maps.

The remains of the island's original fort, **Waterfort**, are located near the mouth of Santa Anna Bay, a block south of Fort Amsterdam. Built in 1634 and renovated two hundred years later, this fort was used by the US army as a military base during World War II (a steel net was dragged across the mouth of the bay to prevent German submarines from entering the deep harbour). A series of stone **waterfront arches**, once used to store gunpowder, are located east of the fort along the waterfront and today house several seaside restaurants.

Situated in the heart of Punda, the **Mikvé Israel-Emanuel Synagogue**, on Hanchi Snoa at Columbusstraat, is one of the Caribbean's most important landmarks and certainly the oldest synagogue still in use in the western hemisphere. Members of the original Jewish community who came here from Europe dedicated the synagogue in 1732. The white sand sprinkled on the floor is said to honour Moses' leading of his people through the desert. Tucked inside is the **Jewish Cultural Museum** (Mon–Fri 9–11.45am & 2.30–4.45pm, Sun 9am–noon; US$2), where you can view an impressive array of Torah scrolls, Hanukah lamps and other religious artefacts.

If you're up at the crack of dawn it's worth a visit to the **floating market**, which lines the canal beside Sha Carpileskade in the northern corner of Punda. Every morning small wooden boats loaded with fresh tropical fruits and vegetables make their way from Venezuela to sell their produce in Willemstad; they typically leave by noon. A few other sights exist nearby, including the popular **Marshe Bieu** (old market), behind the post office, where you can sample inexpensive local cuisine off open charcoal grills.

Directly across the water from the market, in the former Jewish district of Scharloo, you'll find the **Maritime Museum** (Tues–Sat 10am–4pm; US$5.50), which pays homage to Curaçao's rich seafaring history. Ship models, maps and coins from sunken treasures are on display. Nearby is the dock for the **Flamingo Fast Ferry** to Bonaire (see p.804.)

Across the channel and west of the pontoon bridge, Otrobanda has a couple attractions worth looking into. Its main street, **Breedestraat** (not to be confused with the street of the same name in Punda) runs perpendicular from the channel and is chock-full of small shops selling bargain clothing and souvenirs. Be sure to visit the **Kura Hulanda Museum**, just off Breedestraat to the north on Klipstraat 9 (Mon–Sat 10am–5pm; US$5), built in a restored nineteenth-century mansion, for its splendid selection of original art and artefacts from all over Africa. Several permanent exhibits, including one on the slave trade and one on human evolution, are also among the museum's highlights. Across town on the western outskirts of Otrobanda, the smaller **Curaçao Museum**, V Leeuwenhoekstraat (Mon–Fri 9am–noon & 2–5pm, Sun 10am–4pm; US$2.65), is home to a scant collection of traditional and contemporary local art and artefacts.

South of Willemstad

One of the more popular attractions outside of Willemstad is the **Sea Aquarium** (daily 8.30am–5.30pm; US$13, children US$7.25), a twenty-minute drive south of the capital. Touch tanks, aquariums, an underwater shark-feeding observatory and a 3D movie theatre all provide a good preface to perhaps getting underwater yourself: you can swim, snorkel or dive offshore at the entrance to the twenty-kilometre **Curaçao Underwater Park**, which is actually a preserve protecting the delicate marine environment.

A short stroll from the Sea Aquarium leads to a rather large stretch of man-made sandy **beach** fringed with palm trees. An entrance fee of US$3.50 will get you into Kontiki Beach and Mambo Beach as well as the nearby Sea Aquarium Beach. All three are safe for swimming and have bars, restaurants, changing room facilities and plenty of parking. During the evening and on weekends this place comes to life with dance and music (see p.812).

Another smaller but quieter beach can be found at **Zanzibar Beach Resort** in Jan Thiel Bay (US$3), located 4km east of the Sea Aquarium; this also offers snorkelling, diving and swimming possibilities. Beach chairs and mountain bikes (US$20/day) are available for rent.

Many **watersports** activities, including jet skiing, kayaking and windsurfing are offered at nearby **Caracas Bay Island**, a recreation park near the town of Jan Thiel (☎5999/747-0666 or 567-6654).

East of Willemstad

Free tours and liqueur sampling are available at the **Senior & Company Liqueur Distillery** (Mon–Fri 8am–noon & 1–5pm), a few minutes' drive east of Punda at the Landhuis Chobolobo in Saliña. Known for producing the sweet-tasting **Curaçao Blue**, a liqueur made from the peels of the bitter Valencia orange, this small factory bottles more than 20,000 gallons per week. The plant has been in operation since 1896; pick up any of the four varieties – orange, coffee, chocolate or rum raisin – at the on-site gift-shop.

Christoffel National Park and the northern tip

Tucked in the northwest corner of the island is the spectacular **Christoffel National Park**, a 4600-acre wilderness preserve protecting a diverse array of plants and animals. Located 45 minutes from Willemstad and centred around **Mount Christoffel** (375m), the highest point on Curaçao, this former plantation is home to the tiny Curaçao deer as well as numerous species of bats, birds, non-poisonous snakes, iguanas, orchids and cacti. Several well-marked walking and driving routes allow you to explore the rugged and hilly interior at your own pace.

The **main entrance** (Mon–Sat 8am–4pm, Sun 6am–3pm; US$10) is located at the mustard-coloured **Savonet** plantation house, on the right-hand side of the main road leading to Westpunt. A local restaurant and small museum can also be found here. From the main gate it's possible to access any of eight well-marked colour-coded **hiking trails**, which vary in difficulty and can take anywhere from twenty minutes to around five hours to complete. The most strenuous is a steep ascent up Mount Christoffel, which rewards with breathtaking views of the entire island, not to mention the numerous delicate orchids visible along the path. It's also possible to drive through the interior on any one of three well-maintained dirt roads. Trail maps are available at the main entrance, as is a highly recommended guidebook outlining the trails and history of the park (US$6).

Various tours of the park are also on offer, including a two-and-a-half-hour one with park rangers from the main gate on Friday mornings at 10am (US$8.50), and horse-riding and mountain-biking tours; call Rancho Alfin (☎5999/864-0535) for details.

The rugged north coast is best viewed from the tiny **Shete Boka National Park** (US$2), a two-kilometre drive north of the main gate of Christoffel National Park. A series of walking trails on exposed sharp coral wind their way along the coast to several limestone **grottoes**, including **Boka Tabla**, where you can climb inside and watch the waves come crashing in. Keep an eye out for ancient coral formations and fossils along the path, as well as sea turtles swimming in the rough waters – the park was established as a sanctuary for breeding these animals. Swimming is not advisable here; the currents are far too dangerous.

A few kilometres further north, you can easily give **Westpunt** a miss, though you may want to dine at *Jaanchie's* (see review opposite), if you've come up to one of the parks or nearby beaches for the day. Ten minutes south of Westpunt along a winding and hilly coastal road is **Landhuis Knip**, the island's best example of a restored colonial plantation house. Built in the early 1700s and rebuilt in 1830 after a fire, this was one of Curaçao's largest and most prosperous plantations, producing wool, indigo, sorghum, beans and divi divi pods (used in tanning leather). Antique furniture and period pieces decorate the large rooms inside.

Some of the island's best **beaches**, **diving and snorkelling sites** are found along this northwest stretch of Curaçao. If you're coming directly from Willemstad (instead of from the park) head north on the main road to Westpunt and turn left on the road to Santa Cruz at the town of San Pedro; otherwise follow the signs from Westpunt or from Landhuis Knip. The most popular spots, both on Knip Bay, are **Grote Knip** with its calm, turquoise-blue waters and beautiful sandy beach nestled in a protected cove, and the smaller **Kleine Knip**, a few kilometres south of Grote Knip. Both beaches offer superb swimming and snorkelling opportunities and are crowded on weekends and holidays; a small snack bar and changing facilities are available at Grote Knip. Watch out for the poisonous manchineel trees (see p.25) growing by the beach.

As you're making your way back to Willemstad stop by **Landhuis Ascension**, the oldest plantation house, dating back to 1672. Some 5km north of the highway intersection to the beaches, this beautifully restored plantation house is used as a recreation centre for the Dutch marines. There's an open house on the first Sunday of every month, with local music, handicrafts and food.

The rest of the island

The rest of the island has some scattered attractions, most along the lines of **plantation houses** (known as *landhuizen*), though many of these are in fact in disrepair. Ones that have been transformed into restaurants or museums include the lovely **Landhuis Brievengat** (Mon–Fri 9.15am–noon & 3–6pm), north of Willemstad close to the coast and east of the airport, which has a wide selection of local crafts on view, as well as occasional live salsa music (see opposite).

Just a half-kilometre south of the airport are the mysterious limestone **Hato Caves** (daily 10am–4pm; US$6.50), where stunning flowstone formations, stalagmites and stalactites grow in humid chambers. They can be viewed, alongside ancient rock drawings, on the 45-minute guided tours that depart every hour on the hour.

Quite the sight to see as well are the seven hundred or so ostriches penned in at the **Curaçao Ostrich Farm** (Tues–Sun 8am–5pm; US$13; ☎5999/747-2777), situated in the remote eastern corner of the island. Tours (call to be picked up from your hotel) offer the chance to feed these flightless creatures, hold one of the large eggs (equivalent to twenty chicken eggs) and learn a bit of their life cycle.

Eating and drinking

Willemstad

Iguana Café On the waterfront at Handelskade (next to Queen Emma Bridge), Punda ☏5999/461-9866. One of the few places in Punda where you can enjoy a light dinner at a reasonable price. The menu includes sandwiches and Dutch specialties, and it's a great place to watch the cruise ships and tankers pass by. Daily 9am–9pm, closed Sun.

Il Barile Hanchi Snoa 12, Punda ☏5999/461-3025. Don't let appearances fool you; this small street-side restaurant is the best place in Willemstad for home-made Italian food, sandwiches and cappuccinos. Sit outside on the small patio or dine upstairs. Main course US$10–15. Mon–Sat 8am–8pm.

Marshe Bieu The open-air terrace behind the post office, Punda. A popular lunch spot, this market is a great place to sample local dishes such as deep-fried kora (red snapper); Chinese food is also available. Mains US$6. Mon–Sat 11am–3pm.

Plein Café Wilhelmina Wilhelmina Park, Punda ☏5999/461-0461. A pleasant downtown setting for a cold beer and a fresh baguette or "toastie" (toasted cheese). The chicken sate smothered in peanut sauce is also worth trying. Mains around US$10. Mon–Sat 9am–8pm.

Rasta Hut Columbusstraat 6A, Punda. Located across from the synagogue, a friendly place to enjoy wings, chicken and other fast-food dishes while listening to reggae. Mains around US$12. Daily 9am–10pm.

Sarifundy's Marina Spanish Water (east of Punda) ☏5999/767-7643. This restaurant set on a pier overlooking Spanish Water serves fantastic seafood meals and has a wonderfully relaxed atmosphere. Mains US$15–20. Tues–Sun 6–10pm.

Sawasdee Van Eyck v. Voorthuyzenweg 5, Otrobanda ☏5999/462-6361. Across from the entrance to the Curaçao Museum, this cosy place offers excellent Thai dishes. Closed on Mon.

Time Out Café Keukenplein 8, Punda. Tucked into a small courtyard in the heart of Punda's shopping district, this tiny café offers excellent sandwiches plus the catch of the day, and there are internet facilities upstairs. Mon–Fri 9.30am–7pm, Sat 10am–4pm.

Tu Tu Tango Plasa Mundo Merced, Scharloo ☏5999/465-4633. Hidden in a small alley behind The Movies Curaçao theatre, this is one of the few places in the city open for dinner seven days a week. Seafood dishes, steaks and sandwiches run around US$15 and an Indonesian buffet is offered every Wednesday night. Happy hour Fri 6–7pm. Daily 6–11pm.

Zanzibar Lounge and Restaurant Jan Thiel Beach. The best place on the island for pizza, just a ten-minute drive southeast of Willemstad. Both lunch and dinner menus are available serving everything from local to international and seafood dishes. The restaurant terrace, set under an original Moroccan tent, overlooks the beach. Takeout is available. Happy hour Fri 5–6pm. Open daily 10am–11pm.

Northern tip

Jaanchie's On main road in Westpunt ☏5999/864-0126. Delicious local dishes served by friendly staff. Their speciality is wahoo (a fish), served with rice, salad and plantain (about US$13). Watch for the "I Love Jaanchie's" sign on the main road.

Rijsttafel Mercuriusstraat 13–15, close to Chobolobo (home of Senior & Co) ☏5999/461-2606. An elegant and pricey Indonesian restaurant decorated with shadow puppets, batiks and copper pots. Go with a group to enjoy a traditional Indonesian banquet; a vegetarian menu is also available. Mains around US$25. Mon–Sat noon–2pm & 6–9.30pm; reservations recommended.

The rest of the island

Landhuis Brievengat Brievengat ☏5999/565-2156. This historic plantation house, fifteen minutes' drive northeast from Willemstad, is *the* place for salsa and merengue dancing, especially on Friday nights.

Zambezi Restaurant Ostrich Farm, Groot St Joris West ☏5999/747-2777. Ostrich and other African dishes are their specialty. Reservations are recommended. Lunch Tues–Sun noon–5pm, dinner Wed–Sun 6–10pm.

Nightlife

Most of the popular **bars** and **nightclubs** are located outside of downtown Willemstad. Cover charges apply only when a live band is playing.

De Heeren North of Punda next to shopping centre, Zuikertuintje ☎5999/736-0491. Popular hangout on Thursday nights, attracting a fairly young crowd of Dutch locals. Great place to dance, listen to music and have a beer.
De Tropen SBN Doormanweg 37. While there's dancing on Friday and Saturday nights, most come to listen to European music and hang out.
The Living Room Saliña 129. A popular nightspot on Friday and Saturday for listening to music.
Mambo Beach Sea Aquarium Beach, Bapor Kibrá ☎5999/461-8999. Lively after-work bar offering something different every night of the week; movies on Tuesday and dancing every Saturday until 4am. Happy hour Sun 5–6pm.
Wet and Wild Next door to *Mambo Beach* (see above), Bapor Kibrá ☎5999/465-3464. Another beach bar full of weekend energy. On Sunday there's a live DJ and happy hour from 6pm.

Listings

Airlines Aeropostal (☎5999/888-2808); American Airlines (☎5999/869-5707); Avia Air (☎5999/888-1089); Avianca (☎5999/868-0122); Divi Divi Air (☎5999/888-1050); Dutch Caribbean Express, formerly ALM (☎5999/869-5533); and KLM (☎5999/465-2747).
Banks There are many banks located in the shopping district of Punda and Otrobanda. Most of the ATMs at the Maduro & Curiel's Bank dispense US cash or guilders.
Car rental Caribe Rentals (☎5999/461-3089); Casual Car Rental (☎5999/737-4193); Hertz (☎5999/868-1182); and Noordstar (☎5999/737-5616).
Embassies American Consulate General, J.B. Gorsiraweg 1, Willemstad (☎5999/461-3066); Consulate of Canada, Maduro and Curiel's Bank, N.V., Scharlooweg 55, Willemstad (☎5999/466-1115, Ⓕ466-1122).
Internet access *ONCE internet café* (Mon–Sat 9am–6pm; US$6/hr; ☎5999/462-2299) across from the *Pelikaan Hotel* in Otrobanda; in Punda upstairs at *Time Out Café* at Keukenplein 8 (Mon–Fri 9.30am–7pm, Sat 10am–4pm; US$5 for 30min; see review, p.811) and at *C@fe Internet* in the Blue Marlin Building by the Queen Emma Bridge, Handelskade 38 (Mon–Sat 9am–8pm; US$5 for 30min; ☎5999/465-5088). The latter is also the best place to make international calls.
Pharmacies Pharmacies, called *boticas*, are open Monday to Saturday from 8am to 7pm. Botica Brion is across from the post office in Otrobanda (☎5999/462-7027); in Punda try the centrally located Botica Popular at Madurostraat 15 (☎5999/461-1269).
Post office In Punda, Post NV is next to the main market on Waaigatplein 1 (Mon–Fri 7.30am–noon & 1.30–5pm; ☎5999/433-1100). Post NV in Otrobanda is located on the main floor of the large white Landskantoor building on Breedestraat (same hours as above).

index

and small print

Index

Map entries are in colour

INDEX

F

G

H

INDEX

N

O

P

R

S

INDEX

T

U

V

W

Twenty years of Rough Guides

In the summer of 1981, Mark Ellingham, Rough Guides' founder, knocked out the first guide on a typewriter, with a group of friends. Mark had been travelling in Greece after university, and couldn't find a guidebook that really answered his needs.There were heavyweight cultural guides on the one hand – good on museums and classical sites but not on beaches and tavernas – and on the other hand student manuals that were so caught up with how to save money that they lost sight of the country's significance beyond its role as a place for a cool vacation. None of the guides began to address Greece as a country, with its natural and human environment, its politics and its contemporary life.

Having no urgent reason to return home, Mark decided to write his own guide. It was a guide to Greece that tried to combine some erudition and insight with a thoroughly practical approach to travellers' needs. Scrupulously researched listings of places to stay, eat and drink were matched by careful attention to detail on everything from Homer to Greek music, from classical sites to national parks and from nude beaches to monasteries. Back in London, Mark and his friends got their Rough Guide accepted by a farsighted commissioning editor at the publisher Routledge and it came out in 1982.

The Rough Guide to Greece was a student scheme that became a publishing phenomenon. The immediate success of the book – shortlisted for the Thomas Cook award – spawned a series that rapidly covered dozens of countries. The Rough Guides found a ready market among backpackers and budget travellers, but soon acquired a much broader readership that included older and less impecunious visitors. Readers relished the guides' wit and inquisitiveness as much as the enthusiastic, critical approach that acknowledges everyone wants value for money – but not at any price.

Rough Guides soon began supplementing the "rougher" information – the hostel and low-budget listings – with the kind of detail that independent-minded travellers on any budget might expect. These days, the guides – distributed worldwide by the Penguin group – include recommendations spanning the range from shoestring to luxury, and cover more than 200 destinations around the globe. Our growing team of authors, many of whom come to Rough Guides initially as outstandingly good letter-writers telling us about their travels, are spread all over the world, particularly in Europe, the USA and Australia. As well as the travel guides, Rough Guides publishes a series of dictionary phrasebooks covering two dozen major languages, an acclaimed series of music guides running the gamut from Classical to World Music, a series of music CDs in association with World Music Network, and a range of reference books on topics as diverse as the Internet, Pregnancy and Unexplained Phenomena. Visit **www.roughguides.com** to see what's cooking.

Rough Guide credits

Text editors: Yuki Takagaki and Julie Feiner
Series editor: Mark Ellingham
Editorial: Martin Dunford, Jonathan Buckley, Kate Berens, Ann-Marie Shaw, Helena Smith, Judith Bamber, Olivia Swift, Ruth Blackmore, Geoff Howard, Claire Saunders, Gavin Thomas, Alexander Mark Rogers, Polly Thomas, Joe Staines, Richard Lim, Duncan Clark, Peter Buckley, Lucy Ratcliffe, Clifton Wilkinson, Alison Murchie, Matthew Teller, Andrew Dickson, Fran Sandham (UK); Andrew Rosenberg, Stephen Timblin, Yuki Takagaki, Richard Koss, Hunter Slaton, Julie Feiner (US)
Production: Susanne Hillen, Andy Hilliard, Link Hall, Helen Prior, Julia Bovis, Michelle Draycott, Katie Pringle, Zoë Nobes, Rachel Holmes, Andy Turner, Michelle Bhatia
Cartography: Melissa Baker, Maxine Repath, Ed Wright, Katie Lloyd-Jones
Cover art direction: Louise Boulton
Picture research: Sharon Martins, Mark Thomas
Online: Kelly Cross, Anja Mutic-Blessing, Jennifer Gold, Audra Epstein, Suzanne Welles, Cree Lawson (US)
Finance: John Fisher, Gary Singh, Edward Downey, Mark Hall, Tim Bill
Marketing & Publicity: Richard Trillo, Niki Smith, David Wearn, Chloë Roberts, Demelza Dallow, Claire Southern (UK); Simon Carloss, David Wechsler, Megan Kennedy (US)
Administration: Tania Hummel, Julie Sanderson

Publishing information

This first edition published September 2002 by **Rough Guides Ltd**,
62–70 Shorts Gardens, London WC2H 9AH.
Penguin Putnam, Inc. 375 Hudson Street, NY 10014, USA.
Distributed by the Penguin Group
Penguin Books Ltd,
80 Strand, London WC2R 0RL
Penguin Putnam, Inc.
375 Hudson Street, New York, NY 10014, USA
Penguin Books Australia Ltd,
487 Maroondah Highway, PO Box 257, Ringwood, Victoria 3134, Australia
Penguin Books Canada Ltd,
10 Alcorn Avenue, Toronto, Ontario, Canada M4V 1E4
Penguin Books (NZ) Ltd,
182–190 Wairau Road, Auckland 10, New Zealand
Typeset in Bembo and Helvetica to an original design by Henry Iles.
Printed in Italy by LegoPrint S.p.A

856pp includes index
A catalogue record for this book is available from the British Library.

ISBN 1-85828-895-9

Help us update

We've gone to a lot of effort to ensure that the first edition of **The Rough Guide to Caribbean Islands** is accurate and up to date. However, things change – places get "discovered", opening hours are notoriously fickle, restaurants and rooms raise prices or lower standards. If you feel we've got it wrong or left something out, we'd like to know, and if you can remember the address, the price, the time, the phone number, so much the better.

We'll credit all contributions, and send a copy of the next edition (or any other Rough Guide if you prefer) for the best letters. Everyone who writes to us and isn't already a subscriber will receive a copy of our full-colour thrice-yearly newsletter. Please mark letters: "**Rough Guide Caribbean Islands Update**" and send to: Rough Guides, 62–70 Shorts Gardens, London WC2H 9AH, or Rough Guides, 4th Floor, 345 Hudson St, New York, NY 10014. Or send an email to **mail@roughguides.com**

Have your questions answered and tell others about your trip at **www.roughguides.atinfopop.com**

Acknowledgements

Nicky Agate Thanks to Tanya Warner and all at the St Lucia Tourist Board and St Lucia Heritage Tourism, Andrew Davies, Peter Lang, Richard Nisa (for cruise ship advice) and todos at Rough Guides (for keeping me on my toes).

Arabella Bowen Thanks to Élise and Marielle on St Barts; Guadeloupe's Guy-Claude Germain, especially for the automatic car; Muriel Wiltord-Latamie of Martinique; Dominica's Bobby Frederick and Co (never mind Scott Johnson); Yvette and "TC" for rollicking storytelling; Roberta Garzaroli and everyone at St Kitts Tourism for a memorable final week.

Maureen Clarke I'd like to thank Bethzaida García, of the Puerto Rico Tourism Company, for helping me out of a jam that could have aborted my trip to Puerto Rico, and Bruce Walters, for his priceless companionship during my travels.

Dominique De-Light Big up to flatmate Isanna, Polly T, family and friends and nuff respect to Yuki, our hardworking editor. Special thanks to Mark and Zena Puddy, Lisa Kewley, Gaby Hosein and all those who helped in T&T.

Gaylord Dold I would like to acknowledge the many kindnesses shown me by the staff of the Bahamas Ministry of Tourism, and especially those of Craig Woods.

Natalie Folster Thank you very much to Charity Armbrister at the Bahamas Ministry of Tourism and to Carmeta Miller and the Grand Bahama Tourism Board. In the Exumas, thanks go to Warden Ray and Evelyn Darville; David "Blue" Brown; District Administrator Cooper; Mike and Valerie Dudash; Peter and Betty Oxley; North Carolina Outward Bound; and Peterina Hannah and the Exuma Ministry of Tourism Office; and on Eleuthera, the Goede family; Tommy Sands; Charlie Moore; and Mrs Eurene Nottage. Thanks also to Peter Kuska for facilitating my stay on Long Island.

Sean Harvey Thanks to Tim Hall, Iguana Mama, Bob Corbett, Michele Wucker and Martha Davis.

Tom Hutton I'd like to say a huge thank you to Patricia, Richard and all the staff at Iguana Mama. Thanks also to Mike Braden, Udo and Brigitte, Get Wet Mike and of course Gerard, Gundula and Claudia, for their exceptional hospitality. Other help came from Tim Hall, Angie Wolff, Urs at Sunshine, Kim Beddall, David Buglass and Sabrina Cambiaso at the DR Tourist Board in the UK. Also thanks to my partner Steph, for companionship on the research trip, and to Honey and India for stress relief during the writing stage.

Sarah Lazarus Thanks and a big hug to Neale Anderson.

JoAnn Milivojevic Special thanks to the Cayman Islands Department of Tourism.

Matt Norman Matt Norman sends much love to the Havana family: Miriam, Sinai, Ricardo, Hildegard, Abelito, Indira and Bartutis.

Lesley Rose Many thanks to Martin Chester for his research, editing and unfailing support. Thanks also to Lisa at Just Grenada, Carla at the Bequia Tourist Board, the crew of the Jasper for helping me get my sea legs and Betty King for advice on how to fly the return journey.

Nelson Taylor I'd like to thank Bibi Bhajan with FSB Associates for her help with the BVIs and Kelly Campbell with the Martin Agency for her help with the USVIs. I'd also like to thank AnnChristine Gormley for hooking me up with Guana Island's scientists, Lumumba for his "bush tour" of St Croix, and the United States Virgin Islands National Park for working to preserve the natural beauty of the islands.

Polly Thomas Polly Thomas would like to thank the staff of the Jamaica Tourist Board, Sarah Rees at Biss Lancaster and Jean Causewell at Econocars; special thanks also to Mrs Pam Morris, Marjorie Morris and the Morris family; Simone Eshmeier; Victoria Bate; Jan Pauel; Damian "Reds" Parchment; Herbert "Super Herb" Kennedy; Andre McGann; Jason Henzell; and all the friends and family back home.

Claus Vogel Thanks to Pierre and Marjory Mahieu for their invaluable assistance. My trip would not have been possible without the wonderful support of Lisa Blau and Adams Unlimited in New York, the Aruba Tourism Authority, Tourism Corporation Bonaire and the Curaçao Tourism Development Bureau. A

special thanks to my fabulous guides Francis Jacobs, Rolando Marin and Gerrit Brigitha, and my hosts Frank and Ellis Rothweiler. Jadwiga, I really appreciated your constant encouragement and for helping me to get my camera back from the north.

Heartfelt thanks go to Michelle Bhatia, Julia Bovis, Helen Prior and James Morris for their patience and smooth production work, Maxine Repath and The Map Studio, Romsey, Hants, for spot-on mapmaking, Jules Brown, Jeff Dickey and Caroline Osborne for their editorial expertise, Melissa Krupanski for her extensive photo research, Derek Wilde for his proofreading prowess, Arabella Bowen for her diligent indexing and Stephen Timblin and Andrew Rosenberg for overall guidance.

Photo credits

Cover credits

Main front picture St John, Virgin Islands © Stone
Small top photo Beach hut, Rum Point, Grand Cayman © Robert Harding
Small lower photo Yellow snappers © Stone
Back top photo Junkanoo dancers © Robert Harding
Back lower photo St Kitts © John Miller

Colour introduction

Waters near Providenciales, Turks and Caicos © Phil Schermeister/Network Aspen
Market scene, Grenada © Bill Bachmann/Network Aspen
Firecracker flower, Puerto Rico © Dick Meseroll/Eastern Surf
Haitian taxi © Dick Meseroll/Eastern Surf
Bartender making a rum cocktail, St John, USVI © Melissa Krupanski
North Caicos villager, Turks and Caicos © Phil Schermeister/Network Aspen
Divers taking the plunge, Jamaica © Jamaica Tourist Board
Sawfish in the Predator Lagoon of the Atlantis hotel, the Bahamas © Don Nausbaum/Caribphoto
Boats resting on a beach, Dominican Republic © Doug Berry/Telluride Stock
Coconuts, Trinidad © Mike Tauber
Local shop, Dominican Republic © Dick Meseroll/Eastern Surf
Carnival reveller, Trinidad © Nicholas Devore III/Network Aspen

Things not to miss

1. Atlantic spotted dolphin with snorkeller, the Bahamas © Jones & Shimlock/Network Aspen
2. Carnival, Antigua © Antigua/Barbuda Tourist Office
3. Fishing boats near The Pitons, St Lucia © Bill Bachmann/Network Aspen
4. Overview of Saba © Don Nausbaum/Caribphoto
5. Cuban musicians © Don Nausbaum/Caribphoto
6. Boiling Lake, Dominica © Dominica Tourist Department
7. Willemstad, Curaçao © Don Nausbaum/Caribphoto
8. Juvenile queen angelfish © Jones & Shimlock/Network Aspen
9. Seven Mile Beach, Grand Cayman © Cayman Islands Tourism Department
10. Jamaican drummer © Jamaica Tourist Board
11. Rugged Point, Barbados © Dick Meseroll/Eastern Surf
12. Martinique beach © Don Nausbaum/Caribphoto
13. Lobster shack, Bequia, The Grenadines © Chris LaMarca
14. La Soufrière, St Vincent © Nicholas Devore III/Network Aspen
15. Scuba divers at South Caicos, Turks and Caicos © Phil Schermeister/Network Aspen
16. Fish stand, Trinidad and Tobago © Christopher LaMarca
17. Tobago sunset © Christopher LaMarca
18. Old Havana, Cuba © Don Nausbaum/Caribphoto
19. Sea kayakers, the Bahamas © Julian Bajzert/Bahamas Tourist Office
20. Bomba's Surfside Shack, Tortola, BVI © Donald E. Cresitillo
21. The Baths, Virgin Gorda, BVI © Donald E. Cresitillo
22. El Moro, Old San Juan, Puerto Rico © Tom Cunningham
23. Snorkellers in a cove, Dominican Republic © Denise Mattia
24. Windsurfer at Cabarete, Dominican Republic © Dick Meseroll/Eastern Surf
25. Rawlins Plantation, St Kitts © Don Nausbaum/Caribphoto
26. Mount Britton Tower, El Yunque, Puerto Rico © Tom Cunningham
27. Boats in Little Bay, Anguilla © Don Nausbaum/Caribphoto

Black and white photos

Sand patterns, the Bahamas © Mike Tauber (p.104)
Vintage car parked in Habana Vieja, Cuba © Dannielle Hayes (p.186)
Rafting on the Martha Brae River, Jamaica © Dannielle Hayes (p.251)
A fort, Dominican Republic © Don Nausbaum/Caribphoto (p.316)
Muddy road en route to Guajataca, Puerto Rico © Dannielle Hayes (p.370)
Emancipation Garden, St Thomas, USVI © Melissa Krupanski (p.433)
Cannon, St Martin/St Maarten © Don Nausbaum/Caribphoto (p.474)
Picnic table near Pointe-de-la-Grande-Vigie, Guadeloupe © Christopher LaMarca (p.552)
Canoe in Carib Territory, Dominica © Dominica Tourist Department (p.595)
Fisherman casting net, Barbados © Dick Meseroll/Eastern Surf (p.655)
Waterloo Temple, Trinidad © Dominique De-Light (p.766)
Longsnout seahorse, Bonaire © Jones & Shimlock/Network Aspen (p.791)

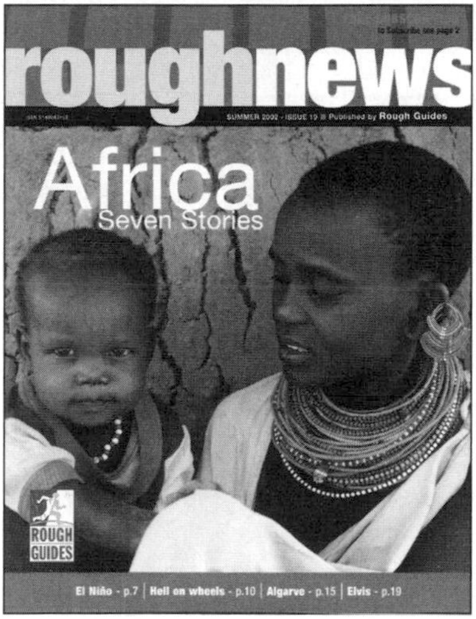